GUITAR
REFERENCE
GUIDE

CHORDS

BY JOE CHARUPAKORN

ISBN 1-57560-198-2

Visit our website at www.cherrylane.com 

PREFACE

This book is the most comprehensive and detailed collection of chords ever published. An enormous range of chords are presented here — from the simplest open varieties to sophisticated ultra-modern voicings.

The chords found in this book will enable you to confidently tackle any style of music. Beginning and intermediate guitarists can take advantage of the unique *Chord-Finder System* to immediately locate any chord, in any key. Advanced guitarists will find a plethora of unorthodox voicings to pique their curiosity.

A book this size can be intimidating at first glance. Don't set out to learn every single chord in the book. Rather, use it as a reference; make note of the chords you like, find other chords that work together, and study the logic behind the chord construction. These are the steps that will lead to mastery.

—Joe Charupakorn

ABOUT THE AUTHOR

Joe Charupakorn is a guitarist, composer, and author. He earned a Master of Fine Arts in Composition from Purchase Conservatory of Music at the State University of New York, where he graduated Magna Cum Laude. Joe has also studied privately with many musical heavyweights—including jazz pianists Richie Beirach and Mike Longo, guitar legend Mike Stern, and contemporary classical composer Ruth Schonthal. He has performed around the world, in places such as Amsterdam, Nice, Barcelona, and Bangkok, and is currently active as a guitarist, composer, and teacher in the New York metropolitan area.

ACKNOWLEDGMENTS

I'd like to thank Arthur Rotfeld and Jack Shneidman, my editors, for their insight, patience, and guidance; Robert Papp for assistance in designing the chord pages; and my family and friends for their unyielding support.

CONTENTS

Introduction

The Chords

Minor 7 Chords

Includes

m7 m7♭5 m(maj7) m(maj7)♭5 m7♯11
m(maj7)♯11
m9 m9♭5 m(maj9) m(maj9)♭5 m9♯11
m(maj9)♯11
m11 m11♭5 m(maj11) m(maj11)♭5
m13 m(maj13) m(maj13)♭5 m13♯11 m(maj13)♯11
m7♭13 m7♭5♭13 m(maj7)♭13 m(maj7)♭5♭13

Dominant-Type Chords

Includes

7 7♭5 7♯5 7♯11 7♯11♯5
9 9♭5 9♯5 9♯11 9♯11♯5
11 13 13♯11
7sus4 9sus4 13sus4 7sus4♭9 13sus4♭9 7sus4♭9♭13
7♭9 7♯9 7♭9♯9 7♭9♯11 7♯9♯11 7♭9♯9♯11
11♭9 13♭9 13♯9 13♭9♯9 13♭9♯11 13♯9♯11
13♭9♯9♯11
7♭13 7♭9♭13 7♯9♭13 7♭9♯9♭13

Non-Tertian Chords

Includes

INTRODUCTION

Chord Construction

Basic Chord Theory

This book is not a harmony text, yet some general knowledge of chord theory is needed to make the best use of this book. Here is a brief overview:

Chords are formed by selecting three or more notes and playing them simultaneously, thus creating harmony, as opposed to melody. When creating chords it is important to know the distance between each note of the chord. The distance between two notes is called an *interval.* From one scale step to the next (C to D, for example), the interval is called a 2nd; two scale steps away (C to E) is a 3rd, etc. Intervals have general and specific names. (The above examples, while generally being labeled a 2nd and 3rd, are specifically defined as a major 2nd and major 3rd, respectively.) There are five categories for labeling specific interval types. The first two come straight from the major scale, the remaining three are alterations.

Major = 2nd, 3rd, 6th, and 7th. (These can also be seen as the 2nd, 3rd, 6th, and 7th notes of a major scale.)

Perfect = Unison, 4th, 5th, and octave. (These can also be seen as the 1st, 4th, 5th, and 8th notes of a major scale.)

Minor = 2nd, 3rd, 6th, and 7th. (These are flatted versions of the major intervals.)

Augmented = A major or perfect interval raised one half-step.

Diminished = A perfect interval flatted one half-step.

C	D	E	F	G	A	B	C
1	2	3	4	5	6	7	8

Triads

The most fundamental type of chord is the triad (a three-note chord, usually constructed in 3rds). There are four basic triads: major, minor, diminished, and augmented.

A major triad is comprised of the 1st, 3rd, and 5th notes of a major scale:

Major = 1 3 5

C Major = C E G

To create the other triads, alter notes of the major triad formula:

Minor = 1 ♭3 5

Diminished = 1 ♭3 ♭5

Augmented =1 3 ♯5

Though not spelled in thirds, there are other triads (in the sense that they are three-note chords), such as sus2 and sus4, in which the 3rd of the chord is replaced with a 2nd and 4th, respectively.

Seventh Chords and Beyond

Seventh chords consist of four notes. These chords are simply triads with the 7th note of the scale added. There are three basic 7th chord qualities; everything else is a modification of one of these.

Major 7 = 1 3 5 7

Minor 7 = 1 ♭3 5 ♭7

Dominant 7 = 1 3 5 ♭7

Extensions are achieved by adding other scale notes (such as the 9th, 11th, and 13th) to triads or 7th chords. *Alterations* are chromatic changes (such as ♭5, ♯9, or ♯11) made to either chord tones or extensions. Chords are named in the following order: letter name, quality, and uppermost extension (Dmaj9, for example). Altered notes are mentioned last (D13♭9, for example).

This book provides precise and exact chord names. However, chord nomenclature is not standardized, and many real-life situations may use shorthand terminology in describing a chord. For example, if you are asked to play a D7 chord in a jazz piece, you can also play D9 or D13—sometimes it's actually expected of you! The D7 label simply tells you which family the chord is from (dominant); you can then choose from any chord that belongs to this family—such as the aforementioned D9 and D13. Study the chord formula chart: note the differences and similarities between chords—if the essential chord tones (3 and 7) are present in a given chord, you can probably use it as a substitute for any other chord in the same family.

Inversions

Inversions are the re-arrangement of chord tones so that the root is not the lowest note. The chord is still the same, but the bass note is a chord tone other than the root. Filling out an application is analogous: some ask for last name, first name; while others ask for first name, last name. Either way, it's still the same name, just a different order. The most common inversions are first inversion, which has the 3rd as the lowest note, second inversion, which has the 5th as the lowest note, and third inversion, which has the 7th as the lowest note.

Chords Without Roots

Some chord voicings have the root omitted, yet can still be easily identified in context. Why leave out roots? Well, depending on the situation, you may not have enough fingers or strings to play every single note of the chord, or you may want a leaner-sounding voicing. Because the 3rd and 7th of the chord provide the necessary harmonic information to define the chord, the root or 5th usually can be omitted without effecting the chord quality.

Chord Formula Chart

Chord Name	Formula	Derived Scale
Triads		
major	1 3 5	Ionian, Lydian
augmented	1 3 ♯5	whole tone, augmented
minor	1 ♭3 5	Aeolian, Dorian
diminished	1 ♭3 ♭5	Locrian, Diminished (Whole/Half)
sus4	1 4 5	Ionian, Mixolydian
sus2	1 2 5	Ionian, Mixolydian
Triads with Added Notes		
add9	1 3 5 9	Ionian, Lydian
madd9	1 ♭3 5 9	Aeolian, Dorian
6	1 3 5 6	Ionian, Lydian
m6	1 ♭3 5 6	Dorian, melodic minor
6/9	1 3 5 6 9	Ionian, Lydian
m6/9	1 ♭3 5 6 9	Dorian, melodic minor
dim7	1 ♭3 ♭5 ♭7	diminished (whole/half)
Major 7 Chords		
Maj7, Δ7, M7		
maj7	1 3 5 7	Ionian, Lydian
maj9	1 3 5 7 9	Ionian, Lydian
maj13	1 3 5 7 9 11 13	Ionian
Maj7♭5, Δ7♭5		
maj7♭5	1 3 ♭5 7	Ionian ♭5
maj9♭5	1 3 ♭5 7 9	Ionian ♭5

CHORD NAME	FORMULA	DERIVED SCALE
Maj7♯5, Δ7♯5		
maj7♯5	1 3 ♯5 7	Lydian augmented
maj9♯5	1 3 ♯5 7 9	Lydian augmented
maj7♯11♯5	1 3 ♯5 7 9 ♯11	Lydian augmented
maj9♯11♯5	1 3 ♯5 7 9 ♯11	Lydian augmented
maj13♯5	1 3 ♯5 7 9 (♯11) 13	Lydian augmented
maj13♯5♯11	1 3 ♯5 7 9 ♯11 13	Lydian augmented
Maj7♯11, Δ7♯11		
maj7♯11	1 3 5 7 9 ♯11	Lydian
maj9♯11	1 3 5 7 9 ♯11	Lydian
maj13♯11	1 3 5 7 9 ♯11 13	Lydian
Maj7♭6, Δ7♭6		
maj7♭6	1 3 5 ♭6 7	harmonic major, augmented scale
maj9♭6	1 3 5 ♭6 7 9	harmonic major
Maj7♯9, Δ7♯9		
maj7♯9	1 3 5 7 ♯9	Lydian ♯ 2
maj7♯9♯11	1 3 5 7 ♯9 ♯11	Lydian ♯ 2
maj7♯9♯5	1 3 ♯5 7 ♯9	Lydian augmented ♯ 2, augmented scale
maj7♯9♯11♯5	1 3 ♯5 7 ♯9 ♯11	Lydian augmented ♯ 2

Minor 7 Chords

m7, min7, –7		
m7	1 ♭3 5 ♭7	Dorian, Aeolian
m9	1 ♭3 5 ♭7 9	Dorian, Aeolian
m11	1 ♭3 5 ♭7 9 11	Dorian, Aeolian
m13	1 ♭3 5 ♭7 9 11 13	Dorian
m7♭13, min7♭13, –7♭13		
m7♭13	1 ♭3 5 ♭7 9 11 ♭13	Aeolian

CHORD NAME	FORMULA	DERIVED SCALE
m(maj7), min/maj7, –Δ7, mΔ7		
m(maj7)	1 ♭3 5 7	melodic minor, harmonic minor
m(maj9)	1 ♭3 5 7 9	melodic minor, harmonic minor
m(maj11)	1 ♭3 5 7 9 11	melodic minor, harmonic minor
m(maj13)	1 ♭3 5 7 9 11 13	melodic minor
m(maj7)♭13	1 ♭3 5 7 9 11 ♭13	harmonic minor
m7♭5, min7♭5, –7♭5, ø		
m7♭5	1 ♭3 ♭5 ♭7	Locrian ♮ 2, Locrian
m9♭5	1 ♭3 ♭5 ♭7 9	Locrian ♮ 2
m11♭5	1 ♭3 ♭5 ♭7 9 11	Locrian ♮ 2
m13♭5	1 ♭3 ♭5 ♭7 9 11 13	Dorian ♭5
m(maj7)♭5, min/maj7♭5, –7Δ♭5, dim/maj7, °maj7, °Δ7		
m(maj7)♭5	1 ♭3 ♭5 7	diminished (whole/half)
m(maj9)♭5	1 ♭3 ♭5 7 9	diminished (whole/half)
m(maj11)♭5	1 ♭3 ♭5 7 9 11	diminished (whole/half)
m(maj13)♭5	1 ♭3 ♭5 7 9 11 13	diminished (whole/half)
m(maj7)♭5♭13	1 ♭3 ♭5 7 9 11 ♭13	diminished (whole/half)
m7♯11, min7♯11, –7♯11		
m7♯11	1 ♭3 5 ♭7 9 ♯11	Dorian ♯ 4
m9♯11	1 ♭3 5 ♭7 9 ♯11	Dorian ♯ 4
m13♯11	1 ♭3 5 ♭7 9 ♯11 13	Dorian ♯ 4
m(maj7)7♯11, min/maj7♯11, –Δ7♯11, mΔ7♯11		
m(maj7)♯11	1 ♭3 5 7 9 ♯11	Lydian ♭3
m(maj9)♯11	1 ♭3 5 7 9 ♯11	Lydian ♭3
m(maj13)♯11	1 ♭3 5 7 9 ♯11 13	Lydian ♭3

Chord Name	Formula	Derived Scale

Dominant-Type Chords

Chord Name	Formula	Derived Scale
7		
7	1 3 5 ♭7	Mixolydian
9	1 3 5 ♭7 9	Mixolydian
11	1 3 5 ♭7 9 11	Mixolydian
13	1 3 5 ♭7 9 (11) 13	Mixolydian
7♭5		
7♭5	1 3 ♭5 ♭7	whole tone, Mixolydian ♭5
9♭5	1 3 ♭5 ♭7 9	whole tone, Mixolydian ♭5
7♯5, 7+5		
7♯5	1 3 ♯5 ♭7	whole tone
7♯5♯11	1 3 ♯5 ♭7 9 ♯11	whole tone
9♯5	1 3 ♯5 ♭7 9	whole tone
9♯5♯11	1 3 ♯5 ♭7 9 ♯11	whole tone
7♯11		
7♯11	1 3 5 ♭7 9 ♯11	Lydian ♭7
9♯11	1 3 5 ♭7 9 ♯11	Lydian ♭7
13♯11	1 3 5 ♭7 9 ♯11 13	Lydian ♭7
7sus4		
7sus4	1 4 5 ♭7	Mixolydian
9sus4	1 4 5 ♭7 9	Mixolydian
13sus4	1 4 5 ♭7 9 13	Mixolydian
7sus4♭9		
7sus4♭9	1 4 5 ♭7 ♭9	Dorian ♭2, Phrygian
13sus4♭9	1 4 5 ♭7 ♭9 13	Dorian ♭2
7sus4♭9♭13	1 4 5 ♭7 ♭9 ♭13	Phrygian dominant

CHORD NAME	FORMULA	DERIVED SCALE
7alt		
7♭9♭5	1 3 ♭5 ♭7 ♭9	Super Locrian
7♭9♭13	1 3 (♭5) ♭7 ♭9 ♭13	Super Locrian
7♭9♭13♭5	1 3 ♭5 ♭7 ♭9 ♭13	Super Locrian
7♯9♭5	1 3 ♭5 ♭7 ♯9	Super Locrian
7♯9♭13	1 3 (♭5) ♭7 ♯9 ♭13	Super Locrian
7♯9♭13♭5	1 3 ♭5 ♭7 ♯9 ♭13	Super Locrian
7♭9♯9♭5	1 3 ♭5 ♭7 ♭9 ♯9	Super Locrian
7♭9♯9♭13	1 3 (♭5) ♭7 ♭9 ♯9 ♭13	Super Locrian
7♭9♯9♭13♭5	1 3 ♭5 ♭7 ♭9 ♯9 ♭13	Super Locrian
7♭9, 13♭9, 7alt (if no 5 or 13 is present)		
7♭9	1 3 5 ♭7 ♭9	diminished (half/whole)
7♯9	1 3 5 ♭7 ♯9	diminished (half/whole)
7♭9♯9	1 3 5 ♭7 ♭9 ♯9	diminished (half/whole)
7♭9♯11	1 3 5 ♭7 ♭9 ♯11	diminished (half/whole)
7♯9♯11	1 3 5 ♭7 ♯9 ♯11	diminished (half/whole)
7♭9♯9♯11	1 3 5 ♭7 ♭9 ♯9 ♯11	diminished (half/whole)
13♭9	1 3 5 ♭7 ♭9 (♯11)13	diminished (half/whole)
13♯9	1 3 5 ♭7 ♯9 (♯11)13	diminished (half/whole)
13♭9♯9	1 3 5 ♭7 ♭9 ♯9 (♯11) 13	diminished (half/whole)
13♭9♯11	1 3 5 ♭7 ♭9 ♯11 13	diminished (half/whole)
13♯9♯11	1 3 5 ♭7 ♯9 ♯11 13	diminished (half/whole)
13♭9♯9♯11	1 3 5 ♭7 ♭9 ♯9 ♯11 13	diminished (half/whole)
11♭9		
11♭9	1 3 5 ♭7 ♭9 11	Phyrgian dominant

How to Use This Book

Reading Chord Diagrams

Chord diagrams are a graphic representation of a small portion of the guitar neck and are used to show the note location and fingering of specific chord voicings. The perspective of a chord diagram is as if you are looking at a guitar on a stand in front of you (see the diagram below). The horizontal lines represent frets and the vertical lines represent strings. (Note: The 6th string is the thickest, lowest-sounding string.) To the right of the diagram is a fret marker, which indicates the specific fret the chord is to be played on. The only time you will not see fret markers is in the open-position, where the lowest fret is the first fret and a nut is shown as part of the chord grid. Directly below the diagram are two sets of characters: The top set indicates the fingering, the bottom set shows the harmonic function of each note as it relates to the *root,* or note the chord is built upon.

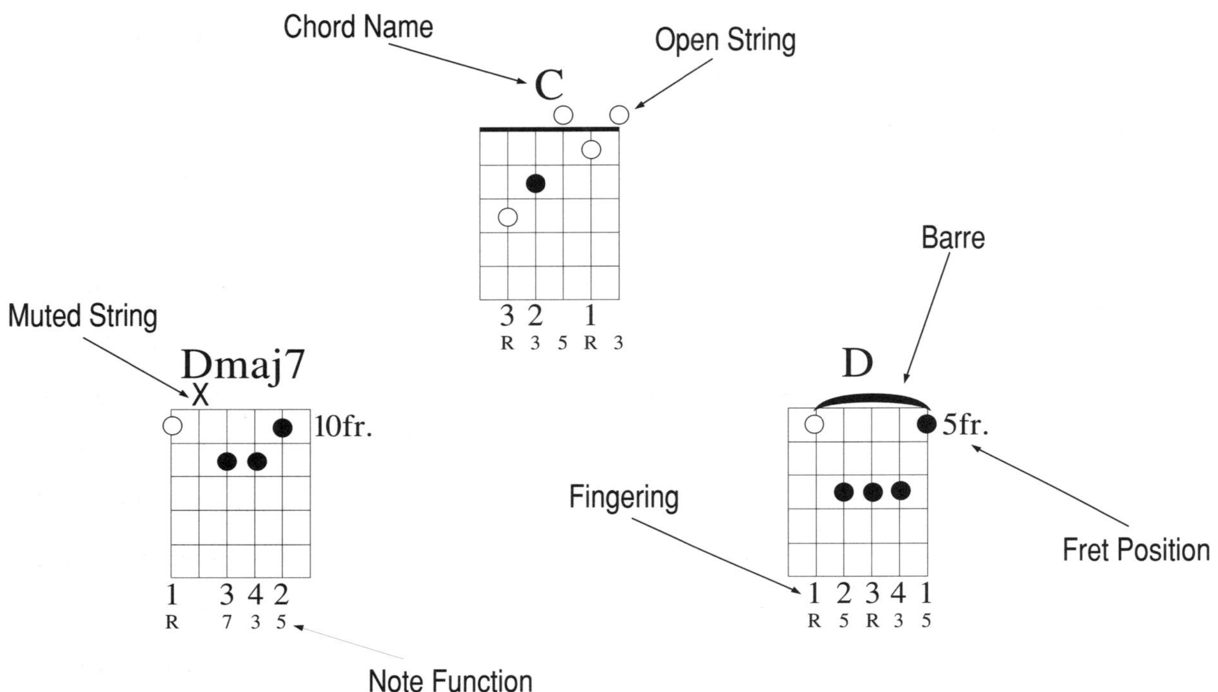

Using the *Chord-Finder System*™

The main purpose of this book is to give you a quick and easy reference to locating the positions of thousands of chords, and for that we have designed the *Chord-Finder System.* This unique tool is shown at the top of every page (of moveable chords) as a display of fret numbers with corresponding notes. Every chord uses D as a root (or, in the case of inversions, as a bass note), which is displayed as a white circle in the chord diagram (and also over the D note location in the *Chord-Finder System* on the top of the page). To move any chord to a different root, find the new root using the *Chord-Finder System.* Say you want to play an Fmaj7 chord: Turn to the page entitled Major 7–Type Chords and choose a Dmaj7 chord shape. Let's suppose you picked a Dmaj7 based on the 5th string, 5th fret. Look at the *Chord-Finder System* and find the location of F on this string, which happens to be the 8th fret. Just move the whole chord from the 5th fret to the 8th fret and you have an Fmaj7 chord!

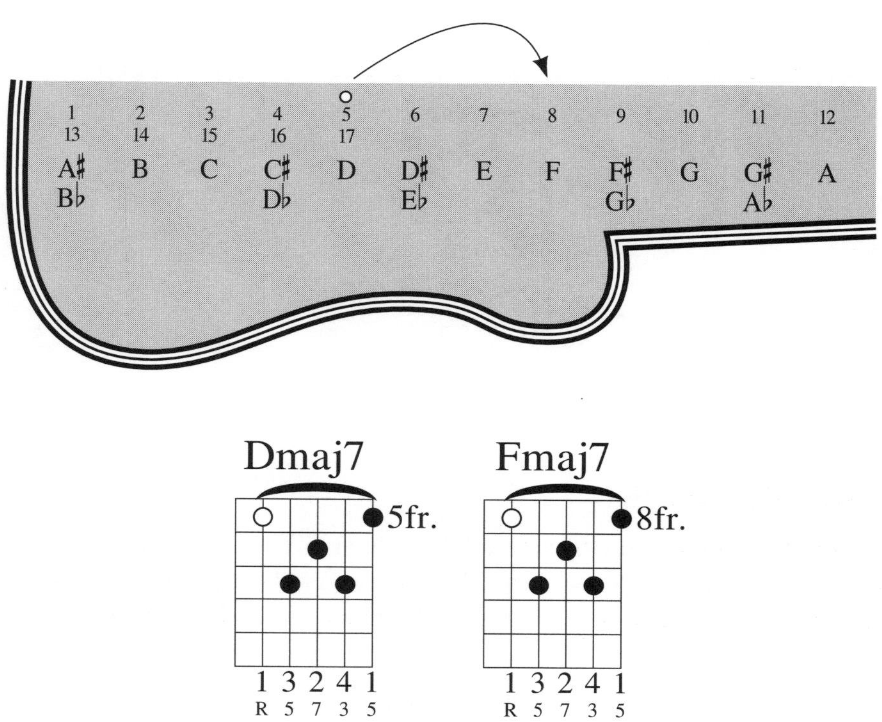

If the chord is an inversion, the note to the left of the slash in the *Chord-Finder System* is the root and the note to the right (which will be your reference) is the bass note.

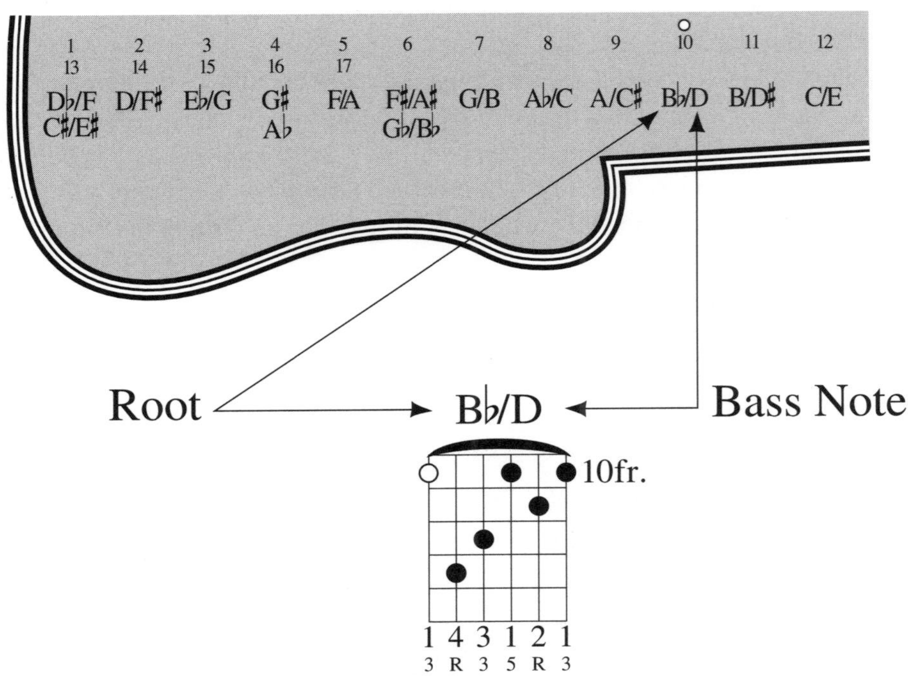

The Presentation of Moveable Chords

Here are some general guidelines to the presentation of moveable chords in this book. (This applies to the headings found in the upper right-hand corner of each page.) There are two general categories of chords—non-7th chords, which include triads and triads with added notes, and 7th chords, which include major 7th, minor 7th, and dominant 7th chords.

The Non-7th Chords

- Non-7th chords include major, minor, diminished, augmented, sus2, sus4, 6, m6, 6/9, m6/9, add9, and madd9 and are grouped by their general quality. For example, as major, 6, 6/9, and add9 chords are all major chords, and sus and aug chords are closely related to them, they are all presented on the same page.
- Inversions of non-7th chords that share the same root and bass note are grouped on the same page. For example, as first inversion minor and first inversion diminished chords have the same root and bass note, they appear on the same page.

The 7th Chords

- All 7th chords are arranged by family (major, minor, dominant).
- Major 7 chords, and their inversions, have a major 3rd and a major 7th.
- Minor 7 chords, and their inversions, have a minor 3rd and a minor or major 7th.*
- Dominant-type chords, and their inversions, have a major 3rd (or in the case of 7sus4-type chords, a perfect 4th) and a minor 7th.

Any of the above chords may have altered 5ths and/or 9ths, and may have extensions and altered extensions, according to common practice.

*Note: When used as a *page heading,* "Minor 7" represents all seventh chords that include a minor 3rd. When used as a *chord name* (m7) it retains its usual definition, that is, the chord 1 ♭3 5 ♭7.

Root Position and Inversions

- Chords are shown in root position and inversions, in the following order:
  Root position on the 6th, 5th, and 4th strings.
  First inversion on the 6th, 5th, and 4th strings.
  Second inversion on the 6th, 5th, and 4th strings.
  Third inversion on the 6th, 5th, and 4th strings.
- All triads (major, minor, diminished, augmented, sus2, sus4) conclude with a 3rd-string root and are shown from root position to second inversion.
- All triads with added notes, except dim7, are shown from root position to second inversion. Dim7 is shown from root position to third inversion.

Choosing Fingerings

Although carefully chosen fingerings have been provided for every chord in this book, you may find the need to re-finger some voicings to suit a particular situation. Here are some general guidelines:

1) Try to minimize finger movement from one chord to the next. If you can keep the same finger on the same note throughout the chord change then do so, otherwise move as little as needed.

2) Always assess the progression and choose a fingering accordingly. What may work for a single isolated chord may not allow for rapid change throughout a progression.

3) Whenever there is a stretch involved, use your outer fingers. First finger for stretches toward the headstock and pinkie for stretches toward the bridge.

4) If two or more notes are on the same fret but different strings you may be able to use a *barre.* (A barre is the straightening of a finger to hold down two or more strings. It is shown in the diagrams as a curved line). The barre should be employed only if it will not obstruct the path of another string being played.

Essential Chords

The "Essential Chords" chapter presents the most prevalent and universal of guitar chords. All guitarists, regardless of style, know them: Learn these first!

Chords Using Open Strings

The "Chords Using Open Strings" chapter is similar to the "Essential Chords" chapter, in that they use one or more open strings and are playable only in their specific location, but this is where the similarities end. In this chapter the chords range from simple embellishments of open chords—such as Cadd9—to more exotic chords—such as D♭7♯11—and can function as substitutes for their open-chord cousins.

Moveable Chords

Moveable chords are the logical evolution of open chords. They are predicated on the fact that all chords of the same quality are exactly the same, regardless of root. Just as your name is still exactly the same whether written with a black pen or a blue pen, a maj7 chord is a maj7 chord, be it Dmaj7 or Fmaj7. This is where the magic of the *Chord-Finder System* comes into play. When you learn one chord, you learn 12 chords, because all 12 chords have the same exact shape—they just start on a different fret. Simply find the fret that corresponds to the desired root and you have your chord.

To experience how moveable chords have evolved from their open chord cousins, try this: Play an open A chord, but re-finger it with 2, 3, and 4 (as opposed to the indicated 1, 2, and 3). Now, move that chord up one fret and play it—sounds pretty cool, but it's not the same kind of sound. Why? Well, every note moved uniformly *except* the open strings, which remained in their original location. This is why we need to use barres. Take your 1st finger and flatten it across the top 5 strings at the first fret. The barre simulates the nut, and creates faux open strings, if you will. The shape and quality of the chord is maintained, it is simply moved to a different location. The root has changed from the open 5th string to the 5th string, 1st fret, which the *Chord-Finder System* tells you is B♭. You now have a B♭ chord!

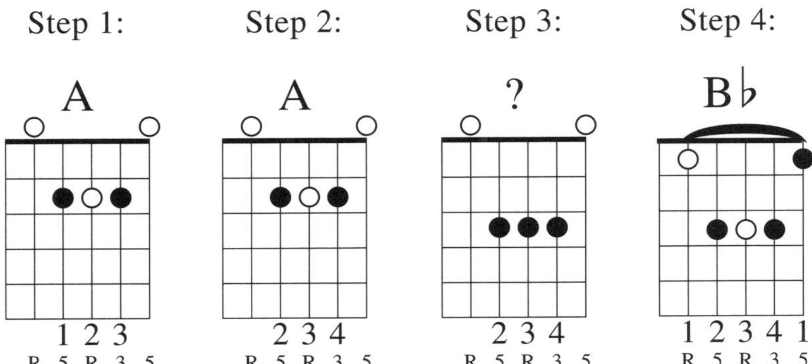

Non-Tertian Chords

Non-tertian chords are not built in thirds: Other intervallic relationships, such as consecutive 4ths (quartal), consecutive 5ths (quintal), and consecutive 2nds (secundal), generate non-tertian harmony. These chords can function as substitutes for tertian chords, or stand alone as valid harmonic entities. Another approach to creating non-tertian voicings is to use different interval combinations—rather than exclusively using 4ths or 5ths—to create an intervallic-structure. Non-tertian chords are used mostly in modal and harmonically less-restrictive music.

The non-tertian chords in this book are all based on a D root for the four most common scales (major, melodic minor, harmonic minor, and harmonic major), and are arranged diatonically from the lowest fret of the lowest string in the voicing. Above each diagram is a number indicating the scale degree of the bass note for the voicing. Try using some of these voicings for chord-soloing—you'll sound like Wes Montgomery meets Allan Holdsworth.

Essential Chords

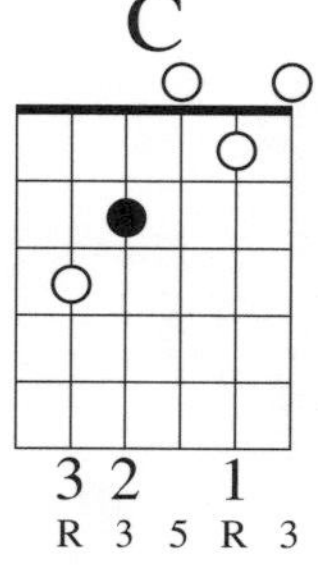

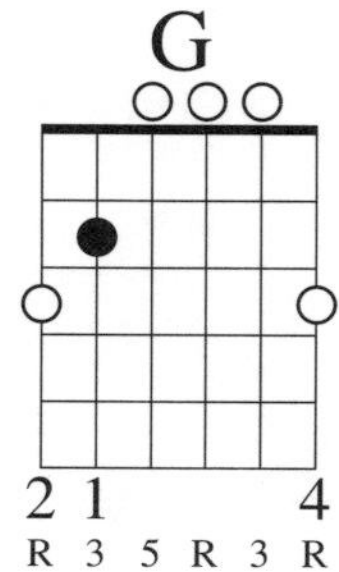

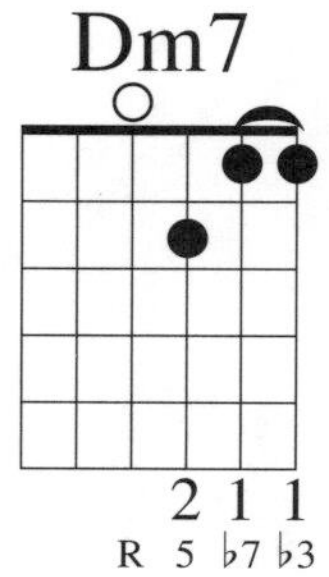

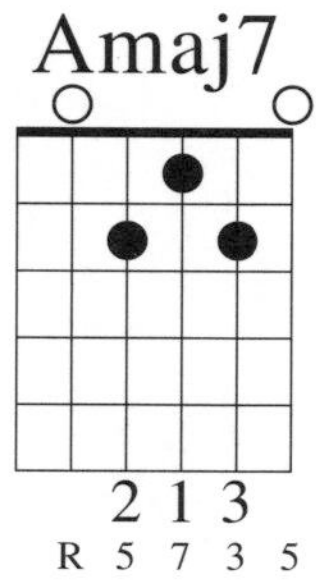

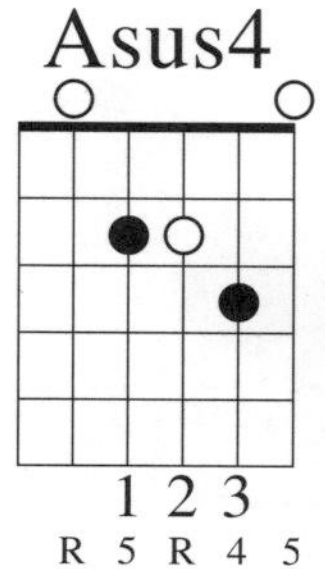

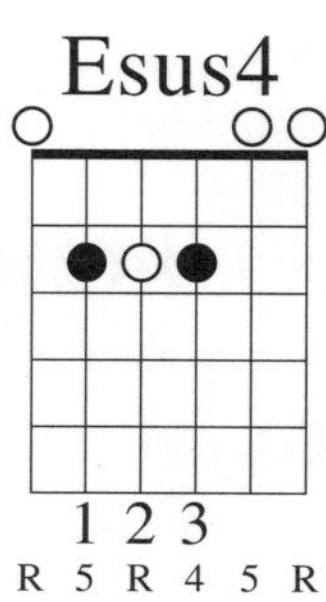

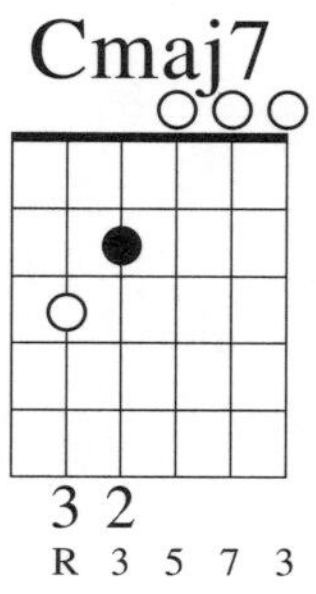

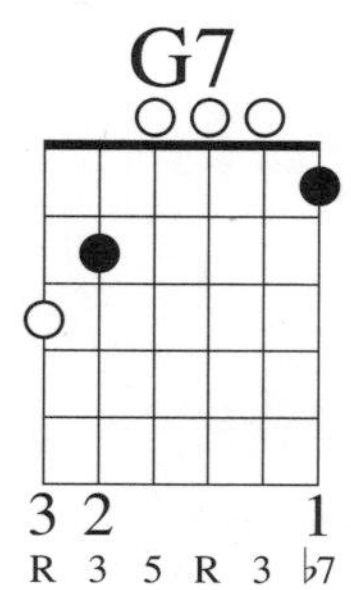

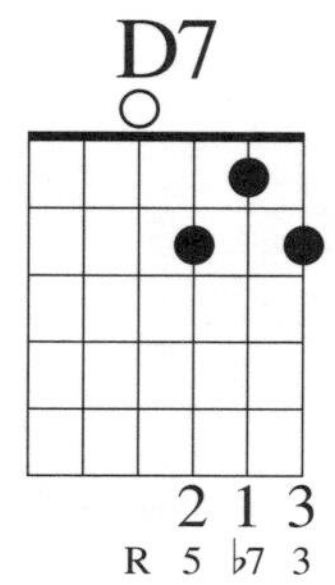

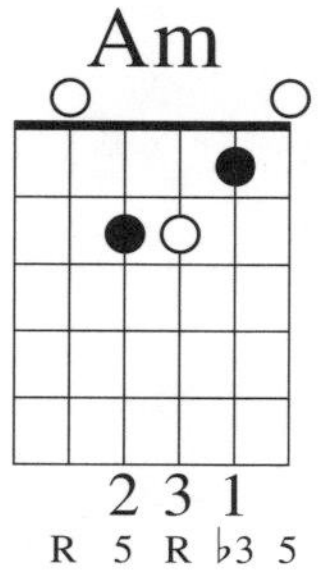

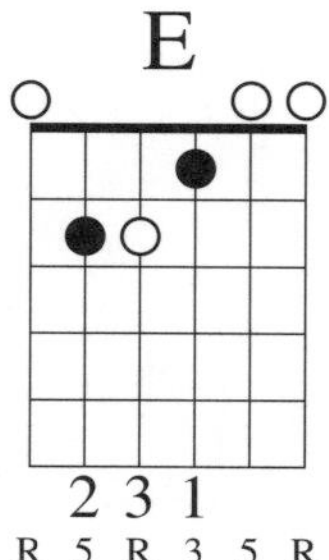

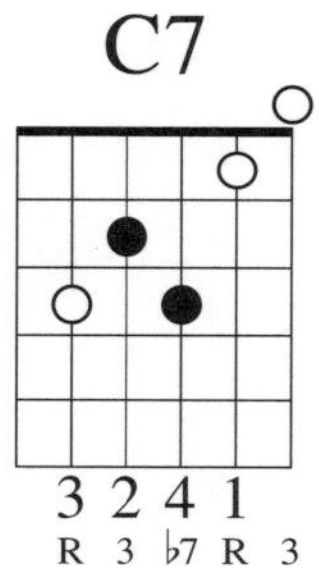

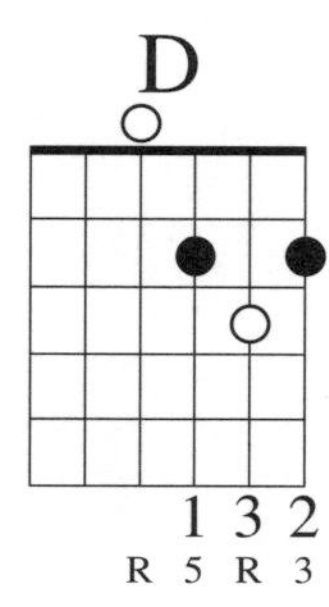

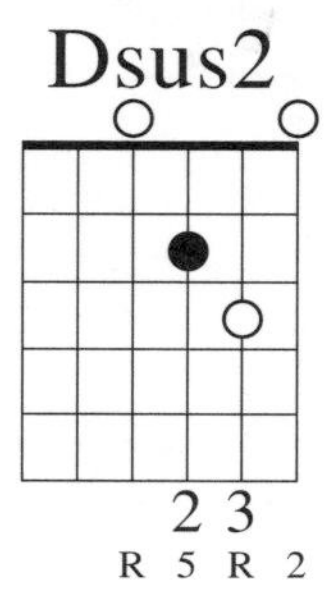

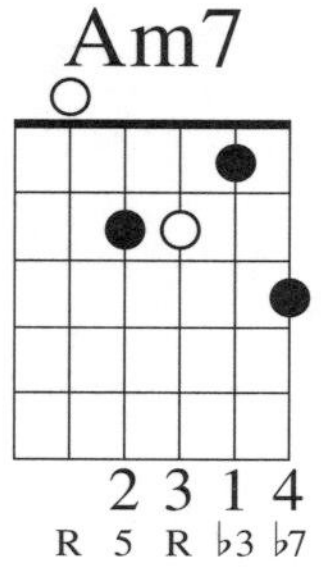

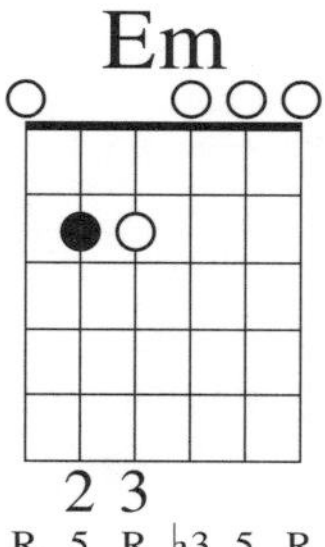

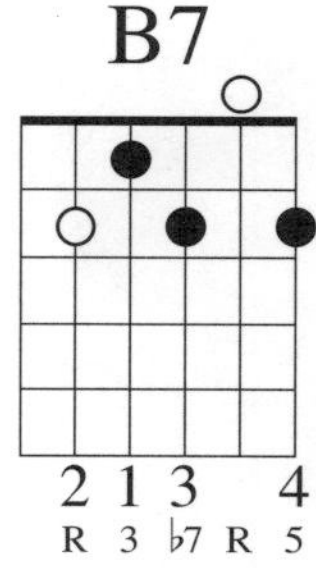

Cm
3 1 2
R ♭3 5 R

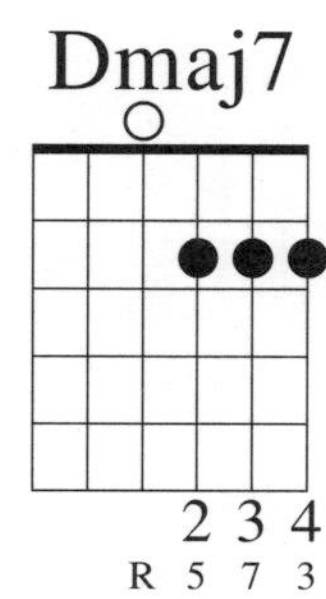

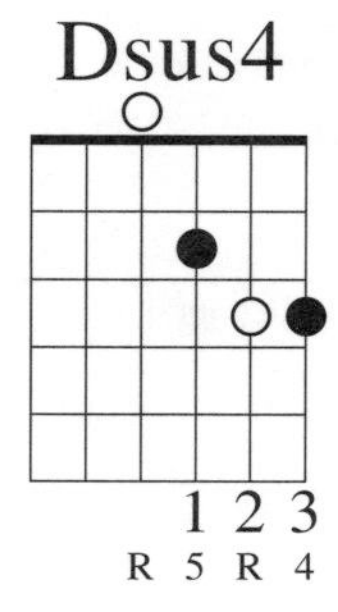

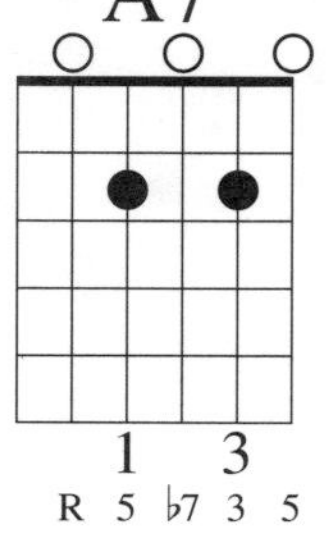

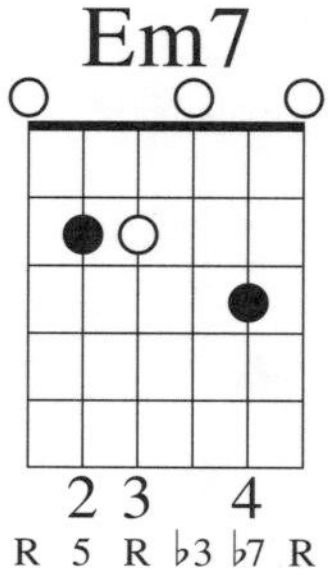

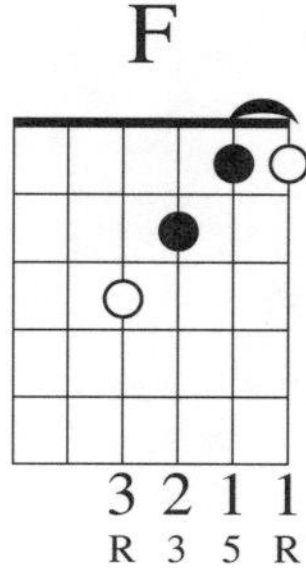

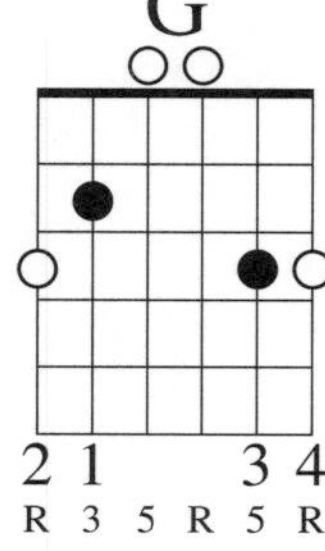

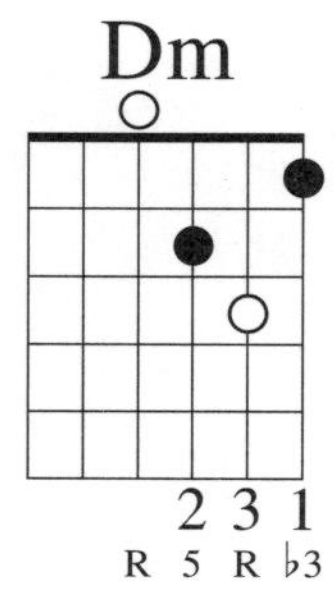

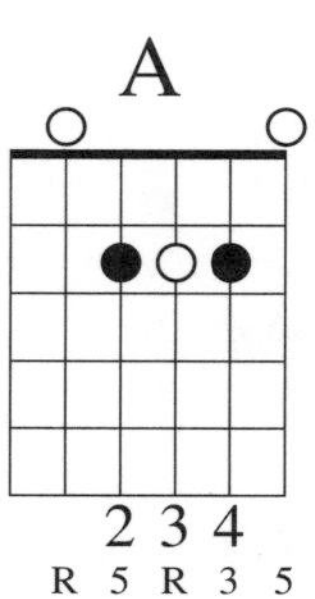

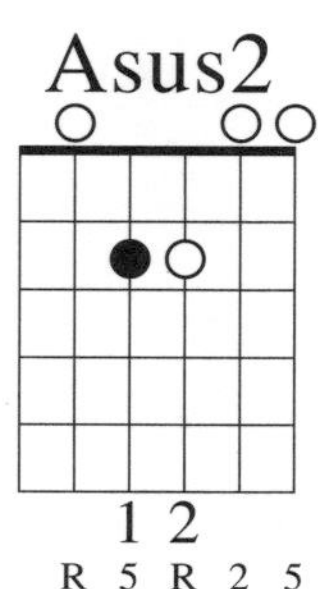

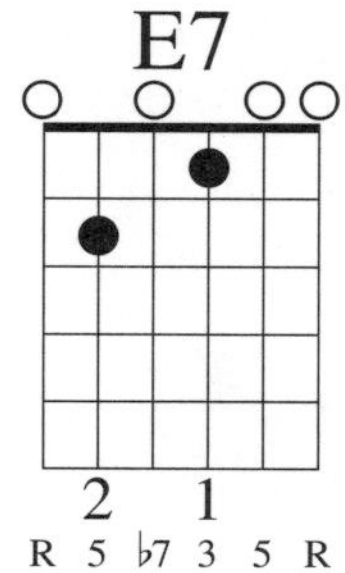

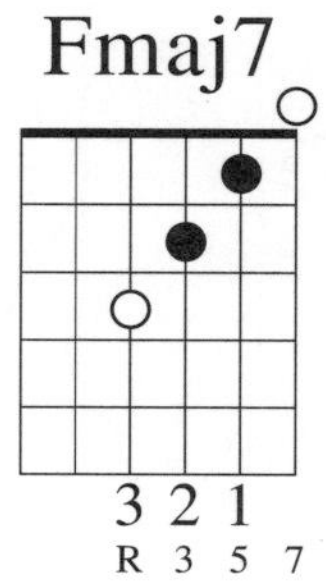

Chords with Open Strings

C Chords

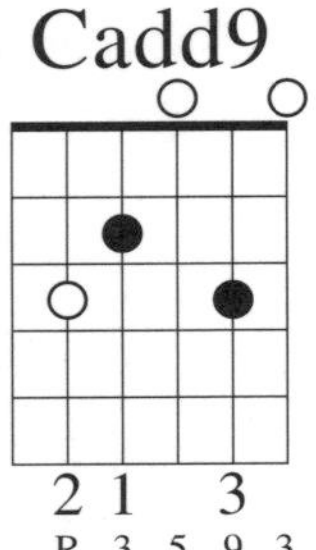

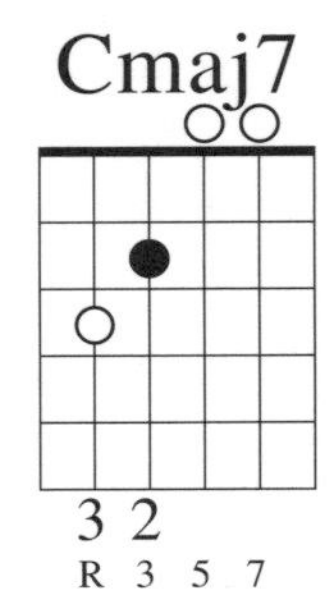

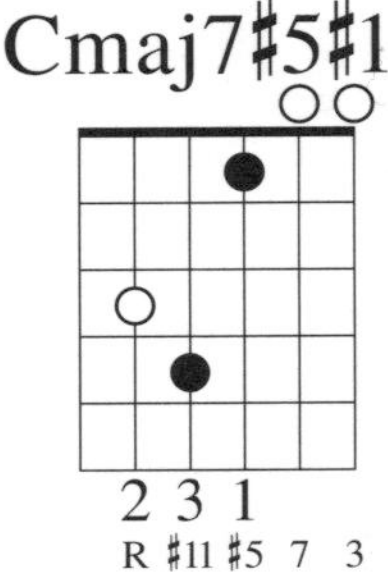

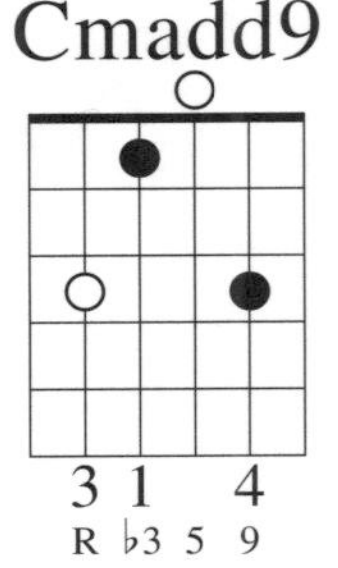

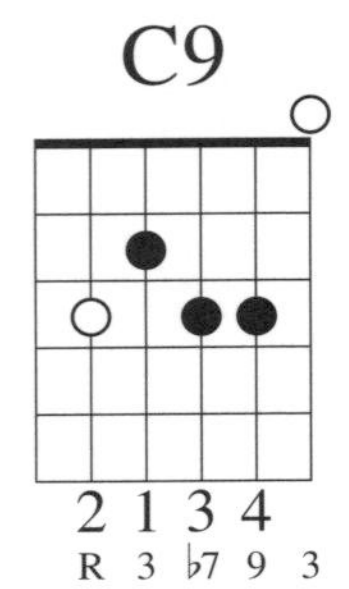

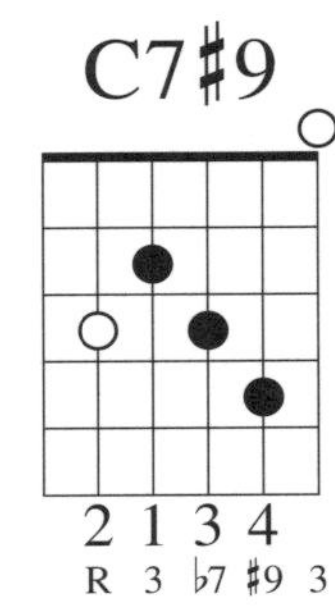

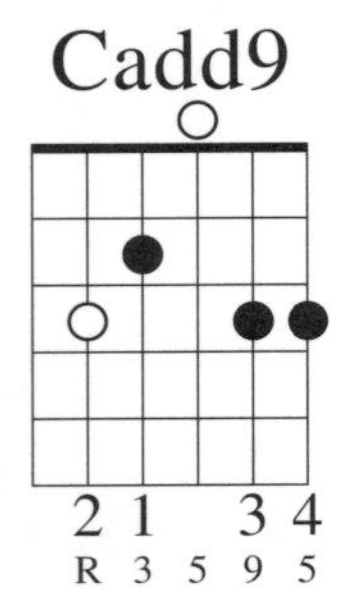

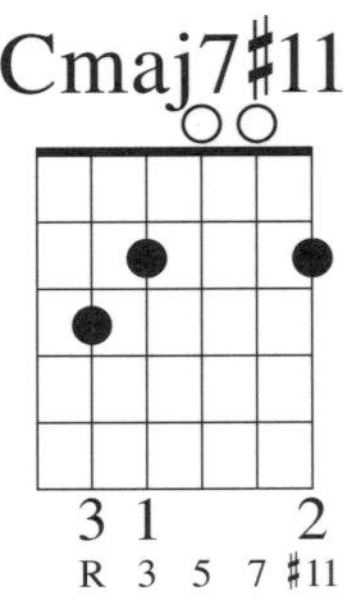

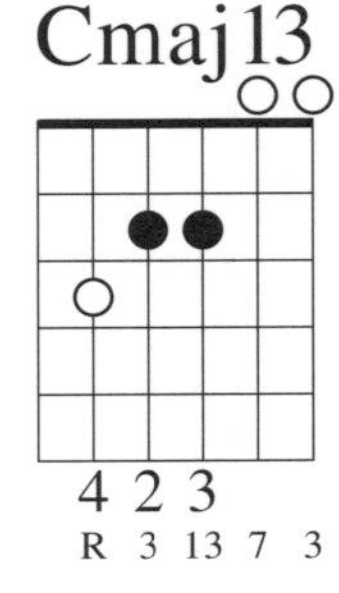

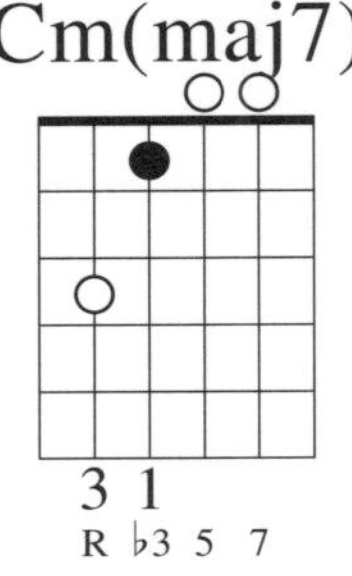

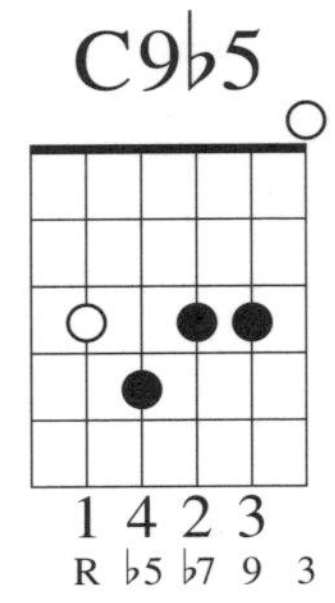

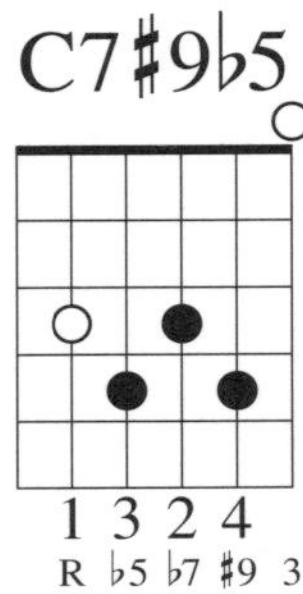

G Chords

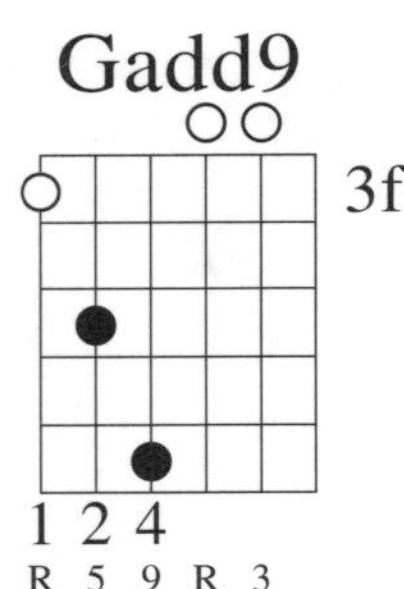

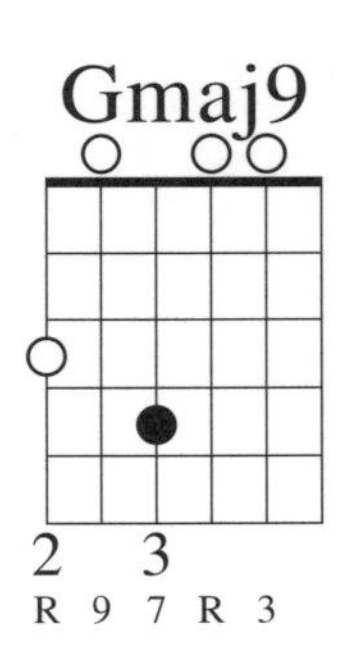

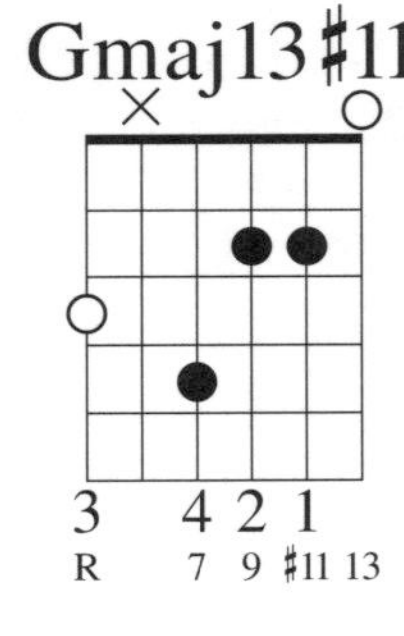

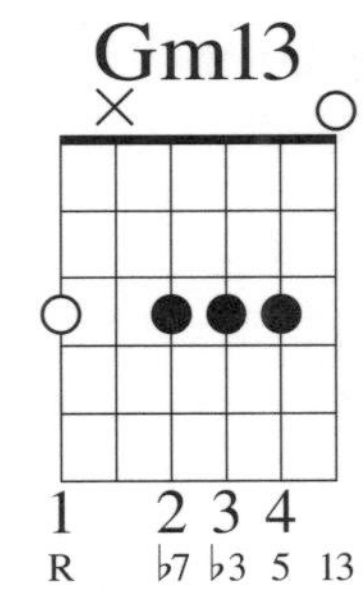

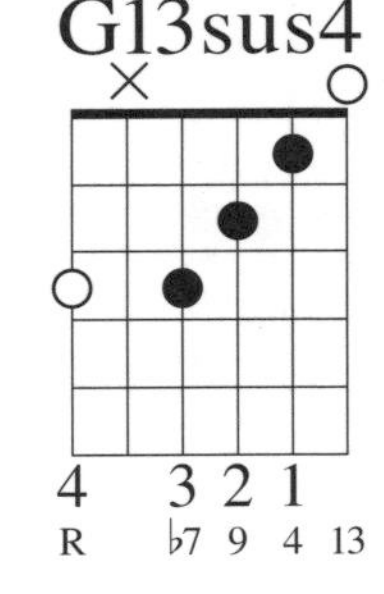

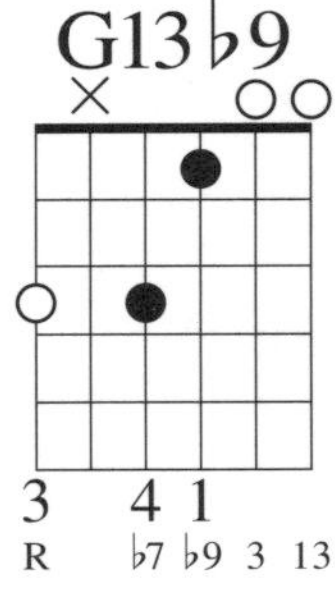

Gmaj7

2 1 3

R 3 5 R 3 7

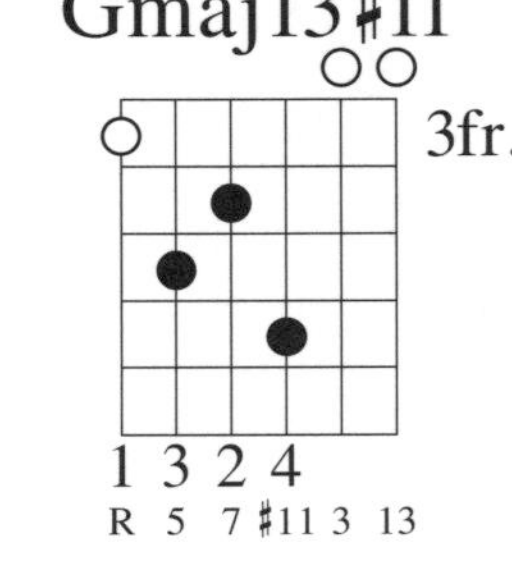

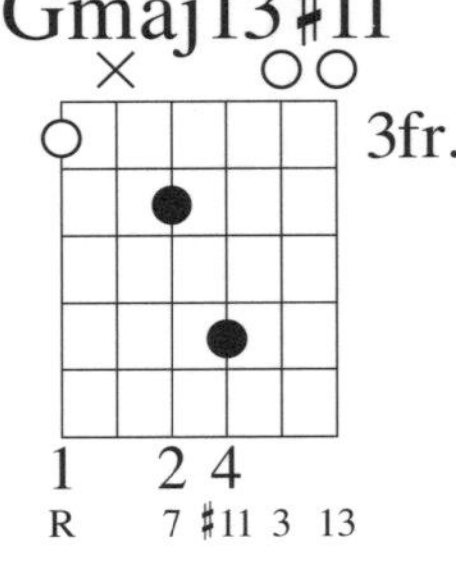

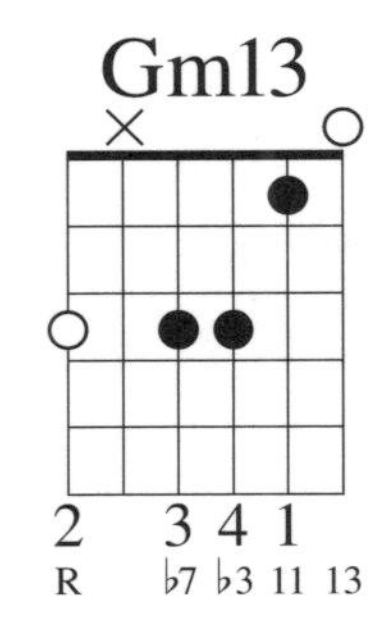

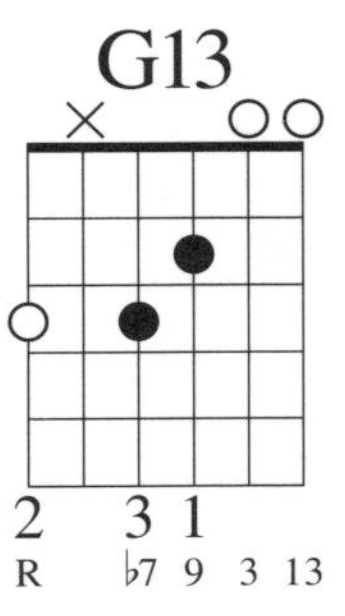

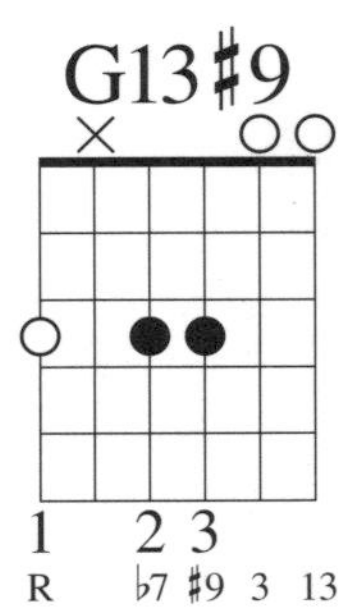

Chords with Open Strings

D Chords

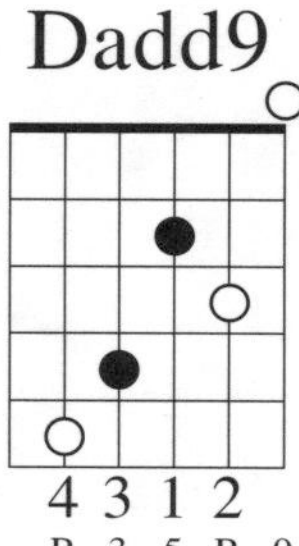

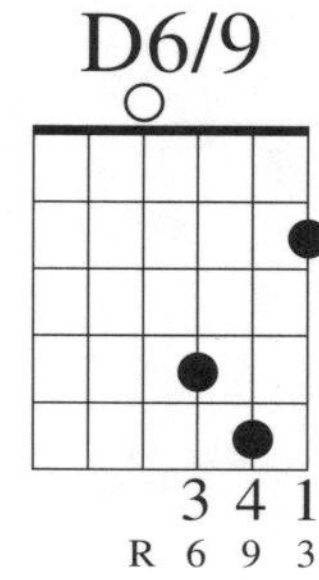

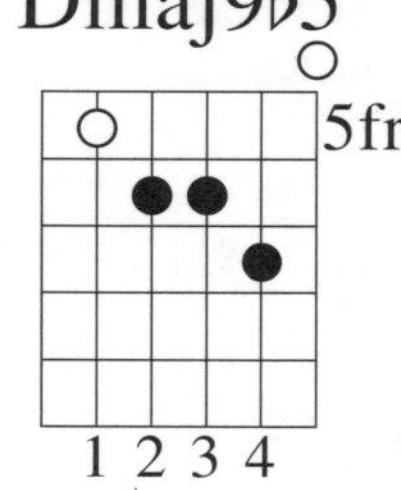

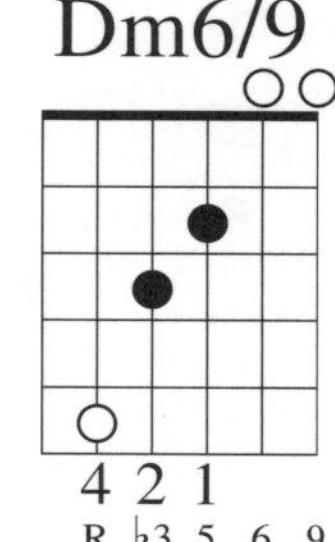

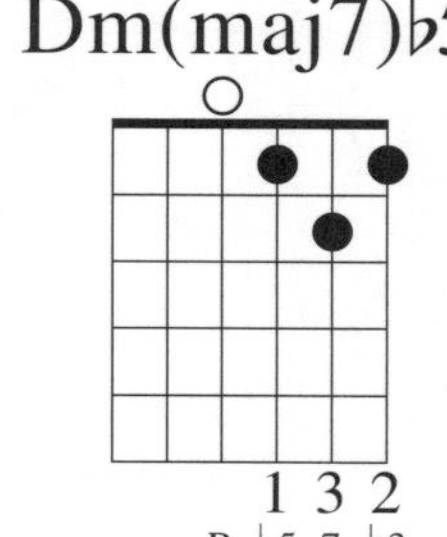

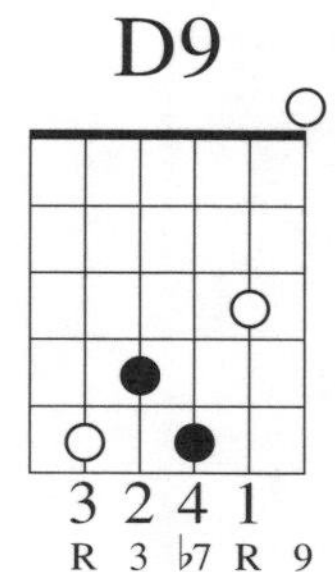

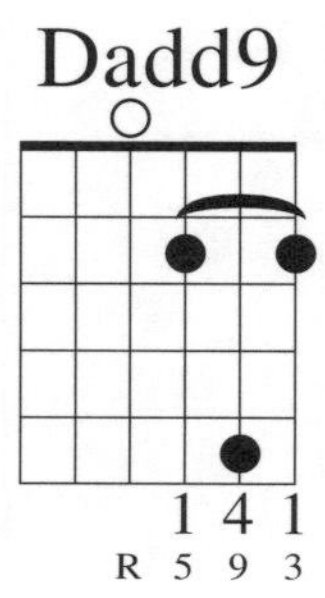

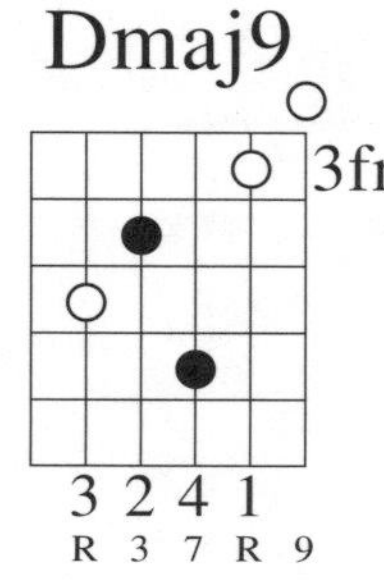

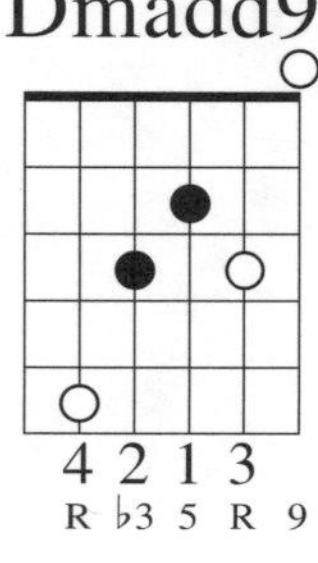

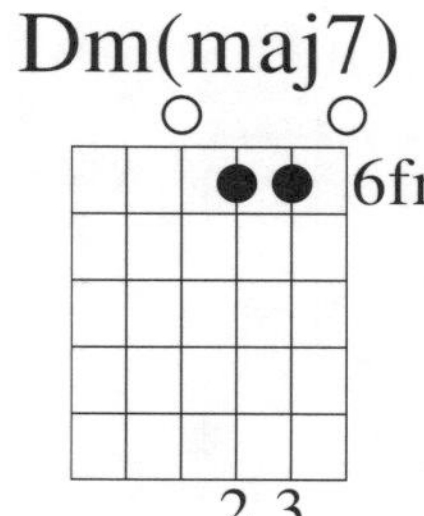

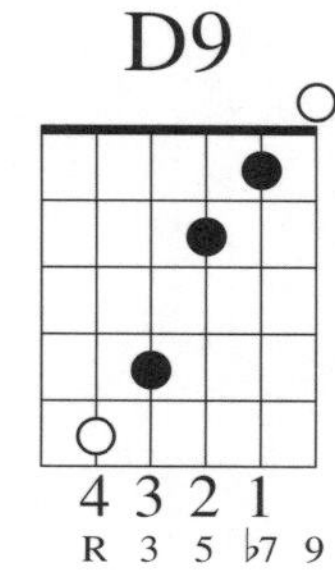

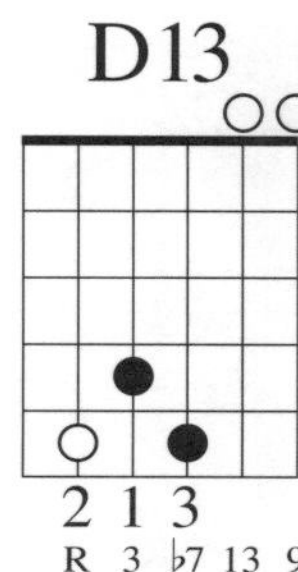

A Chords

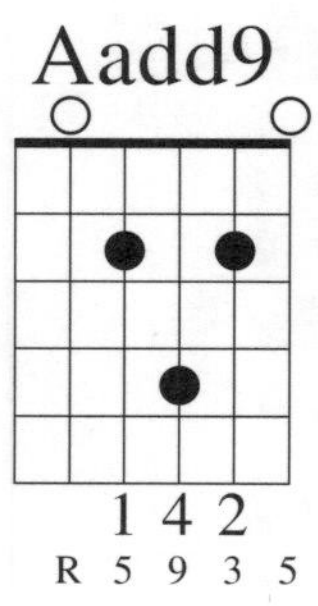

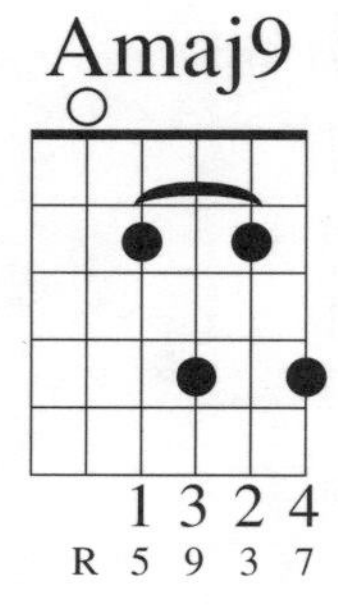

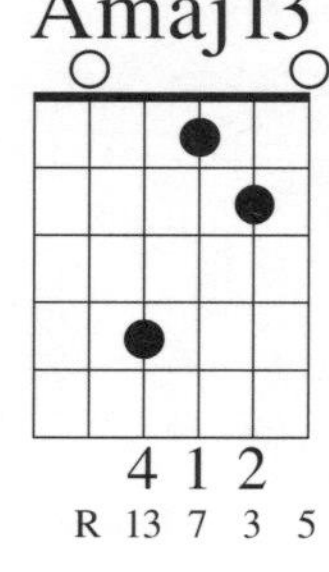

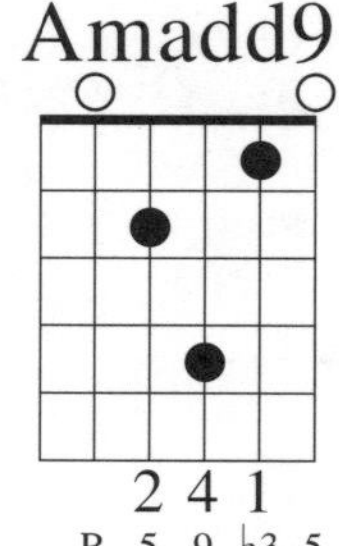

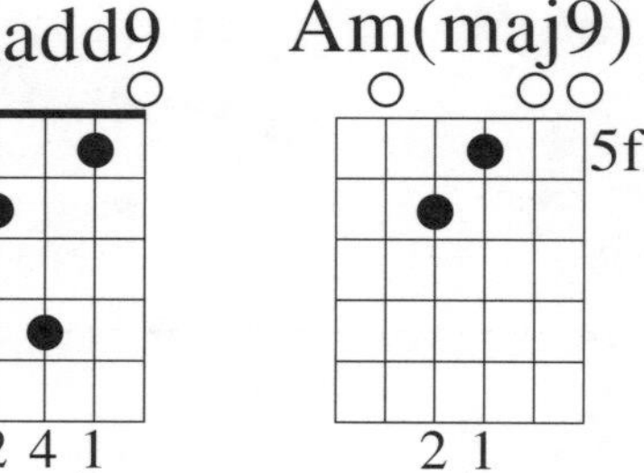

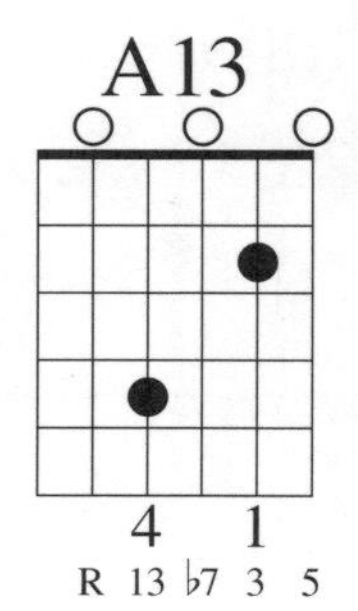

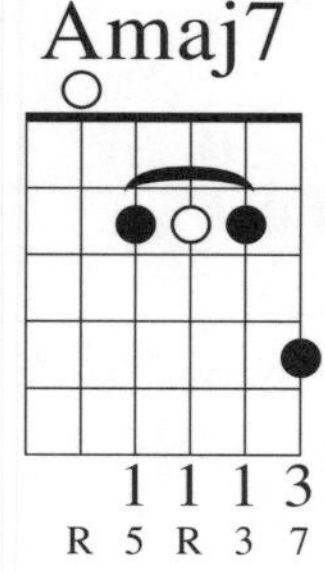

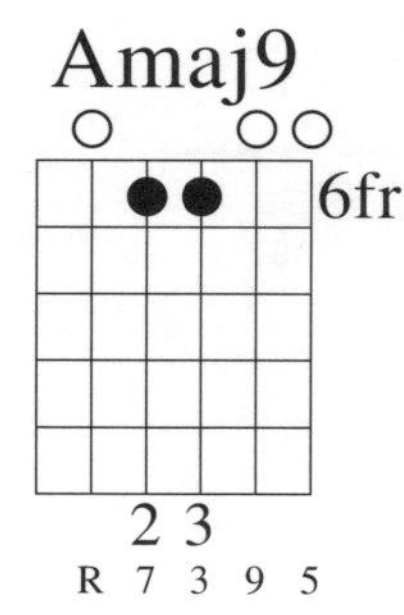

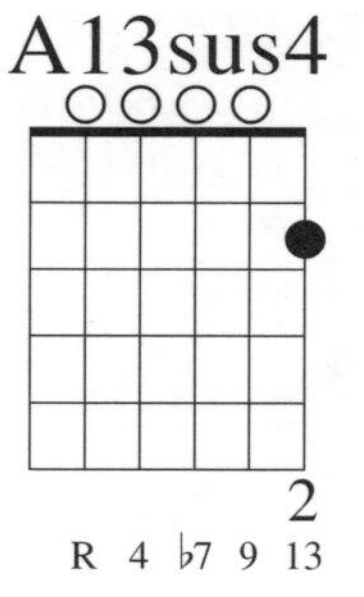

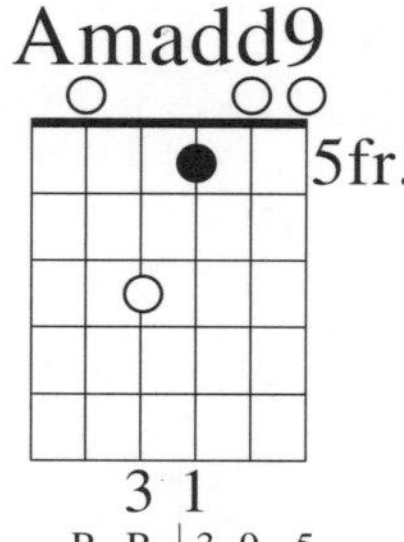

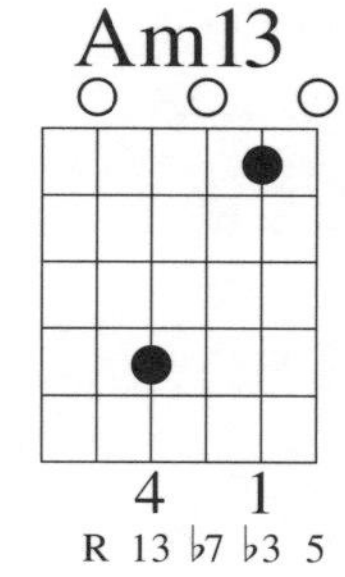

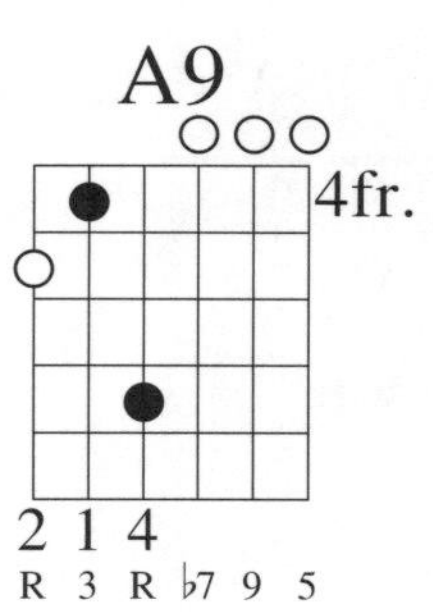

Chords with Open Strings

E Chords

Eadd9

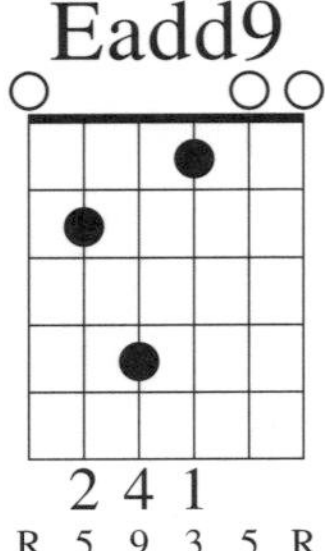

Emaj7♯5

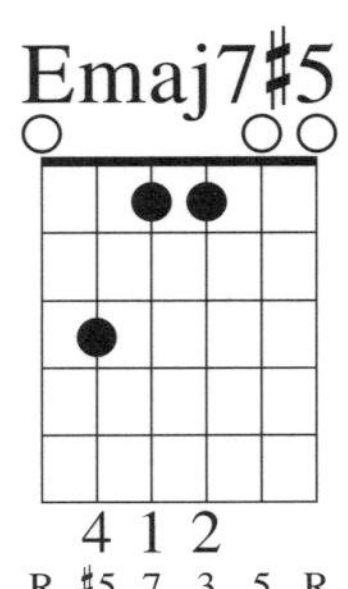

Em6

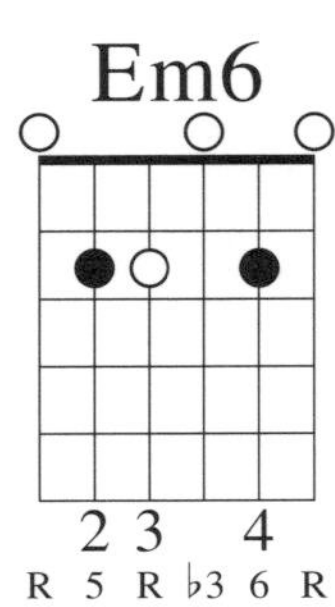

Em11♭5

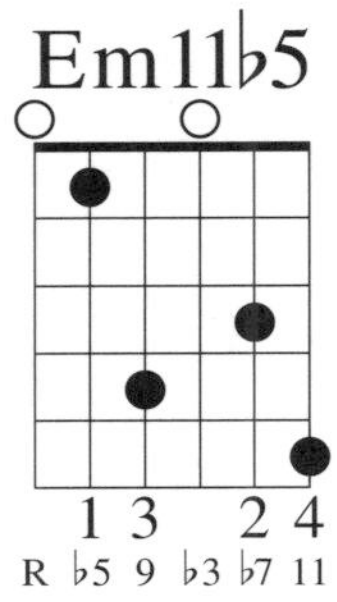

E9

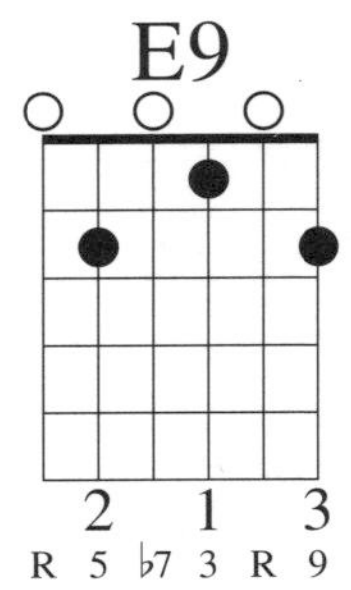

E13♭9

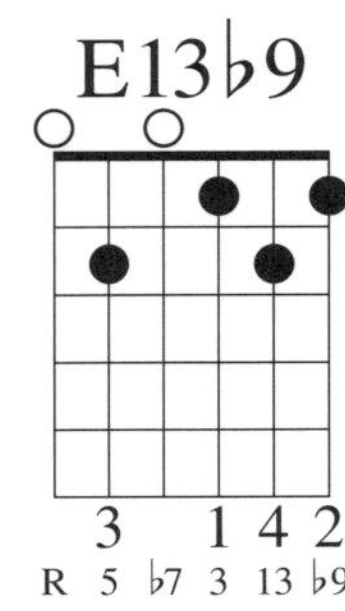

Emaj7

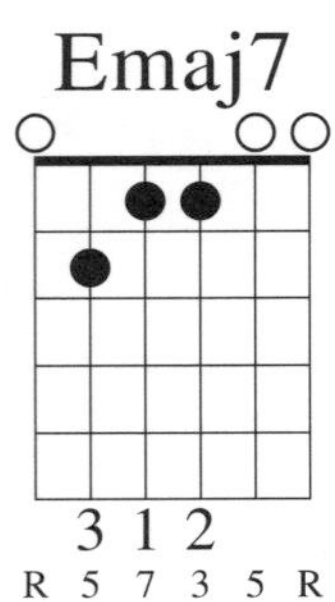

Emadd9

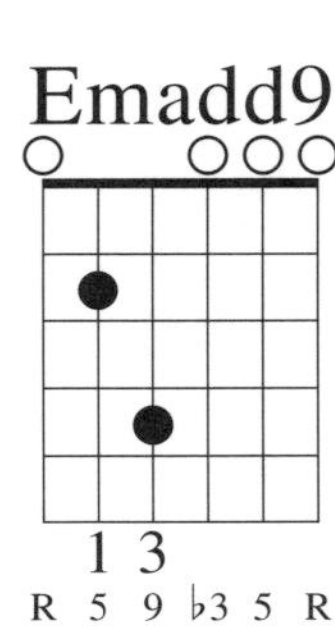

Em11

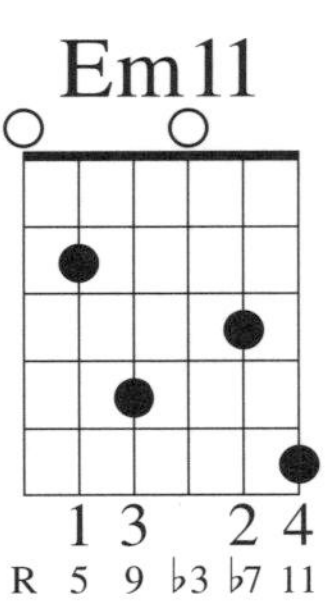

E7sus4

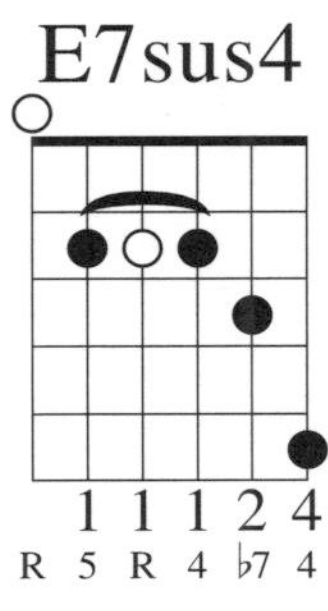

E13

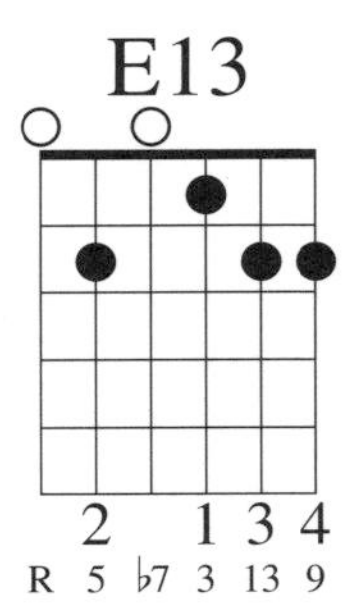

E13♯9

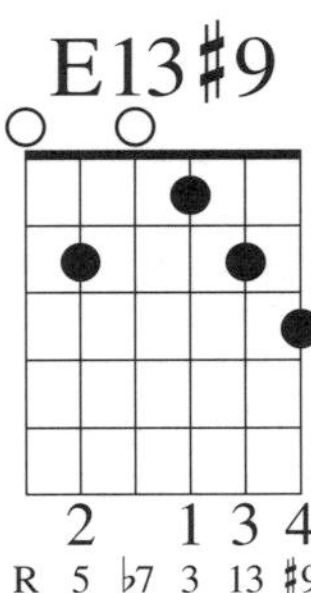

B Chords

Bmaj7

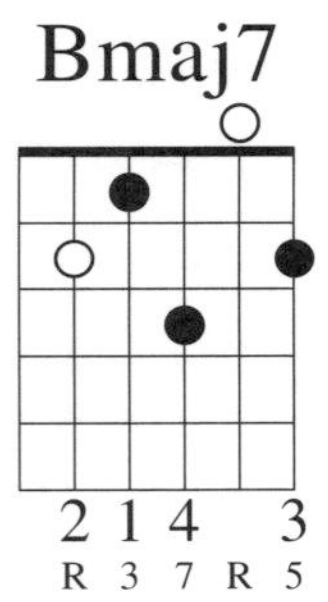

Bmaj9

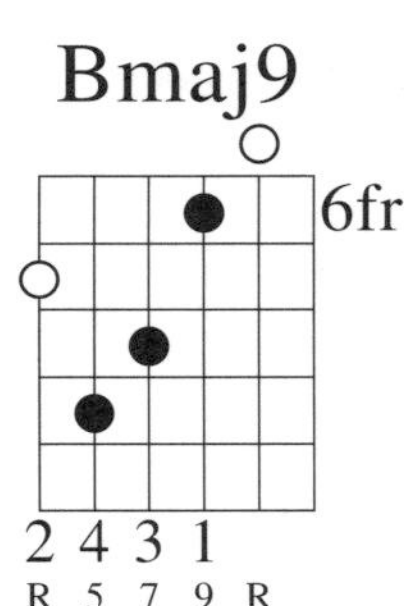

Bm11

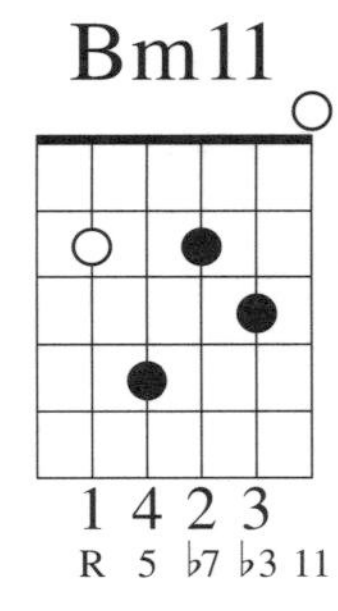

B7sus4

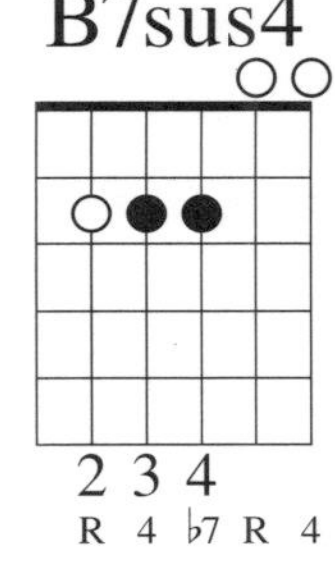

B13sus4

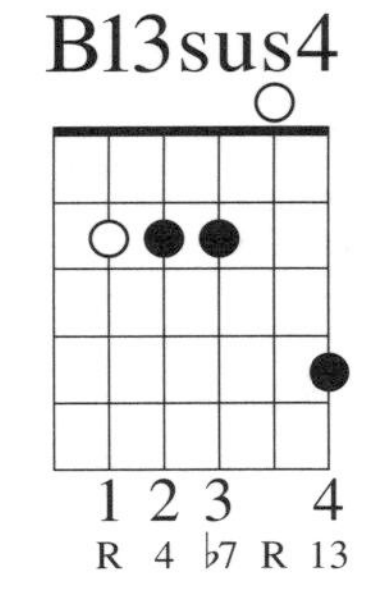

Bm11♭5

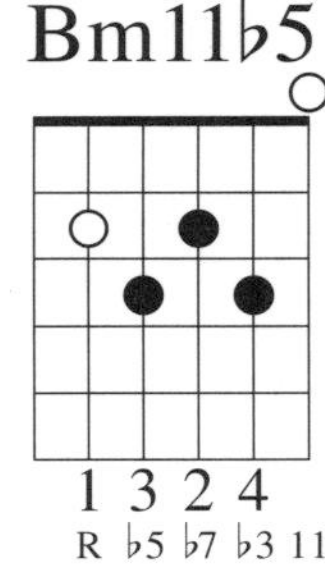

Bmaj13

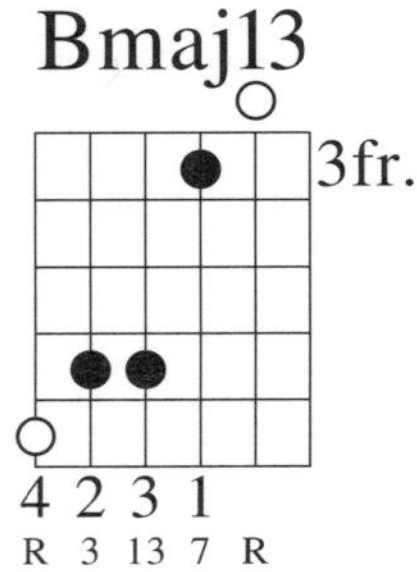

Bm11

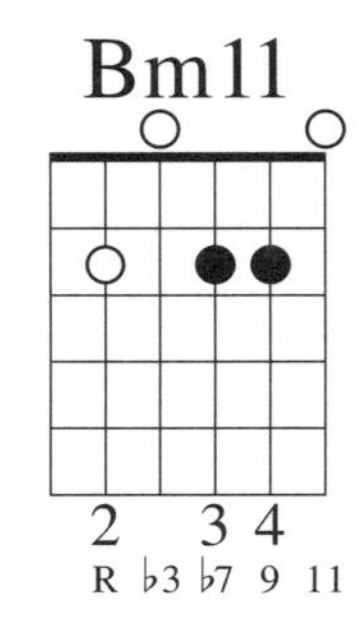

Bm11

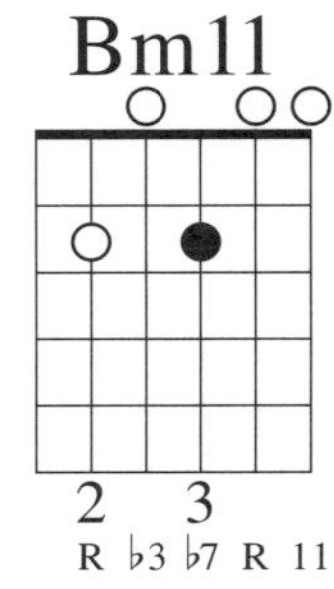

B7sus4

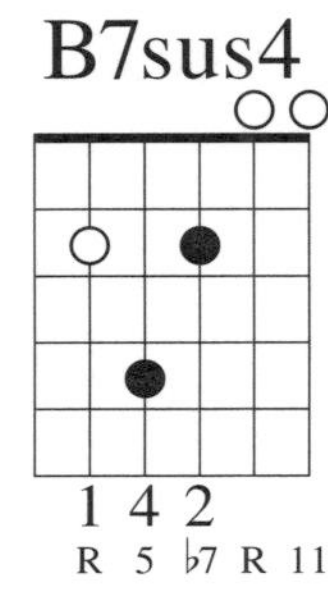

B7♯5

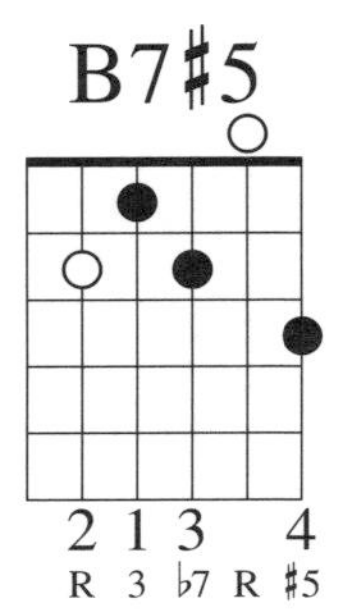

Bm11♭5

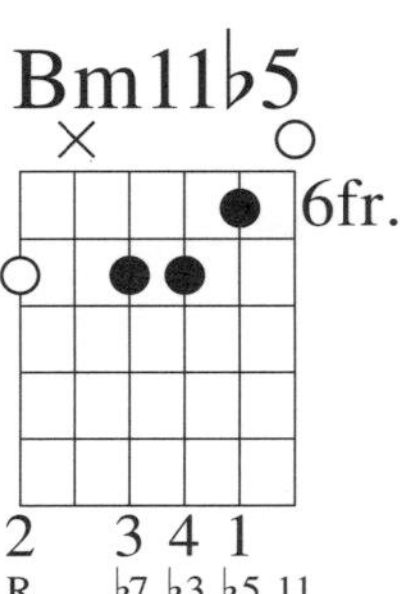

Chords with Open Strings

G♭(F♯) Chords

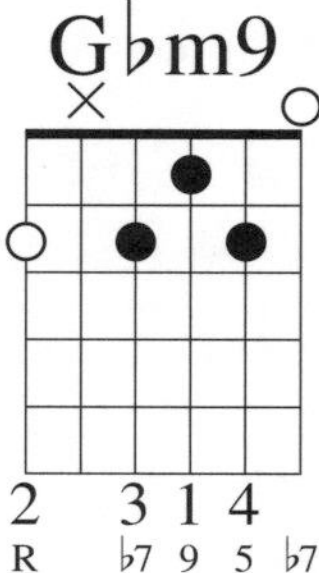

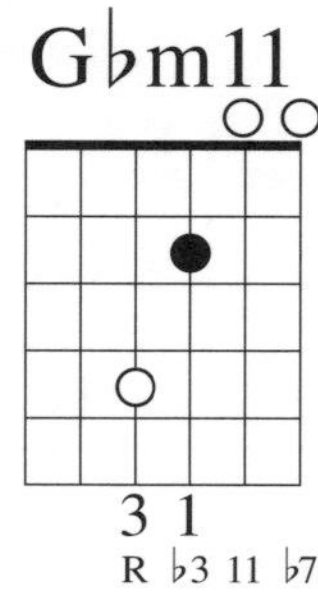

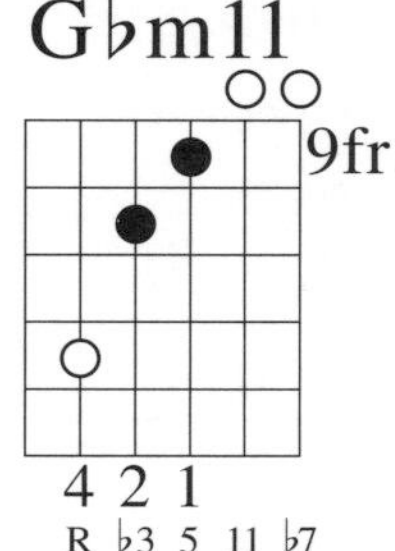

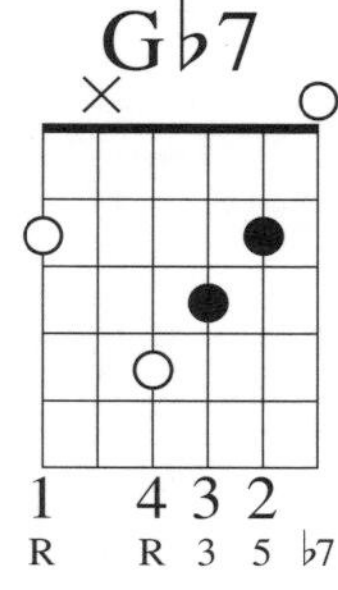

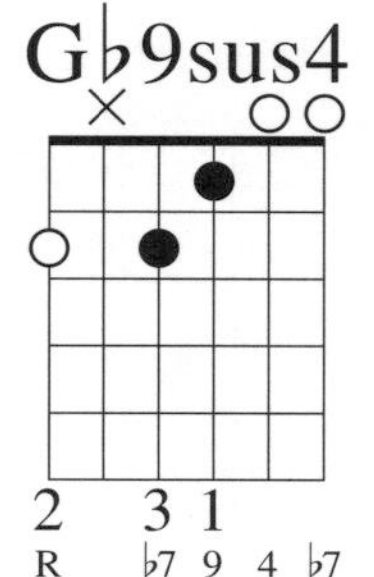

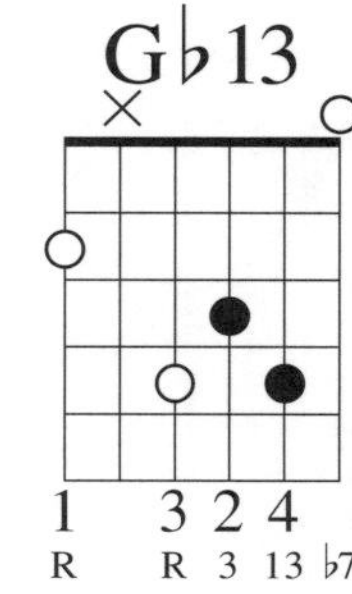

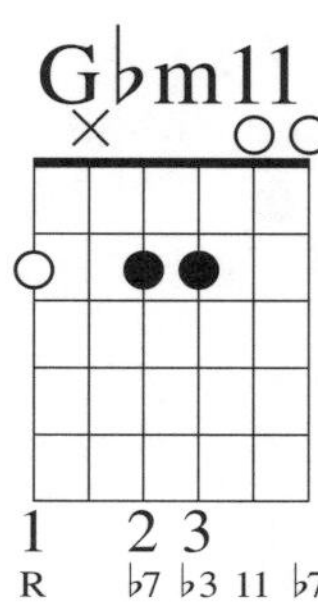

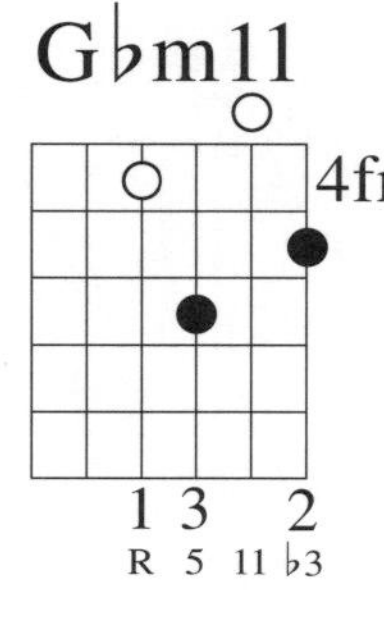

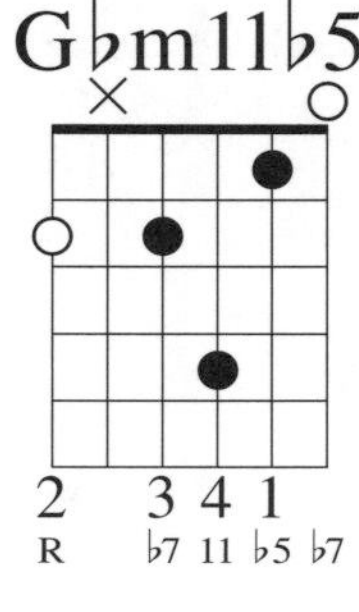

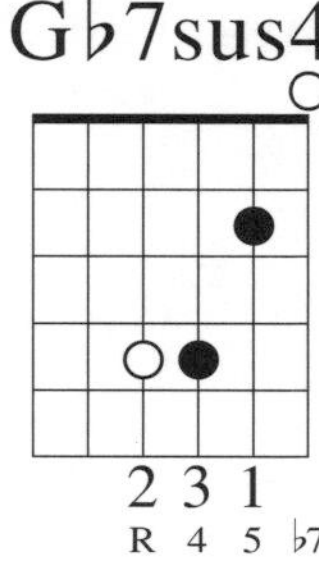

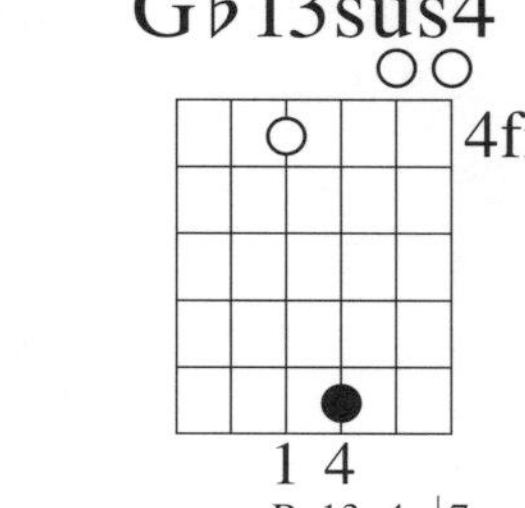

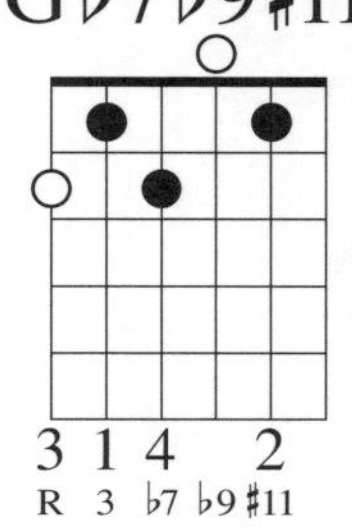

D♭(C♯) Chords

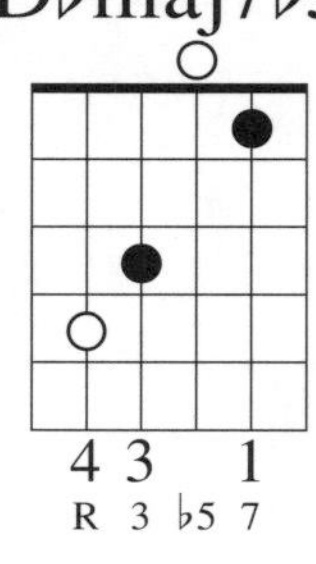

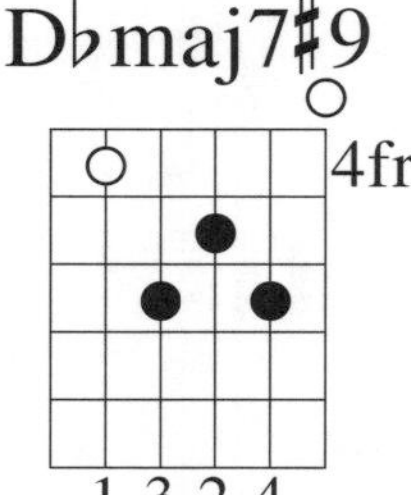

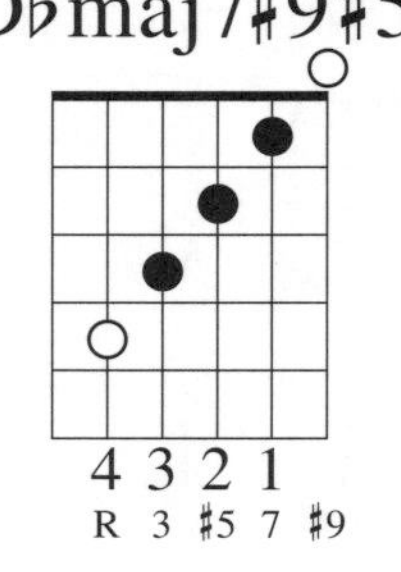

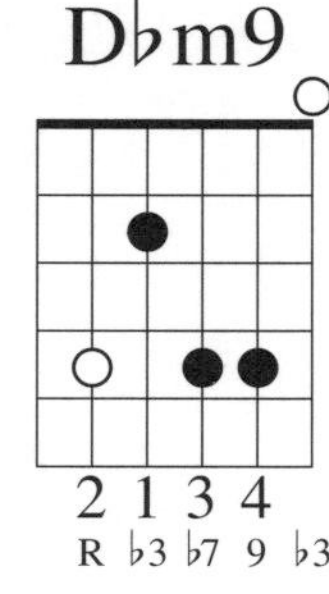

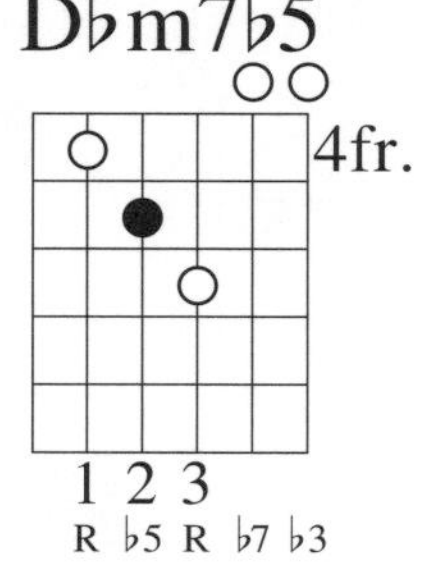

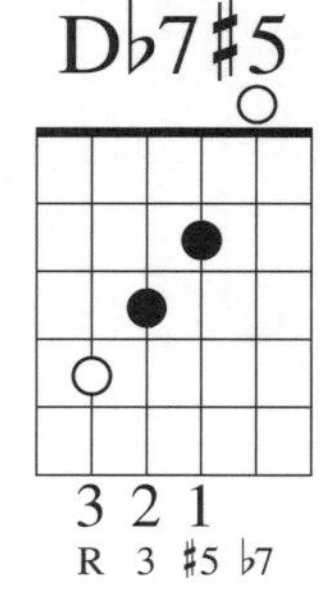

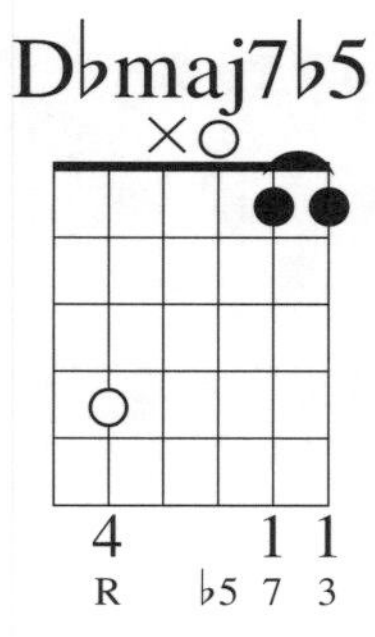

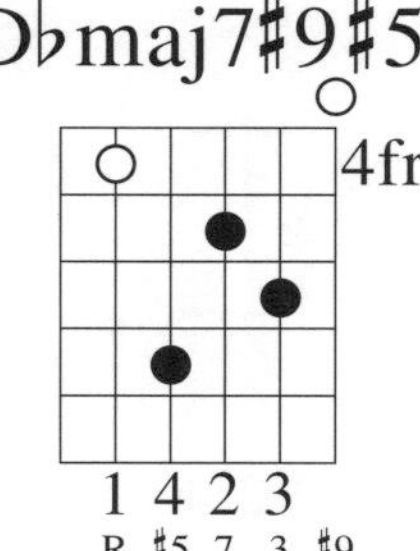

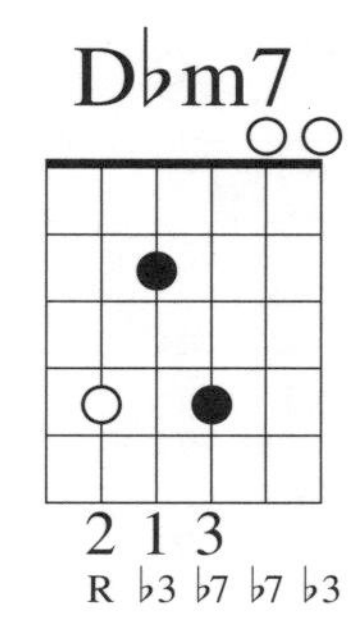

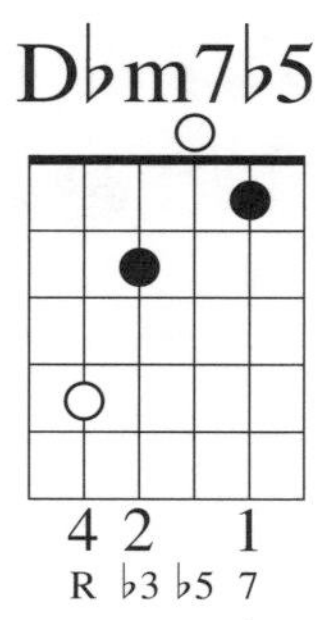

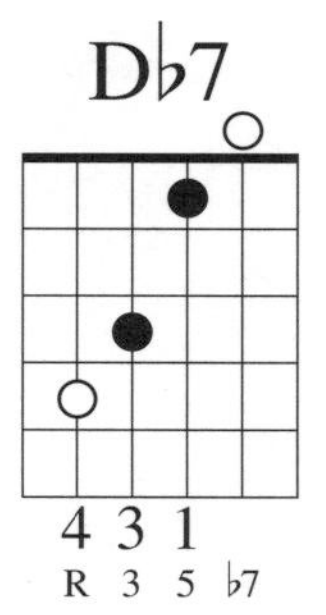

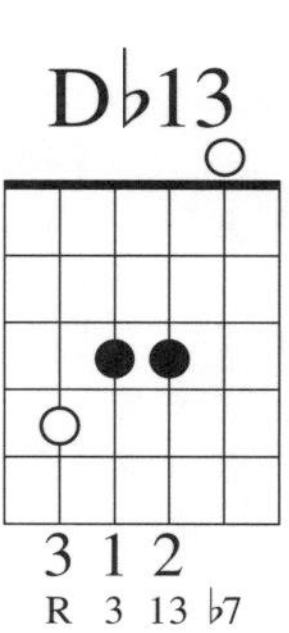

Chords with Open Strings

A♭(G♯) Chords

A♭maj7

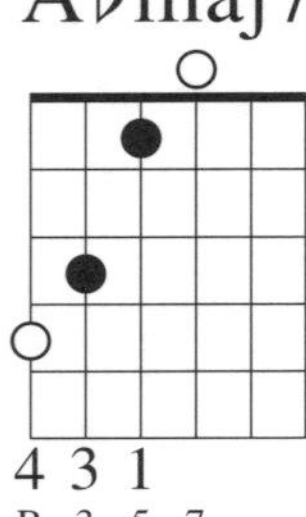

4 3 1
R 3 5 7

A♭maj7♯5

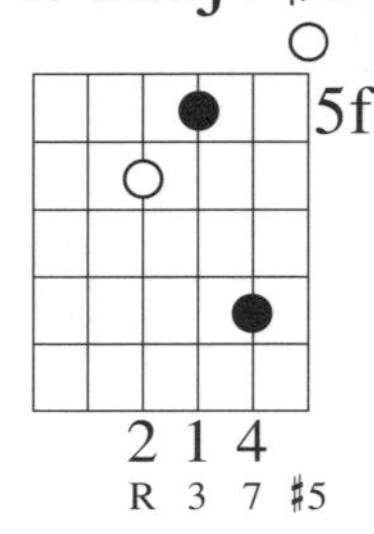

2 1 4
R 3 7 ♯5

A♭maj13♯5

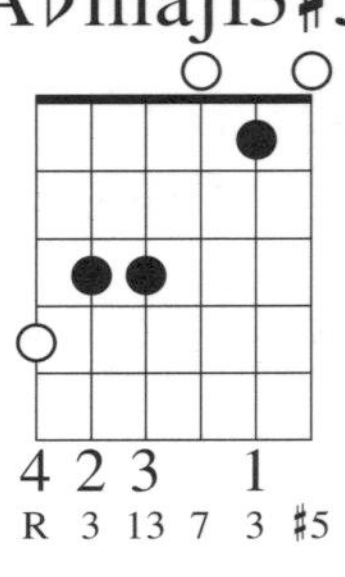

4 2 3 1
R 3 13 7 3 ♯5

A♭maj7♯9♯11

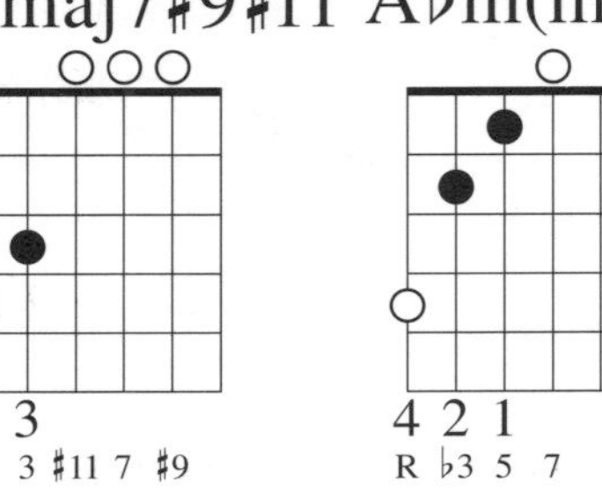

4 3
R 3 ♯11 7 ♯9

A♭m(maj7)

4 2 1
R ♭3 5 7

A♭7♯5♯9

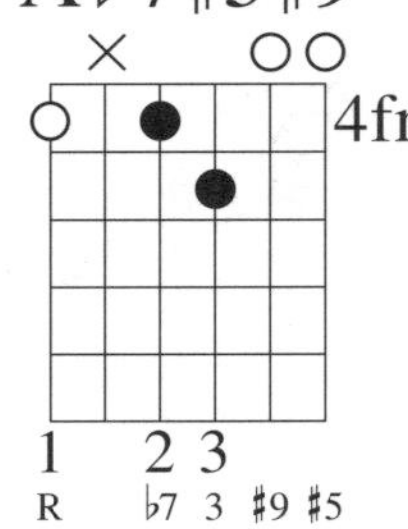

1 2 3
R ♭7 3 ♯9 ♯5

A♭maj7♯5

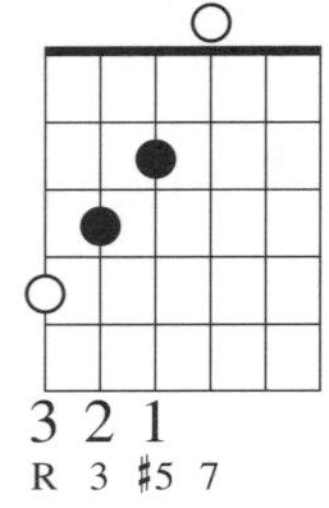

3 2 1
R 3 ♯5 7

A♭maj7♭5

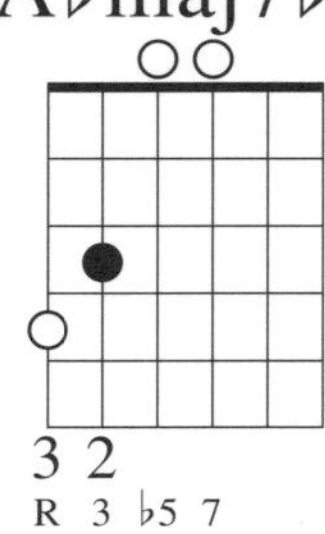

3 2
R 3 ♭5 7

A♭maj7♯9

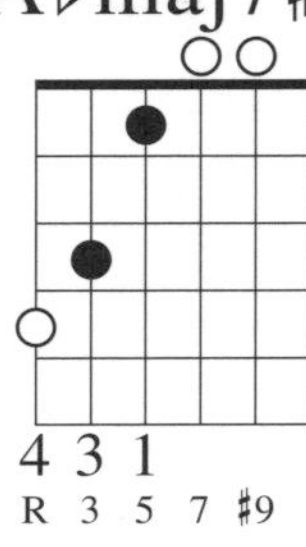

4 3 1
R 3 5 7 ♯9

A♭maj7♯9♯5

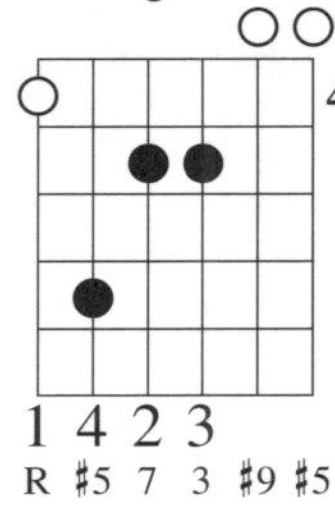

1 4 2 3
R ♯5 7 3 ♯9 ♯5

A♭m(maj7)♭5

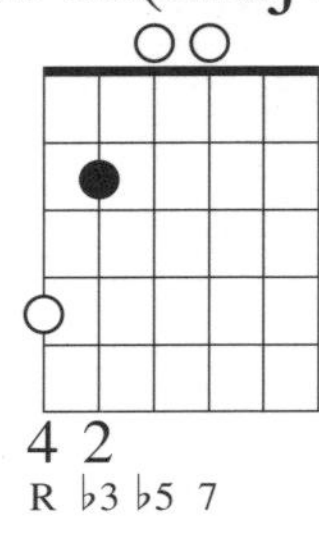

4 2
R ♭3 ♭5 7

A♭7♭5♯9

4fr.

1 3 2 4
R ♭5 ♭7 3 ♯9

E♭(D♯) Chords

E♭maj7♯5

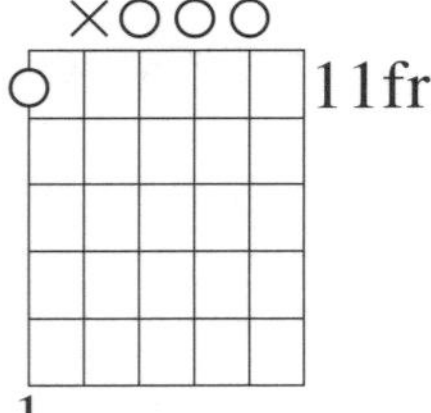

1
R 7 3 ♯5

E♭maj7♯5♯11

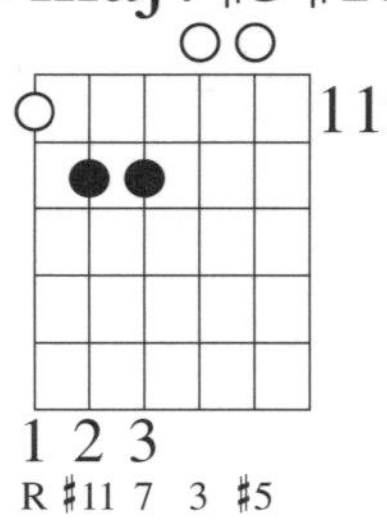

1 2 3
R ♯11 7 3 ♯5

E♭maj7♯9

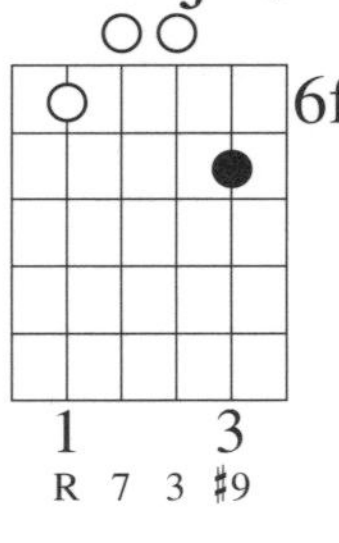

1 3
R 7 3 ♯9

E♭7♯9

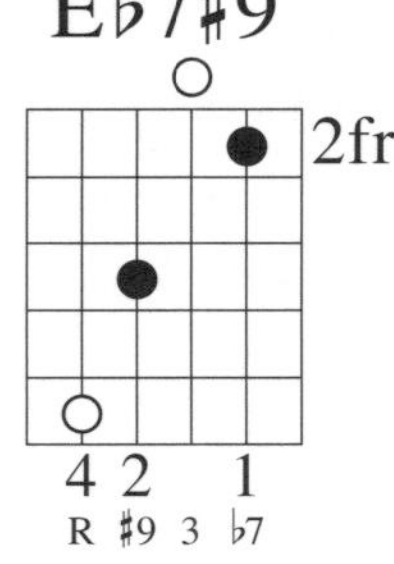

4 2 1
R ♯9 3 ♭7

E♭7♭9♯9

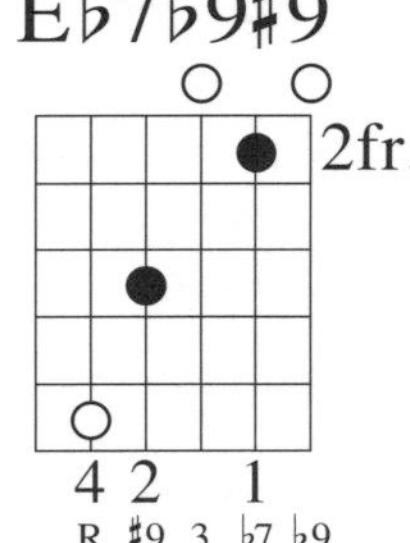

4 2 1
R ♯9 3 ♭7 ♭9

E♭7♯5♭9

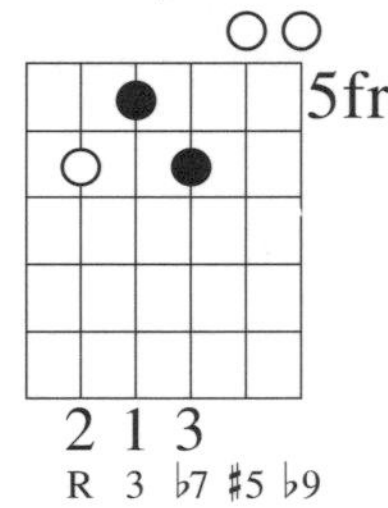

2 1 3
R 3 ♭7 ♯5 ♭9

E♭maj7♯5

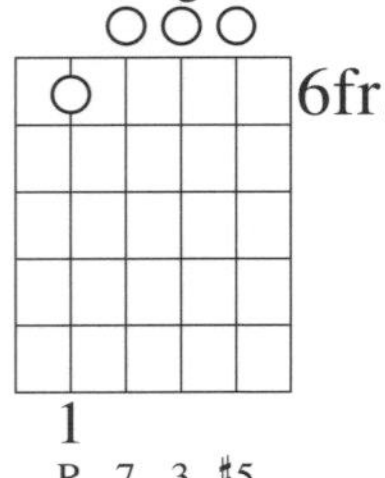

1
R 7 3 ♯5

E♭maj7♯9

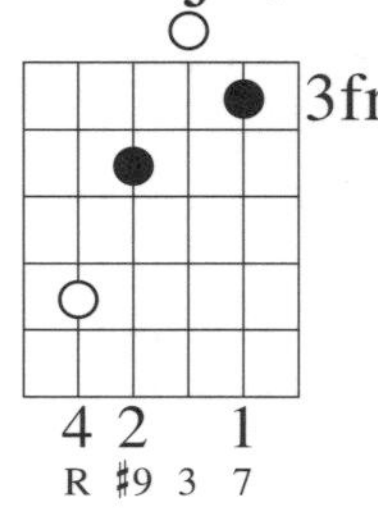

4 2 1
R ♯9 3 7

E♭maj7♯9♯11

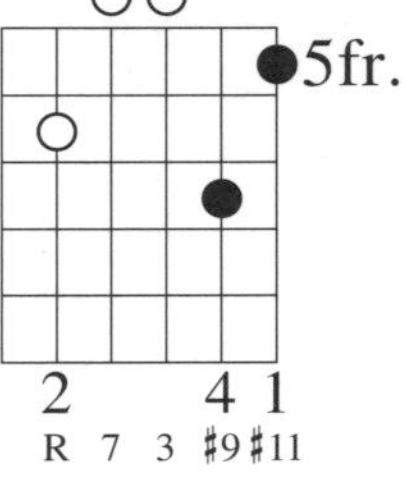

2 4 1
R 7 3 ♯9 ♯11

E♭7♯9

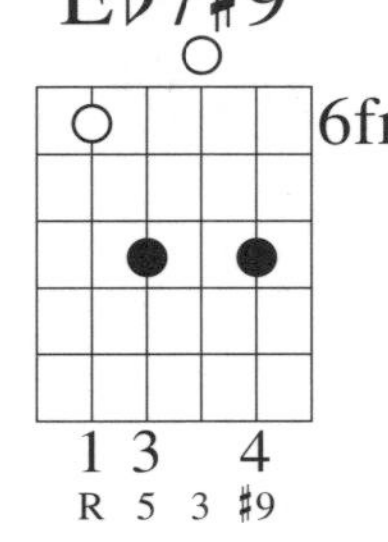

1 3 4
R 5 3 ♯9

E♭7♭5♭9

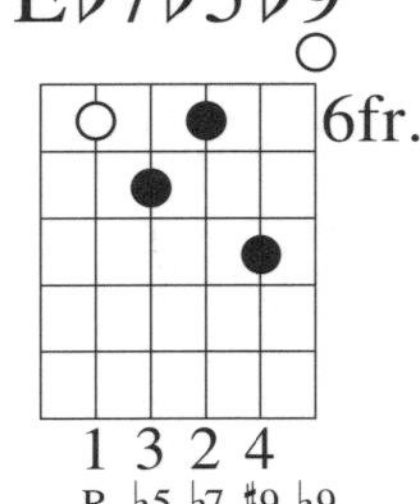

1 3 2 4
R ♭5 ♭7 ♯9 ♭9

E♭7♯9♭5

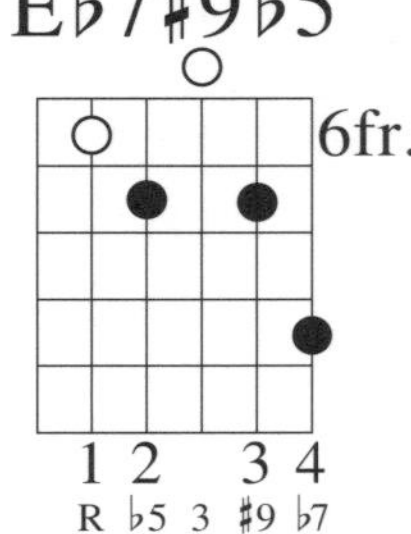

1 2 3 4
R ♭5 3 ♯9 ♭7

B♭(A♯) Chords

B♭maj9

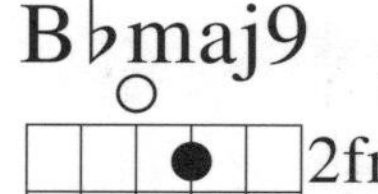
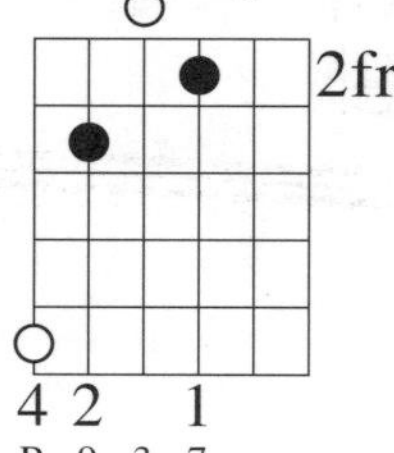

B♭maj9♯11

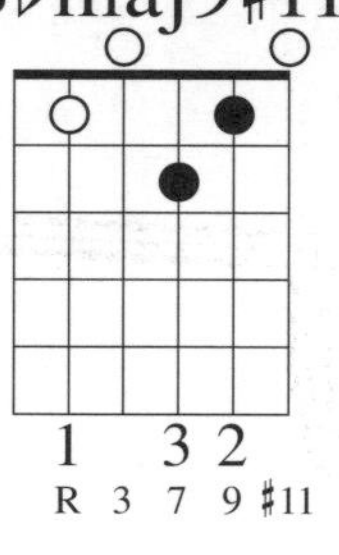

B♭maj9♯5

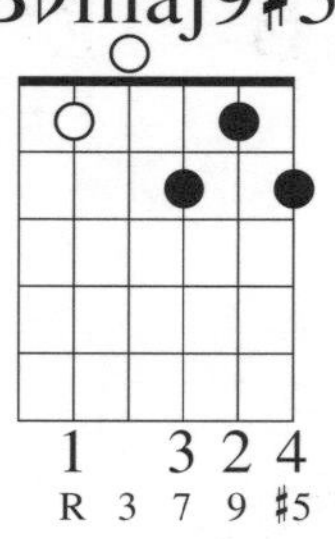

B♭7♯9♯11

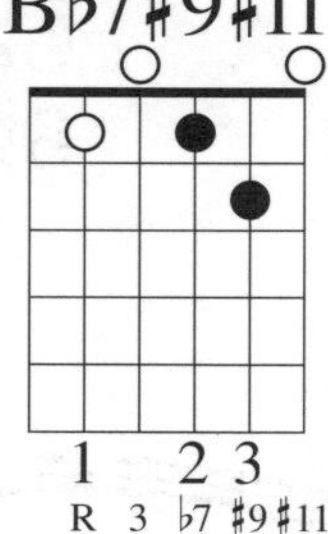

B♭13♭9

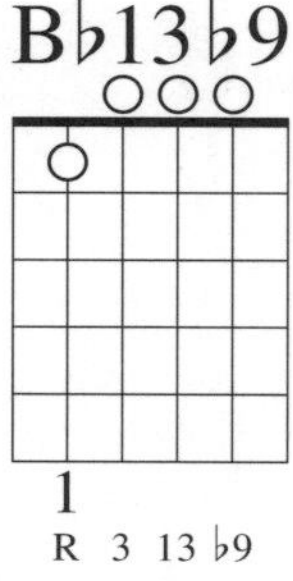

B♭m7♯11

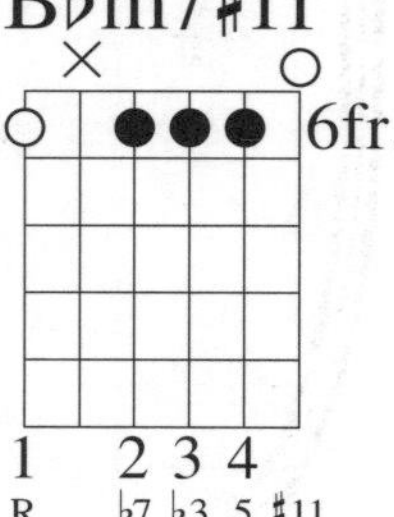

B♭maj7♯11

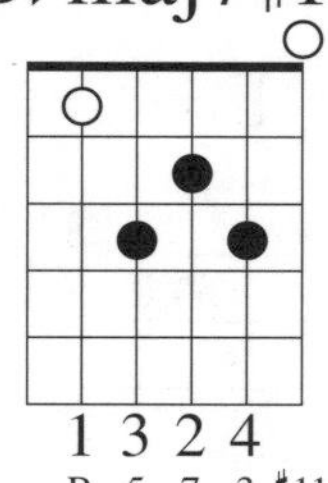

B♭maj9♯11

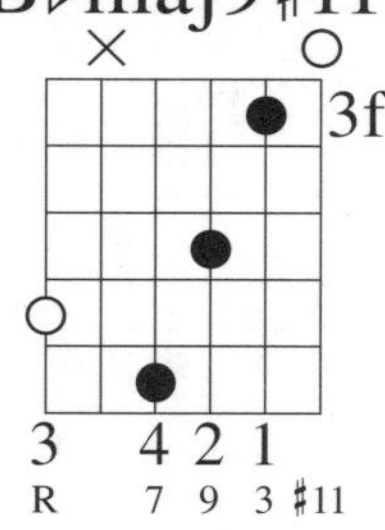

B♭maj7♯9♯11

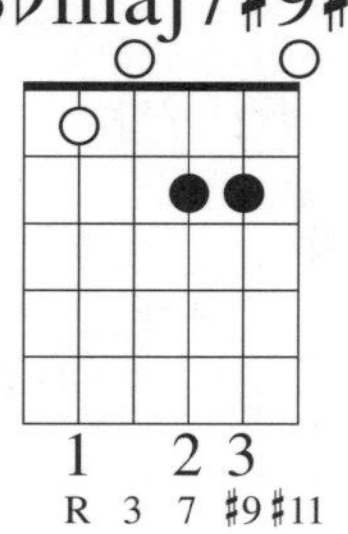

B♭13

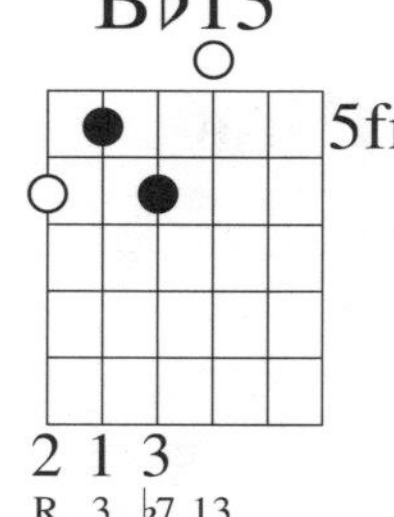

B♭13♭9♯11

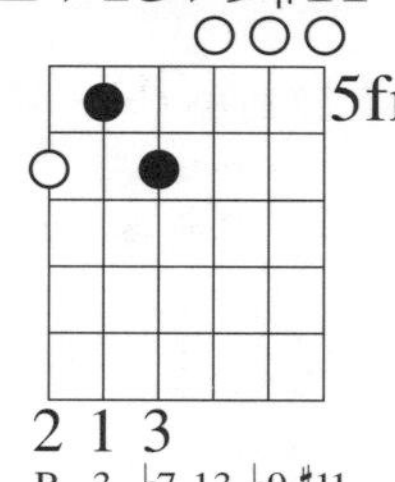

B♭m(maj7)♯11

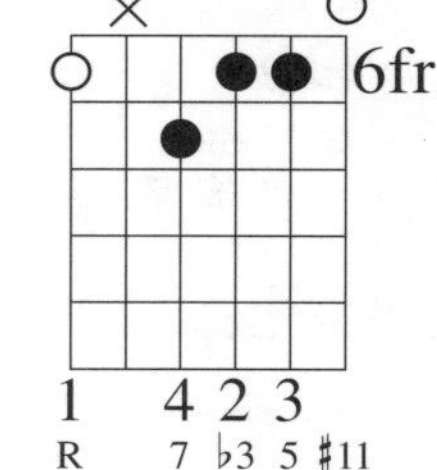

F Chords

Fmaj7♯11

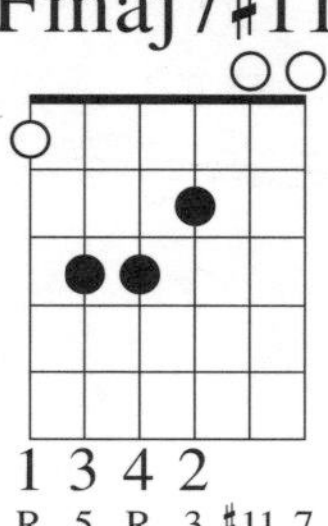

Fmaj7♯5♯11

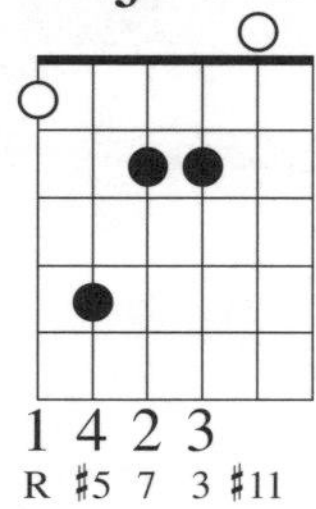

Fmaj13♯11

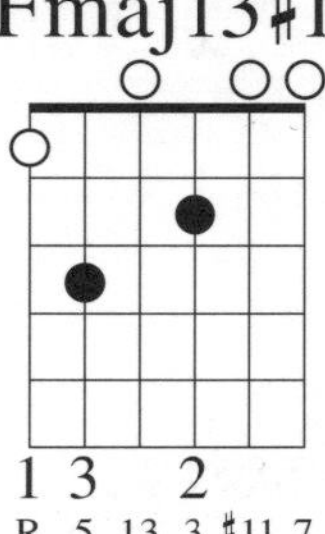

Fmaj7♯9♯11

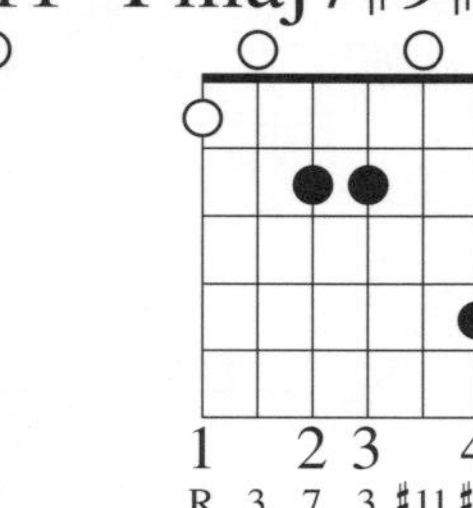

Fm(maj7)♭5

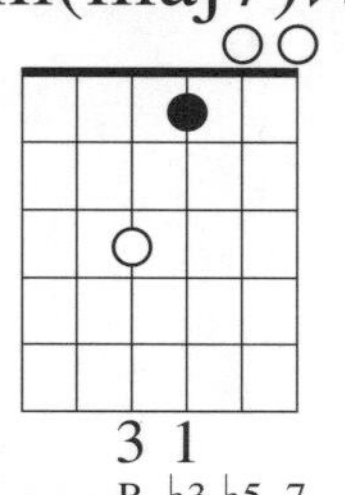

F9♭5

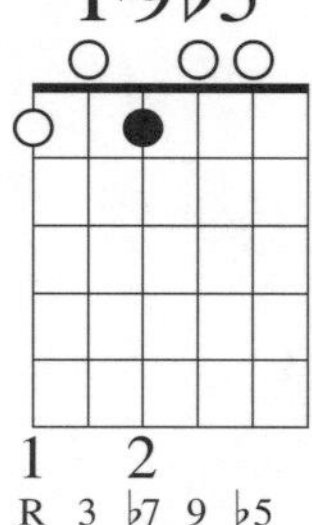

Fmaj7♯5♯11

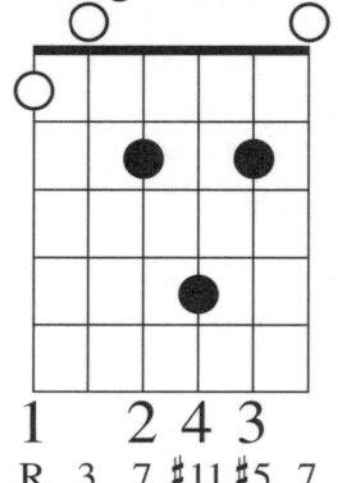

Fmaj9♯5

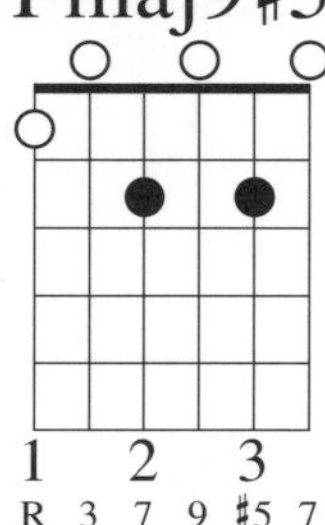

Fmaj7♯9

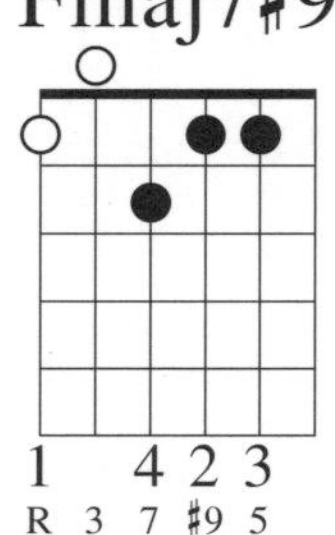

Fm(maj7)

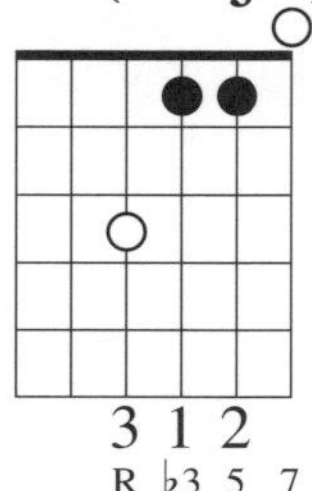

Fm(maj9)♭5

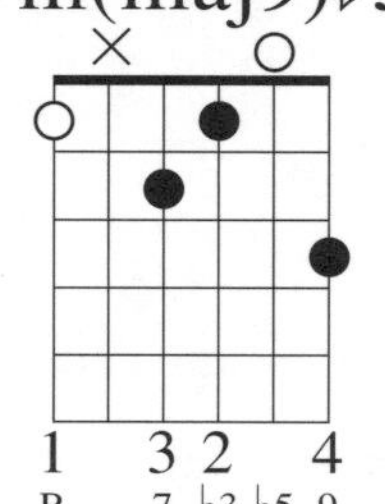

F7♯9♯11

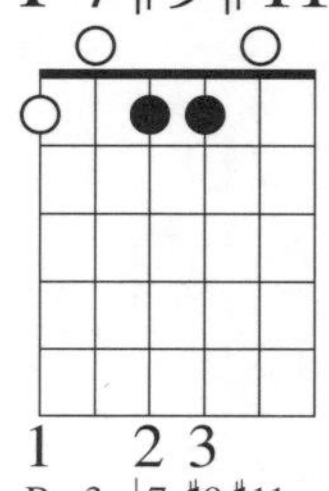

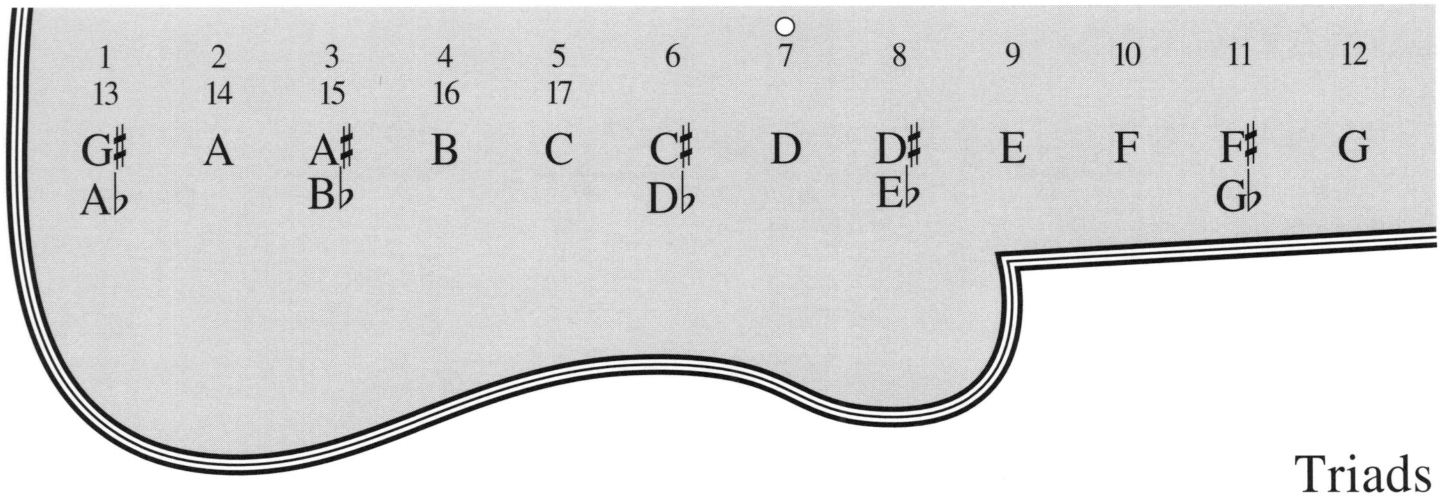

1 13	2 14	3 15	4 16	5 17	6	7	8	9	10	11	12
G♯ A♭	A	A♯ B♭	B	C	C♯ D♭	D	D♯ E♭	E	F	F♯ G♭	G

Triads

D
7fr. 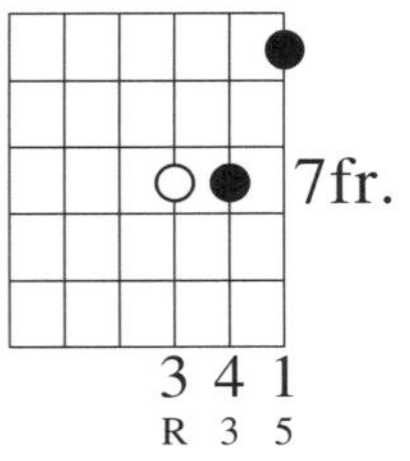
3 4 1
R 3 5

Dsus2
7fr. 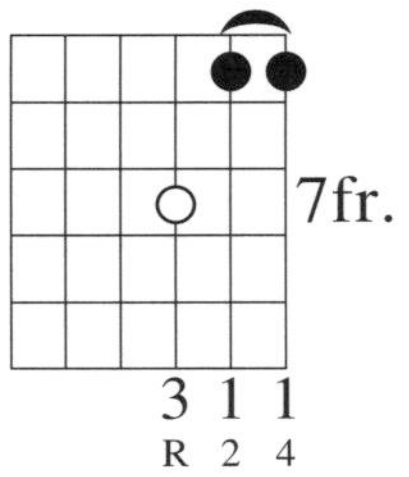
3 1 1
R 2 4

Dsus4
7fr. 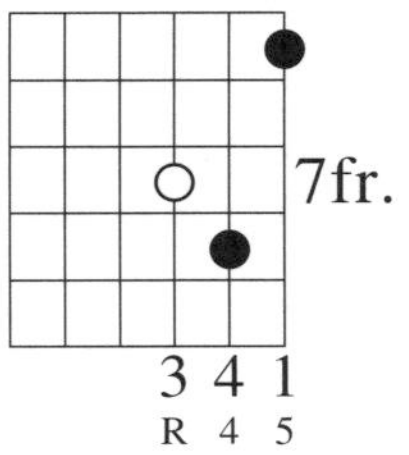
3 4 1
R 4 5

Dm
7fr. 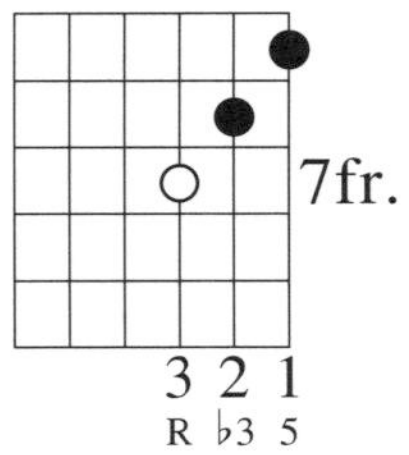
3 2 1
R ♭3 5

D°
7fr. 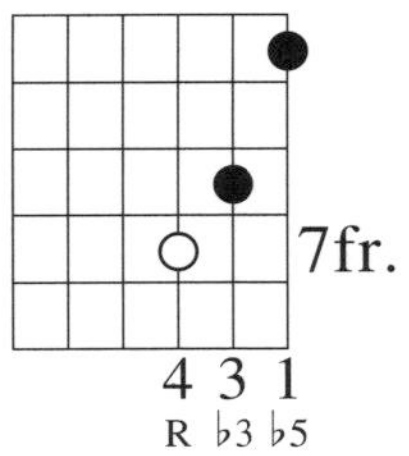
4 3 1
R ♭3 ♭5

D+
7fr. 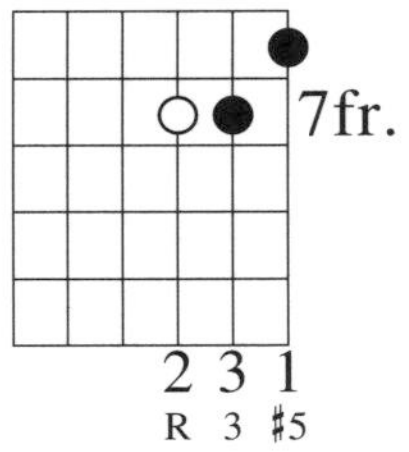
2 3 1
R 3 ♯5

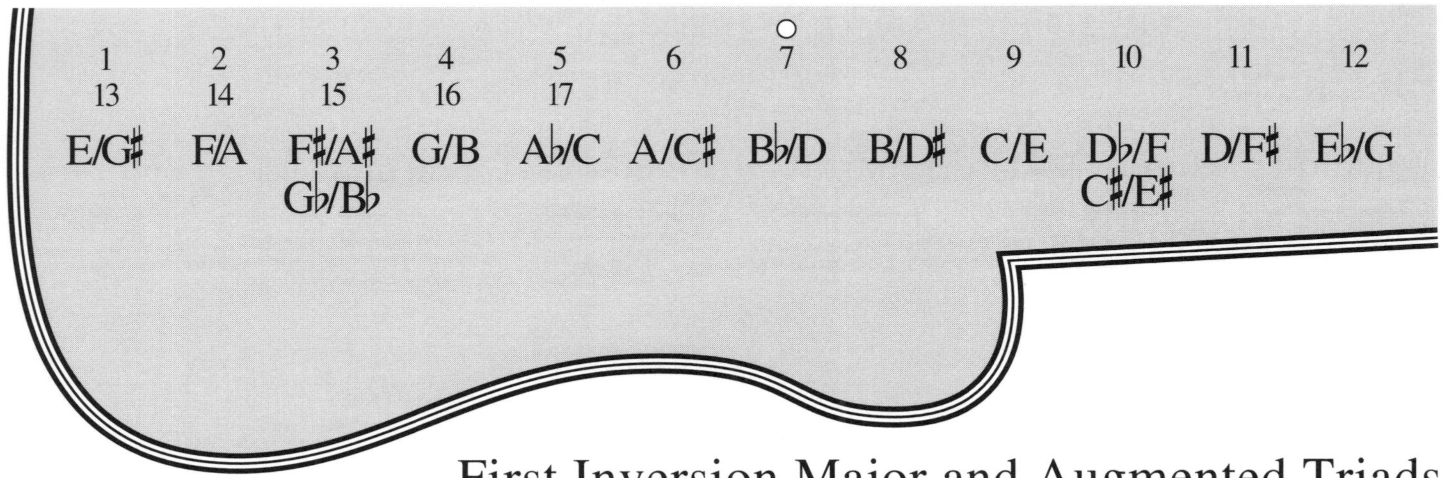

1 13	2 14	3 15	4 16	5 17	6	7	8	9	10	11	12
E/G♯	F/A	F♯/A♯ G♭/B♭	G/B	A♭/C	A/C♯	B♭/D	B/D♯	C/E	D♭/F C♯/E♯	D/F♯	E♭/G

First Inversion Major and Augmented Triads

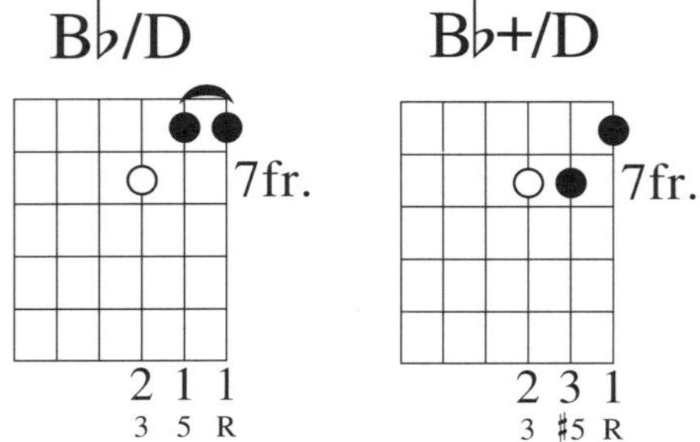

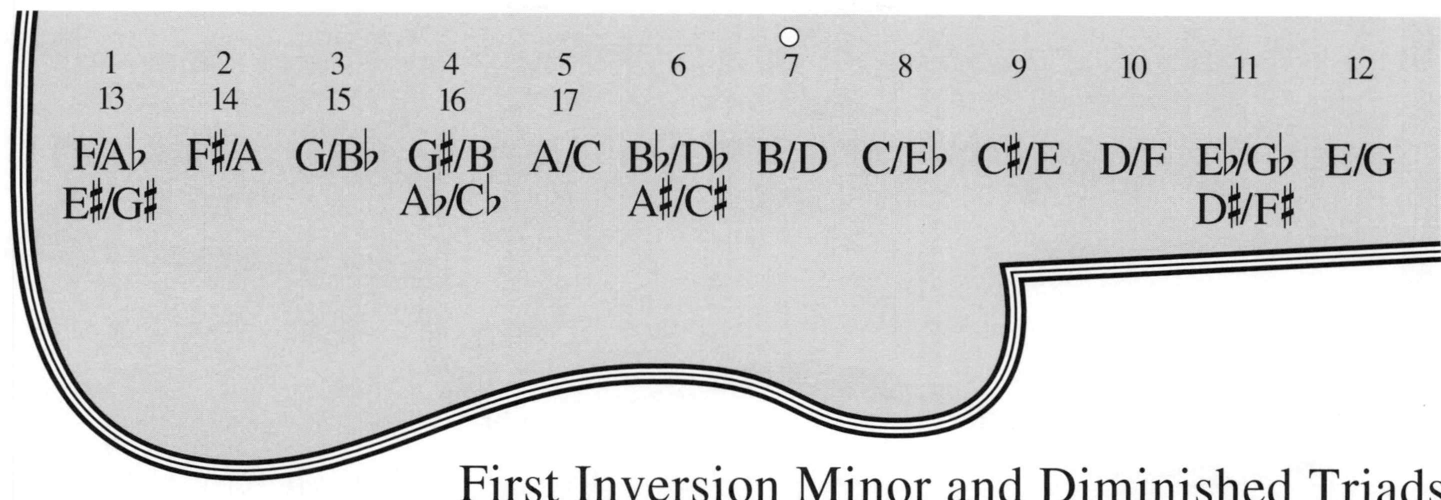

First Inversion Minor and Diminished Triads

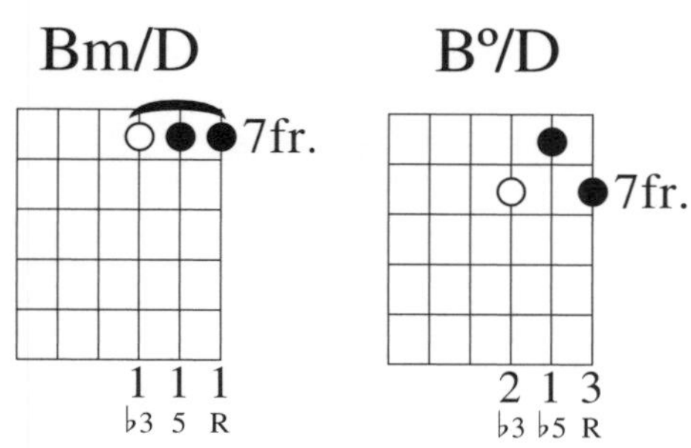

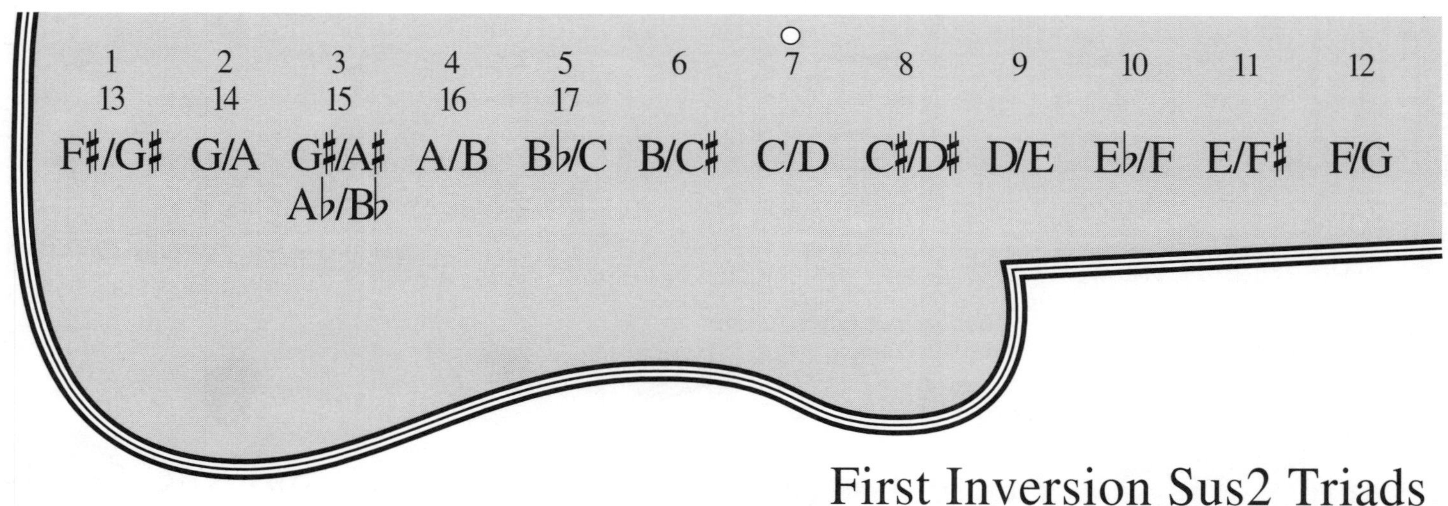

First Inversion Sus2 Triads

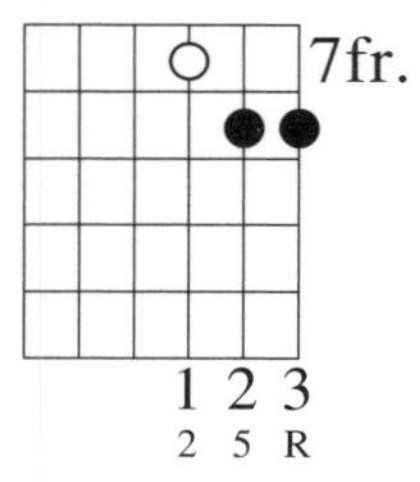

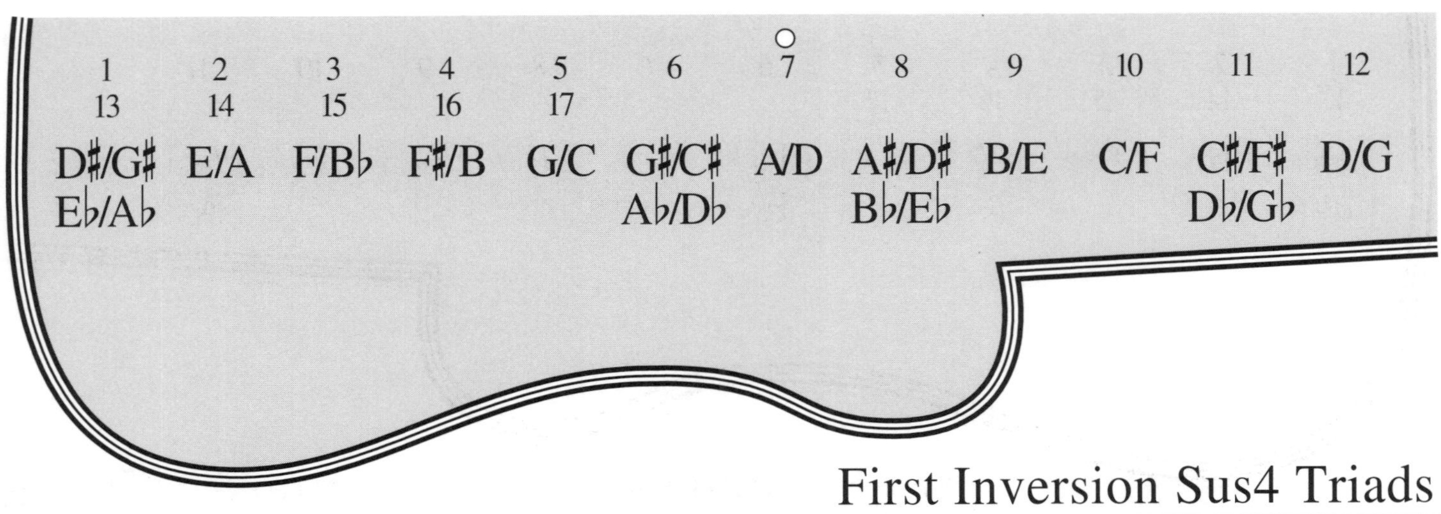

First Inversion Sus4 Triads

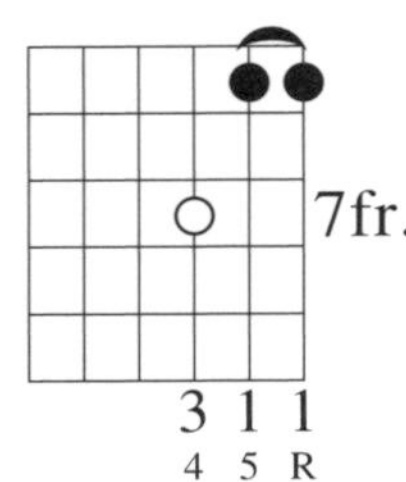

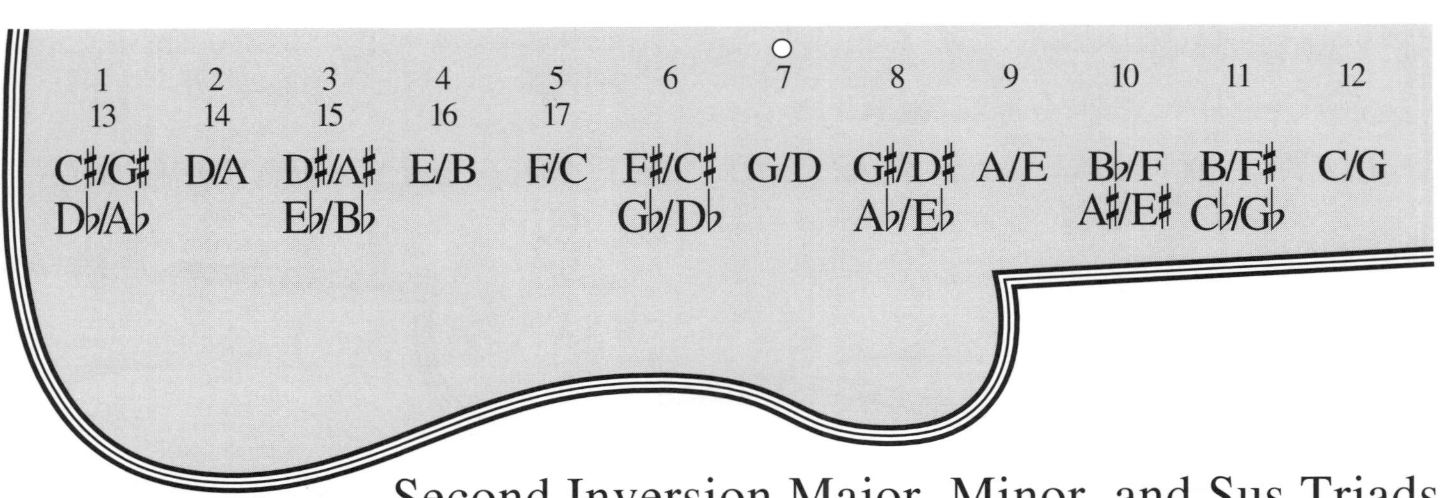

Second Inversion Major, Minor, and Sus Triads

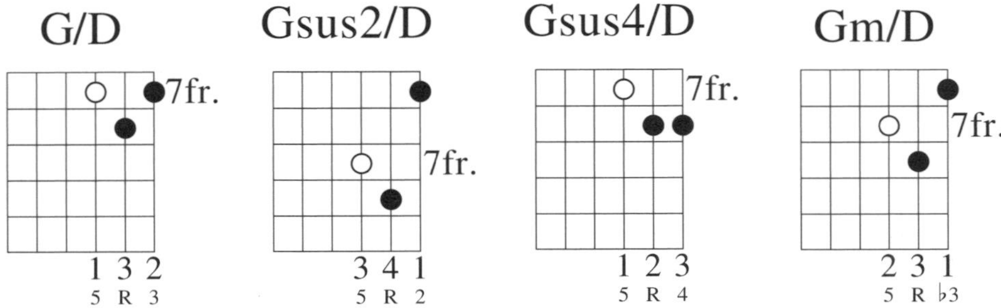

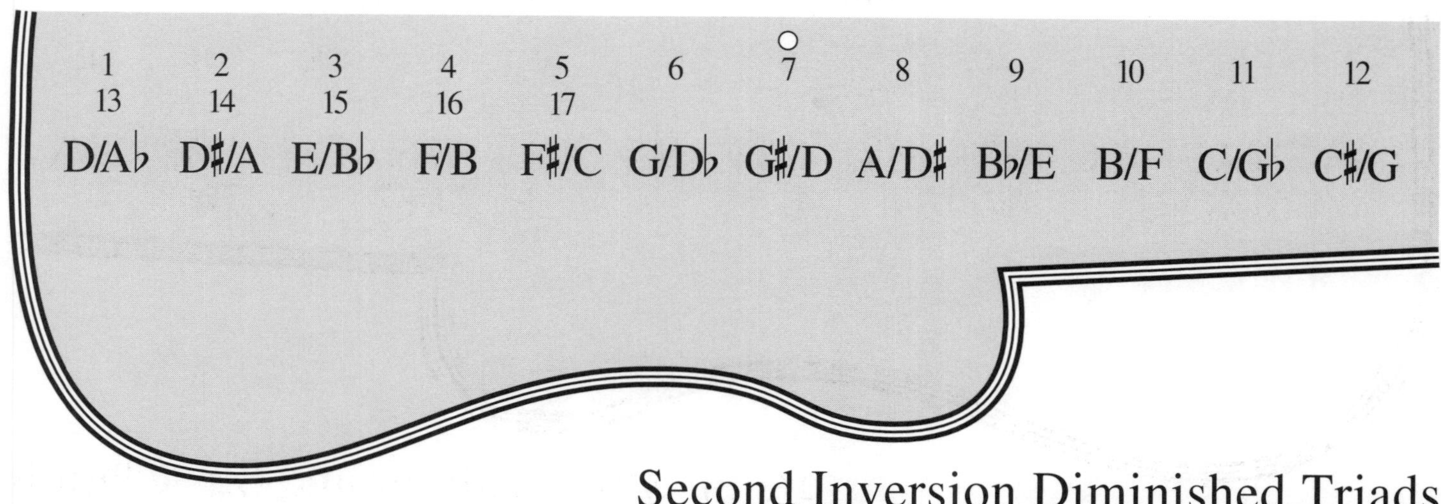

Second Inversion Diminished Triads

G♯°/D

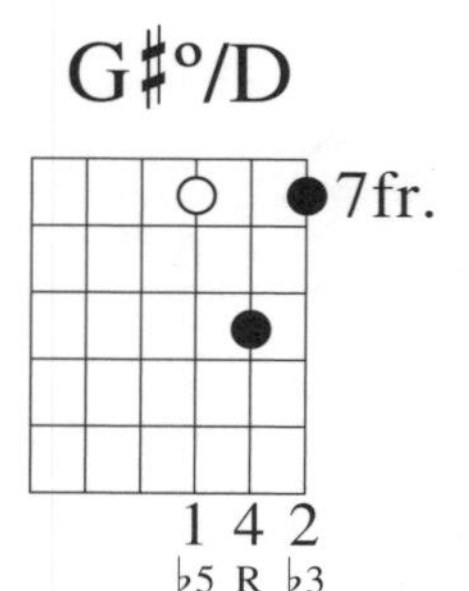

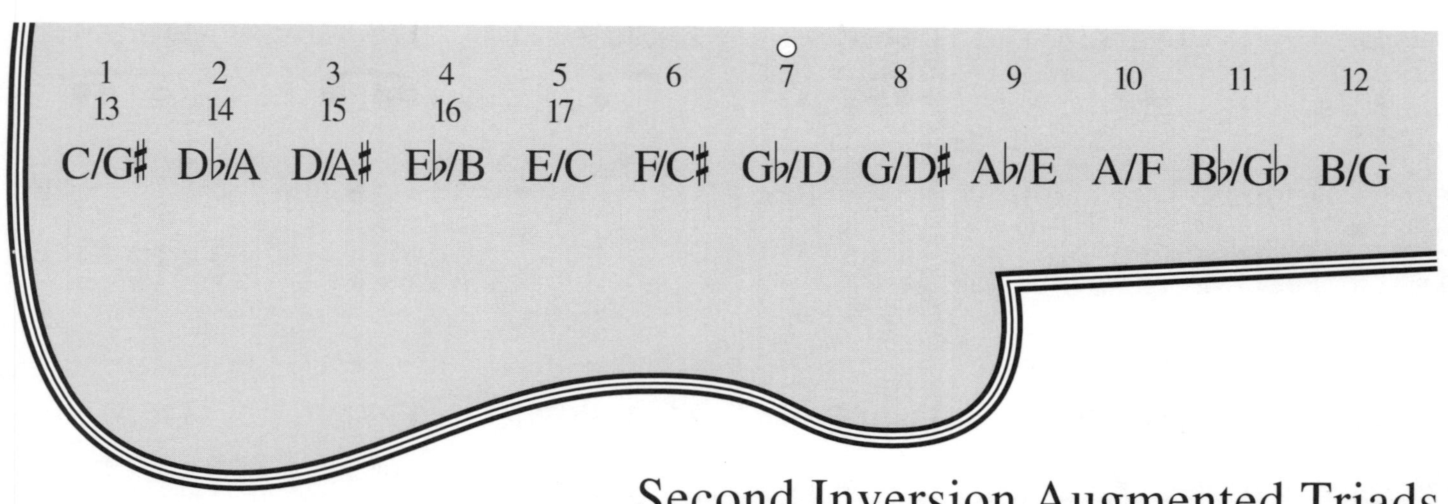

Second Inversion Augmented Triads

G♭+/D

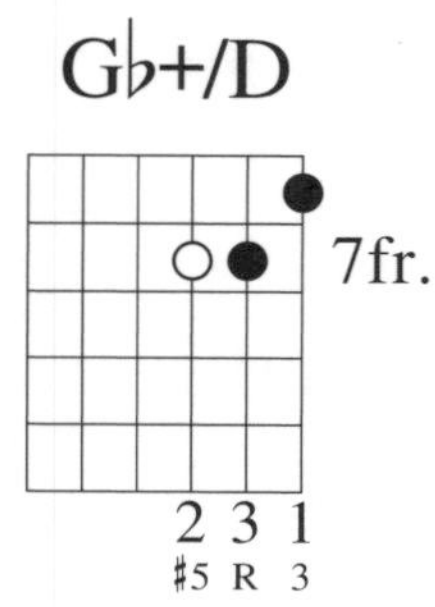

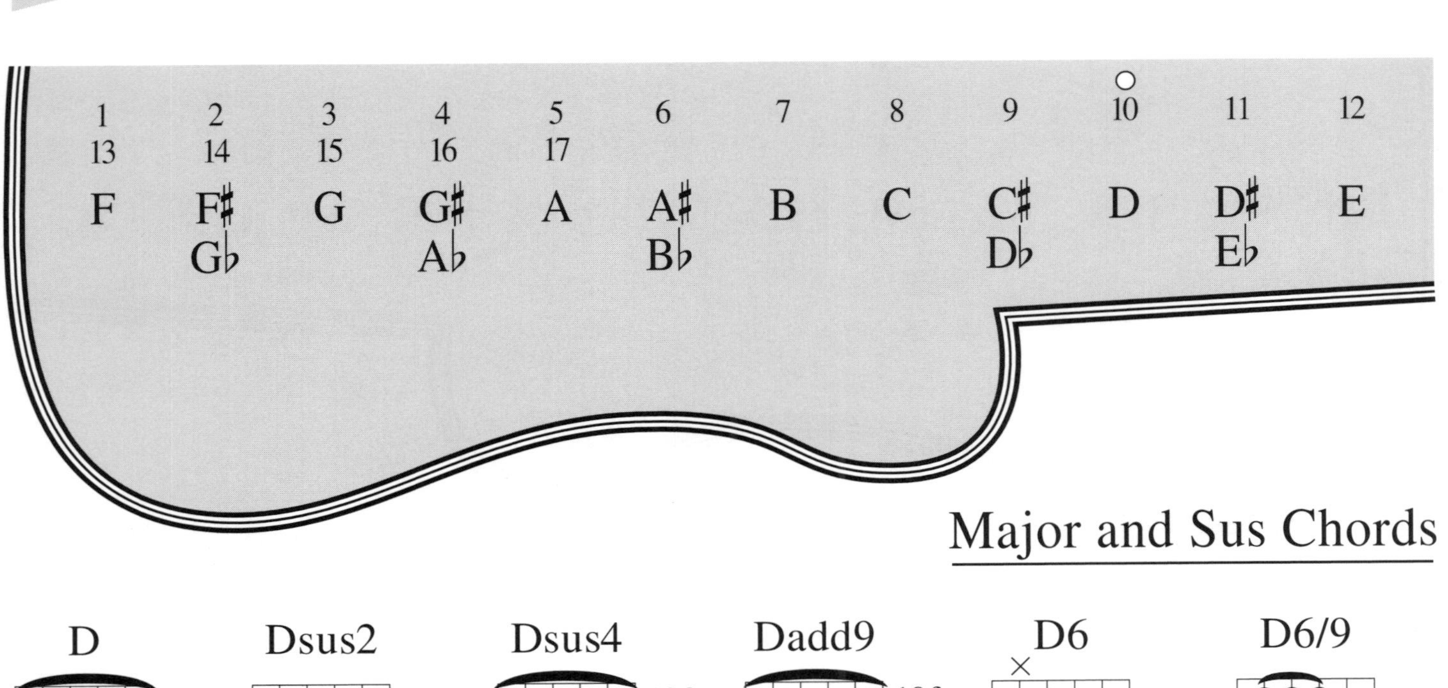

Major and Sus Chords

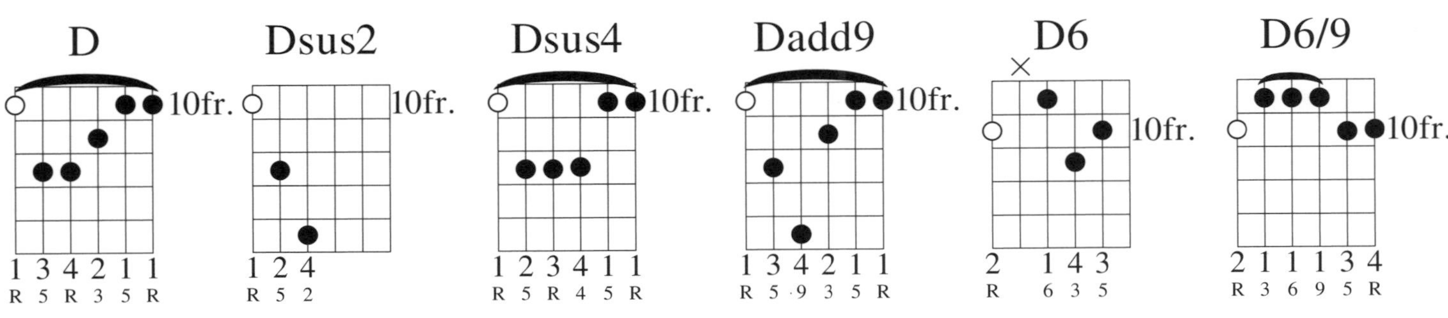

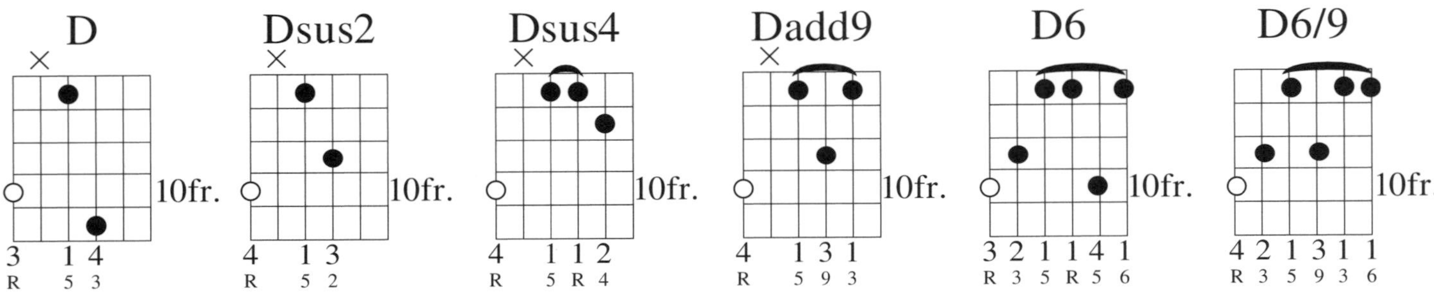

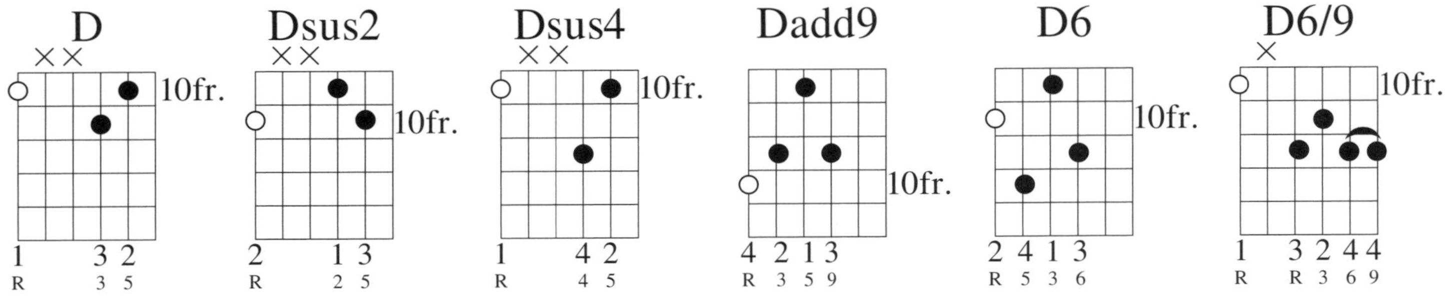

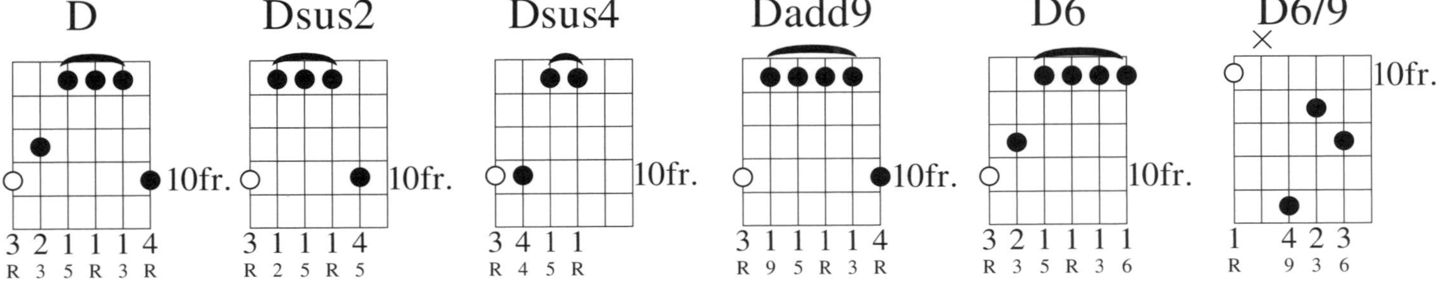

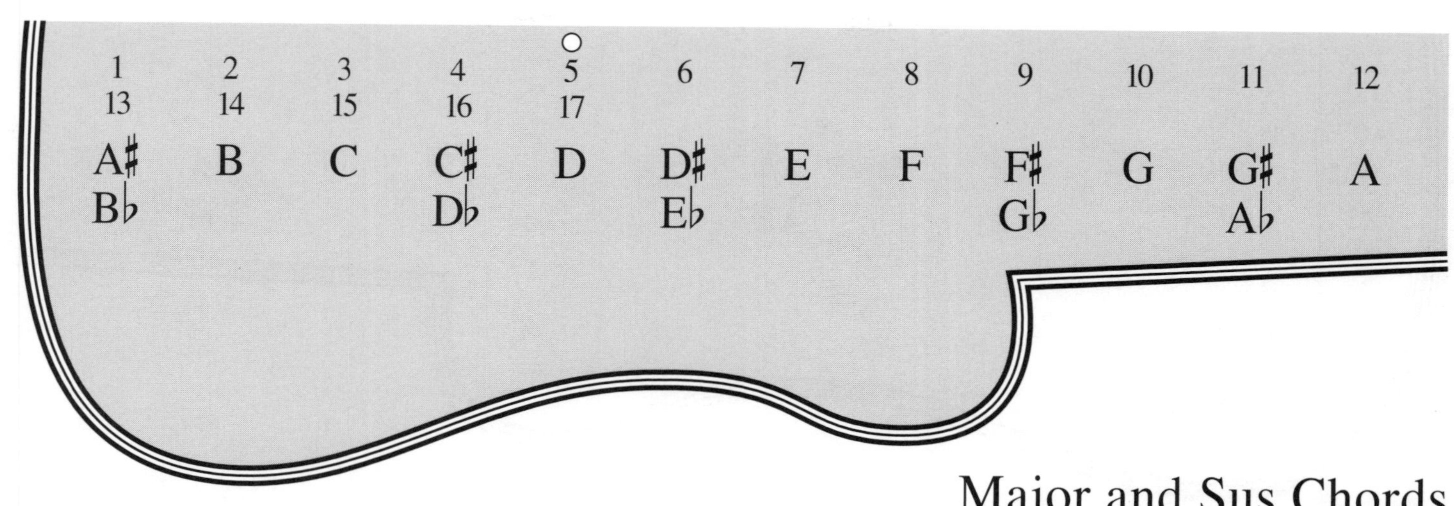

Major and Sus Chords

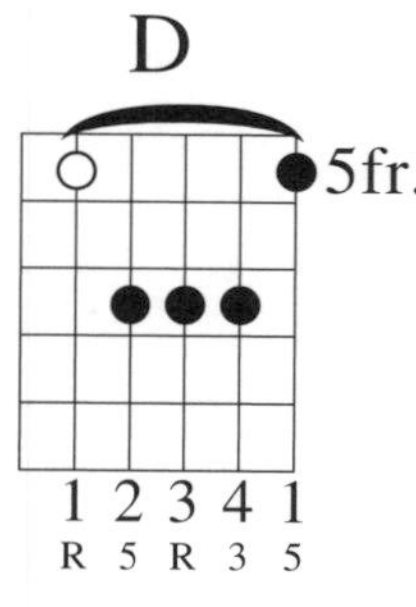

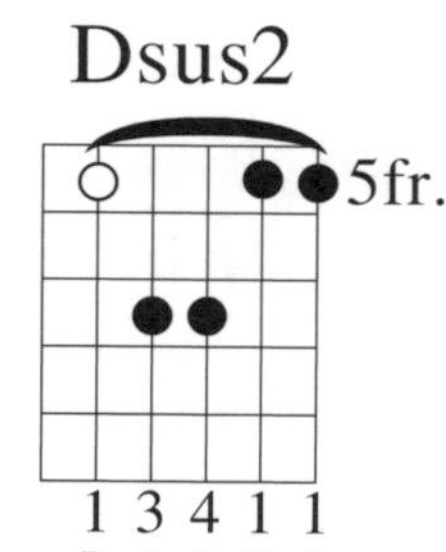

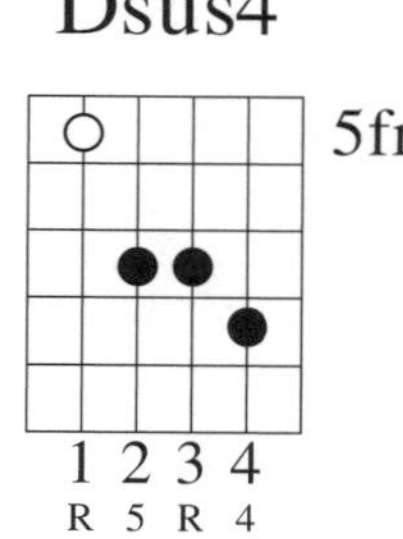

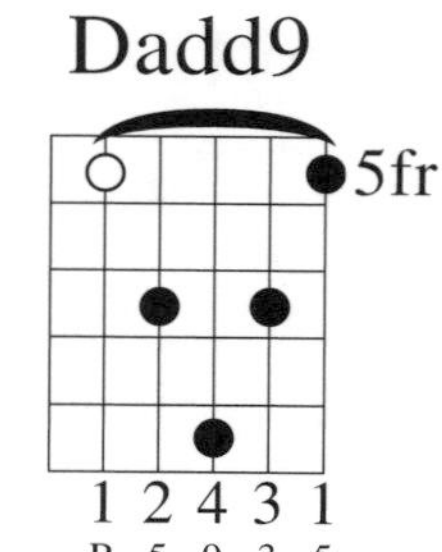

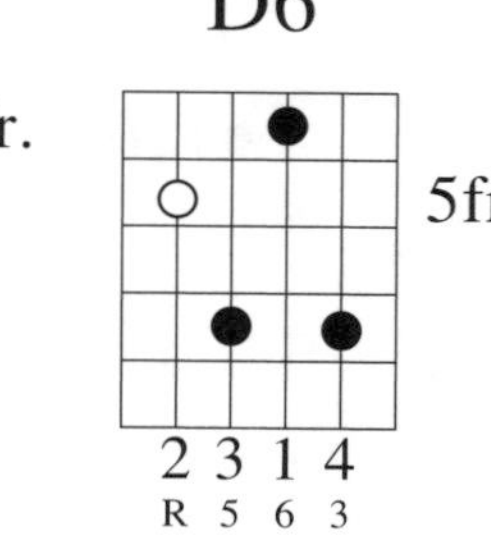

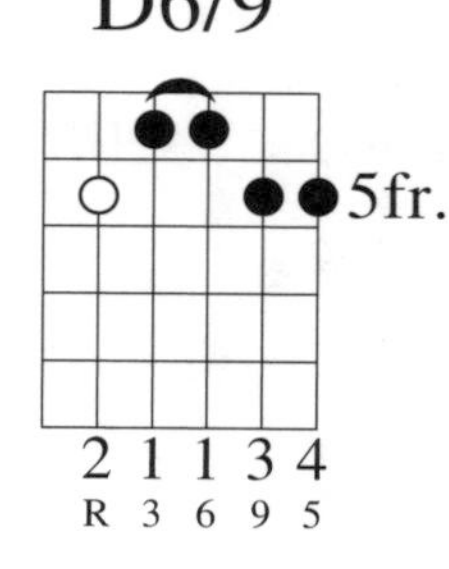

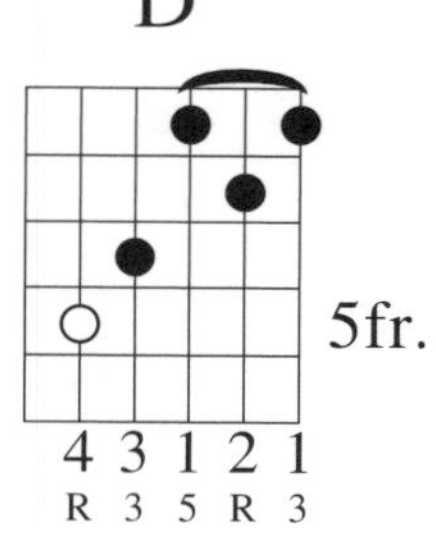

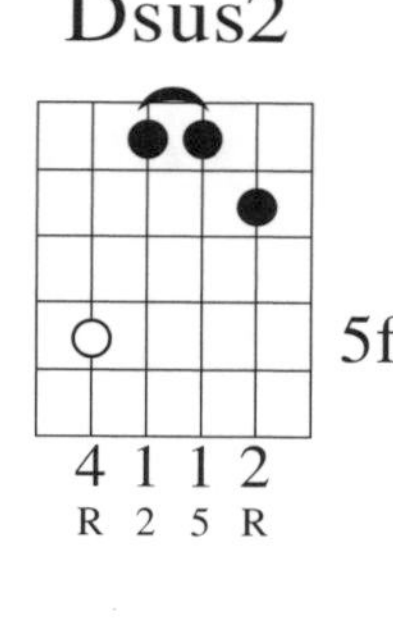

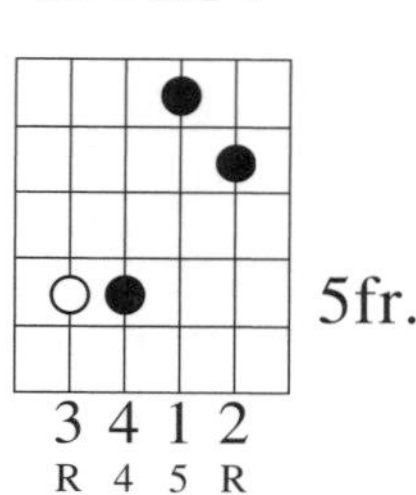

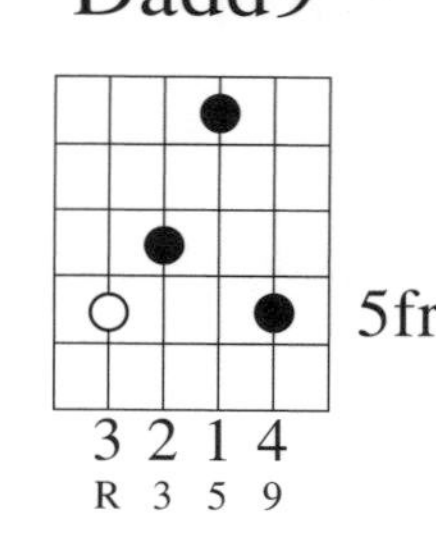

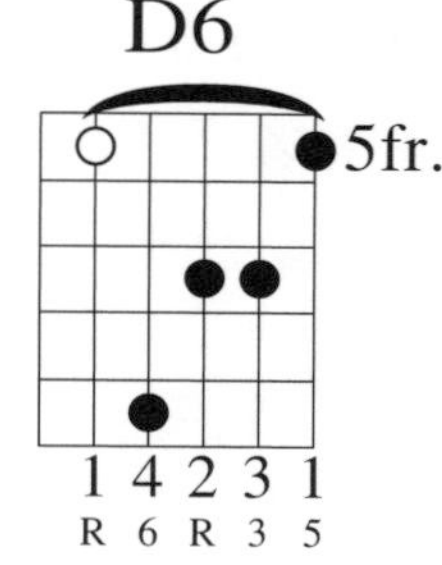

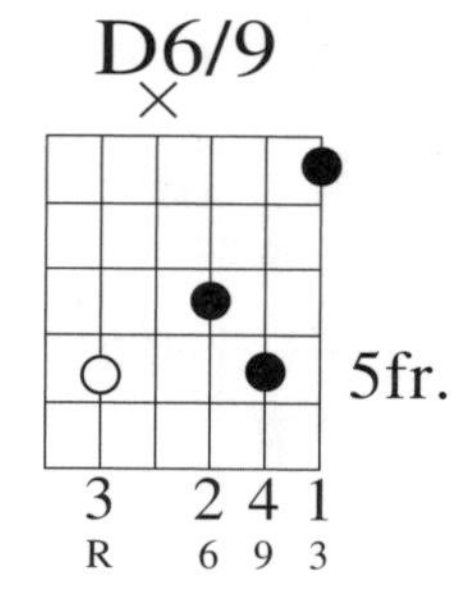

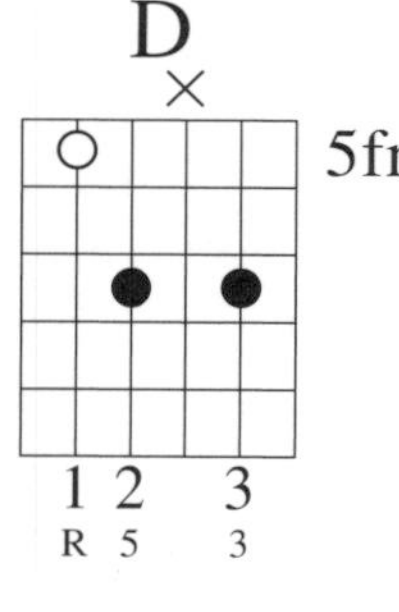

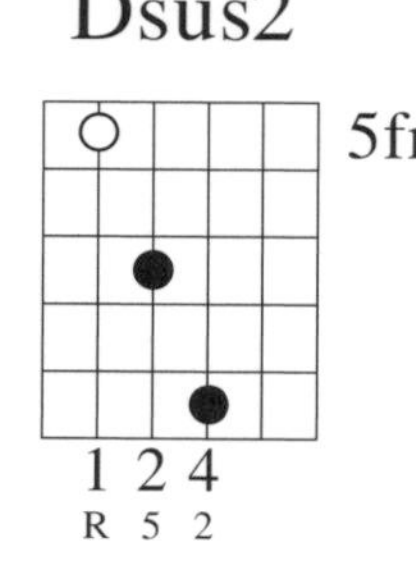

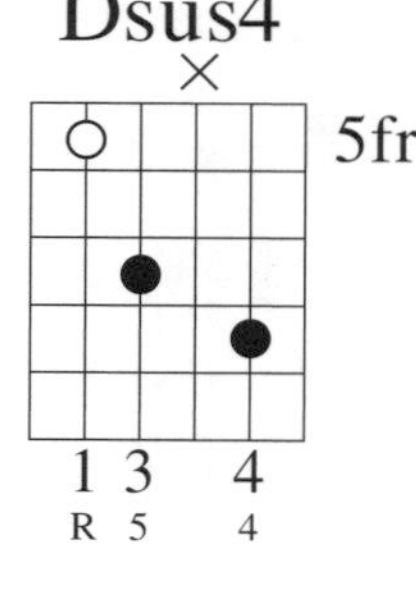

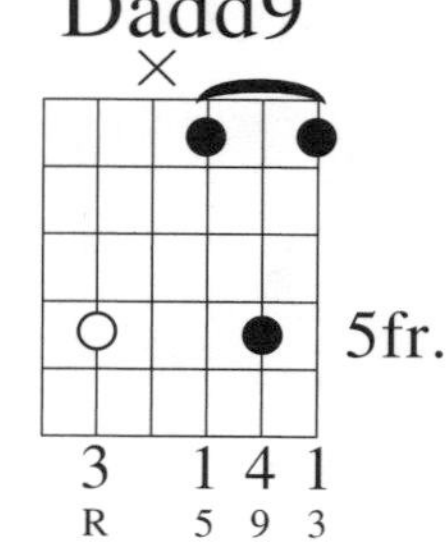

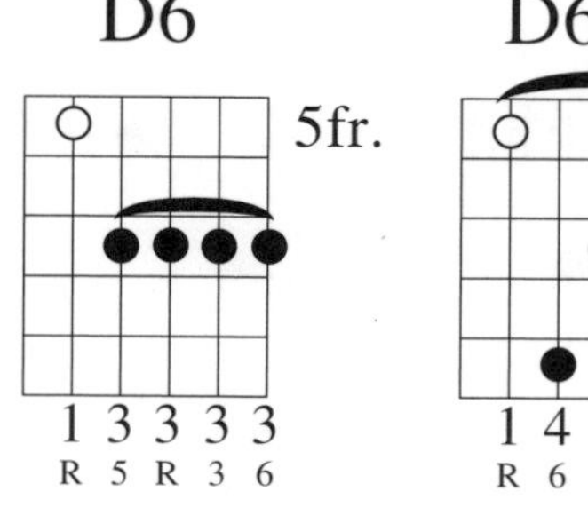

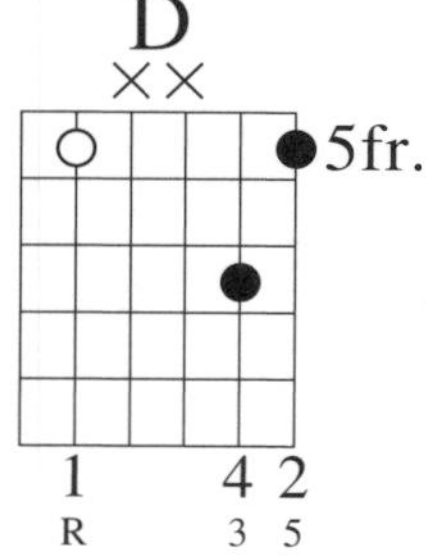

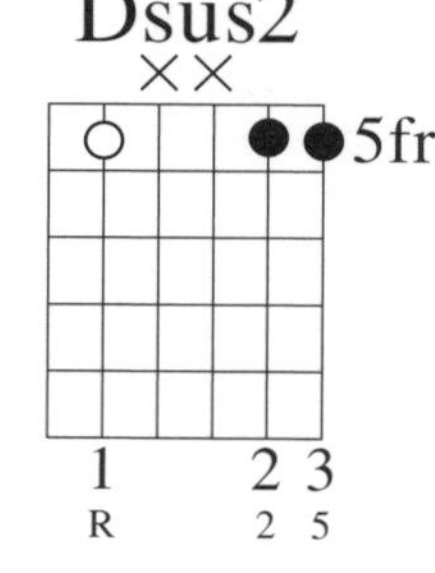

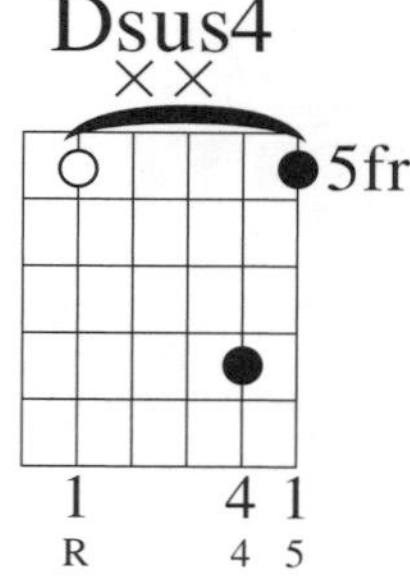

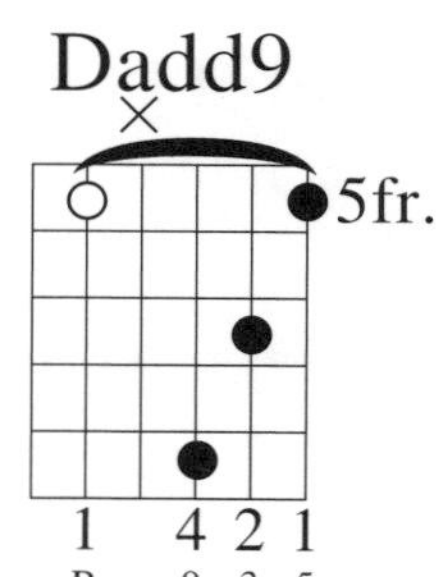

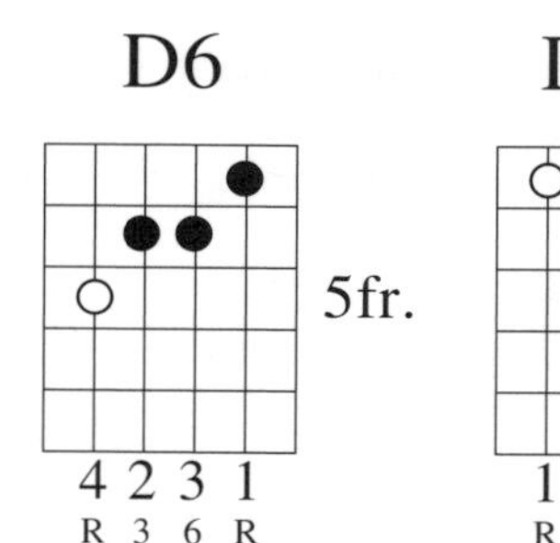

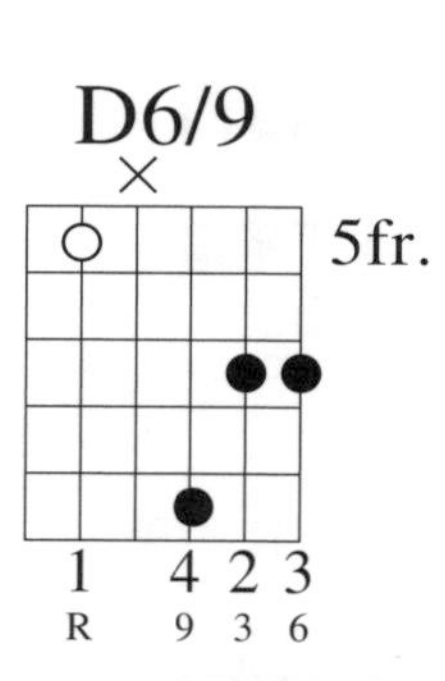

1 13 D♯ E♭
2 14 E
3 15 F
4 16 F♯ G♭
5 17 G
6 G♯ A♭
7 A
8 A♯ B♭
9 B
10 C
11 C♯ D♭
12 D

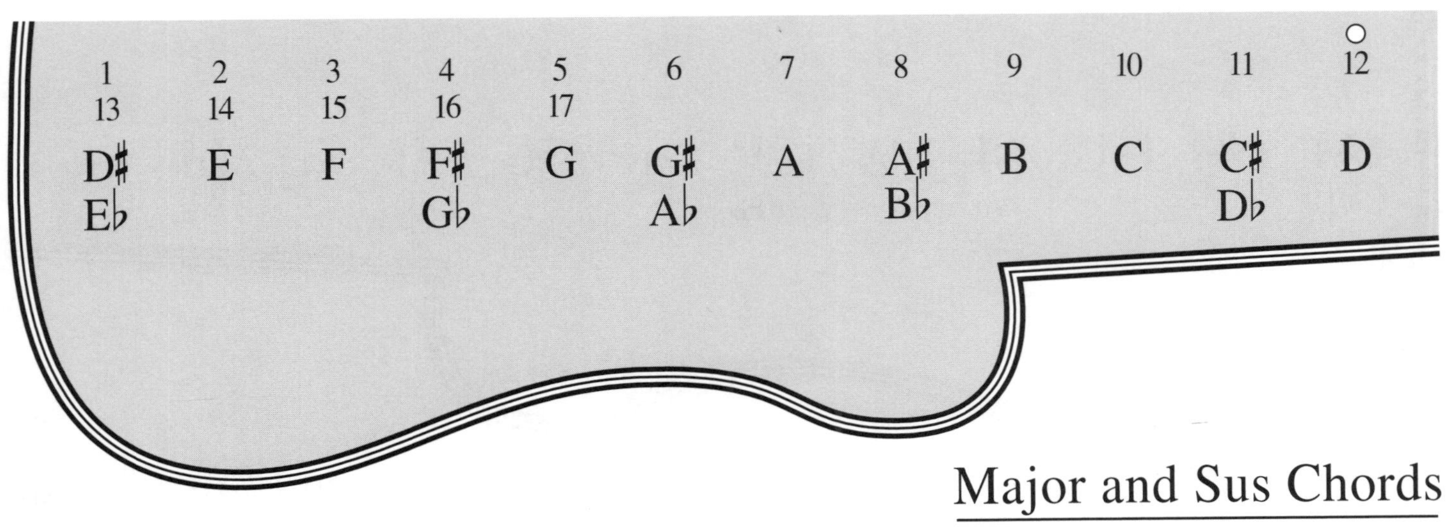

Major and Sus Chords

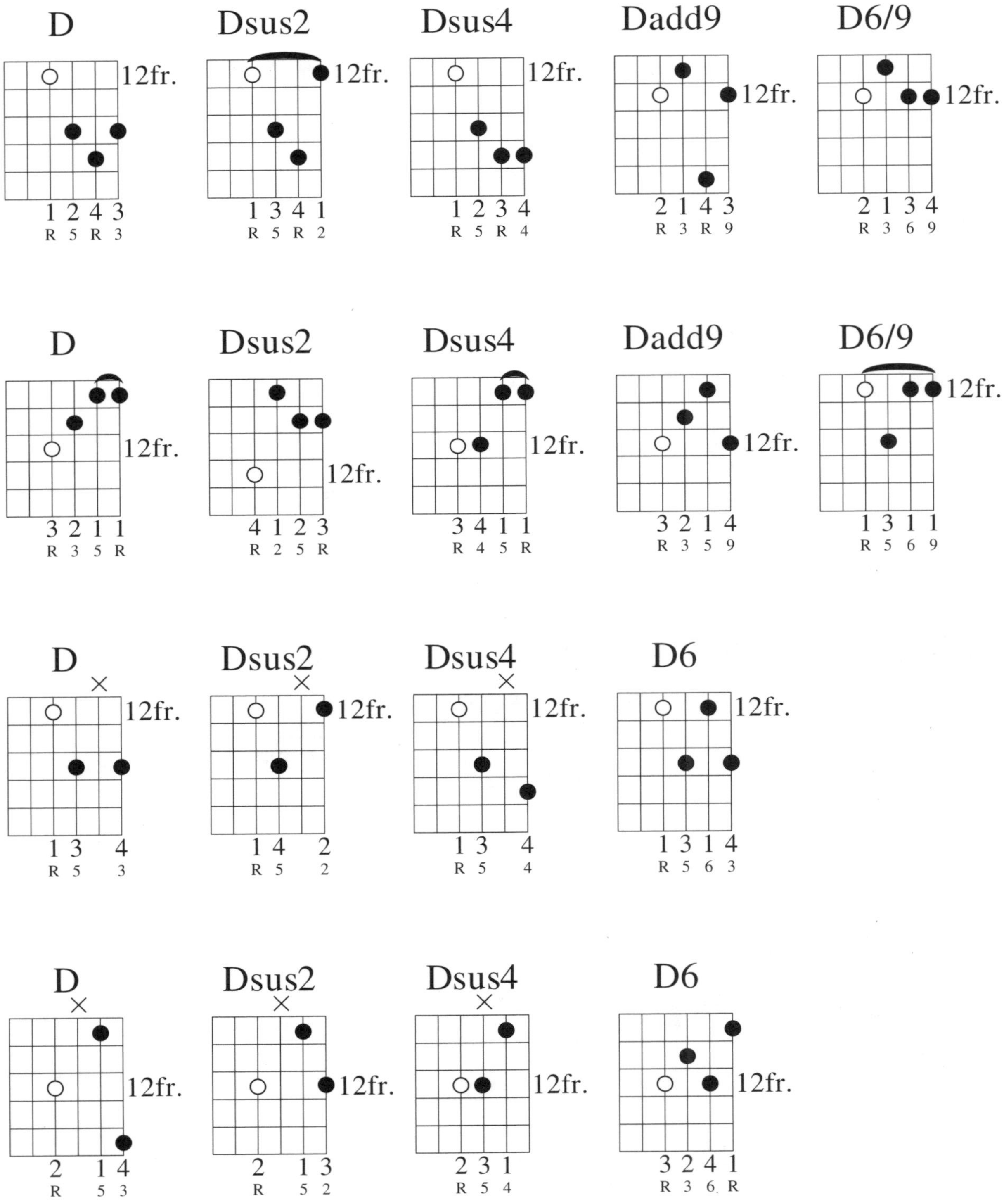

D
12fr.
1 2 4 3
R 5 R 3
Dsus2
12fr.
1 3 4 1
R 5 R 2
Dsus4
12fr.
1 2 3 4
R 5 R 4
Dadd9
12fr.
2 1 4 3
R 3 R 9
D6/9
12fr.
2 1 3 4
R 3 6 9
D
12fr.
3 2 1 1
R 3 5 R
Dsus2
12fr.
4 1 2 3
R 2 5 R
Dsus4
12fr.
3 4 1 1
R 4 5 R
Dadd9
12fr.
3 2 1 4
R 3 5 9
D6/9
12fr.
1 3 1 1
R 5 6 9
D
12fr.
1 3 4
R 5 3
Dsus2
12fr.
1 4 2
R 5 2
Dsus4
12fr.
1 3 4
R 5 4
D6
12fr.
1 3 1 4
R 5 6 3
D
12fr.
2 1 4
R 5 3
Dsus2
12fr.
2 1 3
R 5 2
Dsus4
12fr.
2 3 1
R 5 4
D6
12fr.
3 2 4 1
R 3 6 R

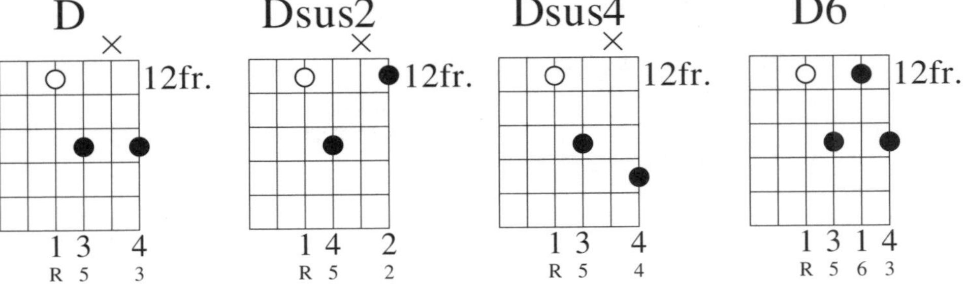

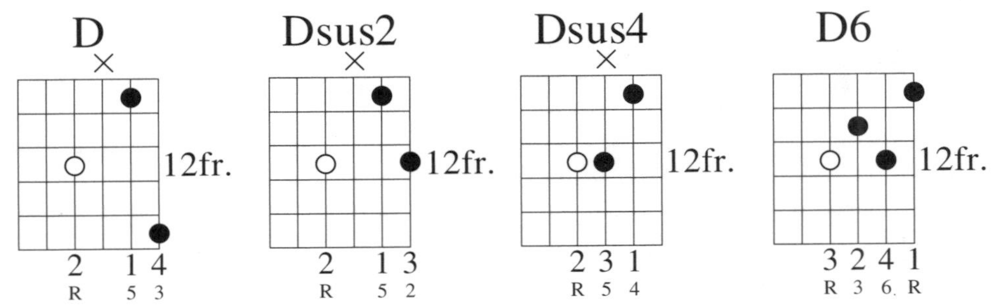

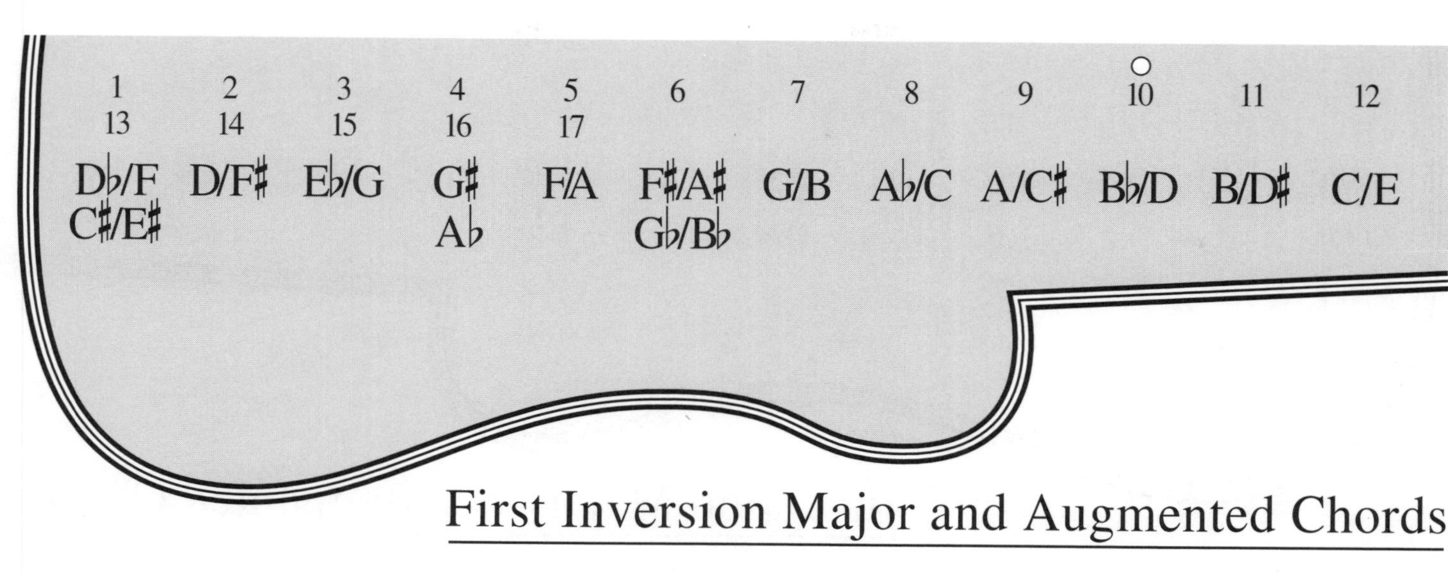

First Inversion Major and Augmented Chords

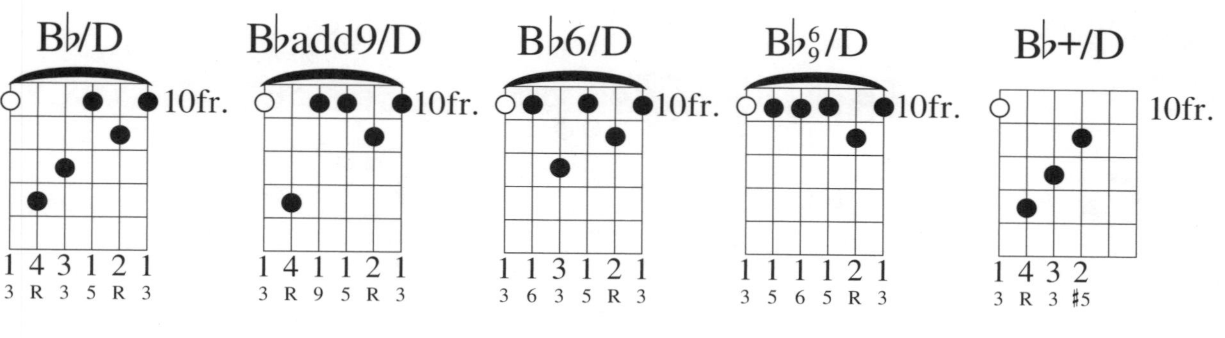

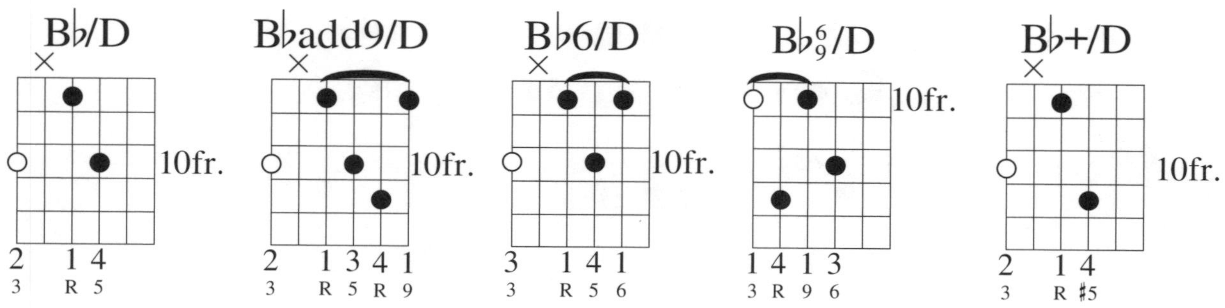

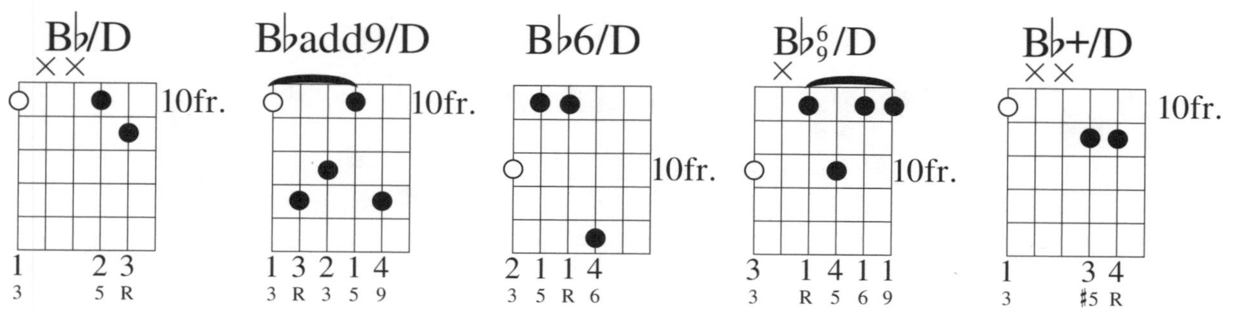

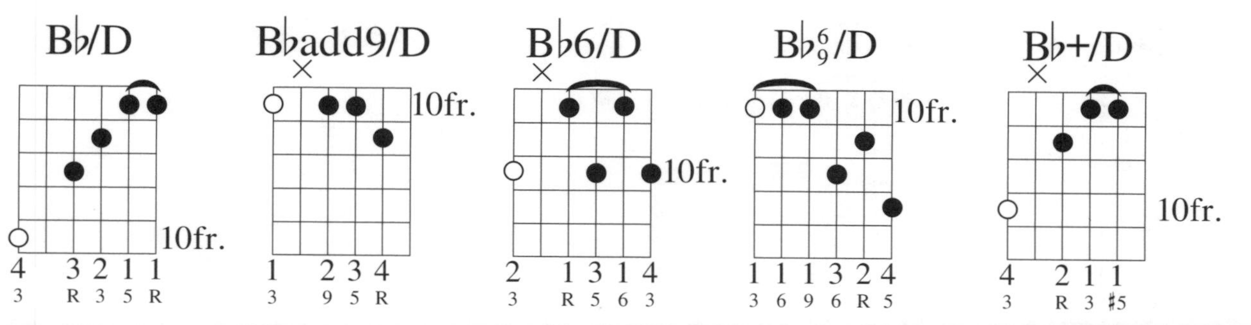

1 13 F♯/A♯ G♭/B♭
2 14 G/B
3 15 A♭/C
4 16 A/C♯
5 17 B♭/D
6 B/D♯
7 C/E
8 D♭/F C♯/E♯
9 D/F♯
10 E♭/G
11 E/G♯
12 F/A

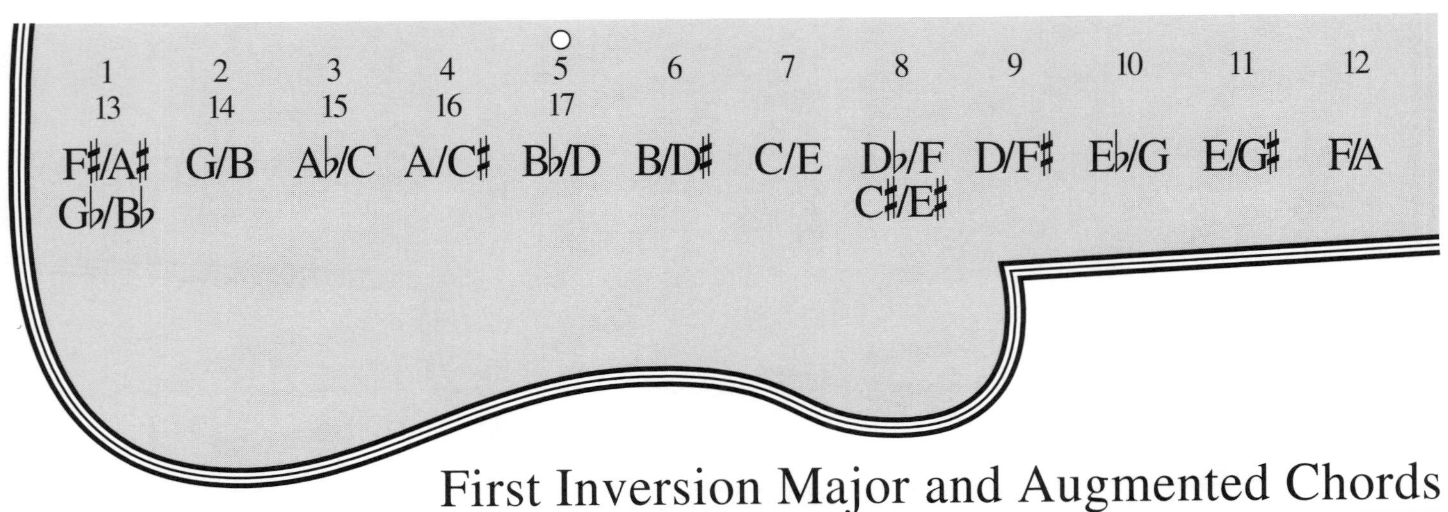

First Inversion Major and Augmented Chords

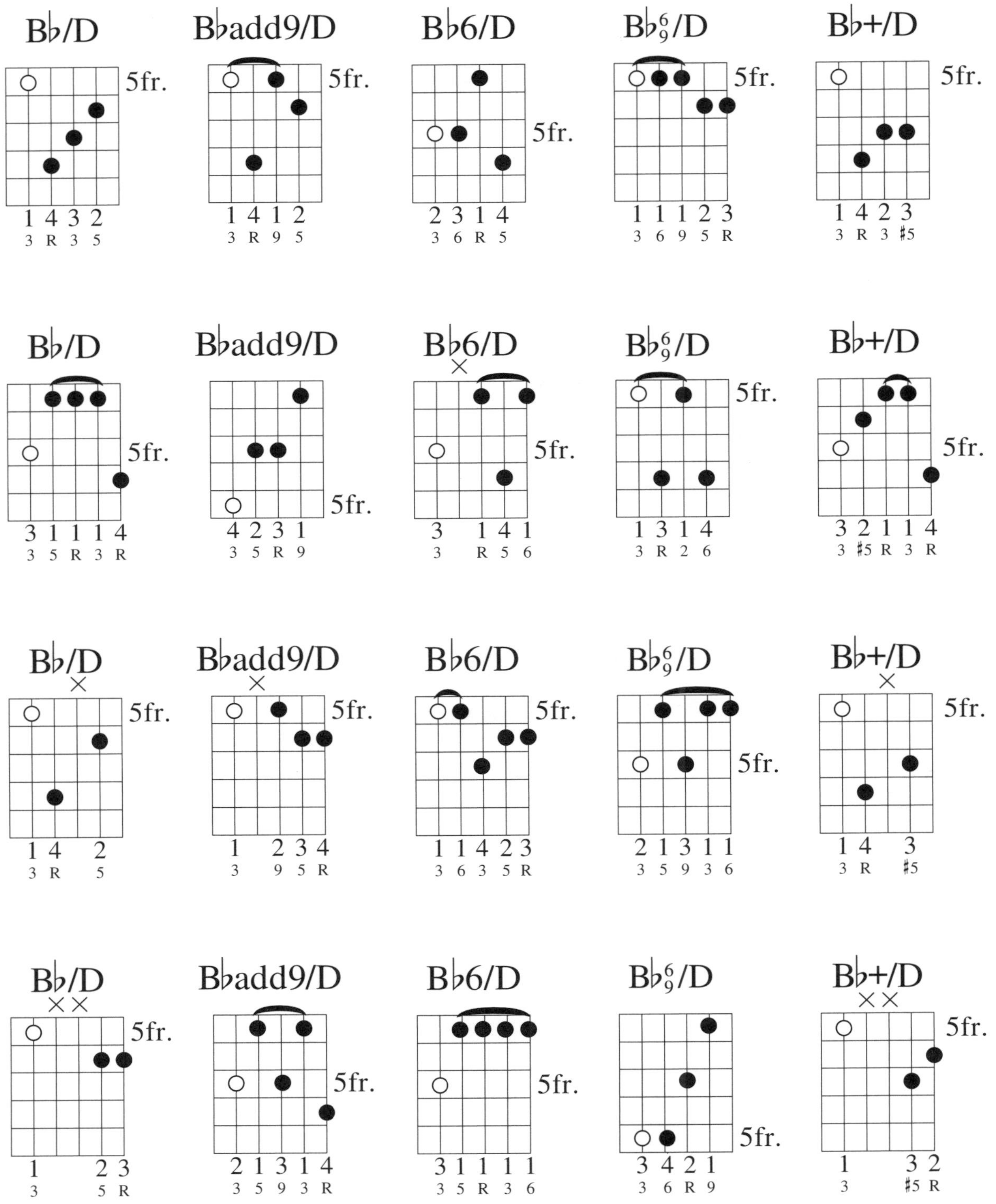

B♭/D 5fr. 1 4 3 2 3 R 3 5
B♭add9/D 5fr. 1 4 1 2 3 R 9 5
B♭6/D 5fr. 2 3 1 4 3 6 R 5
B♭$^6_9$/D 5fr. 1 1 1 2 3 3 6 9 5 R
B♭+/D 5fr. 1 4 2 3 3 R 3 ♯5
B♭/D 5fr. 3 1 1 1 4 3 5 R 3 R
B♭add9/D 5fr. 4 2 3 1 3 5 R 9
B♭6/D 5fr. 3 1 4 1 3 R 5 6
B♭$^6_9$/D 5fr. 1 3 1 4 3 R 2 6
B♭+/D 5fr. 3 2 1 1 4 3 ♯5 R 3 R
B♭/D 5fr. 1 4 2 3 R 5
B♭add9/D 5fr. 1 2 3 4 3 9 5 R
B♭6/D 5fr. 1 1 4 2 3 3 6 3 5 R
B♭$^6_9$/D 5fr. 2 1 3 1 1 3 5 9 3 6
B♭+/D 5fr. 1 4 3 3 R ♯5
B♭/D 5fr. 1 2 3 3 5 R
B♭add9/D 5fr. 2 1 3 1 4 3 5 9 3 R
B♭6/D 5fr. 3 1 1 1 1 3 5 R 3 6
B♭$^6_9$/D 5fr. 3 4 2 1 3 6 R 9
B♭+/D 5fr. 1 3 2 3 ♯5 R

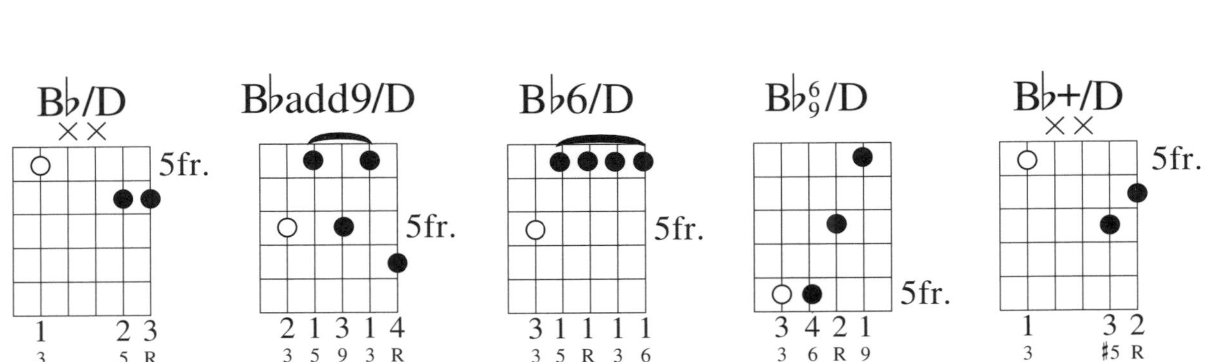

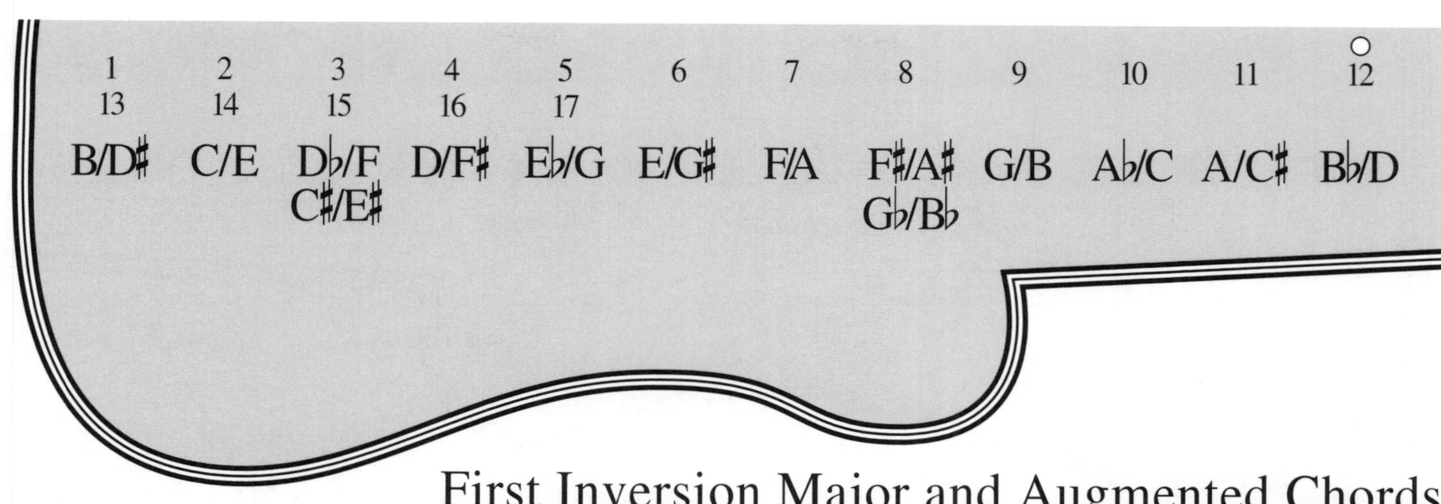

First Inversion Major and Augmented Chords

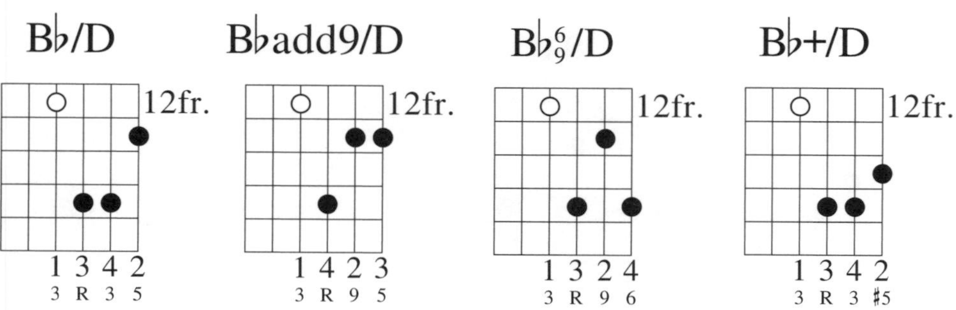

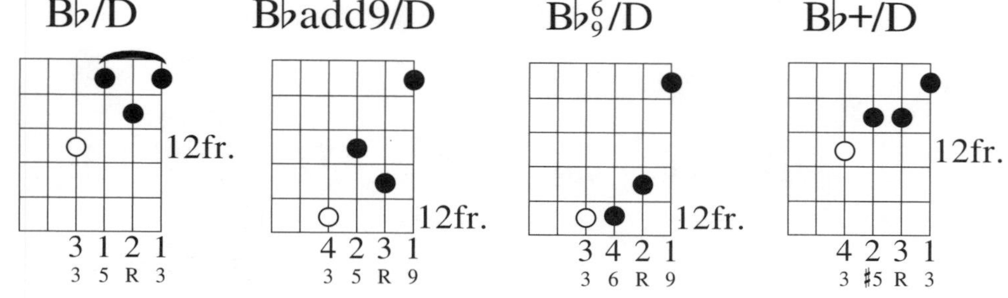

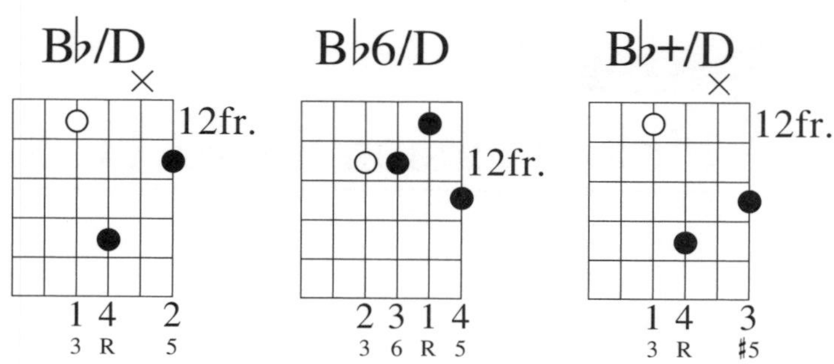

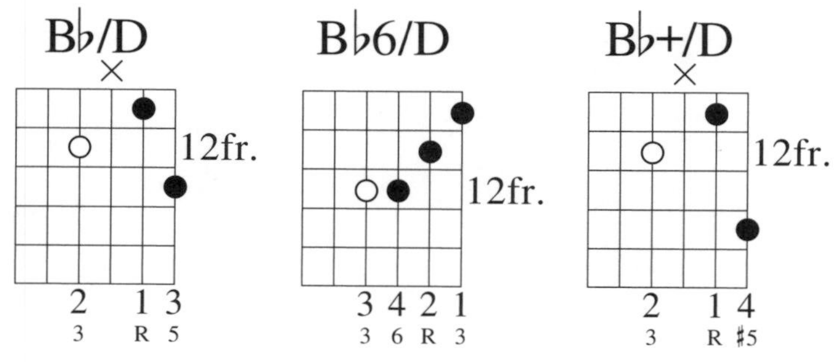

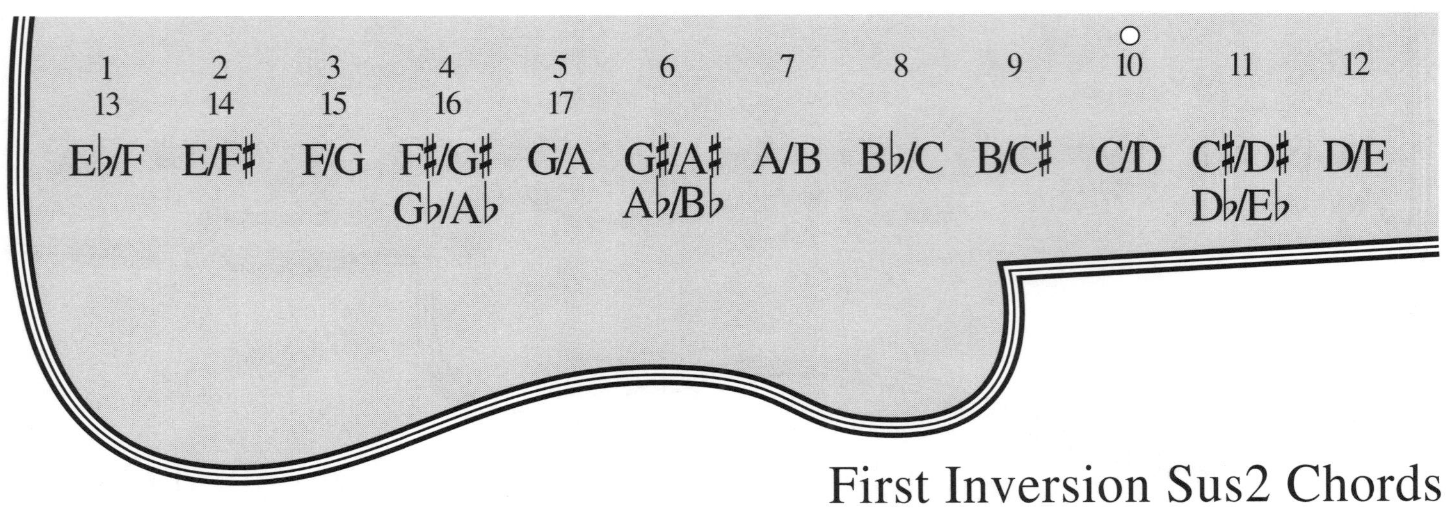

First Inversion Sus2 Chords

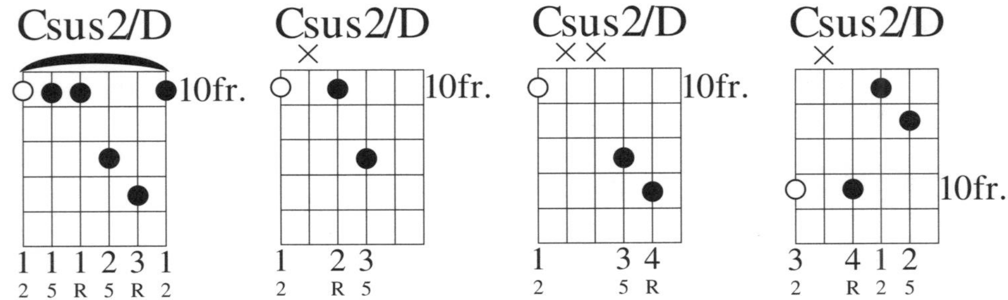

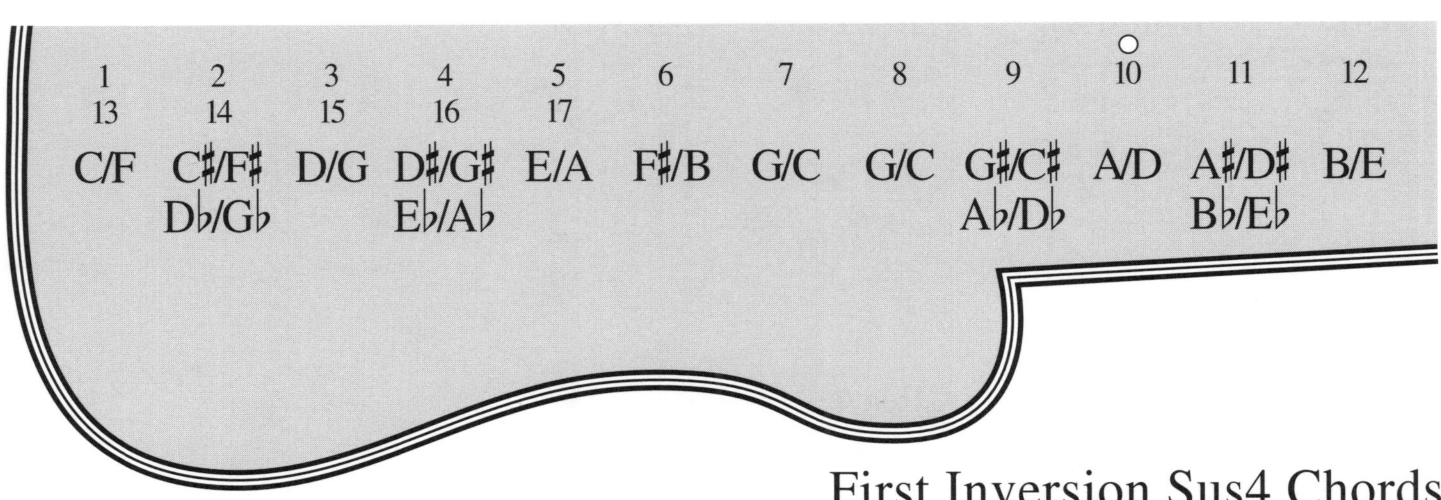

First Inversion Sus4 Chords

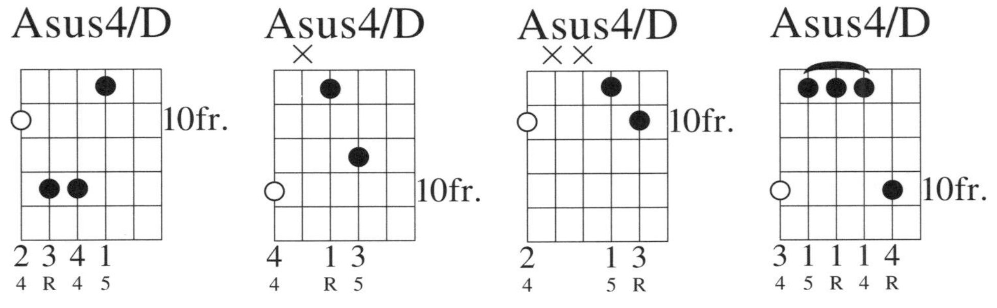

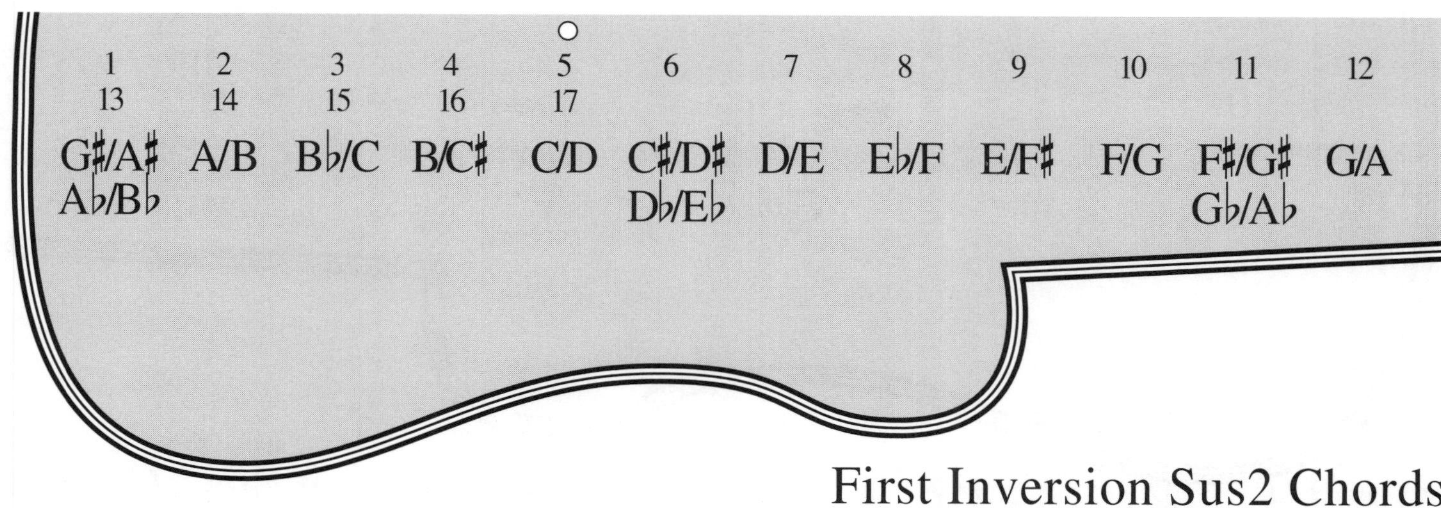

First Inversion Sus2 Chords

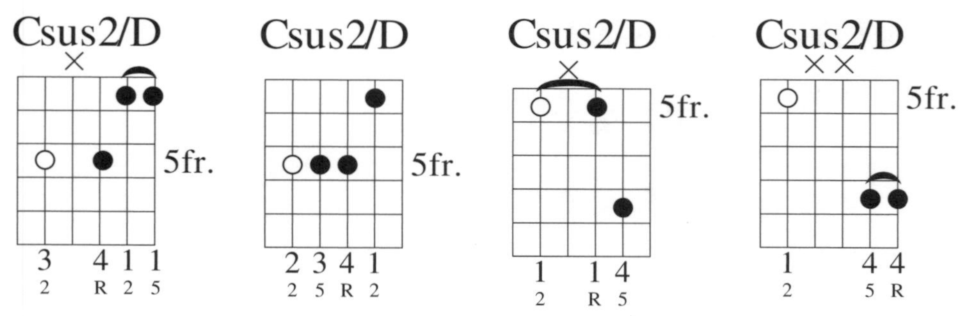

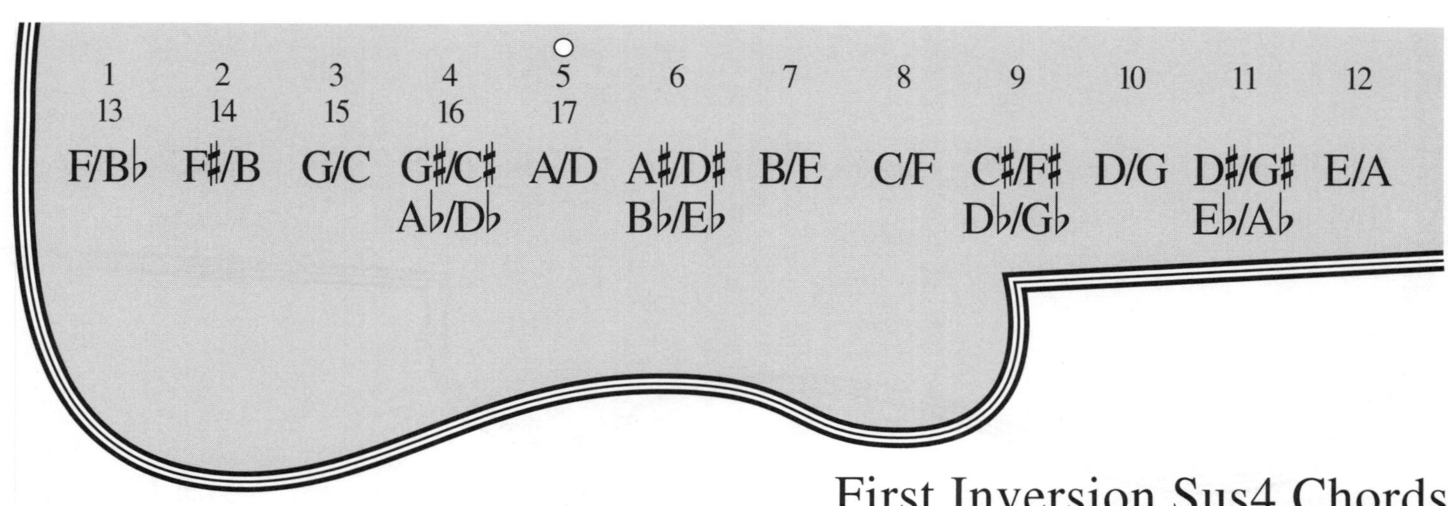

First Inversion Sus4 Chords

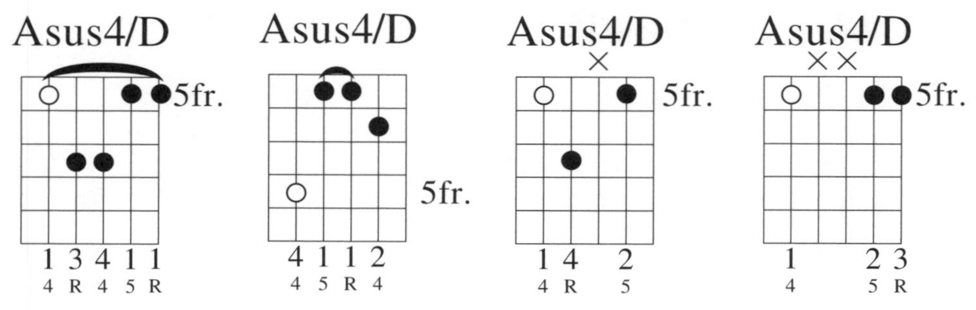

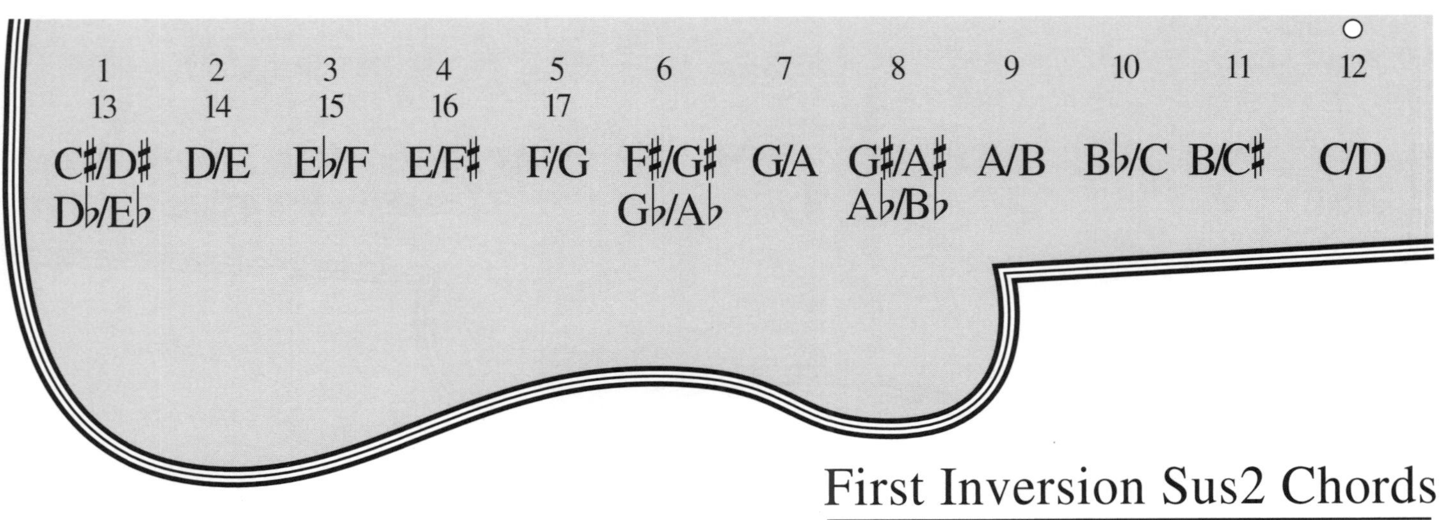

First Inversion Sus2 Chords

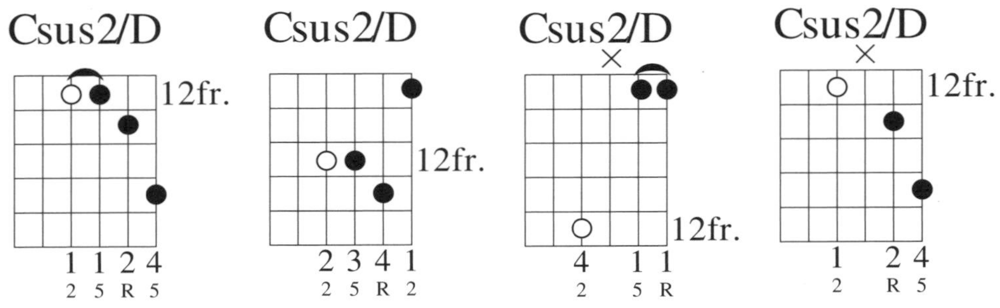

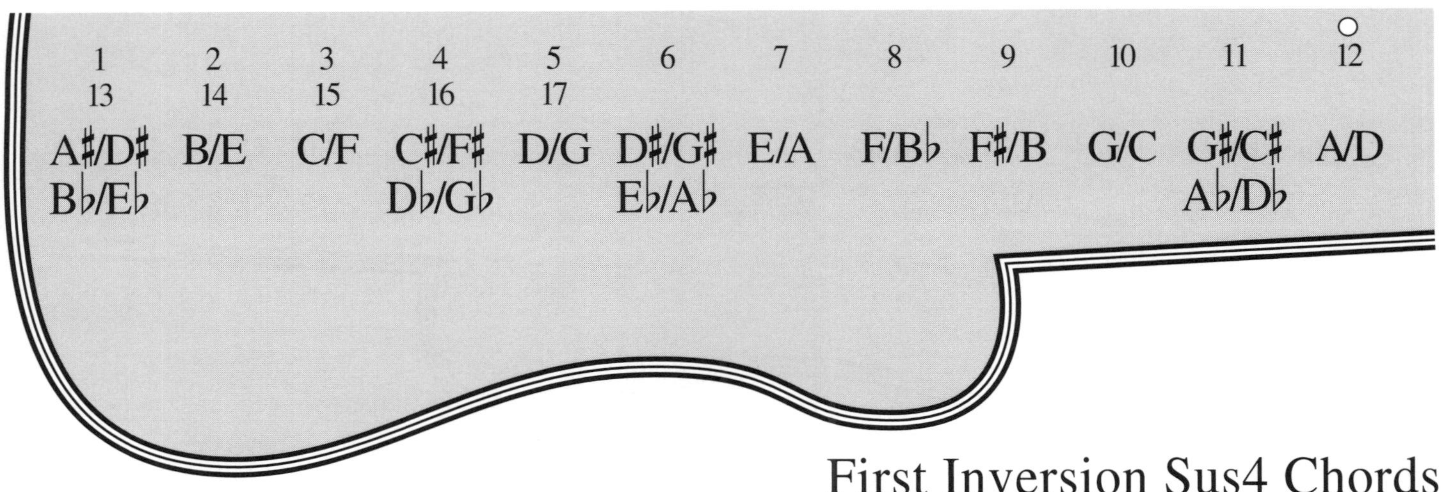

First Inversion Sus4 Chords

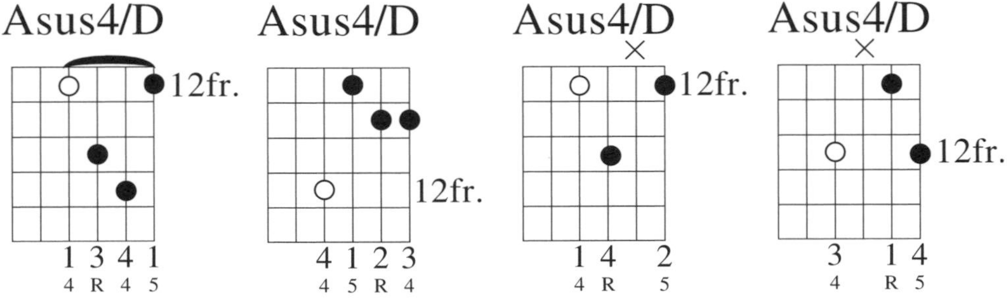

Second Inversion Major and Sus Chords

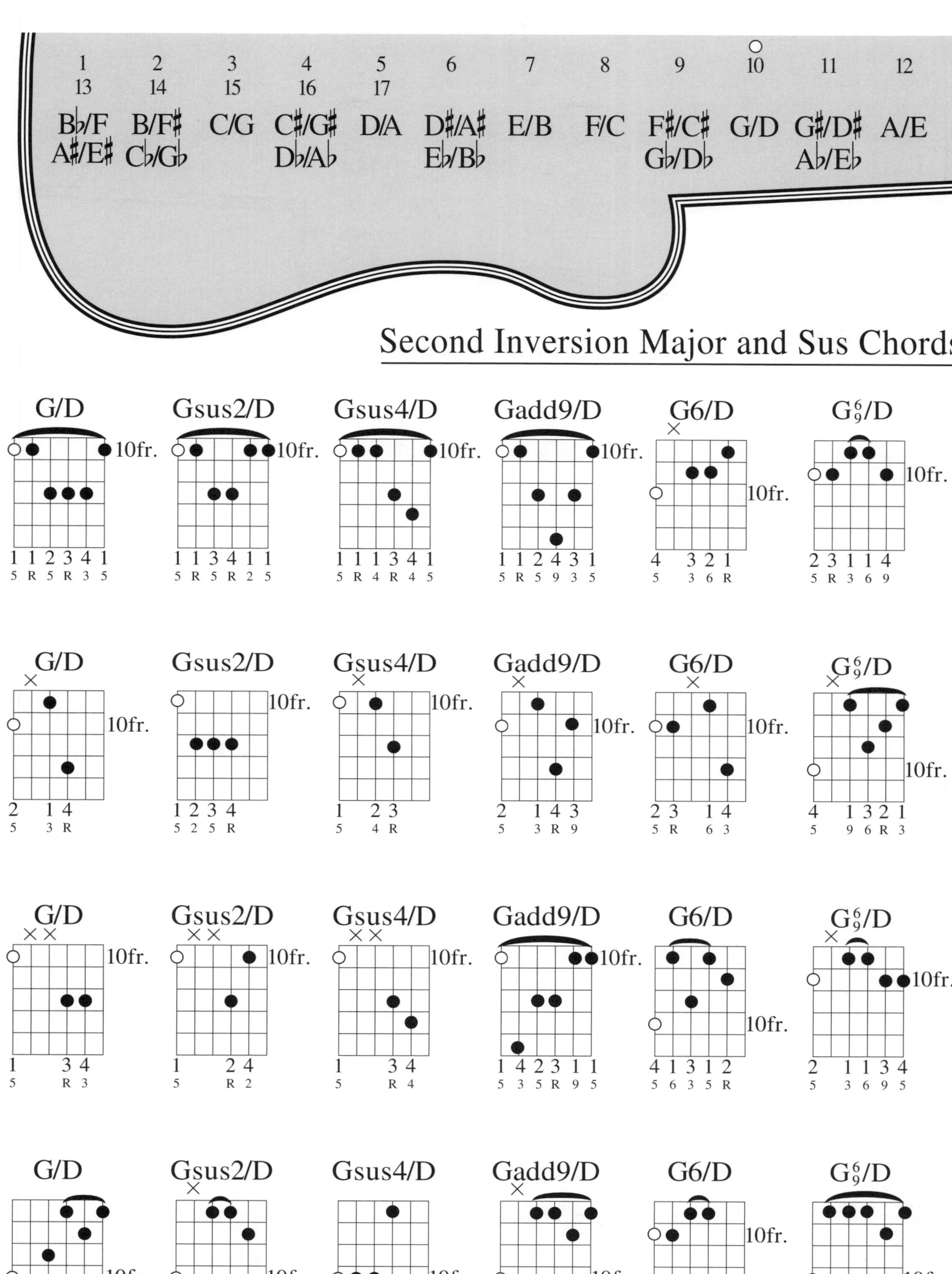

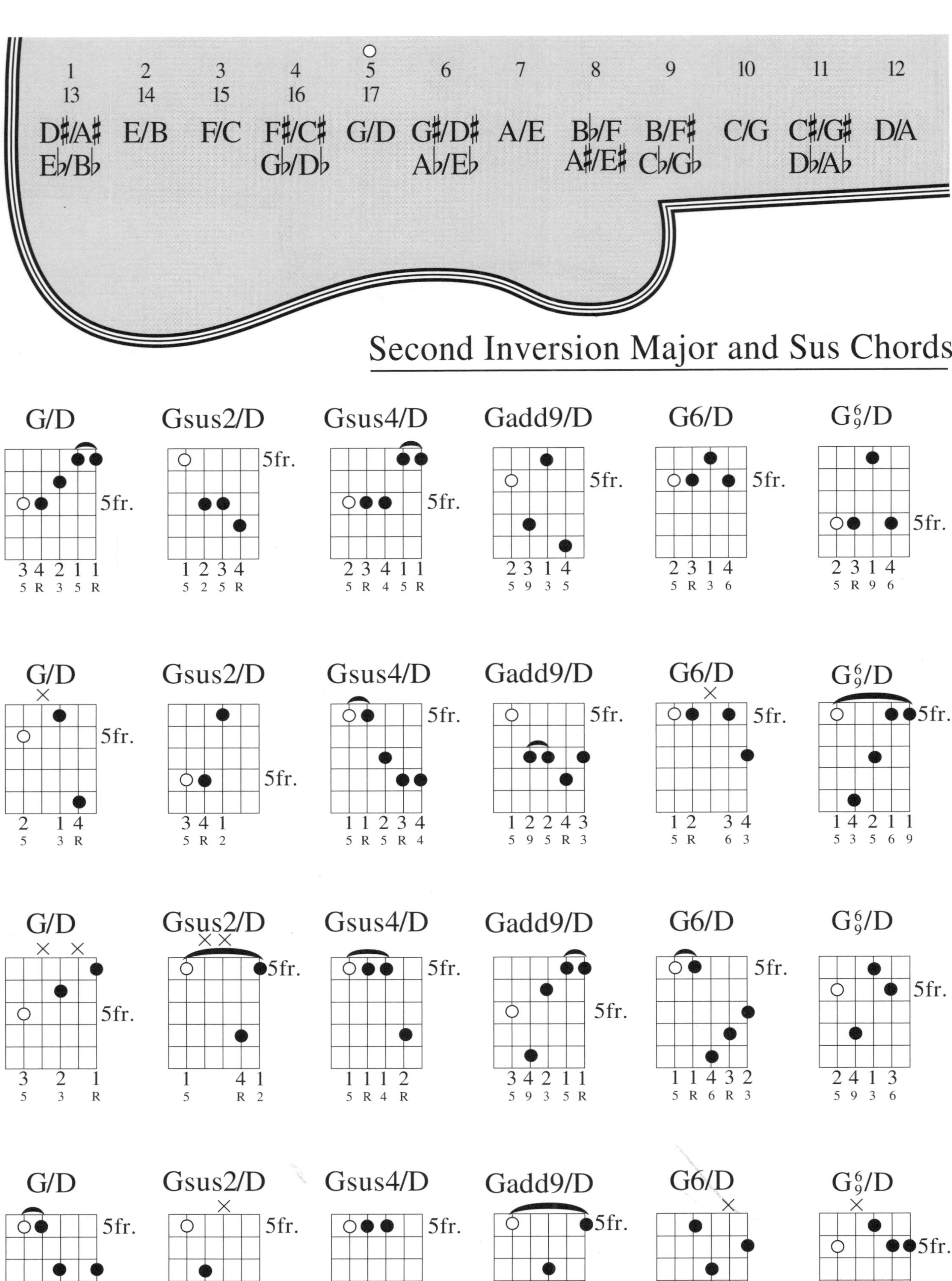
1 13 D♯/A♯ E♭/B♭
2 14 E/B
3 15 F/C
4 16 F♯/C♯ G♭/D♭
5 17 G/D
6 G♯/D♯ A♭/E♭
7 A/E
8 B♭/F A♯/E♯
9 B/F♯ C♭/G♭
10 C/G
11 C♯/G♯ D♭/A♭
12 D/A
Second Inversion Major and Sus Chords
G/D 5fr. 3 4 2 1 1 5 R 3 5 R
Gsus2/D 5fr. 1 2 3 4 5 2 5 R
Gsus4/D 5fr. 2 3 4 1 1 5 R 4 5 R
Gadd9/D 5fr. 2 3 1 4 5 9 3 5
G6/D 5fr. 2 3 1 4 5 R 3 6
G6/9/D 5fr. 2 3 1 4 5 R 9 6
G/D 5fr. 2 1 4 5 3 R
Gsus2/D 5fr. 3 4 1 5 R 2
Gsus4/D 5fr. 1 1 2 3 4 5 R 5 R 4
Gadd9/D 5fr. 1 2 2 4 3 5 9 5 R 3
G6/D 5fr. 1 2 3 4 5 R 6 3
G6/9/D 5fr. 1 4 2 1 1 5 3 5 6 9
G/D 5fr. 3 2 1 5 3 R
Gsus2/D 5fr. 1 4 1 5 R 2
Gsus4/D 5fr. 1 1 1 2 5 R 4 R
Gadd9/D 5fr. 3 4 2 1 1 5 9 3 5 R
G6/D 5fr. 1 1 4 3 2 5 R 6 R 3
G6/9/D 5fr. 2 4 1 3 5 9 3 6
G/D 5fr. 1 1 2 4 3 5 R 5 R 3
Gsus2/D 5fr. 1 3 4 5 2 R
Gsus4/D 5fr. 1 2 3 5 R 4
Gadd9/D 5fr. 1 4 2 3 1 5 3 5 R 9
G6/D 5fr. 4 1 3 2 5 6 3 R
G6/9/D 5fr. 2 1 3 4 5 3 6 9

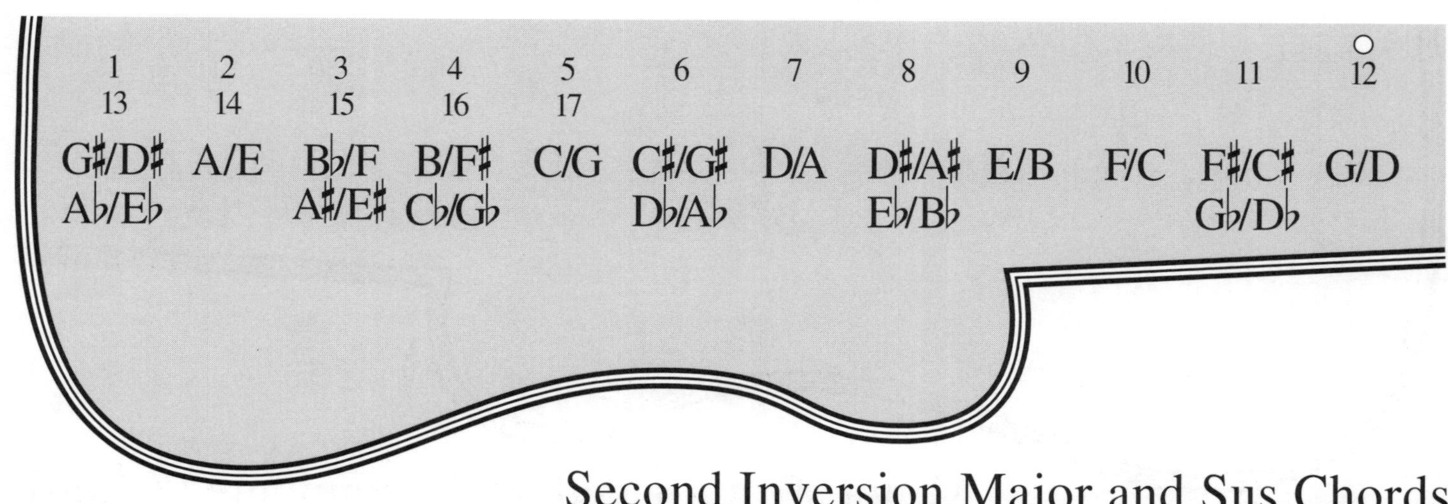

Second Inversion Major and Sus Chords

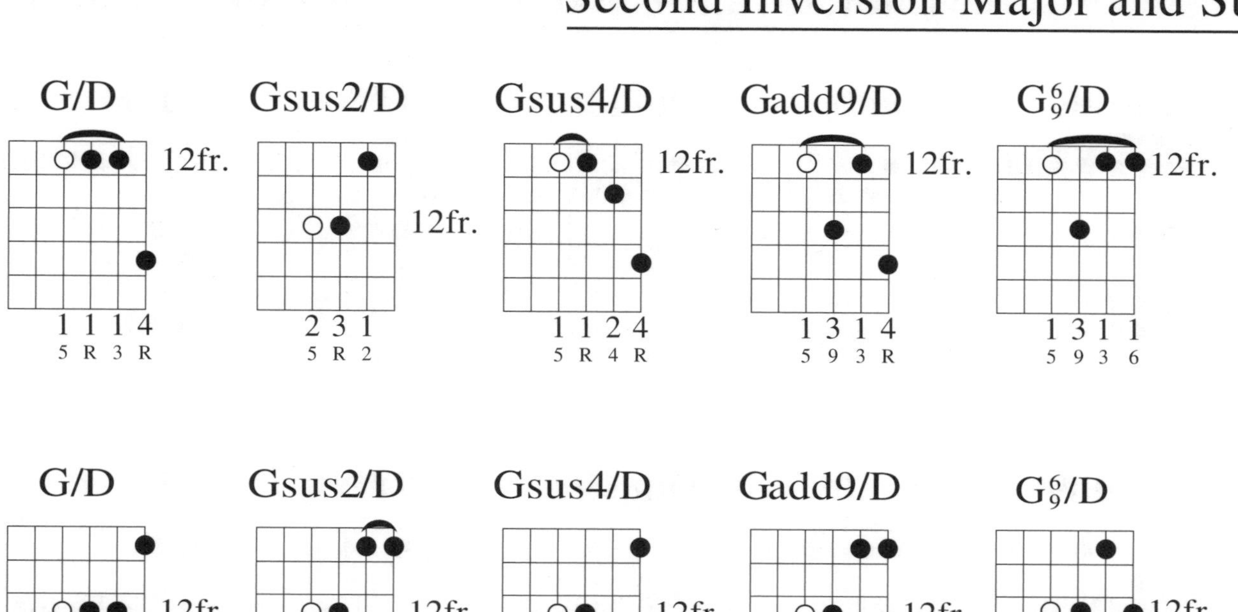

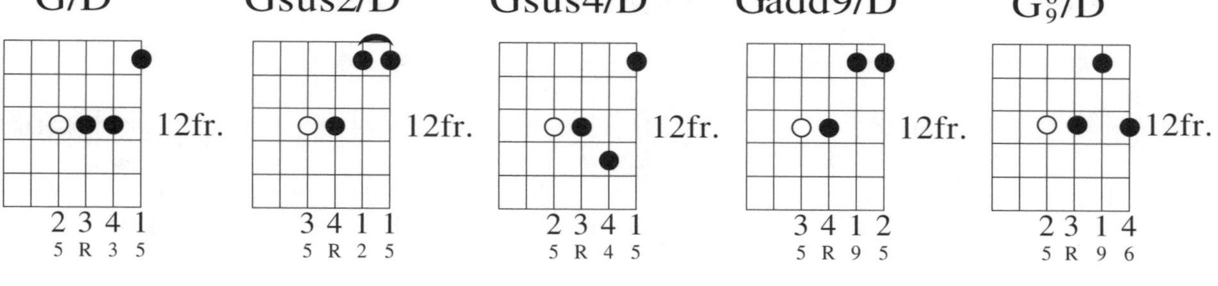

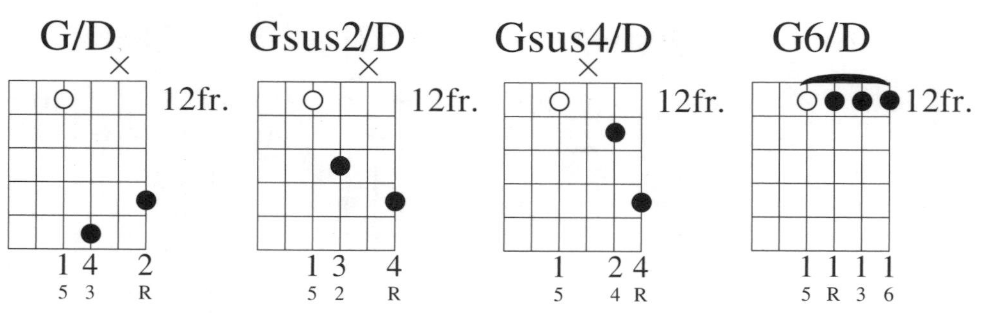

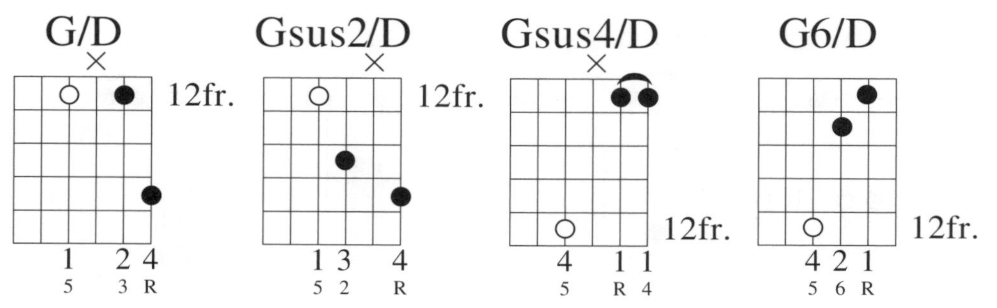

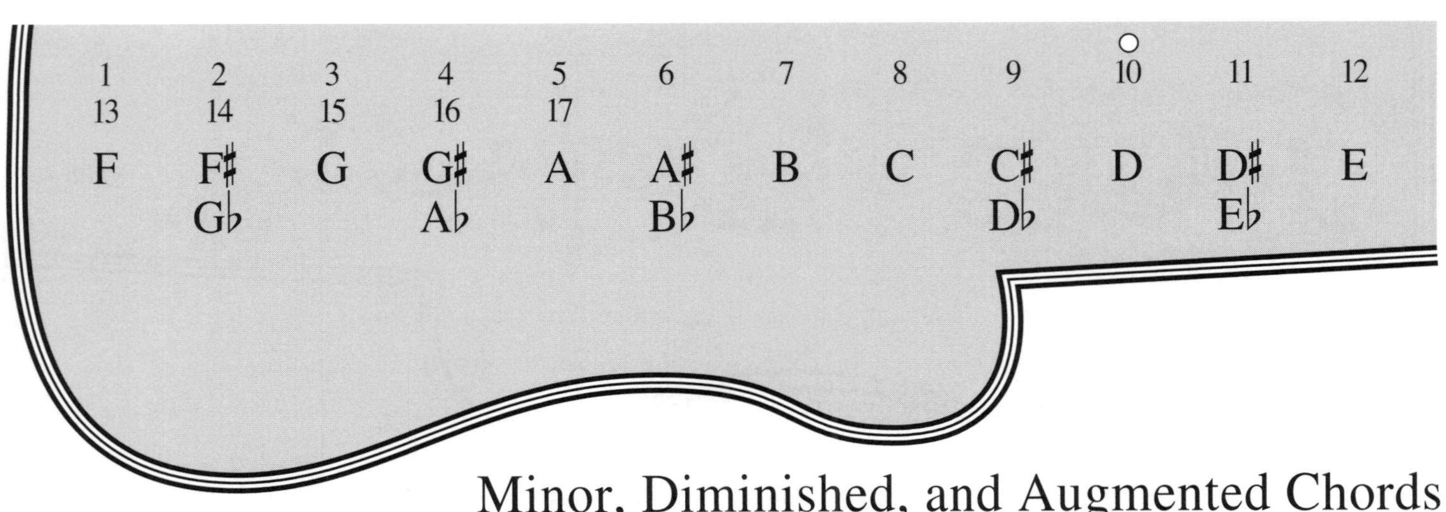

Minor, Diminished, and Augmented Chords

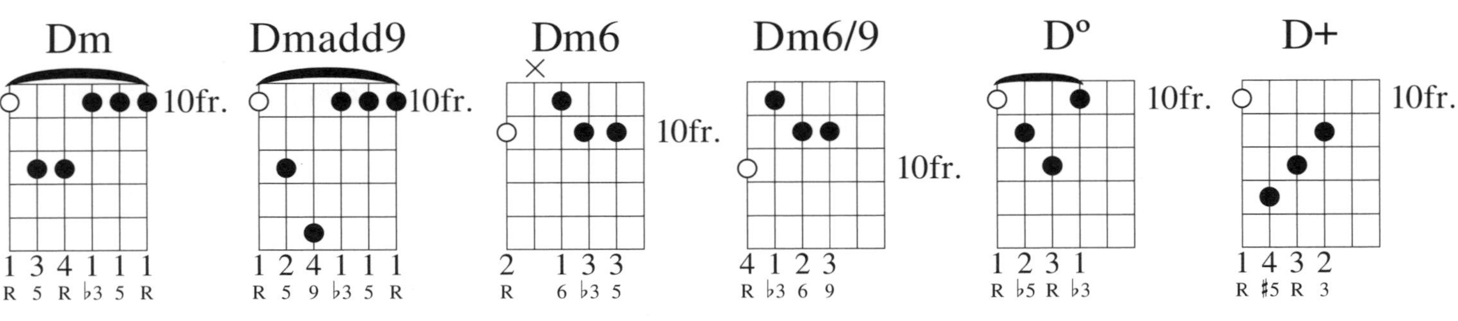

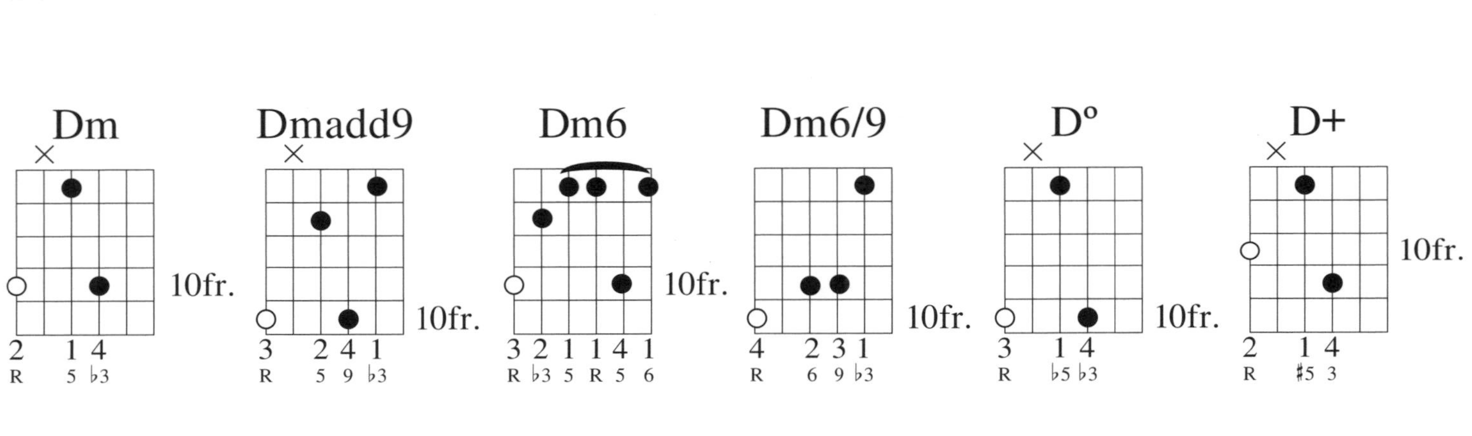

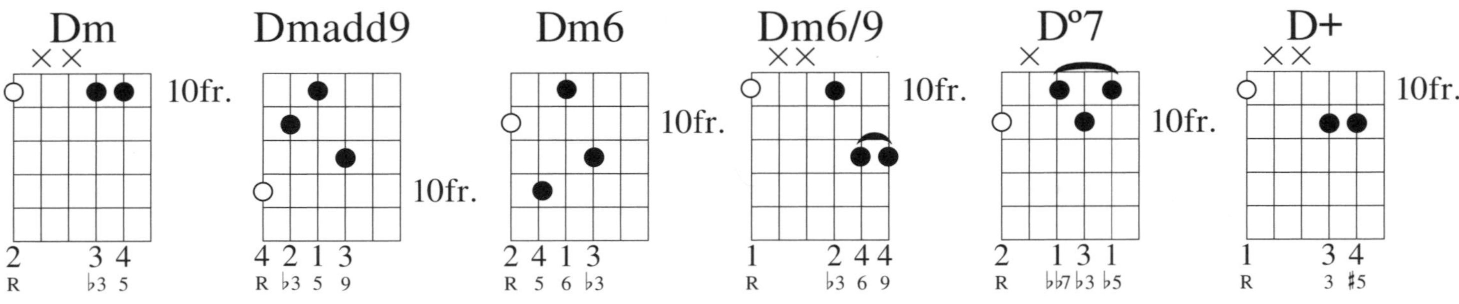

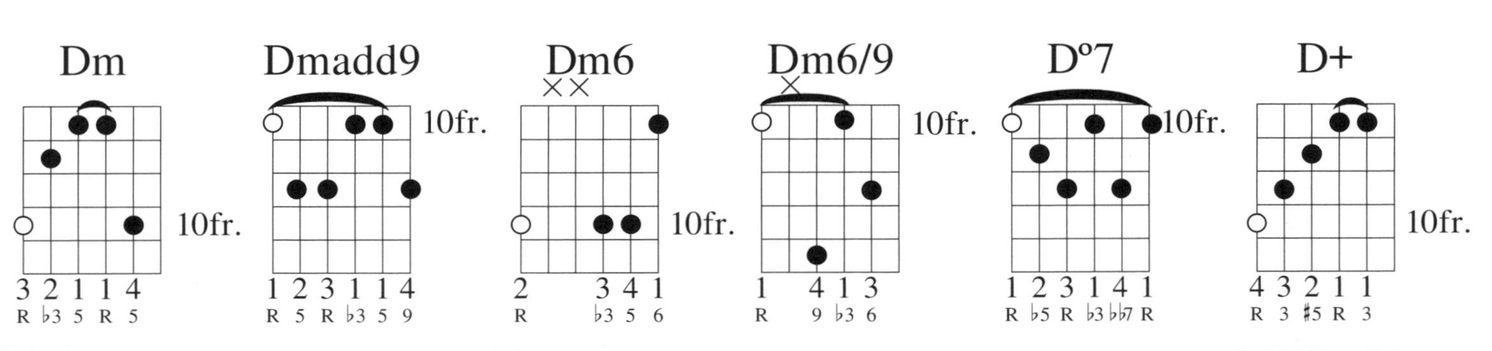

1 13 A♯ B♭
2 14 B
3 15 C
4 16 C♯ D♭
5 17 D
6 D♯ E♭
7 E
8 F
9 F♯ G♭
10 G
11 G♯ A♭
12 A

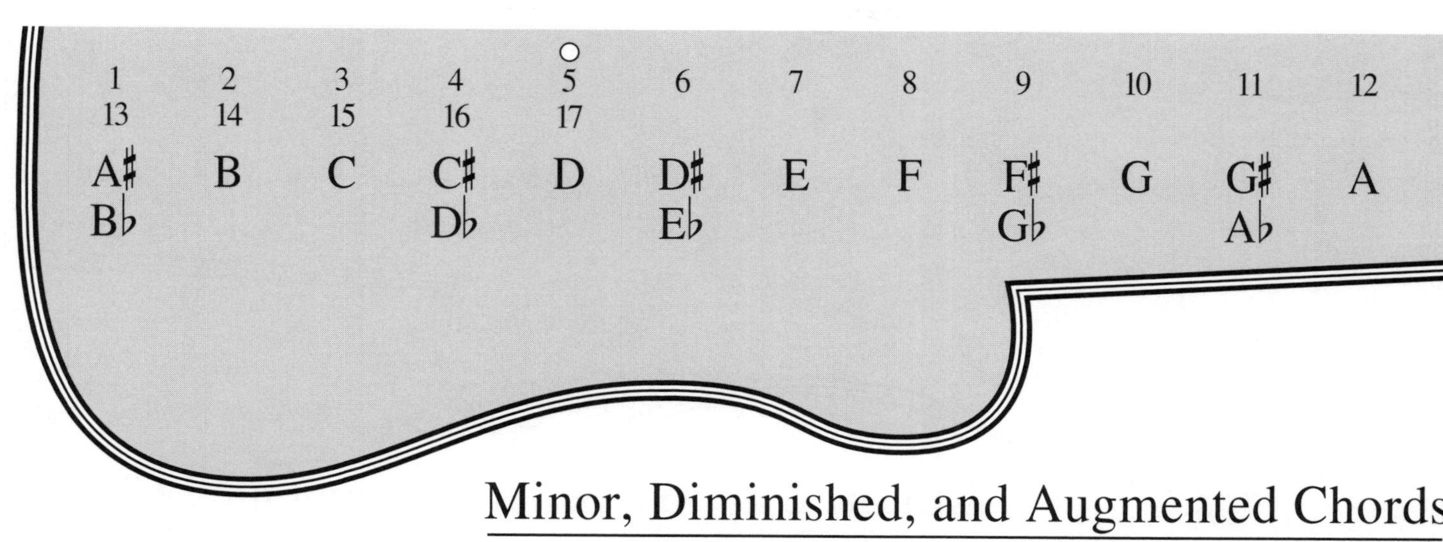

Minor, Diminished, and Augmented Chords

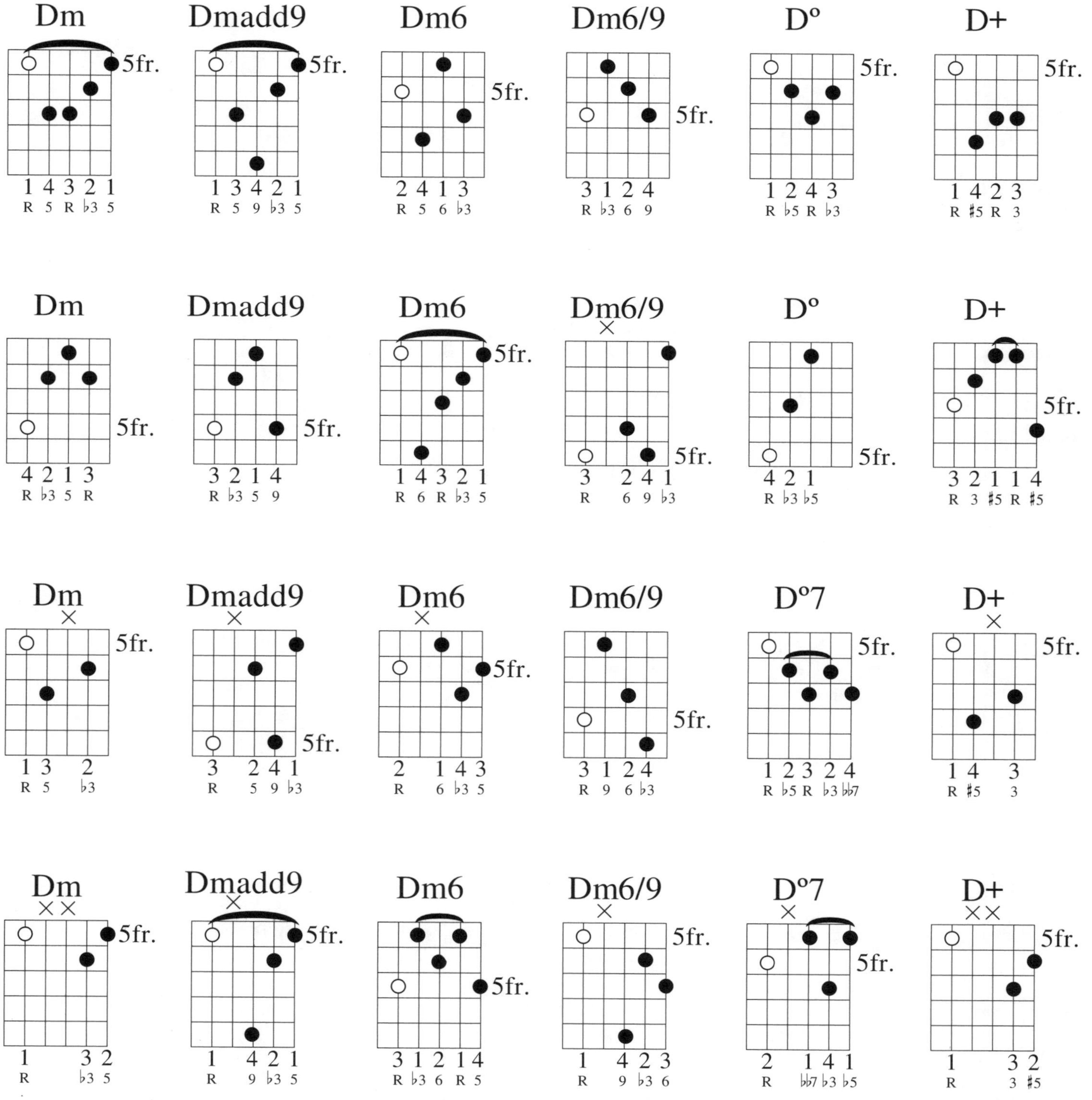

Dm 5fr. 1 4 3 2 1 R 5 R ♭3 5
Dmadd9 5fr. 1 3 4 2 1 R 5 9 ♭3 5
Dm6 5fr. 2 4 1 3 R 5 6 ♭3
Dm6/9 5fr. 3 1 2 4 R ♭3 6 9
D° 5fr. 1 2 4 3 R ♭5 R ♭3
D+ 5fr. 1 4 2 3 R ♯5 R 3
Dm 5fr. 4 2 1 3 R ♭3 5 R
Dmadd9 5fr. 3 2 1 4 R ♭3 5 9
Dm6 5fr. 1 4 3 2 1 R 6 R ♭3 5
Dm6/9 5fr. 3 2 4 1 R 6 9 ♭3
D° 5fr. 4 2 1 R ♭3 ♭5
D+ 5fr. 3 2 1 1 4 R 3 ♯5 R ♯5
Dm 5fr. 1 3 2 R 5 ♭3
Dmadd9 5fr. 3 2 4 1 R 5 9 ♭3
Dm6 5fr. 2 1 4 3 R 6 ♭3 5
Dm6/9 5fr. 3 1 2 4 R 9 6 ♭3
D°7 5fr. 1 2 3 2 4 R ♭5 R ♭3 ♭♭7
D+ 5fr. 1 4 3 R ♯5 3
Dm 5fr. 1 3 2 R ♭3 5
Dmadd9 5fr. 1 4 2 1 R 9 ♭3 5
Dm6 5fr. 3 1 2 1 4 R ♭3 6 R 5
Dm6/9 5fr. 1 4 2 3 R 9 ♭3 6
D°7 5fr. 2 1 4 1 R ♭♭7 ♭3 ♭5
D+ 5fr. 1 3 2 R 3 ♯5

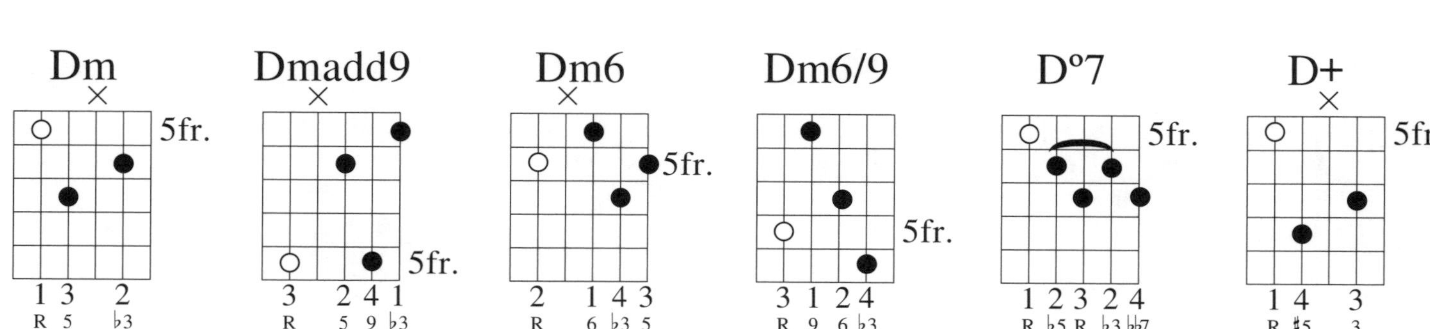

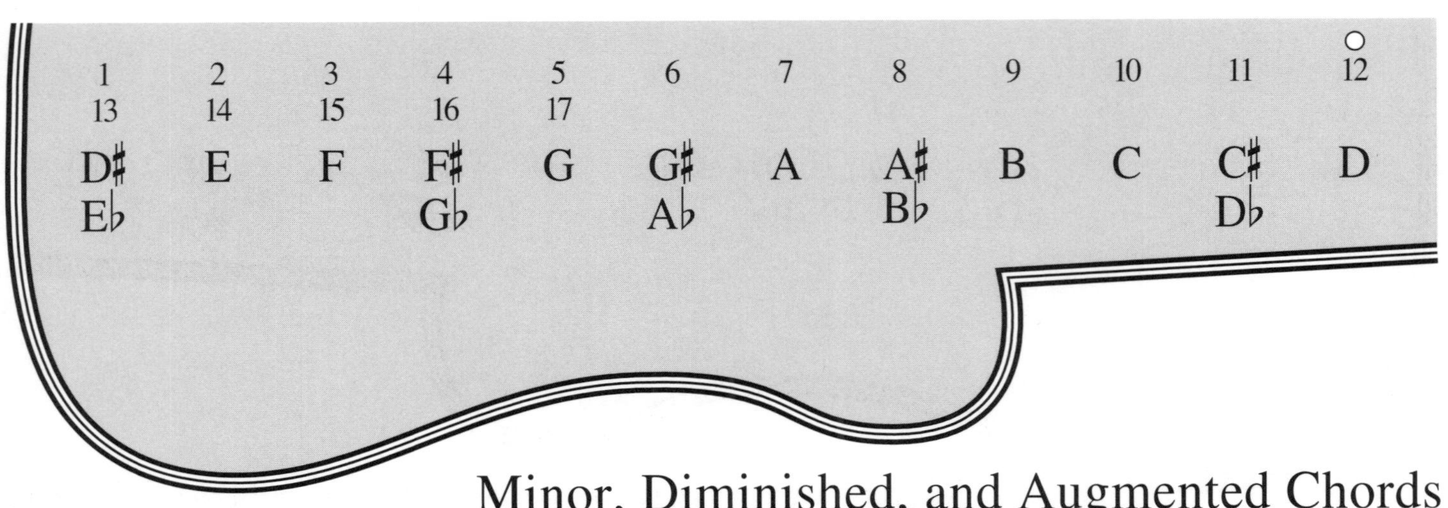

Minor, Diminished, and Augmented Chords

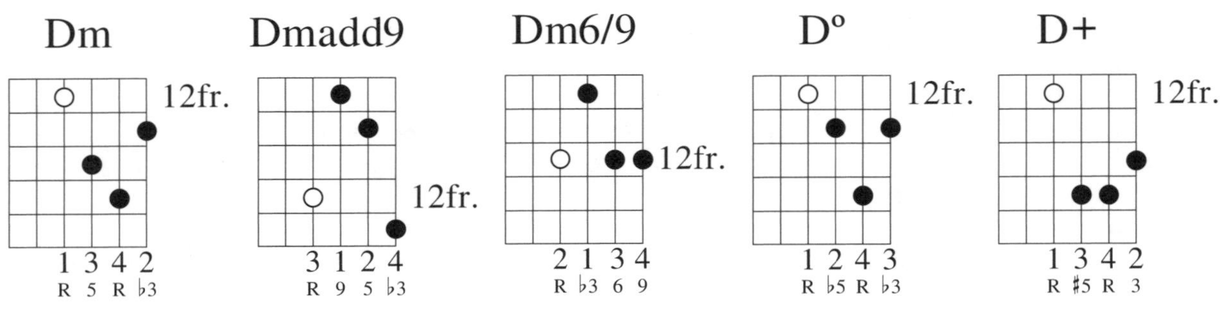

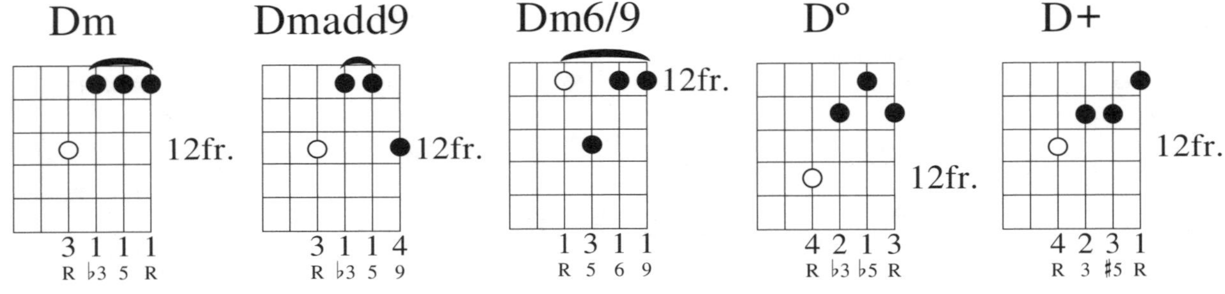

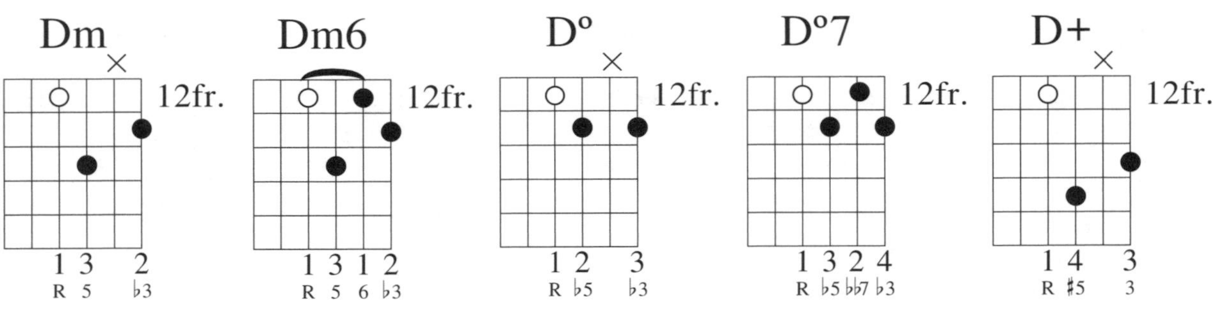

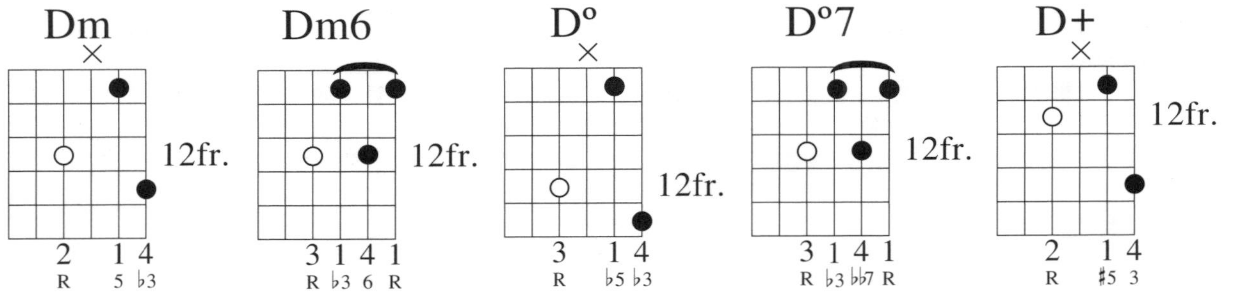

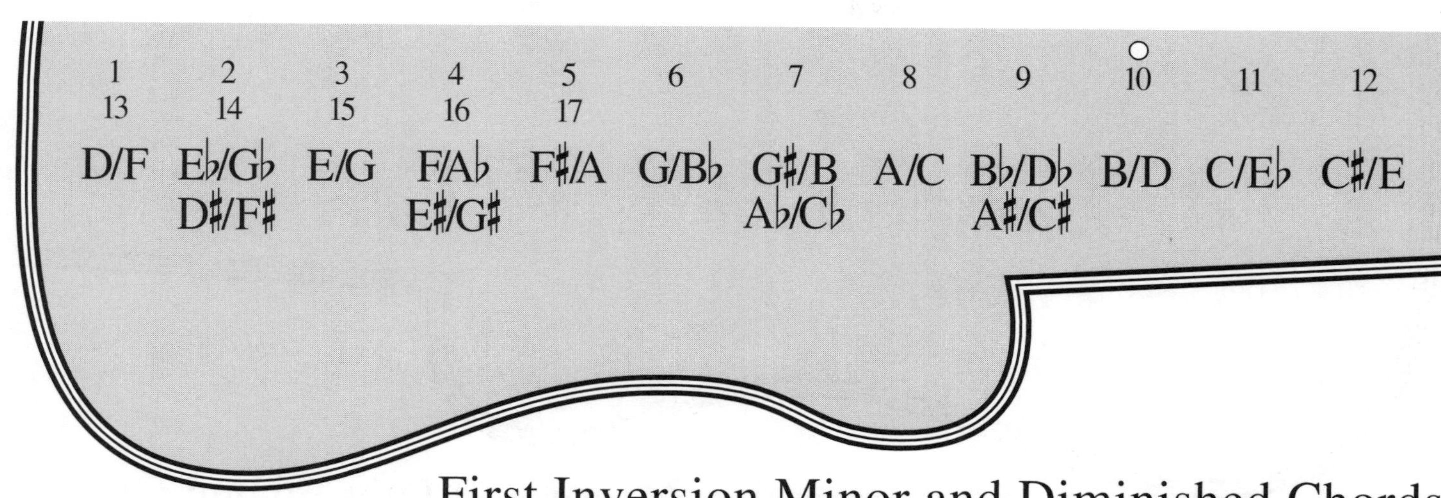

First Inversion Minor and Diminished Chords

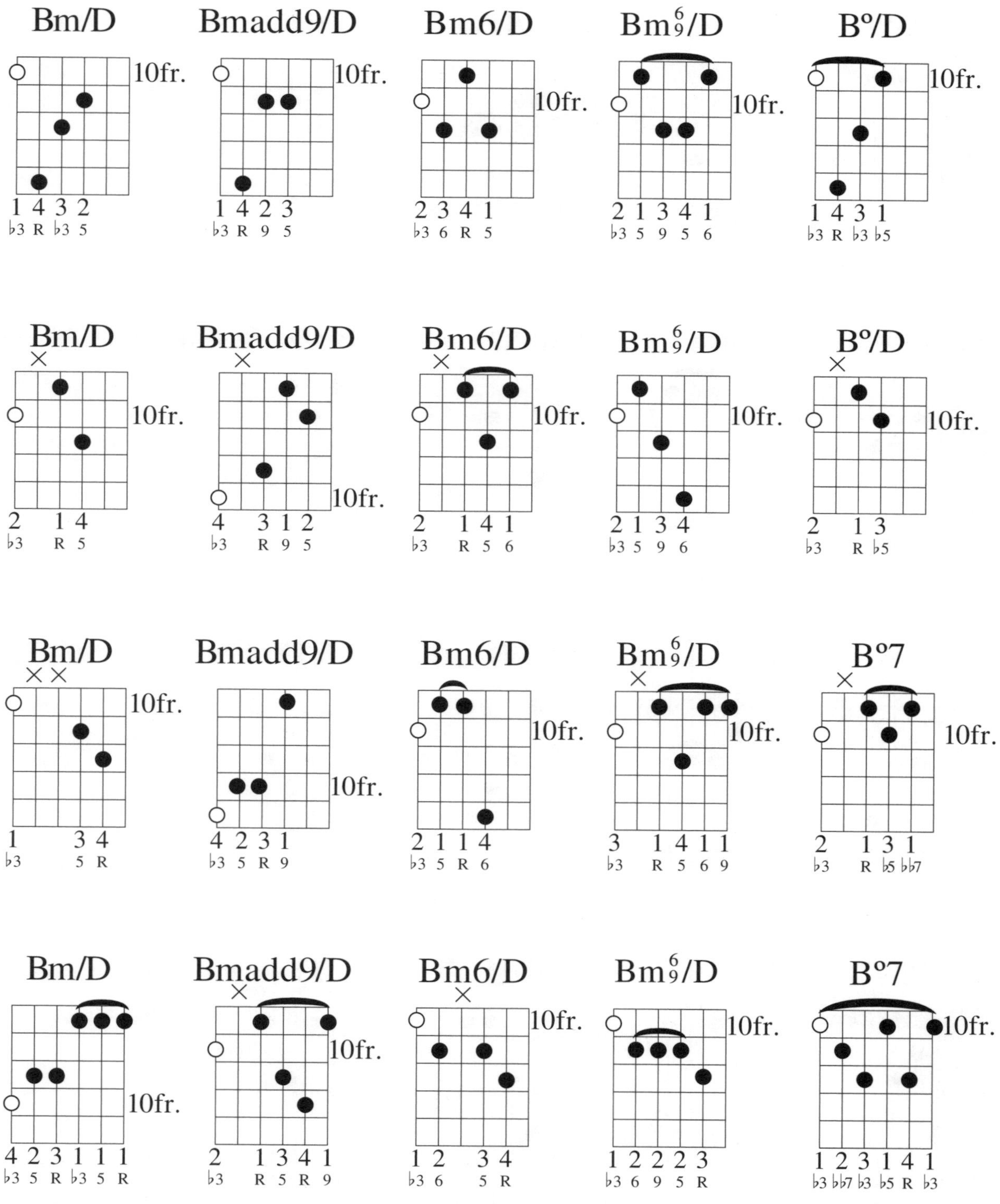

Bm/D
10fr.
1 4 3 2
♭3 R ♭3 5

Bmadd9/D
10fr.
1 4 2 3
♭3 R 9 5

Bm6/D
10fr.
2 3 4 1
♭3 6 R 5

Bm$^{6}_{9}$/D
10fr.
2 1 3 4 1
♭3 5 9 5 6

B°/D
10fr.
1 4 3 1
♭3 R ♭3 ♭5

Bm/D
10fr.
2 1 4
♭3 R 5

Bmadd9/D
10fr.
4 3 1 2
♭3 R 9 5

Bm6/D
10fr.
2 1 4 1
♭3 R 5 6

Bm$^{6}_{9}$/D
10fr.
2 1 3 4
♭3 5 9 6

B°/D
10fr.
2 1 3
♭3 R ♭5

Bm/D
10fr.
1 3 4
♭3 5 R

Bmadd9/D
10fr.
4 2 3 1
♭3 5 R 9

Bm6/D
10fr.
2 1 1 4
♭3 5 R 6

Bm$^{6}_{9}$/D
10fr.
3 1 4 1 1
♭3 R 5 6 9

B°7
10fr.
2 1 3 1
♭3 R ♭5 ♭♭7

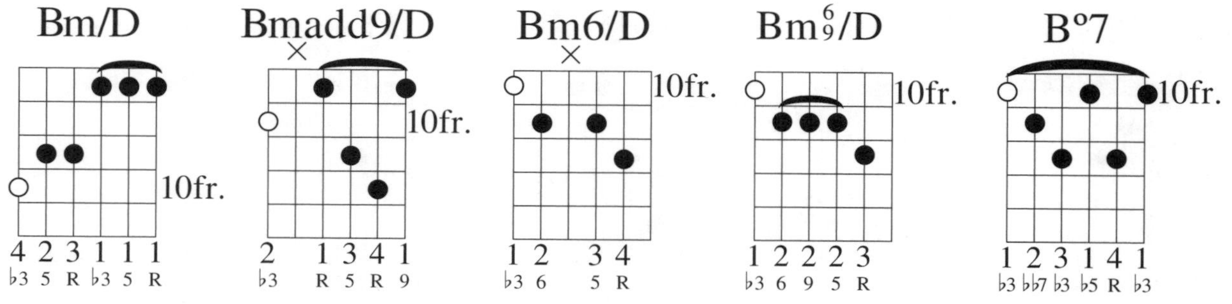

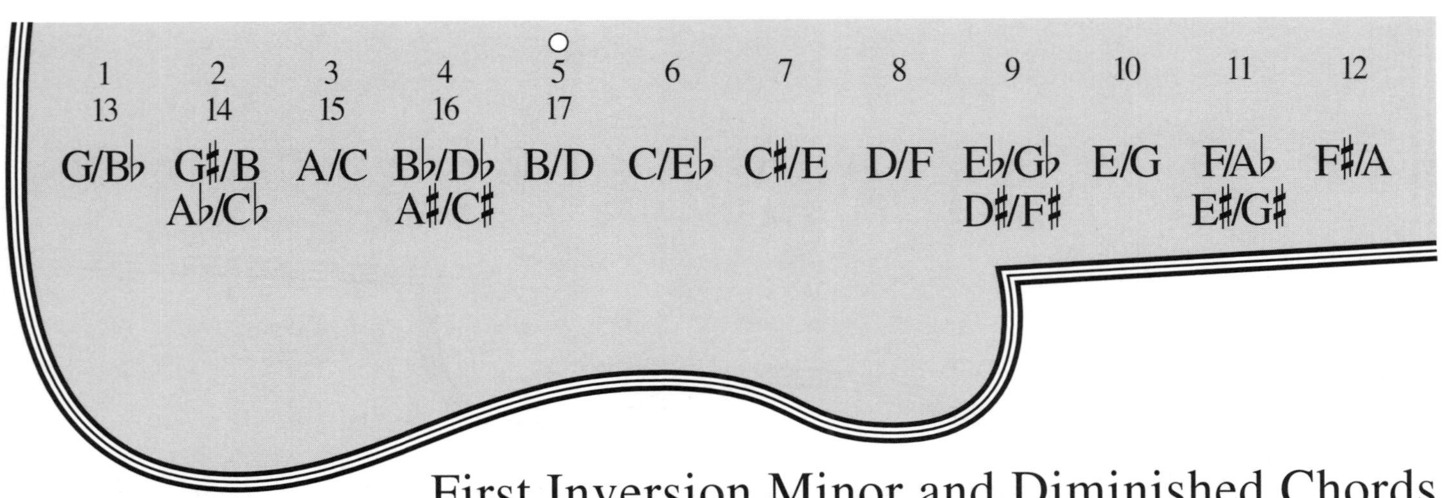

First Inversion Minor and Diminished Chords

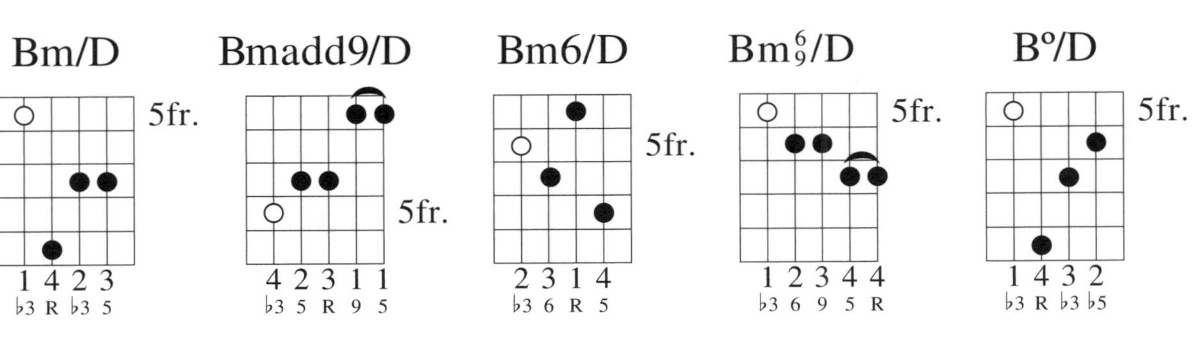

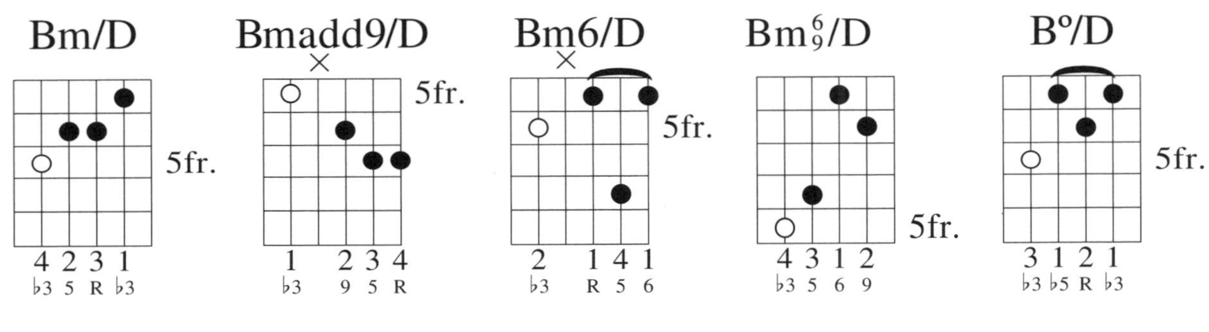

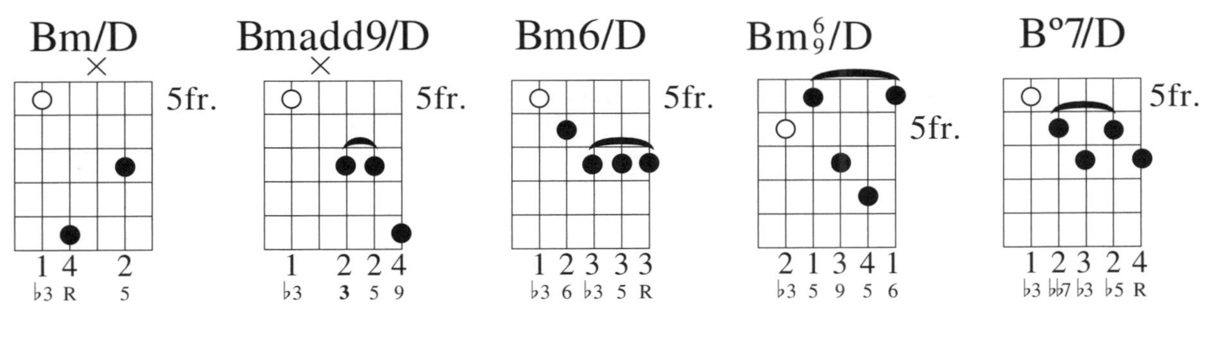

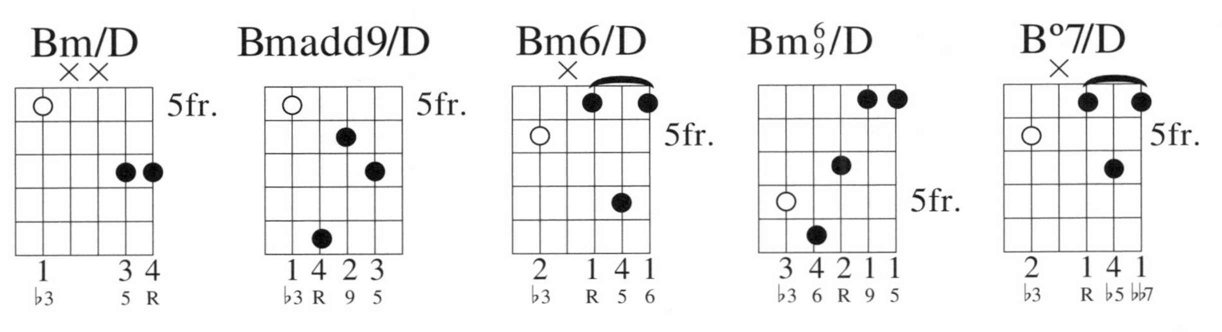

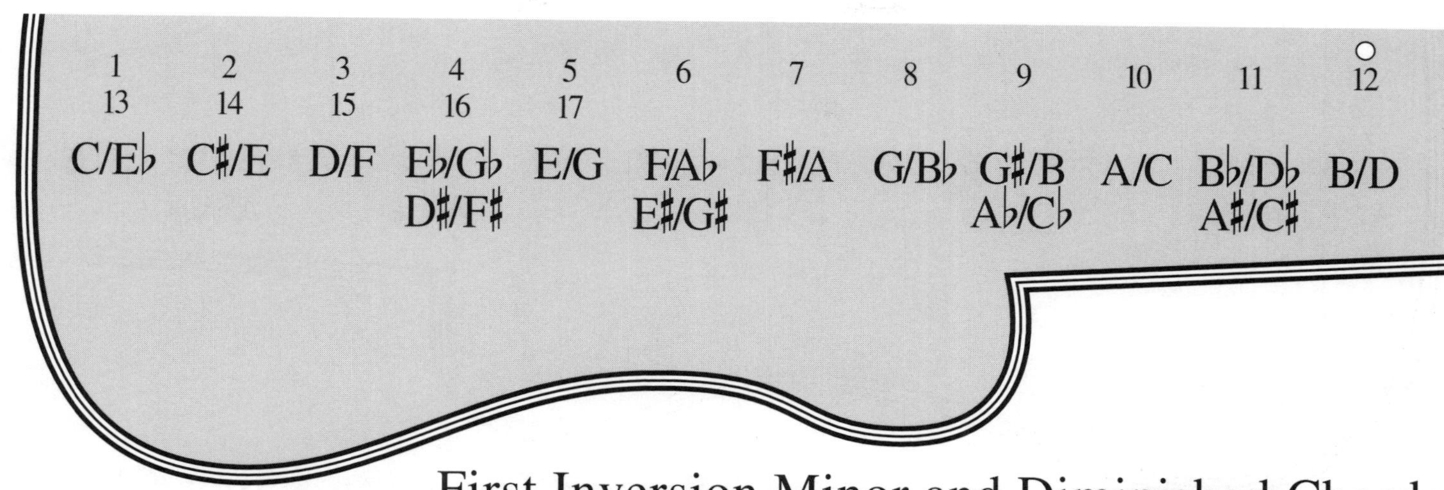

First Inversion Minor and Diminished Chords

Bm/D 12fr. 1 4 3 2 ♭3 R ♭3 5

Bmadd9/D 12fr. 1 4 2 3 ♭3 R 9 5

Bm$^6_9$/D 12fr. 1 2 3 4 ♭3 6 9 5

B°/D 12fr. 1 4 3 2 ♭3 R ♭3 ♭5

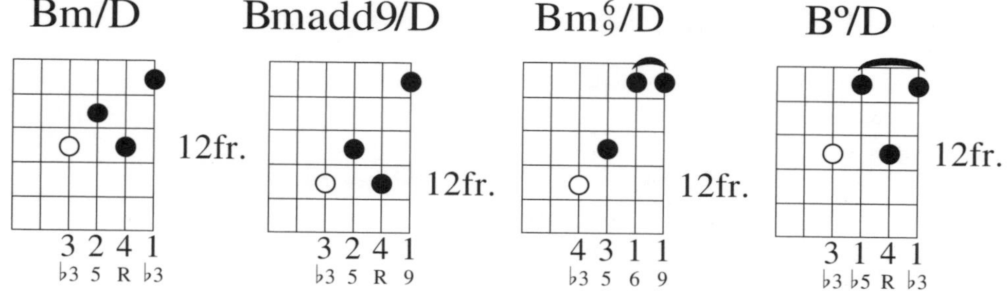

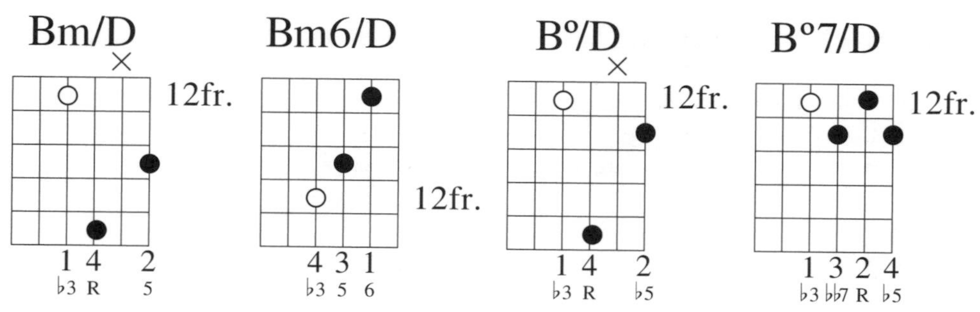

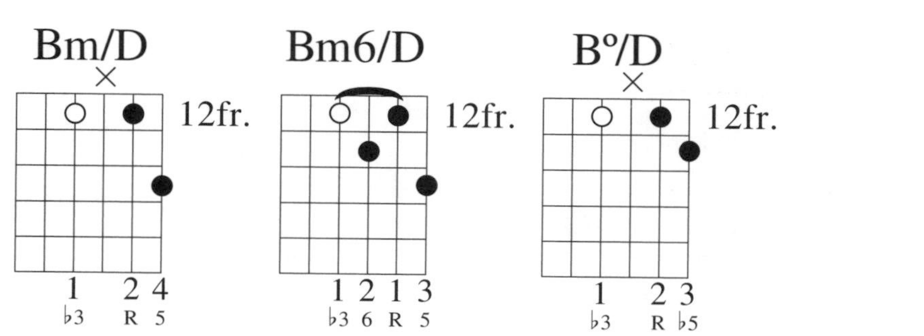

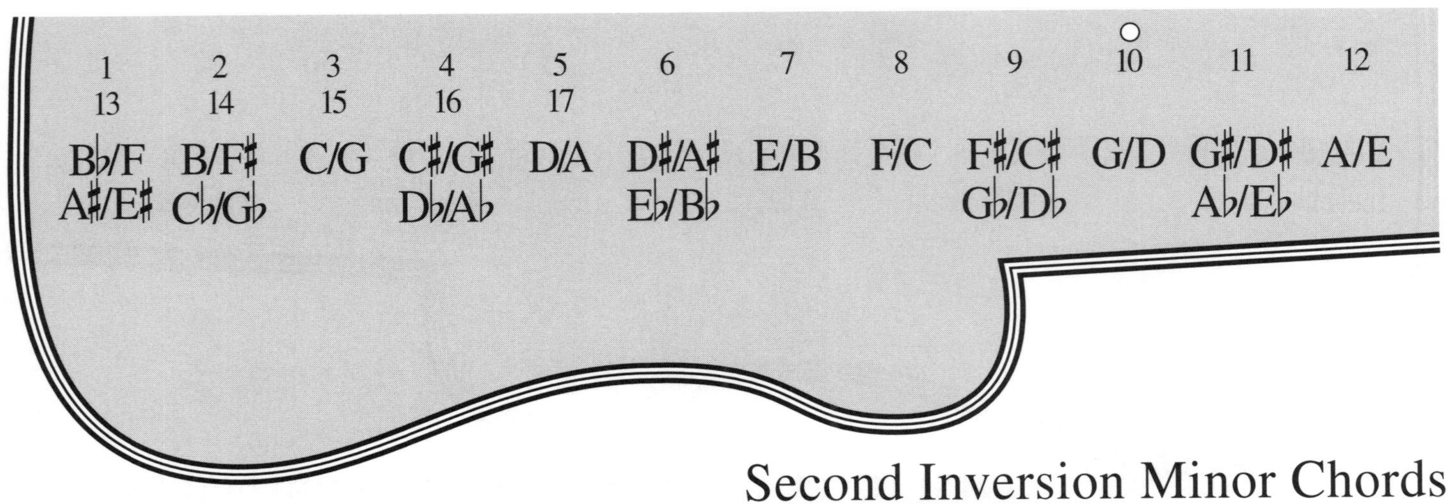

Second Inversion Minor Chords

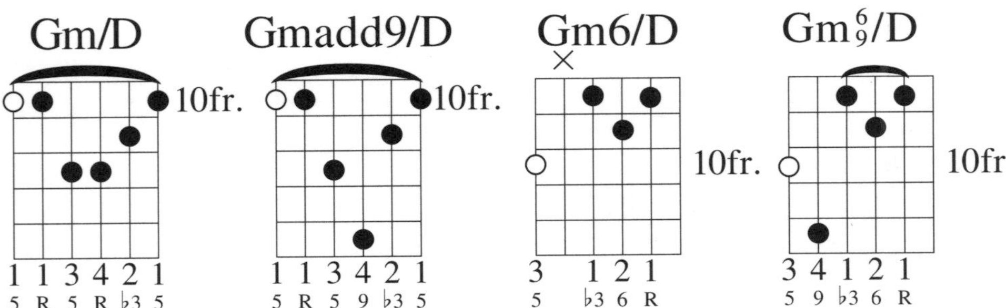

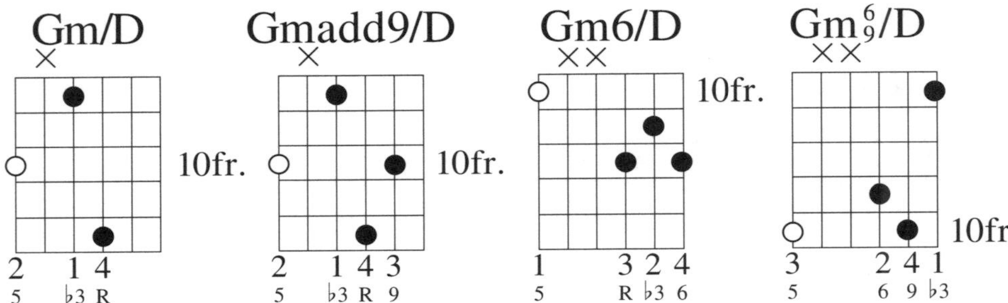

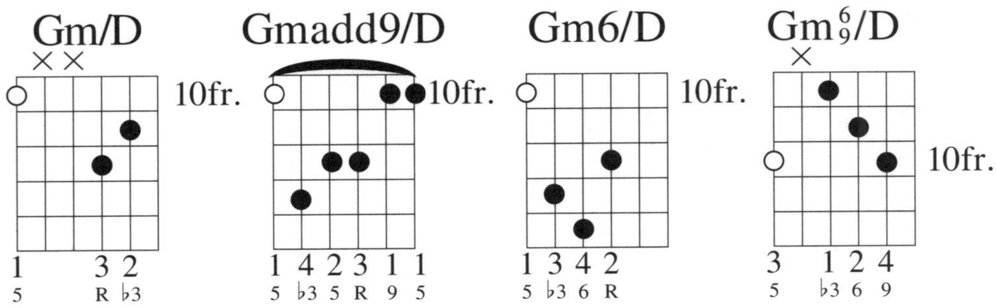

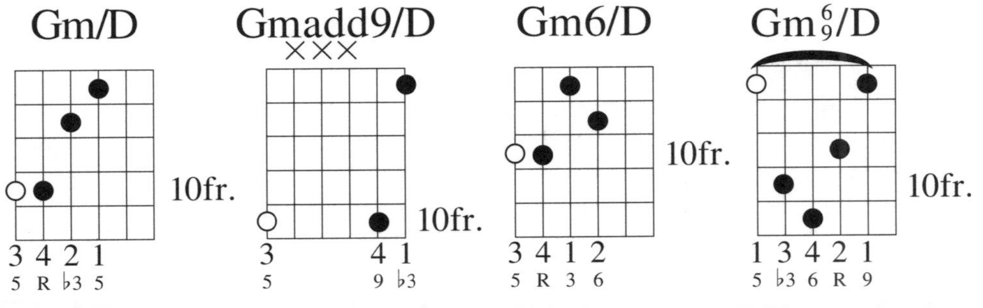

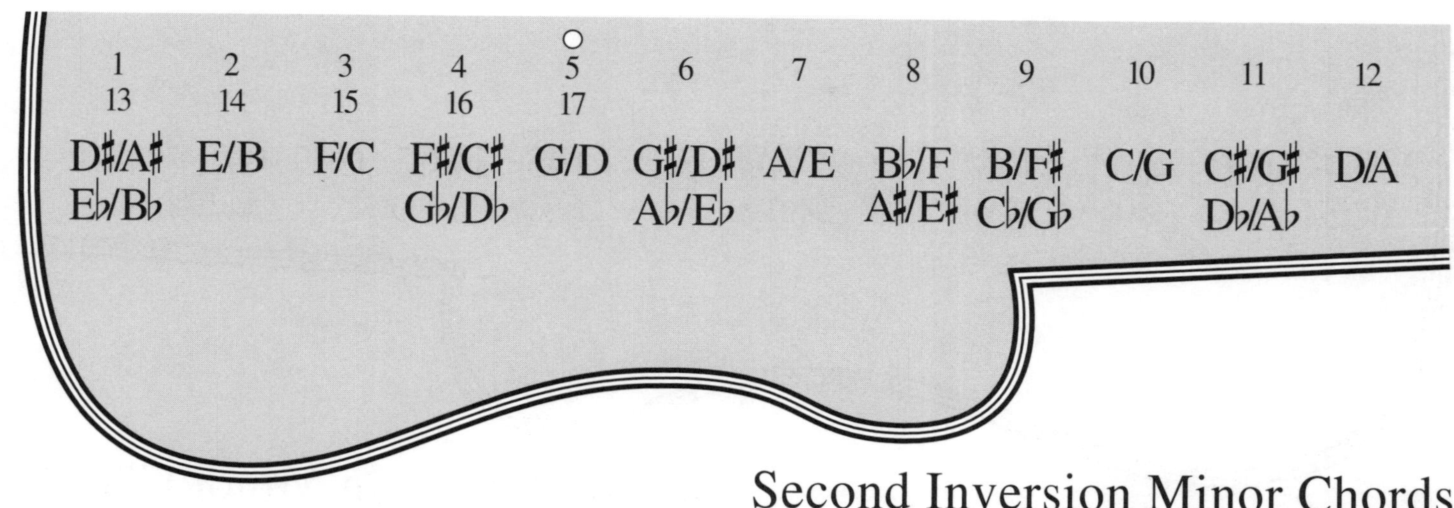

Second Inversion Minor Chords

Gm/D

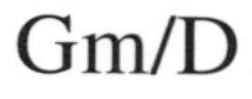

5fr.

1 3 2 4
5 ♭3 5 R

Gmadd9/D

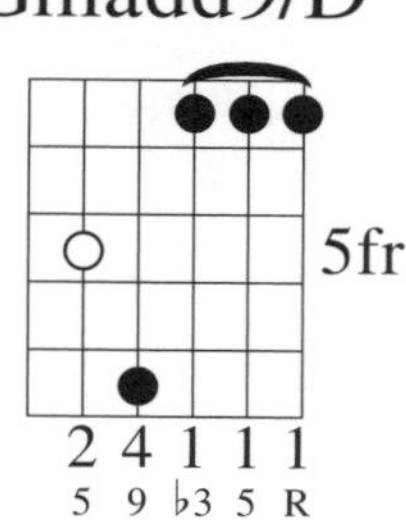

5fr.

2 4 1 1 1
5 9 ♭3 5 R

Gm6/D

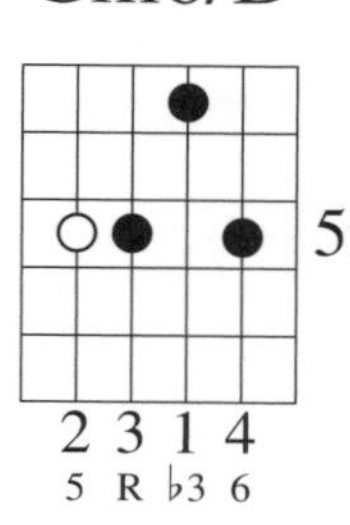

5fr.

2 3 1 4
5 R ♭3 6

Gm$^{6}_{9}$/D

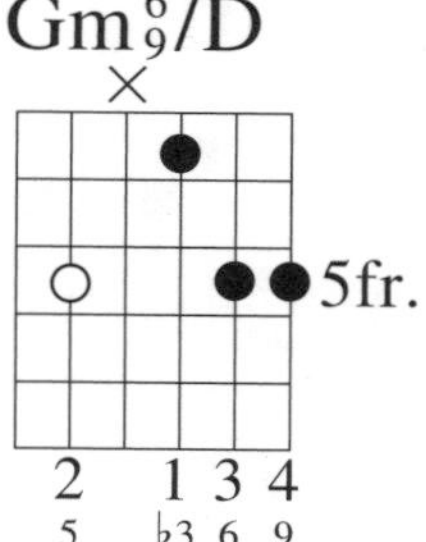

5fr.

2 1 3 4
5 ♭3 6 9

Gm/D

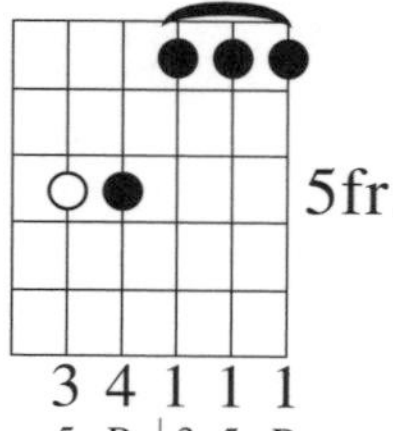

5fr.

3 4 1 1 1
5 R ♭3 5 R

Gmadd9/D

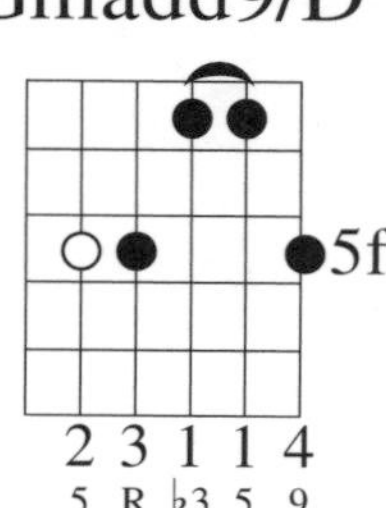

5fr.

2 3 1 1 4
5 R ♭3 5 9

Gm6/D

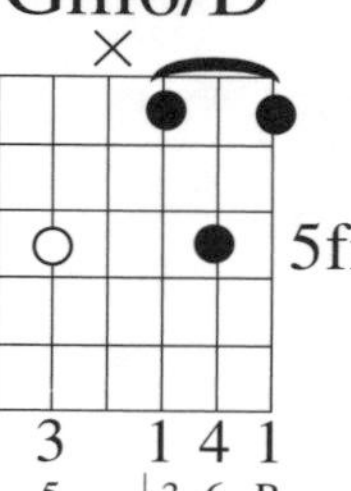

5fr.

3 1 4 1
5 ♭3 6 R

Gm$^{6}_{9}$/D

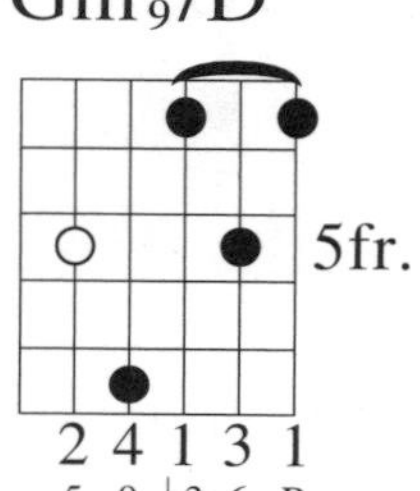

5fr.

2 4 1 3 1
5 9 ♭3 6 R

Gm/D

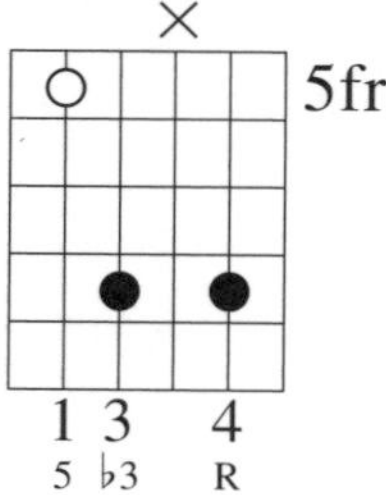

5fr.

1 3 4
5 ♭3 R

Gmadd9/D

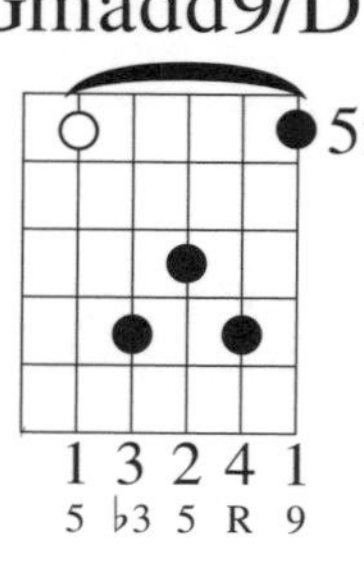

5fr.

1 3 2 4 1
5 ♭3 5 R 9

Gm6/D

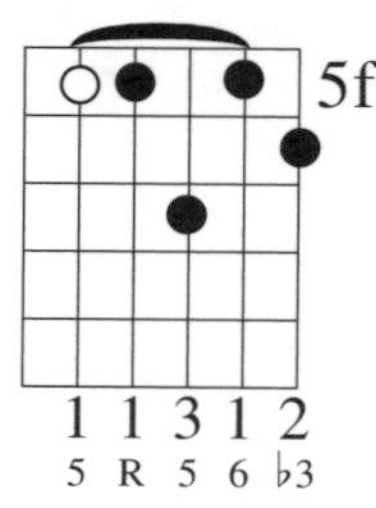

5fr.

1 1 3 1 2
5 R 5 6 ♭3

Gm$^{6}_{9}$/D

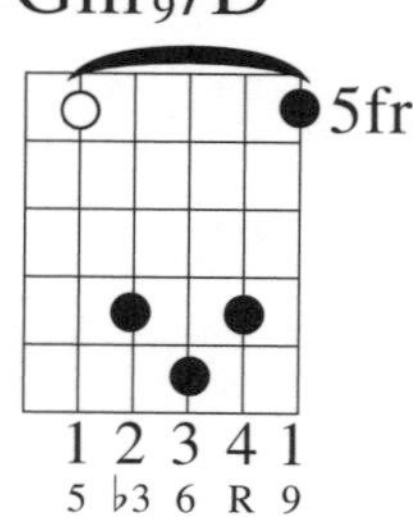

5fr.

1 2 3 4 1
5 ♭3 6 R 9

Gm/D

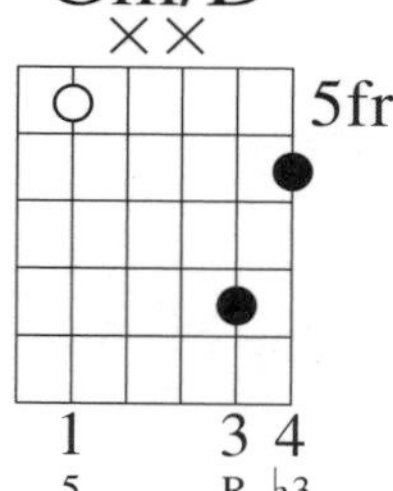

5fr.

1 3 4
5 R ♭3

Gmadd9/D

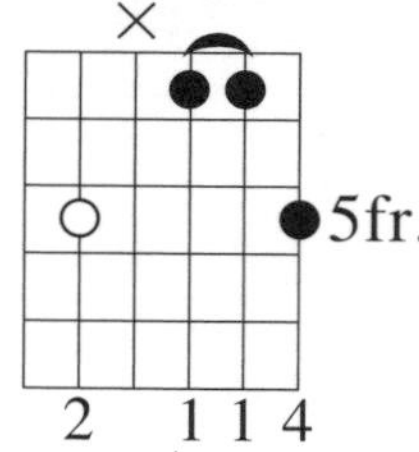

5fr.

2 1 1 4
5 ♭3 5 9

Gm6/D

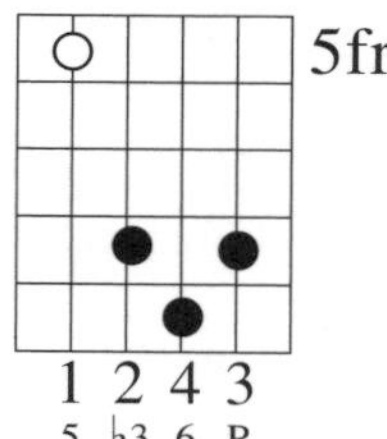

5fr.

1 2 4 3
5 ♭3 6 R

Gm$^{6}_{9}$/D

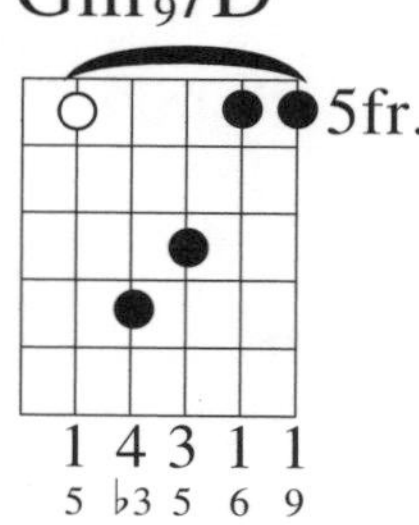

5fr.

1 4 3 1 1
5 ♭3 5 6 9

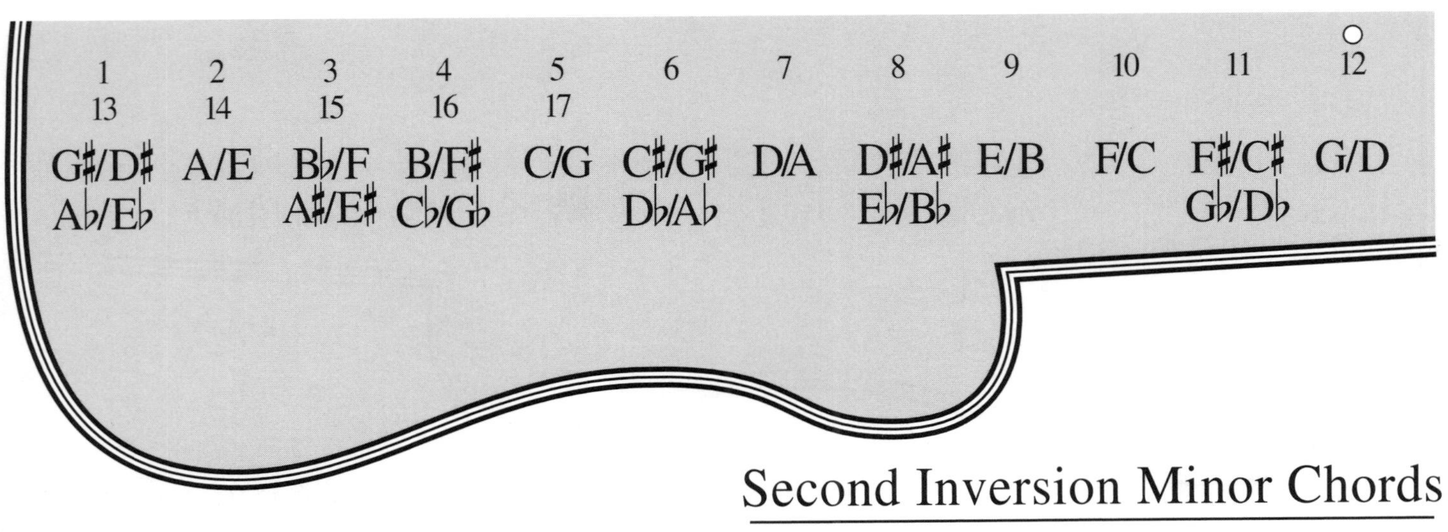

Second Inversion Minor Chords

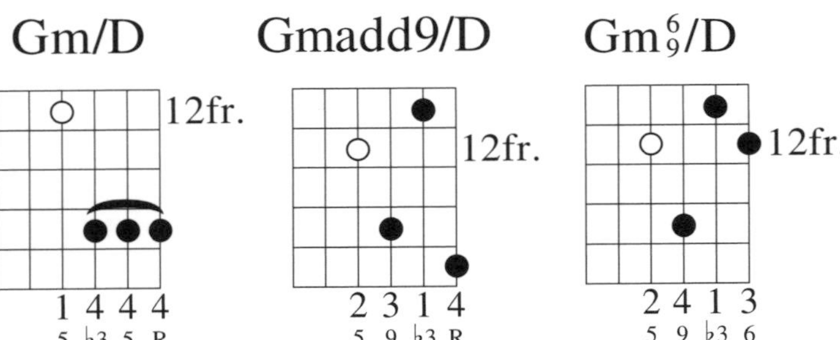

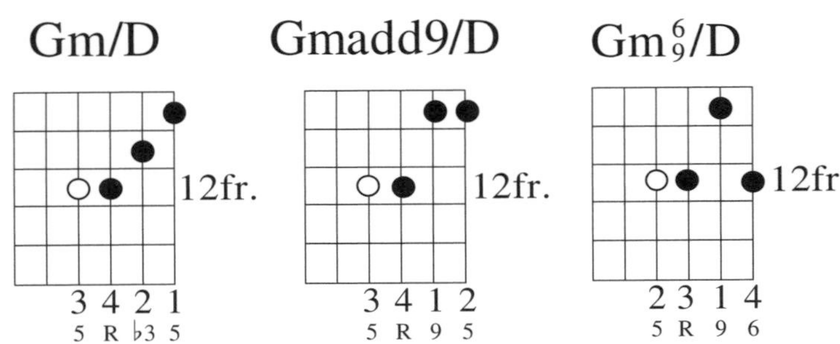

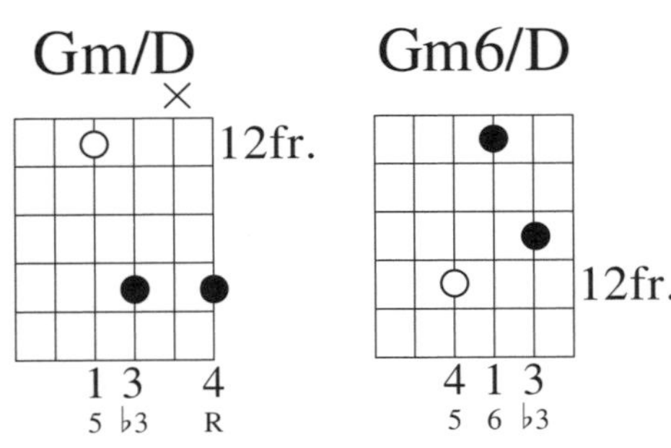

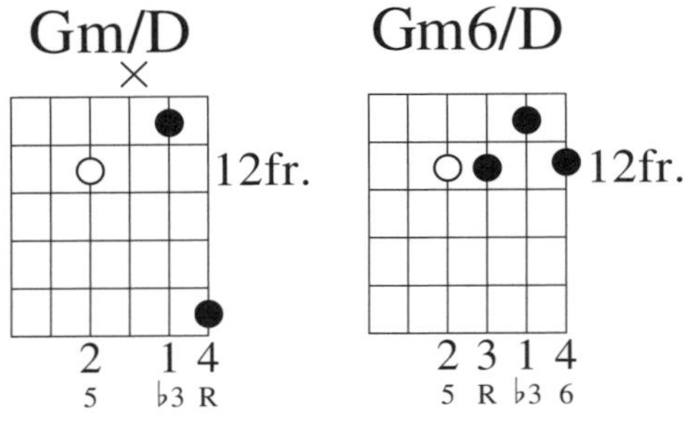

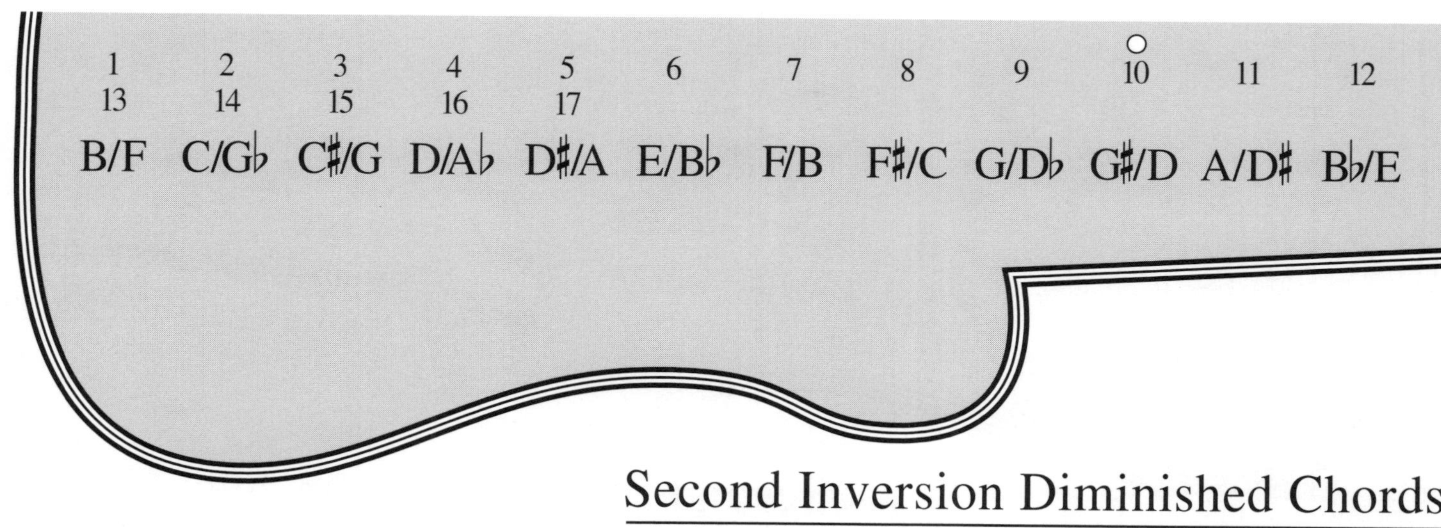

Second Inversion Diminished Chords

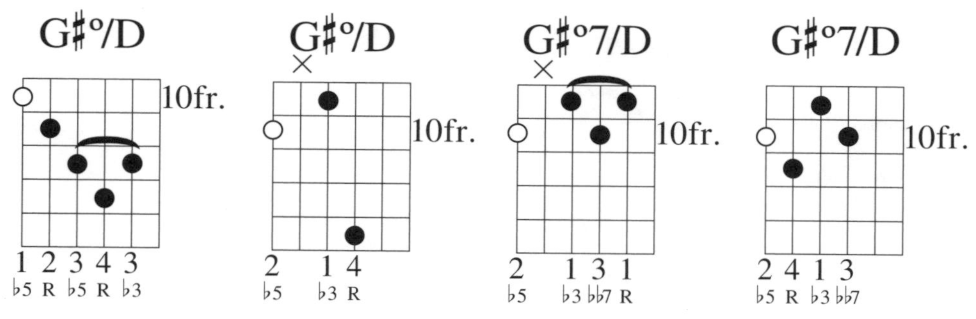

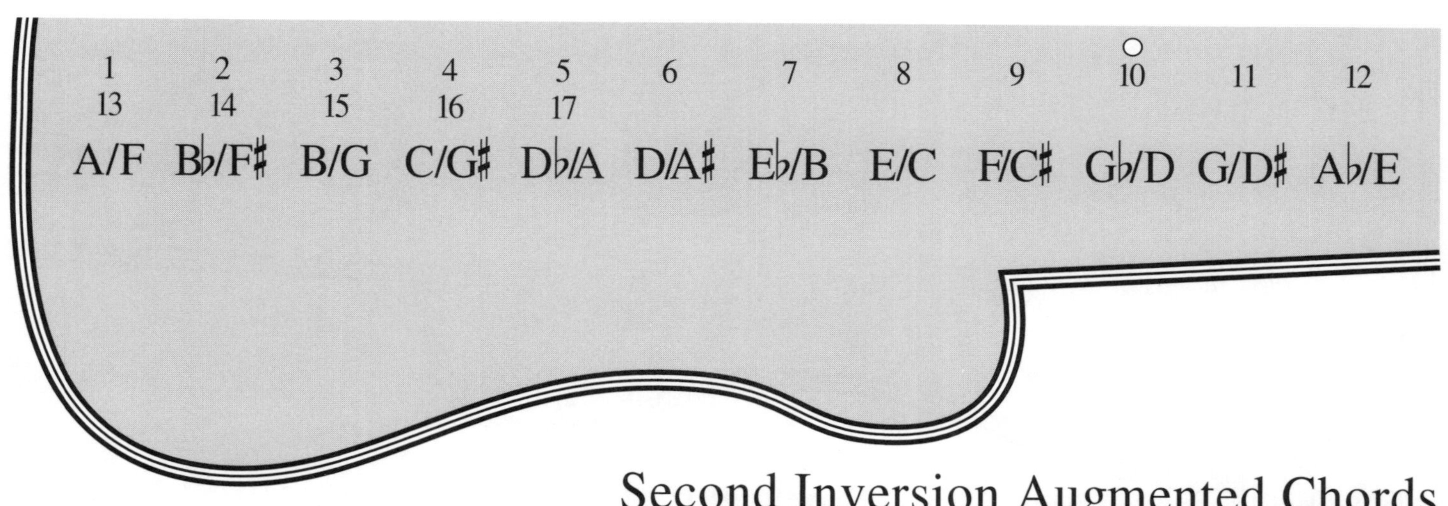

Second Inversion Augmented Chords

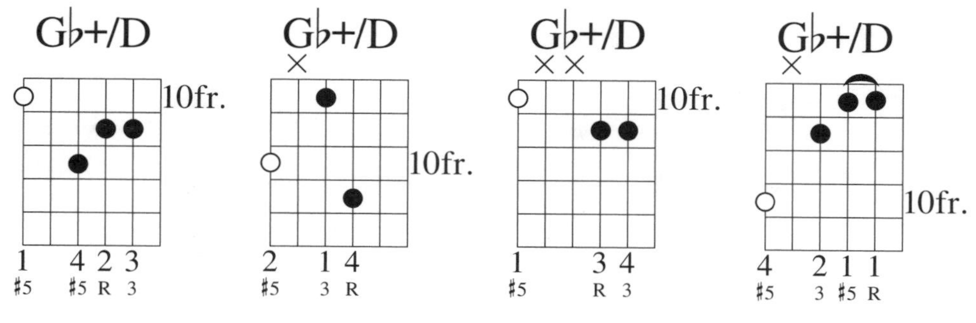

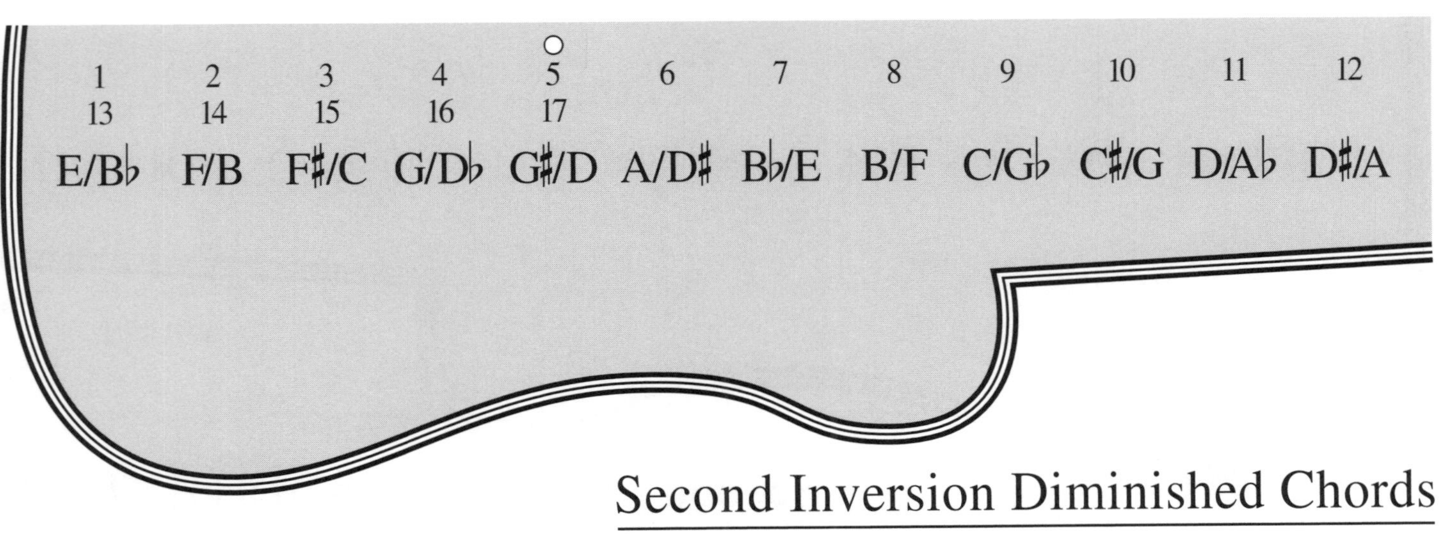

Second Inversion Diminished Chords

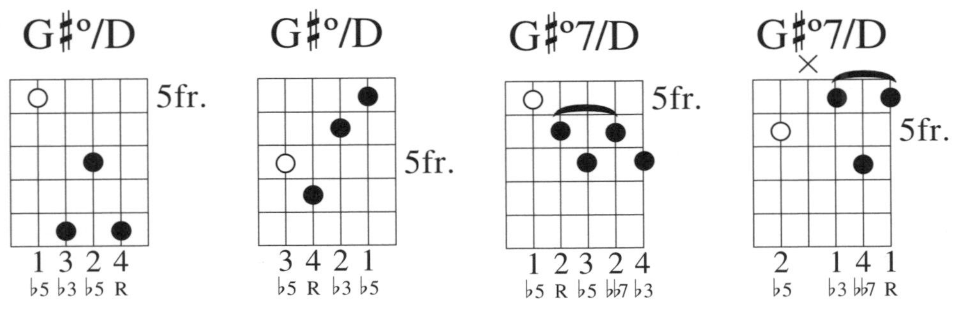

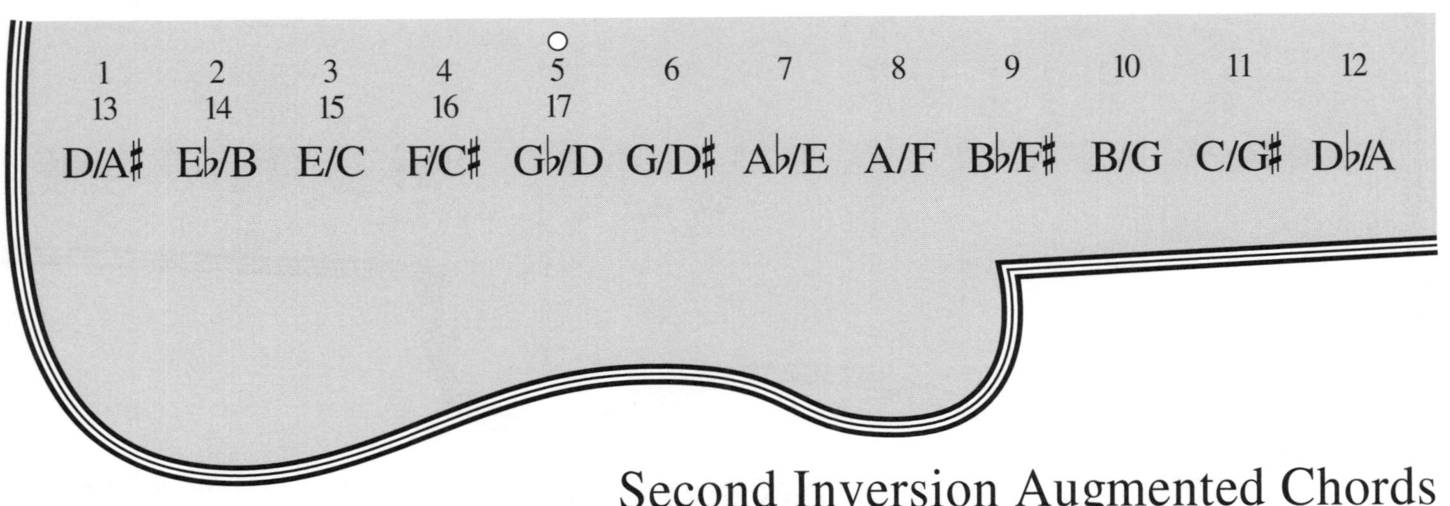

Second Inversion Augmented Chords

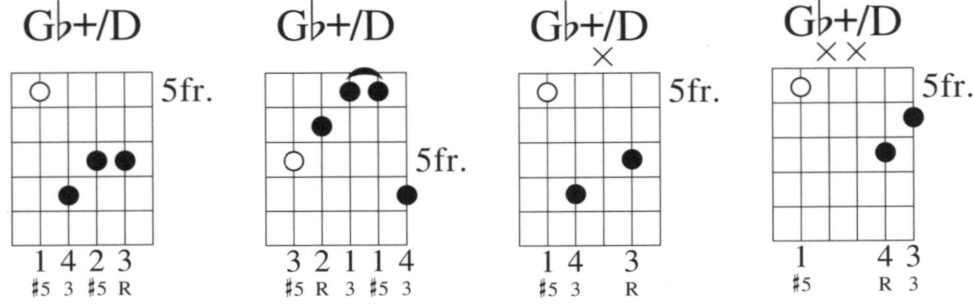

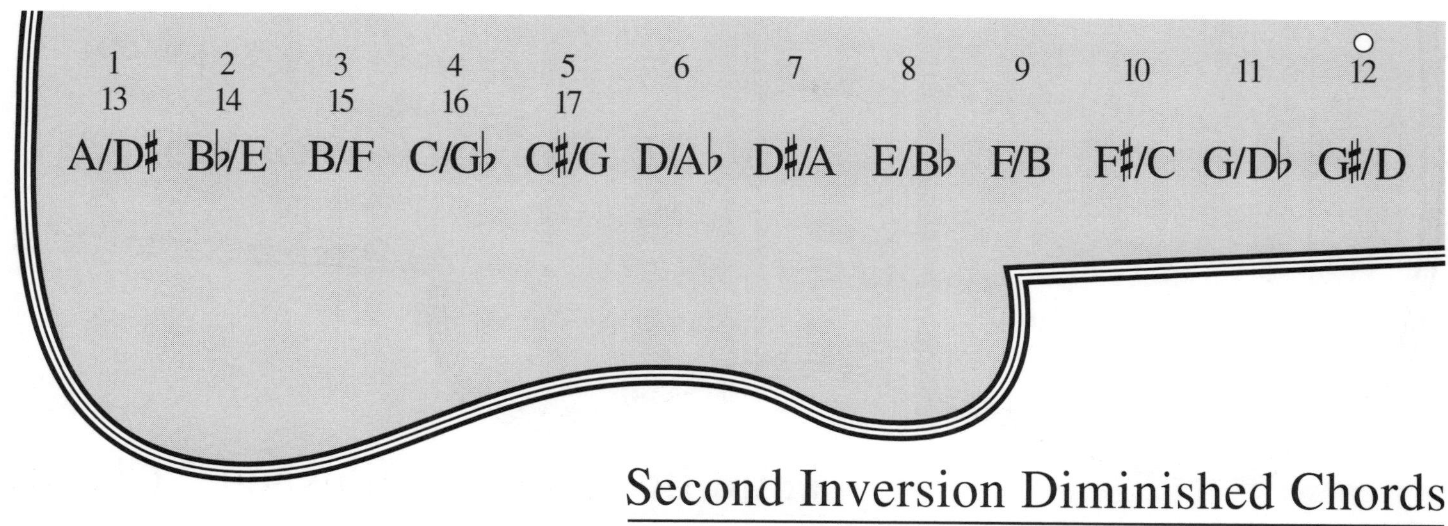

Second Inversion Diminished Chords

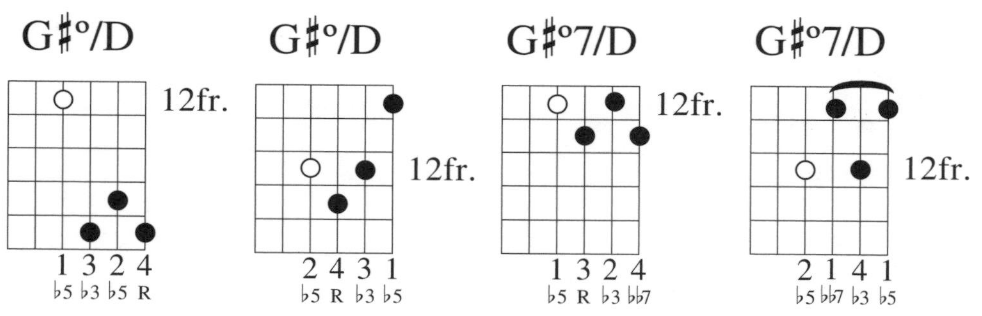

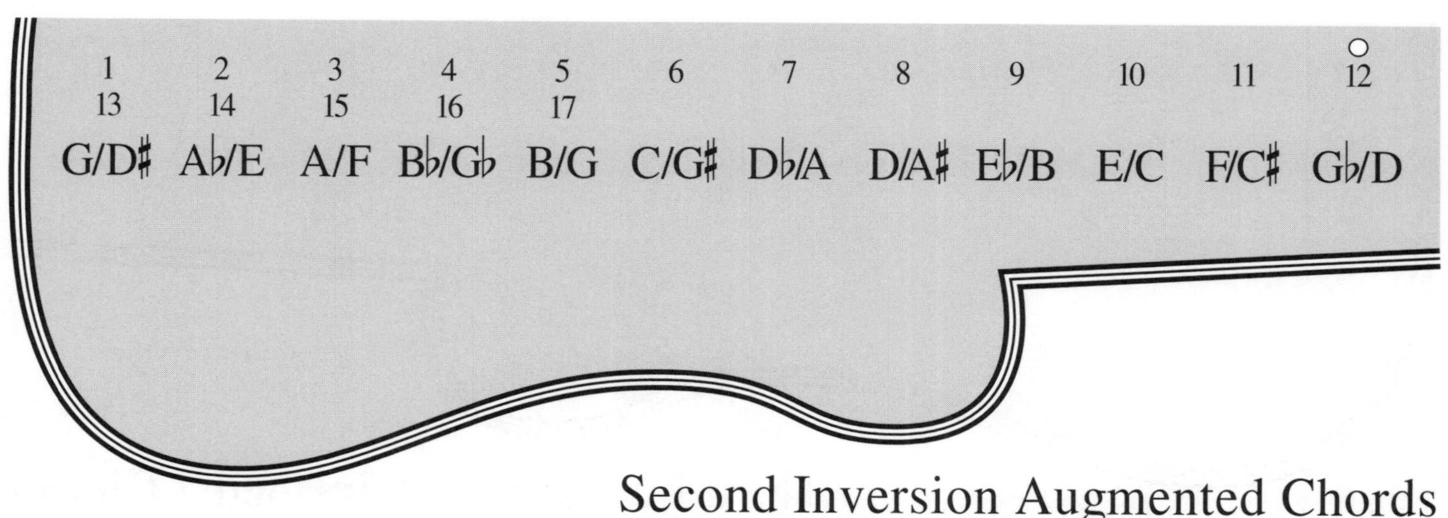

Second Inversion Augmented Chords

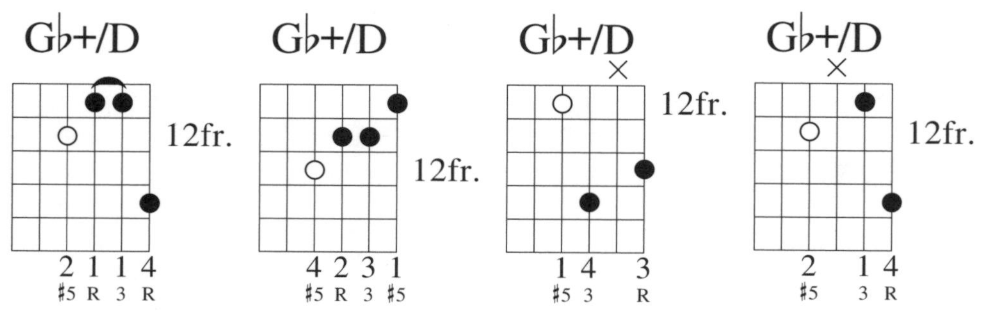

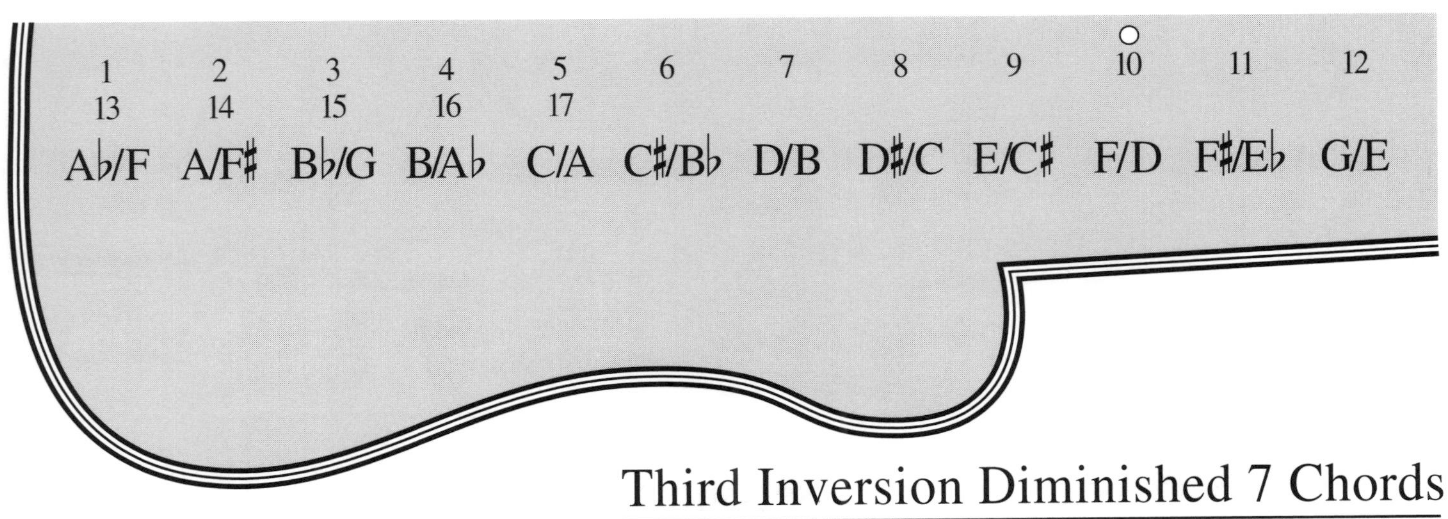

Third Inversion Diminished 7 Chords

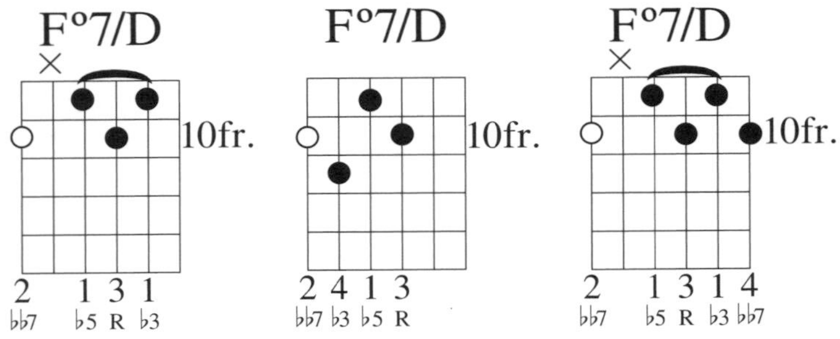

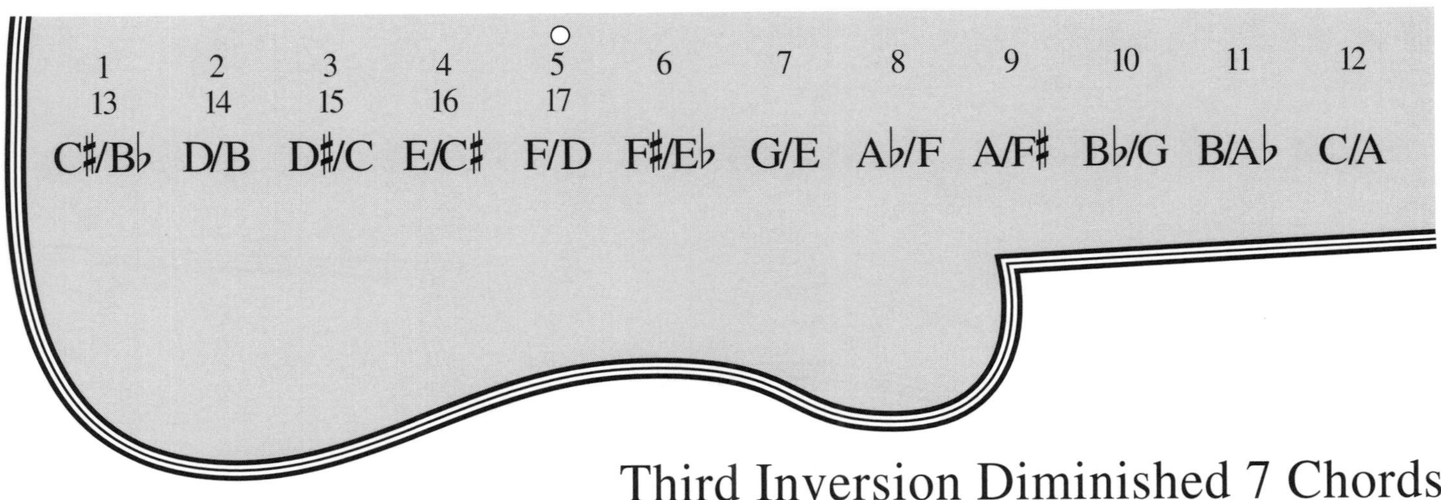

Third Inversion Diminished 7 Chords

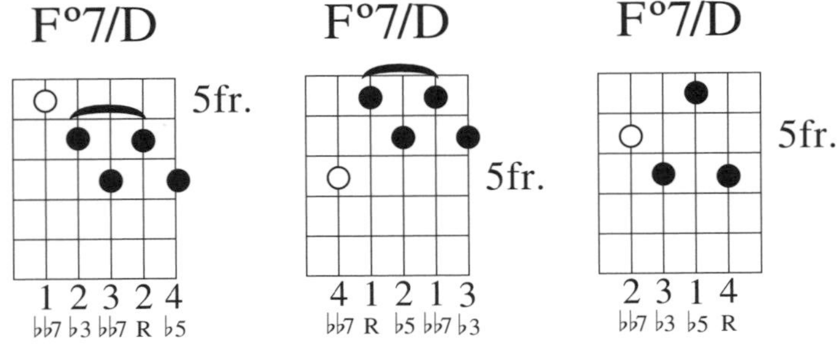

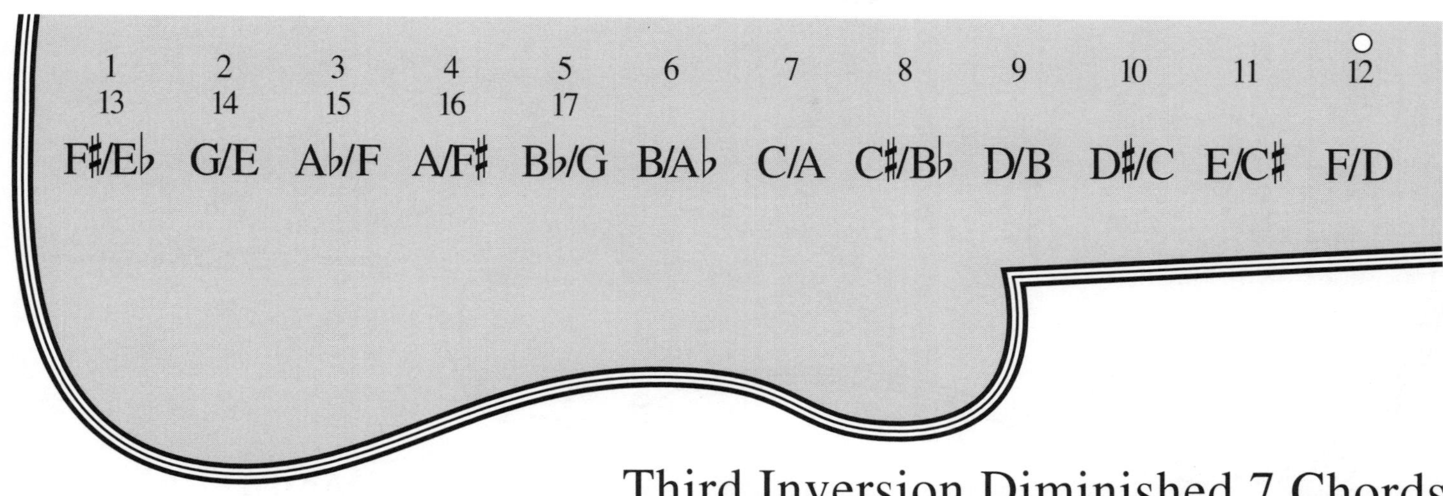

Third Inversion Diminished 7 Chords

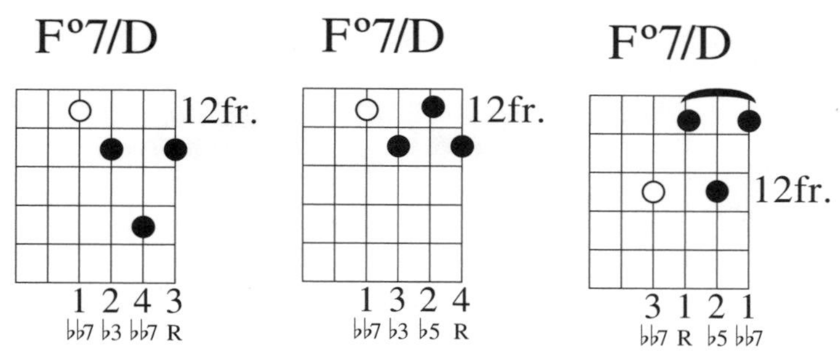

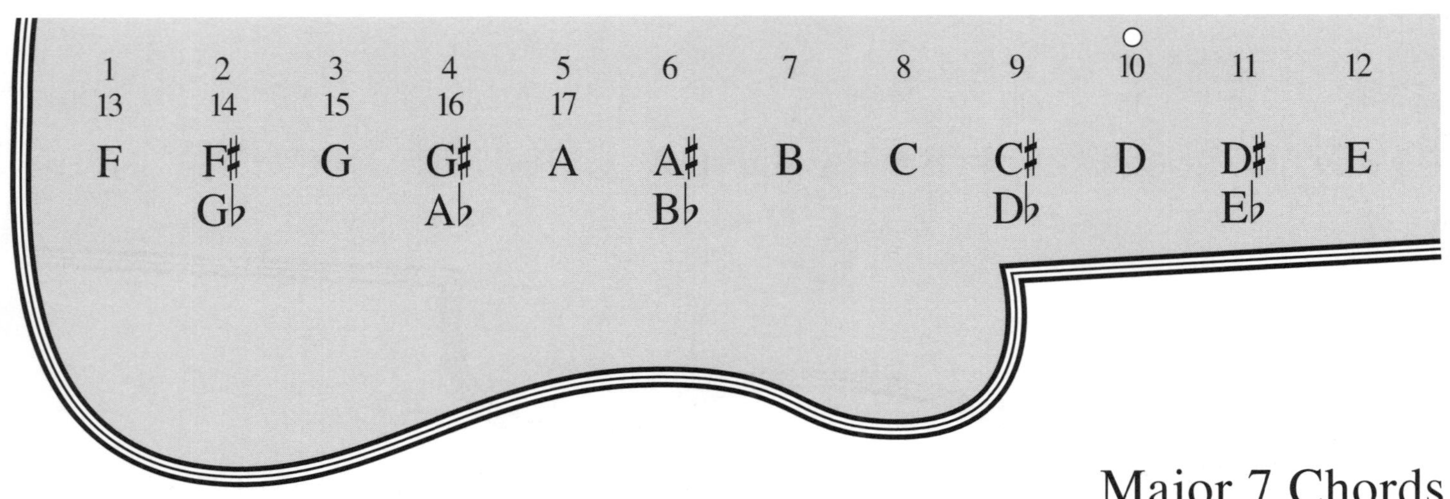

Major 7 Chords

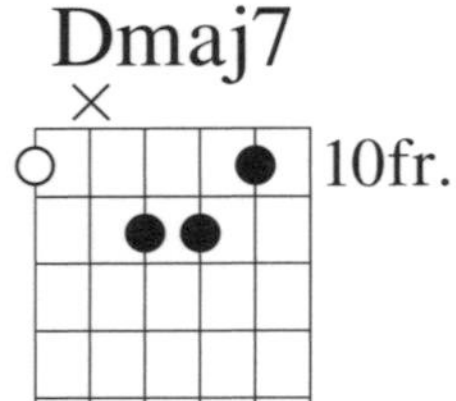

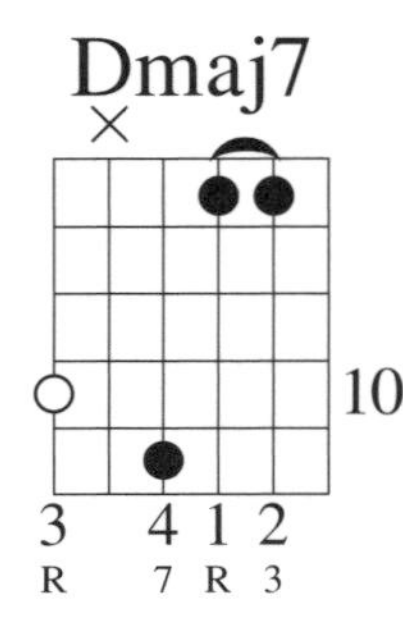

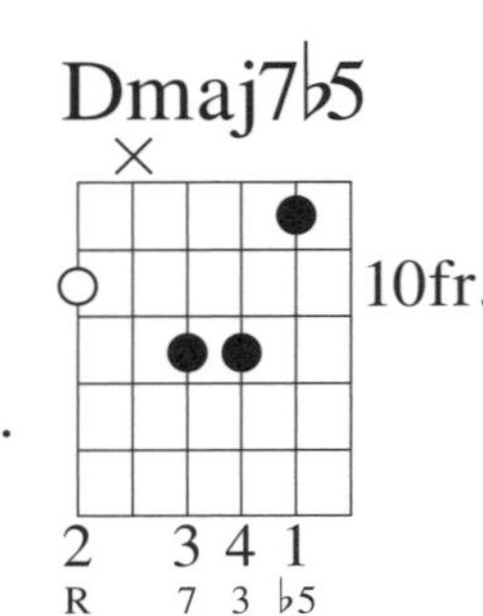

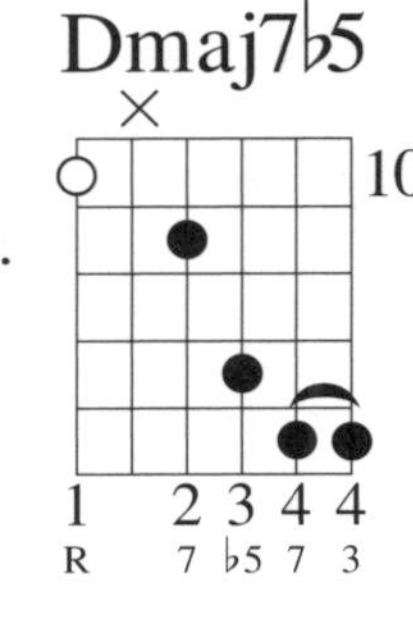

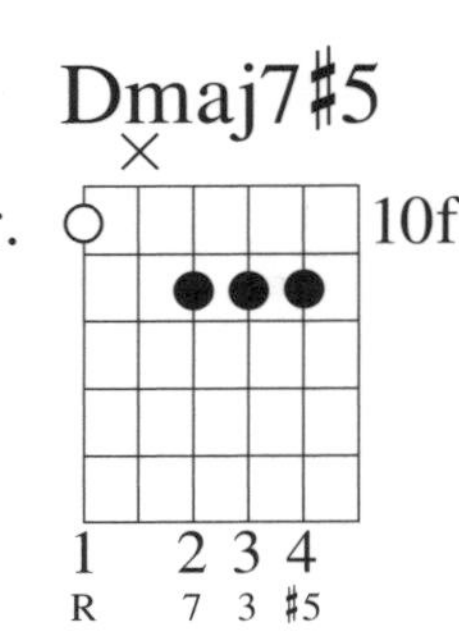

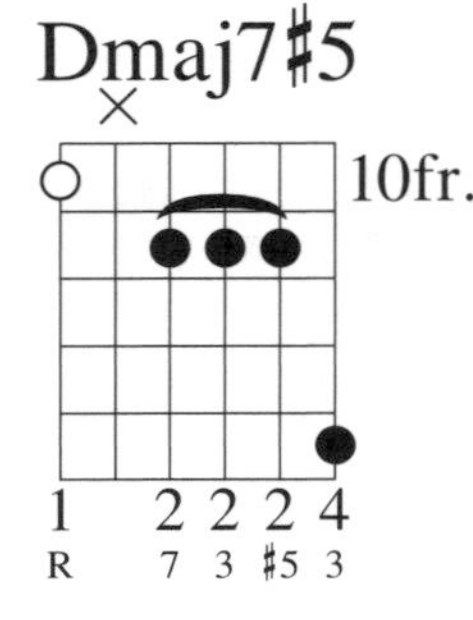

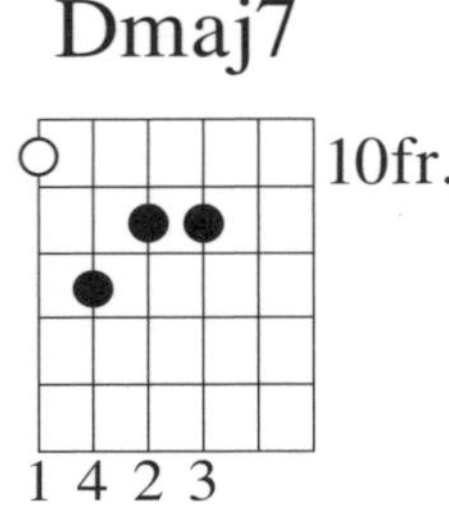

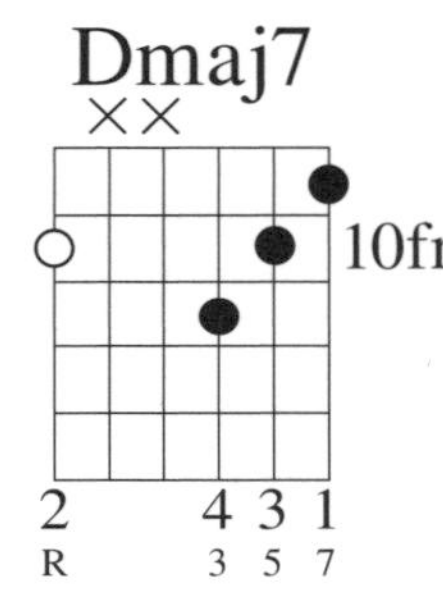

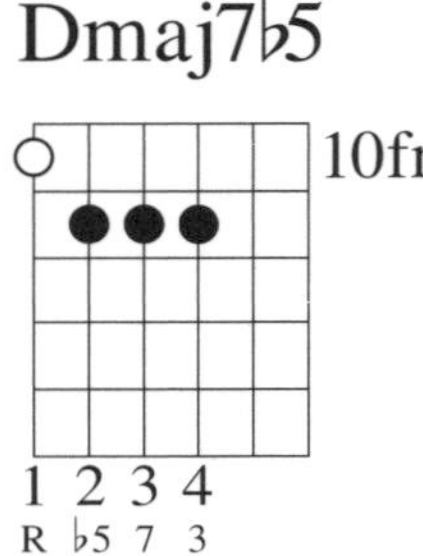

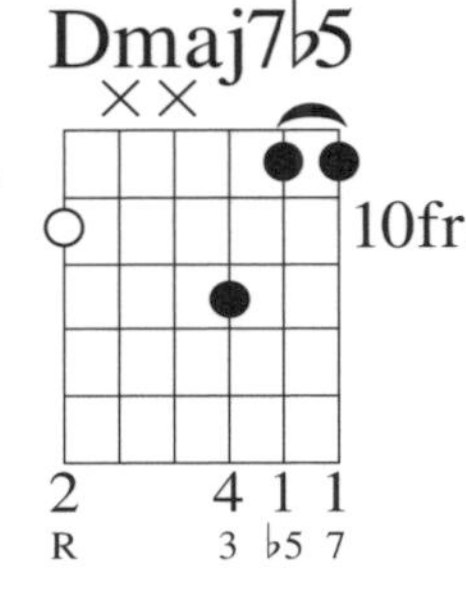

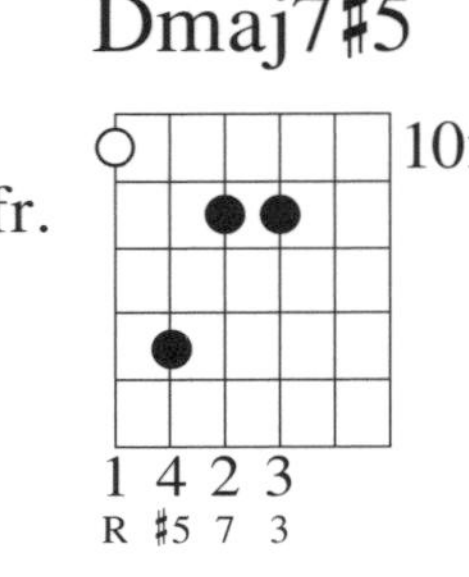

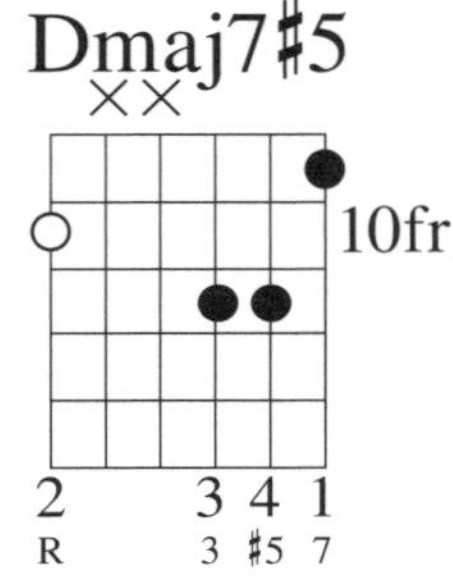

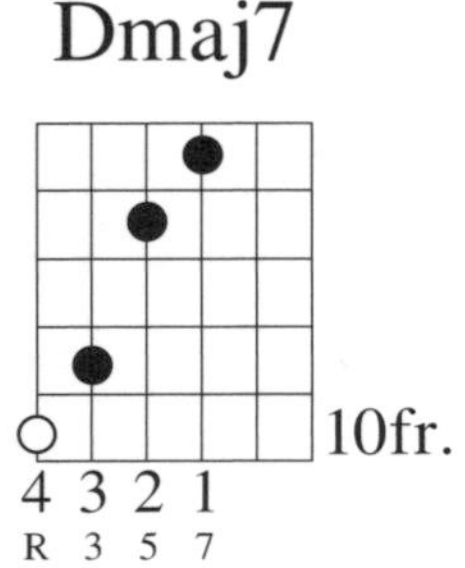

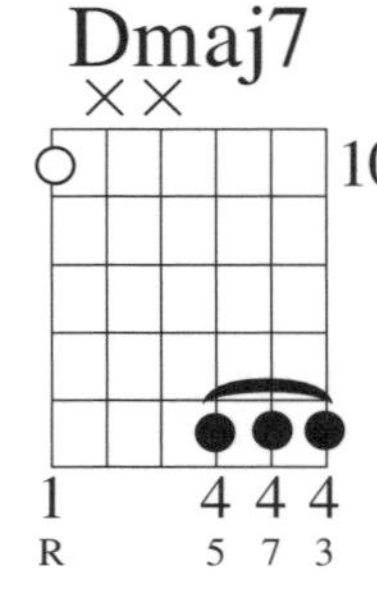

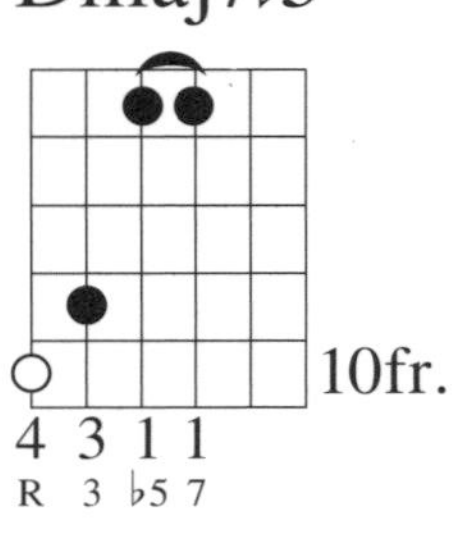

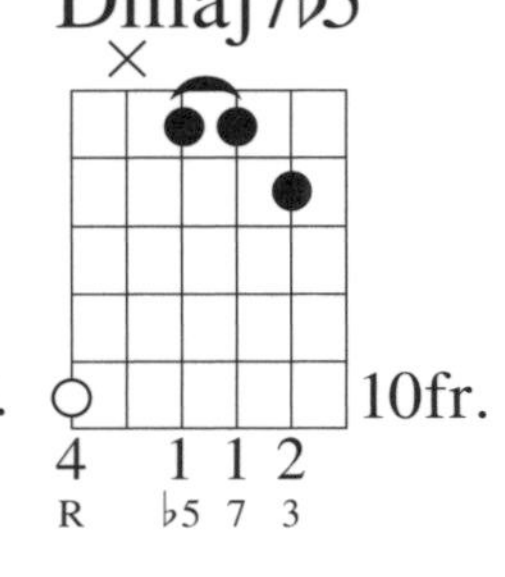

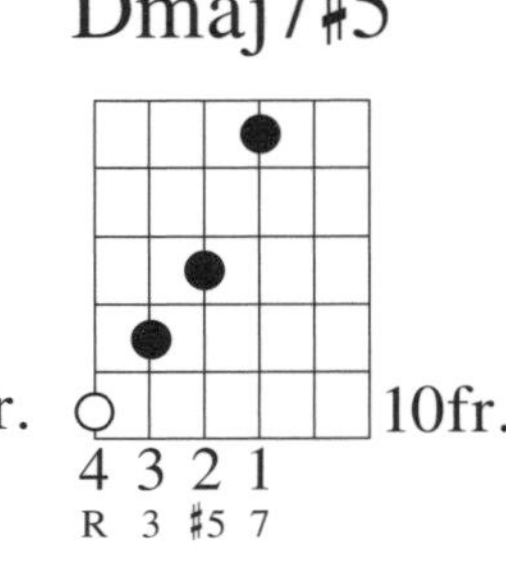

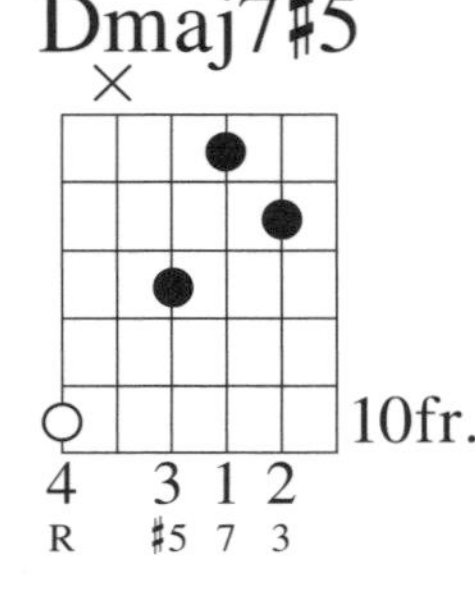

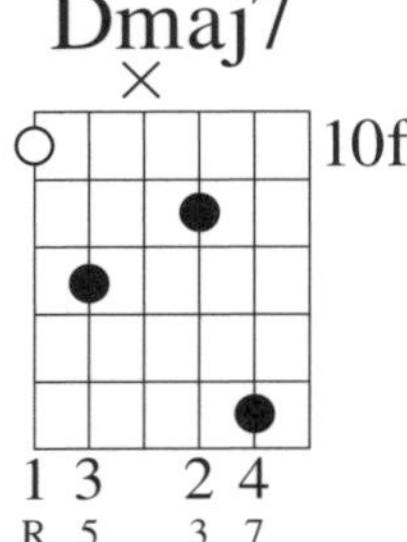

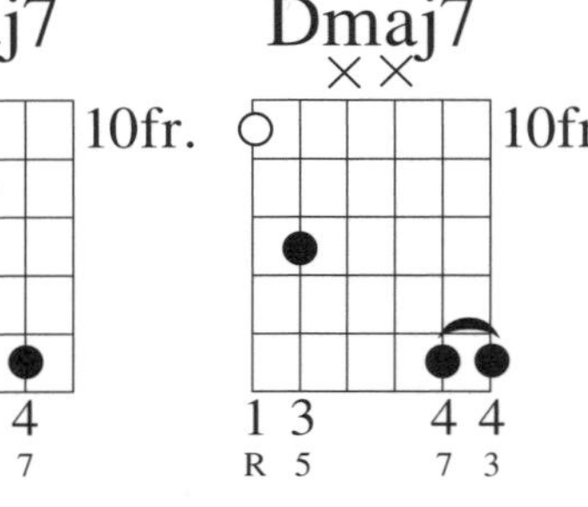

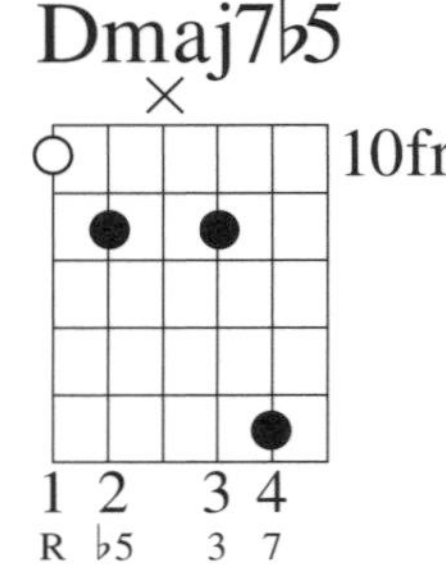

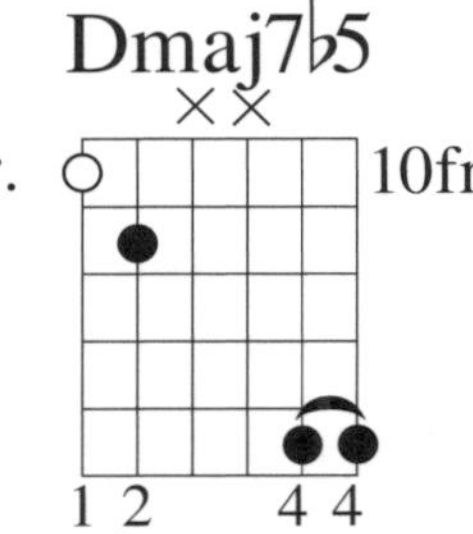

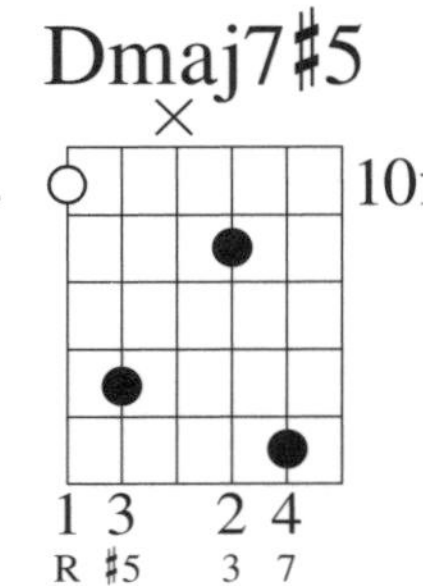

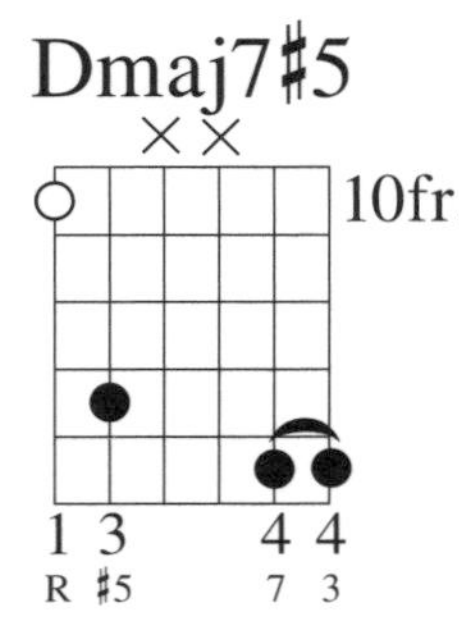

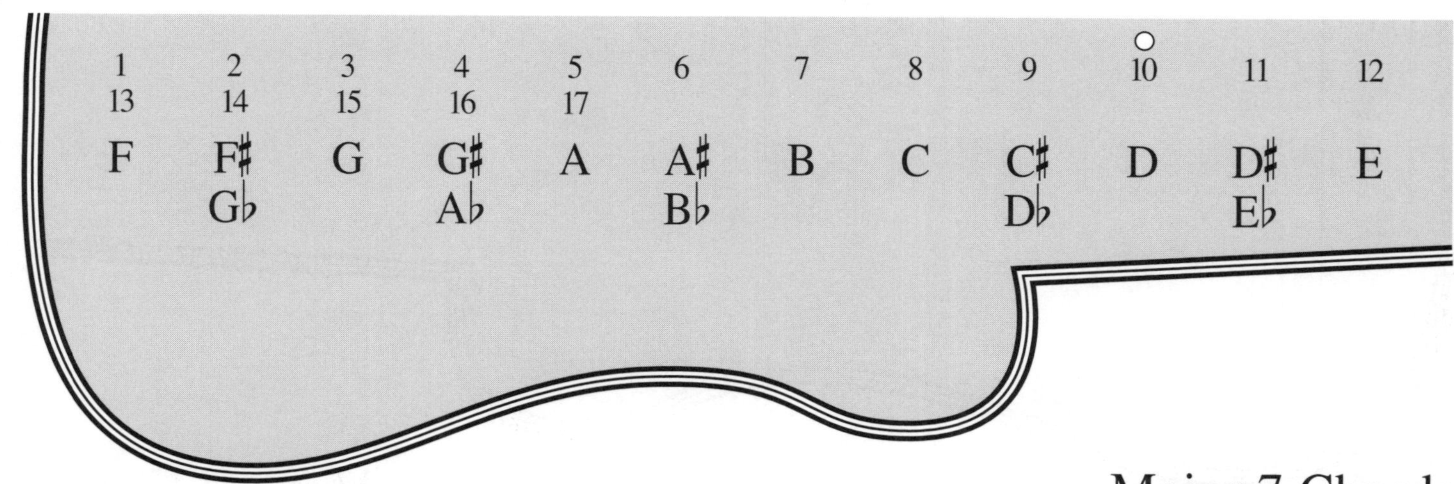

Major 7 Chords

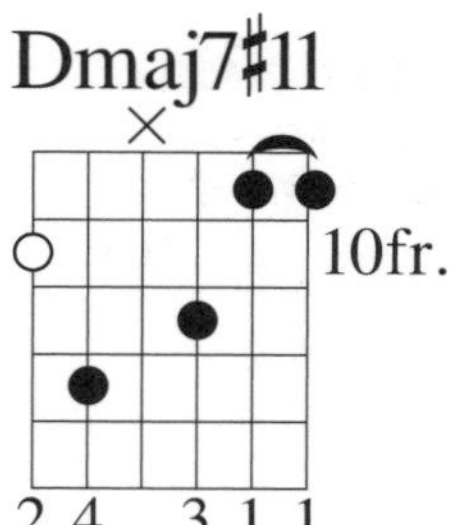

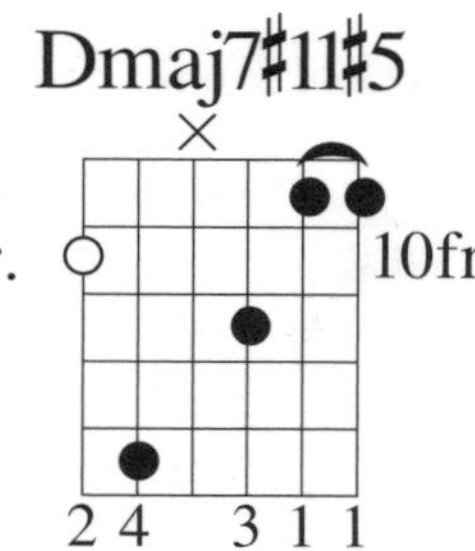

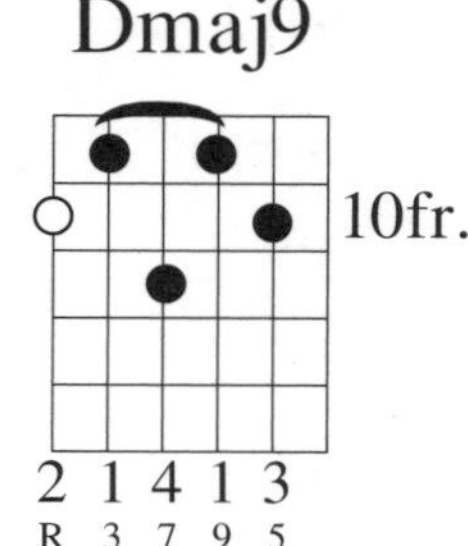

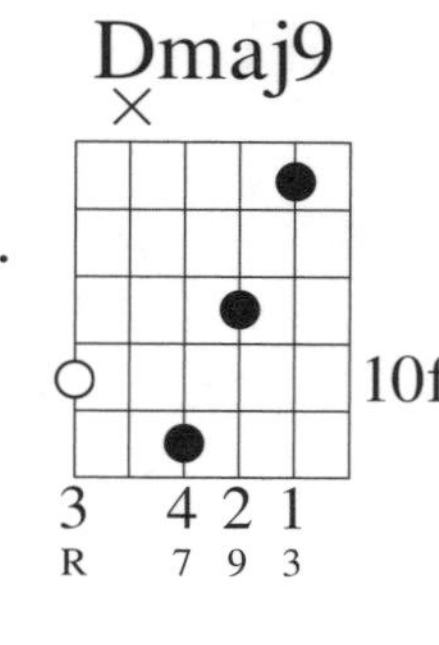

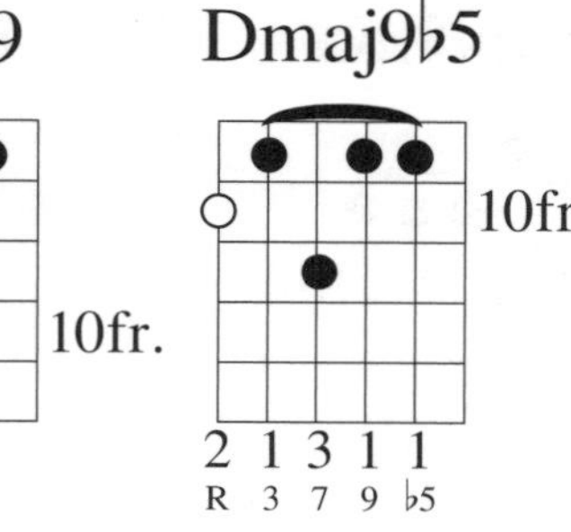

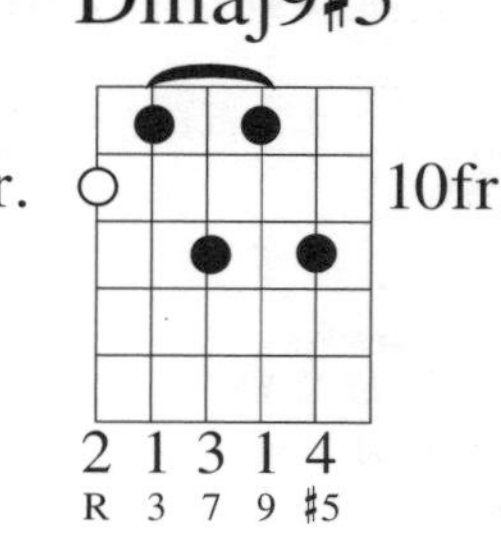

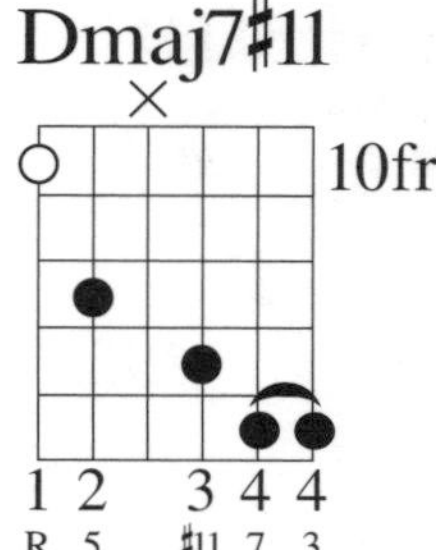

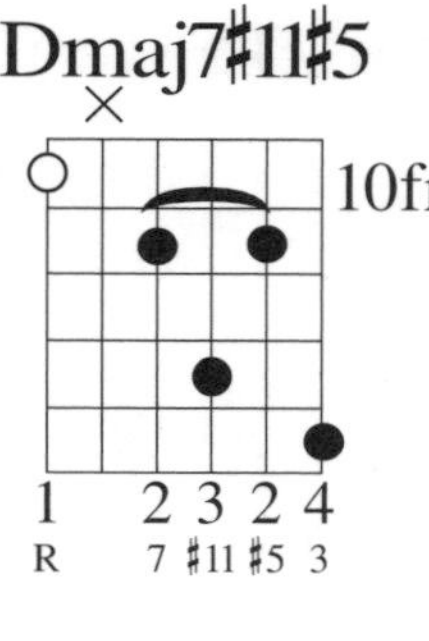

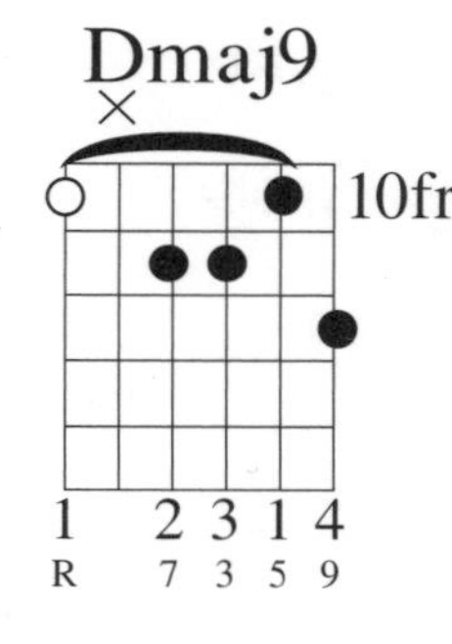

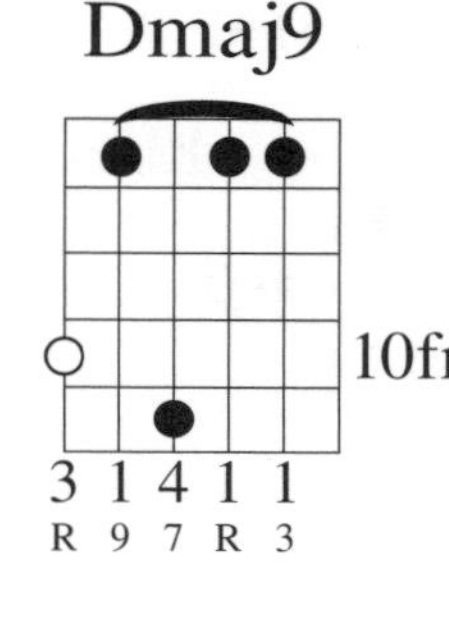

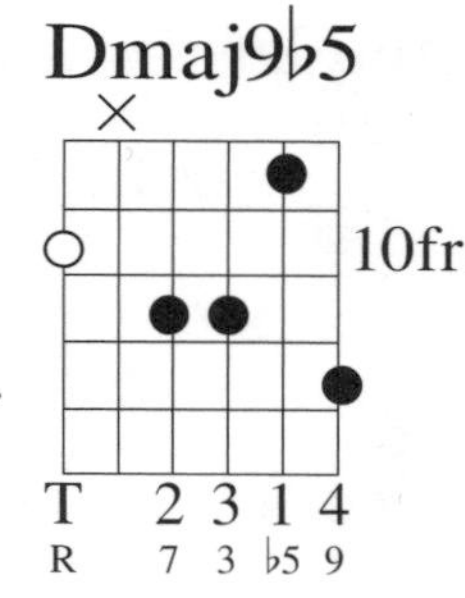

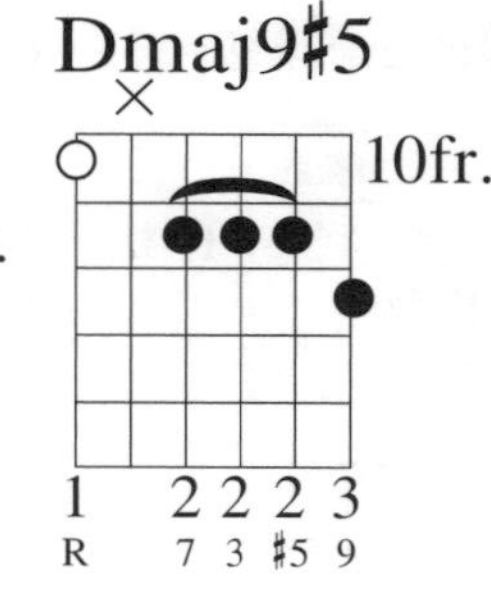

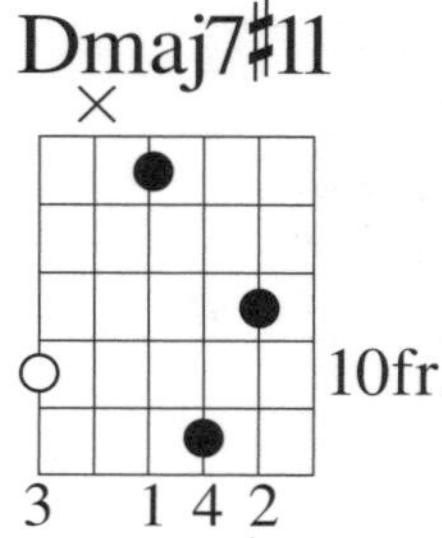

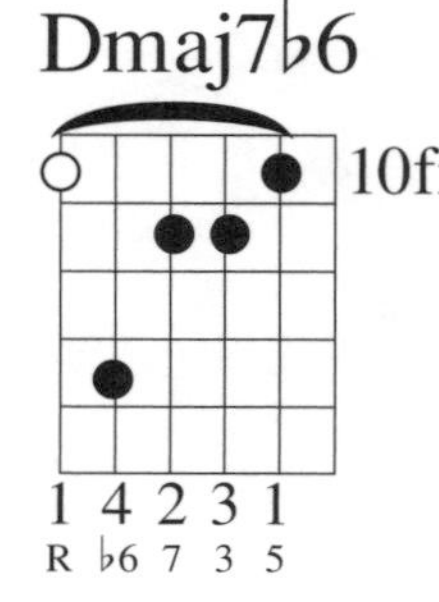

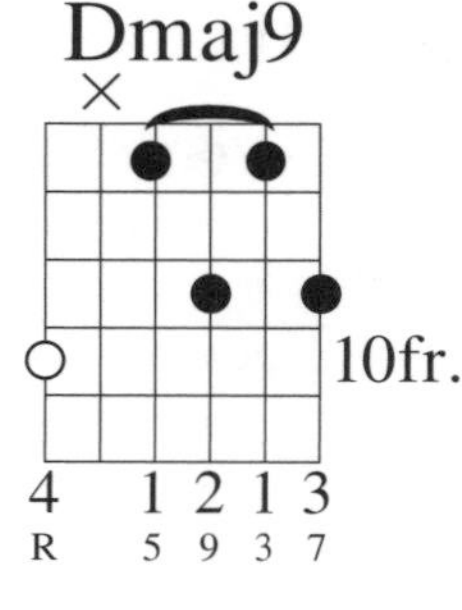

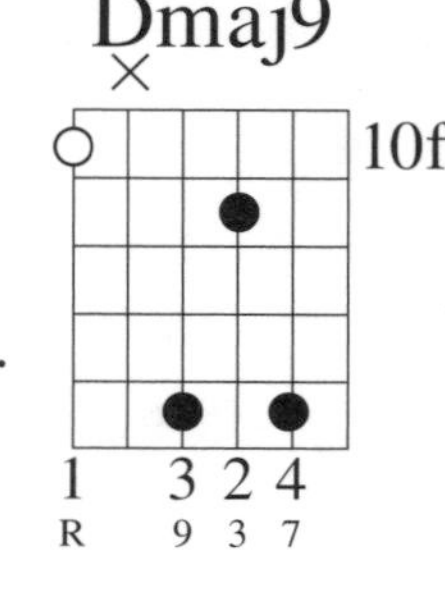

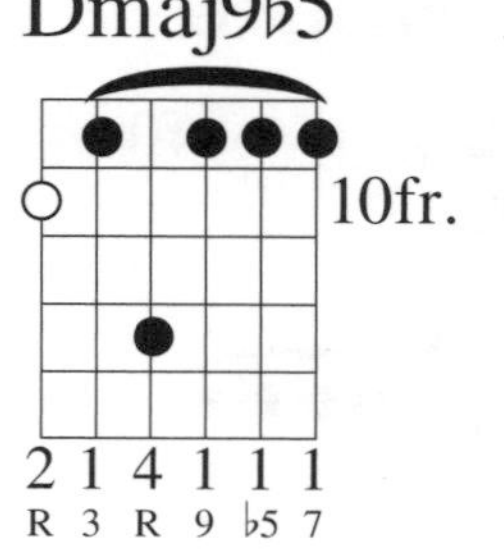

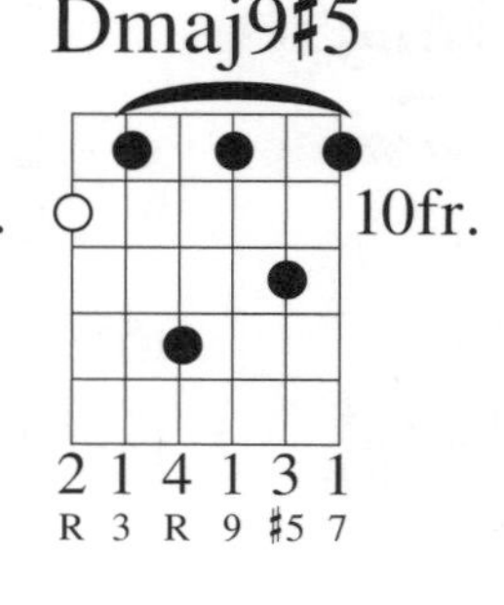

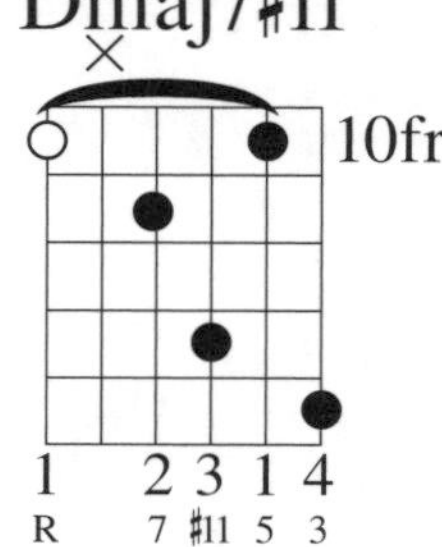

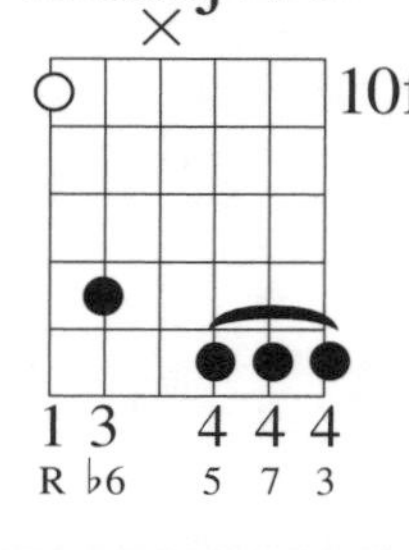

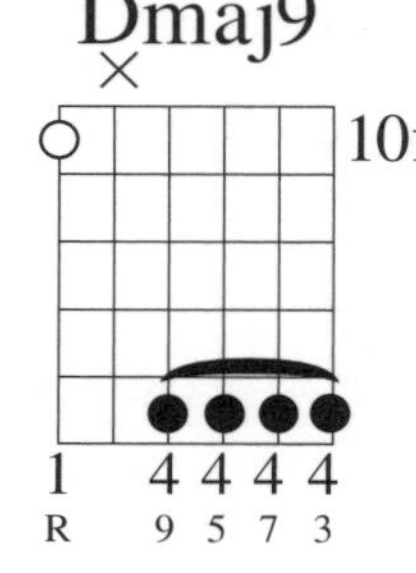

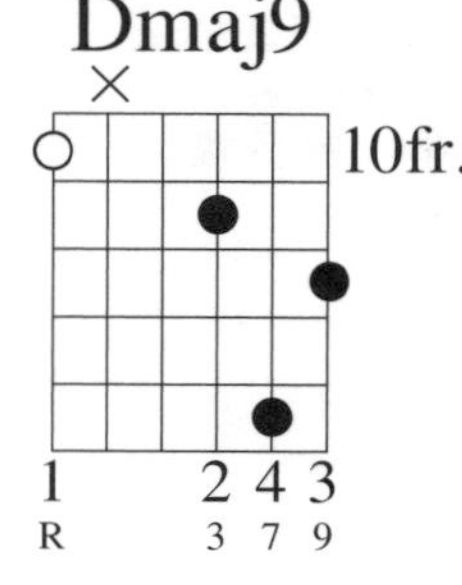

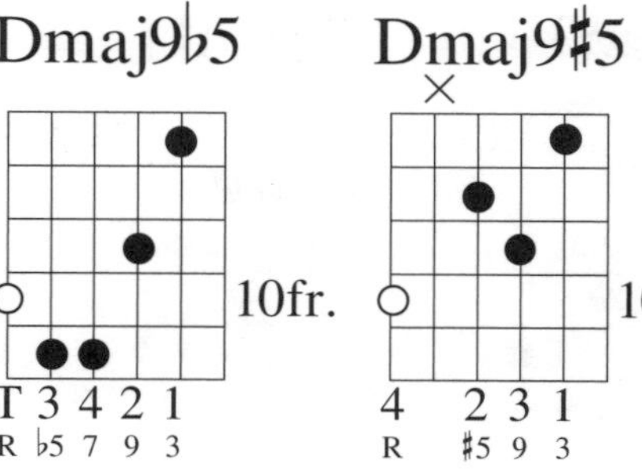

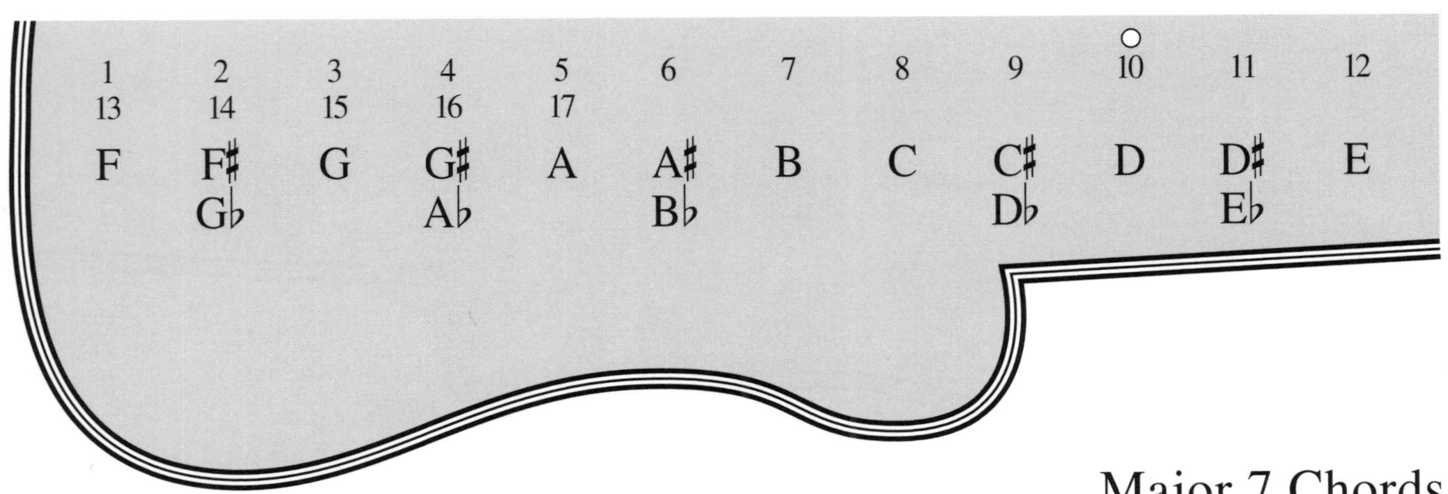

Major 7 Chords

Dmaj9♯11

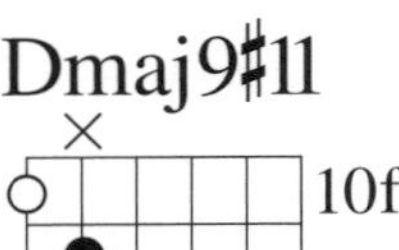

Dmaj9♯11♯5

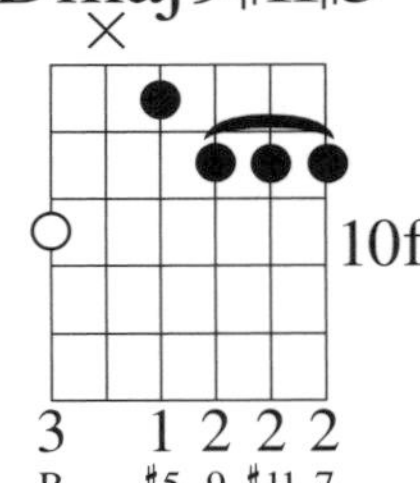

Dmaj13

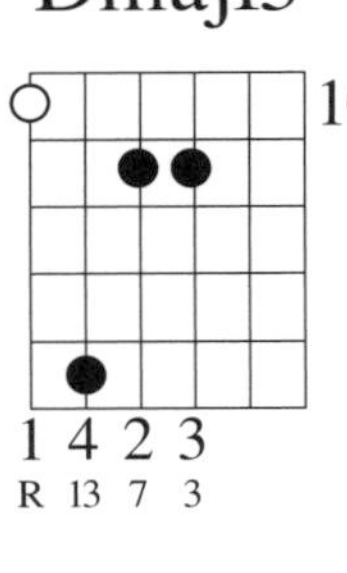

Dmaj13

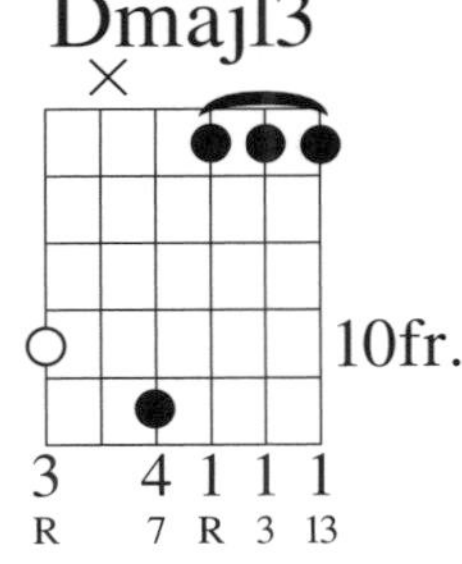

Dmaj13

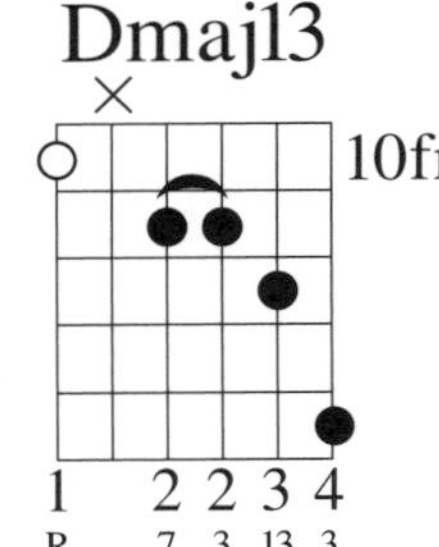

Dmaj13♯11

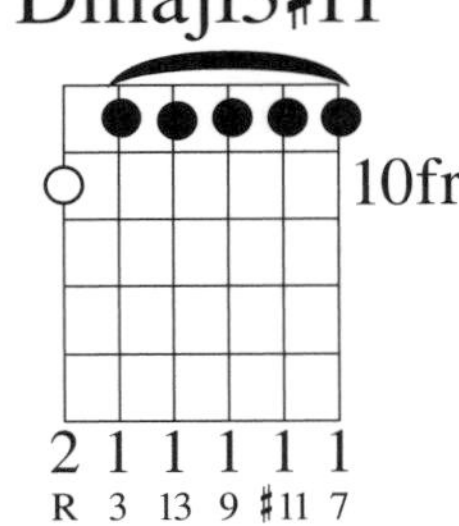

Dmaj9♯11

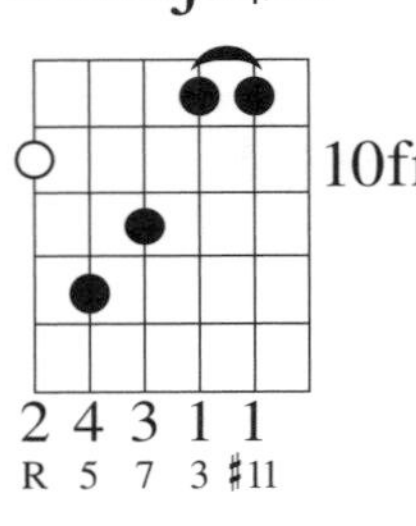

Dmaj9♭6

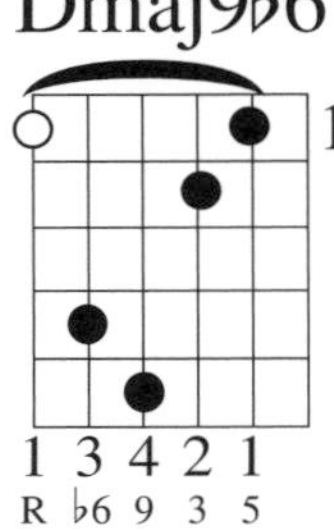

Dmaj13

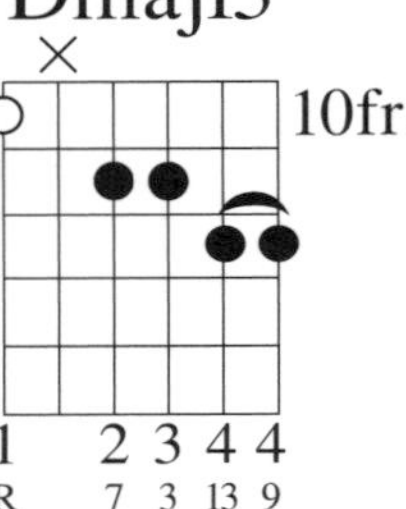

Dmaj13

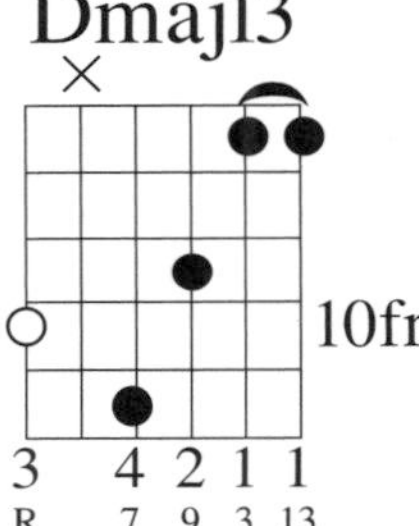

Dmaj13

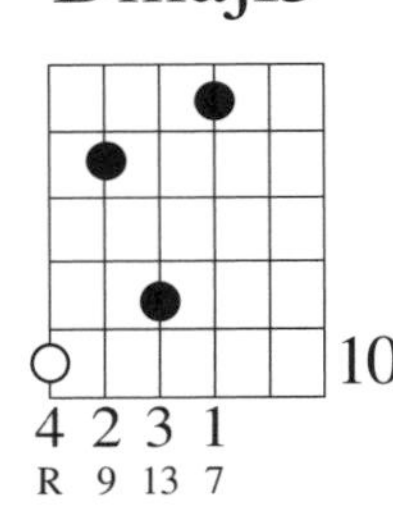

Dmaj13♯11

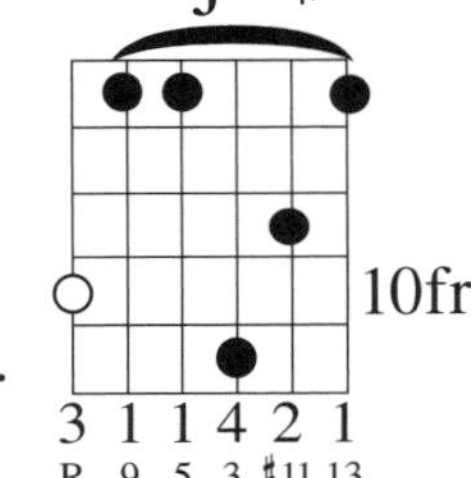

Dmaj9♯11

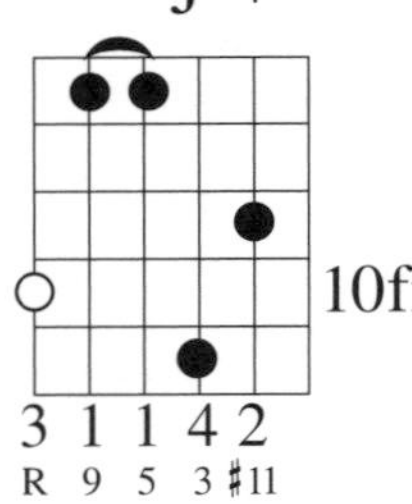

Dmaj9♭6

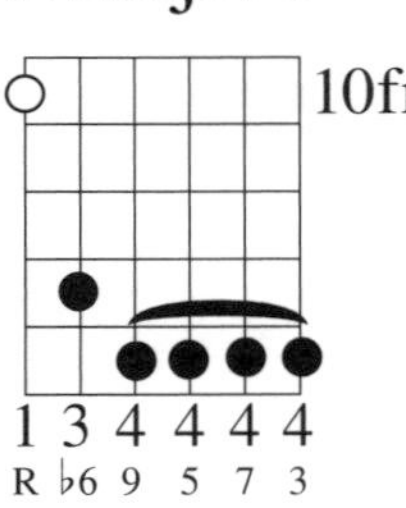

Dmaj13

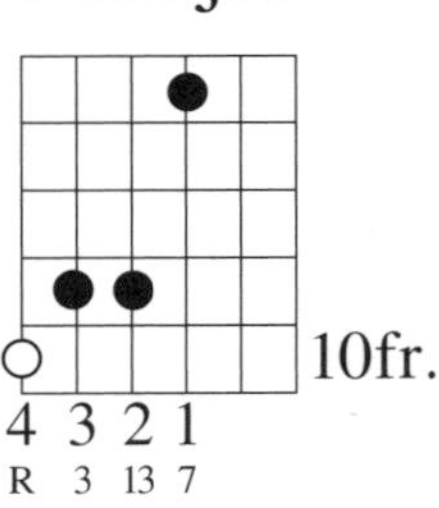

Dmaj13

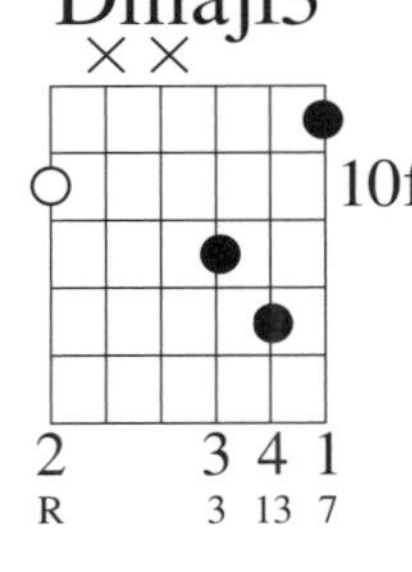

Dmaj13

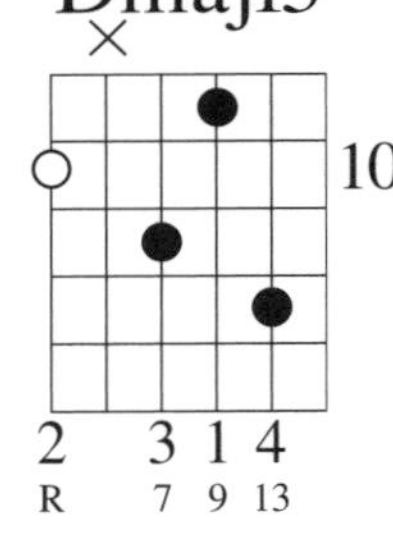

Dmaj13♯11

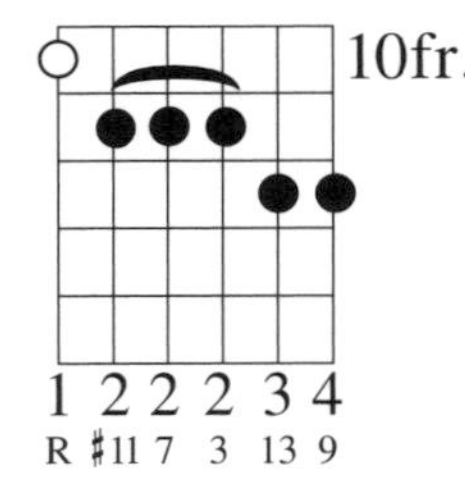

Dmaj9♯11

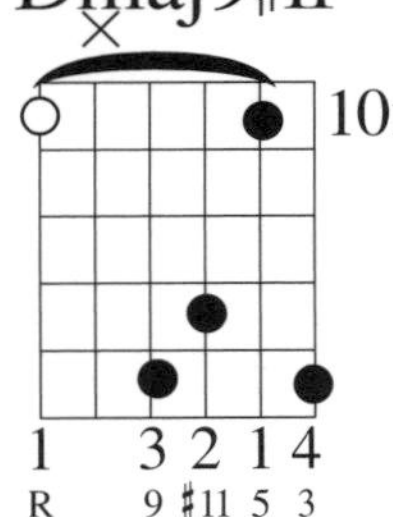

Dmaj13

Dmaj13

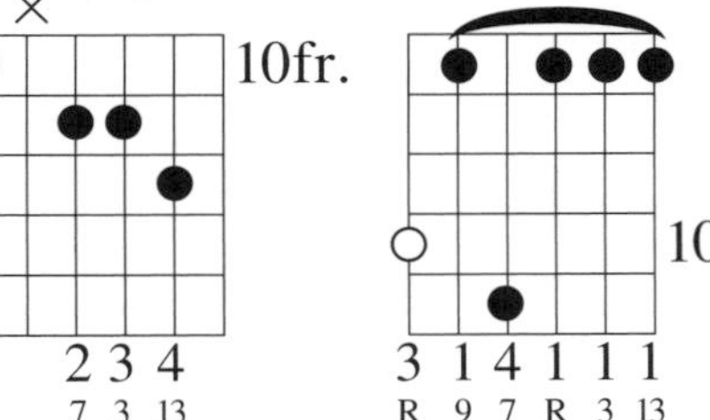

Dmaj13

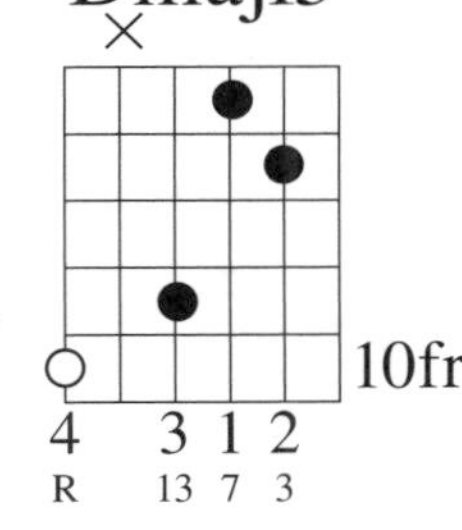

Dmaj13

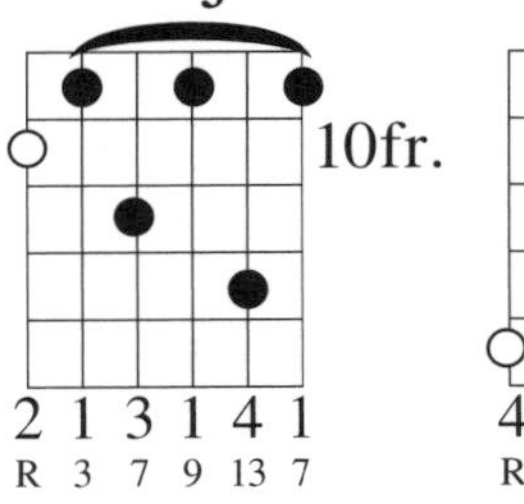

Dmaj13♯5

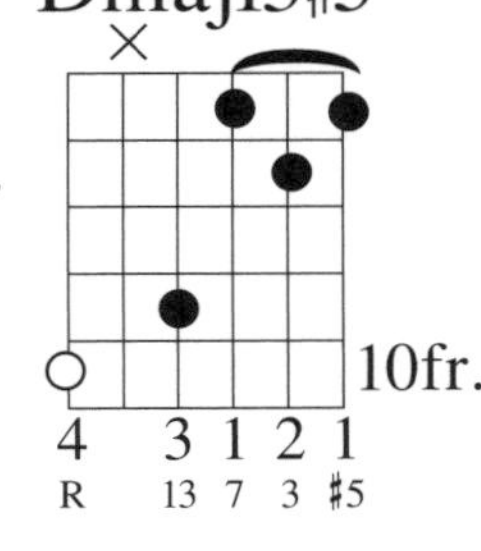

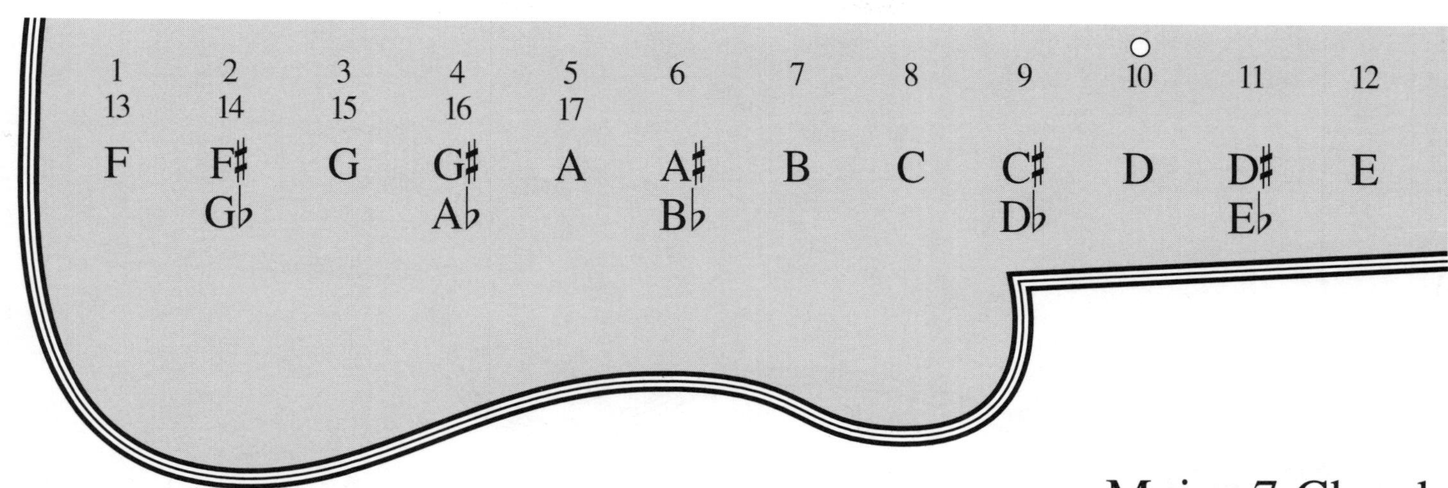

Major 7 Chords

Dmaj13♯5

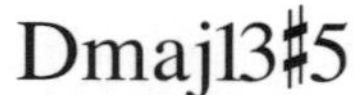

10fr.

2 1 1 1 4 1
R 3 13 9 ♯5 7

Dmaj7♯9

10fr.

2 1 4 3
R 3 7 ♯9

Dmaj7♯9♯11

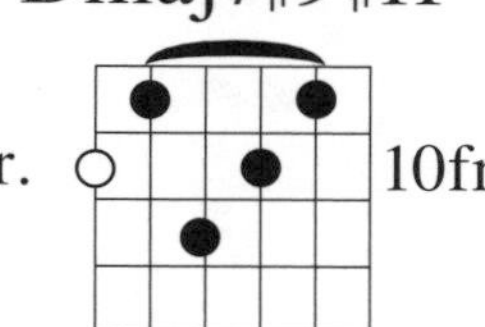

10fr.

2 1 4 3 1
R 3 7 ♯9 ♯11

Dmaj7♯9♯5

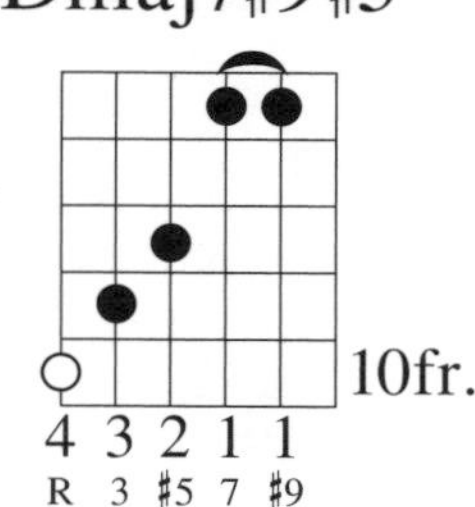

10fr.

4 3 2 1 1
R 3 ♯5 7 ♯9

Dmaj13♯5

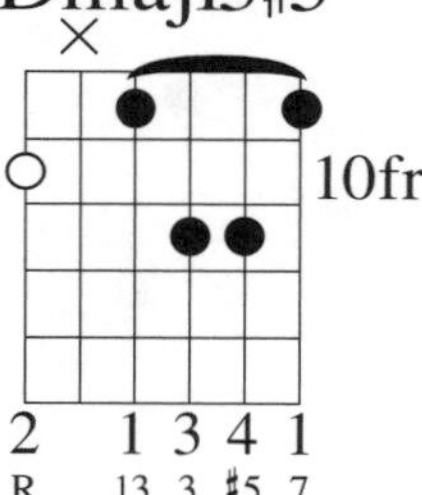

10fr.

2 1 3 4 1
R 13 3 ♯5 7

Dmaj7♯9

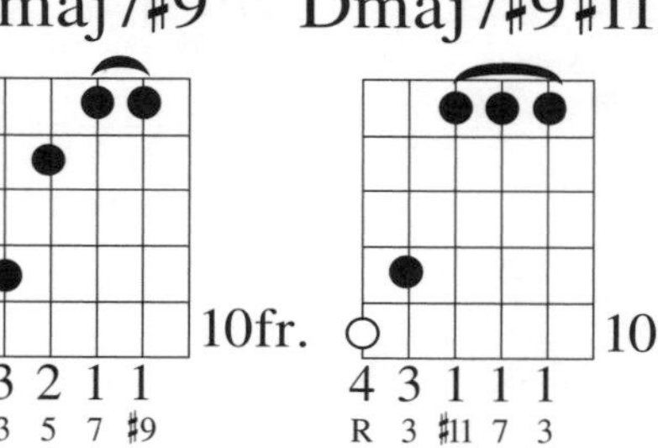

10fr.

4 3 2 1 1
R 3 5 7 ♯9

Dmaj7♯9♯11

10fr.

4 3 1 1 1
R 3 ♯11 7 3

Dmaj7♯9♯11♯5

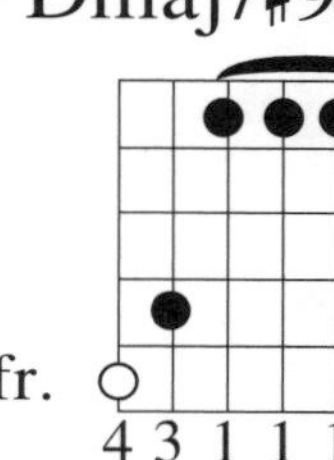

10fr.

4 3 1 1 1 1
R 3 ♯11 7 ♯9 ♯5

Dmaj13♯5

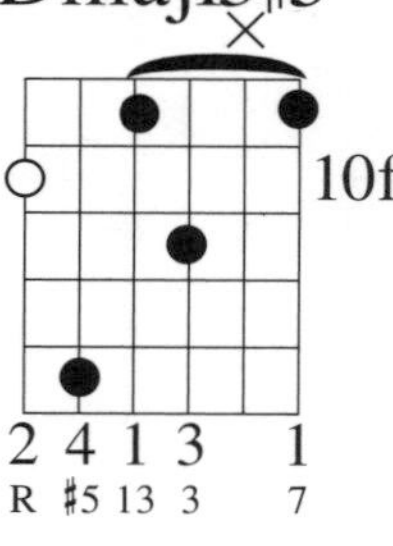

10fr.

2 4 1 3 1
R ♯5 13 3 7

Dmaj7♯9

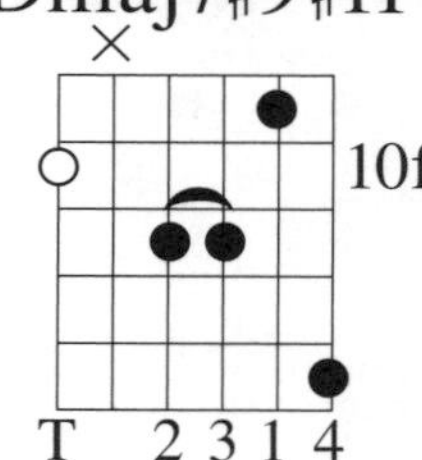

10fr.

1 2 3 1 4
R 7 3 5 ♯9

Dmaj7♯9♯11

10fr.

T 2 3 1 4
R 7 3 ♯11 ♯9

Dmaj7♯9♯11♯5

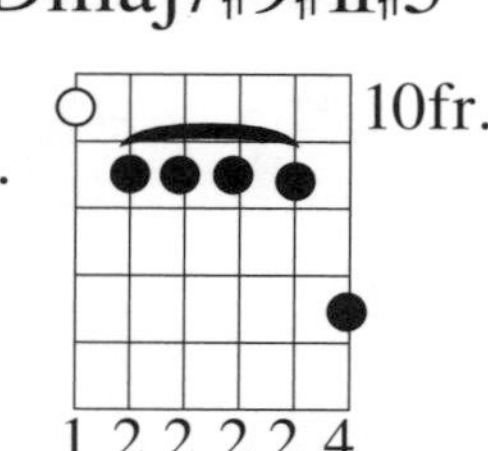

10fr.

1 2 2 2 2 4
R ♯11 7 3 ♯5 ♯9

Dmaj13♯5

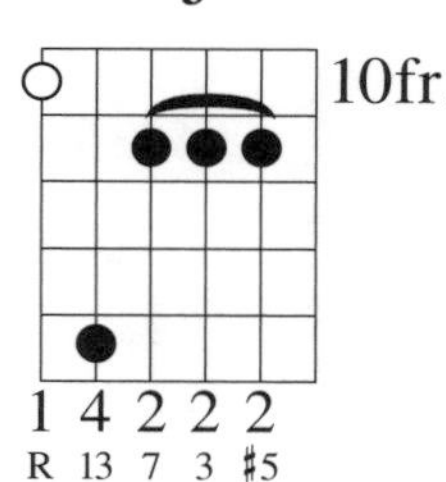

10fr.

1 4 2 2 2
R 13 7 3 ♯5

Dmaj7♯9

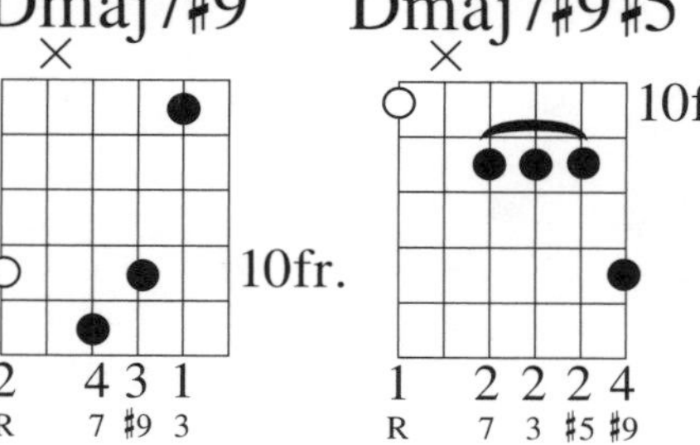

10fr.

2 4 3 1
R 7 ♯9 3

Dmaj7♯9♯5

10fr.

1 2 2 2 4
R 7 3 ♯5 ♯9

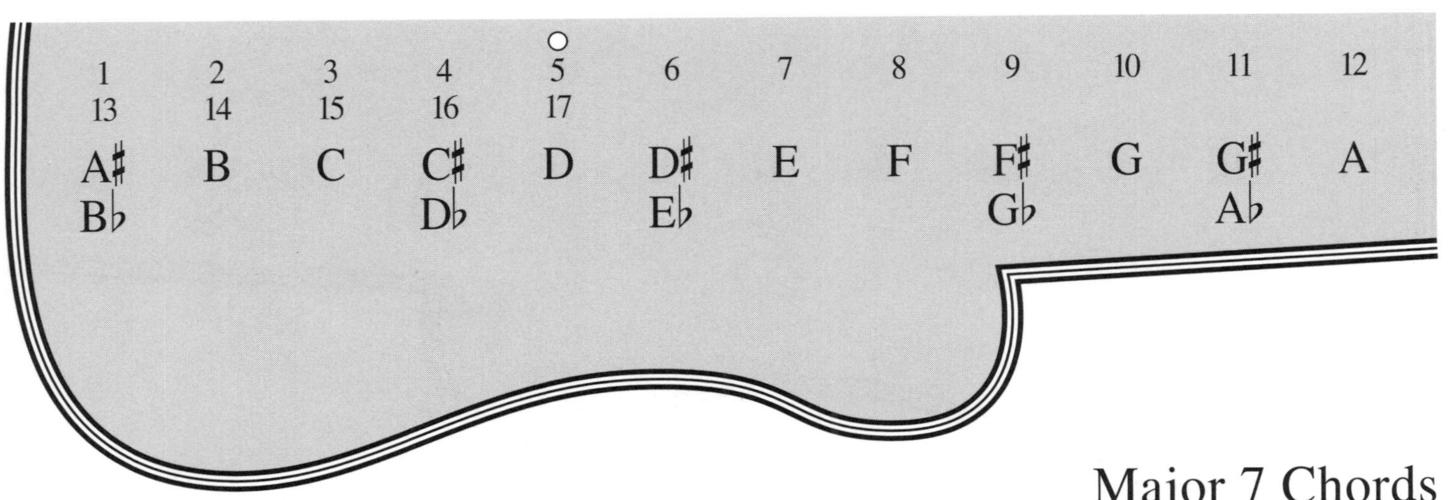

Major 7 Chords

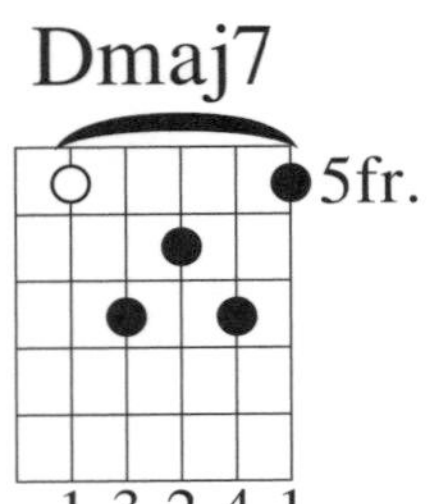

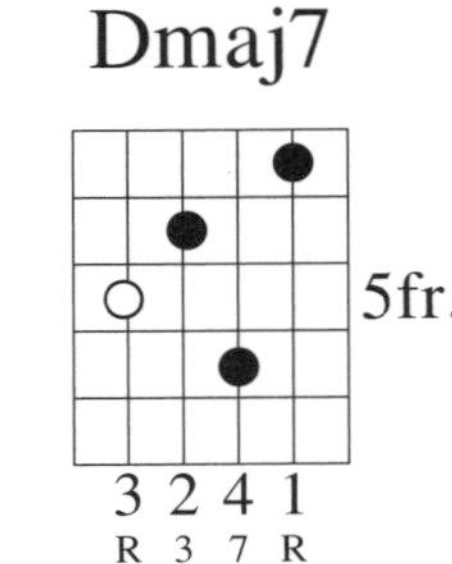

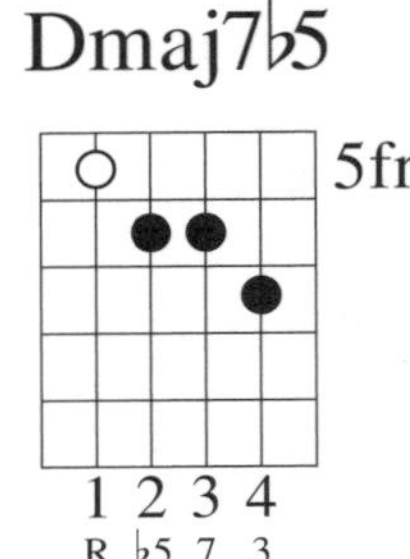

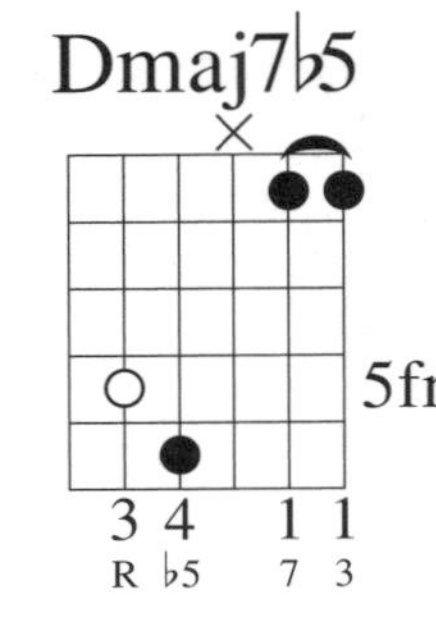

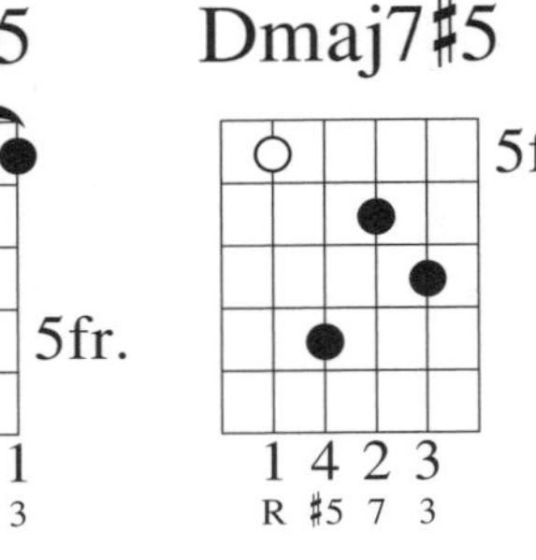

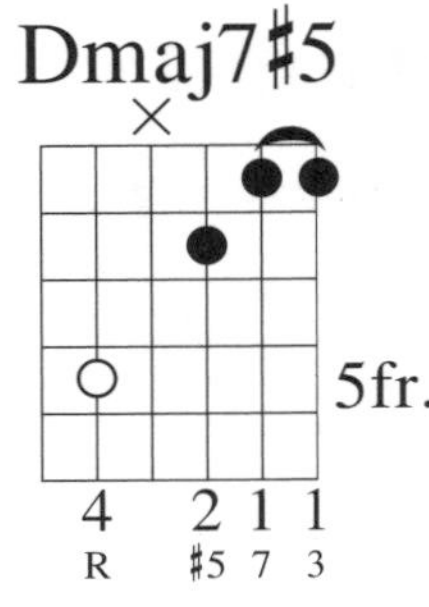

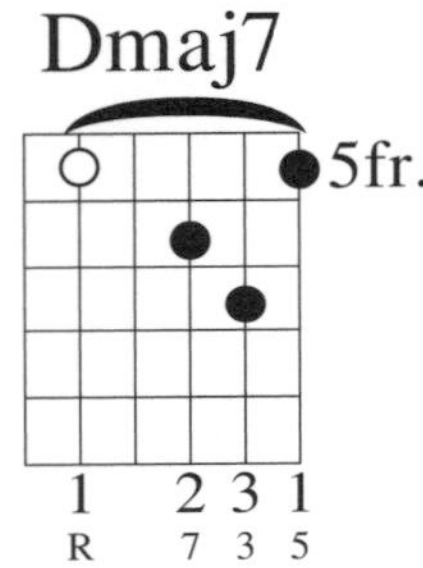

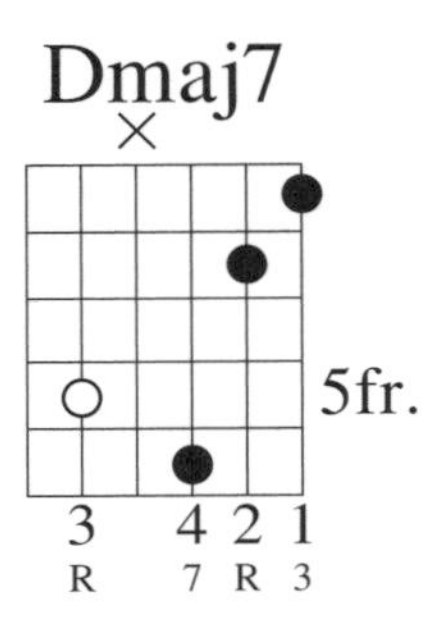

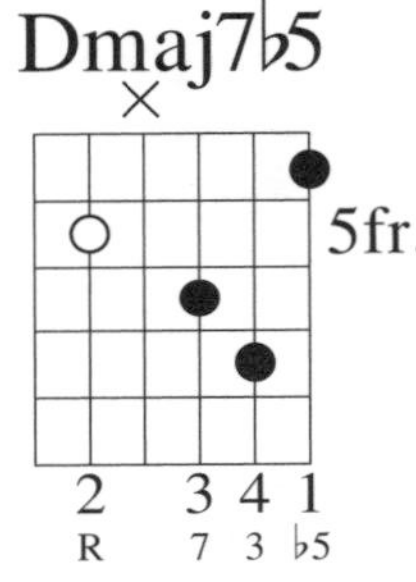

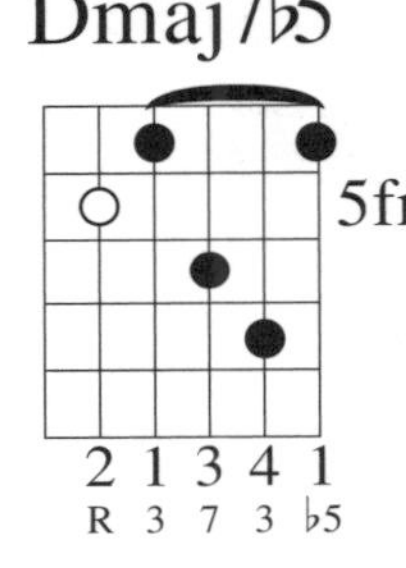

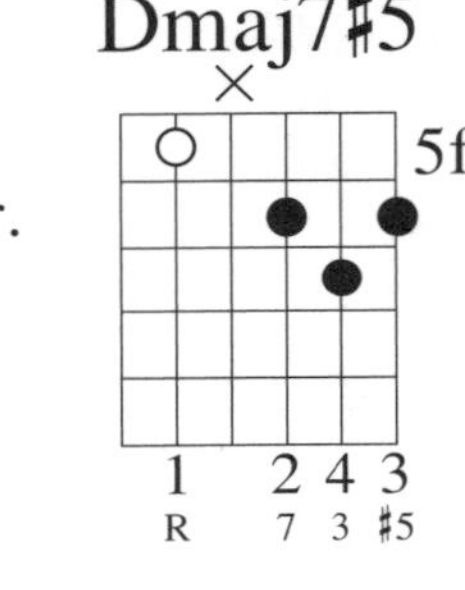

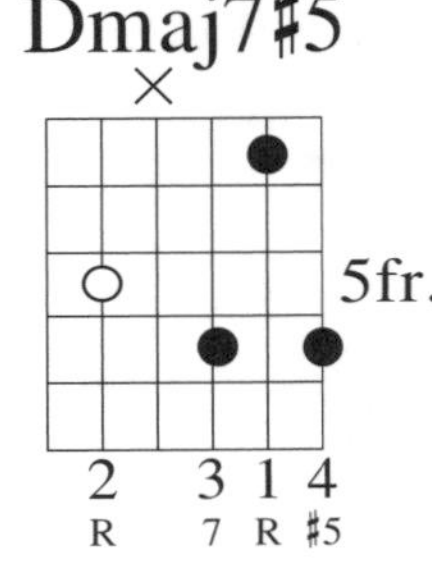

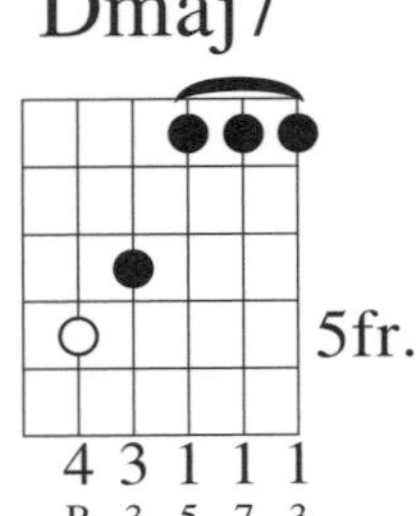

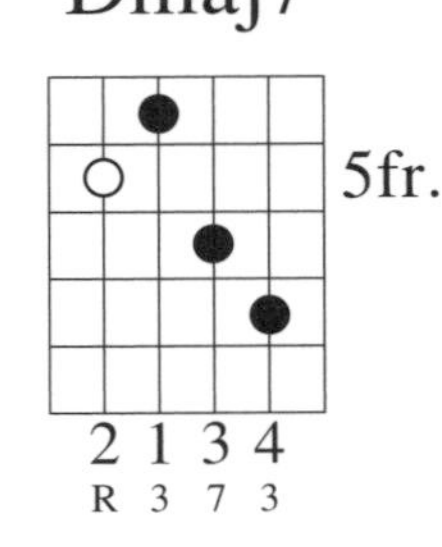

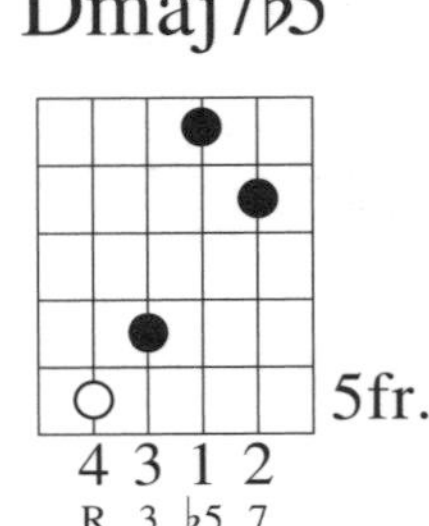

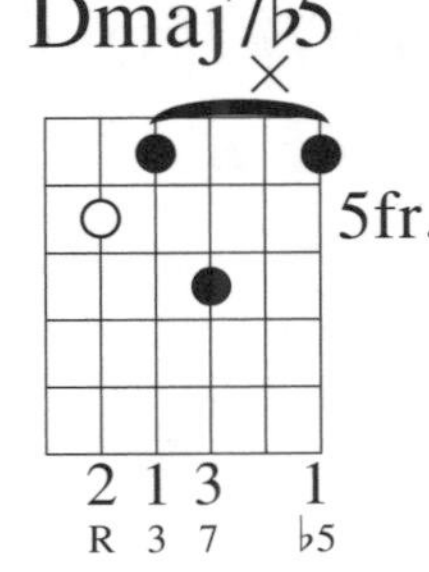

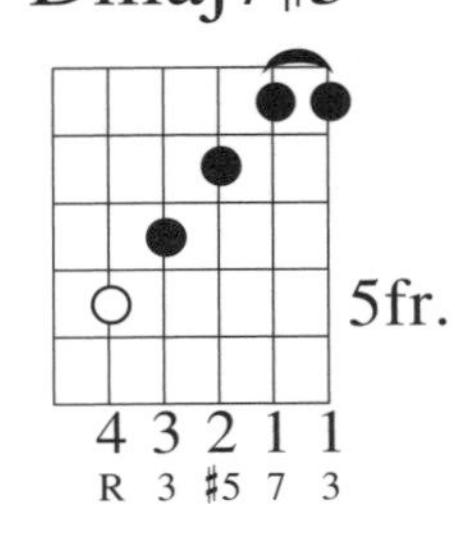

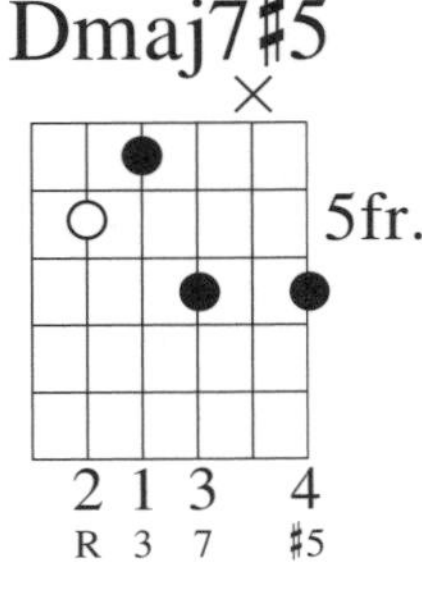

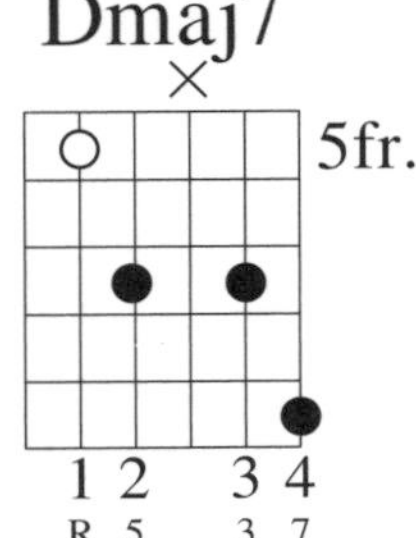

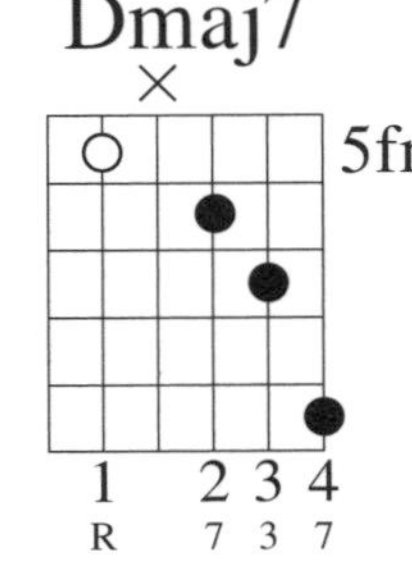

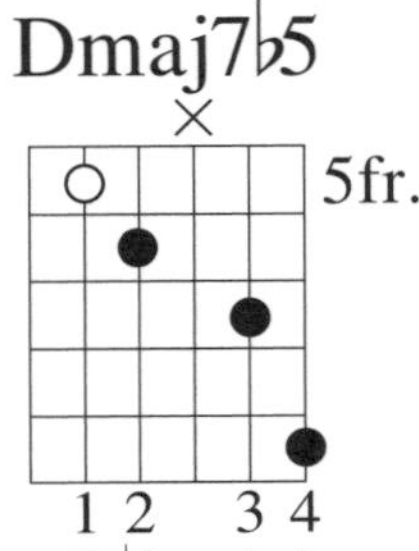

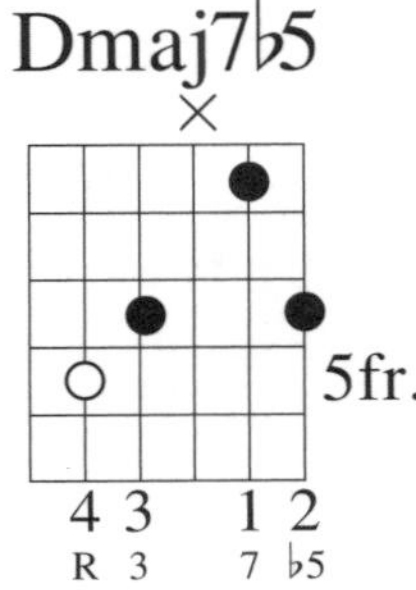

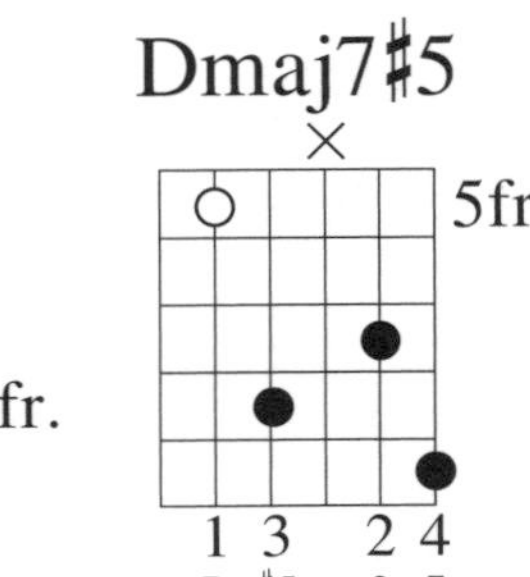

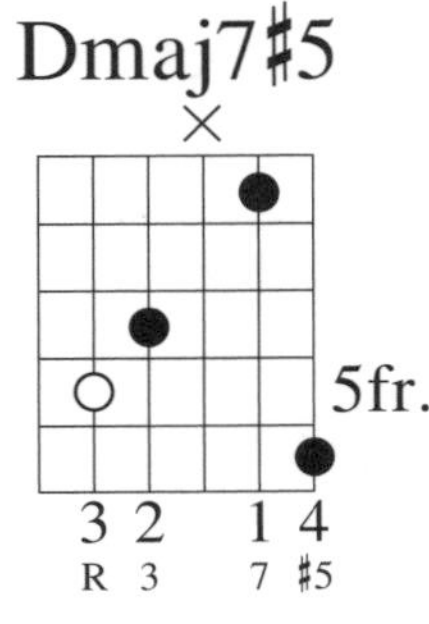

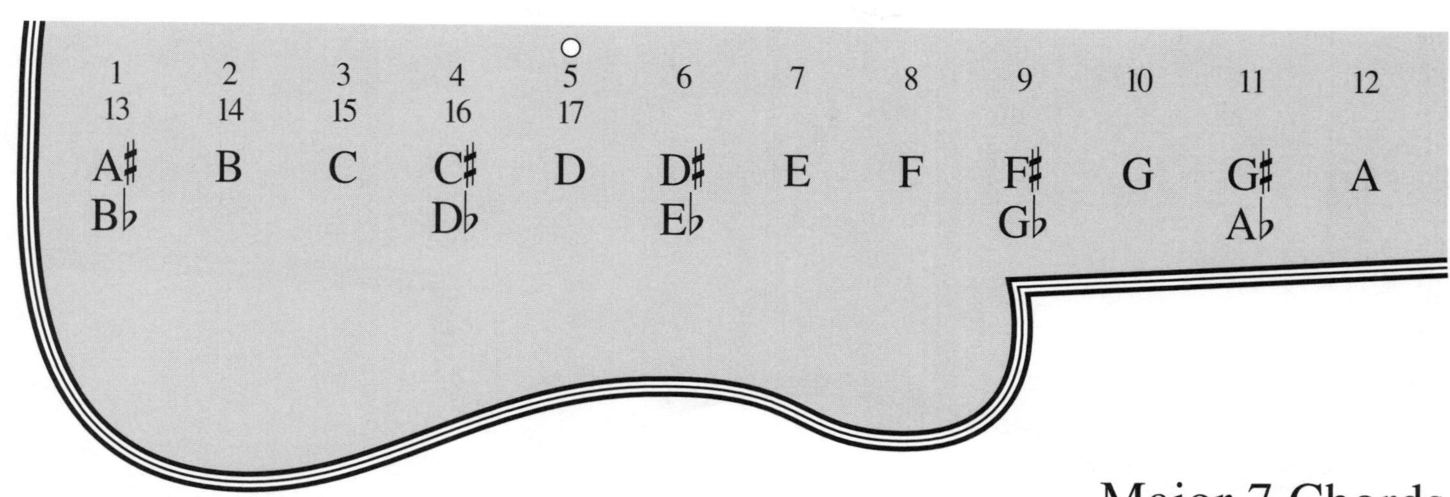

Major 7 Chords

Dmaj7♯11

4 3 1 1 2
R 3 5 7 ♯11

Dmaj7♯11♯5

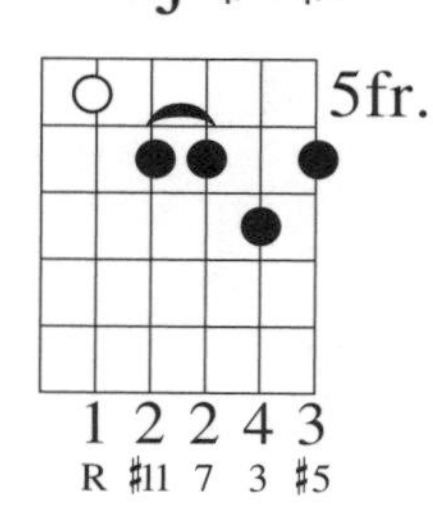

Dmaj9

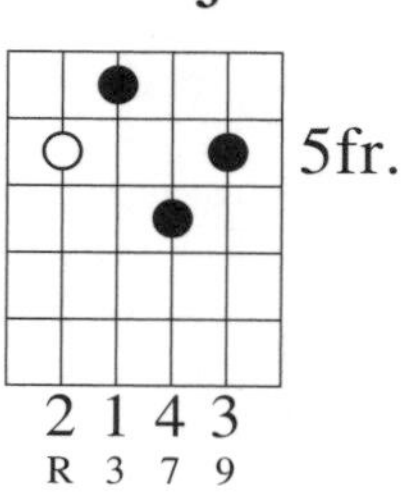

Dmaj9

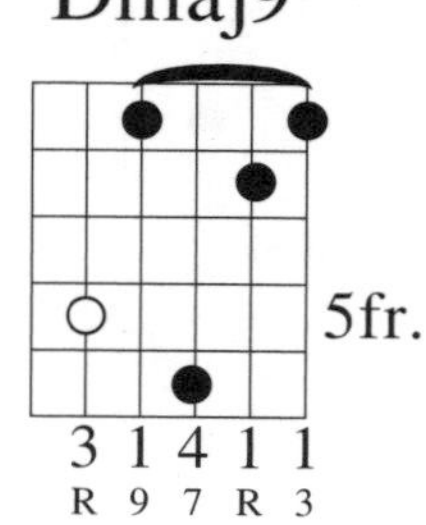

Dmaj9♭5

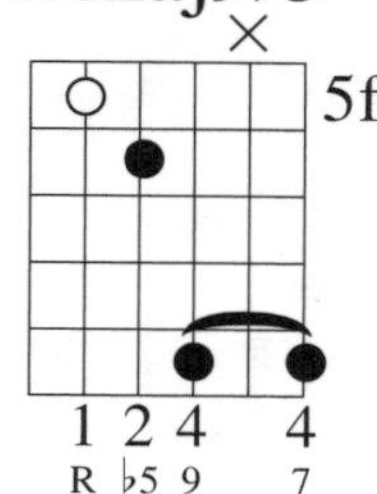

Dmaj9♯11

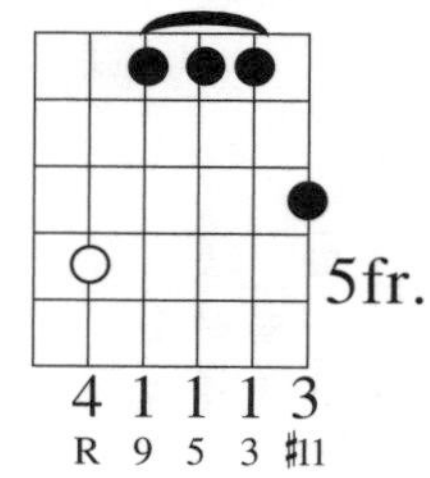

Dmaj7♯11

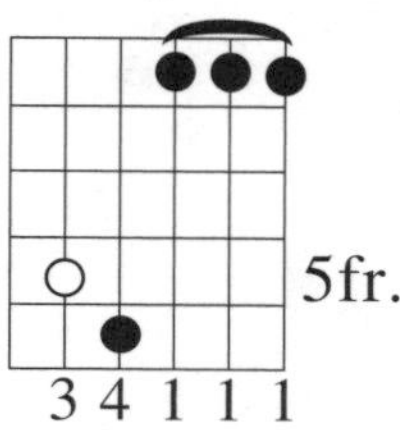

Dmaj7♯11♯5

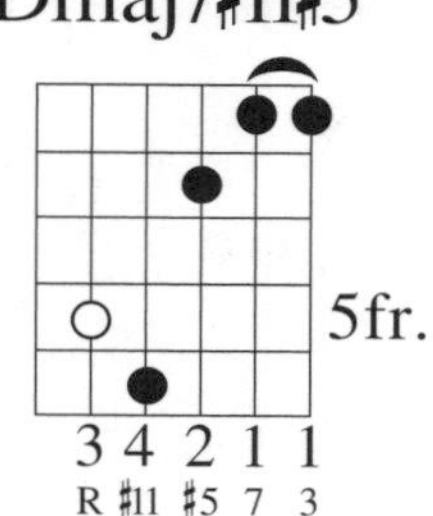

Dmaj9

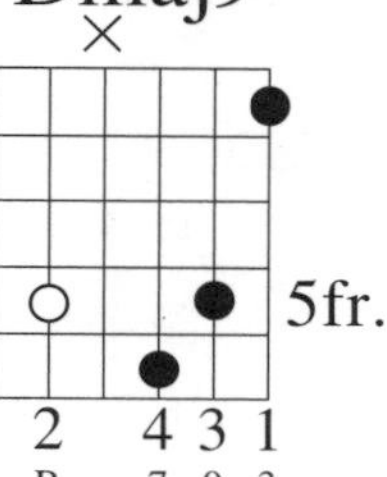

Dmaj9

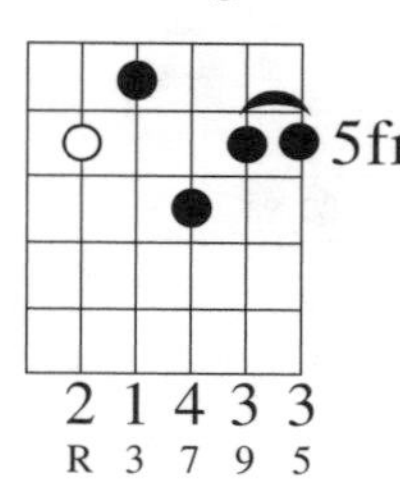

Dmaj9♯5

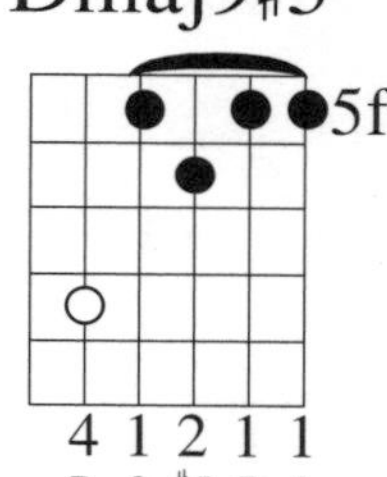

Dmaj9♯11

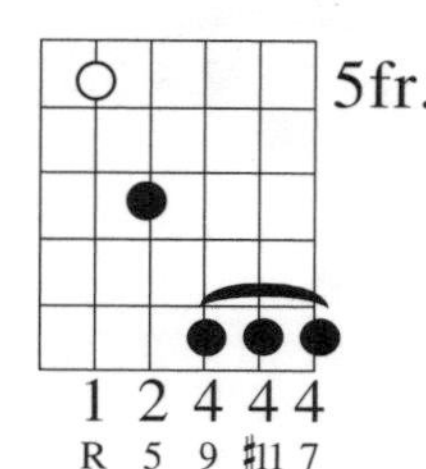

Dmaj7♯11

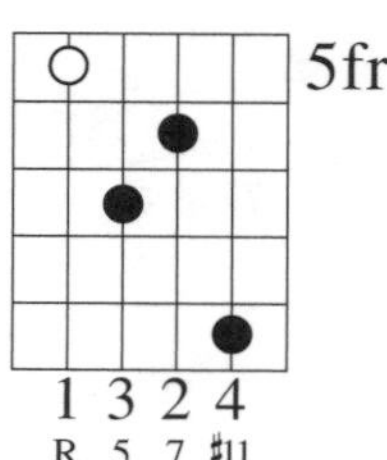

Dmaj7♭6

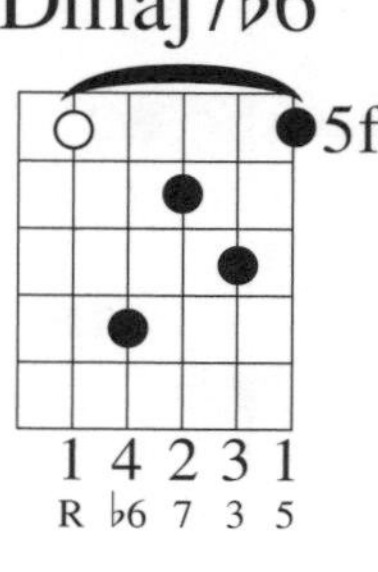

Dmaj9

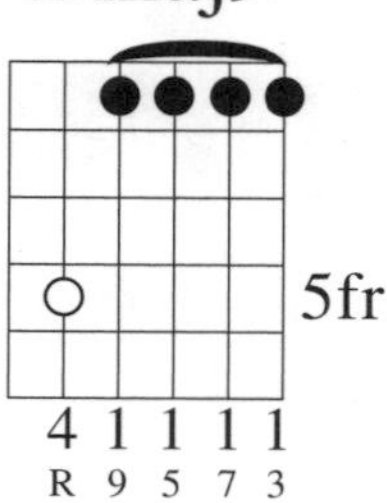

Dmaj9♭5

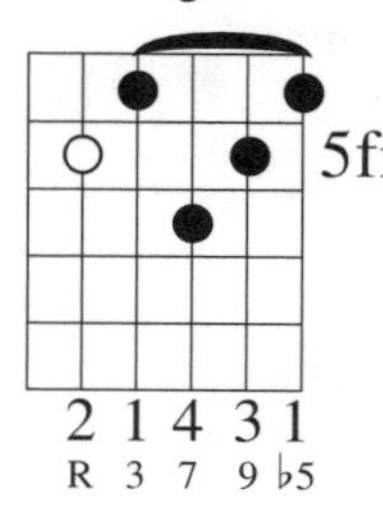

Dmaj9♯5

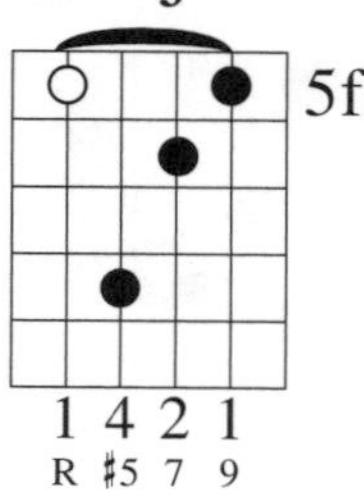

Dmaj9♯11♯5

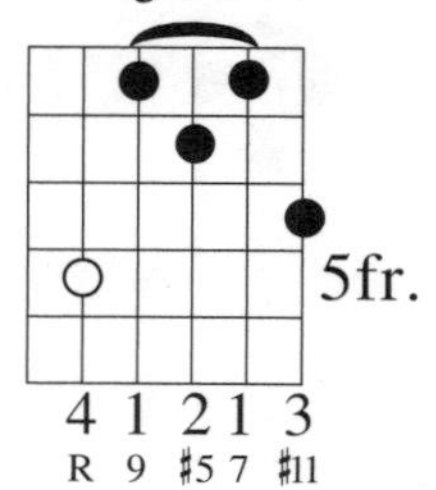

Dmaj7♯11

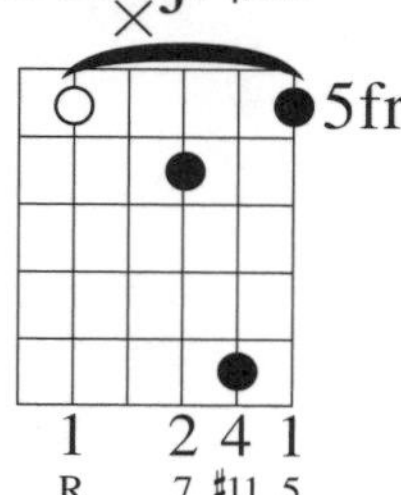

Dmaj7♭6

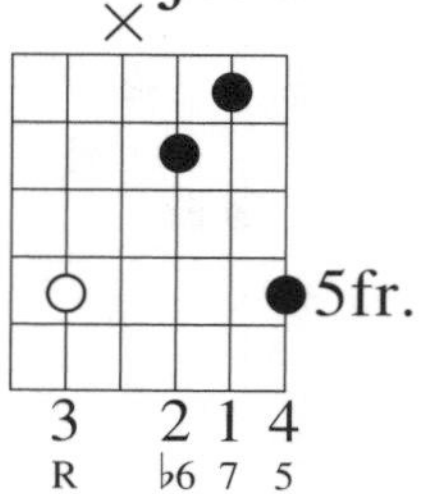

Dmaj9

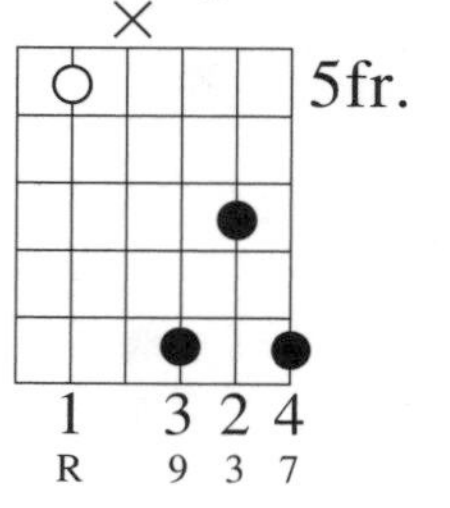

Dmaj9♭5

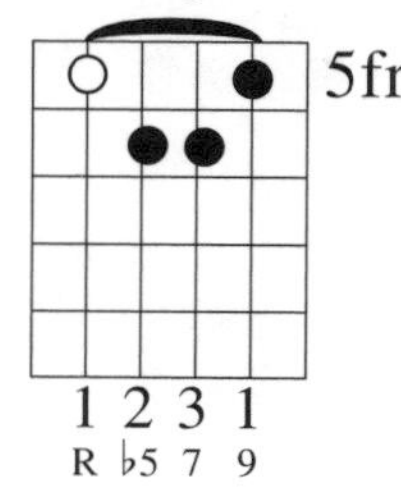

Dmaj9♯5

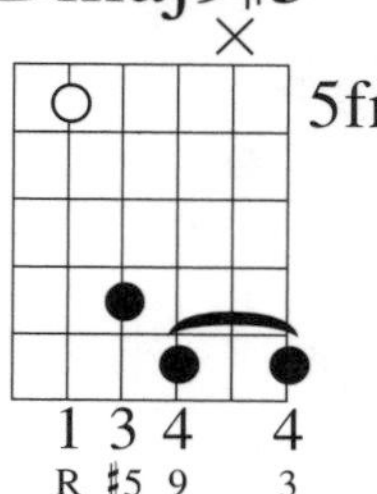

Dmaj9♯11♯5

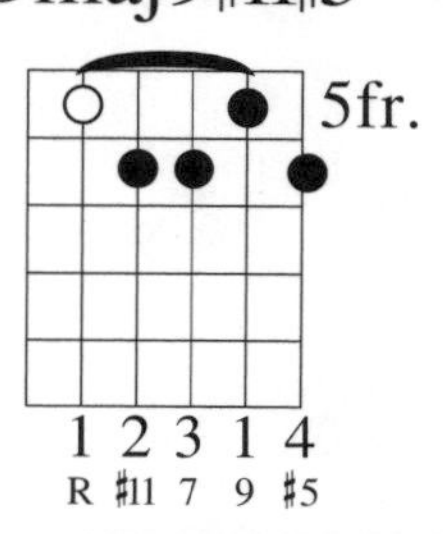

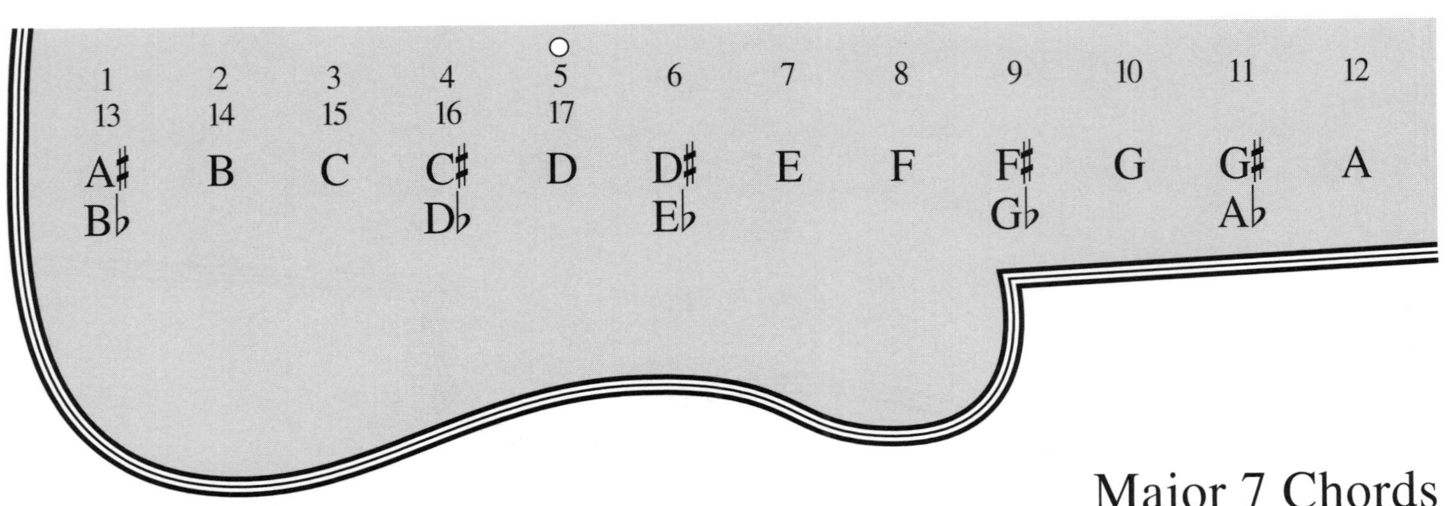

Major 7 Chords

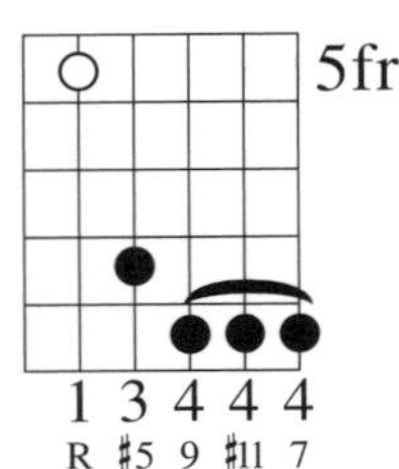

Dmaj9♭6

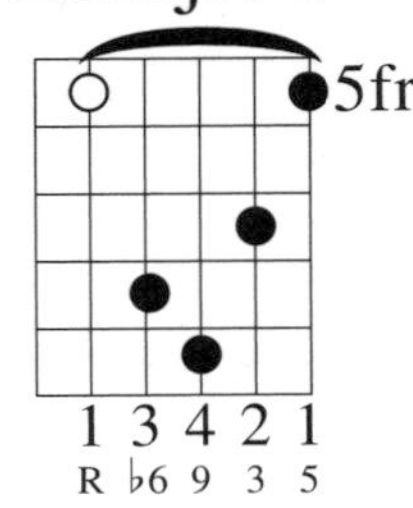

Dmaj13

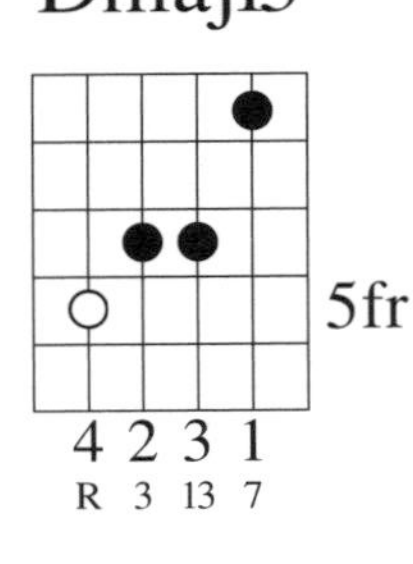

Dmaj13♯11

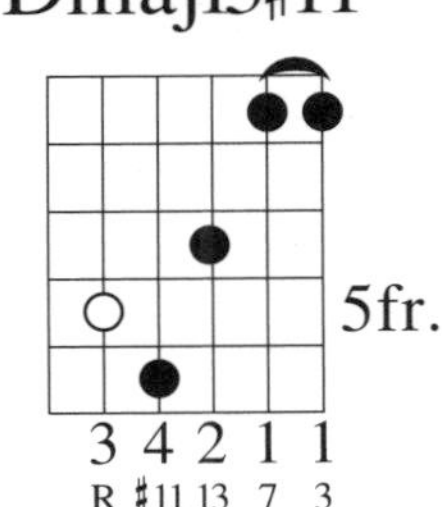

Dmaj13♯5

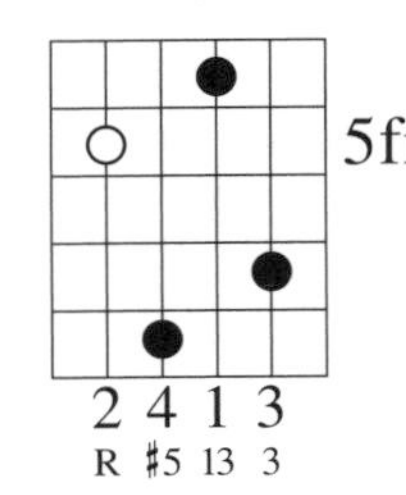

Dmaj7♯9♯11

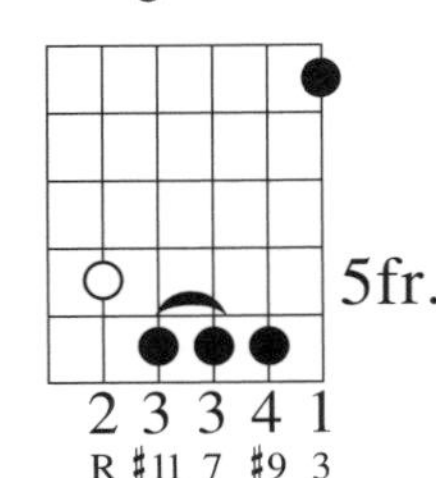

Dmaj9♭6

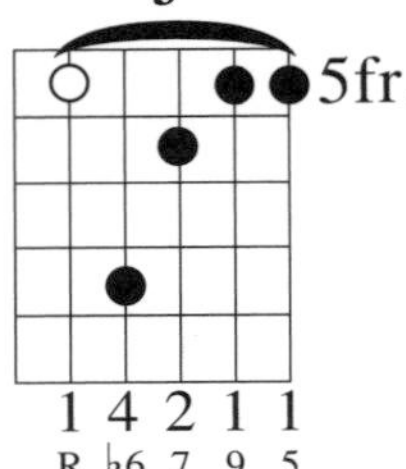

Dmaj13

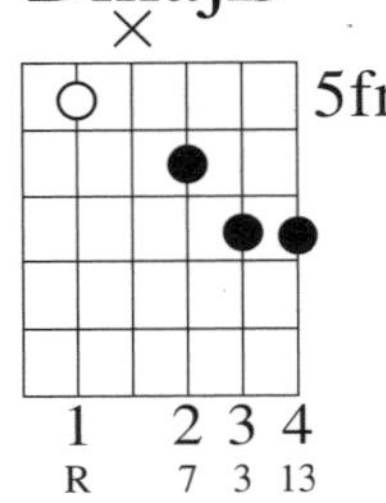

Dmaj13

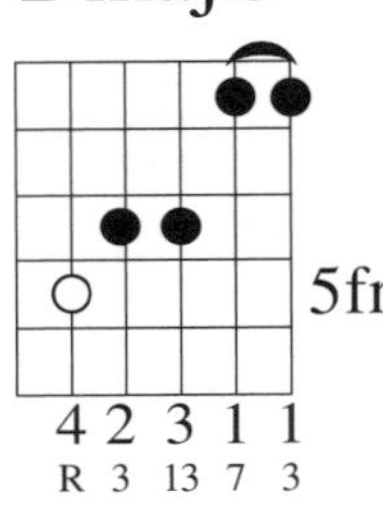

Dmaj13♯11

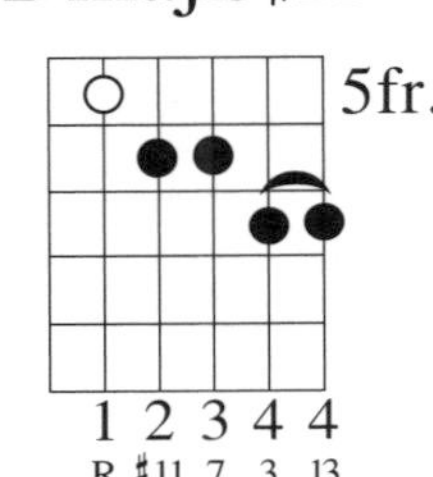

Dmaj7♯9

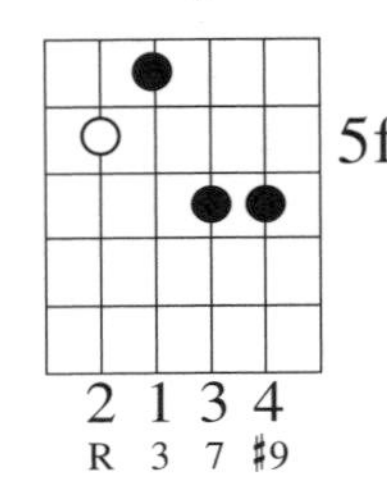

Dmaj7♯9♯11

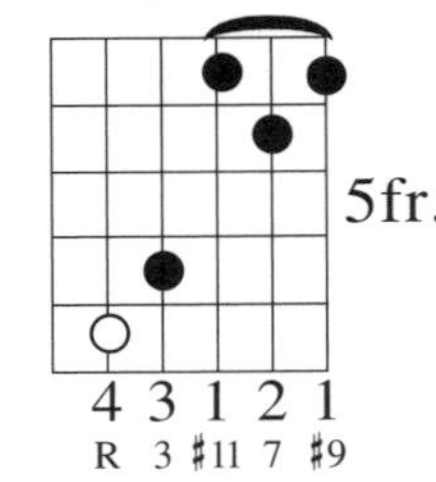

Dmaj9♭6

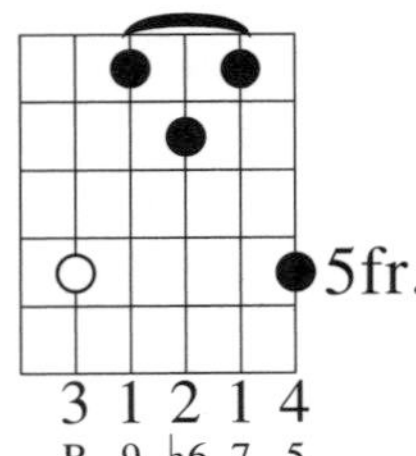

Dmaj13

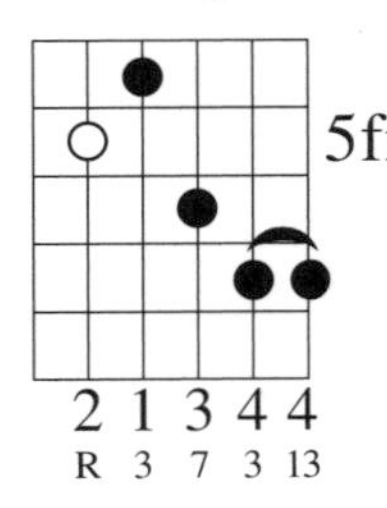

Dmaj13

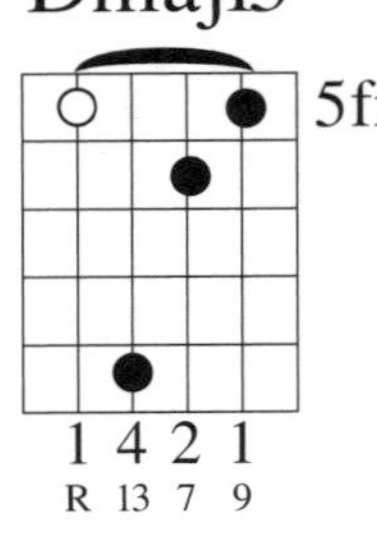

Dmaj13♯11

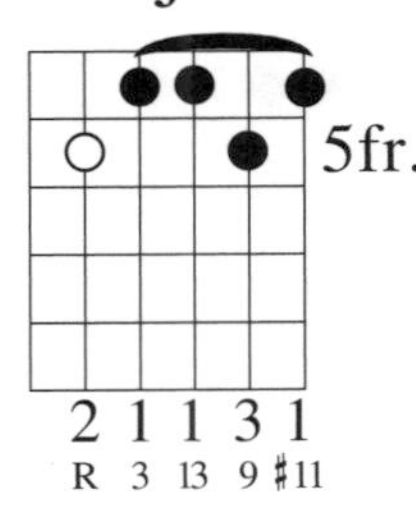

Dmaj7♯9

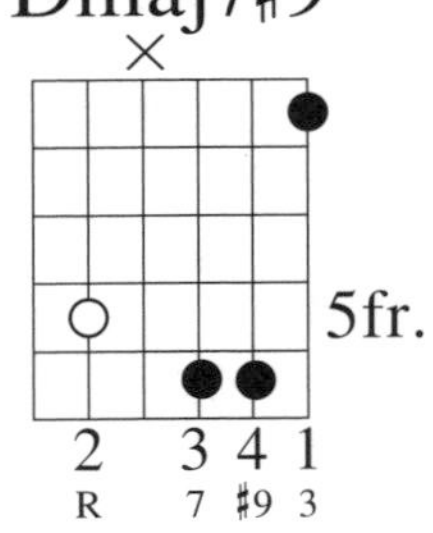

Dmaj7♯9♯5

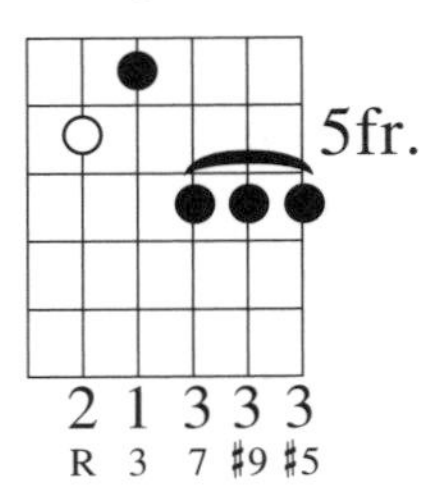

Dmaj9♭6

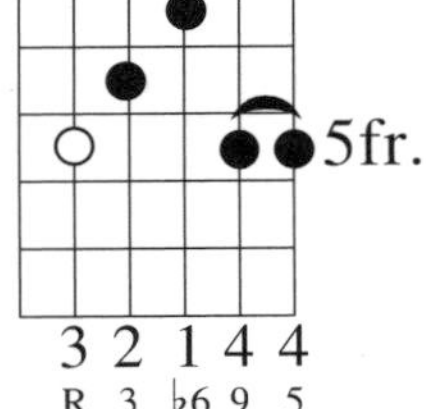

Dmaj13

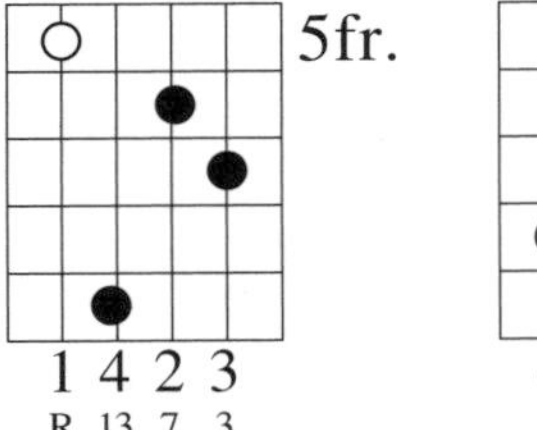

Dmaj13

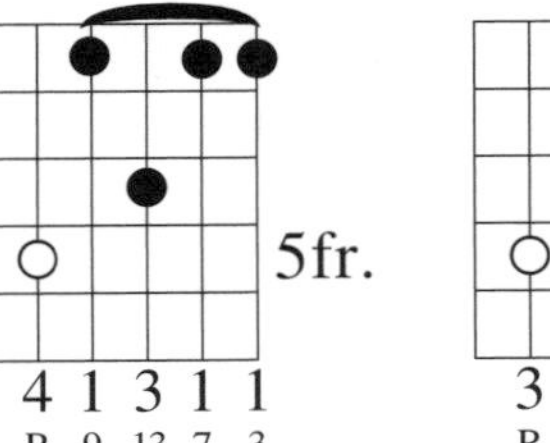

Dmaj13♯5

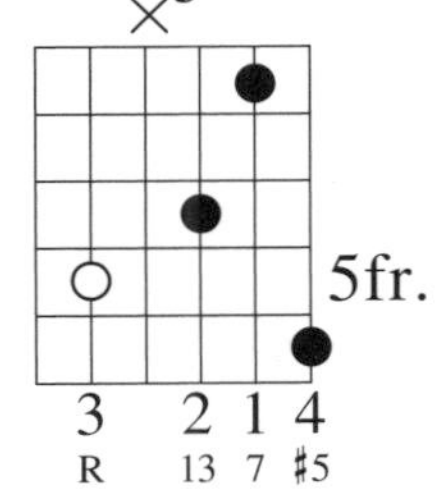

Dmaj7♯9♯11

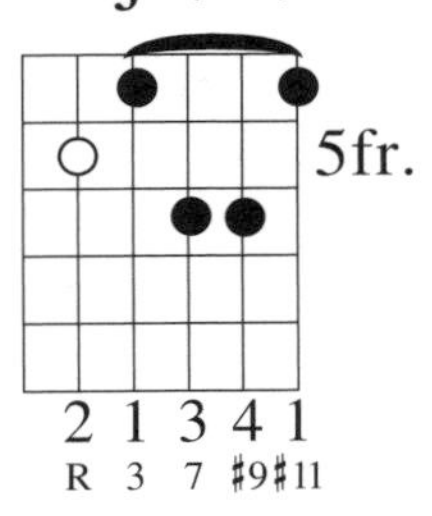

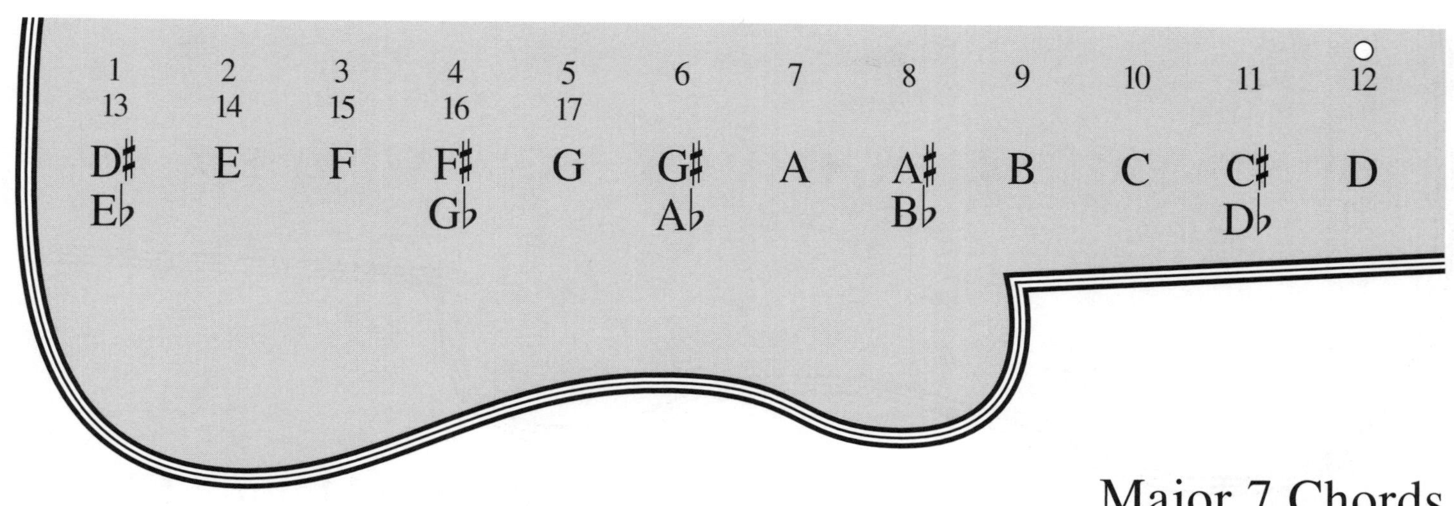

Major 7 Chords

Dmaj7

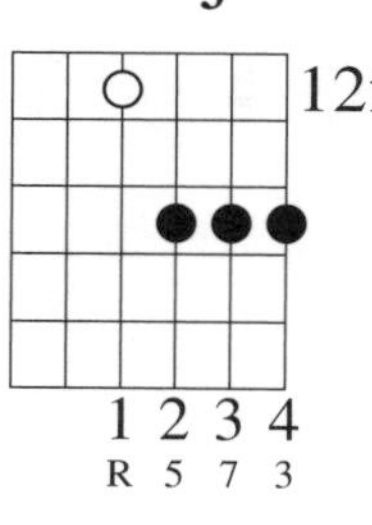

Dmaj7♭5

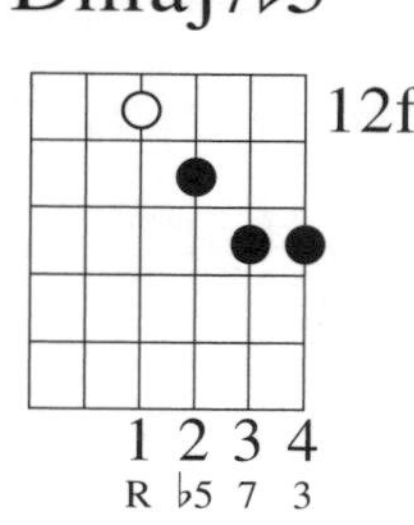

Dmaj9

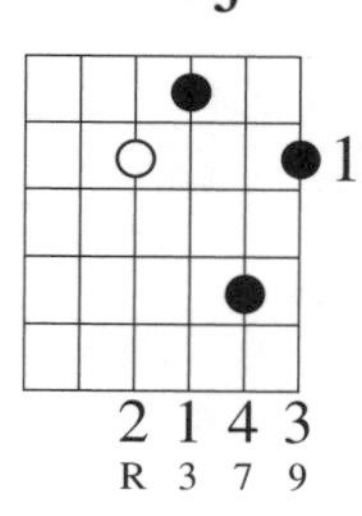

Dmaj9♯5

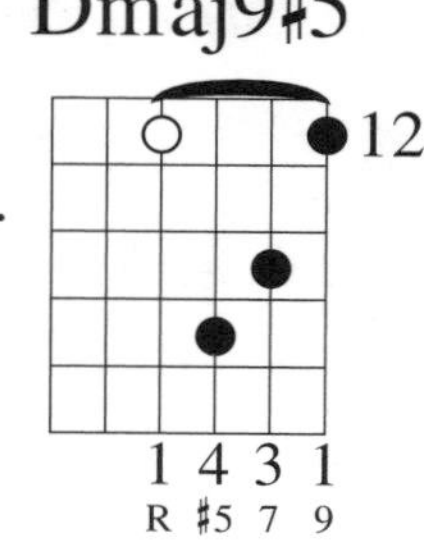

Dmaj13

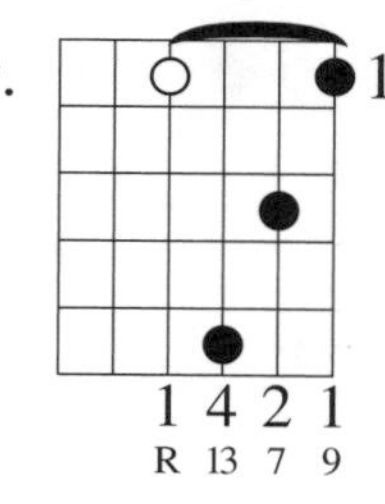

Dmaj13♯5

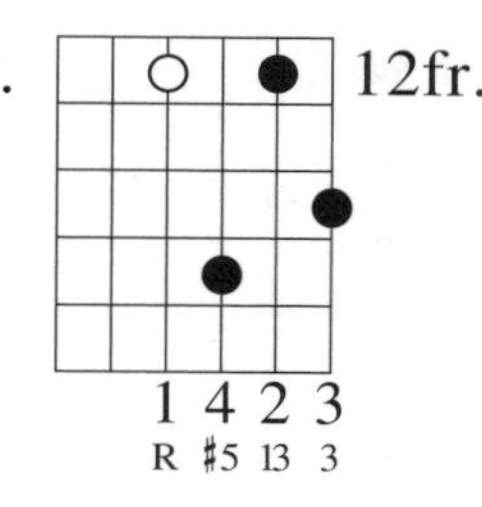

Dmaj7

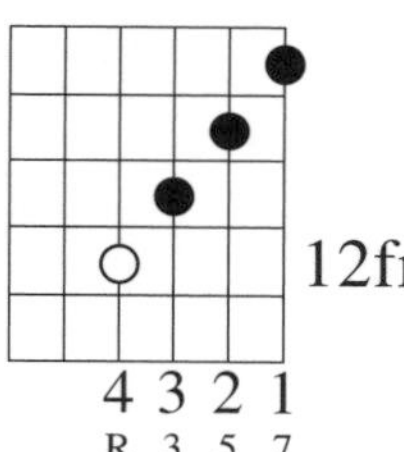

Dmaj7♭5

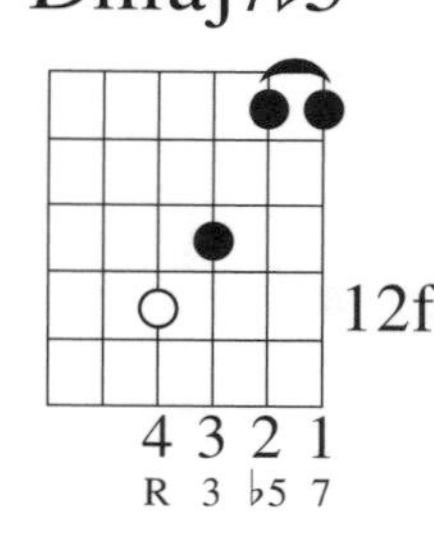

Dmaj9

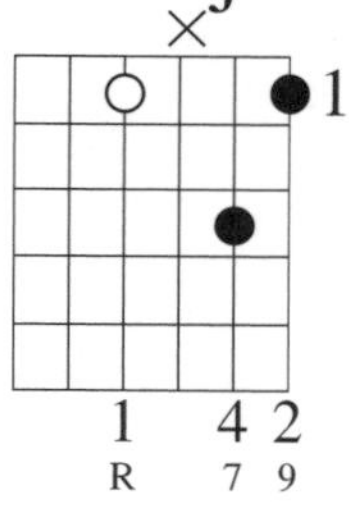

Dmaj9♯5

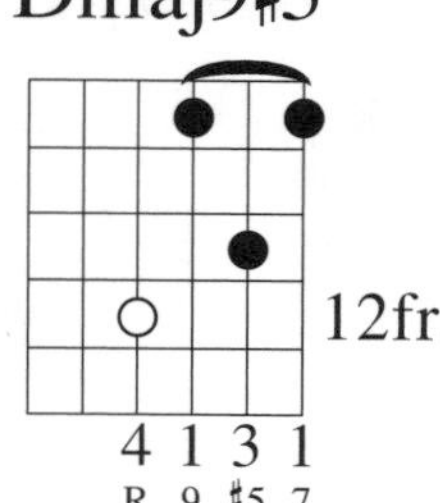

Dmaj13♯11

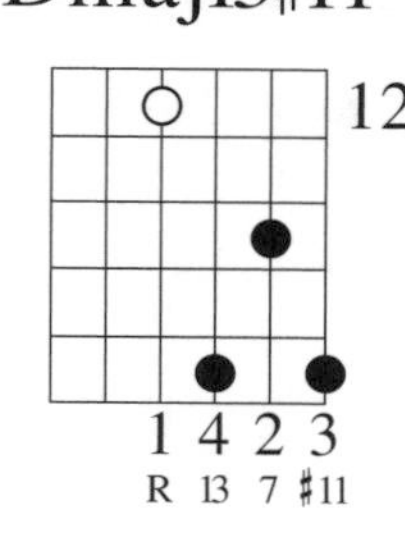

Dmaj7♯9

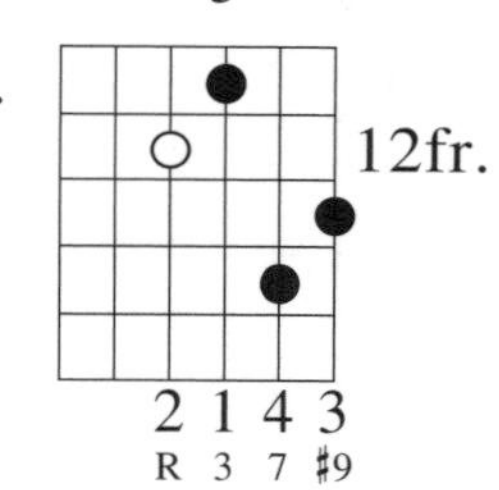

Dmaj7

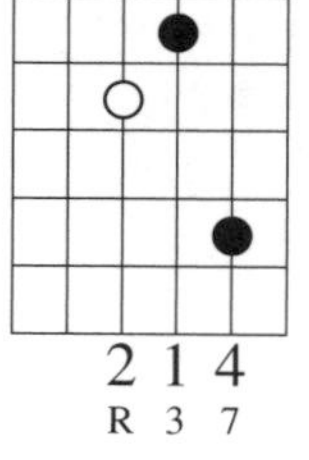

Dmaj7♯5

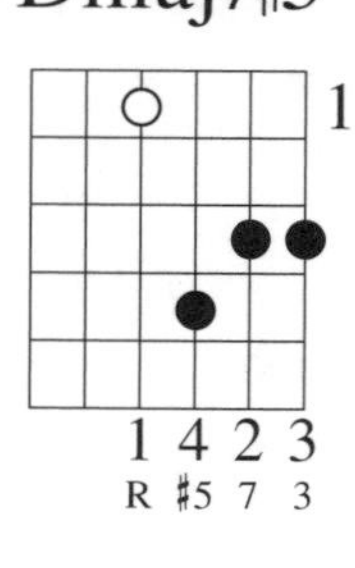

Dmaj9♭5

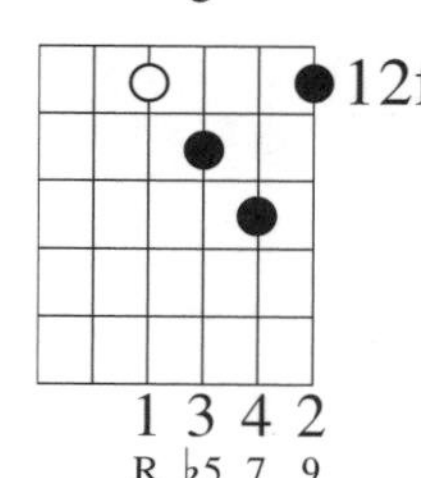

Dmaj9♯11

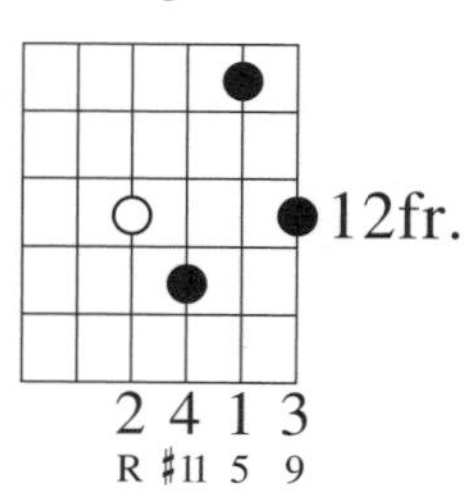

Dmaj13♯11

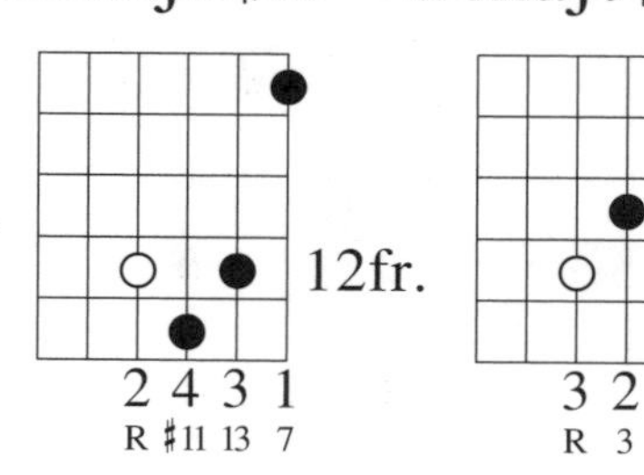

Dmaj7♯9♯11

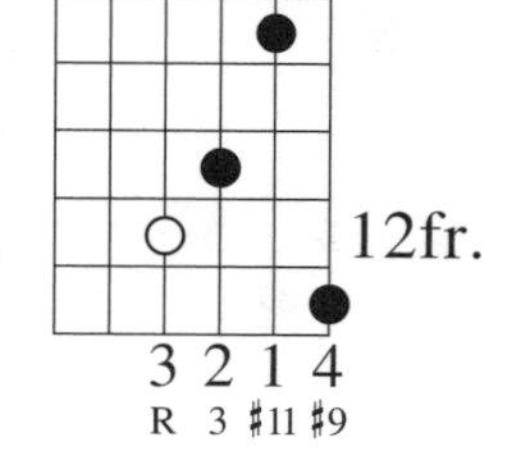

Dmaj7

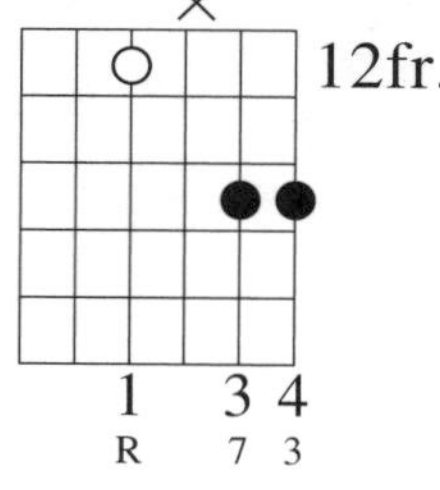

Dmaj7

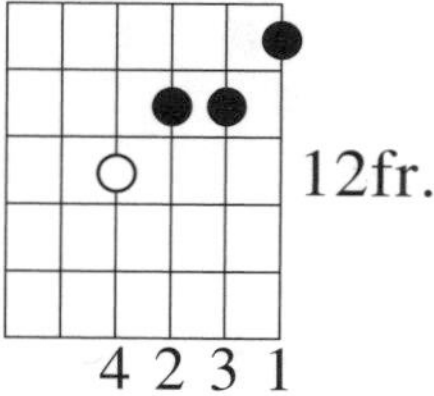

Dmaj9♭5

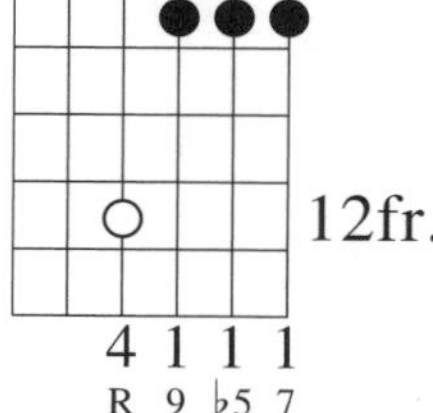

Dmaj13

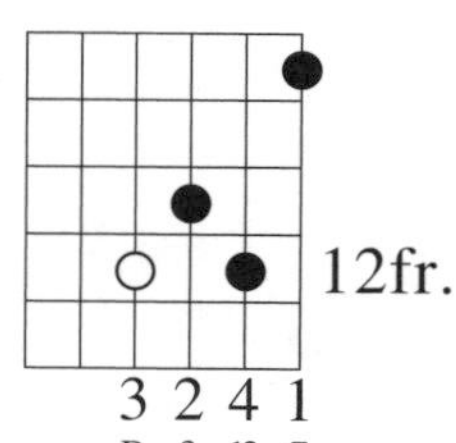

Dmaj13♯11

Dmaj7♯9♯5

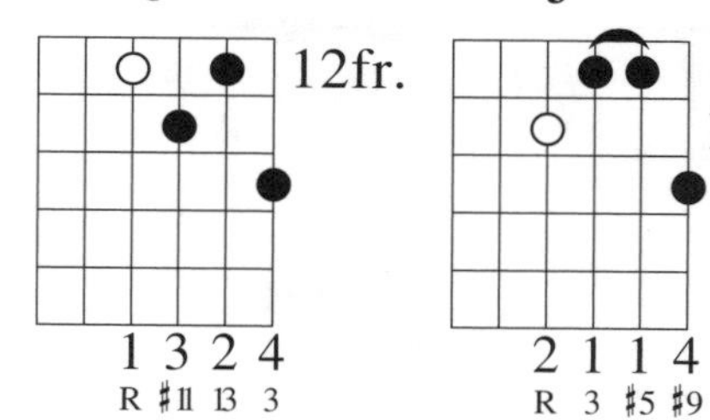

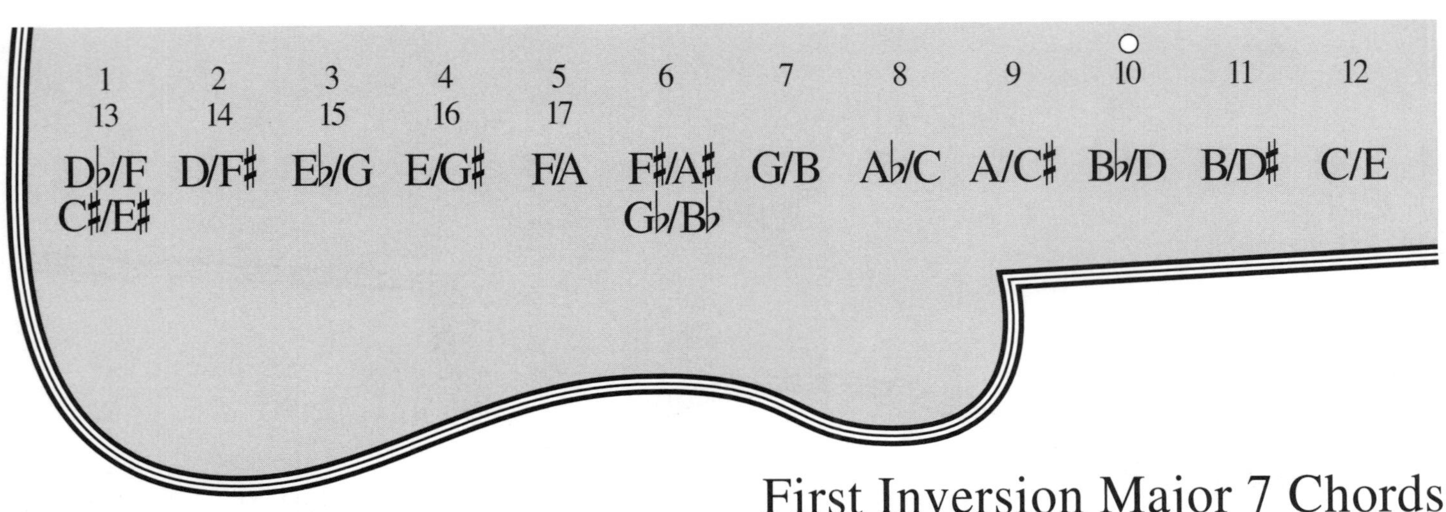

First Inversion Major 7 Chords

B♭maj7/D
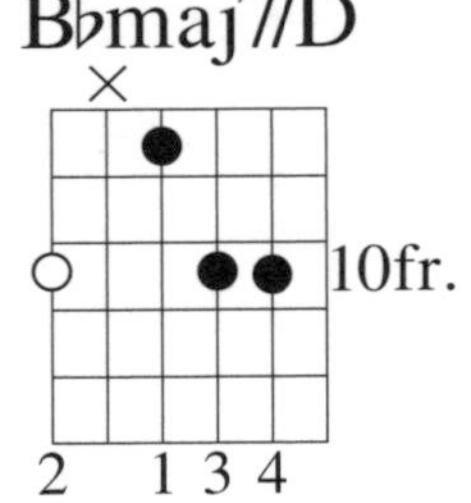

B♭maj7/D
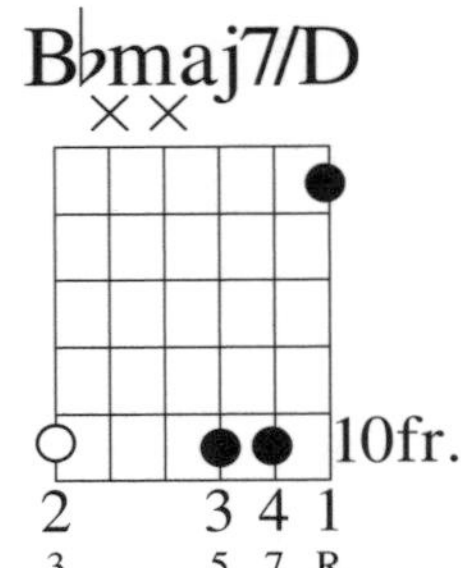

B♭maj7♭5/D
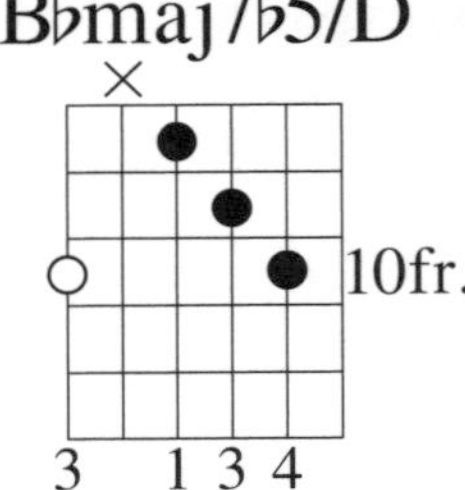

B♭maj7♭5/D
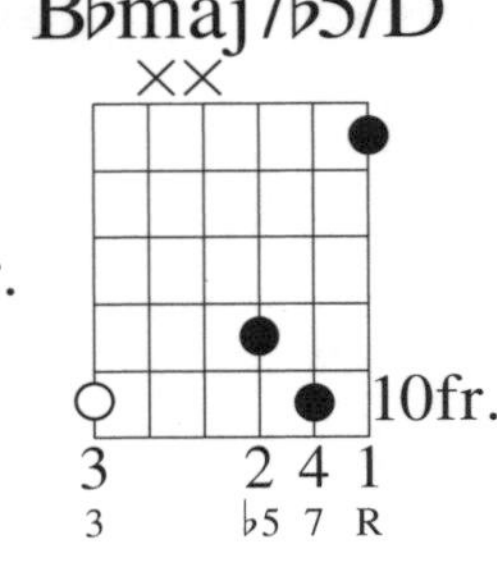

B♭maj7♯5/D
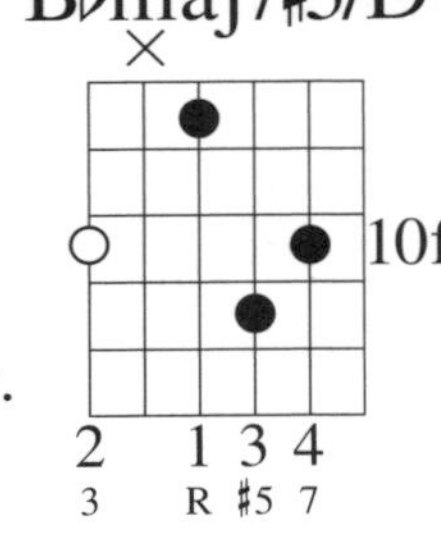

B♭maj7♯5/D
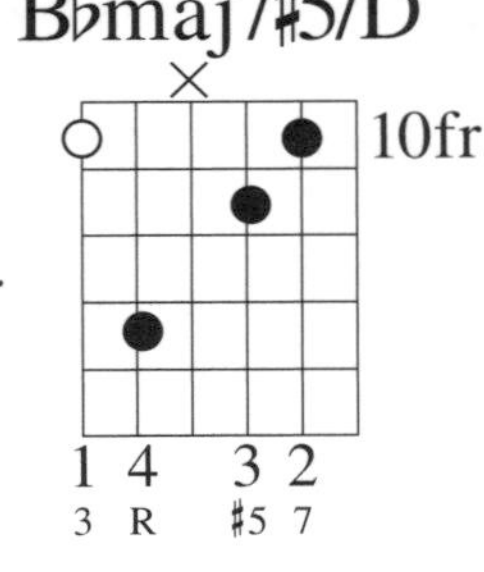

B♭maj7/D
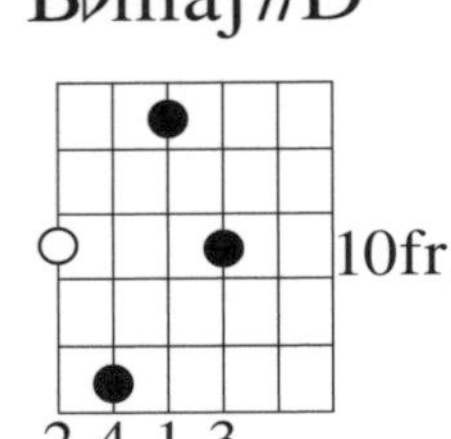

B♭maj7/D
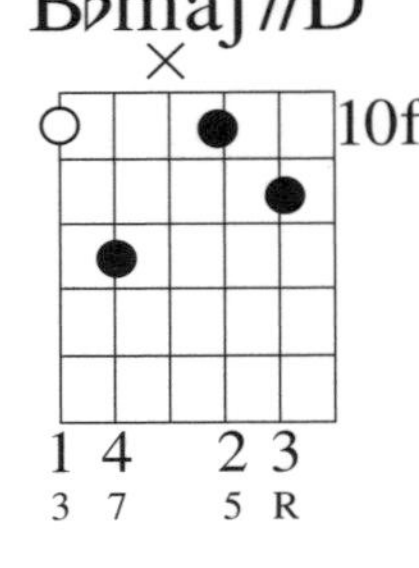

B♭maj7♭5/D
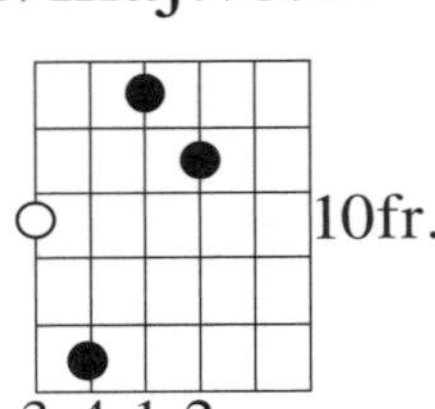

B♭maj7♭5/D
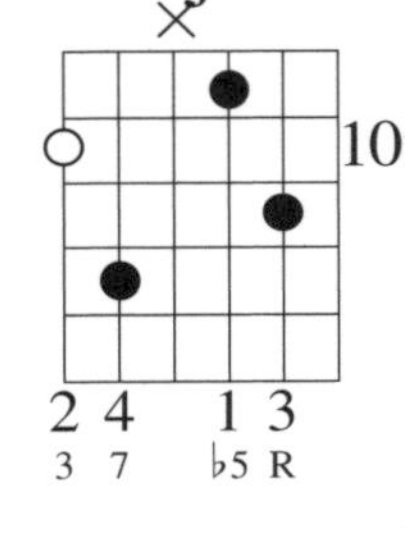

B♭maj7♯5/D
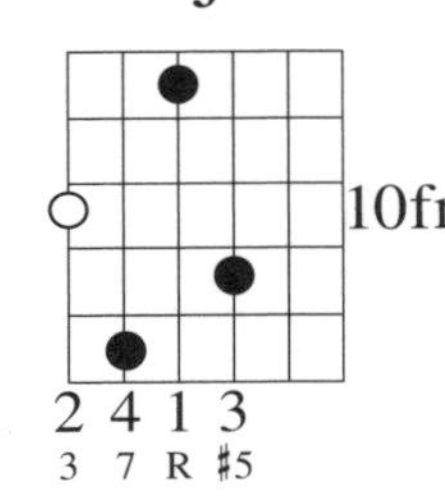

B♭maj7♯5/D
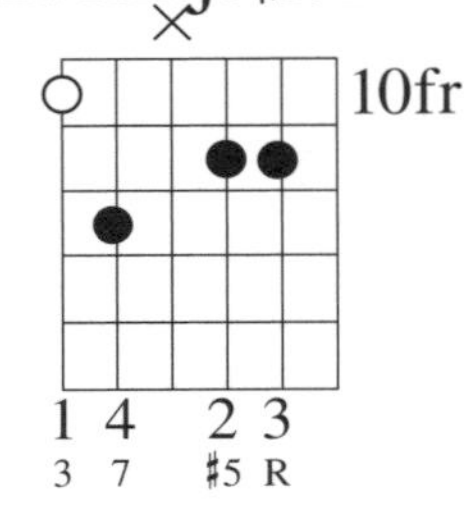

B♭maj7/D
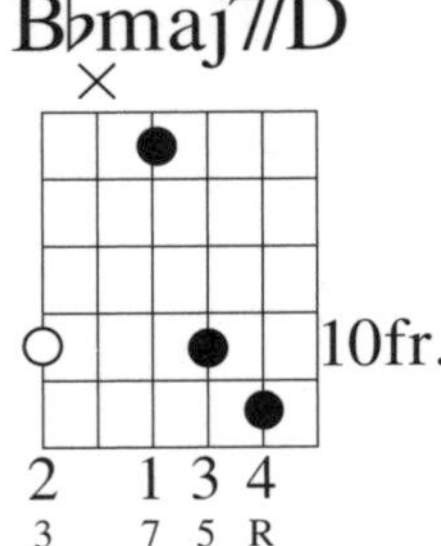

B♭maj7/D
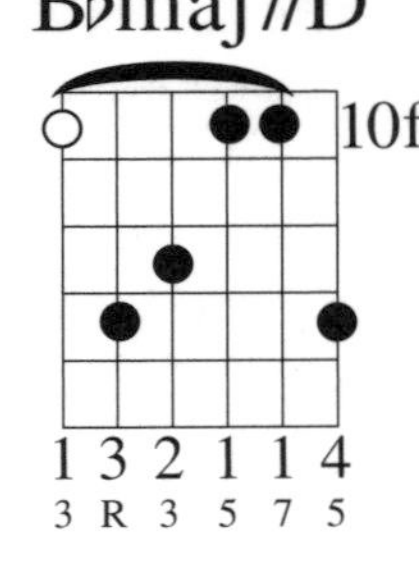

B♭maj7♭5/D
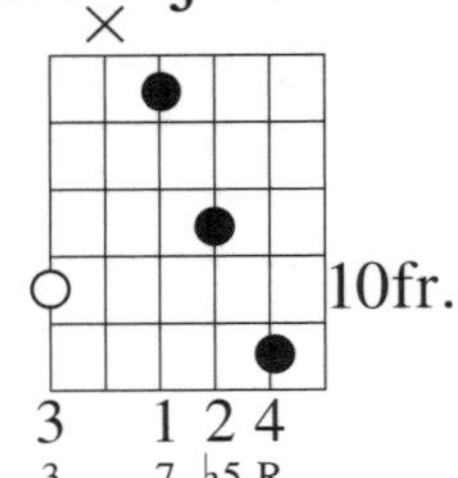

B♭maj7♭5/D
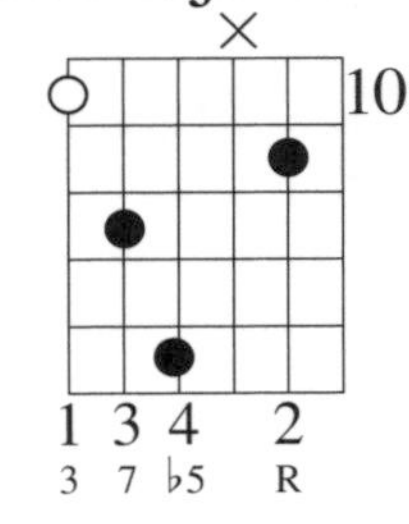

B♭maj7♯5/D
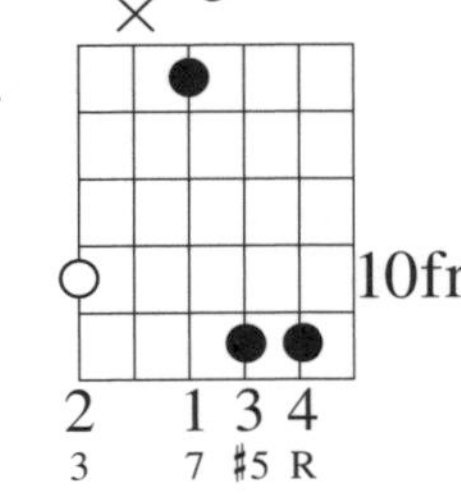

B♭maj7♯11/D
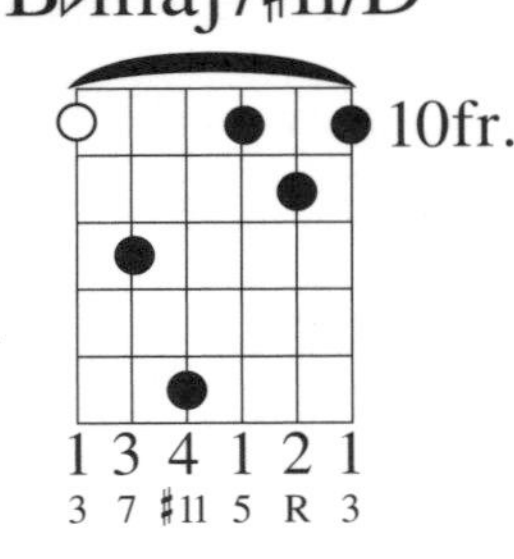

B♭maj7/D
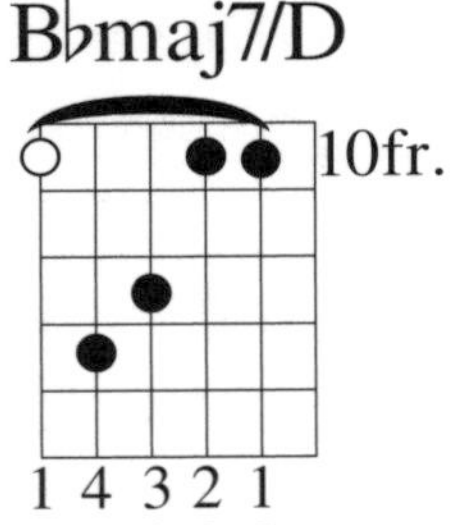

B♭maj7/D
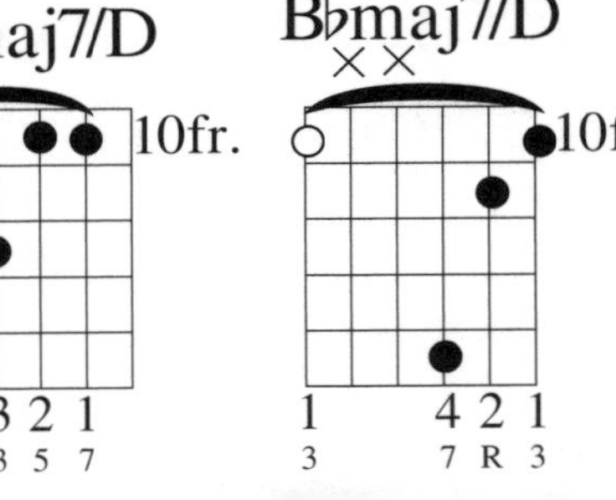

B♭maj7♭5/D
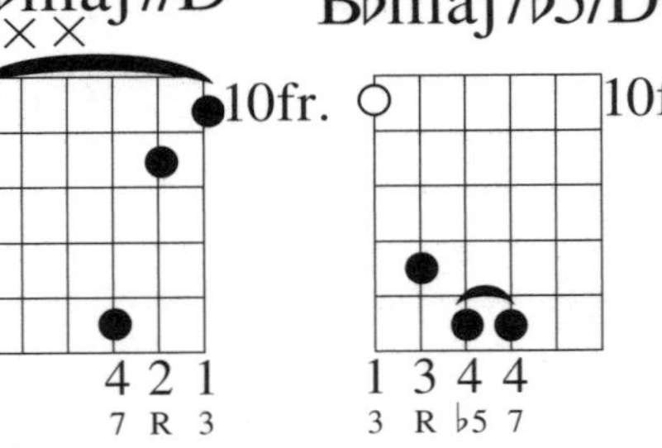

B♭maj7♭5/D
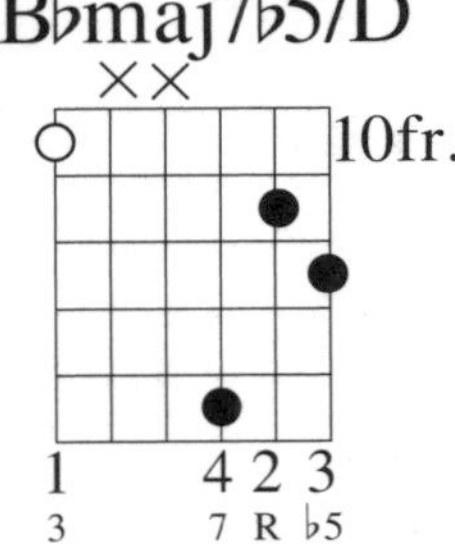

B♭maj7♯5/D
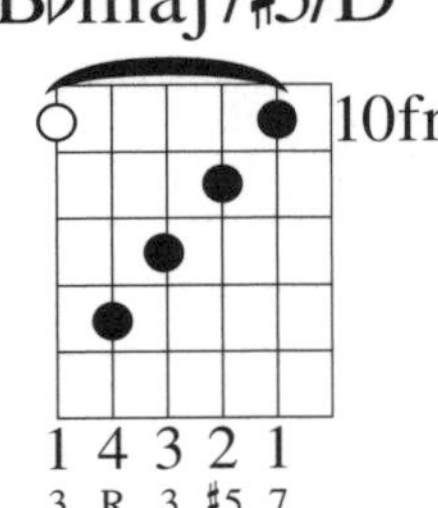

B♭maj7♯11/D
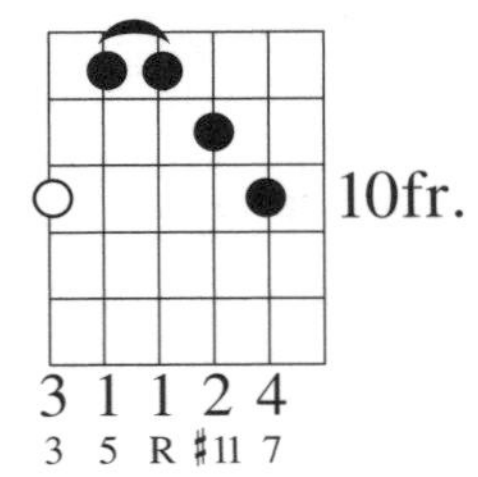

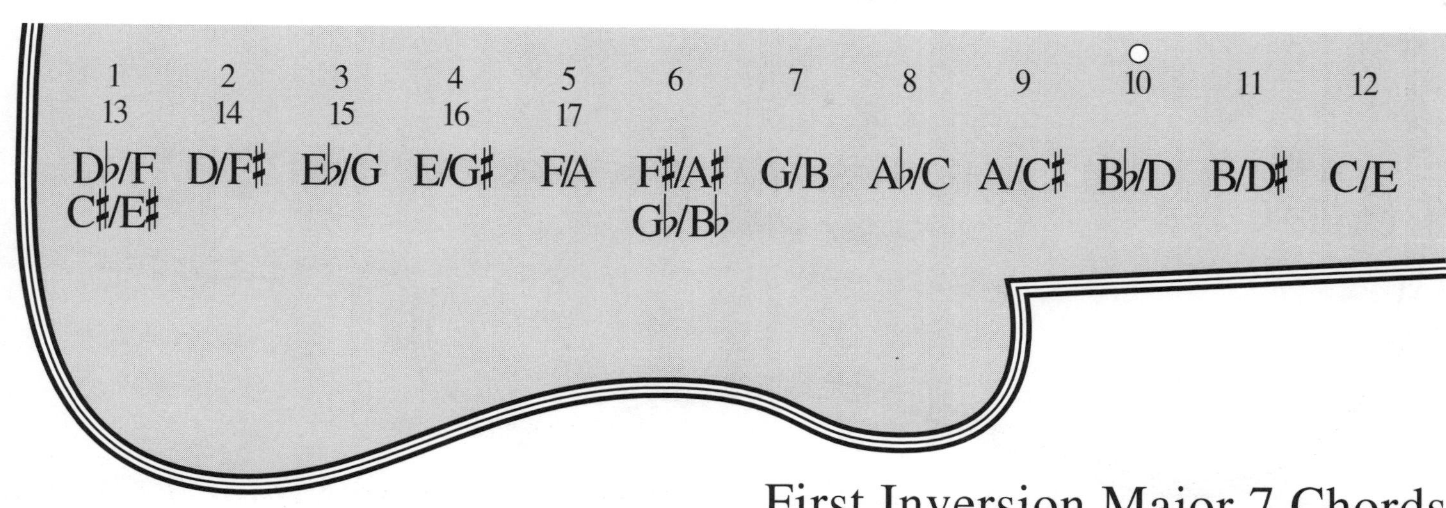

First Inversion Major 7 Chords

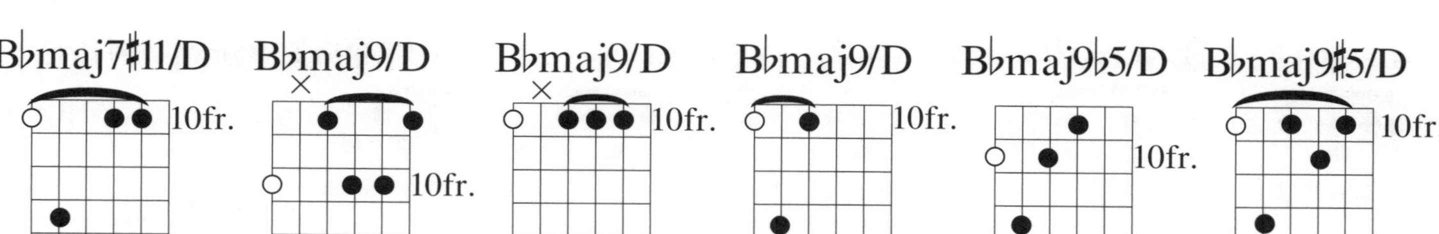

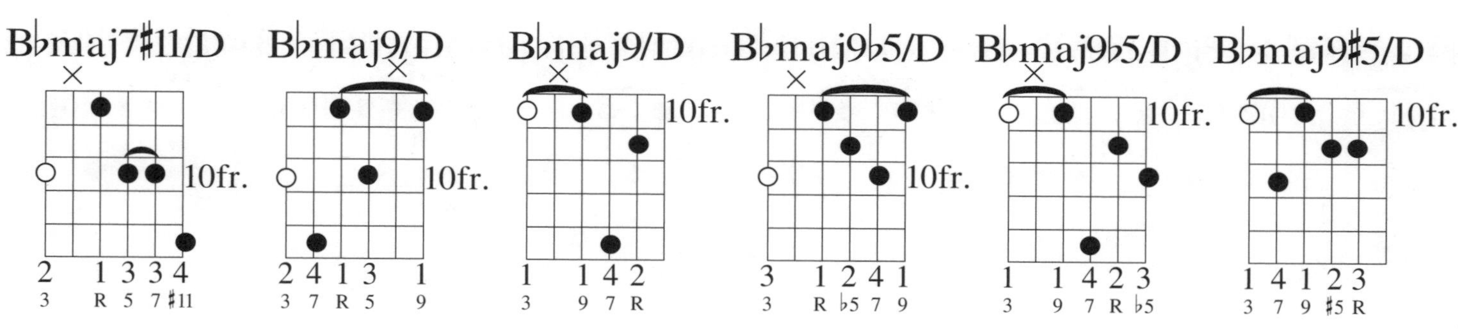

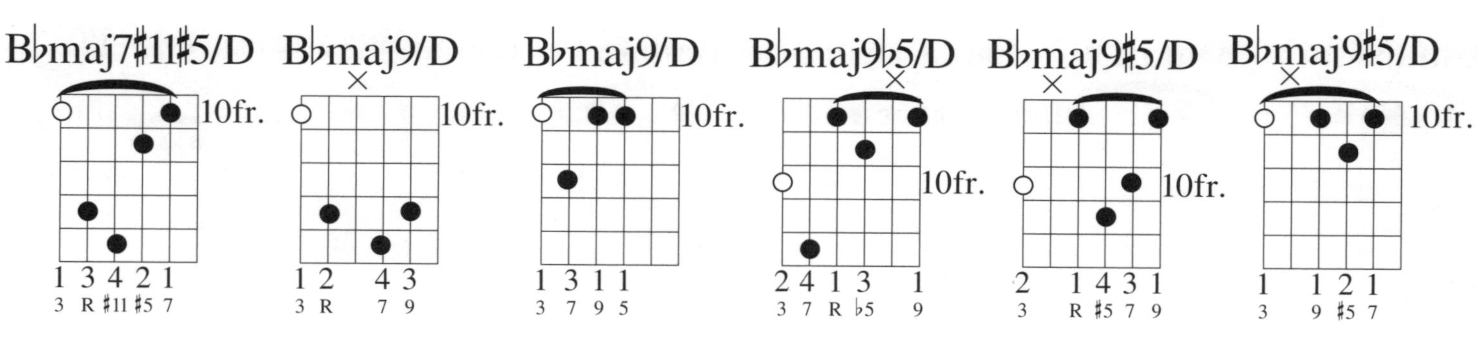

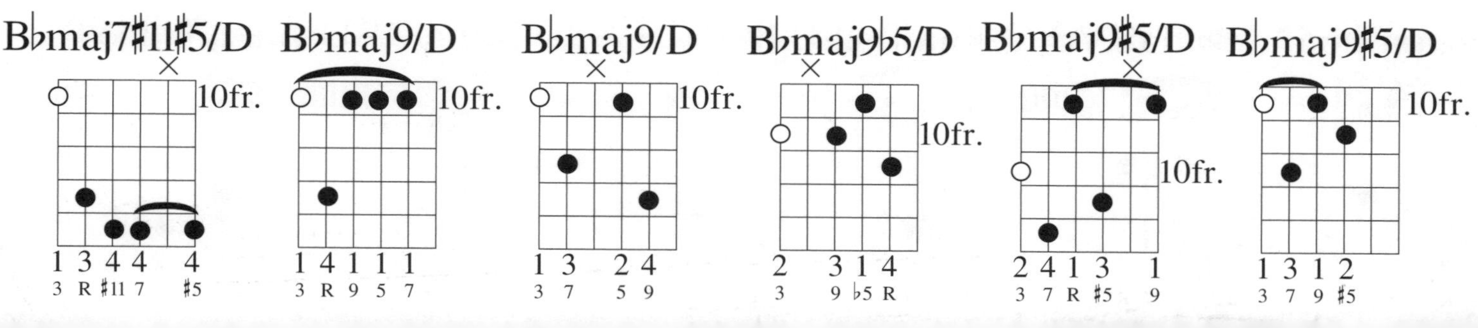

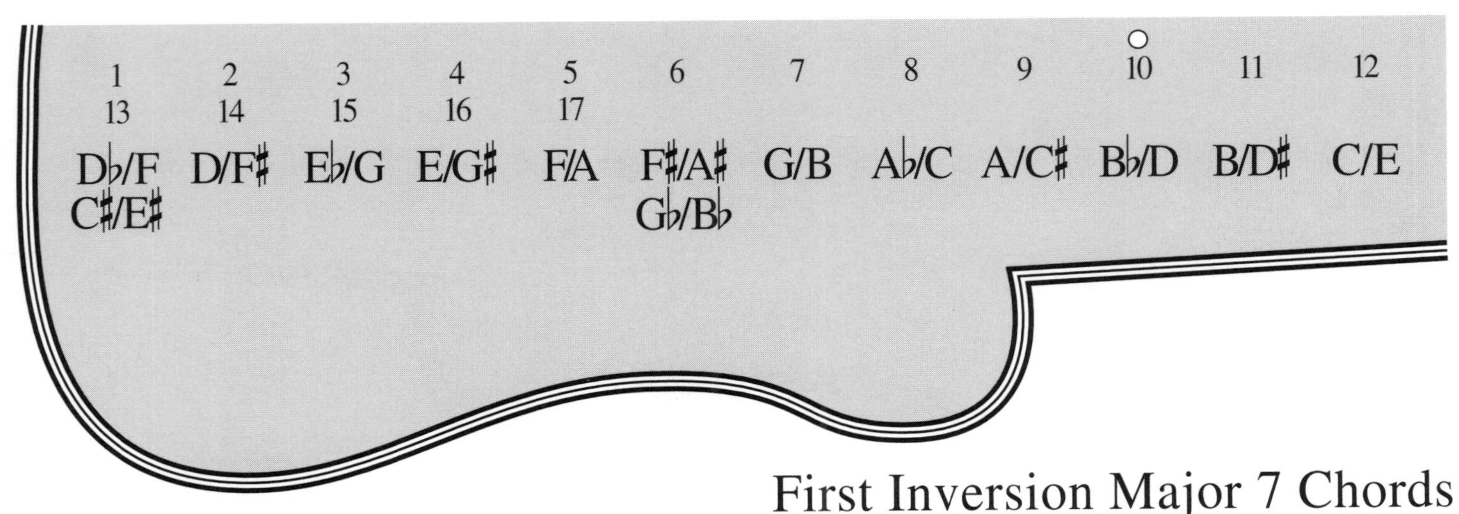

First Inversion Major 7 Chords

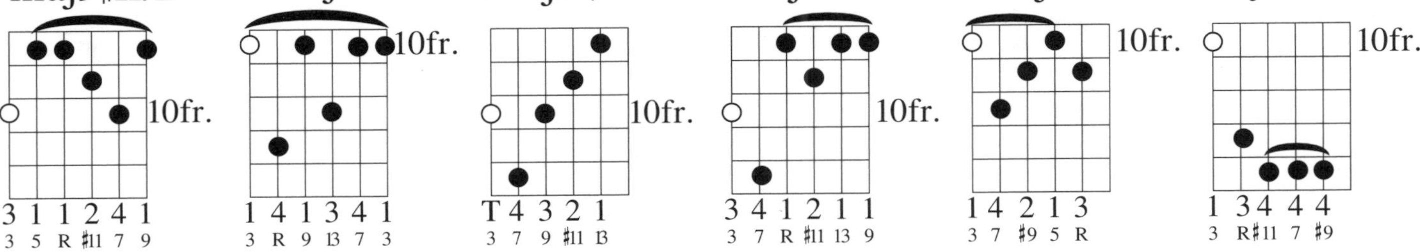

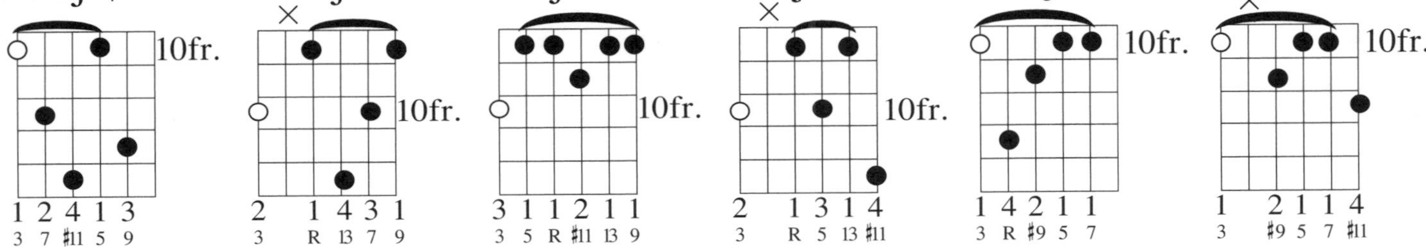

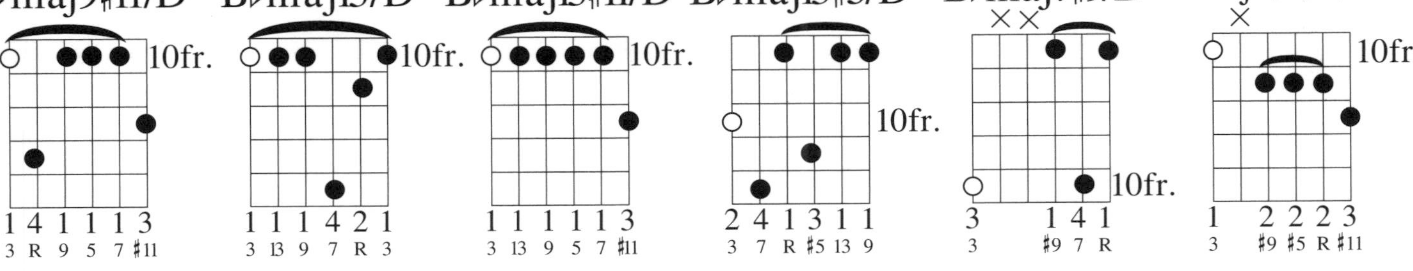

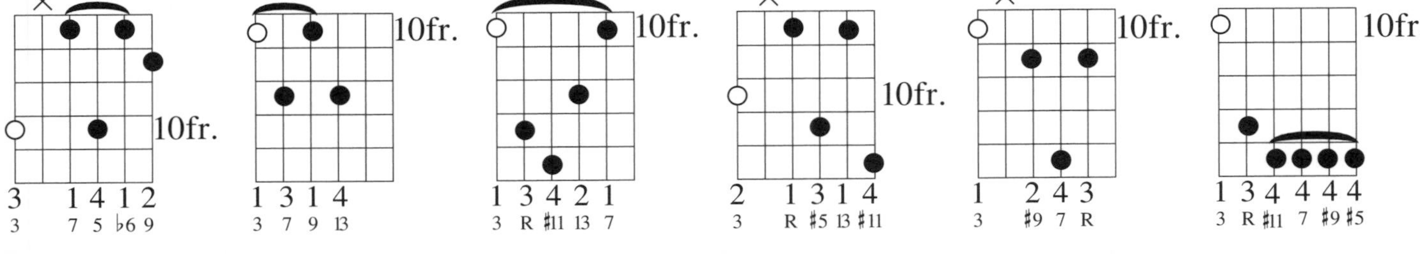

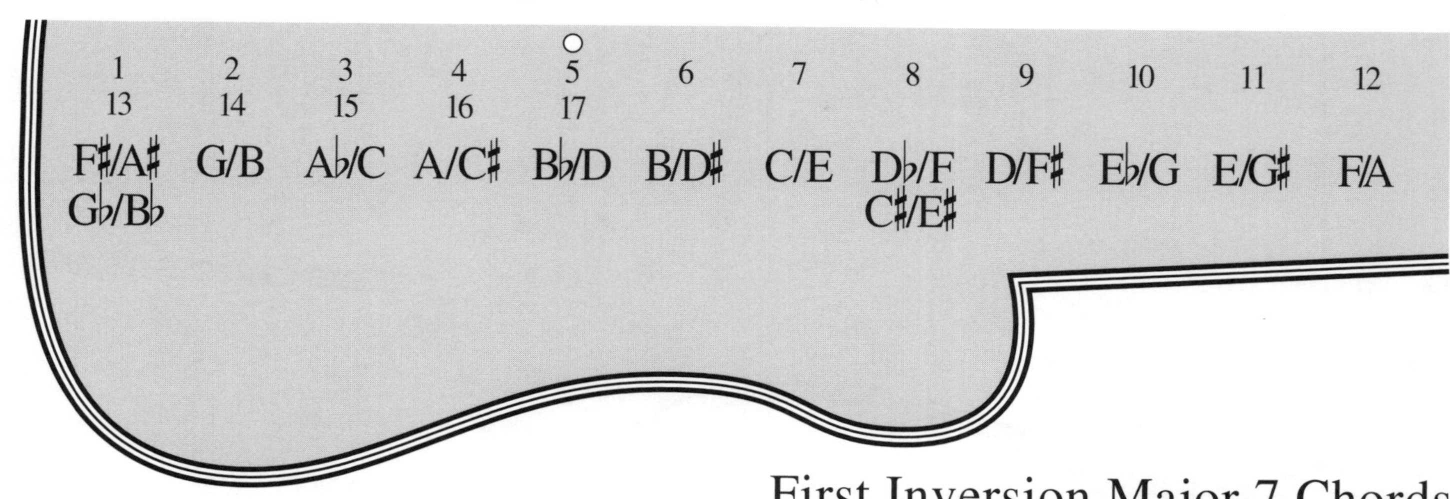

First Inversion Major 7 Chords

B♭maj7/D

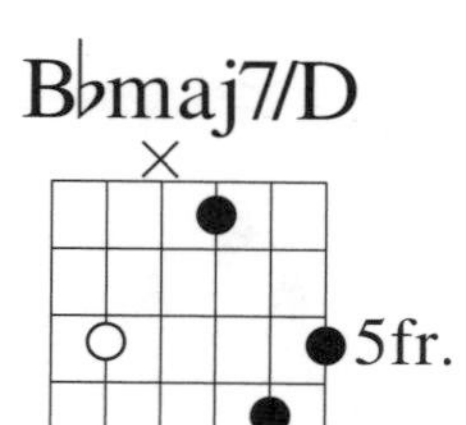

B♭maj7/D

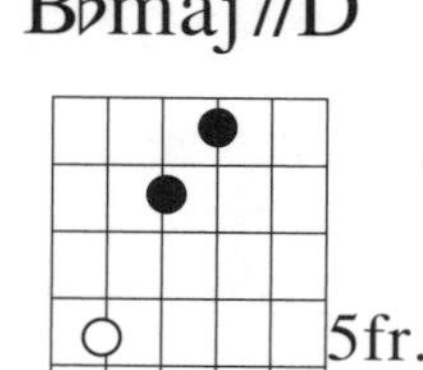

B♭maj7♭5/D

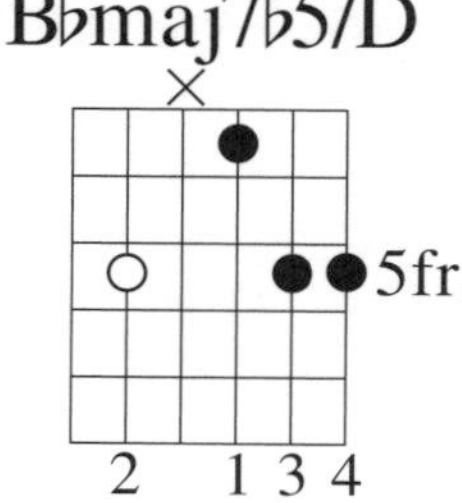

B♭maj7♯5/D

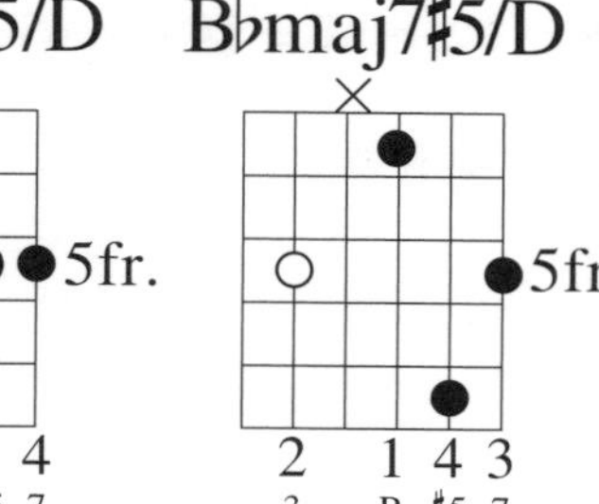

B♭maj7♯5/D

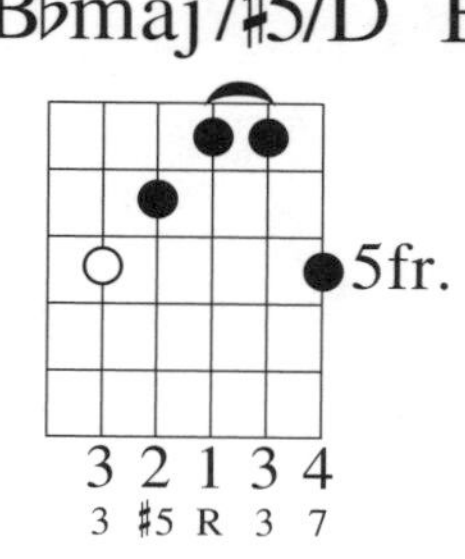

B♭maj7♯11♯5/D

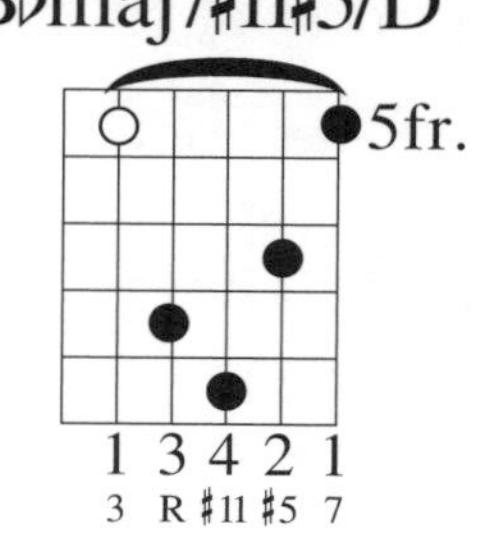

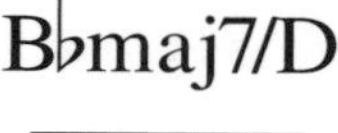

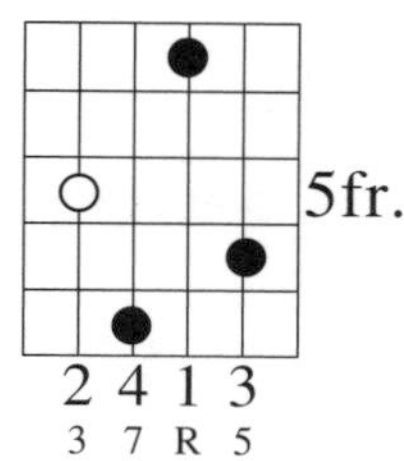

B♭maj7/D

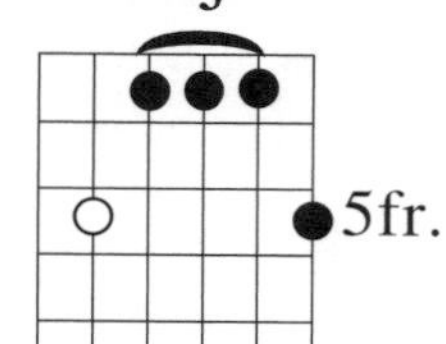

B♭maj7♭5/D

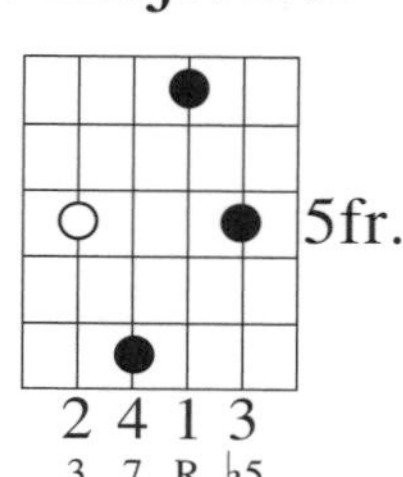

B♭maj7♯5/D

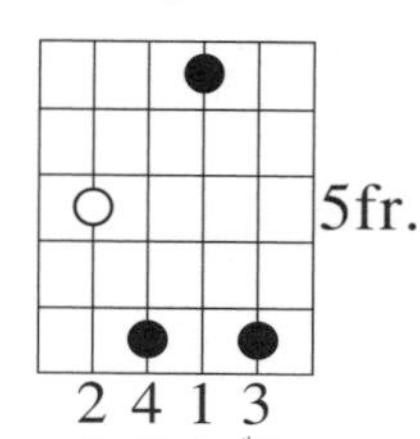

B♭maj7♯11/D

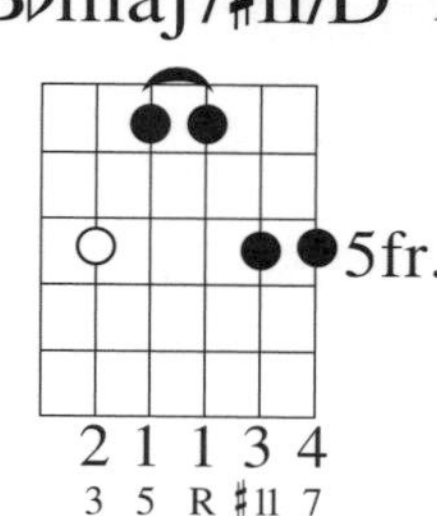

B♭maj7♯11♯5/D

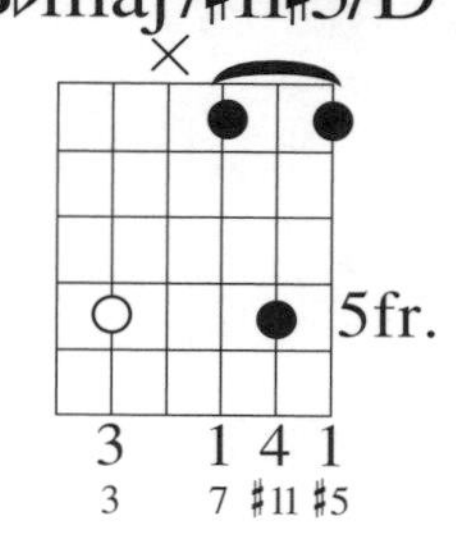

B♭maj7/D

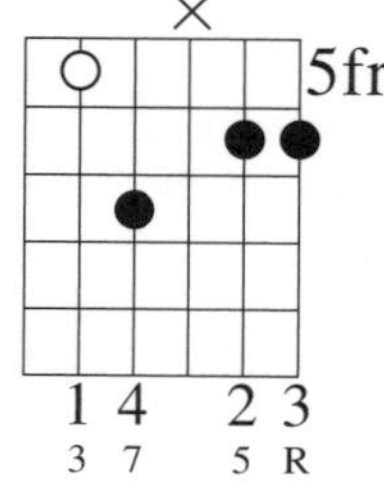

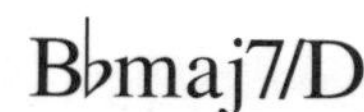

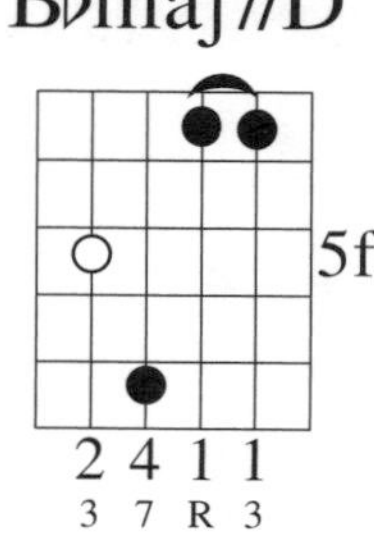

B♭maj7♭5/D

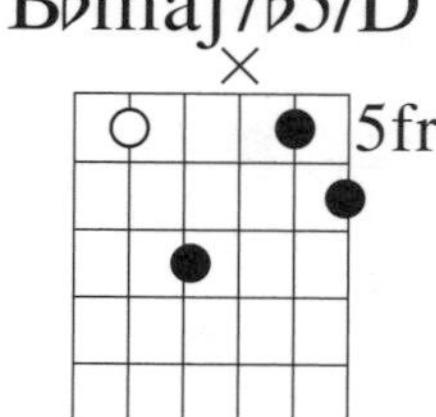

B♭maj7♯5/D

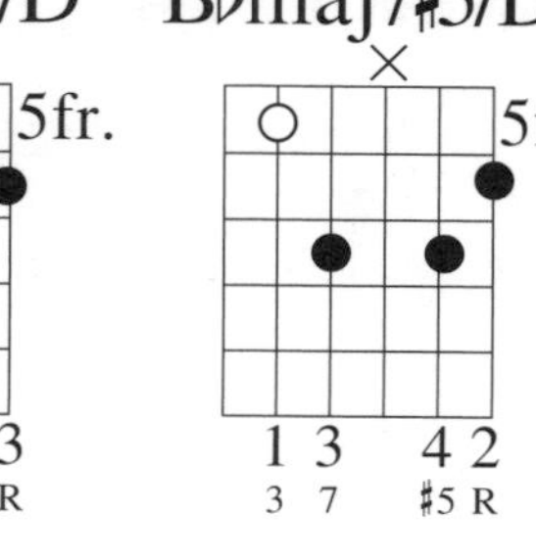

B♭maj7♯11/D

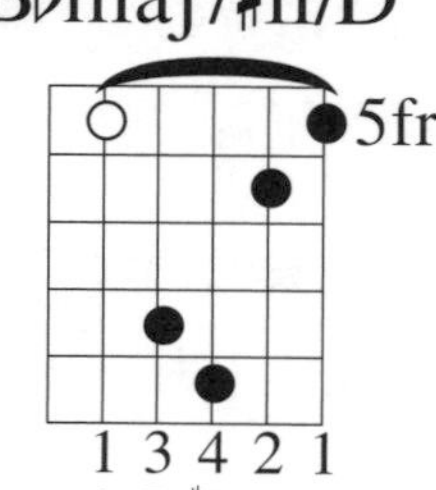

B♭maj7♭6/D

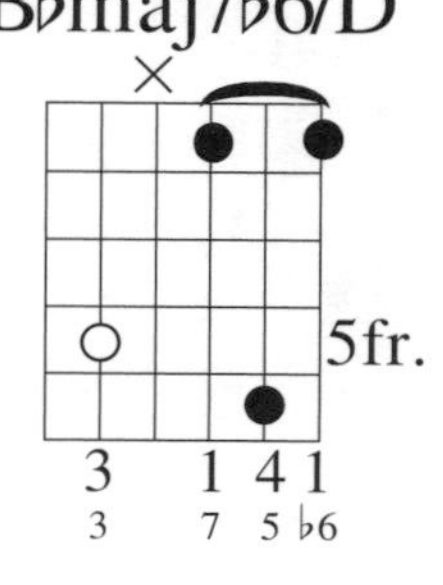

B♭maj7/D

B♭maj7♭5/D

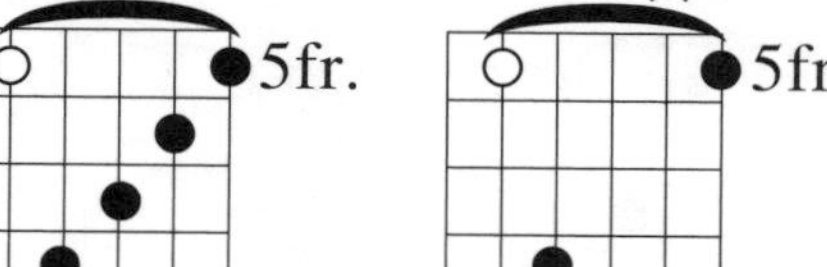

B♭maj7♭5/D

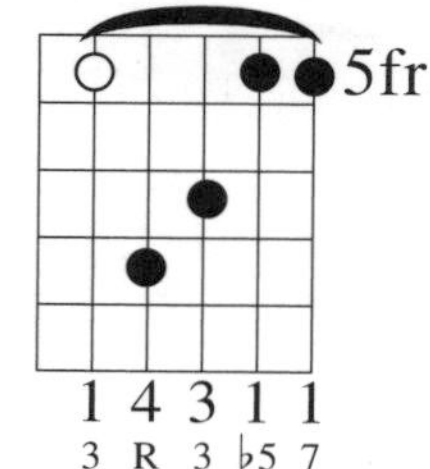

B♭maj7♯5/D

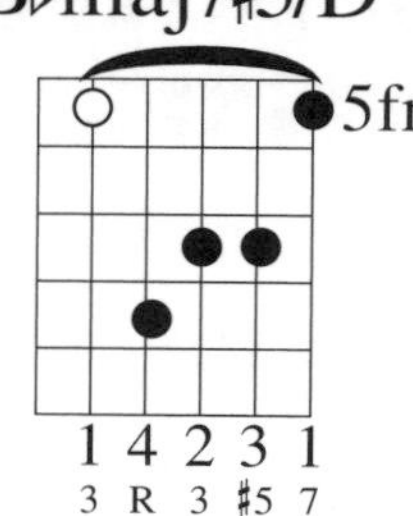

B♭maj7♯11/D

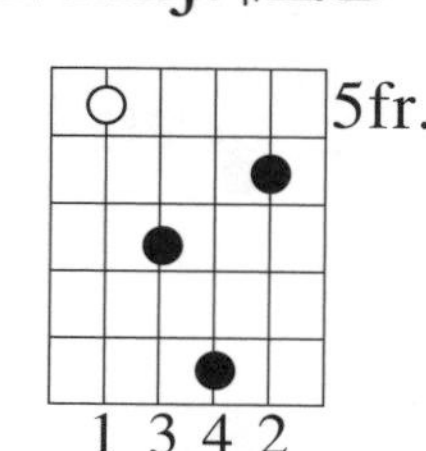

B♭maj7♭6/D

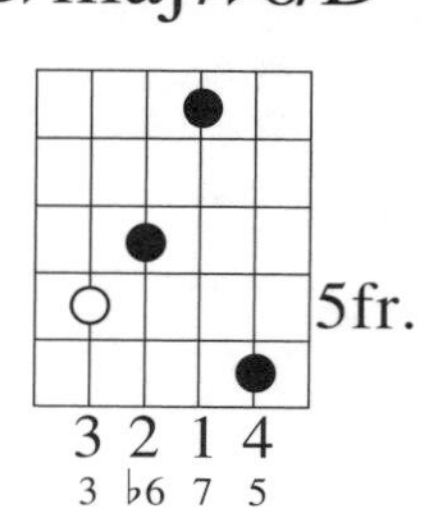

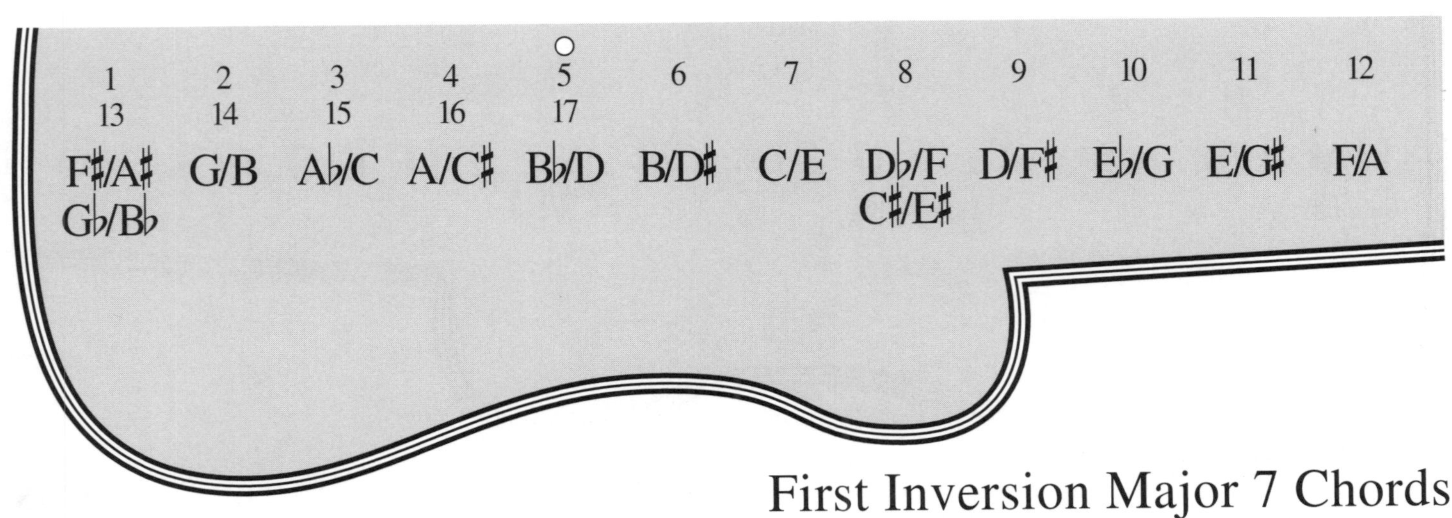

First Inversion Major 7 Chords

B♭maj9/D
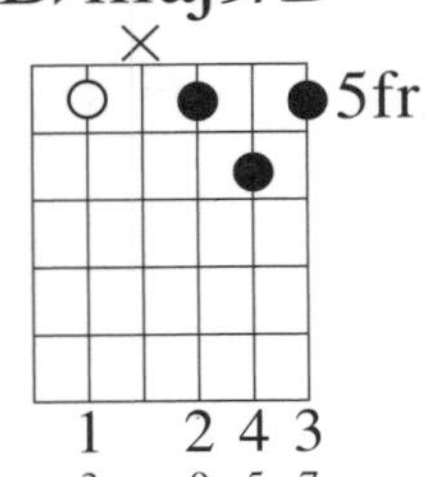

B♭maj9/D
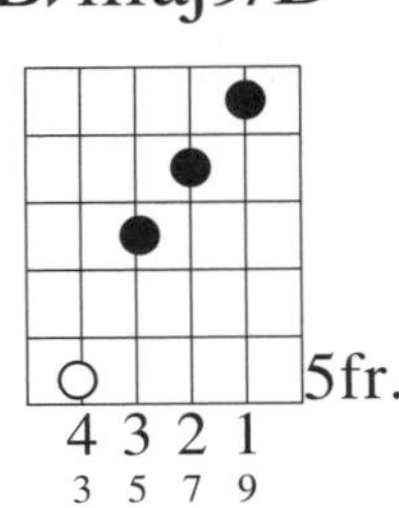

B♭maj9♭5/D
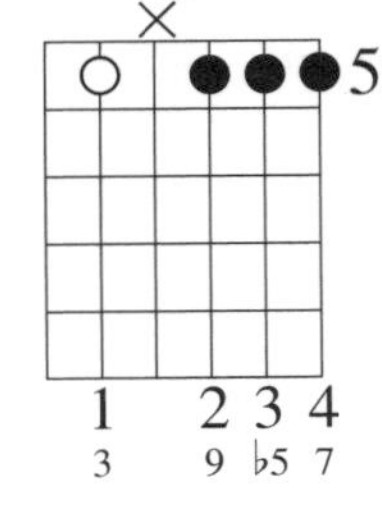

B♭maj9♭5/D
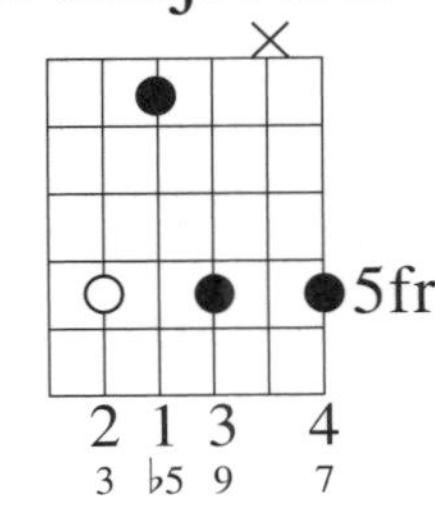

B♭maj9♯5/D
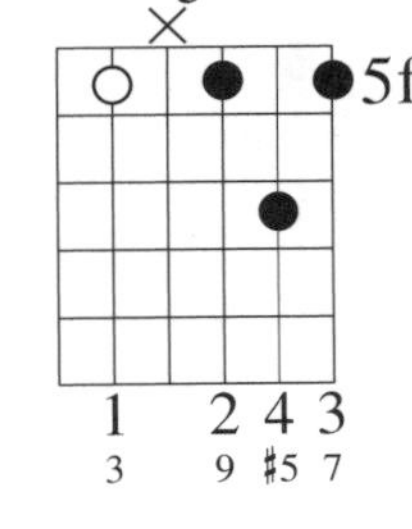

B♭maj9♯5/D
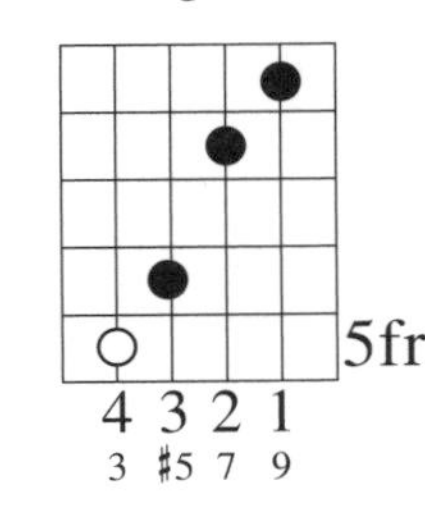

B♭maj9/D
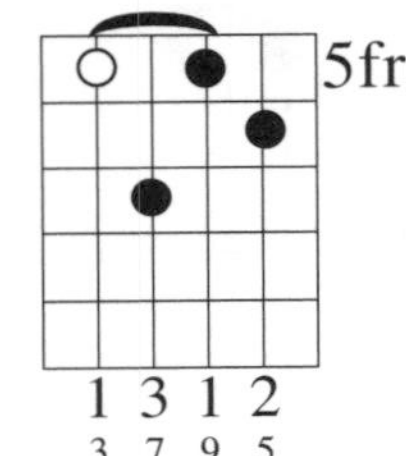

B♭maj9/D
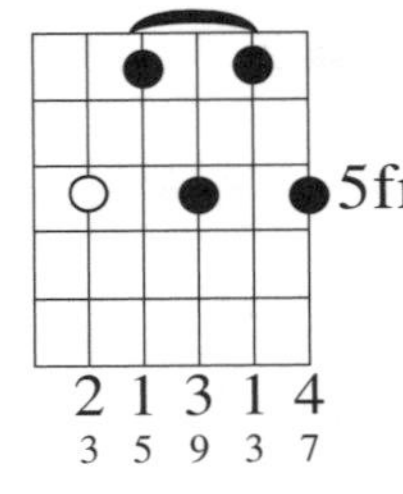

B♭maj9♭5/D
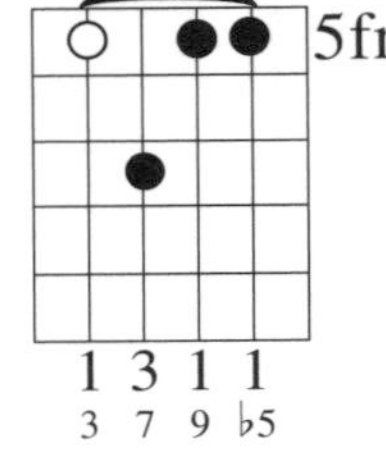

B♭maj9♭5/D
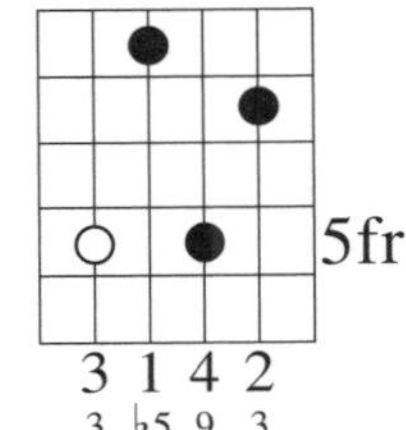

B♭maj9♯5/D
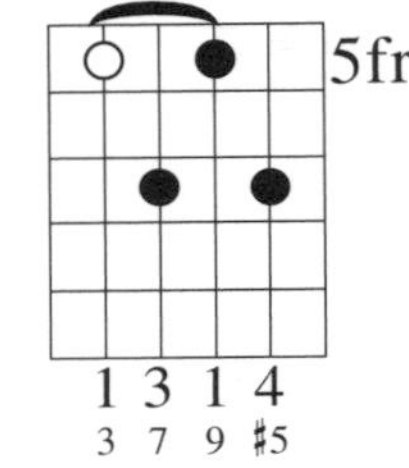

B♭maj9♯11/D
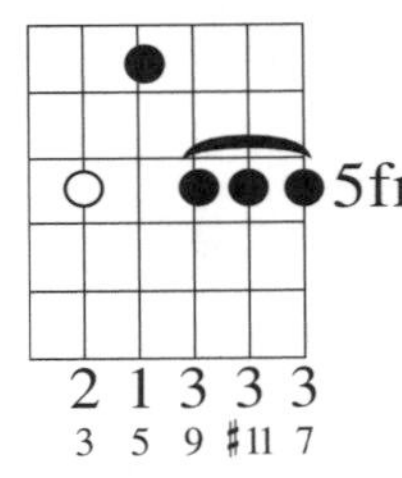

B♭maj9/D
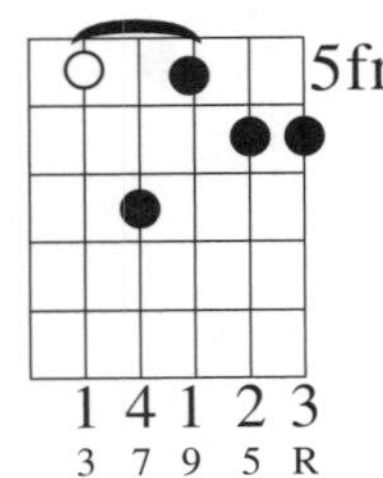

B♭maj9/D
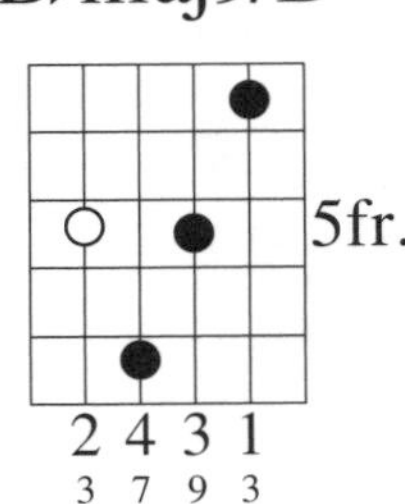

B♭maj9♭5/D
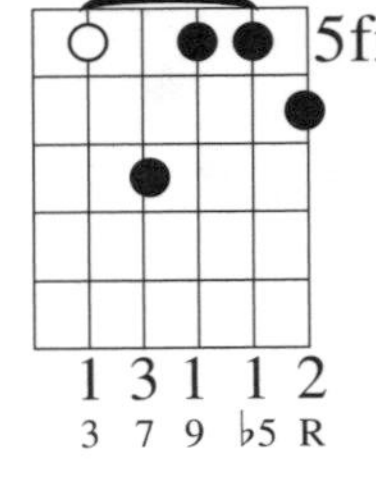

B♭maj9♭5/D
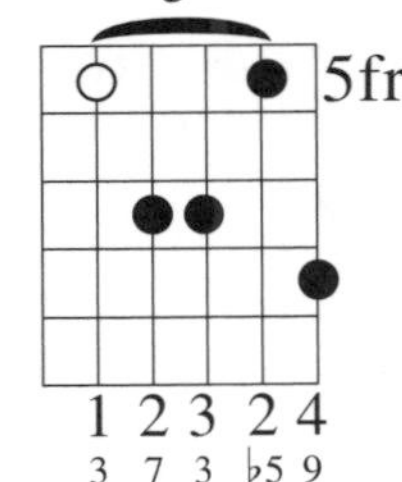

B♭maj9♯5/D
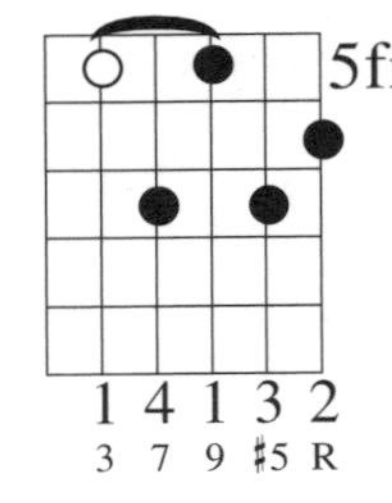

B♭maj9♯11/D
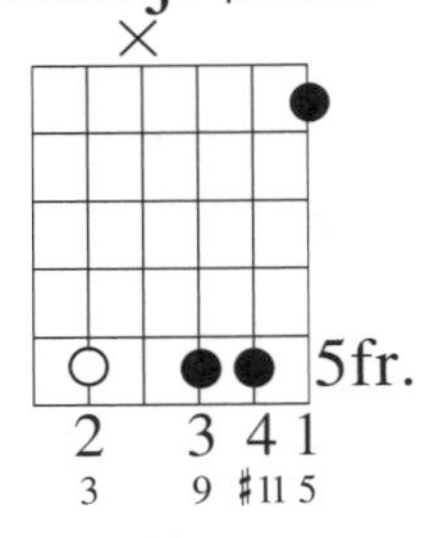

B♭maj9/D
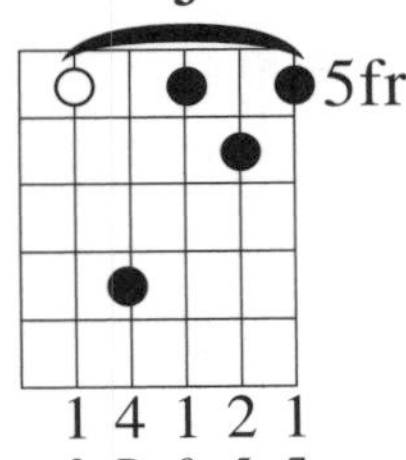

B♭maj9/D
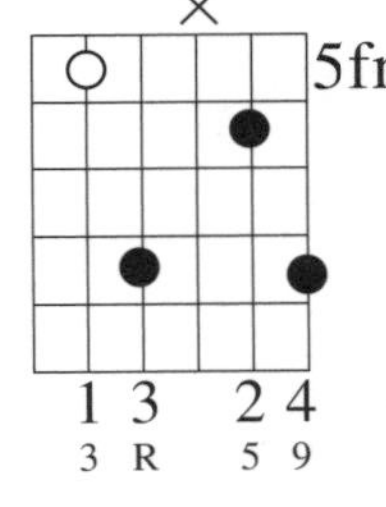

B♭maj9♭5/D
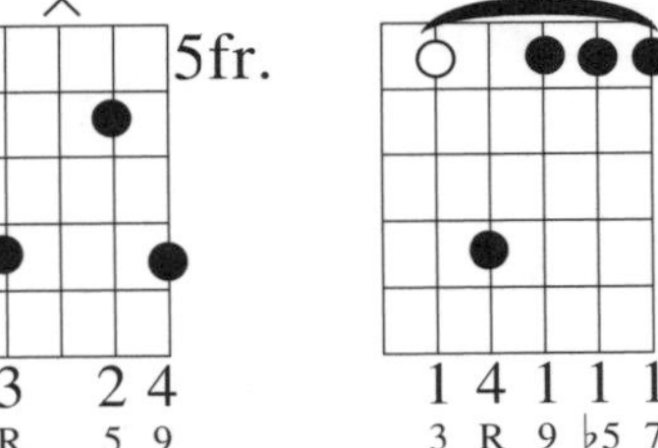

B♭maj9♭5/D
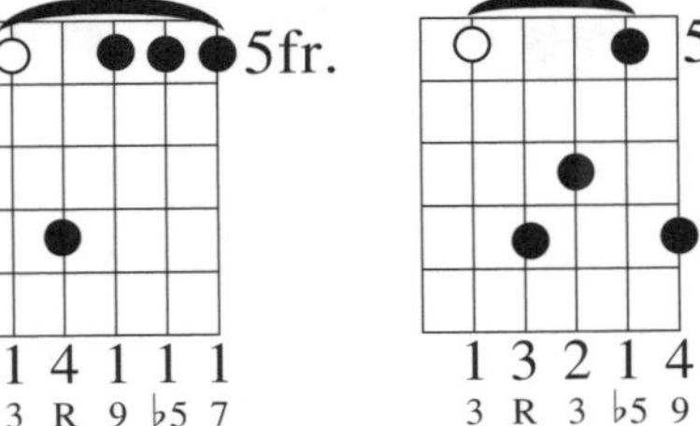

B♭maj9♯5/D
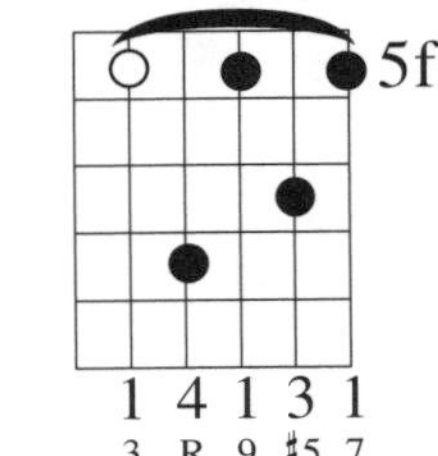

B♭maj9♯11♯5/D
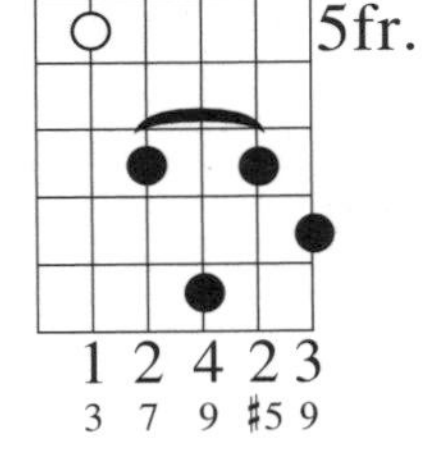

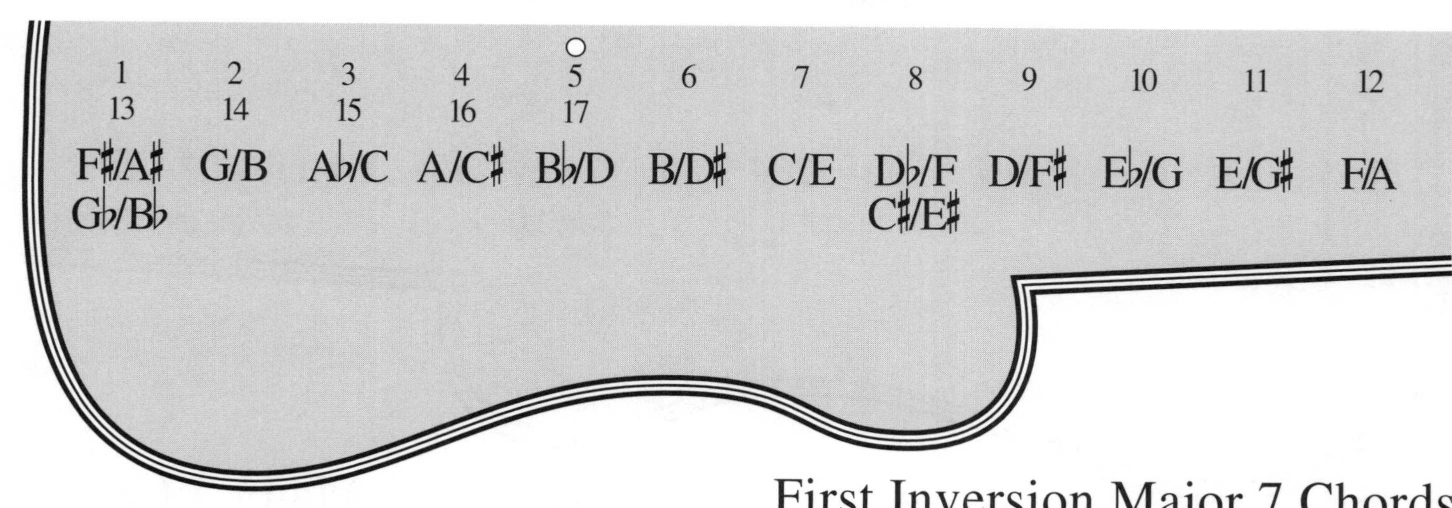

First Inversion Major 7 Chords

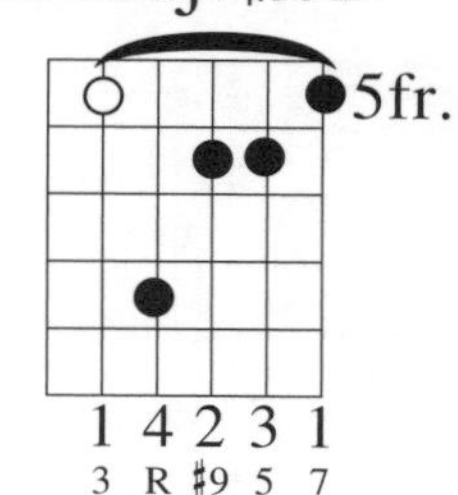

Chord	Fingering	Chord tones
B♭maj13/D	1 1 4 1	3 9 13 7
B♭maj13/D	1 1 1 2 1	3 13 9 5 7
B♭maj13♯11/D	1 2 3 4 1	3 R ♯11 13 7
B♭maj13♯11/D	1 1 1 1 1	3 13 9 ♯11 7
B♭maj13♯5/D	2 3 1 4 1	3 7 R ♯5 13
B♭maj7♯9/D	1 4 2 3 1	3 R ♯9 5 7

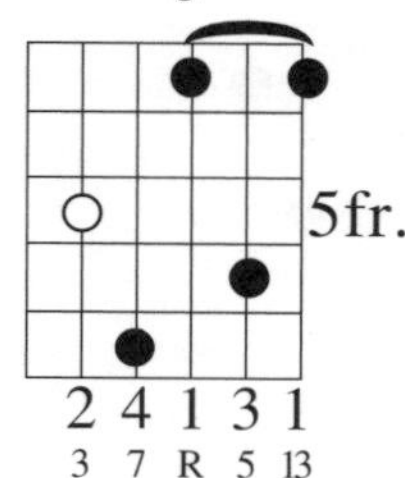
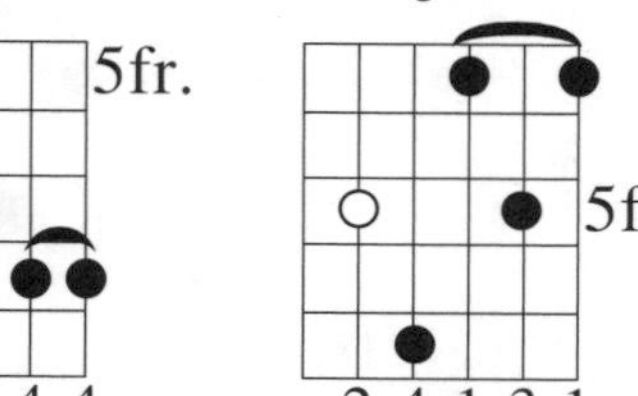
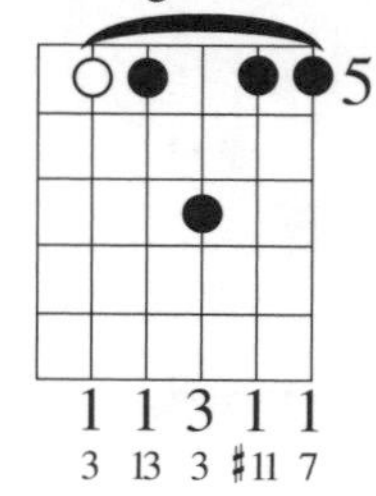
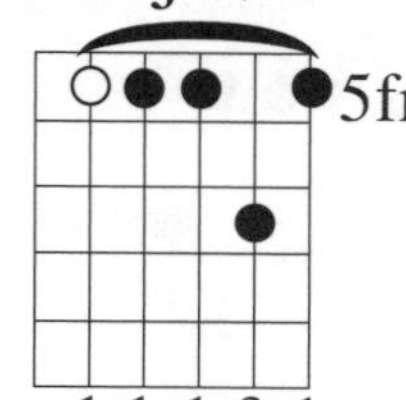
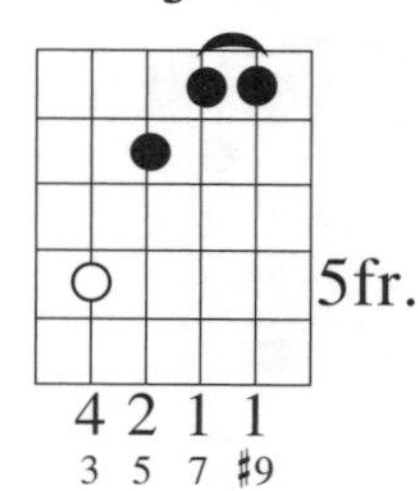

Chord	Fingering	Chord tones
B♭maj13/D	2 4 1 3 1	3 7 R 5 13
B♭maj13/D	1 2 3 4 4	3 7 3 13 9
B♭maj13♯11/D	2 4 1 3 1	3 7 R ♯11 13
B♭maj13♯11/D	1 1 3 1 1	3 13 3 ♯11 7
B♭maj13♯5/D	1 1 1 3 1	3 13 9 ♯5 7
B♭maj7♯9/D	4 2 1 1	3 5 7 ♯9

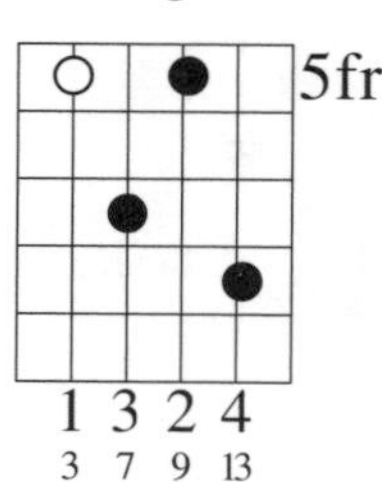
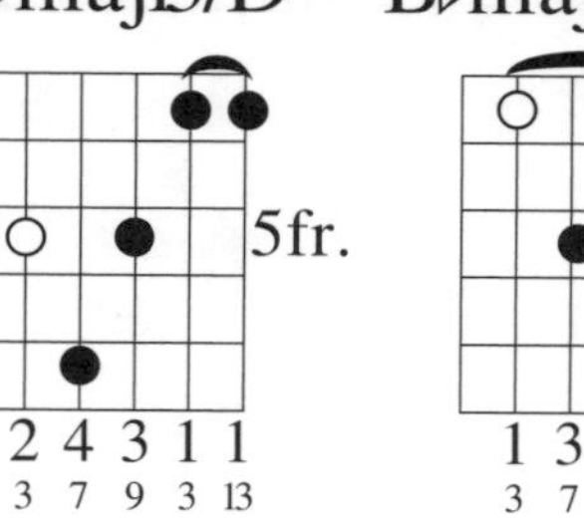
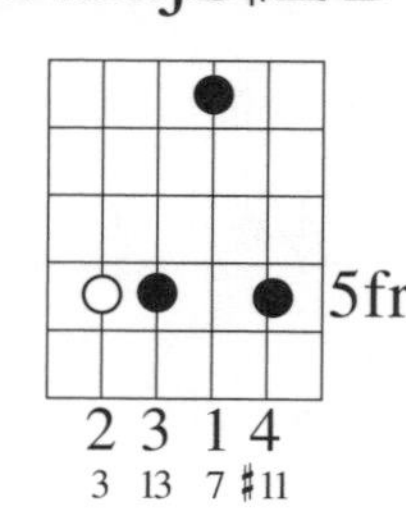
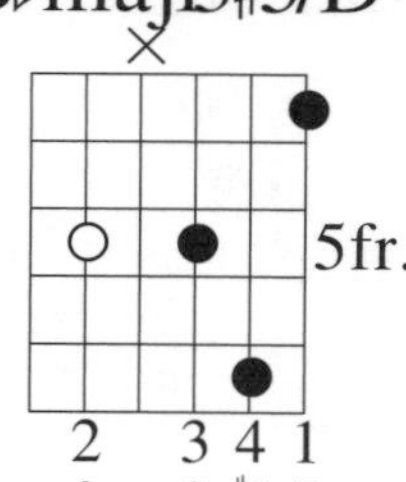
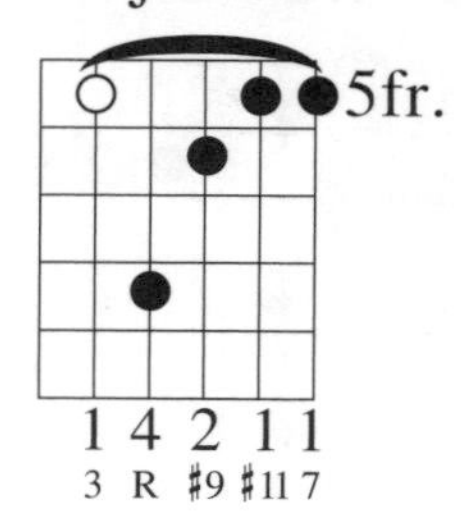

Chord	Fingering	Chord tones
B♭maj13/D	1 3 2 4	3 7 9 13
B♭maj13/D	2 4 3 1 1	3 7 9 3 13
B♭maj13♯11/D	1 3 1 1	3 7 9 ♯11
B♭maj13♯11/D	2 3 1 4	3 13 7 ♯11
B♭maj13♯5/D	2 3 4 1	3 9 ♯5 13
B♭maj7♯9♯11/D	1 4 2 1 1	3 R ♯9 ♯11 7

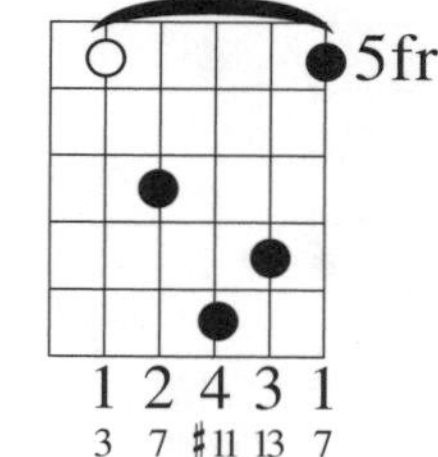
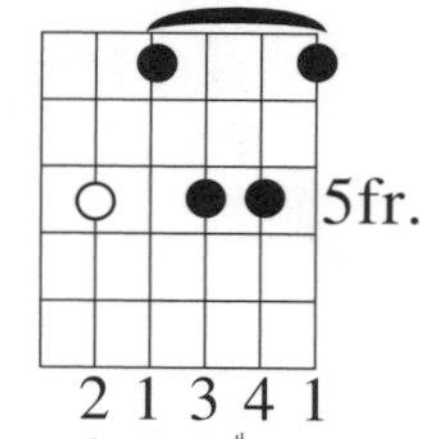
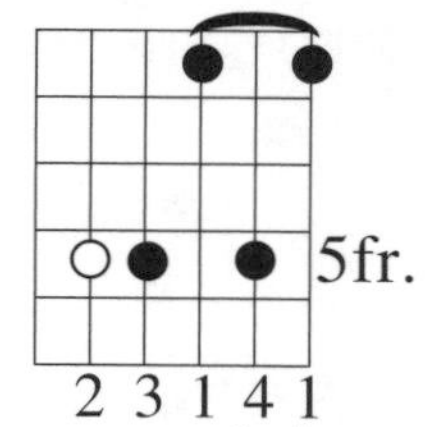
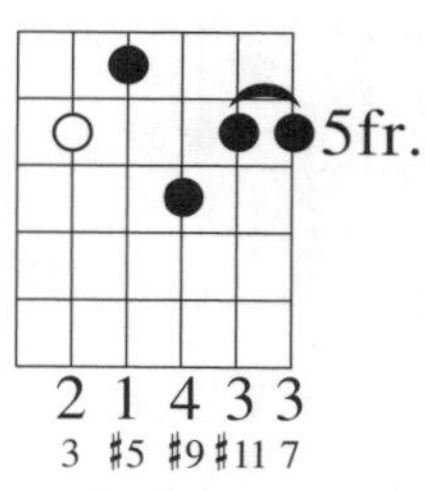

Chord	Fingering	Chord tones
B♭maj13/D	1 3 1 4 1	3 R 9 13 7
B♭maj13/D	2 3 1 4	3 13 7 5
B♭maj13♯11/D	1 2 4 3 1	3 7 ♯11 13 7
B♭maj13♯11/D	2 1 3 4 1	3 5 9 ♯11 13
B♭maj13♯5♯11/D	2 3 1 4 1	3 13 7 ♯11 ♯5
B♭maj7♯9♯11♯5/D	2 1 4 3 3	3 ♯5 ♯9 ♯11 7

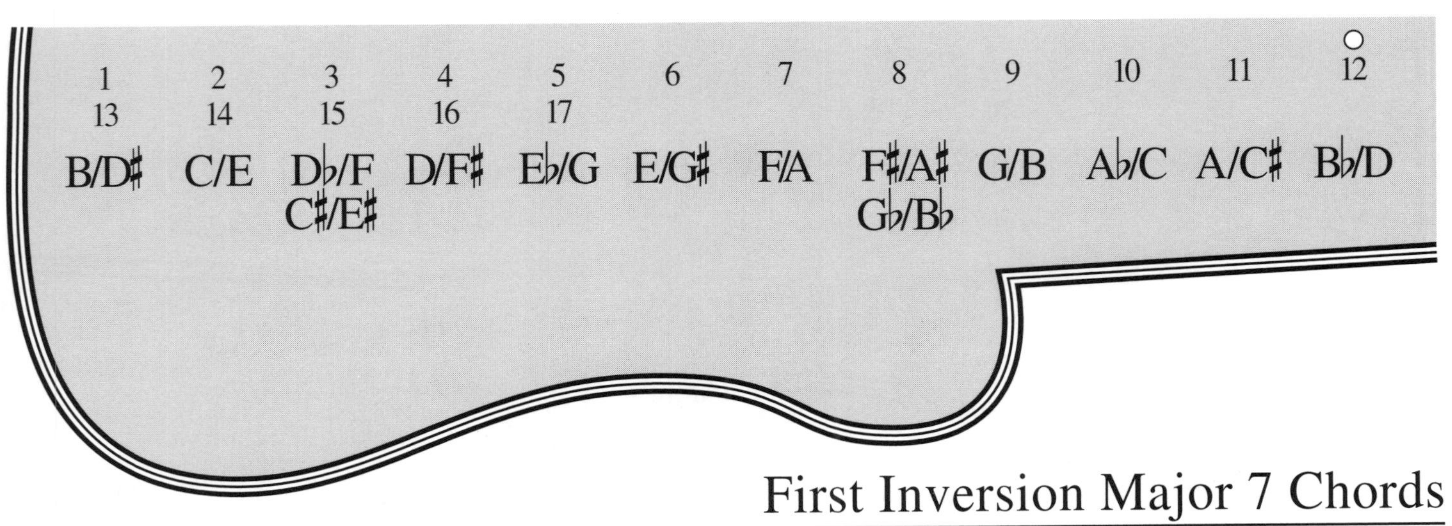

First Inversion Major 7 Chords

B♭maj7/D
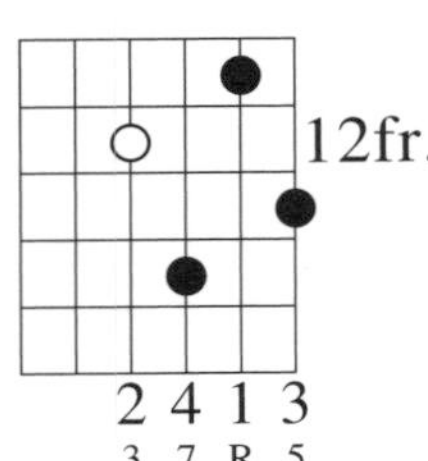

B♭maj7♯5/D
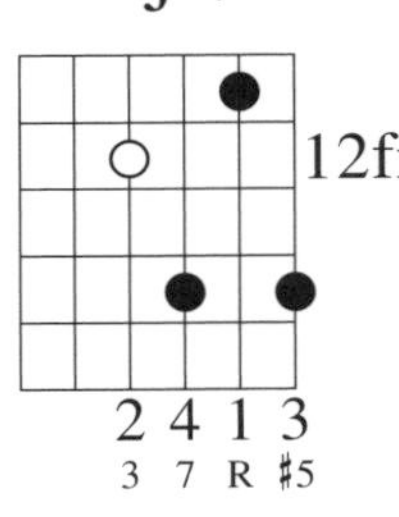

B♭maj7♭6/D
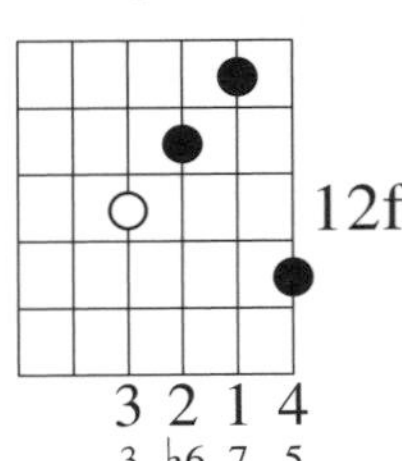

B♭maj9♭5/D
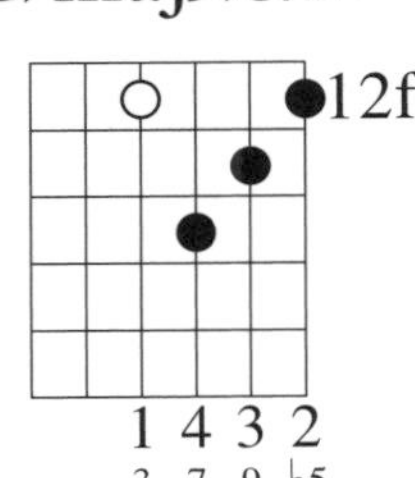

B♭maj9♯11/D
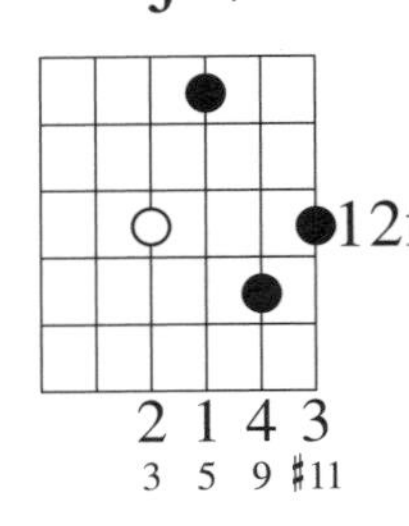

B♭maj13♯11/D
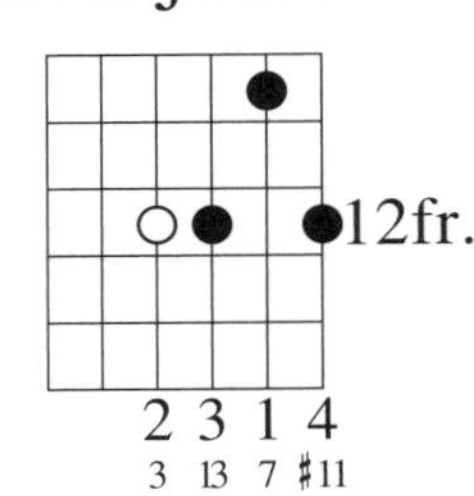

B♭maj7/D
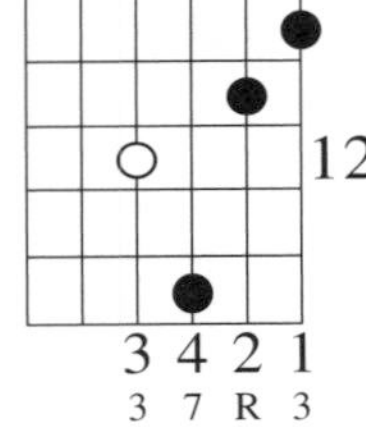

B♭maj7♯11/D
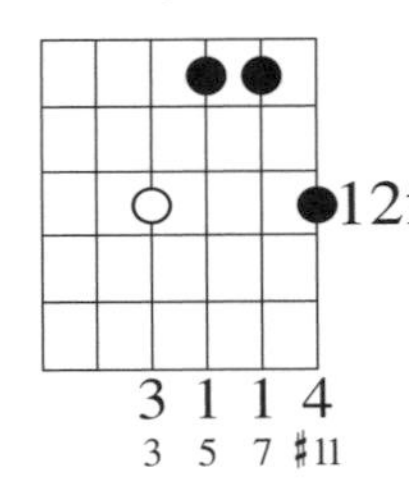

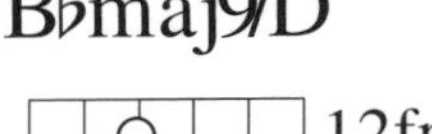

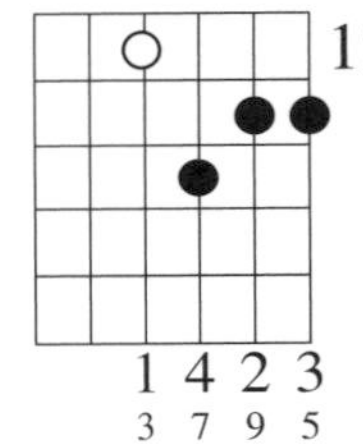

B♭maj9♭5/D
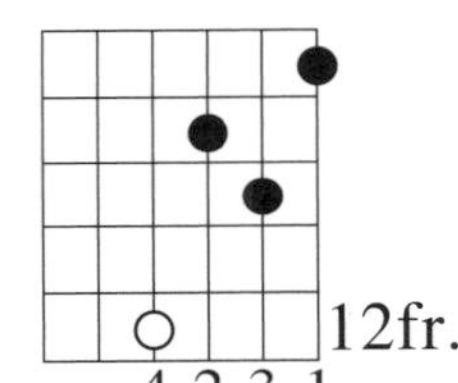

B♭maj9♭6/D
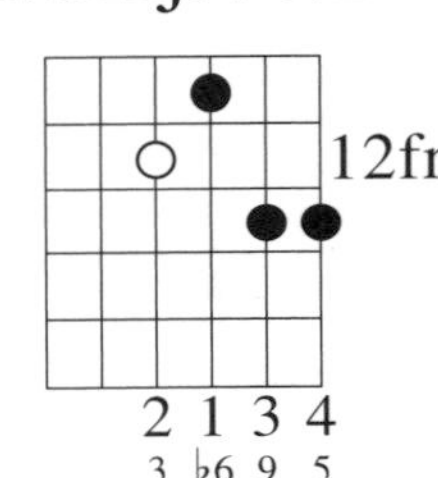

B♭maj13♯5/D
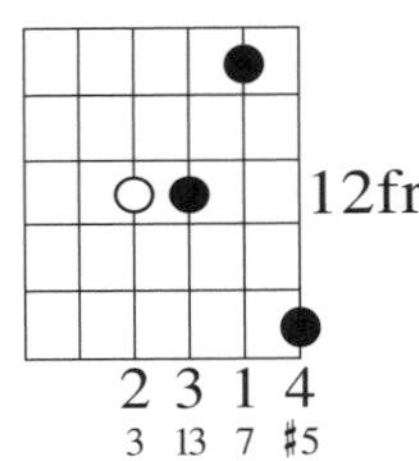

B♭maj7♭5/D
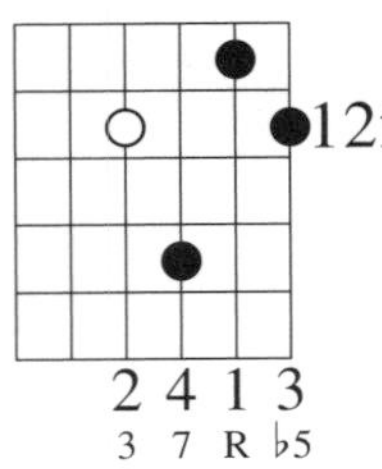

B♭maj7♯11/D
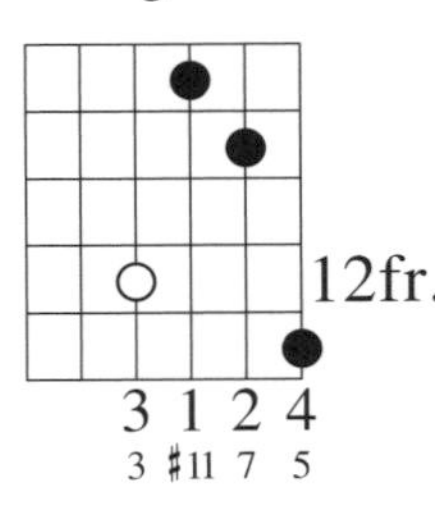

B♭maj9/D
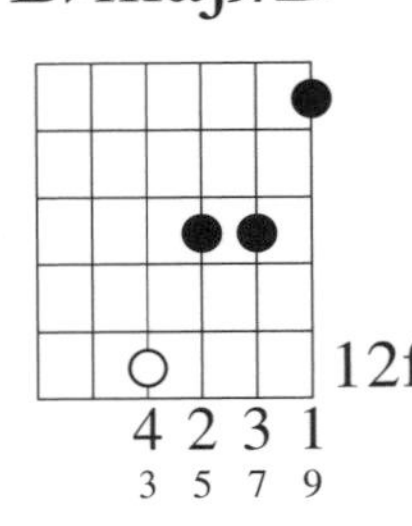

B♭maj9♯5/D
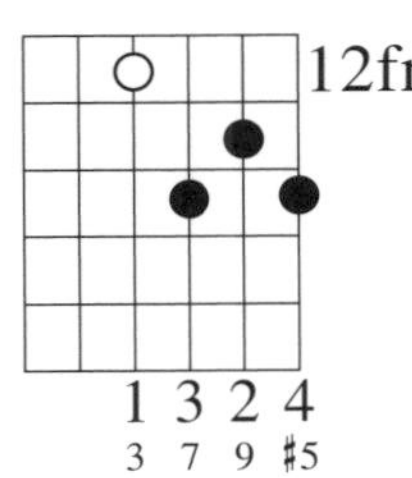

B♭maj13/D
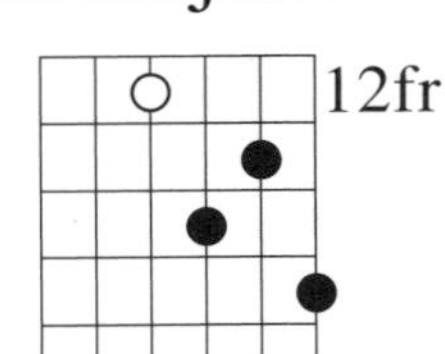

B♭maj7♯9♯11/D
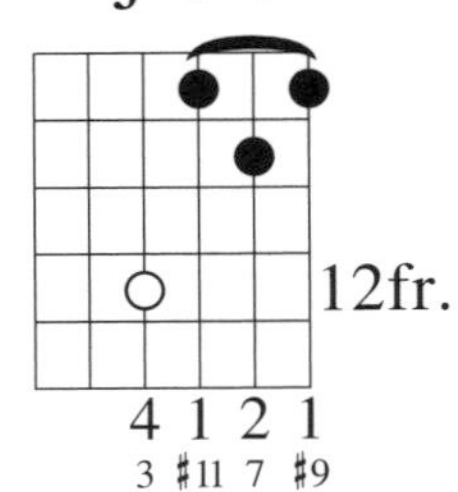

B♭maj7♭5/D B♭maj7♯11♯5/D
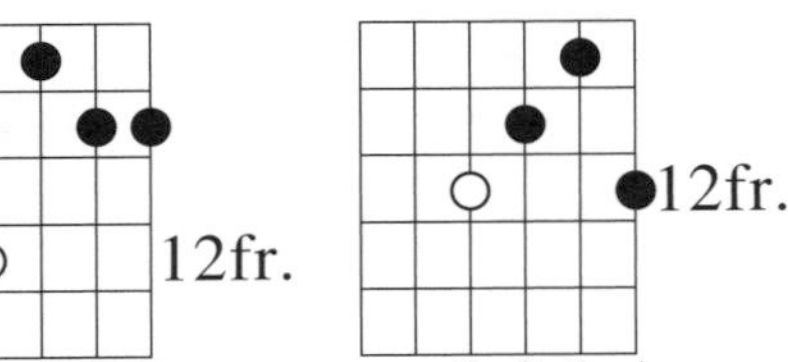

B♭maj9/D
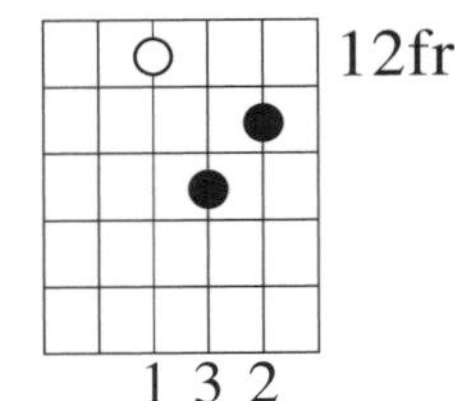

B♭maj9♯5/D
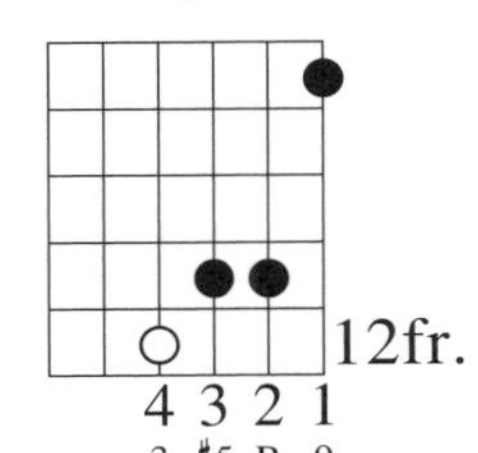

B♭maj13/D
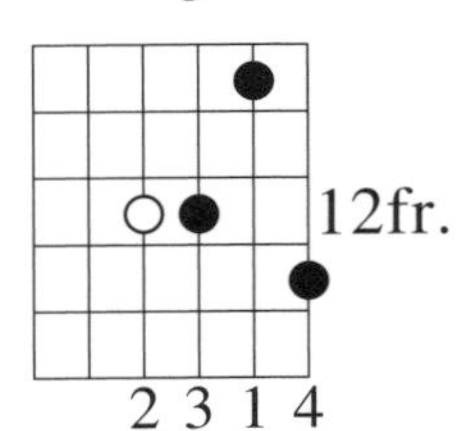

B♭maj7♯9♯5/D
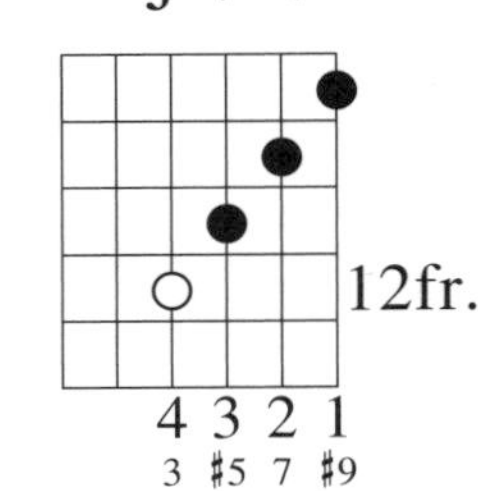

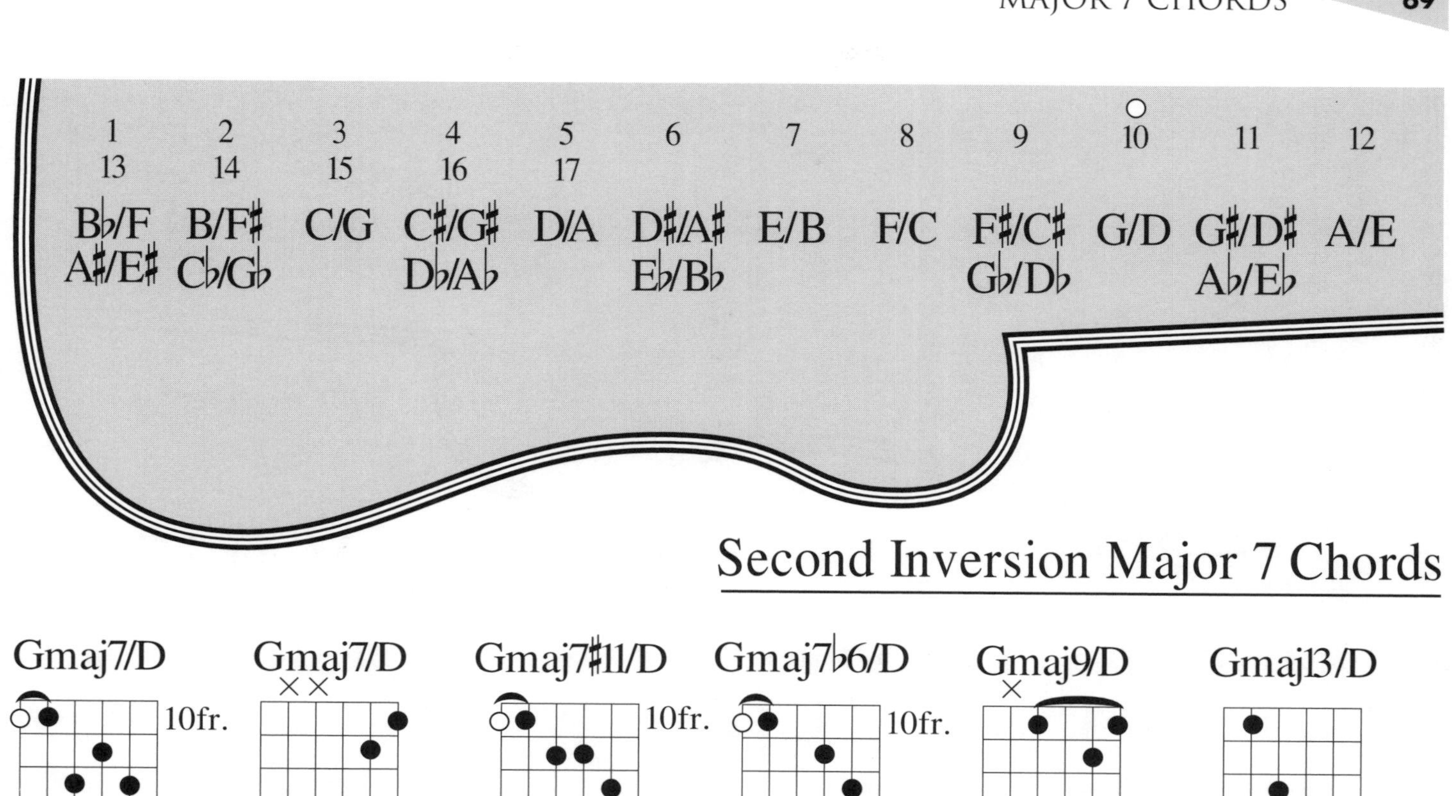

Second Inversion Major 7 Chords

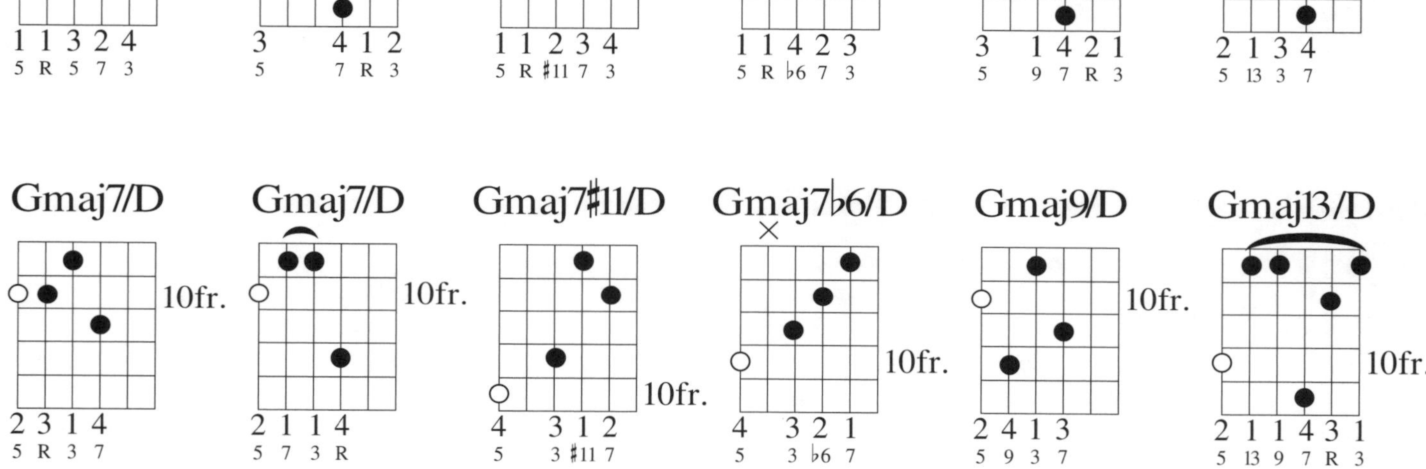

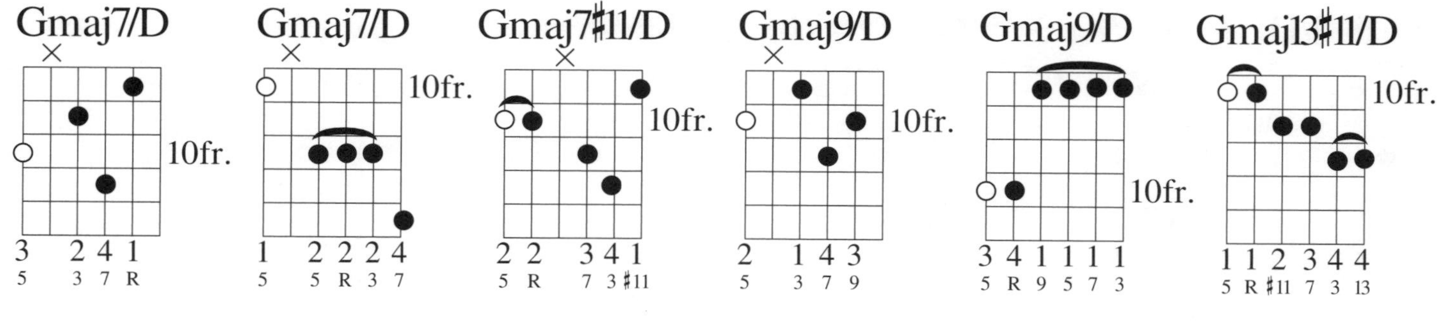

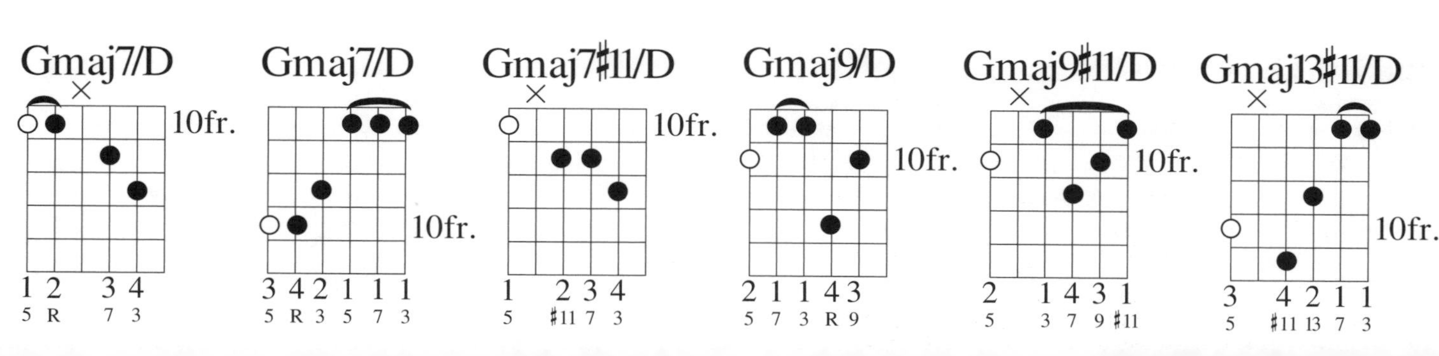

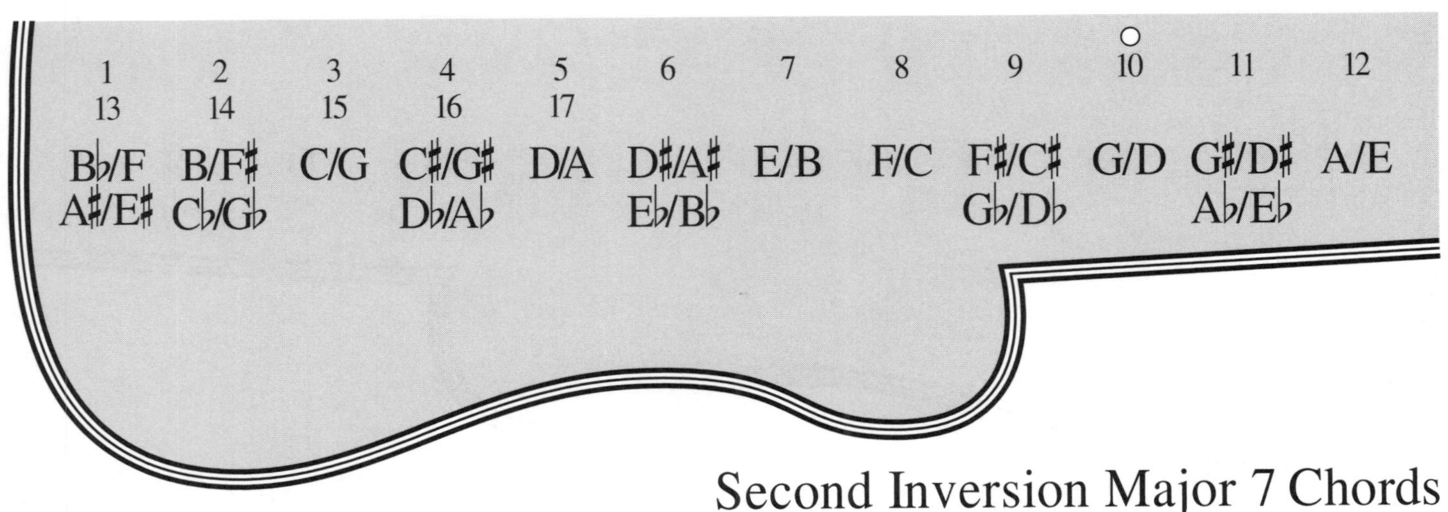

Second Inversion Major 7 Chords

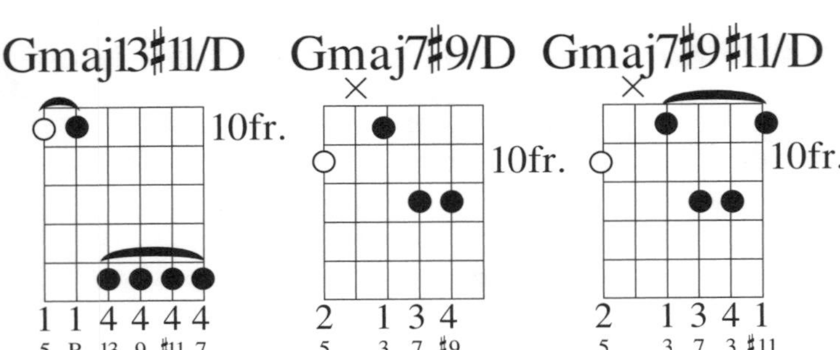

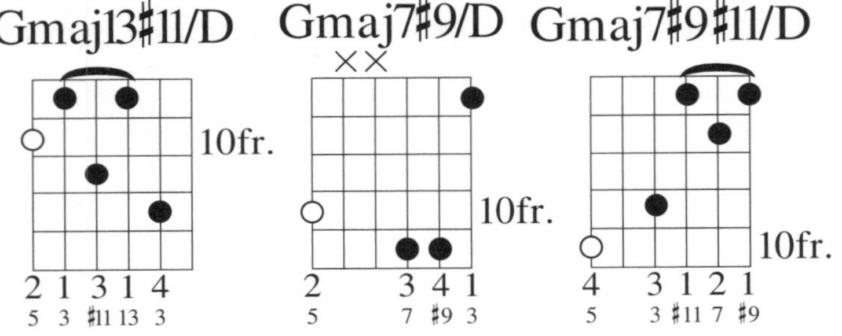

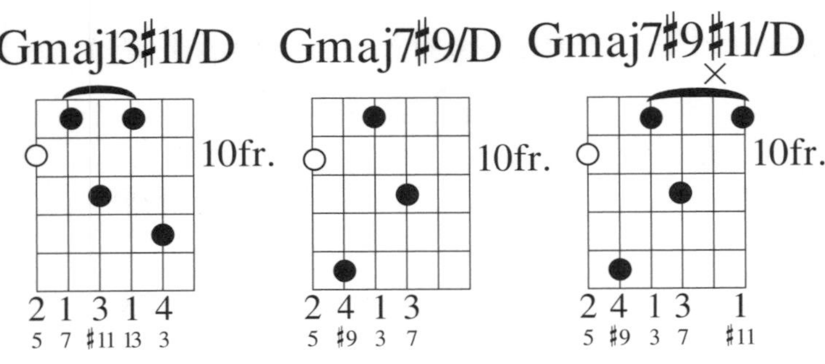

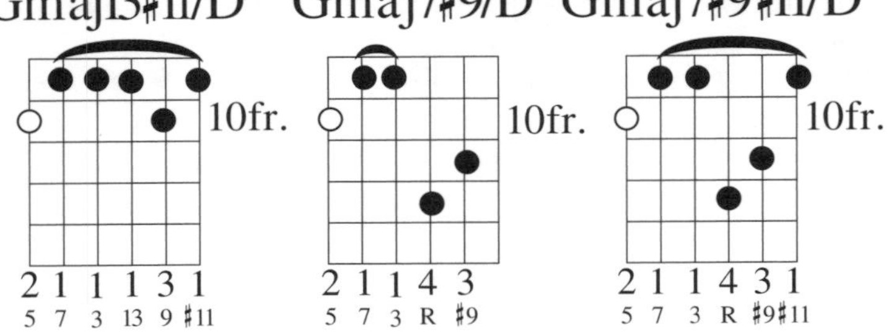

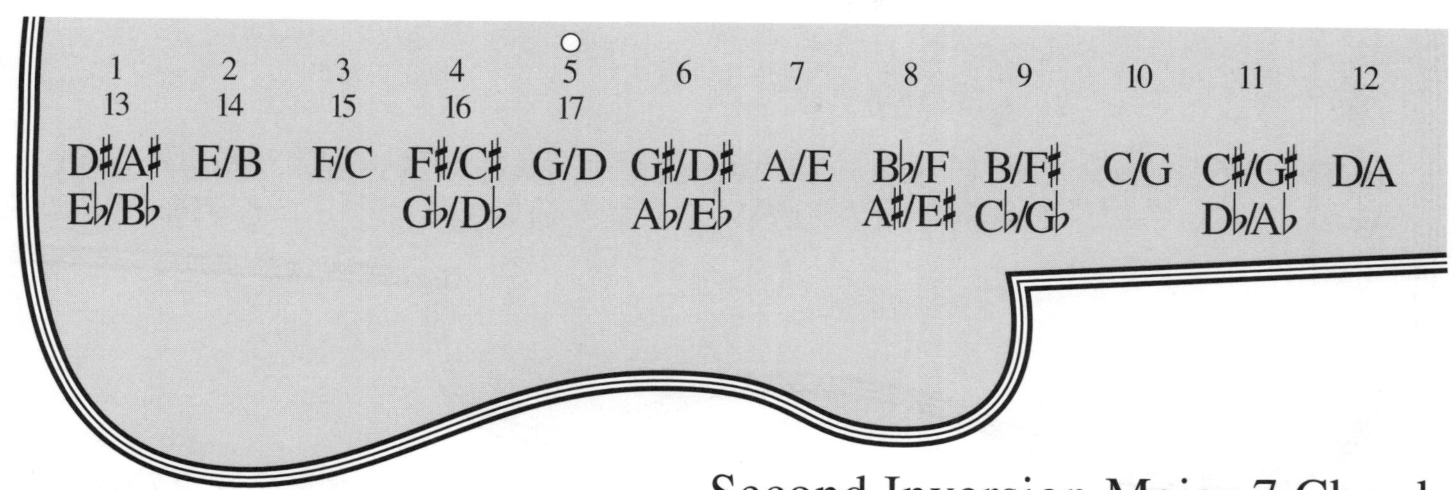

Second Inversion Major 7 Chords

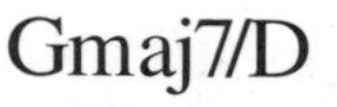

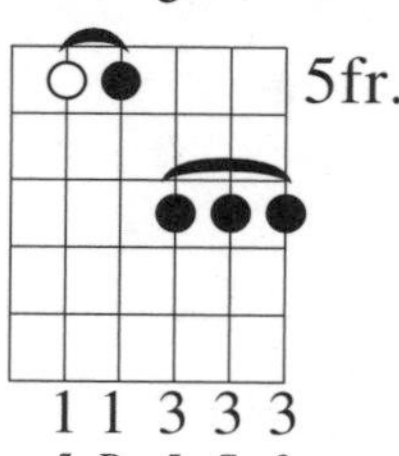

Gmaj7/D
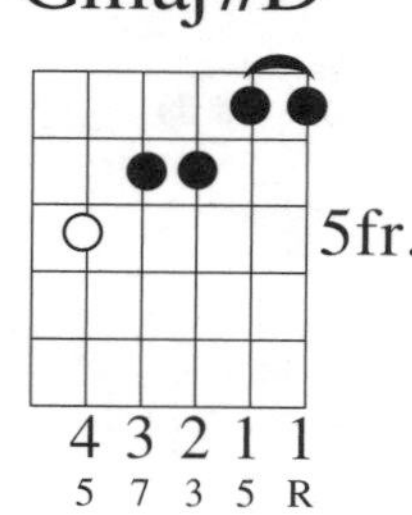

Gmaj7♯11/D
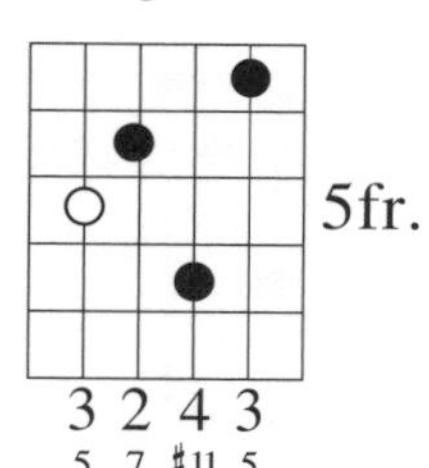

Gmaj7♭6/D
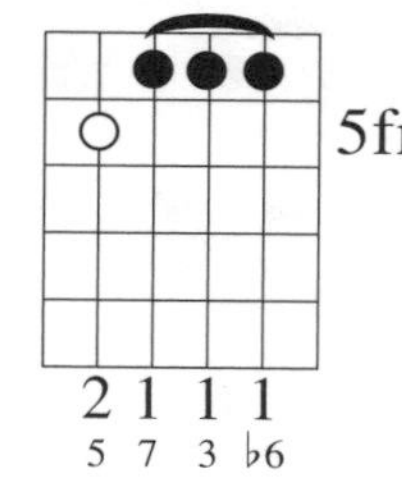

Gmaj9/D
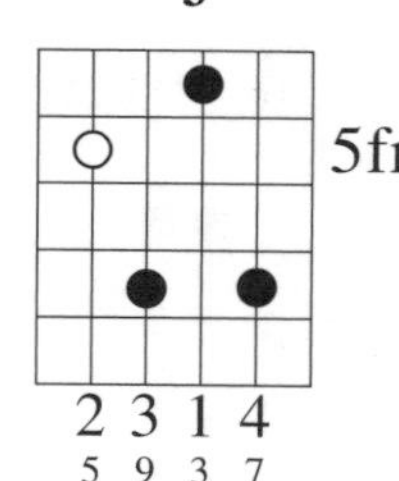

Gmaj13/D
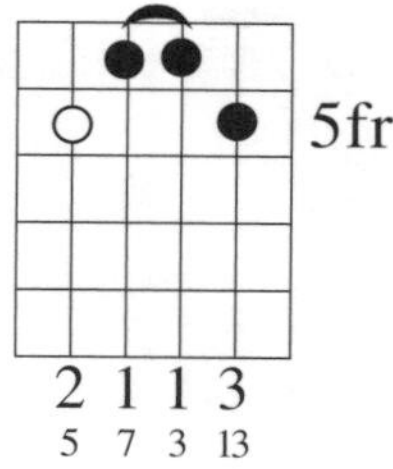

Gmaj7/D
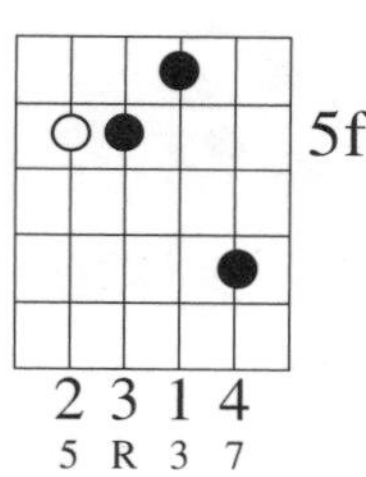

Gmaj7♯11/D
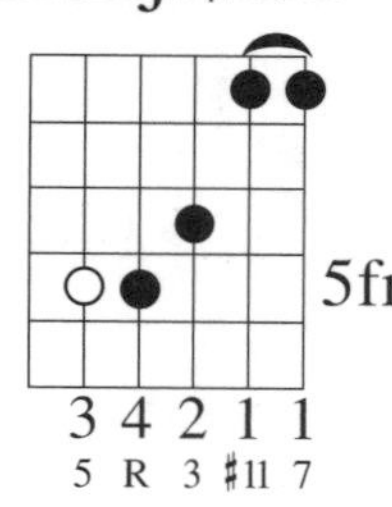

Gmaj7♯11/D
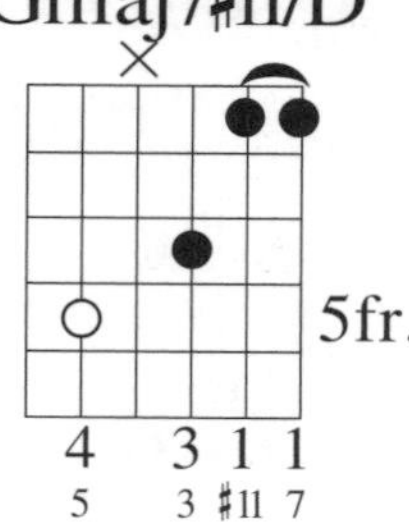

Gmaj7♭6/D
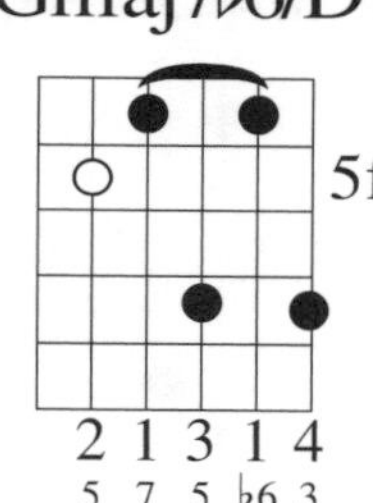

Gmaj9♯11/D
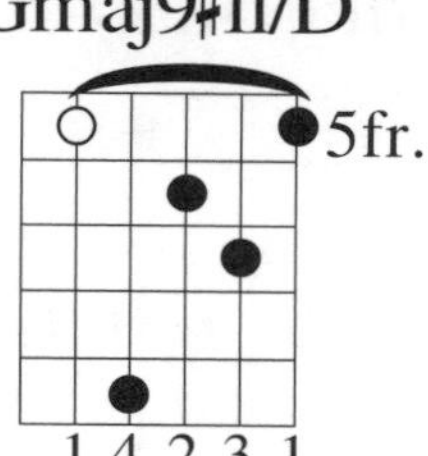

Gmaj13♯11/D
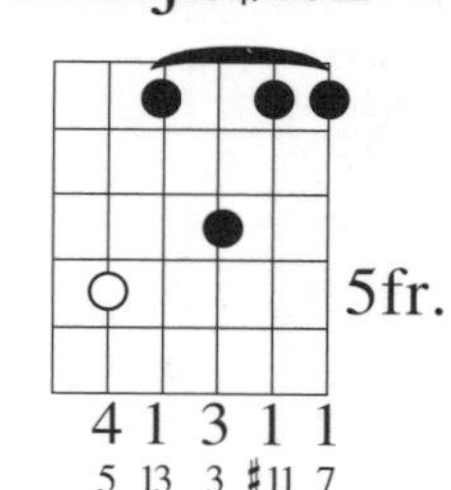

Gmaj7/D
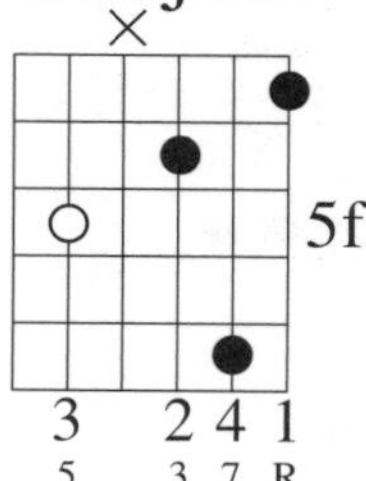

Gmaj7♯11/D
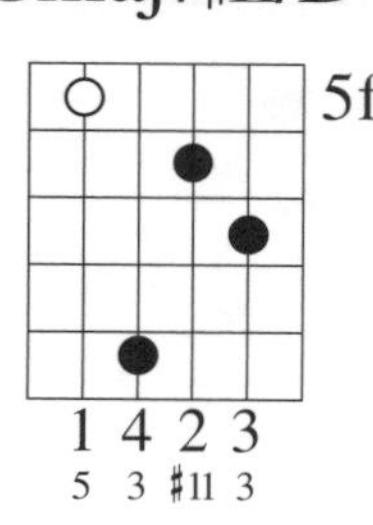

Gmaj7♭6/D
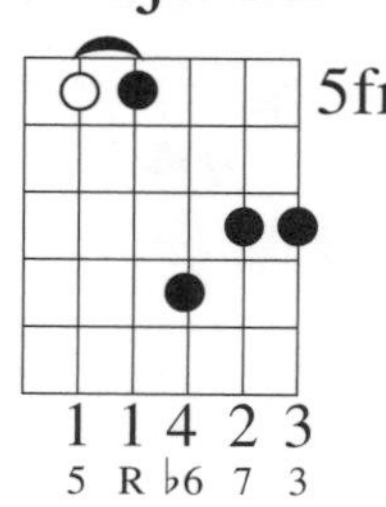

Gmaj9/D
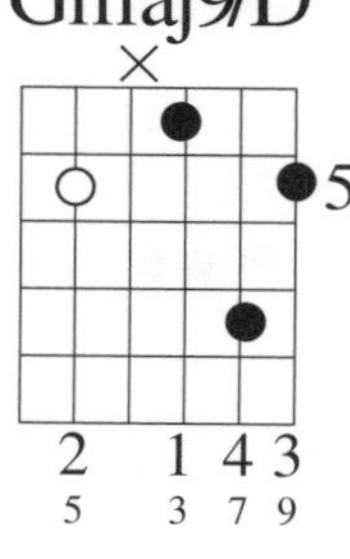

Gmaj9♭6/D
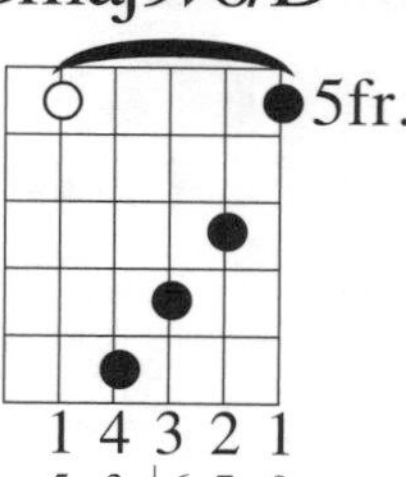

Gmaj7♯9/D
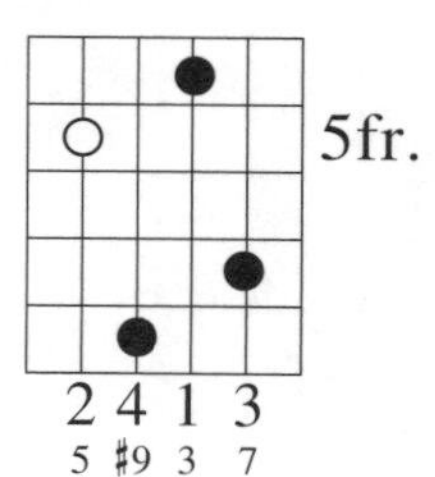

Gmaj7/D
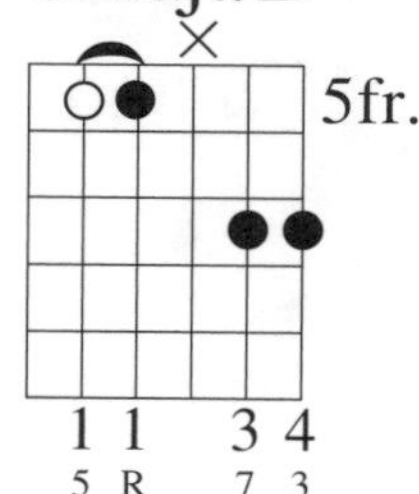

Gmaj7♯11/D
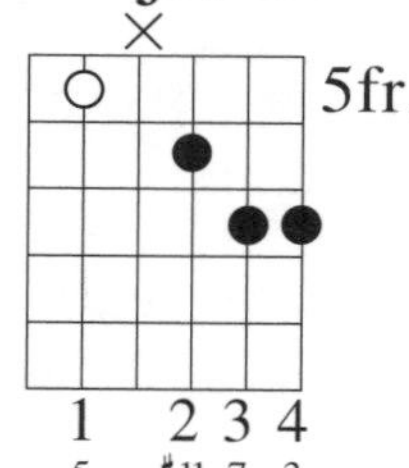

Gmaj7♭6/D
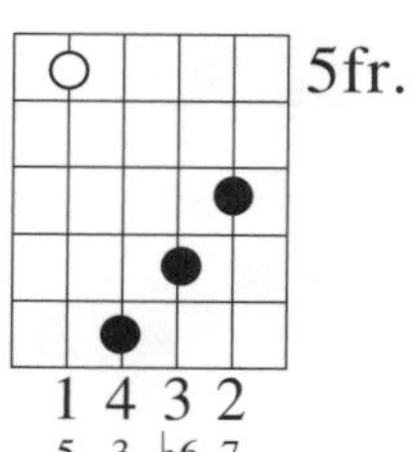

Gmaj9/D
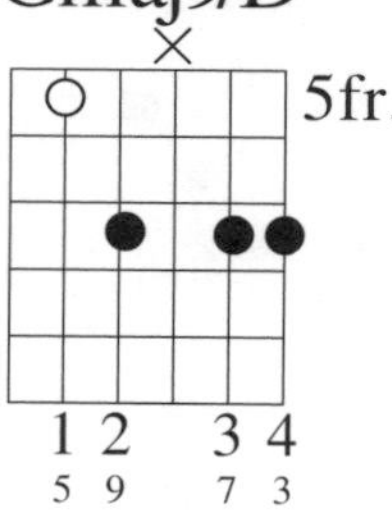

Gmaj13/D
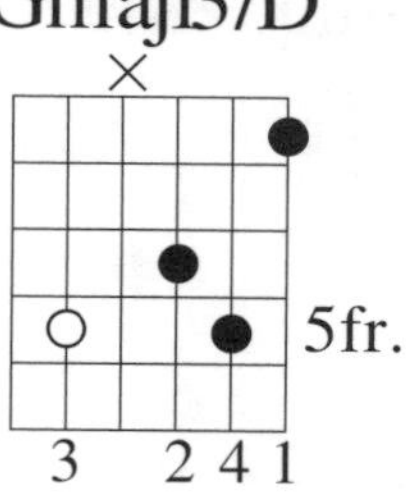

Gmaj7♯9/D
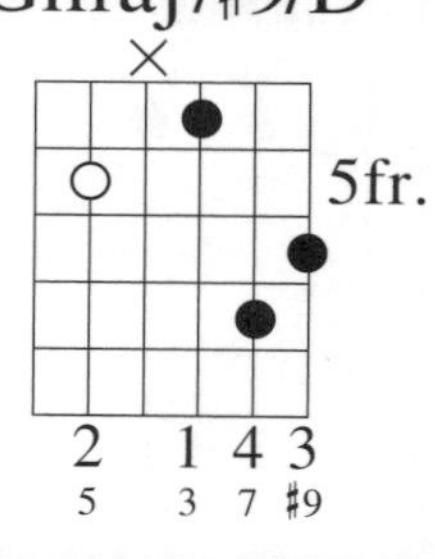

1 13
2 14
3 15
4 16
5 17
6
7
8
9
10
11
12
G♯/D♯ A♭/E♭
A/E
B♭/F A♯/E♯
B/F♯ C♭/G♭
C/G
C♯/G♯ D♭/A♭
D/A
D♯/A♯ E♭/B♭
E/B
F/C
F♯/C♯ G♭/D♭
G/D

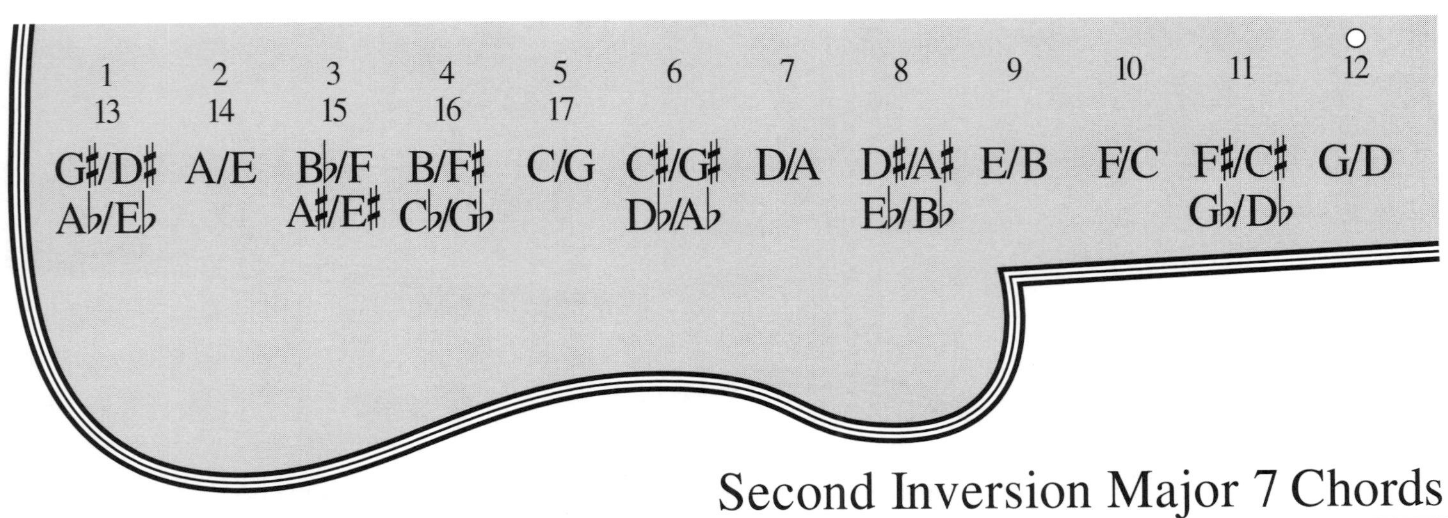

Second Inversion Major 7 Chords

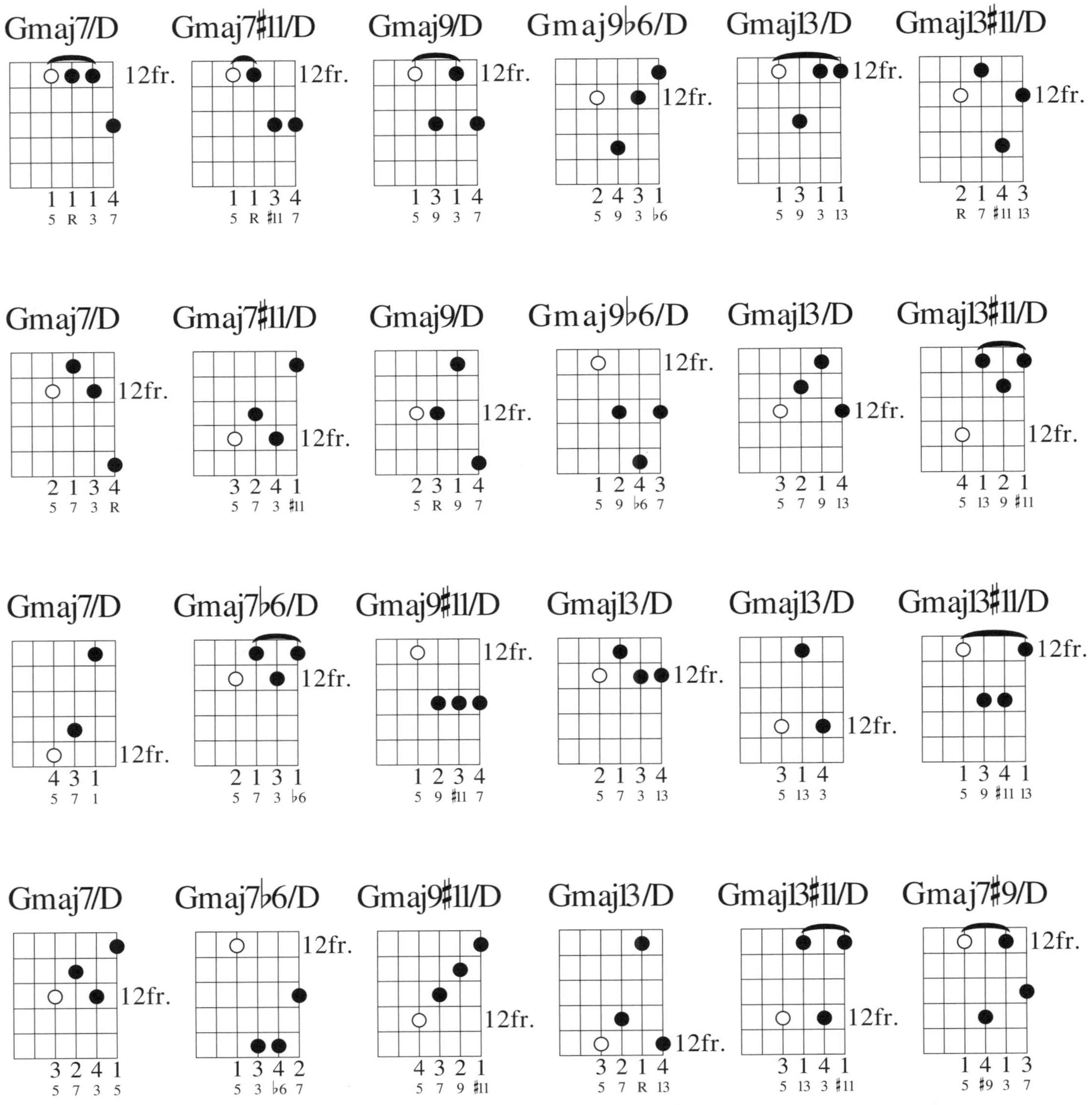

Gmaj7/D
12fr.
1 1 1 4
5 R 3 7
Gmaj7♯11/D
12fr.
1 1 3 4
5 R ♯11 7
Gmaj9/D
12fr.
1 3 1 4
5 9 3 7
Gmaj9♭6/D
12fr.
2 4 3 1
5 9 3 ♭6
Gmaj13/D
12fr.
1 3 1 1
5 9 3 13
Gmaj13♯11/D
12fr.
2 1 4 3
R 7 ♯11 13
Gmaj7/D
12fr.
2 1 3 4
5 7 3 R
Gmaj7♯11/D
12fr.
3 2 4 1
5 7 3 ♯11
Gmaj9/D
12fr.
2 3 1 4
5 R 9 7
Gmaj9♭6/D
12fr.
1 2 4 3
5 9 ♭6 7
Gmaj13/D
12fr.
3 2 1 4
5 7 9 13
Gmaj13♯11/D
12fr.
4 1 2 1
5 13 9 ♯11
Gmaj7/D
12fr.
4 3 1
5 7 1
Gmaj7♭6/D
12fr.
2 1 3 1
5 7 3 ♭6
Gmaj9♯11/D
12fr.
1 2 3 4
5 9 ♯11 7
Gmaj13/D
12fr.
2 1 3 4
5 7 3 13
Gmaj13/D
12fr.
3 1 4
5 13 3
Gmaj13♯11/D
12fr.
1 3 4 1
5 9 ♯11 13
Gmaj7/D
12fr.
3 2 4 1
5 7 3 5
Gmaj7♭6/D
12fr.
1 3 4 2
5 3 ♭6 7
Gmaj9♯11/D
12fr.
4 3 2 1
5 7 9 ♯11
Gmaj13/D
12fr.
3 2 1 4
5 7 R 13
Gmaj13♯11/D
12fr.
3 1 4 1
5 13 3 ♯11
Gmaj7♯9/D
12fr.
1 4 1 3
5 ♯9 3 7

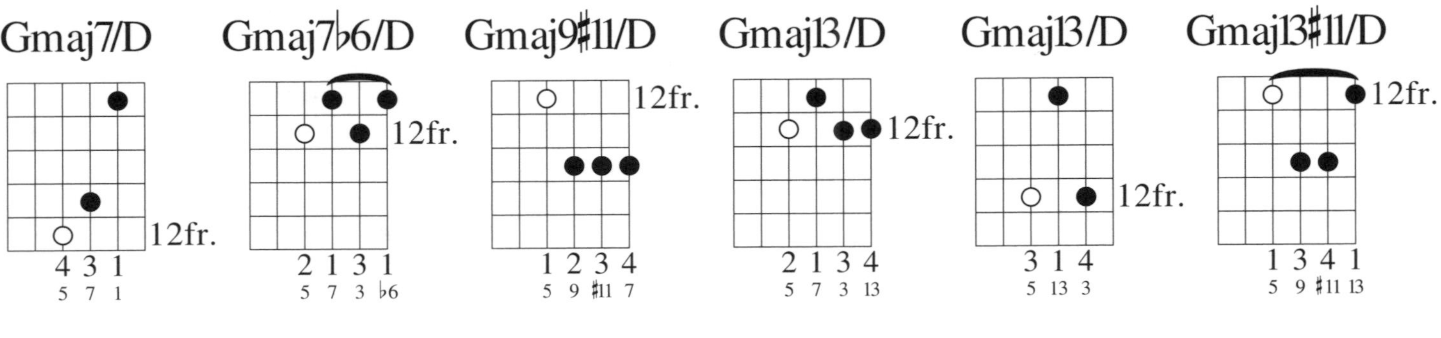

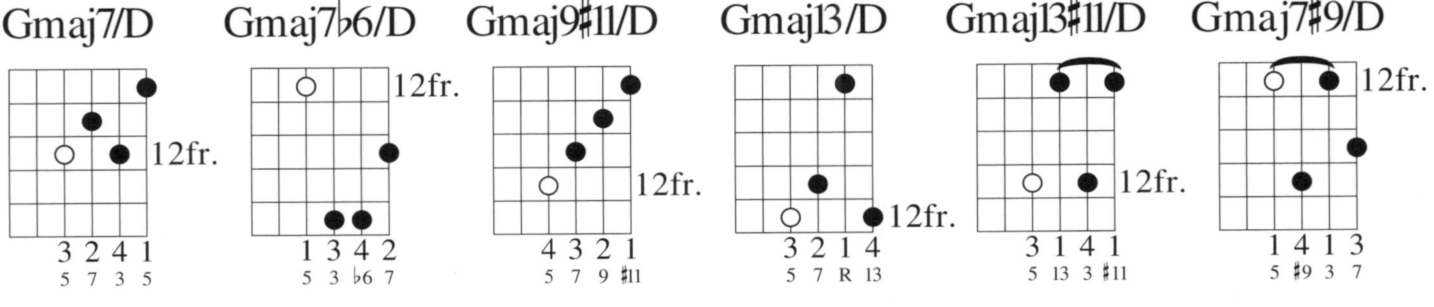

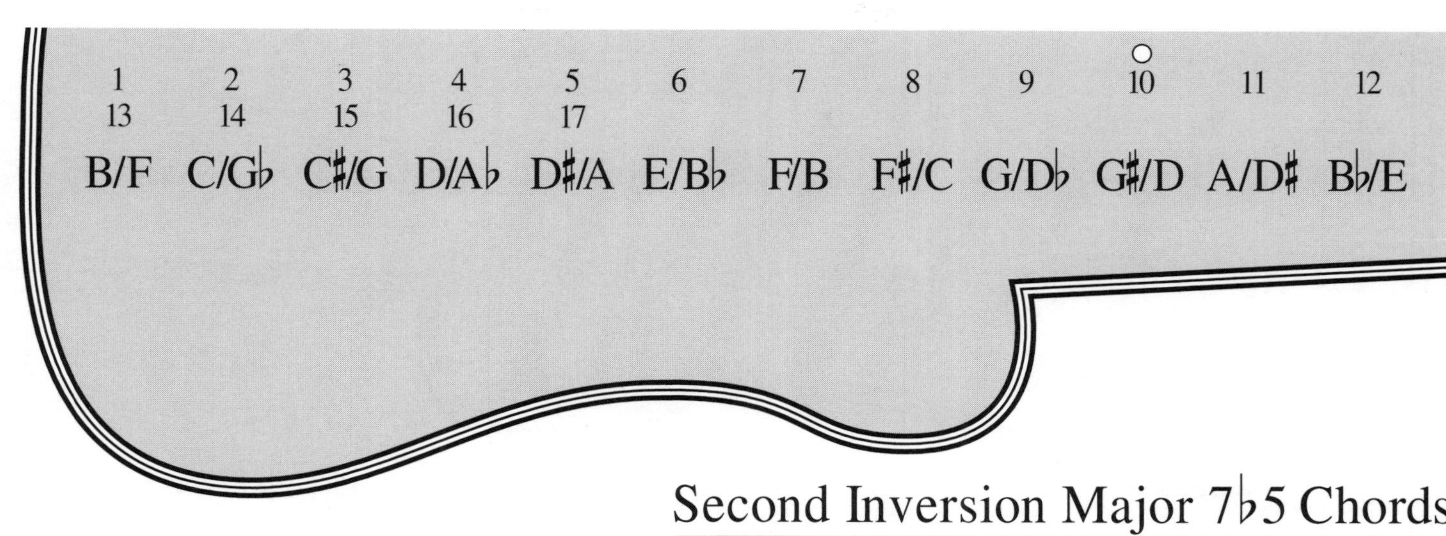

Second Inversion Major 7♭5 Chords

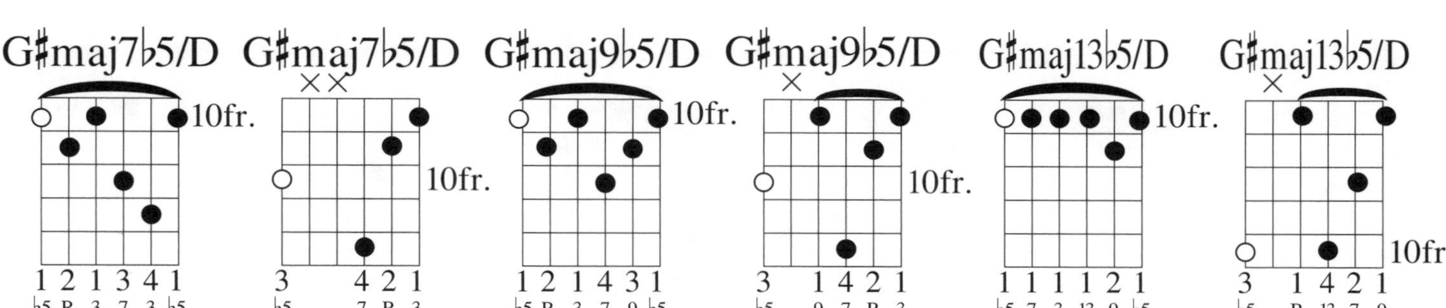

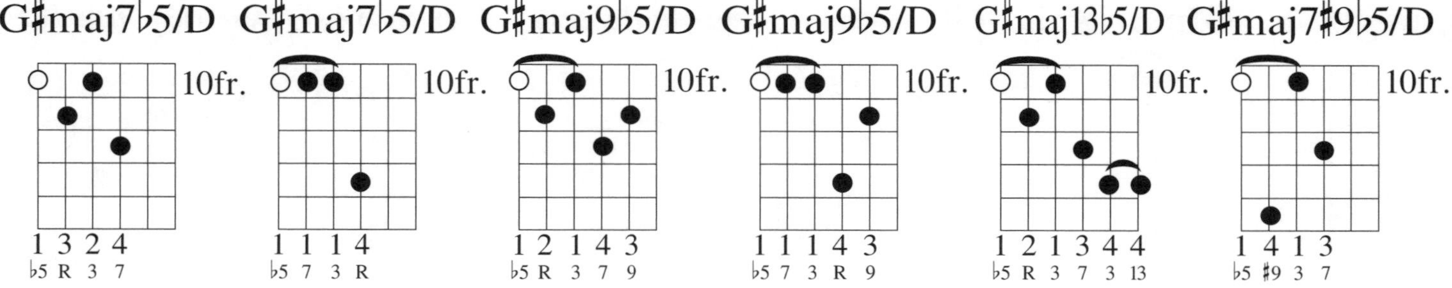

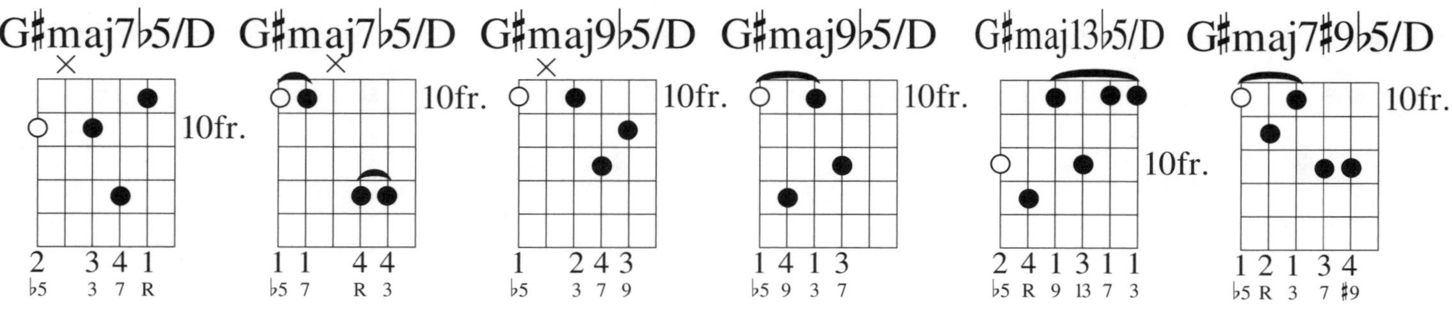

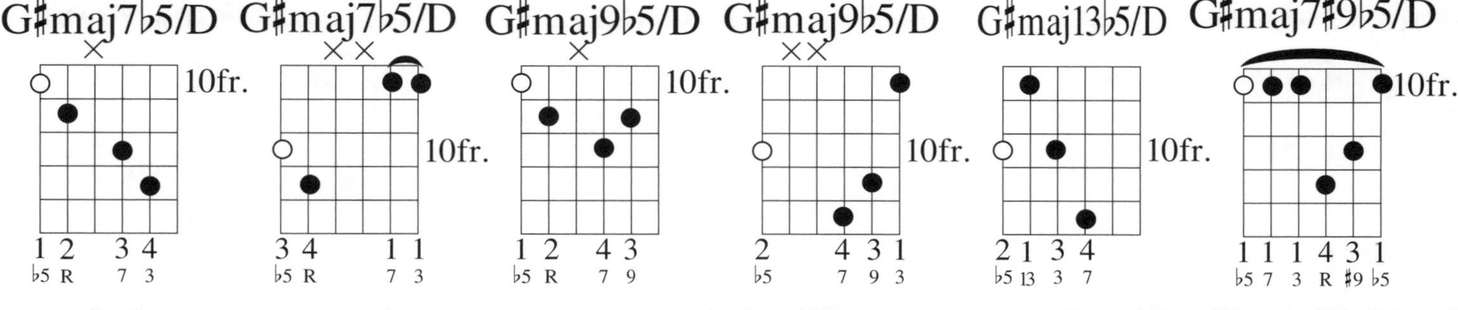

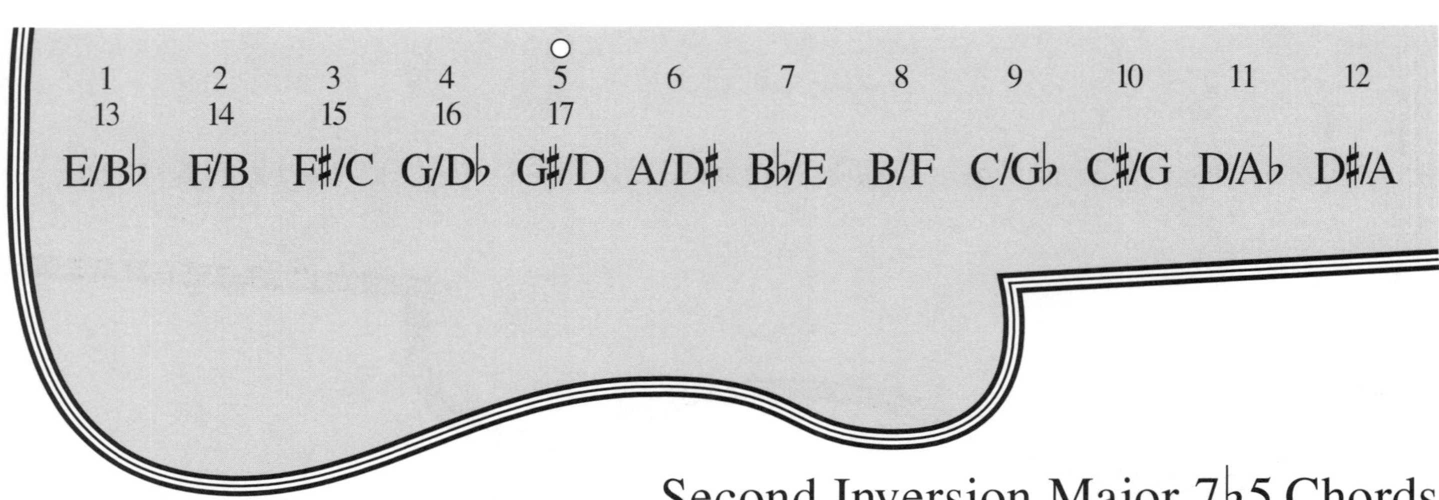

Second Inversion Major 7♭5 Chords

G♯maj7♭5/D | G♯maj7♭5/D | G♯maj9♭5/D | G♯maj13♭5/D | G♯maj13♭5/D | G♯maj7♯9♭5/D

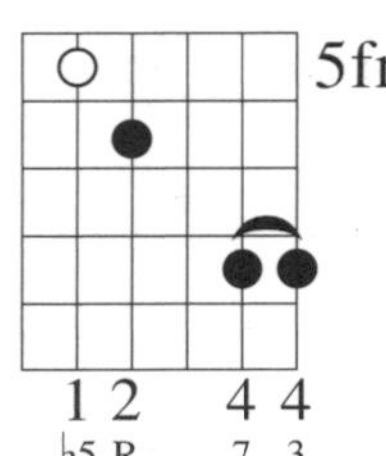

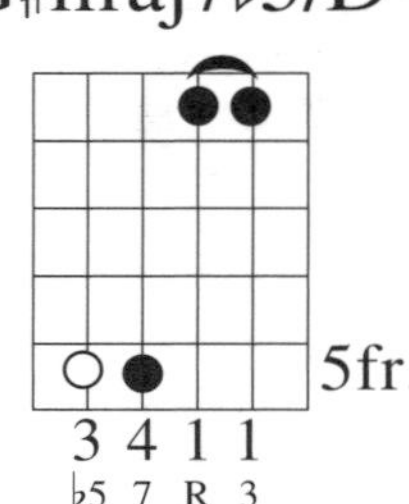

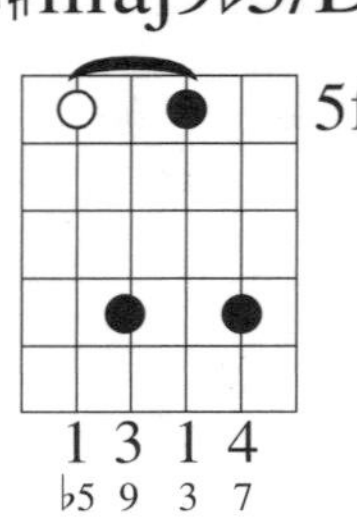

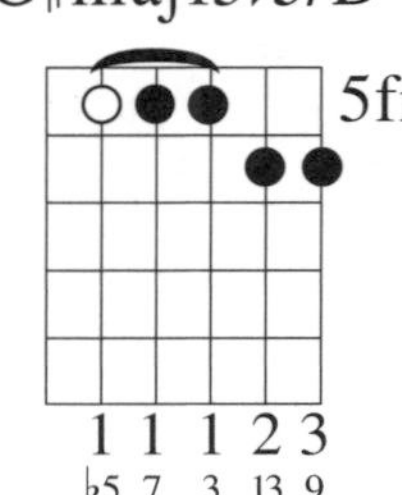

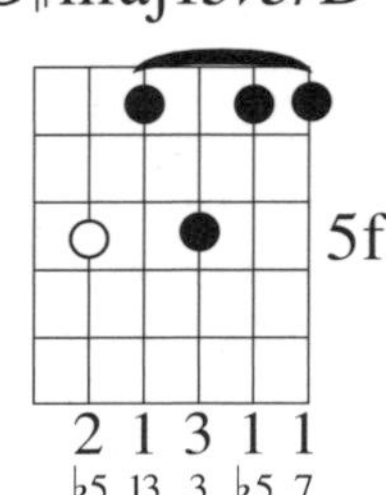

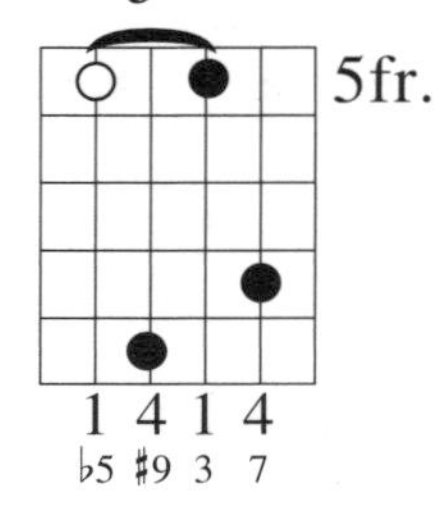

G♯maj7♭5/D | G♯maj7♭5/D | G♯maj9♭5/D | G♯maj13♭5/D | G♯maj13♭5/D | G♯maj7♯9♭5/D

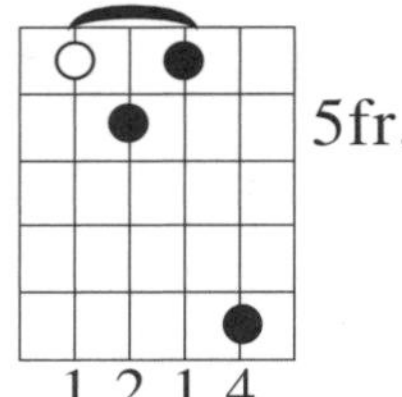

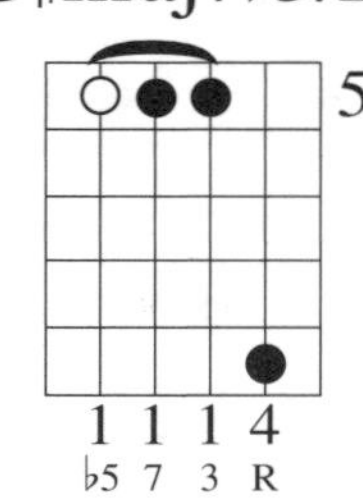

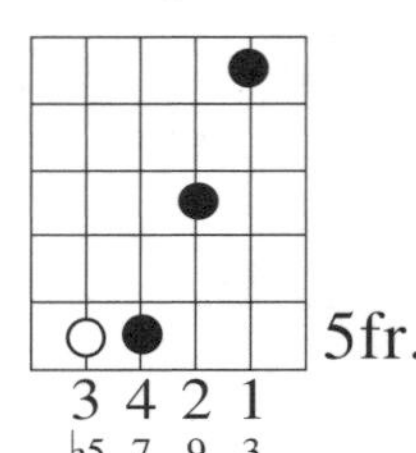

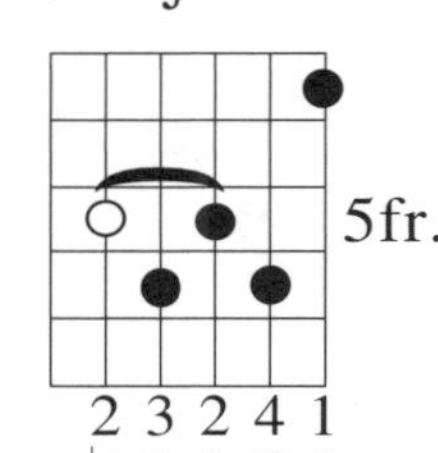

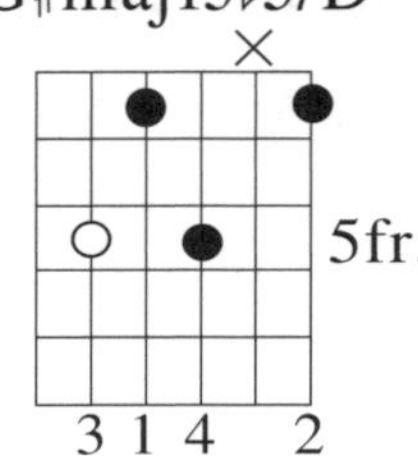

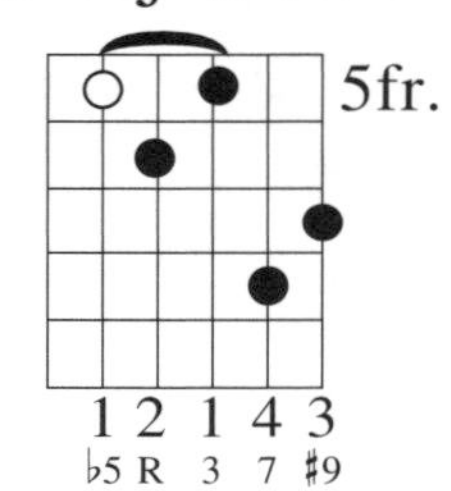

G♯maj7♭5/D | G♯maj7♭5/D | G♯maj9♭5/D | G♯maj13♭5/D |

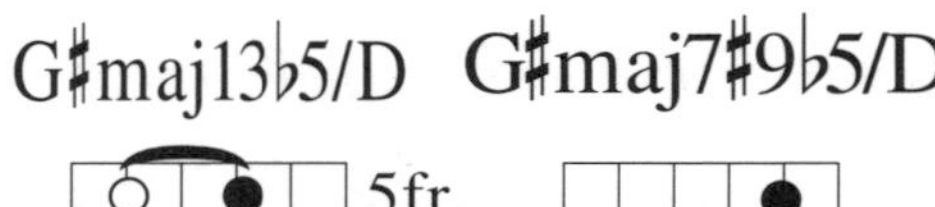
G♯maj13♭5/D | G♯maj7♯9♭5/D

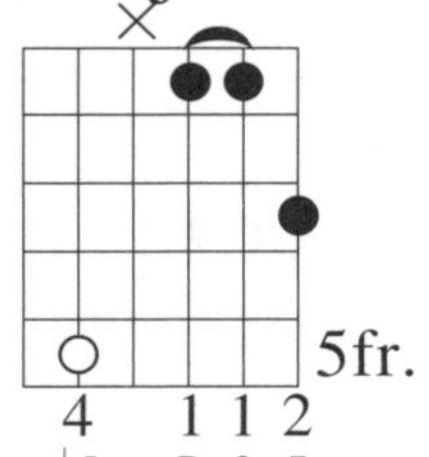

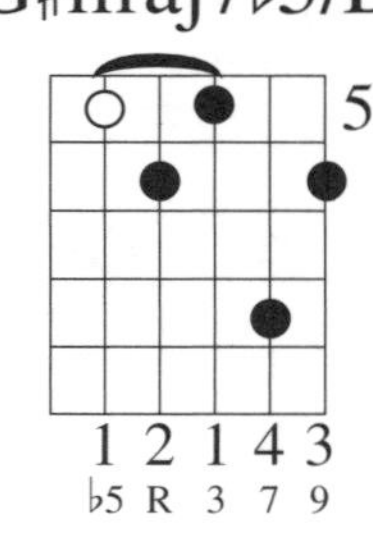

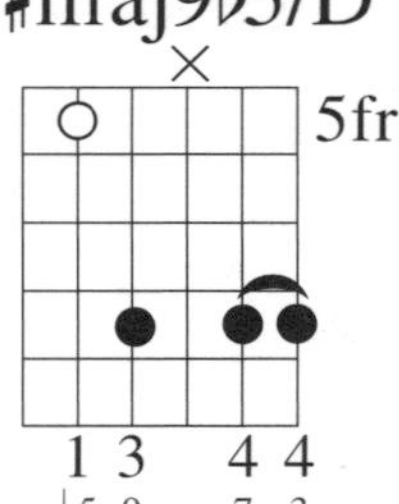

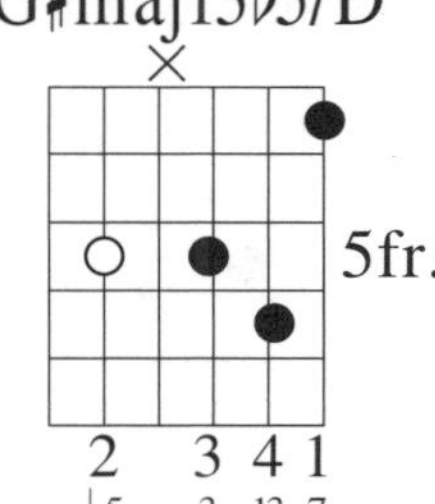

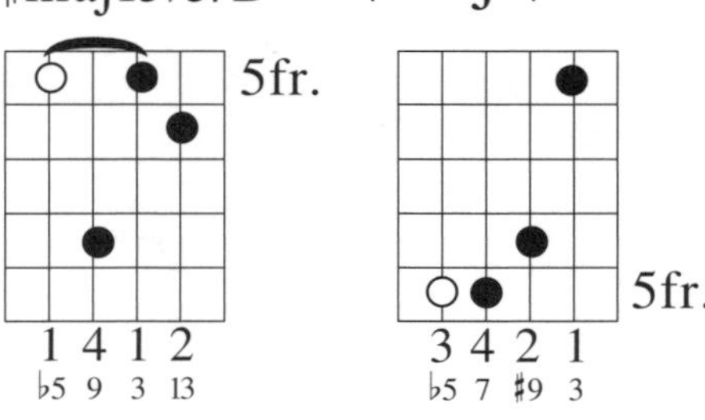

G♯maj7♭5/D | G♯maj9♭5/D | G♯maj9♭5/D | G♯maj13♭5/D | G♯maj13♭5/D | G♯maj7♯9♭5/D

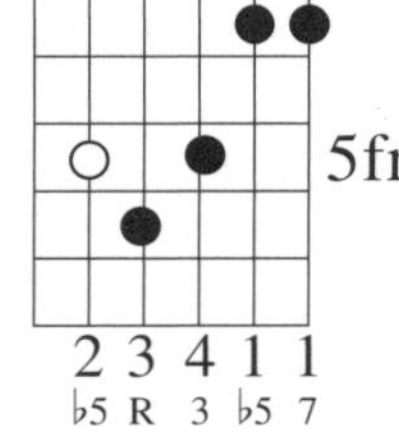

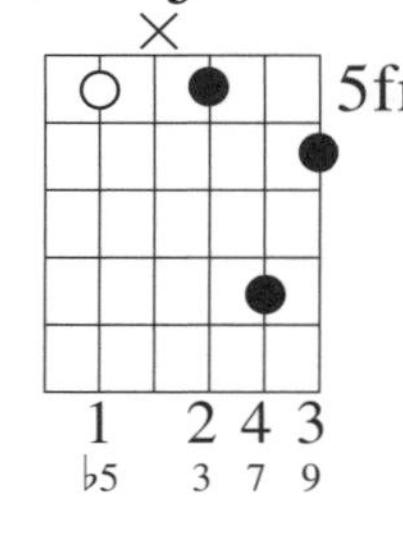

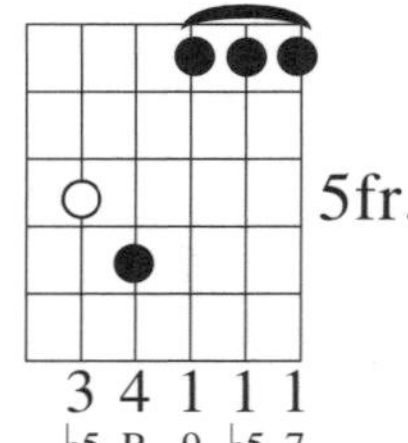

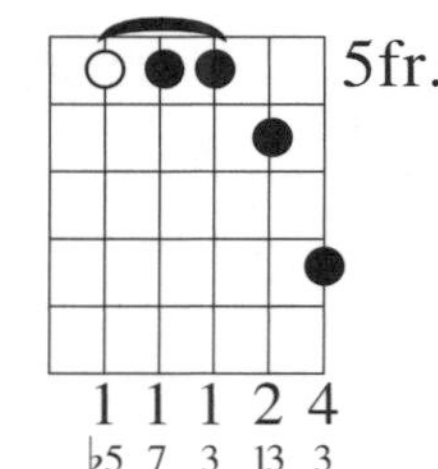

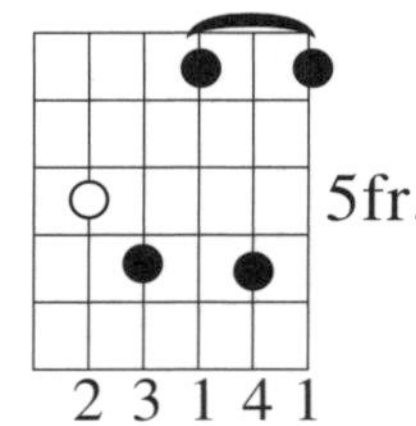

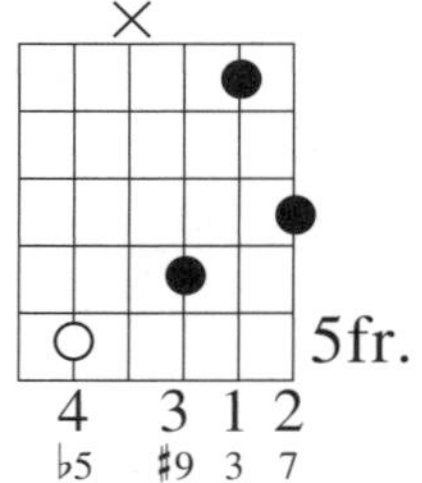

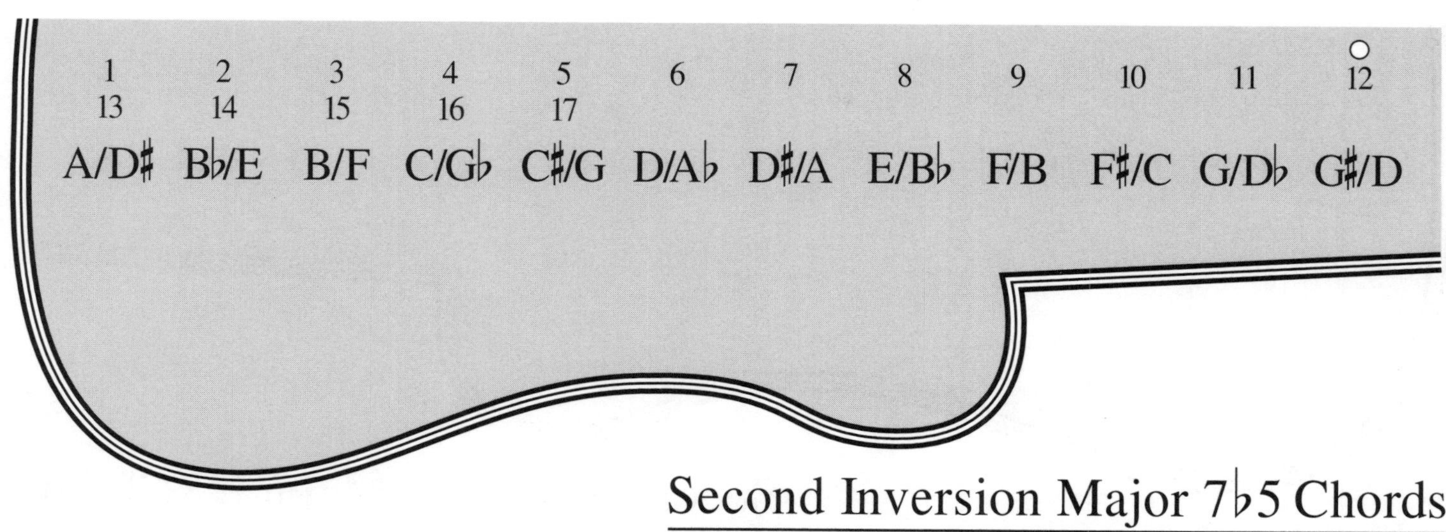

Second Inversion Major 7♭5 Chords

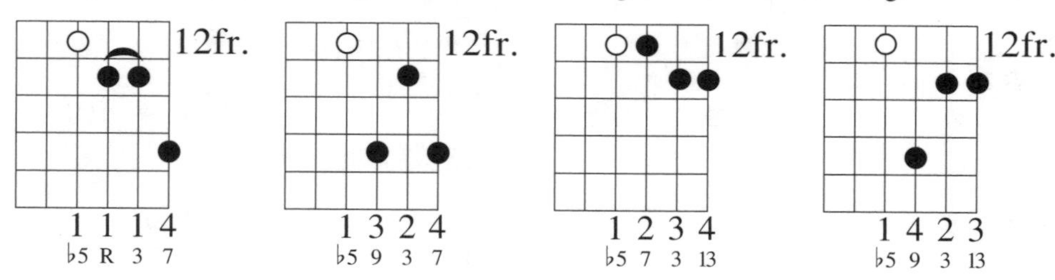

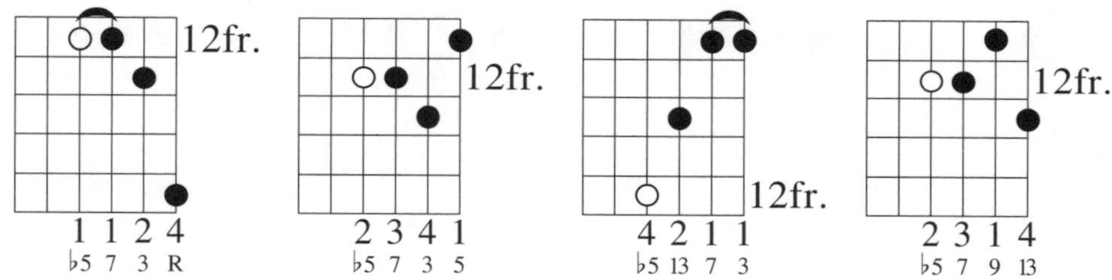

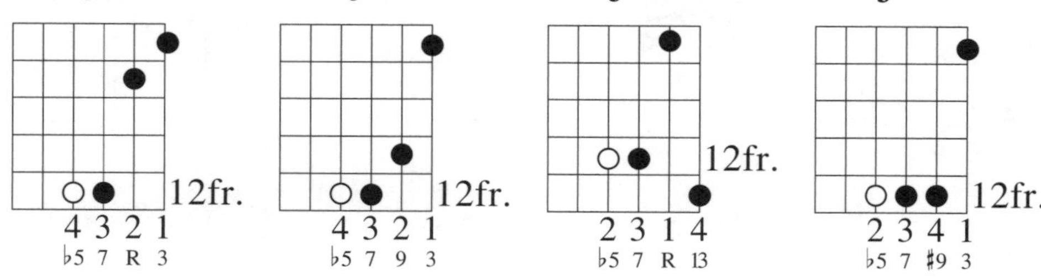

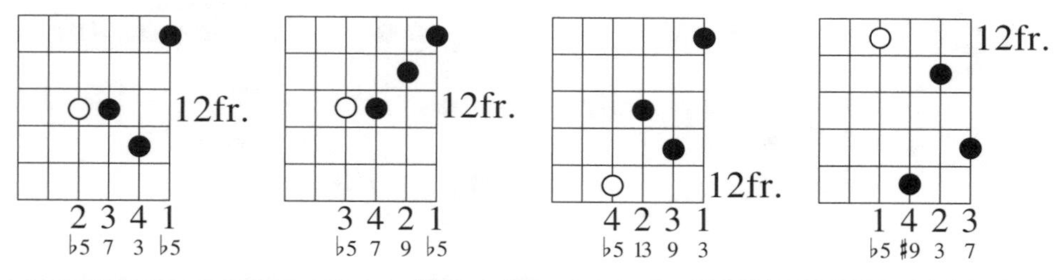

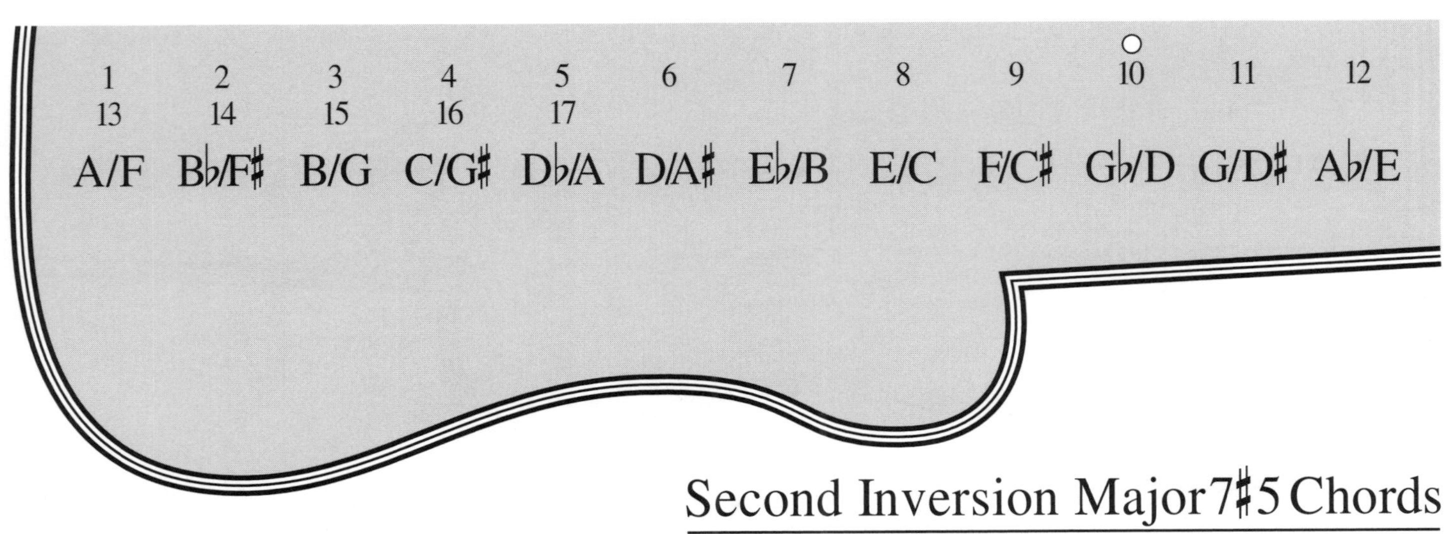

Second Inversion Major7♯5 Chords

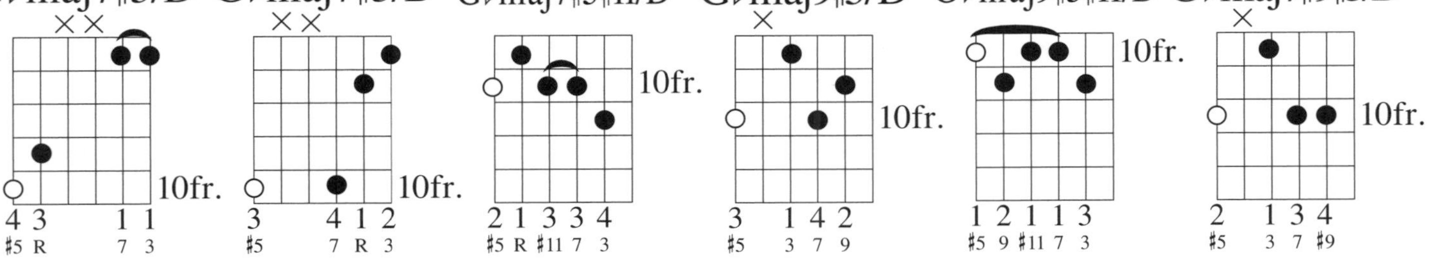

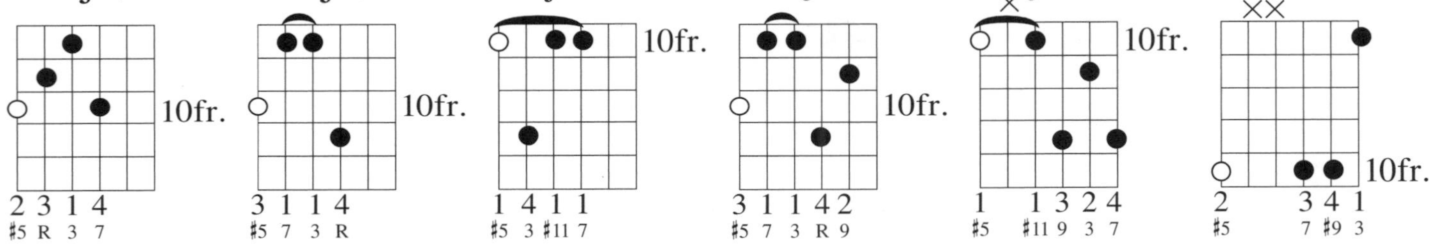

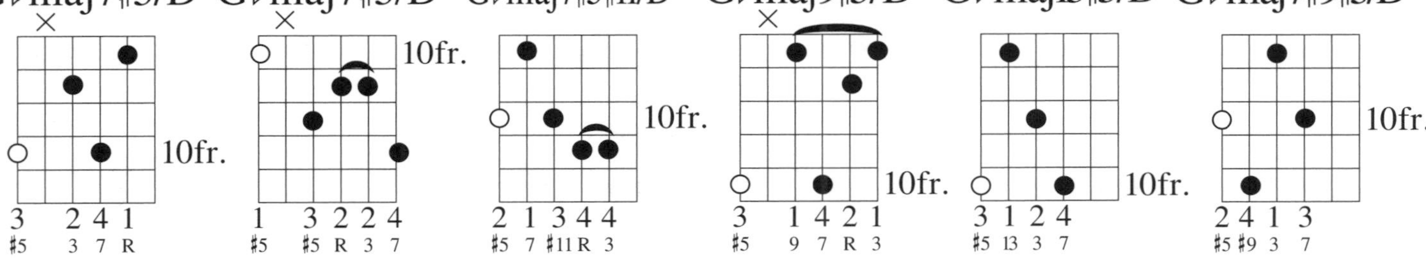

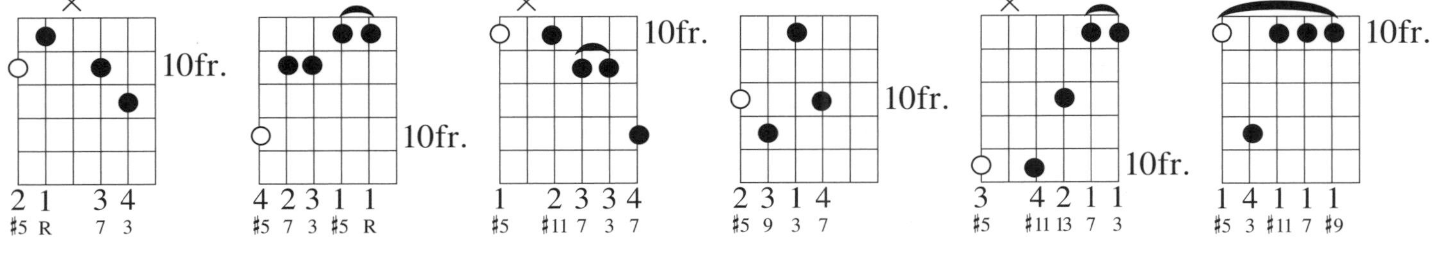

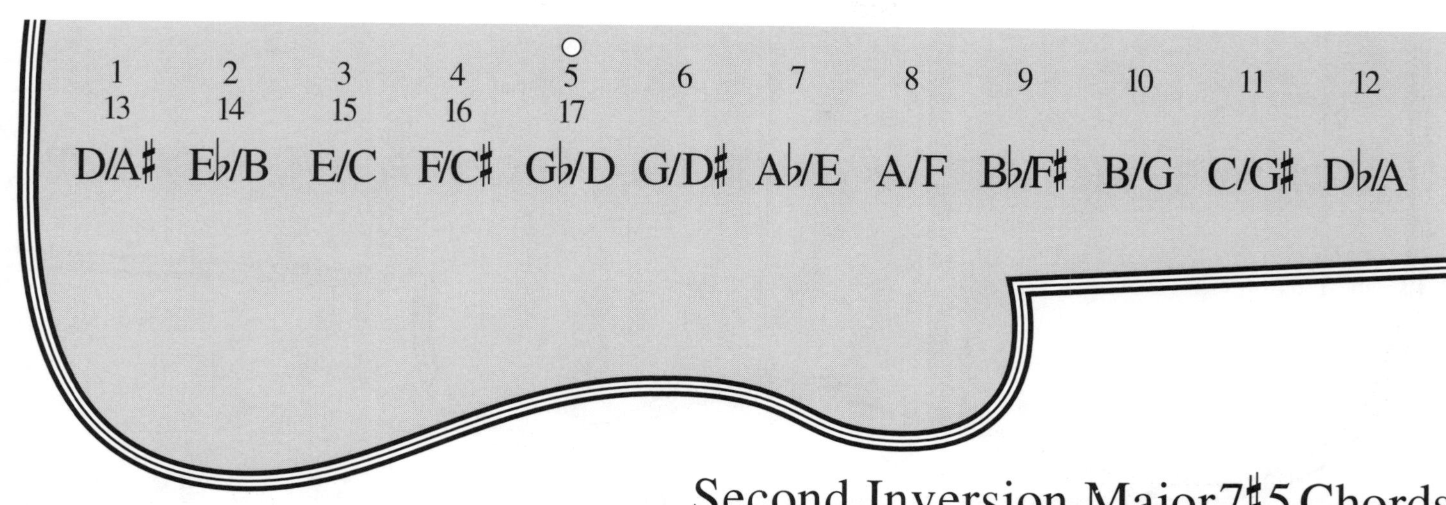

Second Inversion Major7♯5 Chords

G♭maj7♯5/D G♭maj7♯5/D G♭maj7♯5♯11/D G♭maj9♯5/D G♭maj9♯5♯11/D G♭maj7♯9♯5/D

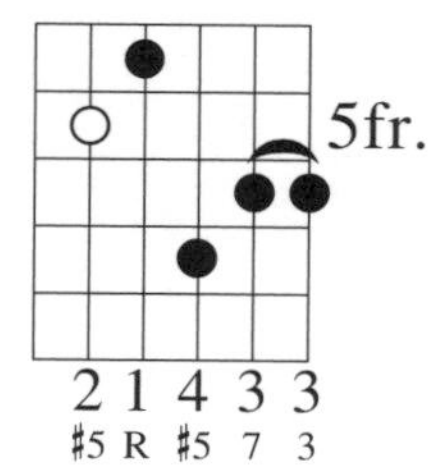

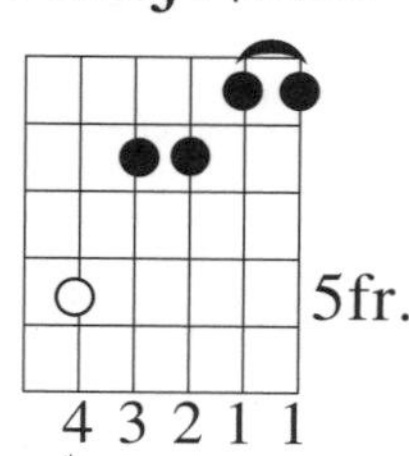

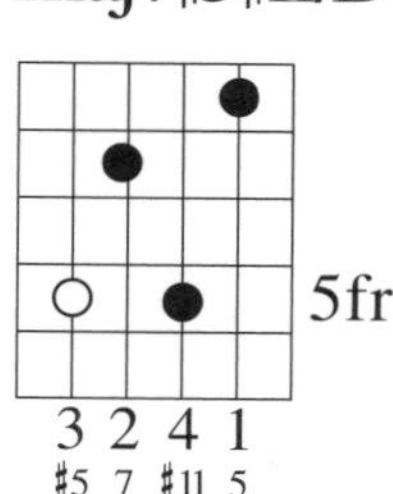

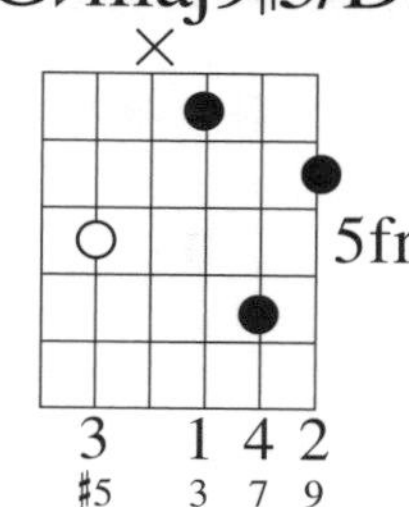

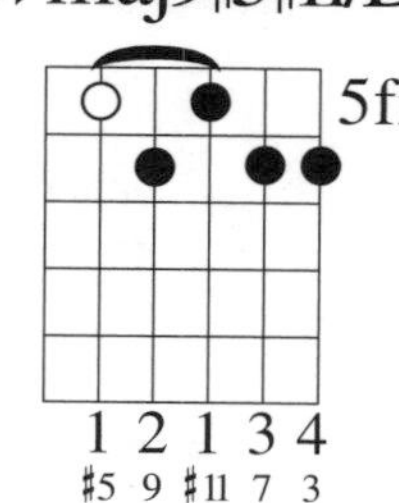

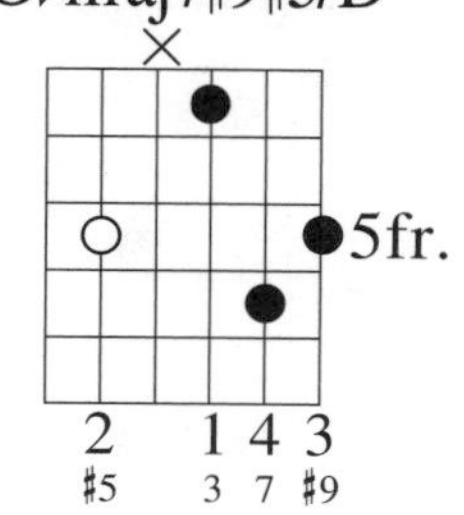

G♭maj7♯5/D G♭maj7♯5/D G♭maj7♯5♯11/D G♭maj9♯5/D G♭maj9♯5♯11/D G♭maj7♯9♯5/D

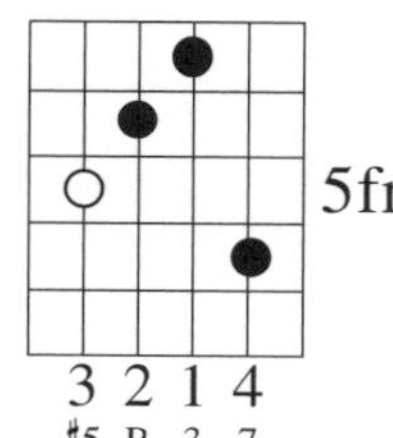

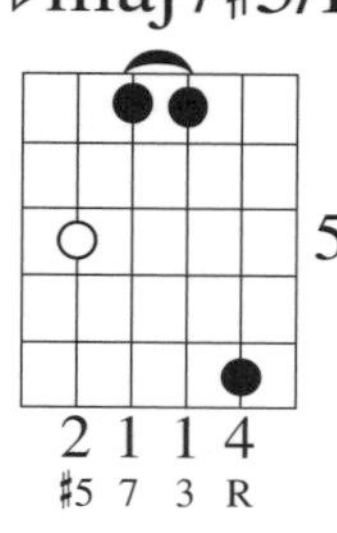

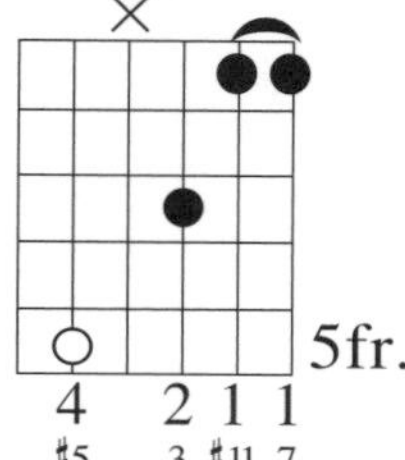

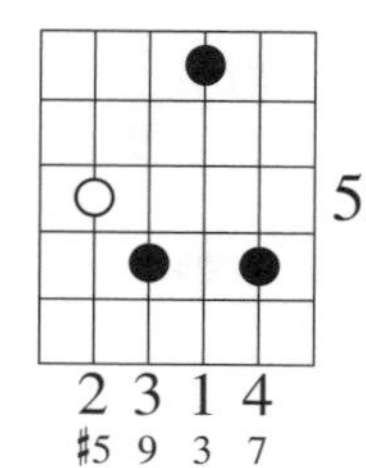

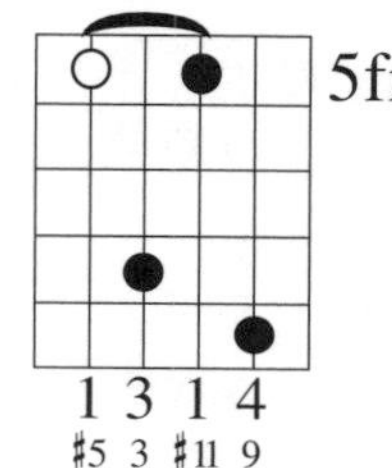

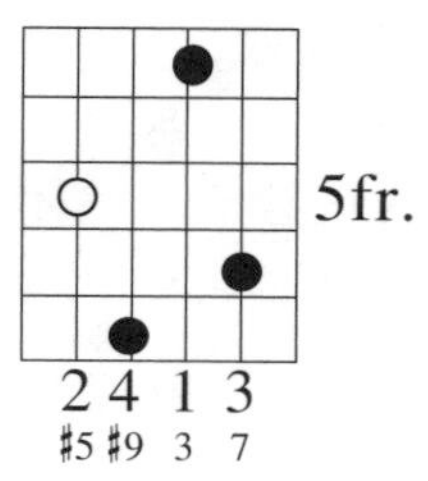

G♭maj7♯5/D G♭maj7♯5/D G♭maj7♯5♯11/D G♭maj9♯5/D G♭maj9♯5♯11/D G♭maj7♯9♯5/D

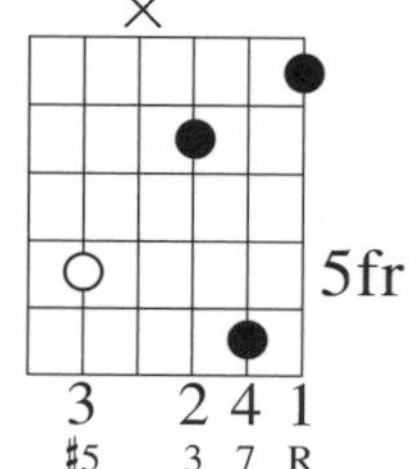

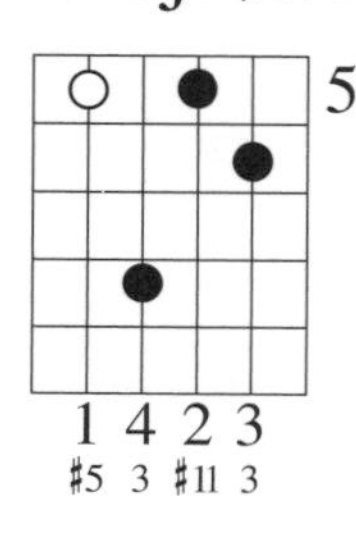

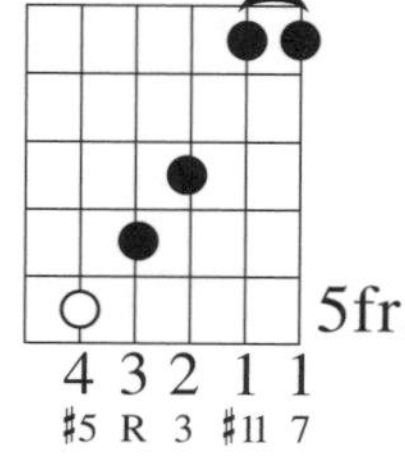

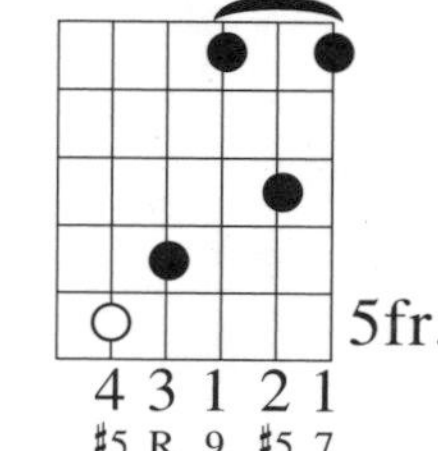

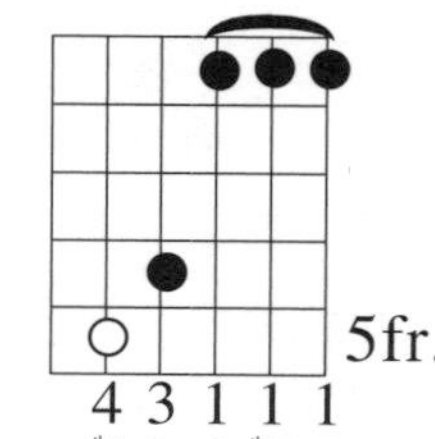

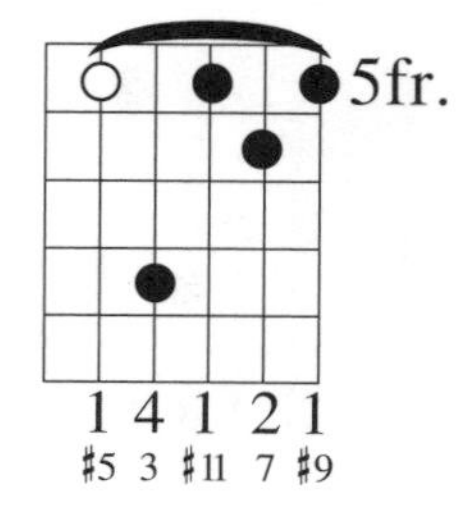

G♭maj7♯5/D G♭maj7♯5♯11/D G♭maj7♯5♯11/D G♭maj9♯5/D G♭maj9♯5♯11/D G♭maj7♯9♯11♯5/D

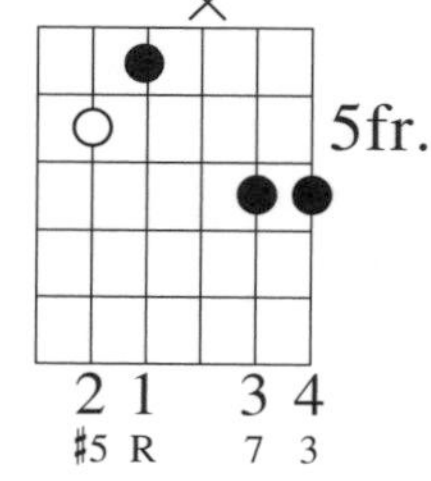

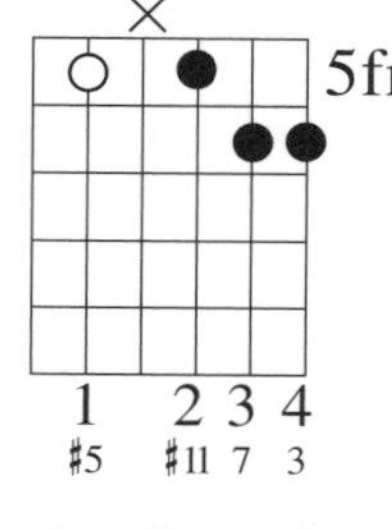

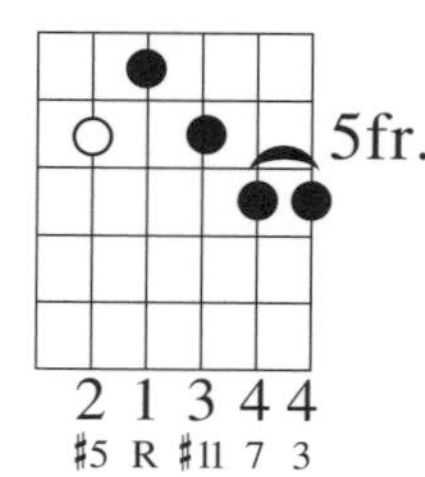

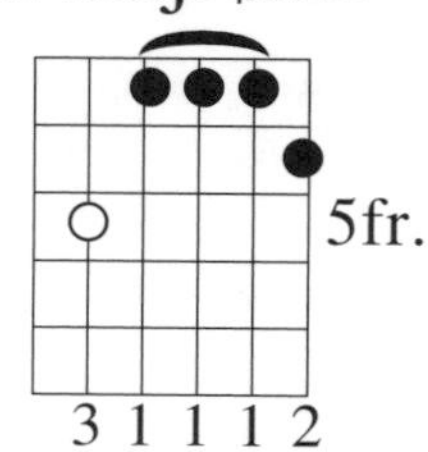

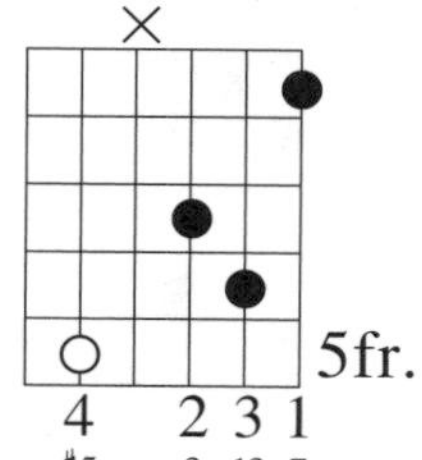

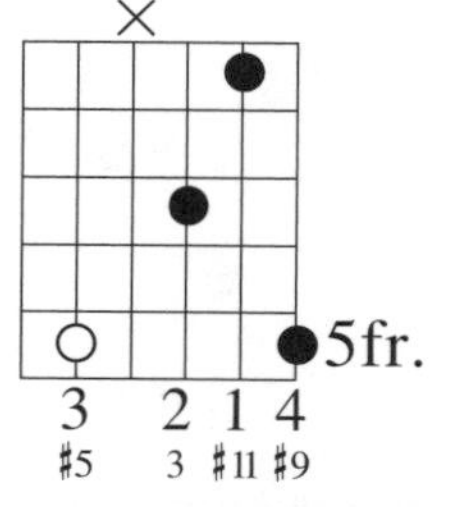

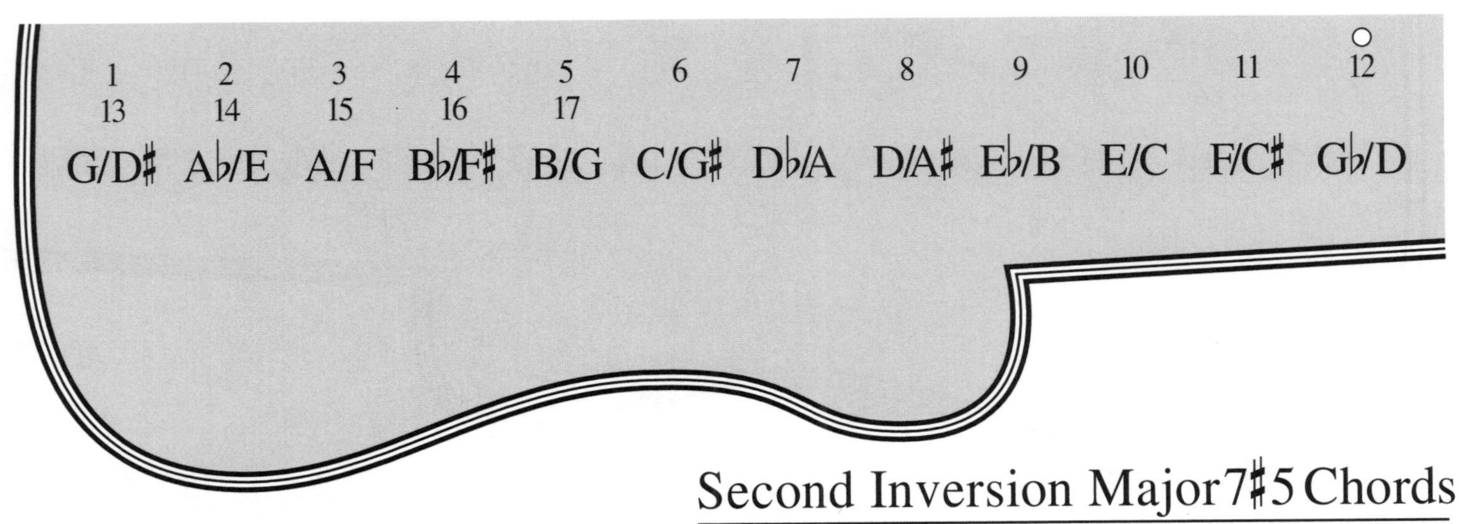

Second Inversion Major7♯5 Chords

G♭maj7♯5/D G♭maj9♯5/D G♭maj13♯11♯5/D

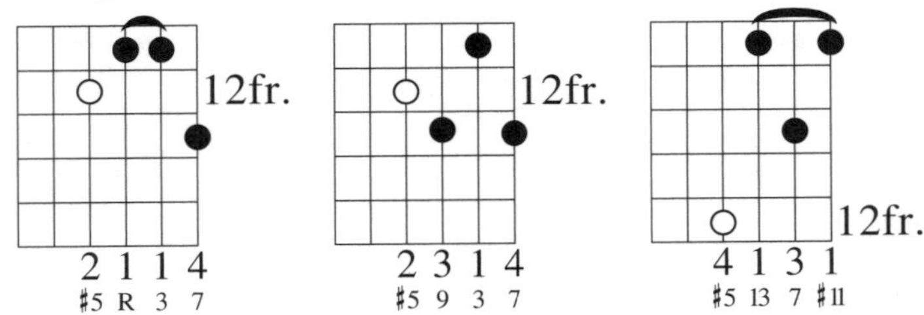

G♭maj7♯5/D G♭maj9♯5♯11/D G♭maj13♯11♯5/D

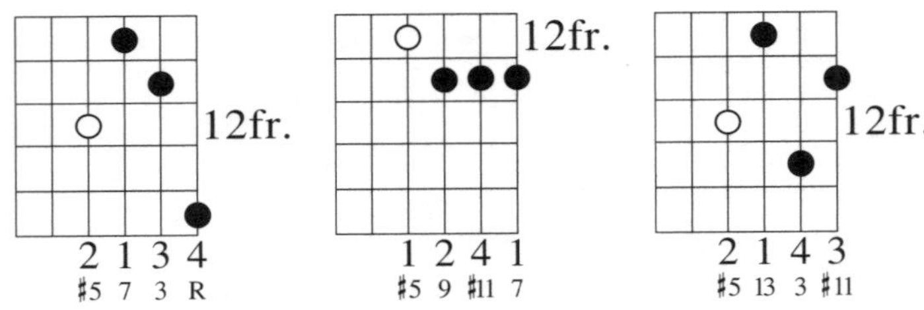

G♭maj7♯5♯11/D G♭maj9♯5♯11/D G♭maj7♯9♯5/D

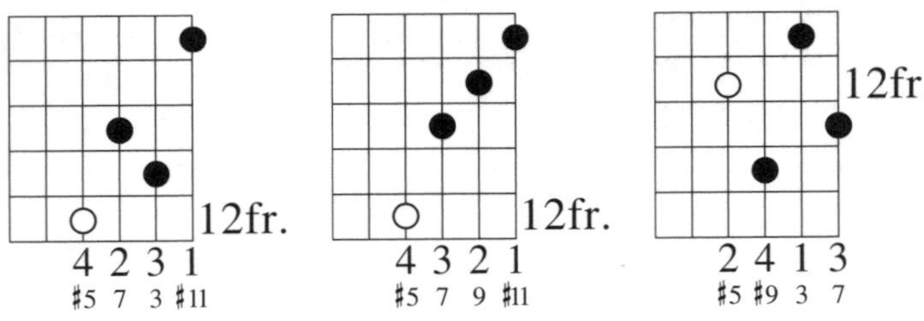

G♭maj7♯5♯11/D G♭maj13♯5/D G♭maj7♯9♯5/D

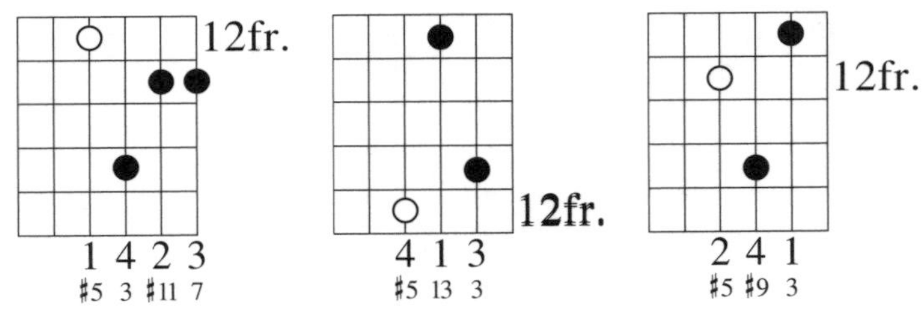

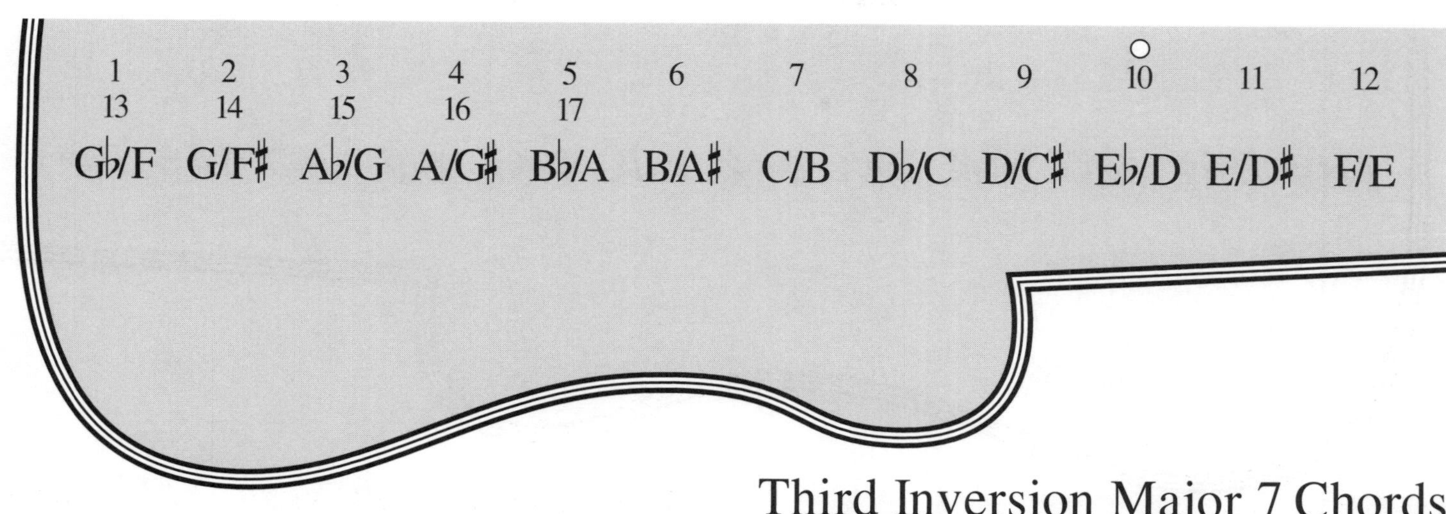

Third Inversion Major 7 Chords

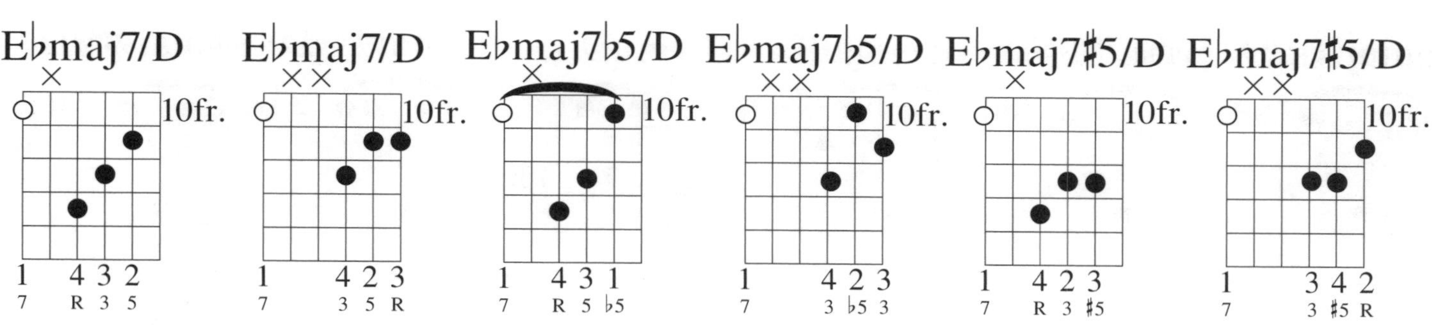

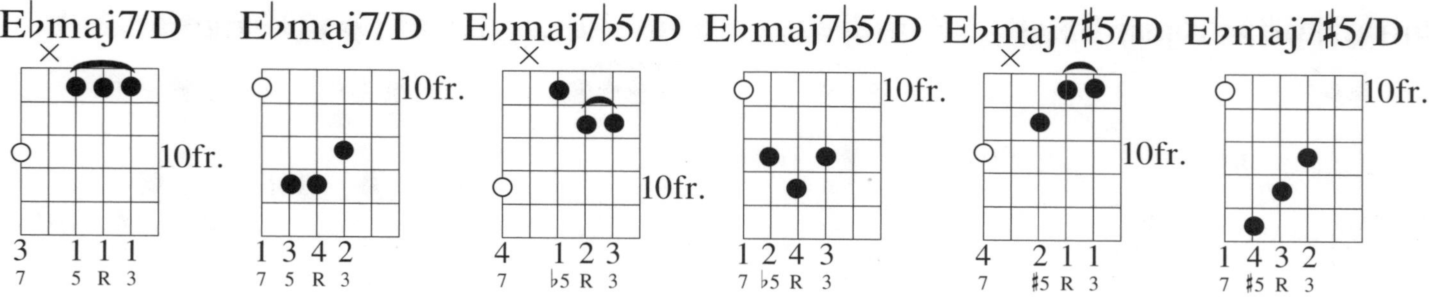

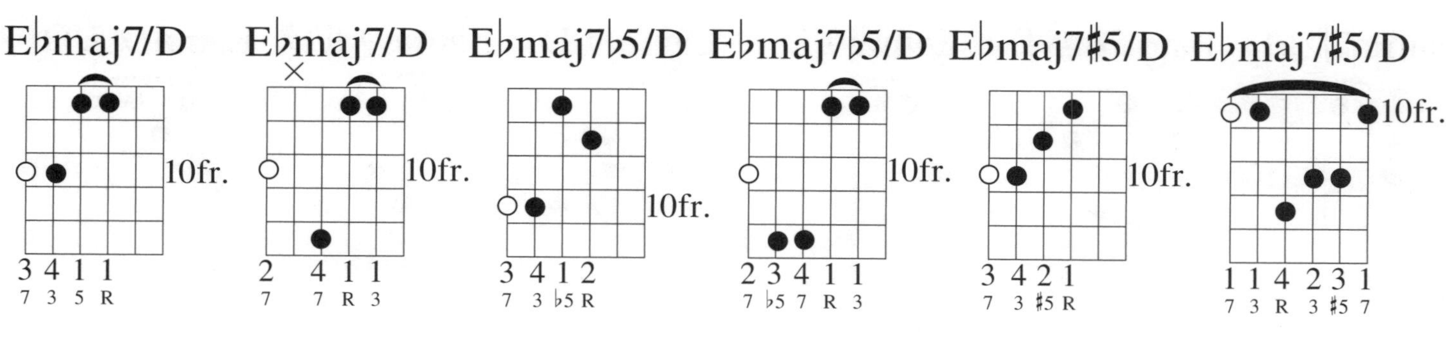

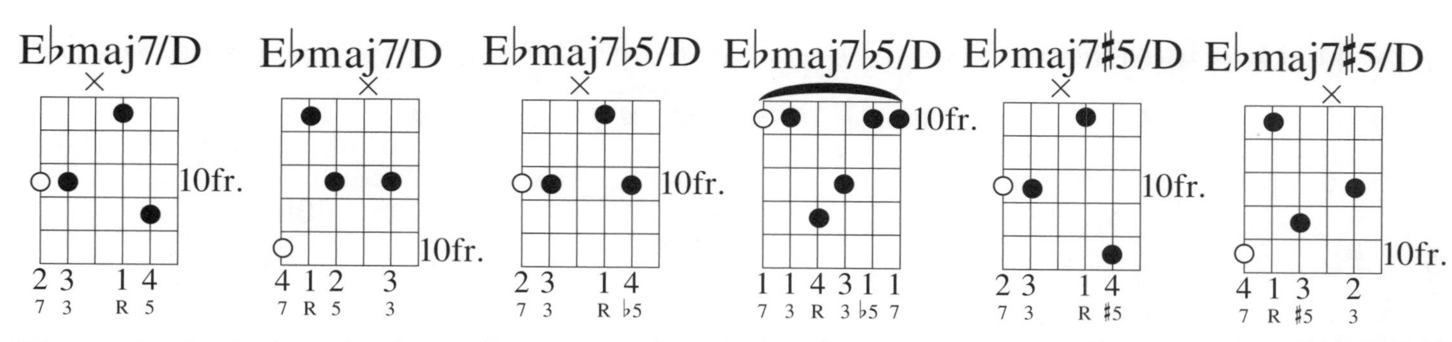

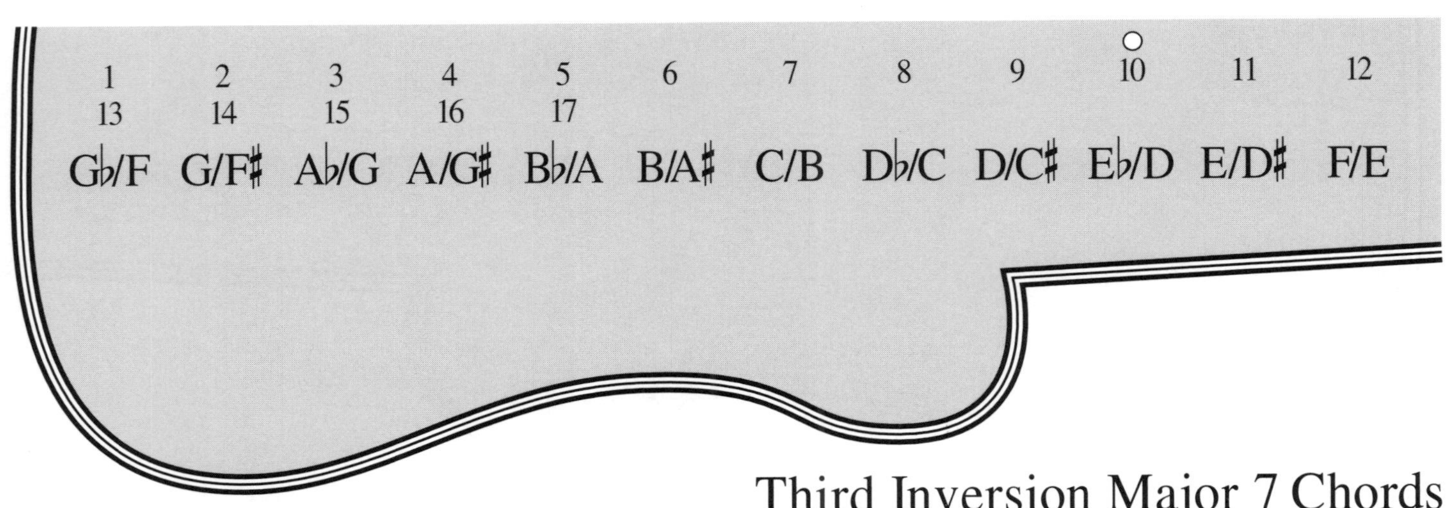

Third Inversion Major 7 Chords

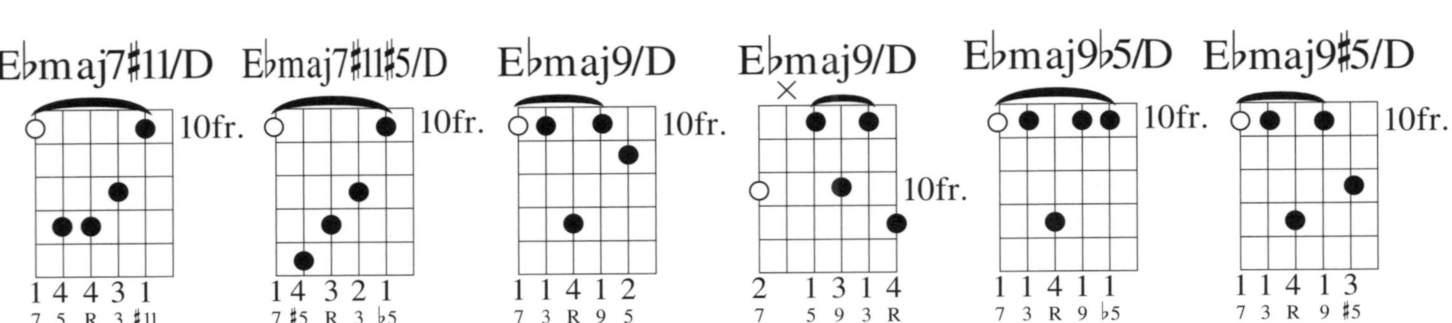

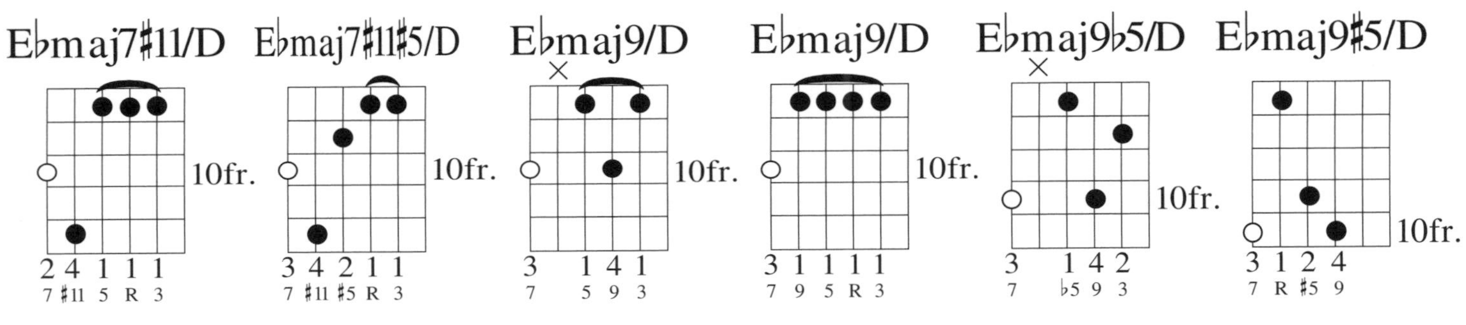

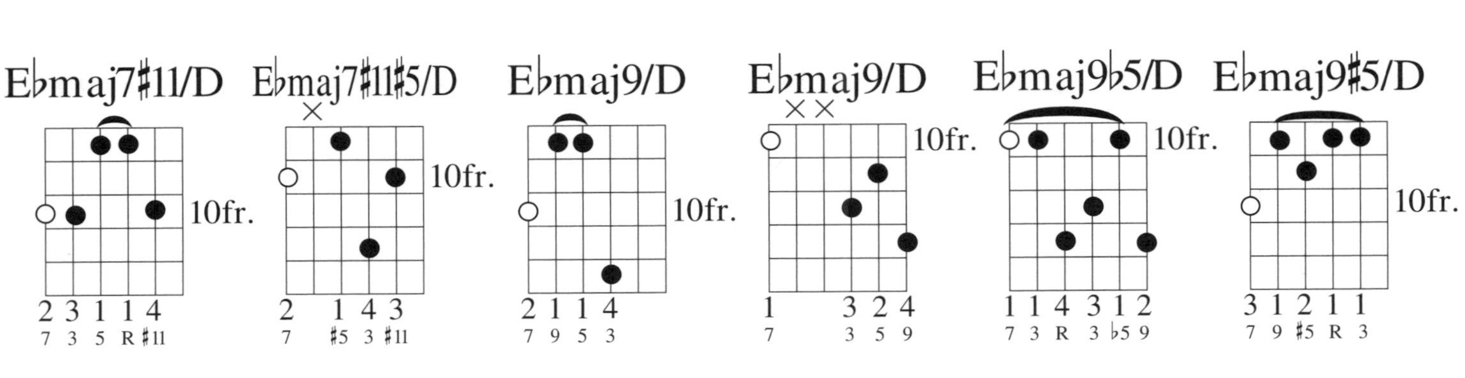

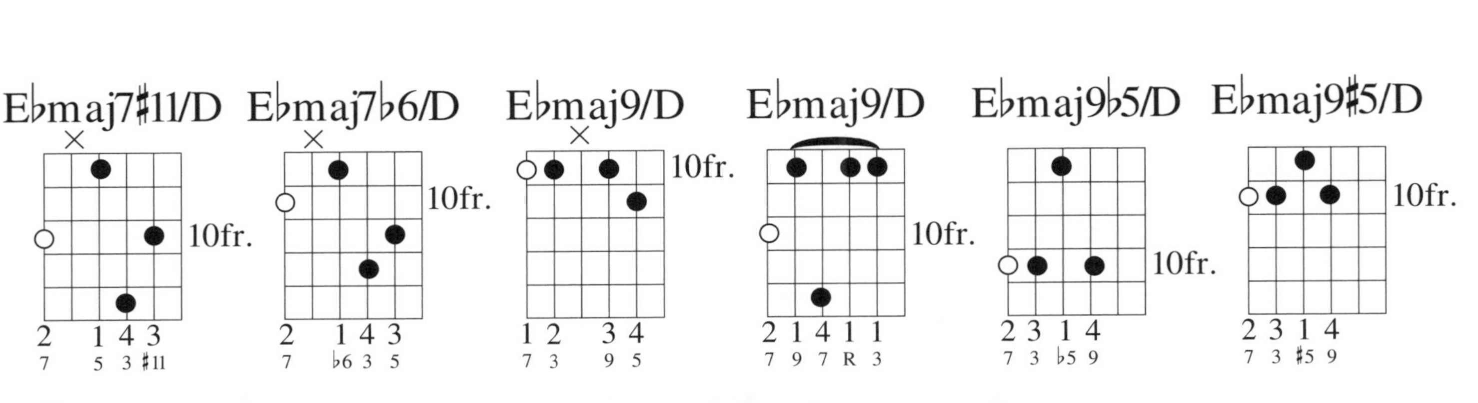

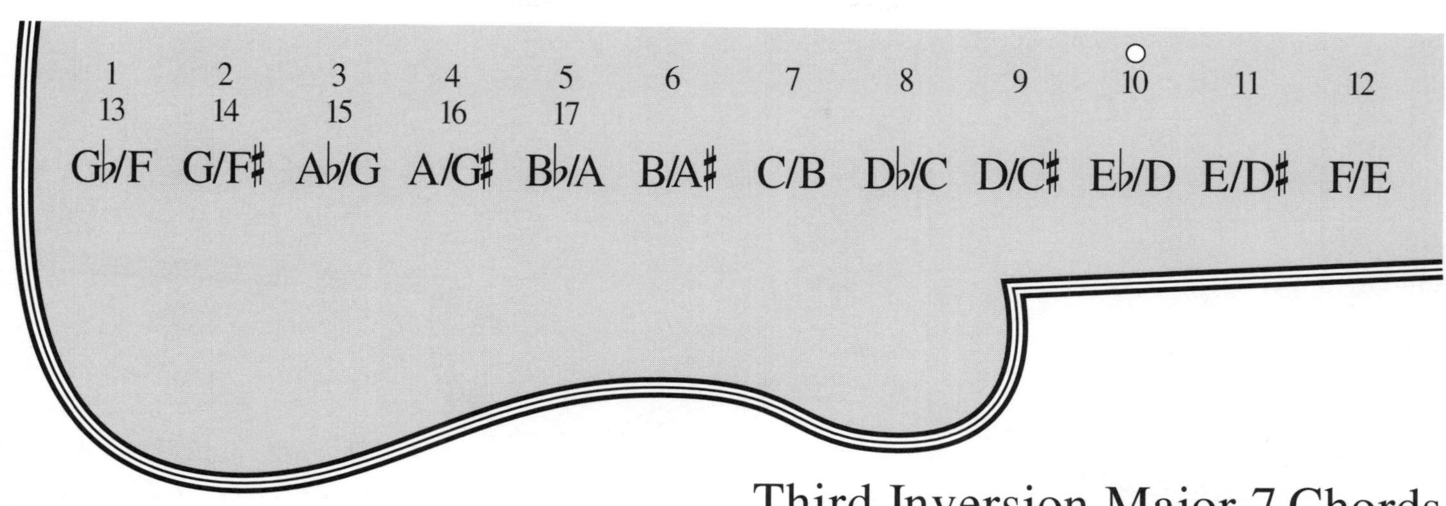

Third Inversion Major 7 Chords

E♭maj9♯11♯5/D E♭maj9♭6/D E♭maj13/D E♭maj13♯11/D E♭maj13♯5/D E♭maj7♯9/D

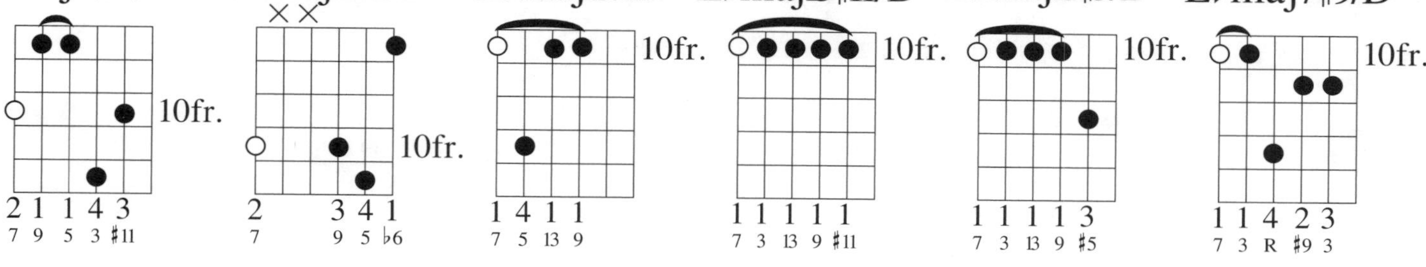

E♭maj9♯11♯5/D E♭maj9♭6/D E♭maj13/D E♭maj13♯11/D E♭maj13♯5/D E♭maj7♯9/D

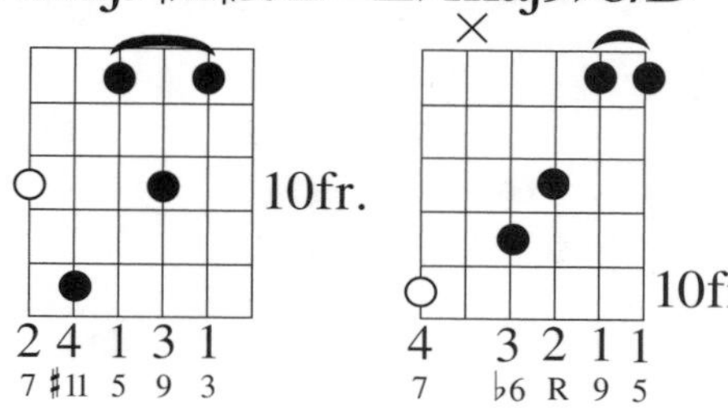

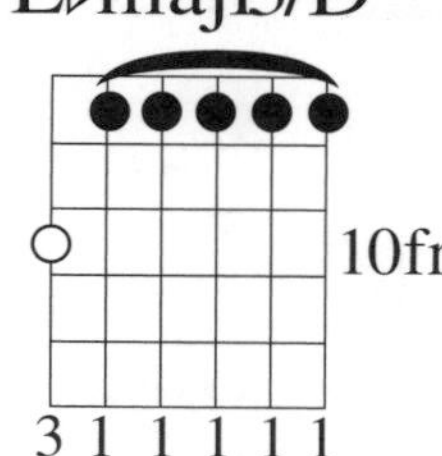

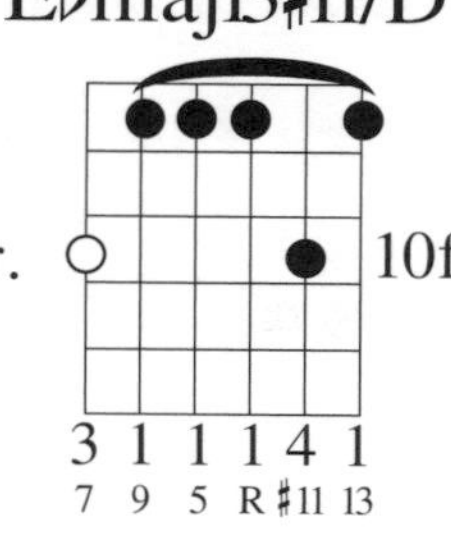

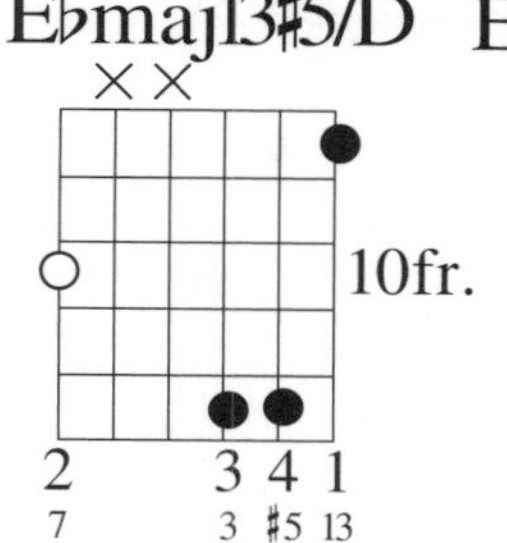

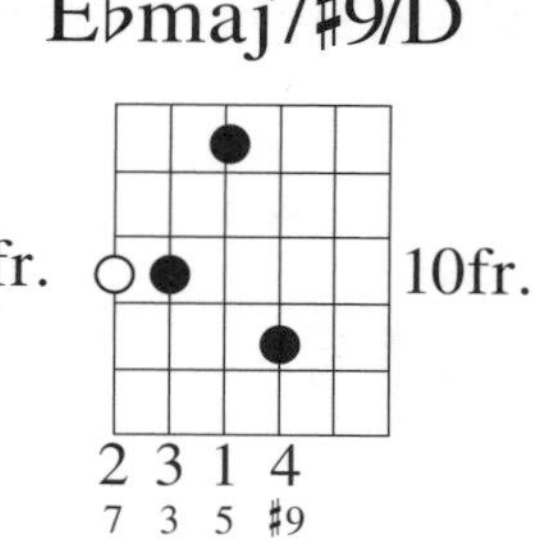

E♭maj9♯11♯5/D E♭maj13/D E♭maj13/D E♭maj13♯11/D E♭maj13♯5/D E♭maj7♯9♯11/D

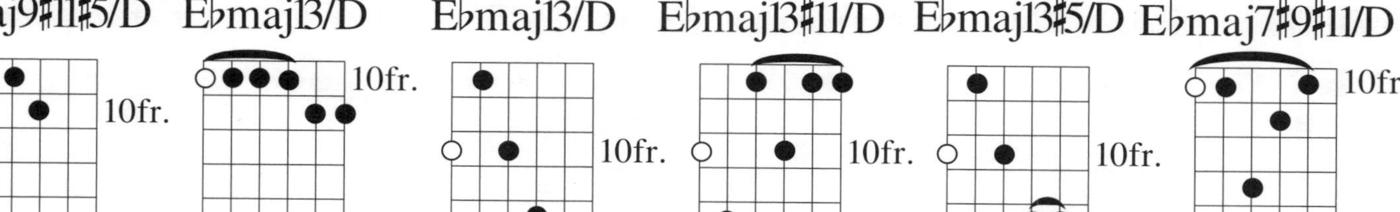

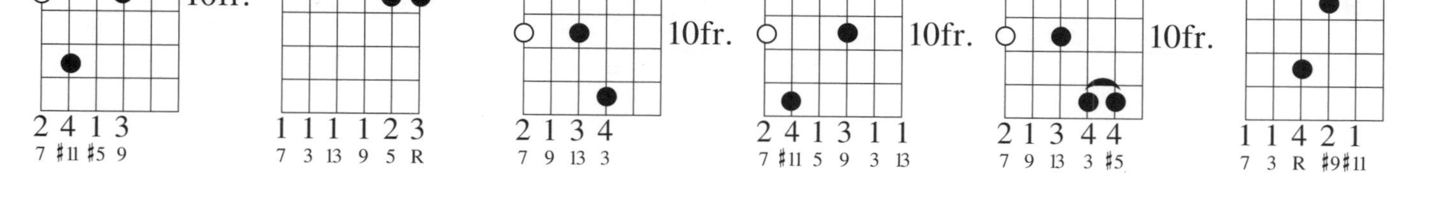

E♭maj9♯11♯5/D E♭maj13/D E♭maj13/D E♭maj13♯11/D E♭maj13♯5♯11/D E♭maj7♯9♯5/D

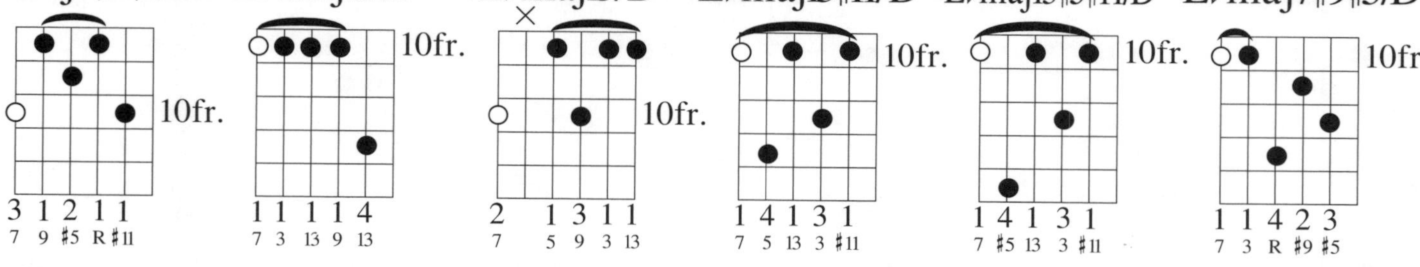

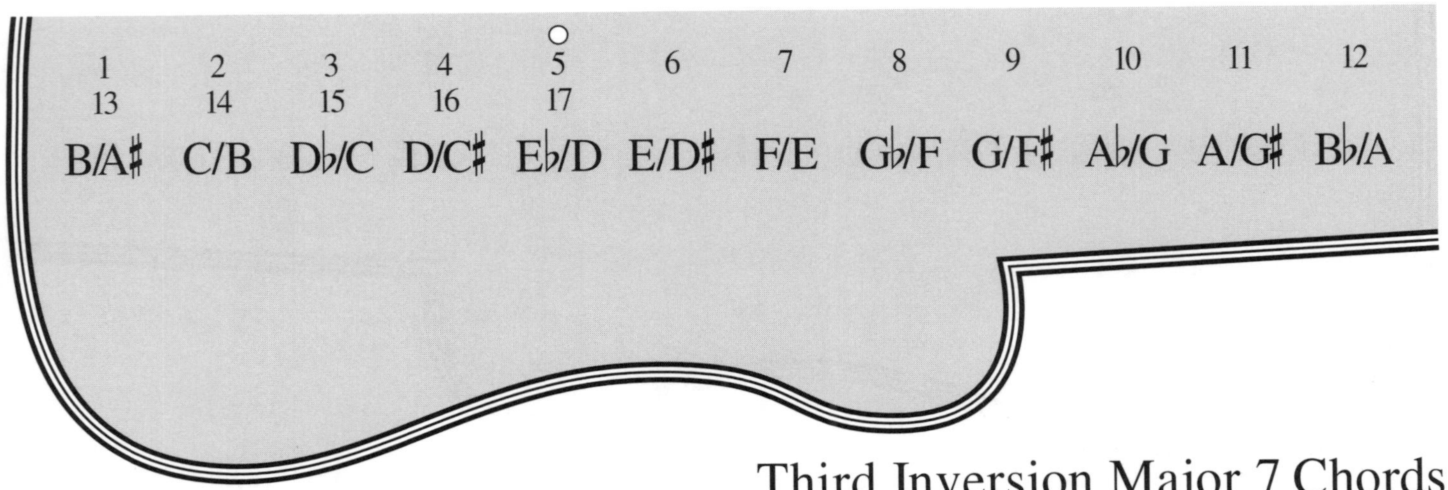

1	2	3	4	5	6	7	8	9	10	11	12
13	14	15	16	17							
B/A♯	C/B	D♭/C	D/C♯	E♭/D	E/D♯	F/E	G♭/F	G/F♯	A♭/G	A/G♯	B♭/A

Third Inversion Major 7 Chords

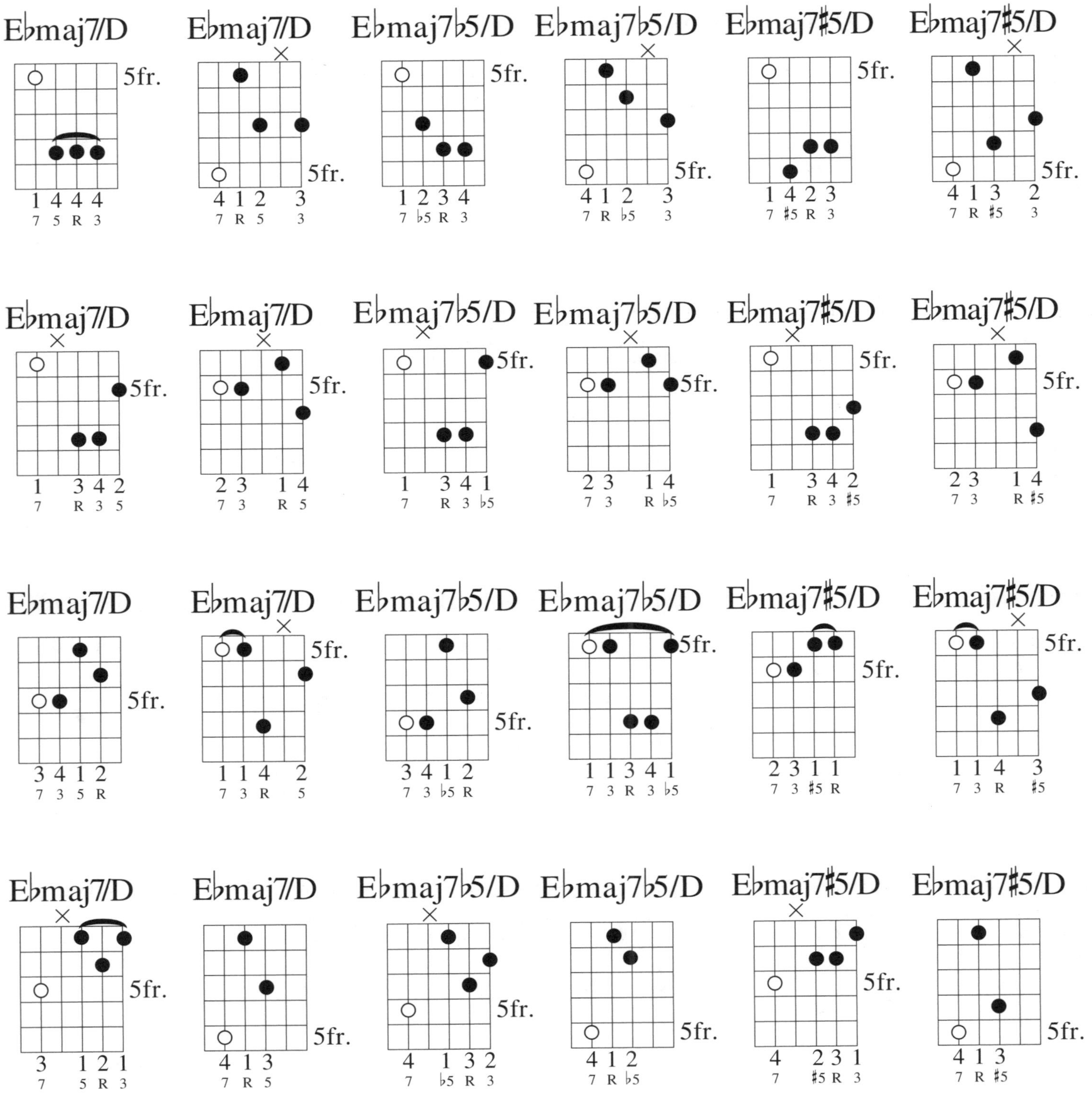

E♭maj7/D
5fr.
1 4 4 4
7 5 R 3

E♭maj7/D
5fr.
4 1 2 3
7 R 5 3

E♭maj7♭5/D
5fr.
1 2 3 4
7 ♭5 R 3

E♭maj7♭5/D
5fr.
4 1 2 3
7 R ♭5 3

E♭maj7♯5/D
5fr.
1 4 2 3
7 ♯5 R 3

E♭maj7♯5/D
5fr.
4 1 3 2
7 R ♯5 3

E♭maj7/D
5fr.
1 3 4 2
7 R 3 5

E♭maj7/D
5fr.
2 3 1 4
7 3 R 5

E♭maj7♭5/D
5fr.
1 3 4 1
7 R 3 ♭5

E♭maj7♭5/D
5fr.
2 3 1 4
7 3 R ♭5

E♭maj7♯5/D
5fr.
1 3 4 2
7 R 3 ♯5

E♭maj7♯5/D
5fr.
2 3 1 4
7 3 R ♯5

E♭maj7/D
5fr.
3 4 1 2
7 3 5 R

E♭maj7/D
5fr.
1 1 4 2
7 3 R 5

E♭maj7♭5/D
5fr.
3 4 1 2
7 3 ♭5 R

E♭maj7♭5/D
5fr.
1 1 3 4 1
7 3 R 3 ♭5

E♭maj7♯5/D
5fr.
2 3 1 1
7 3 ♯5 R

E♭maj7♯5/D
5fr.
1 1 4 3
7 3 R ♯5

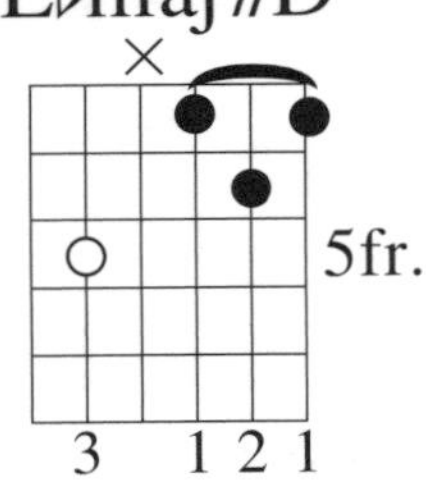

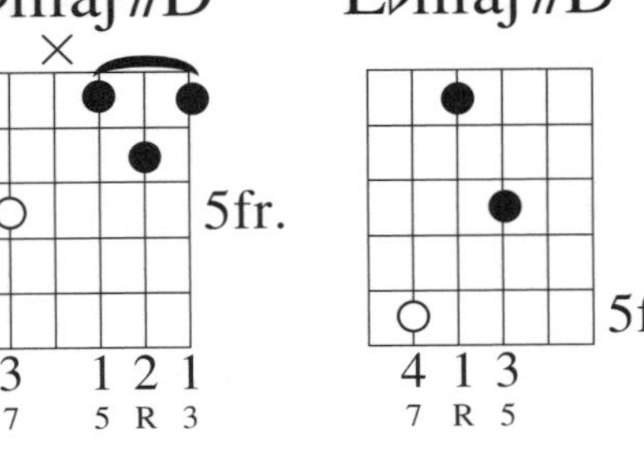

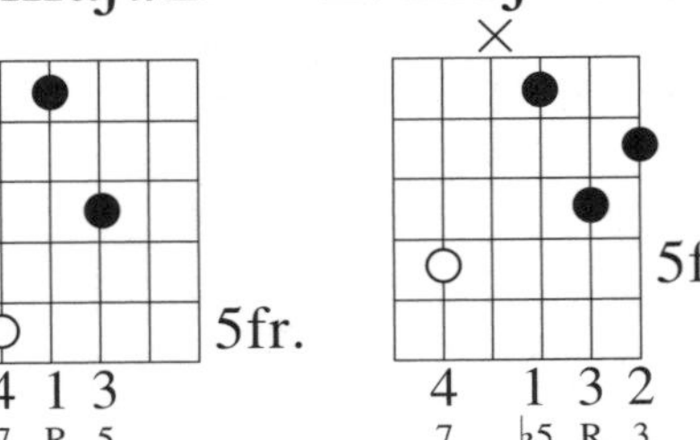

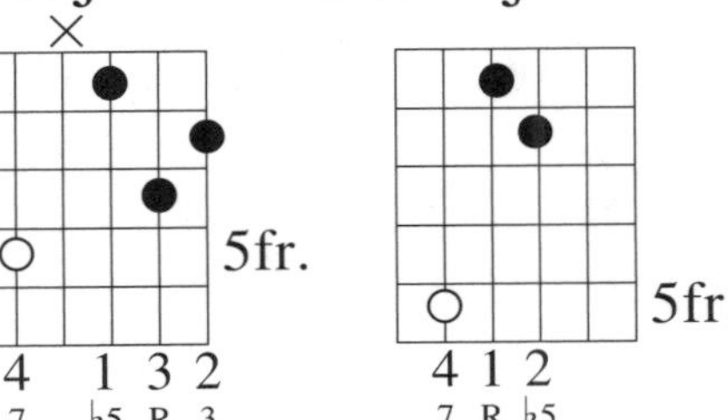

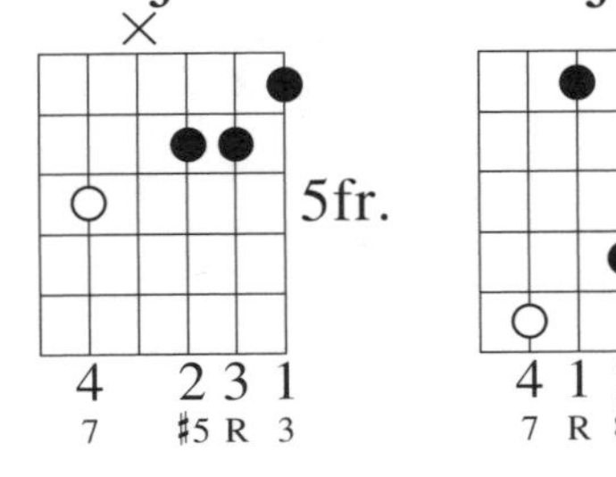

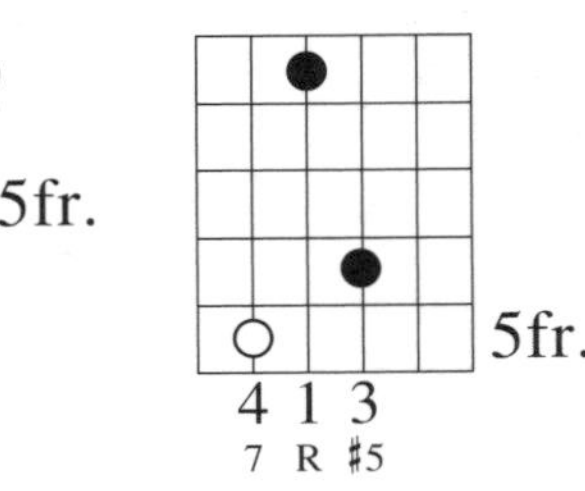

1 13	2 14	3 15	4 16	5 17	6	7	8	9	10	11	12
B/A♯	C/B	D♭/C	D/C♯	E♭/D	E/D♯	F/E	G♭/F	G/F♯	A♭/G	A/G♯	B♭/A

Third Inversion Major 7 Chords

E♭maj7♯11/D
5fr.
1 2 3 4 1
7 5 R 3 ♯11

E♭maj7♯11♯5/D
5fr.
2 3 1 4
7 ♯11 ♯5 3

E♭maj9/D
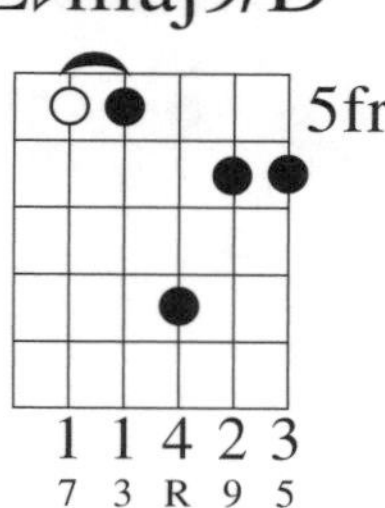
5fr.
1 1 4 2 3
7 3 R 9 5

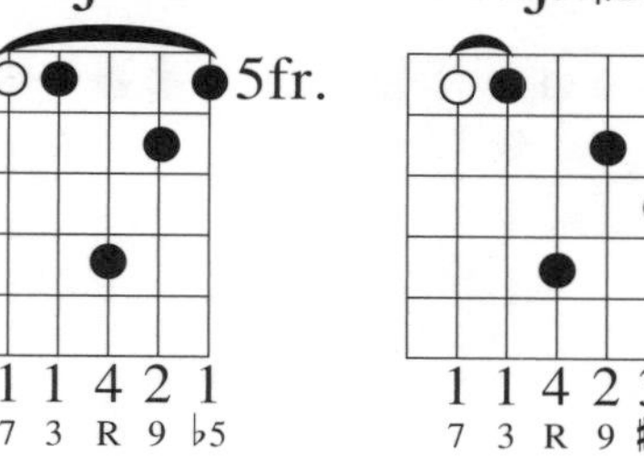
E♭maj9♭5/D
5fr.
1 1 4 2 1
7 3 R 9 ♭5

E♭maj9♯5/D
5fr.
1 1 4 2 3
7 3 R 9 ♯5

E♭maj9♯5/D
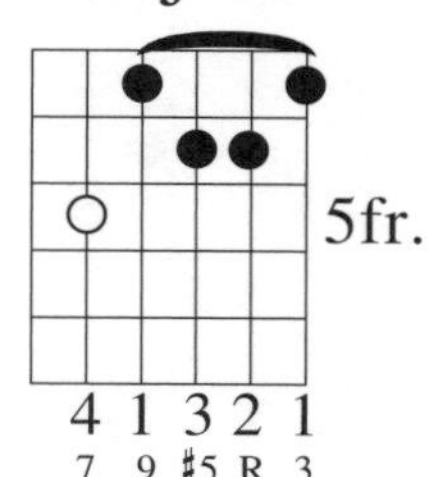
5fr.
4 1 3 2 1
7 9 ♯5 R 3

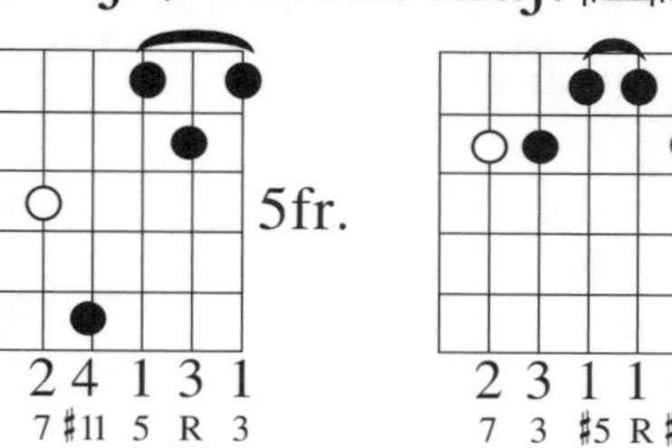
E♭maj7♯11/D
5fr.
2 4 1 3 1
7 ♯11 5 R 3

E♭maj7♯11♯5/D
5fr.
2 3 1 1 4
7 3 ♯5 R ♯11

E♭maj9/D
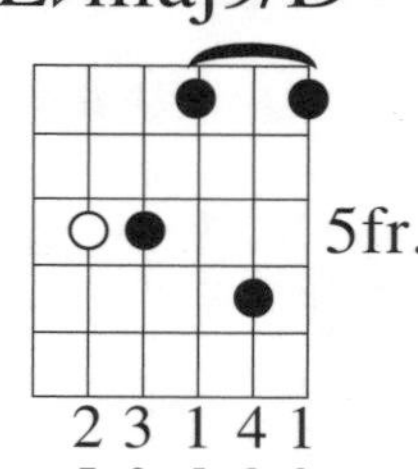
5fr.
2 3 1 4 1
7 3 5 9 3

E♭maj9♭5/D
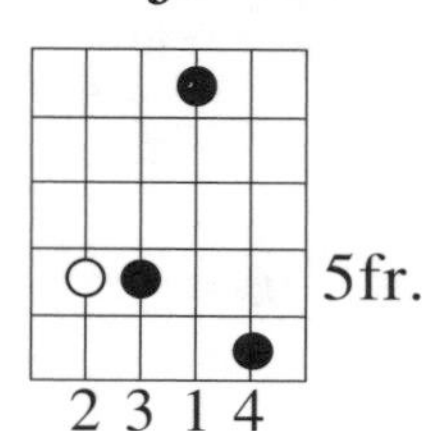
5fr.
2 3 1 4
7 3 ♭5 9

E♭maj9♯5/D
5fr.
2 3 1 4
7 3 ♯5 9

E♭maj9♯11/D
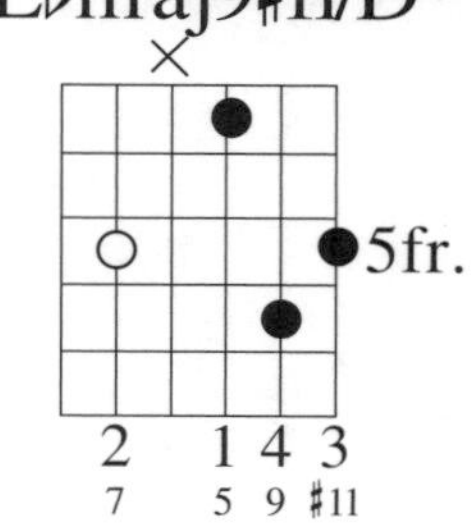
5fr.
2 1 4 3
7 5 9 ♯11

E♭maj7♯11/D
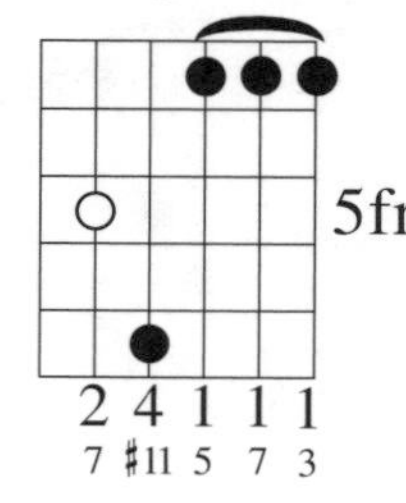
5fr.
2 4 1 1 1
7 ♯11 5 7 3

E♭maj7♭6/D
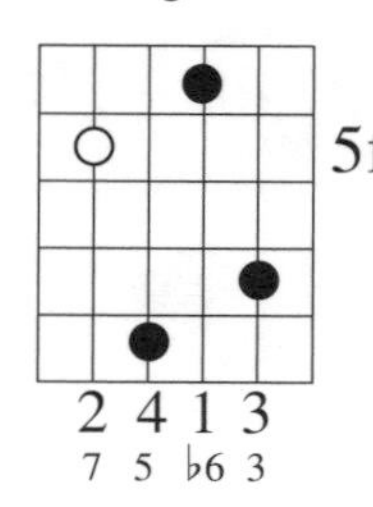
5fr.
2 4 1 3
7 5 ♭6 3

E♭maj9/D
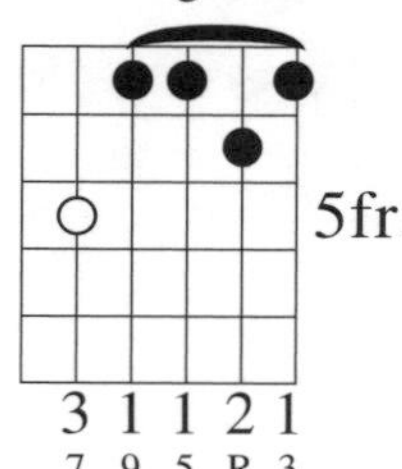
5fr.
3 1 1 2 1
7 9 5 R 3

E♭maj9♭5/D
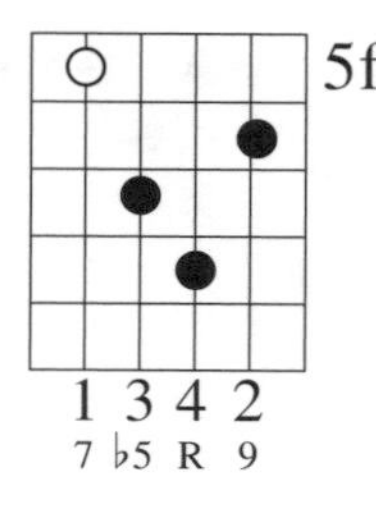
5fr.
1 3 4 2
7 ♭5 R 9

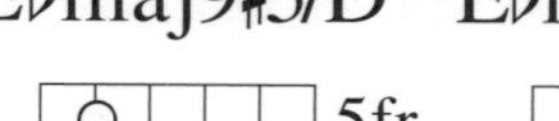
E♭maj9♯5/D
5fr.
1 4 3 2
7 ♯5 R 9

E♭maj9♯11/D
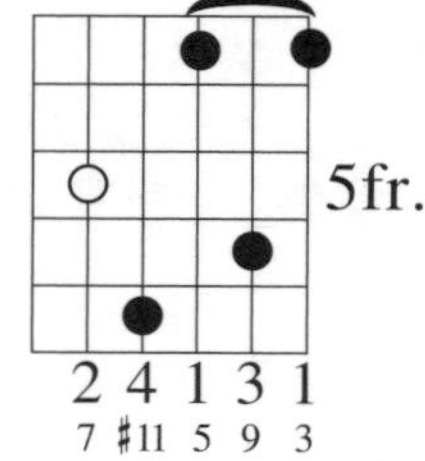
5fr.
2 4 1 3 1
7 ♯11 5 9 3

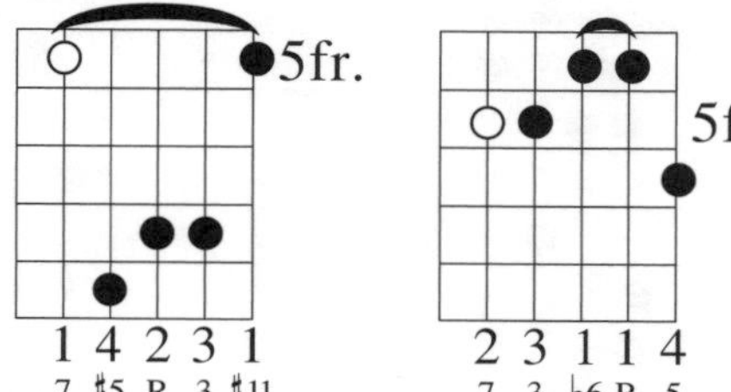
E♭maj7♯11♯5/D
5fr.
1 4 2 3 1
7 ♯5 R 3 ♯11

E♭maj7♭6/D
5fr.
2 3 1 1 4
7 3 ♭6 R 5

E♭maj9/D
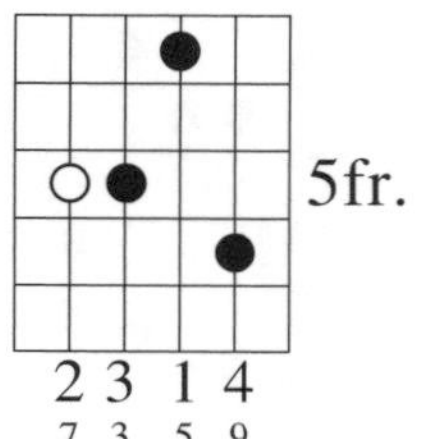
5fr.
2 3 1 4
7 3 5 9

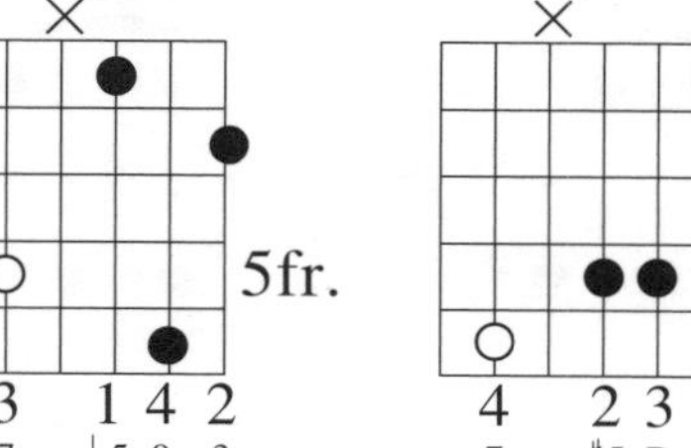
E♭maj9♭5/D
5fr.
3 1 4 2
7 ♭5 9 3

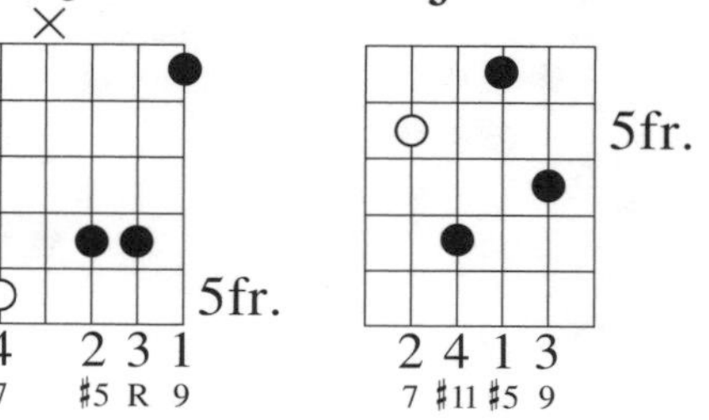
E♭maj9♯5/D
5fr.
4 2 3 1
7 ♯5 R 9

E♭maj9♯11♯5/D
5fr.
2 4 1 3
7 ♯11 ♯5 9

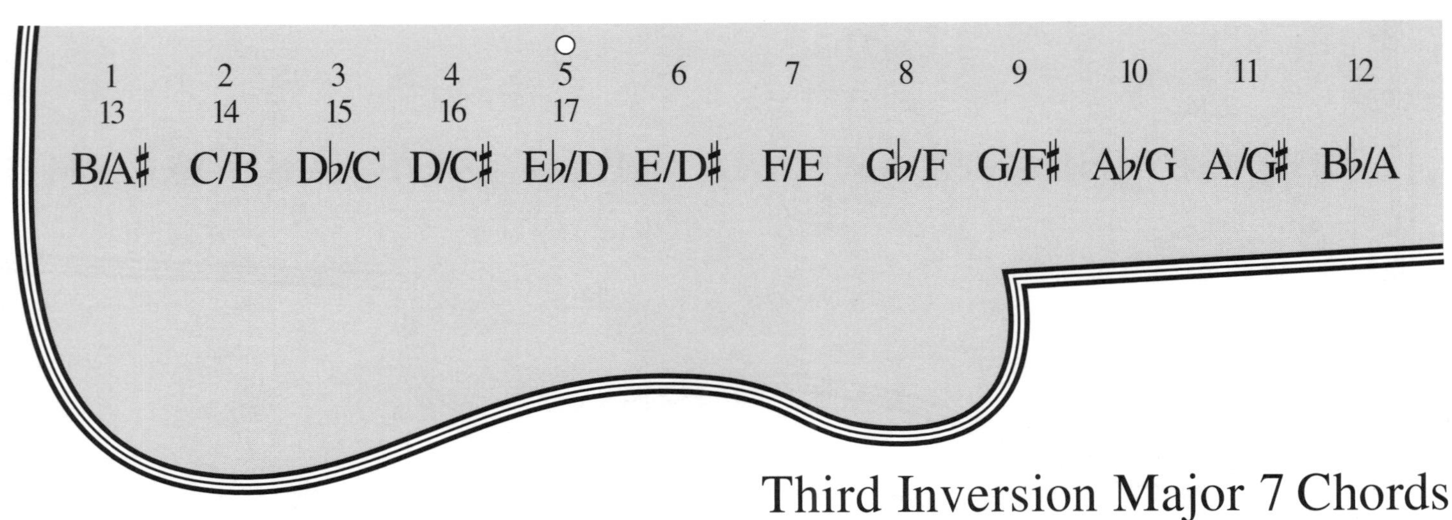

Third Inversion Major 7 Chords

E♭maj9♯11♯5/D

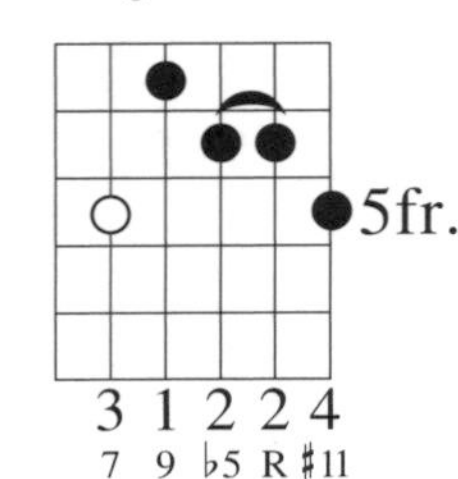

E♭maj13/D

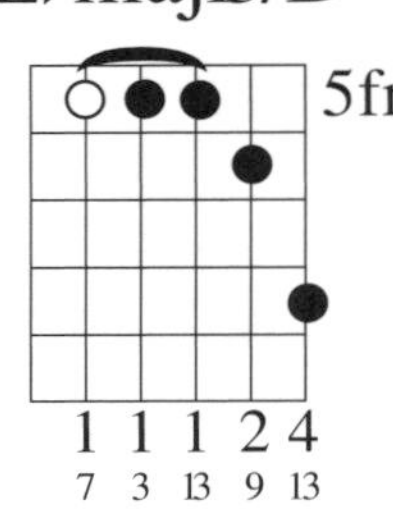

E♭maj13♯11/D

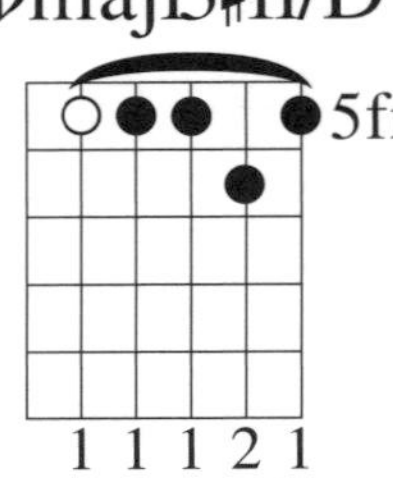

E♭maj13♯11/D

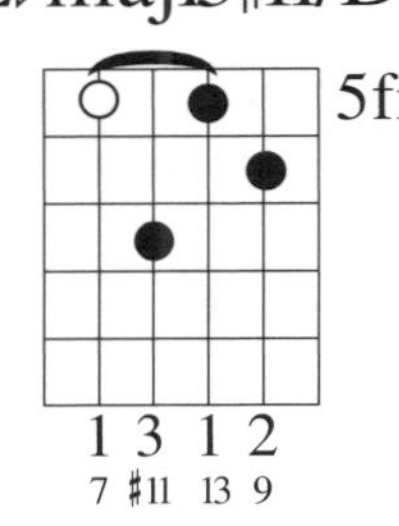

E♭maj13♯5/D

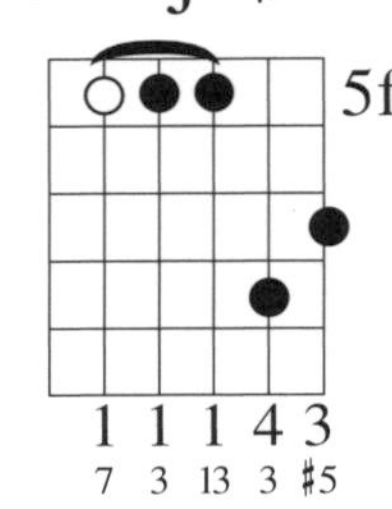

E♭maj13♯5/D

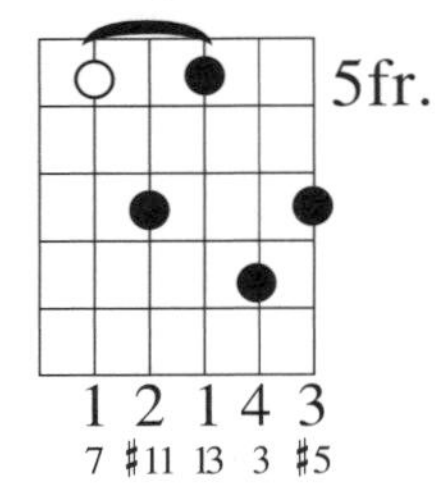

E♭maj9♭6/D

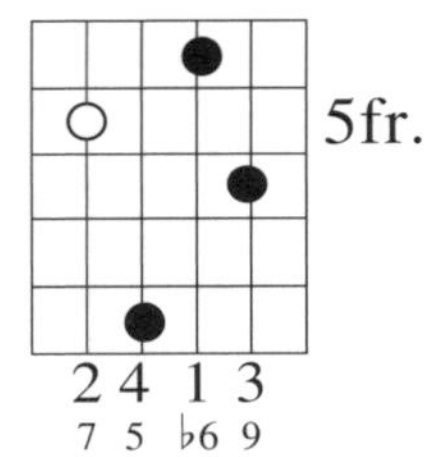

E♭maj13/D

E♭maj13♯11/D

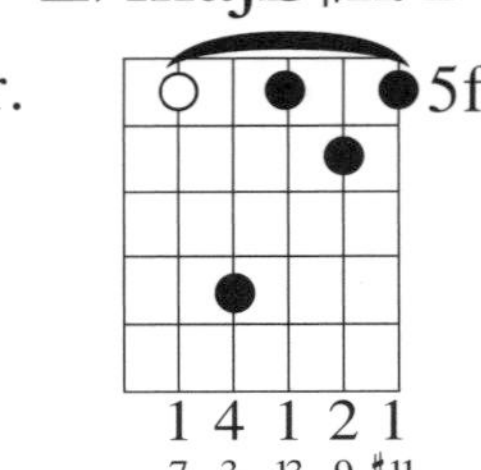

E♭maj13♯11/D

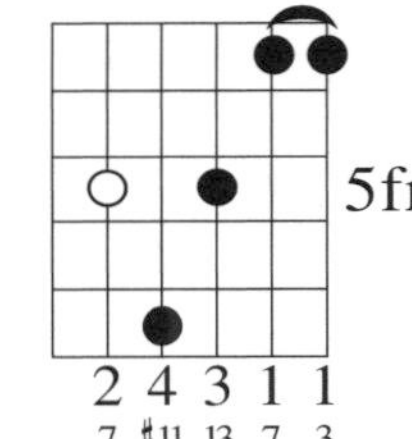

E♭maj13♯5/D

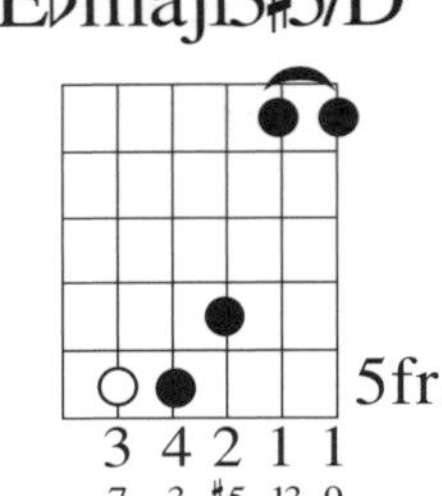

E♭maj7♯9/D

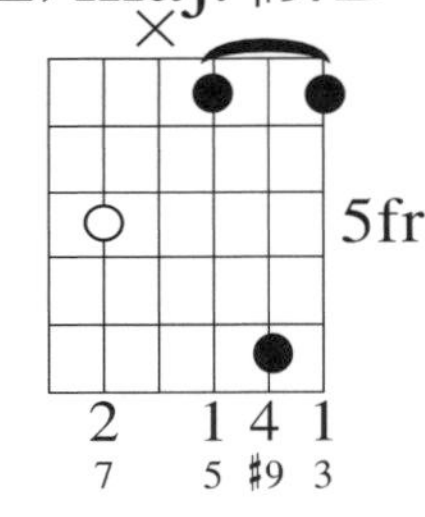

E♭maj9♭6/D

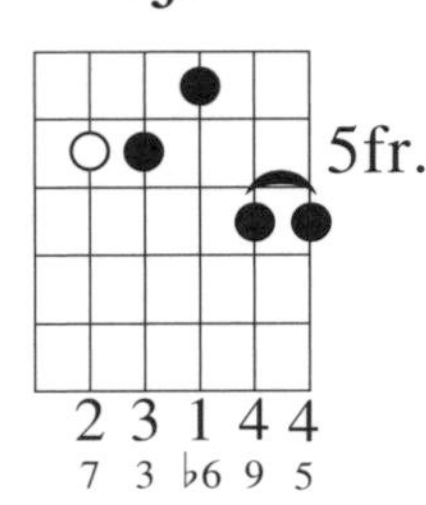

E♭maj13/D

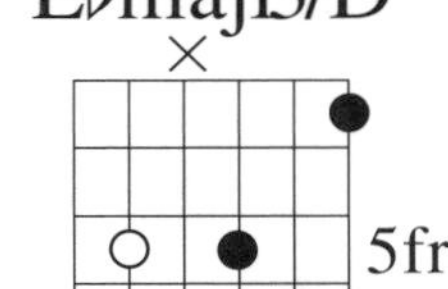

E♭maj13♯11/D

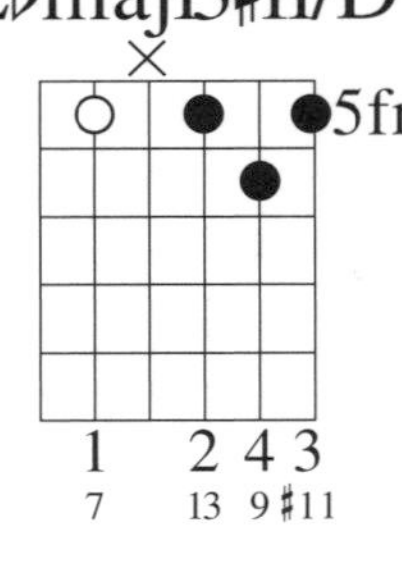

E♭maj13♯5/D

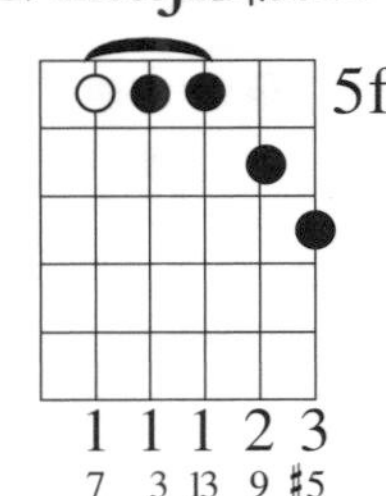

E♭maj13♯5/D

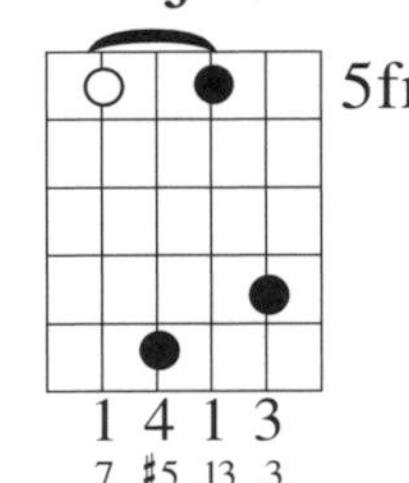

E♭maj7♯9♯11/D

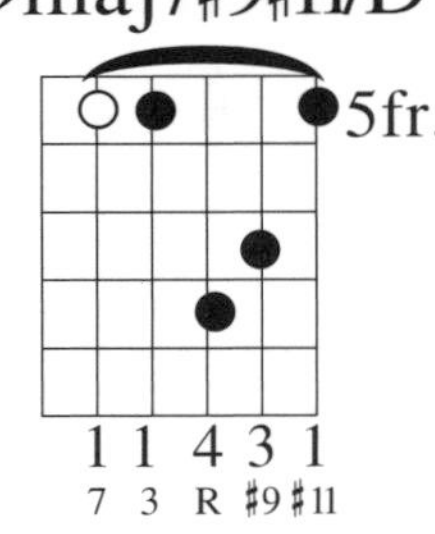

E♭maj13/D

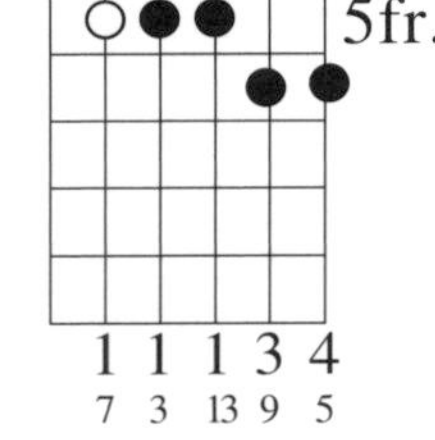

E♭maj13/D

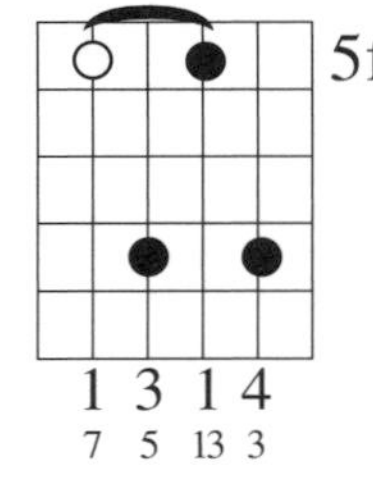

E♭maj13♯11/D

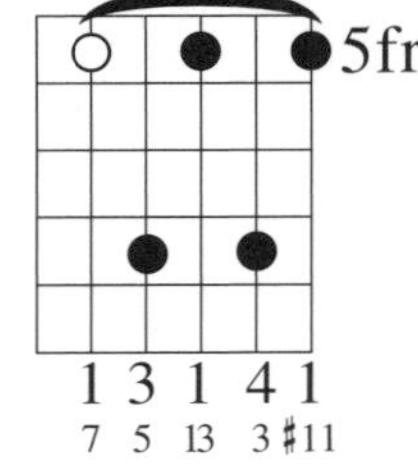

E♭maj13♯5/D

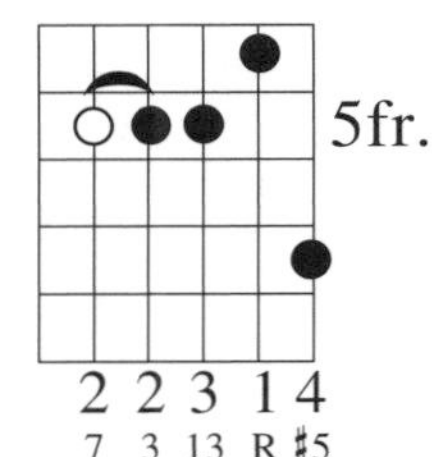

E♭maj13♯5♯11/D

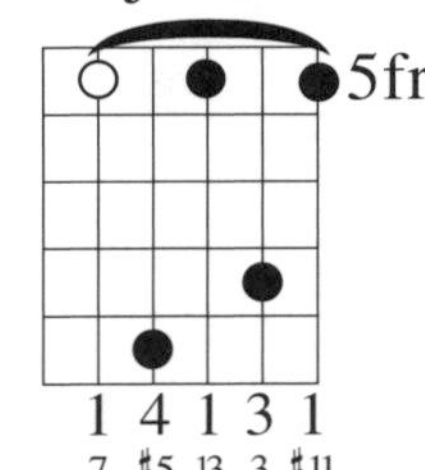

E♭maj7♯9♯5/D

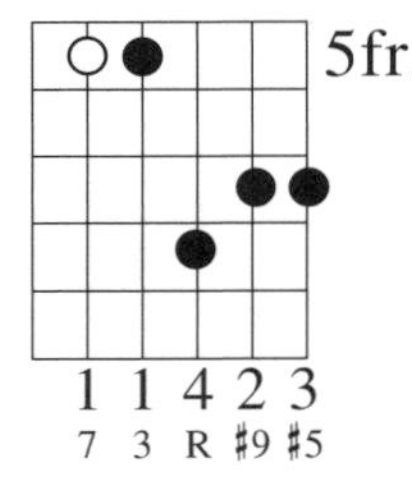

1	2	3	4	5	6	7	8	9	10	11	12
13	14	15	16	17							
E/D♯	F/E	G♭/F	G/F♯	A♭/G	A/G♯	B♭/A	B/A♯	C/B	D♭/C	D/C♯	E♭/D

Third Inversion Major 7 Chords

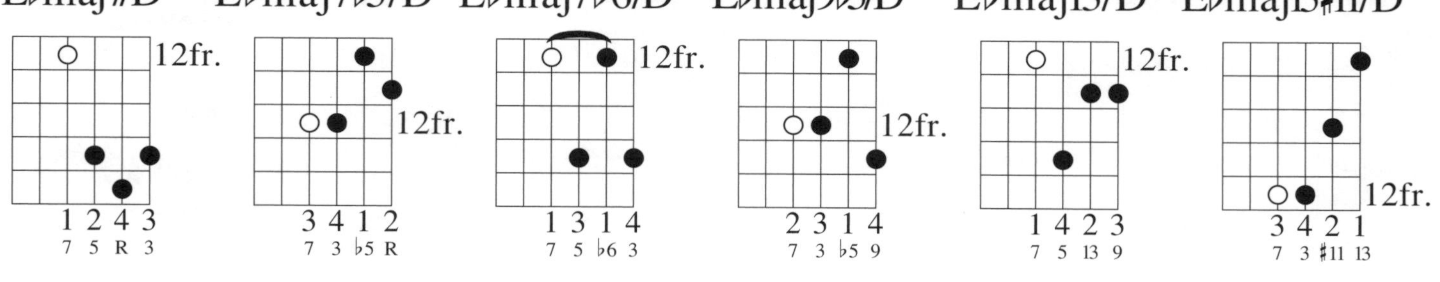

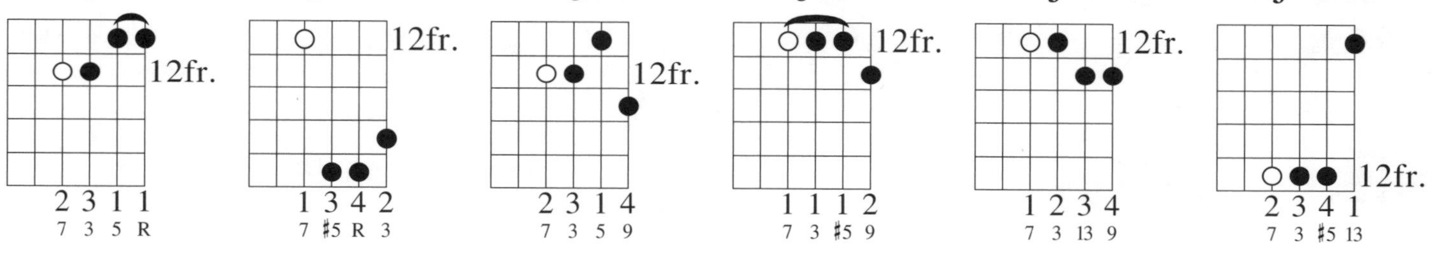

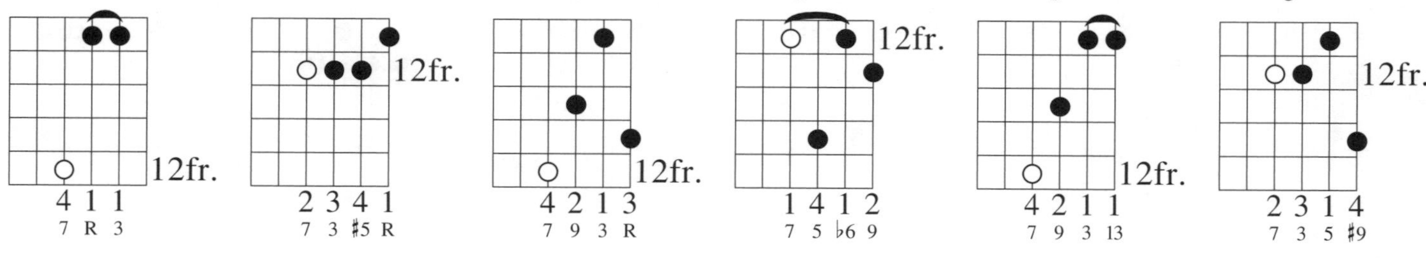

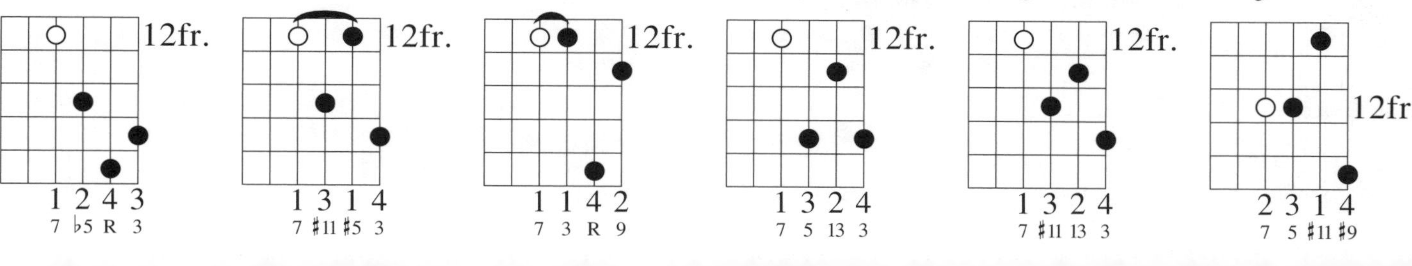

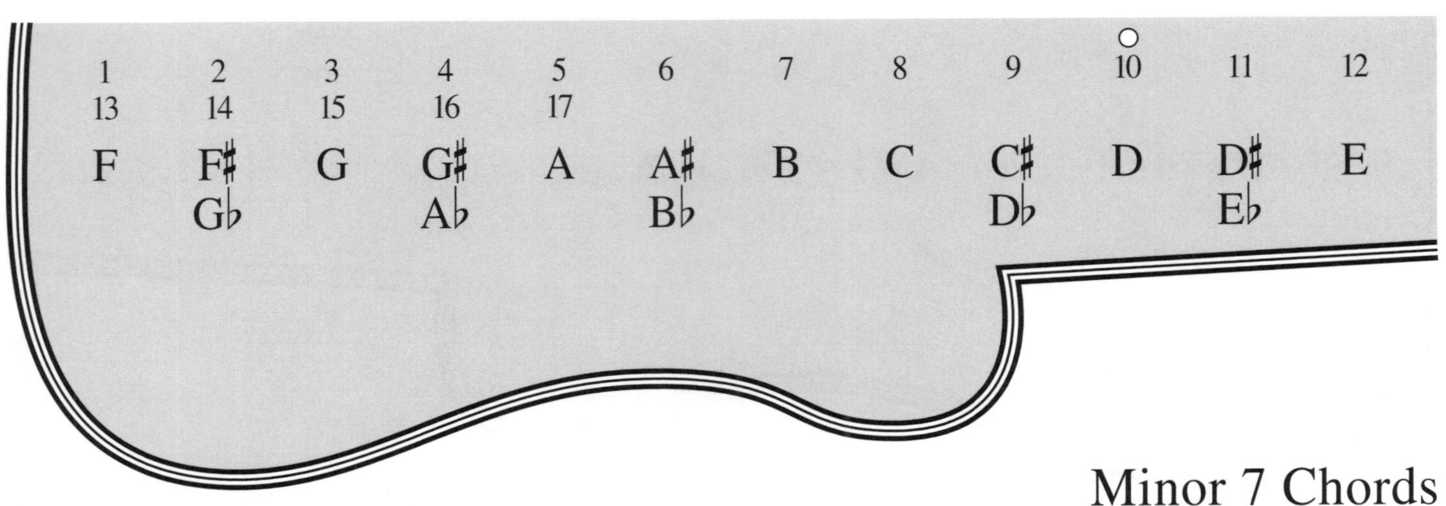

Minor 7 Chords

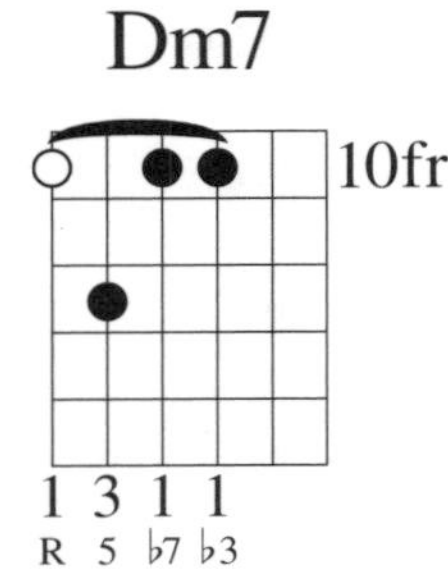

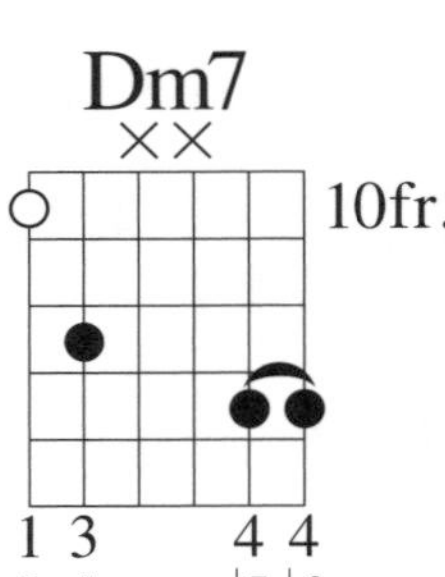

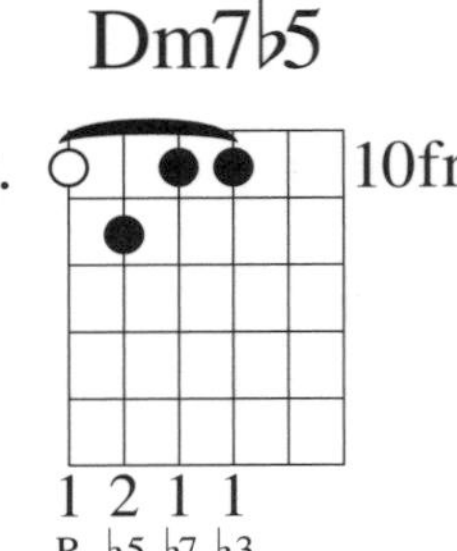

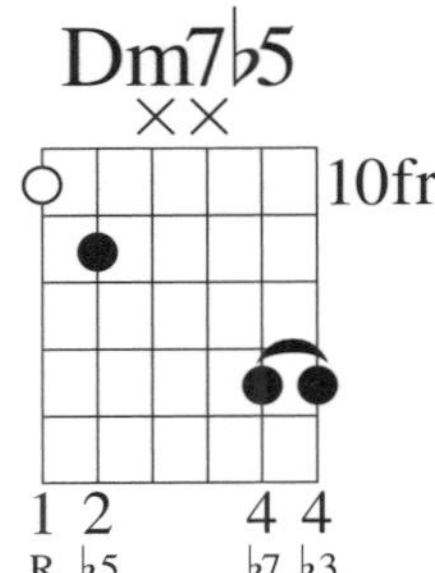

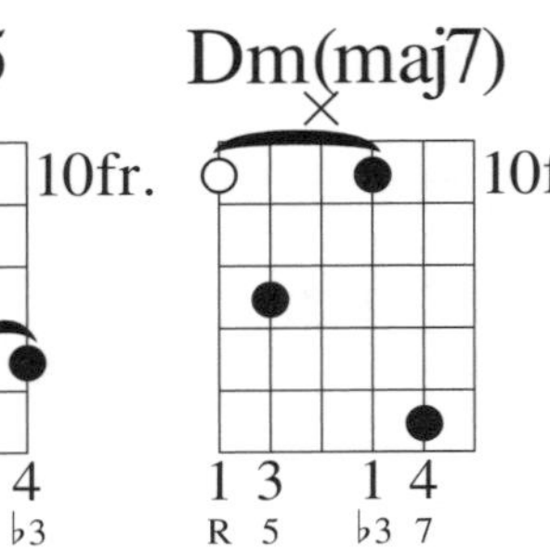

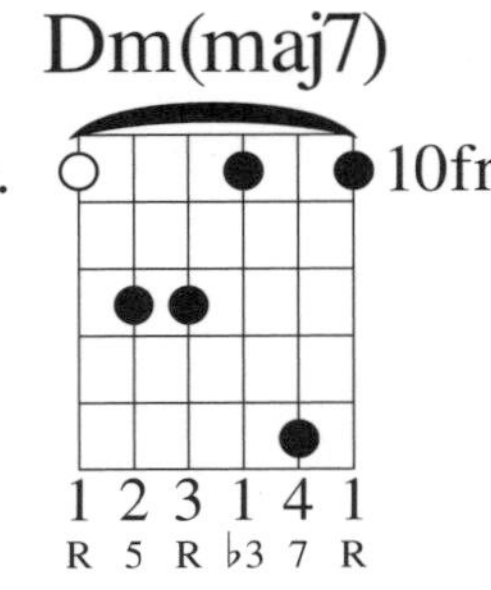

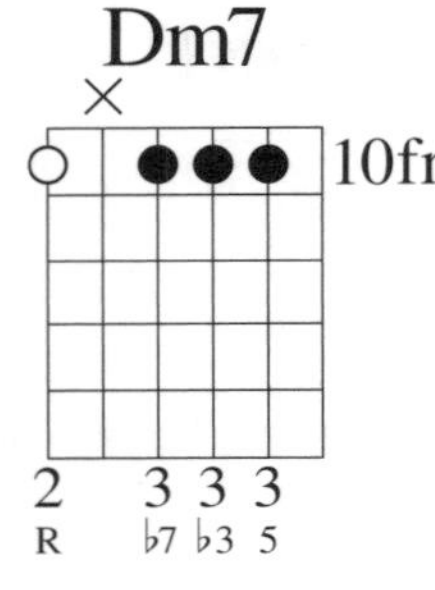

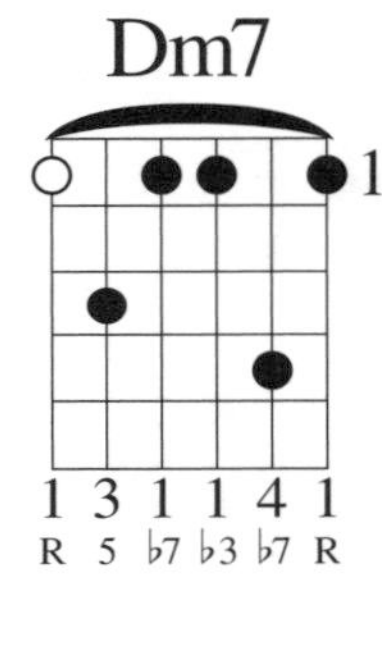

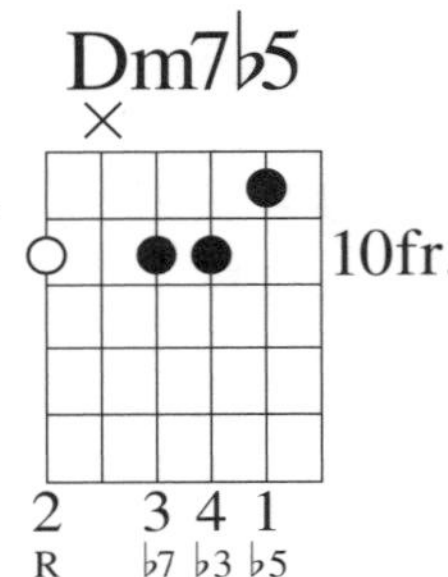

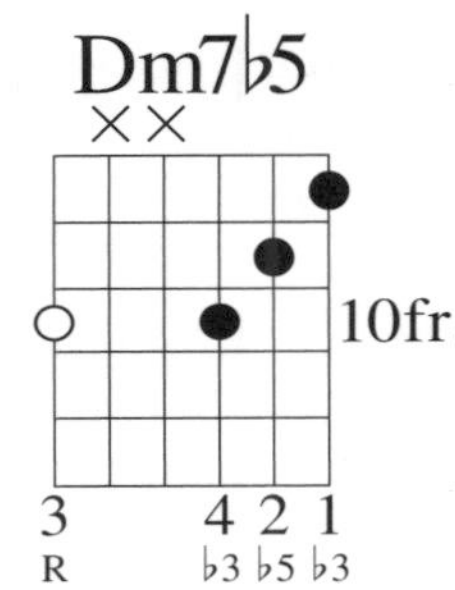

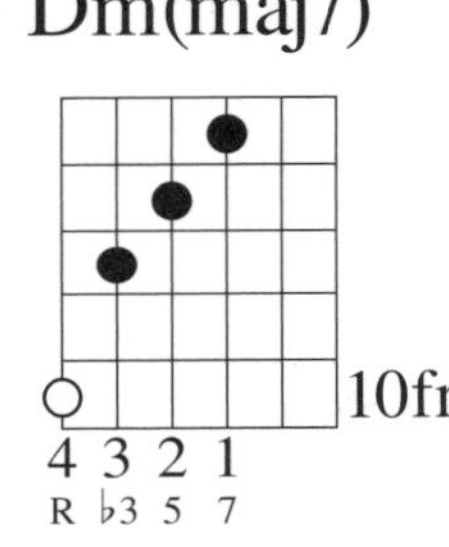

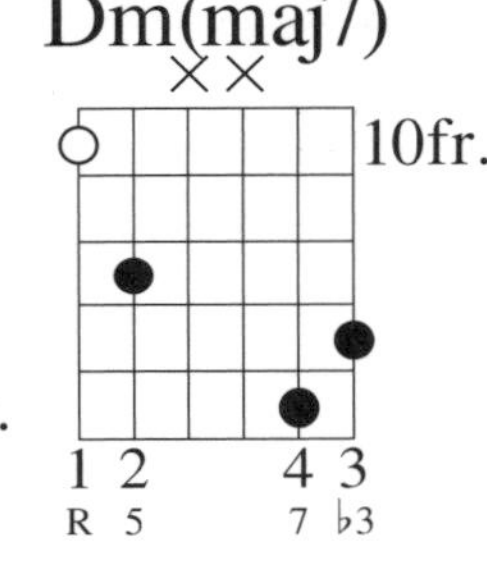

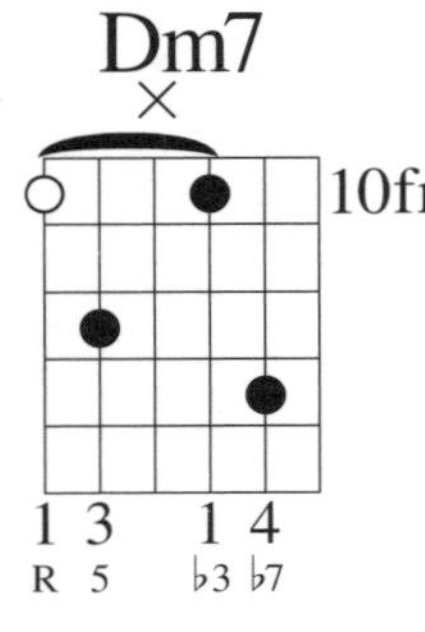

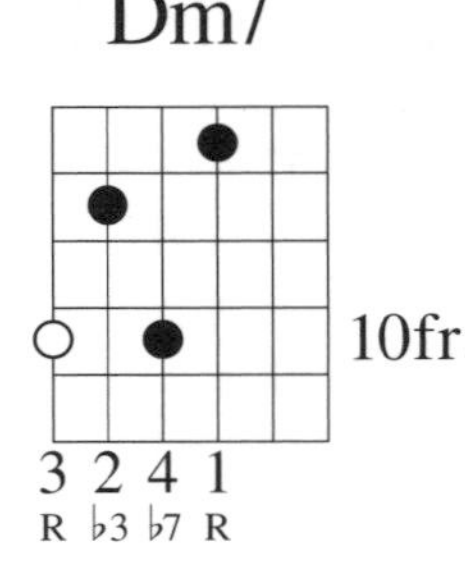

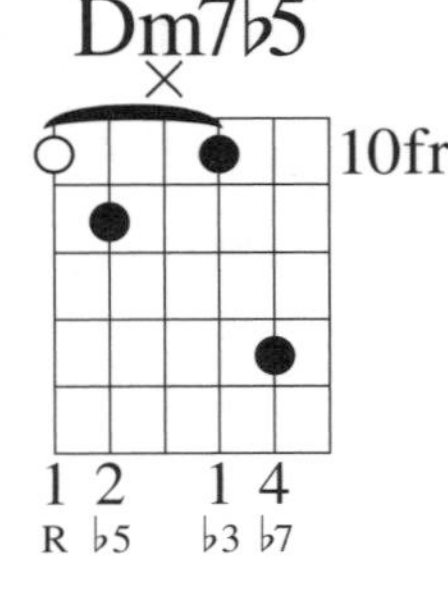

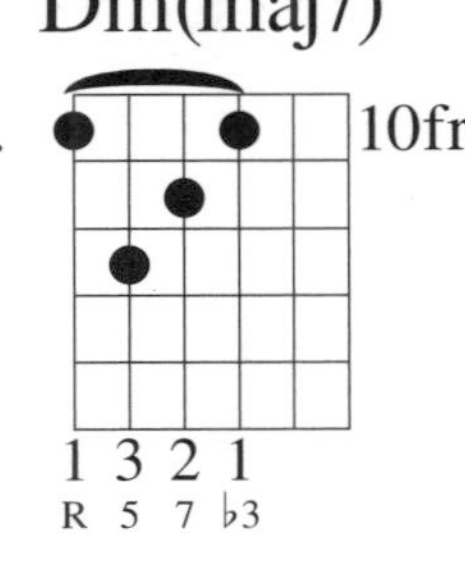

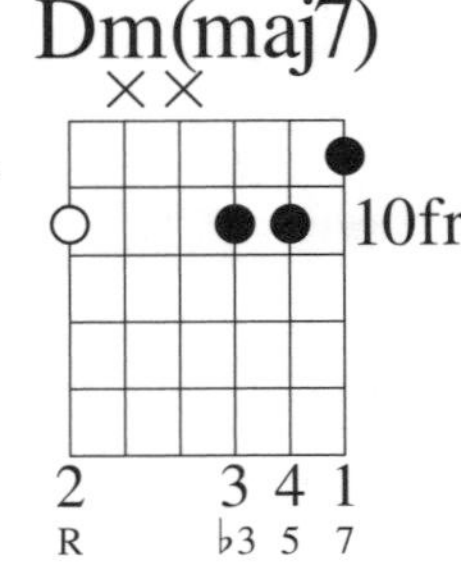

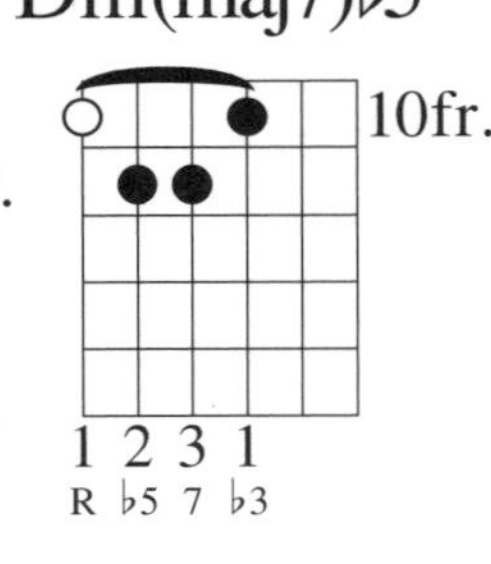

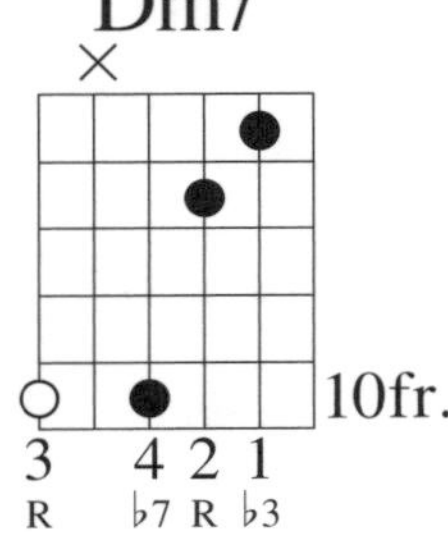

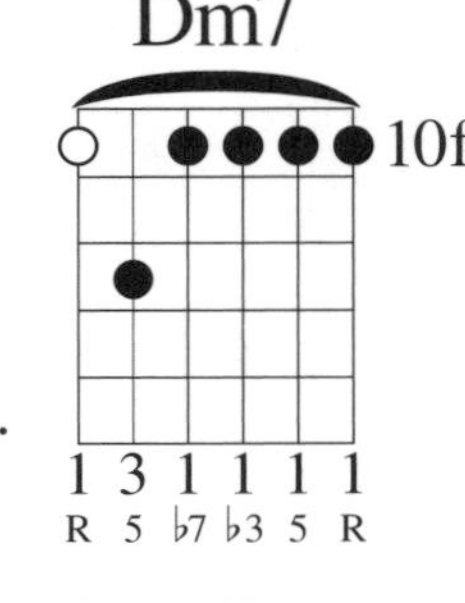

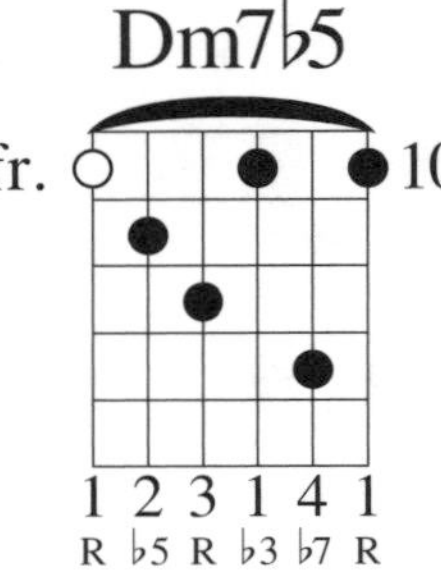

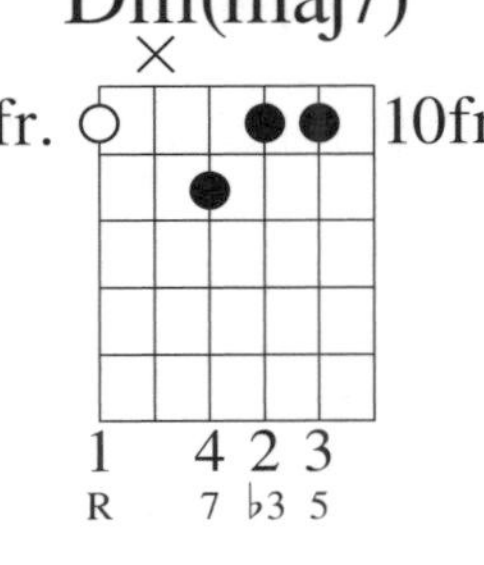

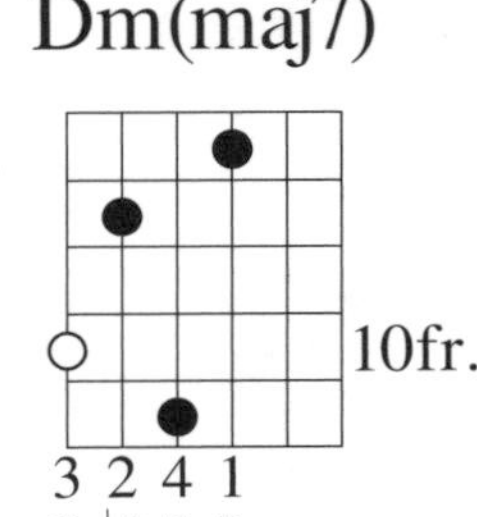

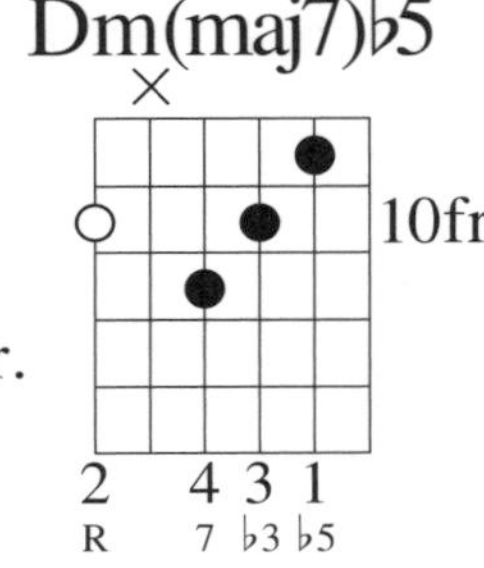

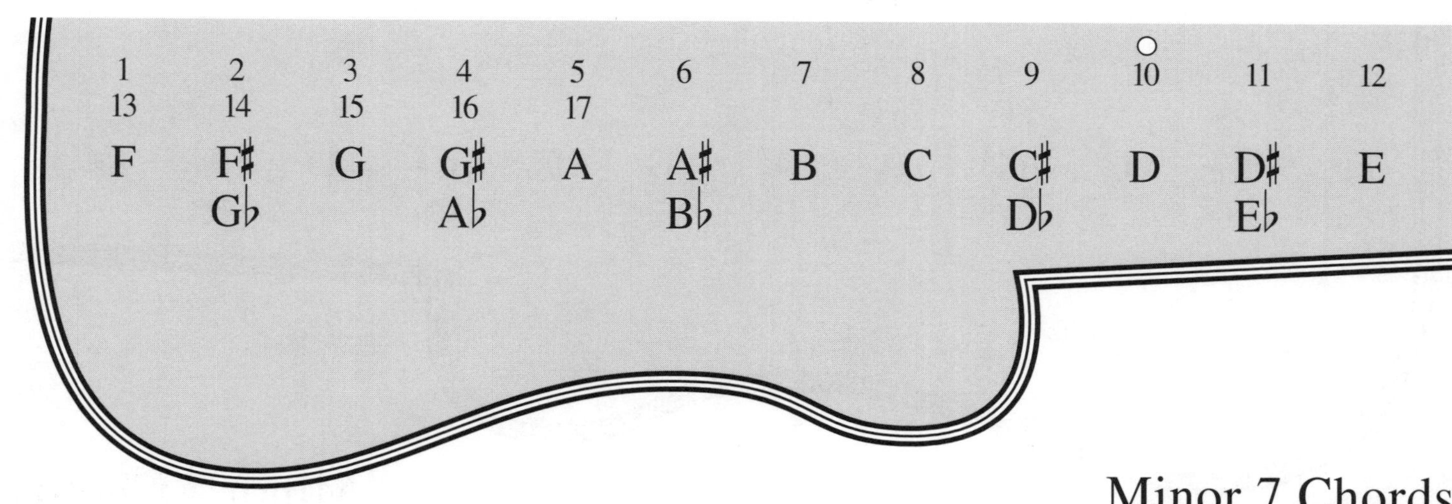

Minor 7 Chords

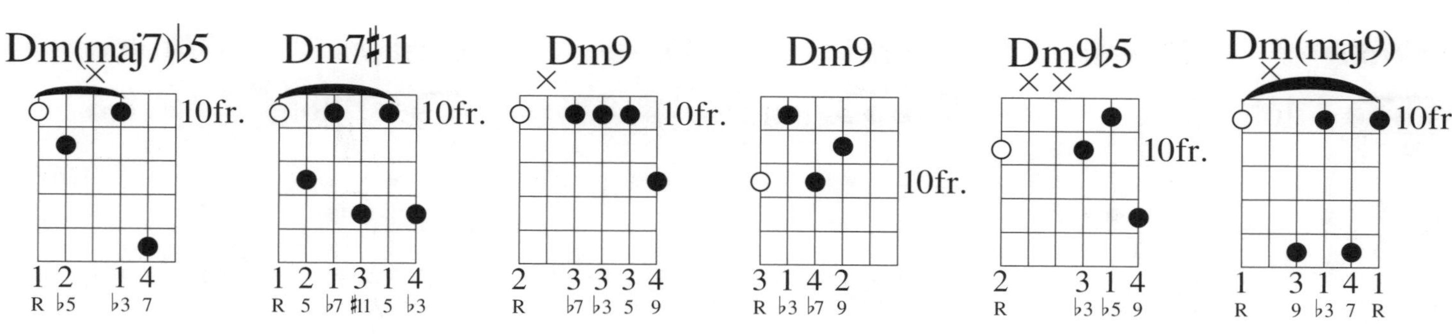

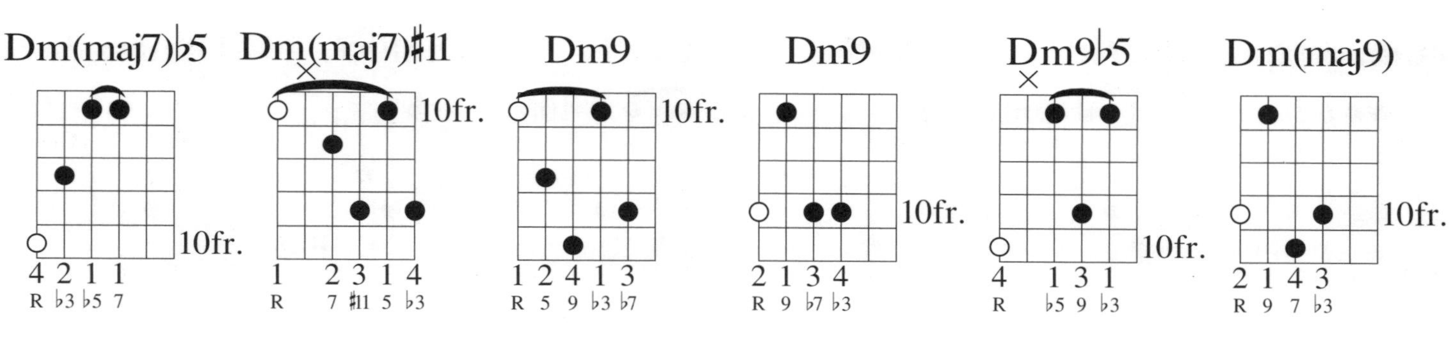

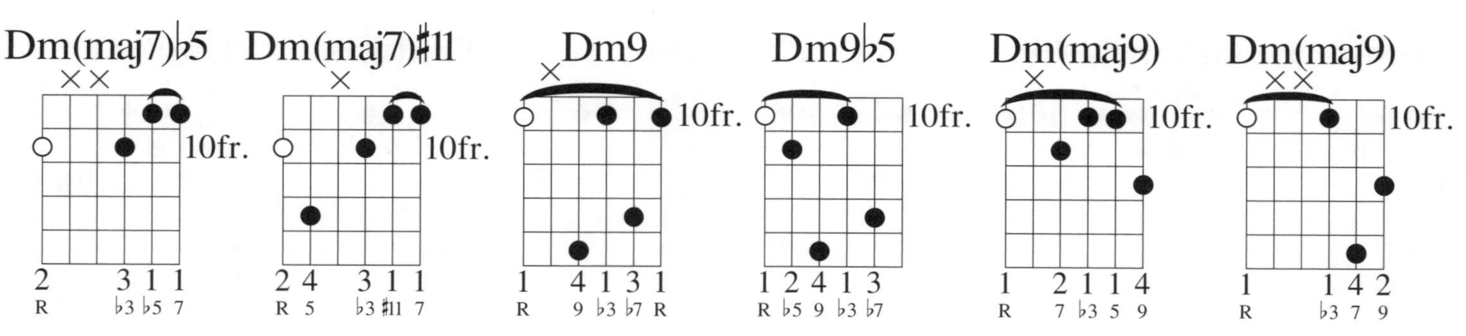

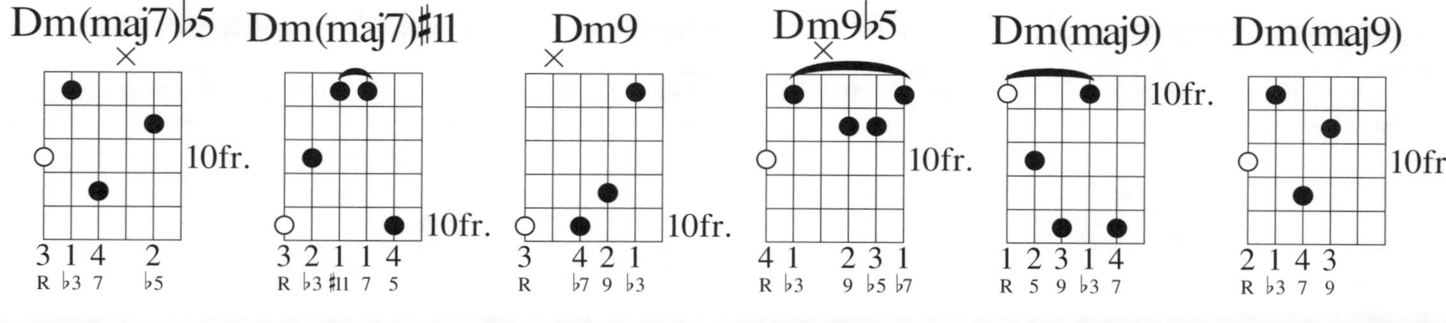

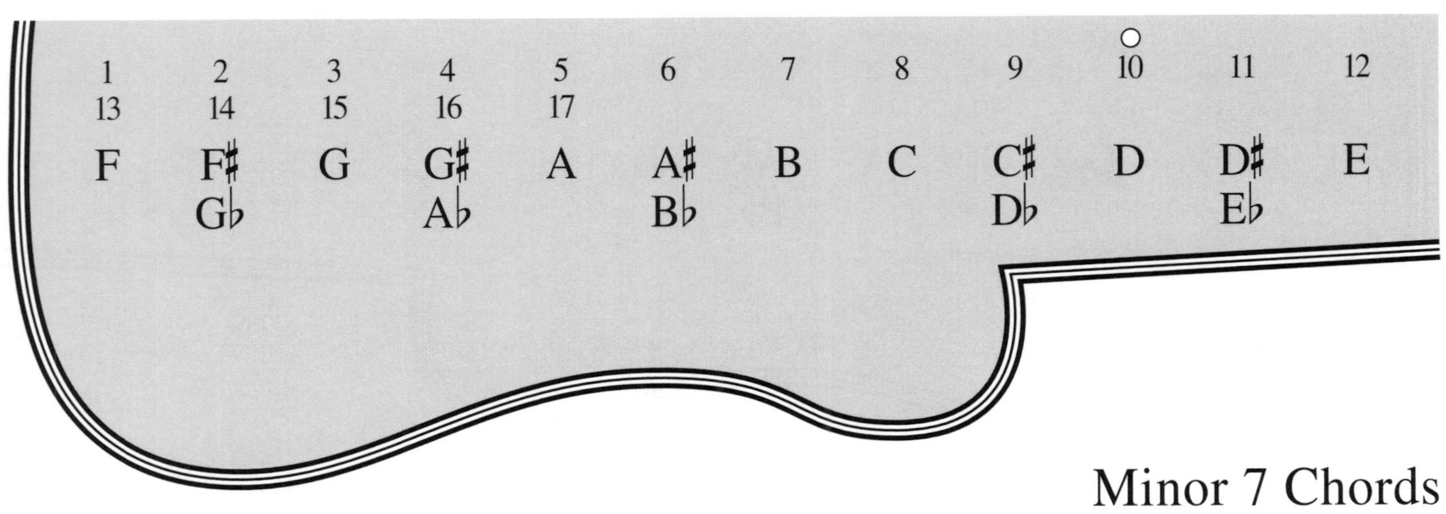

Minor 7 Chords

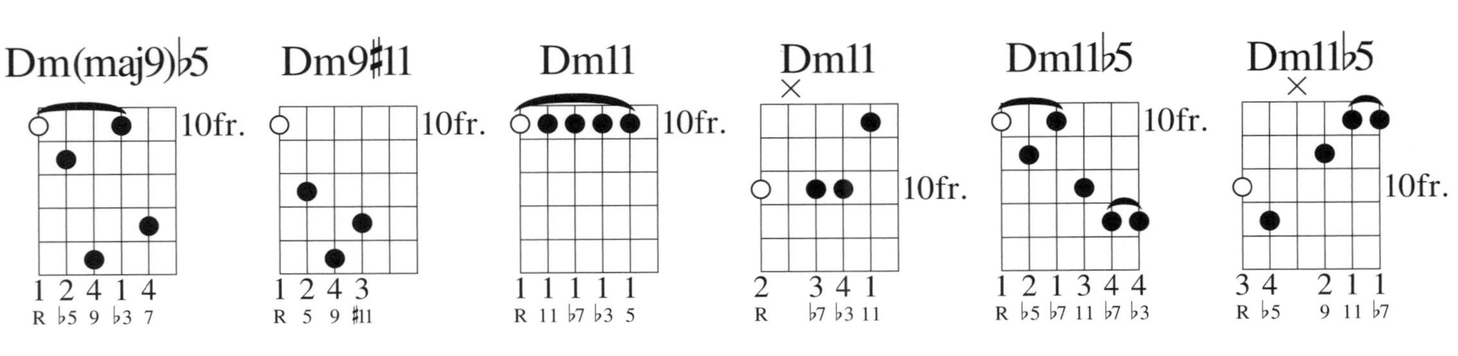

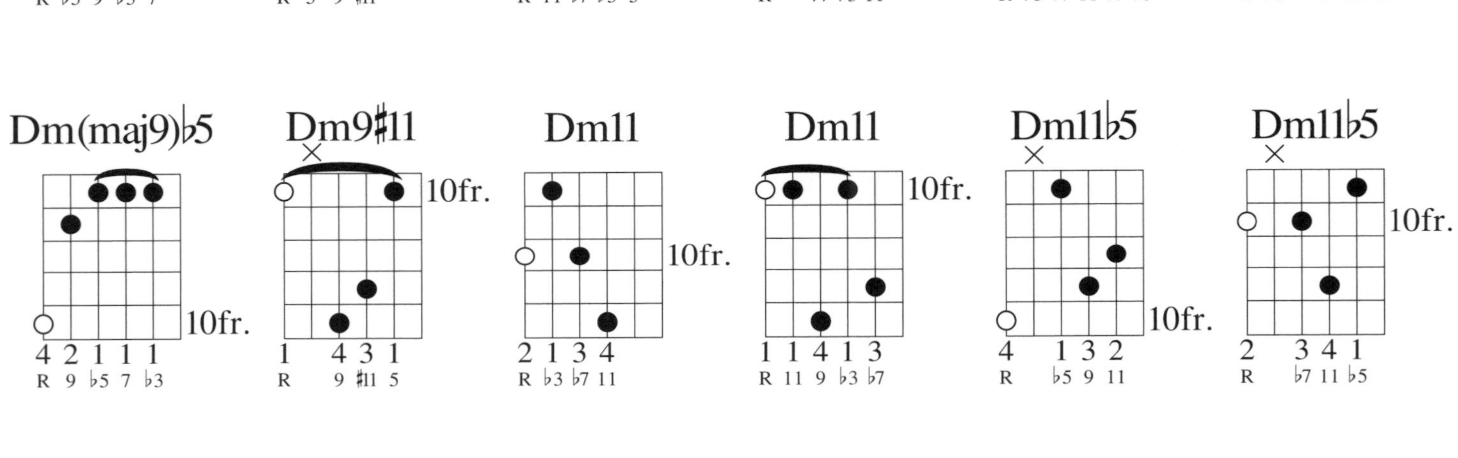

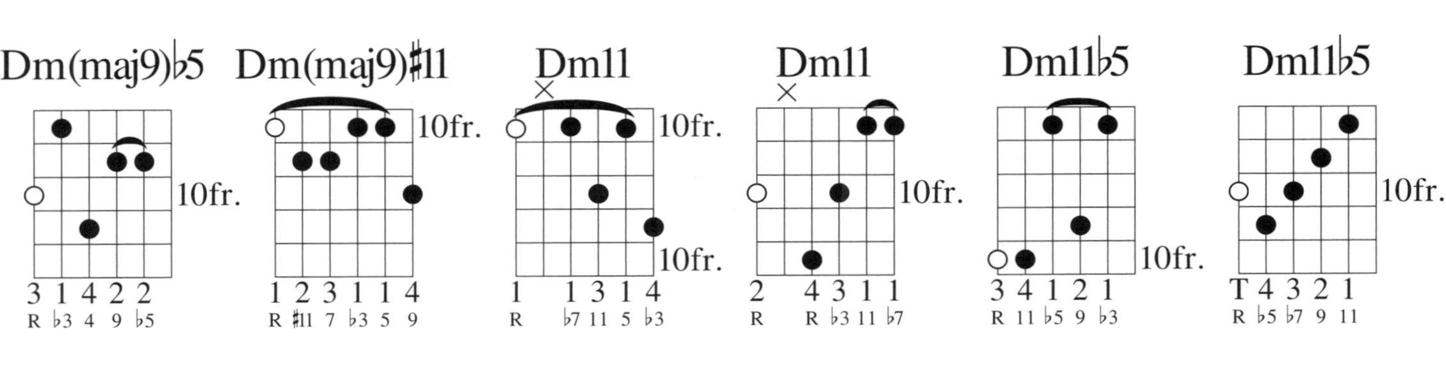

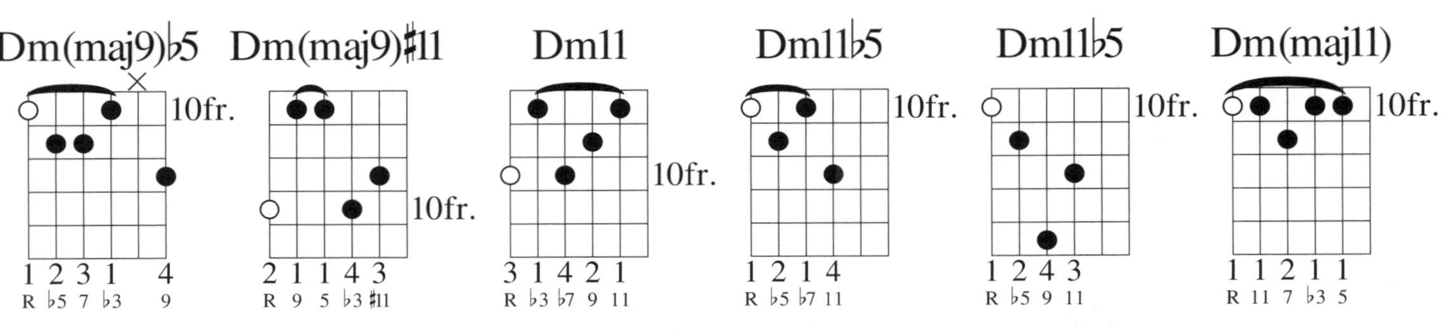

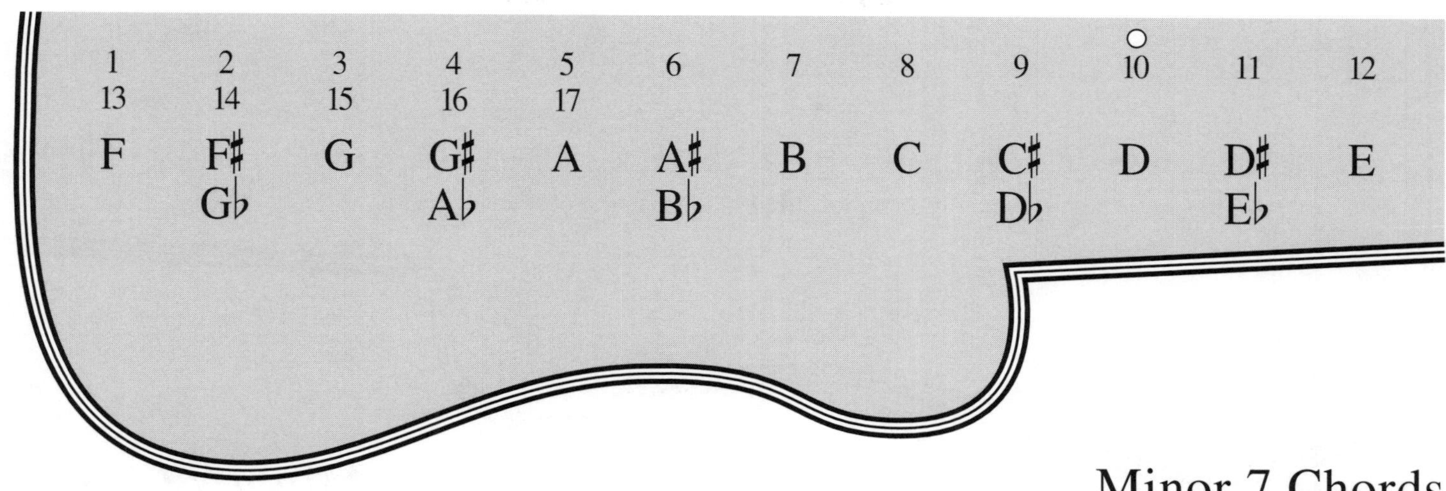

Minor 7 Chords

Dm(maj11) Dm(maj11) Dm(maj11)♭5 Dm13♯11 Dm(maj13)♯11 Dm13

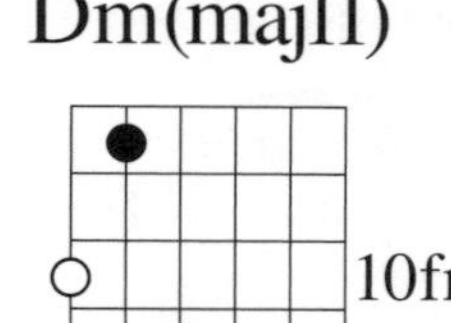

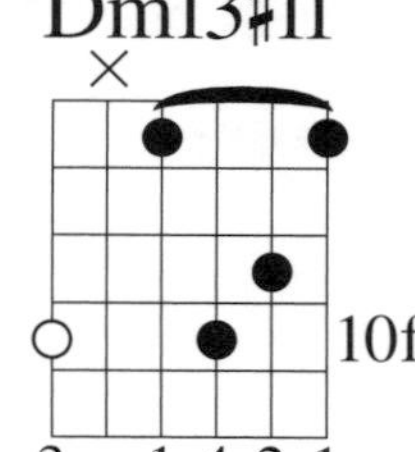

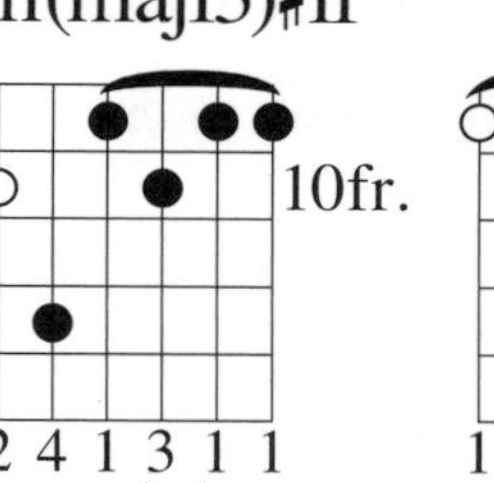

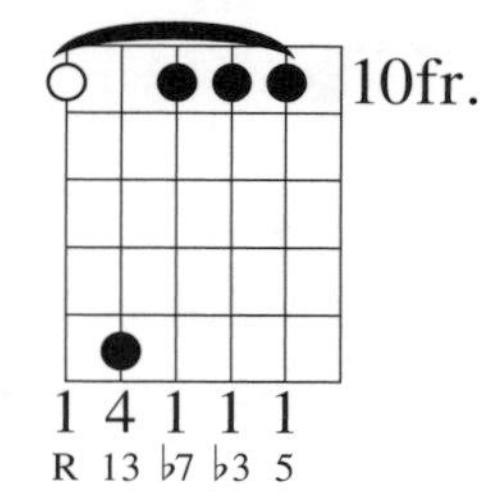

Dm(maj11) Dm(maj11)♭5 Dm(maj11)♭5 Dm13♯11 Dm(maj13)♯11 Dm13

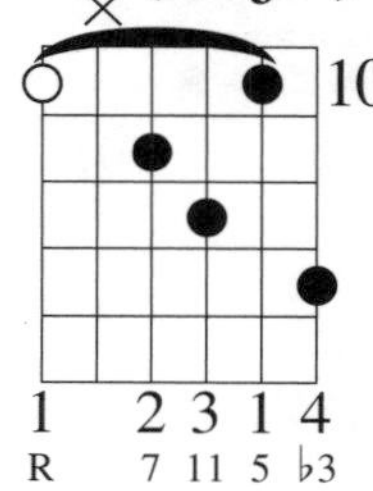

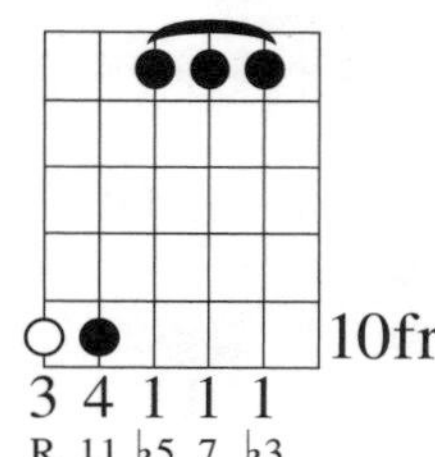

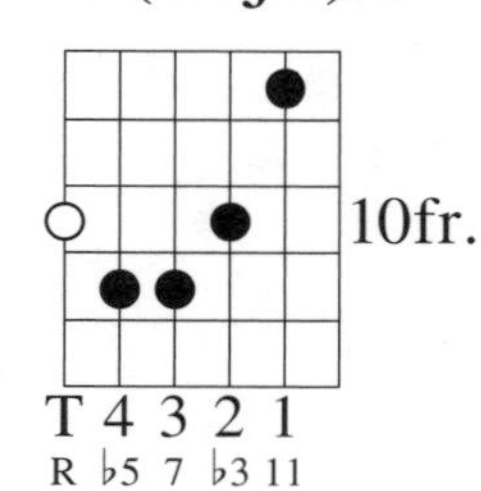

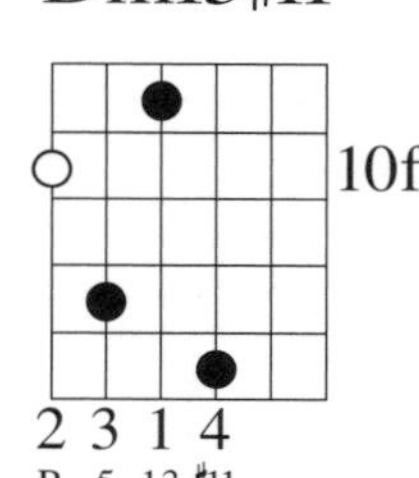

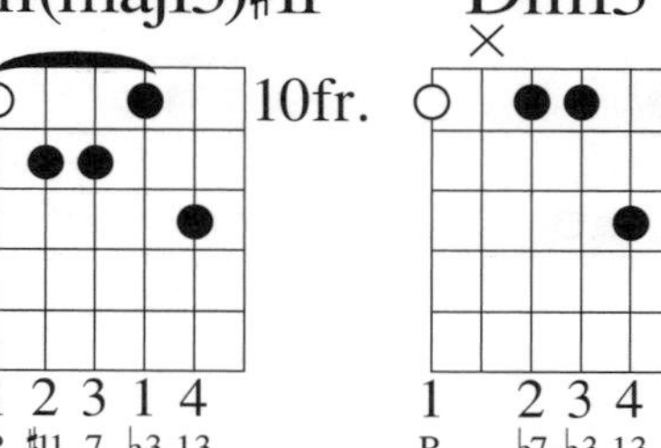

Dm(maj11) Dm(maj11)♭5 Dm13♯11 Dm13♯11 Dm(maj13)♯11 Dm13

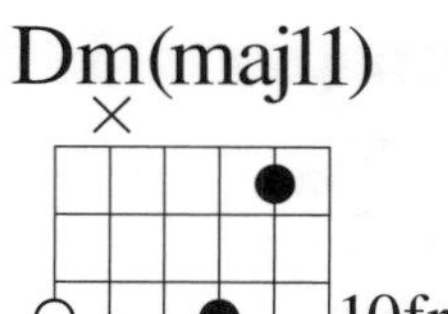

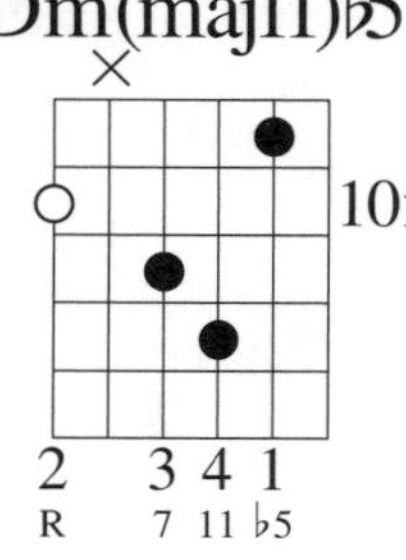

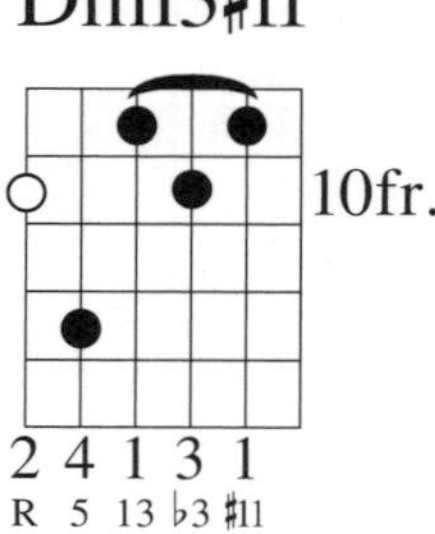

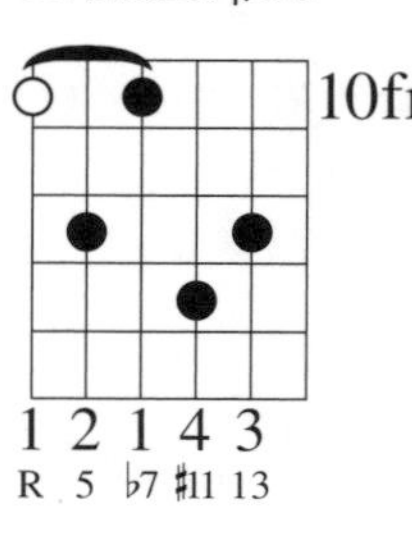

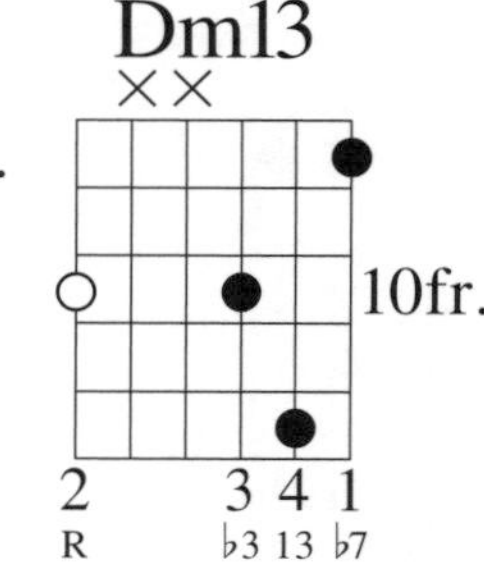

Dm(maj11) Dm(maj11)♭5 Dm13♯11 Dm13♯11 Dm(maj13)♯11 Dm13

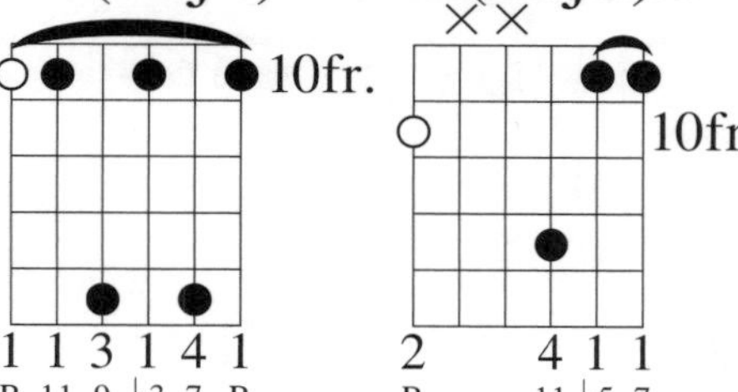

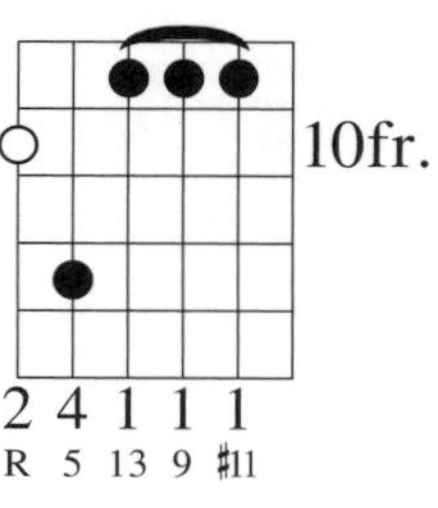

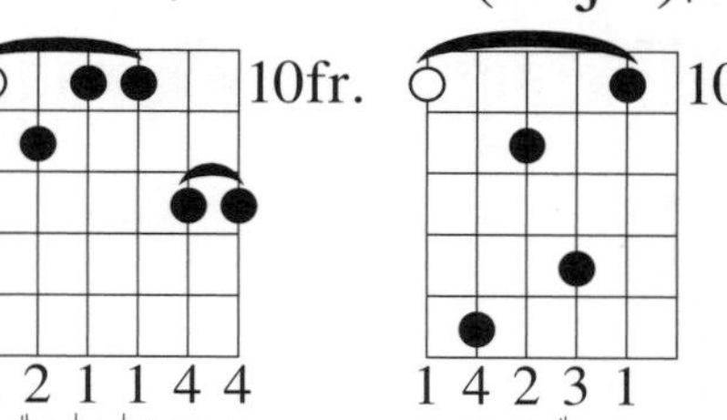

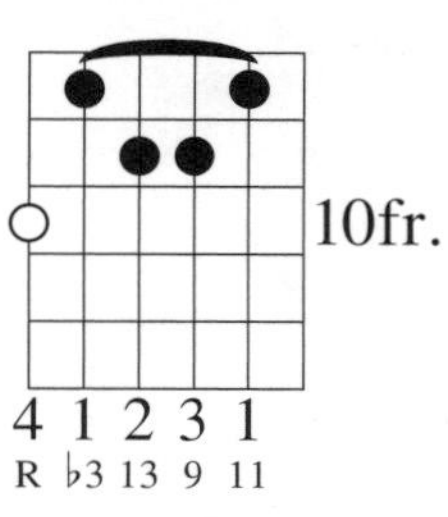

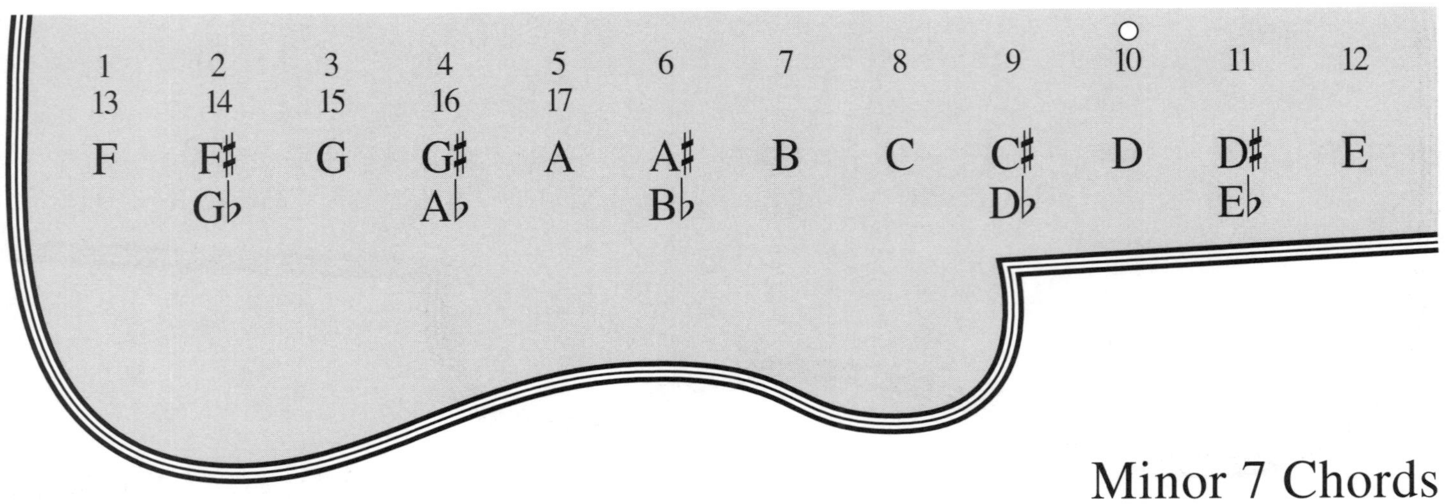

Minor 7 Chords

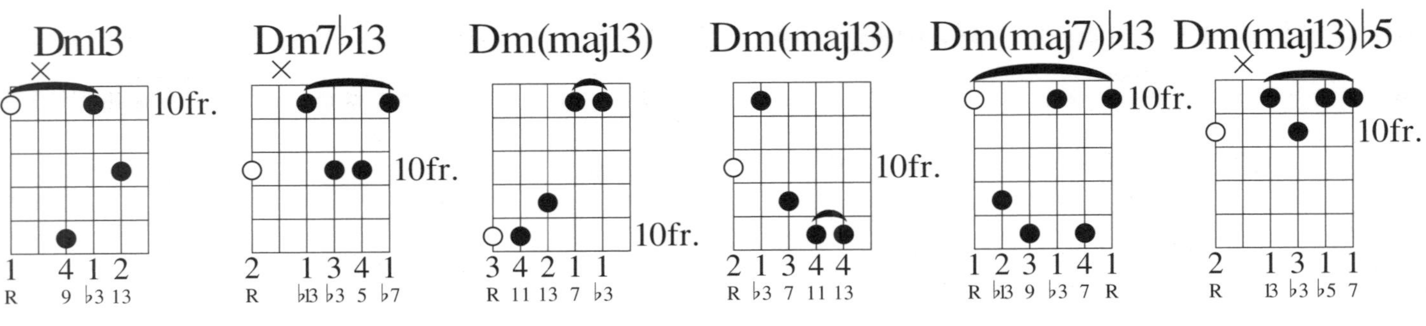

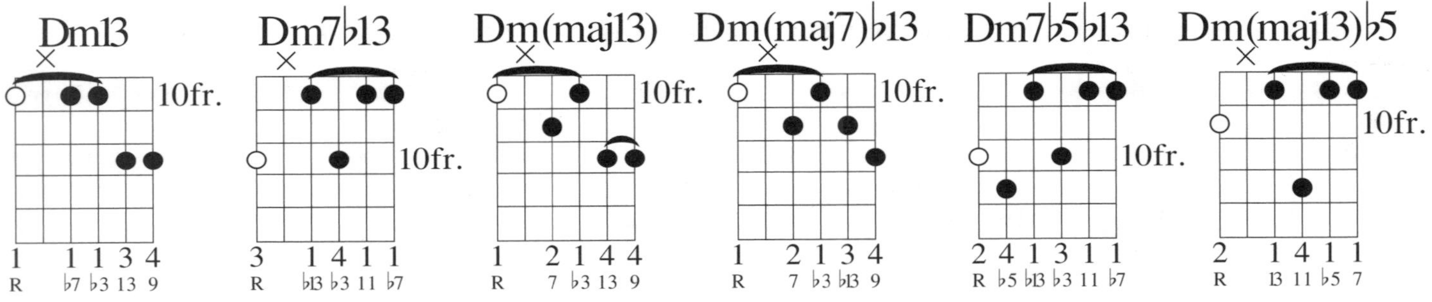

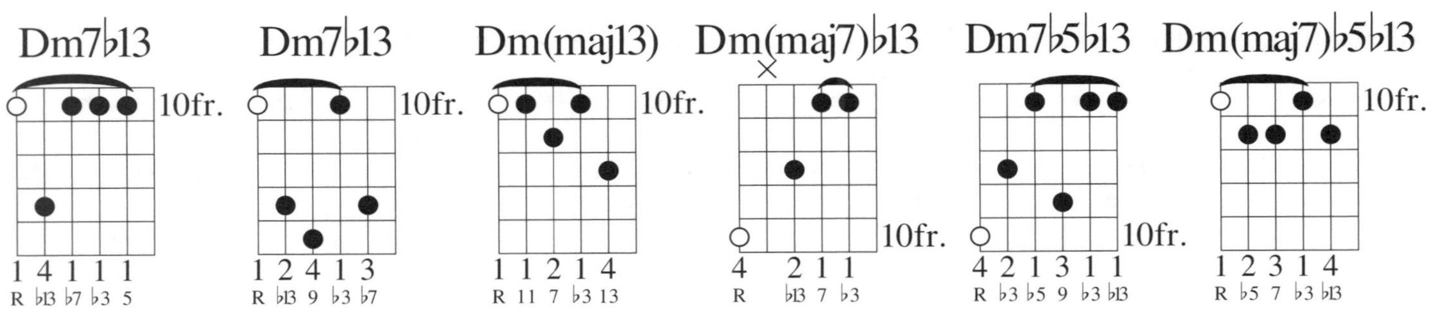

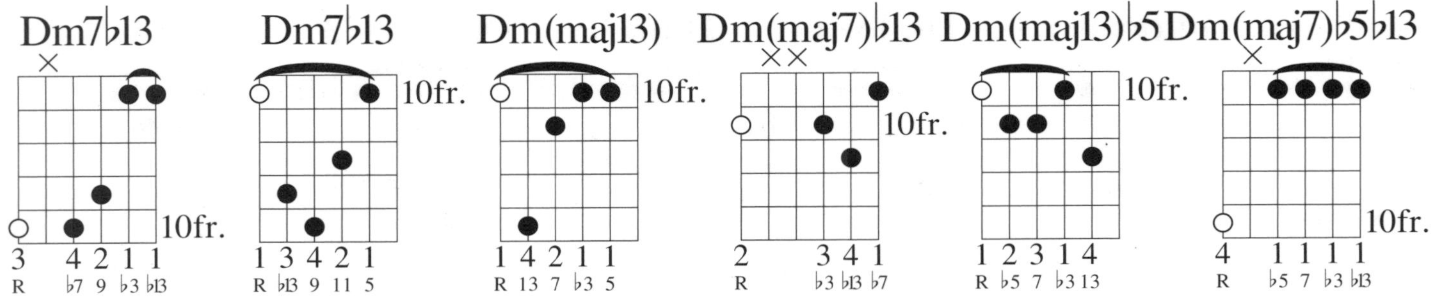

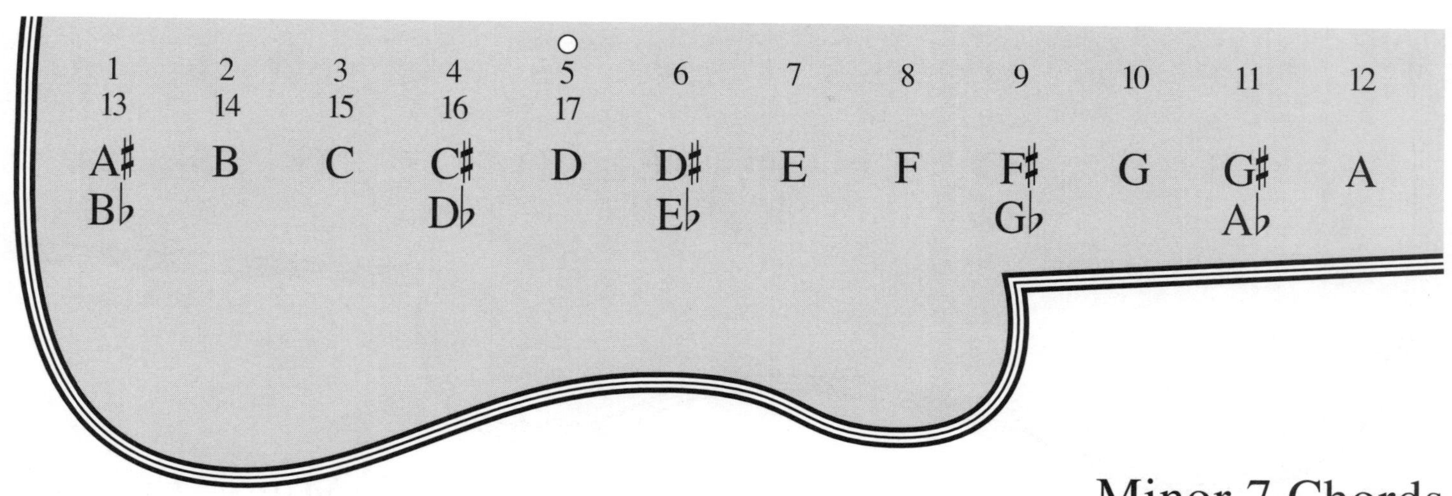

Minor 7 Chords

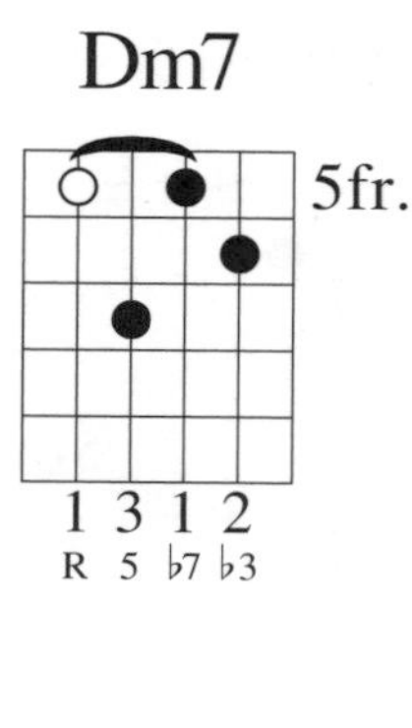

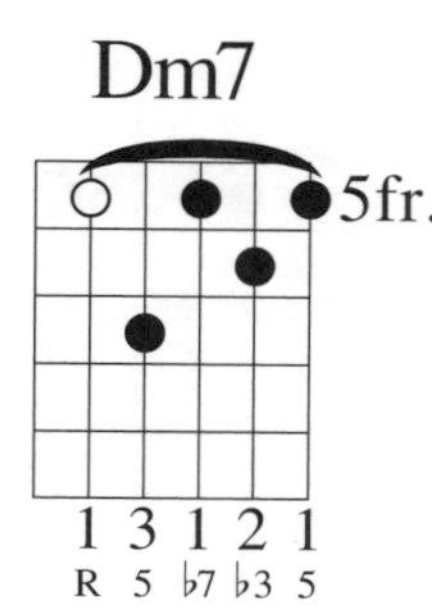

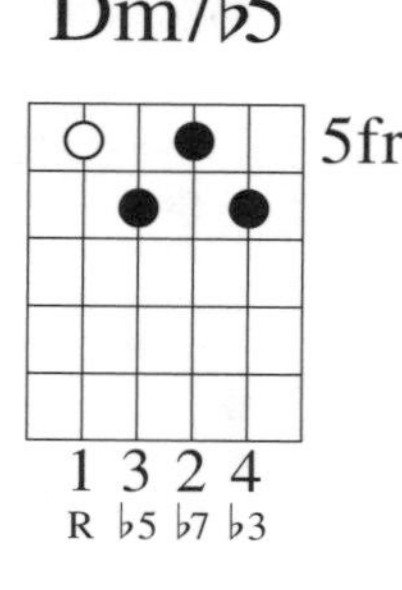

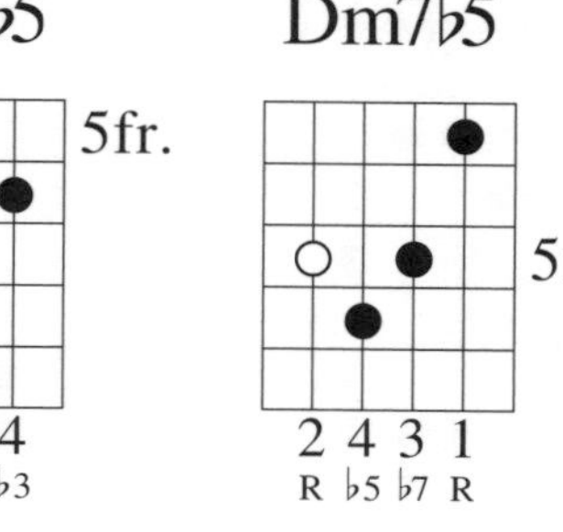

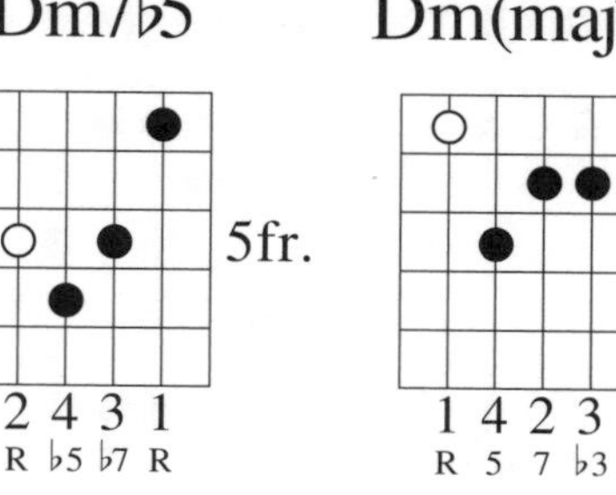

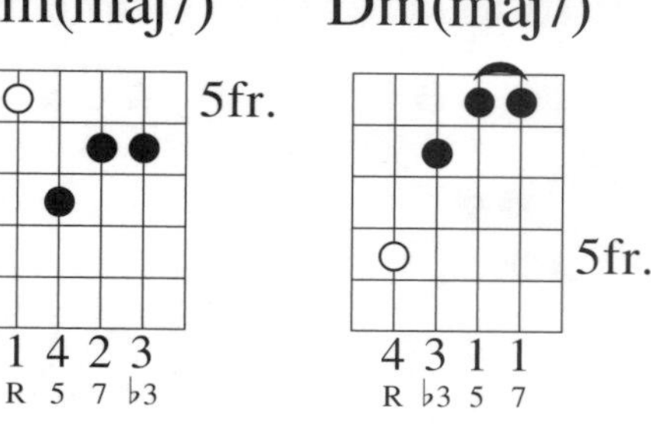

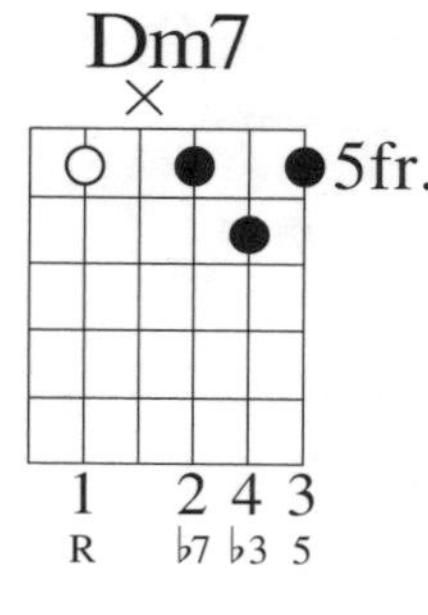

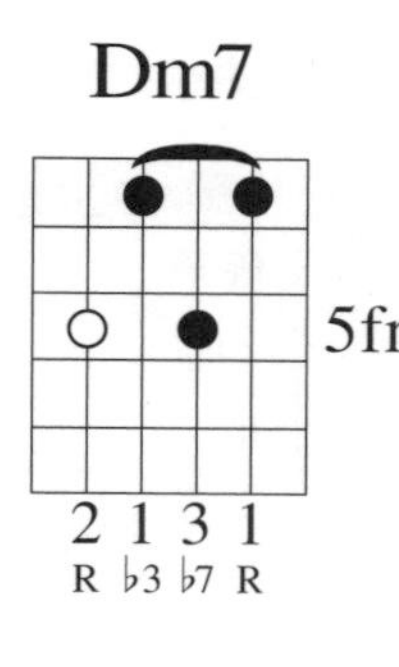

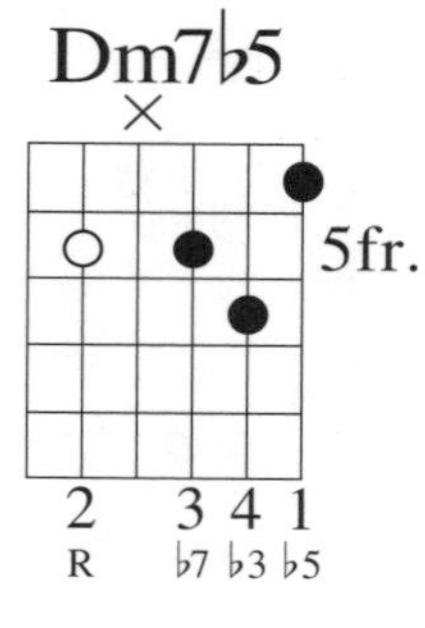

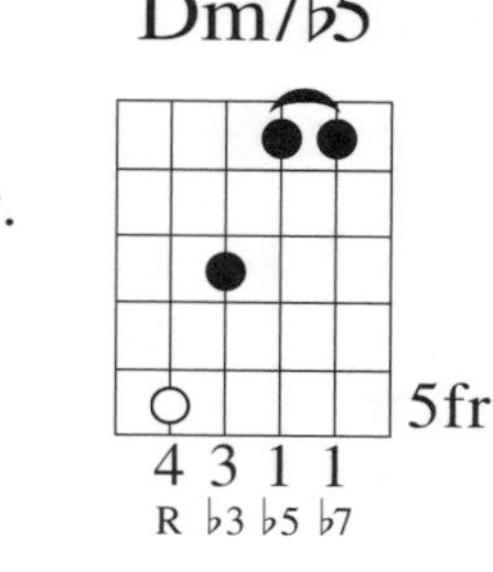

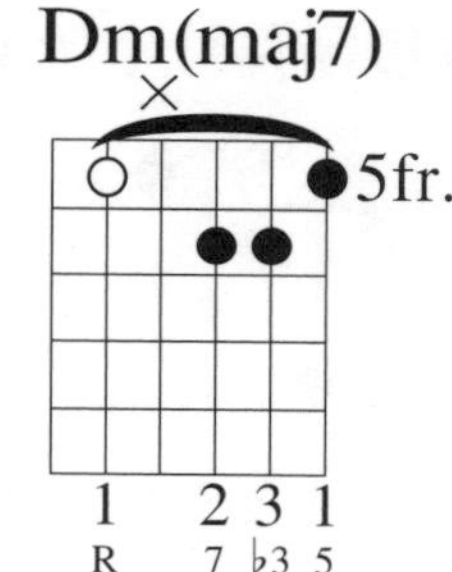

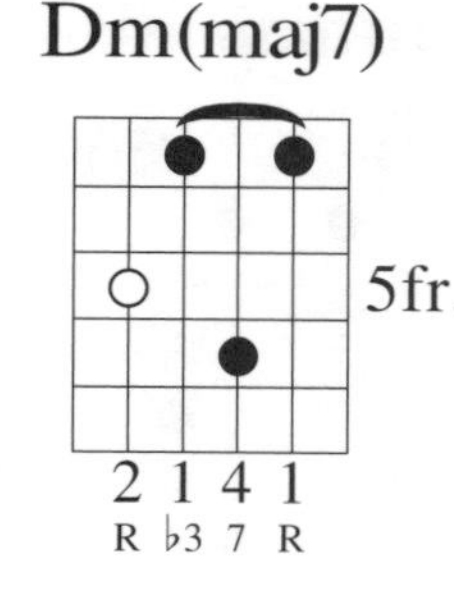

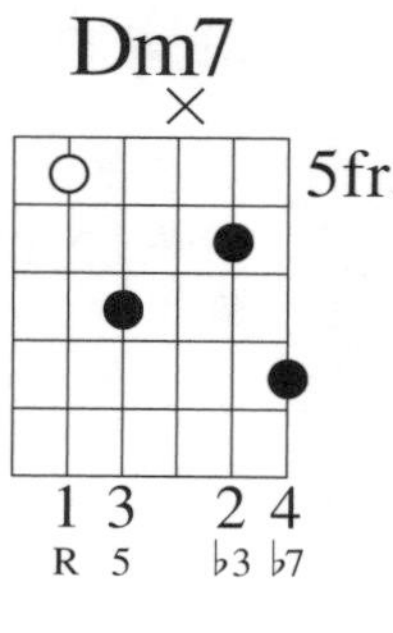

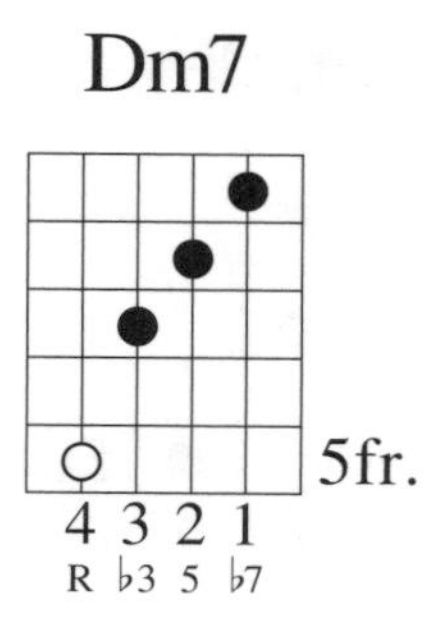

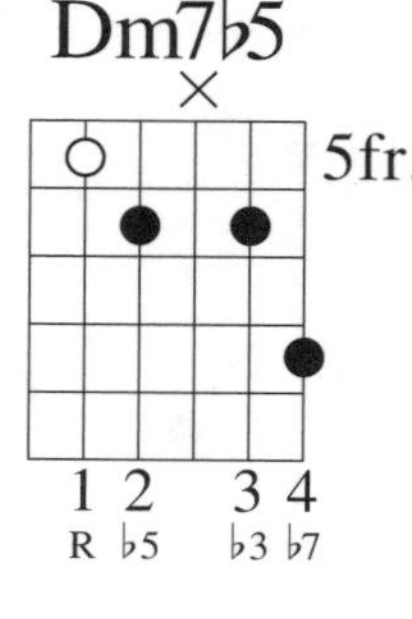

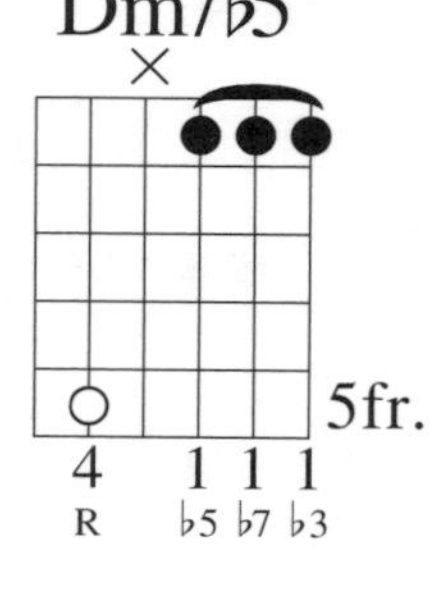

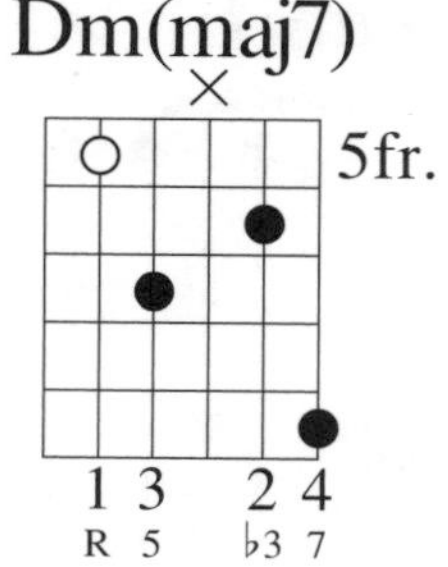

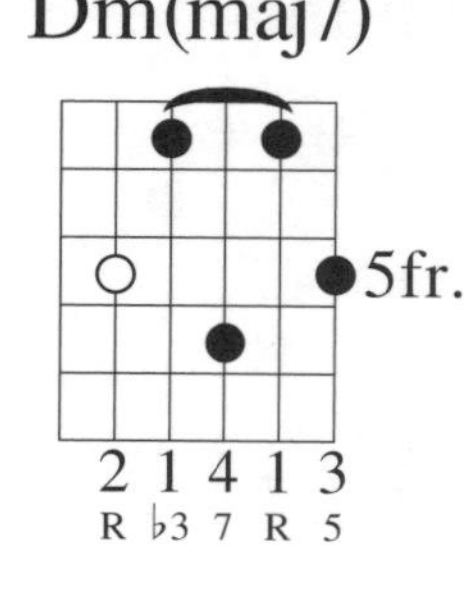

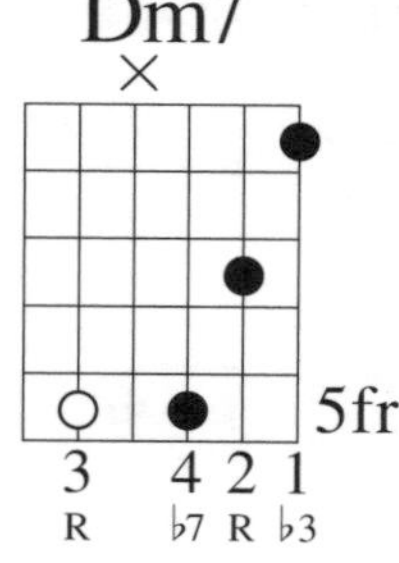

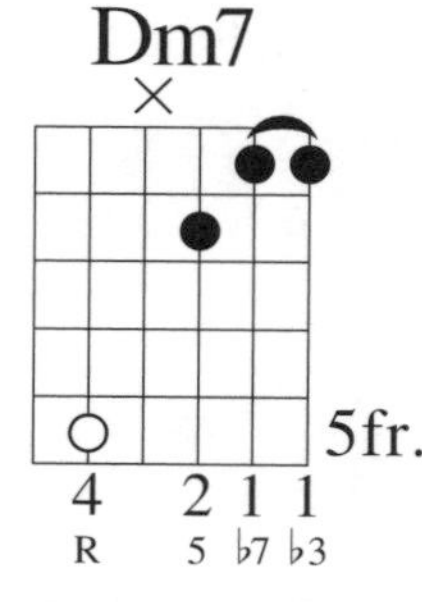

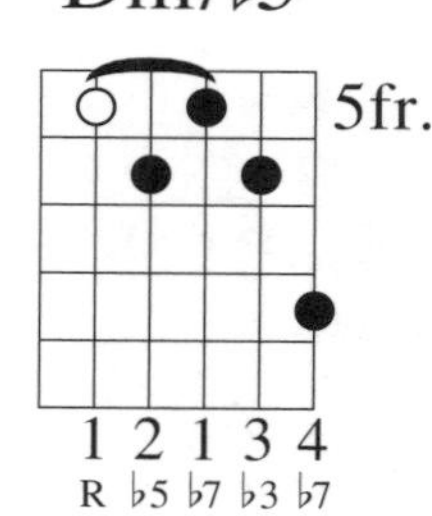

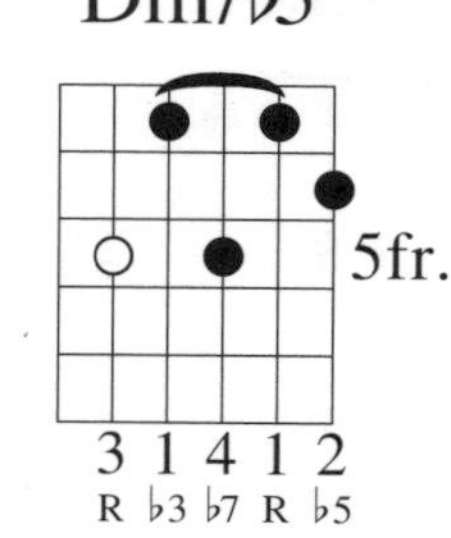

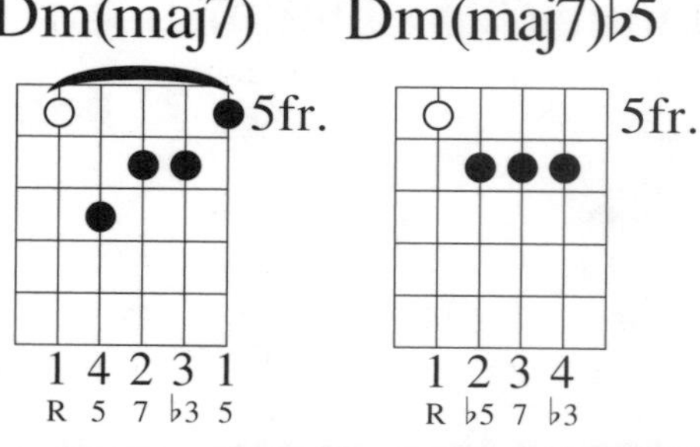

Minor 7 Chords

Dm(maj7)♭5

Dm(maj7)♭5

Dm(maj7)♯11

Dm9

Dm9♭5

Dm9♭5

Dm(maj7)♭5

Dm7♯11

Dm(maj7)♯11

Dm9

Dm9♭5

Dm(maj9)♭5

Dm(maj7)♭5

Dm7♯11

Dm9

Dm9

Dm9♭5

Dm(maj9)♭5

Dm(maj7)♭5

Dm(maj7)♯11

Dm9

Dm9

Dm9♭5

Dm(maj9)♭5

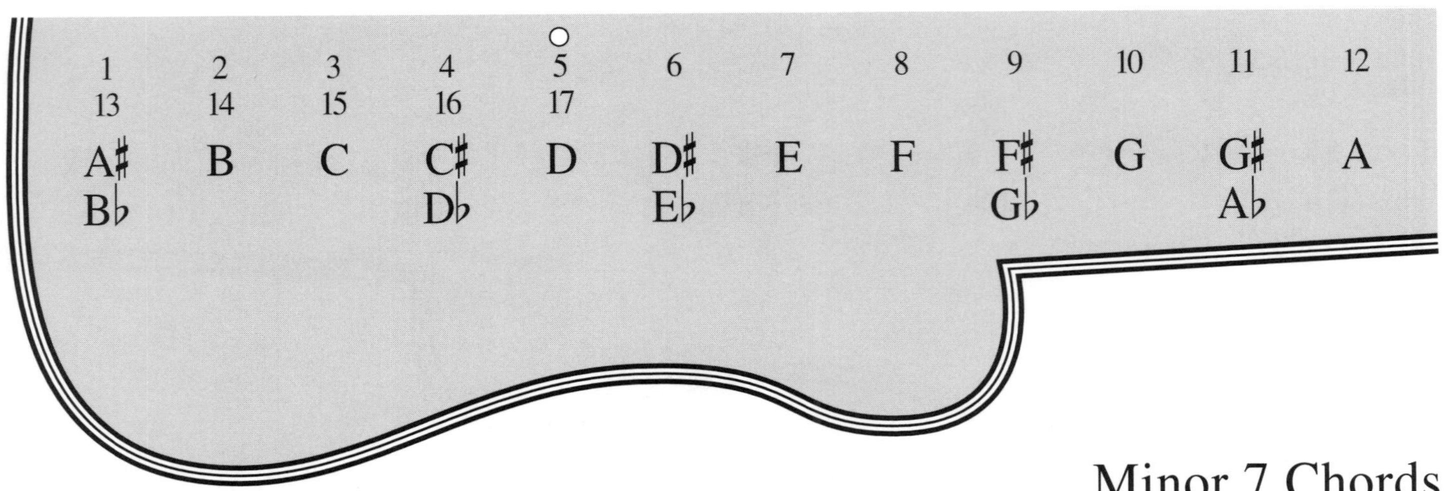

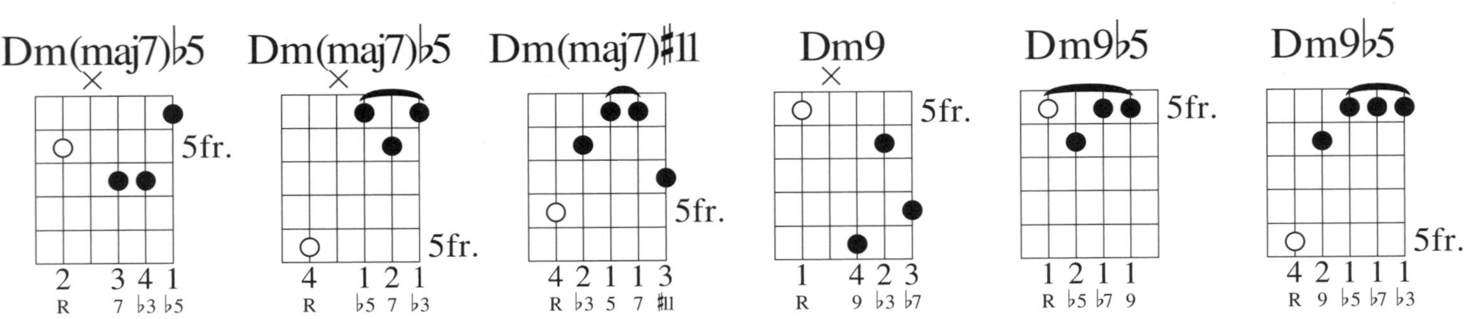

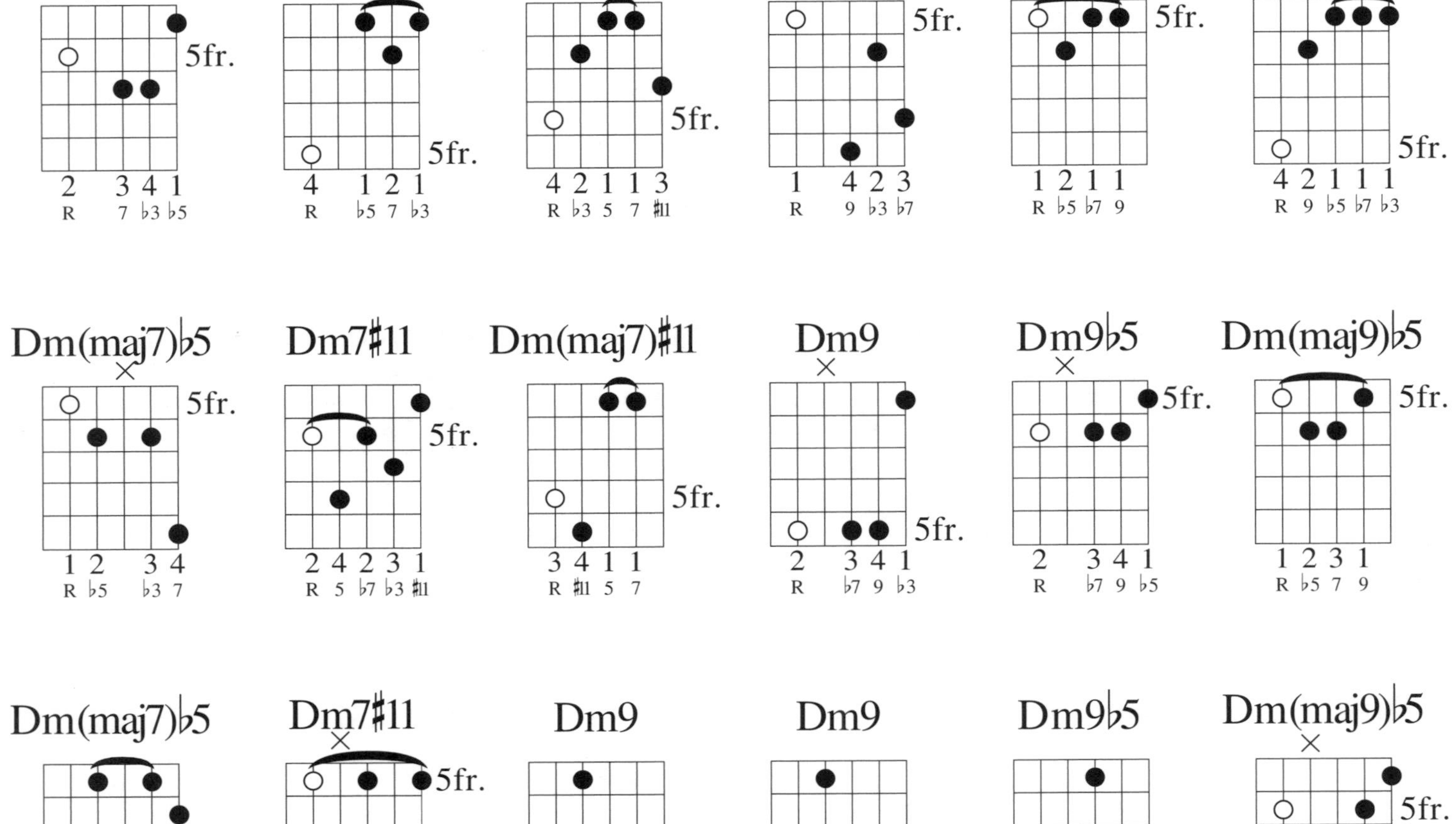

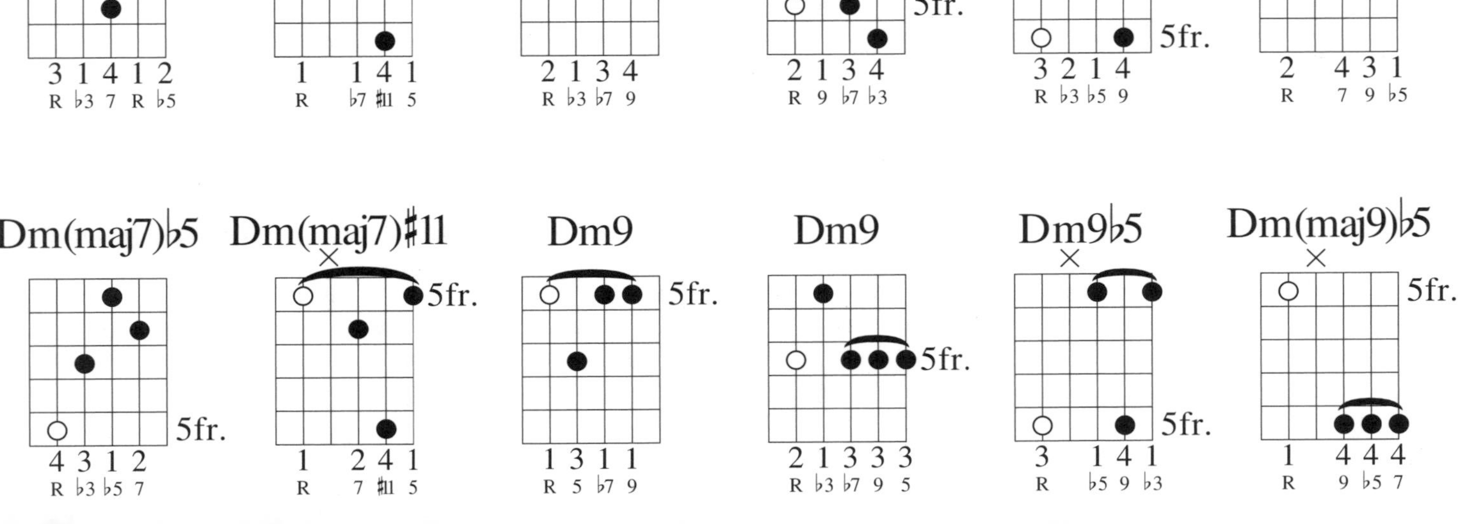

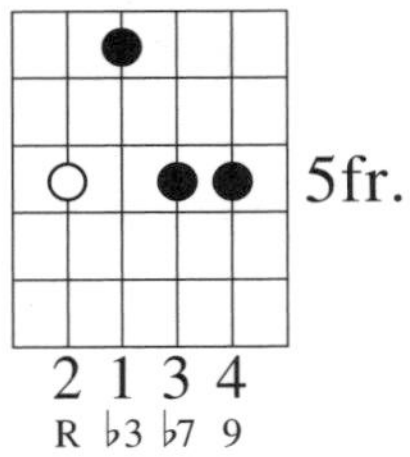

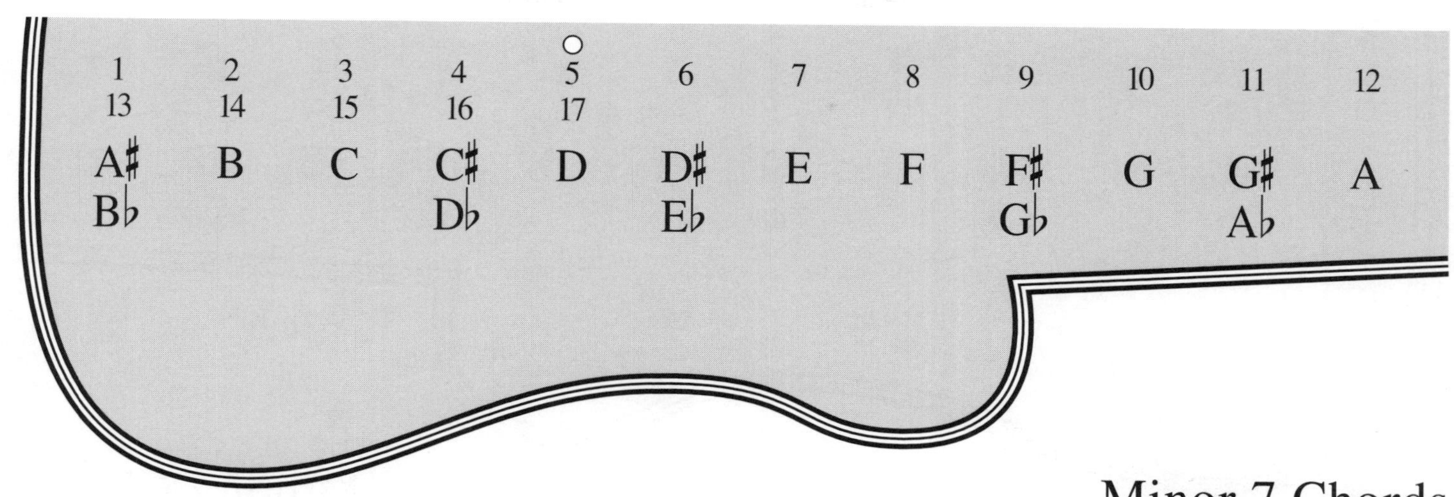

Minor 7 Chords

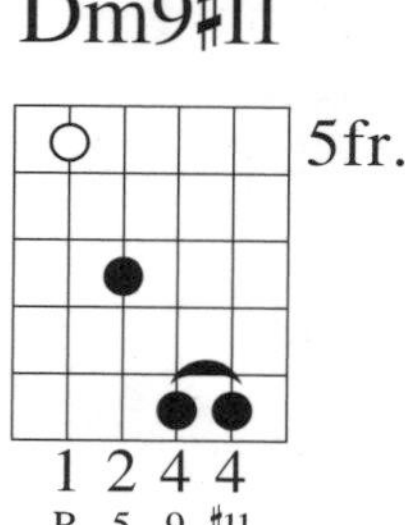

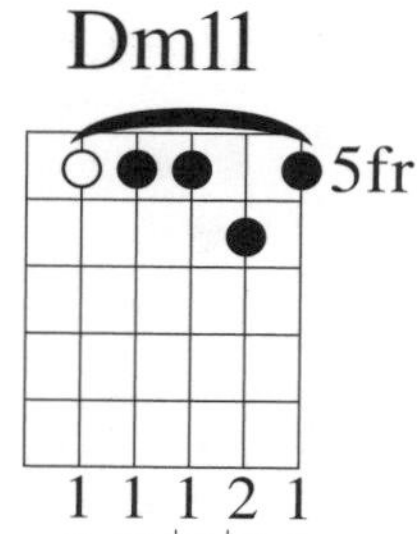

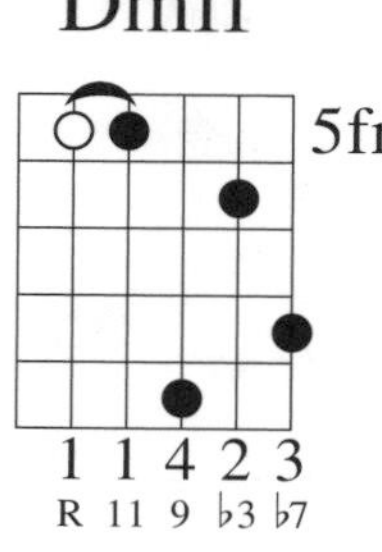

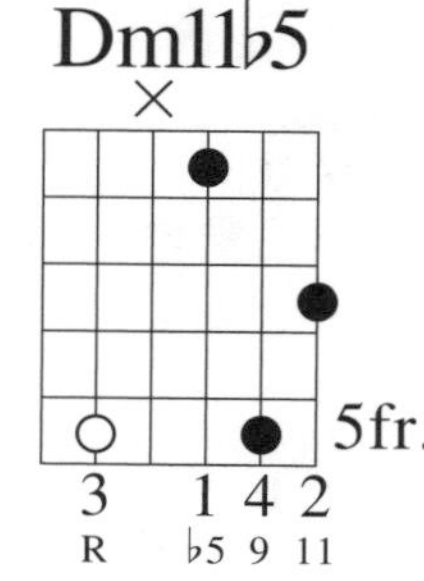

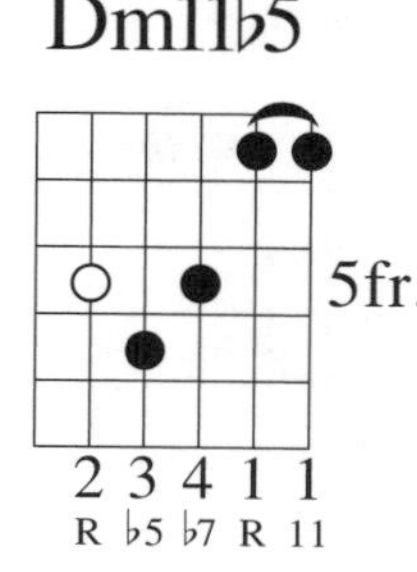

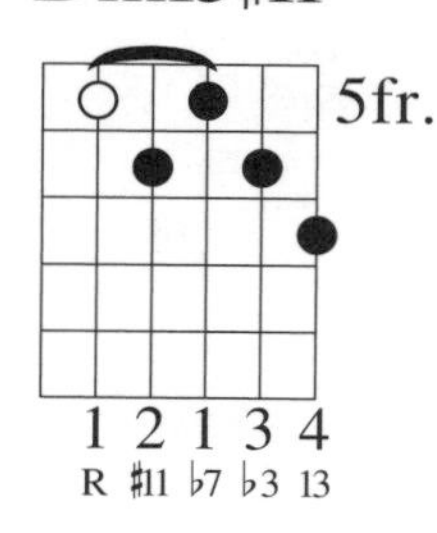

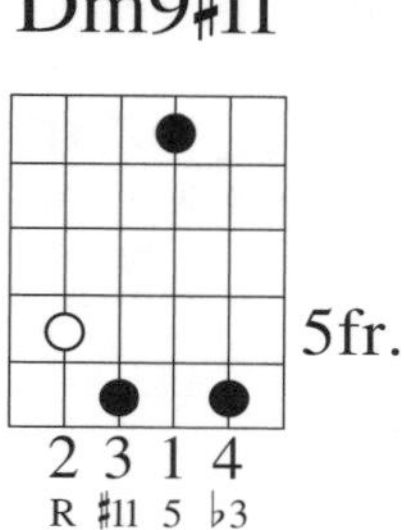

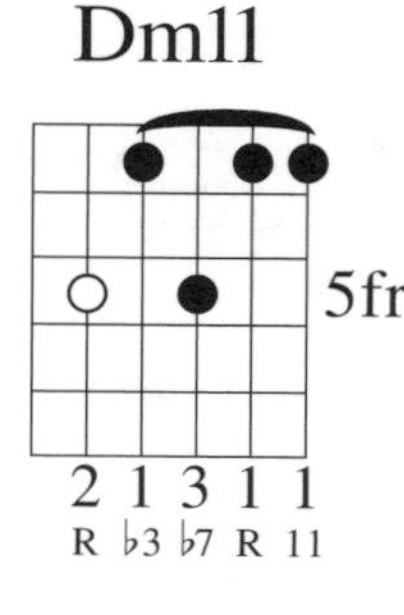

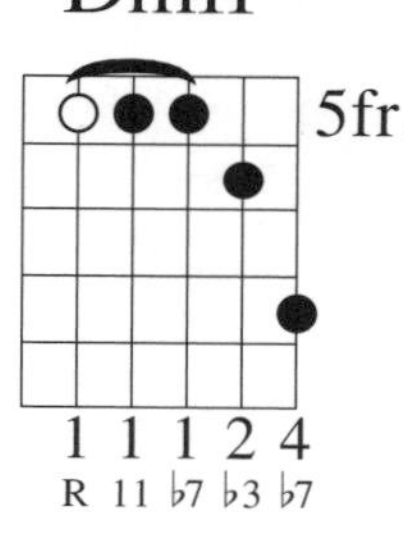

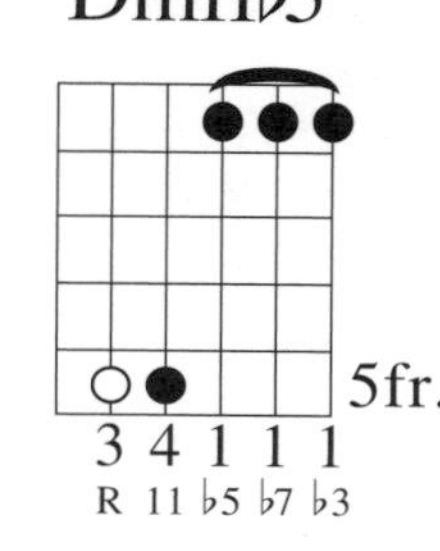

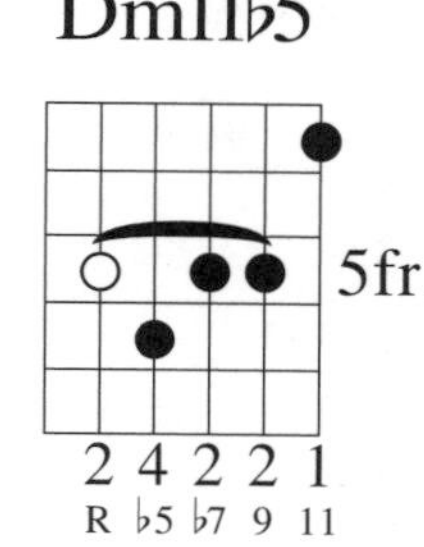

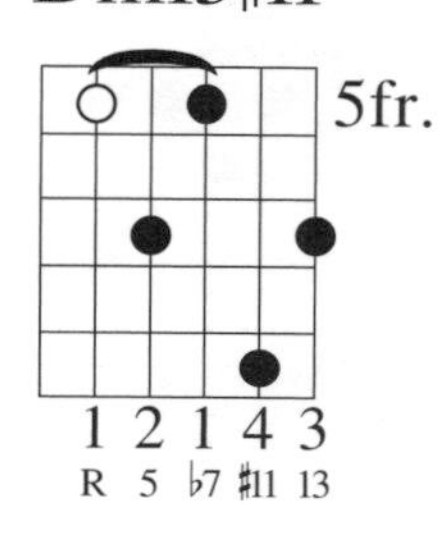

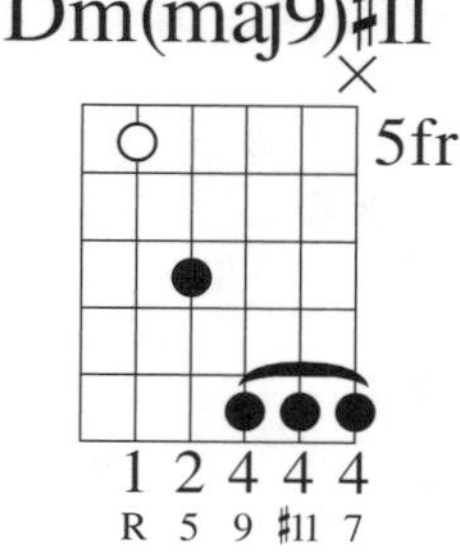

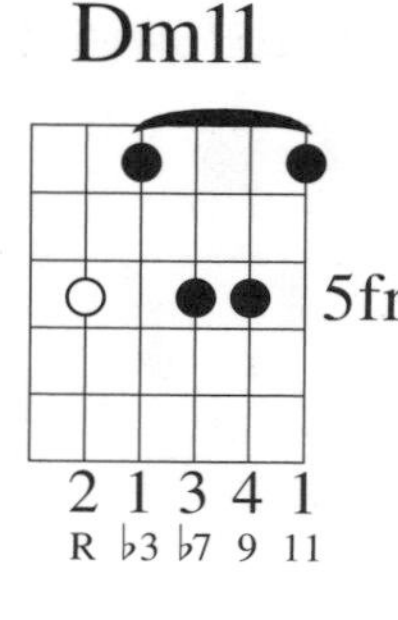

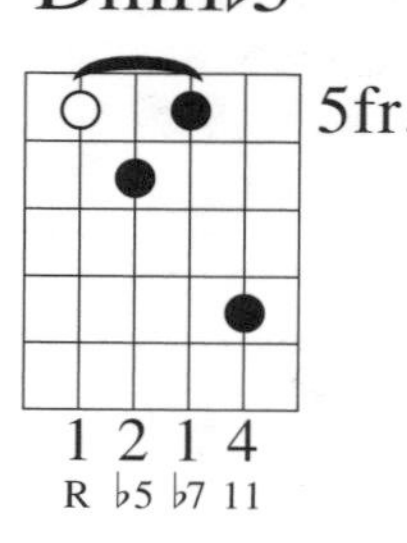

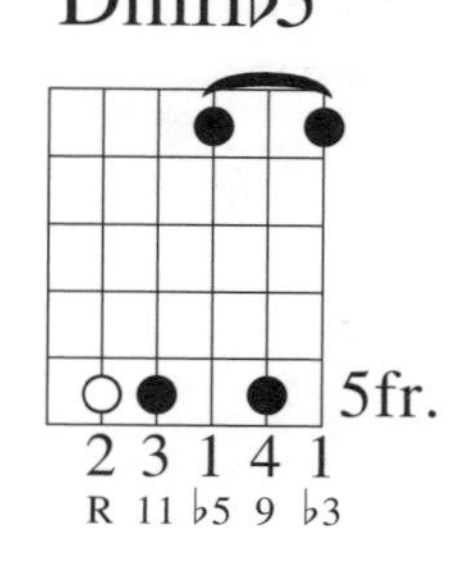

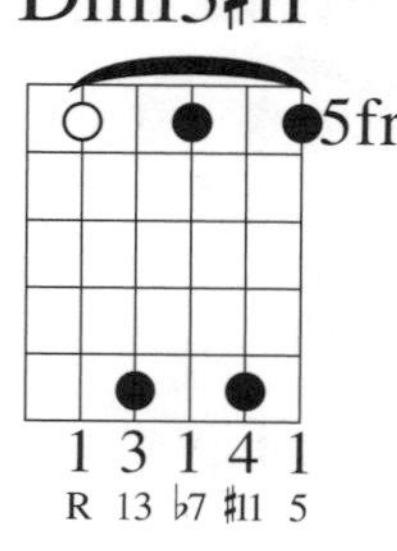

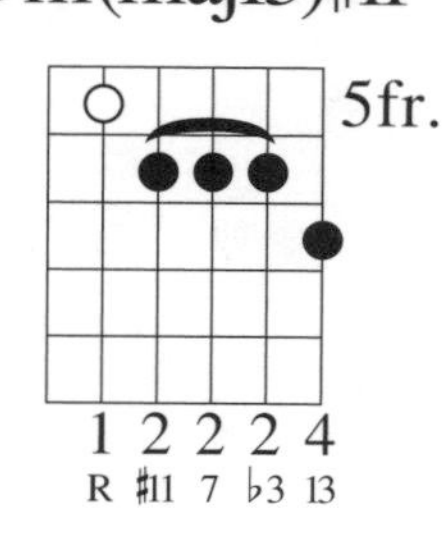

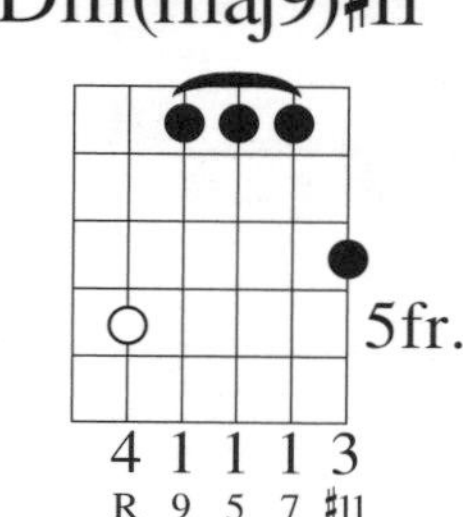

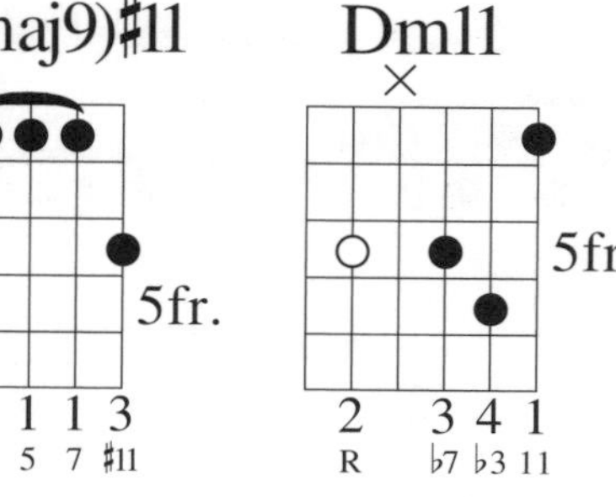

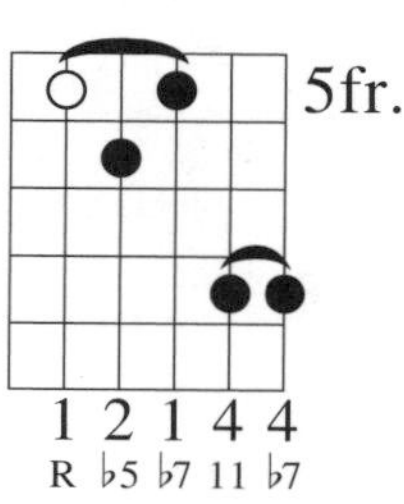

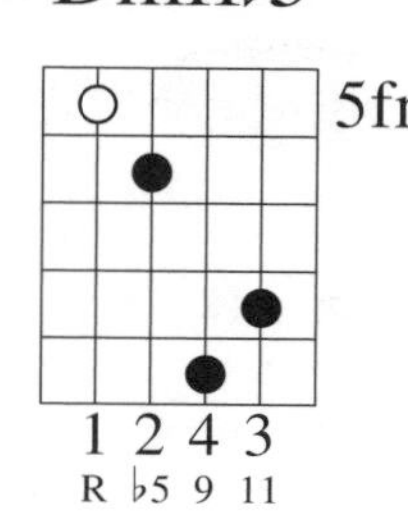

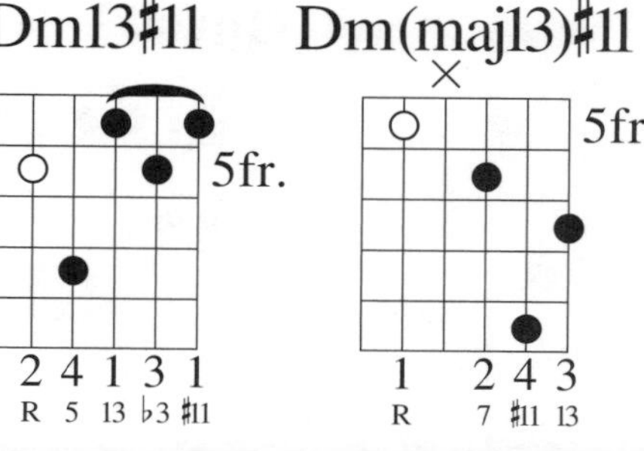

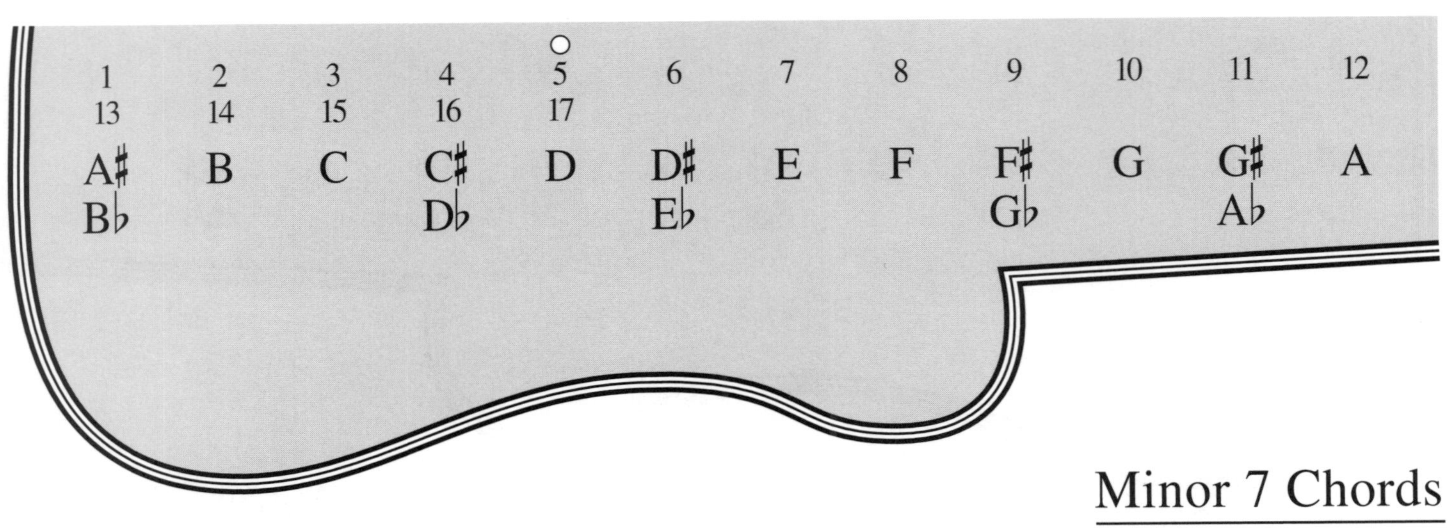

Minor 7 Chords

Dm13

Dm13

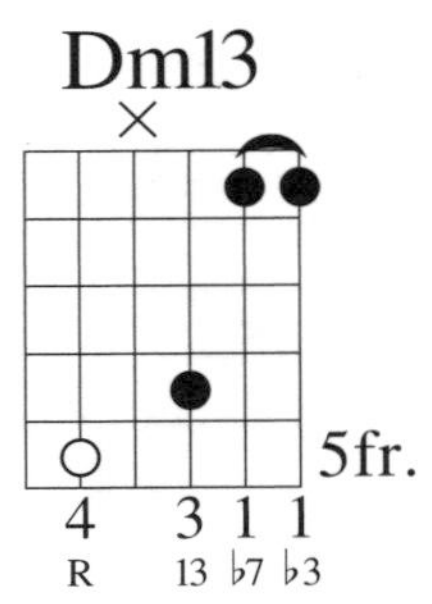

Dm7♭13

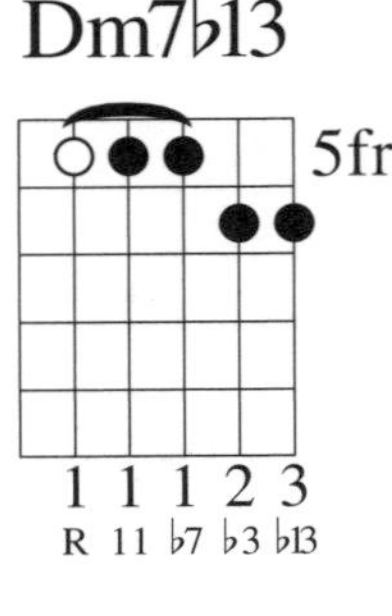

Dm(maj13)

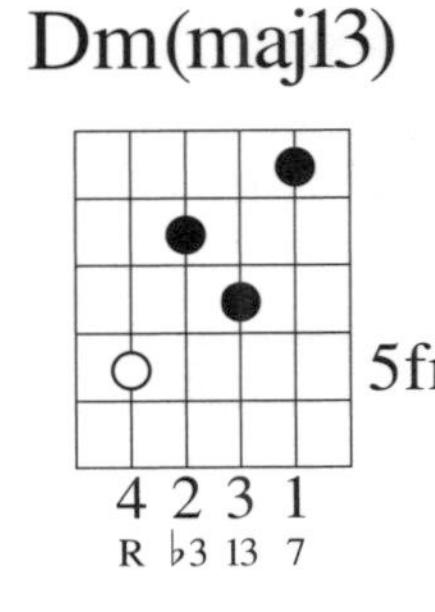

Dm(maj7)♭13

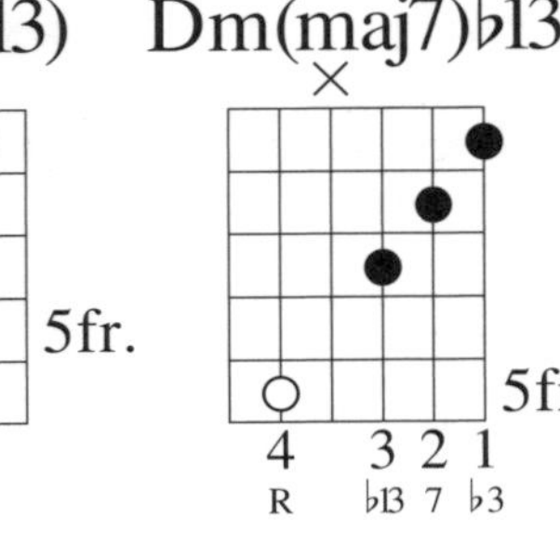

Dm7♭5♭13

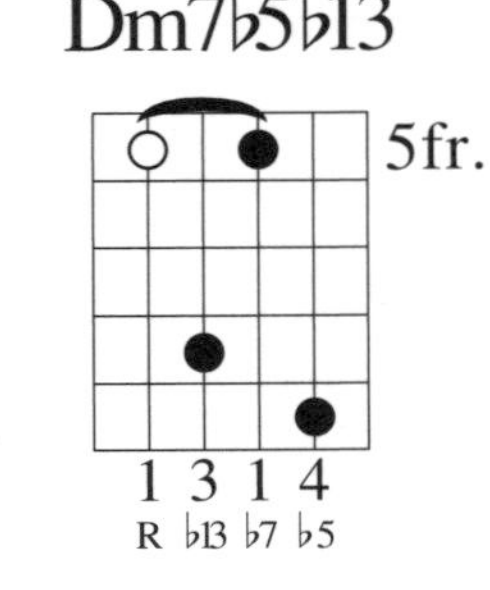

Dm13

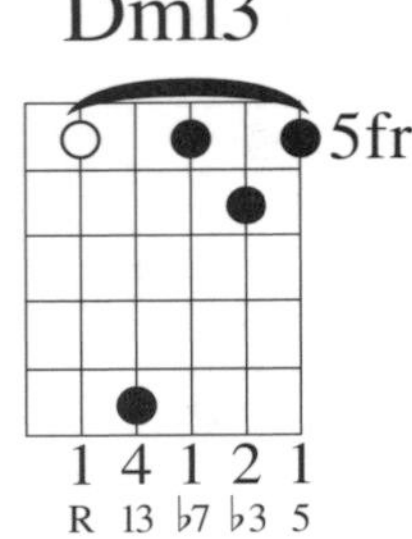

Dm13

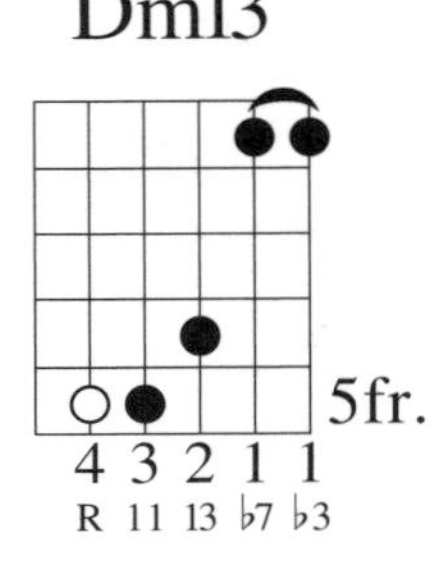

Dm7♭13

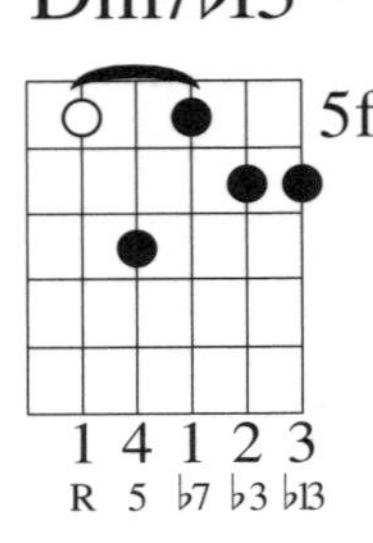

Dm(maj13)

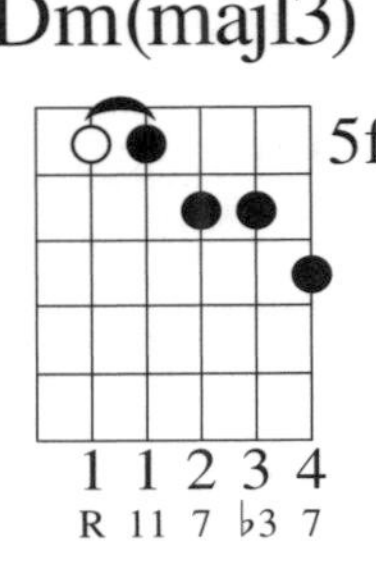

Dm(maj7)♭13

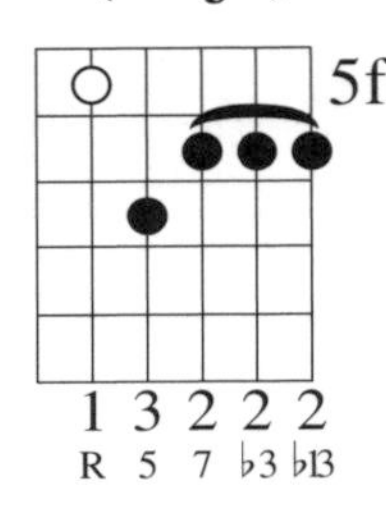

Dm(maj13)♭5

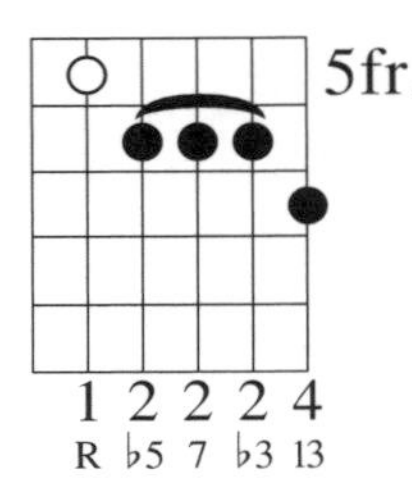

Dm13

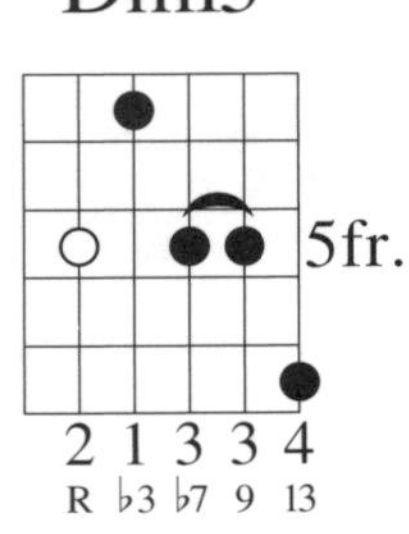

Dm7♭13

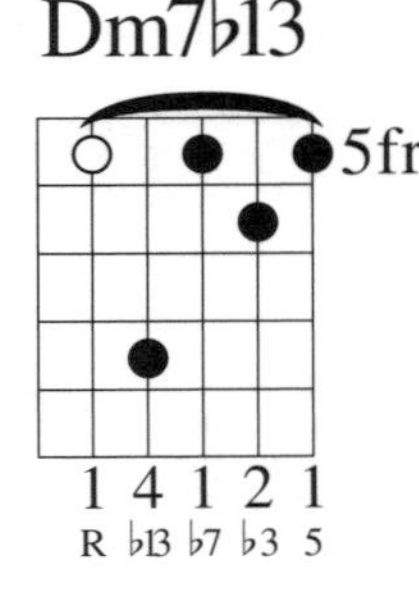

Dm7♭13

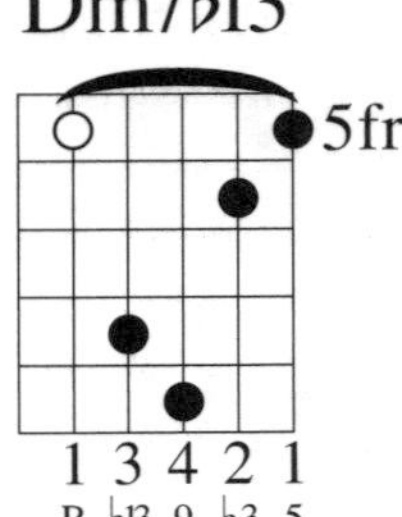

Dm(maj13)

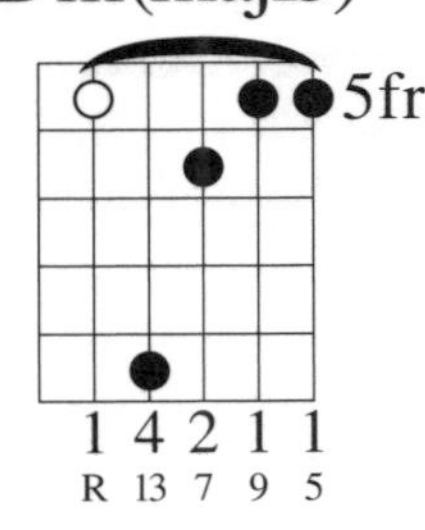

Dm(maj7)♭13

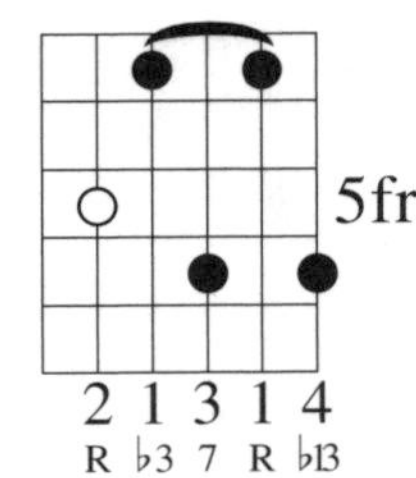

Dm(maj7)♭5♭13

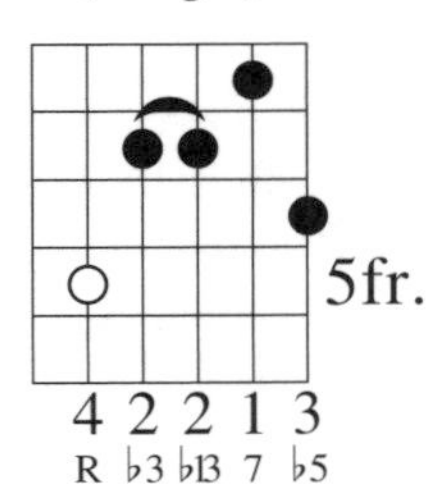

Dm13

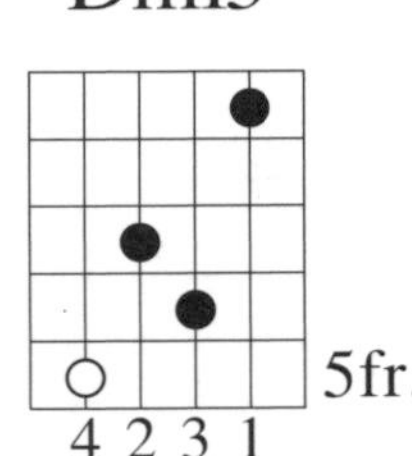

Dm7♭13

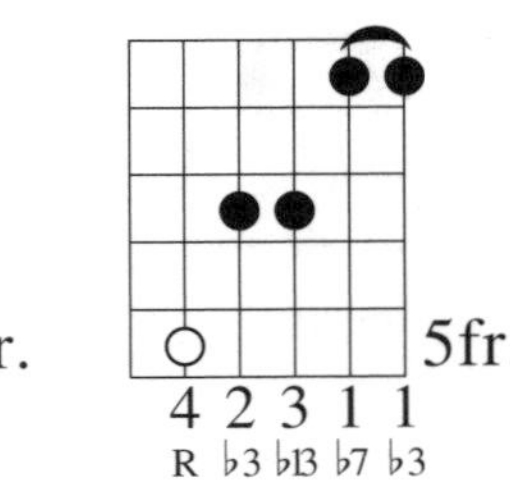

Dm7♭13

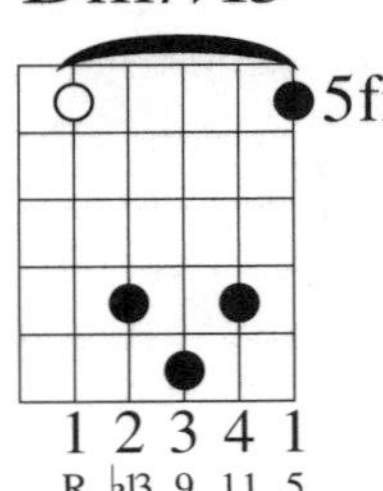

Dm(maj7)♭13

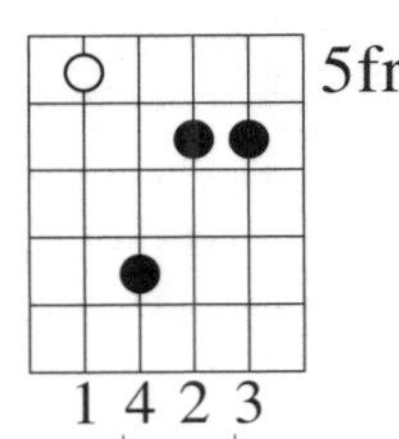

Dm7♭5♭13

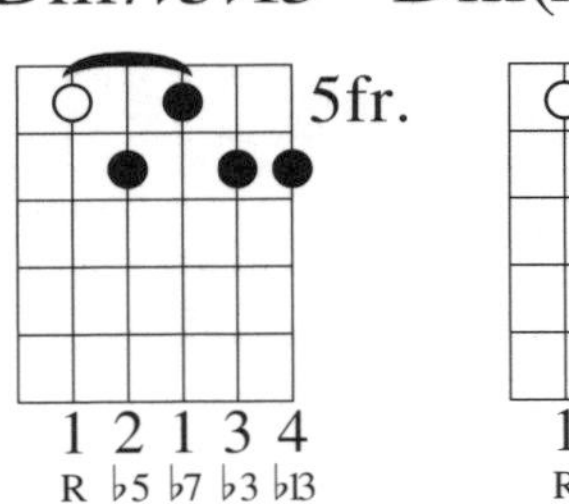

Dm(maj7)♭5♭13

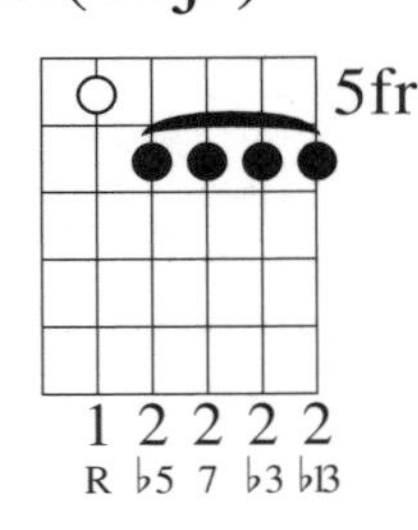

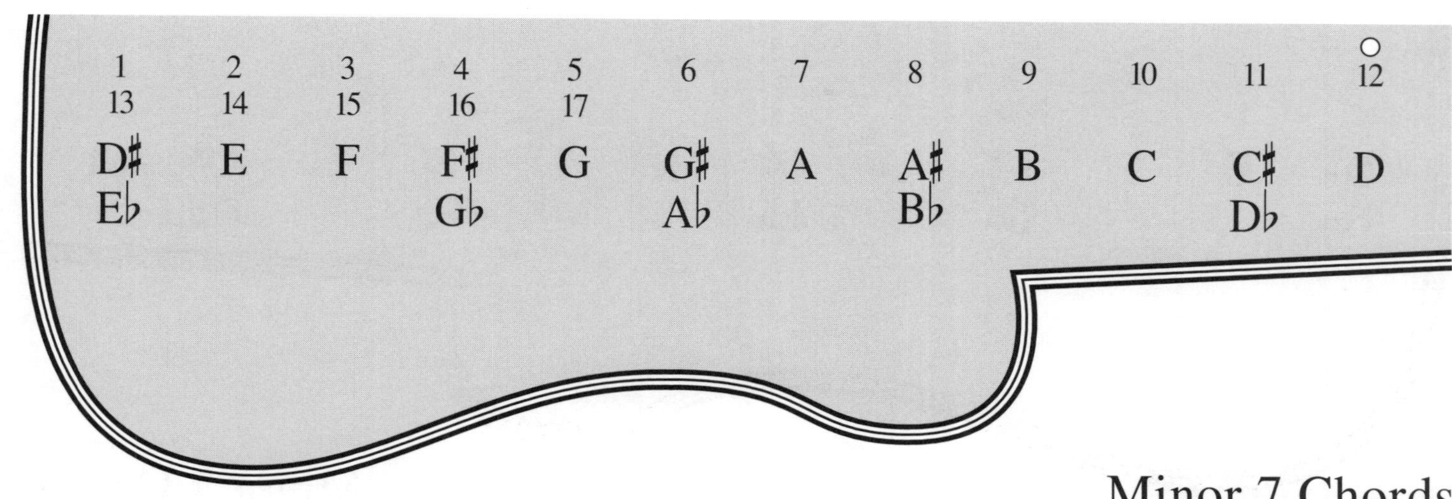

Minor 7 Chords

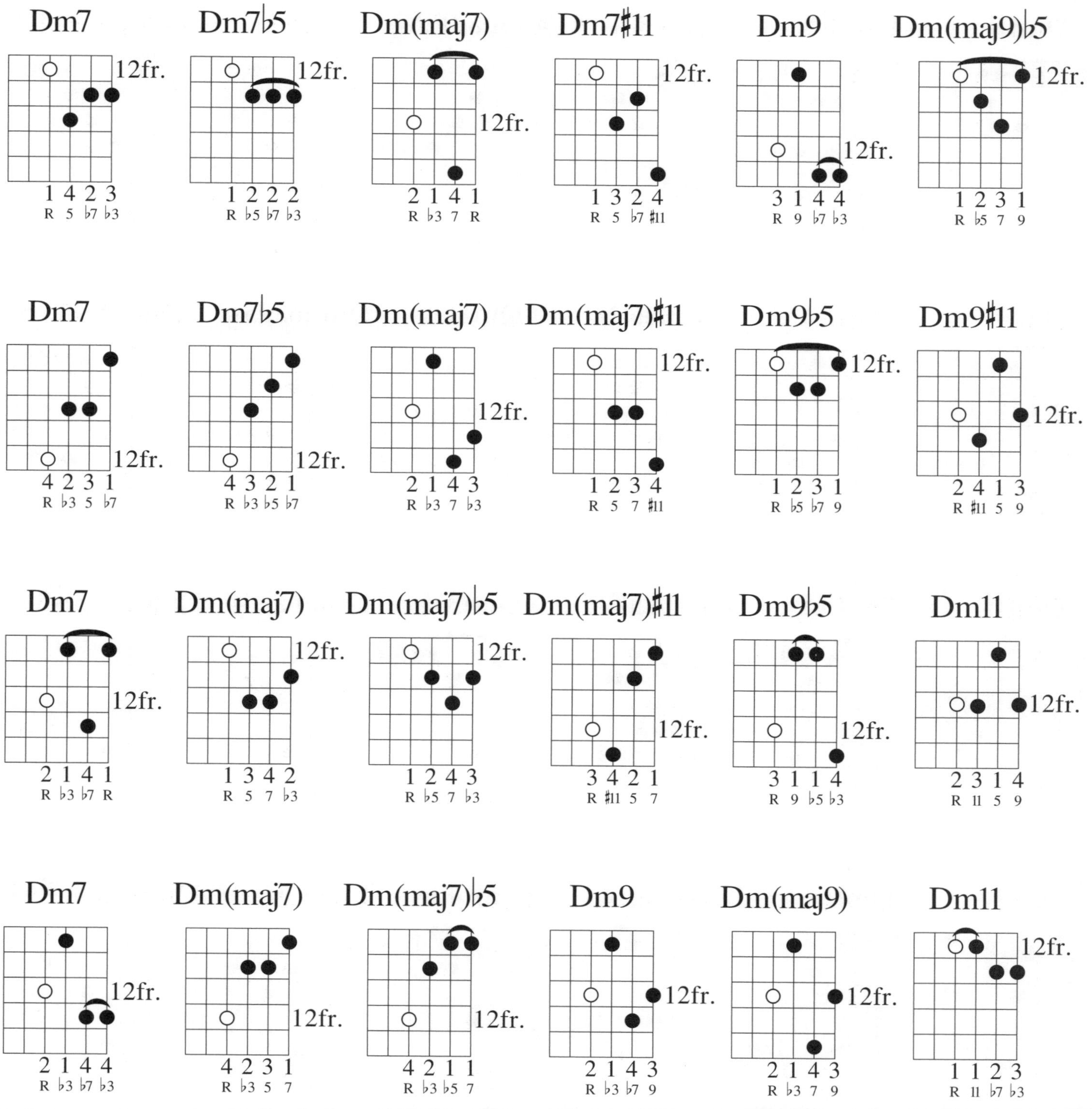

Dm7	Dm7♭5	Dm(maj7)	Dm7♯11	Dm9	Dm(maj9)♭5
12fr.	12fr.	12fr.	12fr.	12fr.	12fr.
1 4 2 3	1 2 2 2	2 1 4 1	1 3 2 4	3 1 4 4	1 2 3 1
R 5 ♭7 ♭3	R ♭5 ♭7 ♭3	R ♭3 7 R	R 5 ♭7 ♯11	R 9 ♭7 ♭3	R ♭5 7 9

Dm7	Dm7♭5	Dm(maj7)	Dm(maj7)♯11	Dm9♭5	Dm9♯11
12fr.	12fr.	12fr.	12fr.	12fr.	12fr.
4 2 3 1	4 3 2 1	2 1 4 3	1 2 3 4	1 2 3 1	2 4 1 3
R ♭3 5 ♭7	R ♭3 ♭5 ♭7	R ♭3 7 ♭3	R 5 7 ♯11	R ♭5 ♭7 9	R ♯11 5 9

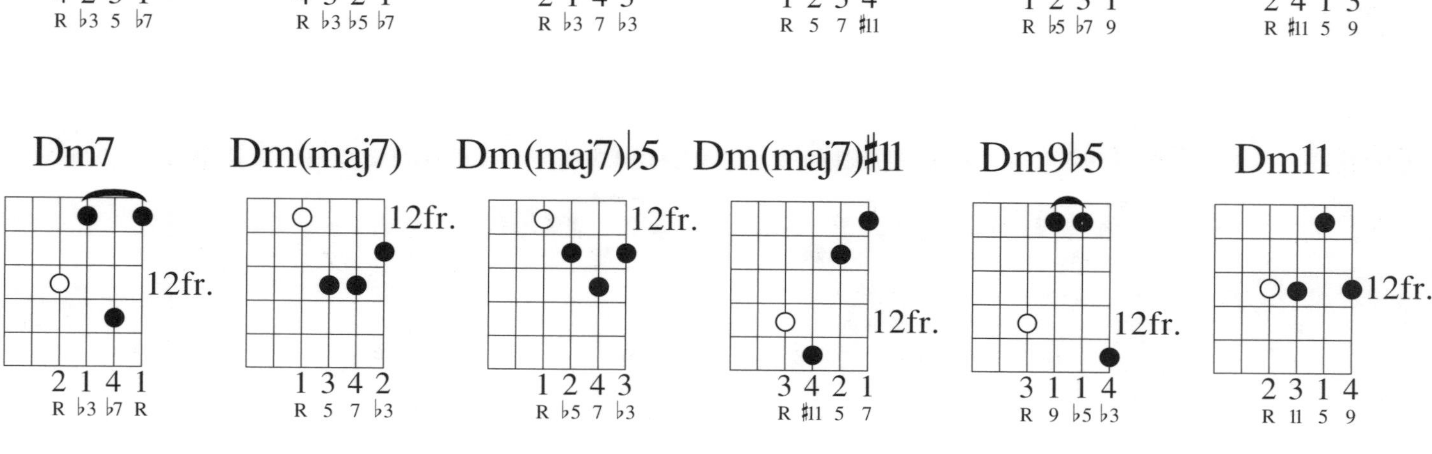

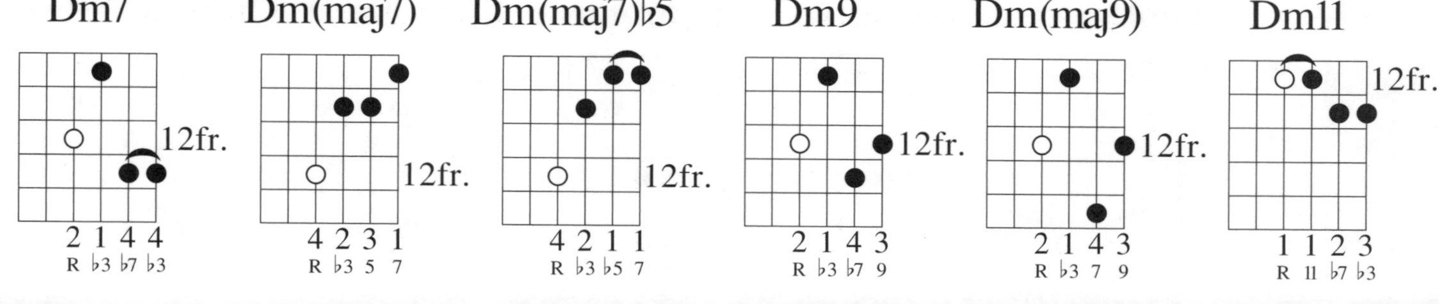

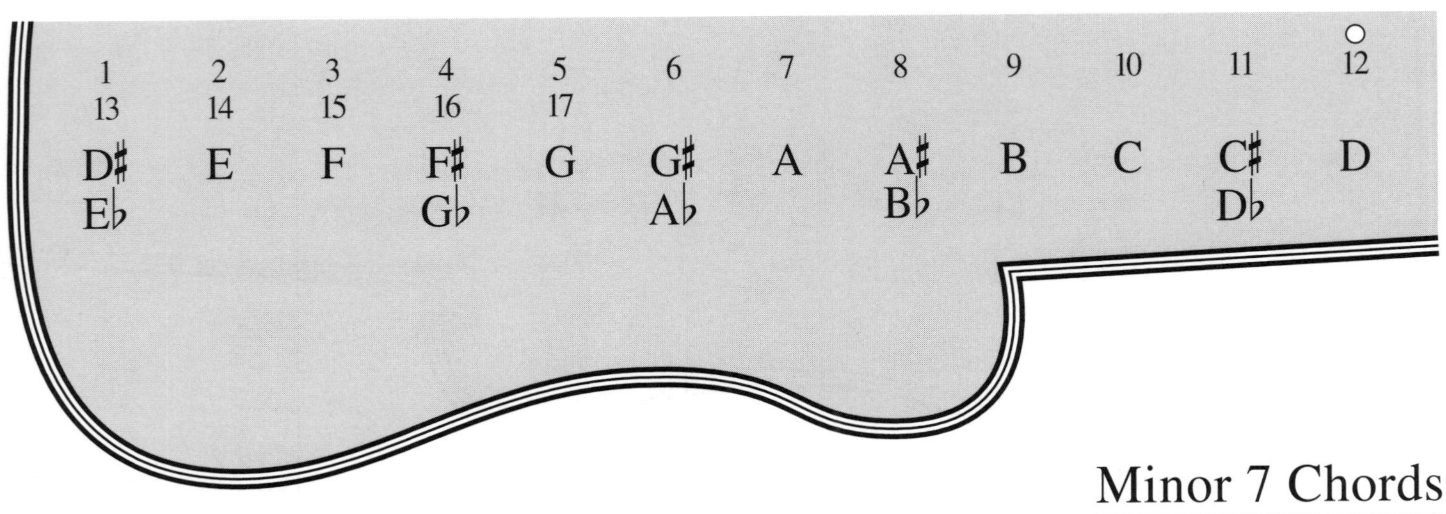

Minor 7 Chords

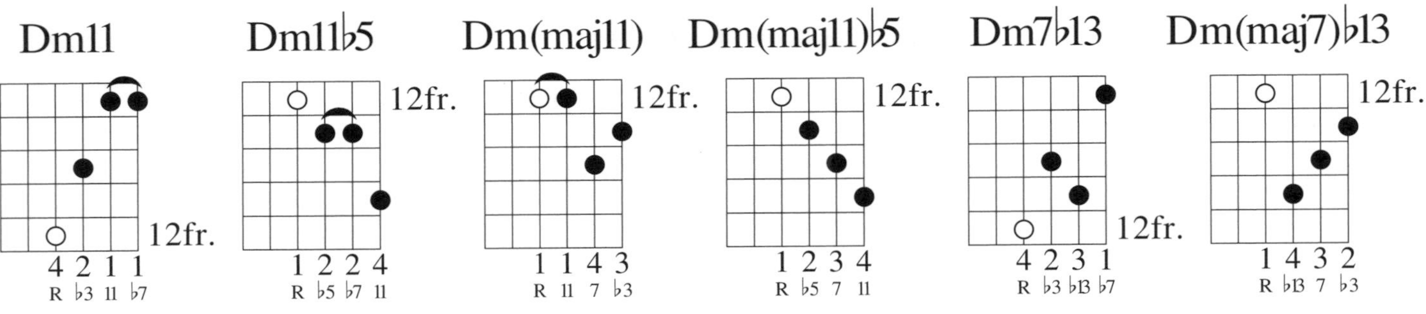

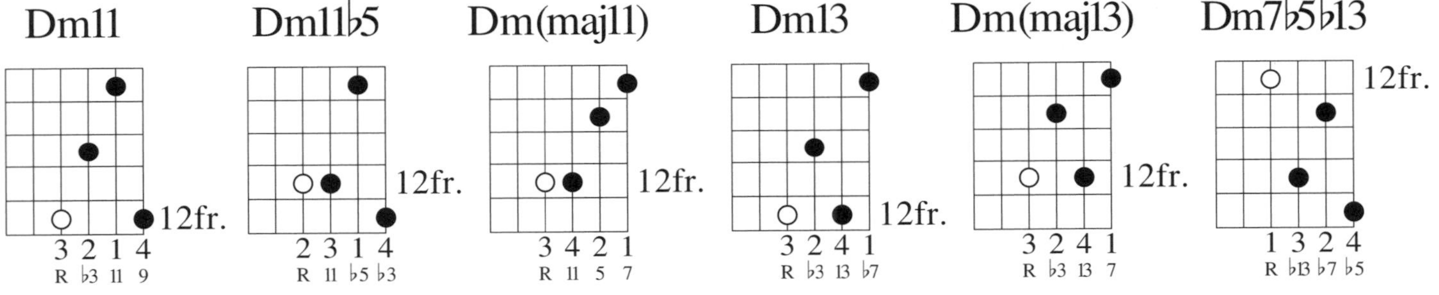

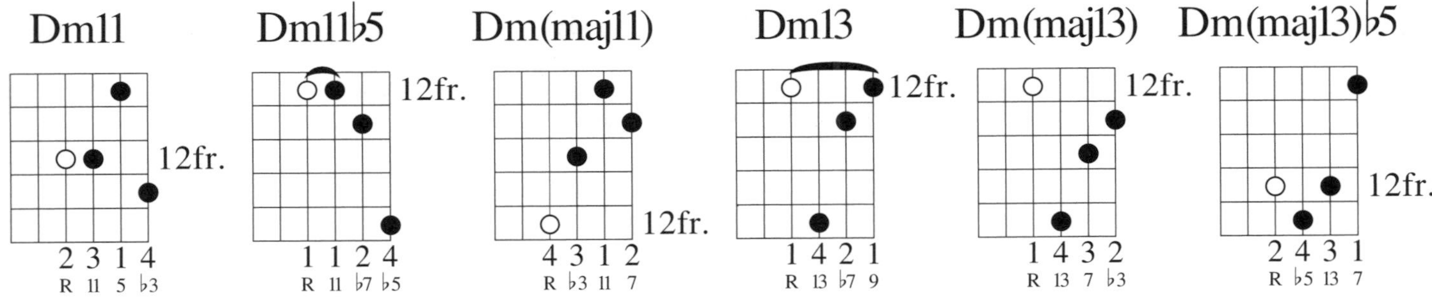

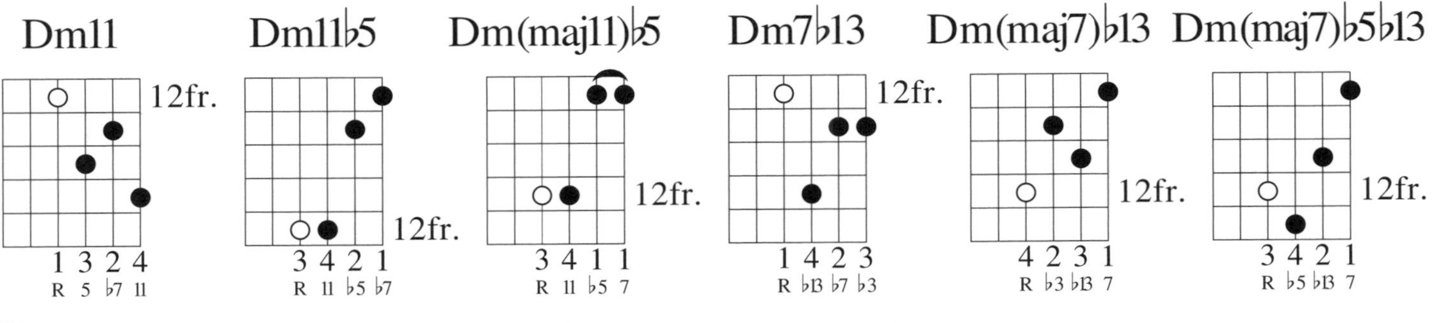

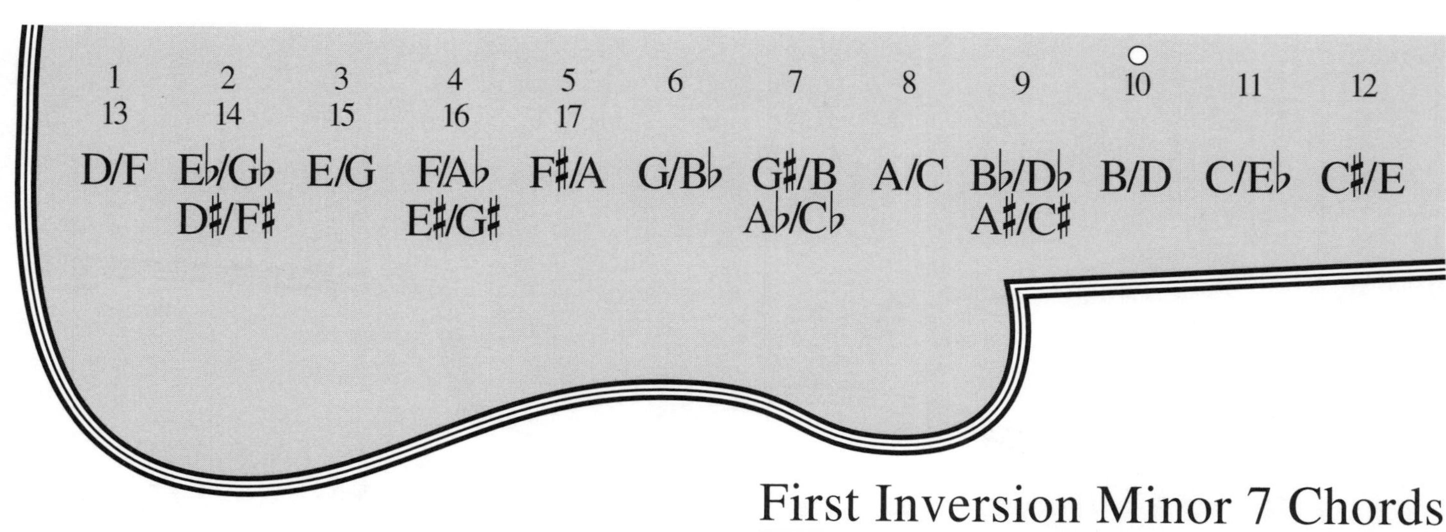

First Inversion Minor 7 Chords

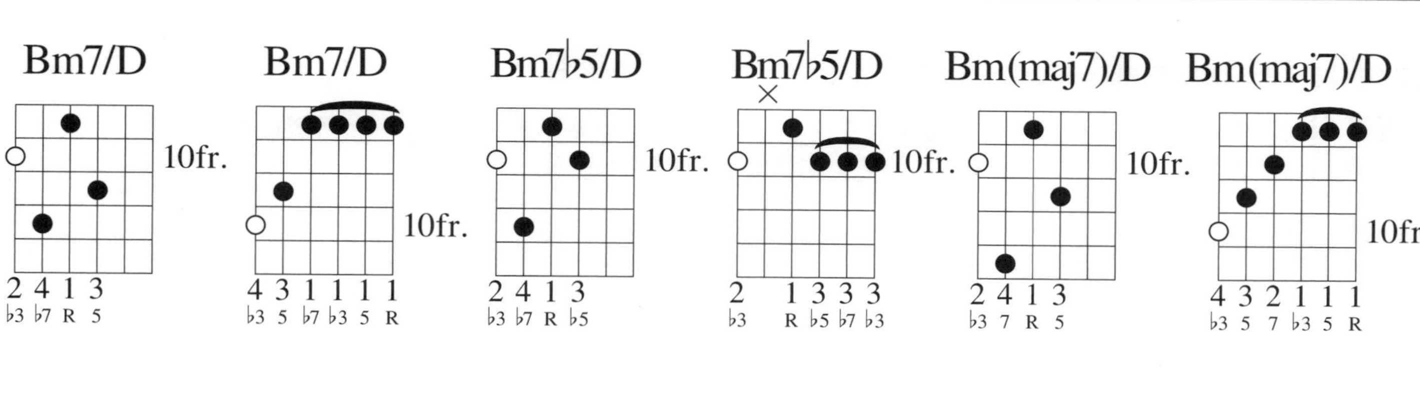

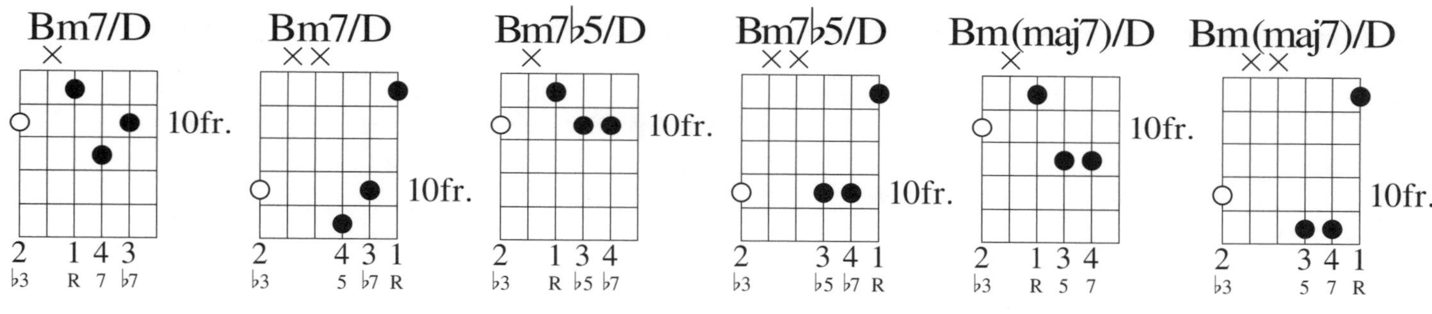

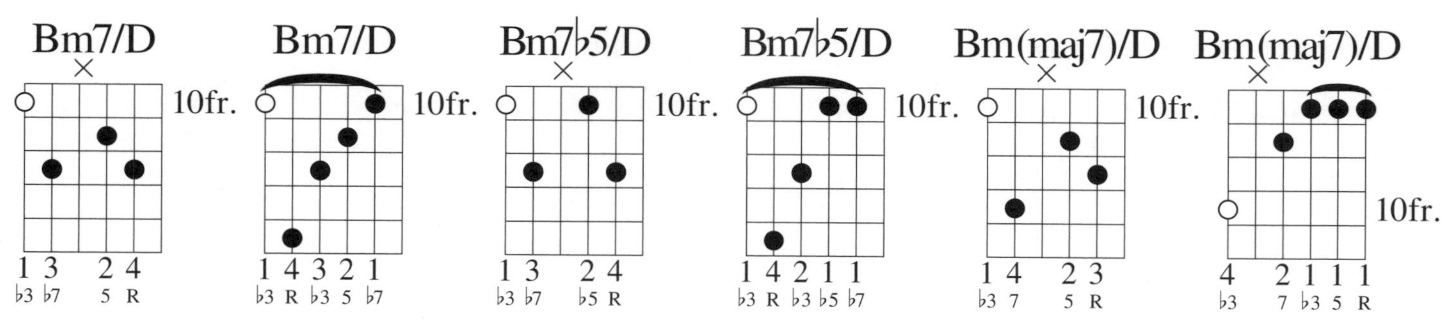

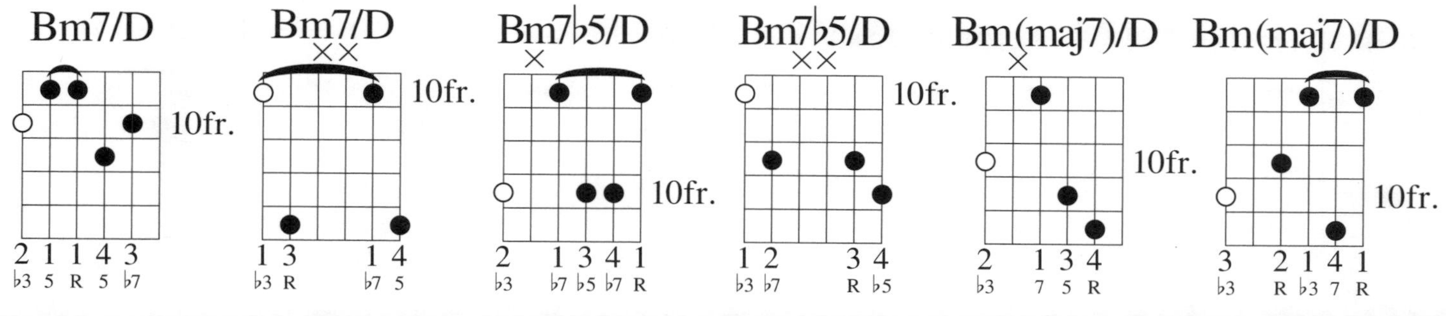

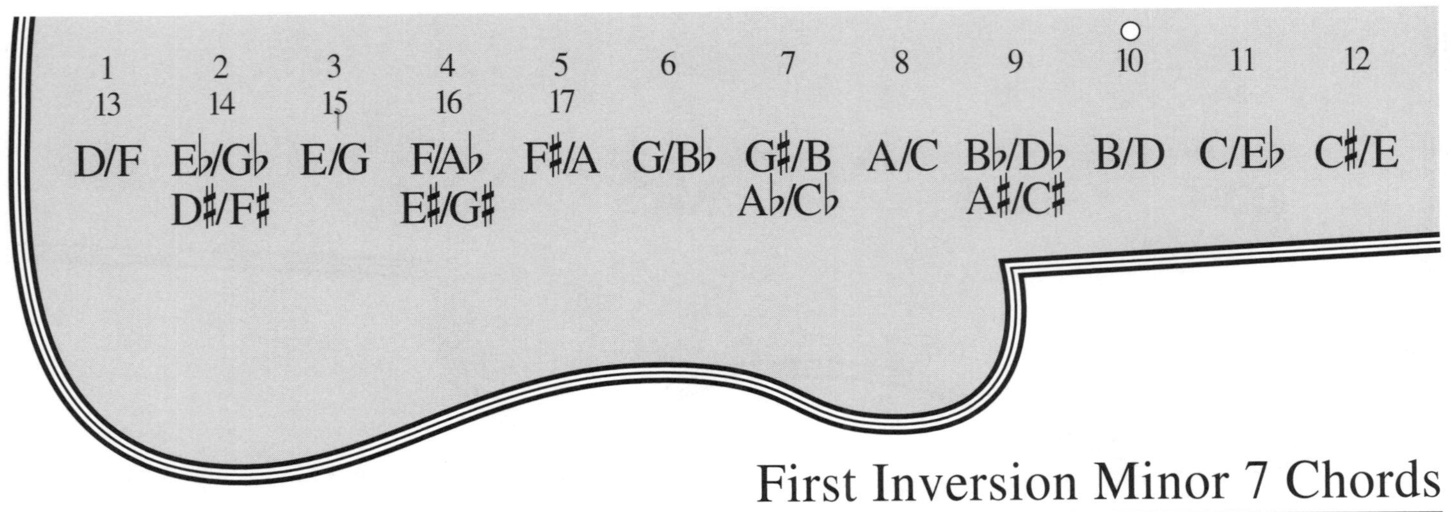

First Inversion Minor 7 Chords

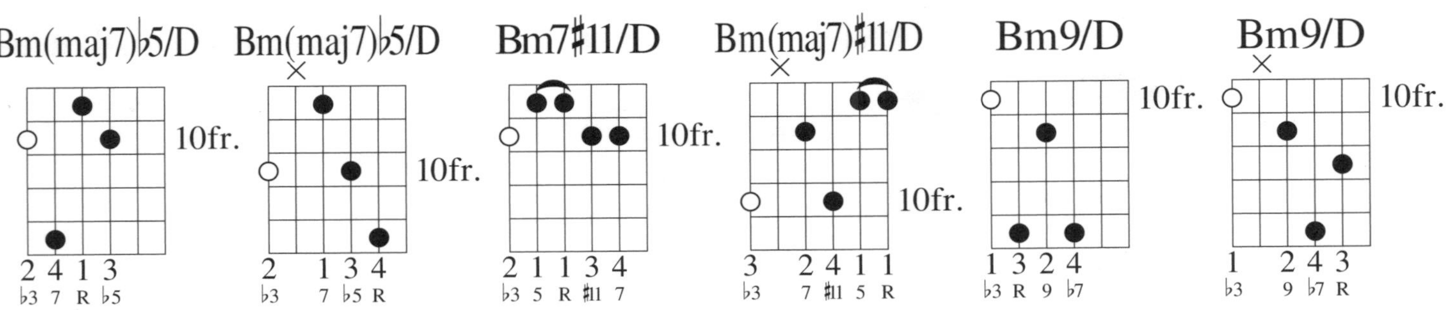

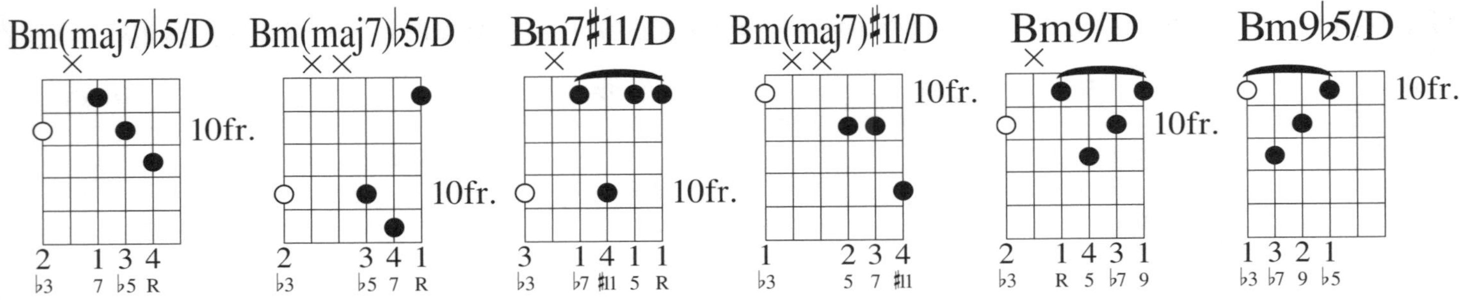

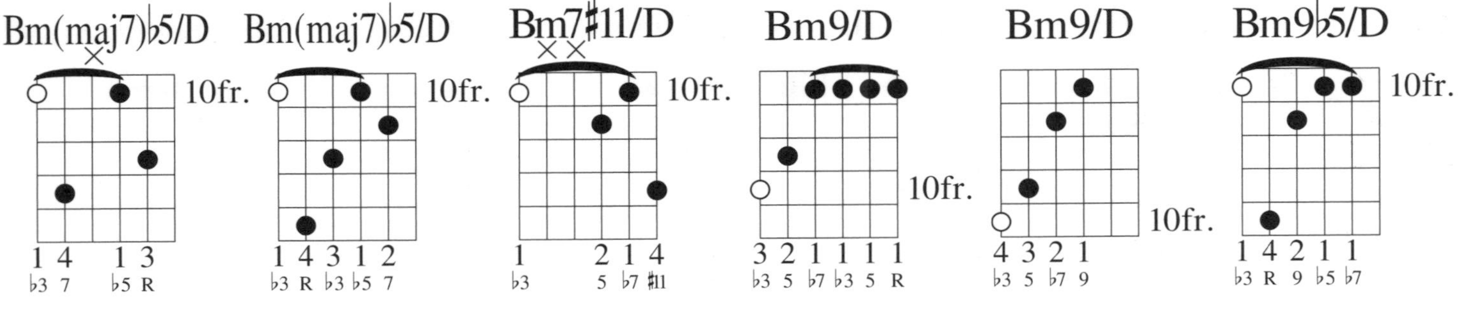

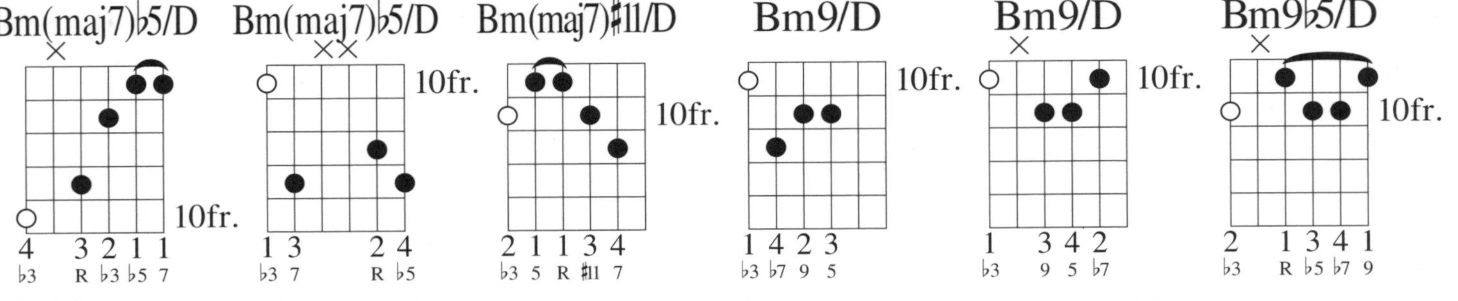

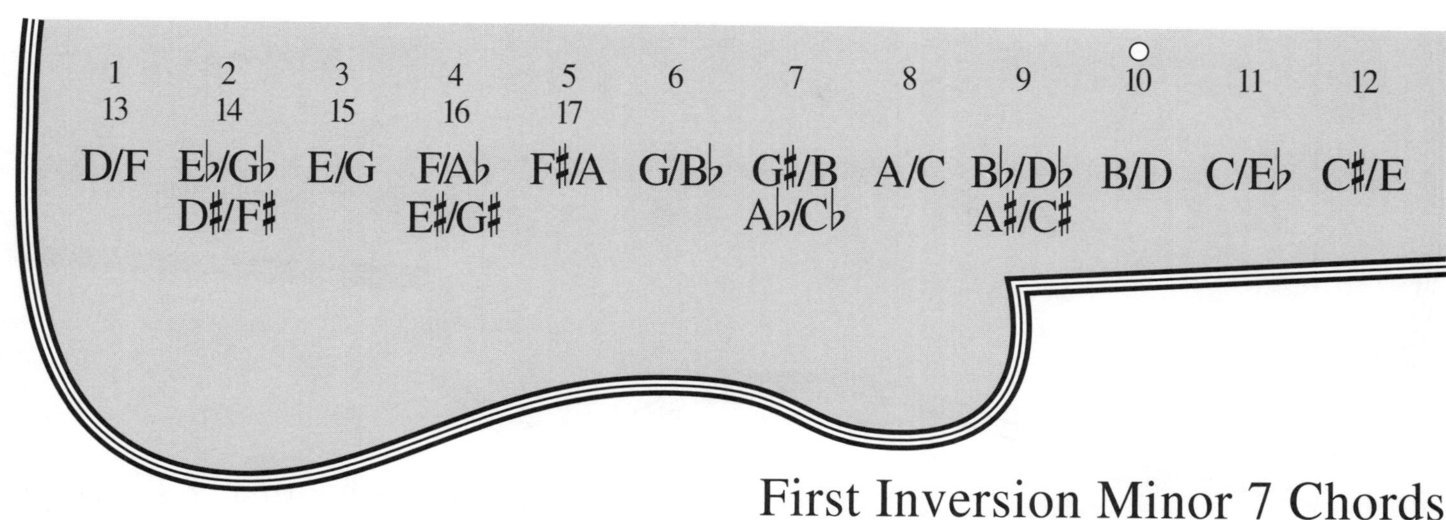

First Inversion Minor 7 Chords

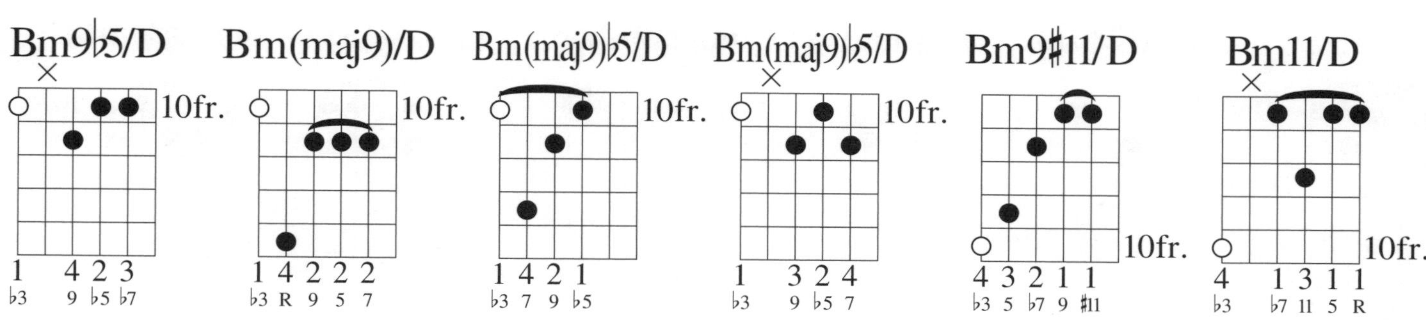

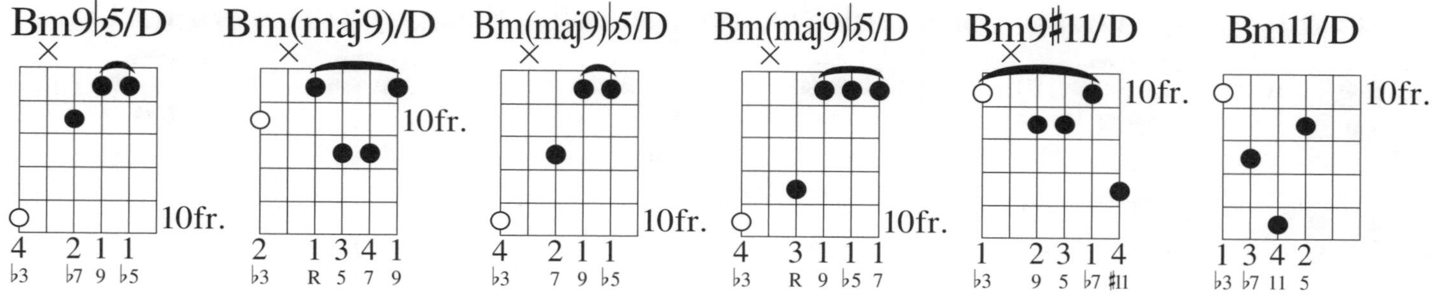

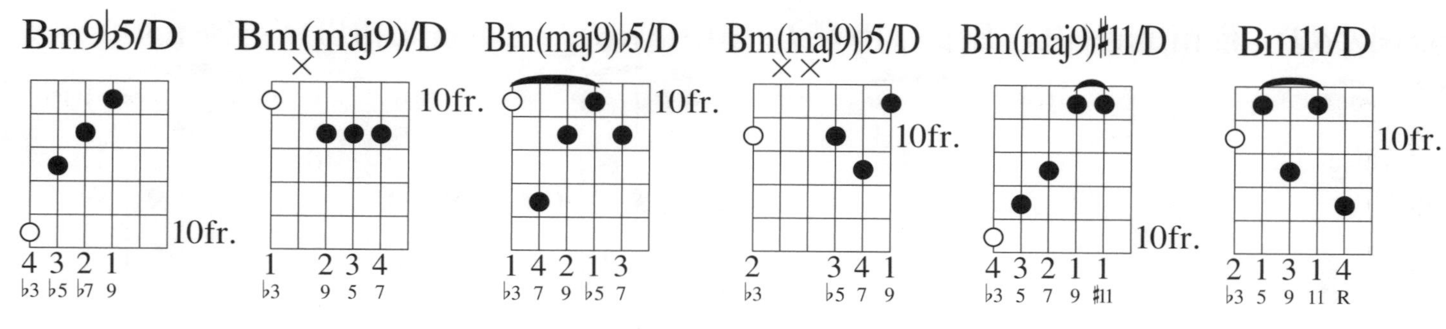

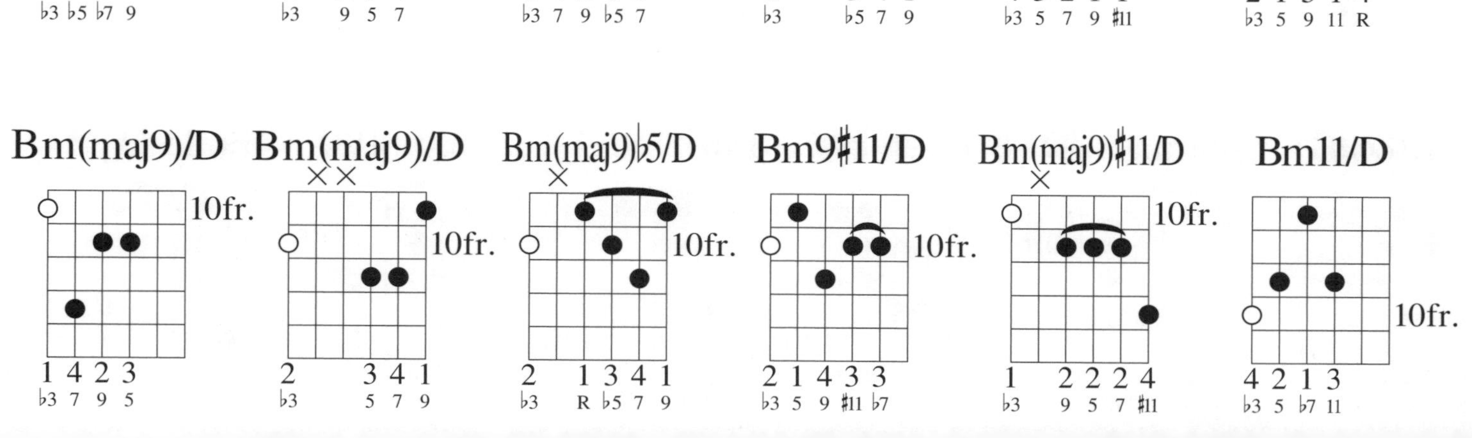

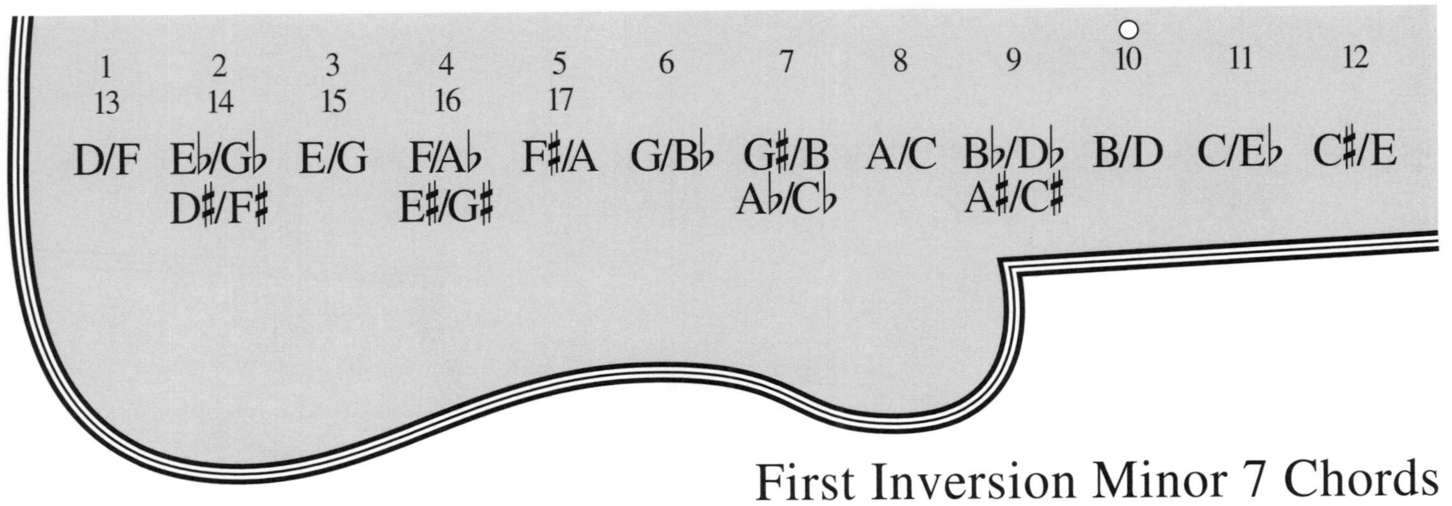

First Inversion Minor 7 Chords

Bm11/D

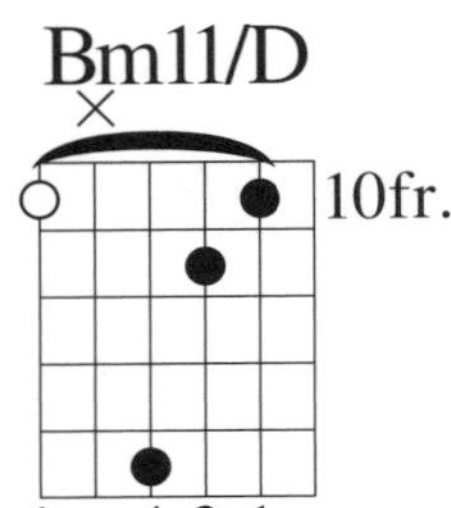
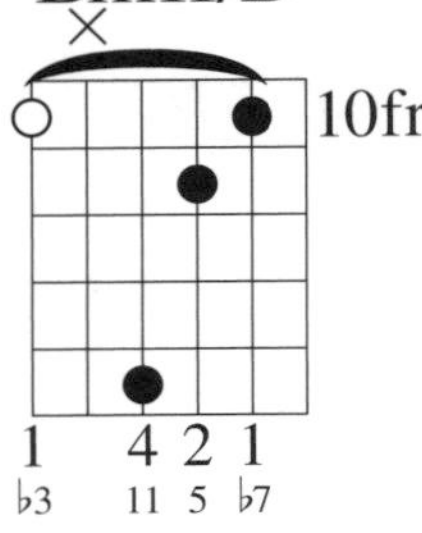

Bm11♭5/D

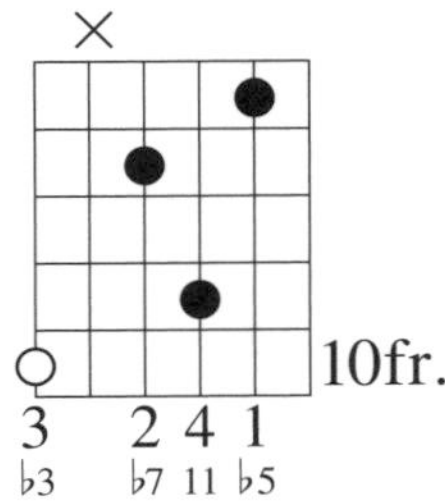

Bm(maj11)/D

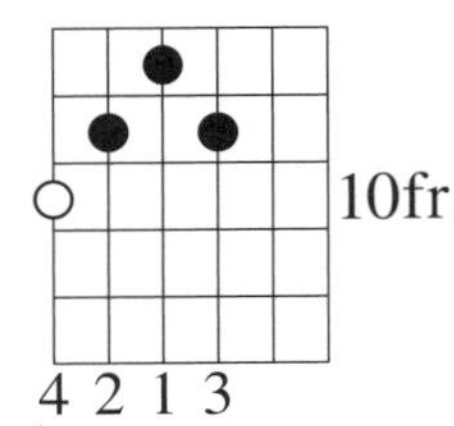

Bm(maj11)♭5/D

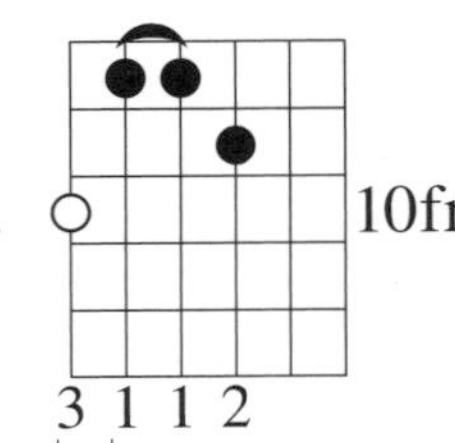

Bm13♯11/D

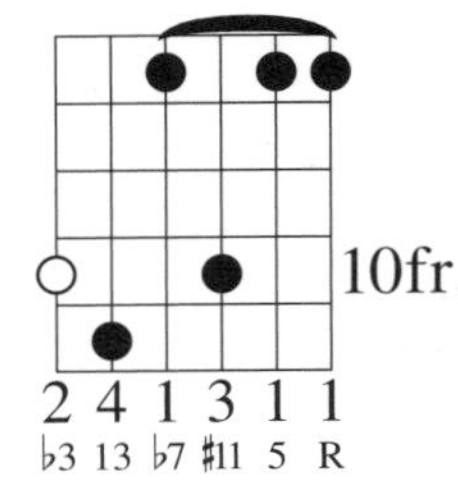

Bm(maj13)♯11/D

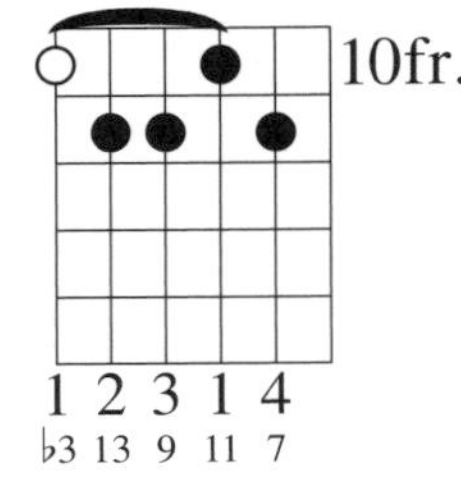

Bm11♭5/D

Bm11♭5/D

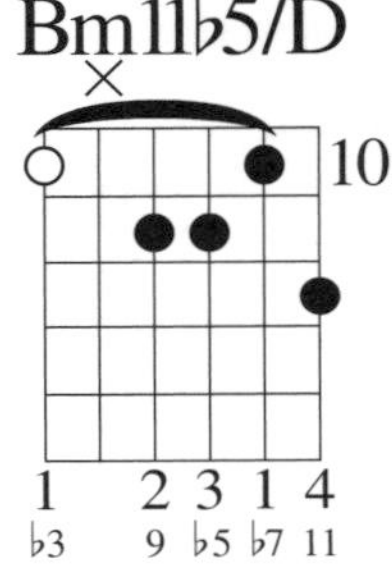

Bm(maj11)/D

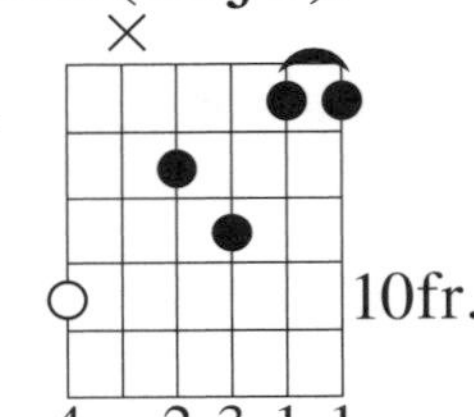

Bm(maj11)♭5/D

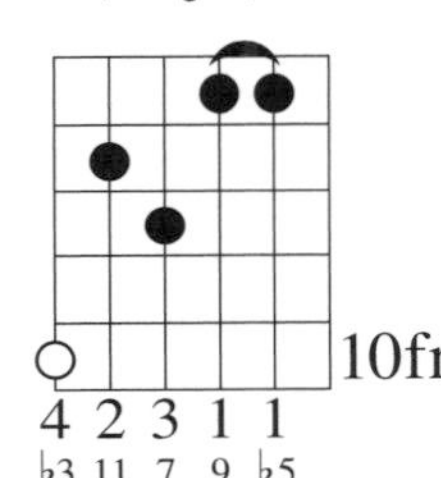

Bm(maj13)♯11/D

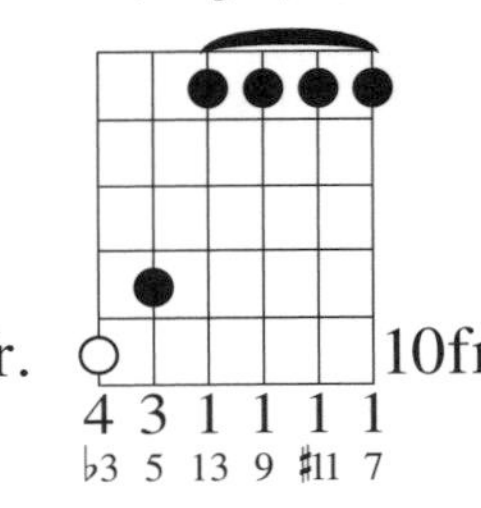

Bm13/D

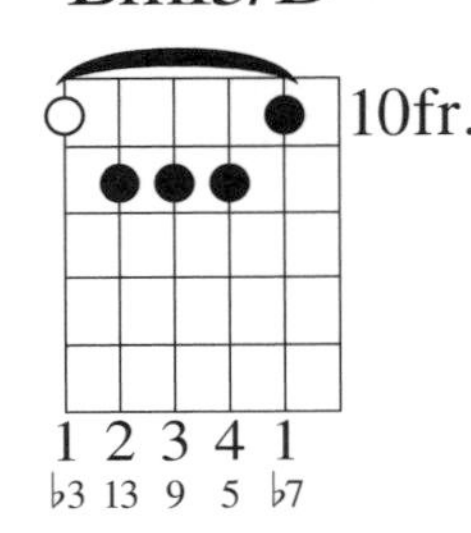

Bm11♭5/D

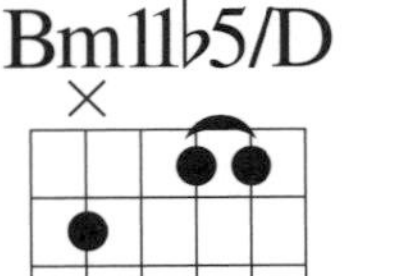
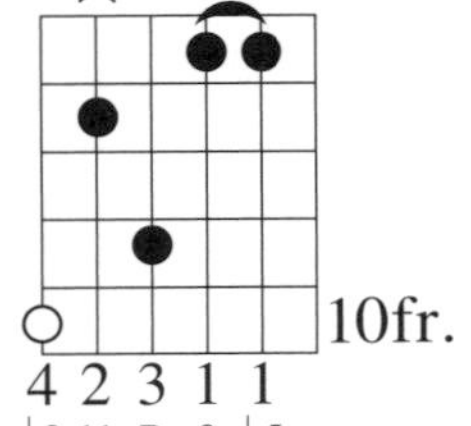

Bm(maj11)/D

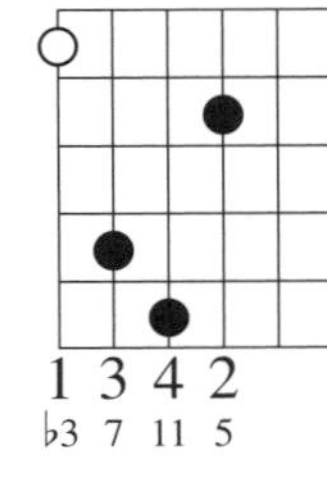

Bm(maj11)♭5/D

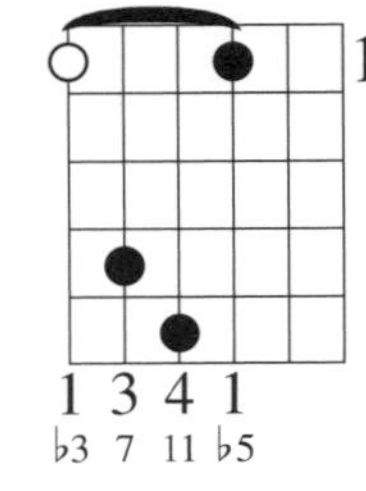

Bm13♯11/D

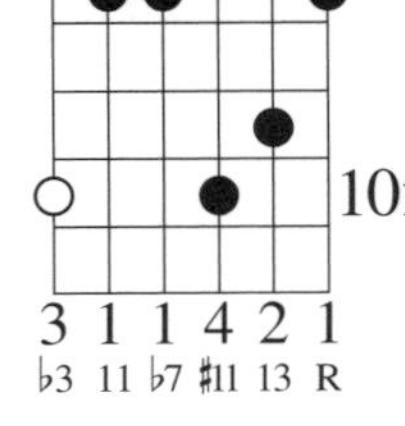

Bm(maj13)♯11/D

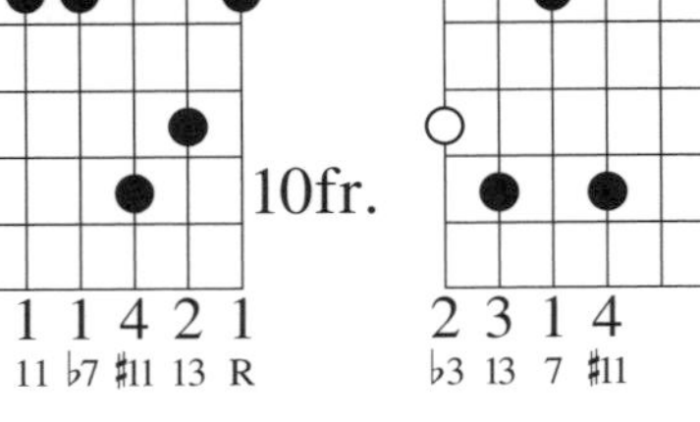

Bm13/D

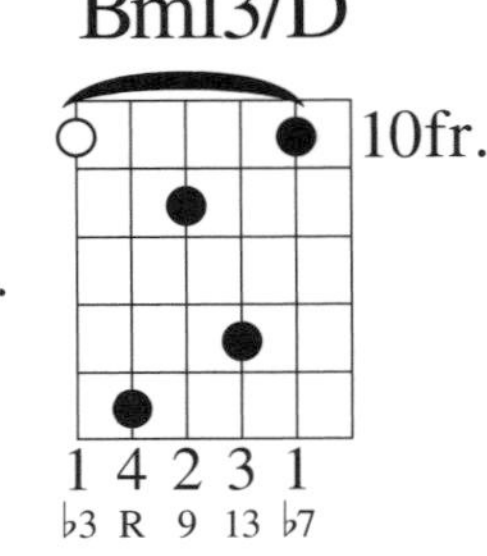

Bm11♭5/D

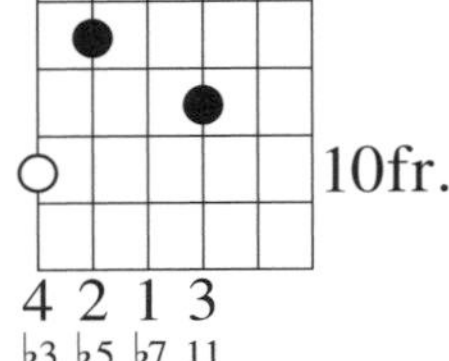

Bm(maj11)/D

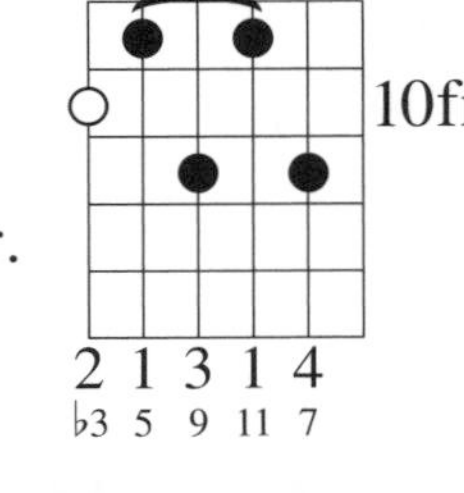

Bm(maj11)♭5/D

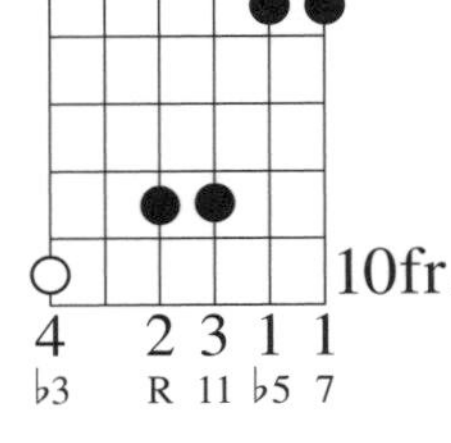

Bm13♯11/D

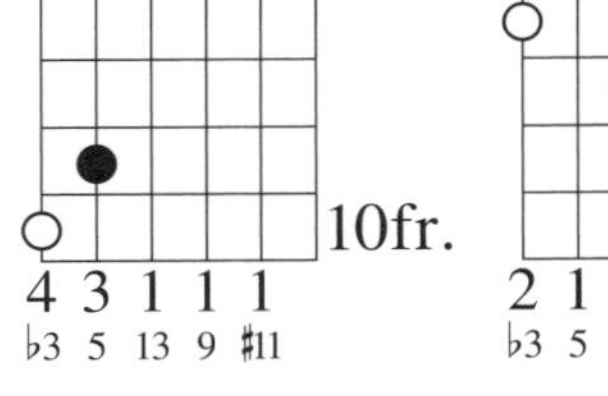

Bm(maj13)♯11/D

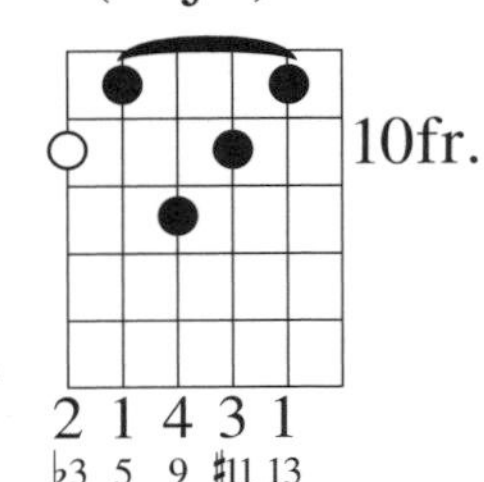

Bm13/D

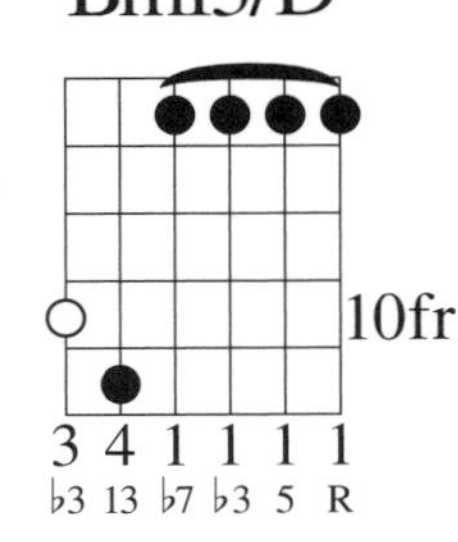

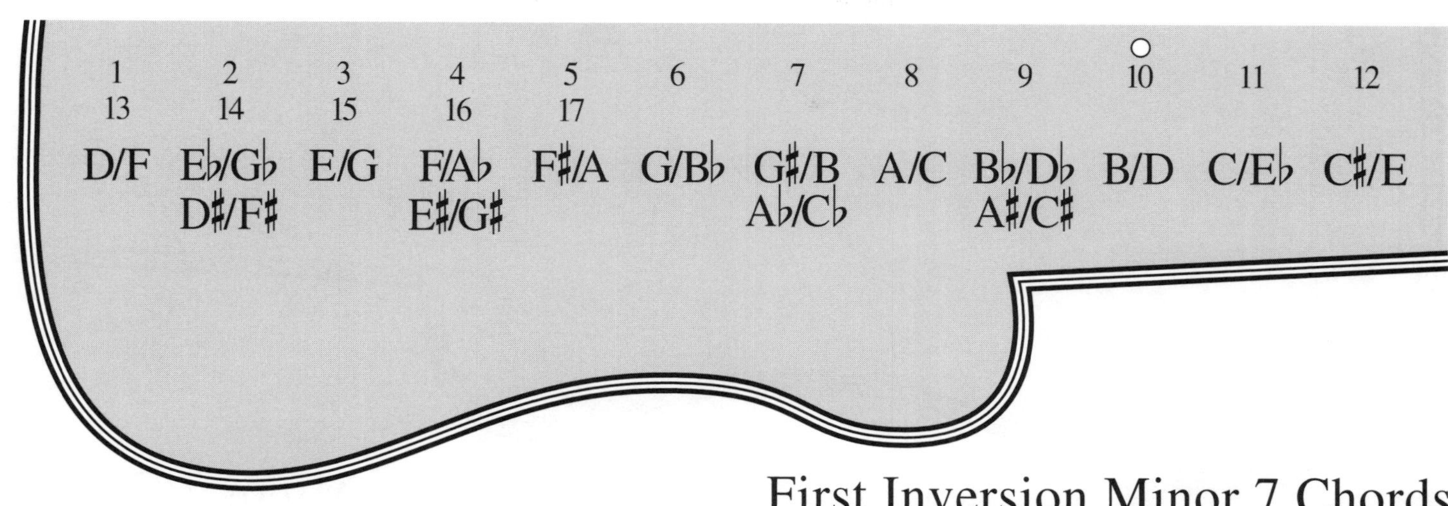

First Inversion Minor 7 Chords

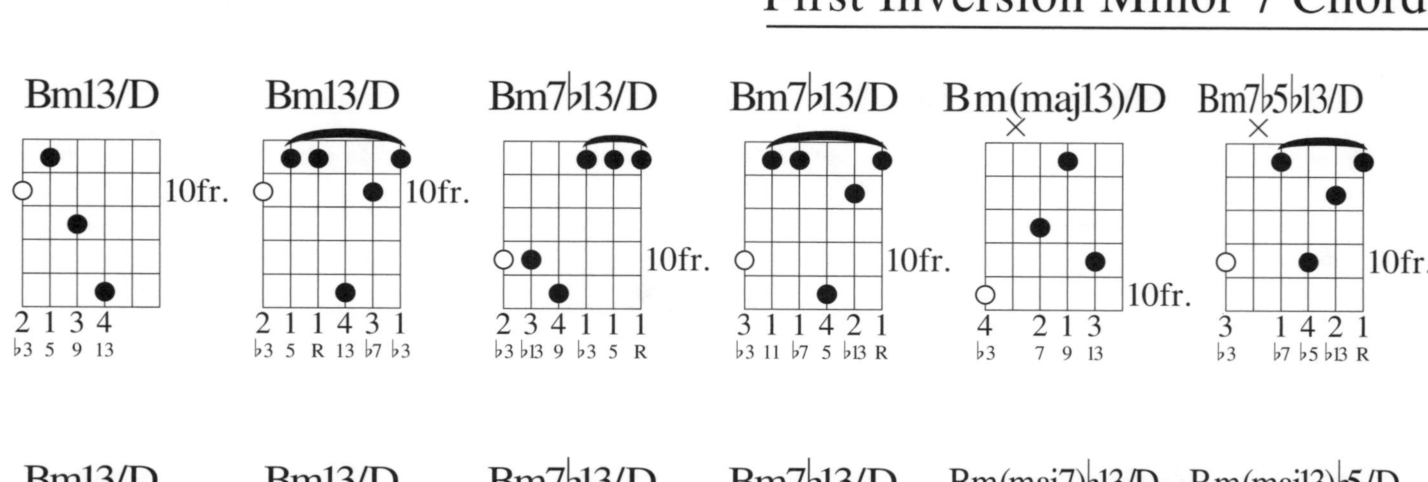

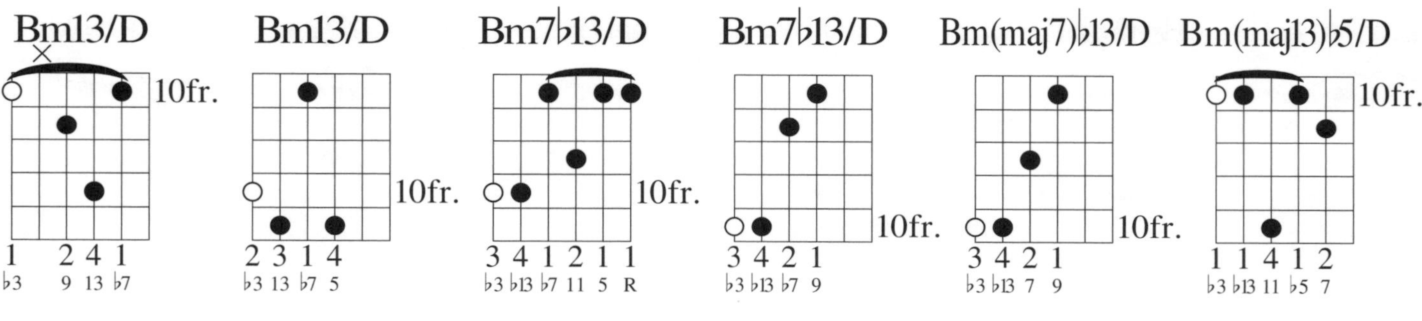

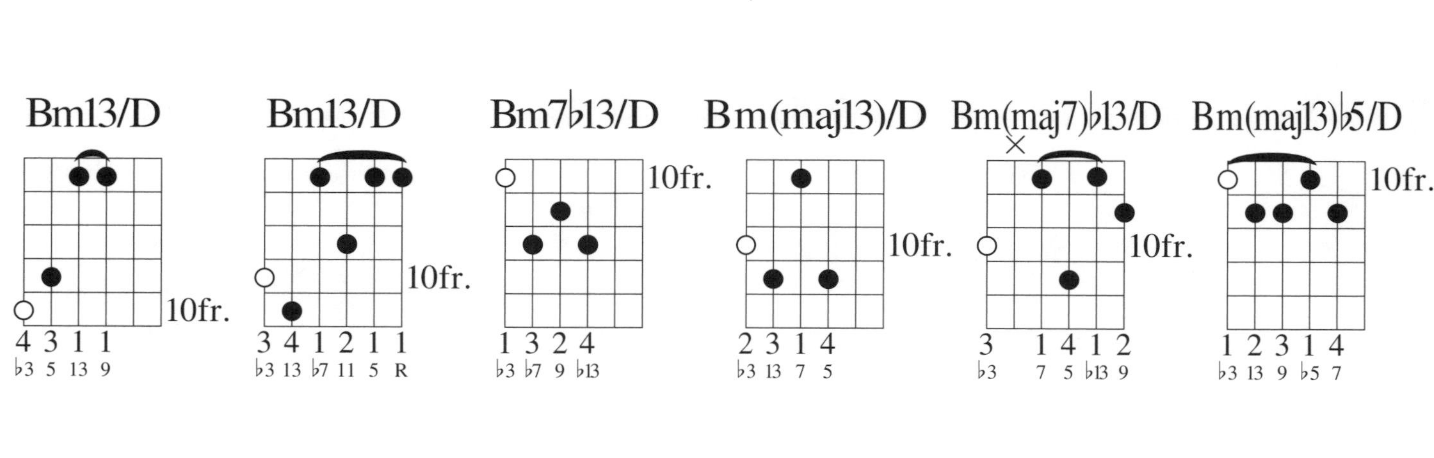

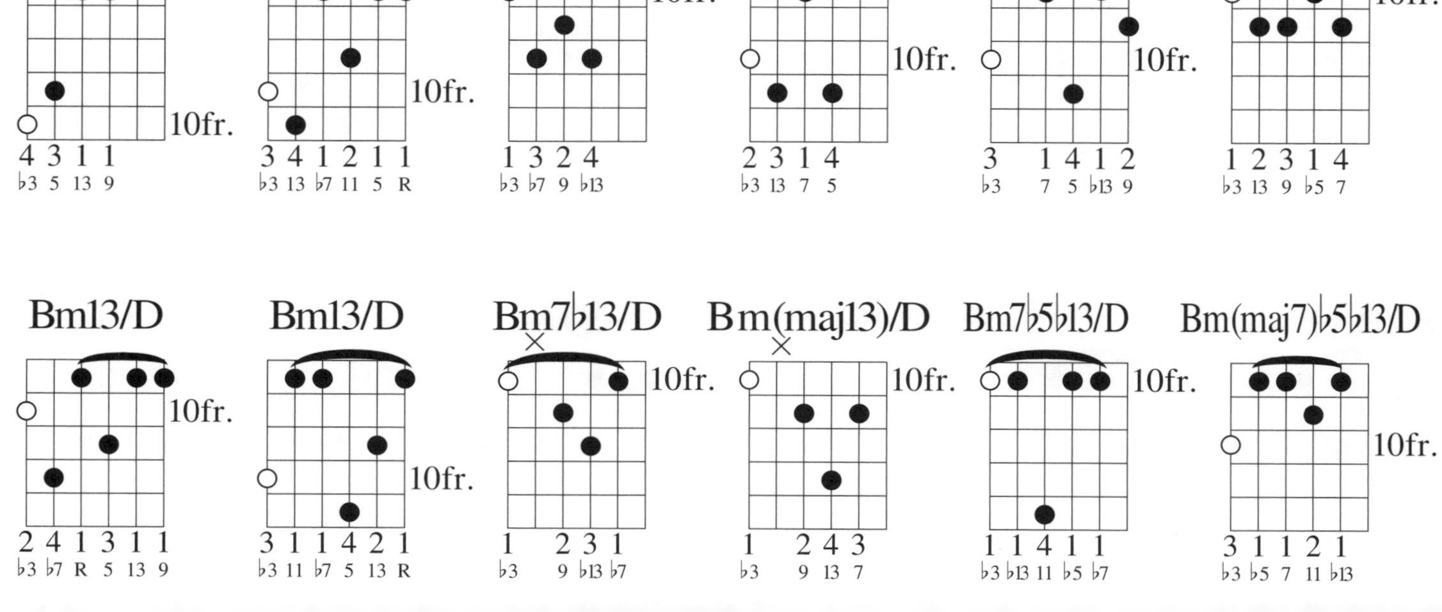

1 13 G/B♭
2 14 G♯/B A♭/C♭
3 15 A/C
4 16 B♭/D♭ A♯/C♯
5 17 B/D
6 C/E♭
7 C♯/E
8 D/F
9 E♭/G♭ D♯/F♯
10 E/G
11 F/A♭ E♯/G♯
12 F♯/A

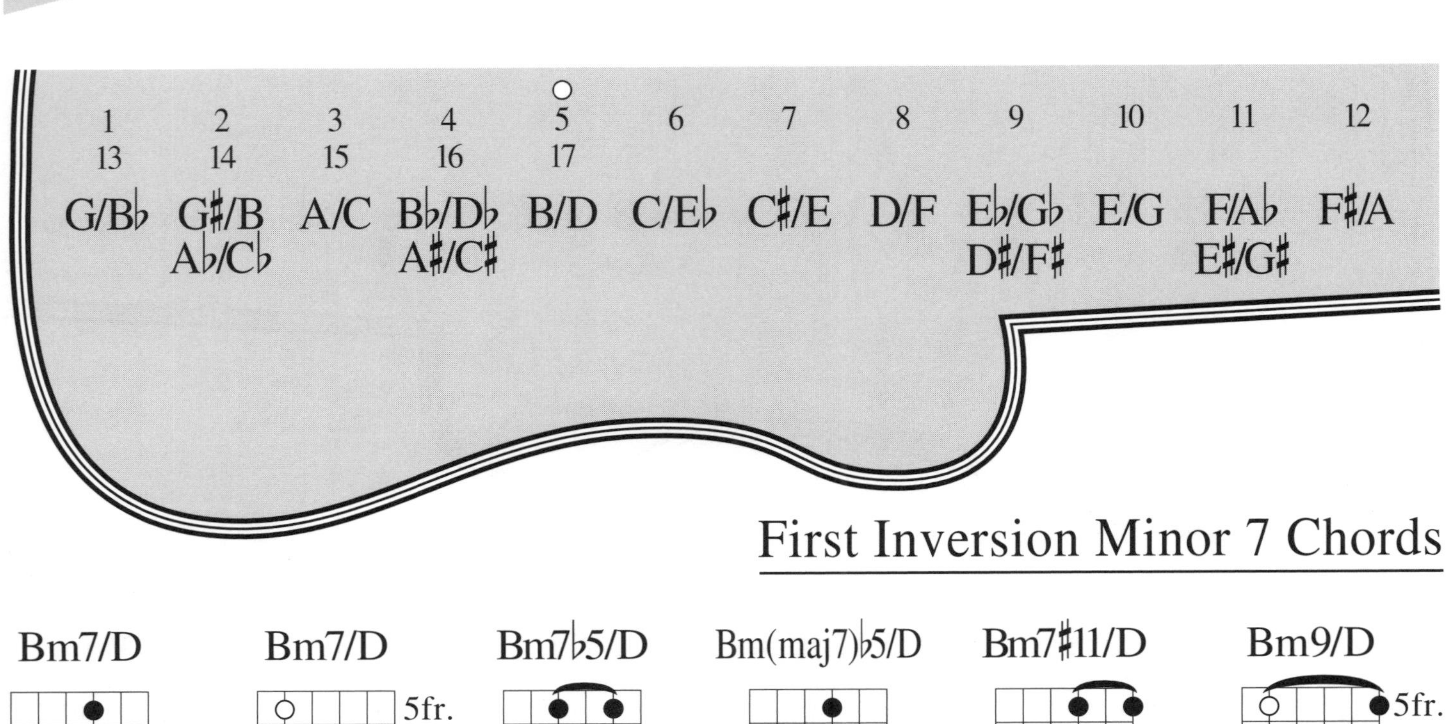

First Inversion Minor 7 Chords

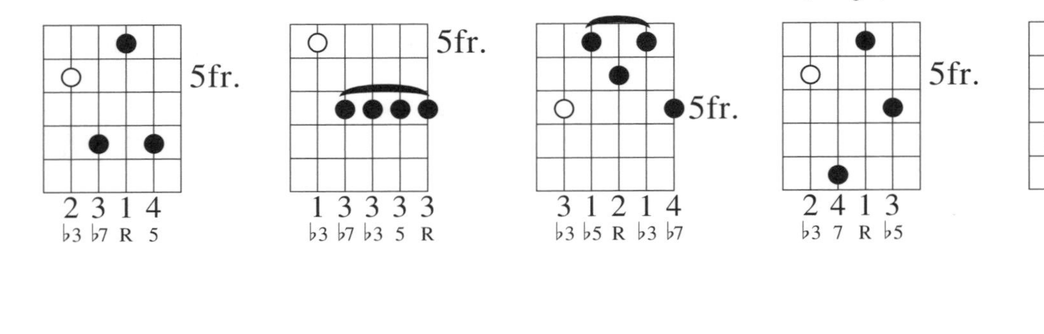

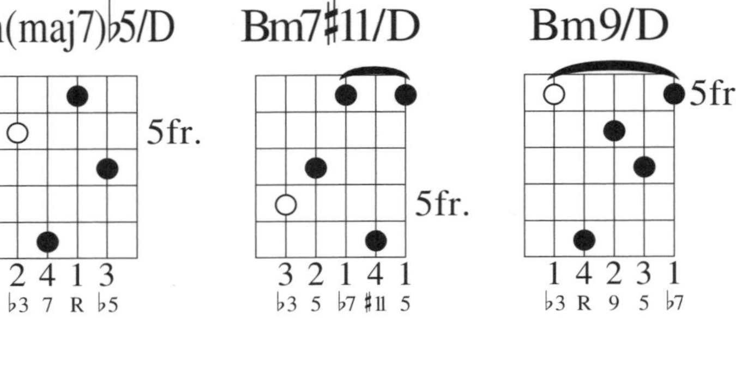

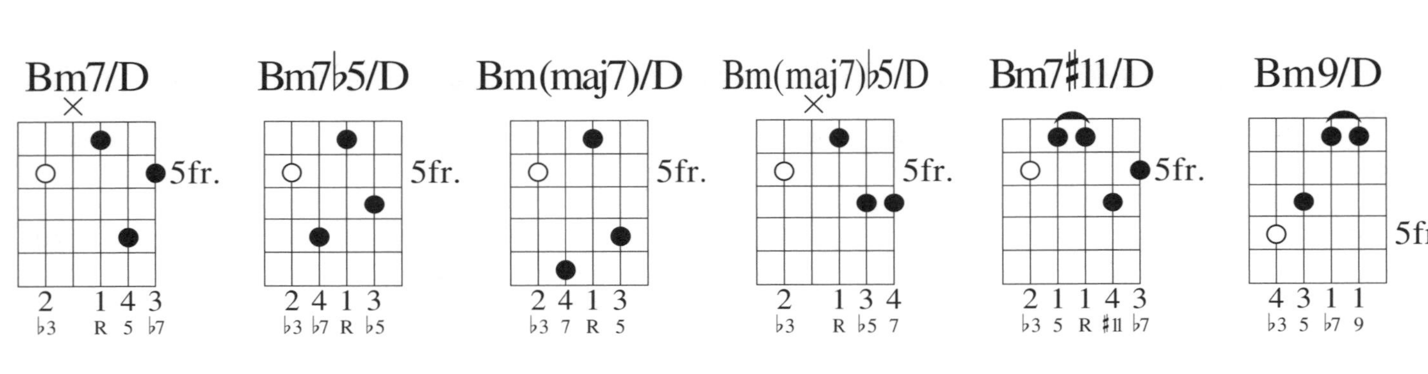

Bm7/D | Bm7/D | Bm7♭5/D | Bm(maj7)♭5/D | Bm7♯11/D | Bm9/D

5fr. 2 3 1 4 ♭3 ♭7 R 5
5fr. 1 3 3 3 3 ♭3 ♭7 ♭3 5 R
5fr. 3 1 2 1 4 ♭3 ♭5 R ♭3 ♭7
5fr. 2 4 1 3 ♭3 7 R ♭5
5fr. 3 2 1 4 1 ♭3 5 ♭7 ♯11 5
5fr. 1 4 2 3 1 ♭3 R 9 5 ♭7

Bm7/D | Bm7♭5/D | Bm(maj7)/D | Bm(maj7)♭5/D | Bm7♯11/D | Bm9/D

5fr. 2 1 4 3 ♭3 R 5 ♭7
5fr. 2 4 1 3 ♭3 ♭7 R ♭5
5fr. 2 4 1 3 ♭3 7 R 5
5fr. 2 1 3 4 ♭3 R ♭5 7
5fr. 2 1 1 4 3 ♭3 5 R ♯11 ♭7
5fr. 4 3 1 1 ♭3 5 ♭7 9

Bm7/D | Bm7♭5/D | Bm(maj7)/D | Bm(maj7)♭5/D | Bm7♯11/D | Bm9/D

5fr. 1 2 3 4 ♭3 ♭7 5 R
5fr. 1 3 2 4 ♭3 ♭7 ♭5 R
5fr. 2 1 4 3 ♭3 R 5 7
5fr. 1 4 2 3 ♭3 7 ♭5 R
5fr. 3 1 4 1 ♭3 ♭7 ♯11 5
5fr. 1 4 2 3 ♭3 ♭7 9 5

Bm7/D | Bm7♭5/D | Bm(maj7)/D | Bm(maj7)♭5/D | Bm(maj7)♯11/D | Bm9/D

5fr. 1 4 2 3 1 ♭3 R ♭3 5 ♭7
5fr. 1 4 3 2 1 ♭3 R ♭3 ♭5 ♭7
5fr. 1 4 2 3 ♭3 7 5 R
5fr. 2 1 3 1 4 ♭3 ♭5 R ♭3 7
5fr. 2 1 1 3 4 ♭3 5 R ♯11 7
5fr. 1 3 2 4 4 ♭3 ♭7 9 5 R

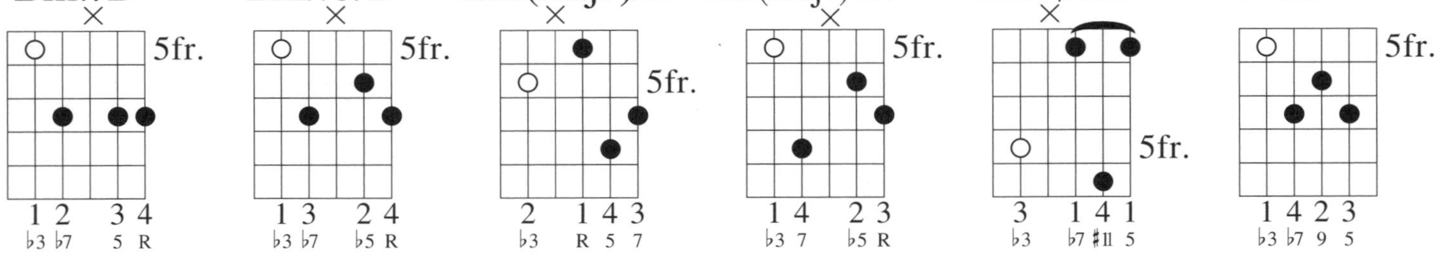

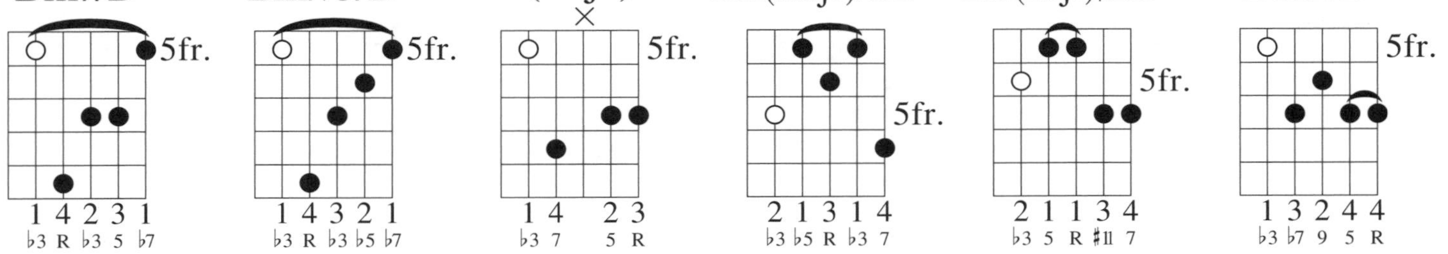

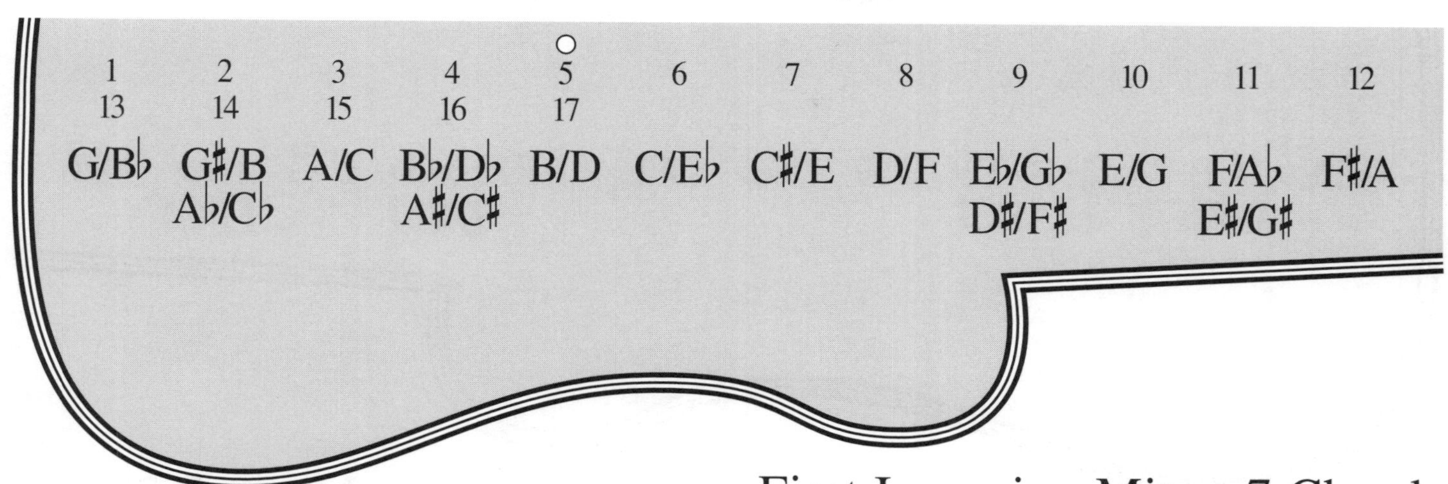

First Inversion Minor 7 Chords

Bm9♭5/D	Bm(maj9)/D	Bm(maj9)♭5/D	Bm9♯11/D	Bm11/D	Bm11/D
 5fr.	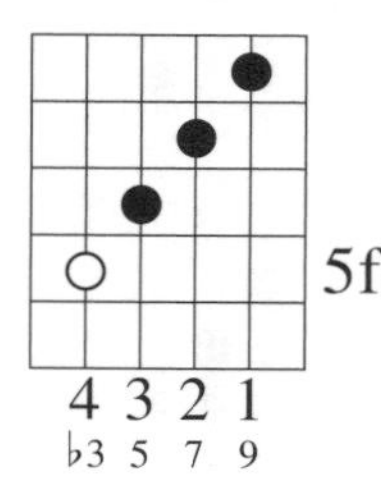 5fr.	5fr.	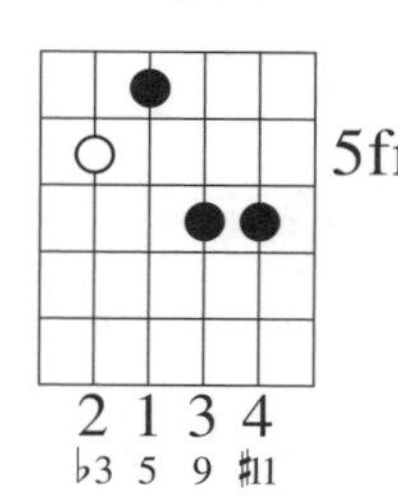 5fr.	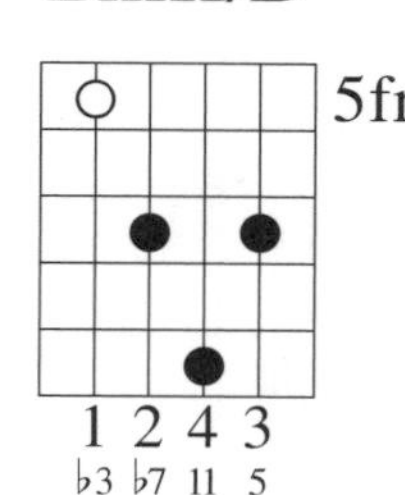 5fr.	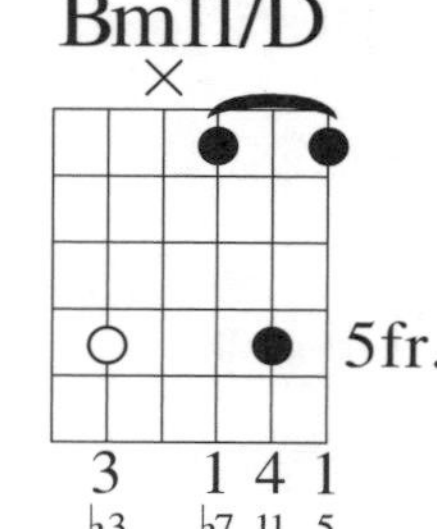 5fr.
4 2 1 1	4 3 2 1	4 2 3 1	2 1 3 4	1 2 4 3	3 1 4 1
♭3 ♭5 ♭7 9	♭3 5 7 9	♭3 ♭5 7 9	♭3 5 9 ♯11	♭3 ♭7 11 5	♭3 ♭7 11 5

Bm9♭5/D	Bm(maj9)/D	Bm(maj9)♭5/D	Bm9♯11/D	Bm11/D	Bm11/D
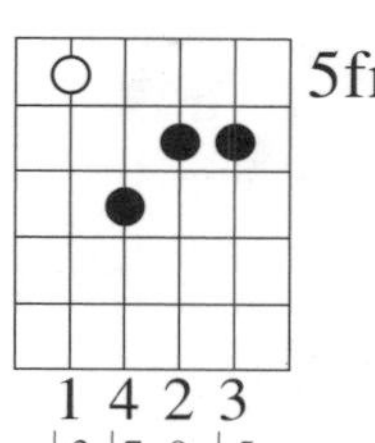 5fr.	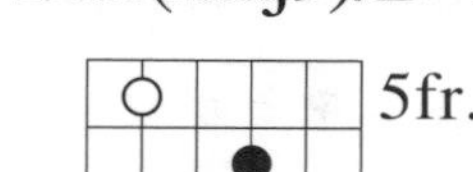 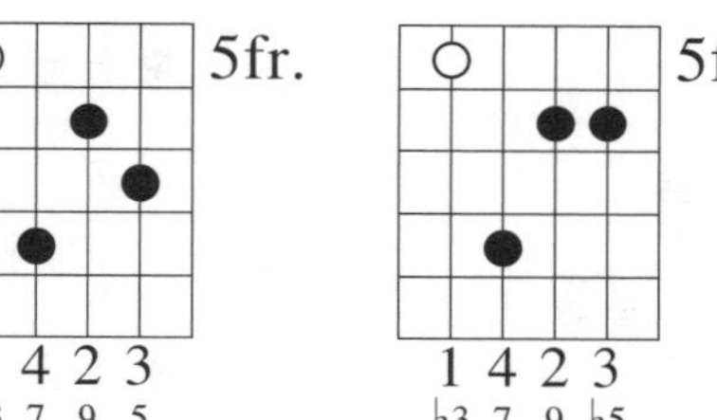 5fr.	5fr.	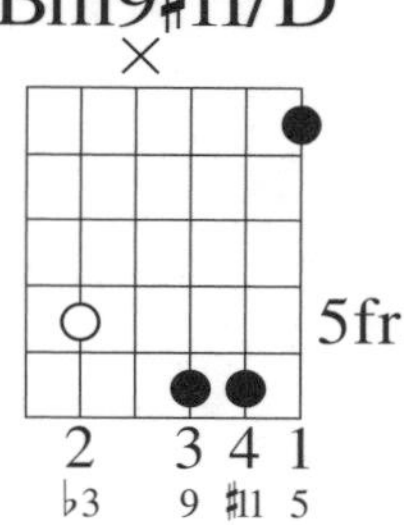 5fr.	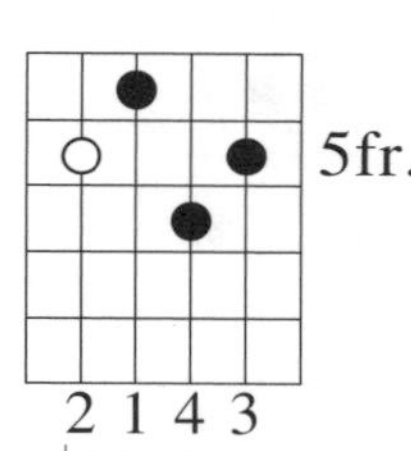 5fr.	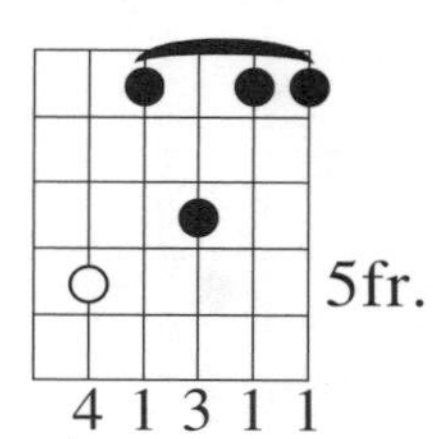 5fr.
1 4 2 3	1 4 2 3	1 4 2 3	2 3 4 1	2 1 4 3	4 1 3 1 1
♭3 ♭7 9 ♭5	♭3 7 9 5	♭3 7 9 ♭5	♭3 9 ♯11 5	♭3 5 9 11	♭3 11 R 9 5

Bm9♭5/D	Bm(maj9)/D	Bm(maj9)♭5/D	Bm(maj9)♯11/D	Bm11/D	Bm11/D
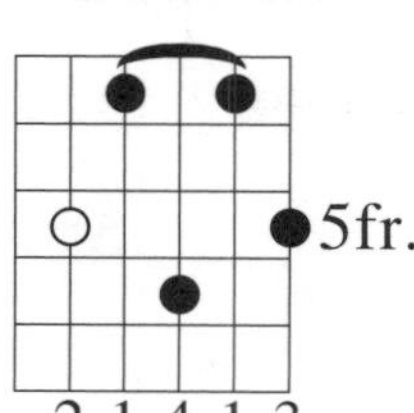 5fr.	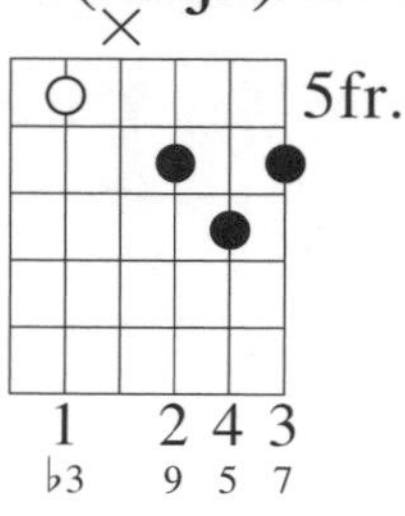 5fr.	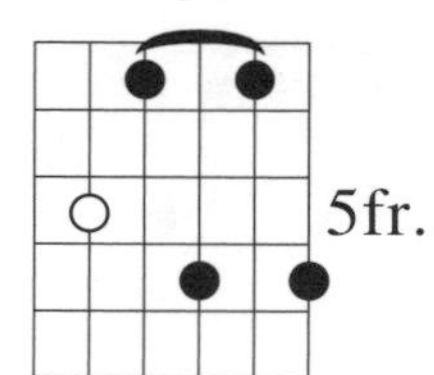 5fr.	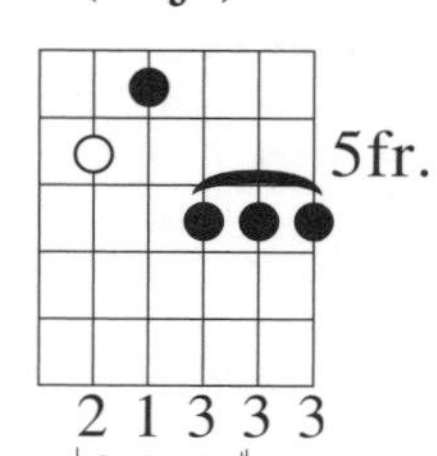 5fr.	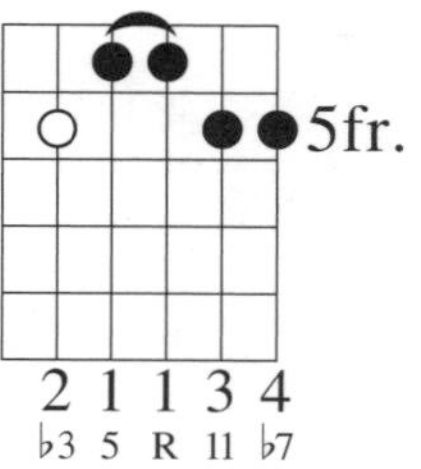 5fr.	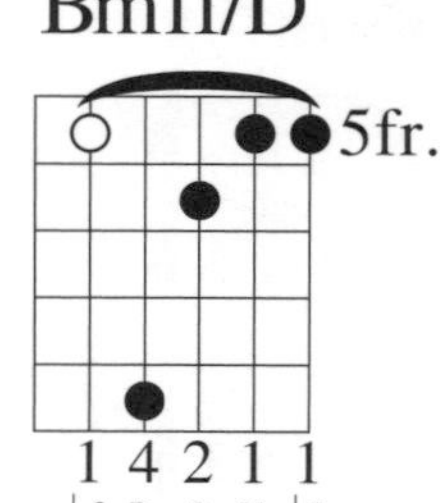 5fr.
2 1 4 1 3	1 2 4 3	2 1 3 1 4	2 1 3 3 3	2 1 1 3 4	1 4 2 1 1
♭3 ♭5 9 ♭3 ♭7	♭3 9 5 7	♭3 ♭5 9 ♭3 7	♭3 5 9 ♯11 7	♭3 5 R 11 ♭7	♭3 R 9 11 ♭7

Bm9♭5/D	Bm(maj9)/D	Bm(maj9)♭5/D	Bm11/D	Bm11/D	Bm11♭5/D
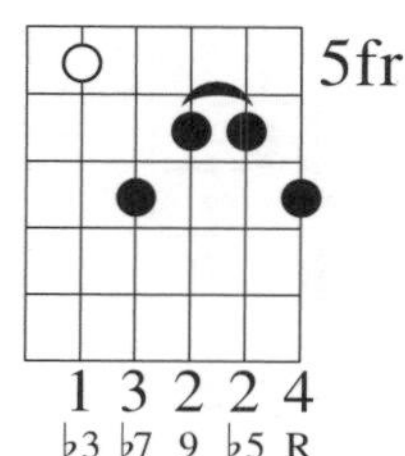 5fr.	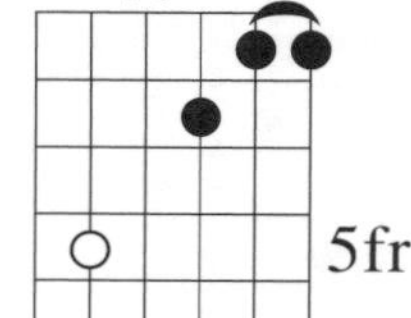 5fr.	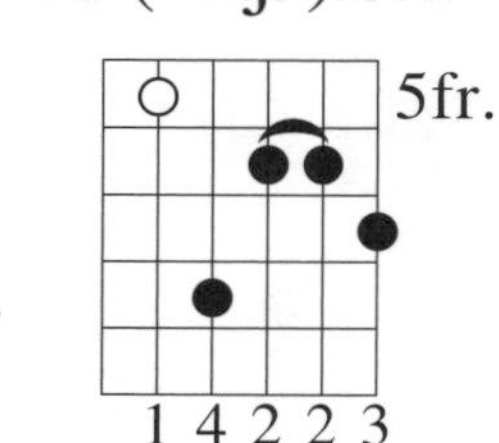 5fr.	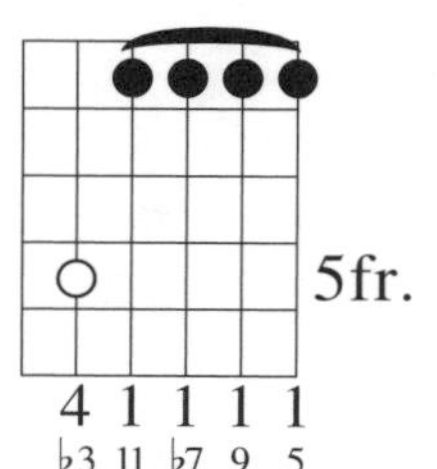 5fr.	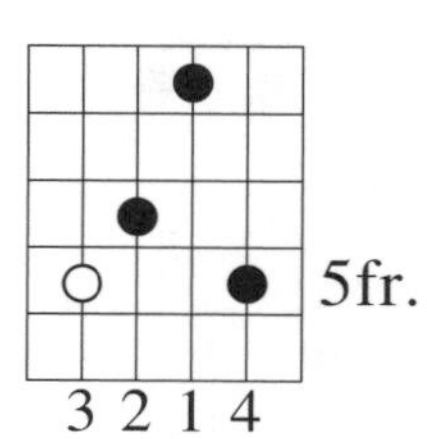 5fr.	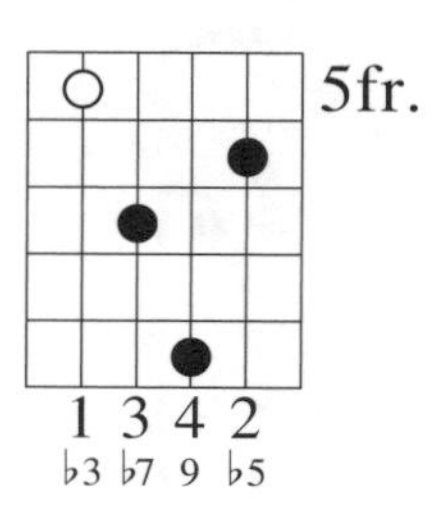 5fr.
1 3 2 2 4	4 2 1 1	1 4 2 2 3	4 1 1 1 1	3 2 1 4	1 3 4 2
♭3 ♭7 9 ♭5 R	♭3 7 9 5	♭3 7 9 ♭5 R	♭3 11 ♭7 9 5	♭3 5 ♭7 11	♭3 ♭7 9 ♭5

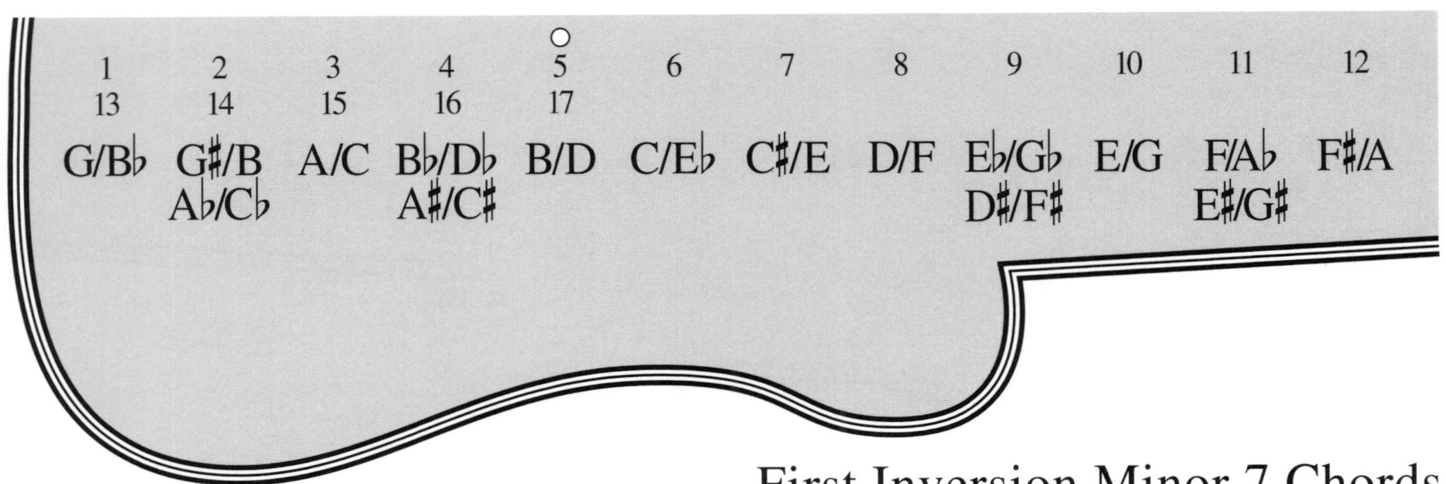

First Inversion Minor 7 Chords

Bm11♭5/D

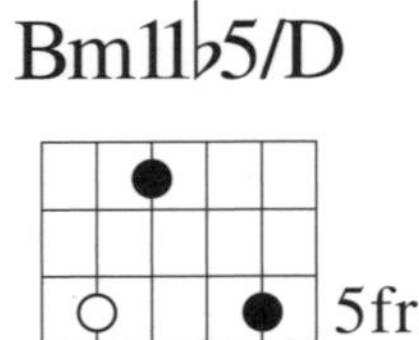
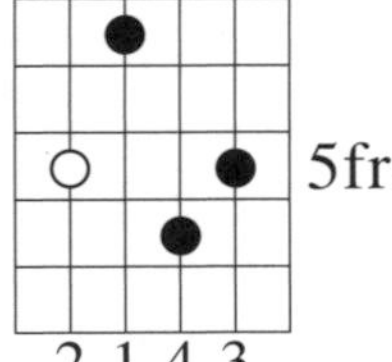

5fr.

2 1 4 3
♭3 ♭5 9 11

Bm(maj11)♭5/D

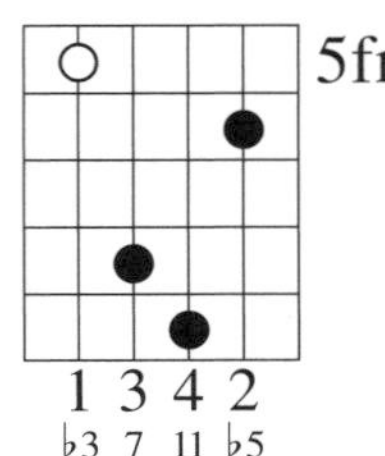

5fr.

1 3 4 2
♭3 7 11 ♭5

Bm13♯11/D

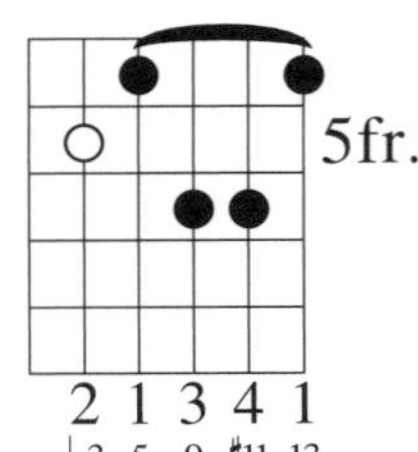

5fr.

2 1 3 4 1
♭3 5 9 ♯11 13

Bm13/D

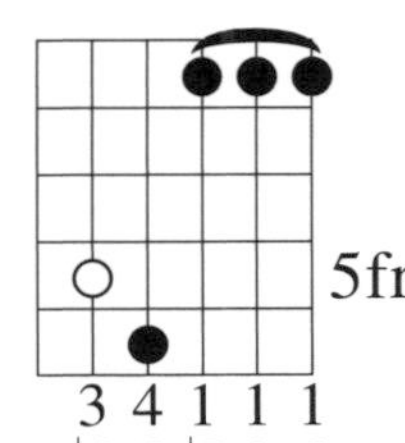

5fr.

3 4 1 1 1
♭3 13 ♭7 9 5

Bm7♭13/D

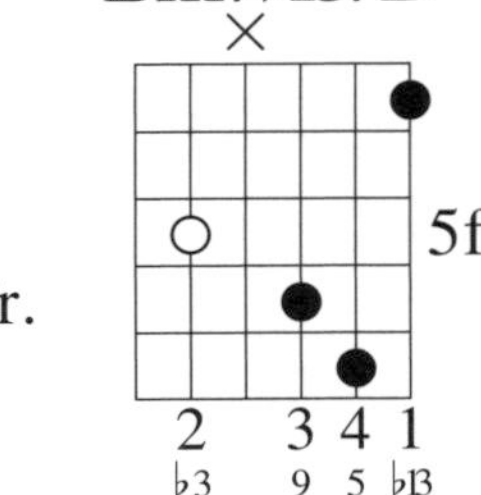

5fr.

2 3 4 1
♭3 9 5 ♭13

Bm(maj13)/D

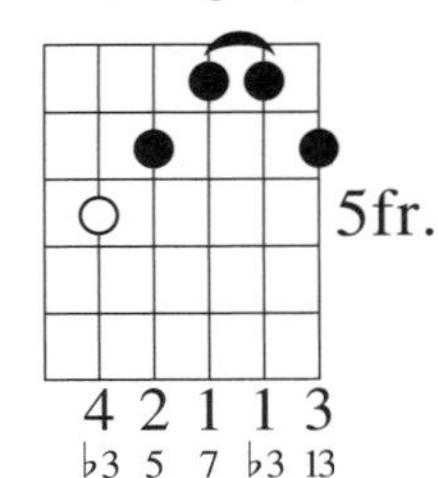

5fr.

4 2 1 1 3
♭3 5 7 ♭3 13

Bm11♭5/D

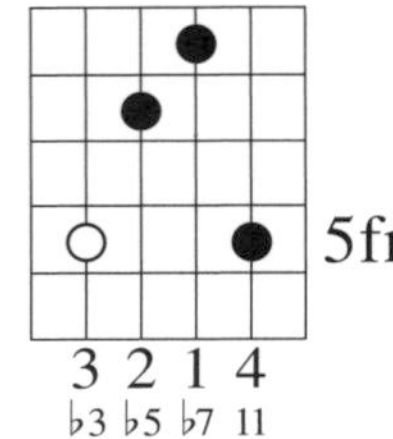

5fr.

3 2 1 4
♭3 ♭5 ♭7 11

Bm(maj11)♭5/D

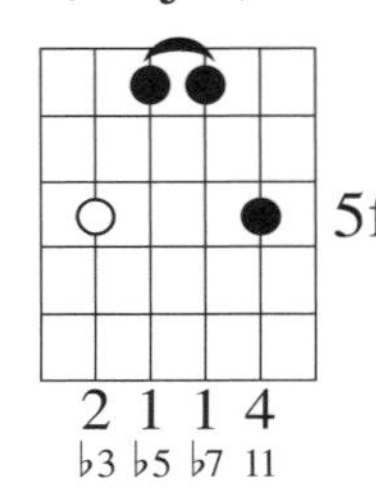

5fr.

2 1 1 4
♭3 ♭5 ♭7 11

Bm13/D

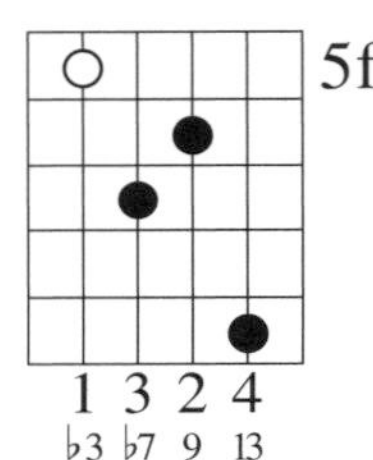

5fr.

1 3 2 4
♭3 ♭7 9 13

Bm13/D

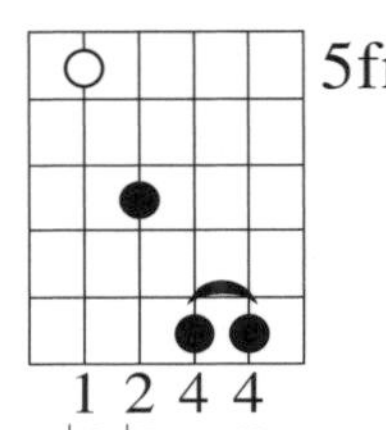

5fr.

1 2 4 4
♭3 ♭7 11 13

Bm7♭13/D

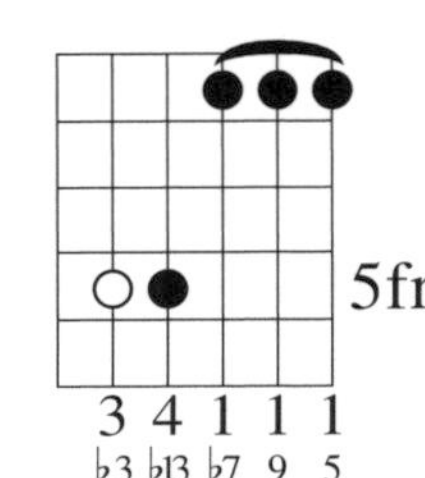

5fr.

3 4 1 1 1
♭3 ♭13 ♭7 9 5

Bm(maj13)/D

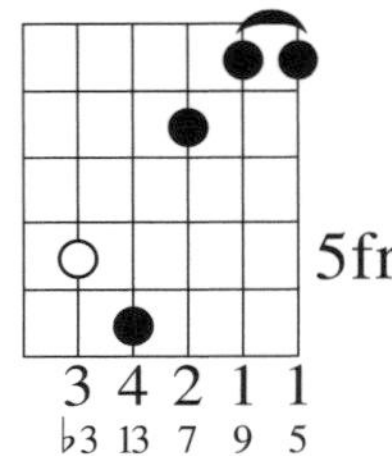

5fr.

3 4 2 1 1
♭3 13 7 9 5

Bm11♭5/D

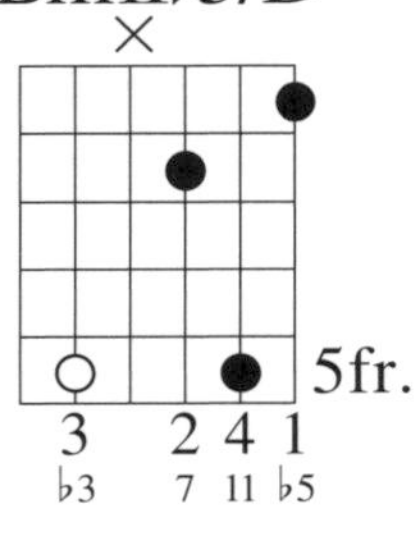

5fr.

3 2 4 1
♭3 7 11 ♭5

Bm(maj11)♭5/D

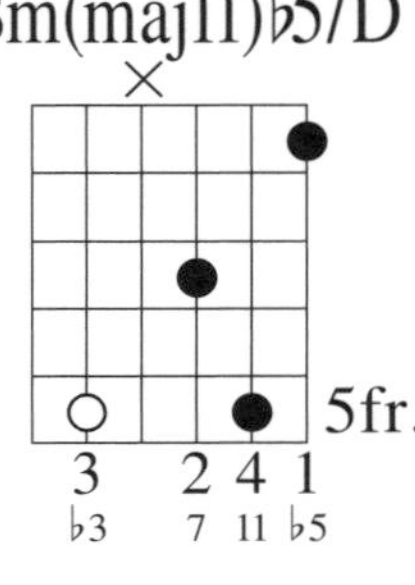

5fr.

3 2 4 1
♭3 7 11 ♭5

Bm13/D

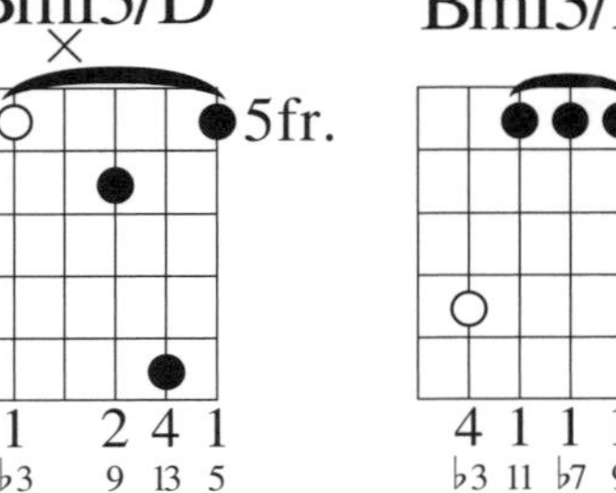

5fr.

1 2 4 1
♭3 9 13 5

Bm13/D

5fr.

4 1 1 1 3
♭3 11 ♭7 9 13

Bm7♭13/D

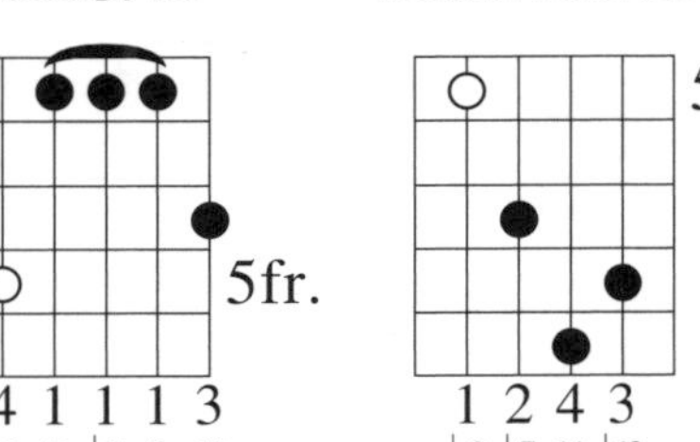

5fr.

1 2 4 3
♭3 ♭7 11 ♭13

Bm(maj13)/D

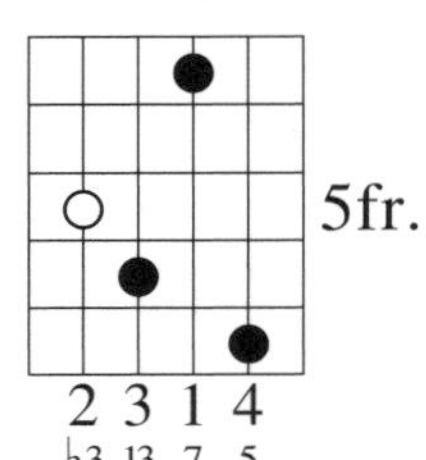

5fr.

2 3 1 4
♭3 13 7 5

Bm11♭5/D

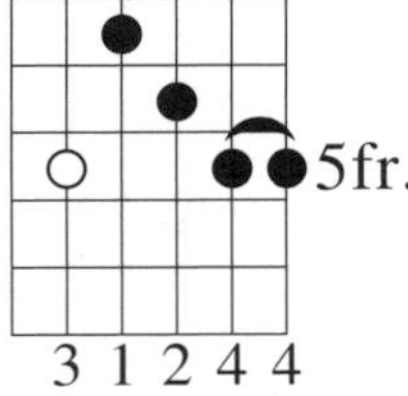

5fr.

3 1 2 4 4
♭3 ♭5 R 11 ♭7

Bm13♯11/D

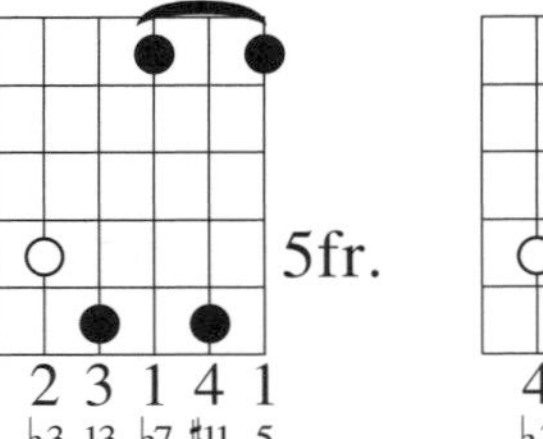

5fr.

2 3 1 4 1
♭3 13 ♭7 ♯11 5

Bm13/D

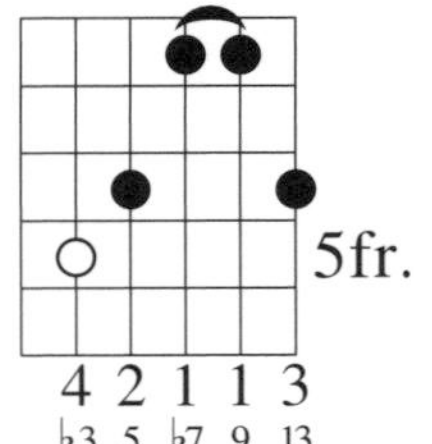

5fr.

4 2 1 1 3
♭3 5 ♭7 9 13

Bm7♭13/D

5fr.

1 3 2 4
♭3 ♭7 9 ♭13

Bm(maj13)/D

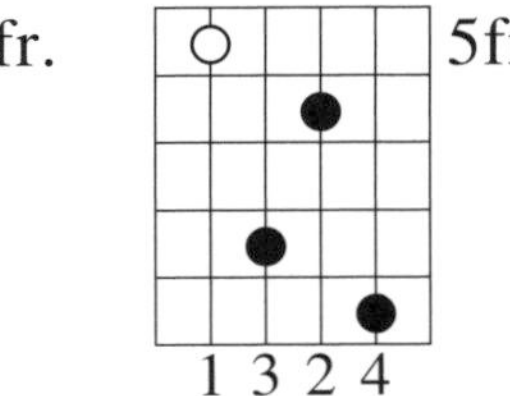

5fr.

1 3 2 4
♭3 7 9 13

Bm(maj7)♭13/D

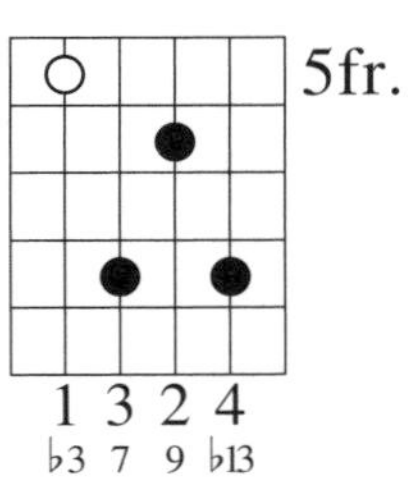

5fr.

1 3 2 4
♭3 7 9 ♭13

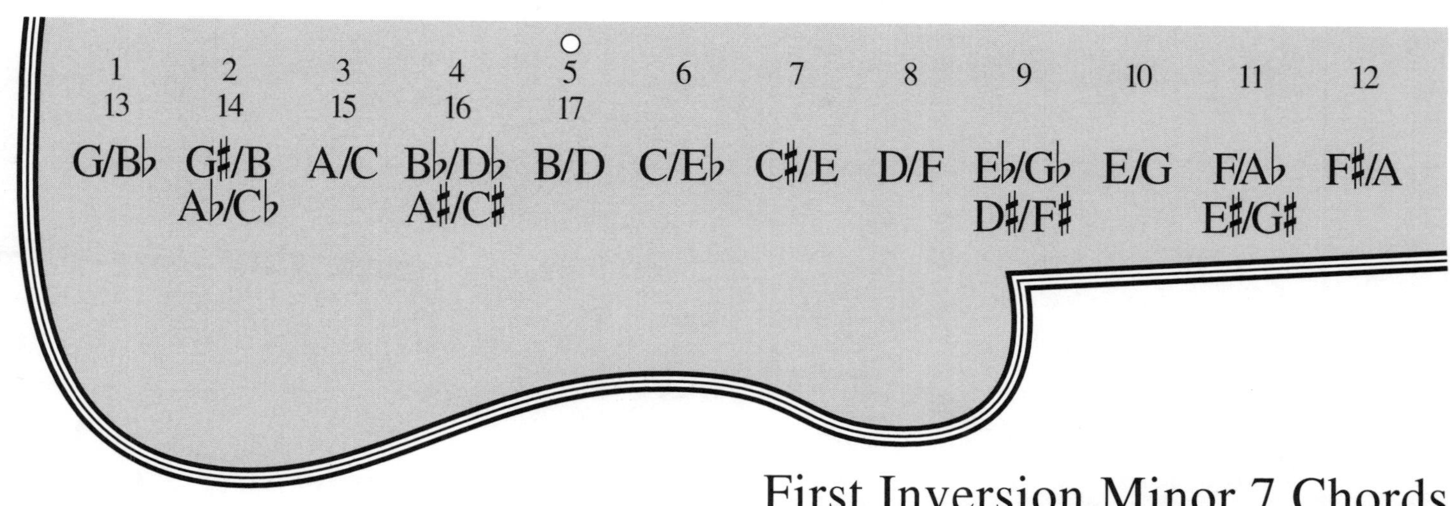

First Inversion Minor 7 Chords

Bm(maj7)♭13/D

3 2 1 4 1
♭3 5 7 11 ♭13

Bm7♭5♭13/D Bm(maj13)♭5/D

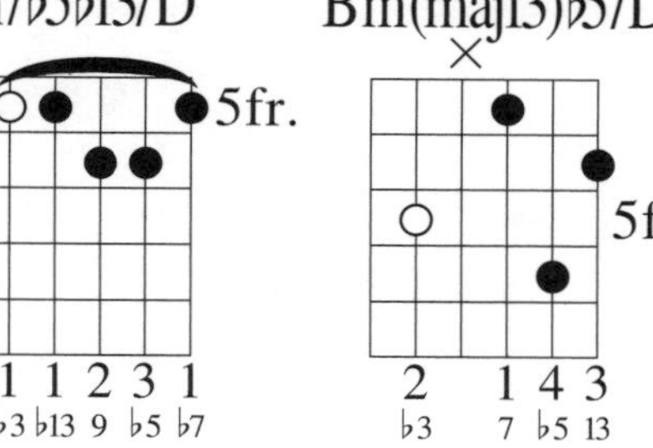

Bm(maj7)♭13/D

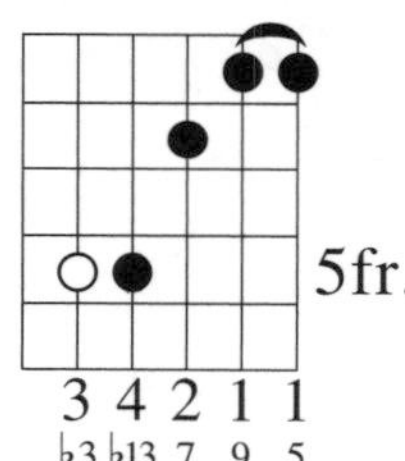

Bm7♭5♭13/D Bm(maj7)♭5♭13/D

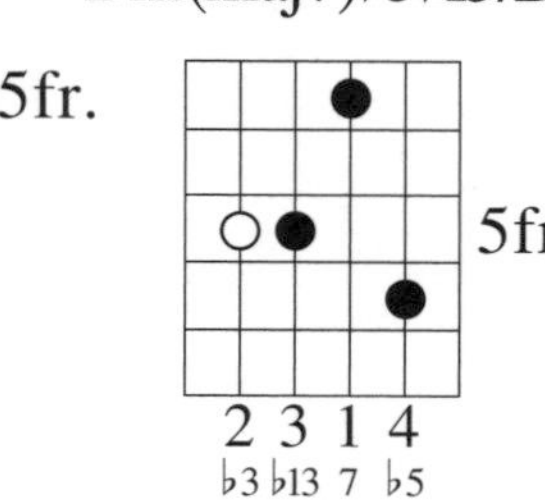

Bm(maj7)♭13/D

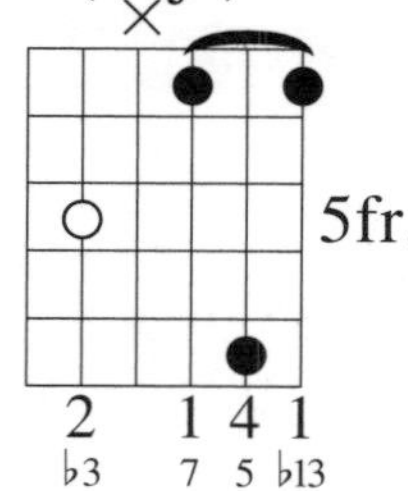

Bm(maj13)♭5/D

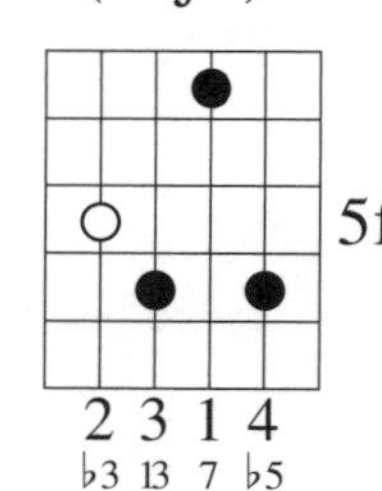

Bm(maj7)♭5♭13/D

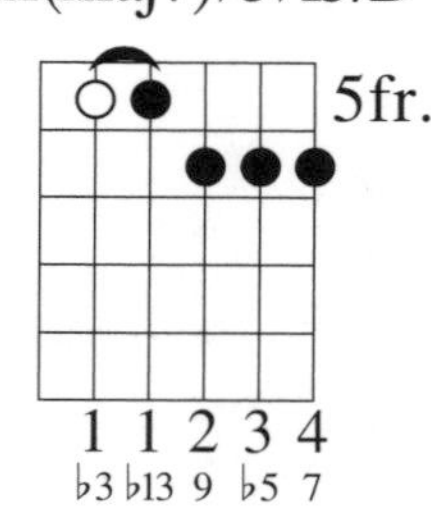

Bm7♭5♭13/D

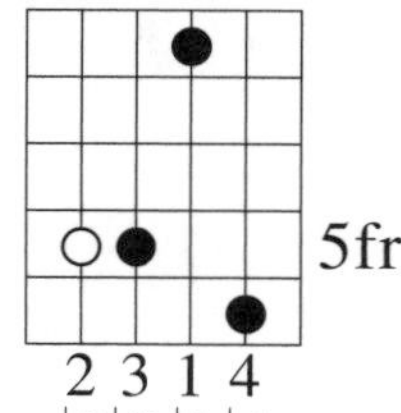

Bm(maj13)♭5/D

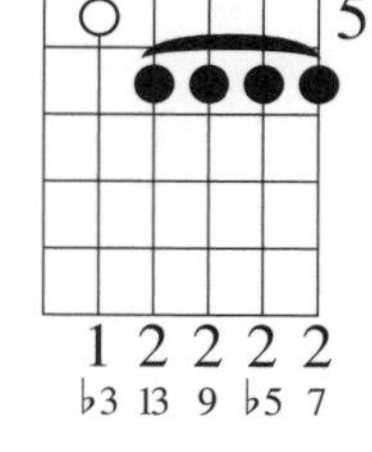

Bm(maj7)♭5♭13/D

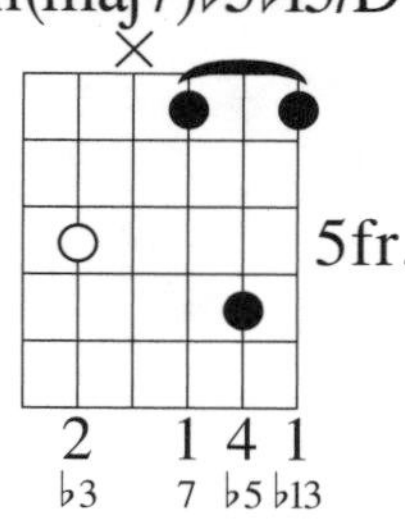

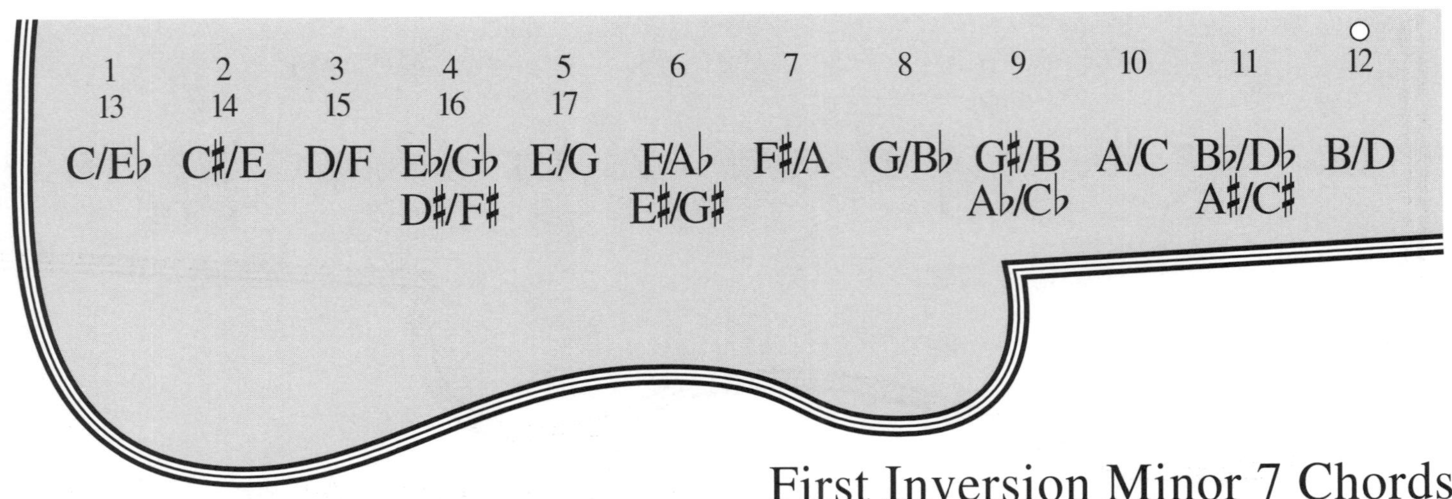

First Inversion Minor 7 Chords

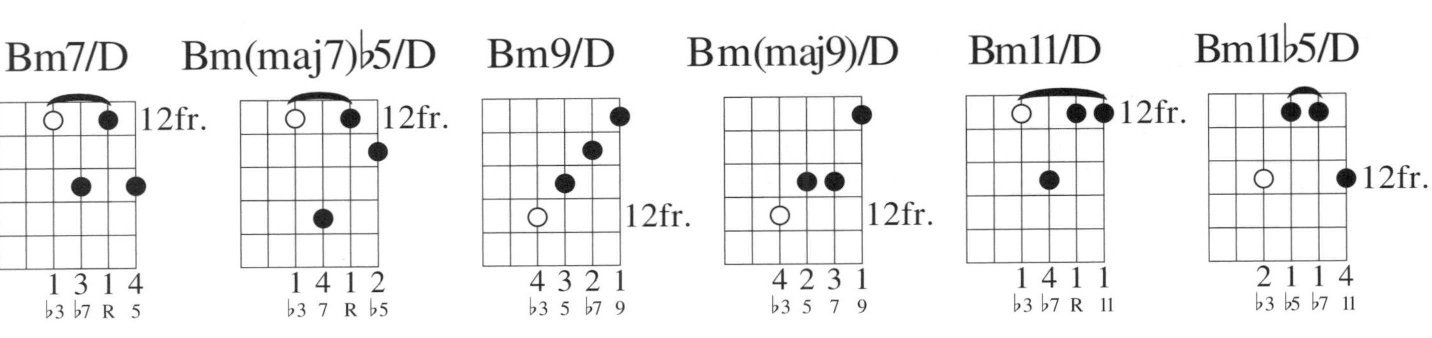

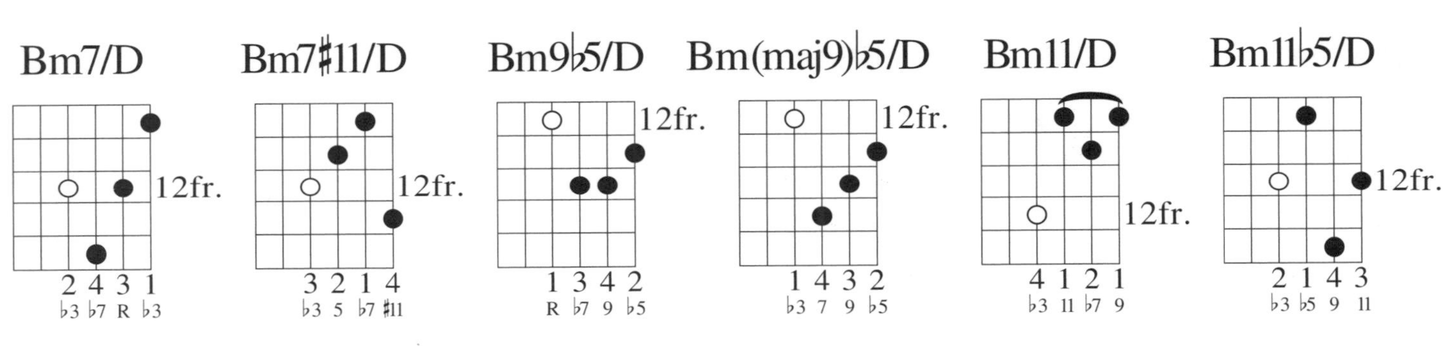

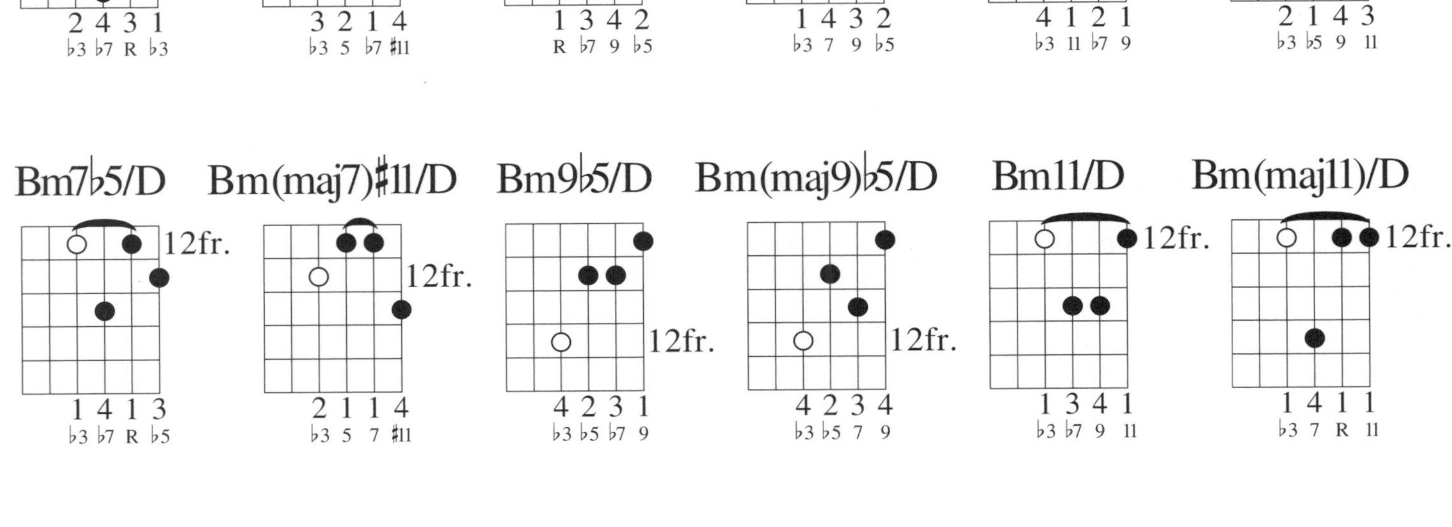

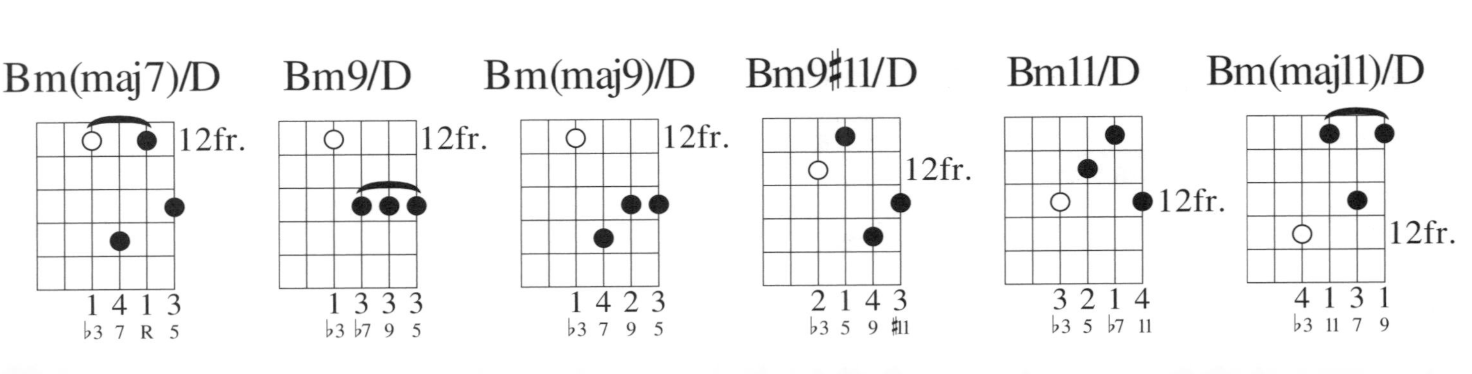

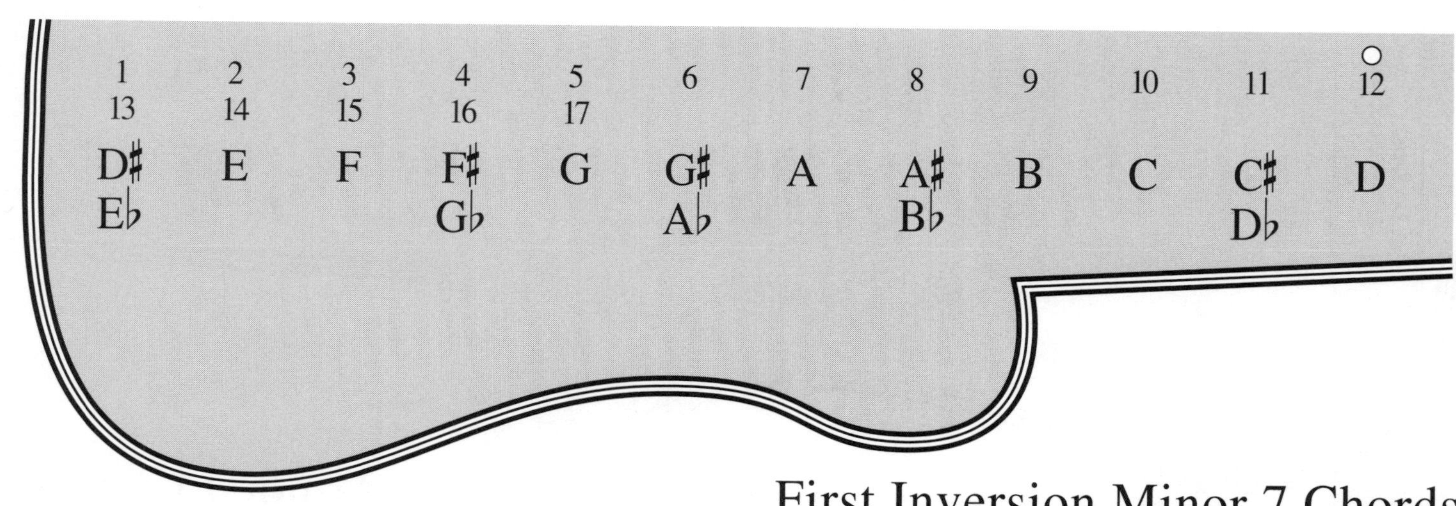

First Inversion Minor 7 Chords

Bm(maj11)/D | Bm13/D | Bm7♭13/D | Bm7♭13/D | Bm(maj7)♭13/D | Bm7♭5♭13/D

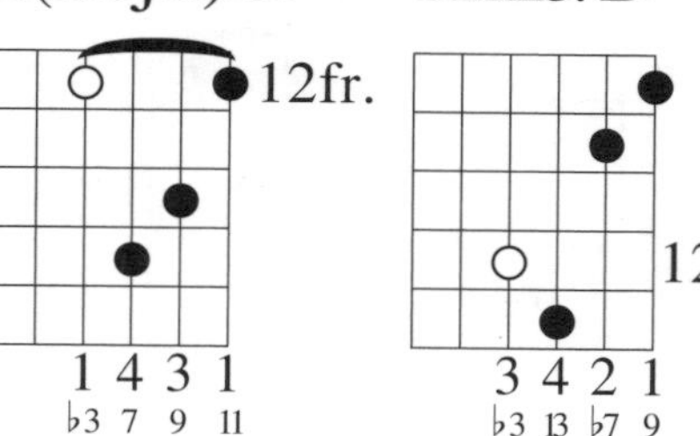

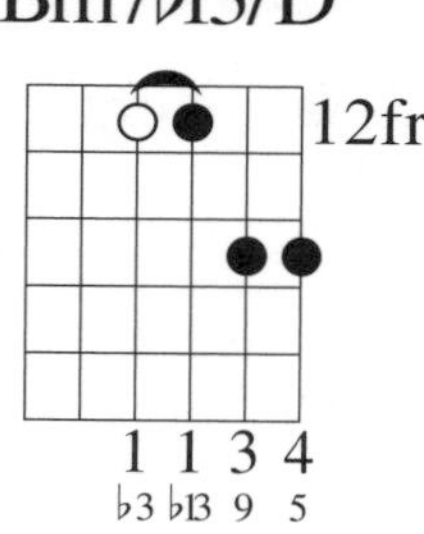

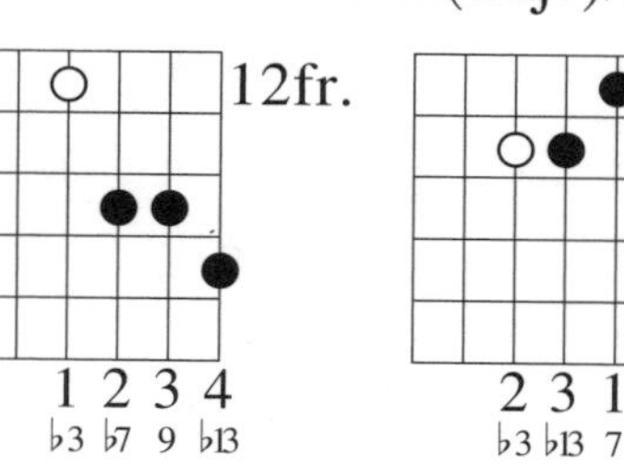

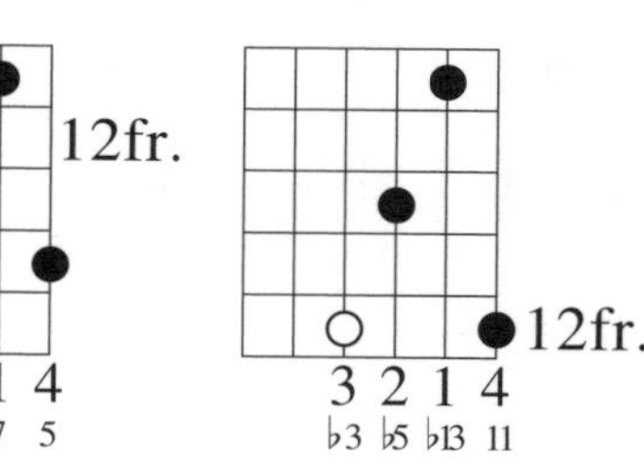

Bm(maj11)♭5/D | Bm13/D | Bm7♭13/D | Bm(maj13)/D | Bm(maj7)♭13/D | Bm7♭5♭13/D

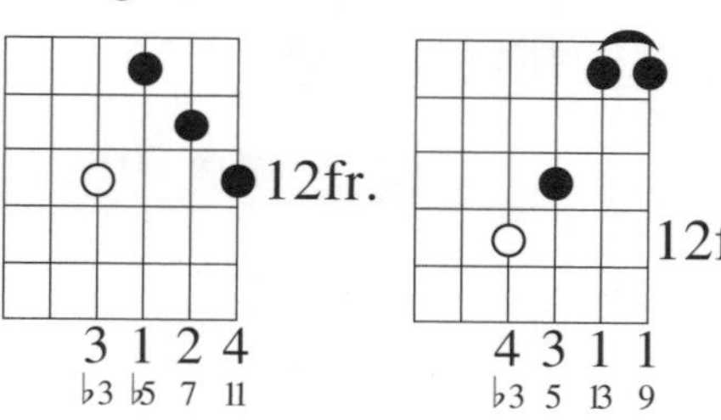

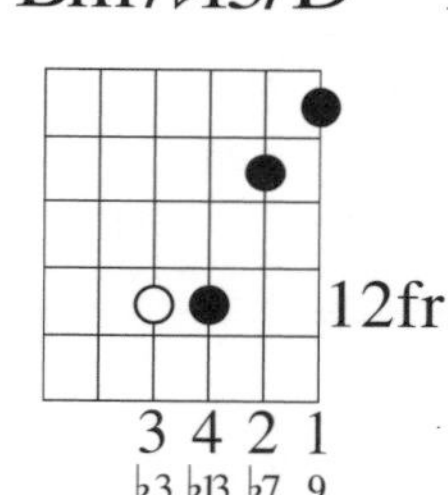

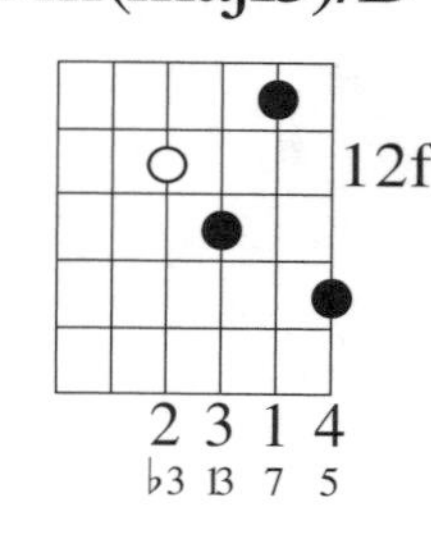

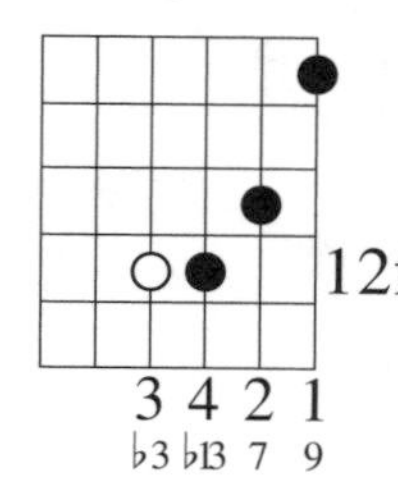

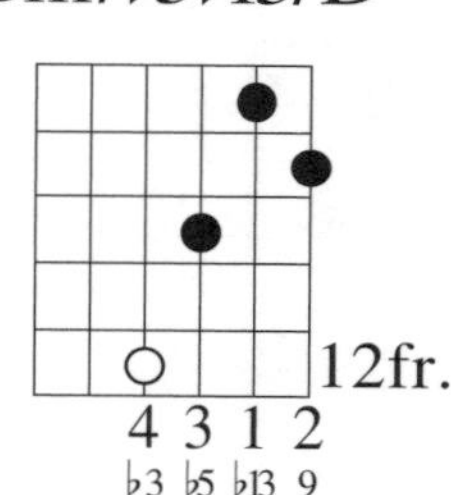

Bm13♯11/D | Bm13/D | Bm7♭13/D | Bm(maj13)/D | Bm(maj7)♭13/D | Bm(maj13)♭5/D

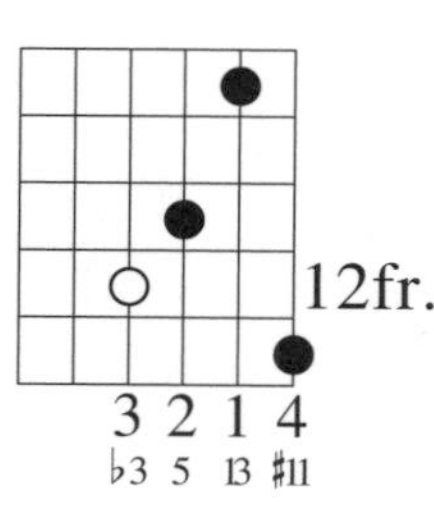

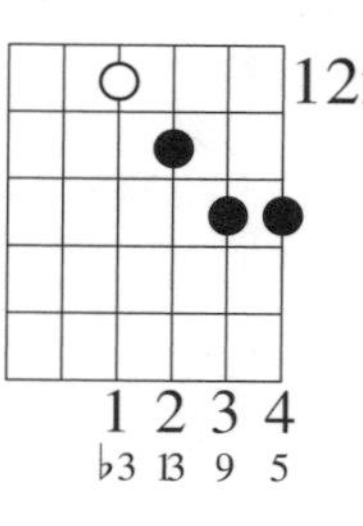

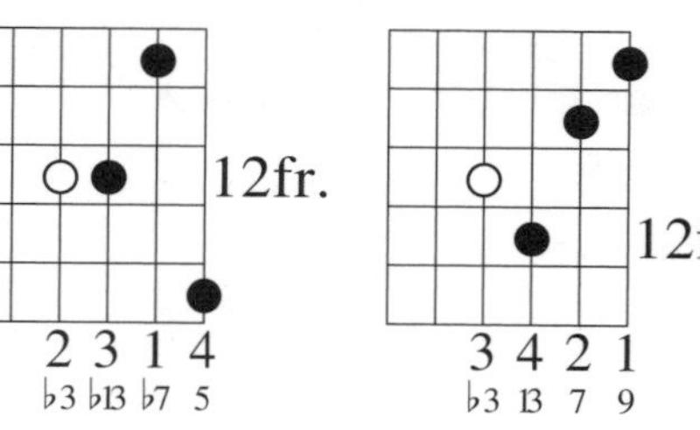

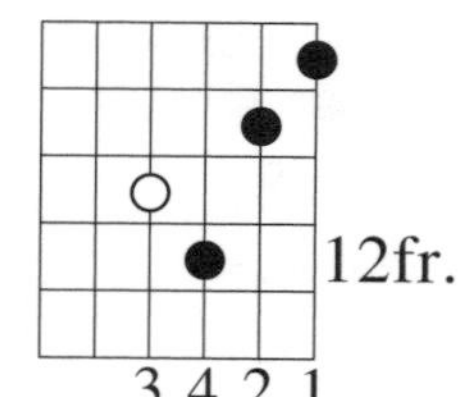
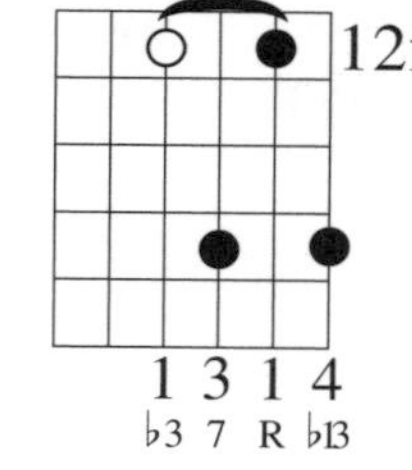

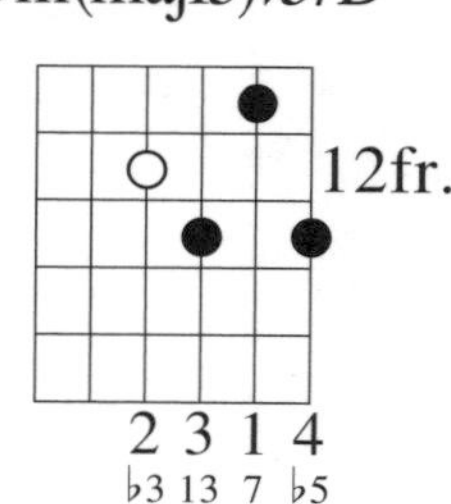

Bm13/D | Bm13/D | Bm7♭13/D | Bm(maj13)/D | Bm(maj7)♭13/D | Bm(maj7)♭5♭13/D

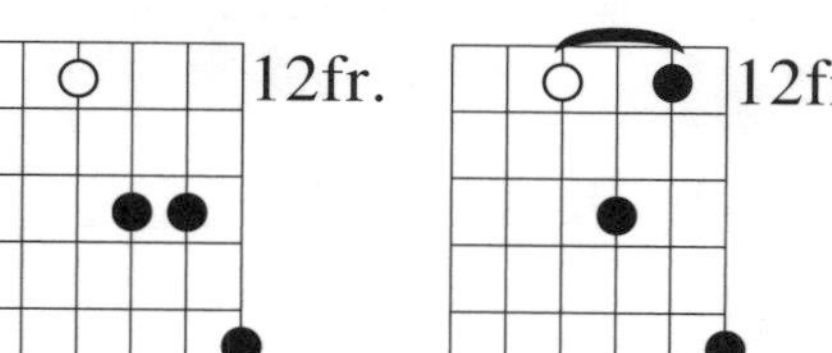

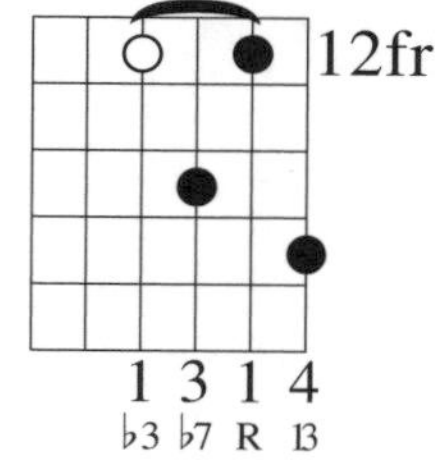
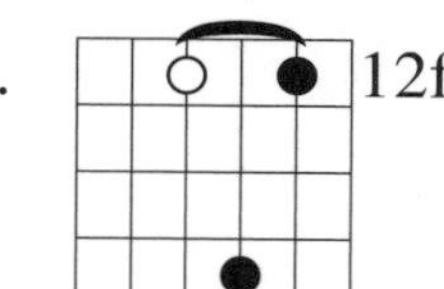
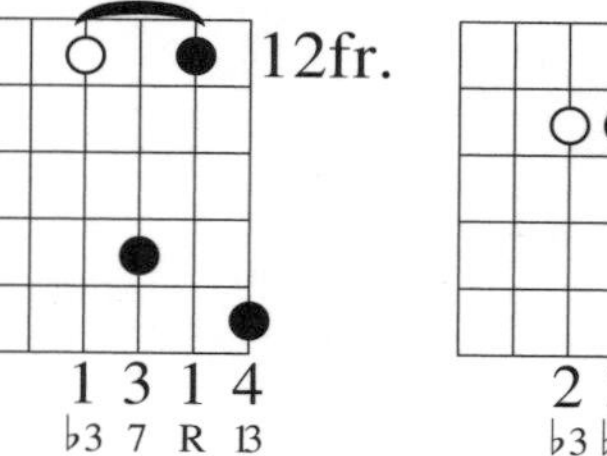

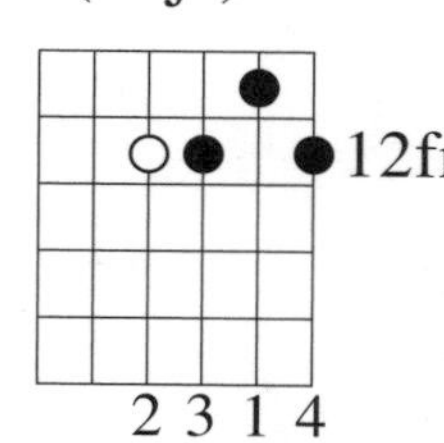

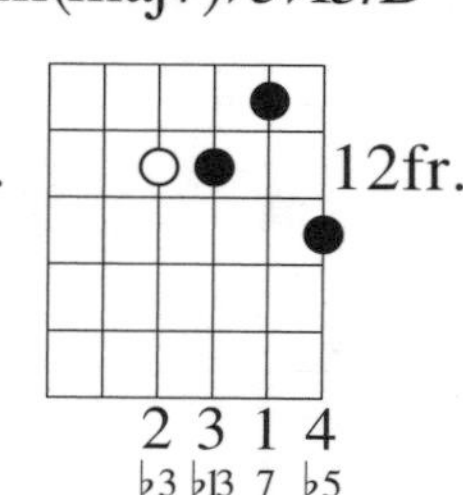

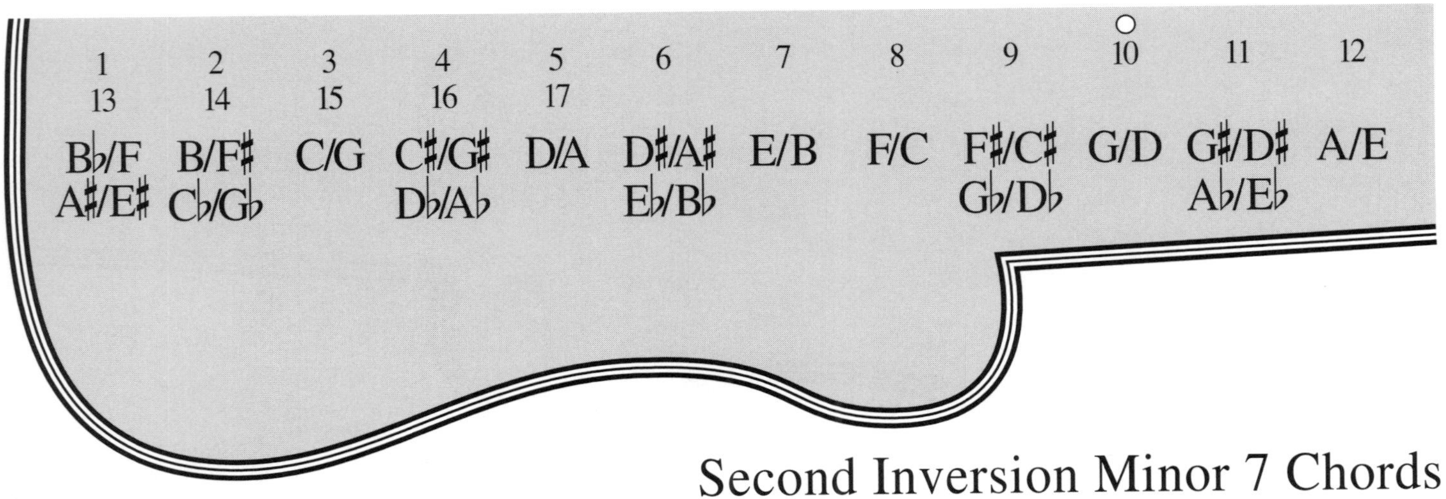

Second Inversion Minor 7 Chords

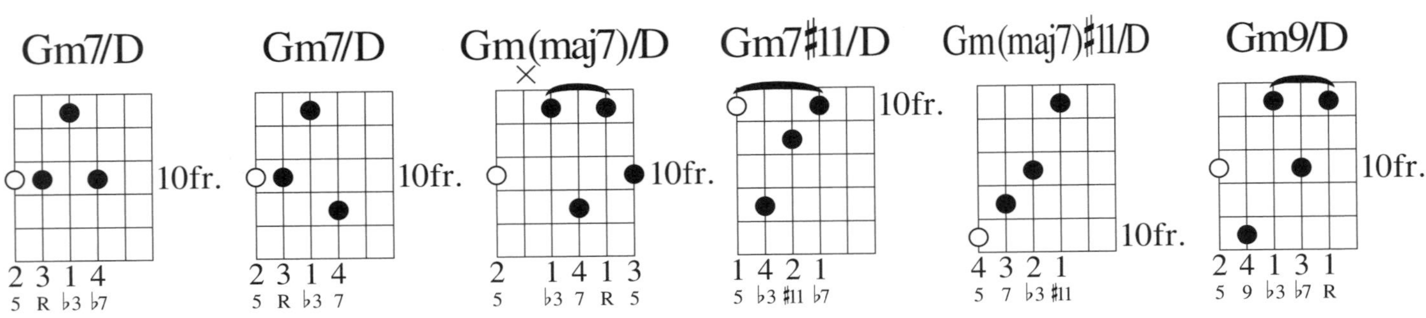

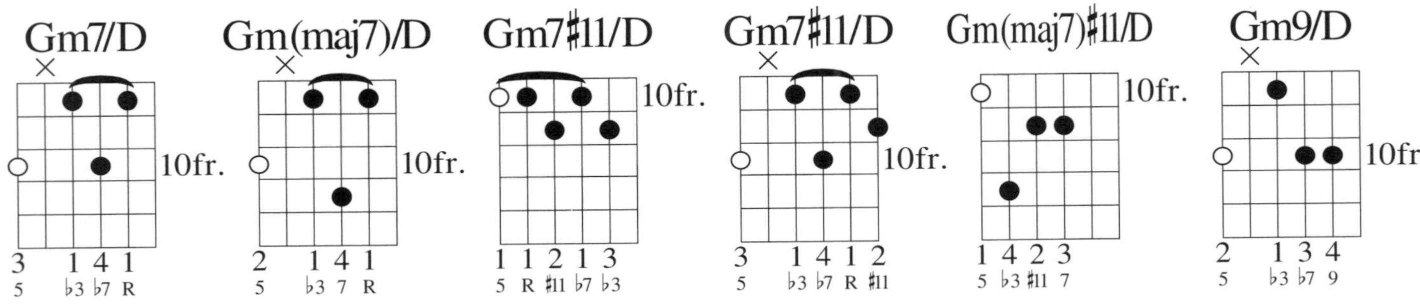

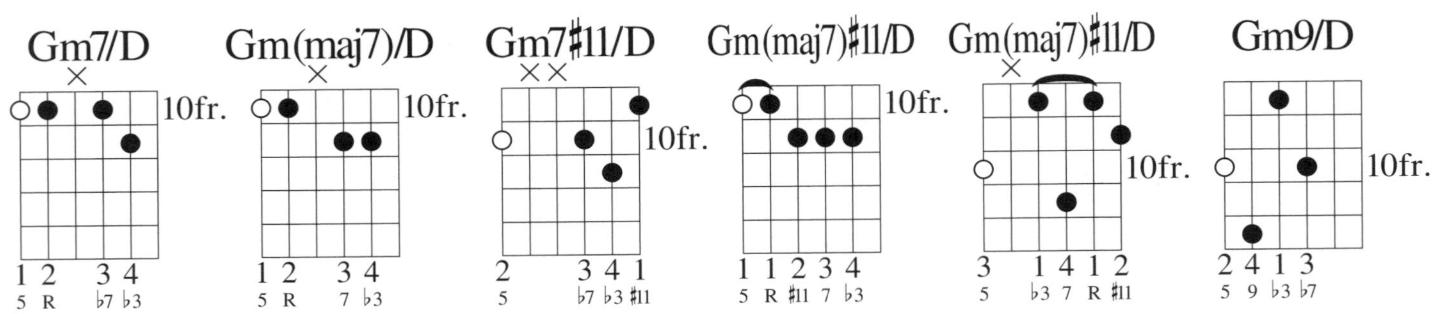

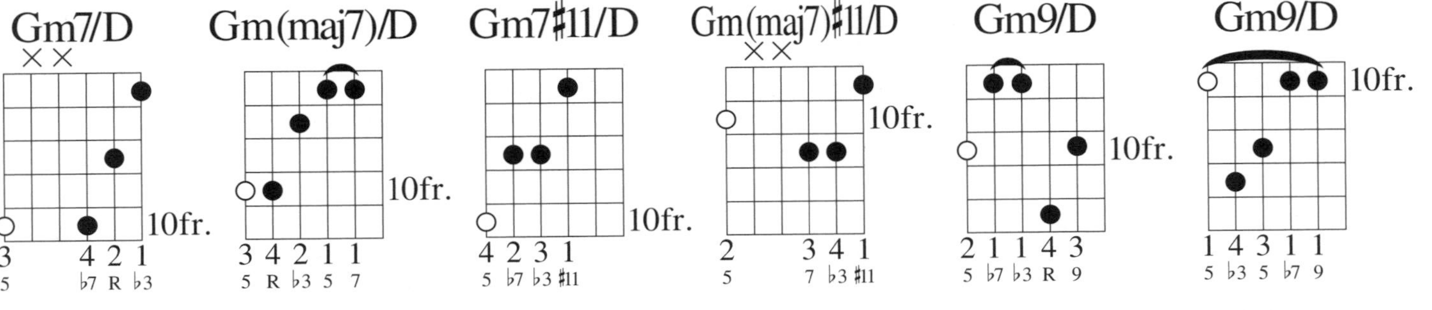

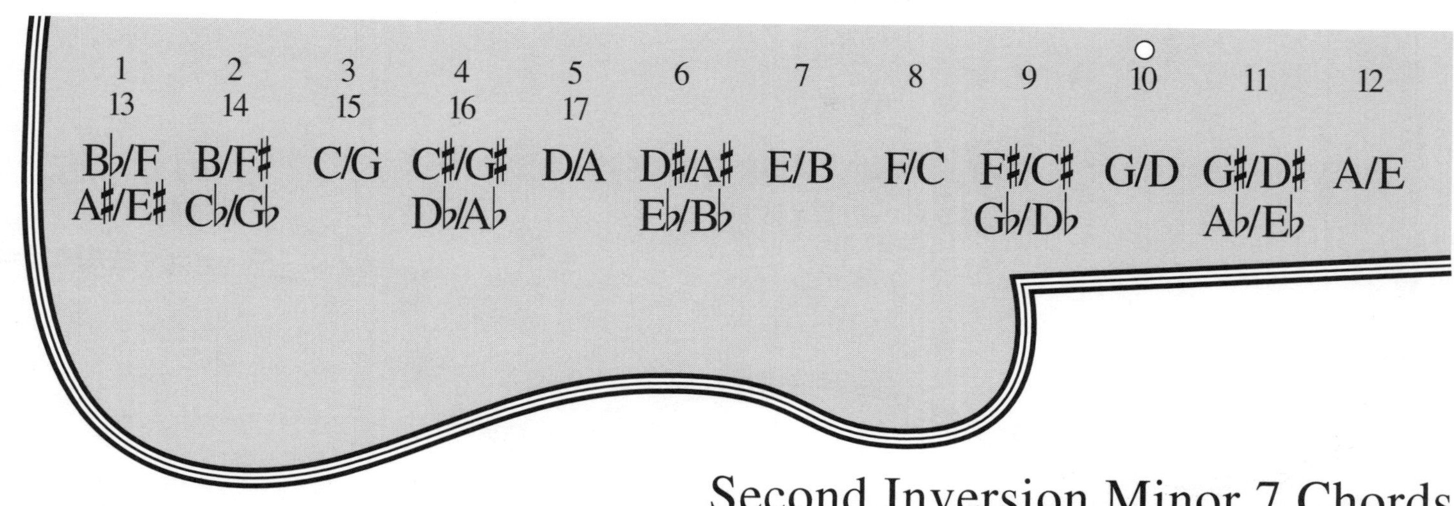

Second Inversion Minor 7 Chords

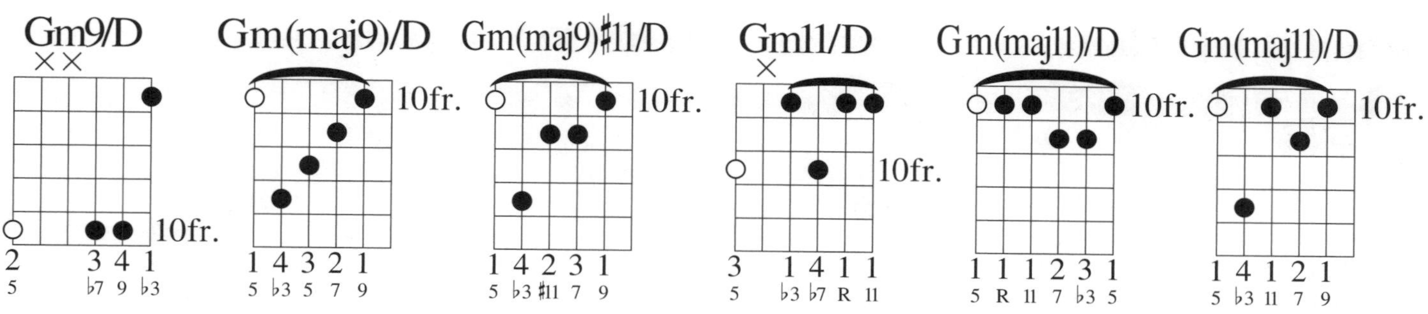

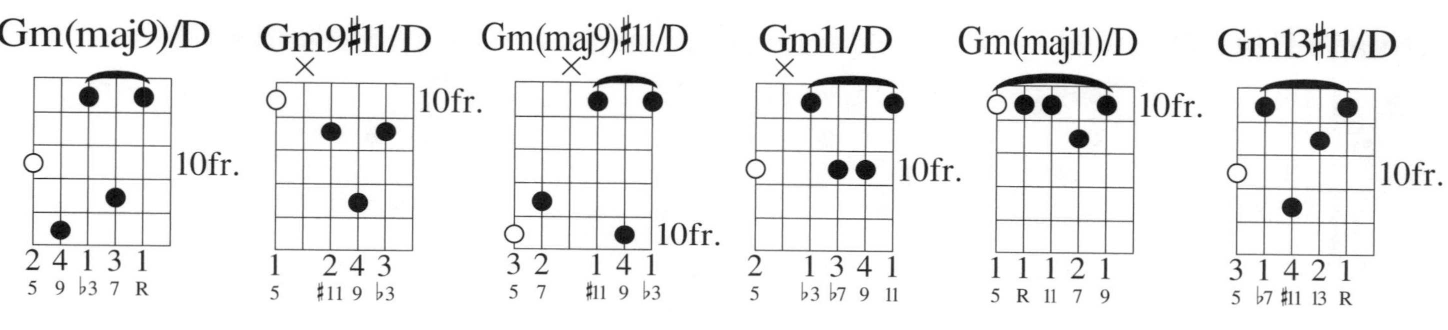

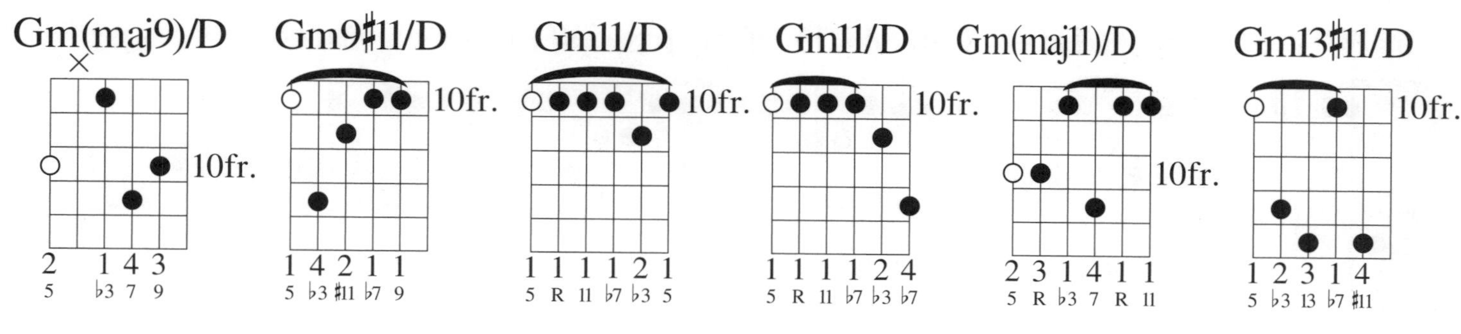

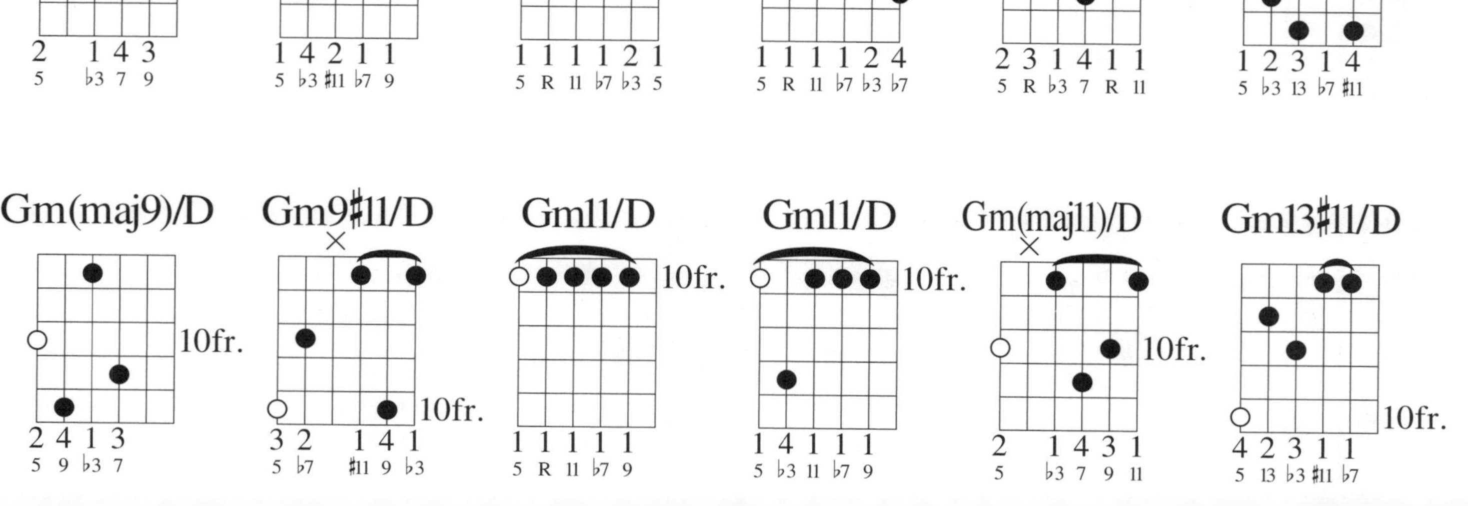

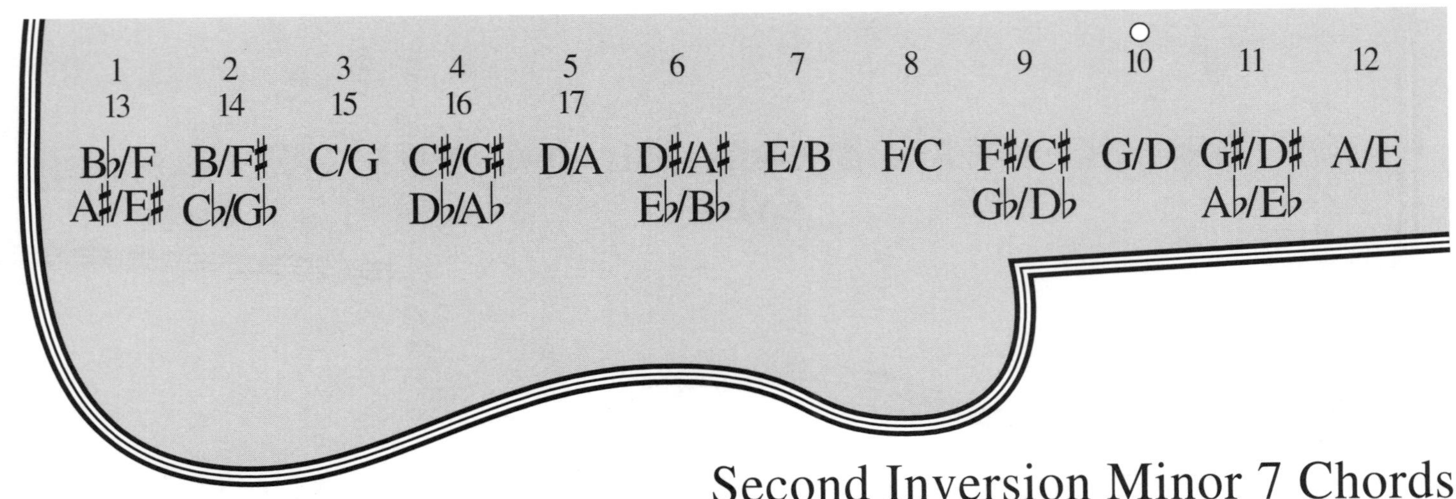

Second Inversion Minor 7 Chords

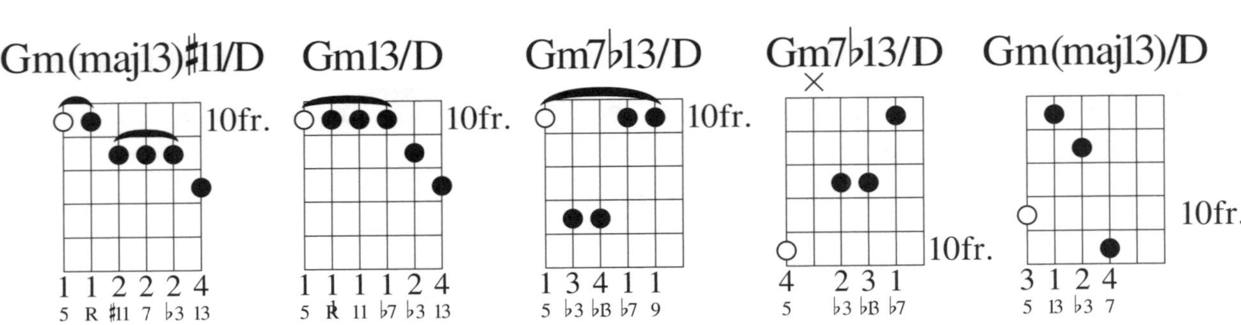

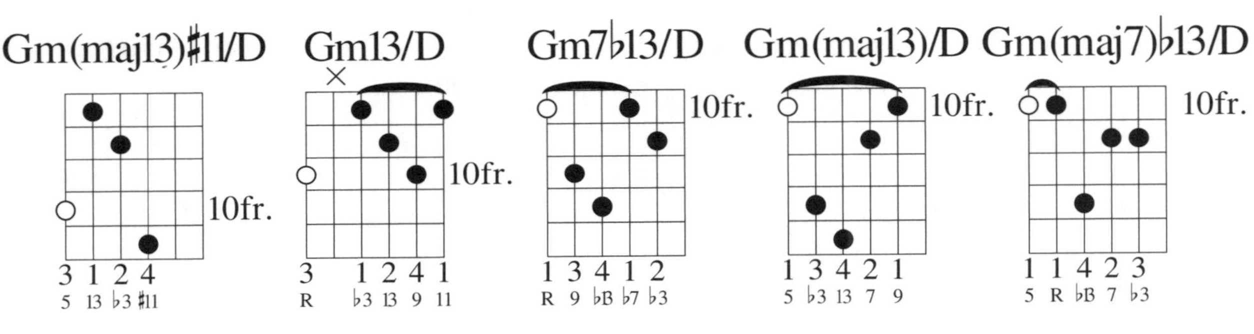

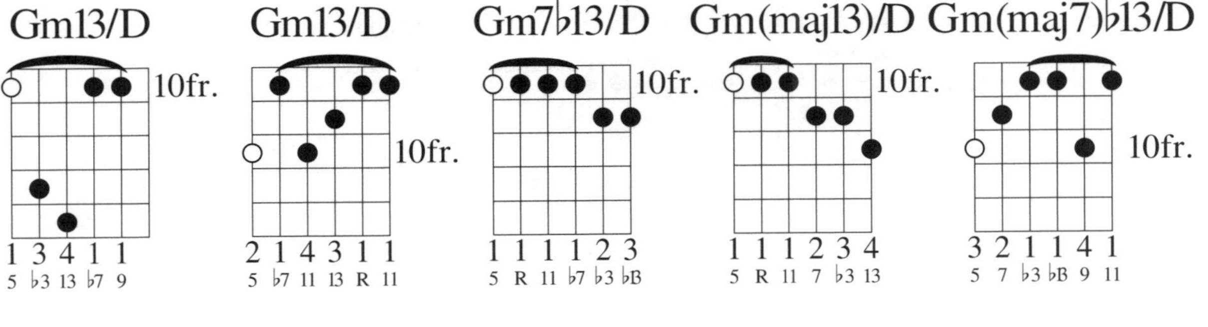

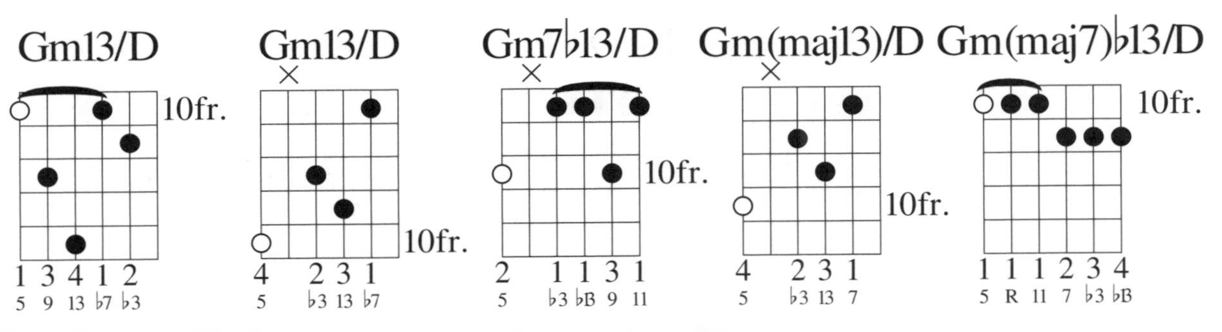

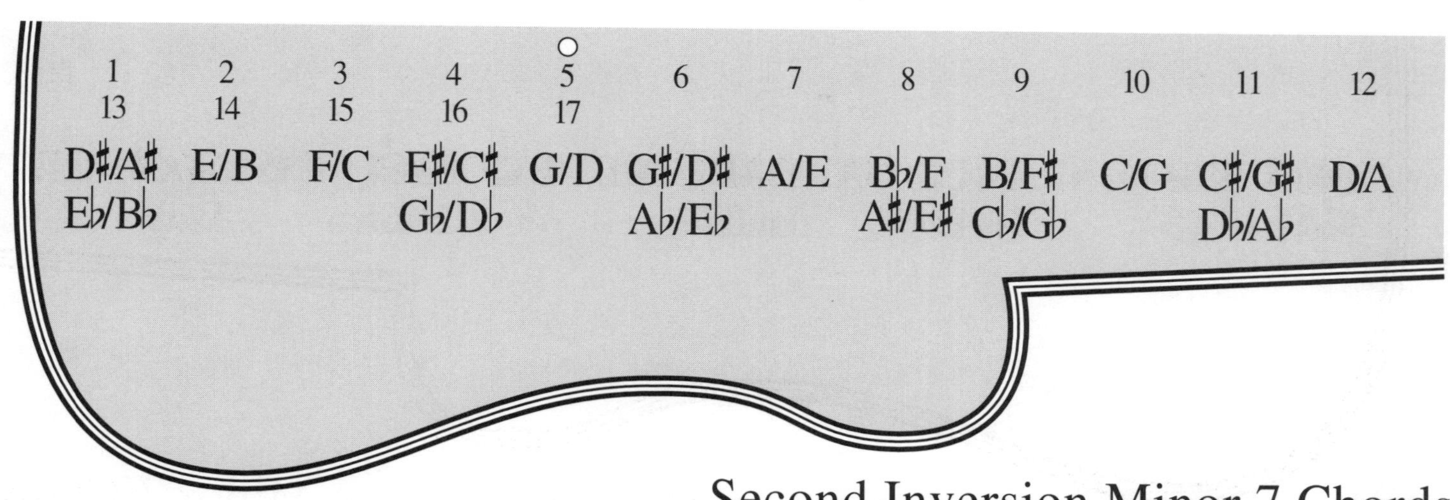

Second Inversion Minor 7 Chords

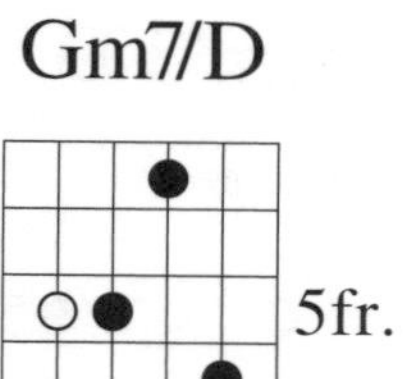

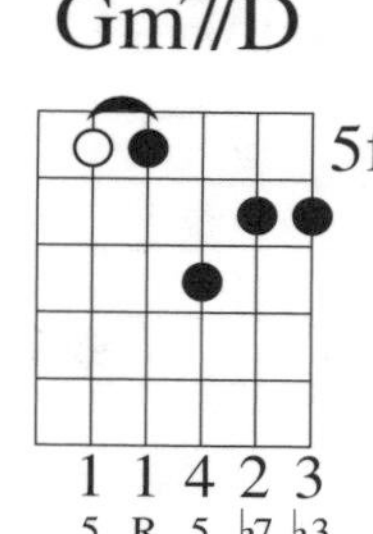

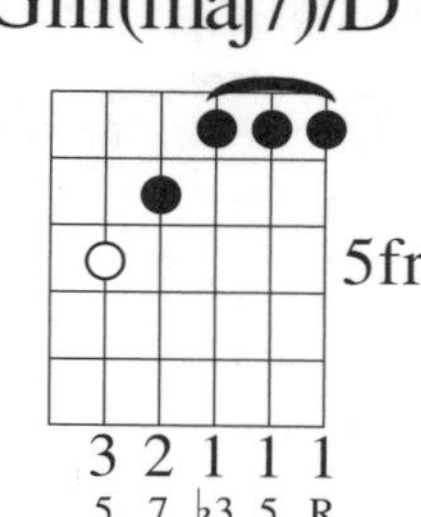

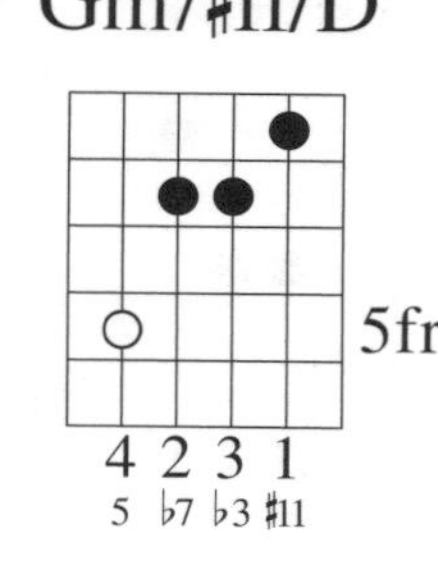

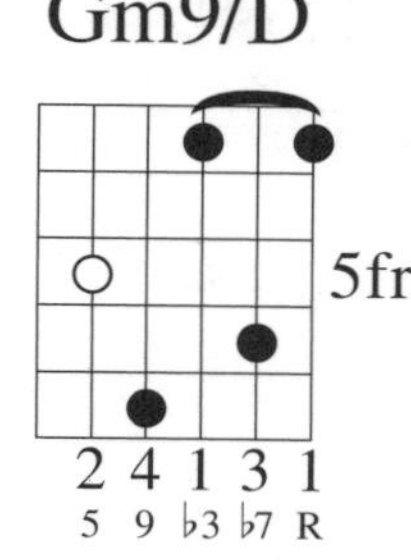

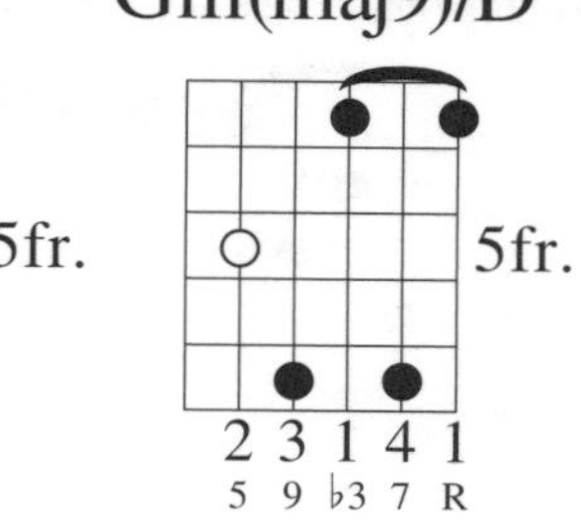

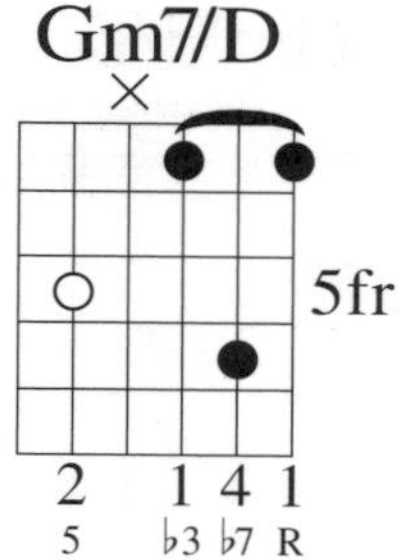

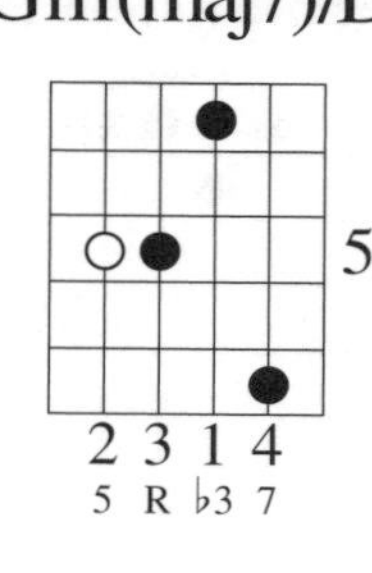

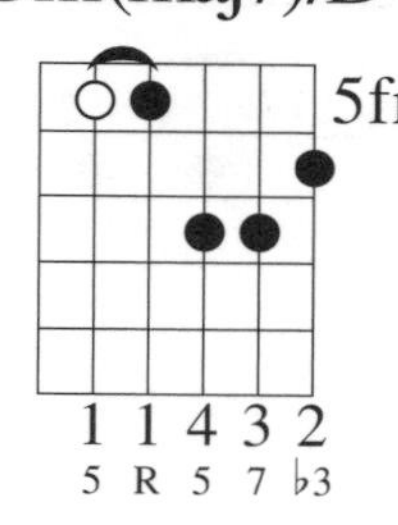

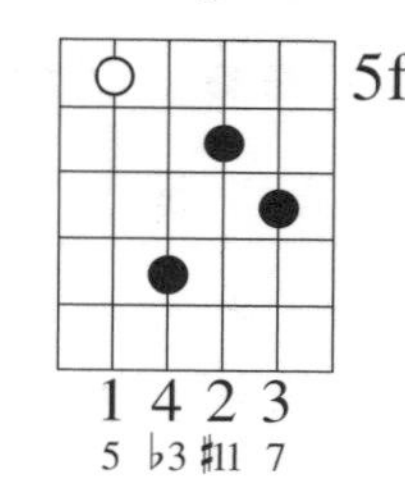

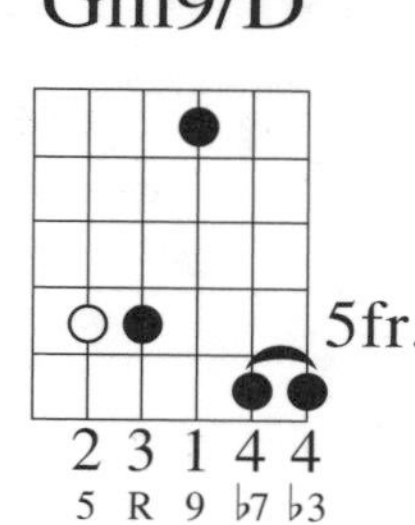

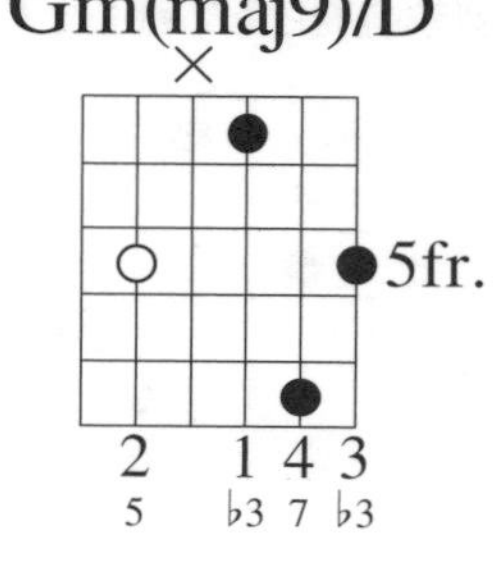

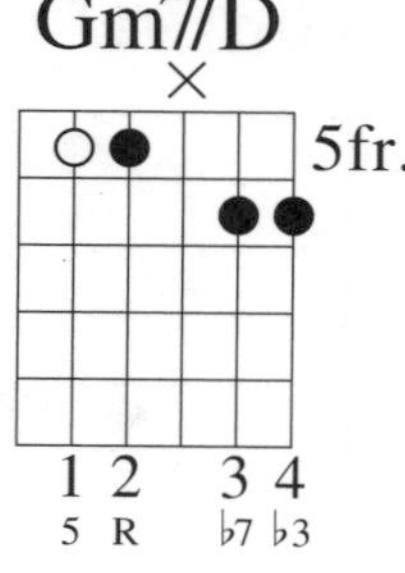

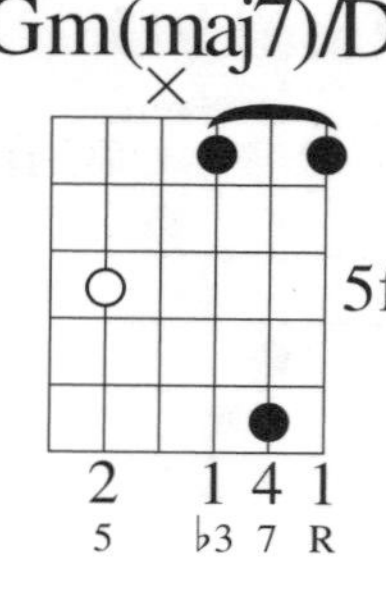

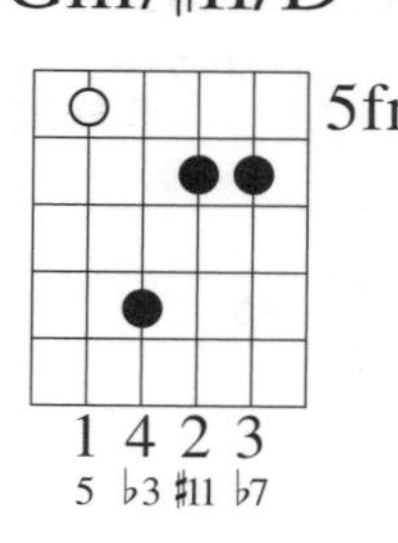

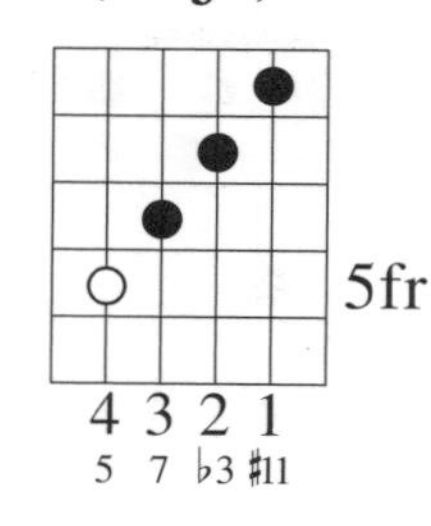

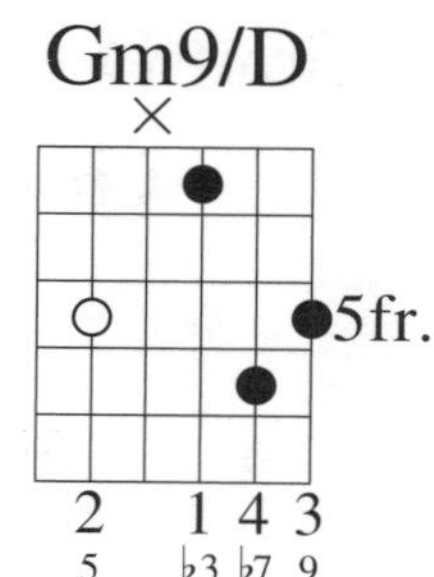

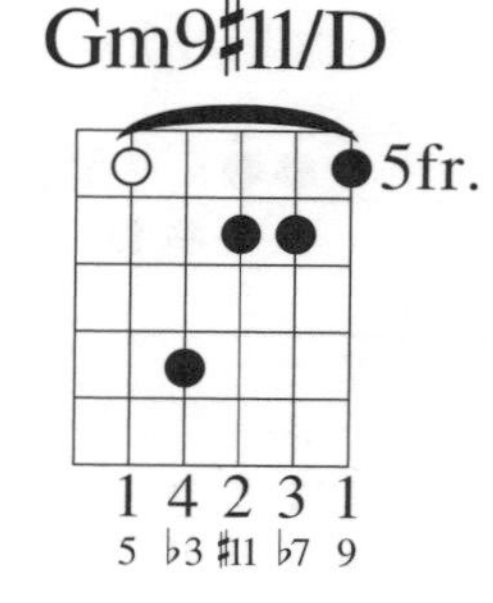

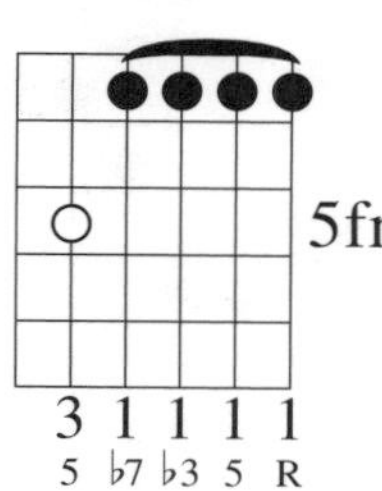

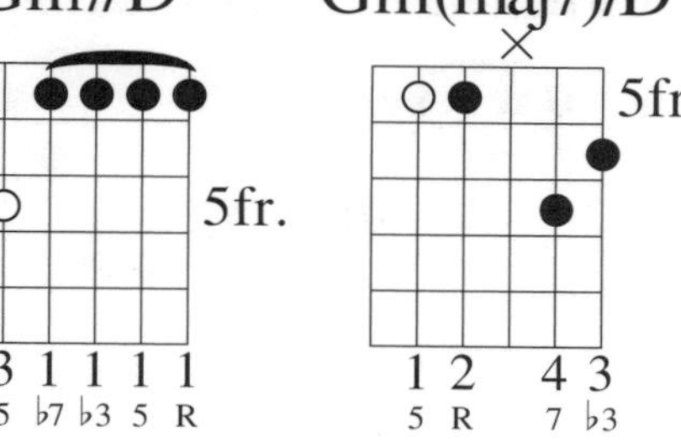

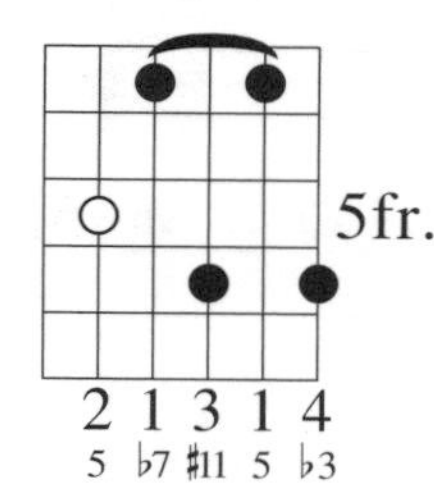

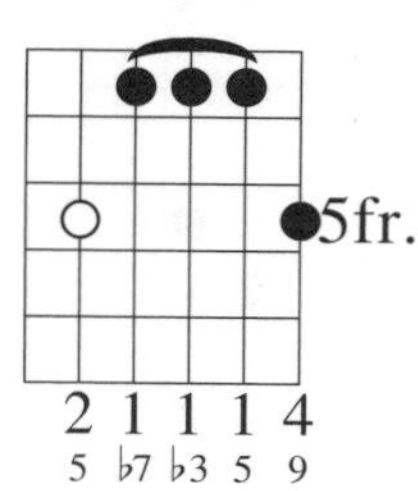

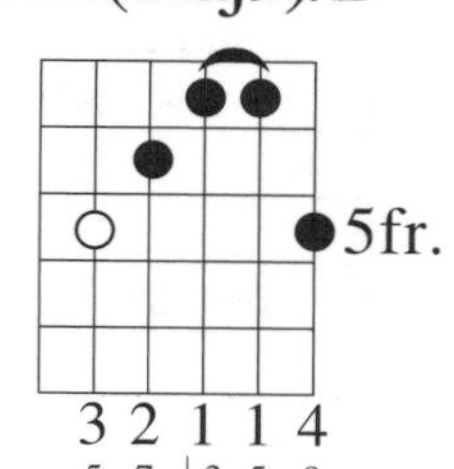

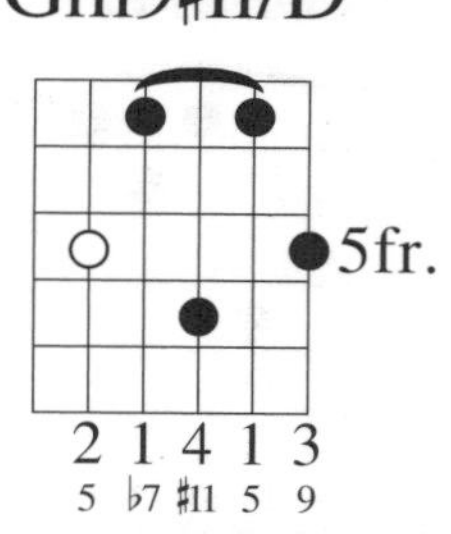

1 2 3 4 5 6 7 8 9 10 11 12
13 14 15 16 17
D♯/A♯ E/B F/C F♯/C♯ G/D G♯/D♯ A/E B♭/F B/F♯ C/G C♯/G♯ D/A
E♭/B♭ G♭/D♭ A♭/E♭ A♯/E♯ C♭/G♭ D♭/A♭

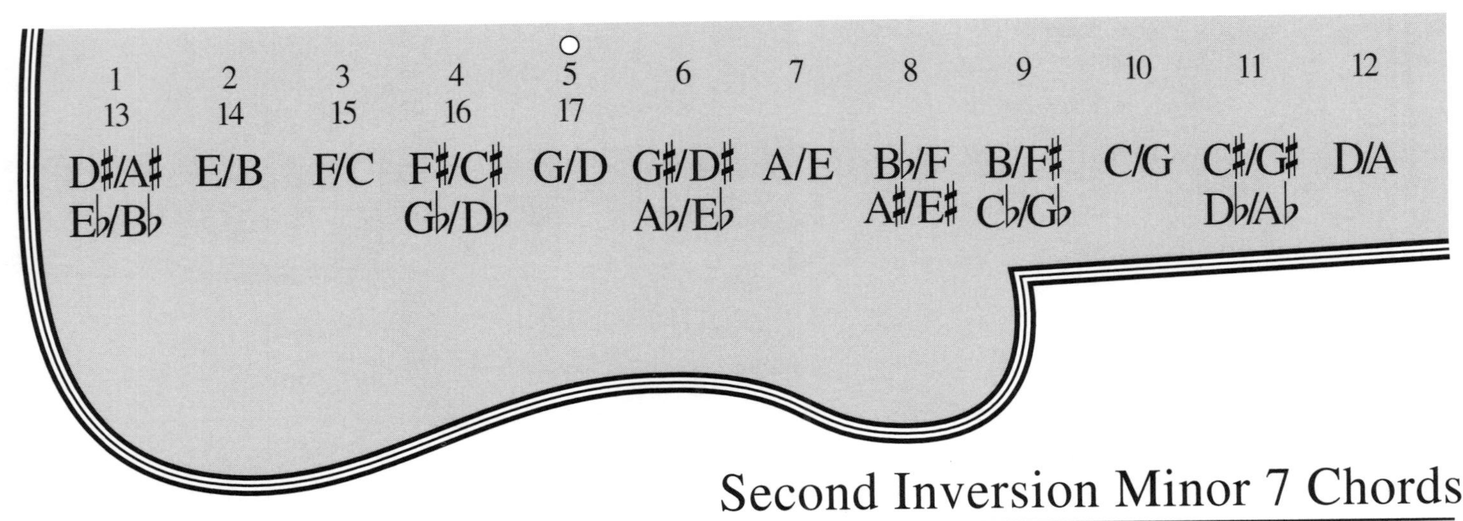

Second Inversion Minor 7 Chords

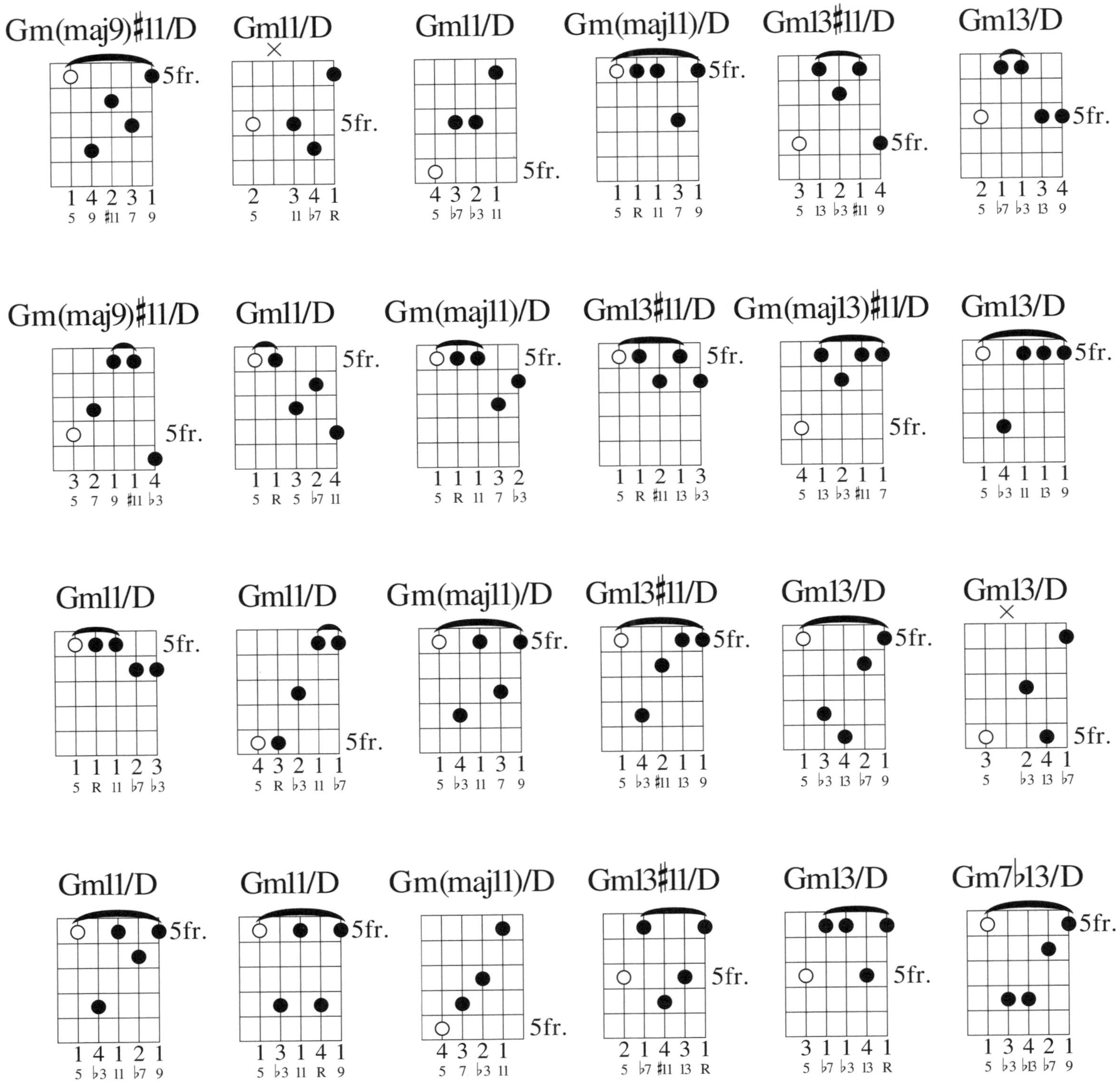

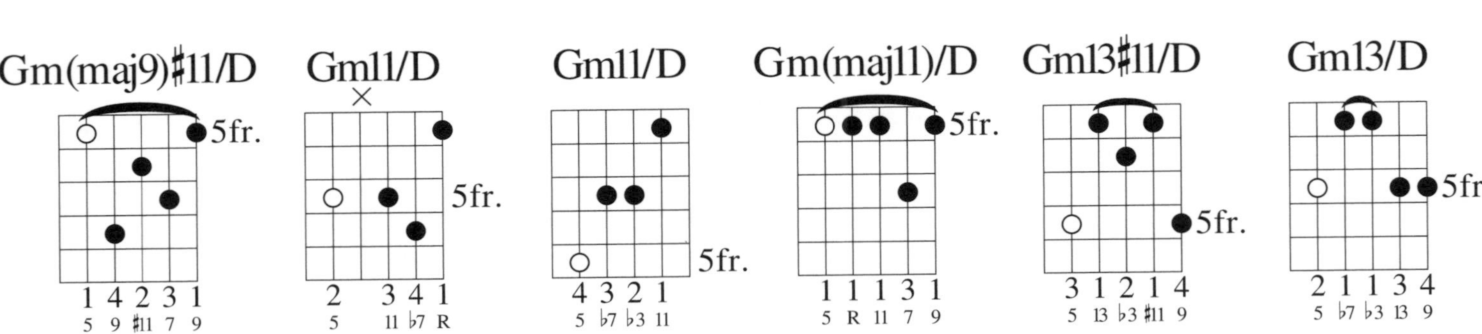

Gm(maj9)♯11/D
5fr.
1 4 2 3 1
5 9 ♯11 7 9
Gm11/D
5fr.
2 3 4 1
5 11 ♭7 R
Gm11/D
5fr.
4 3 2 1
5 ♭7 ♭3 11
Gm(maj11)/D
5fr.
1 1 1 3 1
5 R 11 7 9
Gm13♯11/D
5fr.
3 1 2 1 4
5 13 ♭3 ♯11 9
Gm13/D
5fr.
2 1 1 3 4
5 ♭7 ♭3 13 9
Gm(maj9)♯11/D
5fr.
3 2 1 1 4
5 7 9 ♯11 ♭3
Gm11/D
5fr.
1 1 3 2 4
5 R 5 ♭7 11
Gm(maj11)/D
5fr.
1 1 1 3 2
5 R 11 7 ♭3
Gm13♯11/D
5fr.
1 1 2 1 3
5 R ♯11 13 ♭3
Gm(maj13)♯11/D
5fr.
4 1 2 1 1
5 13 ♭3 ♯11 7
Gm13/D
5fr.
1 4 1 1 1
5 ♭3 11 13 9
Gm11/D
5fr.
1 1 1 2 3
5 R 11 ♭7 ♭3
Gm11/D
5fr.
4 3 2 1 1
5 R ♭3 11 ♭7
Gm(maj11)/D
5fr.
1 4 1 3 1
5 ♭3 11 7 9
Gm13♯11/D
5fr.
1 4 2 1 1
5 ♭3 ♯11 13 9
Gm13/D
5fr.
1 3 4 2 1
5 ♭3 13 ♭7 9
Gm13/D
5fr.
3 2 4 1
5 ♭3 13 ♭7
Gm11/D
5fr.
1 4 1 2 1
5 ♭3 11 ♭7 9
Gm11/D
5fr.
1 3 1 4 1
5 ♭3 11 R 9
Gm(maj11)/D
5fr.
4 3 2 1
5 7 ♭3 11
Gm13♯11/D
5fr.
2 1 4 3 1
5 ♭7 ♯11 13 R
Gm13/D
5fr.
3 1 1 4 1
5 ♭7 ♭3 13 R
Gm7♭13/D
5fr.
1 3 4 2 1
5 ♭3 ♭13 ♭7 9

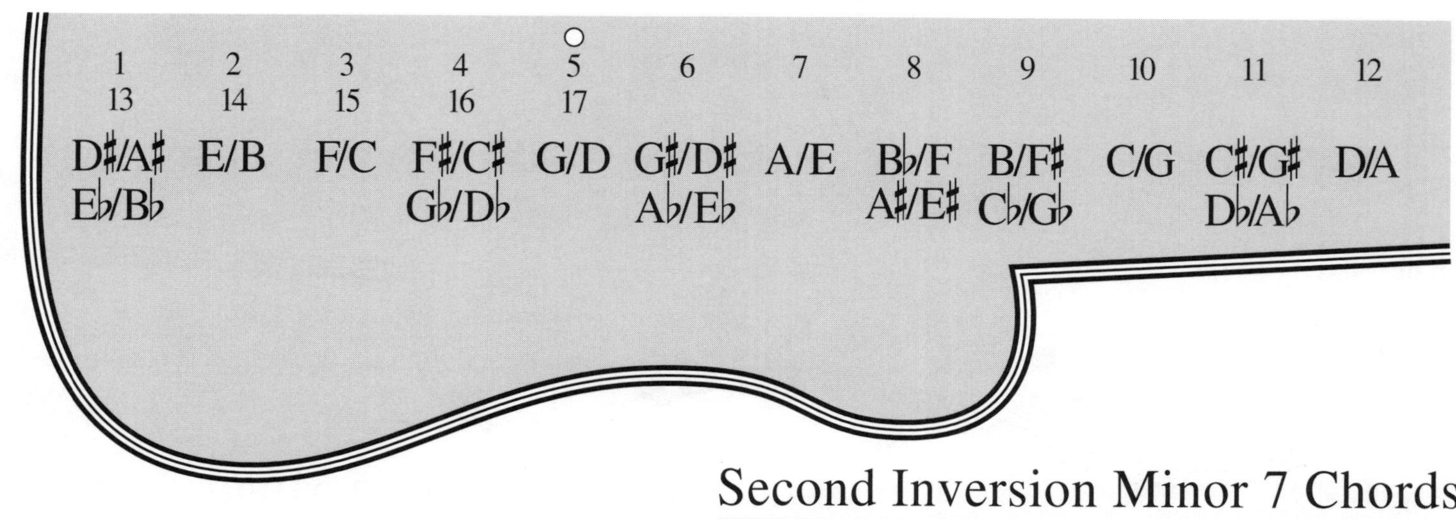

Second Inversion Minor 7 Chords

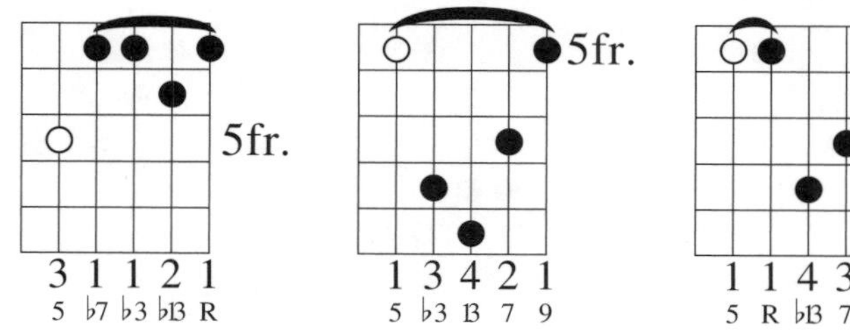

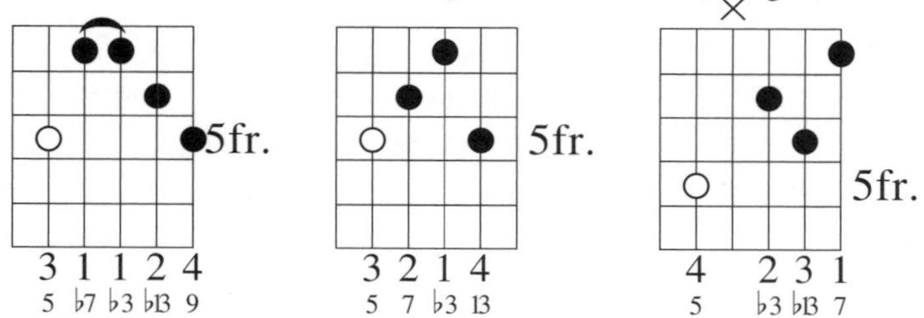

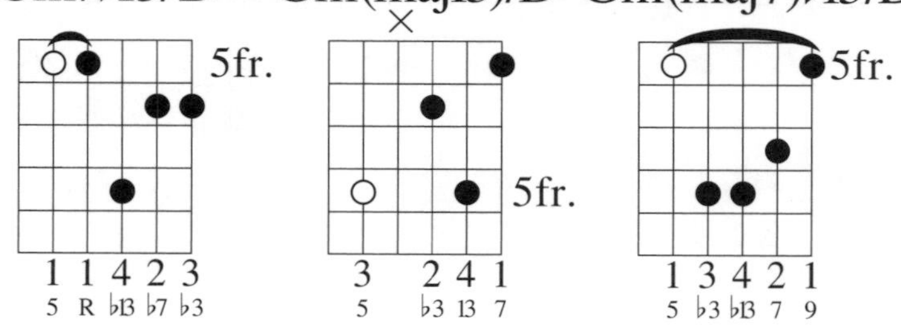

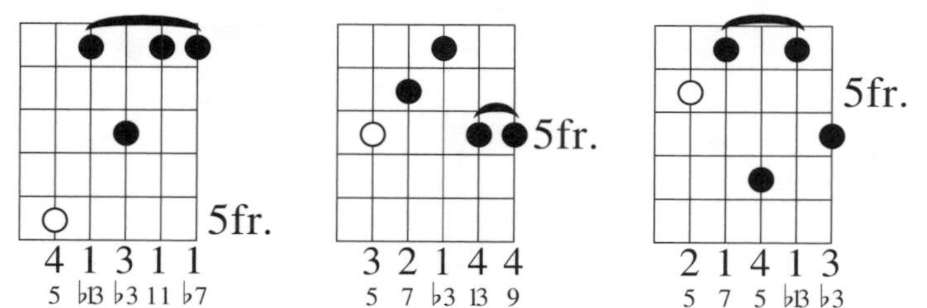

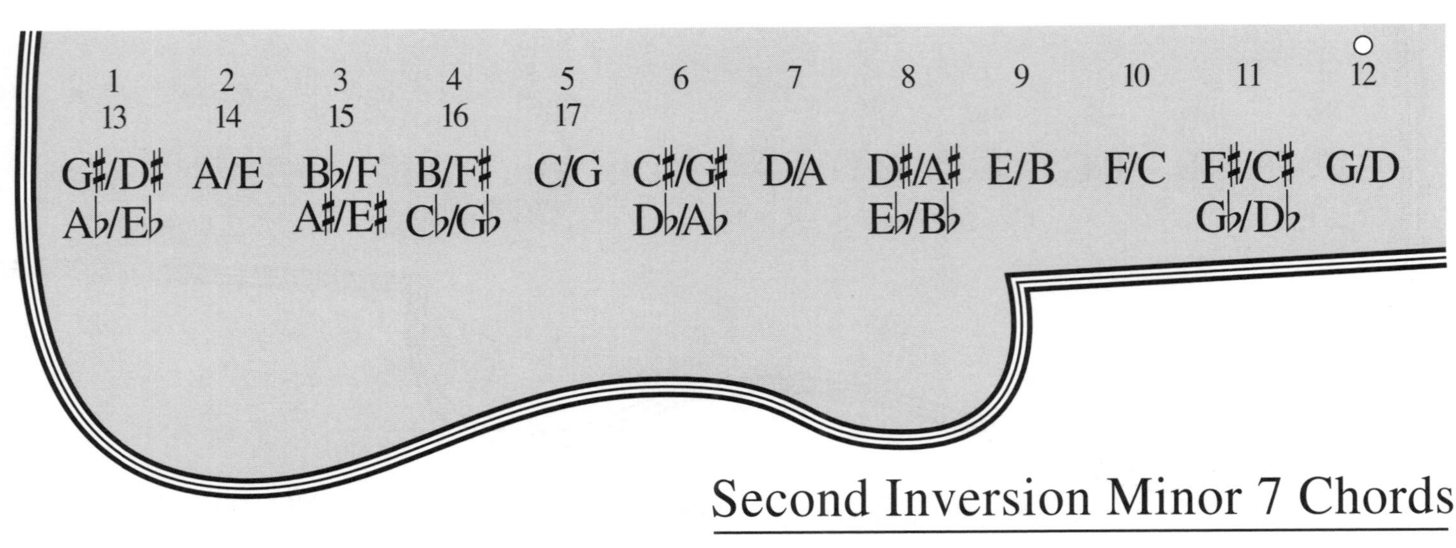

Second Inversion Minor 7 Chords

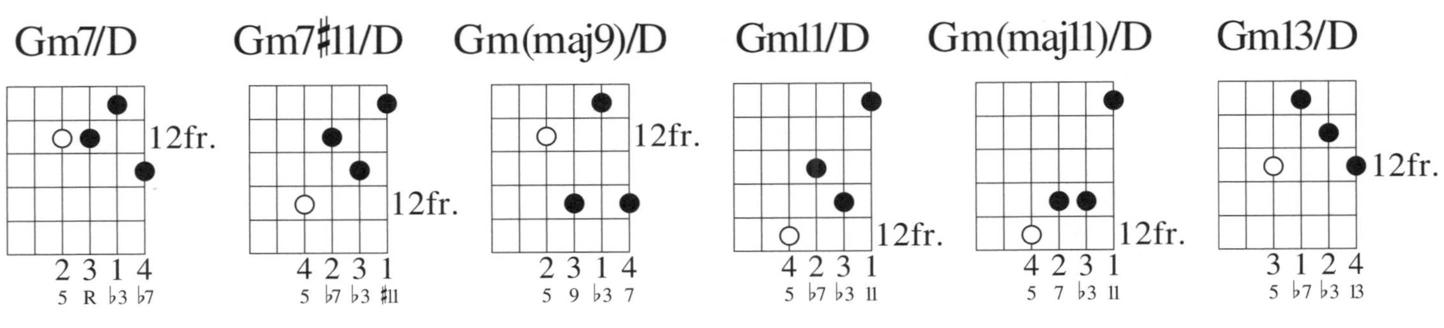

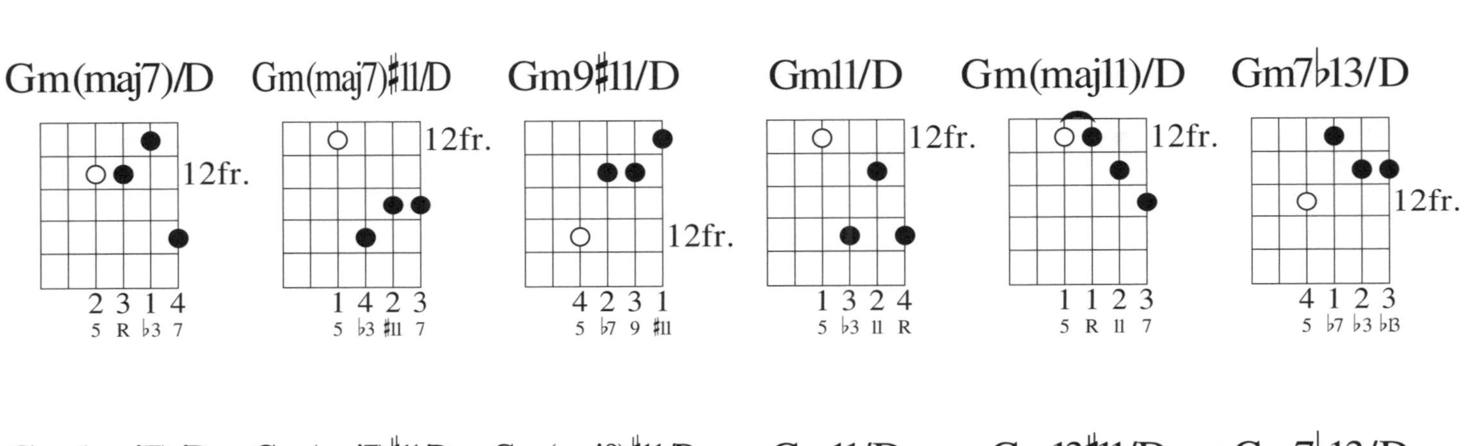

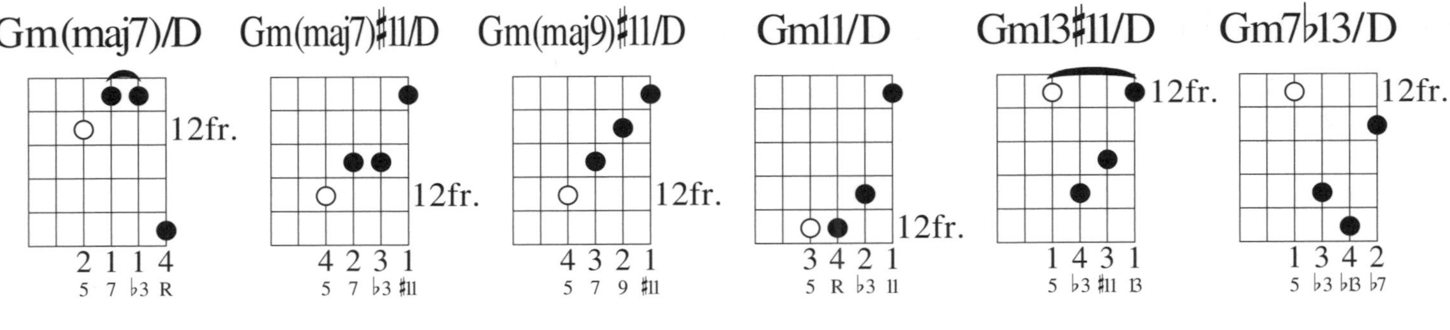

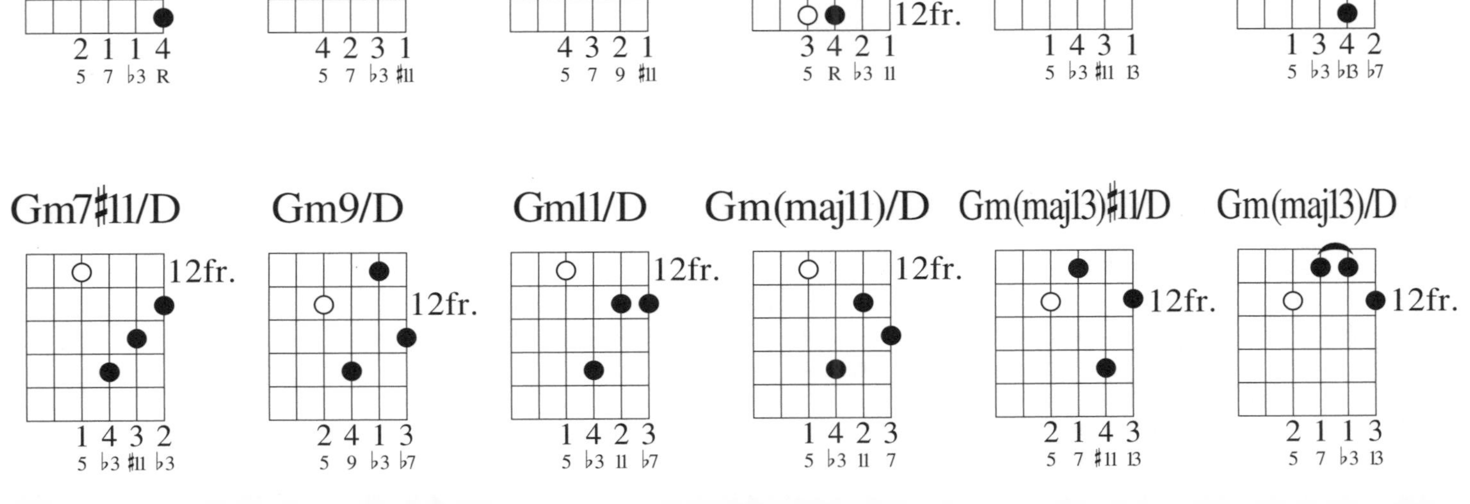

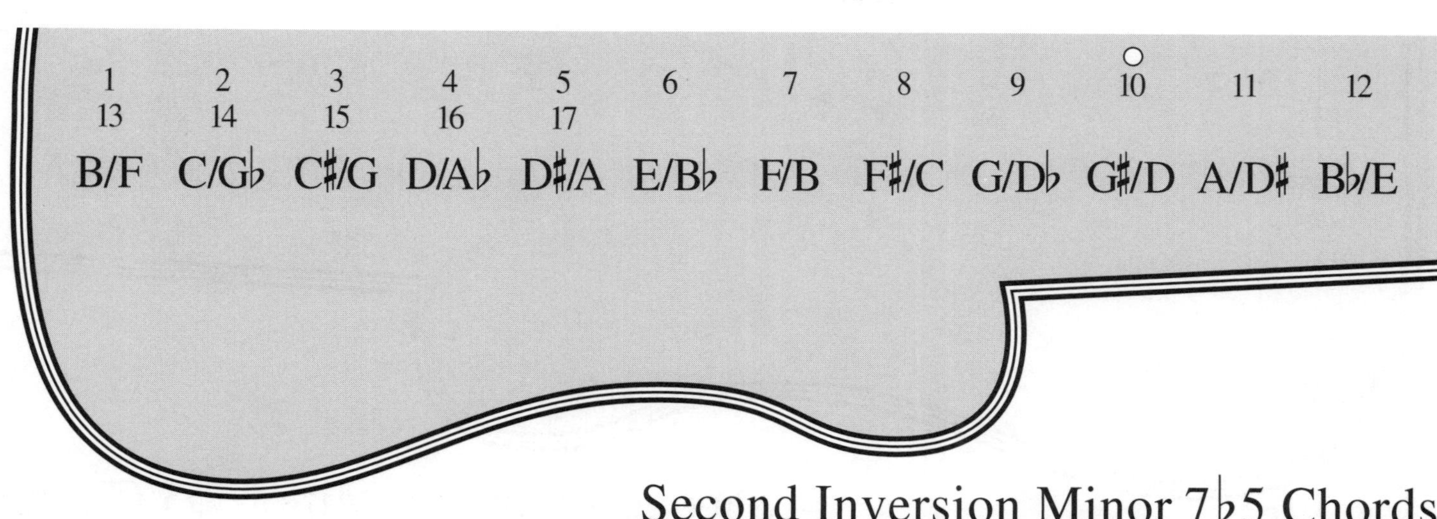

Second Inversion Minor 7♭5 Chords

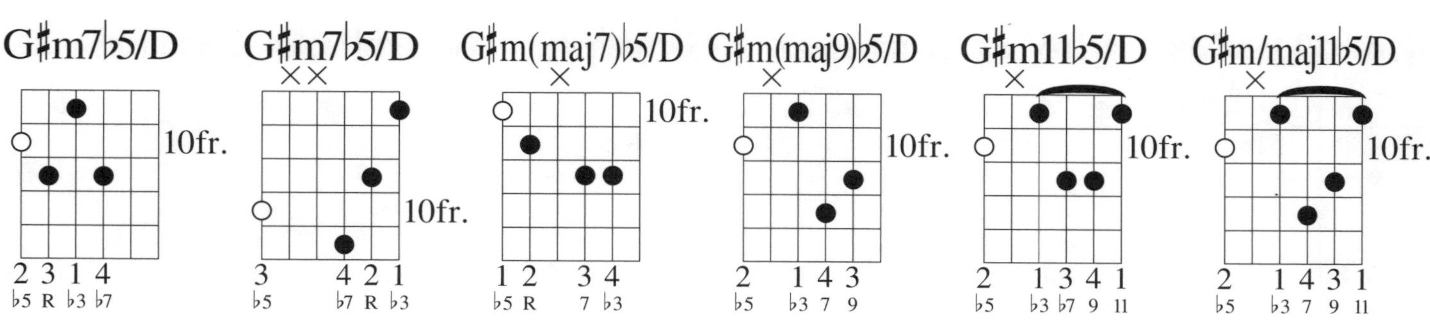

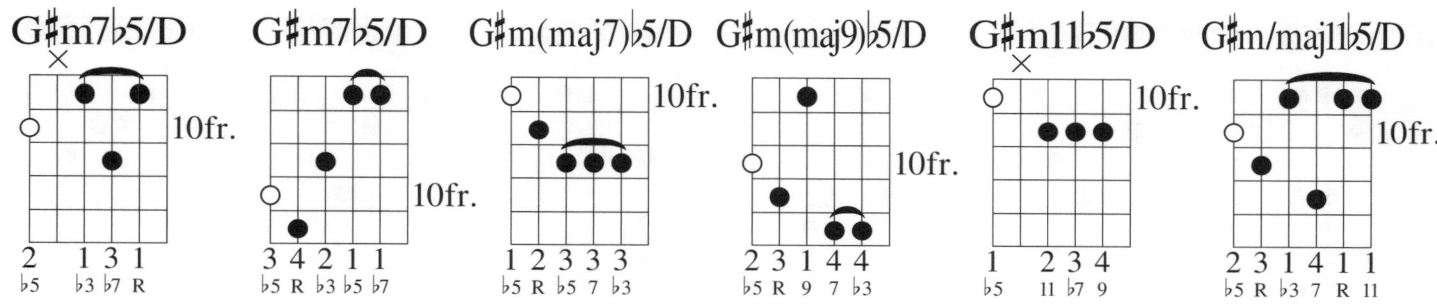

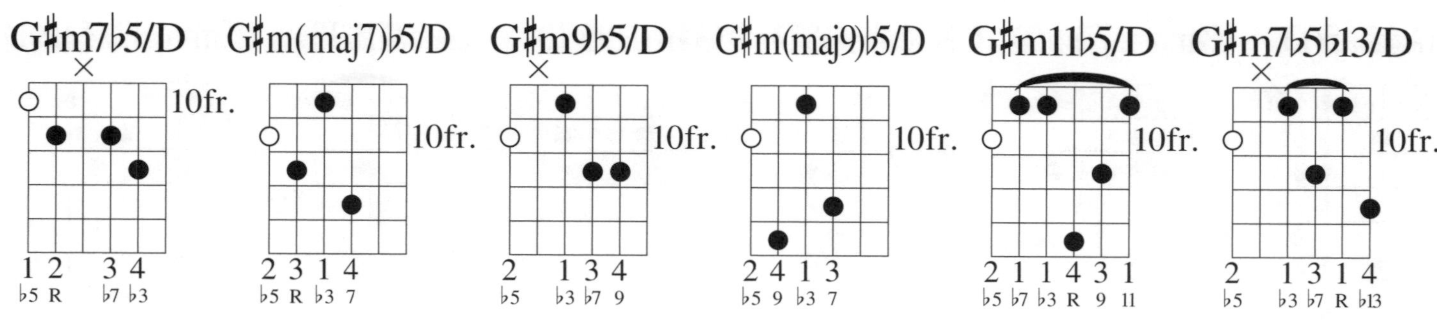

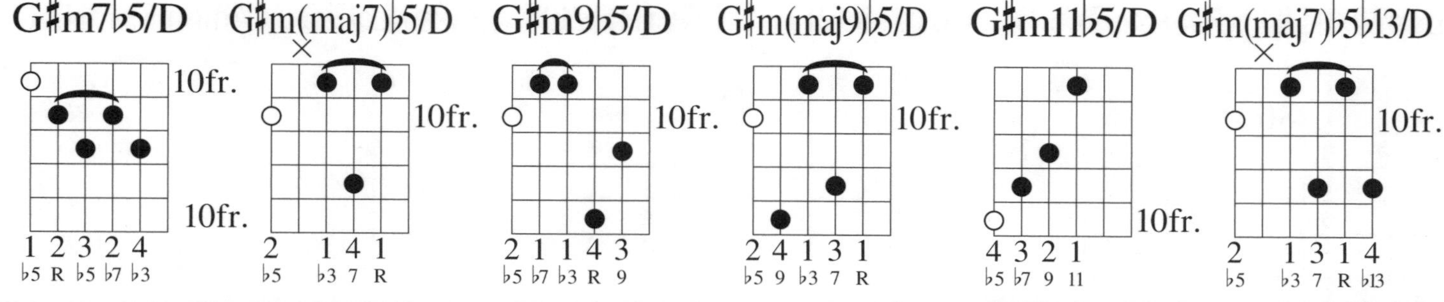

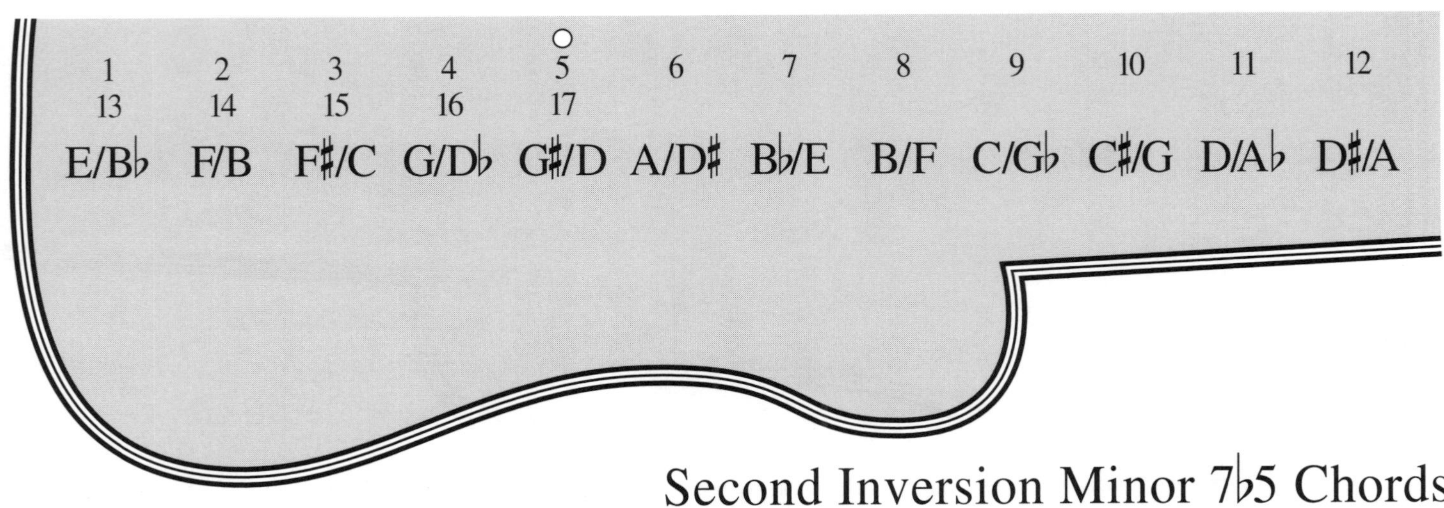

Second Inversion Minor 7♭5 Chords

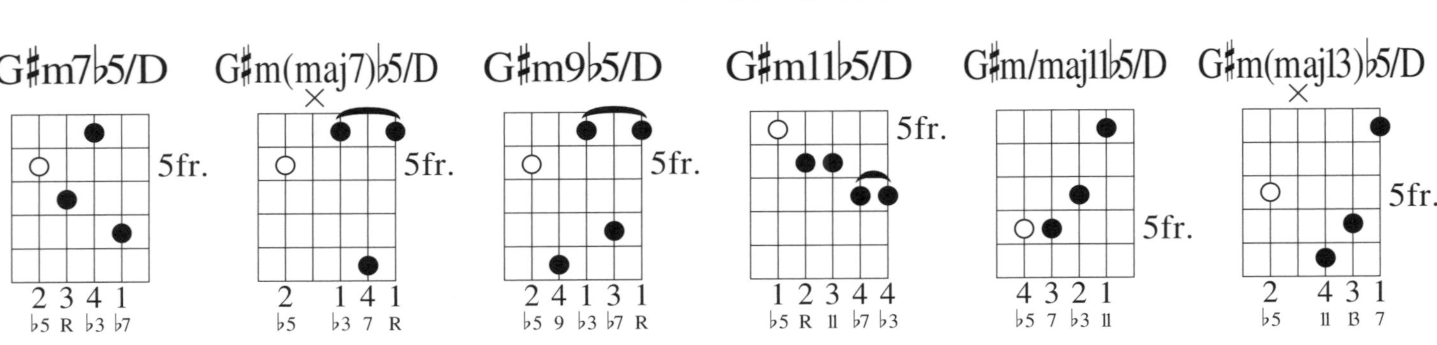

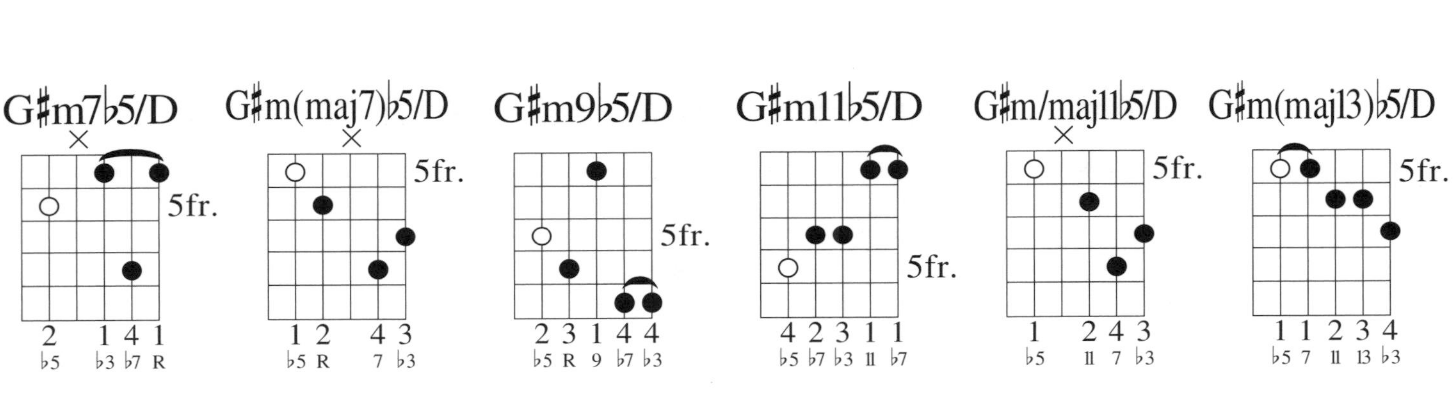

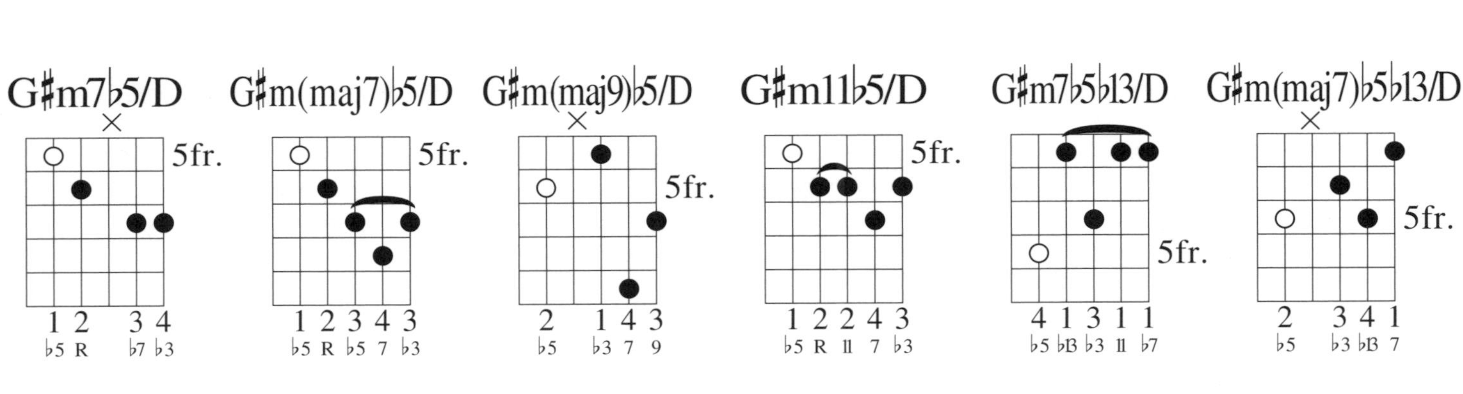

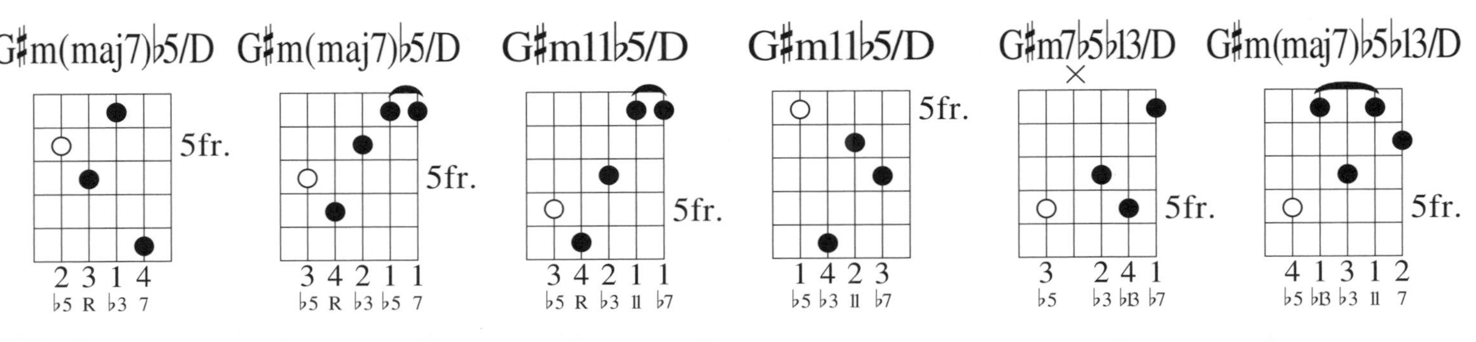

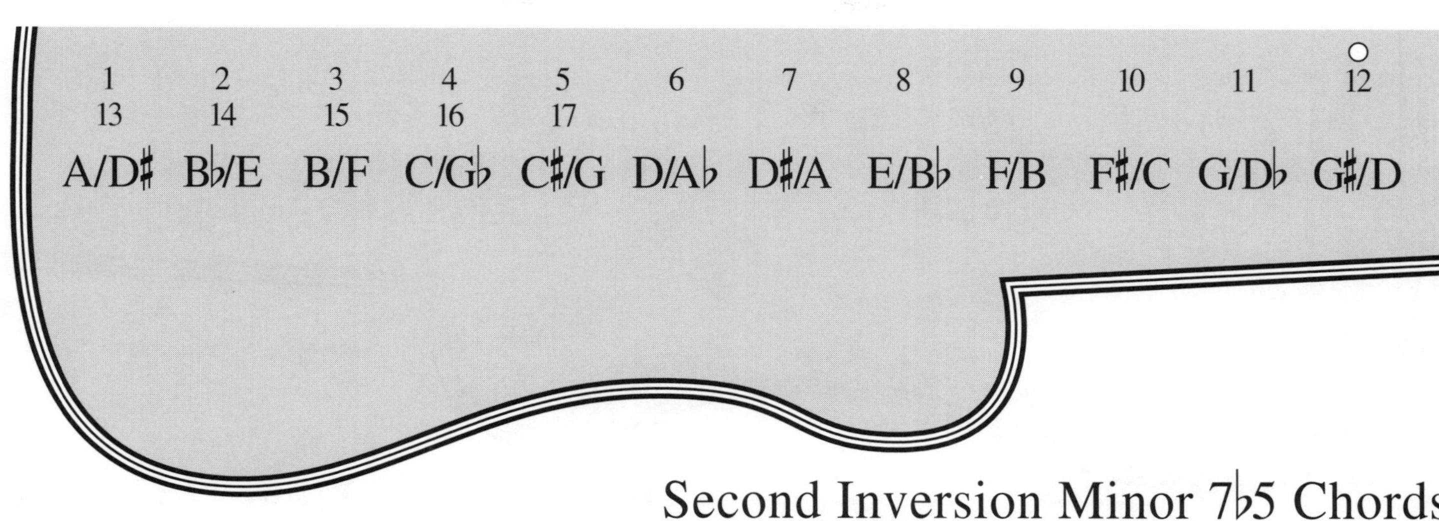

Second Inversion Minor 7♭5 Chords

G♯m7♭5/D

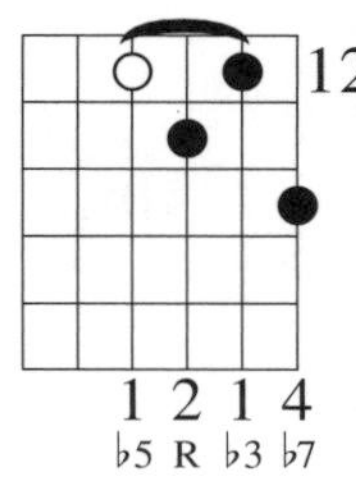

G♯m9♭5/D

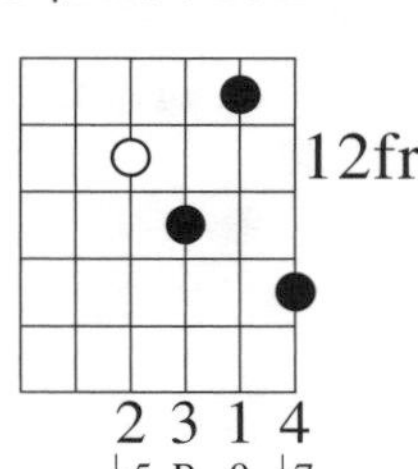

G♯m11♭5/D

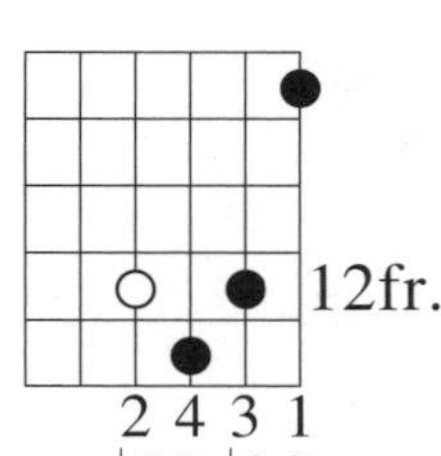

G♯m/maj11♭5/D

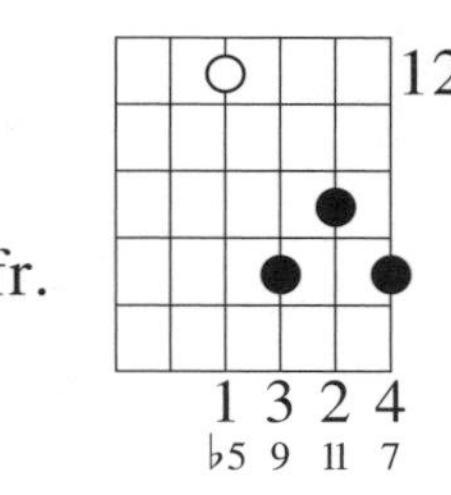

G♯m7♭5♭13/D

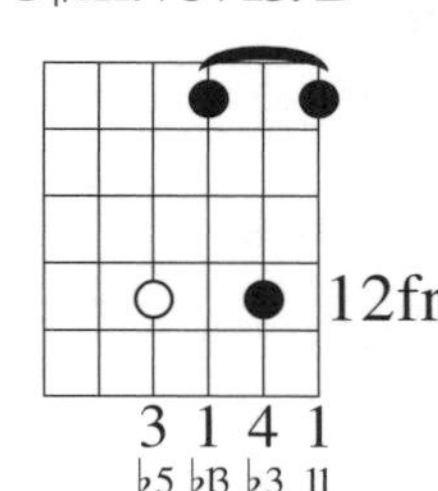

G♯m(maj13)♭5/D

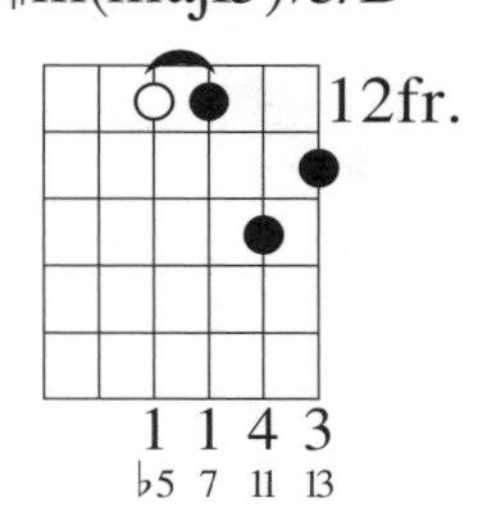

G♯m(maj7)♭5/D

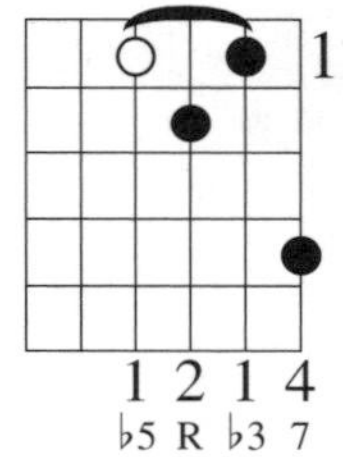

G♯m(maj9)♭5/D

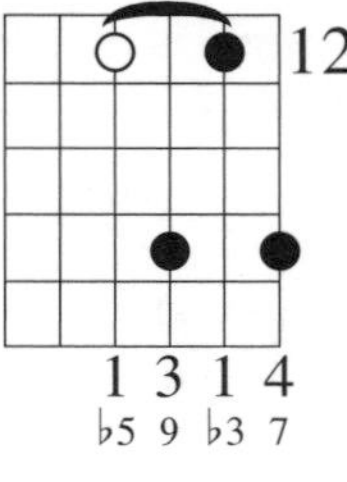

G♯m11♭5/D

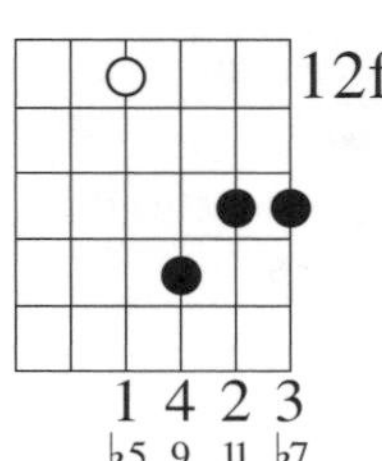

G♯m/maj11♭5/D

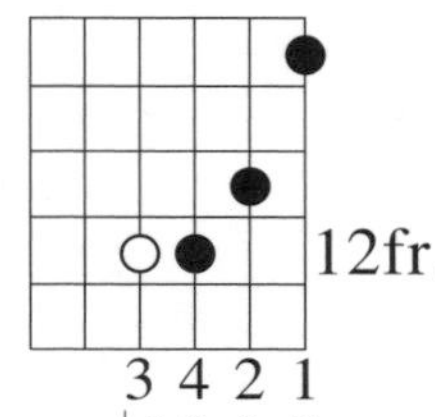

G♯m7♭5♭13/D

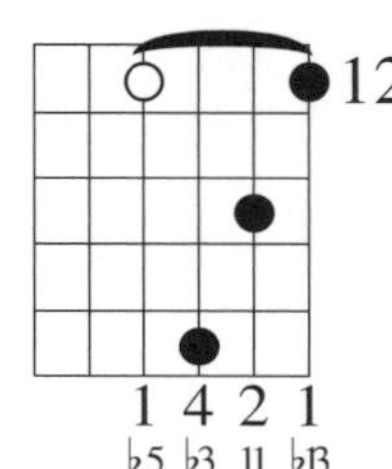

G♯m(maj13)♭5/D

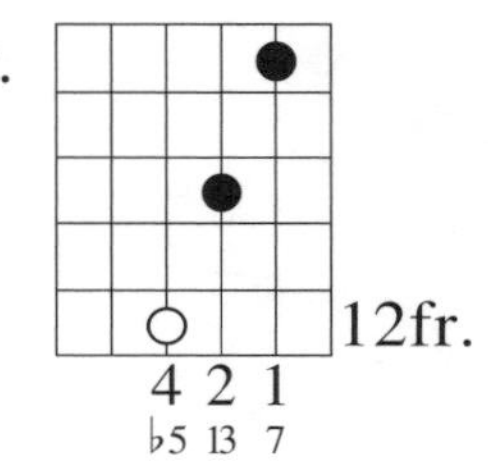

G♯m(maj7)♭5/D

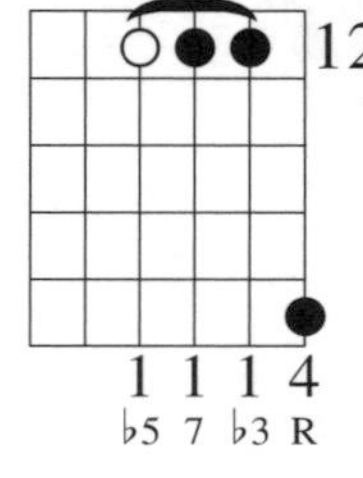

G♯m(maj9)♭5/D

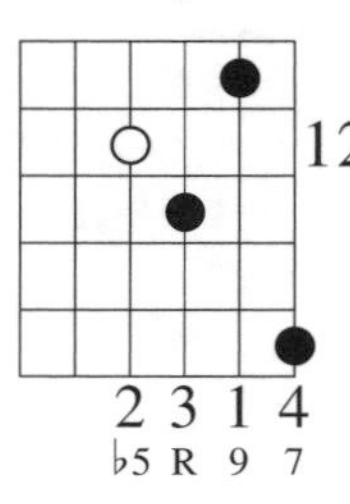

G♯m11♭5/D

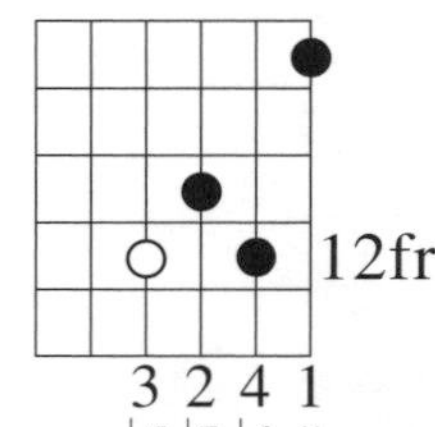

G♯m/maj11♭5/D

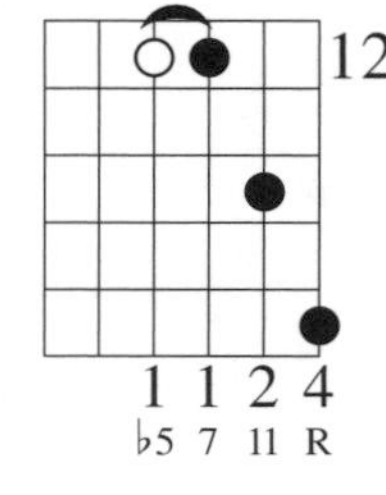

G♯m7♭5♭13/D

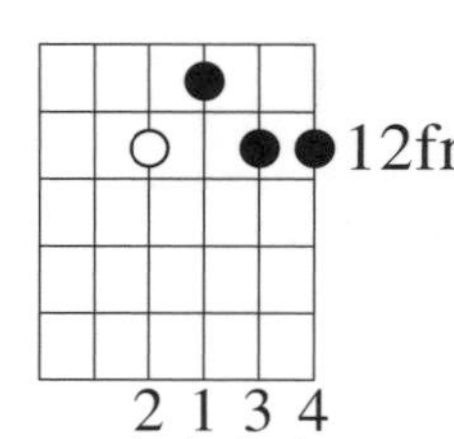

G♯m(maj7)♭5♭13/D

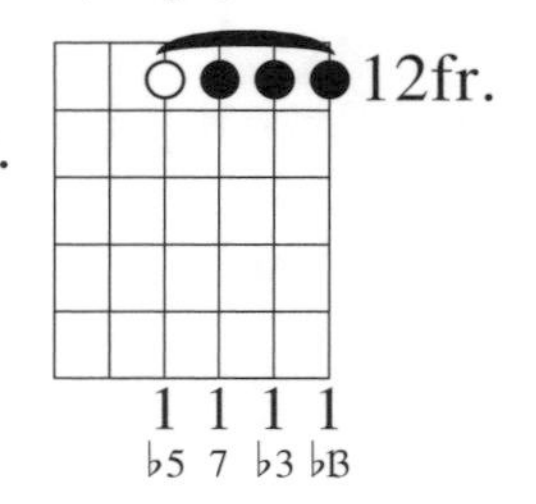

G♯m9♭5/D

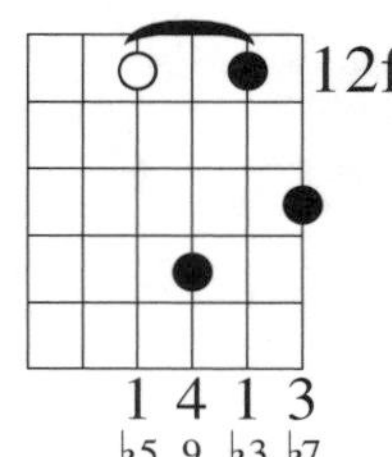

G♯m11♭5/D

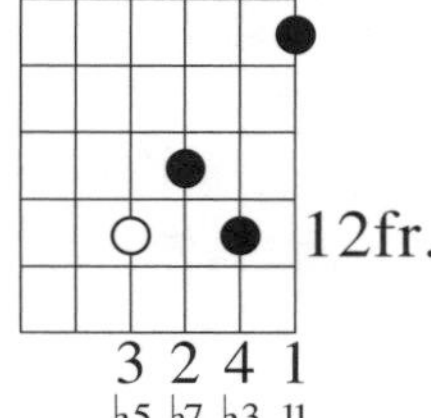

G♯m/maj11♭5/D

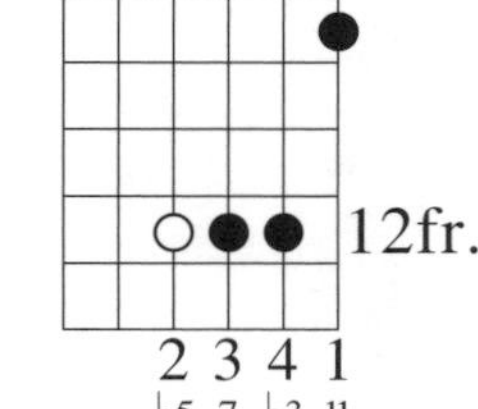

G♯m/maj11♭5/D

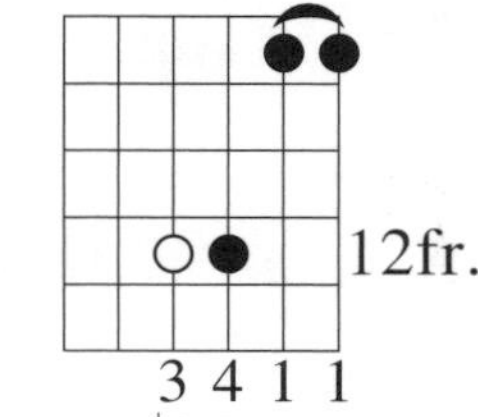

G♯m7♭5♭13/D

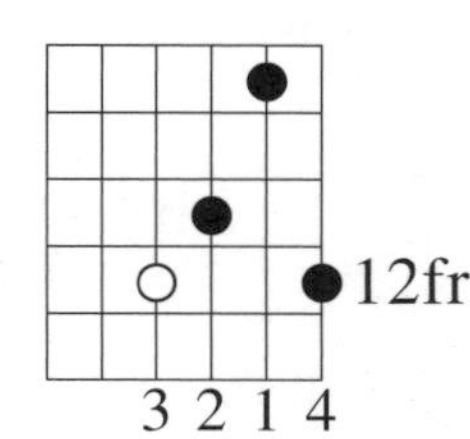

G♯m(maj7)♭5♭13/D

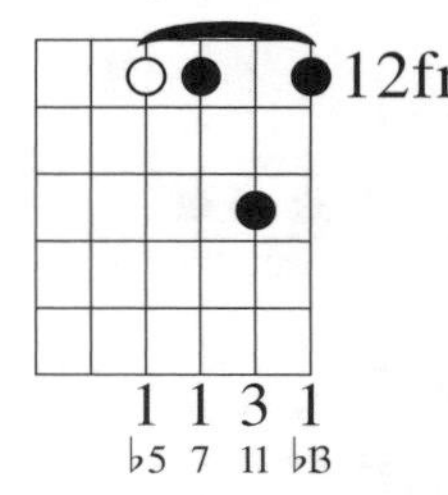

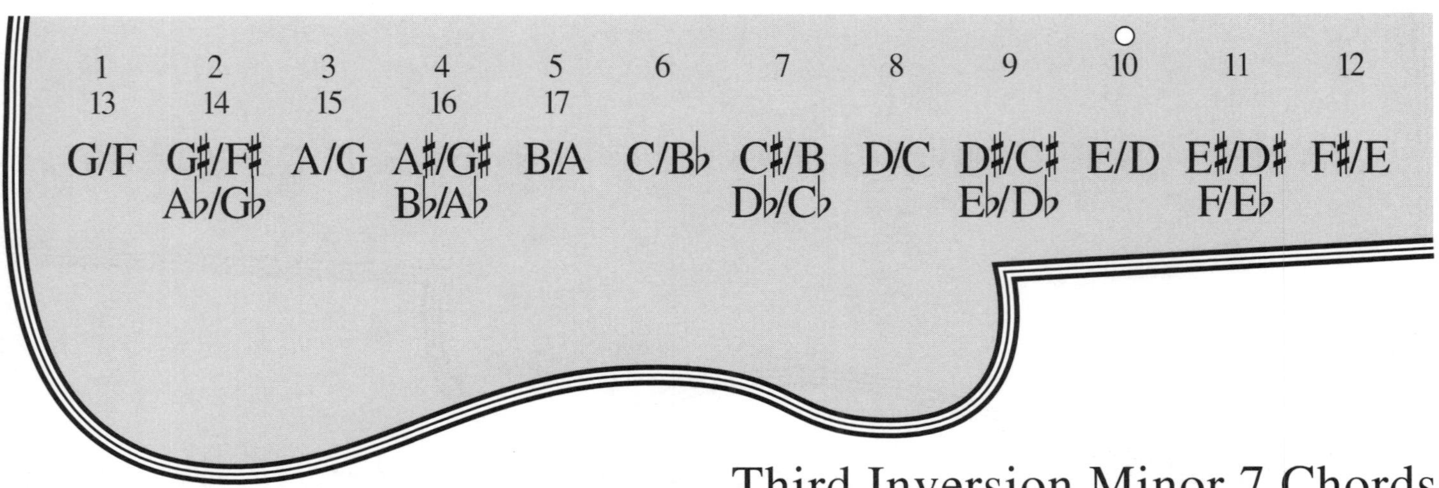

Third Inversion Minor 7 Chords

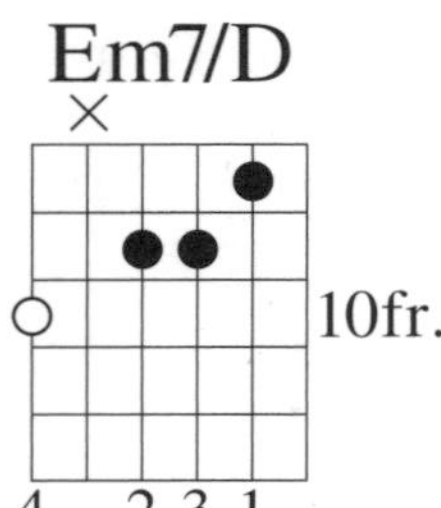

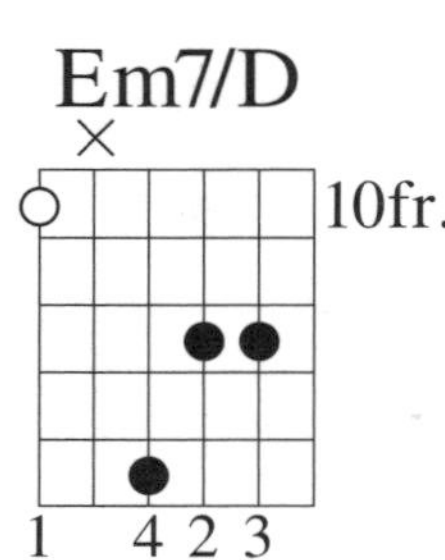

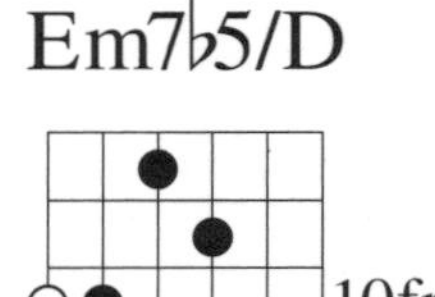

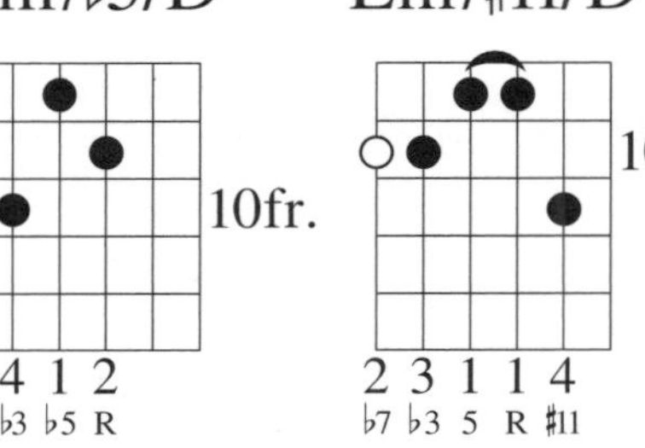

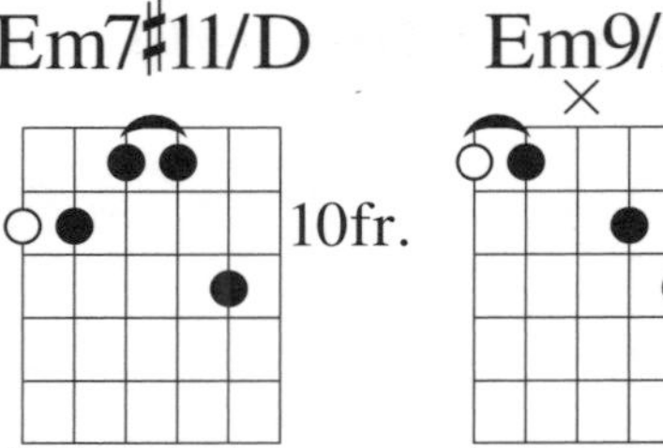

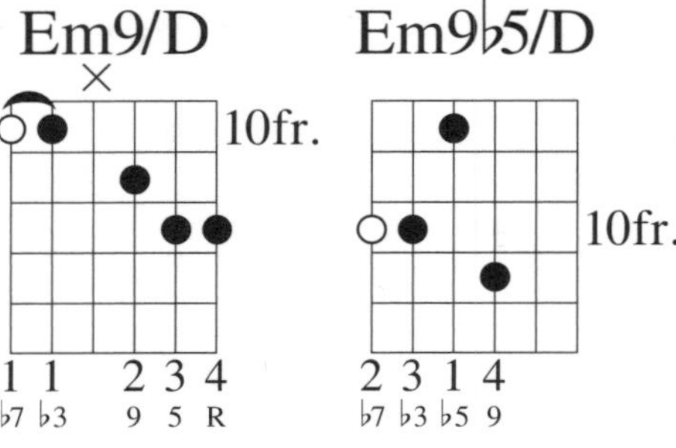

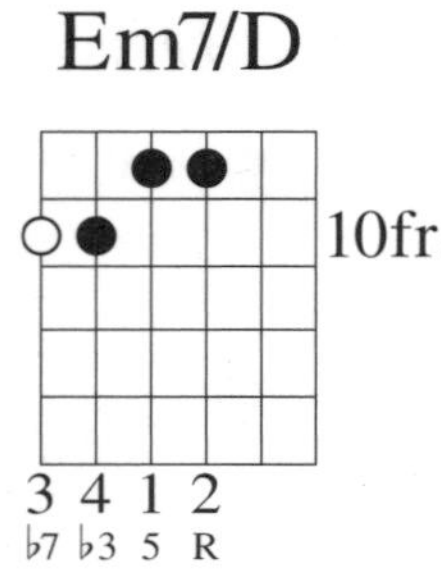

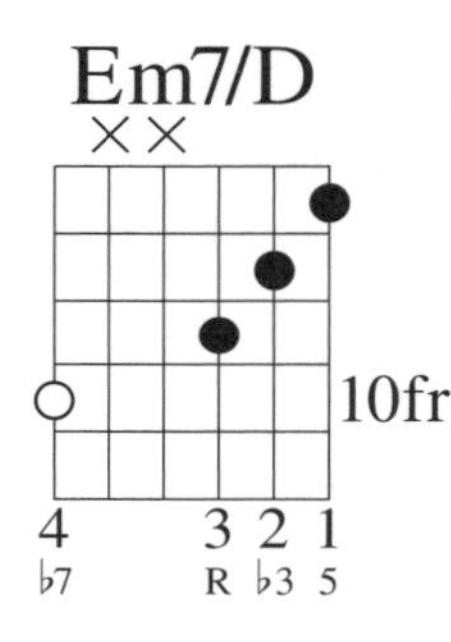

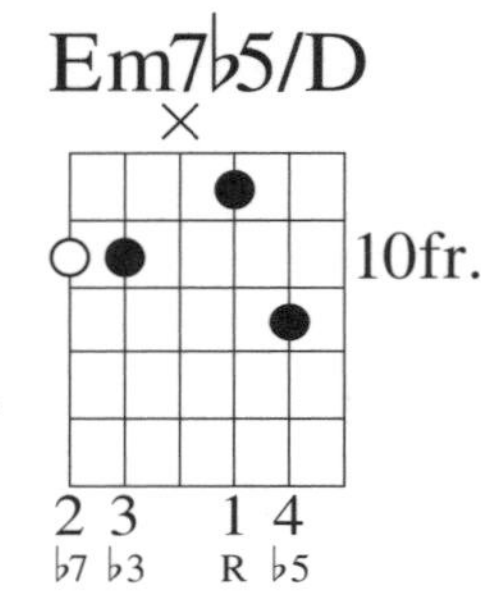

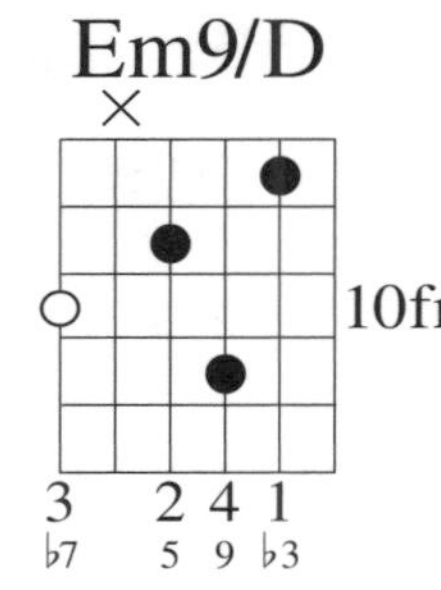

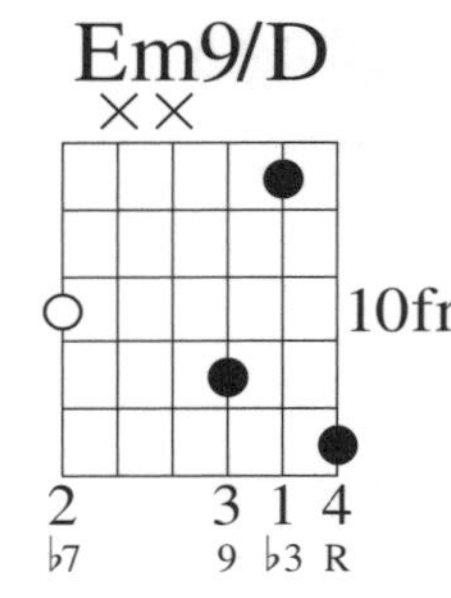

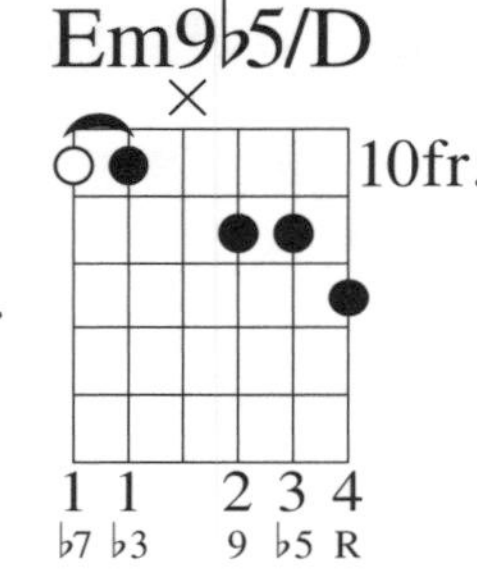

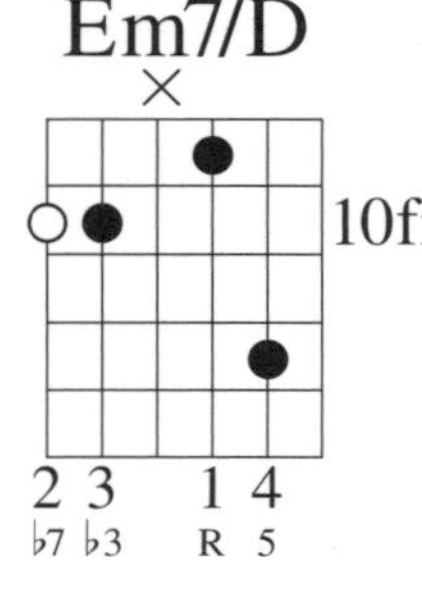

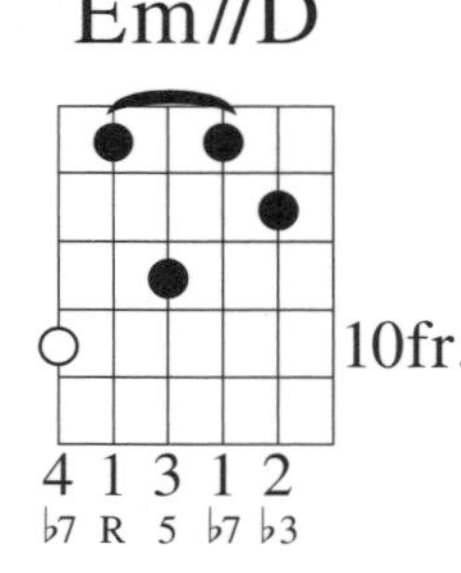

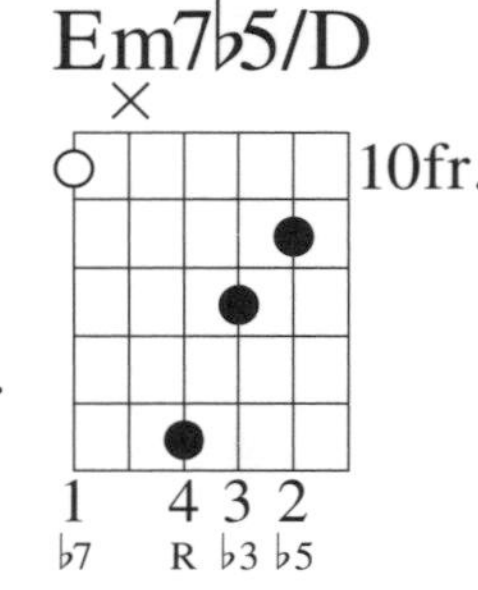

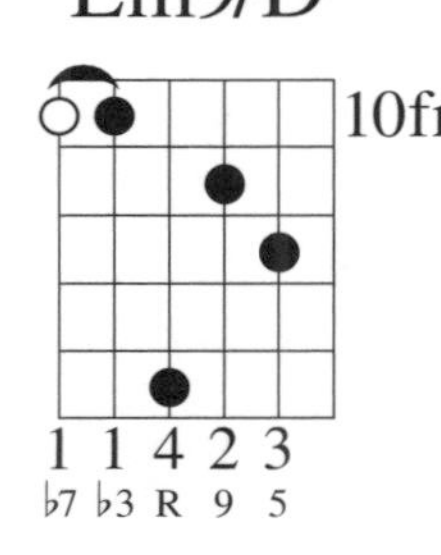

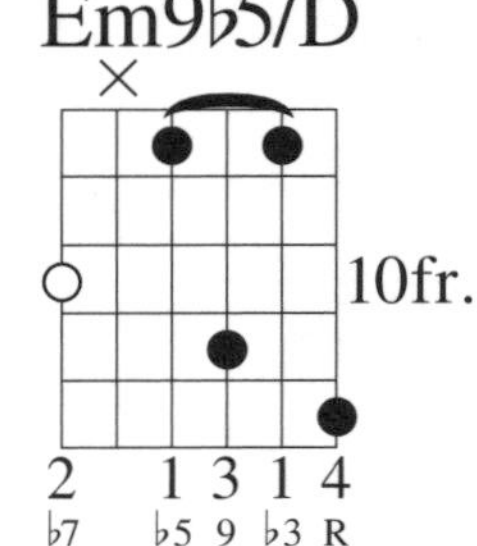

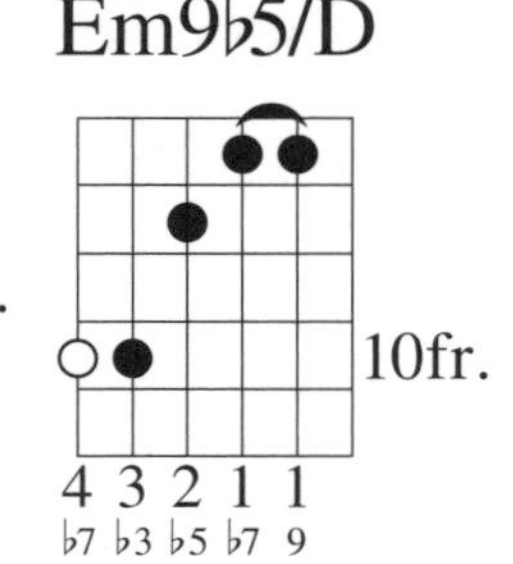

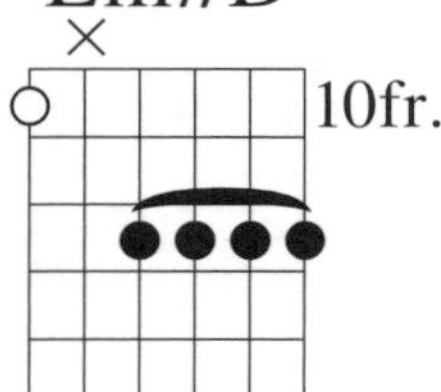

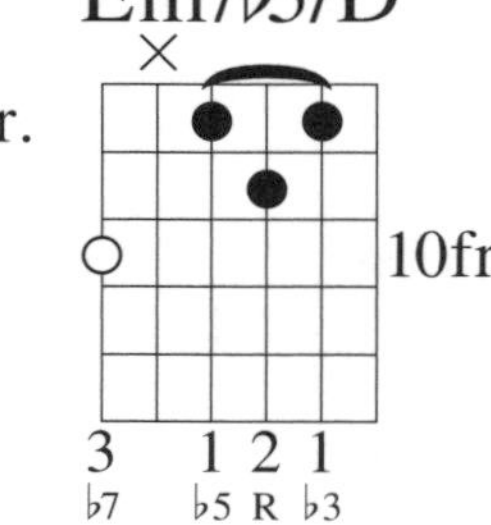

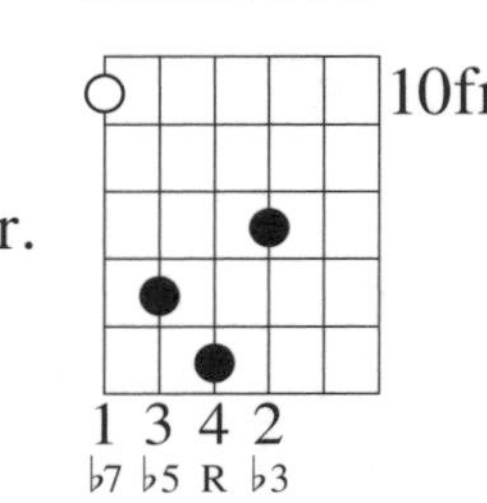

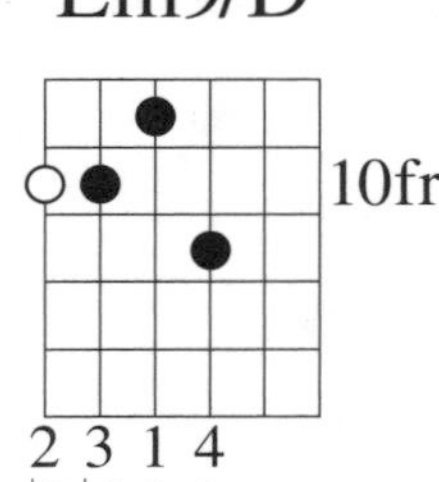

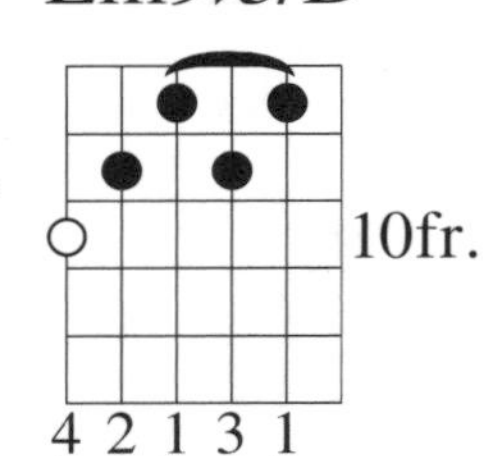

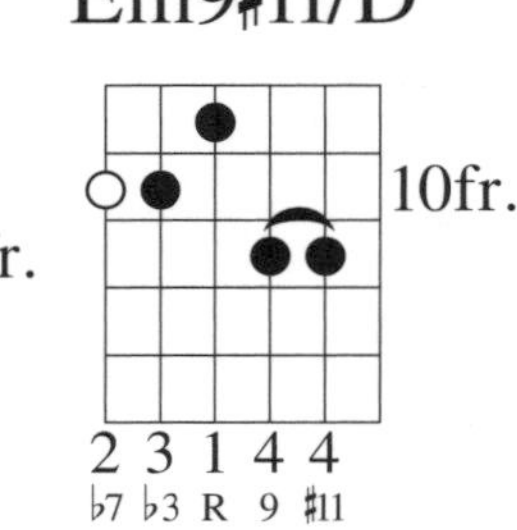

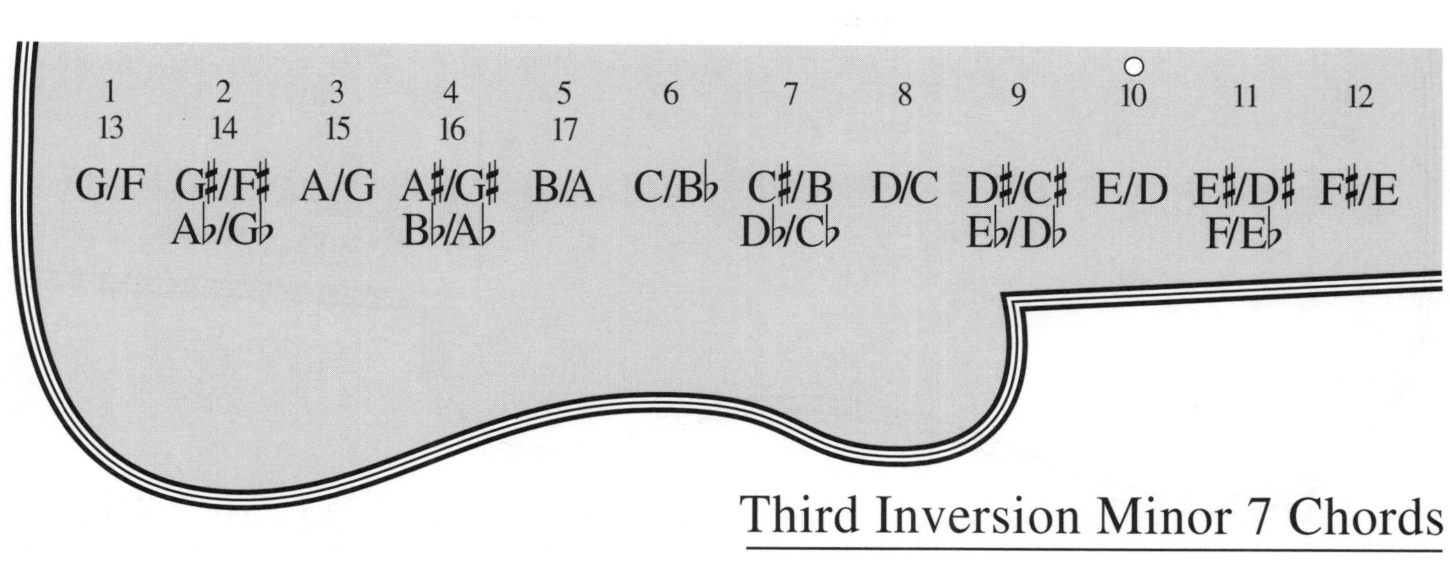

Third Inversion Minor 7 Chords

Em11/D

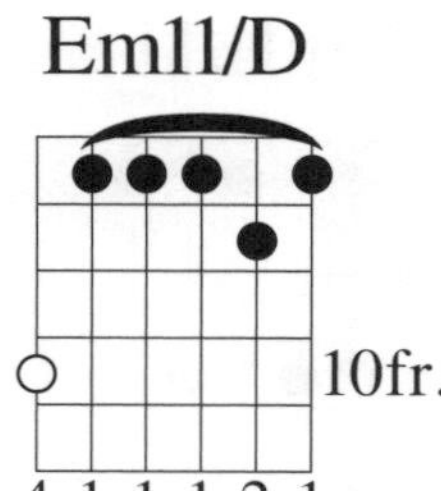

Em11/D

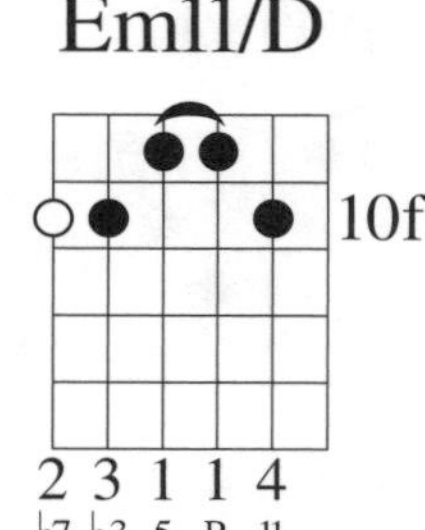

Em11♭5/D

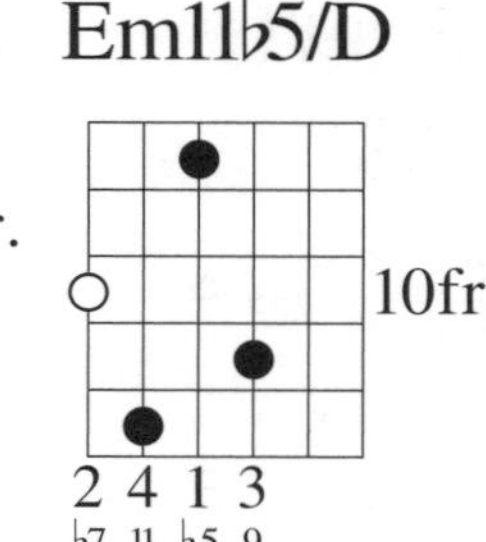

Em13♯11/D

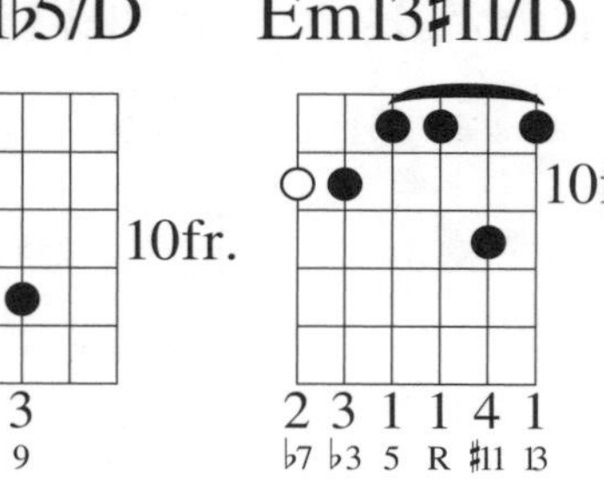

Em13/D

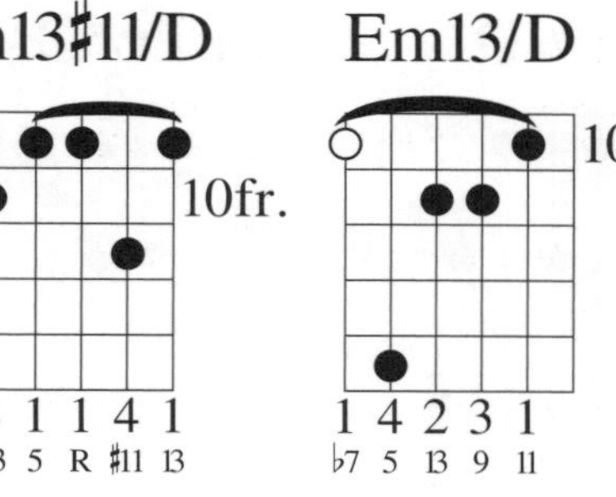

Em7♭13/D

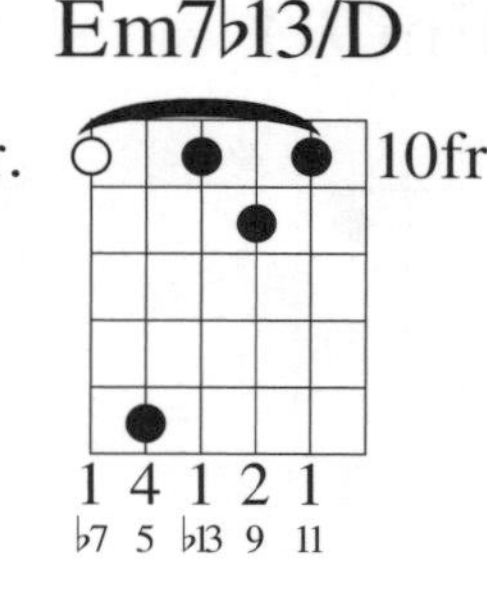

Em11/D

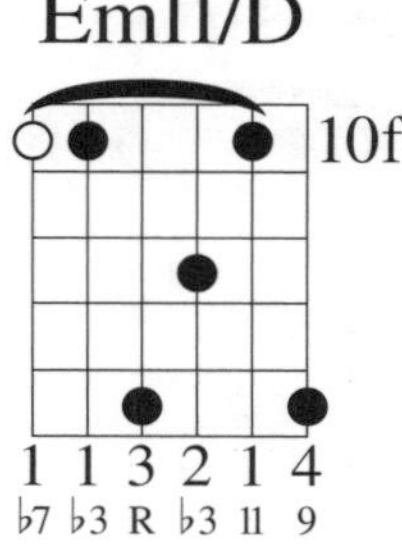

Em11♭5/D

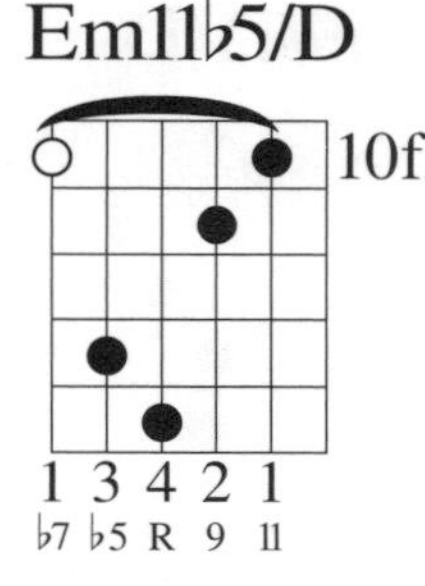

Em13♯11/D

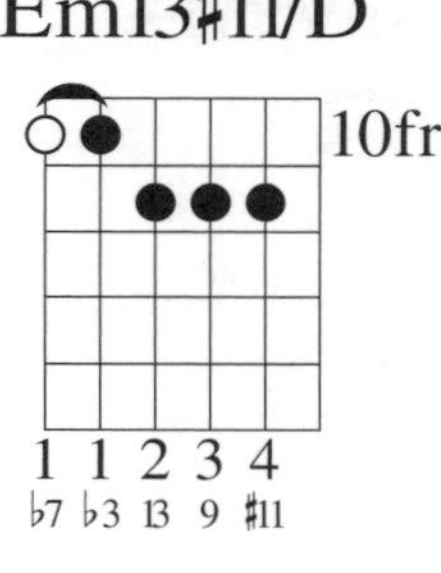

Em13/D

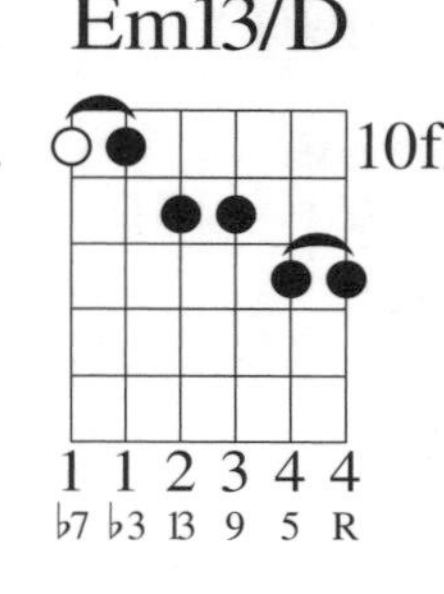

Em7♭13/D

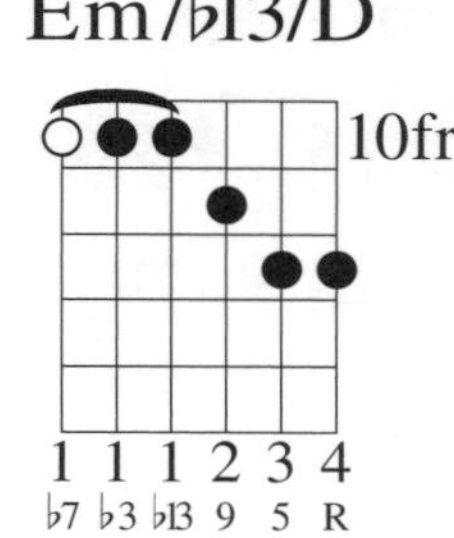

Em7♭13/D

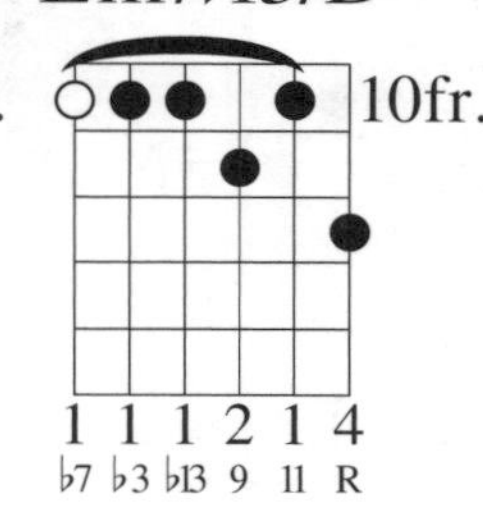

Em11/D

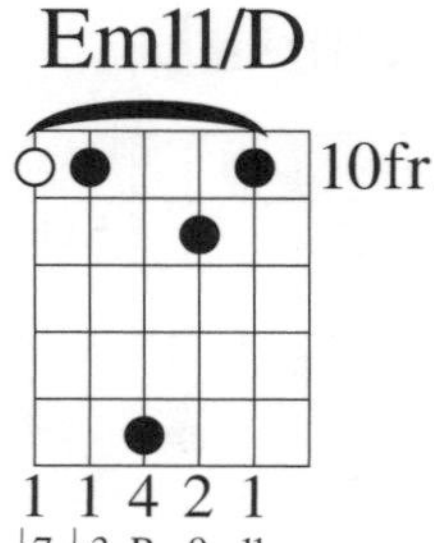

Em11♭5/D

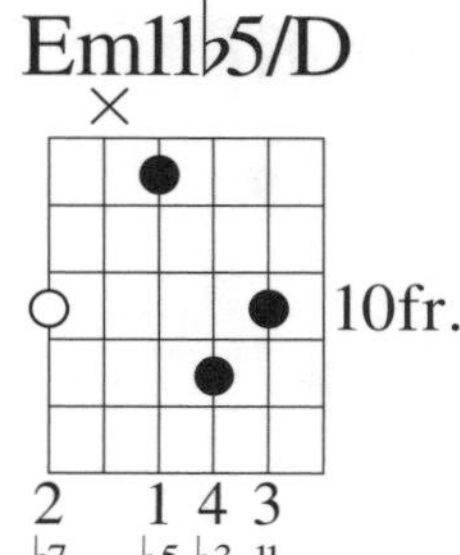

Em13♯11/D

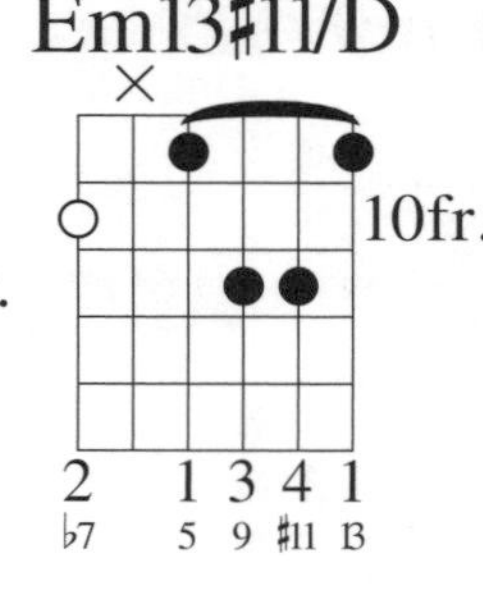

Em13/D

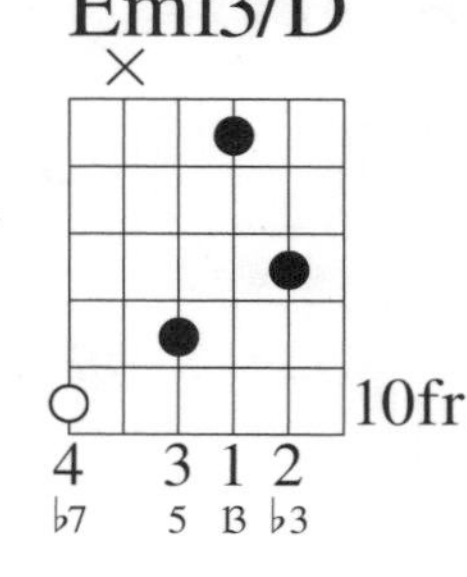

Em7♭13/D

Em7♭5♭13/D

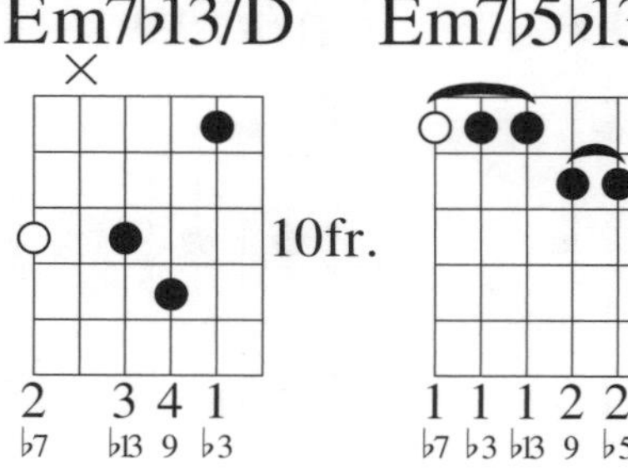

Em11/D

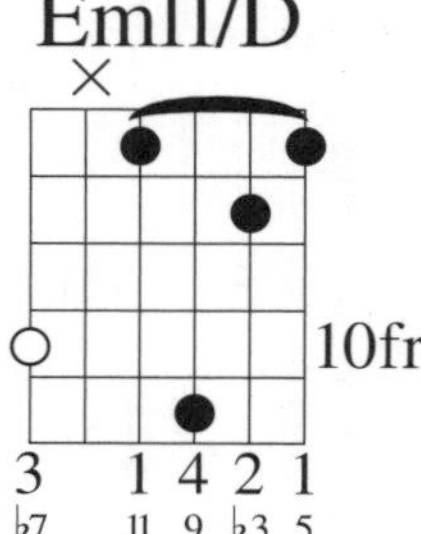

Em11♭5/D

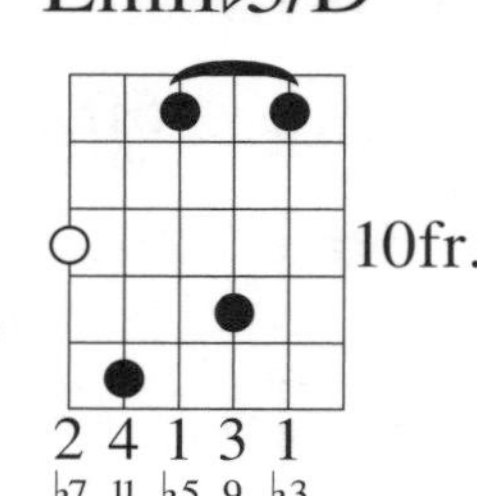

Em13♯11/D

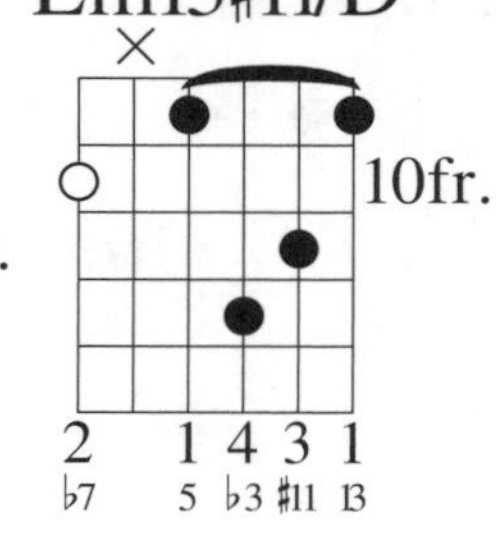

Em13/D

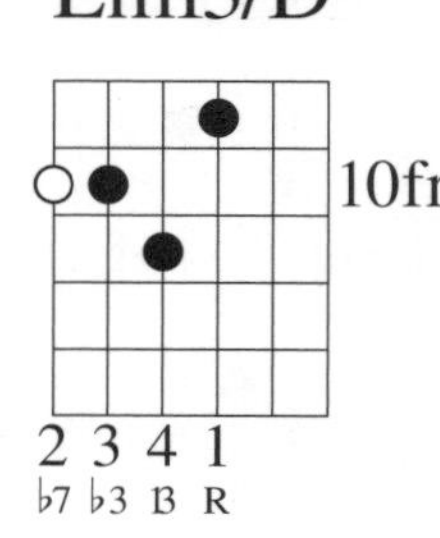

Em7♭13/D

Em7♭5♭13/D

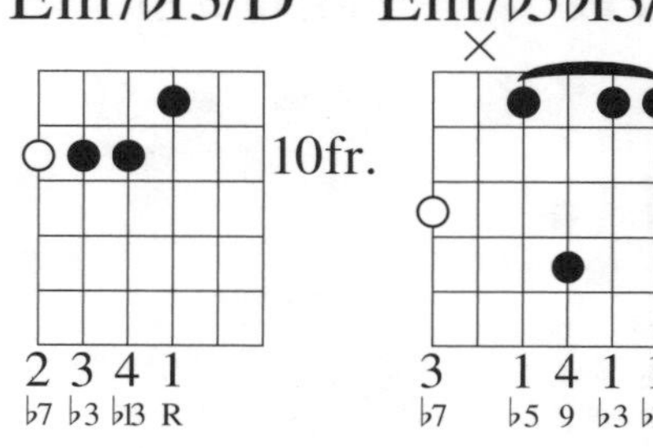

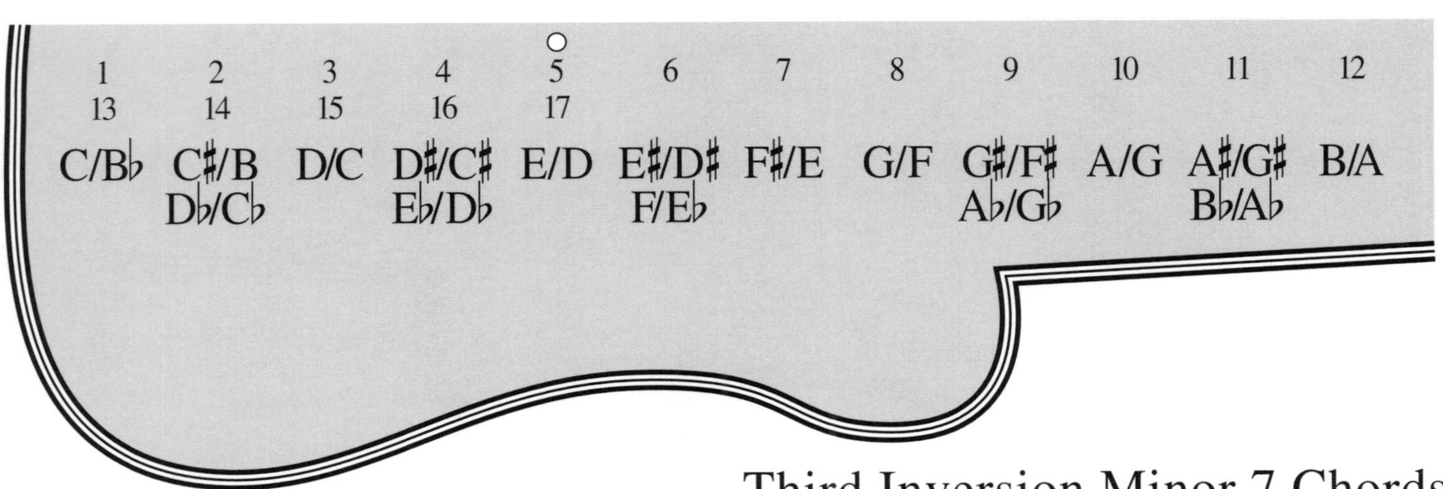

Third Inversion Minor 7 Chords

Em7/D
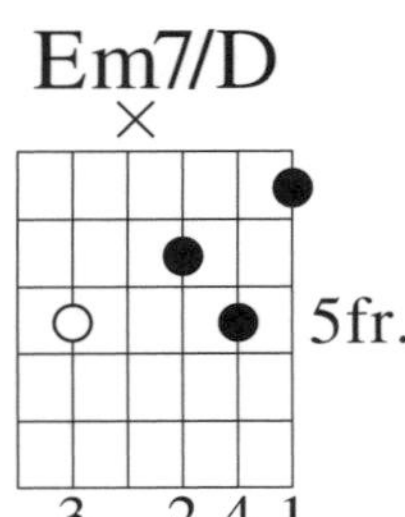

Em7/D
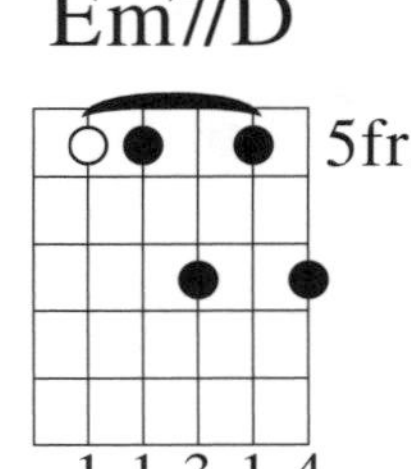

Em7♭5/D
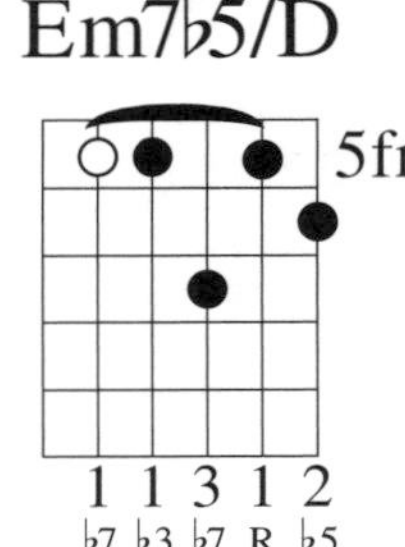

Em9/D
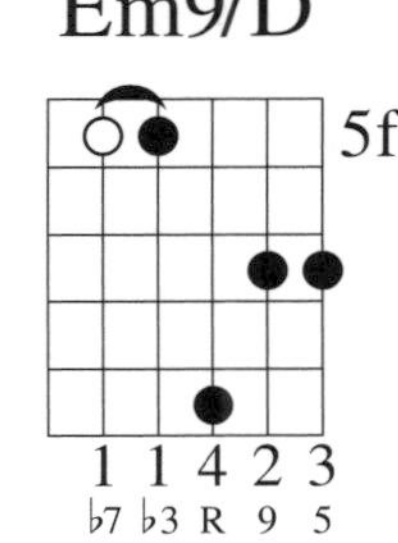

Em9♭5/D
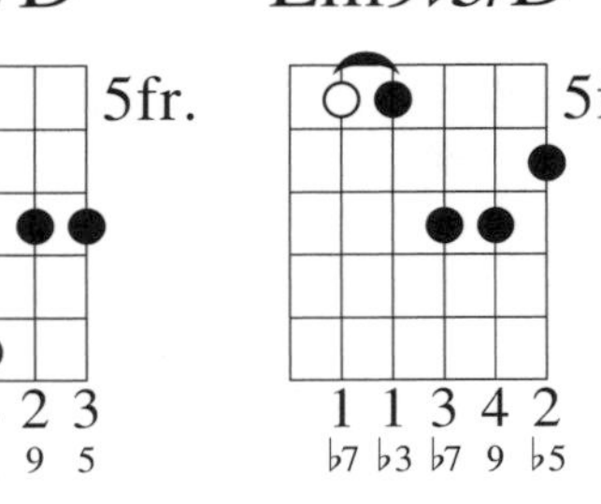

Em11/D
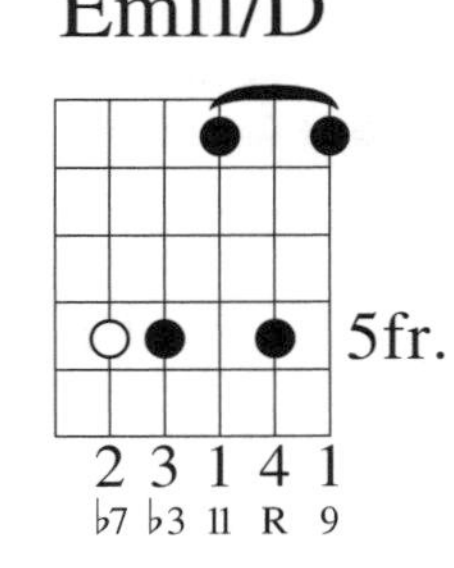

Em7/D
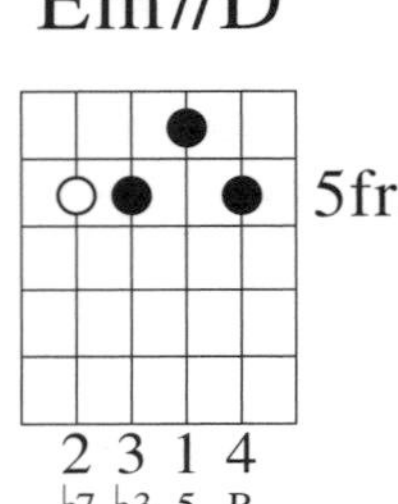

Em7♭5/D
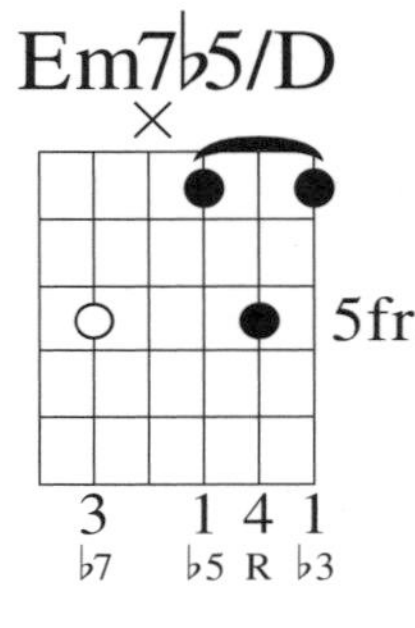

Em9/D
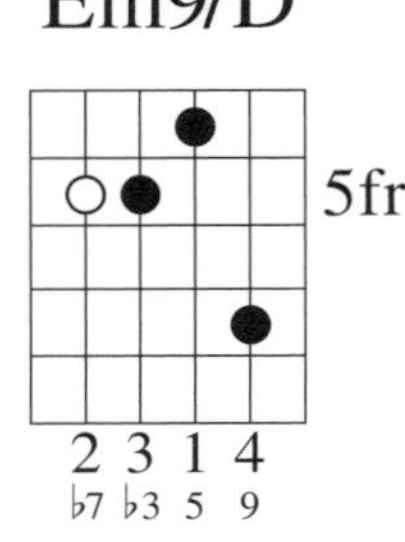

Em9♭5/D
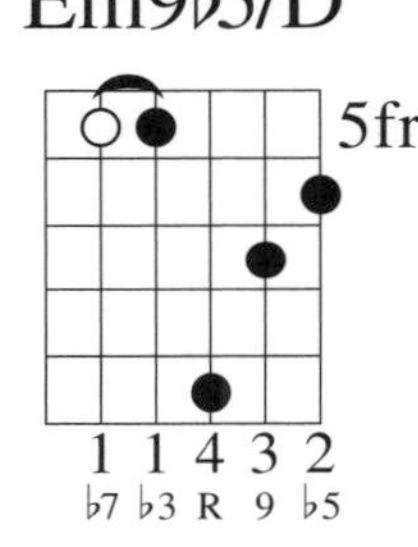

Em9♯11/D
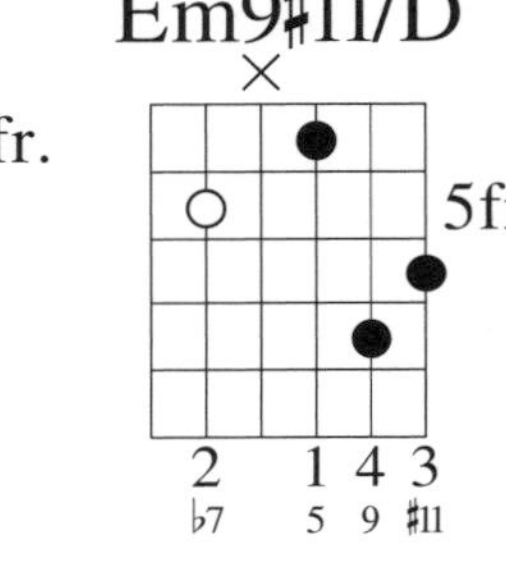

Em11/D
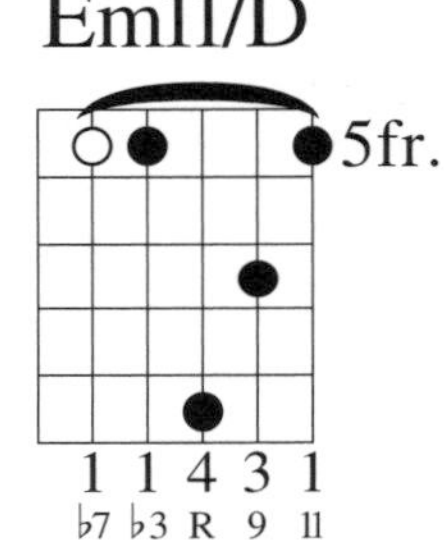

Em7/D
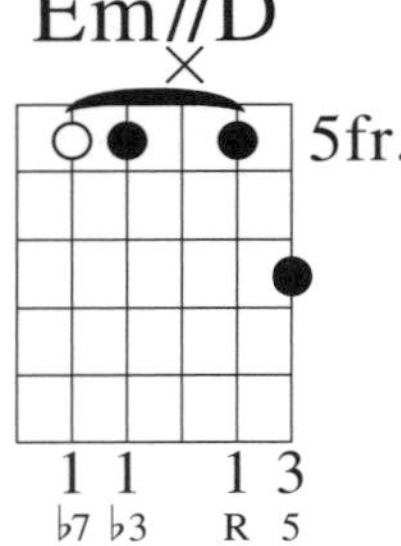

Em7♭5/D
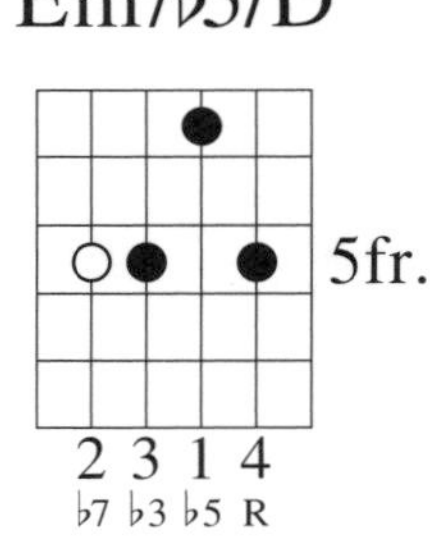

Em9/D
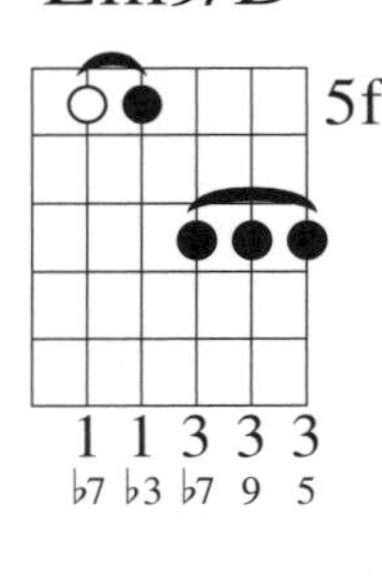

Em9♭5/D
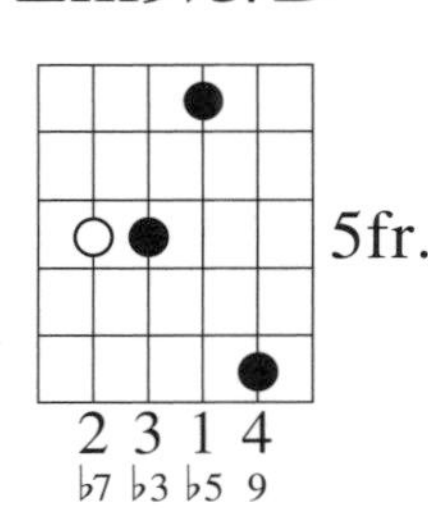

Em11/D
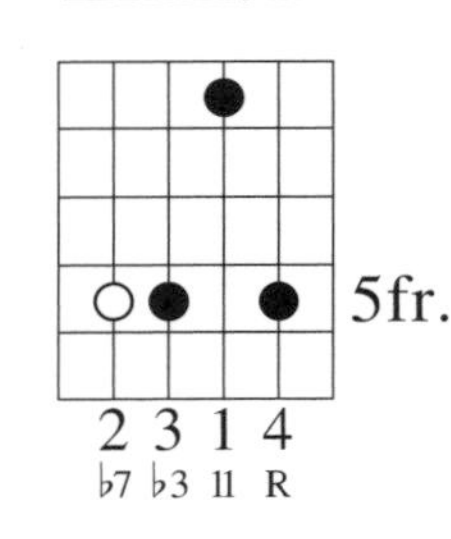

Em11/D
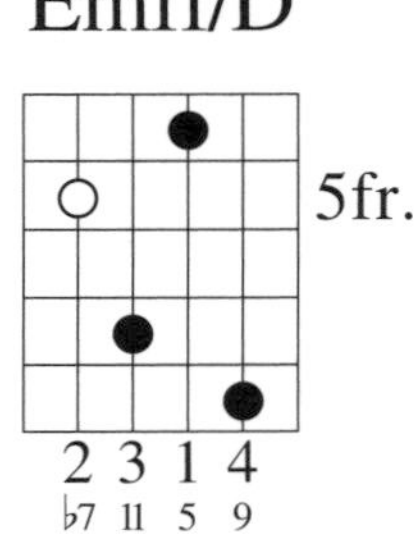

Em7/D
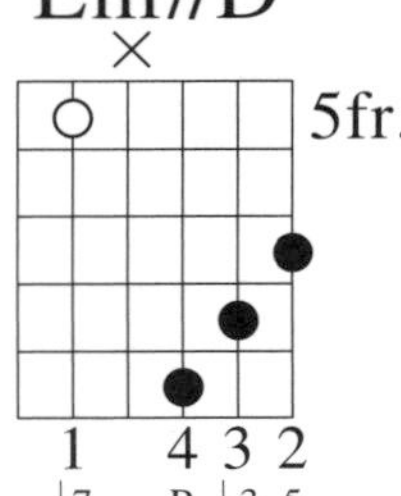

Em7♭5/D
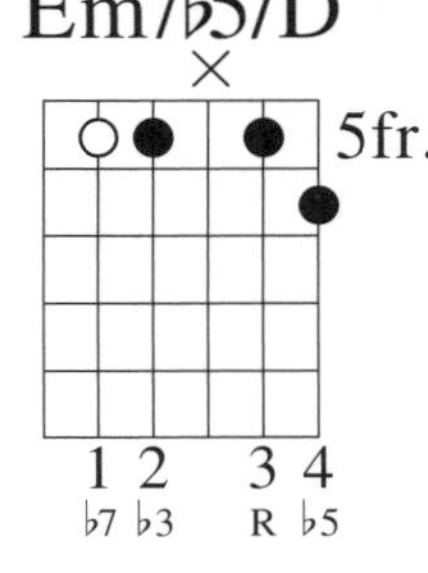

Em9/D
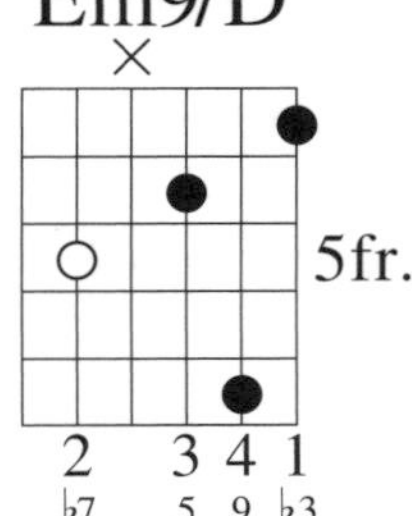

Em9♭5/D
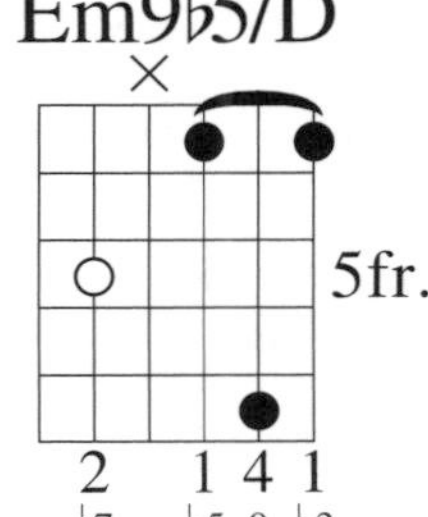

Em11/D
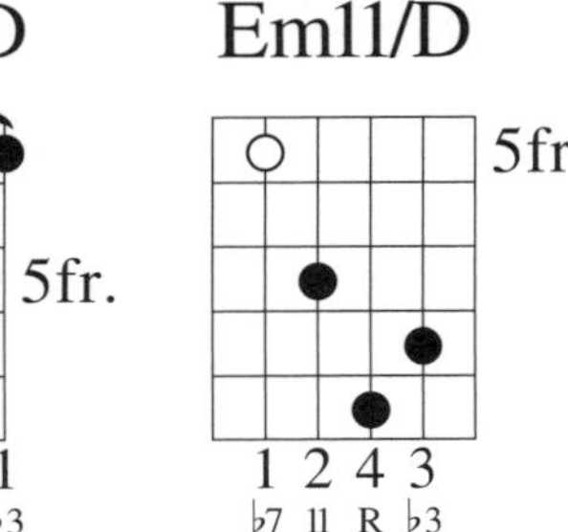

Em11/D
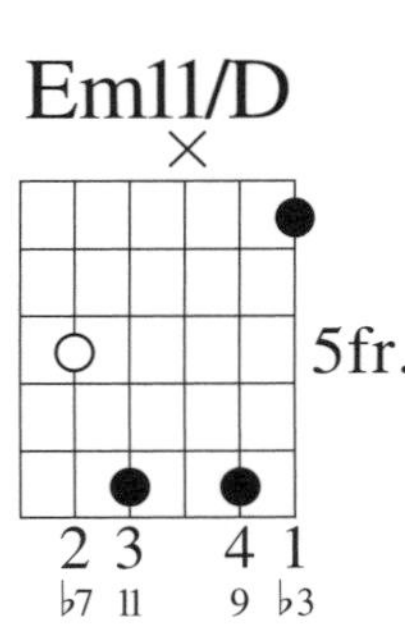

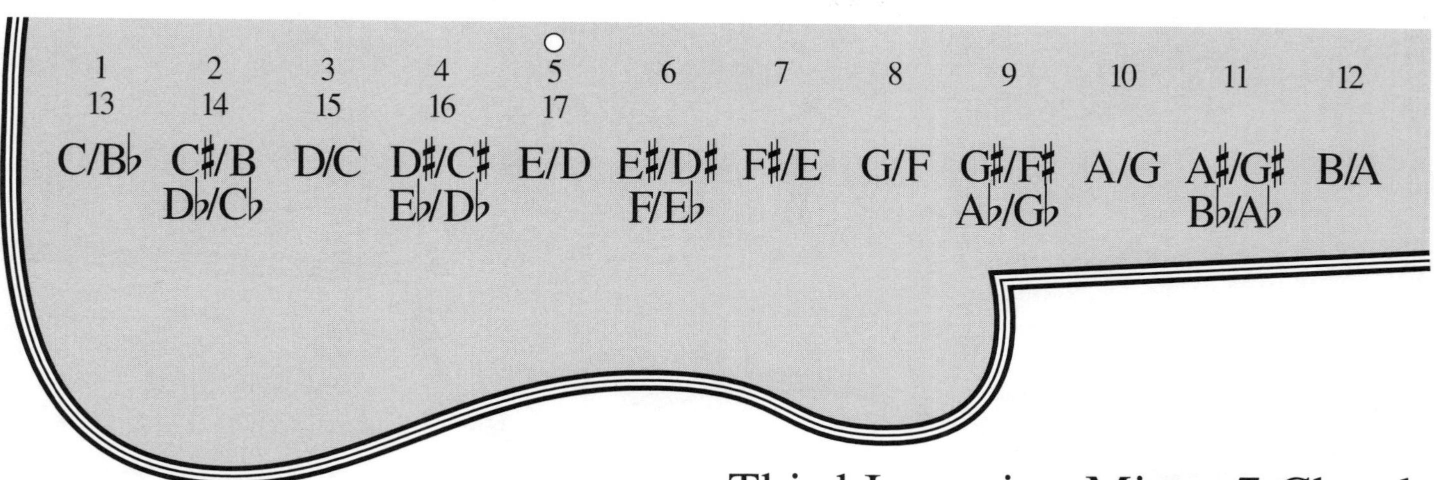

Third Inversion Minor 7 Chords

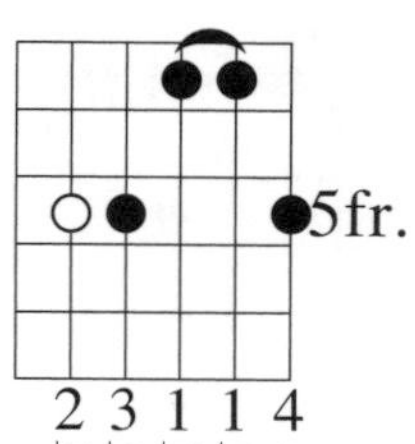

Em11♭5/D

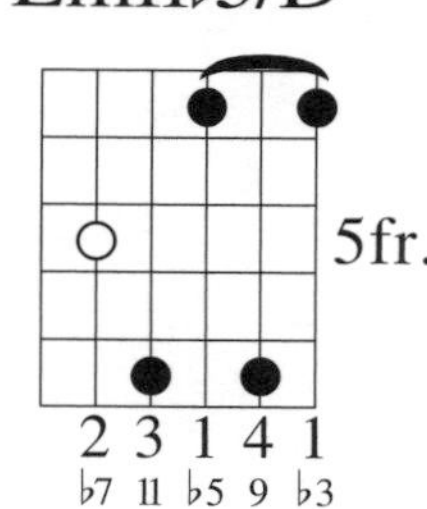

Em13/D

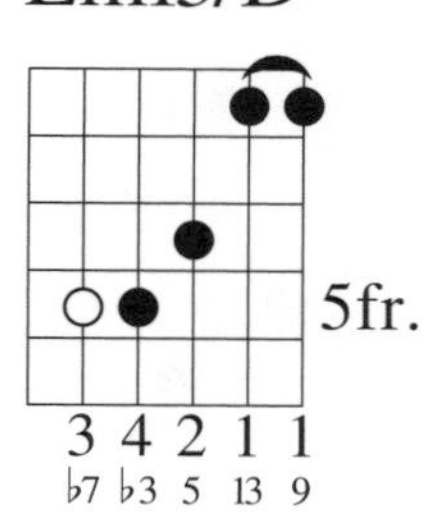

Em13/D

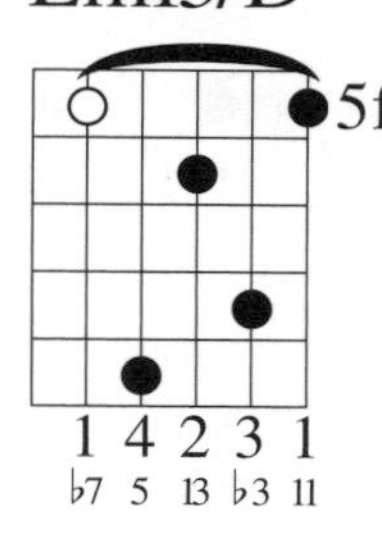

Em7♭13/D

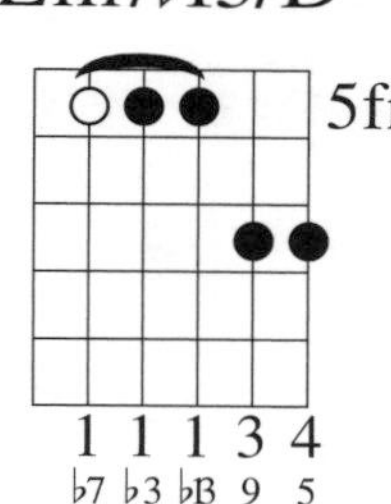

Em7♭13/D

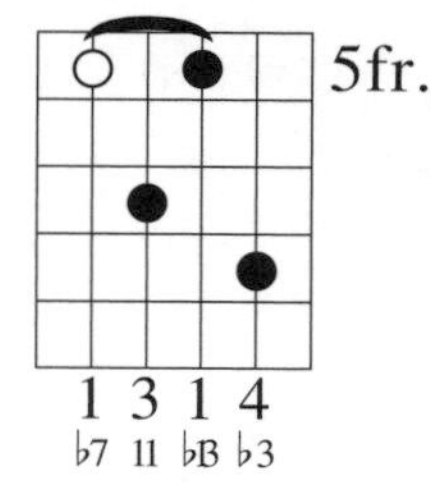

Em11♭5/D

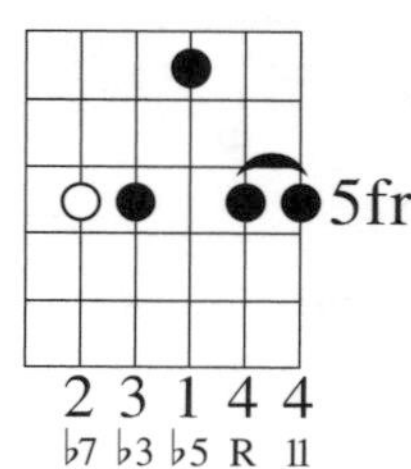

Em11♭5/D

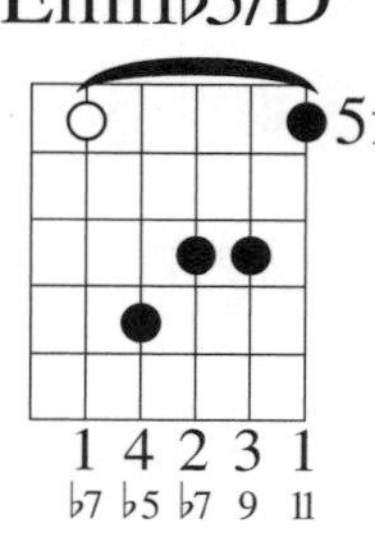

Em13/D

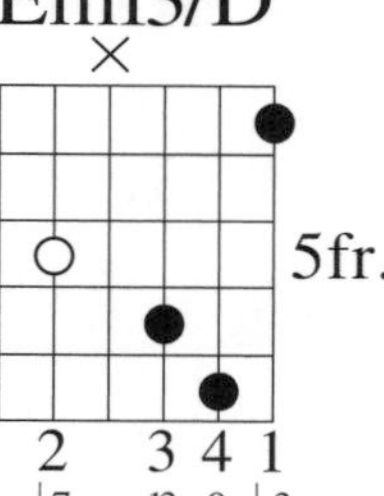

Em13/D

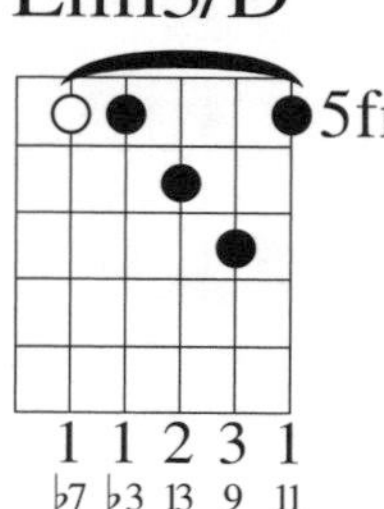

Em7♭13/D

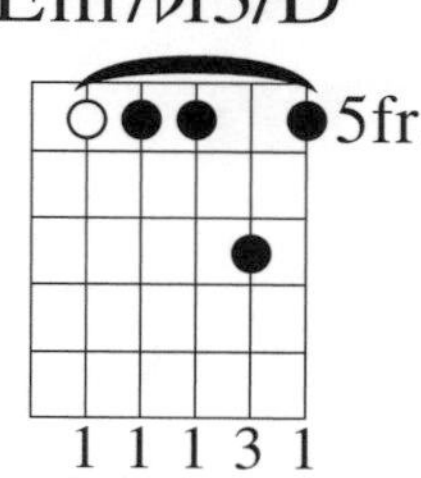

Em7♭5♭13/D

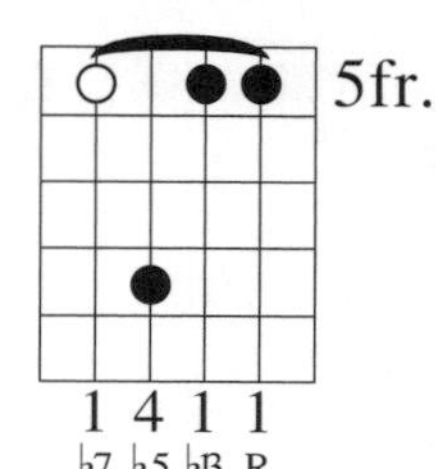

Em11♭5/D

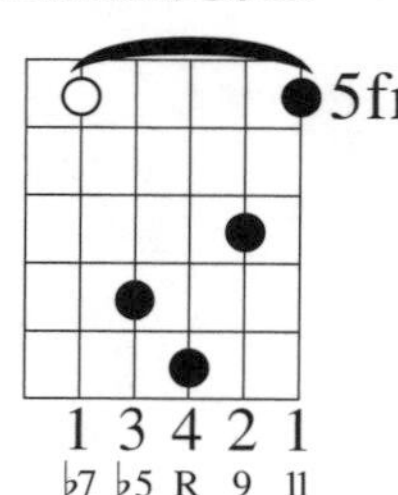

Em11♭5/D

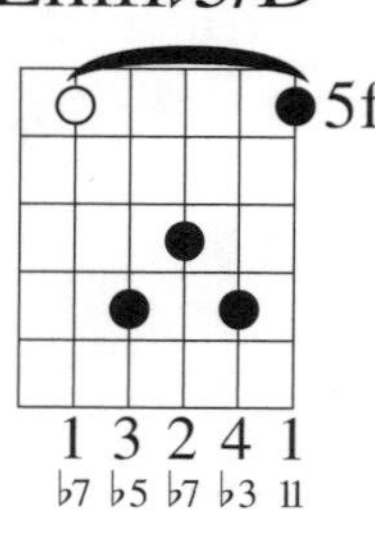

Em13/D

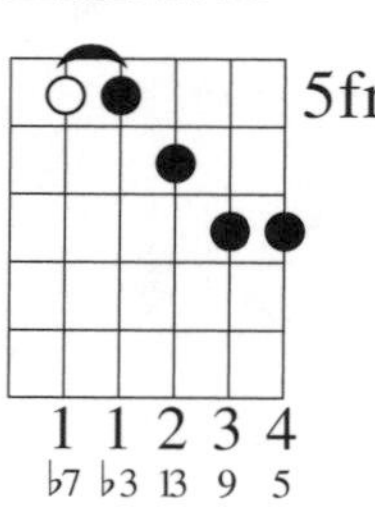

Em13/D

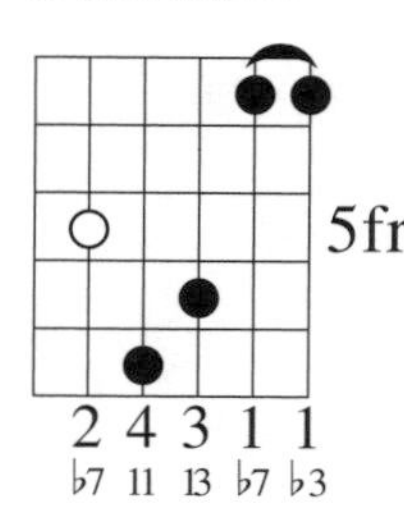

Em7♭13/D

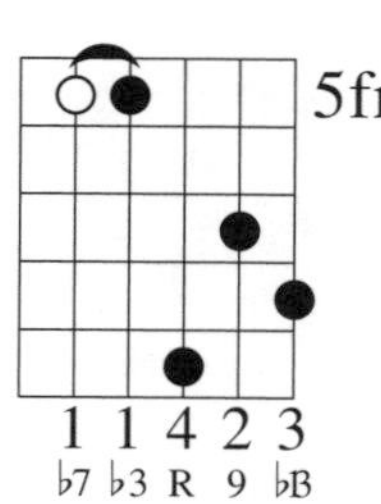

Em7♭5♭13/D

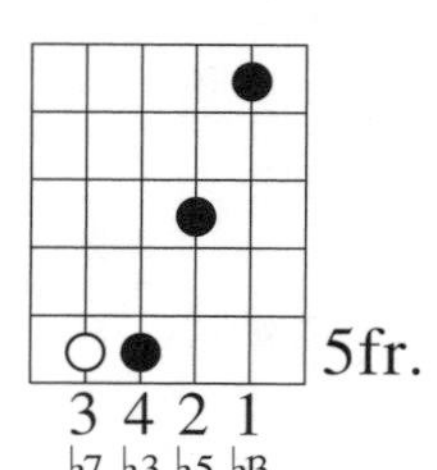

Em11♭5/D

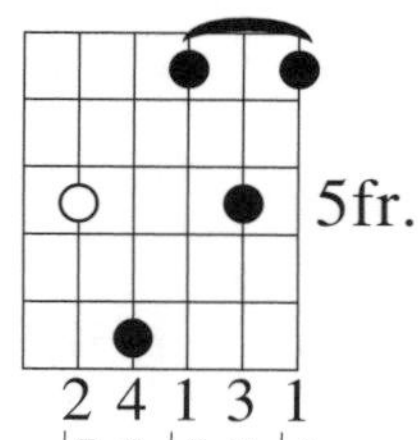

Em13♯11/D

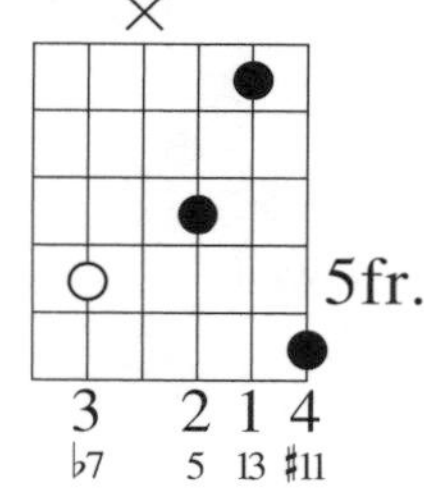

Em13/D

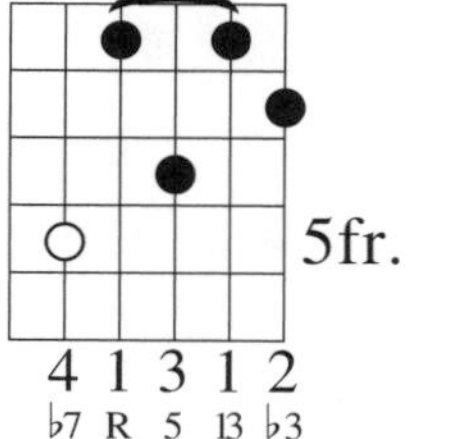

Em7♭13/D

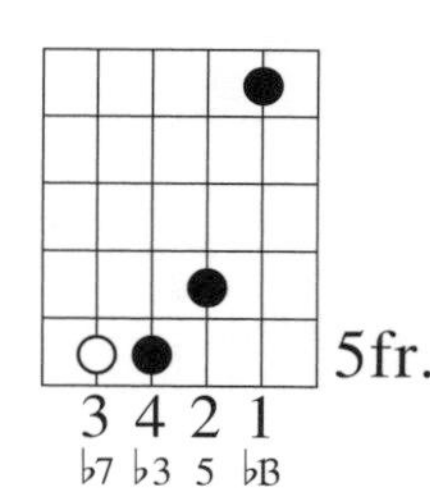

Em7♭13/D

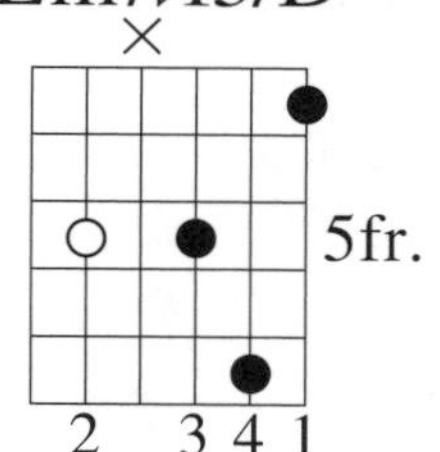

Em7♭5♭13/D

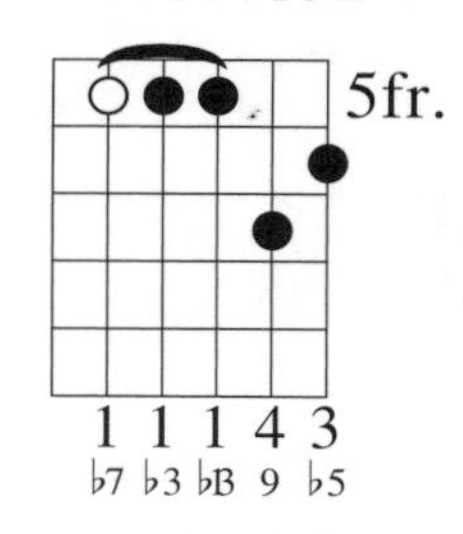

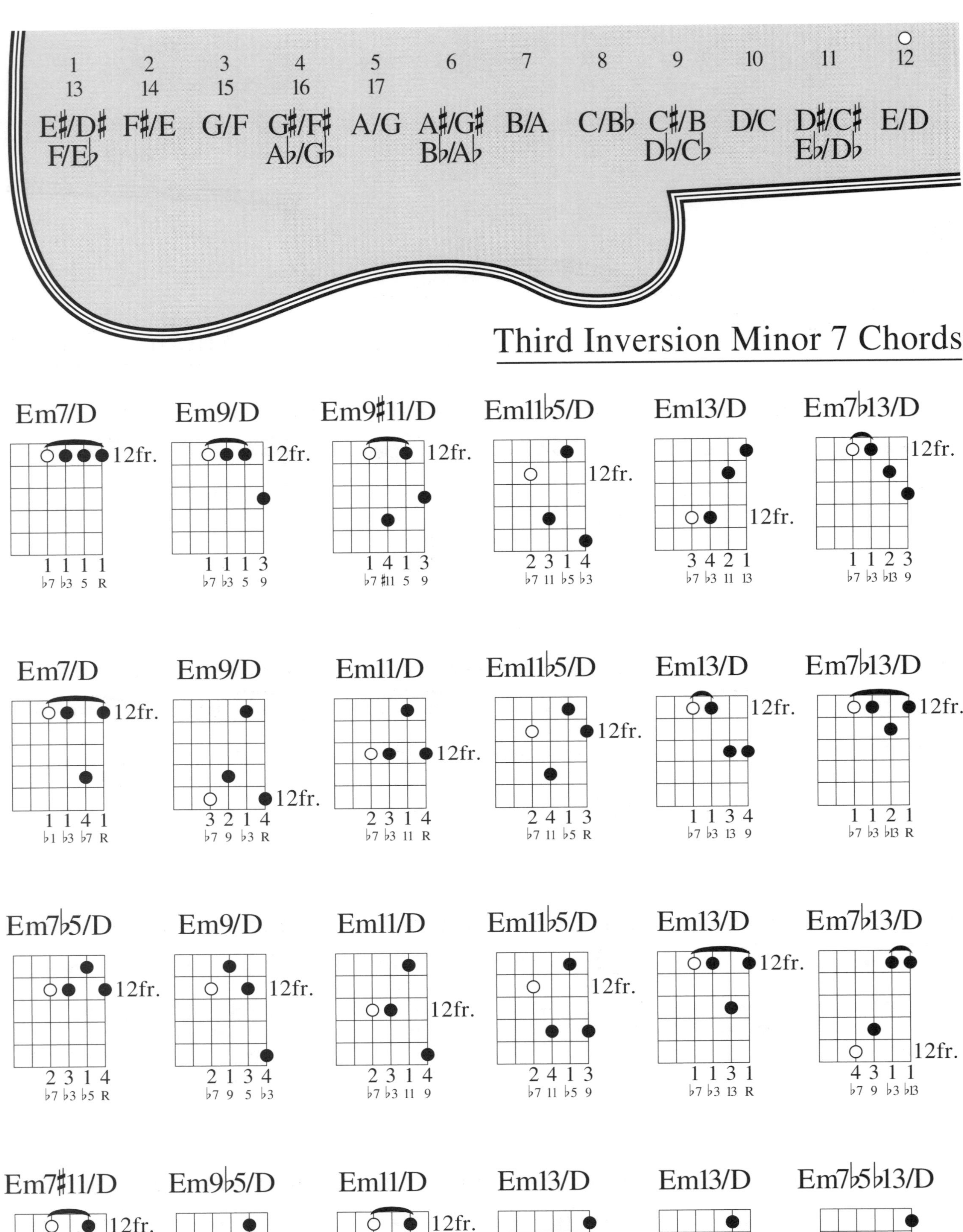

1 13 E♯/D♯ F/E♭
2 14 F♯/E
3 15 G/F
4 16 G♯/F♯ A♭/G♭
5 17 A/G
6 A♯/G♯ B♭/A♭
7 B/A
8 C/B♭
9 C♯/B D♭/C♭
10 D/C
11 D♯/C♯ E♭/D♭
12 E/D
Third Inversion Minor 7 Chords
Em7/D 12fr. 1 1 1 1 ♭7 ♭3 5 R
Em9/D 12fr. 1 1 1 3 ♭7 ♭3 5 9
Em9♯11/D 12fr. 1 4 1 3 ♭7 ♯11 5 9
Em11♭5/D 12fr. 2 3 1 4 ♭7 11 ♭5 ♭3
Em13/D 12fr. 3 4 2 1 ♭7 ♭3 11 13
Em7♭13/D 12fr. 1 1 2 3 ♭7 ♭3 ♭13 9
Em7/D 12fr. 1 1 4 1 ♭1 ♭3 ♭7 R
Em9/D 12fr. 3 2 1 4 ♭7 9 ♭3 R
Em11/D 12fr. 2 3 1 4 ♭7 ♭3 11 R
Em11♭5/D 12fr. 2 4 1 3 ♭7 11 ♭5 R
Em13/D 12fr. 1 1 3 4 ♭7 ♭3 13 9
Em7♭13/D 12fr. 1 1 2 1 ♭7 ♭3 ♭13 R
Em7♭5/D 12fr. 2 3 1 4 ♭7 ♭3 ♭5 R
Em9/D 12fr. 2 1 3 4 ♭7 9 5 ♭3
Em11/D 12fr. 2 3 1 4 ♭7 ♭3 11 9
Em11♭5/D 12fr. 2 4 1 3 ♭7 11 ♭5 9
Em13/D 12fr. 1 1 3 1 ♭7 ♭3 13 R
Em7♭13/D 12fr. 4 3 1 1 ♭7 9 ♭3 ♭13
Em7♯11/D 12fr. 1 3 1 4 ♭7 ♯11 5 ♭3
Em9♭5/D 12fr. 2 3 1 4 ♭7 ♭3 ♭5 9
Em11/D 12fr. 1 3 1 4 ♭7 11 5 ♭3
Em13/D 12fr. 2 3 4 1 ♭7 ♭3 5 13
Em13/D 12fr. 4 3 1 2 ♭7 9 ♭3 13
Em7♭5♭13/D 12fr. 3 4 2 1 ♭7 ♭3 ♭5 ♭13

1 13	2 14	3 15	4 16	5 17	6	7	8	9	○ 10	11	12
G♭/F	G/F♯	A♭/G	A/G♯	B♭/A	B/A♯	C/B	D♭/C	D/C♯	E♭/D	E/D♯	F/E

Third Inversion Minor/Major 7 Chords

E♭m(maj7)/D 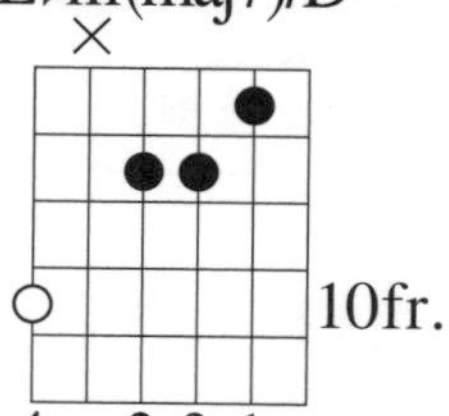
10fr.
4 2 3 1
7 5 R ♭3

E♭m(maj7)/D 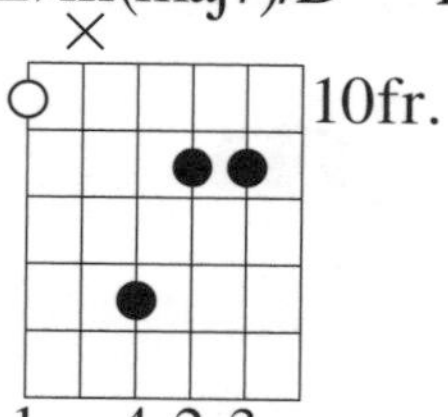
10fr.
1 4 2 3
7 R ♭3 5

E♭m(maj7)♭5/D 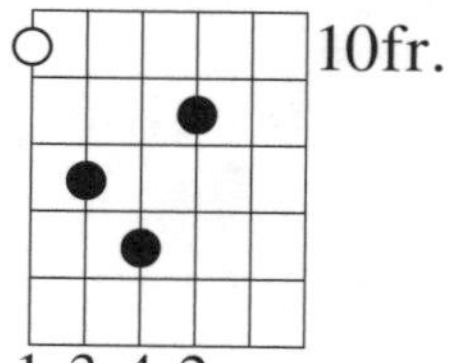
10fr.
1 3 4 2
7 ♭5 R ♭3

E♭m(maj7)♯11/D 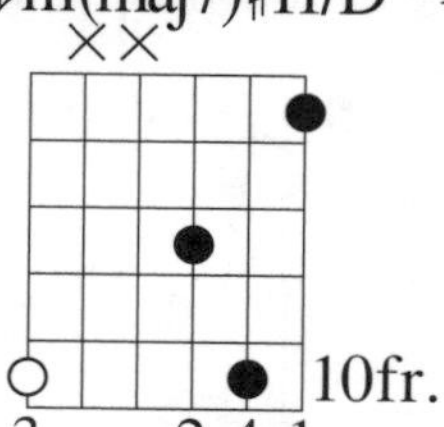
10fr.
3 2 4 1
7 R ♯11 5

E♭m(maj9)♭5/D 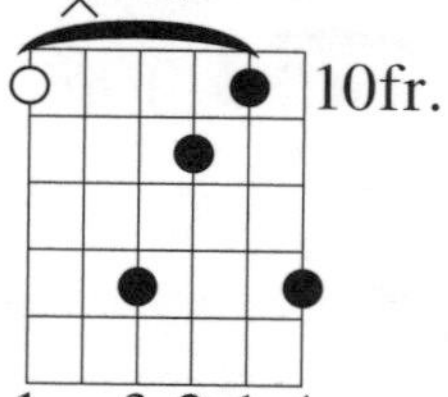
10fr.
1 3 2 1 4
7 R ♭3 ♭5 9

E♭m(maj9)♯11/D 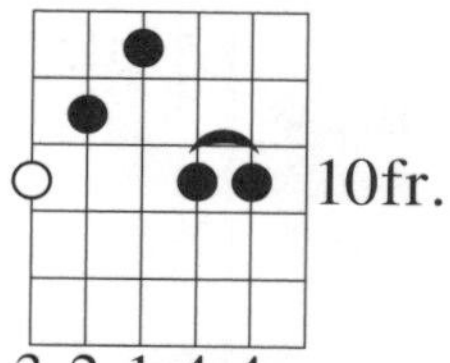
10fr.
3 2 1 4 4
7 ♭3 5 9 ♯11

E♭m(maj7)/D 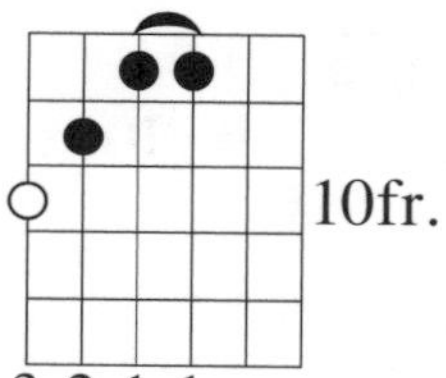
10fr.
3 2 1 1
7 ♭3 5 R

E♭m(maj7)♭5/D 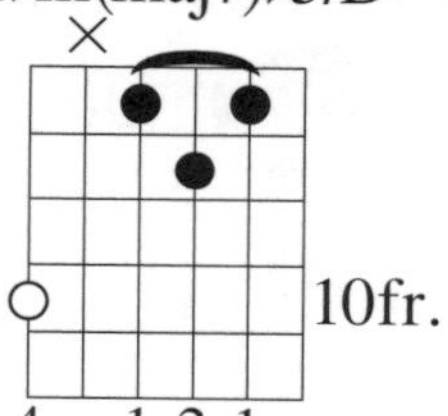
10fr.
4 1 2 1
7 ♭5 R ♭3

E♭m(maj7)♭5/D 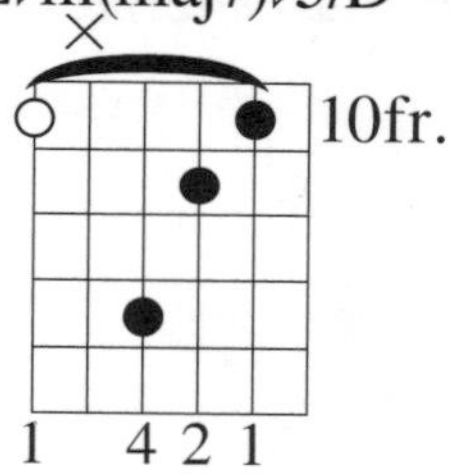
10fr.
1 4 2 1
7 R ♭3 ♭5

E♭m(maj9)/D 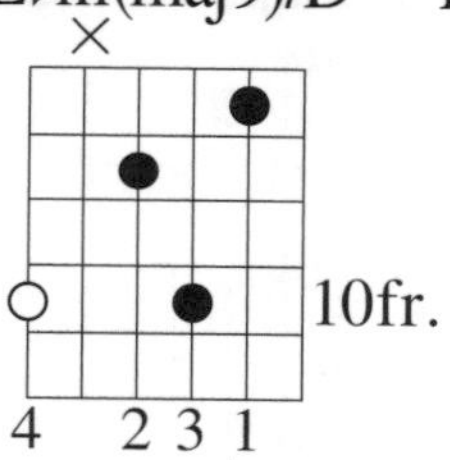
10fr.
4 2 3 1
7 5 9 ♭3

E♭m(maj9)♭5/D 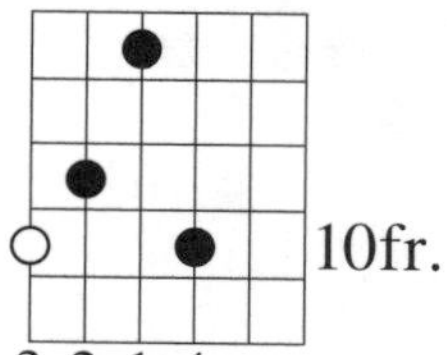
10fr.
3 2 1 4
7 ♭3 ♭5 9

E♭m(maj9)♯11/D 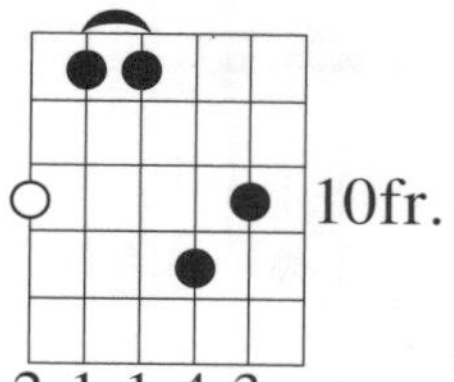
10fr.
2 1 1 4 3
7 9 5 ♭3 ♯11

E♭m(maj7)/D 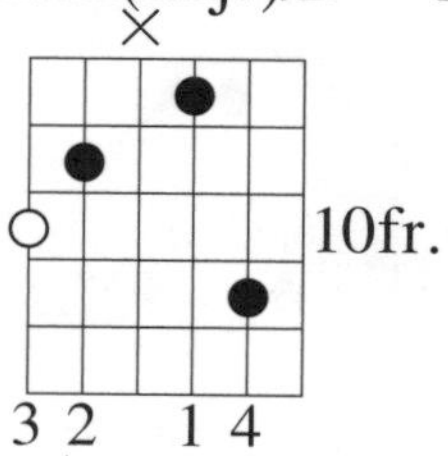
10fr.
3 2 1 4
7 ♭3 R 5

E♭m(maj7)♭5/D 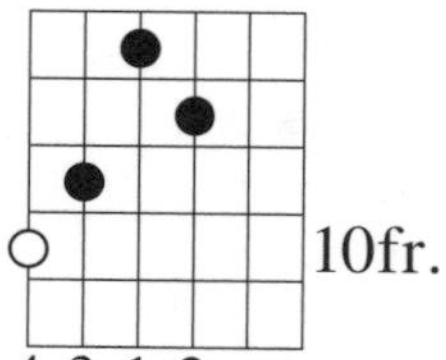
10fr.
4 3 1 2
7 ♭3 ♭5 R

E♭m(maj7)♯11/D 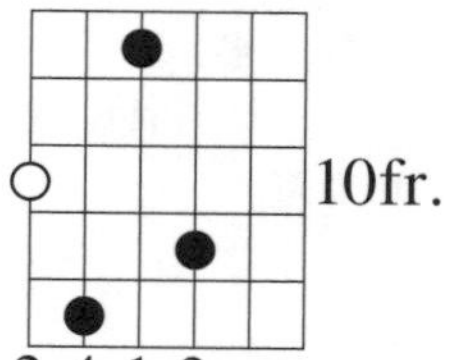
10fr.
2 4 1 3
7 ♯11 5 ♭3

E♭m(maj9)/D 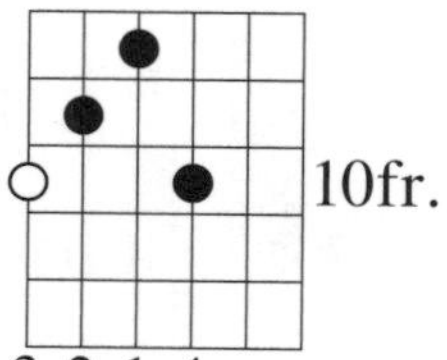
10fr.
3 2 1 4
7 ♭3 R 9

E♭m(maj9)♭5/D 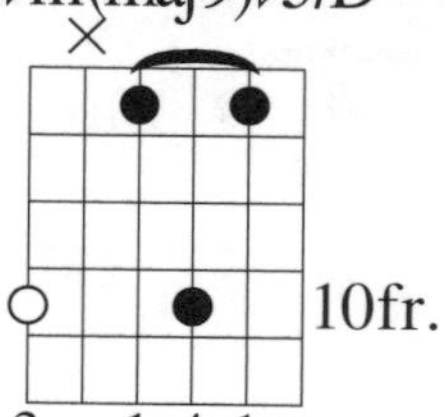
10fr.
3 1 4 1
7 ♭5 9 ♭3

E♭m(maj11)/D 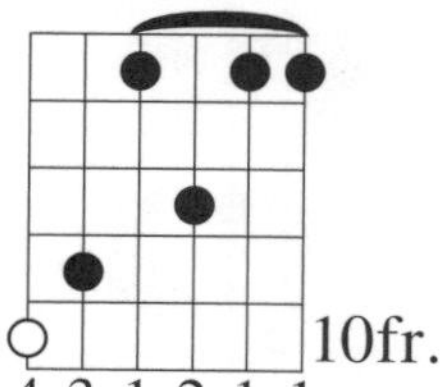
10fr.
4 3 1 2 1 1
7 ♭3 11 R 9 5

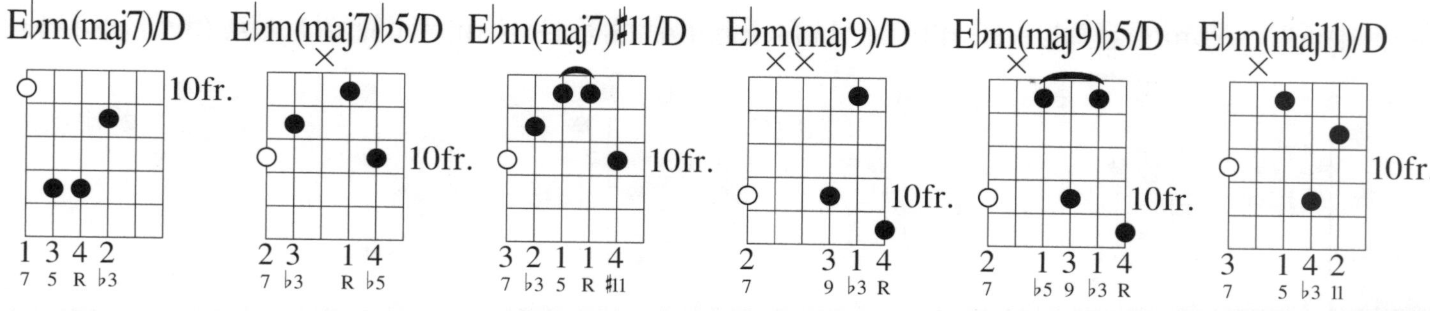

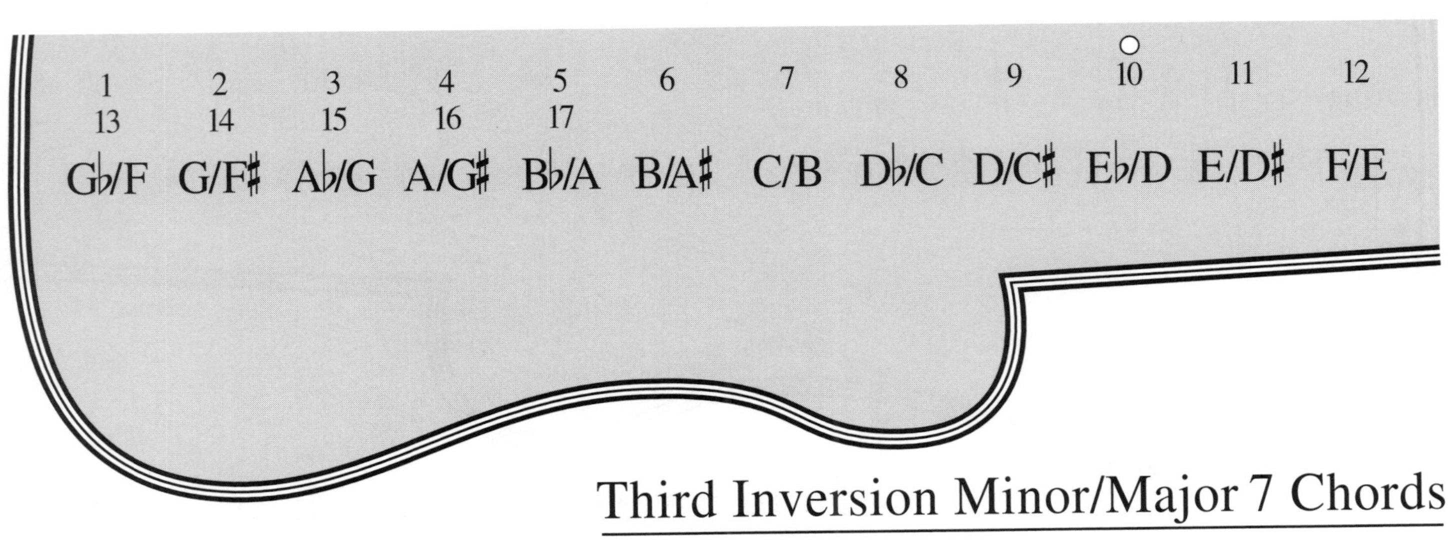

Third Inversion Minor/Major 7 Chords

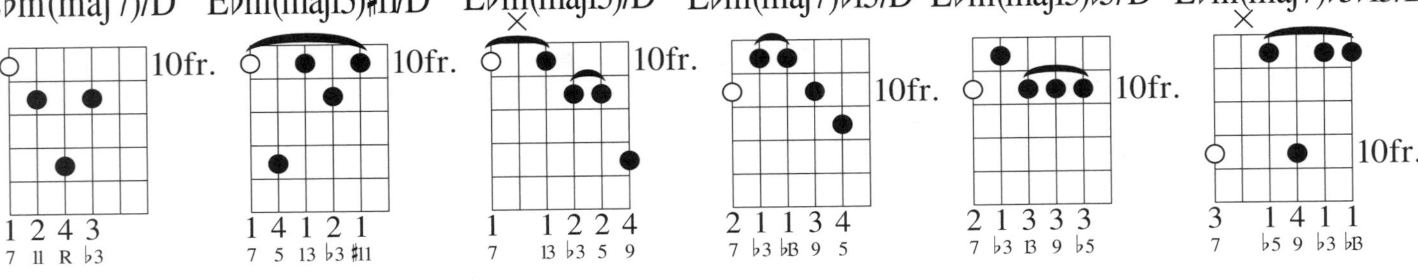

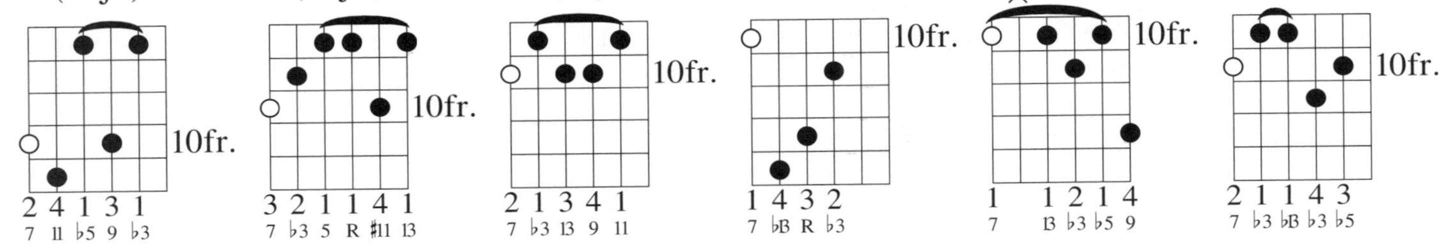

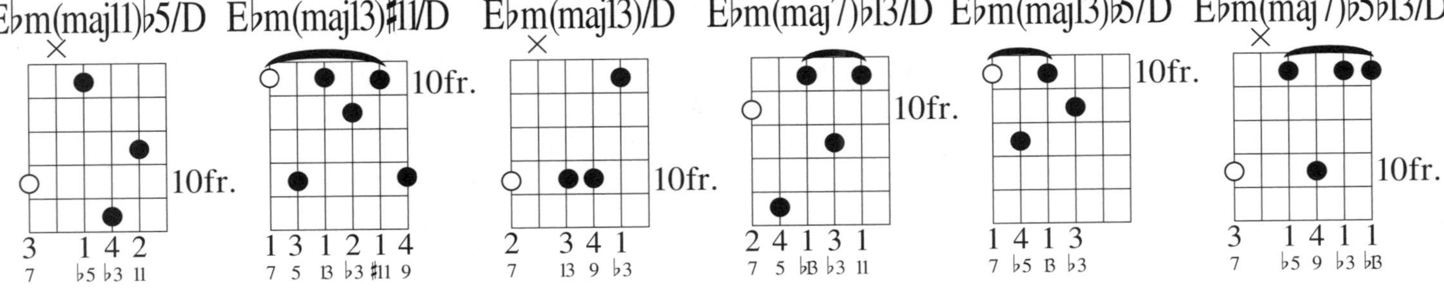

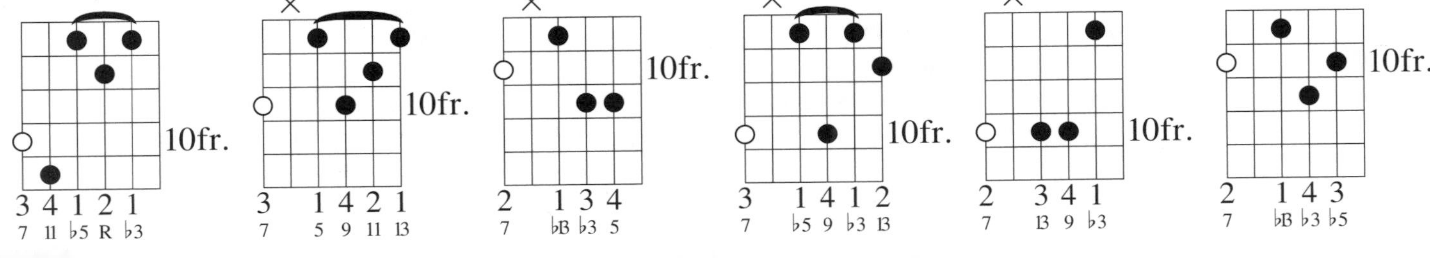

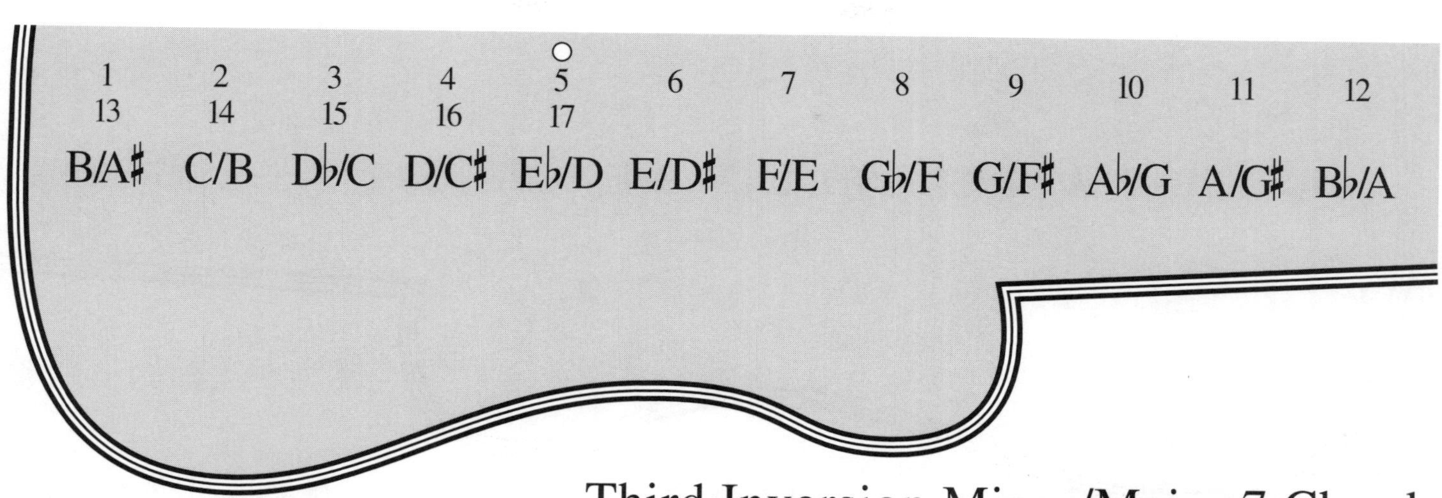

Third Inversion Minor/Major 7 Chords

Chord	Fingering	Intervals
E♭m(maj7)/D	4 2 3 1	7 5 R ♭3
E♭m(maj7)/D	2 1 4 1 3	7 ♭3 7 R 5
E♭m(maj7)♭5/D	1 2 4 3	7 ♭5 R ♭3
E♭m(maj9)/D	3 2 4 1	7 5 9 ♭3
E♭m(maj9)♭5/D	3 2 1 4 1	7 ♭3 ♭5 9 ♭3
E♭m(maj11)/D	4 2 1 3 1	7 ♭3 11 R 9

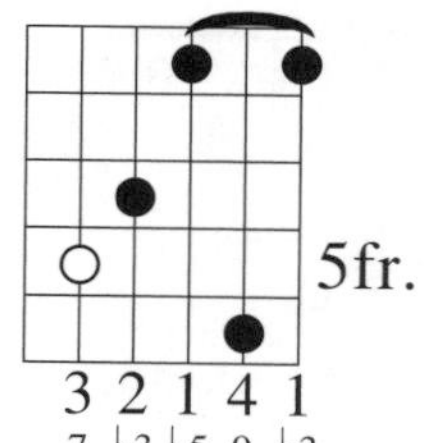
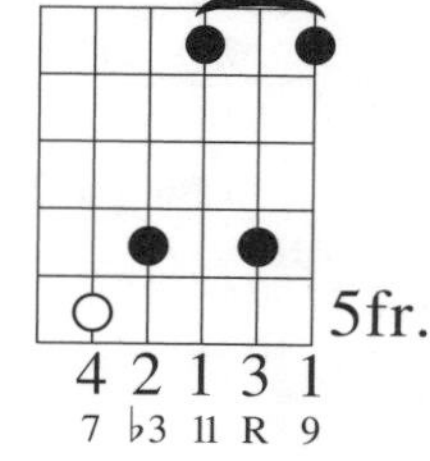

Chord	Fingering	Intervals
E♭m(maj7)/D	4 2 1 3	7 ♭3 5 R
E♭m(maj7)♭5/D	4 1 3 1	7 ♭5 R ♭3
E♭m(maj7)♭5/D	2 1 4 1 3	7 ♭3 7 R ♭5
E♭m(maj9)/D	3 2 1 4	7 ♭3 5 9
E♭m(maj9)♭5/D	4 2 1 3 1	7 9 ♭5 R ♭3
E♭m(maj11)/D	1 2 4 3 2	7 11 R ♭3 5

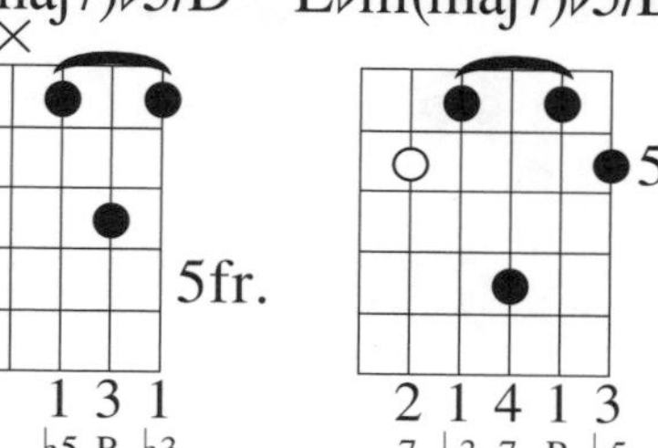
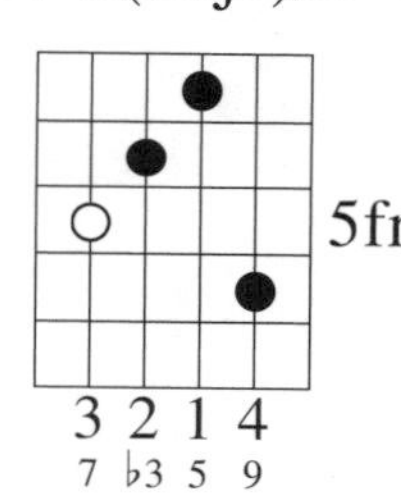
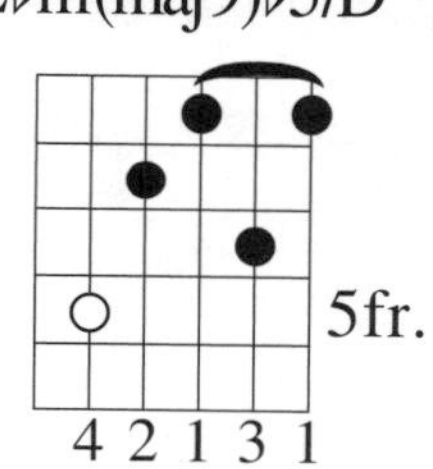
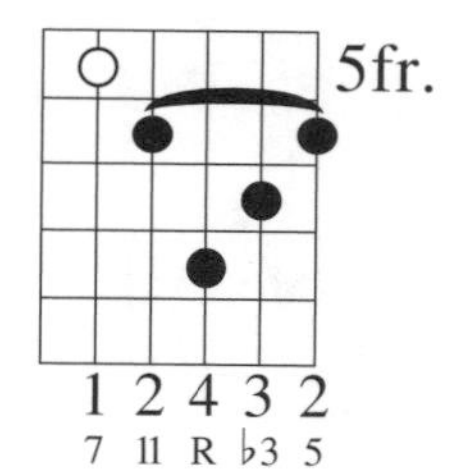

Chord	Fingering	Intervals
E♭m(maj7)/D	2 1 3 4	7 ♭3 R 5
E♭m(maj7)♭5/D	4 2 1 3	7 ♭3 ♭5 R
E♭m(maj7)♯11/D	1 3 4 2 1	7 5 R ♭3 ♯11
E♭m(maj9)♭5/D	3 2 1 4	7 ♭3 ♭5 9
E♭m(maj9)♯11/D	3 2 1 4 4	7 ♭3 ♯11 9 5
E♭m(maj11)♭5/D	2 3 1 4 1	7 11 ♭5 9 ♭3

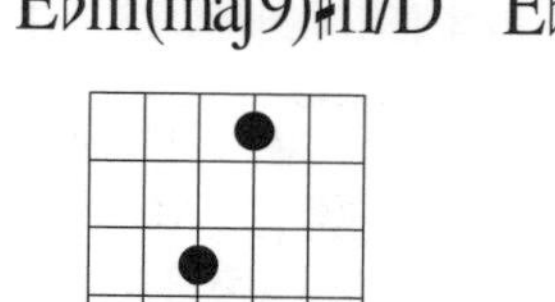
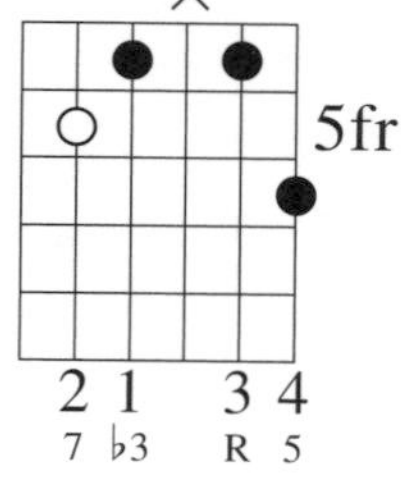
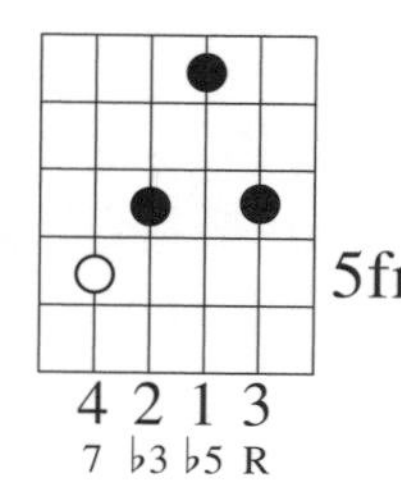
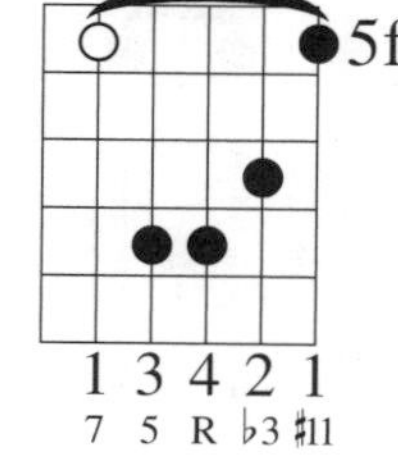
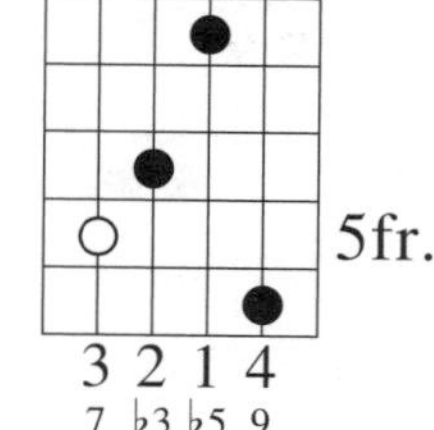
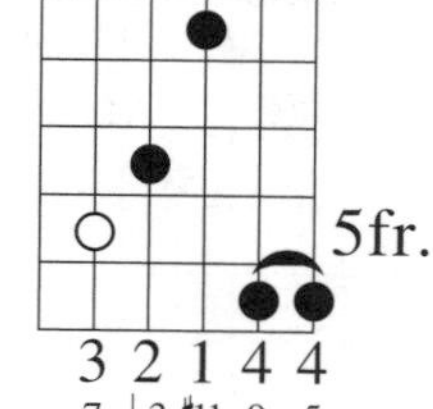
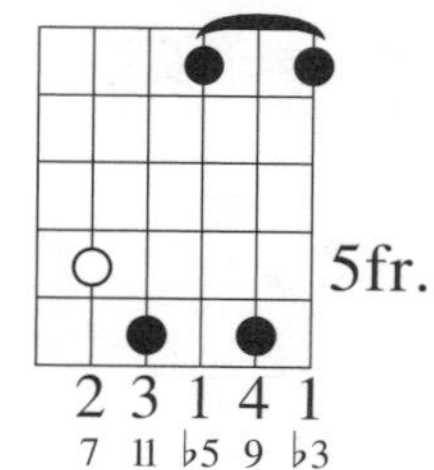

Chord	Fingering	Intervals
E♭m(maj7)/D	1 3 4 2	7 5 R ♭3
E♭m(maj7)♭5/D	2 1 3 4	7 ♭3 R ♭5
E♭m(maj7)♯11/D	2 1 4 3	7 5 ♭3 ♯11
E♭m(maj9)♭5/D	3 1 4 1	7 ♭5 9 ♭3
E♭m(maj11)/D	1 2 4 3	7 11 R ♭3
E♭m(maj11)♭5/D	2 4 3 1	7 ♭5 ♭3 11

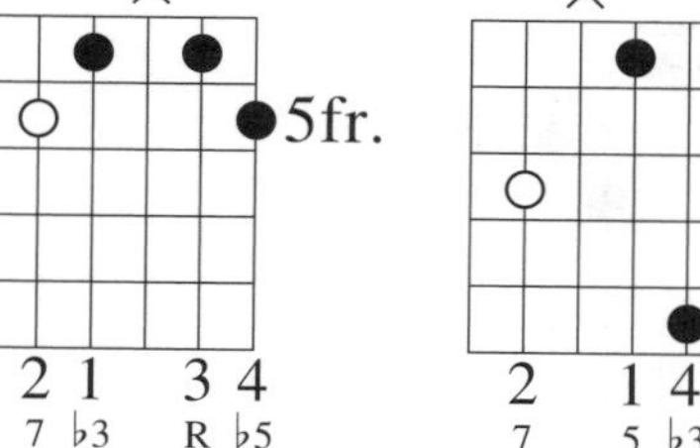
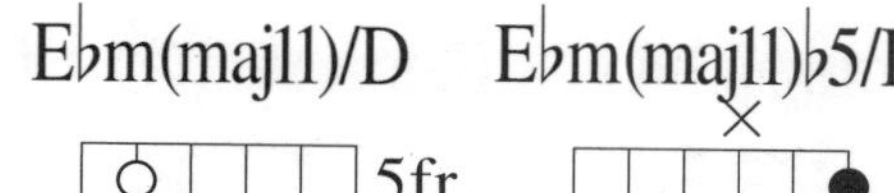
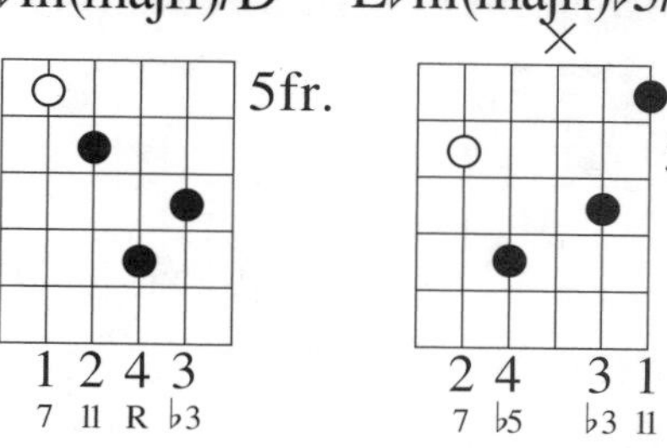

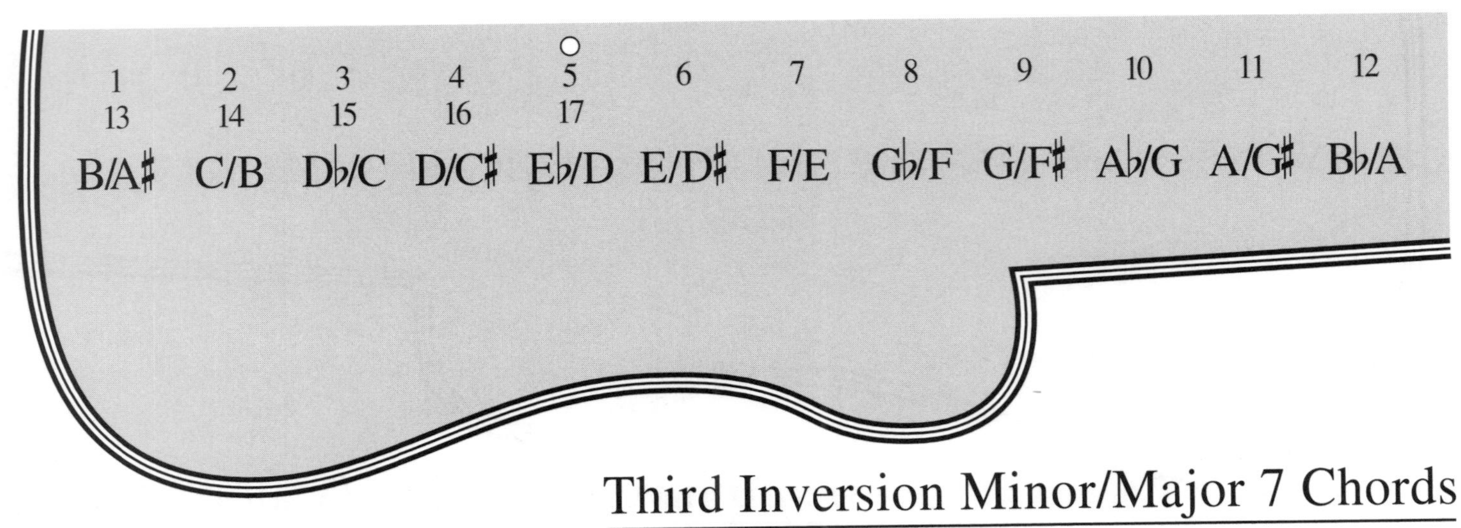

Third Inversion Minor/Major 7 Chords

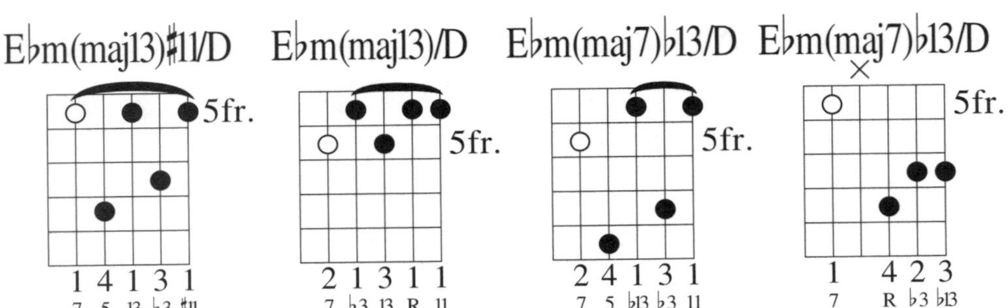

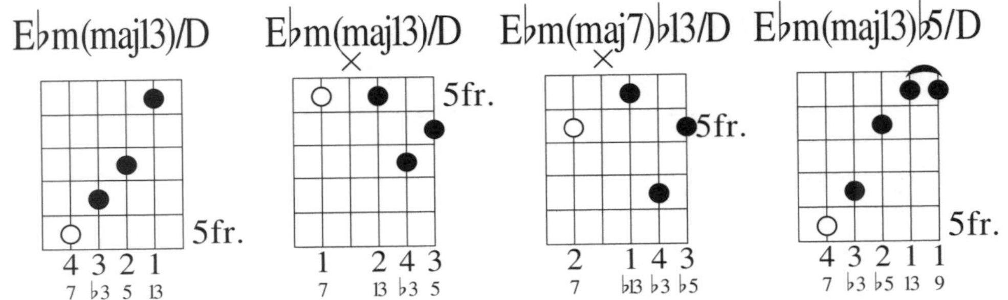

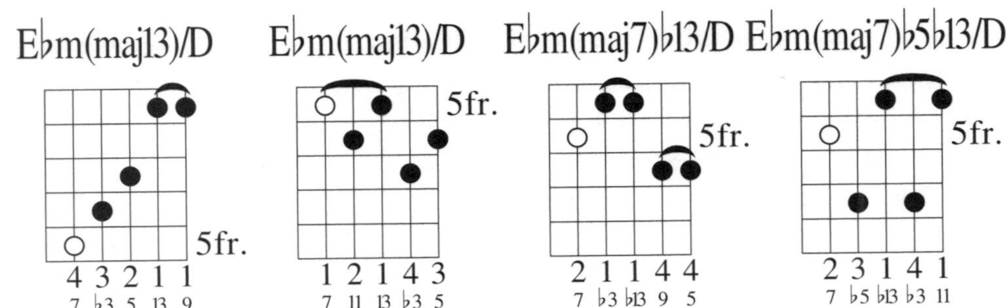

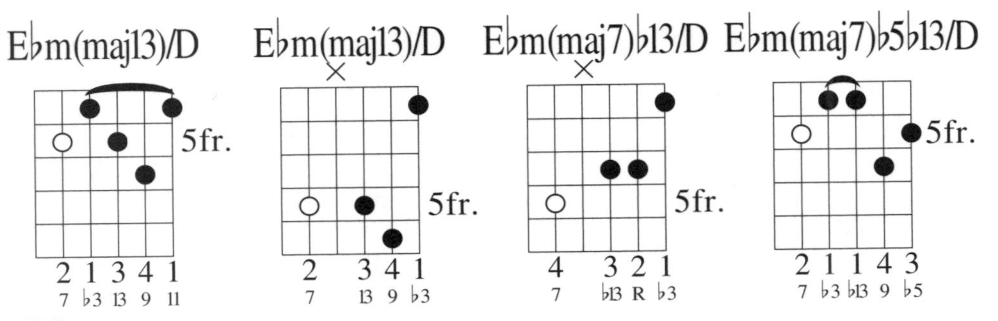

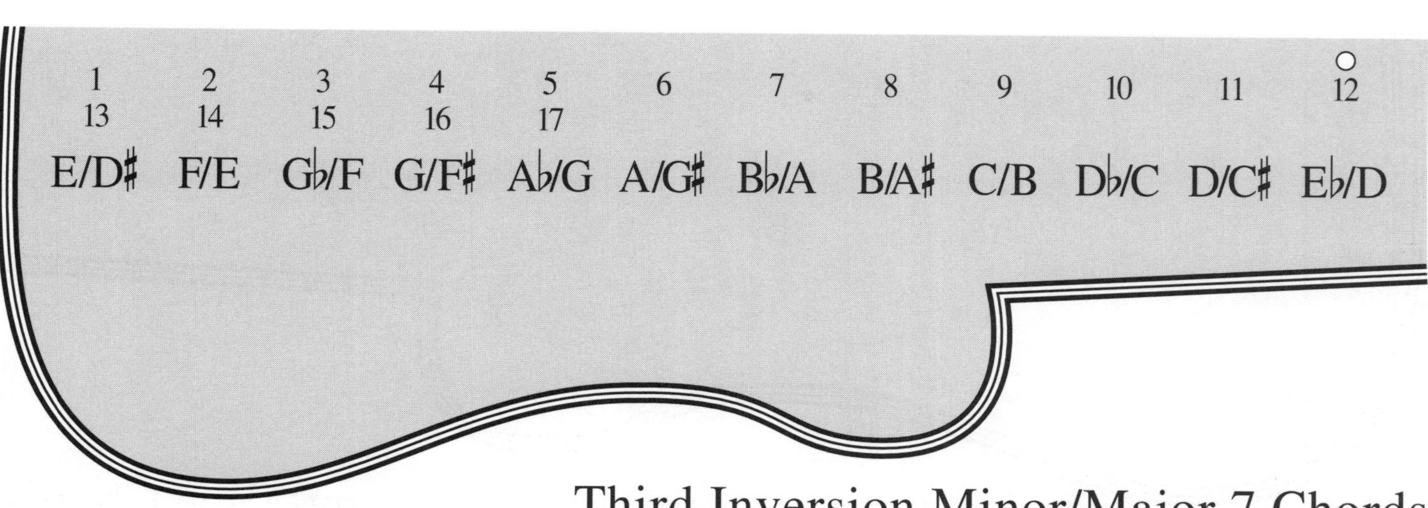

Third Inversion Minor/Major 7 Chords

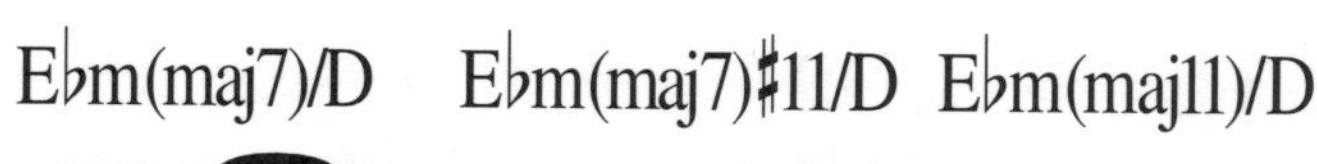

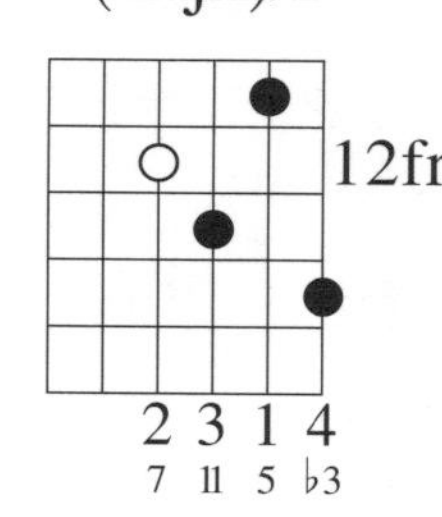
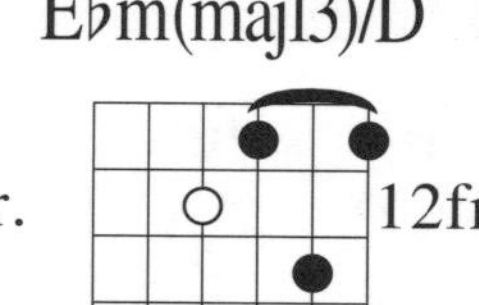
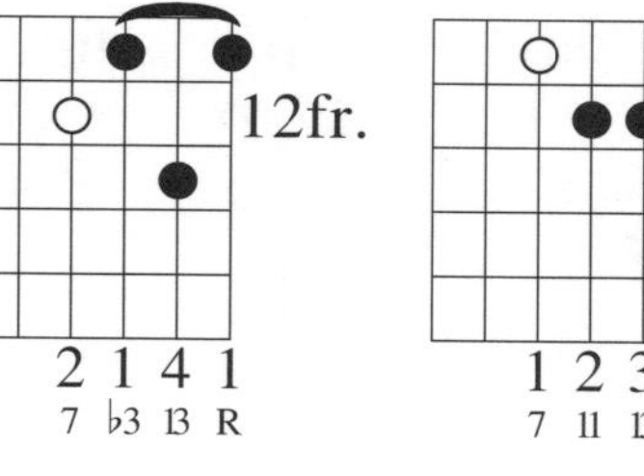
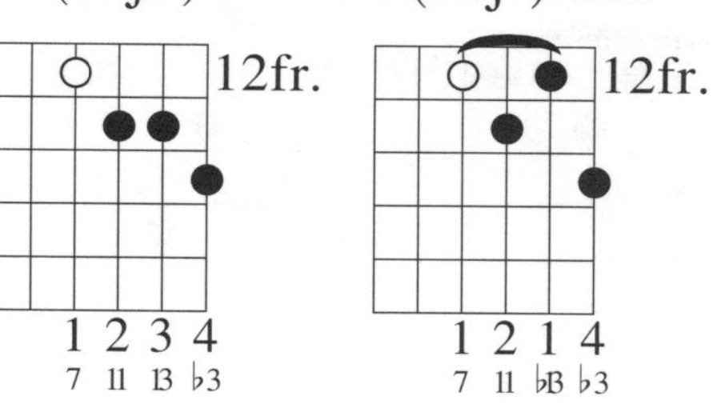

Chord	Fingering	Intervals	Fret
E♭m(maj7)/D	2 1 1 1	7 ♭3 5 R	12fr.
E♭m(maj7)♯11/D	2 4 1 3	7 ♯11 5 ♭3	12fr.
E♭m(maj11)/D	2 3 1 4	7 11 5 ♭3	12fr.
E♭m(maj13)/D	2 1 4 1	7 ♭3 13 R	12fr.
E♭m(maj13)/D	1 2 3 4	7 11 13 ♭3	12fr.
E♭m(maj7)♭13/D	1 2 1 4	7 11 ♭13 ♭3	12fr.

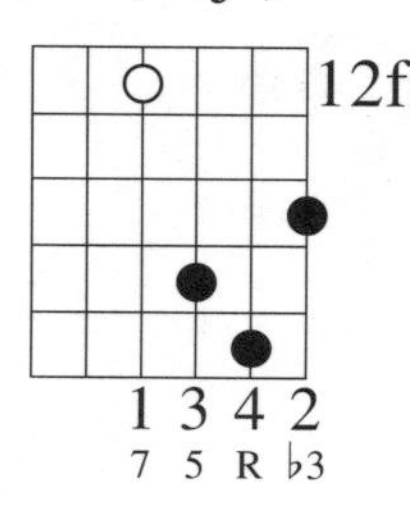
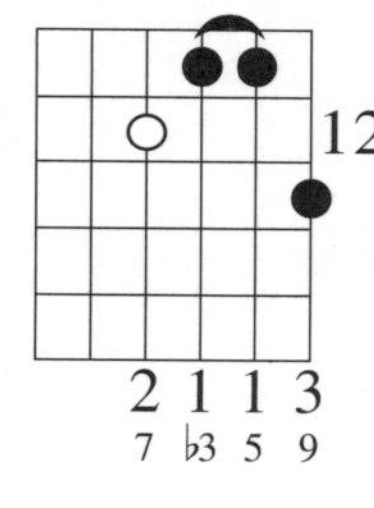
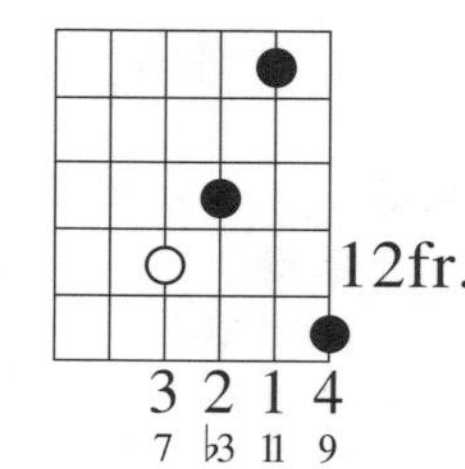
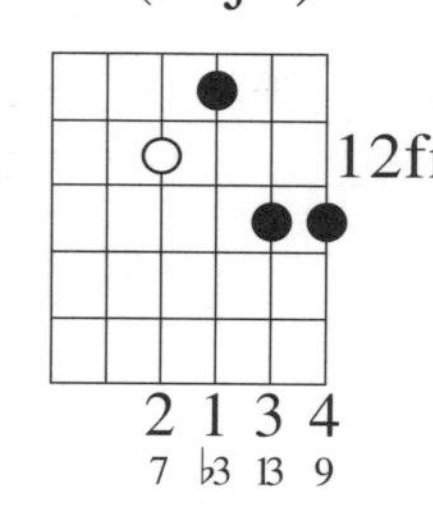
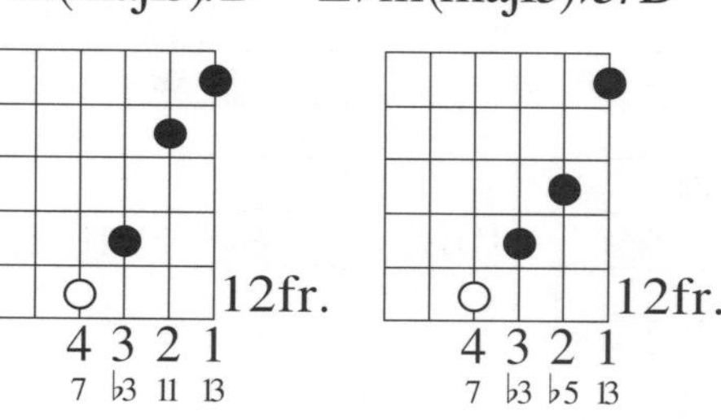

Chord	Fingering	Intervals	Fret
E♭m(maj7)/D	1 3 4 2	7 5 R ♭3	12fr.
E♭m(maj9)/D	2 1 1 3	7 ♭3 5 9	12fr.
E♭m(maj11)/D	3 2 1 4	7 ♭3 11 9	12fr.
E♭m(maj13)/D	2 1 3 4	7 ♭3 13 9	12fr.
E♭m(maj13)/D	4 3 2 1	7 ♭3 11 13	12fr.
E♭m(maj13)♭5/D	4 3 2 1	7 ♭3 ♭5 13	12fr.

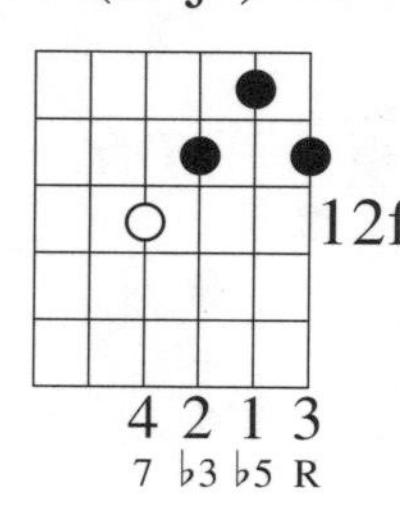
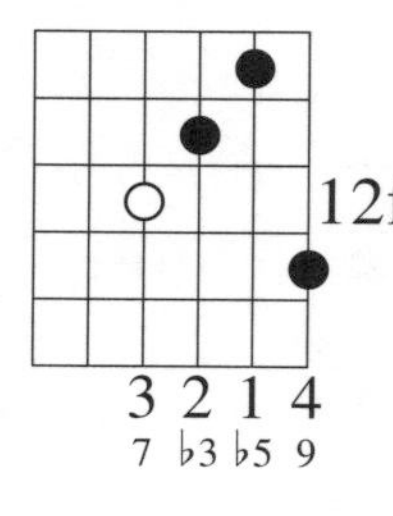
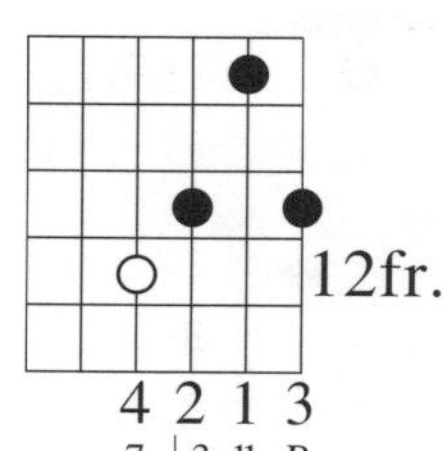
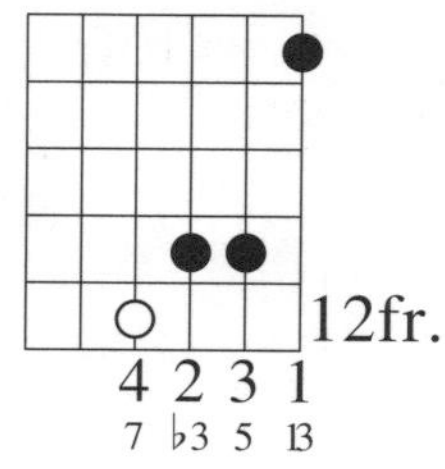
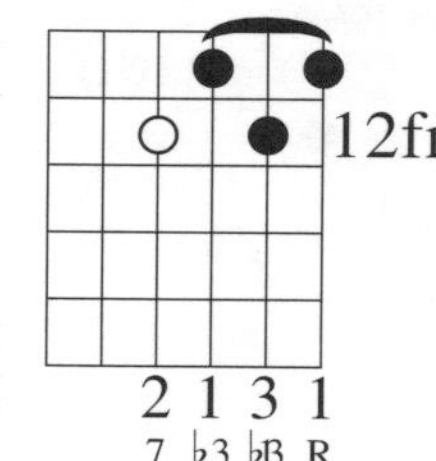
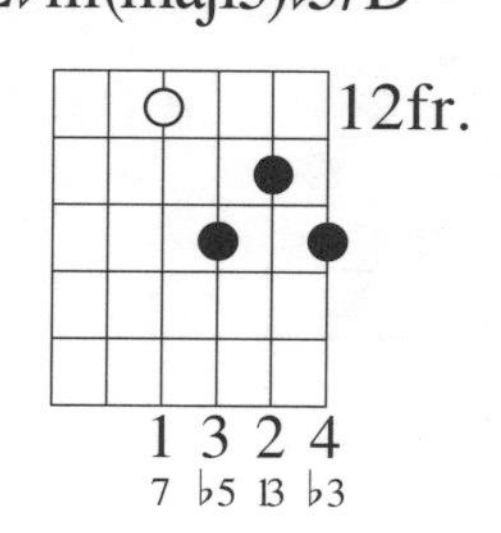

Chord	Fingering	Intervals	Fret
E♭m(maj7)♭5/D	4 2 1 3	7 ♭3 ♭5 R	12fr.
E♭m(maj9)♭5/D	3 2 1 4	7 ♭3 ♭5 9	12fr.
E♭m(maj11)/D	4 2 1 3	7 ♭3 11 R	12fr.
E♭m(maj13)/D	4 2 3 1	7 ♭3 5 13	12fr.
E♭m(maj7)♭13/D	2 1 3 1	7 ♭3 ♭13 R	12fr.
E♭m(maj13)♭5/D	1 3 2 4	7 ♭5 13 ♭3	12fr.

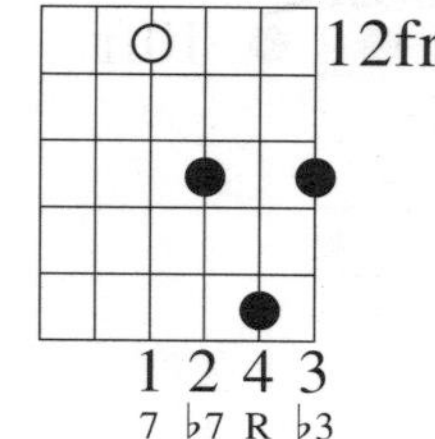
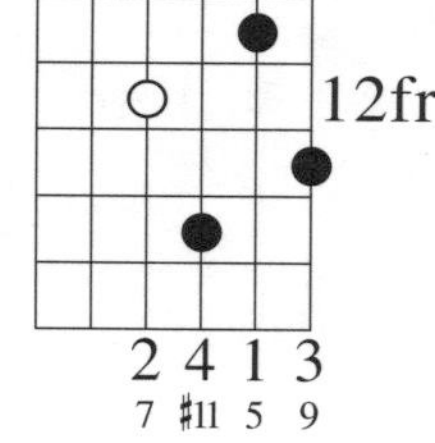
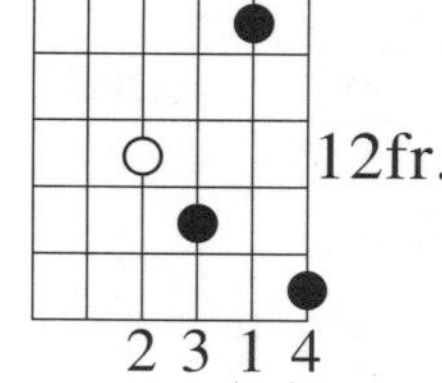
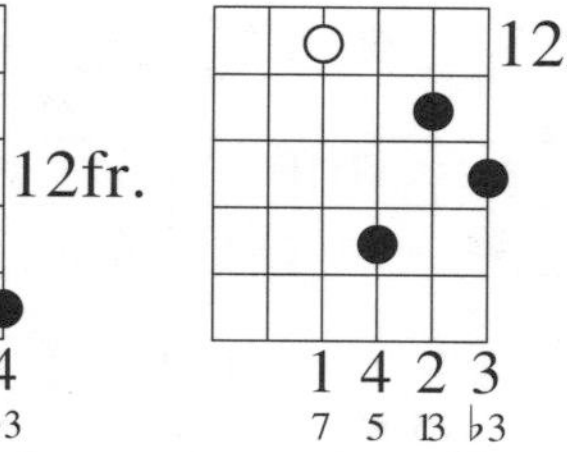
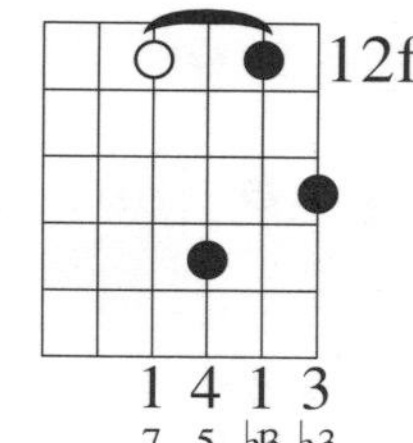
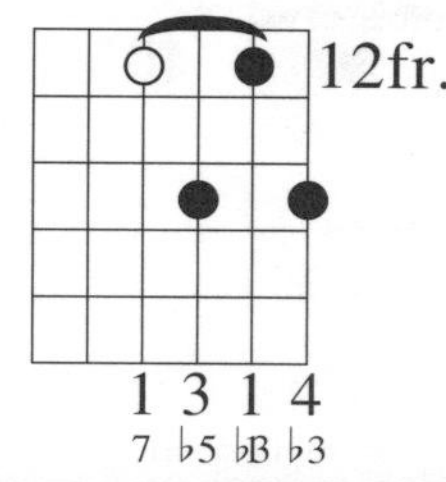

Chord	Fingering	Intervals	Fret
E♭m(maj7)♭5/D	1 2 4 3	7 ♭7 R ♭3	12fr.
E♭m(maj9)♯11/D	2 4 1 3	7 ♯11 5 9	12fr.
E♭m(maj11)♭5/D	2 3 1 4	7 11 ♭5 ♭3	12fr.
E♭m(maj13)/D	1 4 2 3	7 5 13 ♭3	12fr.
E♭m(maj7)♭13/D	1 4 1 3	7 5 ♭13 ♭3	12fr.
E♭m(maj7)♭5♭13/D	1 3 1 4	7 ♭5 ♭13 ♭3	12fr.

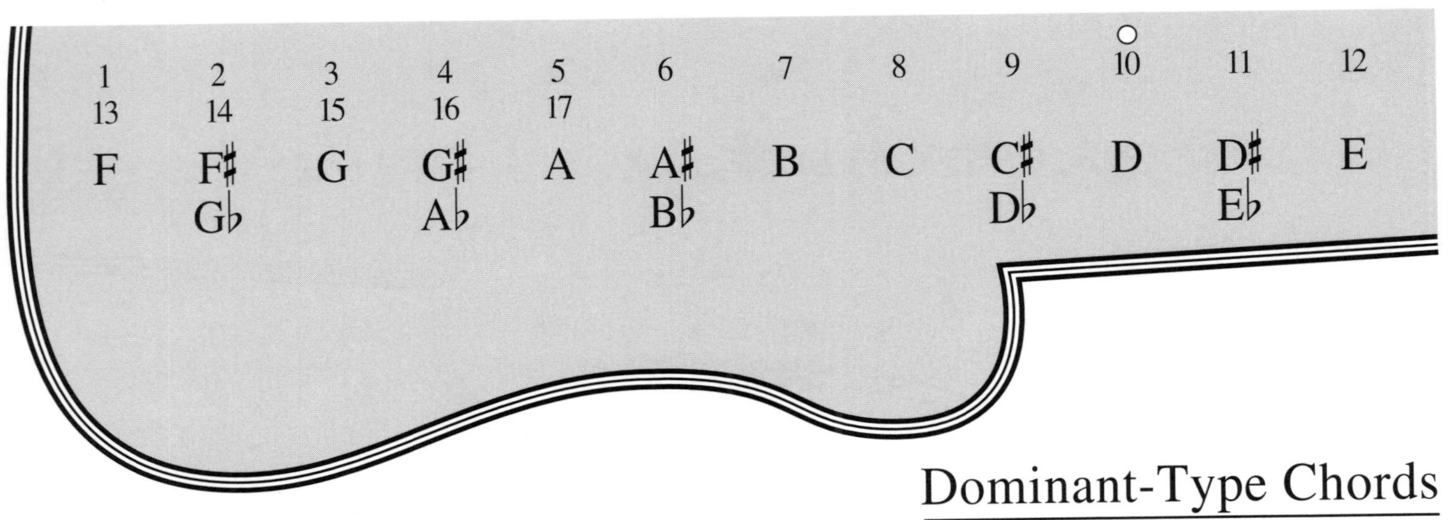

Dominant-Type Chords

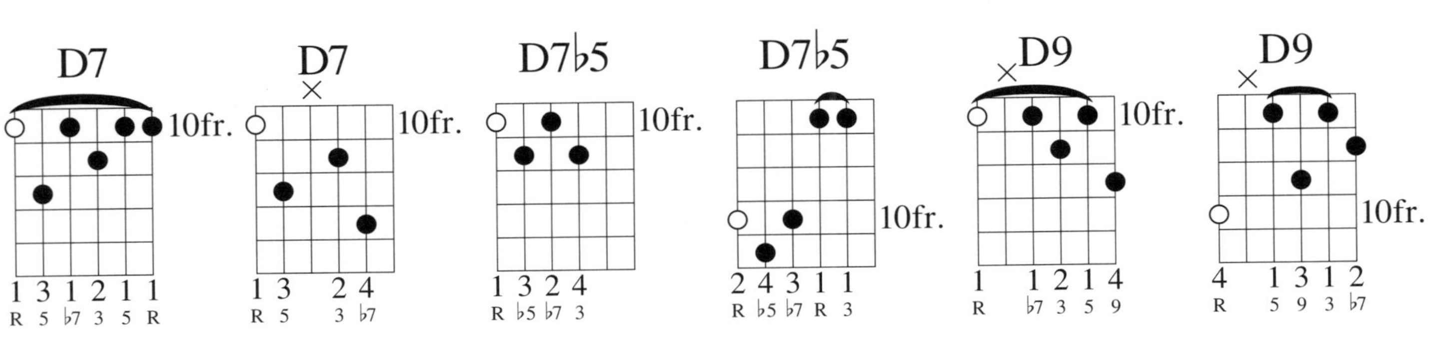

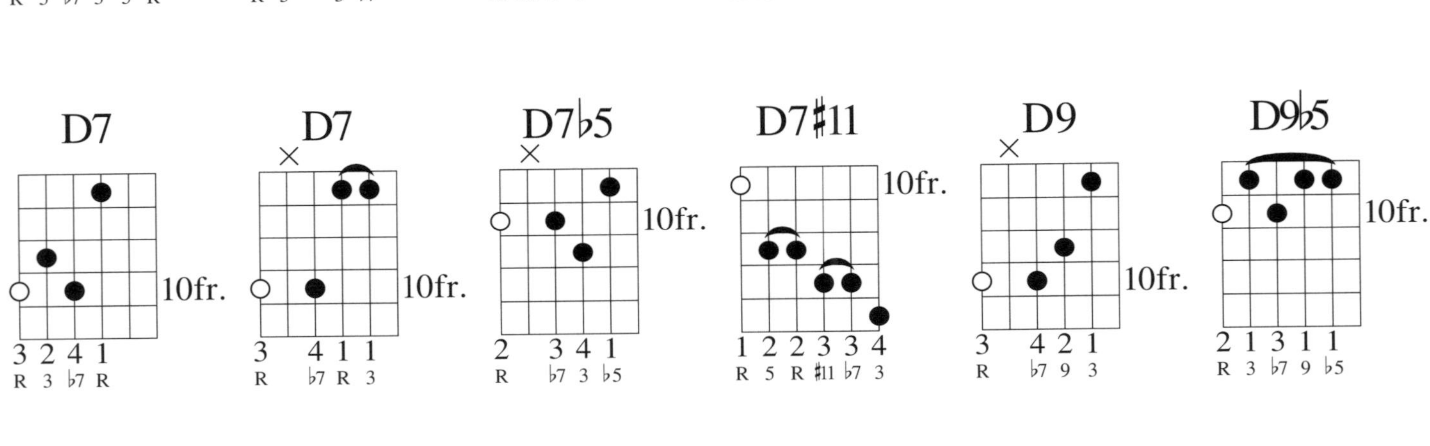

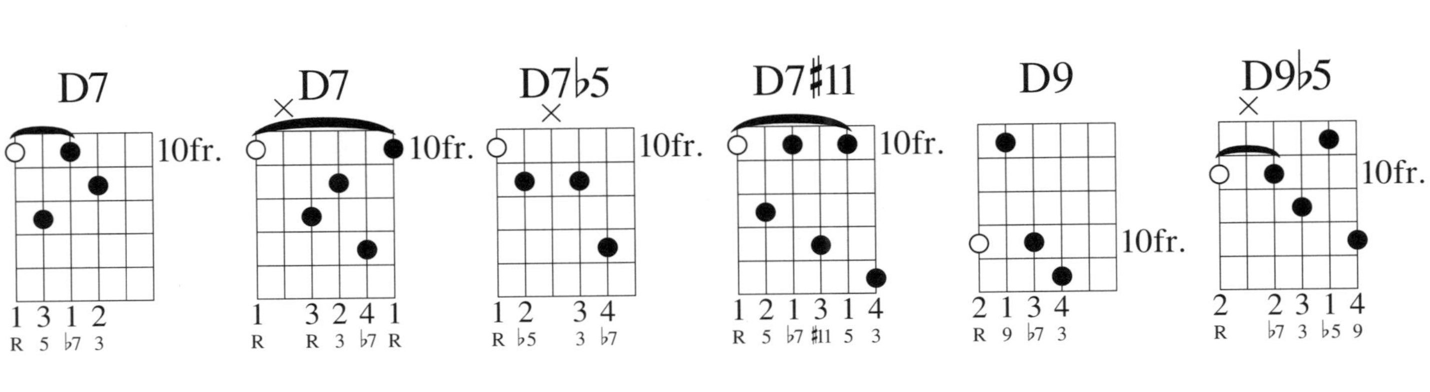

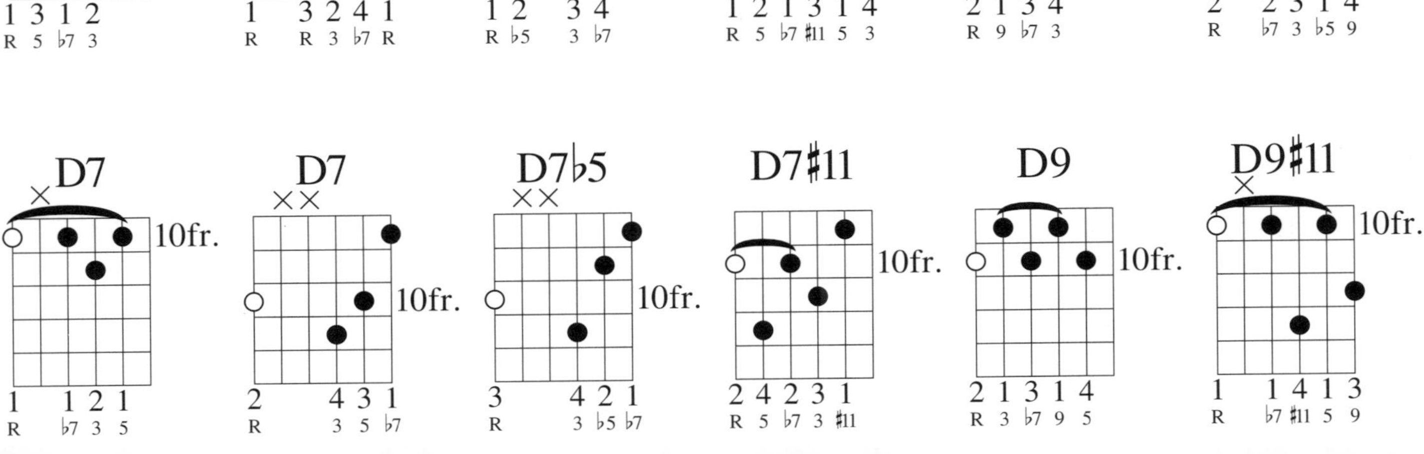

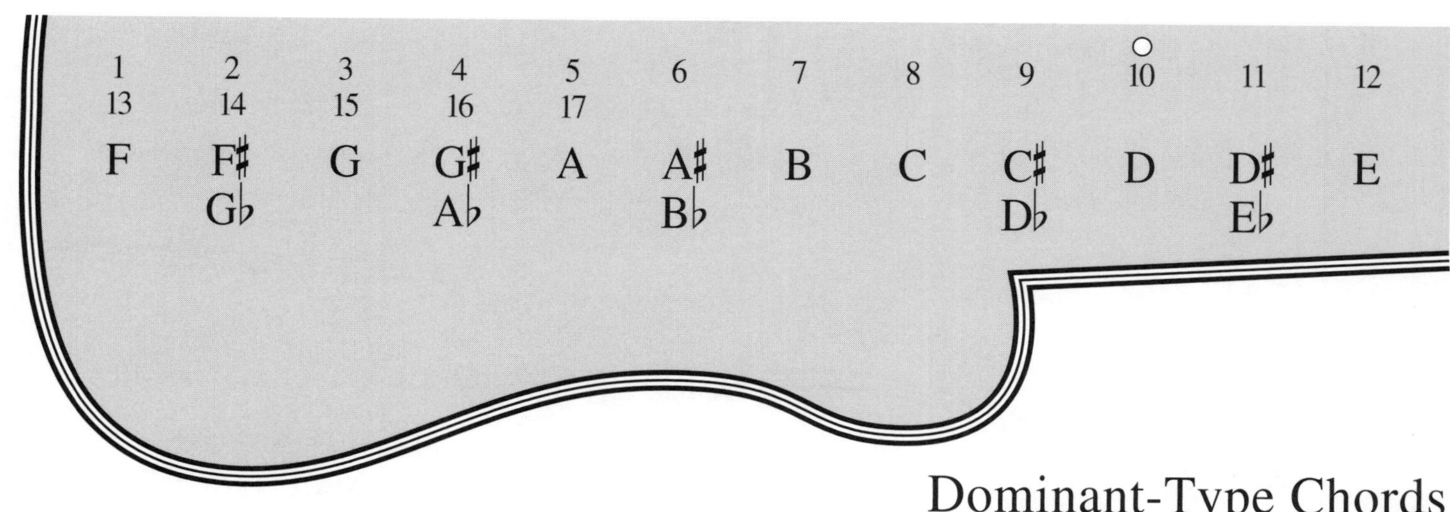

Dominant-Type Chords

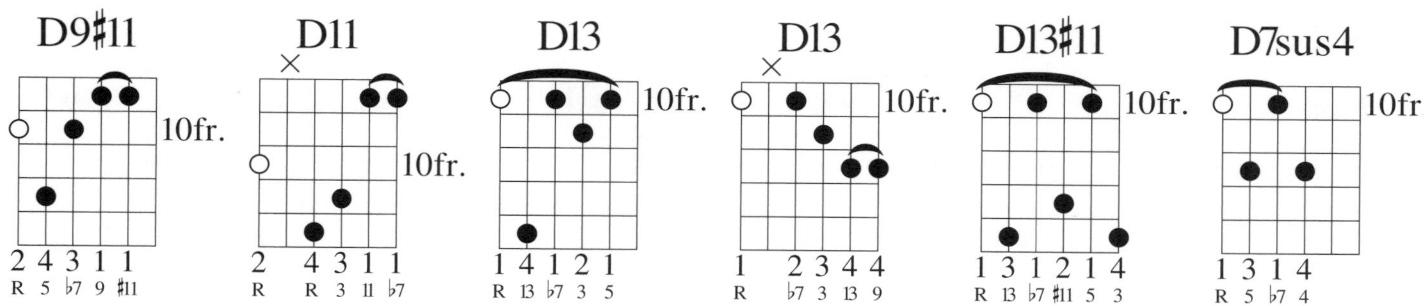

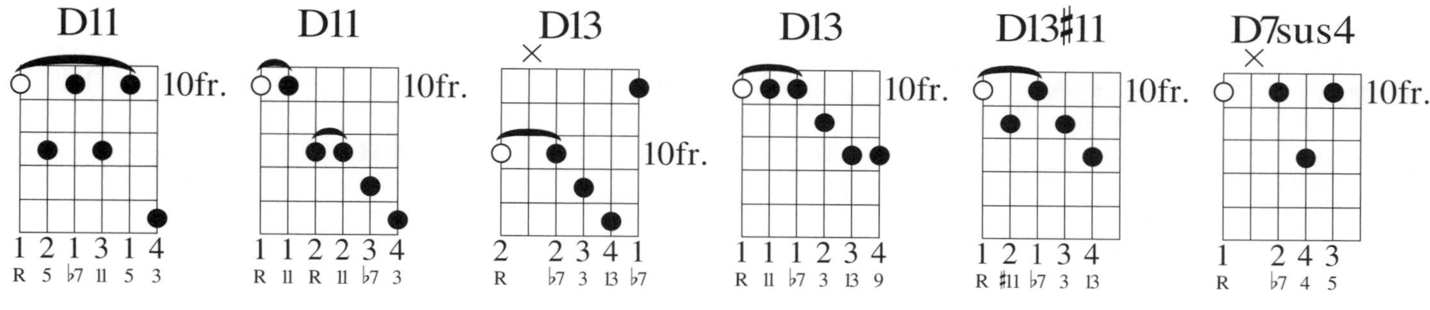

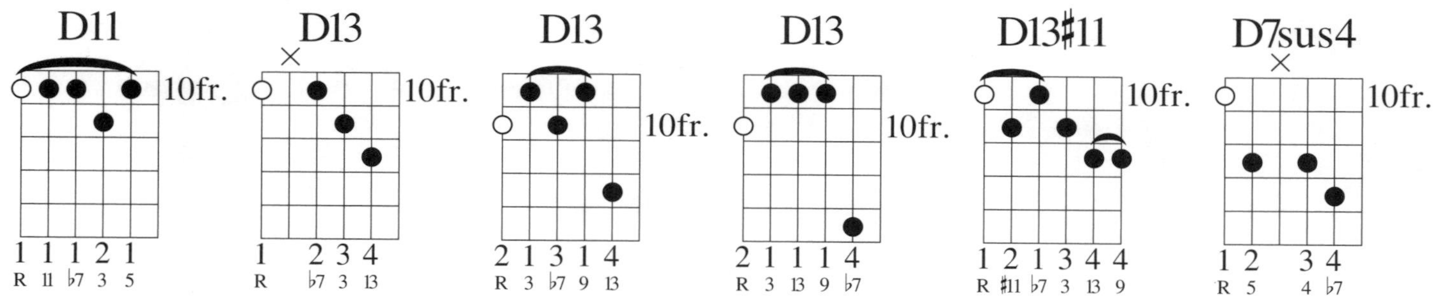

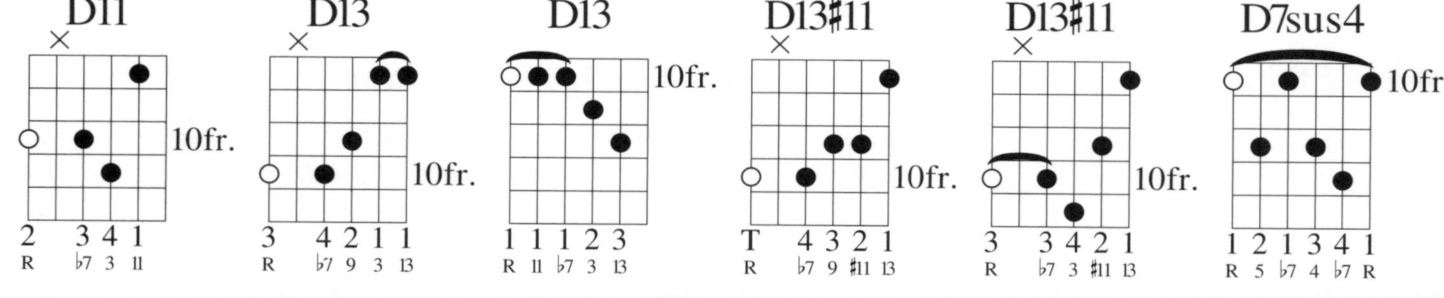

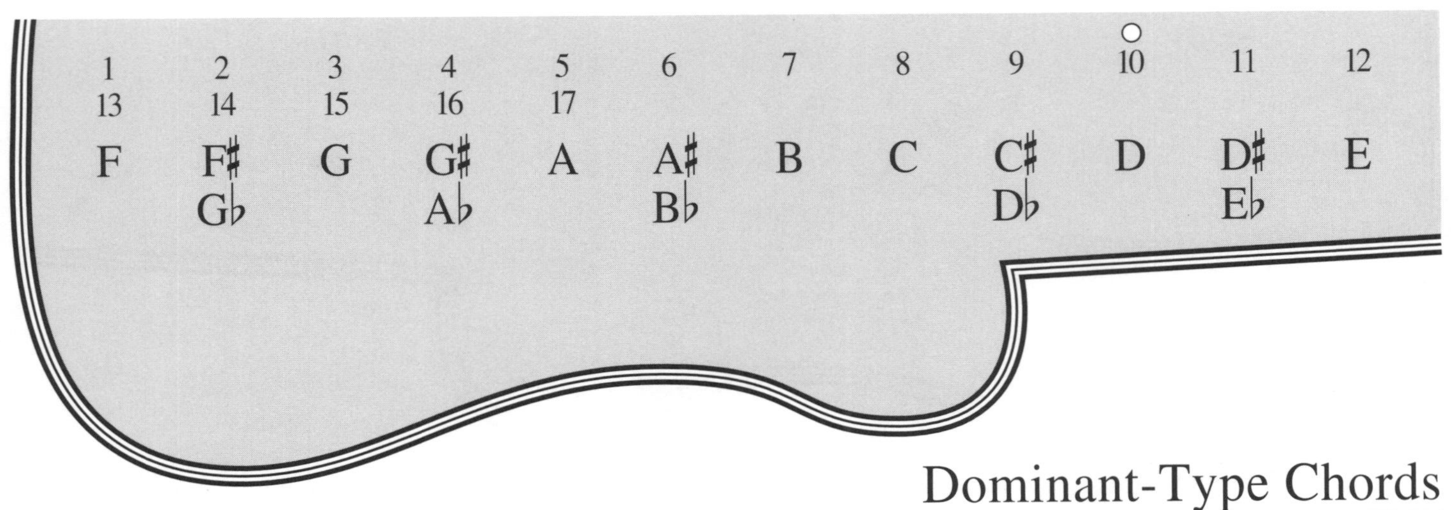

Dominant-Type Chords

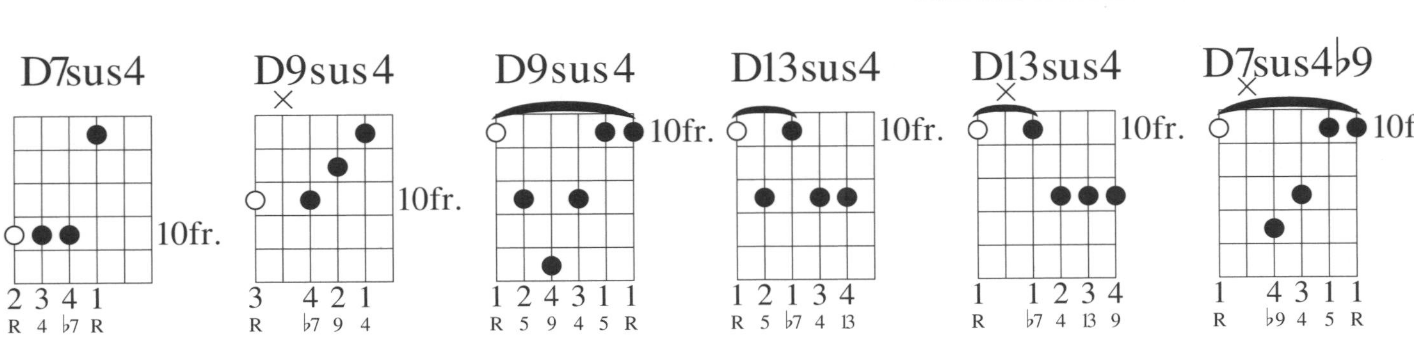

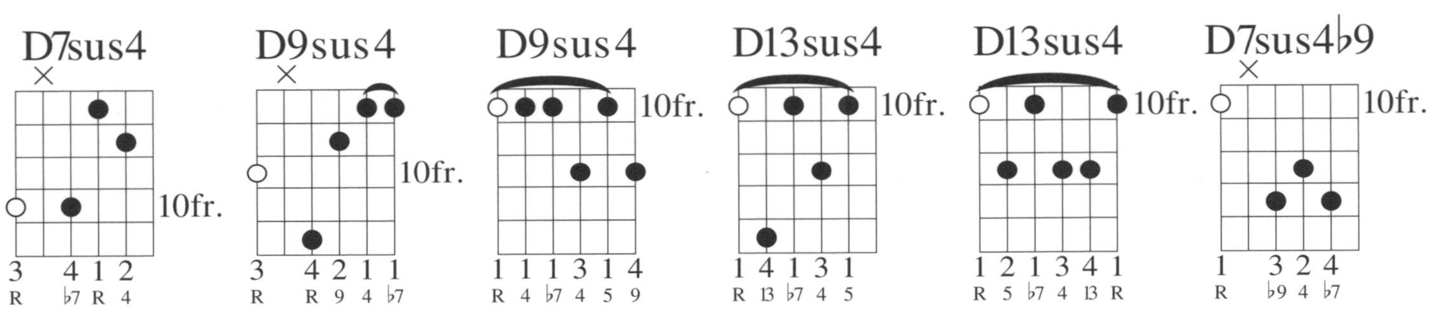

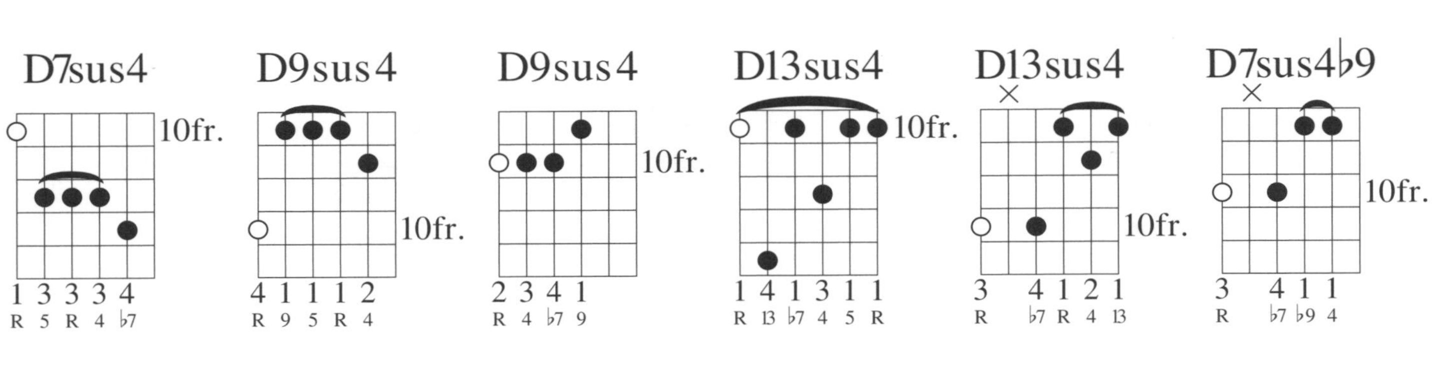

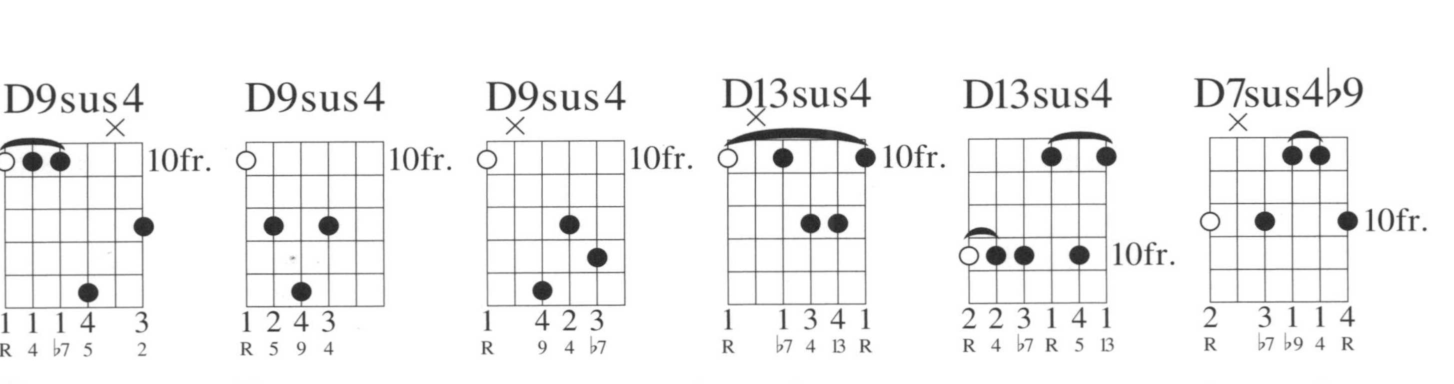

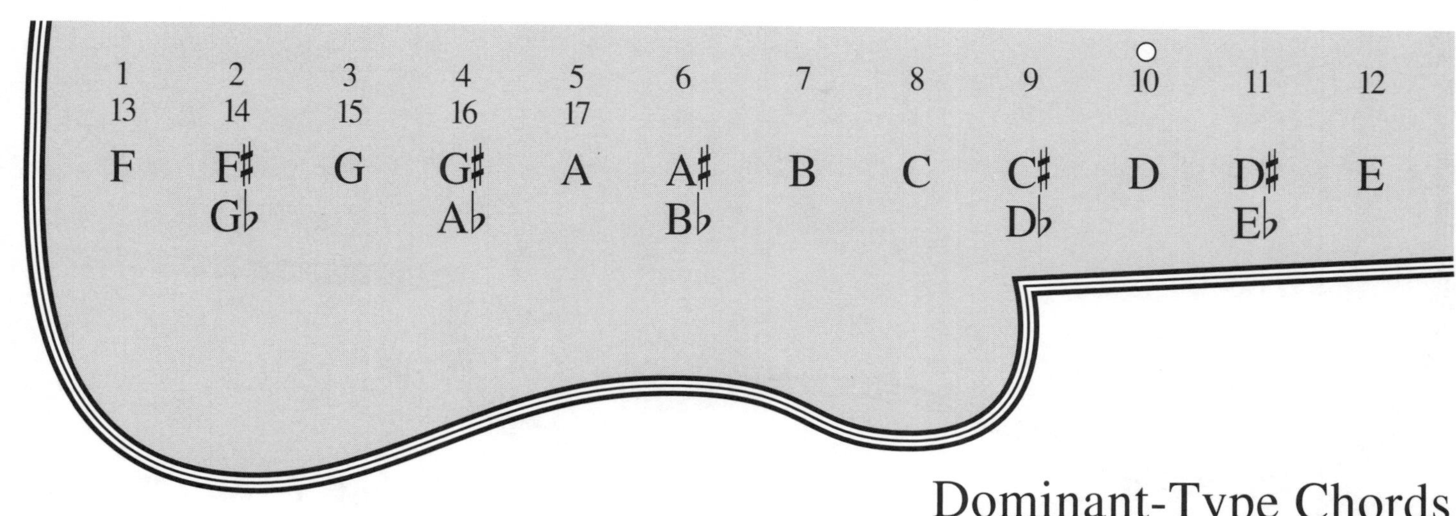

Dominant-Type Chords

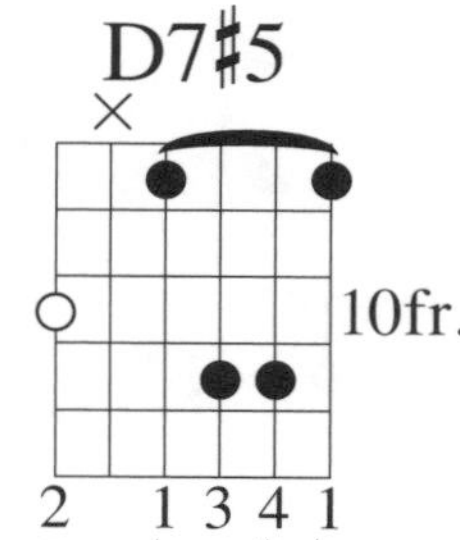

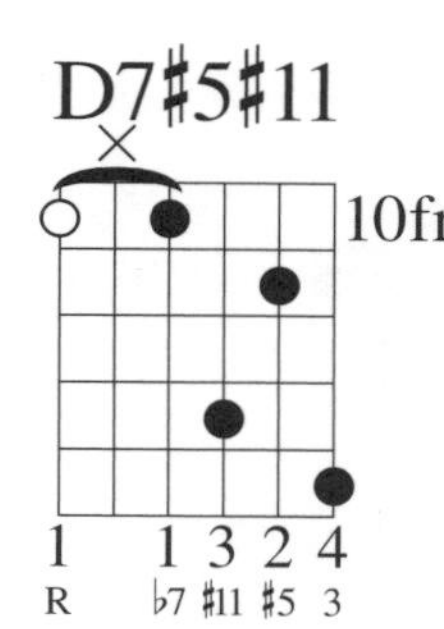

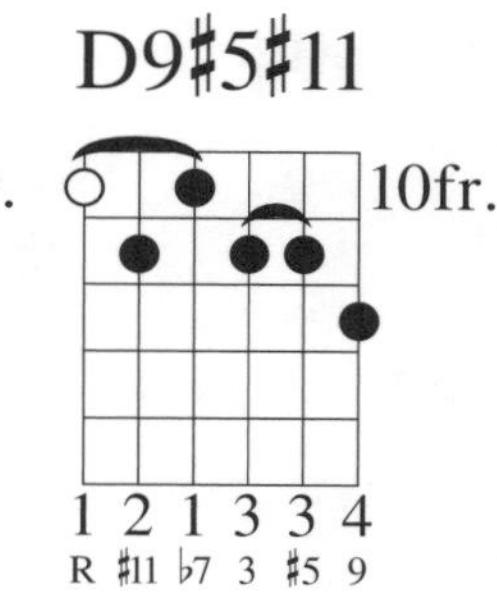

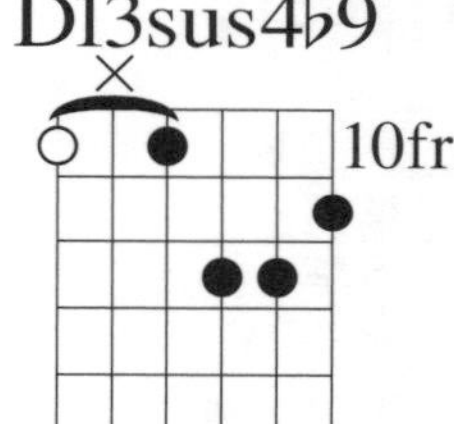

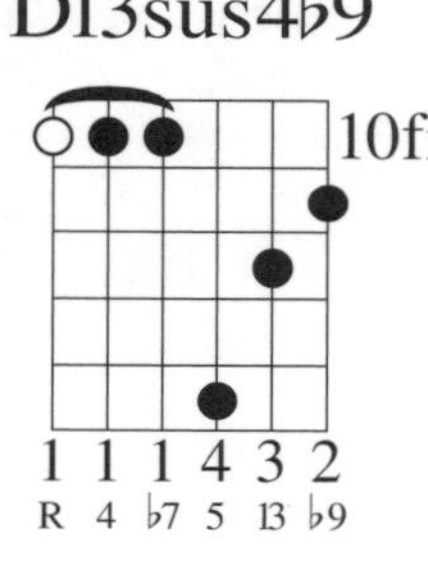

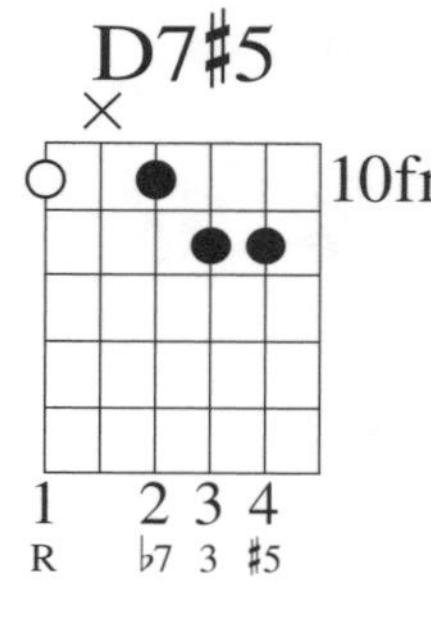

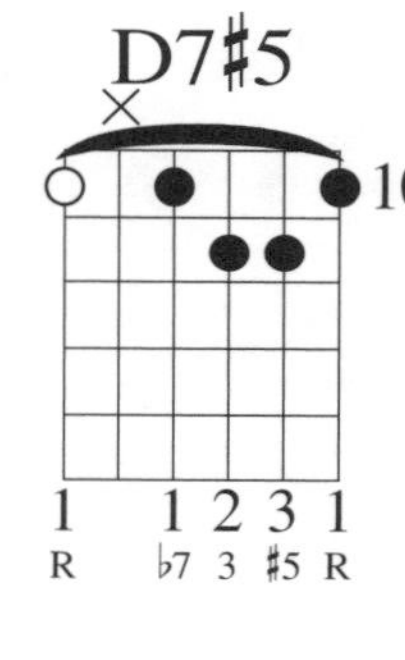

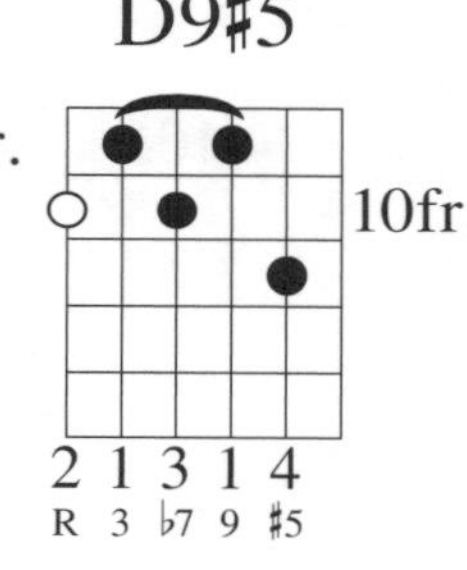

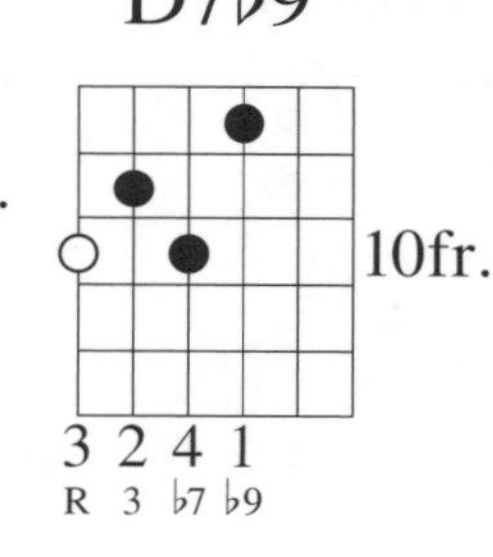

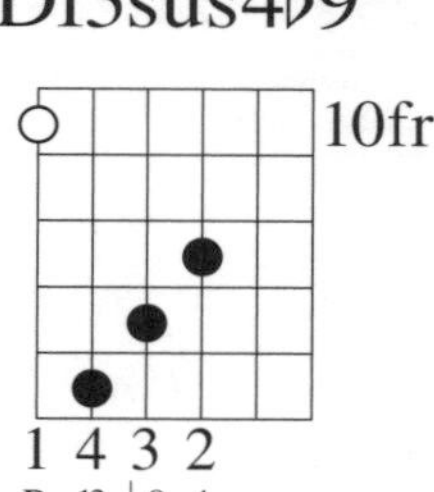

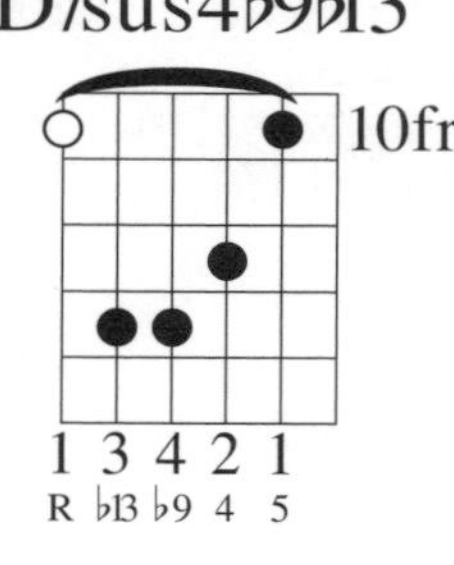

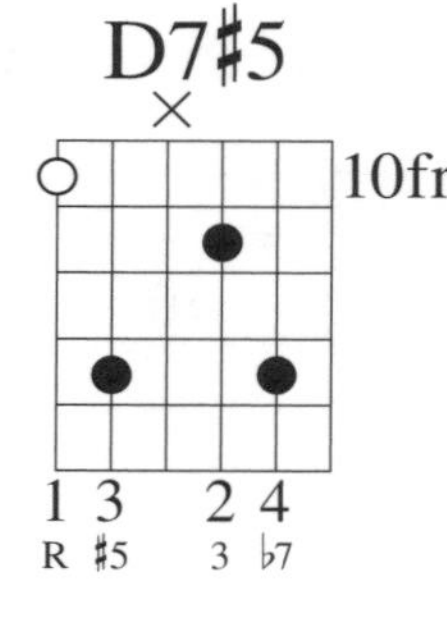

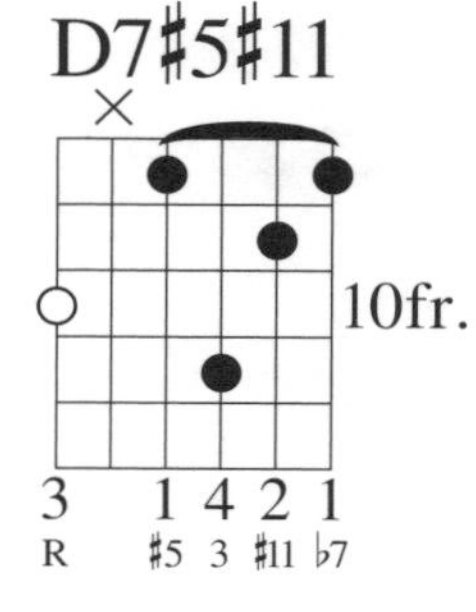

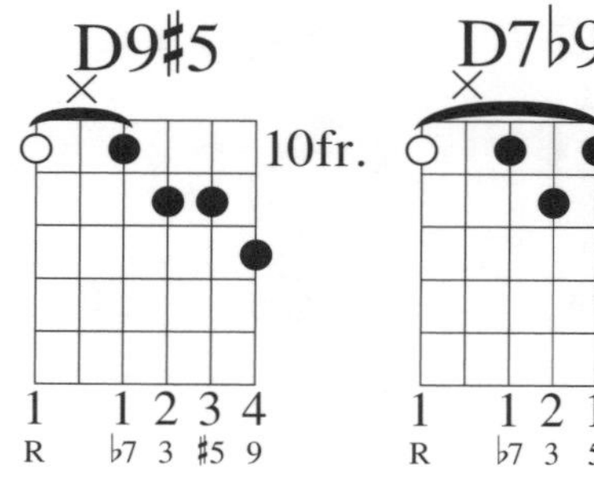

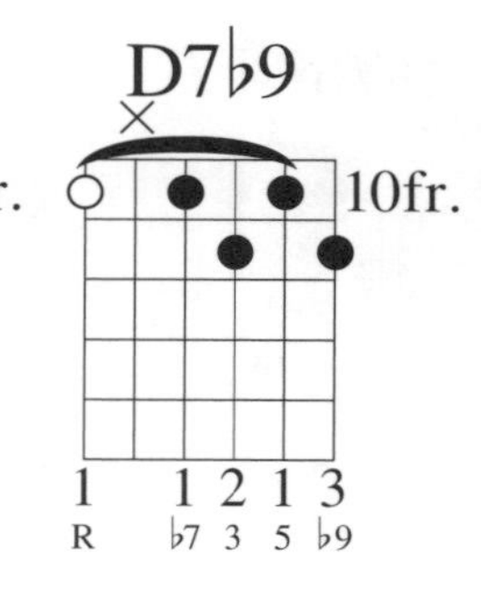

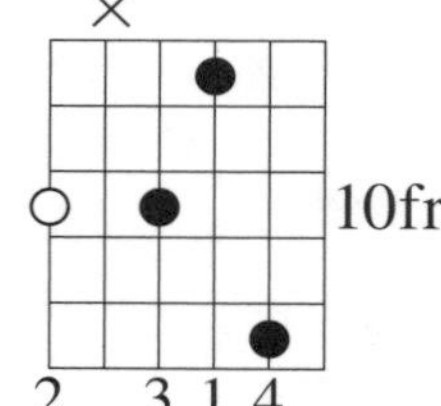

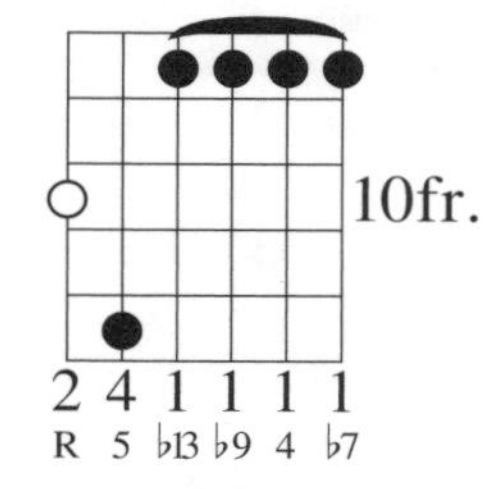

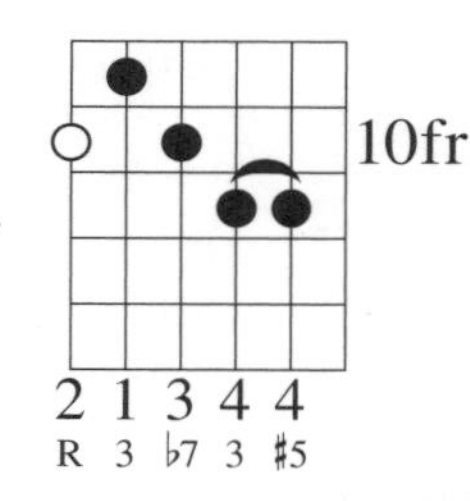

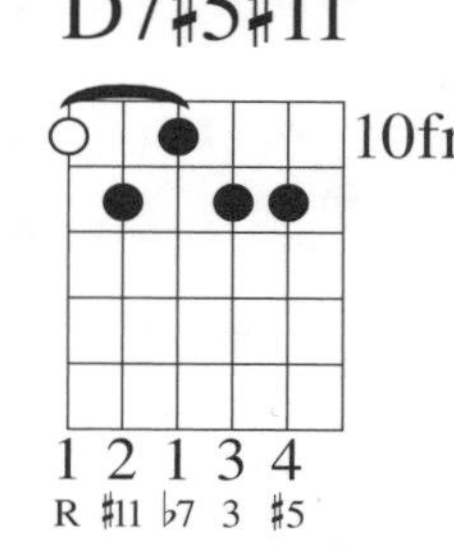

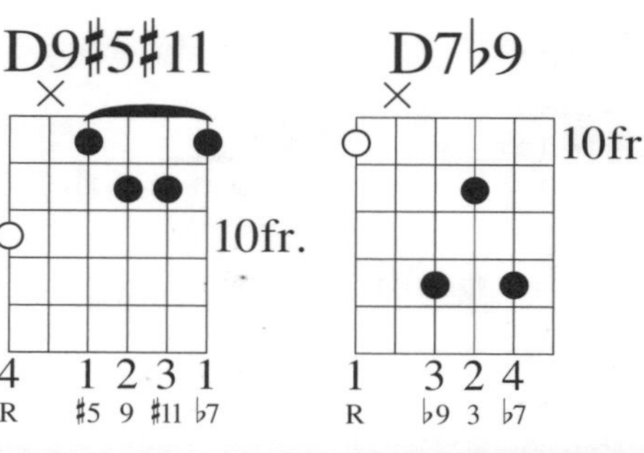

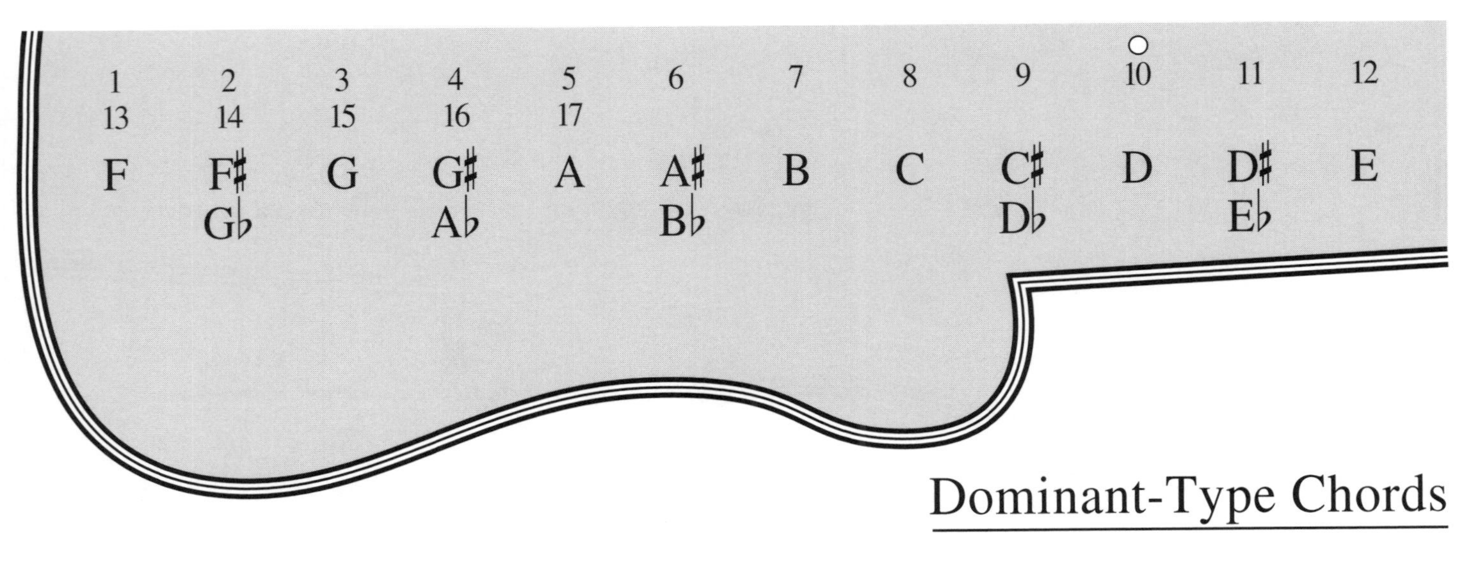

Dominant-Type Chords

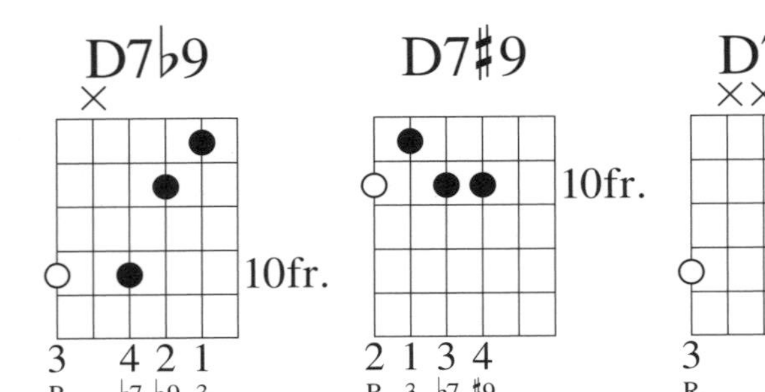
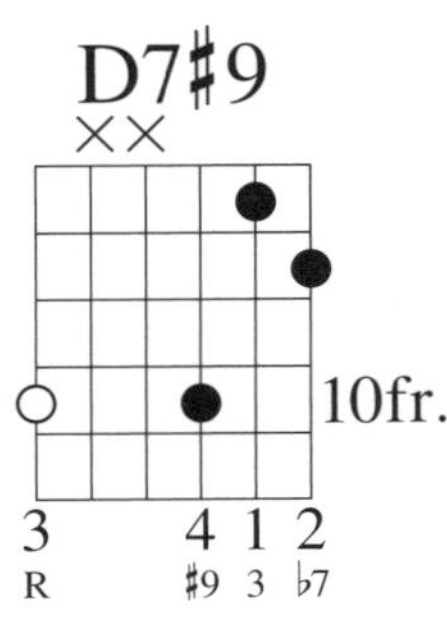
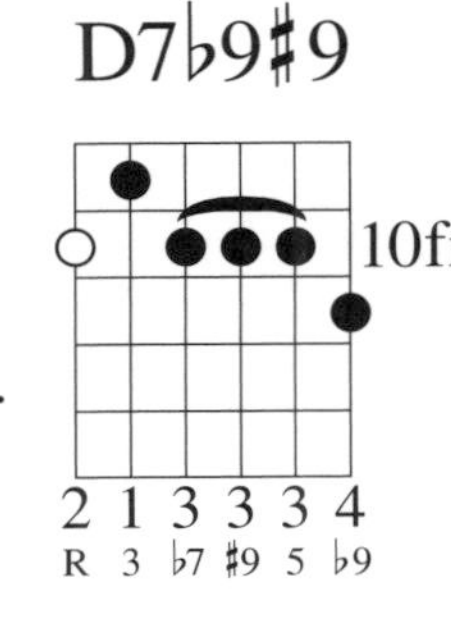
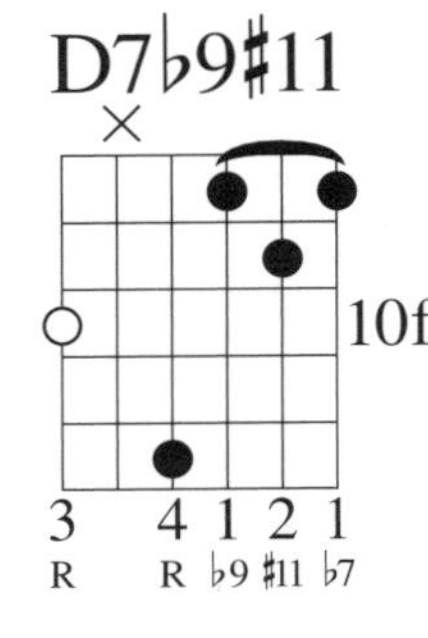
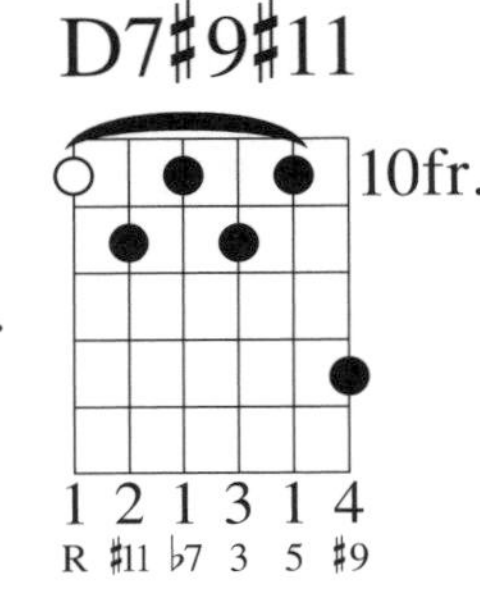
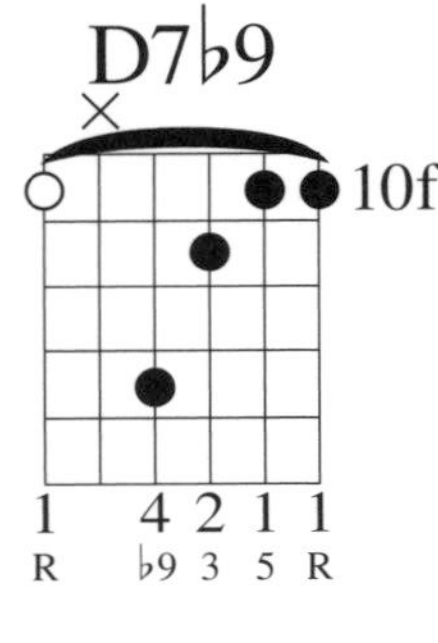
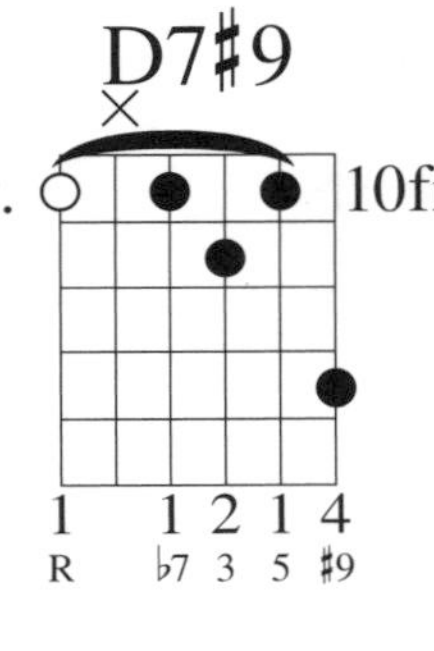
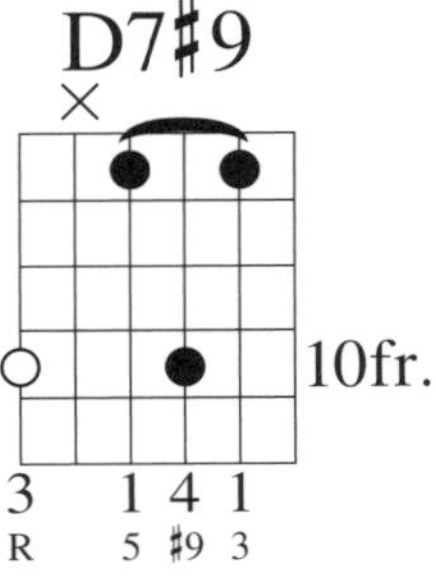
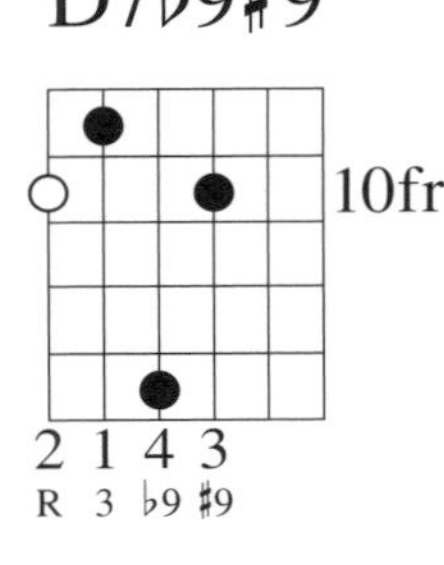
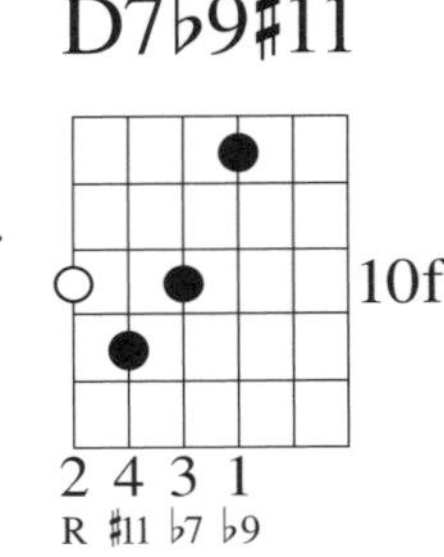
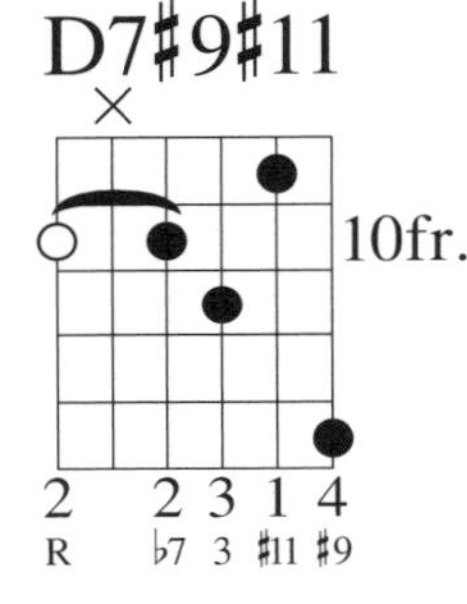
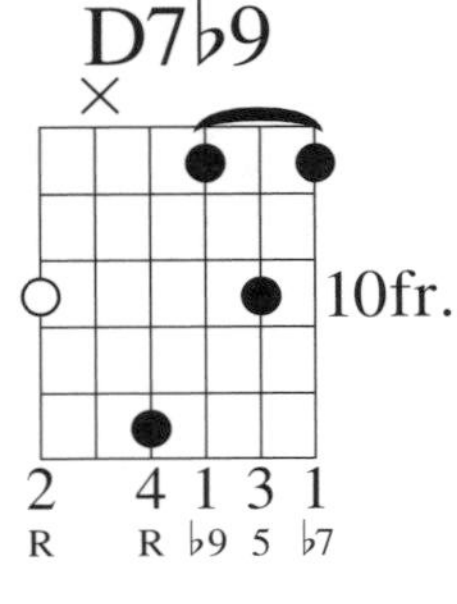
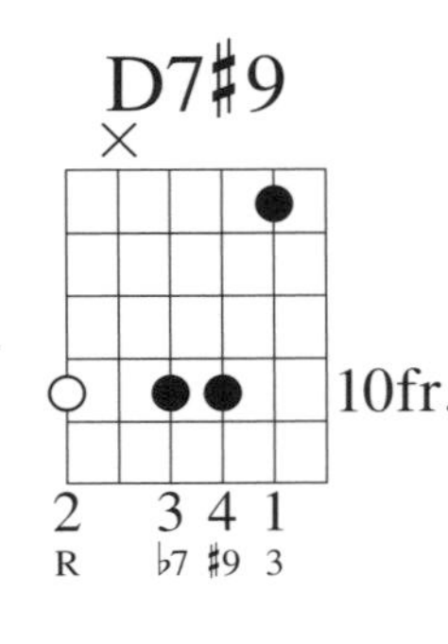
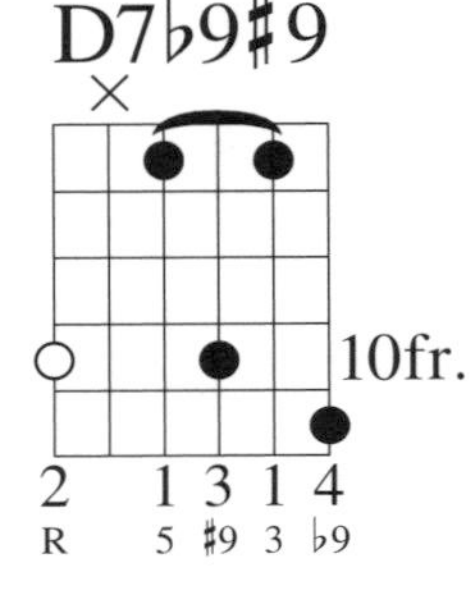
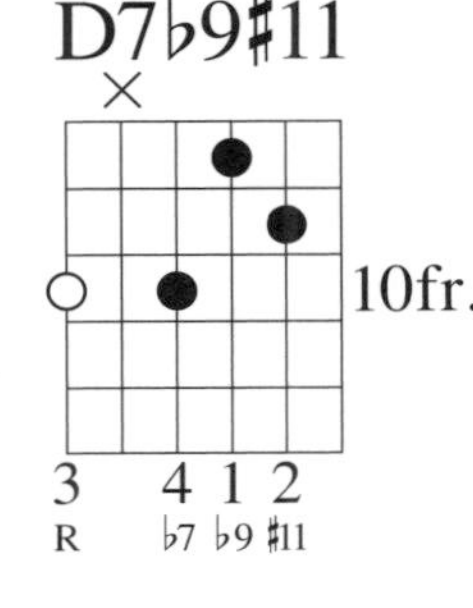
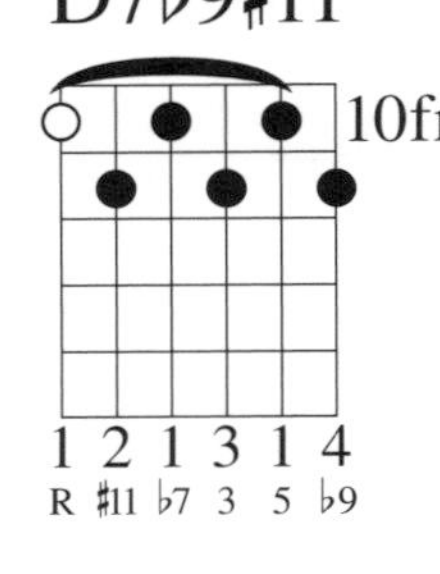
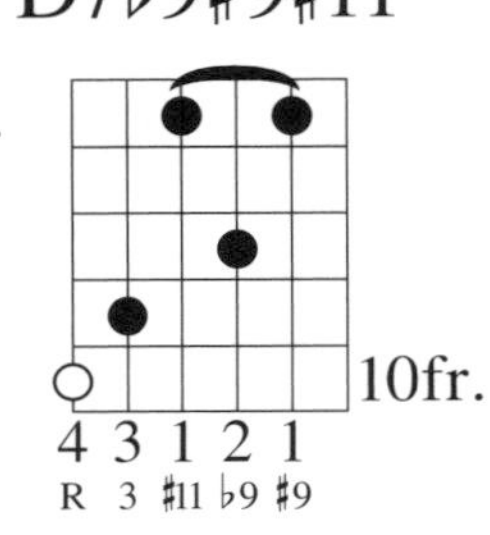
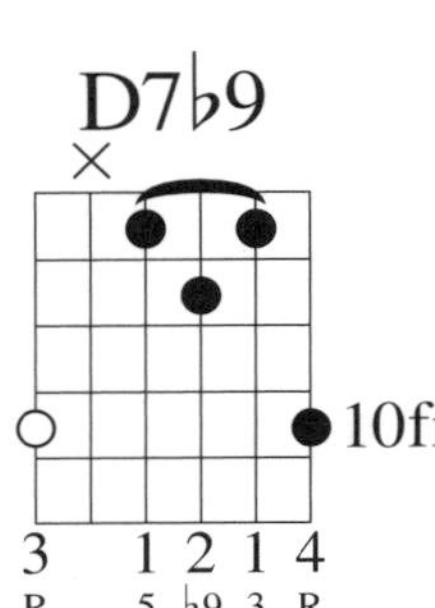
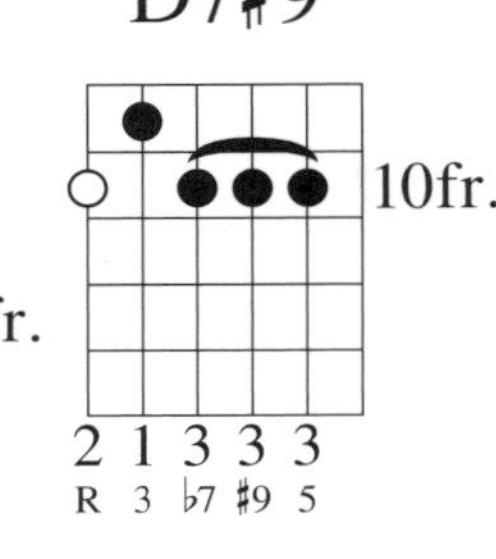
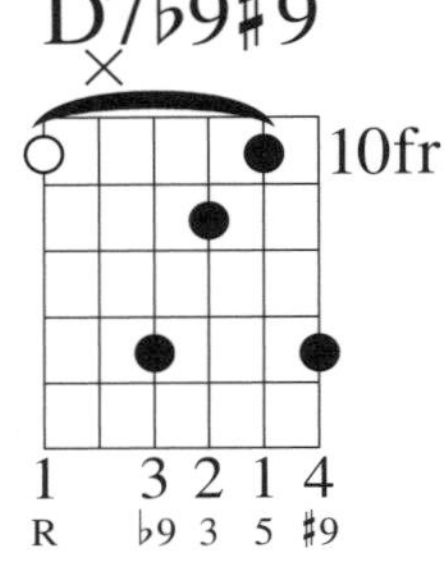
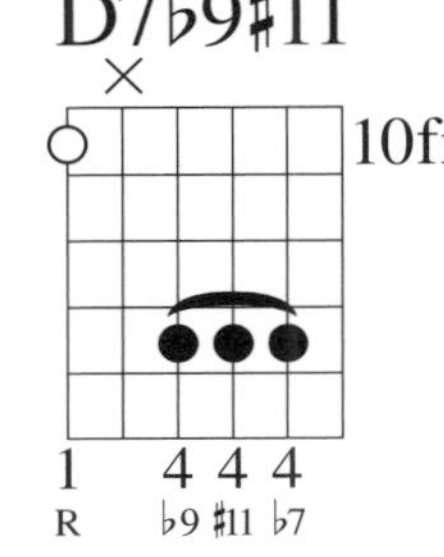
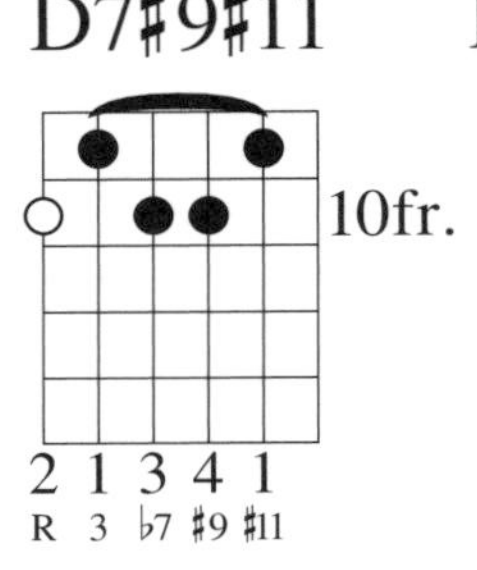
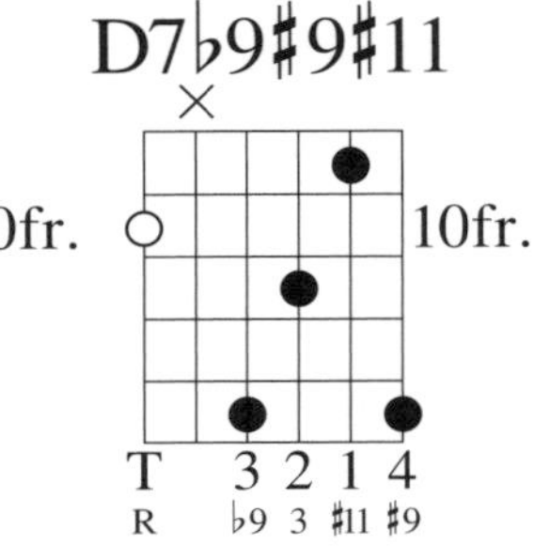

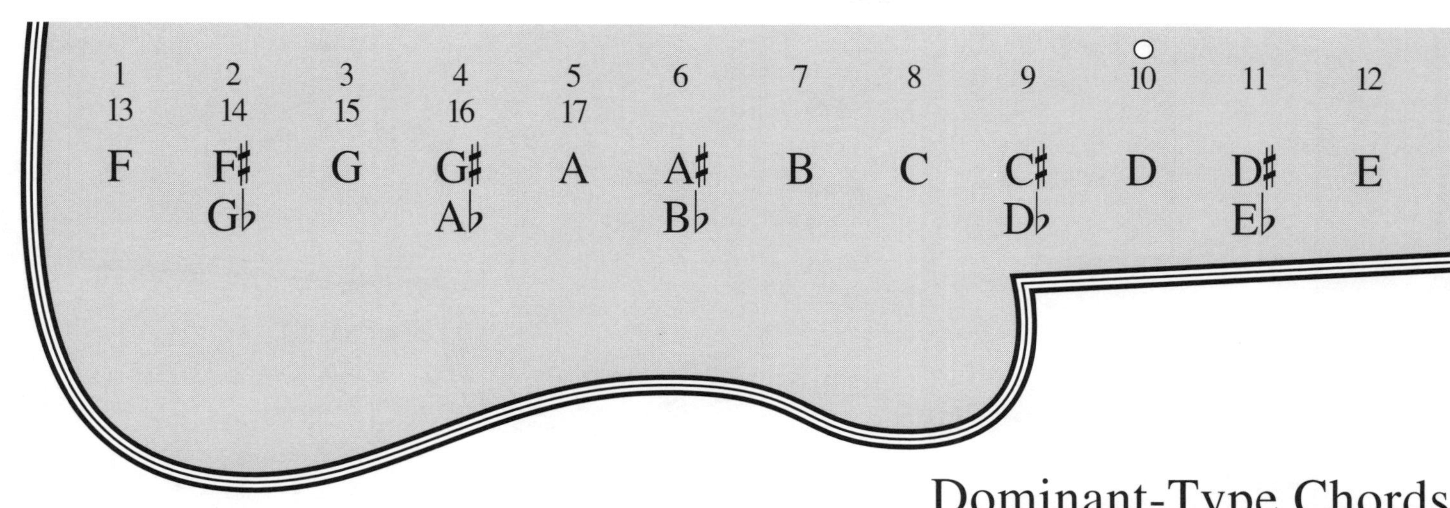

Dominant-Type Chords

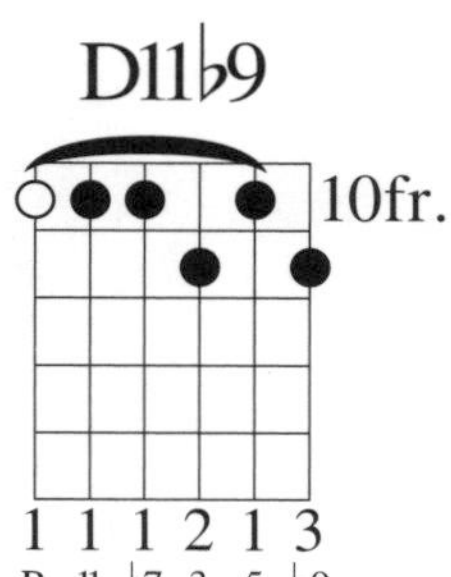

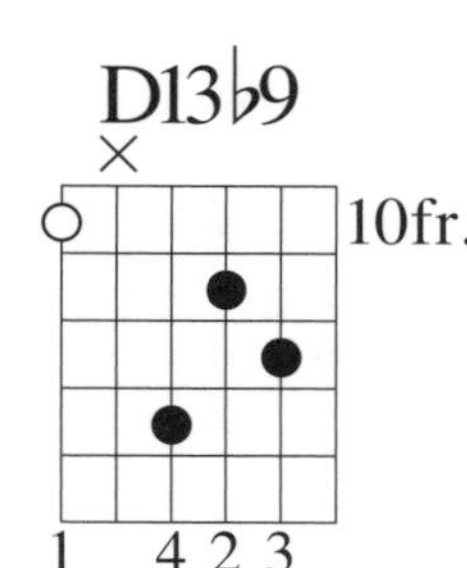

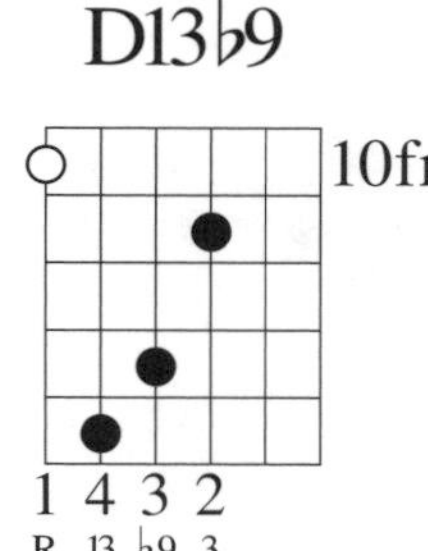

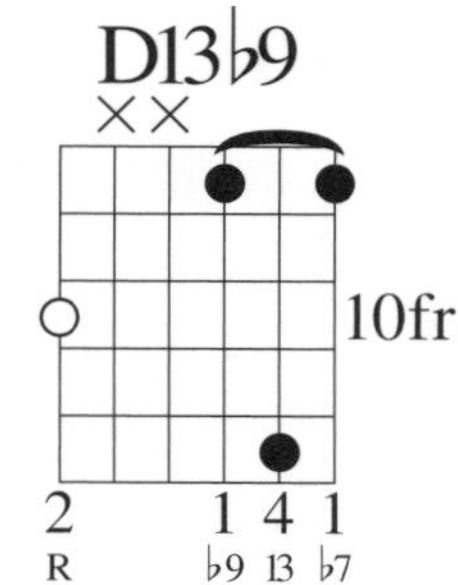

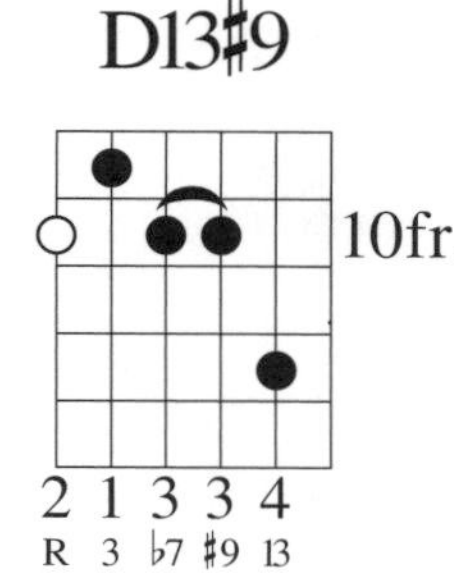

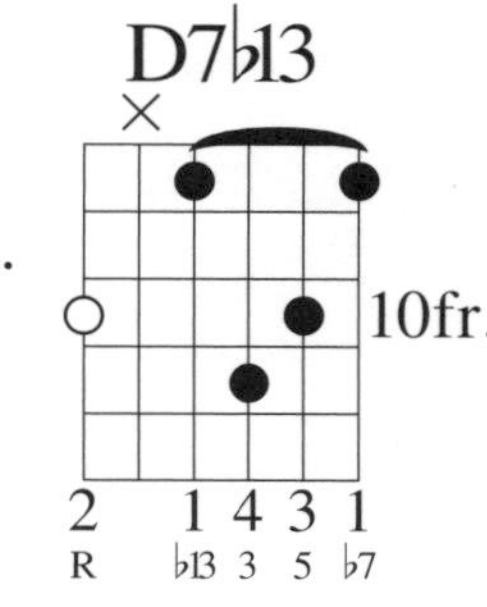

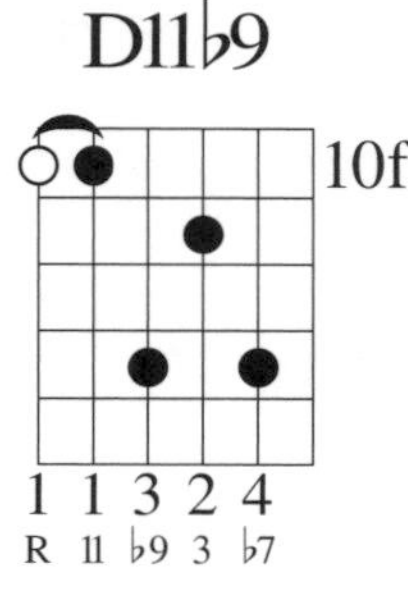

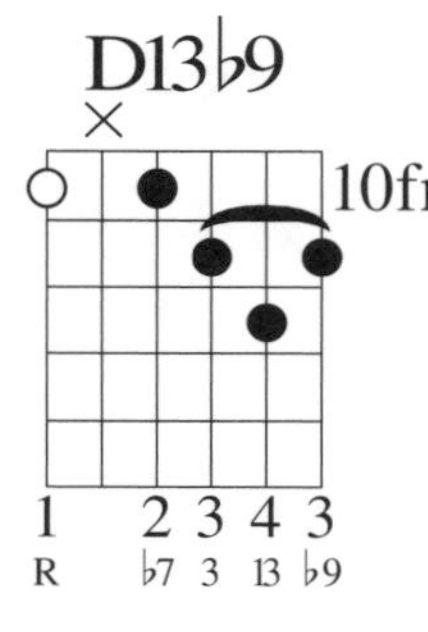

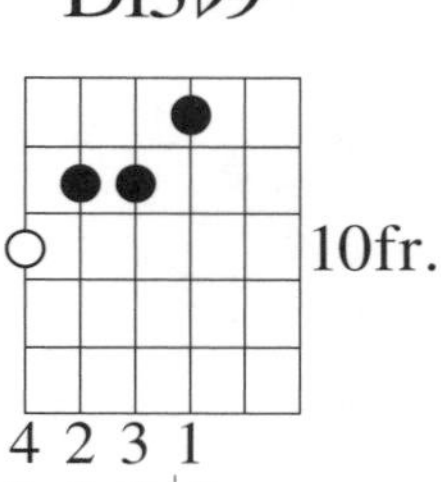

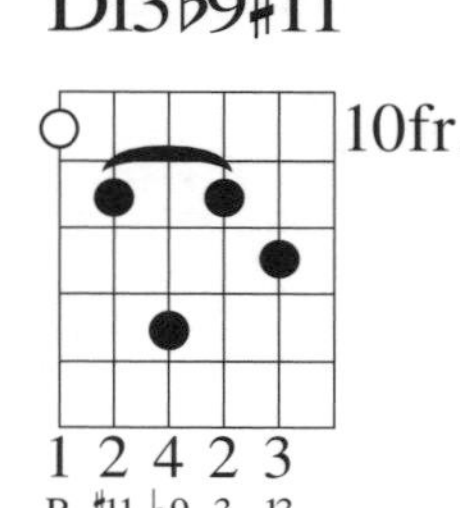

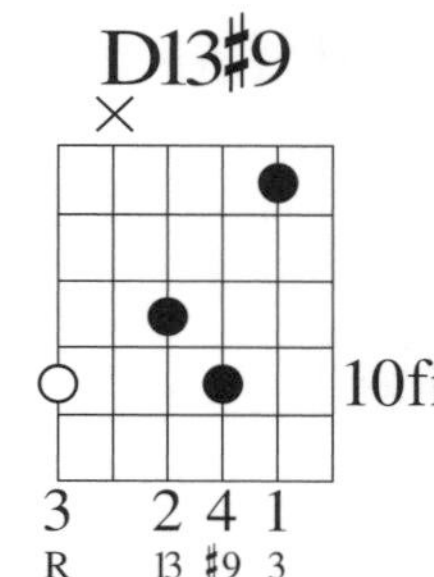

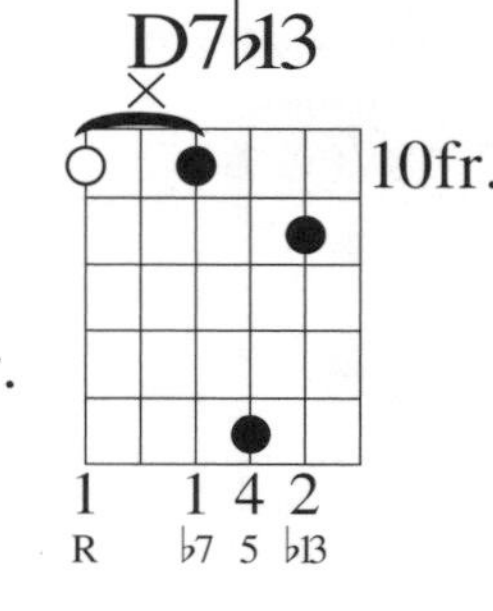

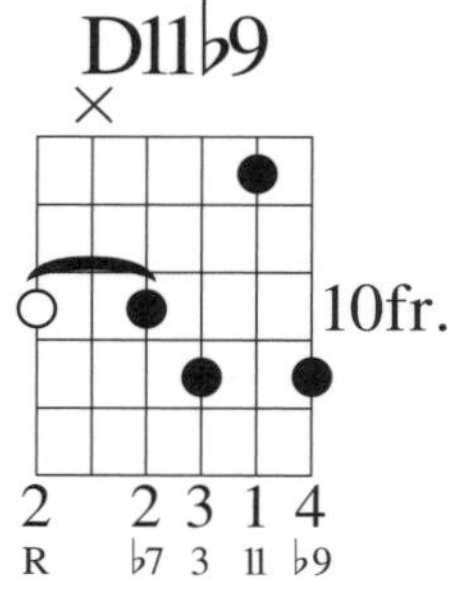

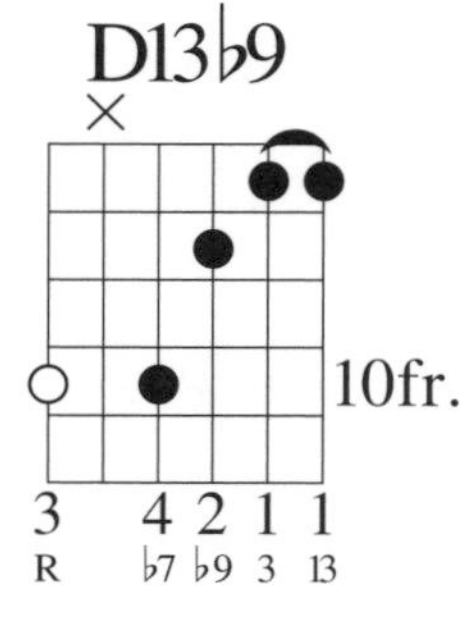

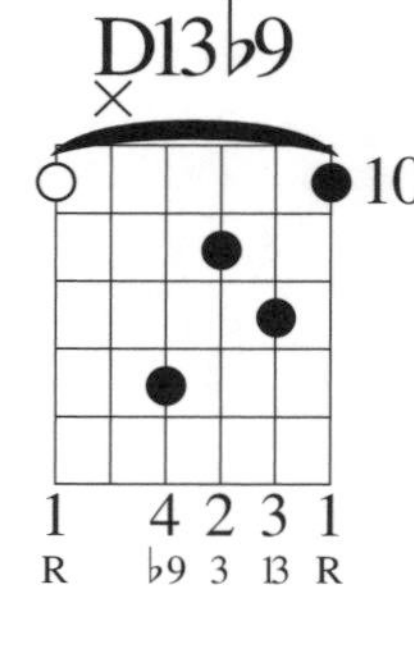

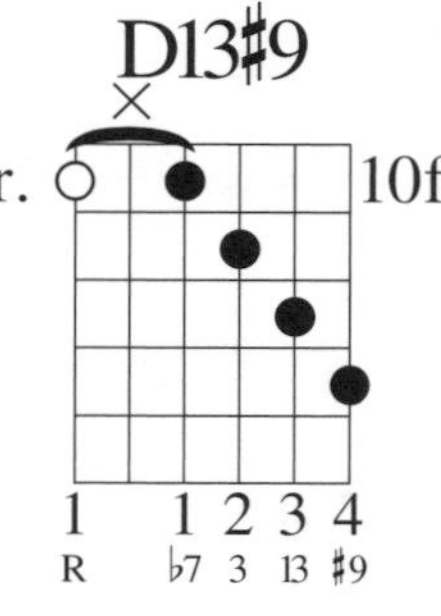

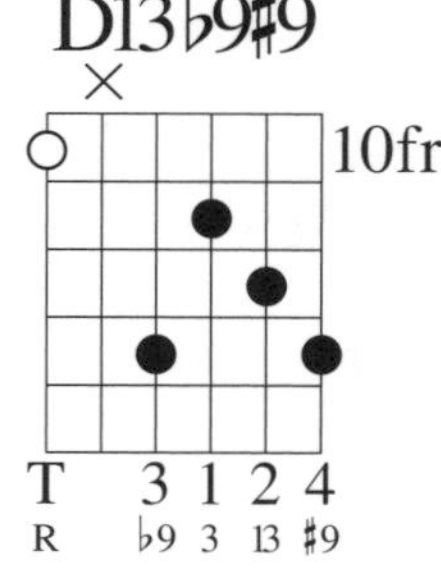

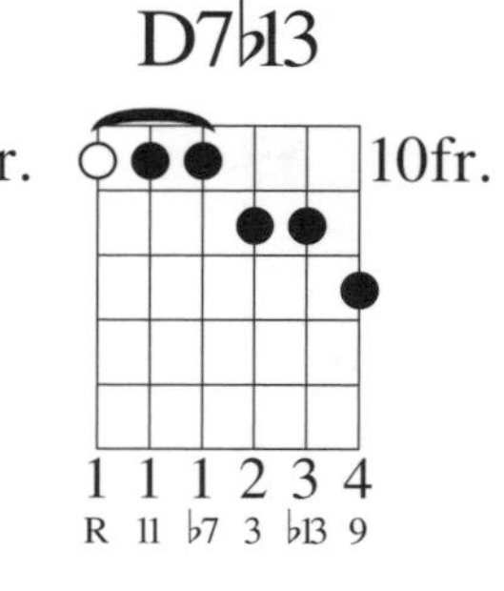

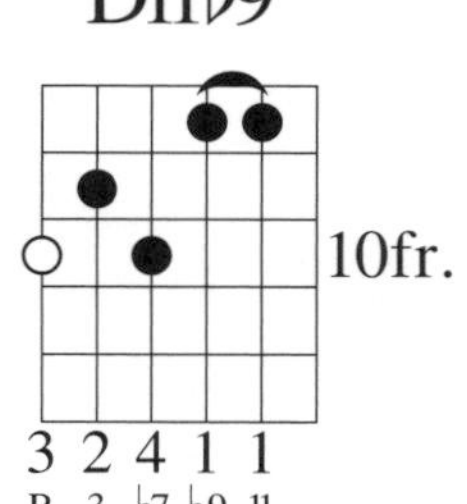

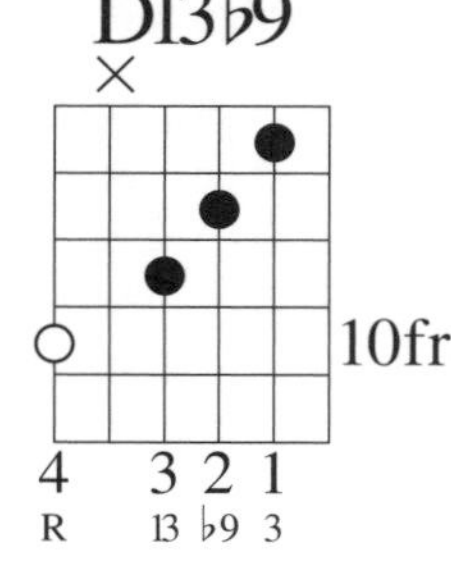

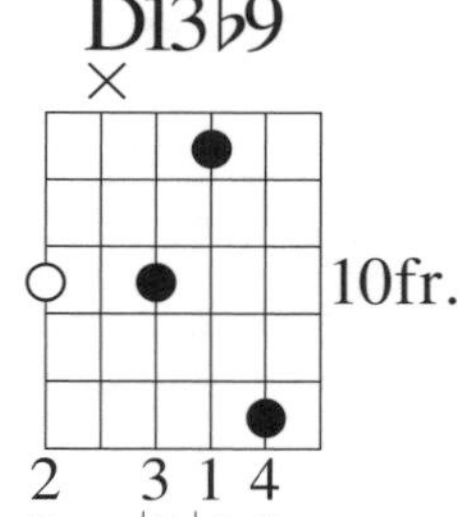

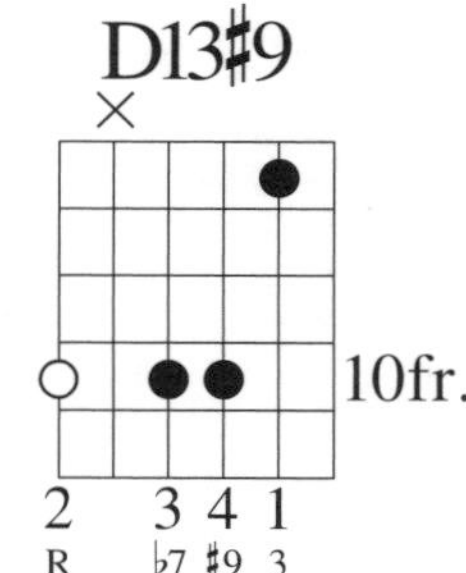

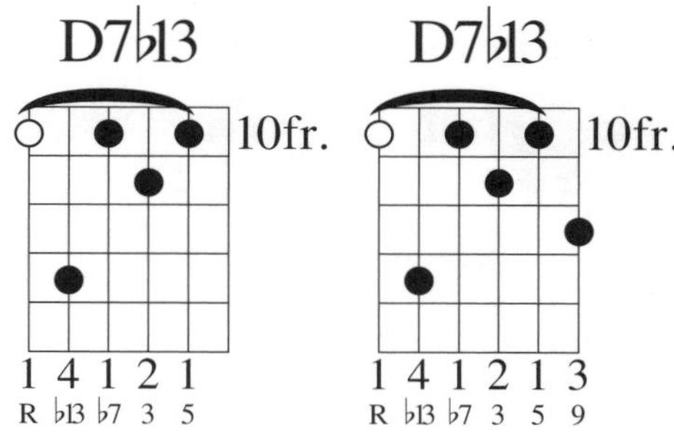

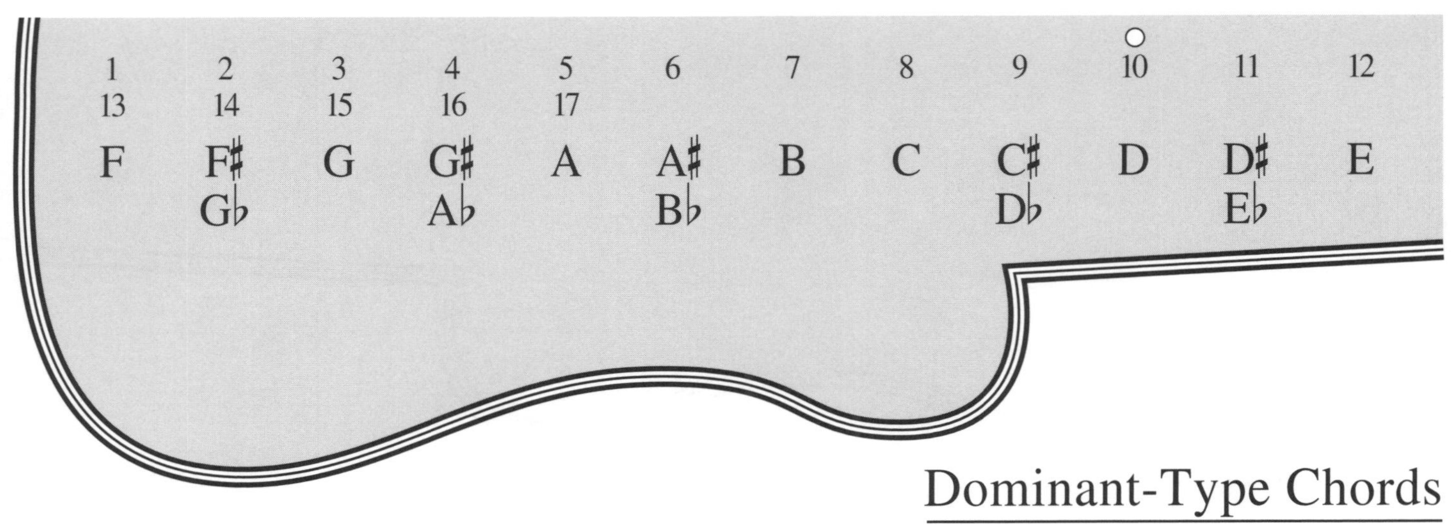

Dominant-Type Chords

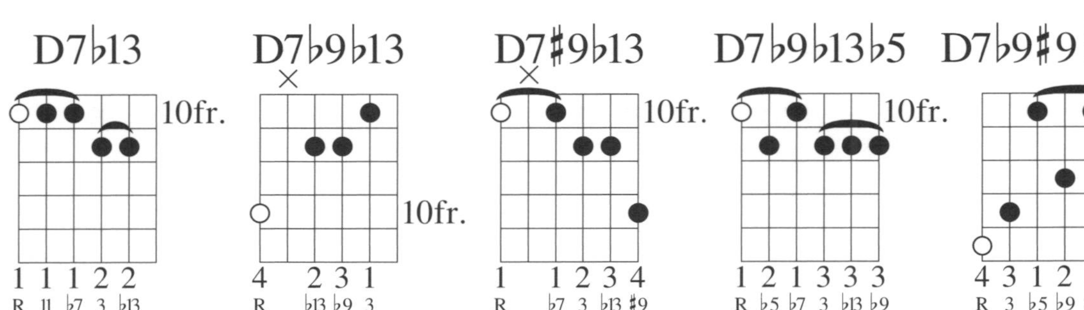

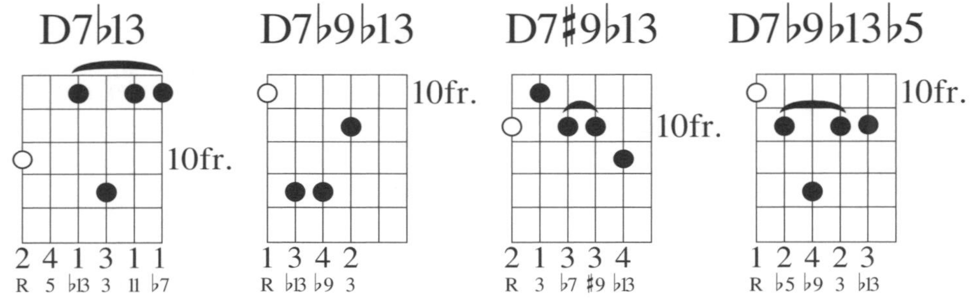

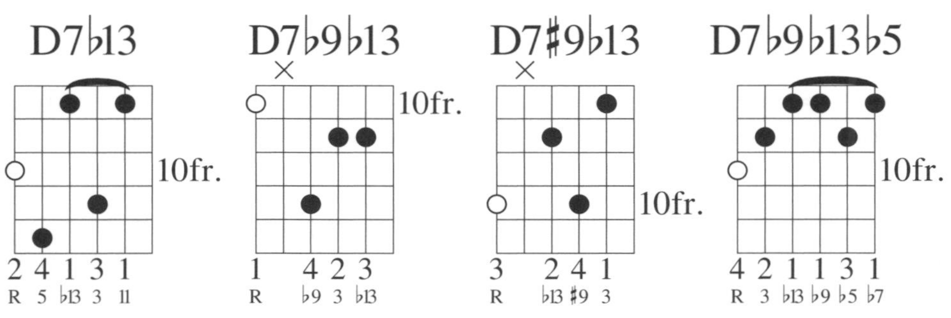

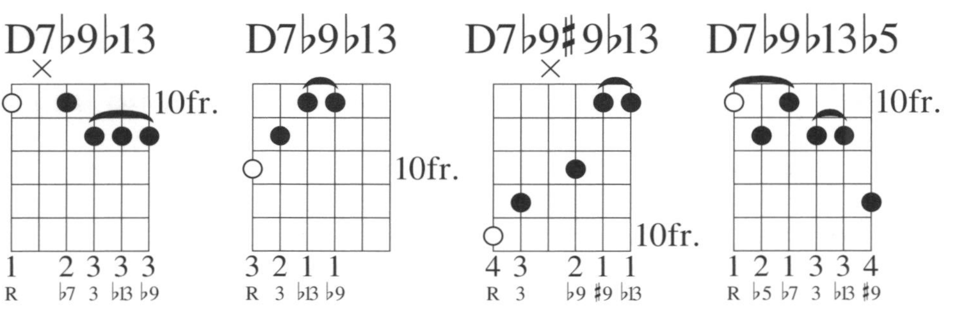

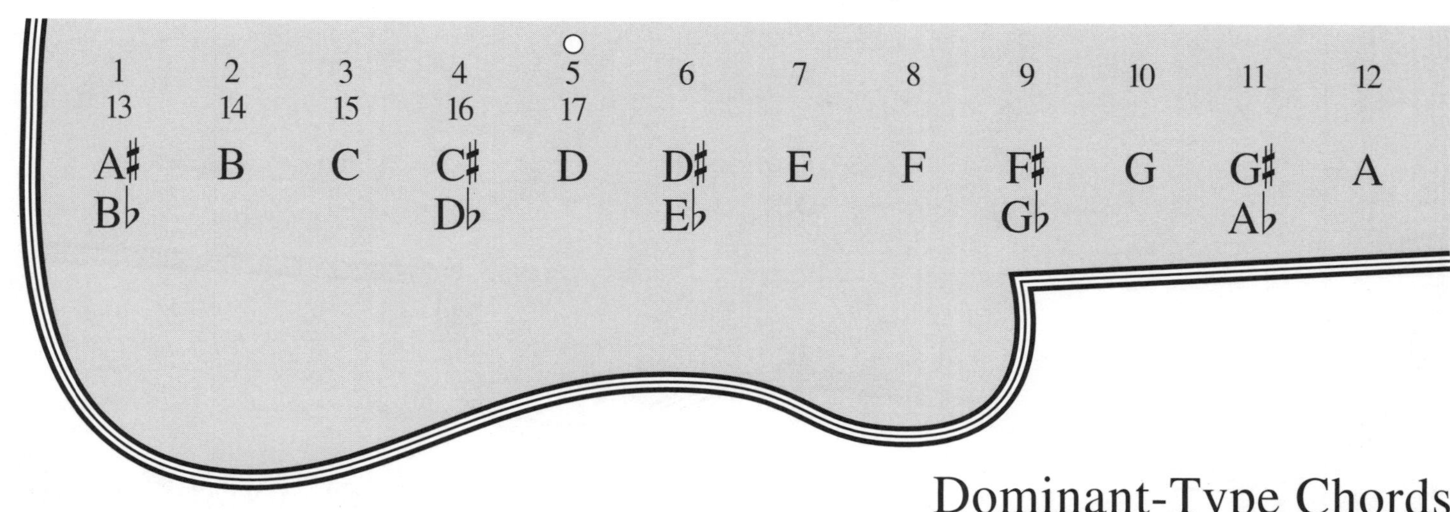

Dominant-Type Chords

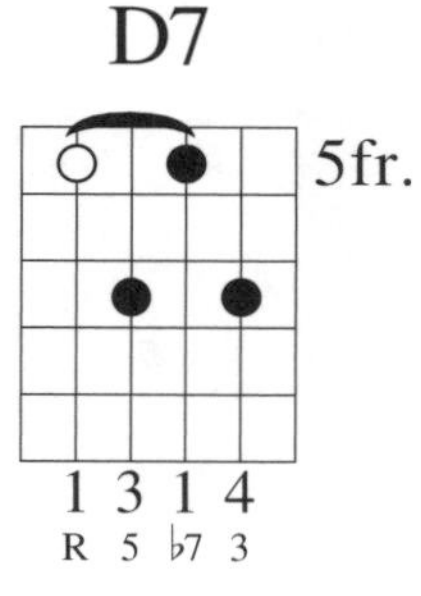

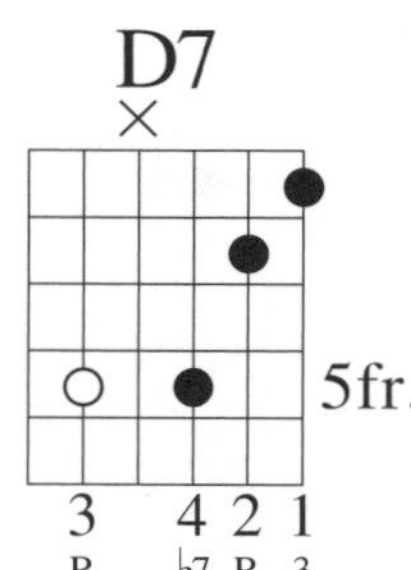

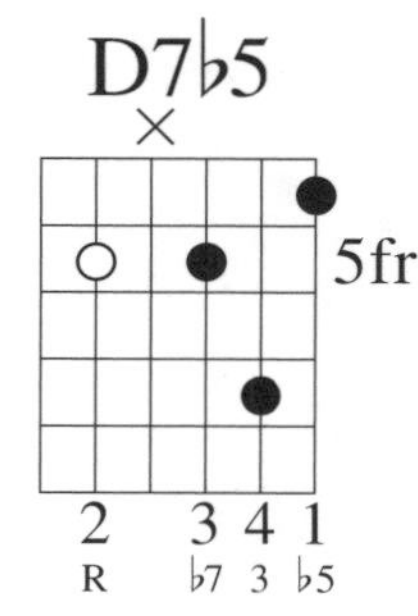

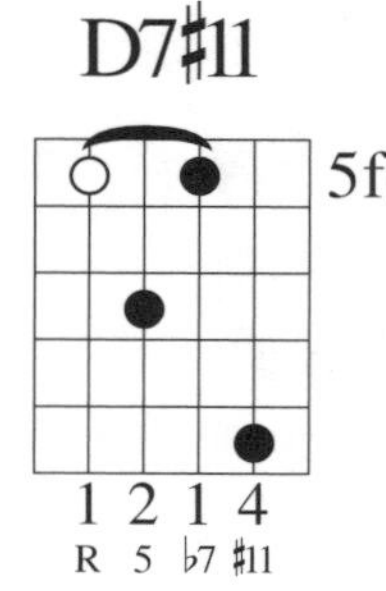

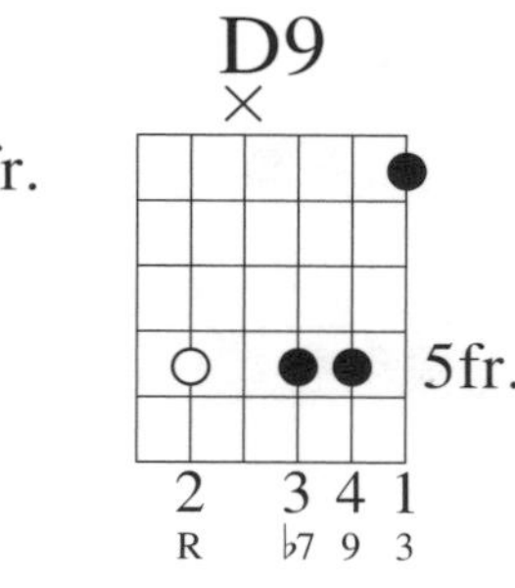

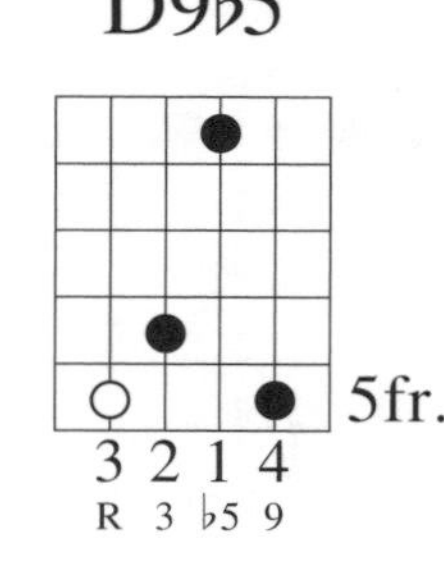

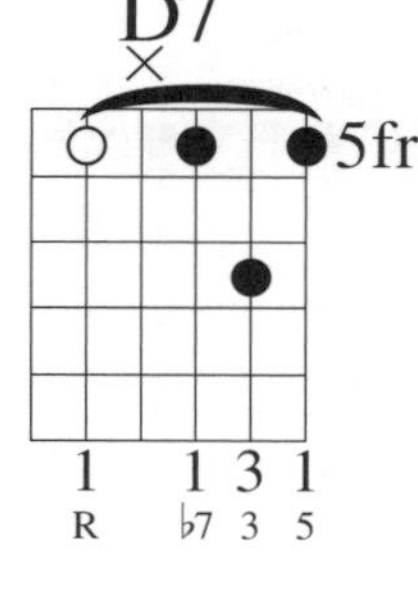

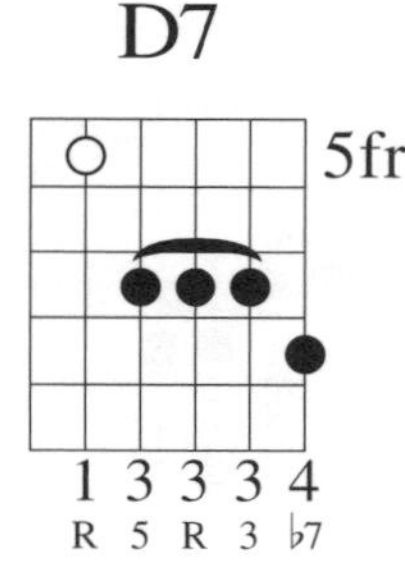

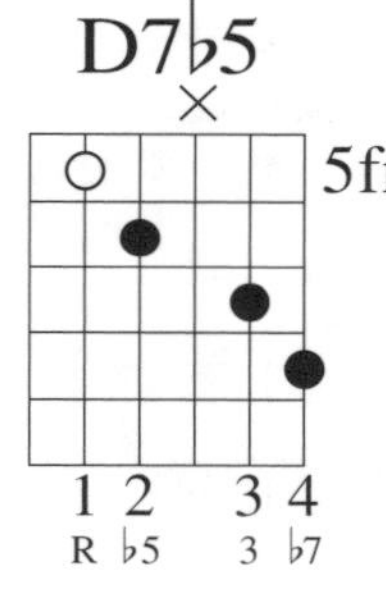

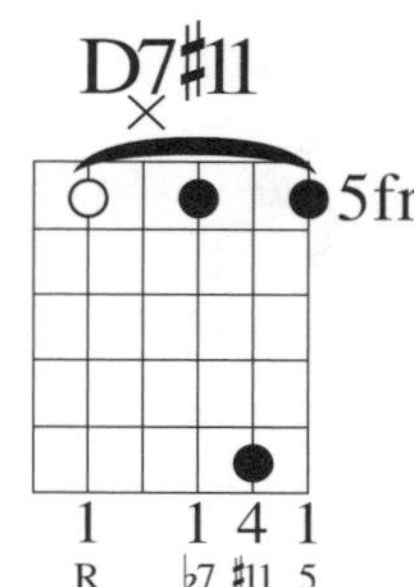

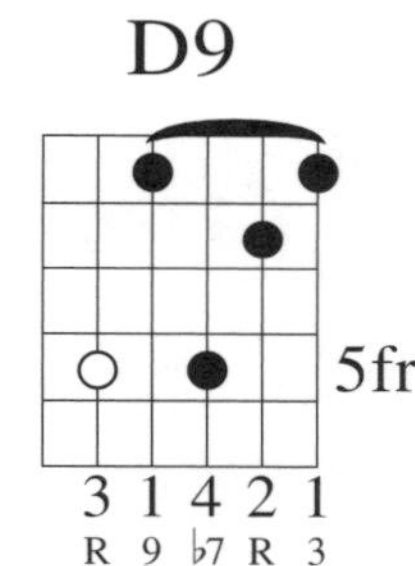

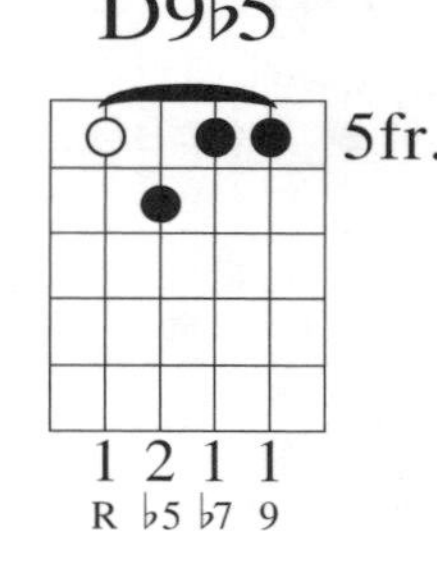

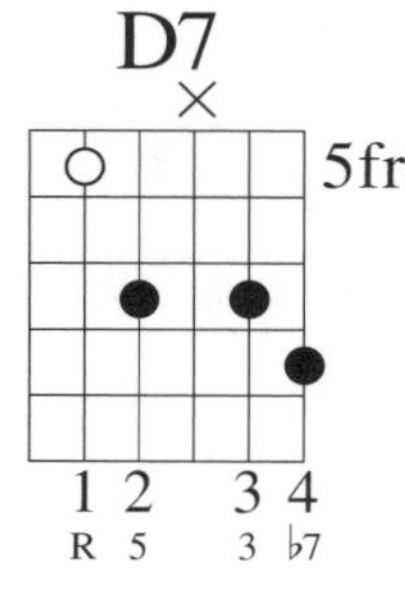

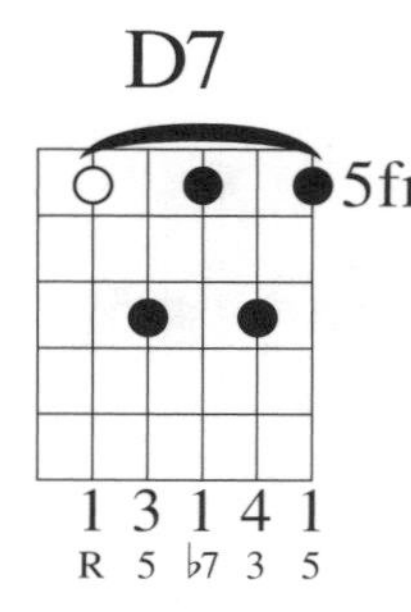

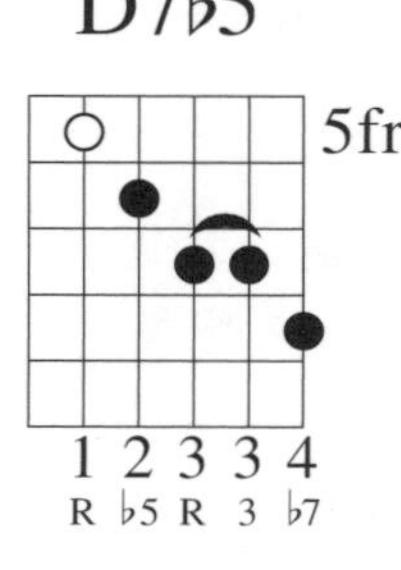

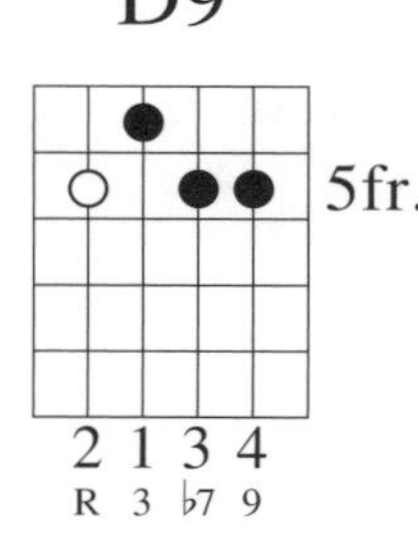

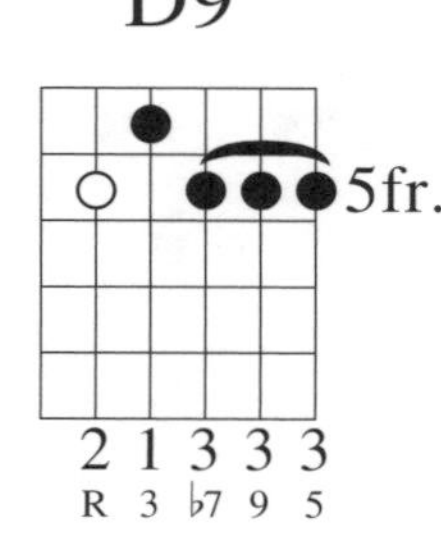

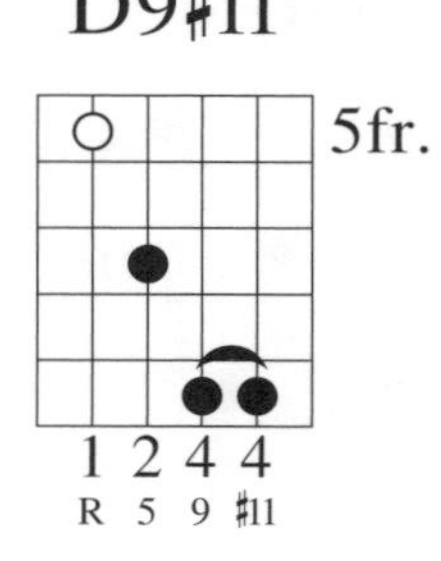

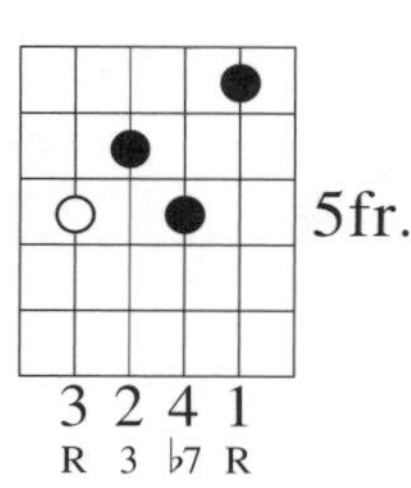

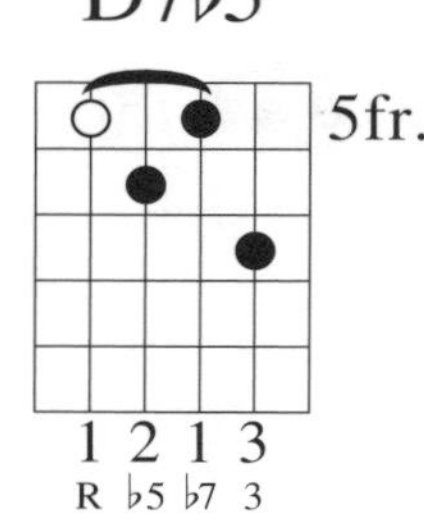

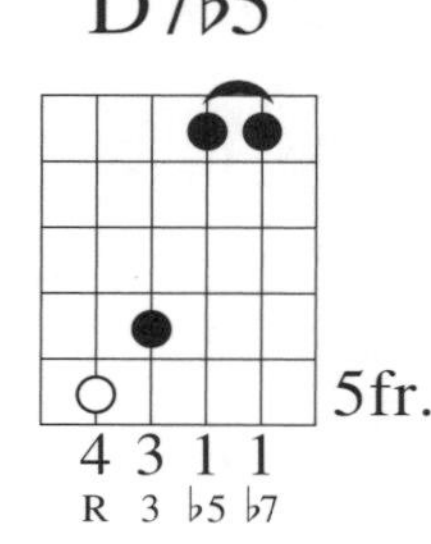

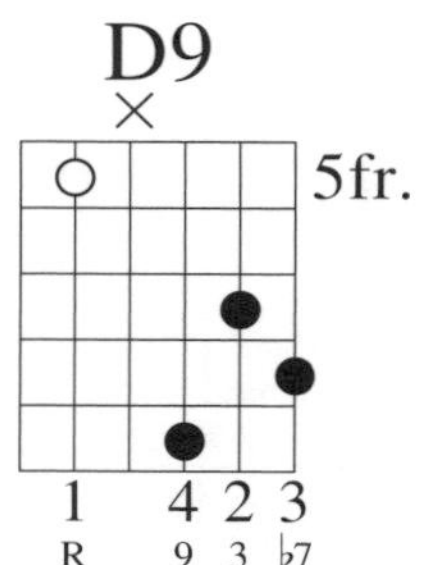

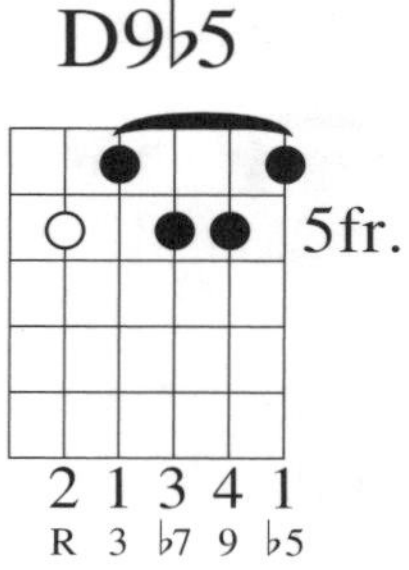

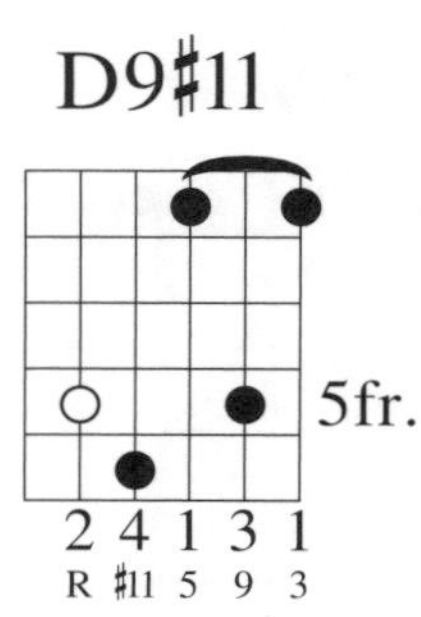

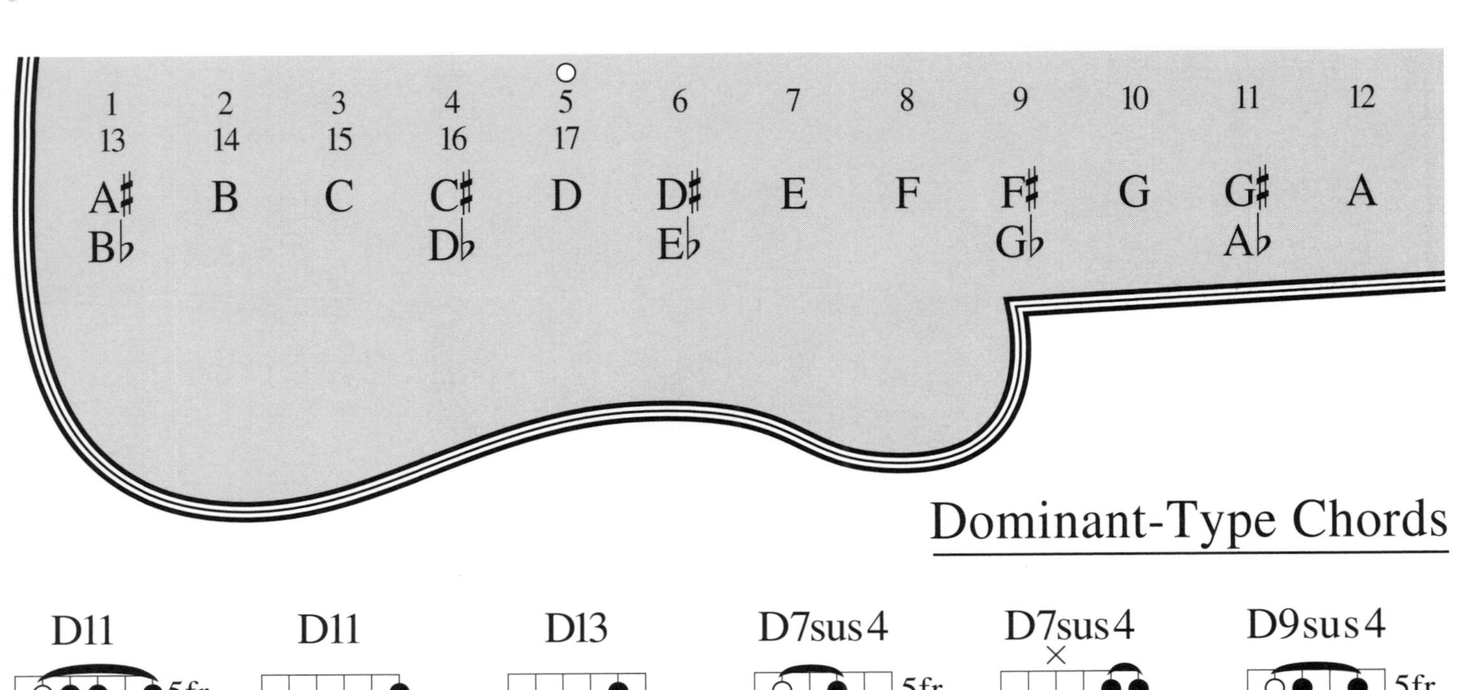

Dominant-Type Chords

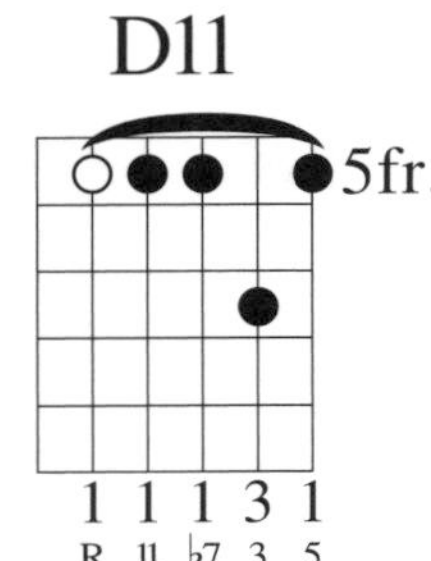

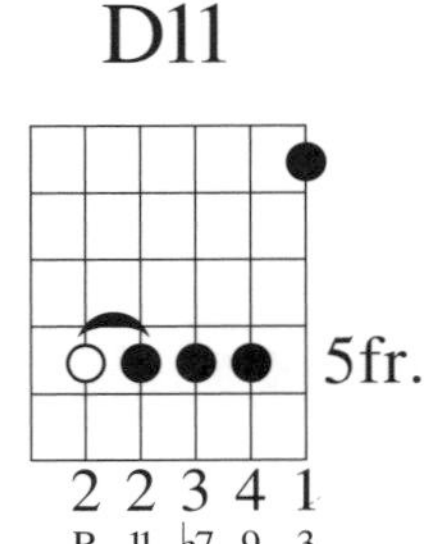

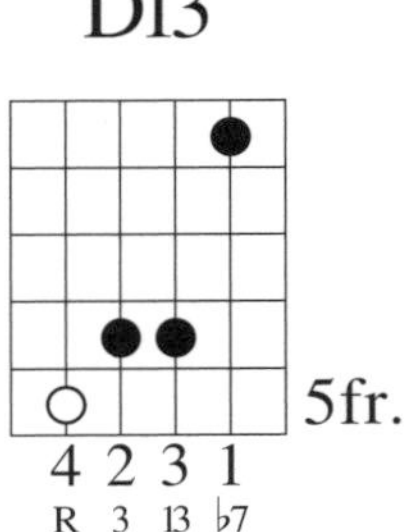

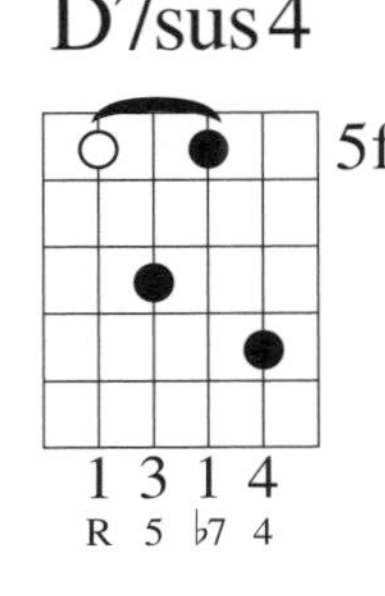

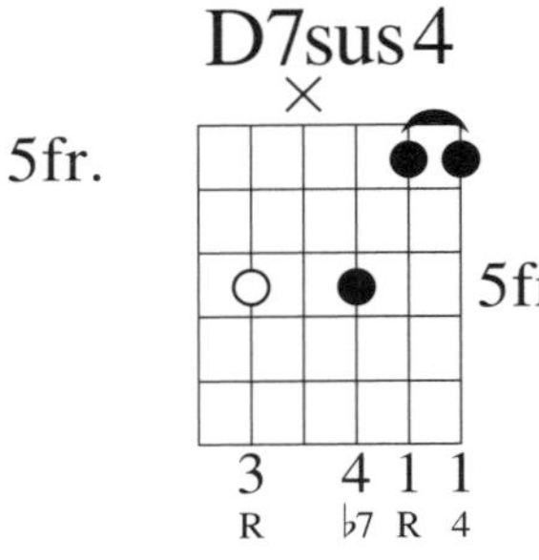

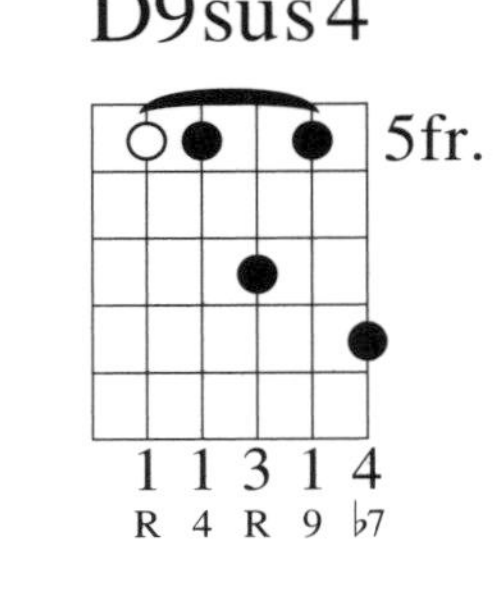

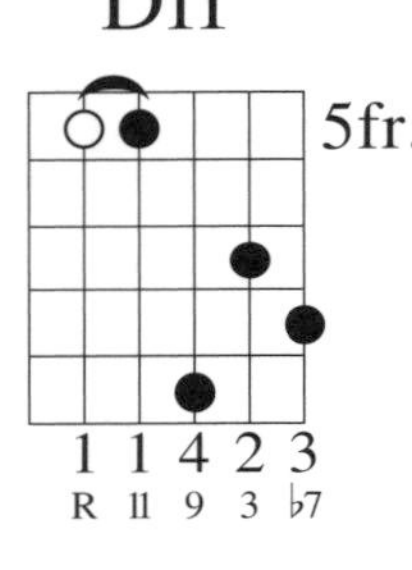

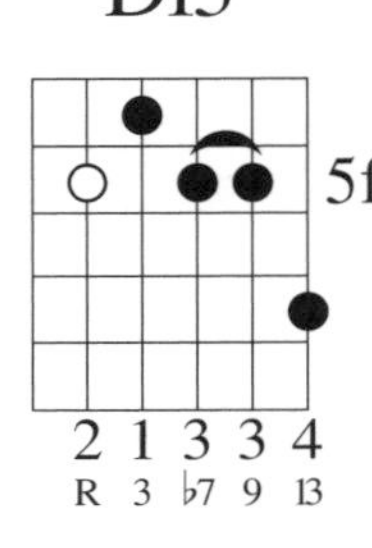

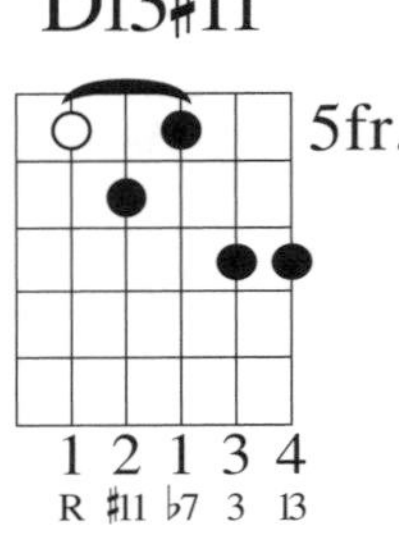

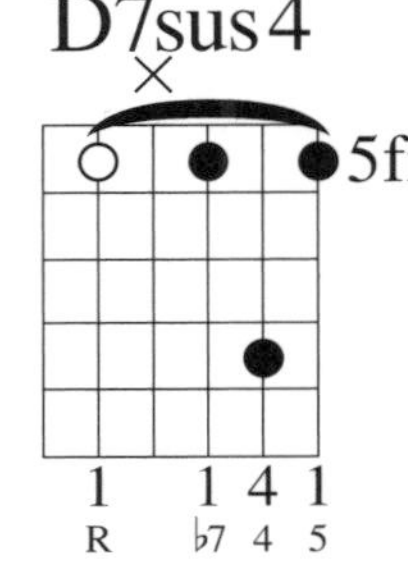

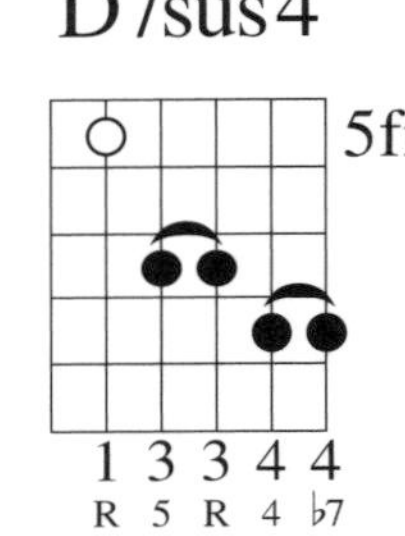

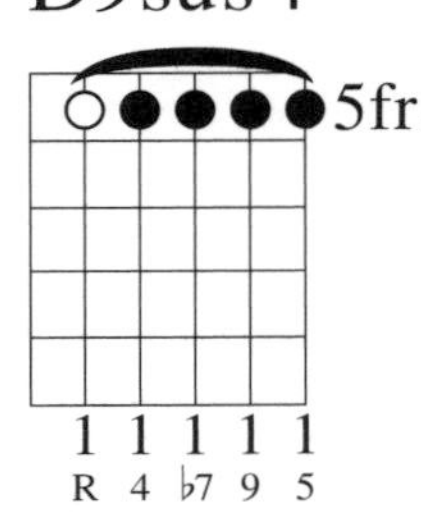

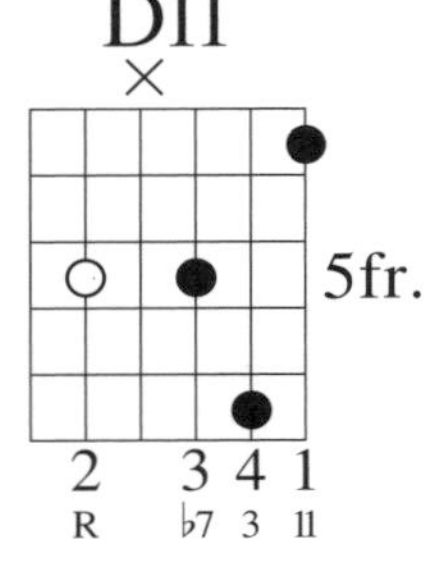

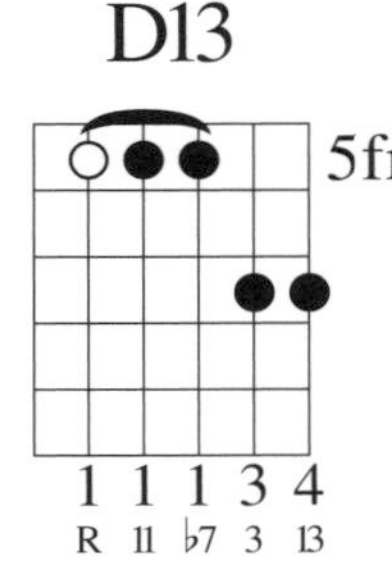

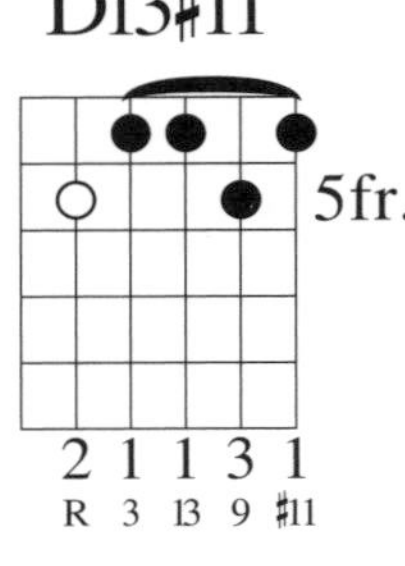

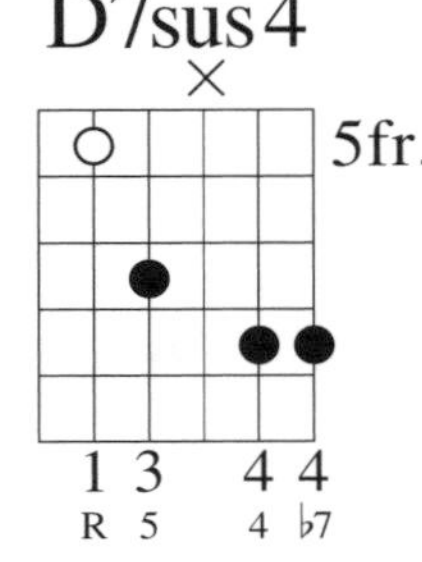

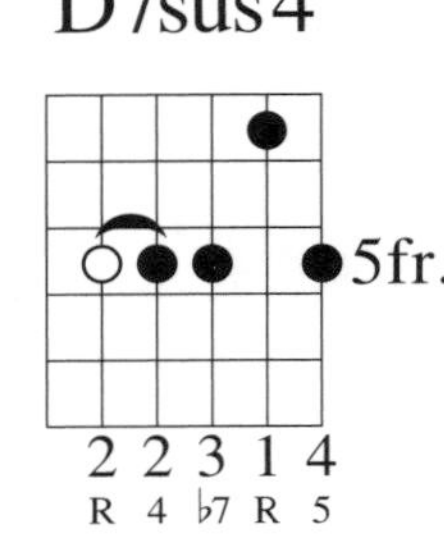

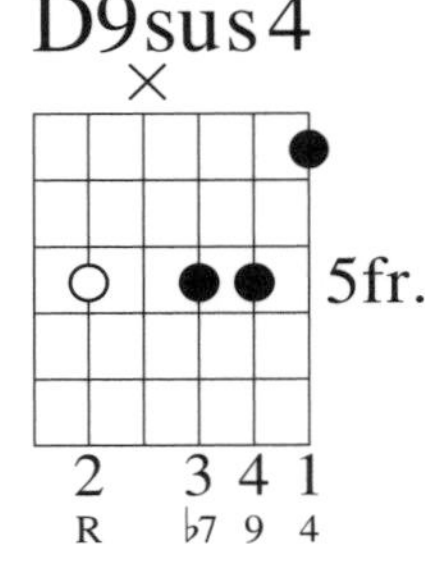

D11

5fr.

3 2 4 1 1

R 3 ♭7 R 11

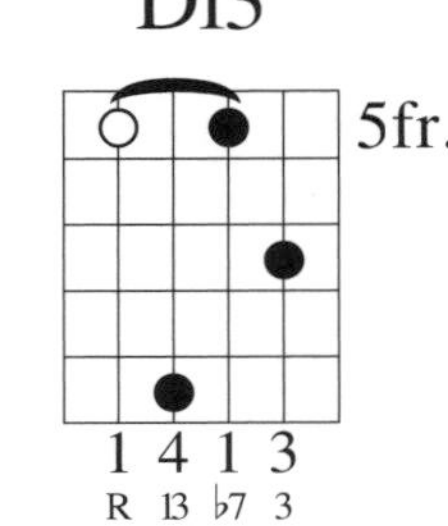

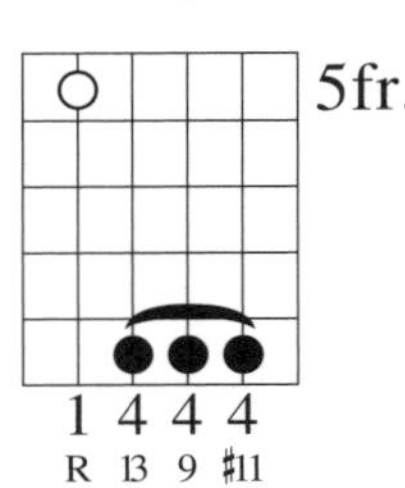

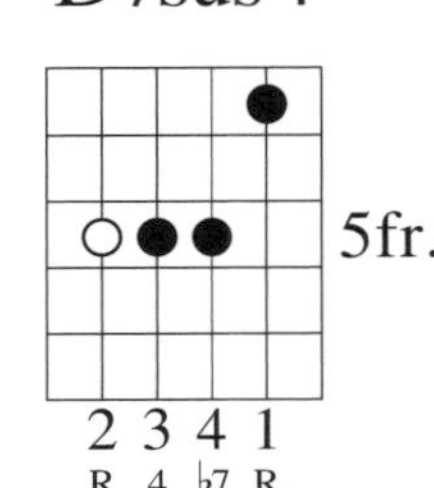

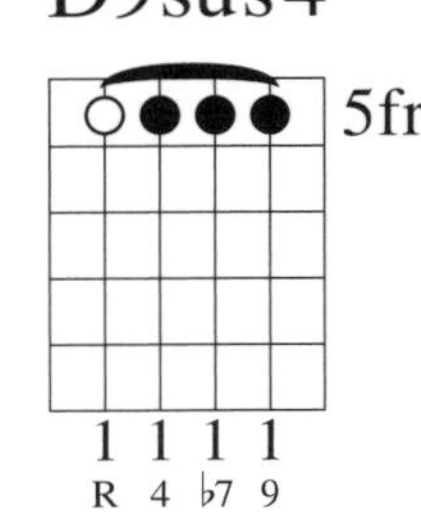

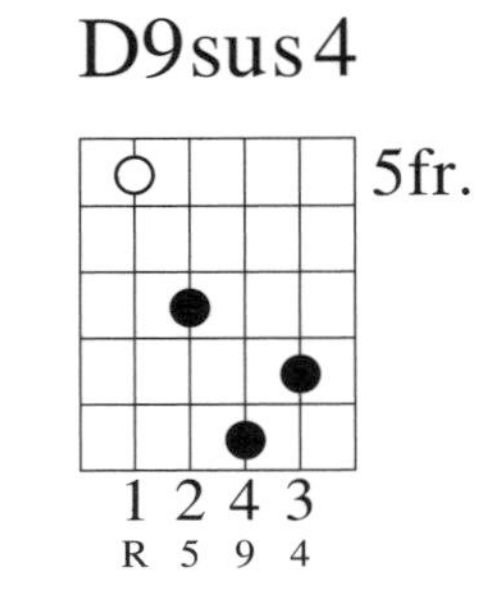

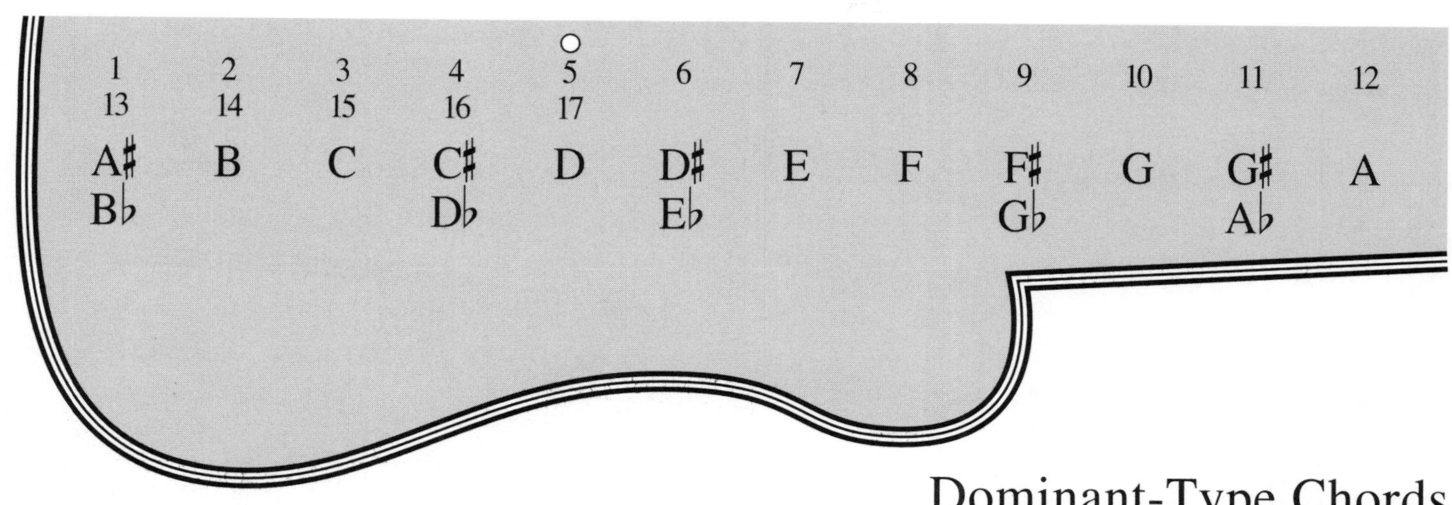

Dominant-Type Chords

D13sus4

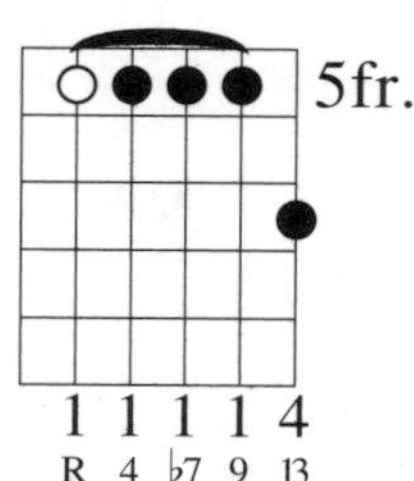

D7sus4♭9

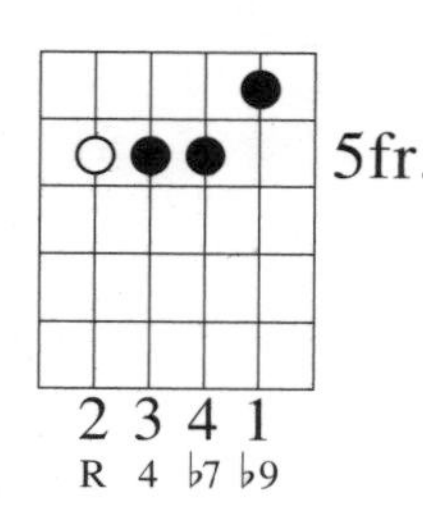

D7sus4♭9

D7sus4♭9♭13

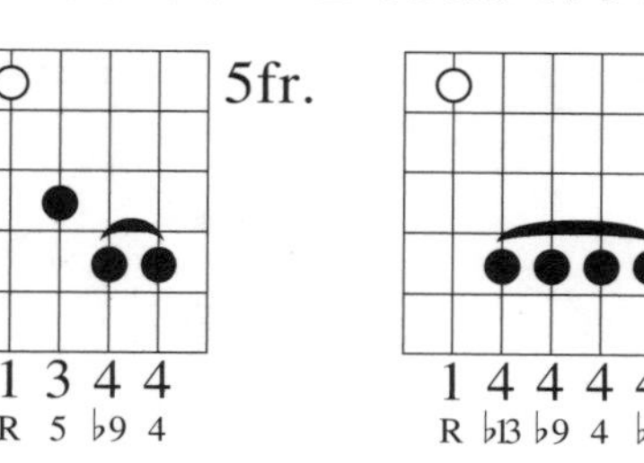

D7♯5

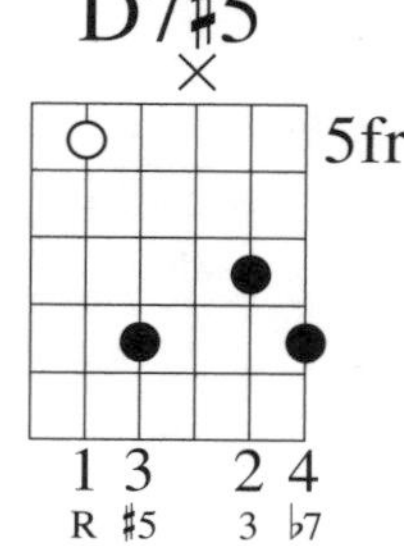

D9♯5

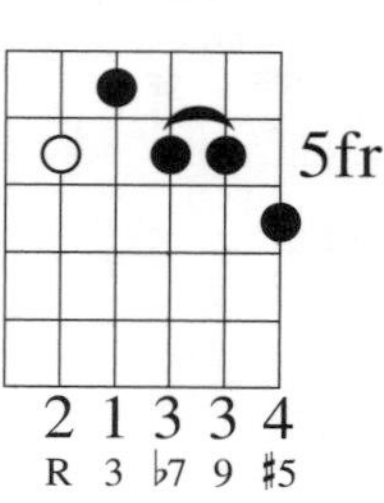

D13sus4

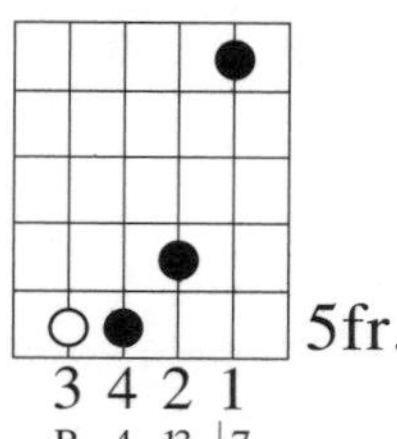

D7sus4♭9

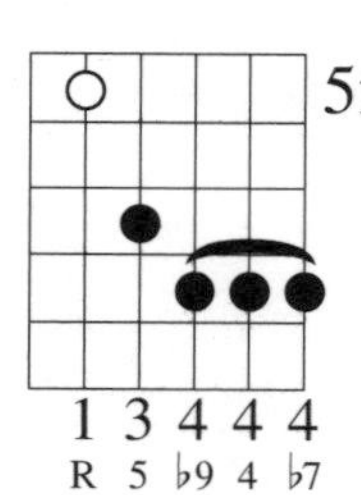

D7sus4♭9

D7sus4♭9♭13

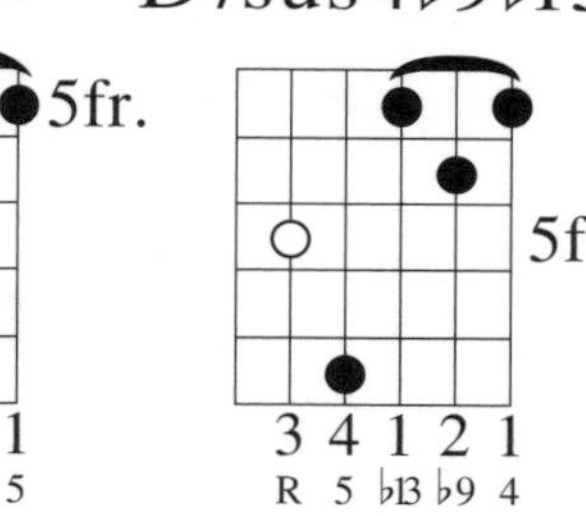

D7♯5

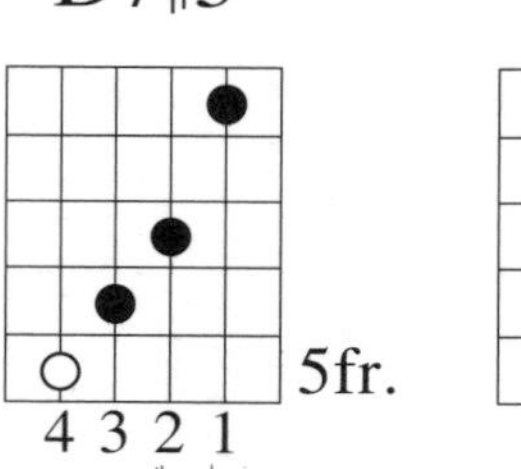

D9♯5

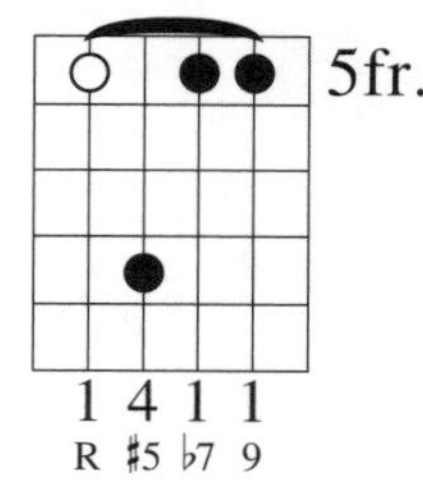

D13sus4

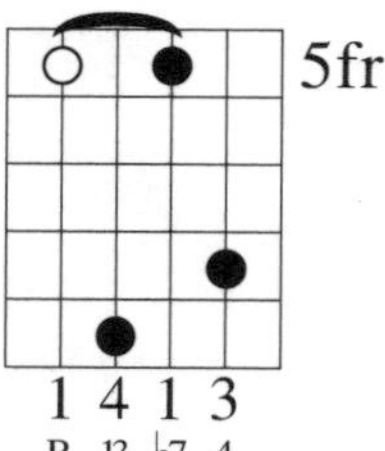

D7sus4♭9

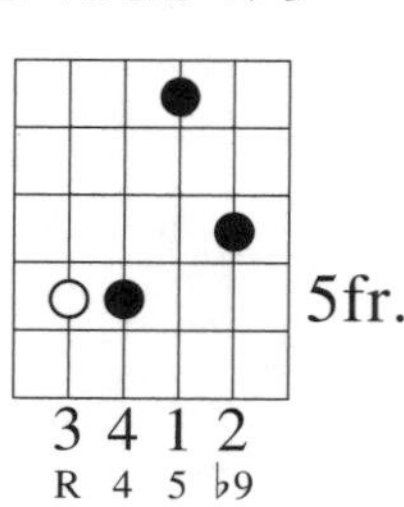

D13sus4♭9

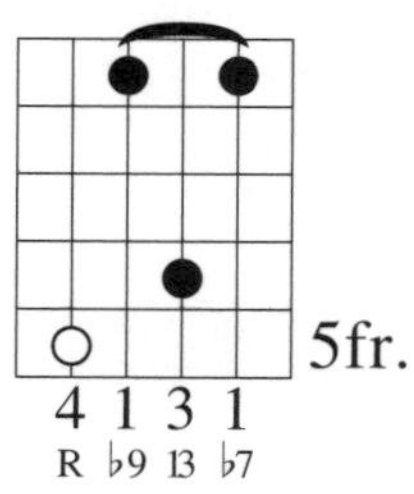

D7♯5

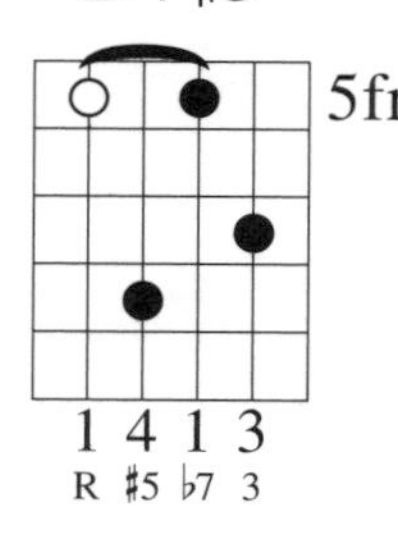

D7♯5♯11

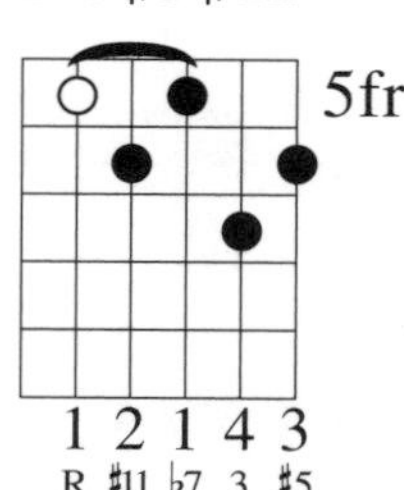

D9♯5

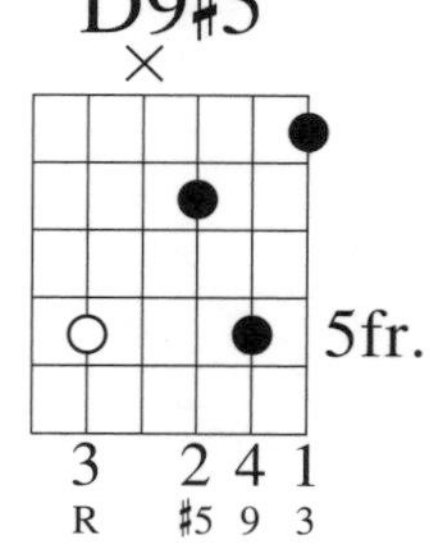

D13sus4

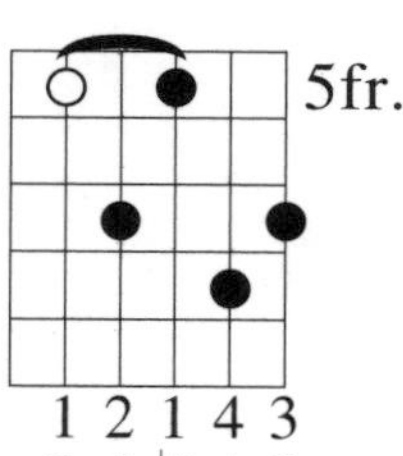

D7sus4♭9

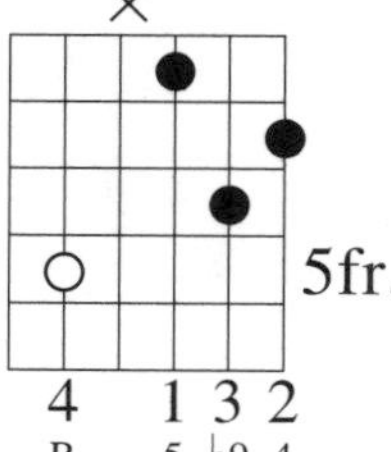

D13sus4♭9

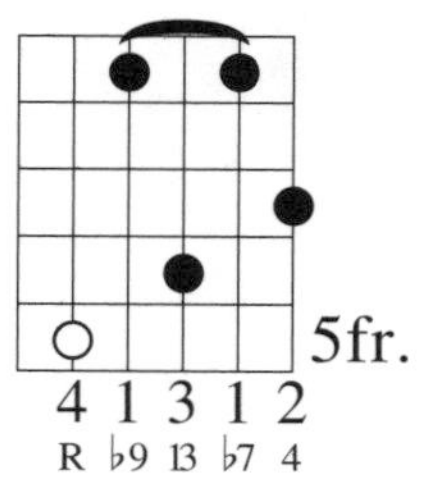

D7♯5

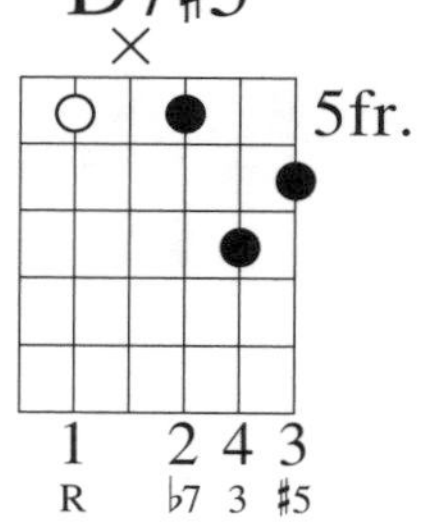

D7♯5♯11

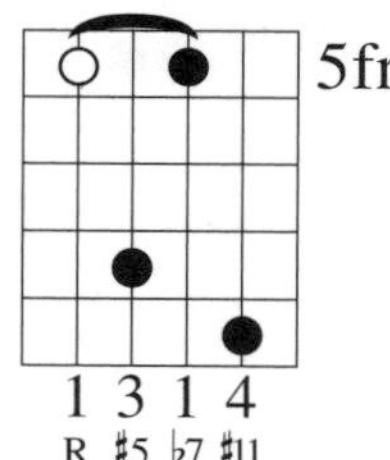

D9♯5♯11

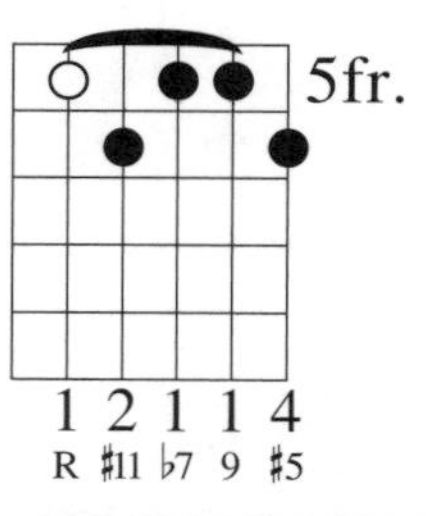

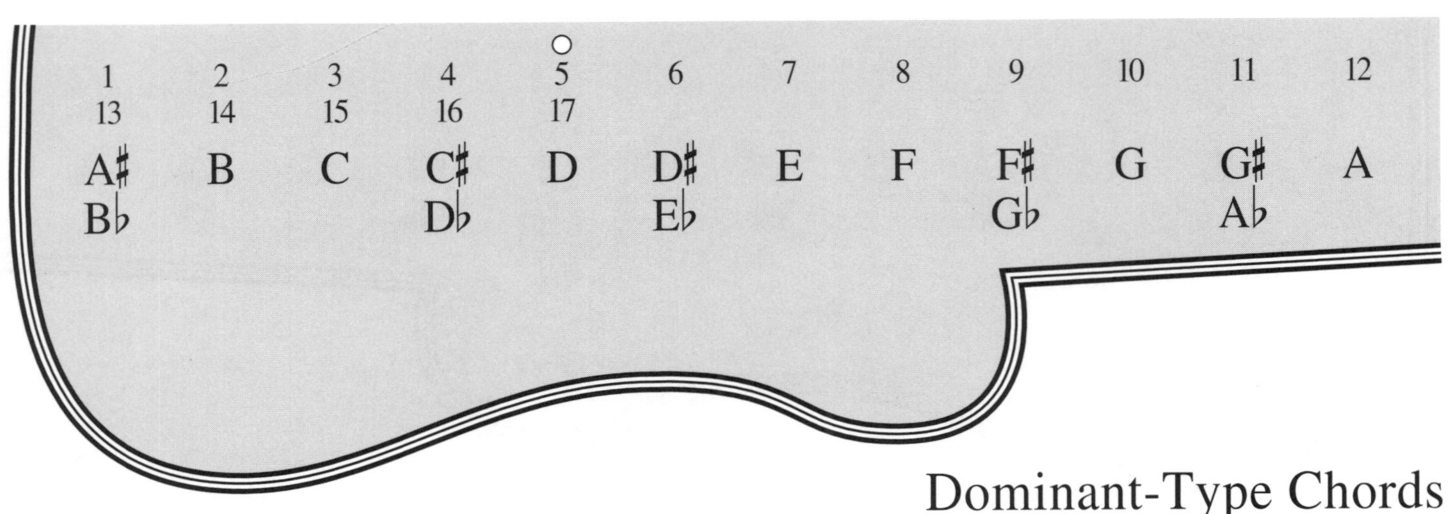

Dominant-Type Chords

D7♭9
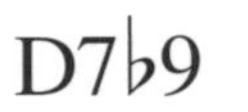
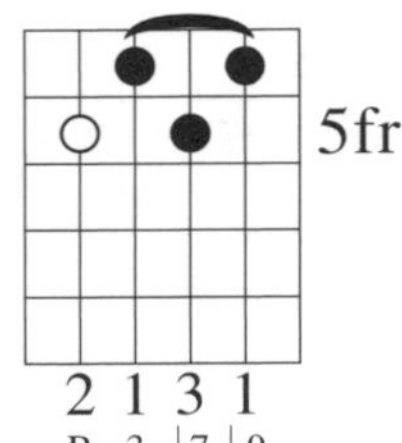

D7♯9
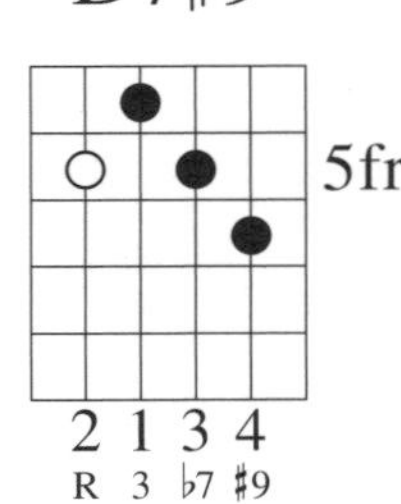

D7♭9♯9
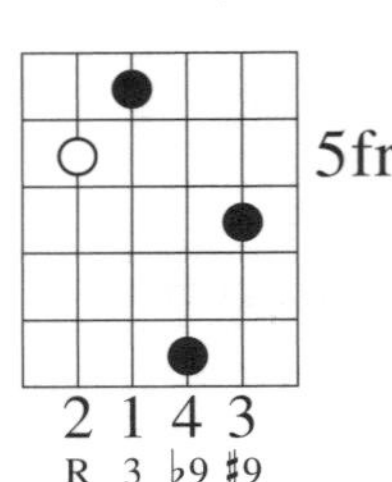

D7♯9♯11
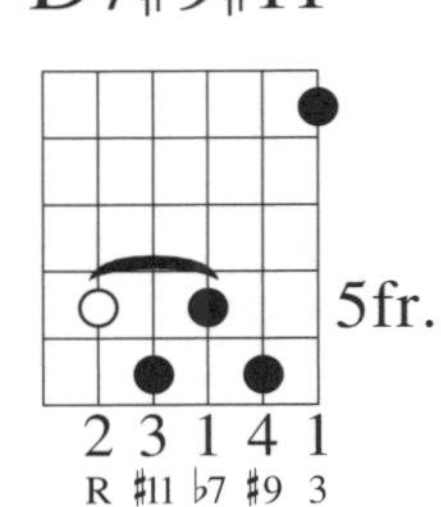

D13♭9
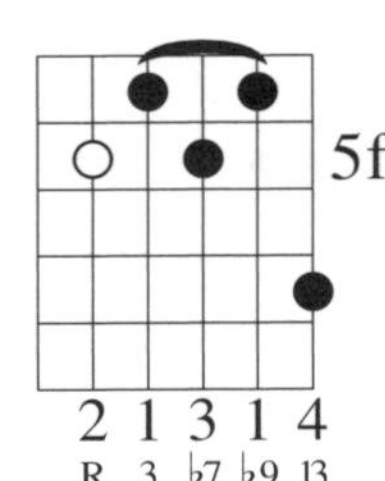

D13♭9
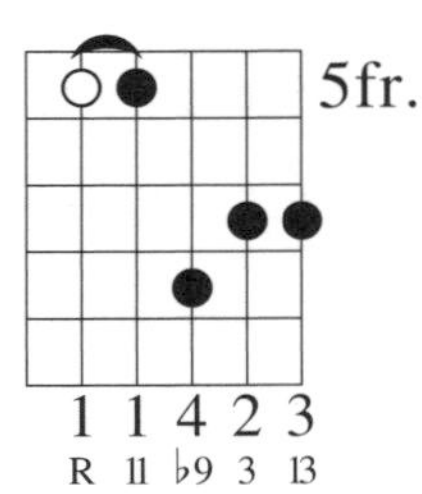

D7♭9
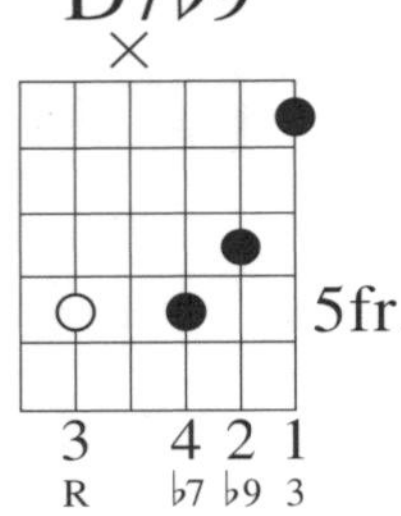

D7♯9
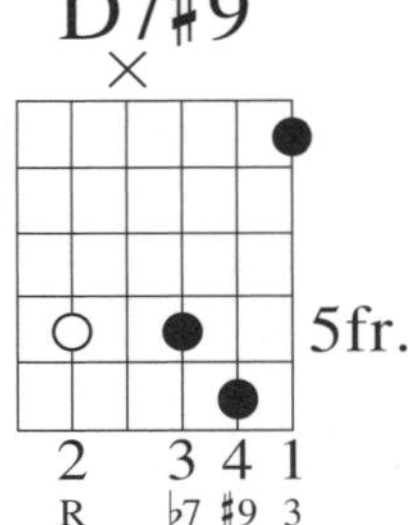

D7♭9♯11
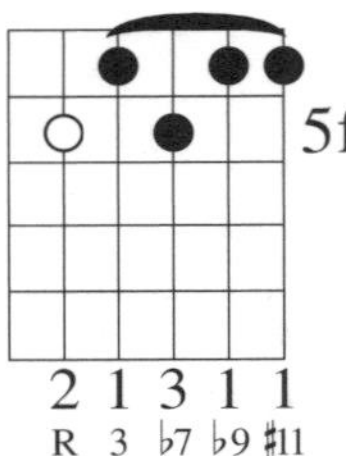

D7♭9♯9♯11
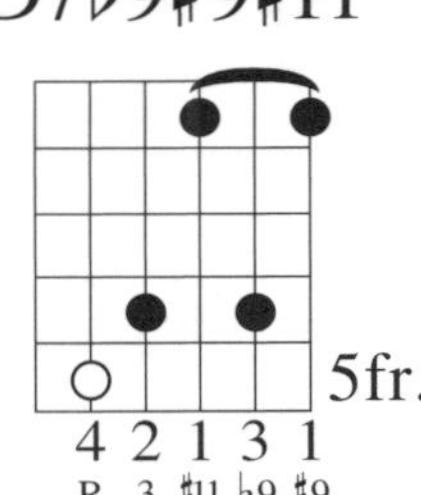

D13♭9
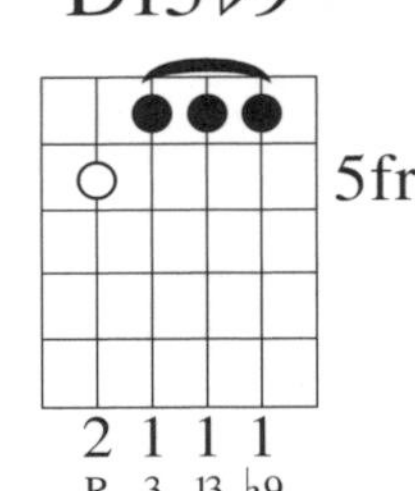

D13♭9♯11
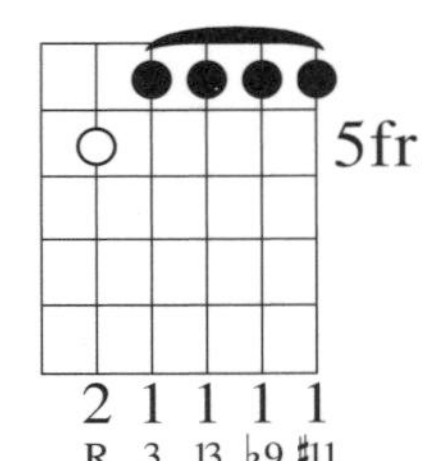

D7♭9
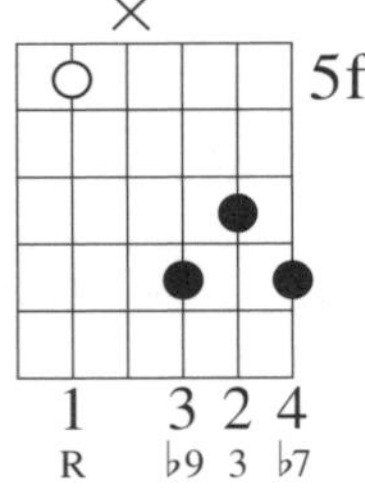

D7♯9
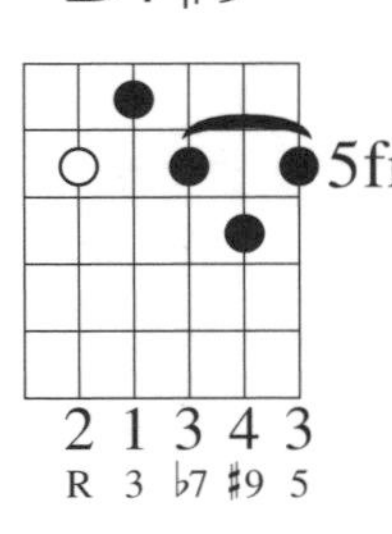

D7♭9♯11
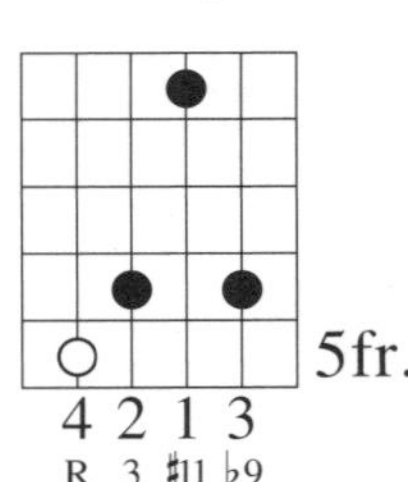

D7♭9♯9♯11
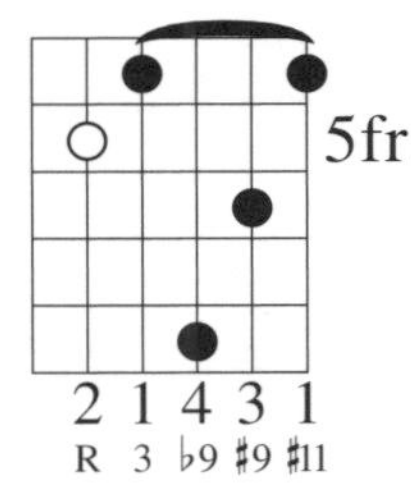

D13♭9
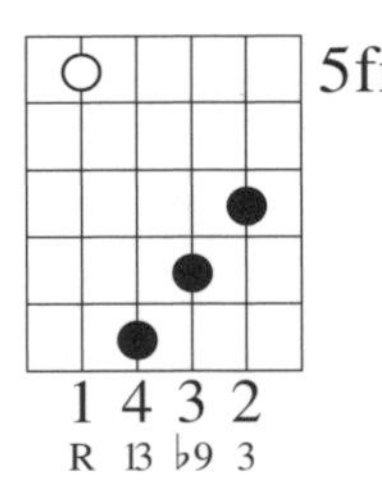

D13♭9♯11
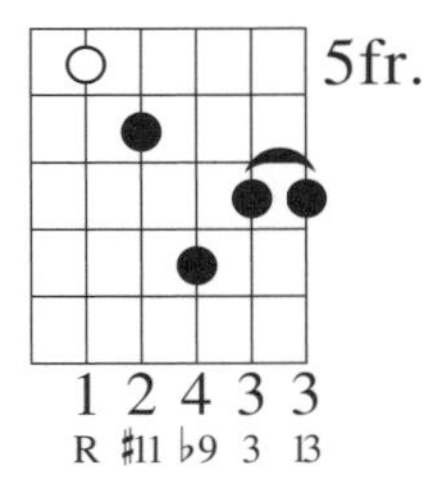

D7♭9
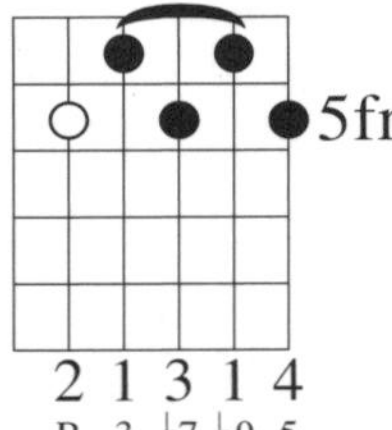

D7♯9
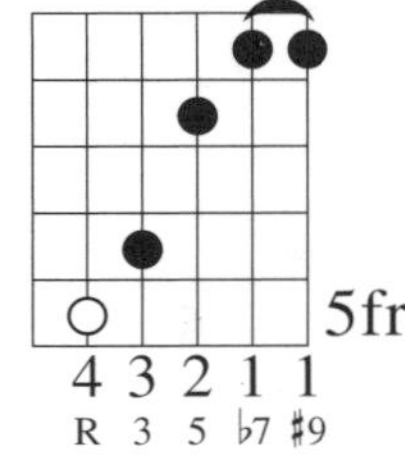

D7♯9♯11
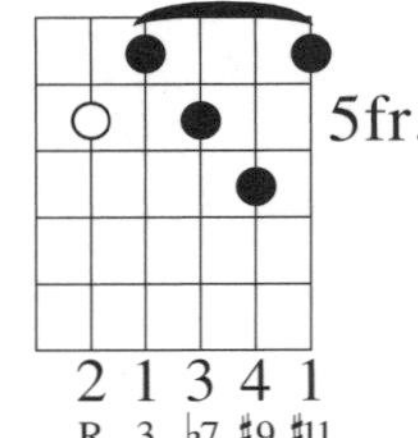

D11♭9
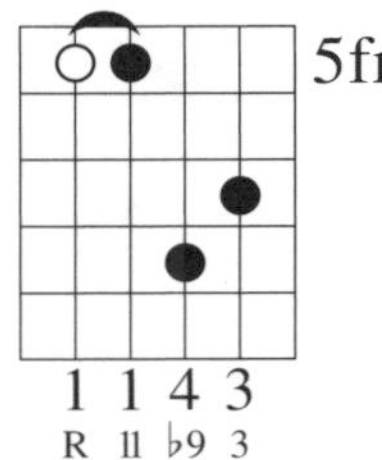

D13♭9
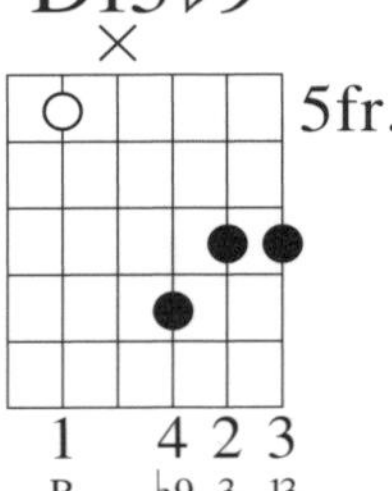

D13♯9
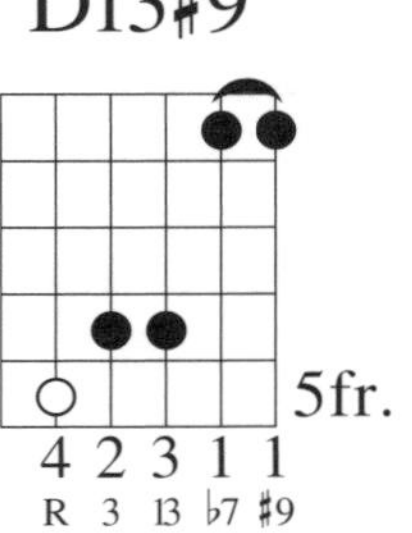

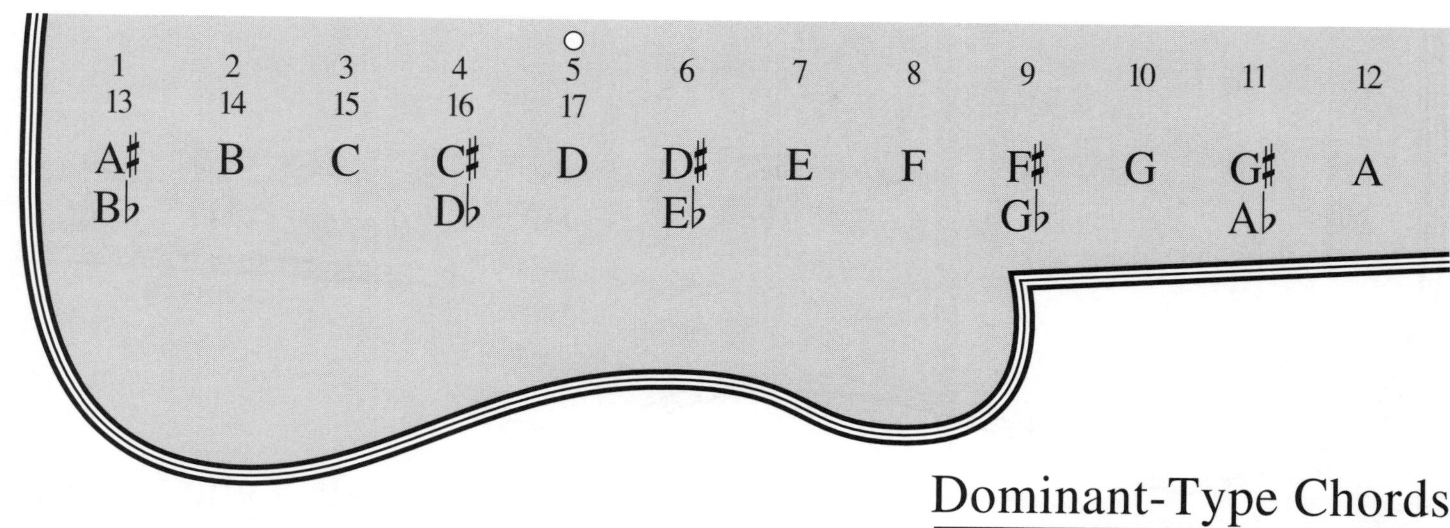

Dominant-Type Chords

D13♯9

D7♭9♭13

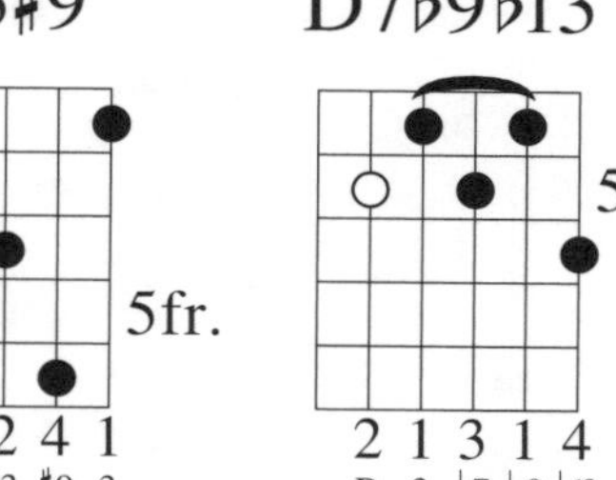

D7♯9♭13

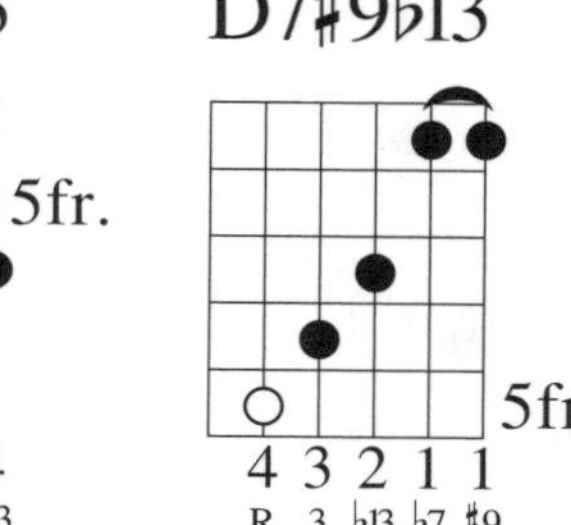

D7♭9♯9♭13

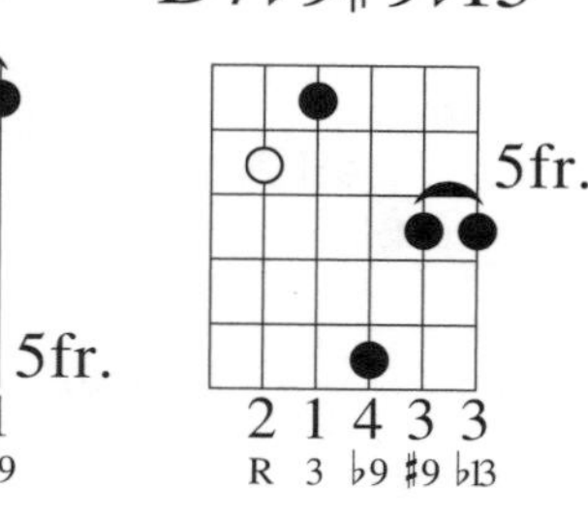

D13♭9♯9

5fr.
4 2 2 3 1
R 3 13 ♭9 ♯9

D7♭9♭13

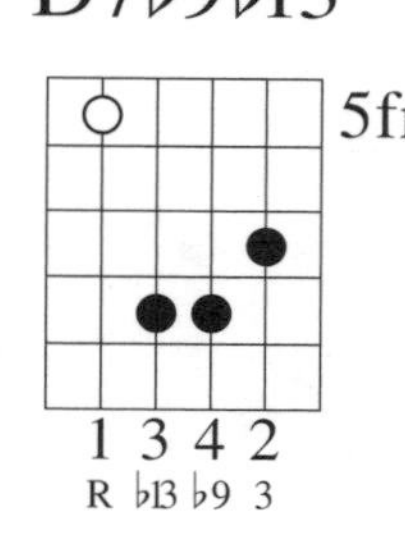

D7♯9♭13

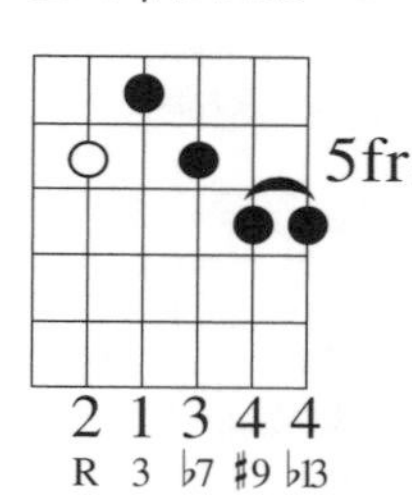

D7♯9♭13♭5

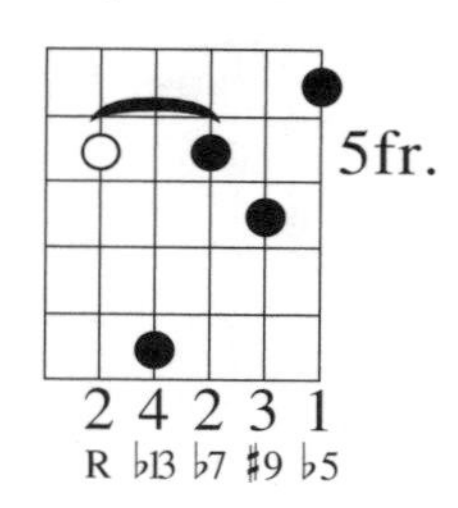

D7♭13

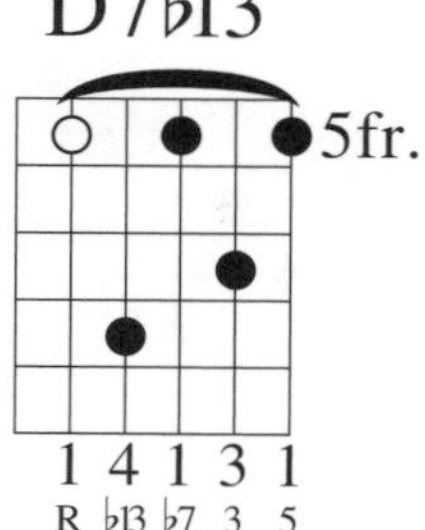

D7♭9♭13

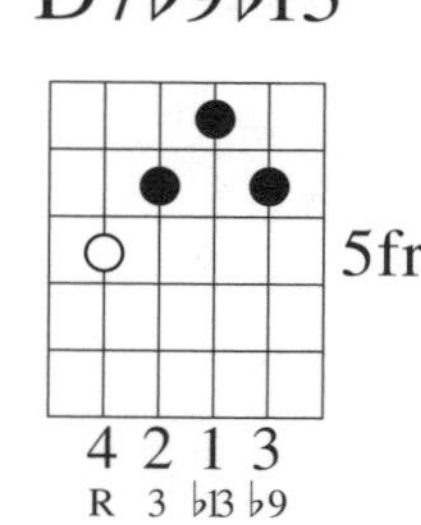

D7♯9♭13

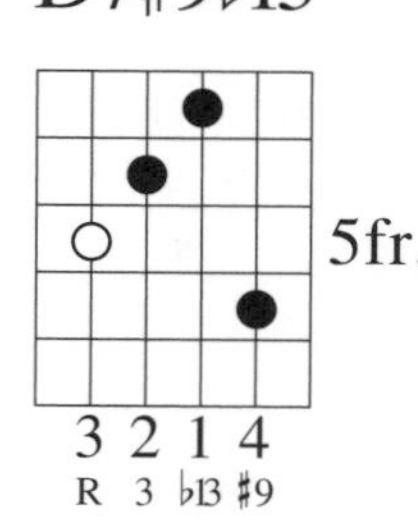

D7♭13

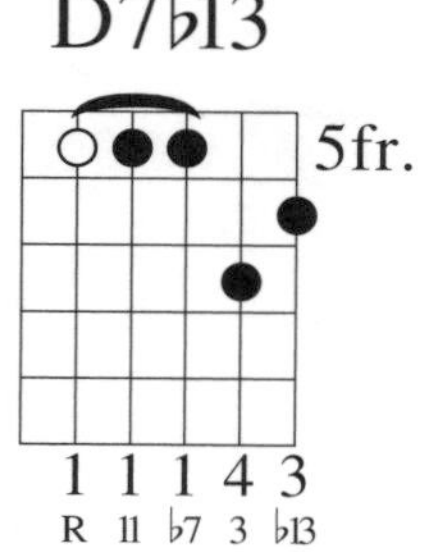

D7♭9♭13

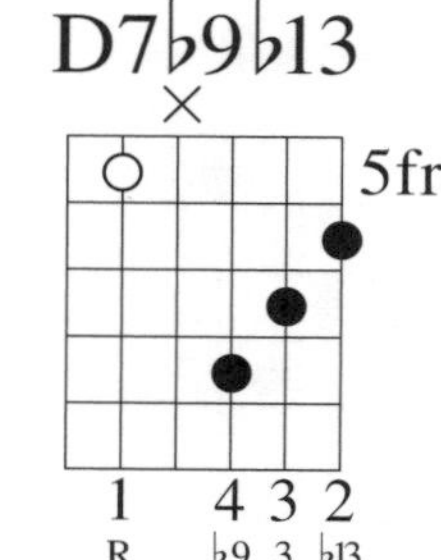

D7♯9♭13

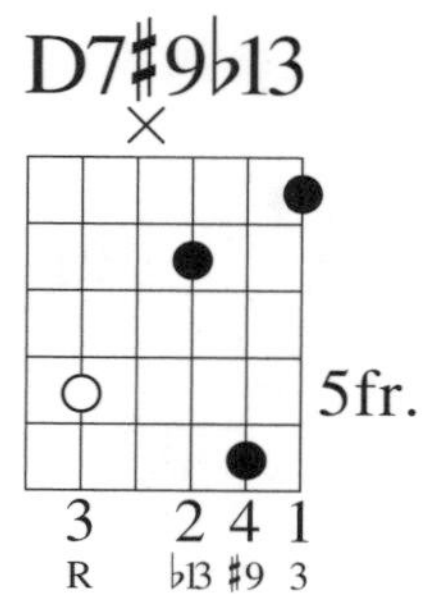

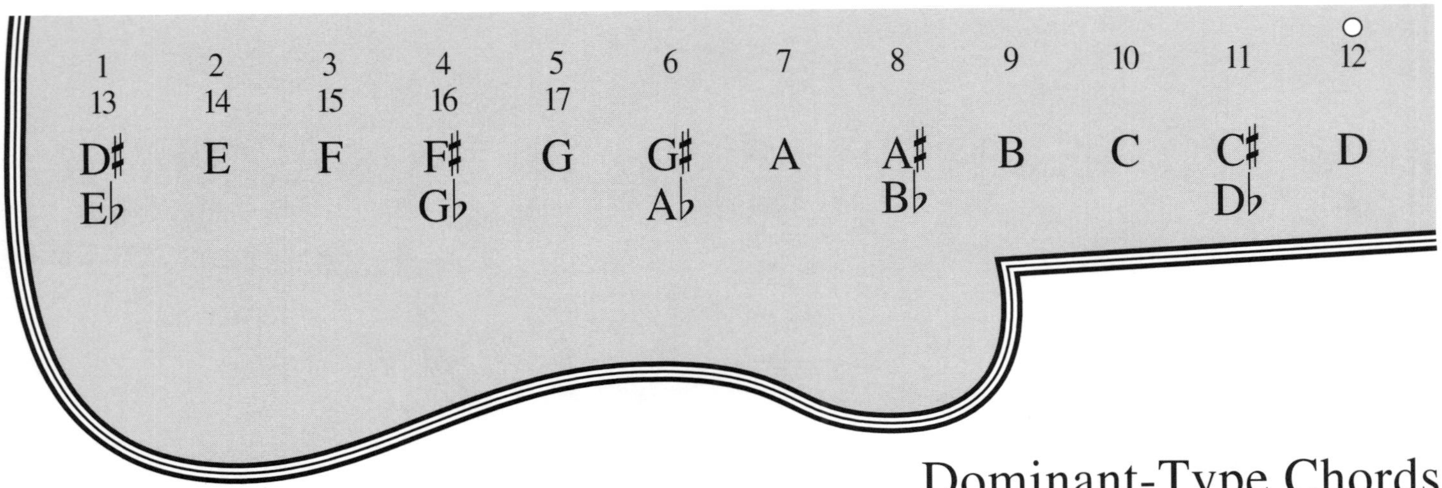

1 13	2 14	3 15	4 16	5 17	6	7	8	9	10	11	12
D♯ E♭	E	F	F♯ G♭	G	G♯ A♭	A	A♯ B♭	B	C	C♯ D♭	D

Dominant-Type Chords

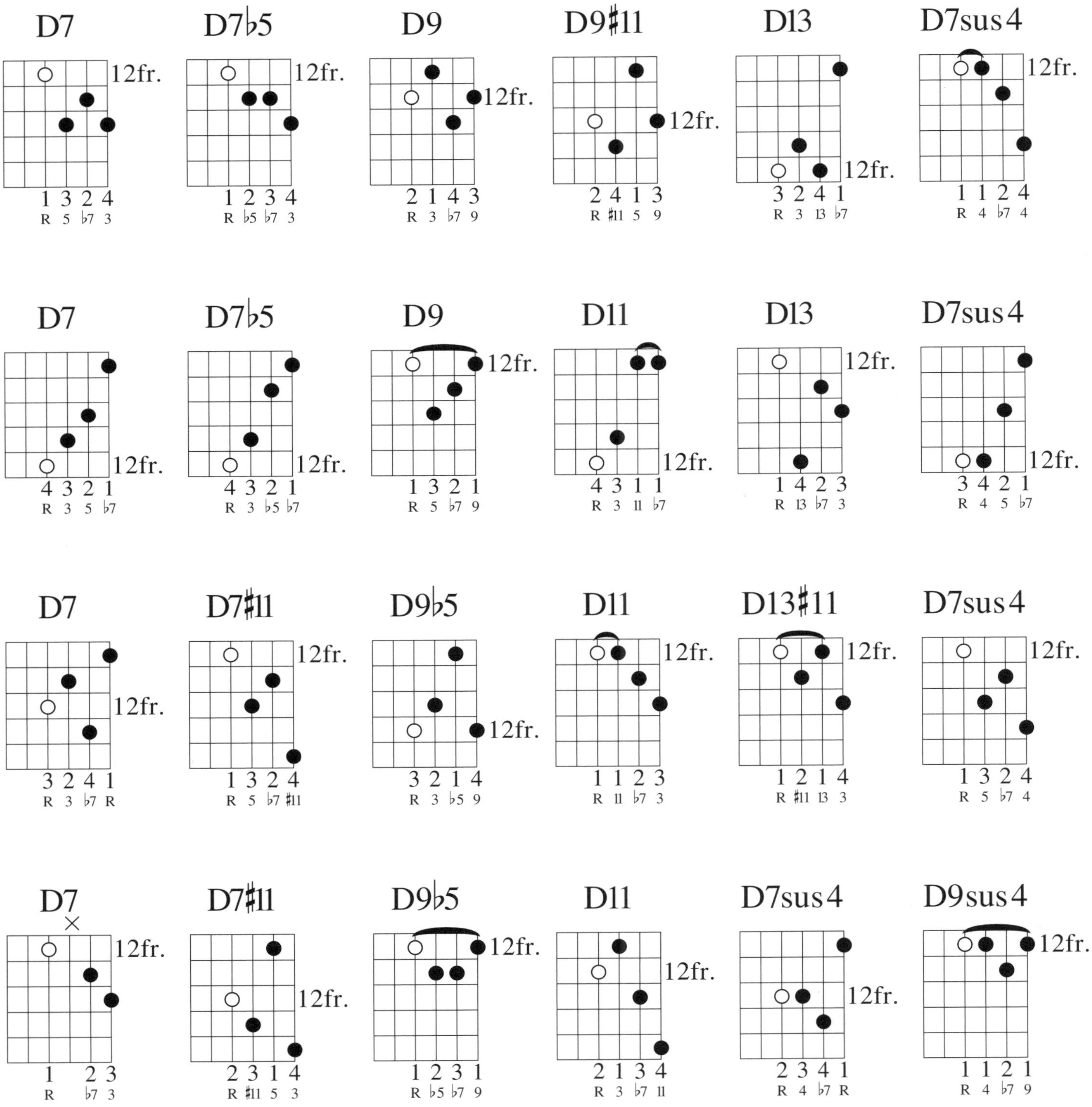

D7
12fr.
1 3 2 4
R 5 ♭7 3

D7♭5
12fr.
1 2 3 4
R ♭5 ♭7 3

D9
12fr.
2 1 4 3
R 3 ♭7 9

D9♯11
12fr.
2 4 1 3
R ♯11 5 9

D13
12fr.
3 2 4 1
R 3 13 ♭7

D7sus4
12fr.
1 1 2 4
R 4 ♭7 4

D7
12fr.
4 3 2 1
R 3 5 ♭7

D7♭5
12fr.
4 3 2 1
R 3 ♭5 ♭7

D9
12fr.
1 3 2 1
R 5 ♭7 9

D11
12fr.
4 3 1 1
R 3 11 ♭7

D13
12fr.
1 4 2 3
R 13 ♭7 3

D7sus4
12fr.
3 4 2 1
R 4 5 ♭7

D7
12fr.
3 2 4 1
R 3 ♭7 R

D7♯11
12fr.
1 3 2 4
R 5 ♭7 ♯11

D9♭5
12fr.
3 2 1 4
R 3 ♭5 9

D11
12fr.
1 1 2 3
R 11 ♭7 3

D13♯11
12fr.
1 2 1 4
R ♯11 13 3

D7sus4
12fr.
1 3 2 4
R 5 ♭7 4

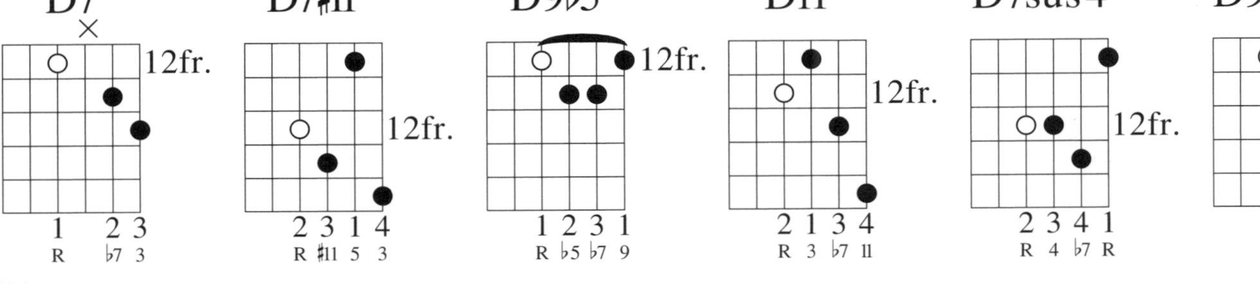

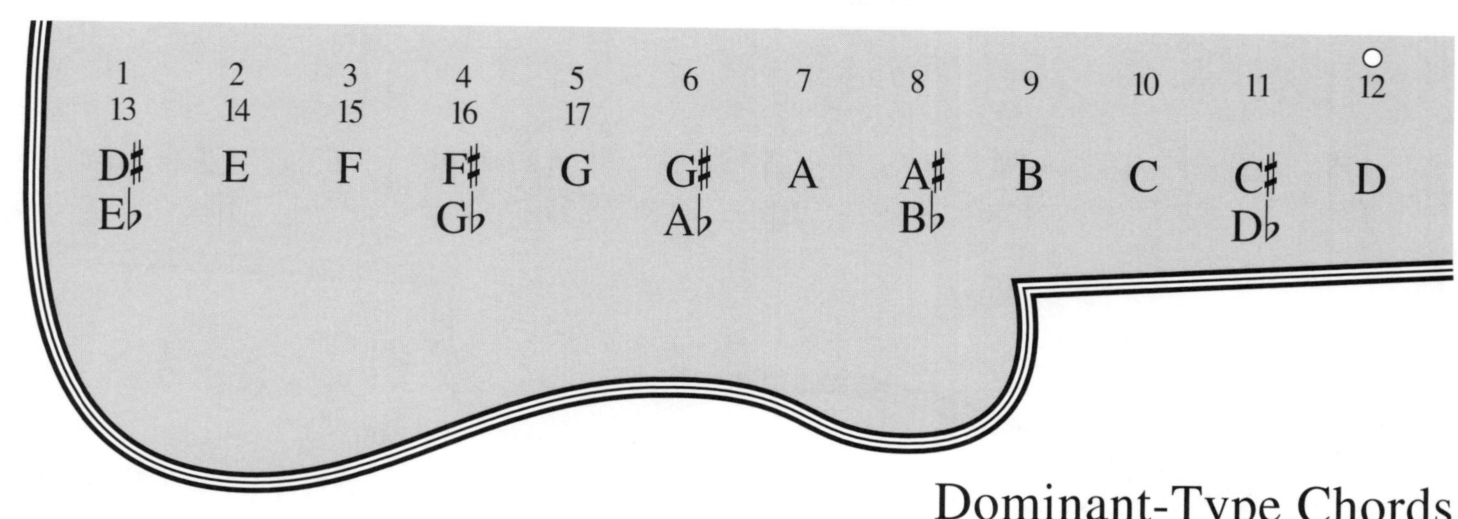

Dominant-Type Chords

D9sus4

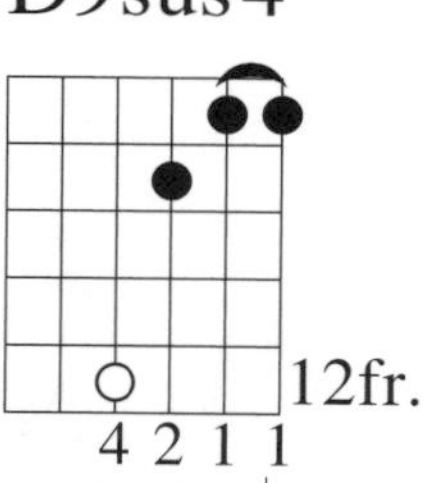

D7sus4♭9

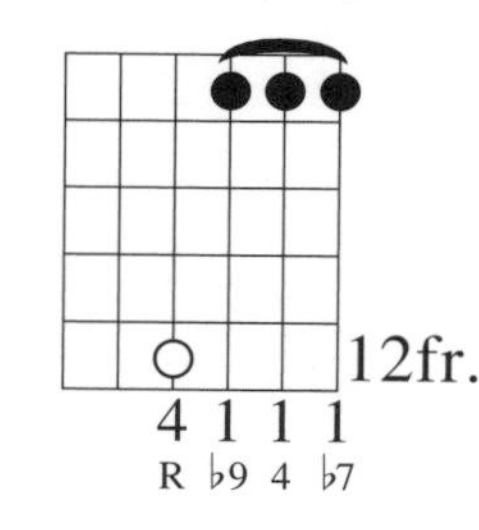

D7♯5

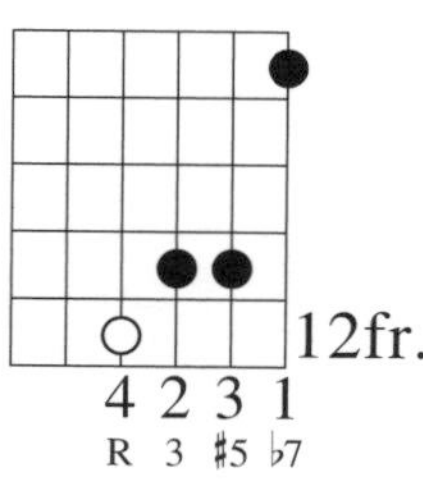

D7♭9

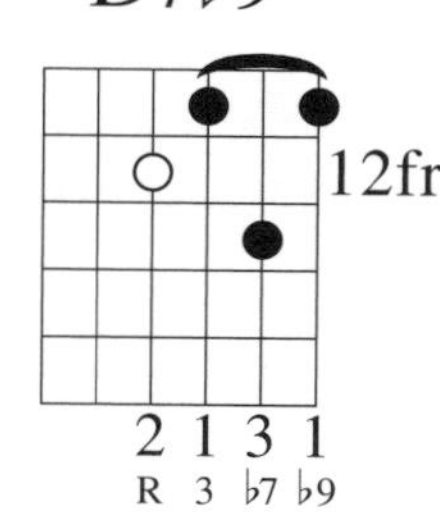

D7♯9

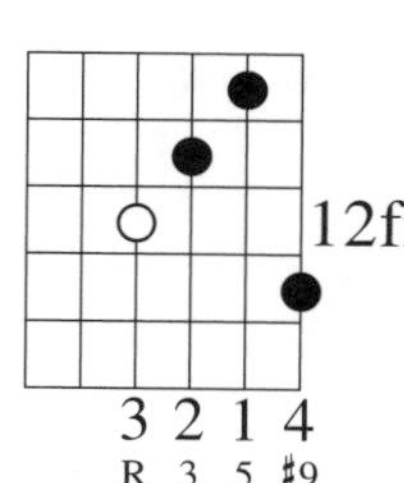

D7♭9♯9♯11

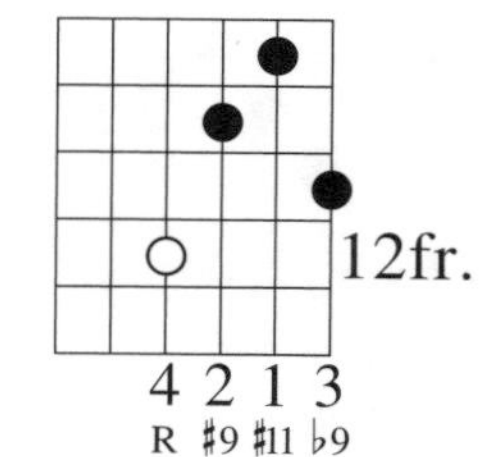

D13sus4

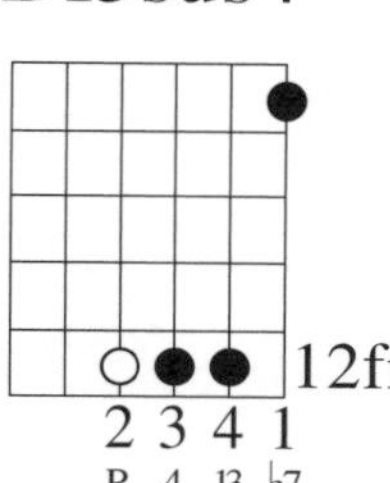

D13sus4♭9

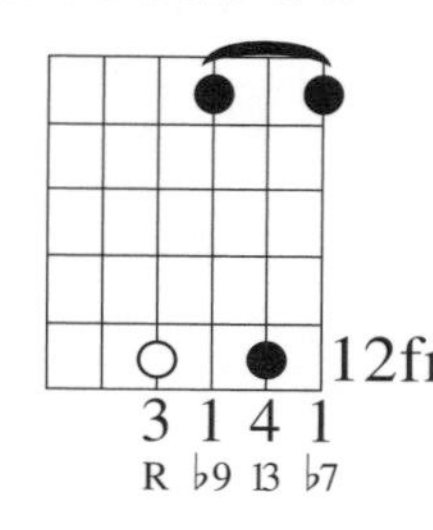

D7♯5♯11

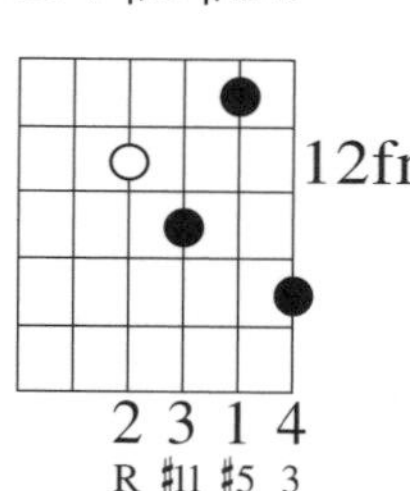

D7♭9

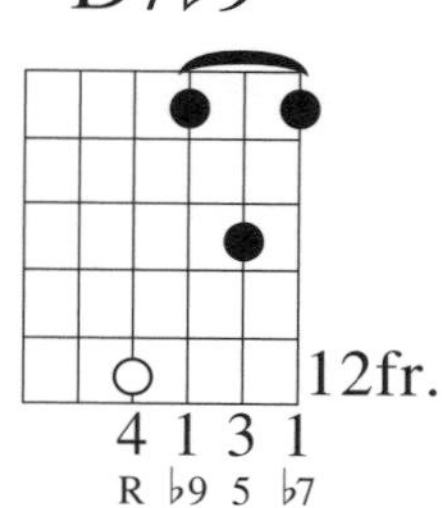

D7♭9♯11

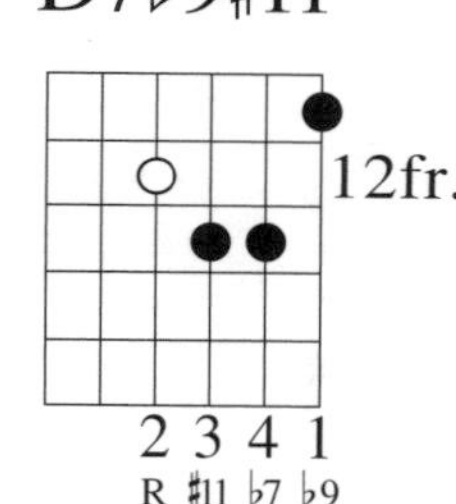

D11♭9

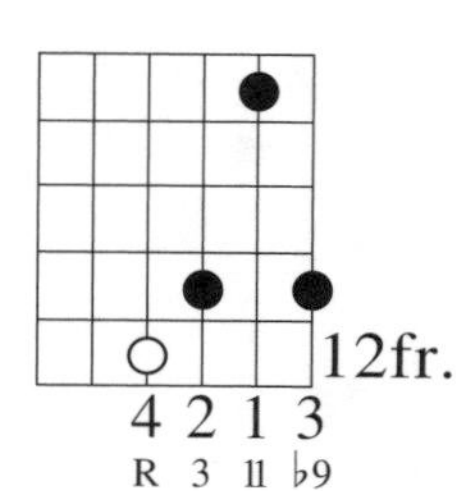

D13sus4 D7sus4♭9♭13

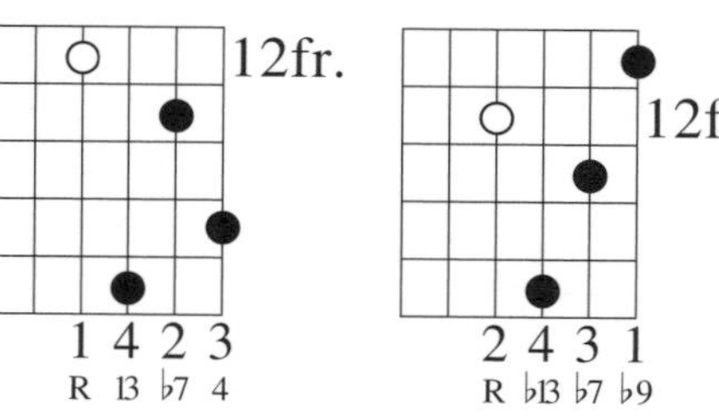

D9♯5

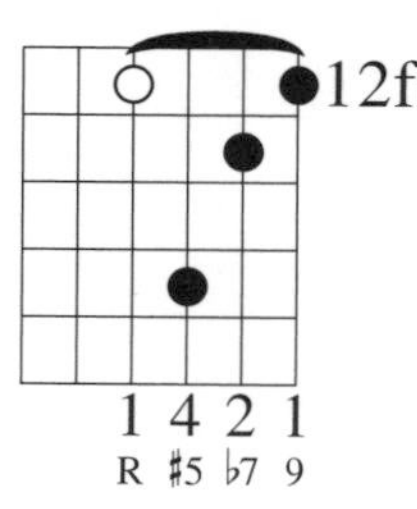

D7♭9

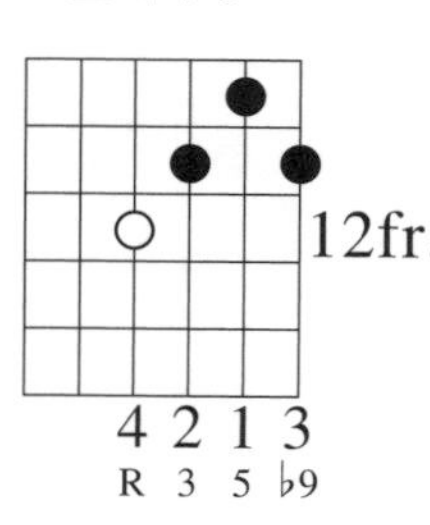

D7♭9♯11

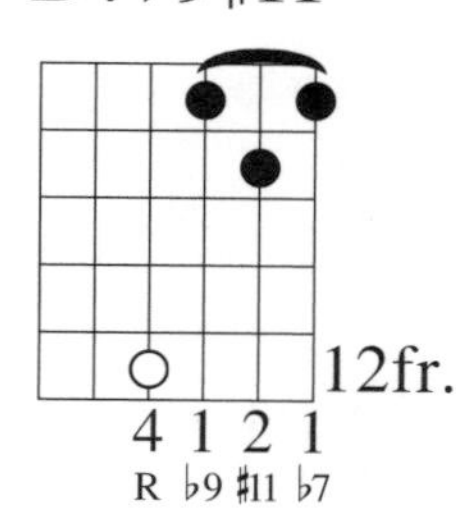

D11♭9

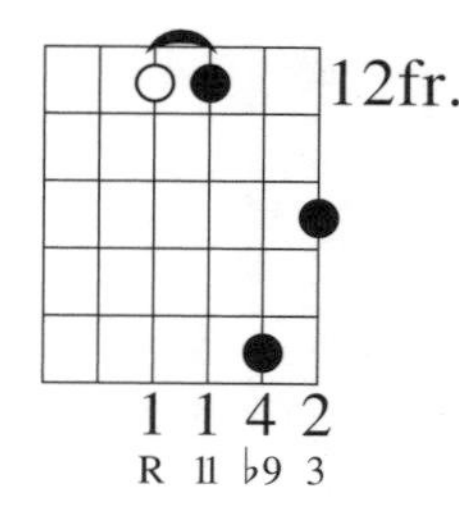

D7sus4♭9

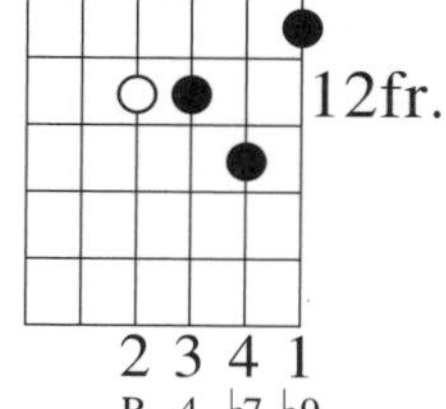

D7♯5

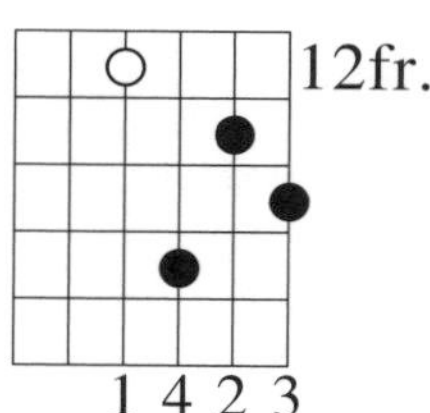

D9♯5♯11

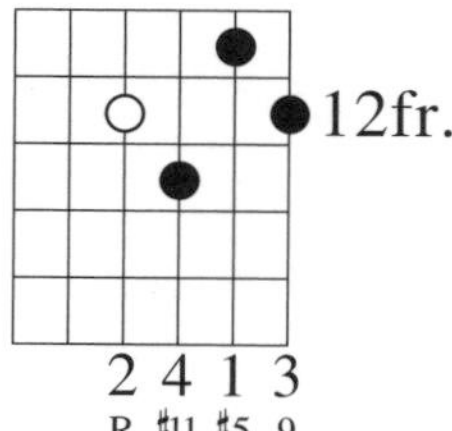

D7♭9

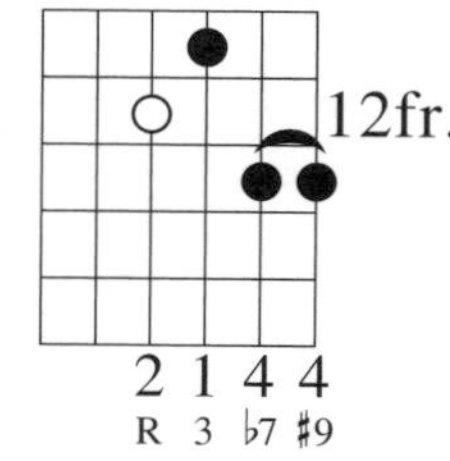

D7♯9♯11

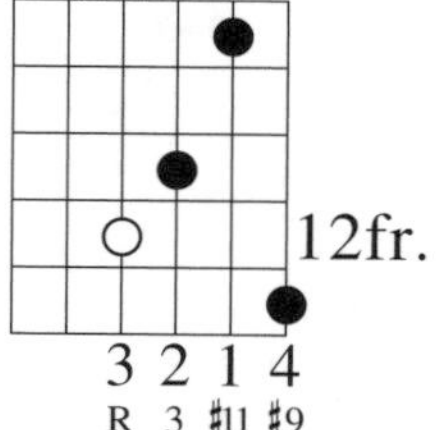

D13♭9

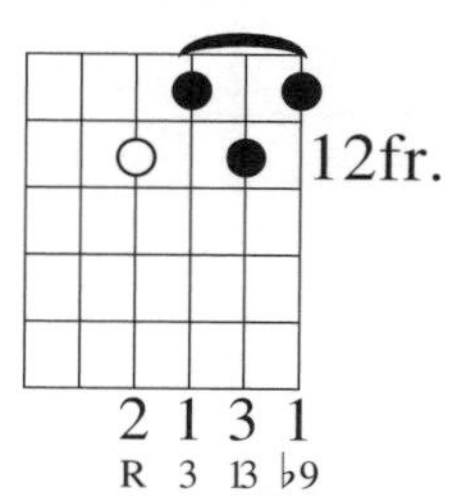

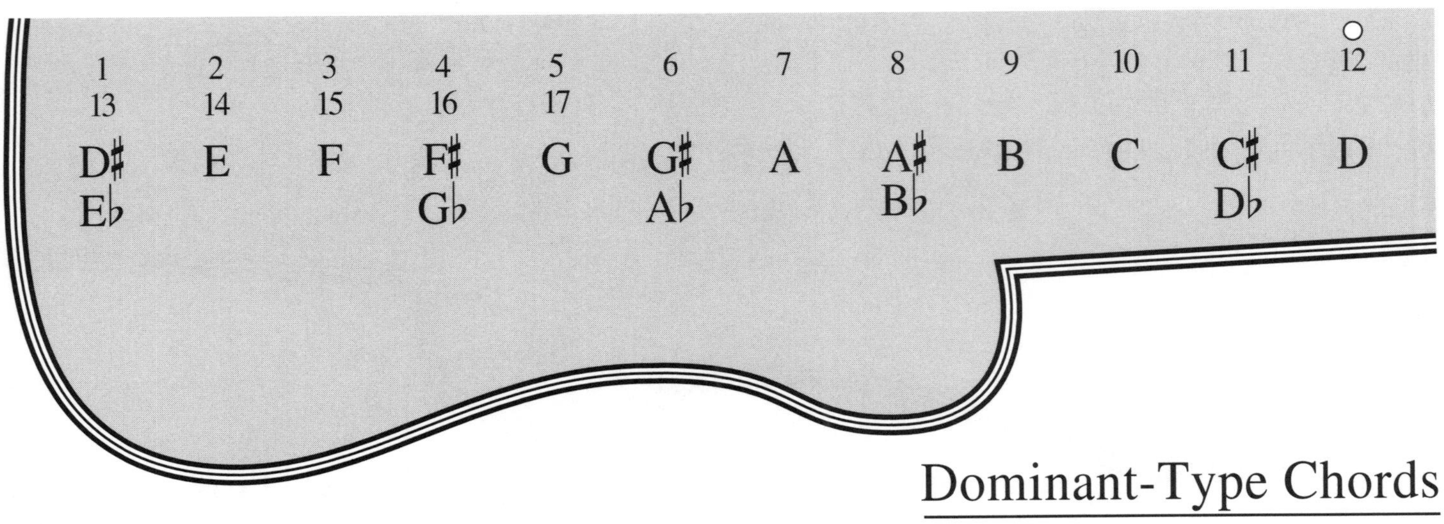

Dominant-Type Chords

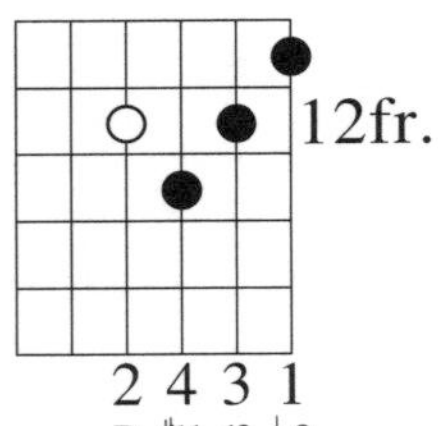

D7♭9♭13

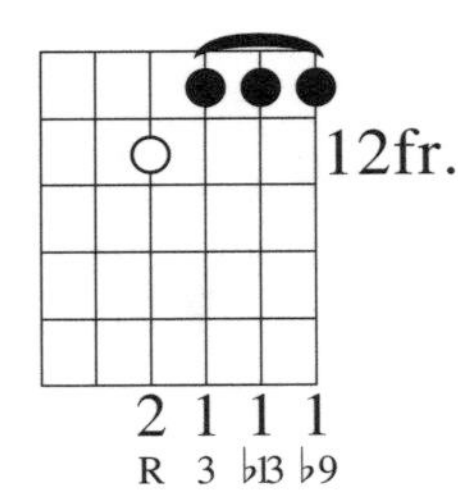

D13♯9

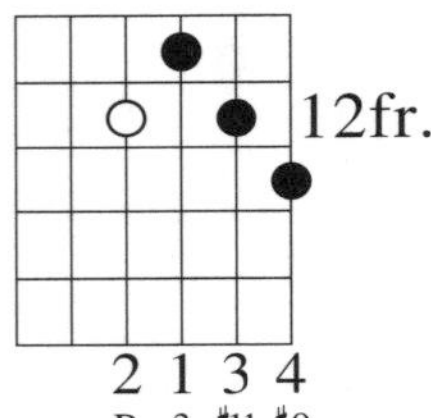

D7♭9♭13

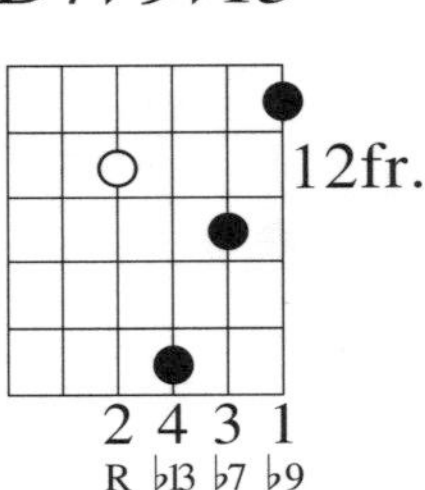

D13♯9

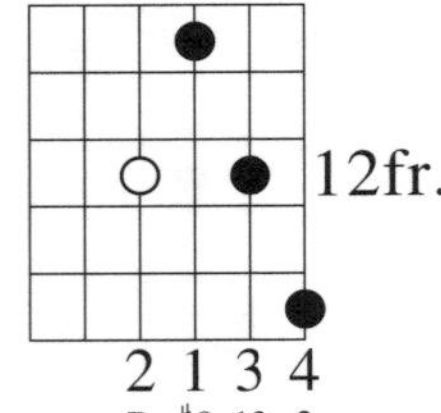

D7♯9♭13

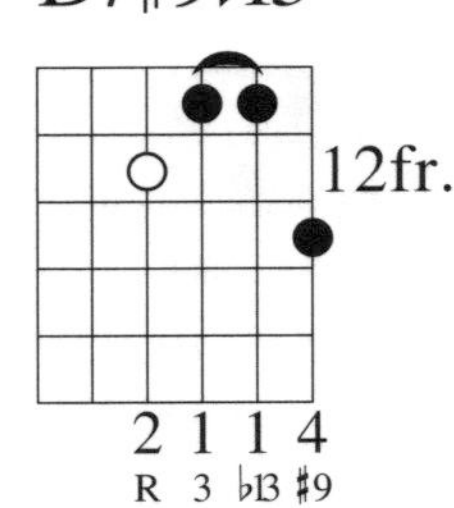

D7♭13

D7♭9♭13♭5

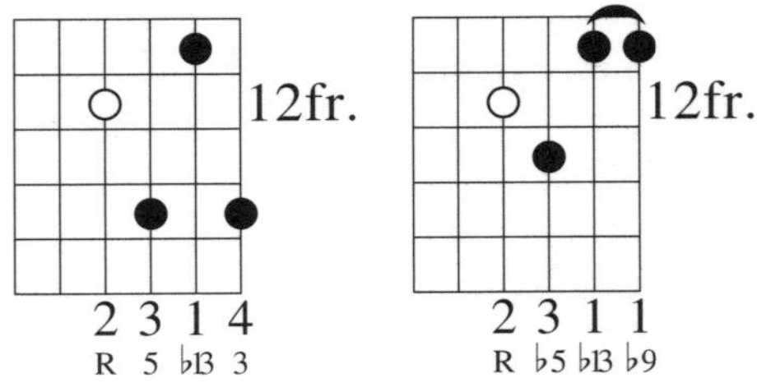

1 13
2 14
3 15
4 16
5 17
6
7
8
9
10
11
12
D♭/F C♯/E♯
D/F♯
E♭/G
E/G♯
F/A
F♯/A♯ G♭/B♭
G/B
A♭/C
A/C♯
B♭/D
B/D♯
C/E

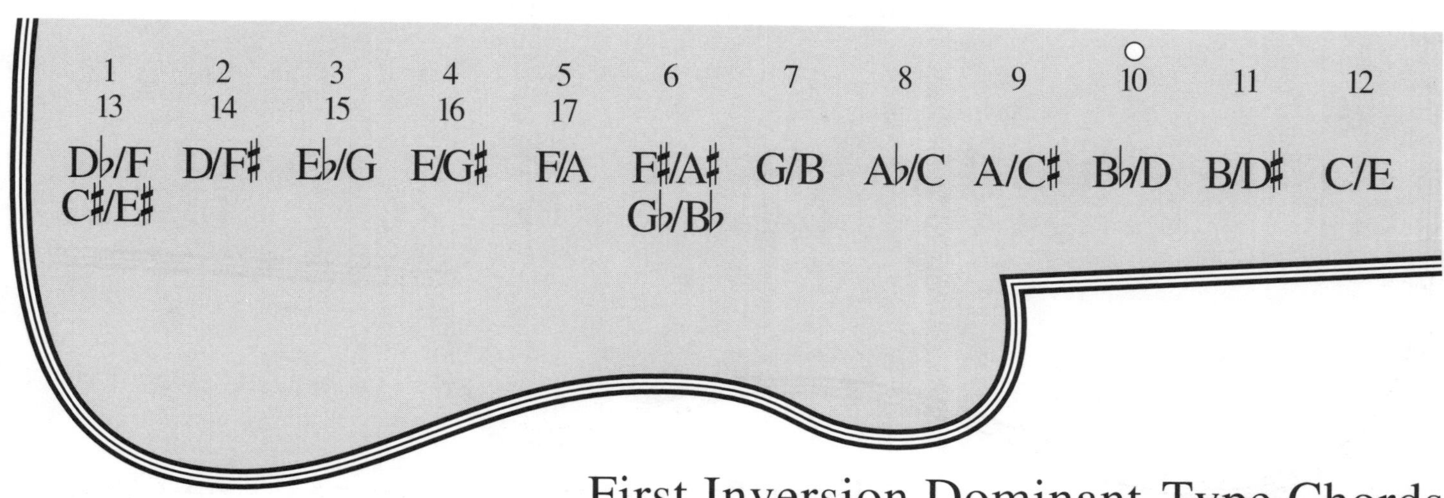

First Inversion Dominant-Type Chords

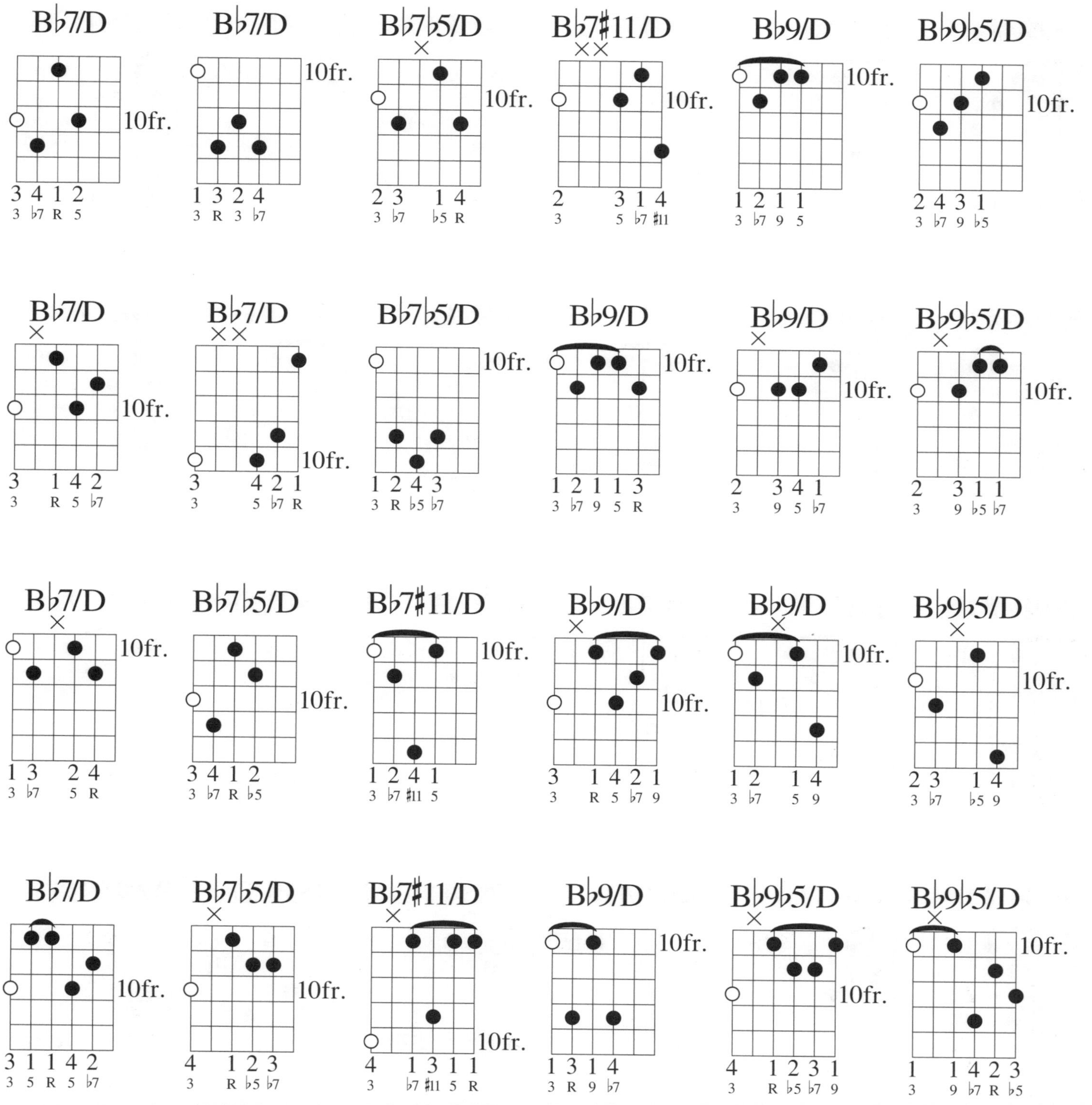

B♭7/D
10fr.
3 4 1 2
3 ♭7 R 5
B♭7/D
10fr.
1 3 2 4
3 R 3 ♭7
B♭7♭5/D
10fr.
2 3 1 4
3 ♭7 ♭5 R
B♭7♯11/D
10fr.
2 3 1 4
3 5 ♭7 ♯11
B♭9/D
10fr.
1 2 1 1
3 ♭7 9 5
B♭9♭5/D
10fr.
2 4 3 1
3 ♭7 9 ♭5
B♭7/D
10fr.
3 1 4 2
3 R 5 ♭7
B♭7/D
10fr.
3 4 2 1
3 5 ♭7 R
B♭7♭5/D
10fr.
1 2 4 3
3 R ♭5 ♭7
B♭9/D
10fr.
1 2 1 1 3
3 ♭7 9 5 R
B♭9/D
10fr.
2 3 4 1
3 9 5 ♭7
B♭9♭5/D
10fr.
2 3 1 1
3 9 ♭5 ♭7
B♭7/D
10fr.
1 3 2 4
3 ♭7 5 R
B♭7♭5/D
10fr.
3 4 1 2
3 ♭7 R ♭5
B♭7♯11/D
10fr.
1 2 4 1
3 ♭7 ♯11 5
B♭9/D
10fr.
3 1 4 2 1
3 R 5 ♭7 9
B♭9/D
10fr.
1 2 1 4
3 ♭7 5 9
B♭9♭5/D
10fr.
2 3 1 4
3 ♭7 ♭5 9
B♭7/D
10fr.
3 1 1 4 2
3 5 R 5 ♭7
B♭7♭5/D
10fr.
4 1 2 3
3 R ♭5 ♭7
B♭7♯11/D
10fr.
4 1 3 1 1
3 ♭7 ♯11 5 R
B♭9/D
10fr.
1 3 1 4
3 R 9 ♭7
B♭9♭5/D
10fr.
4 1 2 3 1
3 R ♭5 ♭7 9
B♭9♭5/D
10fr.
1 1 4 2 3
3 9 ♭7 R ♭5

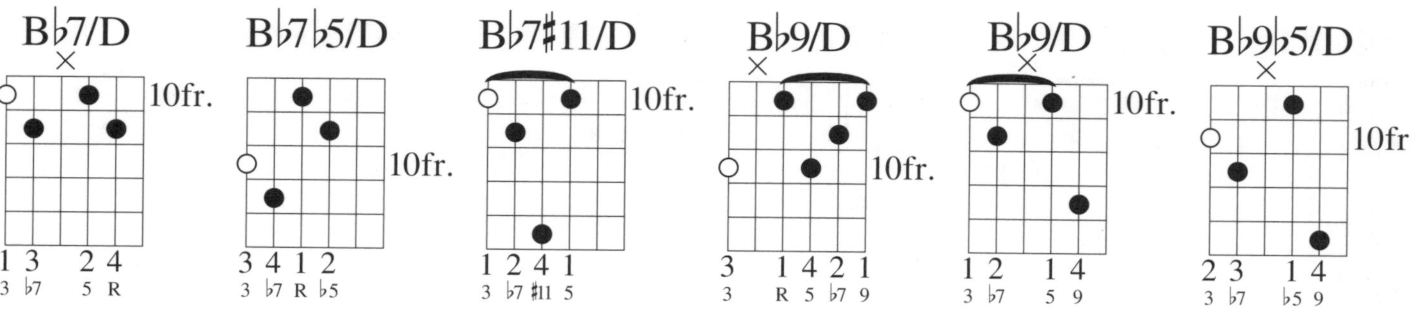

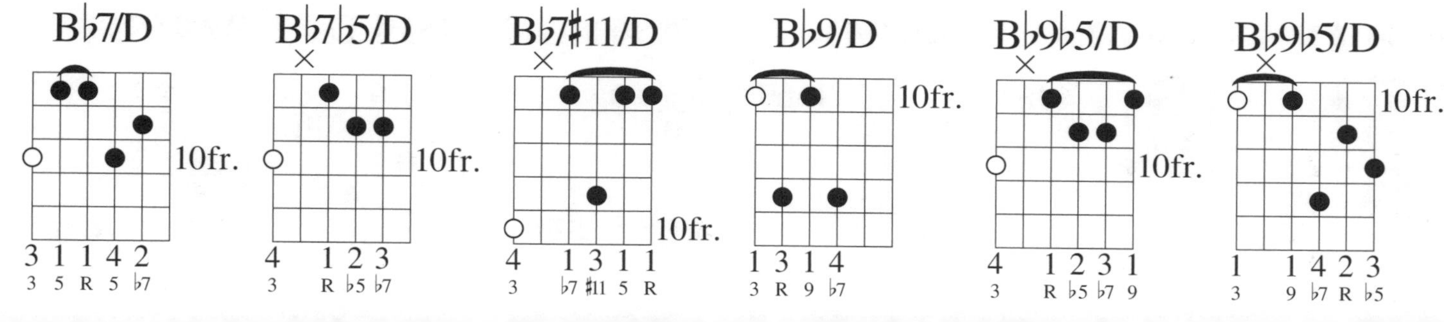

1 2 3 4 5 6 7 8 9 10 11 12
13 14 15 16 17
D♭/F D/F♯ E♭/G E/G♯ F/A F♯/A♯ G/B A♭/C A/C♯ B♭/D B/D♯ C/E
C♯/E♯
G♭/B♭

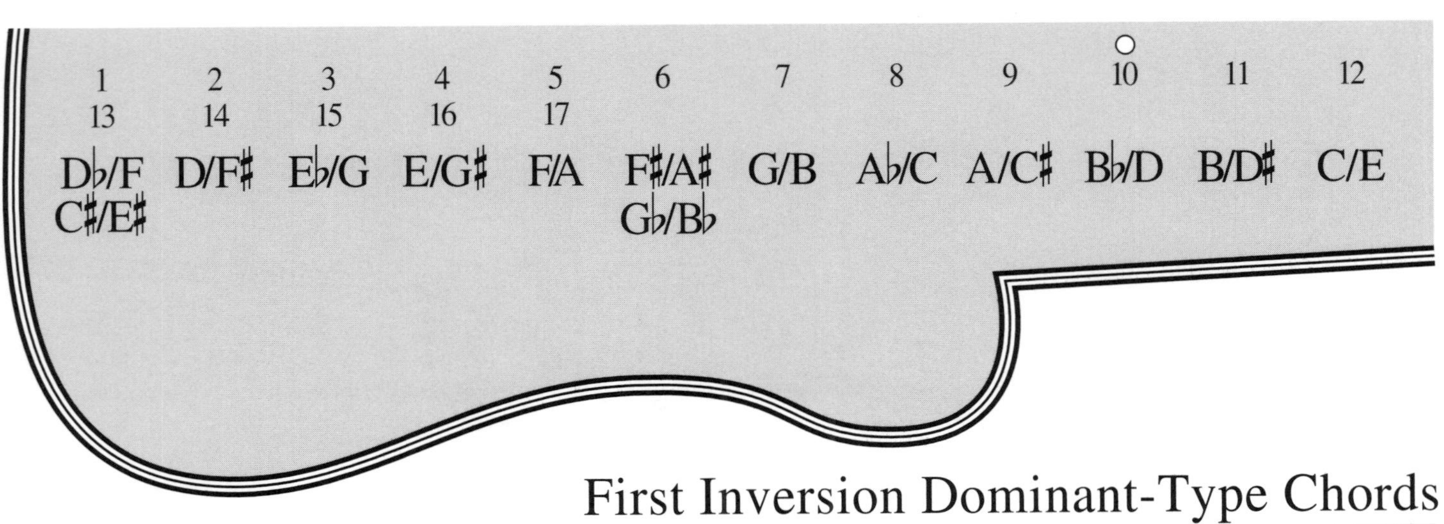

First Inversion Dominant-Type Chords

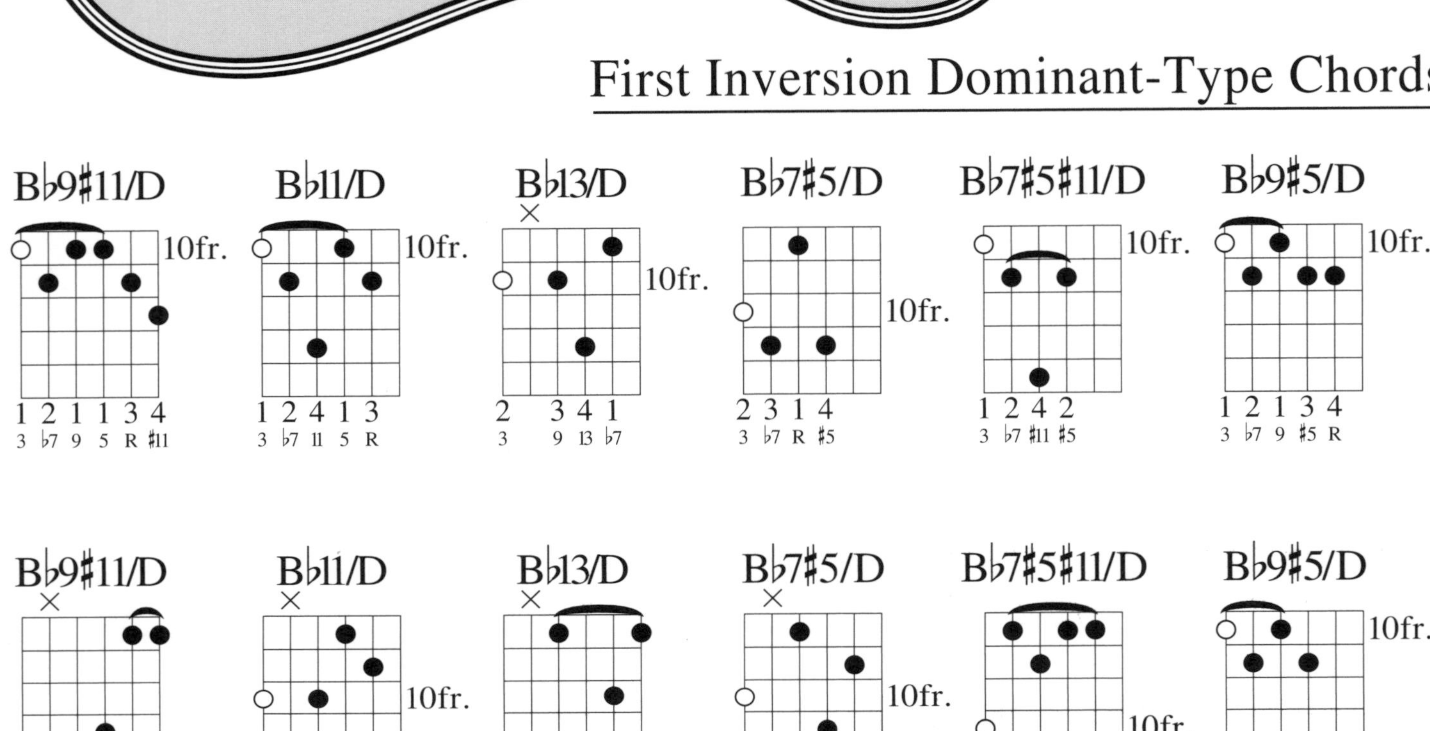

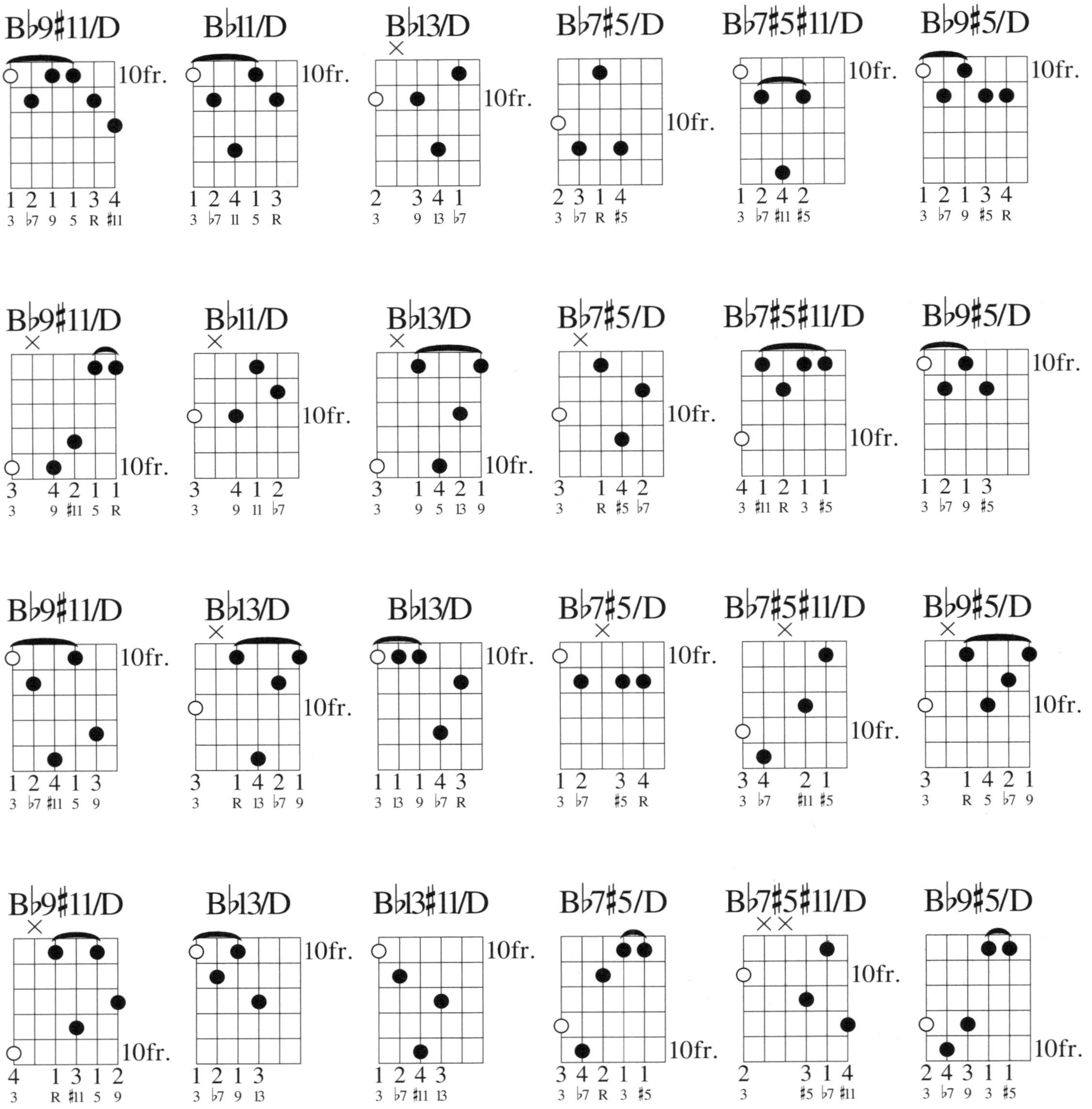

B♭9♯11/D
10fr.
1 2 1 1 3 4
3 ♭7 9 5 R ♯11
B♭11/D
10fr.
1 2 4 1 3
3 ♭7 11 5 R
B♭13/D
10fr.
2 3 4 1
3 9 13 ♭7
B♭7♯5/D
10fr.
2 3 1 4
3 ♭7 R ♯5
B♭7♯5♯11/D
10fr.
1 2 4 2
3 ♭7 ♯11 ♯5
B♭9♯5/D
10fr.
1 2 1 3 4
3 ♭7 9 ♯5 R
B♭9♯11/D
10fr.
3 4 2 1 1
3 9 ♯11 5 R
B♭11/D
10fr.
3 4 1 2
3 9 11 ♭7
B♭13/D
10fr.
3 1 4 2 1
3 9 5 13 9
B♭7♯5/D
10fr.
3 1 4 2
3 R ♯5 ♭7
B♭7♯5♯11/D
10fr.
4 1 2 1 1
3 ♯11 R 3 ♯5
B♭9♯5/D
10fr.
1 2 1 3
3 ♭7 9 ♯5
B♭9♯11/D
10fr.
1 2 4 1 3
3 ♭7 ♯11 5 9
B♭13/D
10fr.
3 1 4 2 1
3 R 13 ♭7 9
B♭13/D
10fr.
1 1 1 4 3
3 13 9 ♭7 R
B♭7♯5/D
10fr.
1 2 3 4
3 ♭7 ♯5 R
B♭7♯5♯11/D
10fr.
3 4 2 1
3 ♭7 ♯11 ♯5
B♭9♯5/D
10fr.
3 1 4 2 1
3 R 5 ♭7 9
B♭9♯11/D
10fr.
4 1 3 1 2
3 R ♯11 5 9
B♭13/D
10fr.
1 2 1 3
3 ♭7 9 13
B♭13♯11/D
10fr.
1 2 4 3
3 ♭7 ♯11 13
B♭7♯5/D
10fr.
3 4 2 1 1
3 ♭7 R 3 ♯5
B♭7♯5♯11/D
10fr.
2 3 1 4
3 ♯5 ♭7 ♯11
B♭9♯5/D
10fr.
2 4 3 1 1
3 ♭7 9 3 ♯5

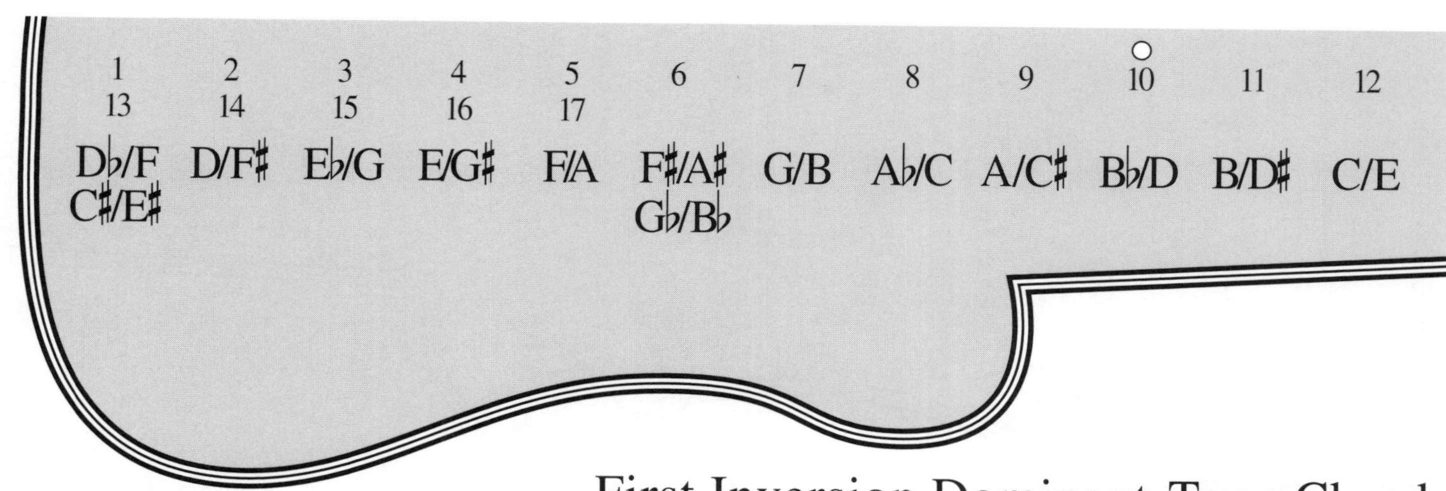

First Inversion Dominant-Type Chords

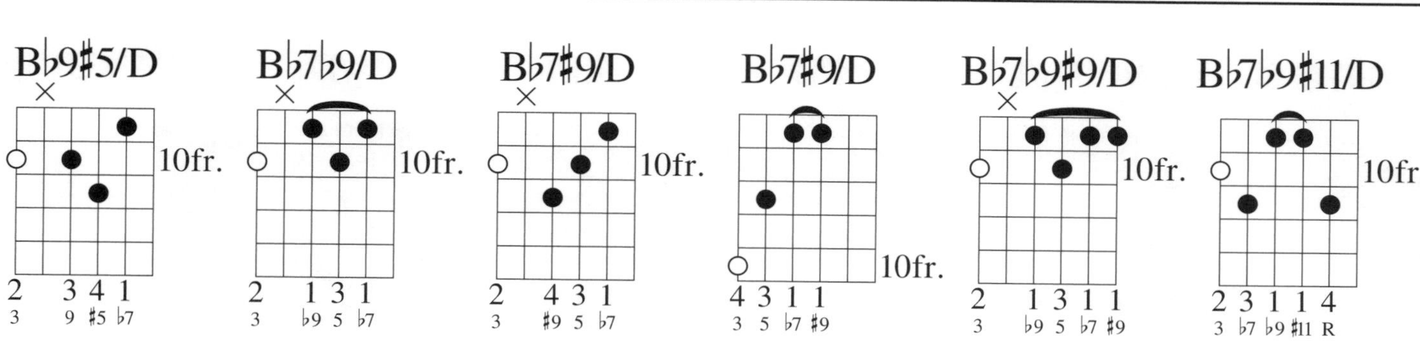

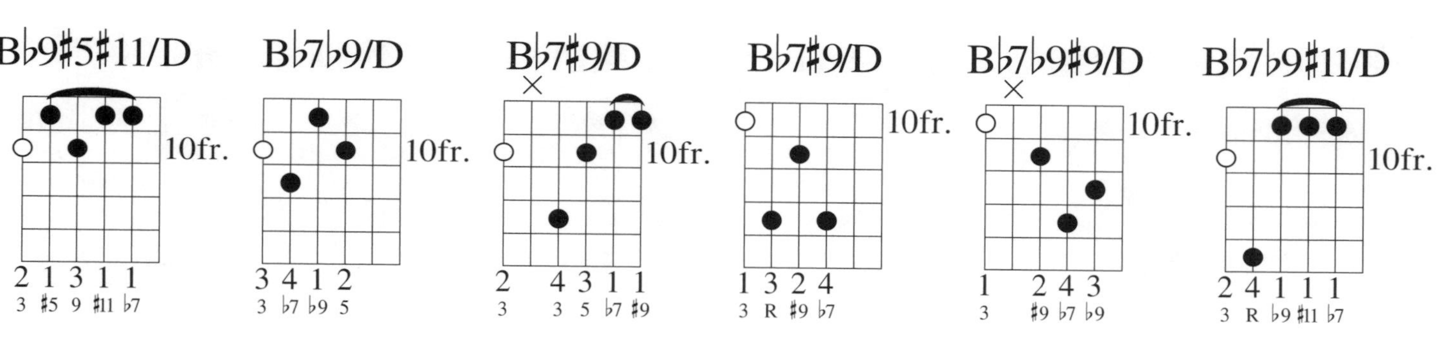

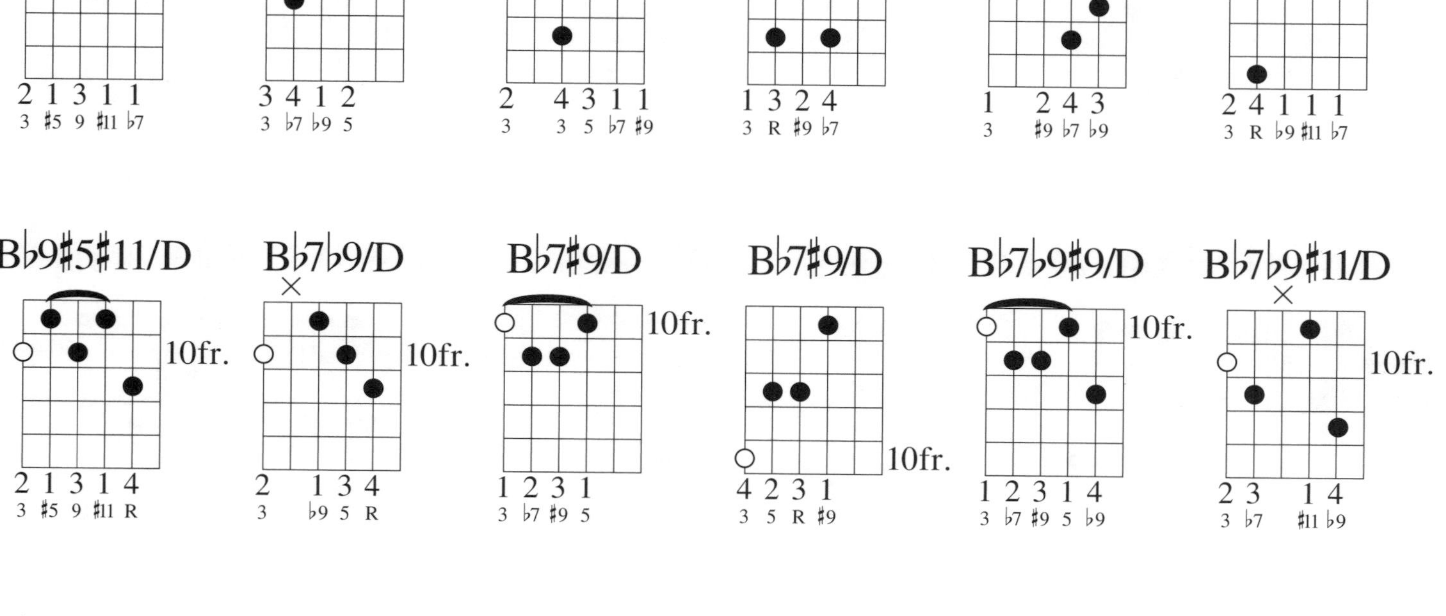

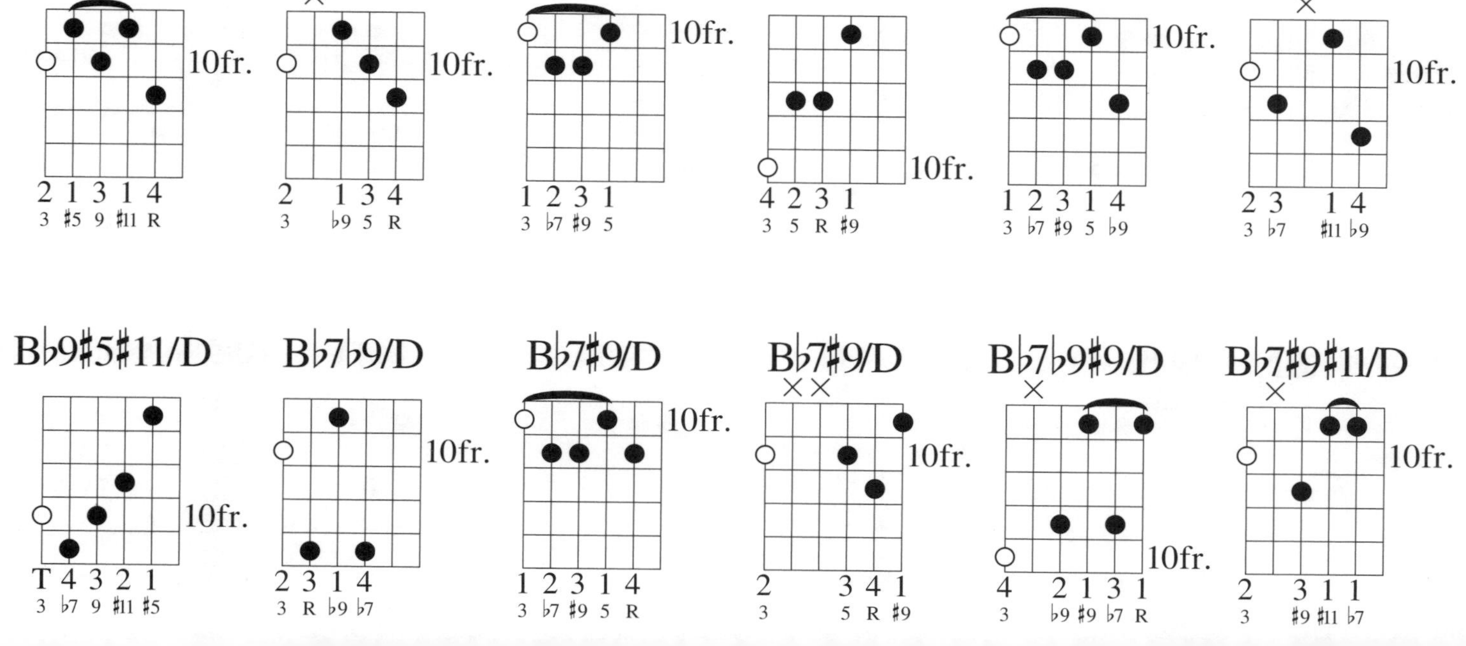

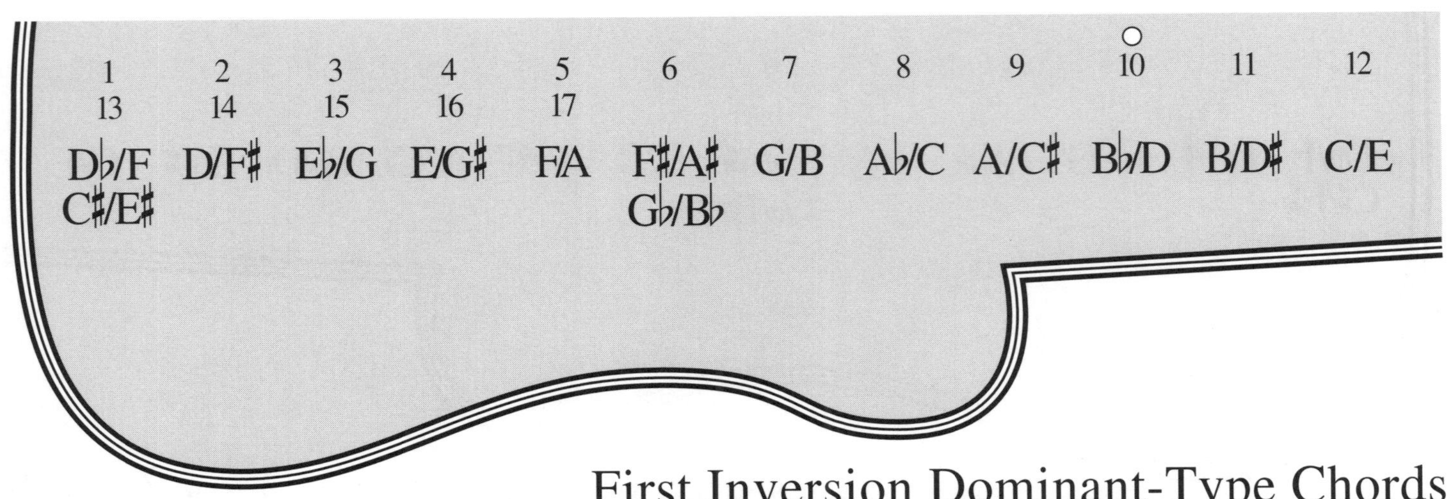

First Inversion Dominant-Type Chords

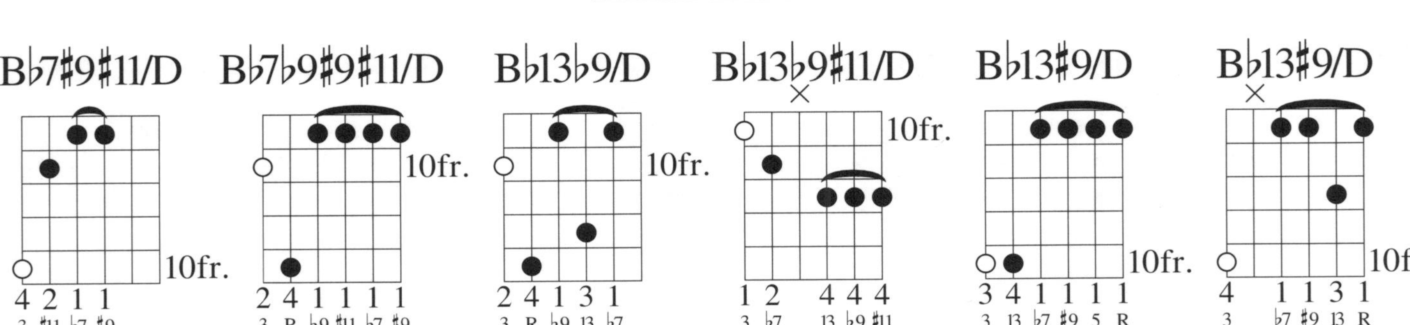

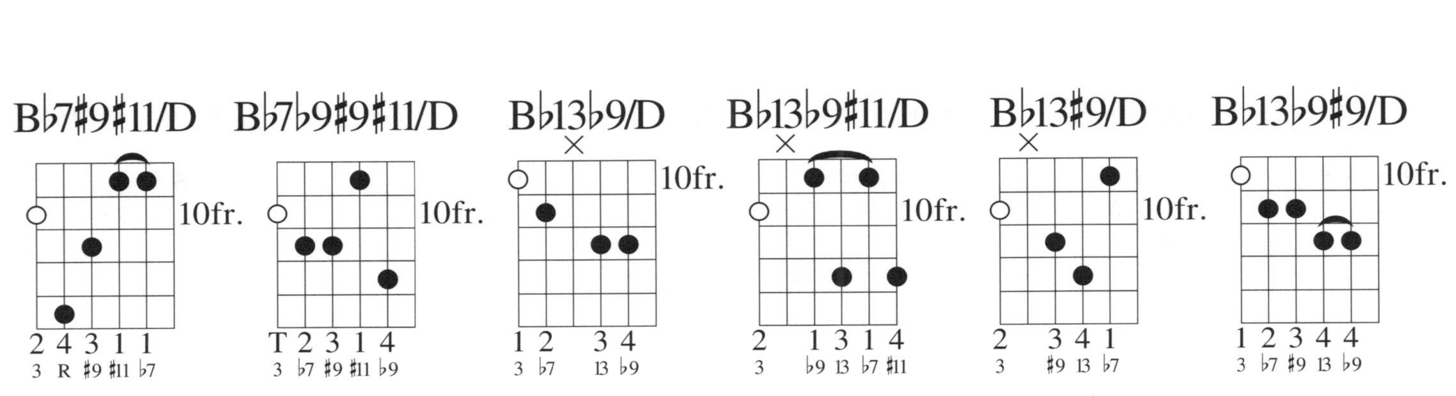

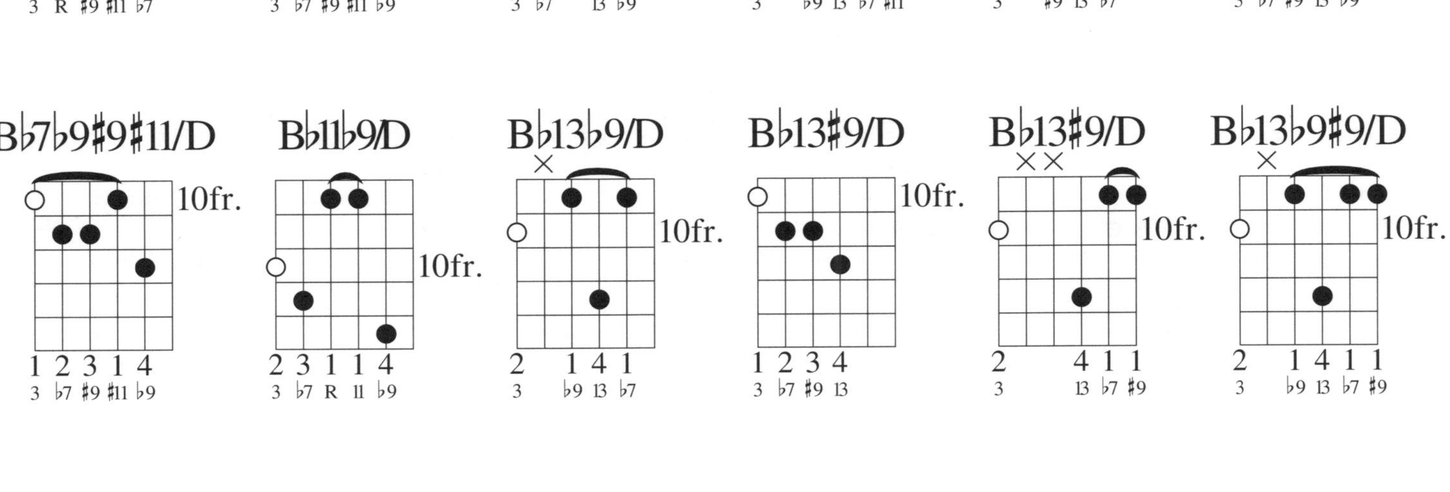

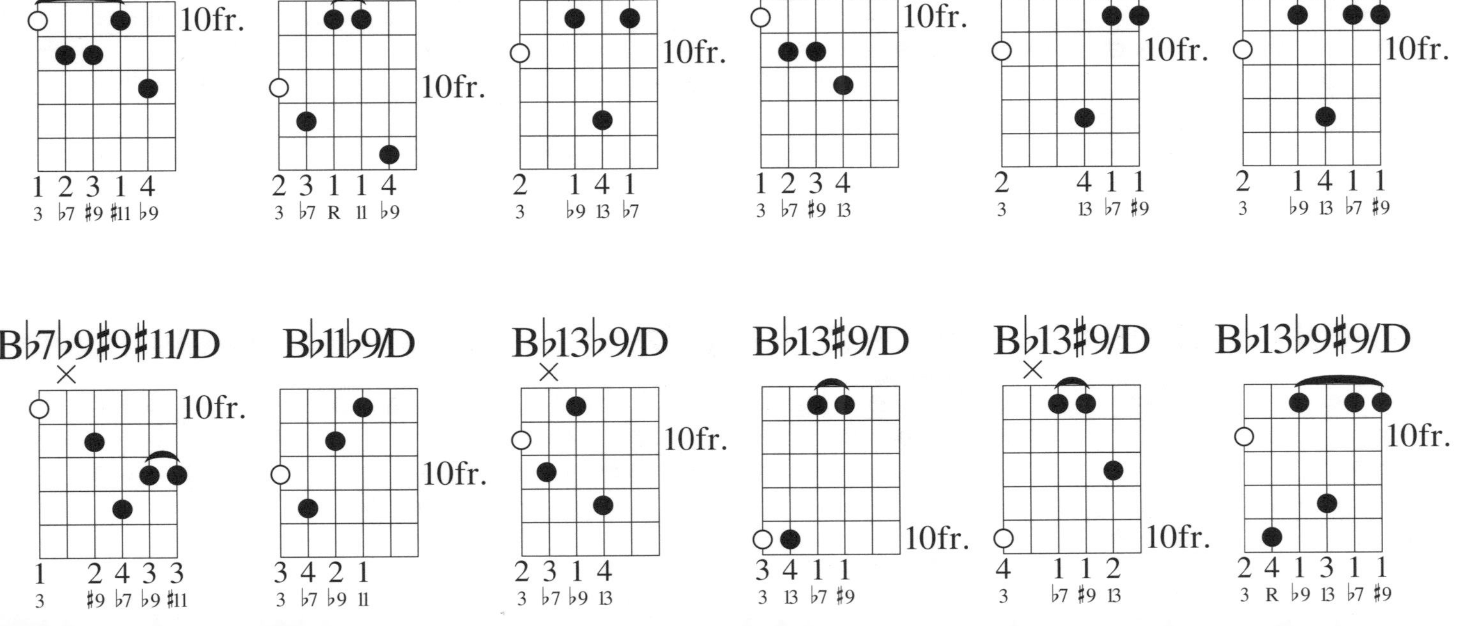

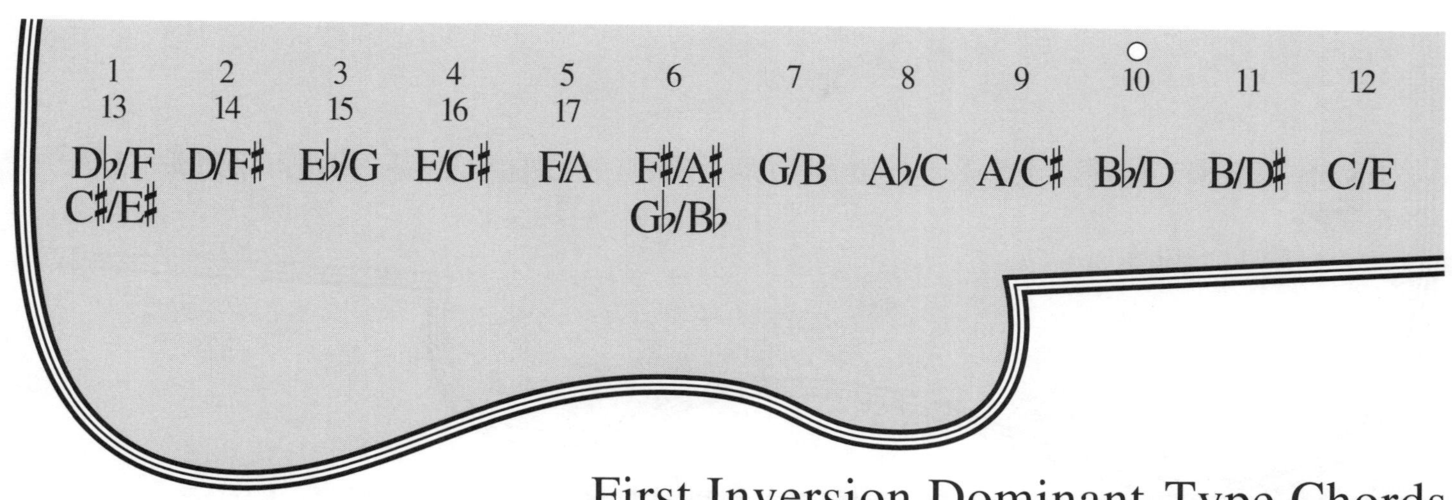

First Inversion Dominant-Type Chords

B♭7♭13/D

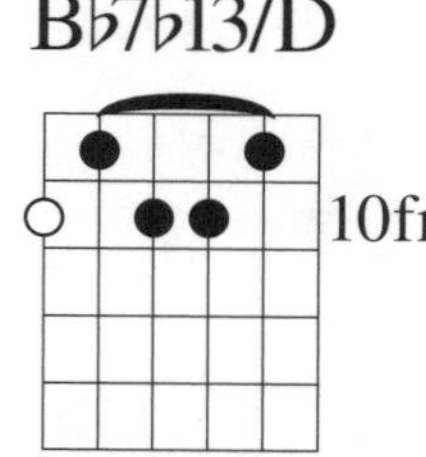

B♭7♭9♭13/D

10fr.
2 1 3 1
3 ♭9 ♭13 ♭7

B♭7♯9♭13/D

10fr.
2 3 4 1
3 ♯9 ♭13 ♭7

B♭7♭9♯9♭13/D

10fr.
4 2 3 1
3 ♭13 ♭9 ♯9

B♭7♭9♭13♭5/D

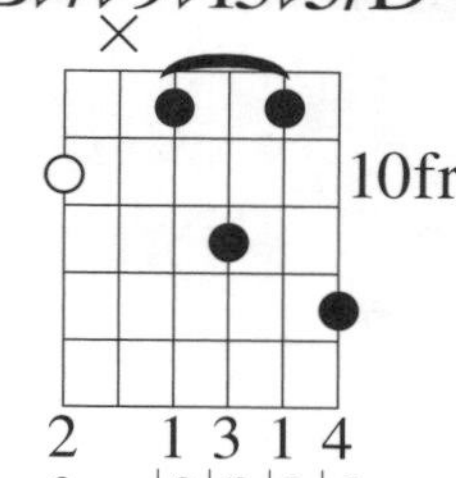

B♭7♯9♭13♭5/D

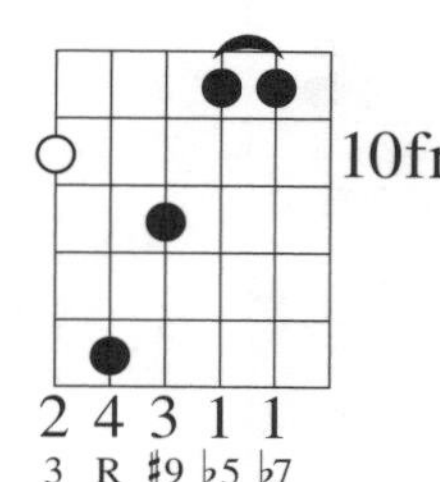

B♭7♭13/D

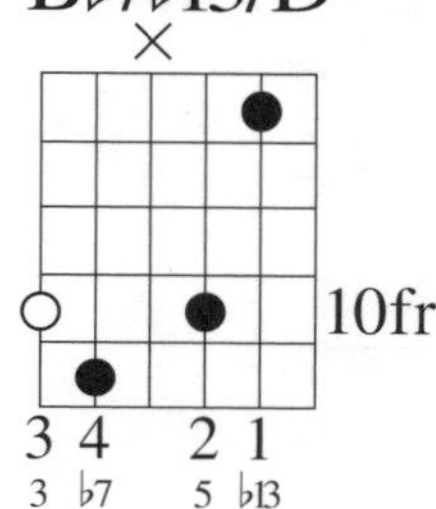

B♭7♯9♭13/D

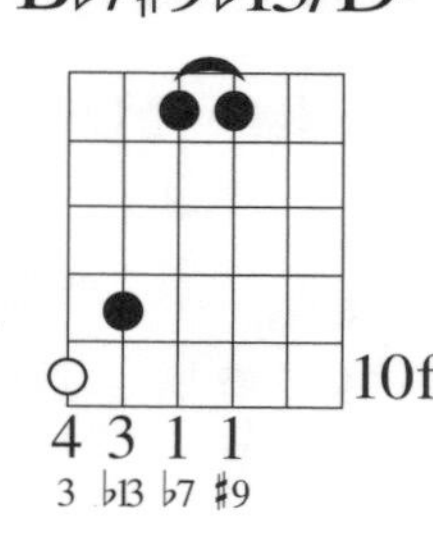

B♭7♯9♭13/D

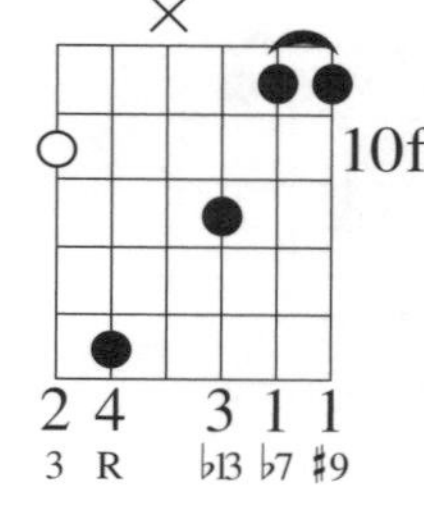

B♭7♭9♯9♭13/D

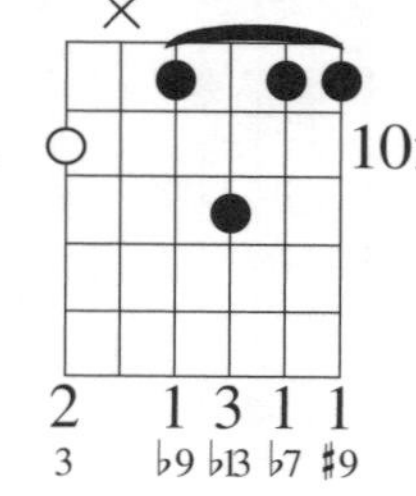

B♭7♭9♭13♭5/D

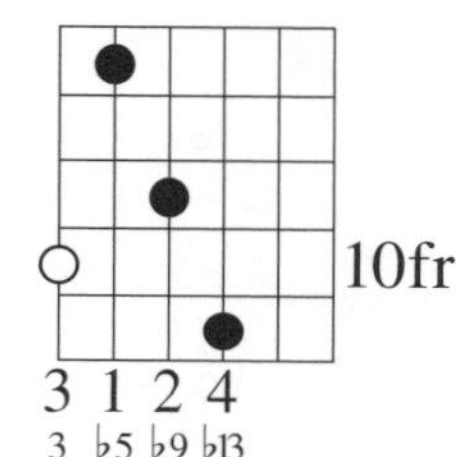

B♭7♯9♭13♭5/D

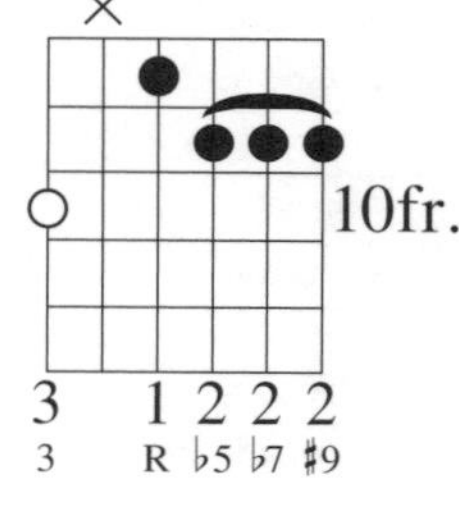

B♭7♭9♭13/D

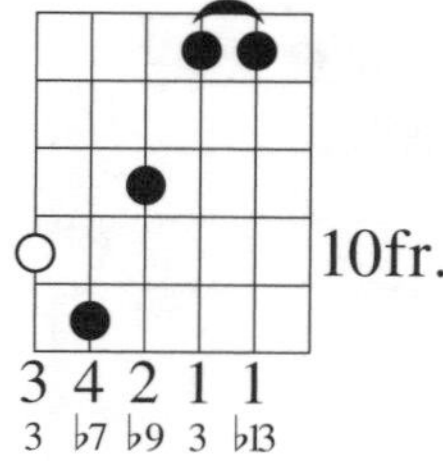

B♭7♯9♭13/D

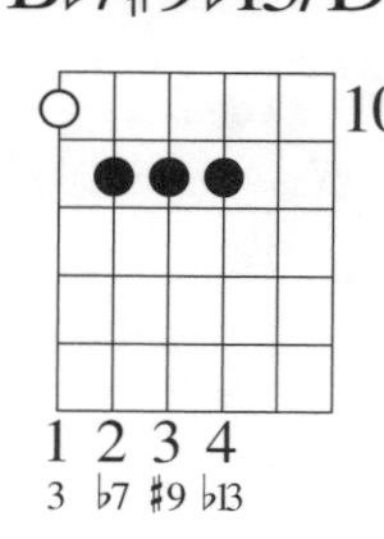

B♭7♭9♯9♭13/D

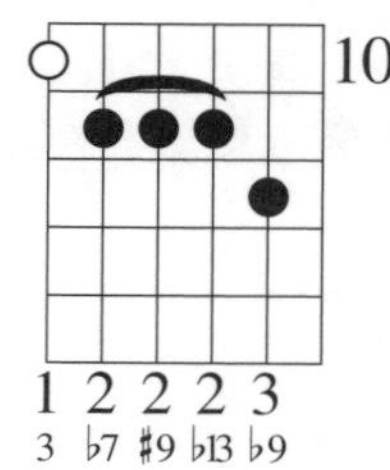

B♭7♭9♭13♭5/D

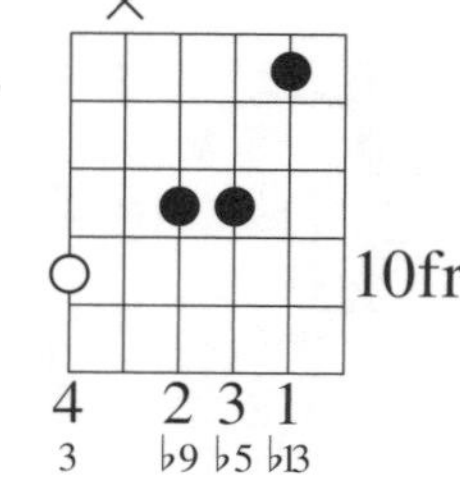

B♭7♭9♭13♭5/D

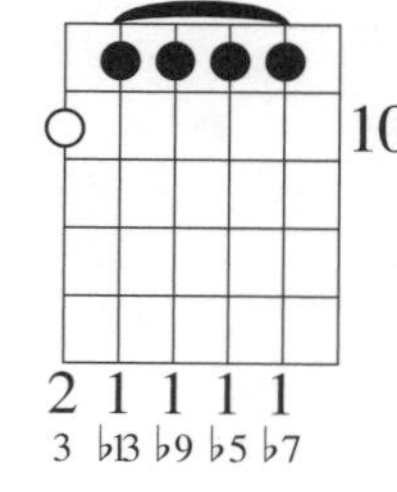

B♭7♭9♯9♭13♭5/D

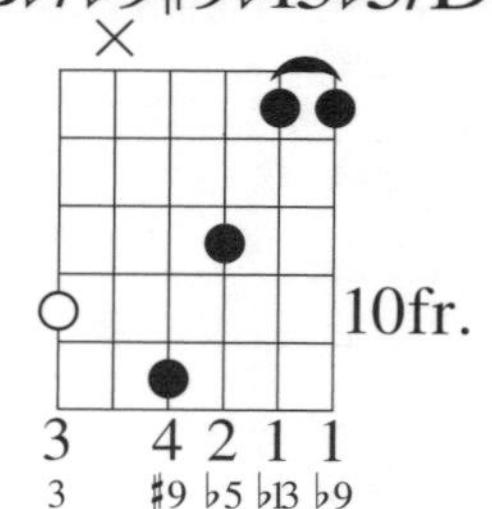

B♭7♭9♭13/D

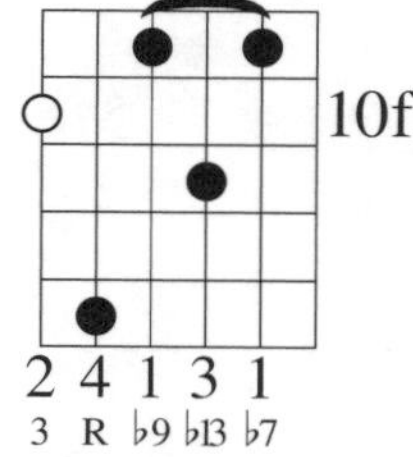

B♭7♯9♭13/D

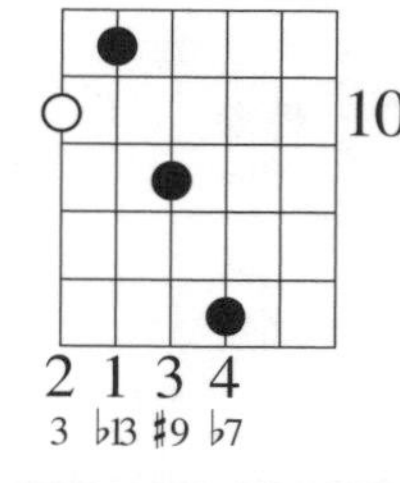

B♭7♭9♯9♭13/D

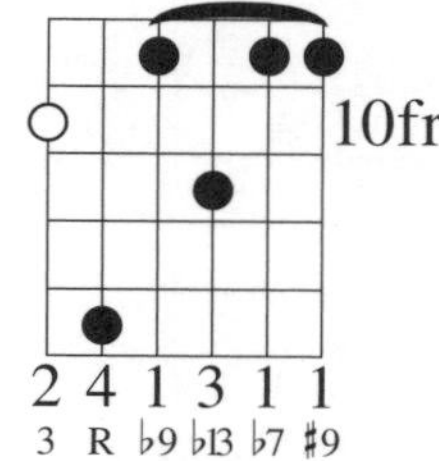

B♭7♭9♭13♭5/D

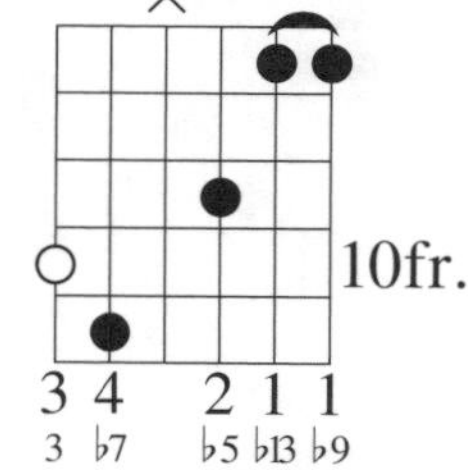

B♭7♯9♭13♭5/D

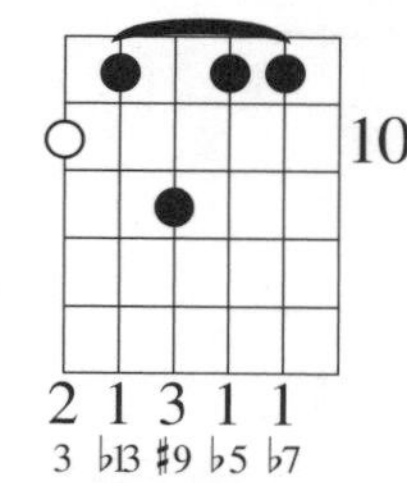

B♭7♭9♯9♭13♭5/D

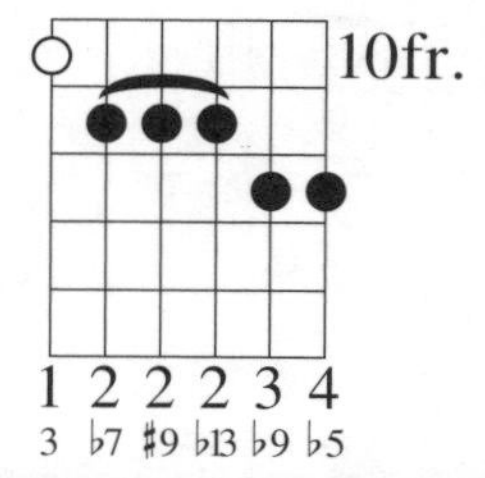

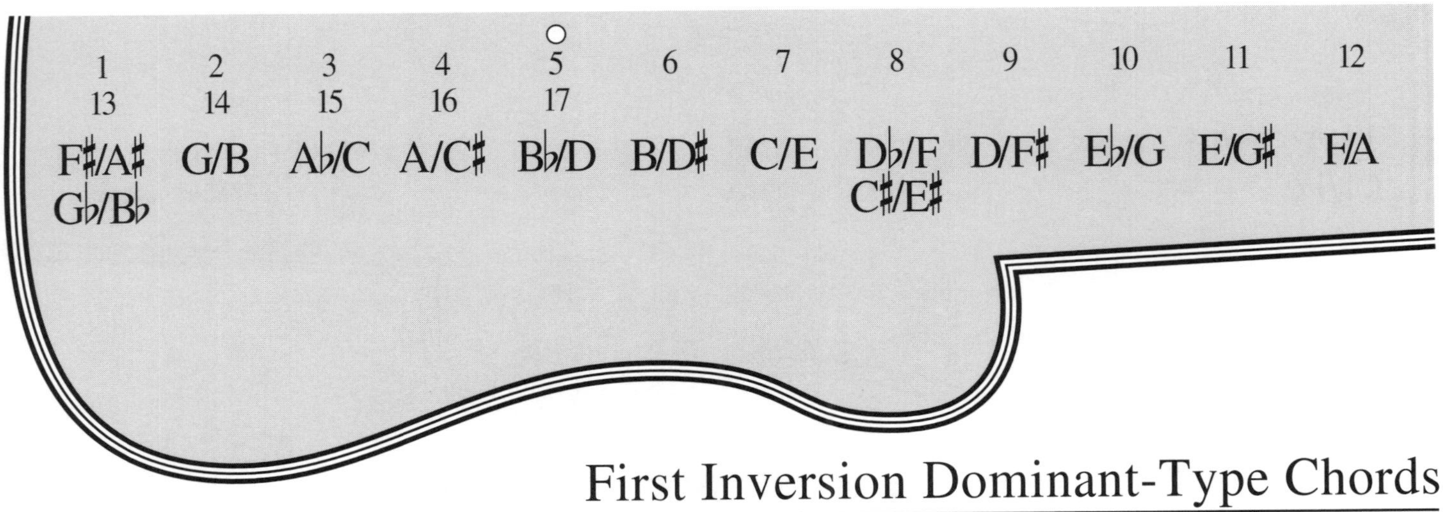

1	2	3	4	5	6	7	8	9	10	11	12
13	14	15	16	17							
F♯/A♯ G♭/B♭	G/B	A♭/C	A/C♯	B♭/D	B/D♯	C/E	D♭/F C♯/E♯	D/F♯	E♭/G	E/G♯	F/A

First Inversion Dominant-Type Chords

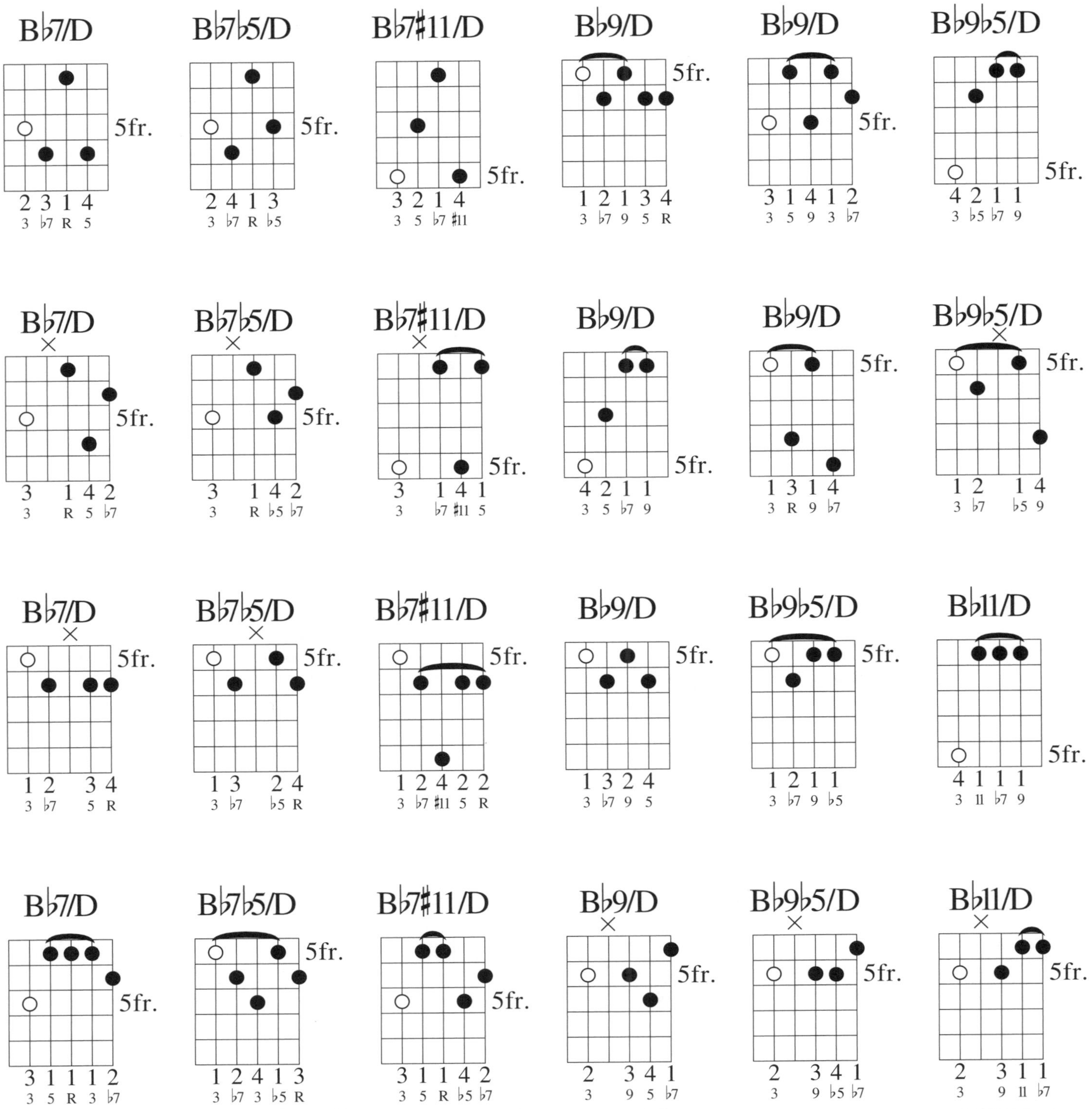

B♭7/D
5fr.
2 3 1 4
3 ♭7 R 5

B♭7♭5/D
5fr.
2 4 1 3
3 ♭7 R ♭5

B♭7♯11/D
5fr.
3 2 1 4
3 5 ♭7 ♯11

B♭9/D
5fr.
1 2 1 3 4
3 ♭7 9 5 R

B♭9/D
5fr.
3 1 4 1 2
3 5 9 3 ♭7

B♭9♭5/D
5fr.
4 2 1 1
3 ♭5 ♭7 9

B♭7/D
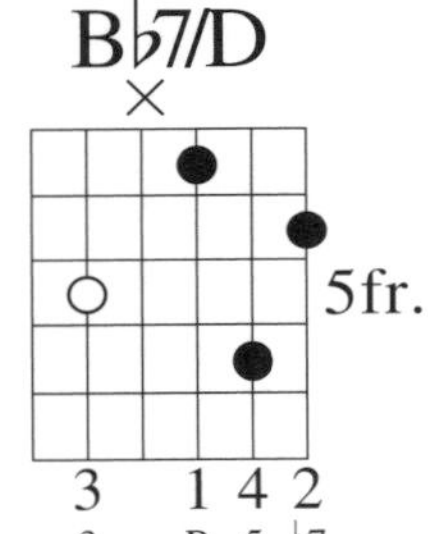

B♭7♭5/D
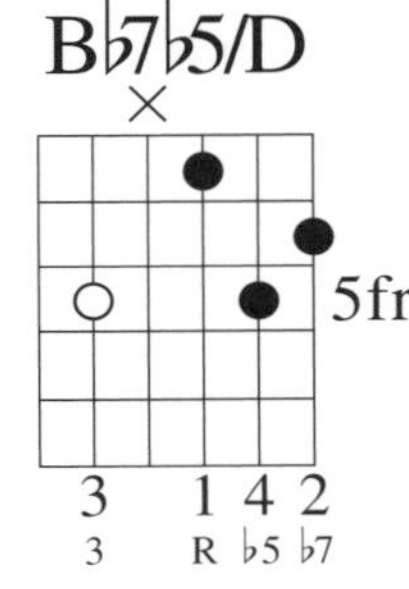

B♭7♯11/D
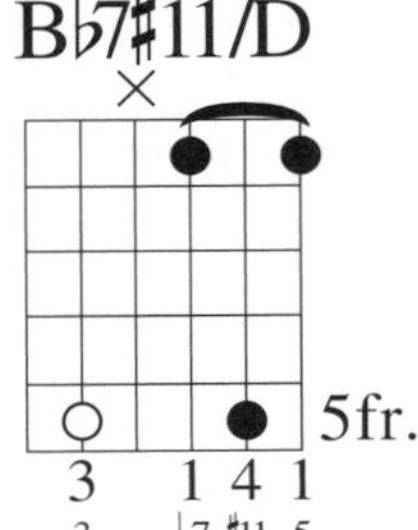

B♭9/D
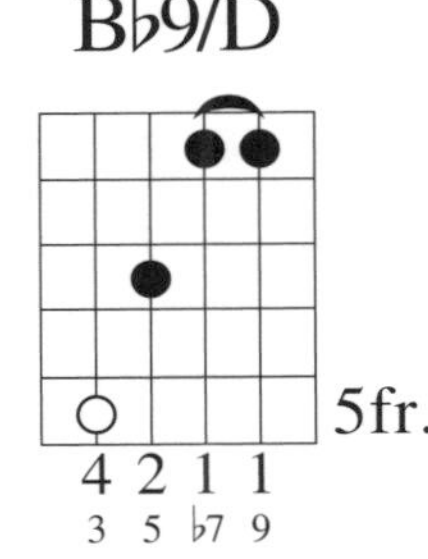

B♭9/D
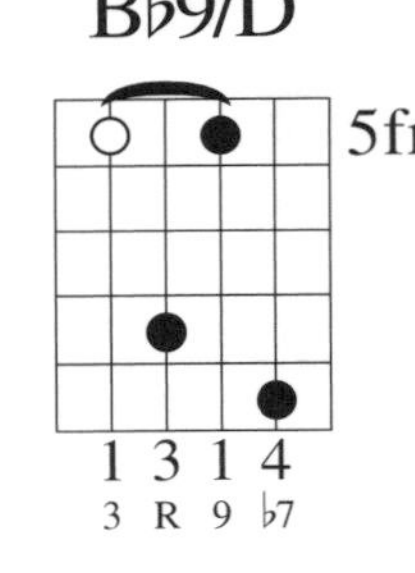

B♭9♭5/D
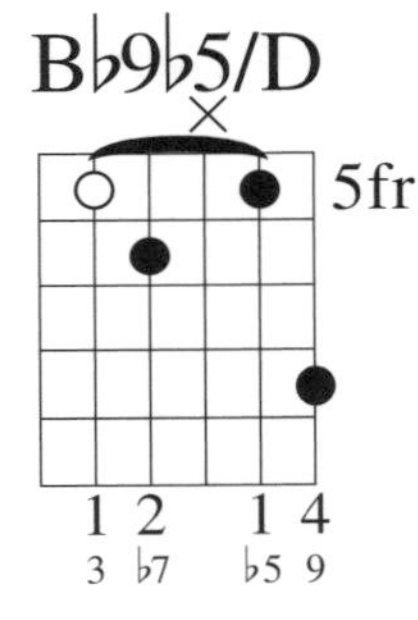

B♭7/D
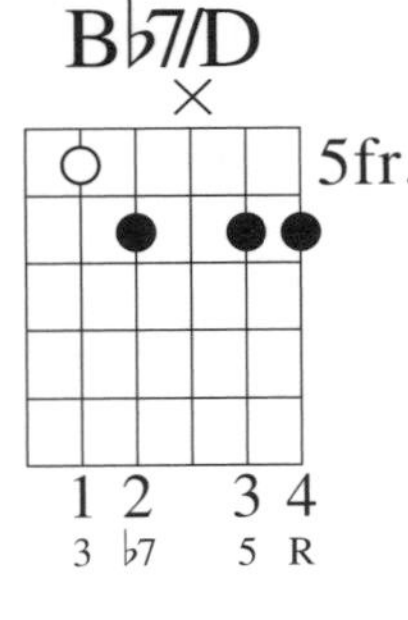

B♭7♭5/D
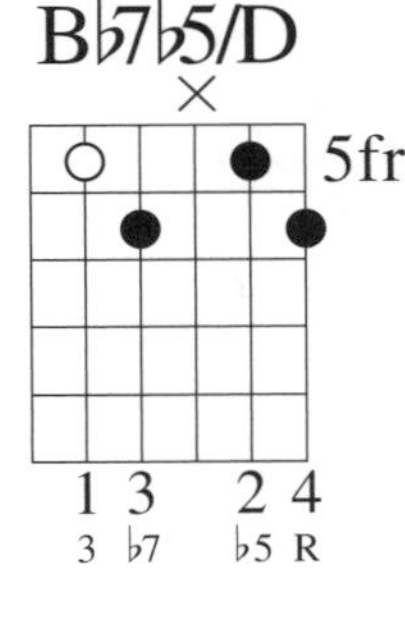

B♭7♯11/D
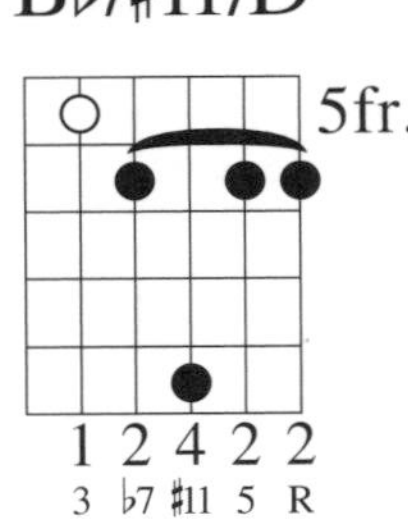

B♭9/D
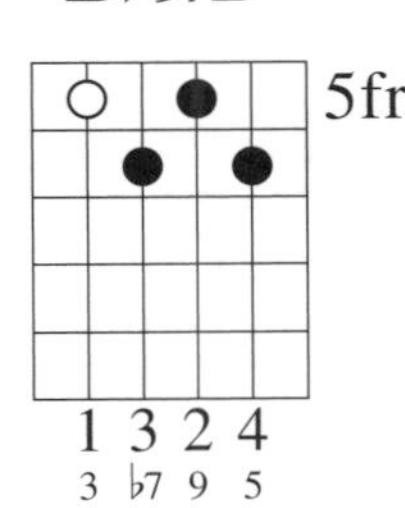

B♭9♭5/D
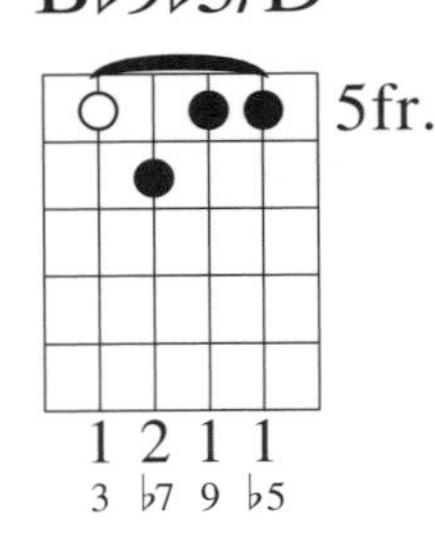

B♭11/D
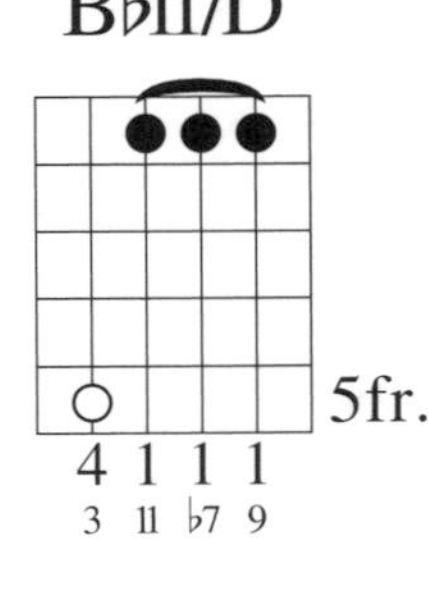

B♭7/D
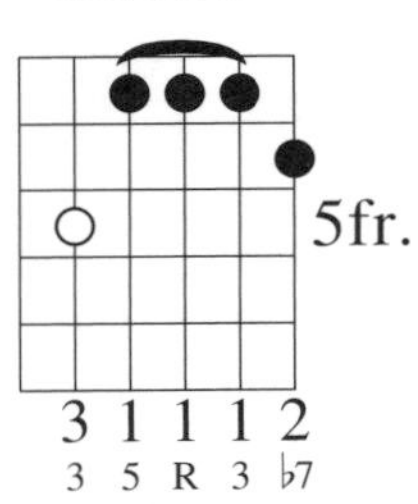

B♭7♭5/D
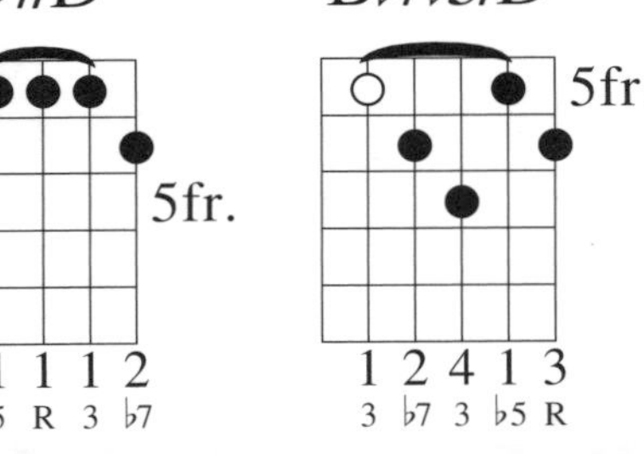

B♭7♯11/D
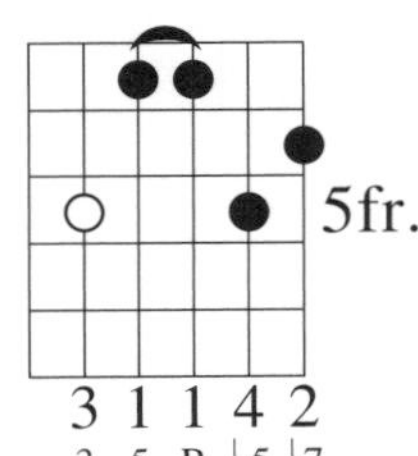

B♭9/D
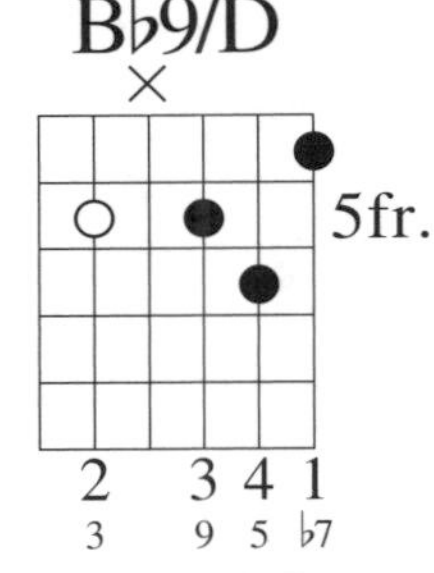

B♭9♭5/D
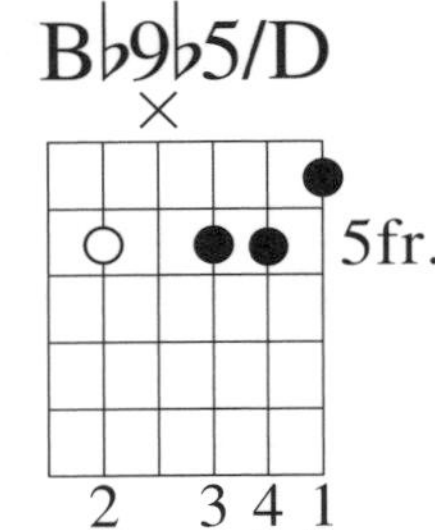

B♭11/D
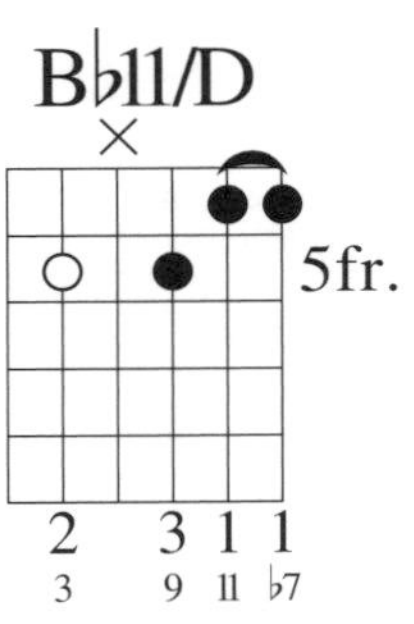

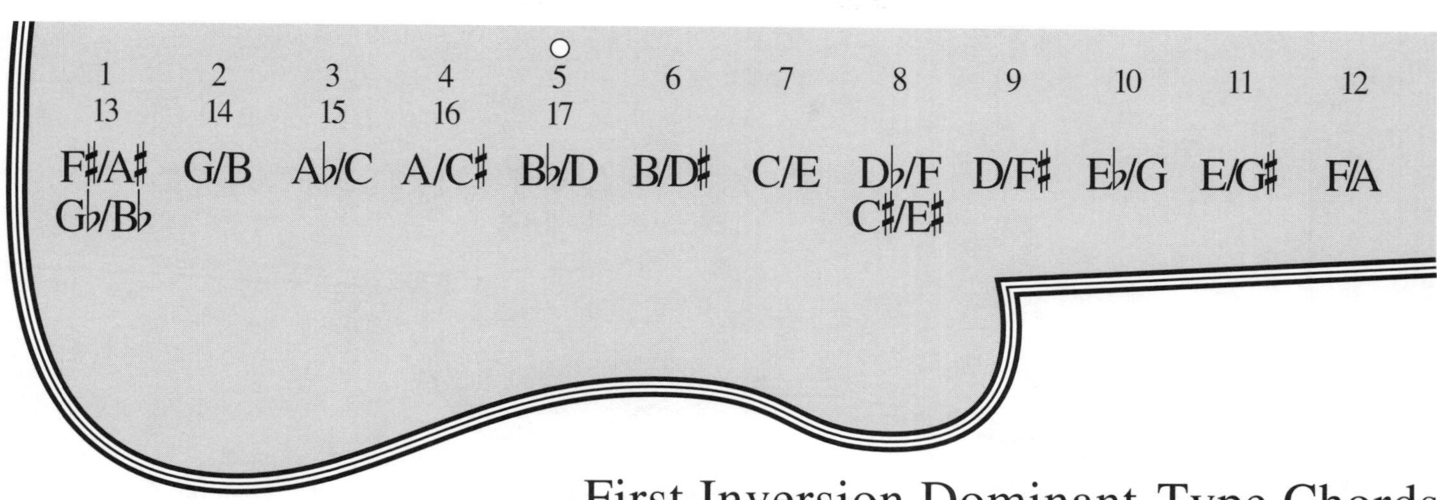

First Inversion Dominant-Type Chords

B♭13/D
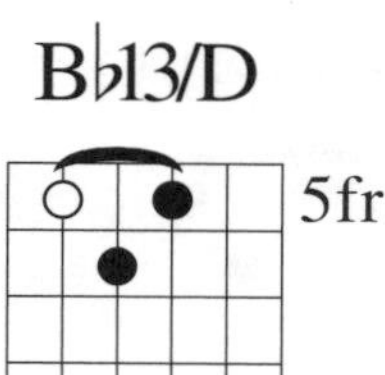
5fr.
1 2 1 4
3 ♭7 9 13

B♭13/D
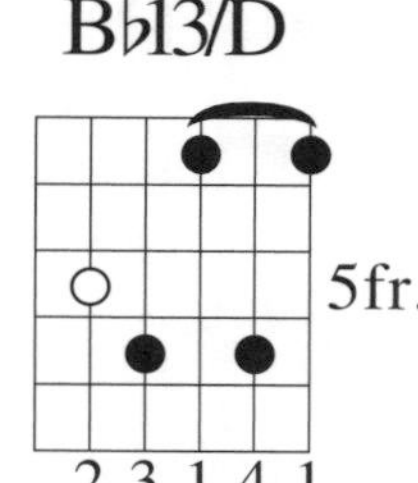
5fr.
2 3 1 4 1
3 ♭7 R 5 13

B♭7♯5/D
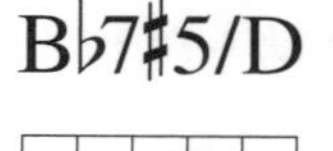
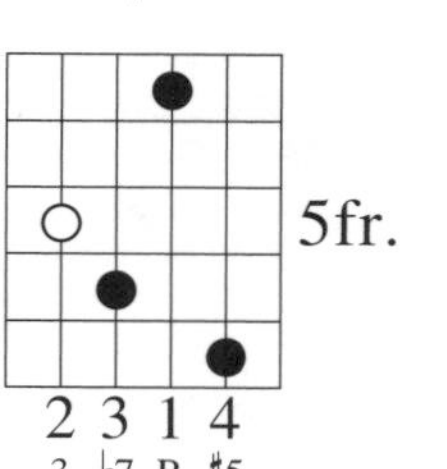
5fr.
2 3 1 4
3 ♭7 R ♯5

B♭7♯5♯11/D
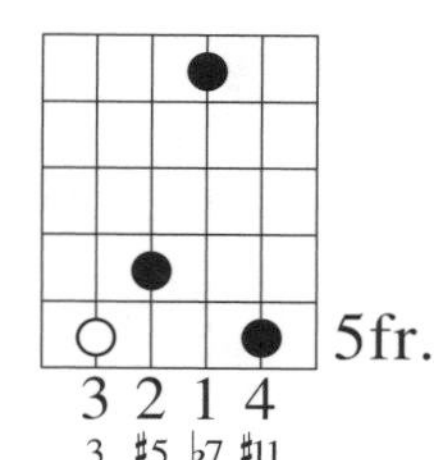
5fr.
3 2 1 4
3 ♯5 ♭7 ♯11

B♭9♯5/D
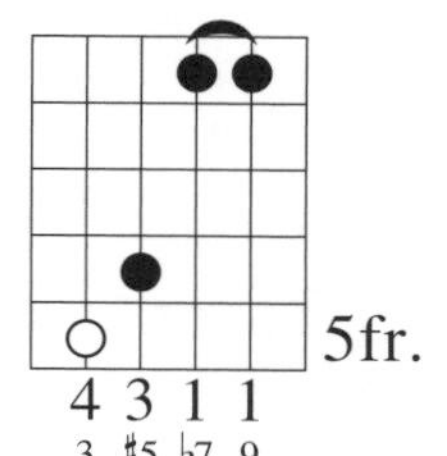
5fr.
4 3 1 1
3 ♯5 ♭7 9

B♭9♯5/D

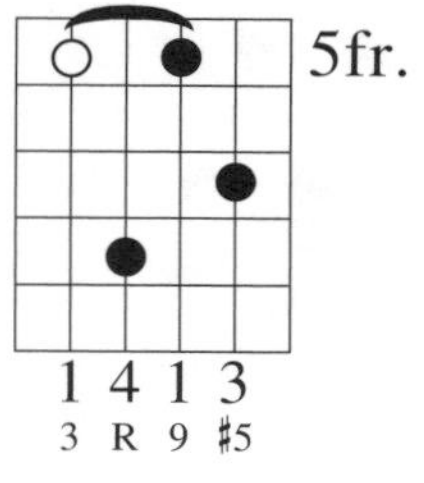
5fr.
1 4 1 3
3 R 9 ♯5

B♭13/D
5fr.
2 4 3 1 1
3 ♭7 9 3 13

B♭13/D
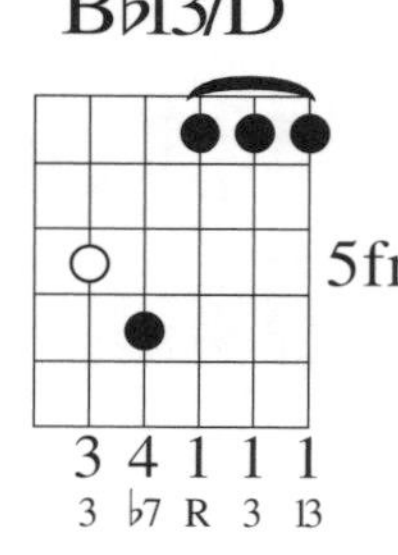
5fr.
3 4 1 1 1
3 ♭7 R 3 13

B♭7♯5/D
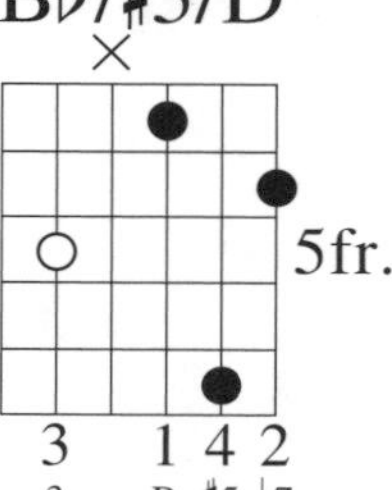
5fr.
3 1 4 2
3 R ♯5 ♭7

B♭7♯5♯11/D
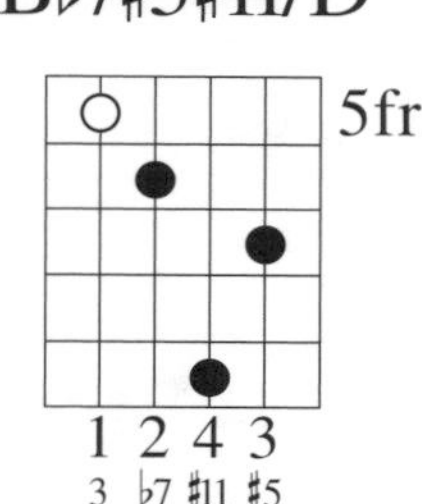
5fr.
1 2 4 3
3 ♭7 ♯11 ♯5

B♭9♯5/D
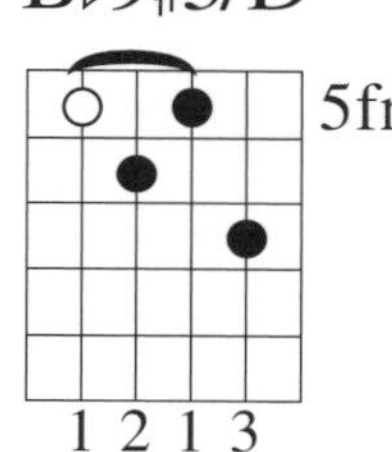
5fr.
1 2 1 3
3 ♭7 9 ♯5

B♭9♯5/D
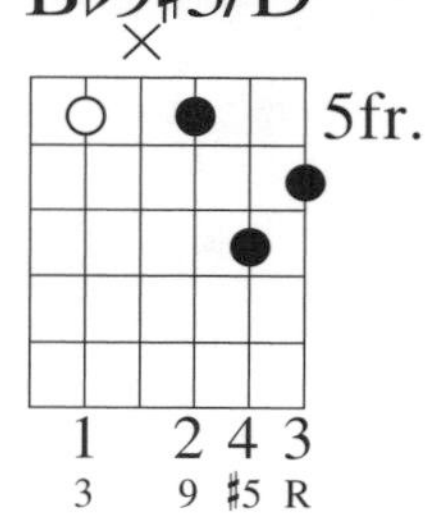
5fr.
1 2 4 3
3 9 ♯5 R

B♭13/D
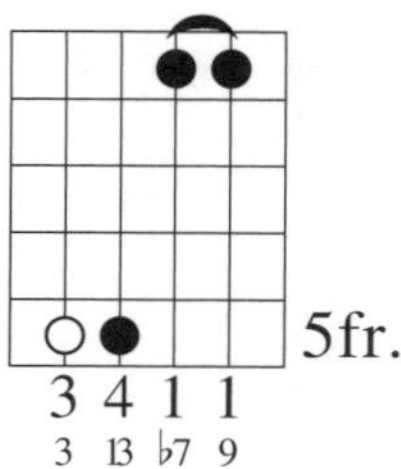
5fr.
3 4 1 1
3 13 ♭7 9

B♭13♯11/D
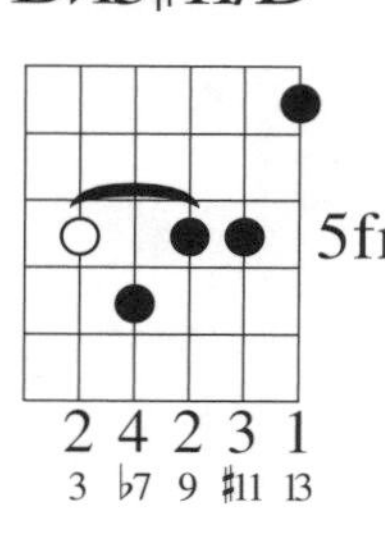
5fr.
2 4 2 3 1
3 ♭7 9 ♯11 13

B♭7♯5/D
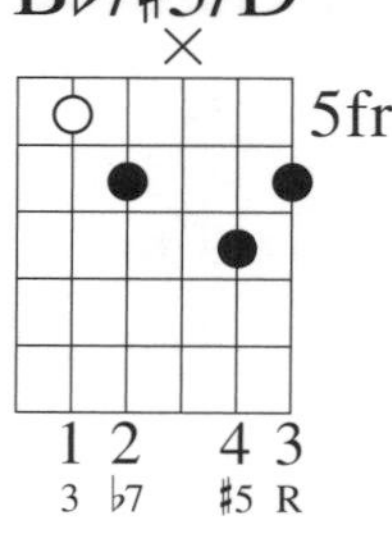
5fr.
1 2 4 3
3 ♭7 ♯5 R

B♭7♯5♯11/D
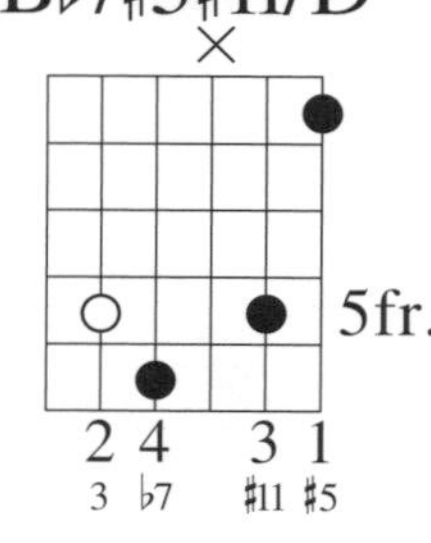
5fr.
2 4 3 1
3 ♭7 ♯11 ♯5

B♭9♯5/D
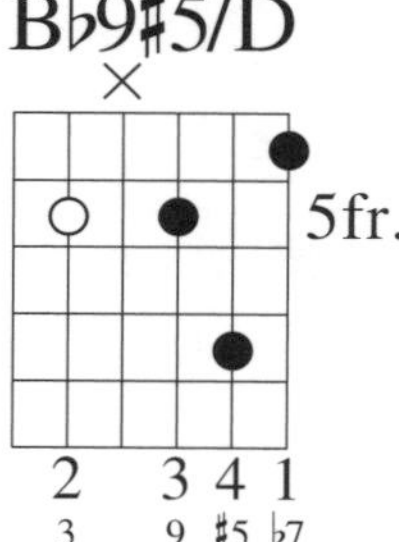
5fr.
2 3 4 1
3 9 ♯5 ♭7

B♭9♯5♯11/D
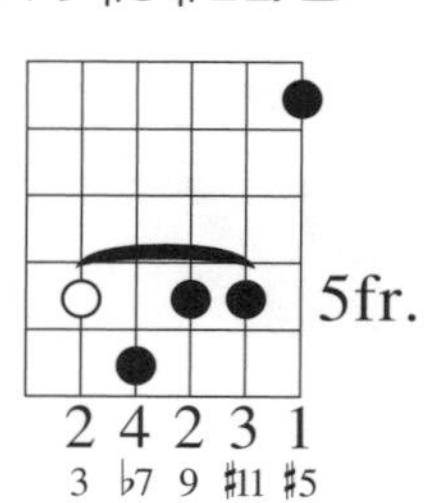
5fr.
2 4 2 3 1
3 ♭7 9 ♯11 ♯5

B♭13/D
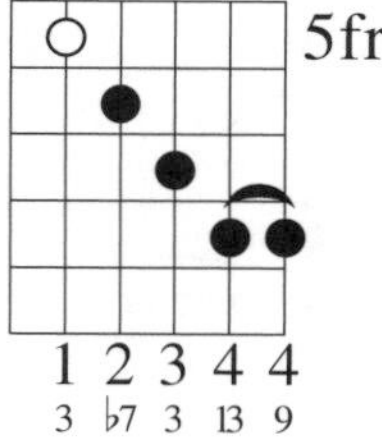
5fr.
1 2 3 4 4
3 ♭7 3 13 9

B♭13♯11/D
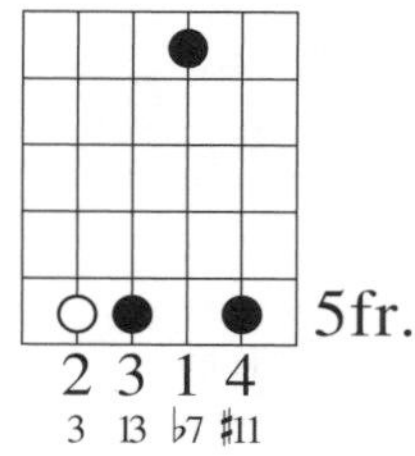
5fr.
2 3 1 4
3 13 ♭7 ♯11

B♭7♯5/D
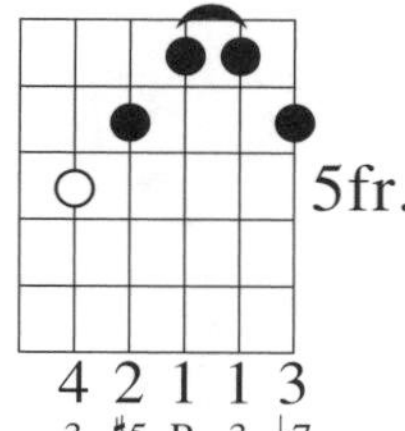
5fr.
4 2 1 1 3
3 ♯5 R 3 ♭7

B♭7♯5♯11/D
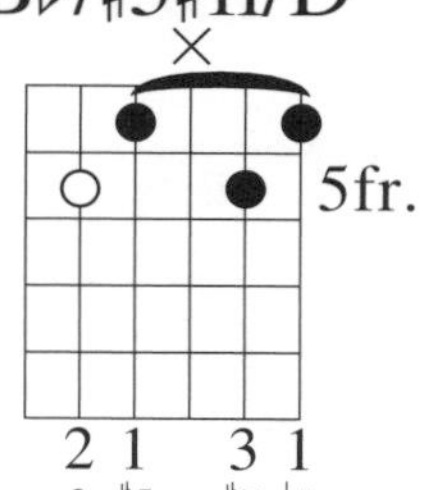
5fr.
2 1 3 1
3 ♯5 ♯11 ♭7

B♭9♯5/D
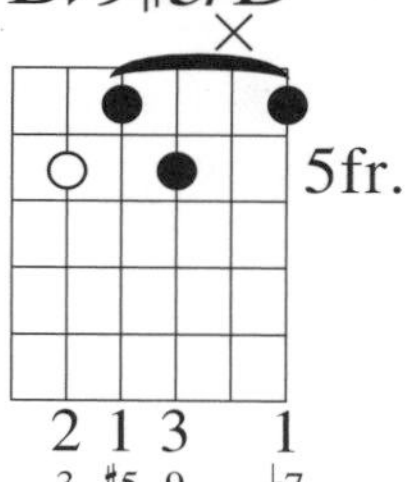
5fr.
2 1 3 1
3 ♯5 9 ♭7

B♭9♯5♯11/D
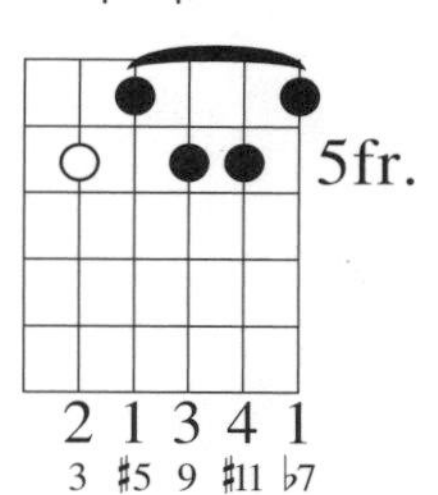
5fr.
2 1 3 4 1
3 ♯5 9 ♯11 ♭7

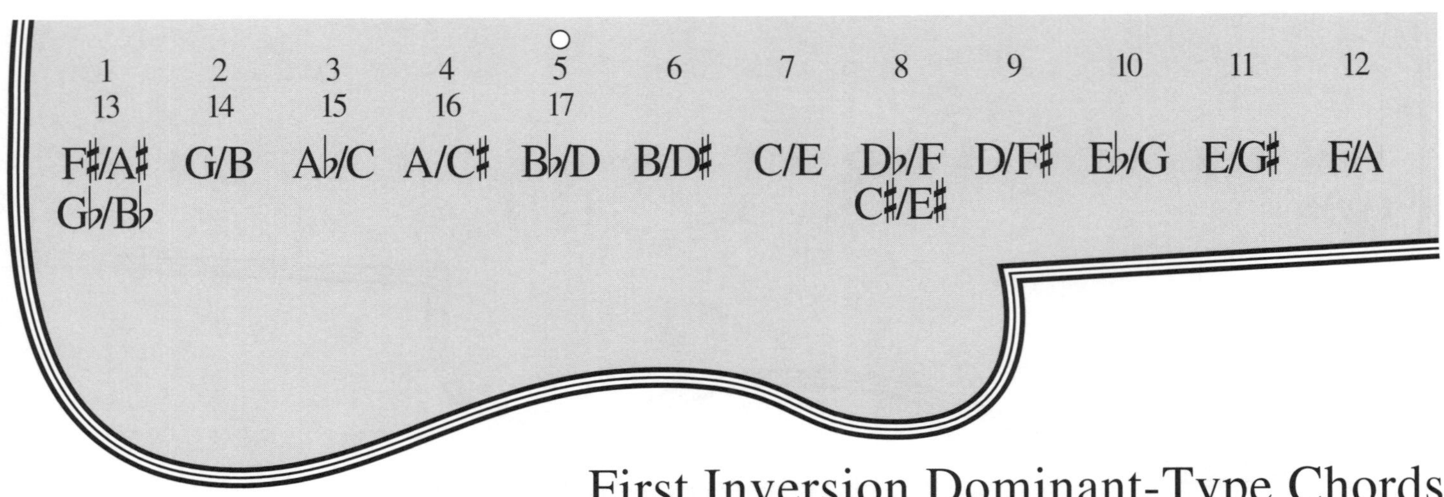

First Inversion Dominant-Type Chords

B♭7♭9/D

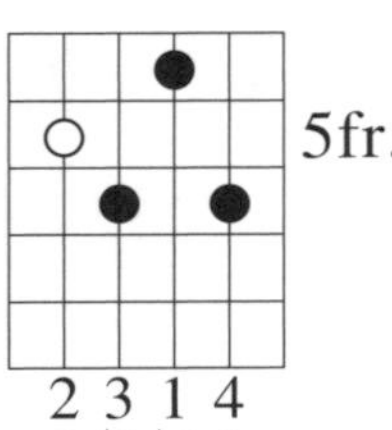

B♭7♯9/D
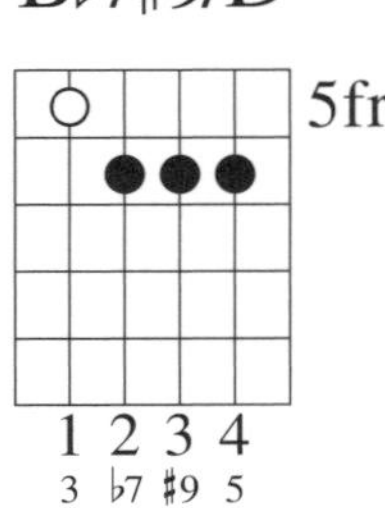

B♭7♯9/D
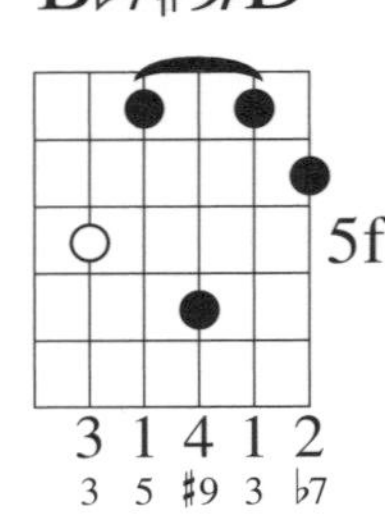

B♭7♭9♯9/D
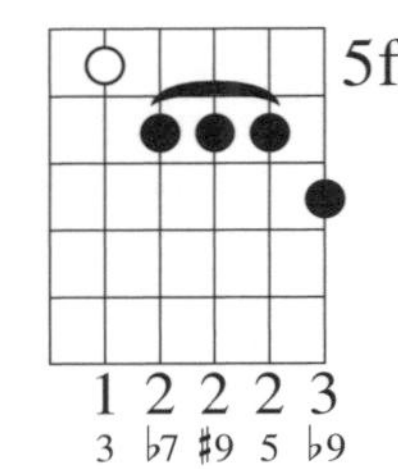

B♭7♭9♯11/D
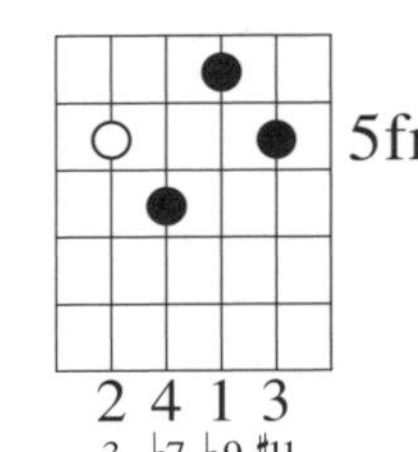

B♭7♯9♯11/D
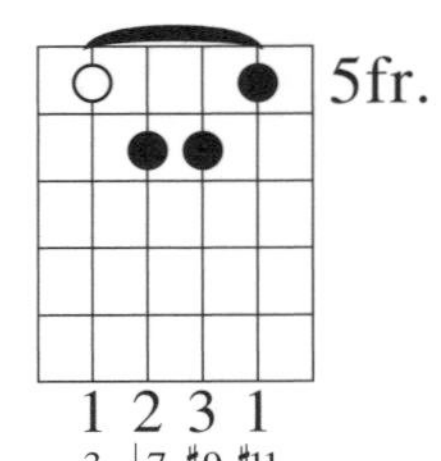

B♭7♭9/D
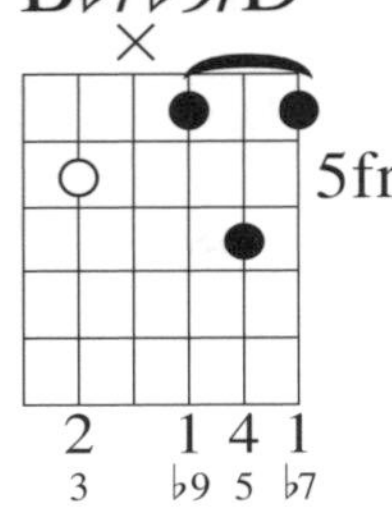

B♭7♯9/D
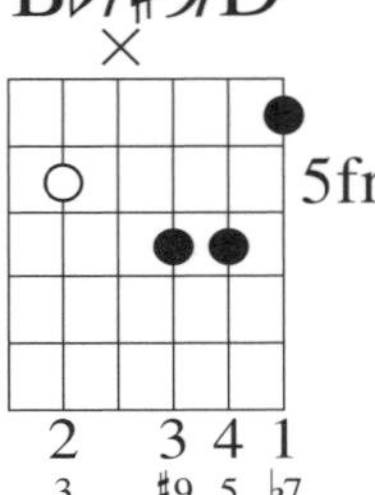

B♭7♯9/D
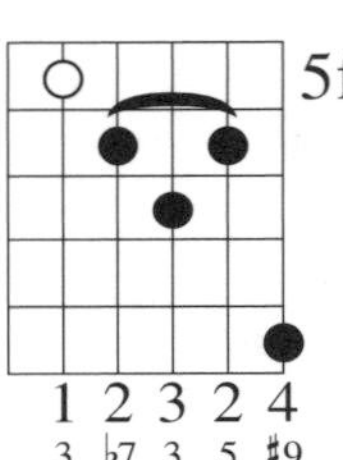

B♭7♭9♯9/D
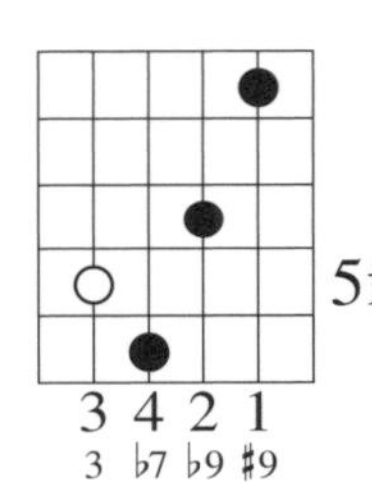

B♭7♭9♯11/D
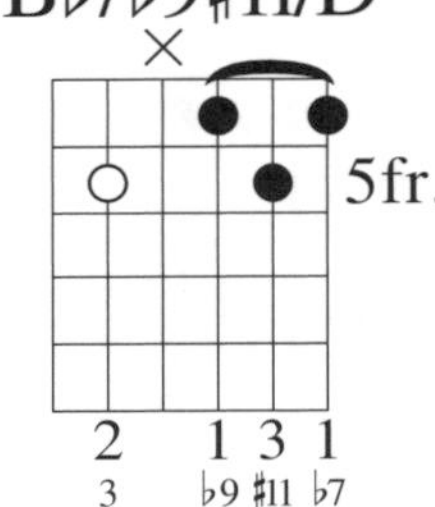

B♭7♯9♯11/D
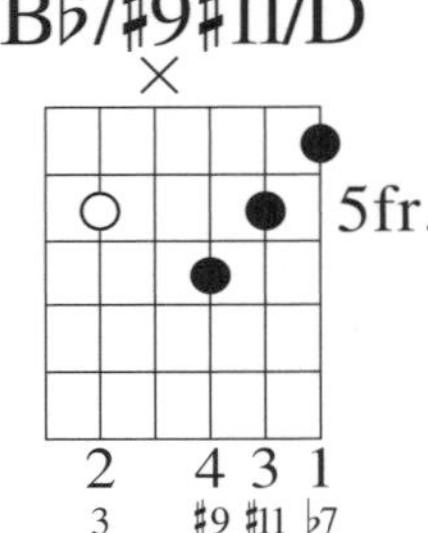

B♭7♭9/D
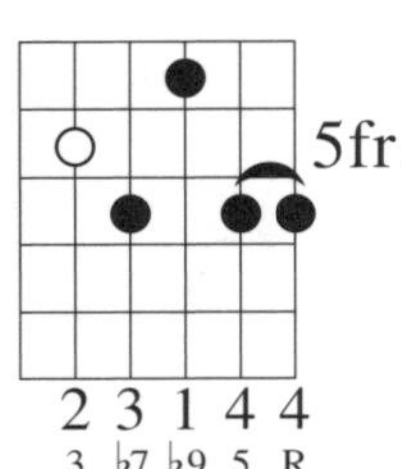

B♭7♯9/D
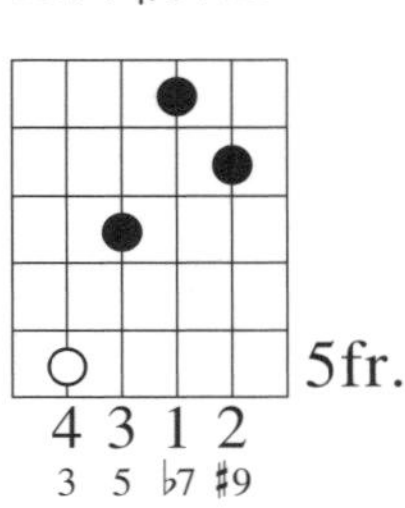

B♭7♯9/D
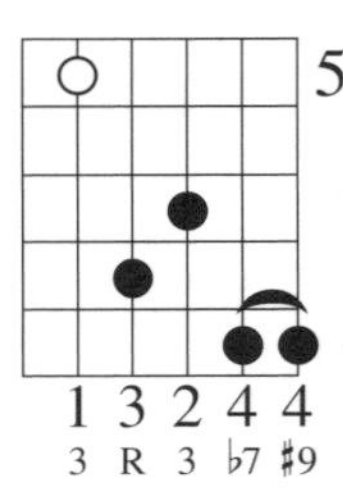

B♭7♭9♯9/D
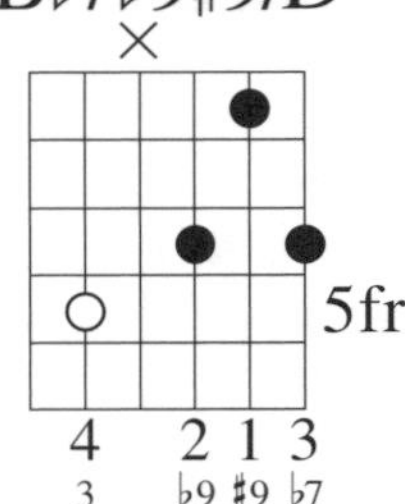

B♭7♭9♯11/D
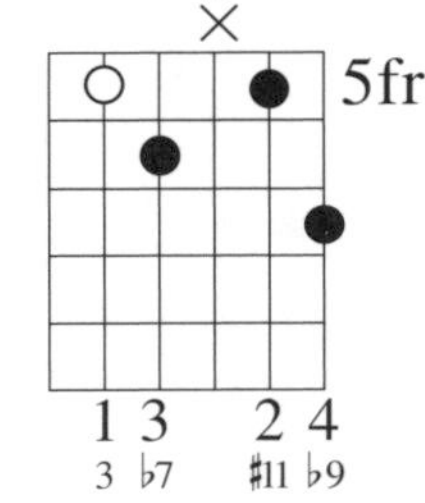

B♭7♯9♯11/D
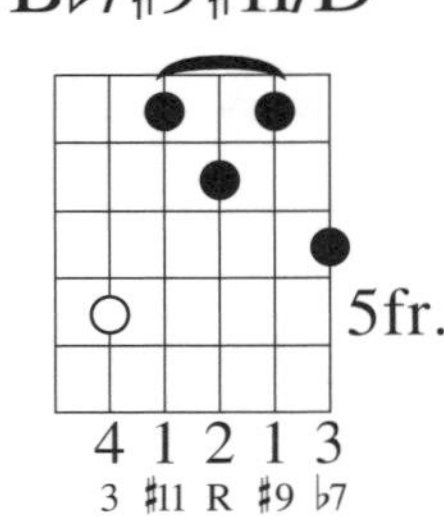

B♭7♭9/D
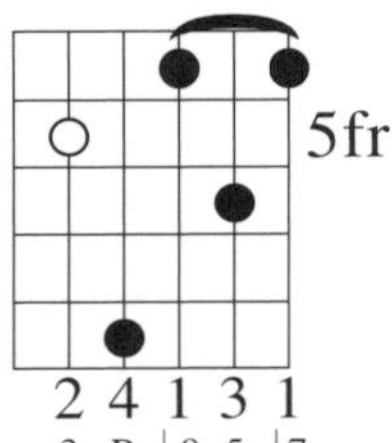

B♭7♯9/D
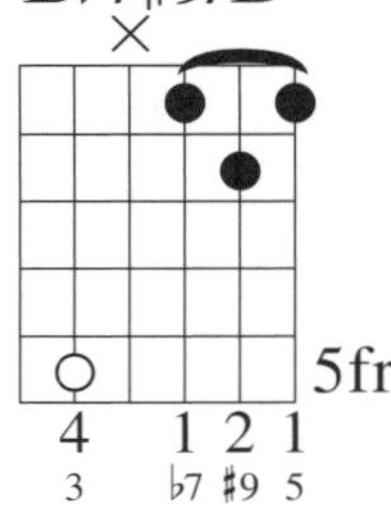

B♭7♯9/D
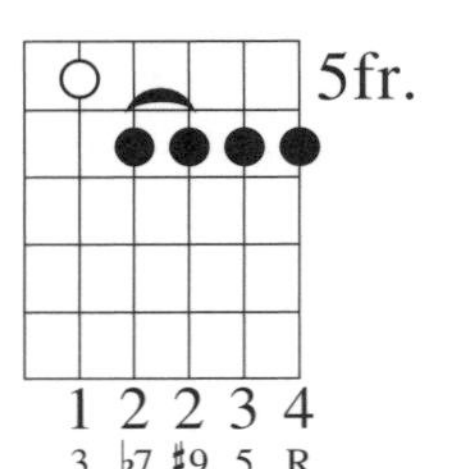

B♭7♭9♯9/D
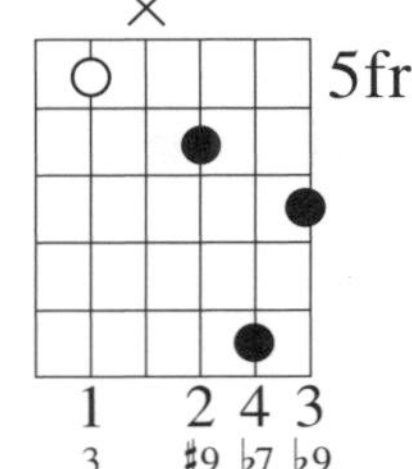

B♭7♭9♯11/D
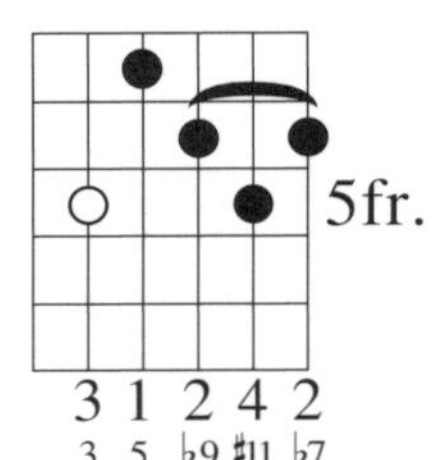

B♭7♯9♯11/D
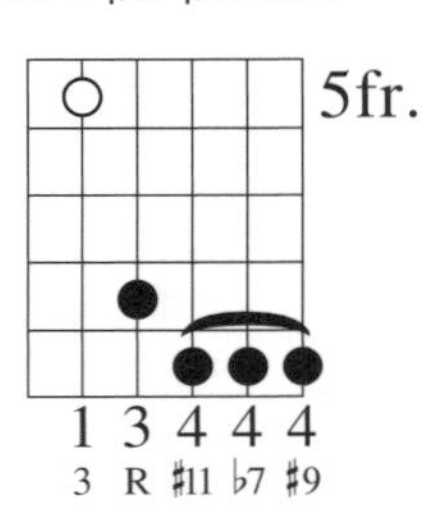

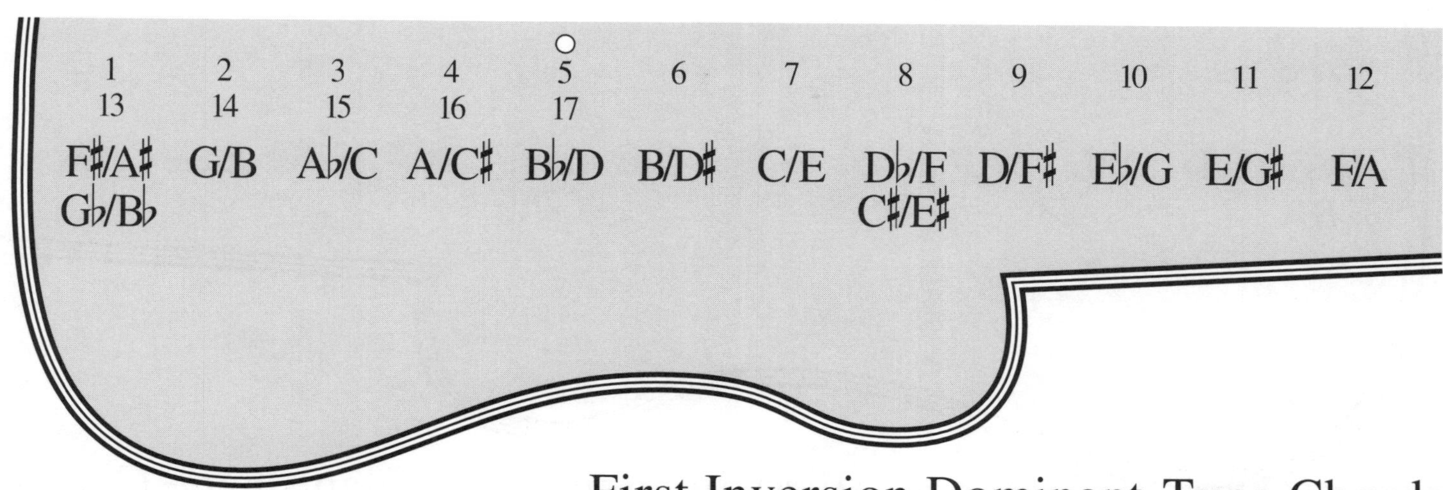

First Inversion Dominant-Type Chords

B♭7♭9♯9♯11/D
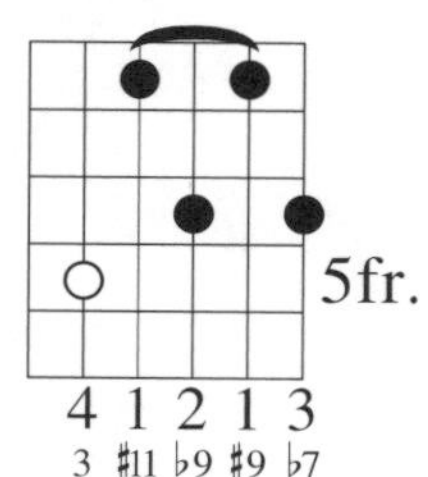

B♭11♭9/D
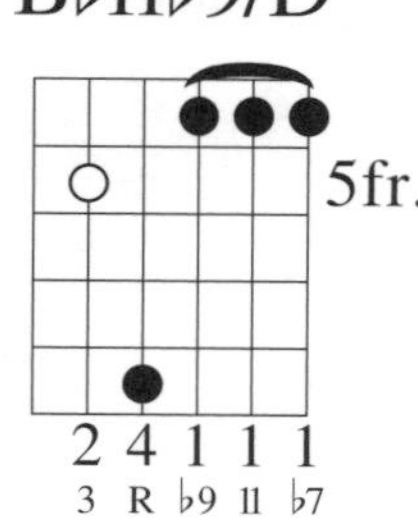

B♭13♯9/D
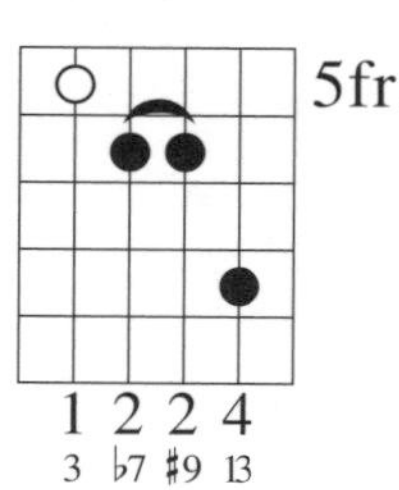

B♭13♭9♯9/D
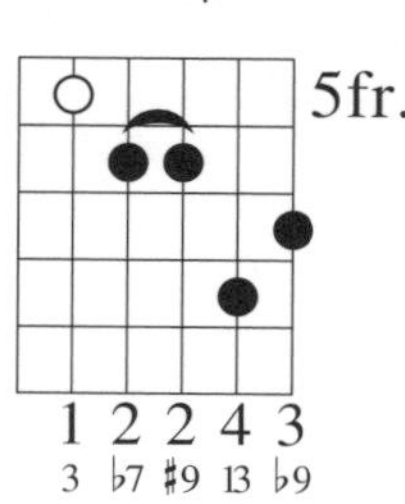

B♭7♭13/D
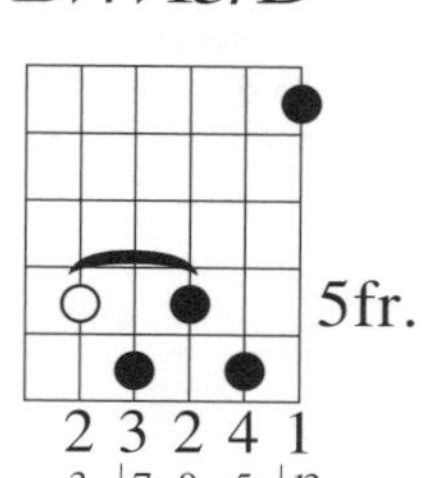

B♭7♭9♭13/D
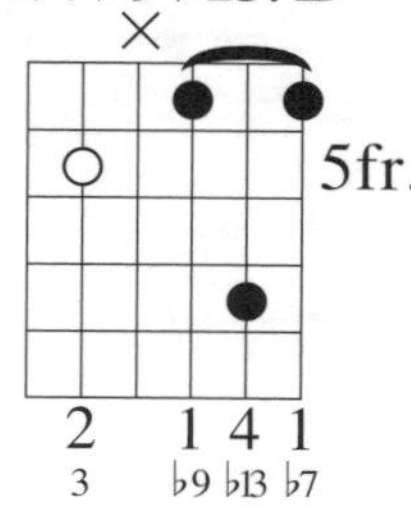

B♭7♭9♯9♯11/D
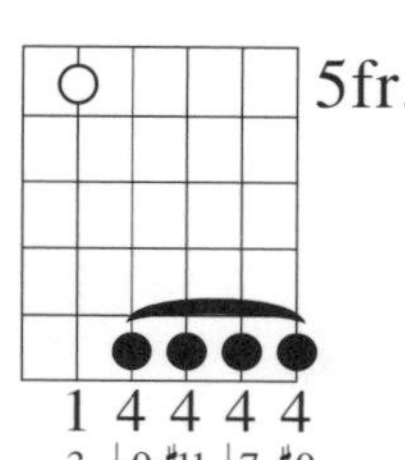

B♭13♭9/D
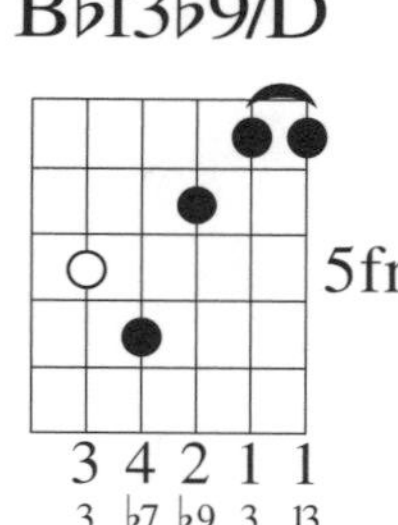

B♭13♯9/D
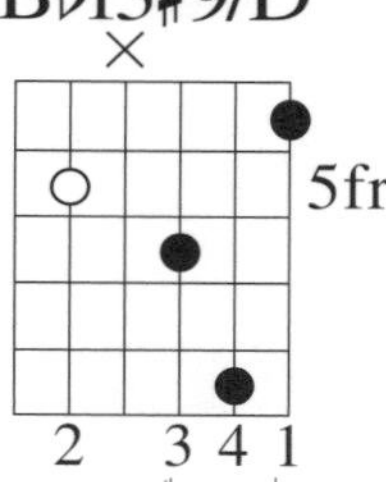

B♭13♭9♯9♯11/D
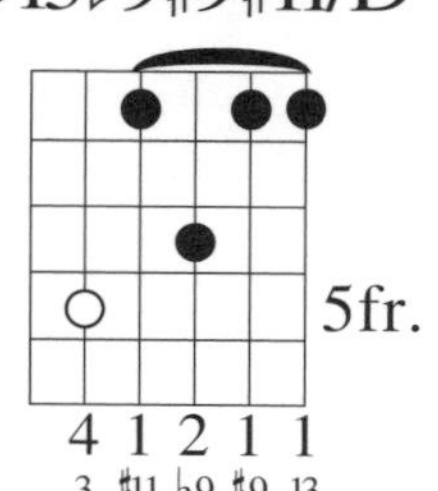

B♭7♭9♭13/D
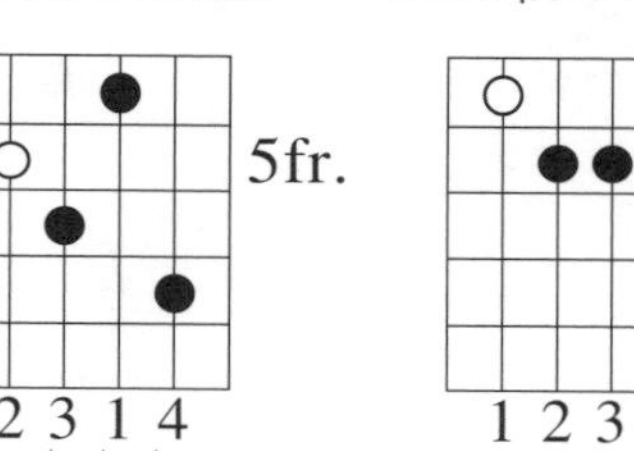

B♭7♯9♭13/D
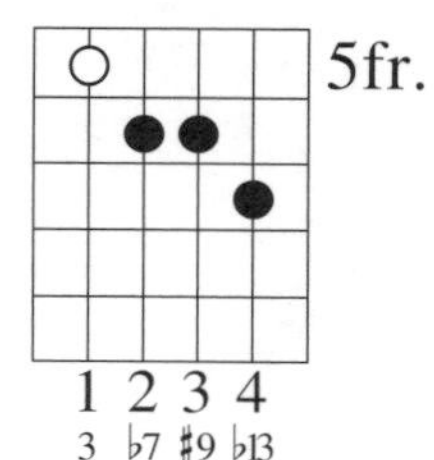

B♭7♭9♯9♯11/D
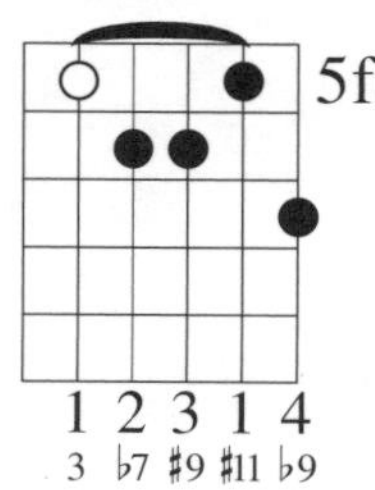

B♭13♭9/D
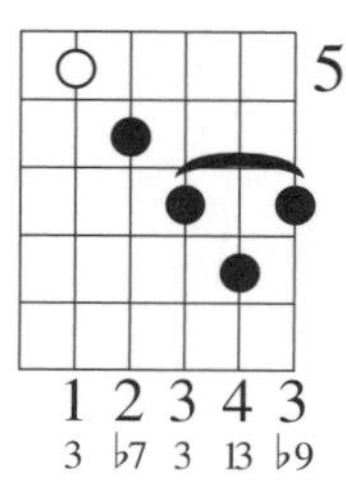

B♭13♯9/D
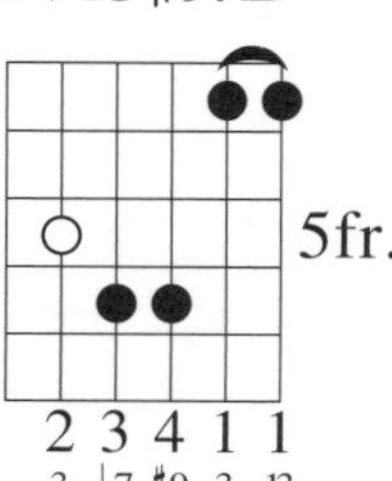

B♭13♭9♯9♯11/D
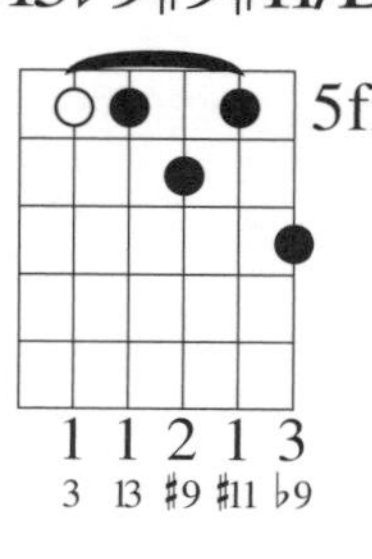

B♭7♭9♭13/D
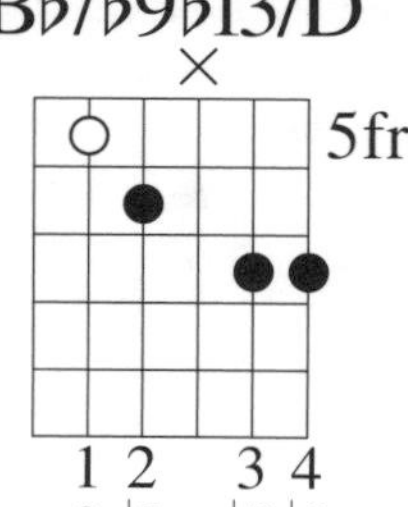

B♭7♯9♭13/D
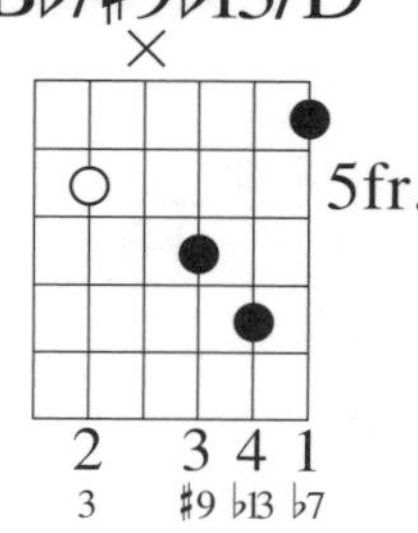

B♭11♭9/D
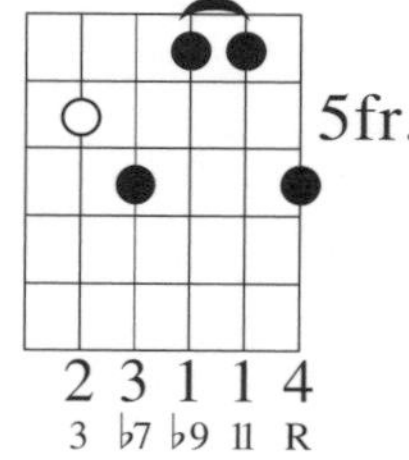

B♭13♭9/D
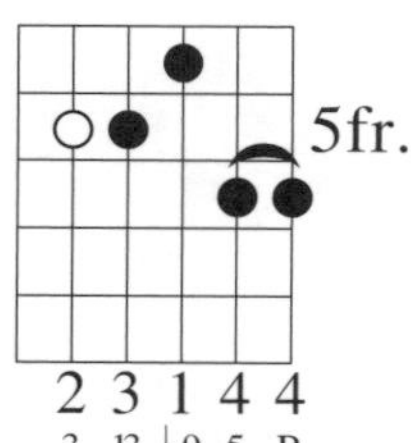

B♭13♯9/D
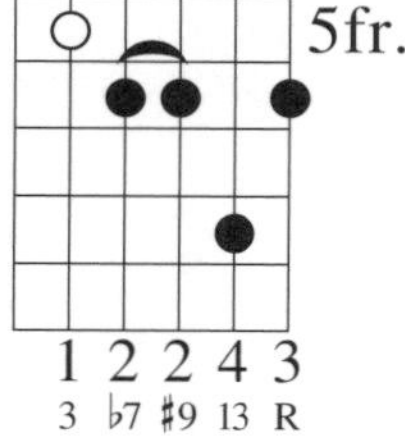

B♭7♭13/D
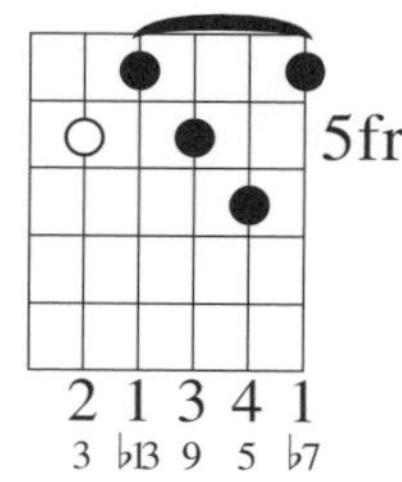

B♭7♭9♭13/D
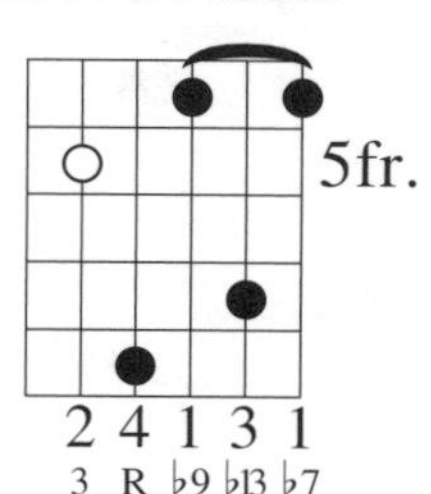

B♭7♯9♭13/D
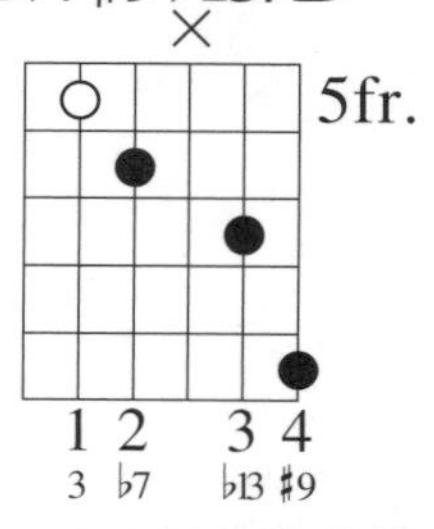

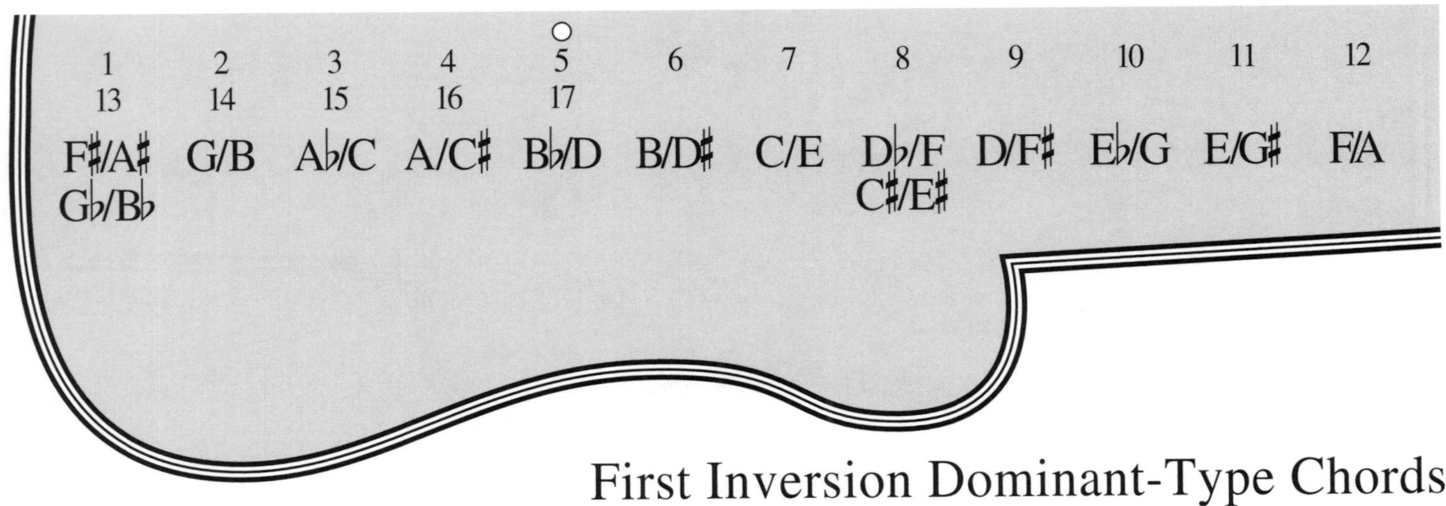

First Inversion Dominant-Type Chords

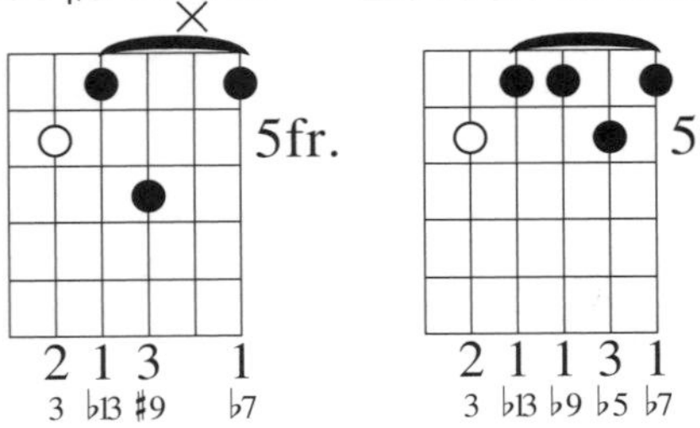

B♭7♯9♭13/D B♭7♭9♭13♭5/D

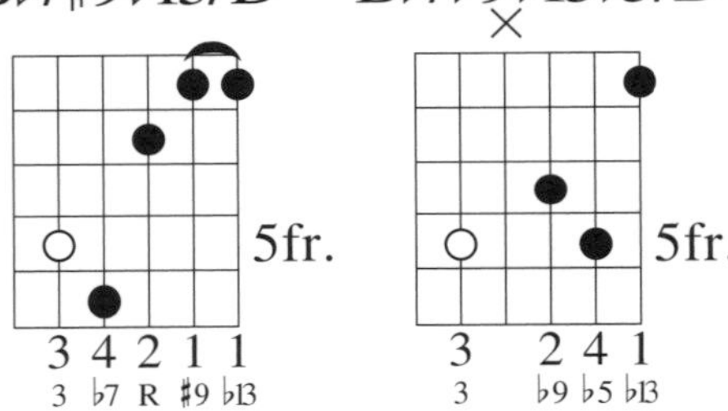

B♭7♭9♯9♭13/D B♭7♯9♭13♭5/D

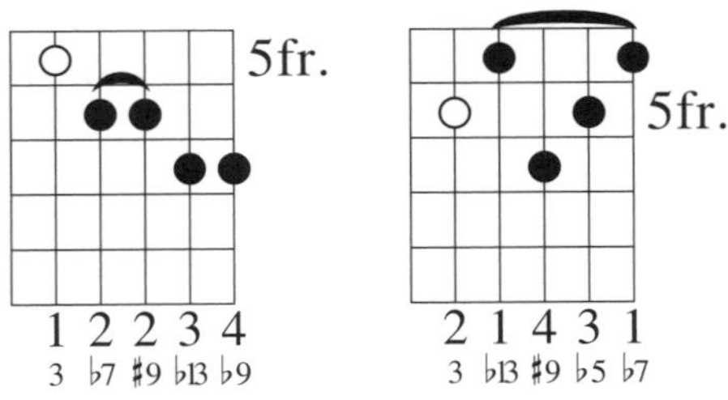

B♭7♭9♯9♭13/D B♭7♭9♯9♭13♭5/D

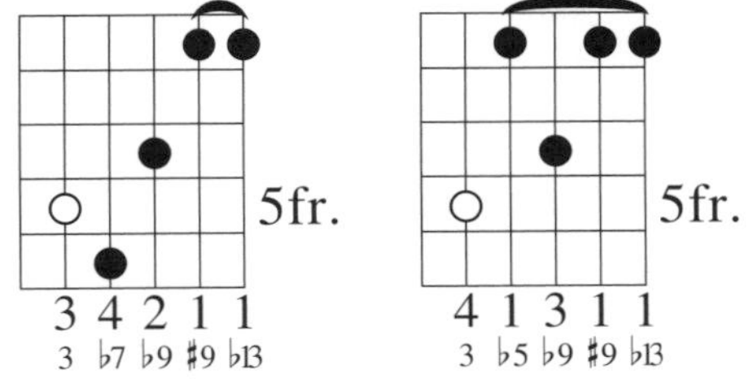

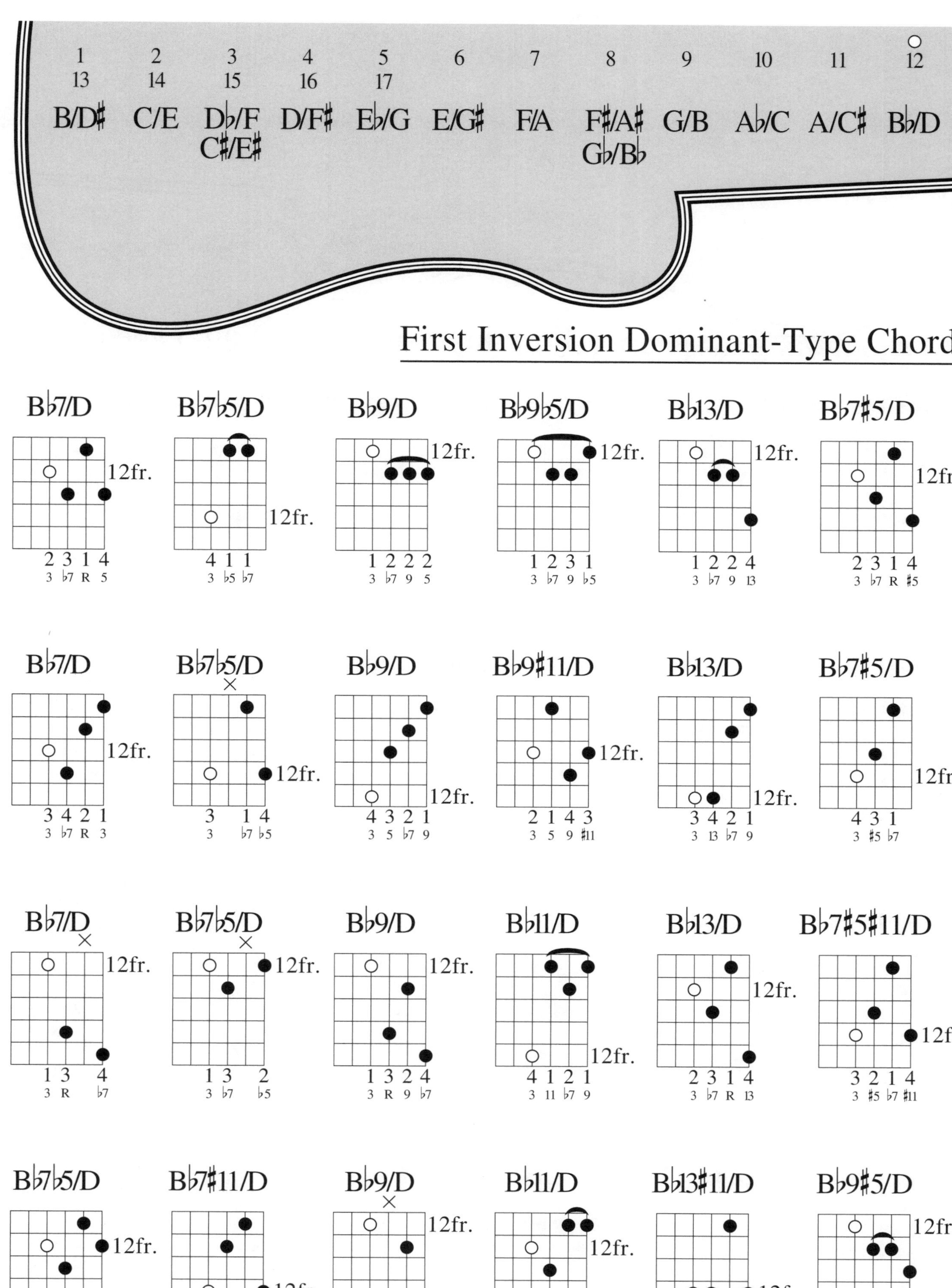
1 13 B/D♯
2 14 C/E
3 15 D♭/F C♯/E♯
4 16 D/F♯
5 17 E♭/G
6 E/G♯
7 F/A
8 F♯/A♯ G♭/B♭
9 G/B
10 A♭/C
11 A/C♯
12 B♭/D
First Inversion Dominant-Type Chords
B♭7/D 12fr. 2 3 1 4 3 ♭7 R 5
B♭7♭5/D 12fr. 4 1 1 3 ♭5 ♭7
B♭9/D 12fr. 1 2 2 2 3 ♭7 9 5
B♭9♭5/D 12fr. 1 2 3 1 3 ♭7 9 ♭5
B♭13/D 12fr. 1 2 2 4 3 ♭7 9 13
B♭7♯5/D 12fr. 2 3 1 4 3 ♭7 R ♯5
B♭7/D 12fr. 3 4 2 1 3 ♭7 R 3
B♭7♭5/D 12fr. 3 1 4 3 ♭7 ♭5
B♭9/D 12fr. 4 3 2 1 3 5 ♭7 9
B♭9♯11/D 12fr. 2 1 4 3 3 5 9 ♯11
B♭13/D 12fr. 3 4 2 1 3 13 ♭7 9
B♭7♯5/D 12fr. 4 3 1 3 ♯5 ♭7
B♭7/D 12fr. 1 3 4 3 R ♭7
B♭7♭5/D 12fr. 1 3 2 3 ♭7 ♭5
B♭9/D 12fr. 1 3 2 4 3 R 9 ♭7
B♭11/D 12fr. 4 1 2 1 3 11 ♭7 9
B♭13/D 12fr. 2 3 1 4 3 ♭7 R 13
B♭7♯5♯11/D 12fr. 3 2 1 4 3 ♯5 ♭7 ♯11
B♭7♭5/D 12fr. 2 3 1 4 3 ♭7 R ♭5
B♭7♯11/D 12fr. 3 2 1 4 3 5 ♭7 ♯11
B♭9/D 12fr. 1 2 4 3 9 ♭7
B♭11/D 12fr. 2 3 1 1 3 ♭7 R 11
B♭13♯11/D 12fr. 2 3 1 4 3 13 ♭7 ♯11
B♭9♯5/D 12fr. 1 2 2 3 3 ♭7 9 ♯5

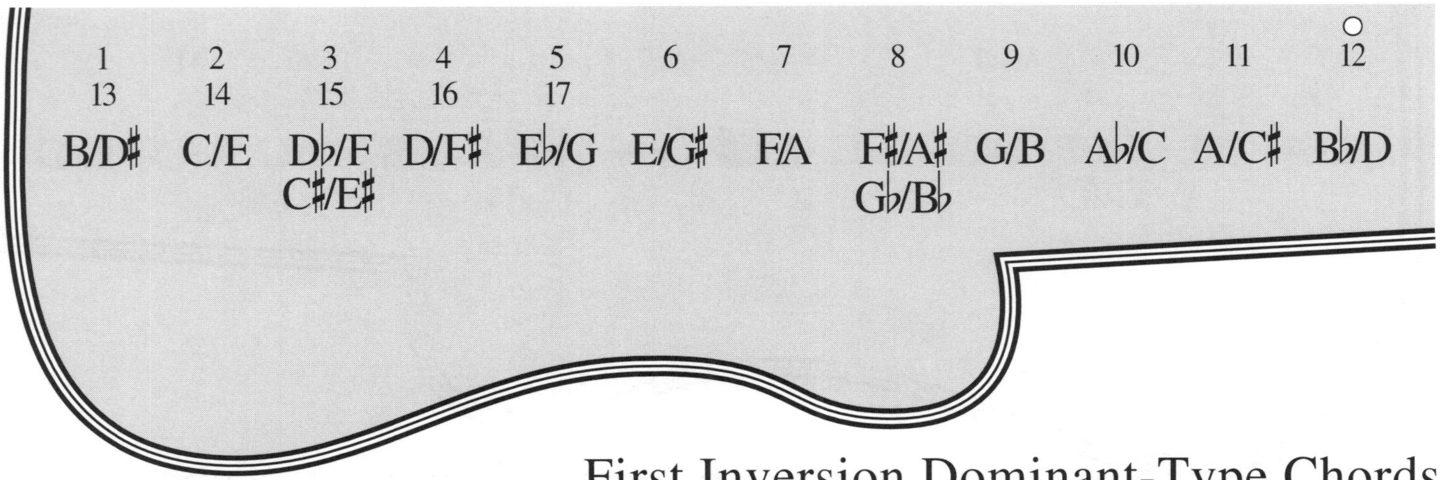

1 13	2 14	3 15	4 16	5 17	6	7	8	9	10	11	12
B/D♯	C/E	D♭/F C♯/E♯	D/F♯	E♭/G	E/G♯	F/A	F♯/A♯ G♭/B♭	G/B	A♭/C	A/C♯	B♭/D

First Inversion Dominant-Type Chords

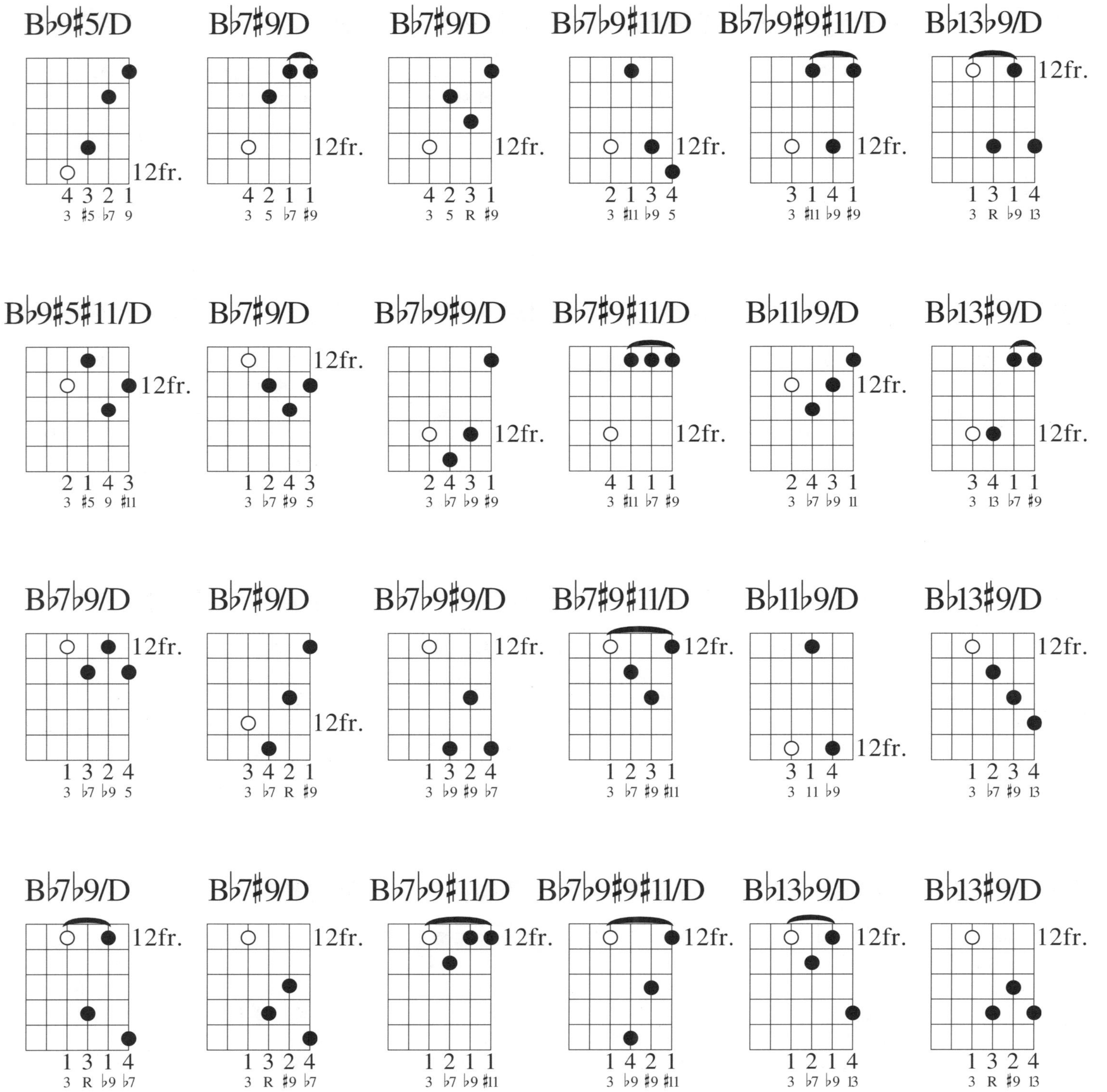

B♭9♯5/D
12fr.
4 3 2 1
3 ♯5 ♭7 9

B♭7♯9/D
12fr.
4 2 1 1
3 5 ♭7 ♯9

B♭7♯9/D
12fr.
4 2 3 1
3 5 R ♯9

B♭7♭9♯11/D
12fr.
2 1 3 4
3 ♯11 ♭9 5

B♭7♭9♯9♯11/D
12fr.
3 1 4 1
3 ♯11 ♭9 ♯9

B♭13♭9/D
12fr.
1 3 1 4
3 R ♭9 13

B♭9♯5♯11/D
12fr.
2 1 4 3
3 ♯5 9 ♯11

B♭7♯9/D
12fr.
1 2 4 3
3 ♭7 ♯9 5

B♭7♭9♯9/D
12fr.
2 4 3 1
3 ♭7 ♭9 ♯9

B♭7♯9♯11/D
12fr.
4 1 1 1
3 ♯11 ♭7 ♯9

B♭11♭9/D
12fr.
2 4 3 1
3 ♭7 ♭9 11

B♭13♯9/D
12fr.
3 4 1 1
3 13 ♭7 ♯9

B♭7♭9/D
12fr.
1 3 2 4
3 ♭7 ♭9 5

B♭7♯9/D
12fr.
3 4 2 1
3 ♭7 R ♯9

B♭7♭9♯9/D
12fr.
1 3 2 4
3 ♭9 ♯9 ♭7

B♭7♯9♯11/D
12fr.
1 2 3 1
3 ♭7 ♯9 ♯11

B♭11♭9/D
12fr.
3 1 4
3 11 ♭9

B♭13♯9/D
12fr.
1 2 3 4
3 ♭7 ♯9 13

B♭7♭9/D
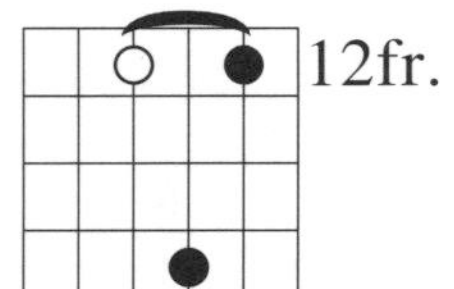
12fr.
1 3 1 4
3 R ♭9 ♭7

B♭7♯9/D
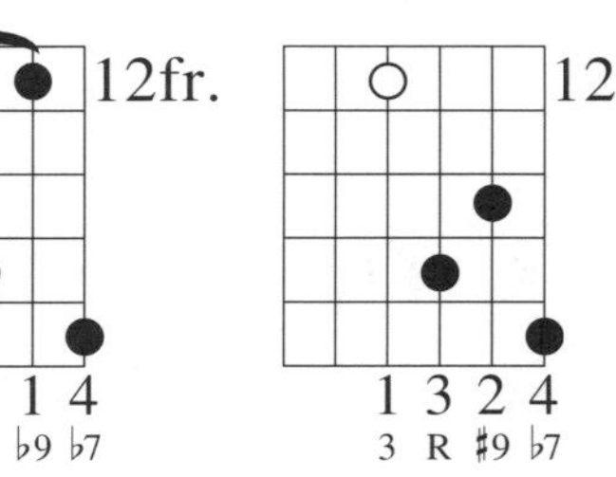
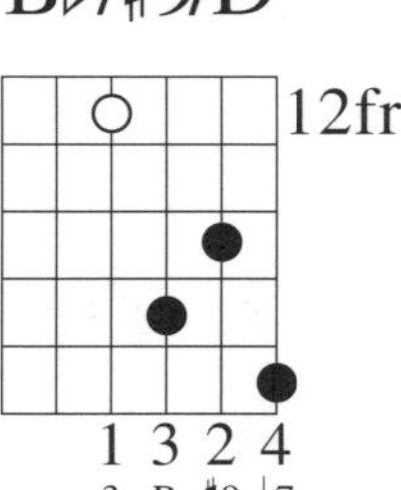
12fr.
1 3 2 4
3 R ♯9 ♭7

B♭7♭9♯11/D
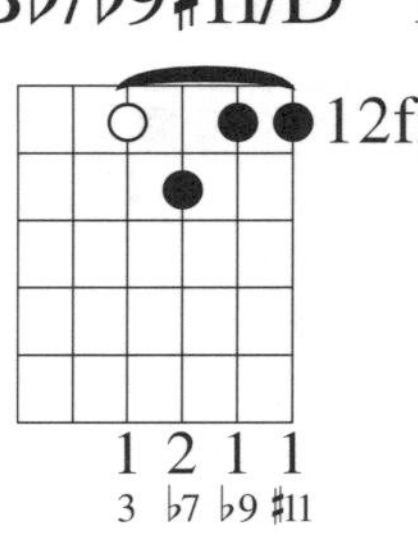
12fr.
1 2 1 1
3 ♭7 ♭9 ♯11

B♭7♭9♯9♯11/D
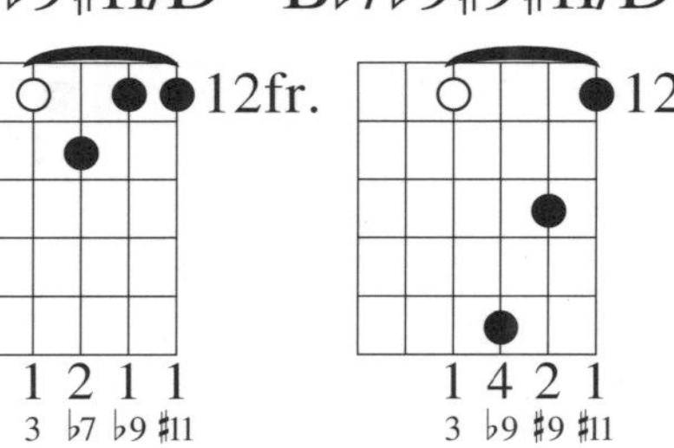
12fr.
1 4 2 1
3 ♭9 ♯9 ♯11

B♭13♭9/D
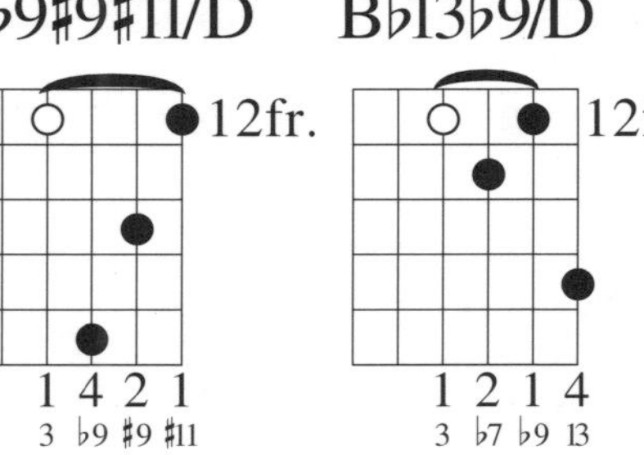
12fr.
1 2 1 4
3 ♭7 ♭9 13

B♭13♯9/D
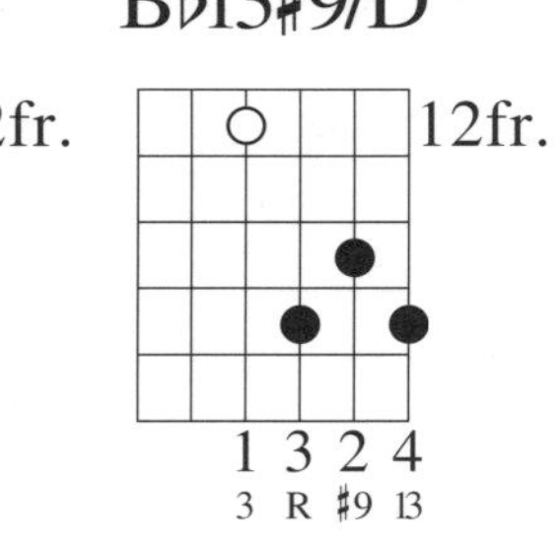
12fr.
1 3 2 4
3 R ♯9 13

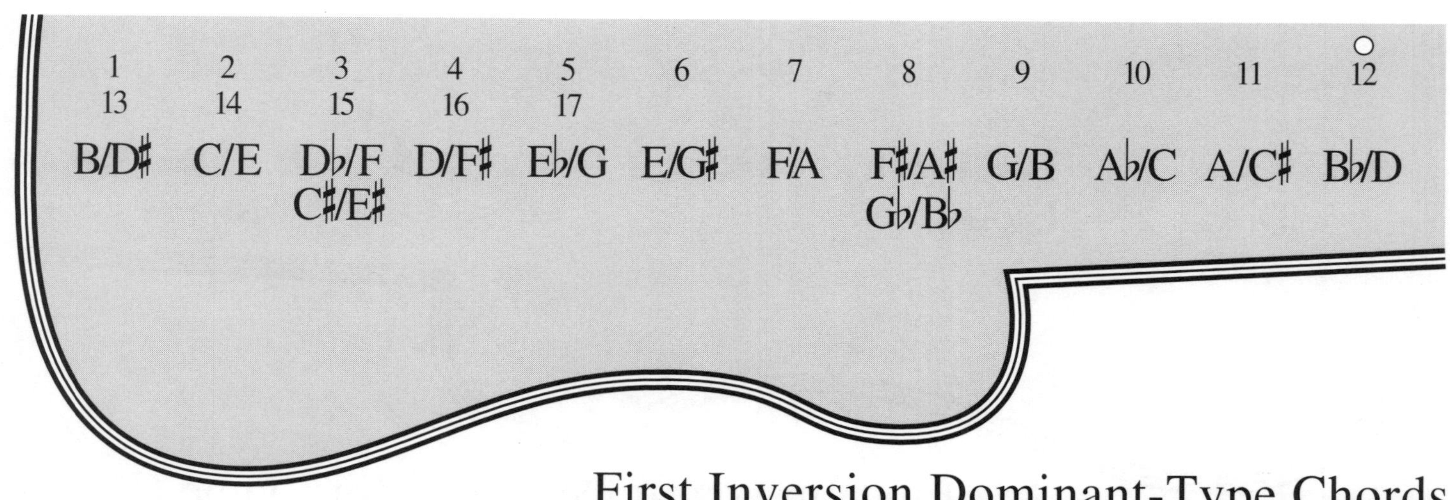

First Inversion Dominant-Type Chords

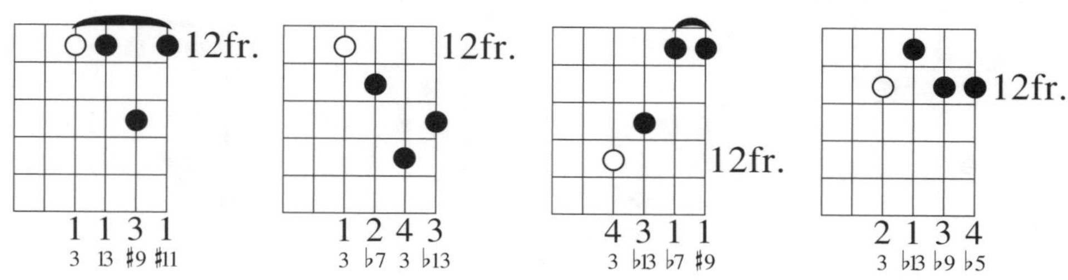

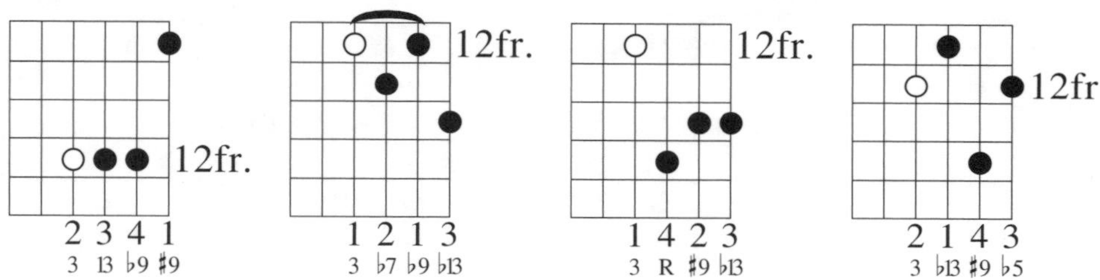

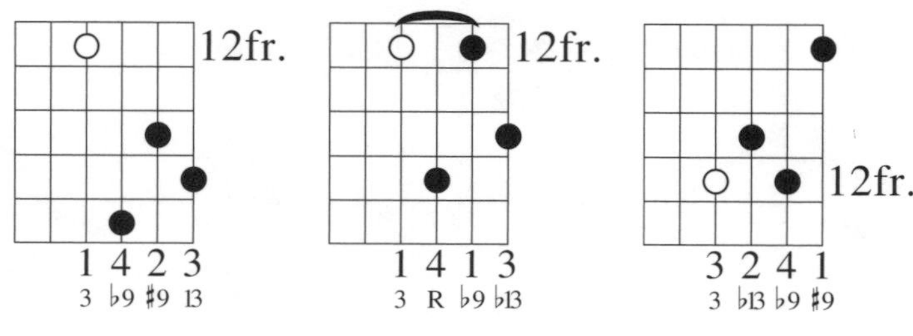

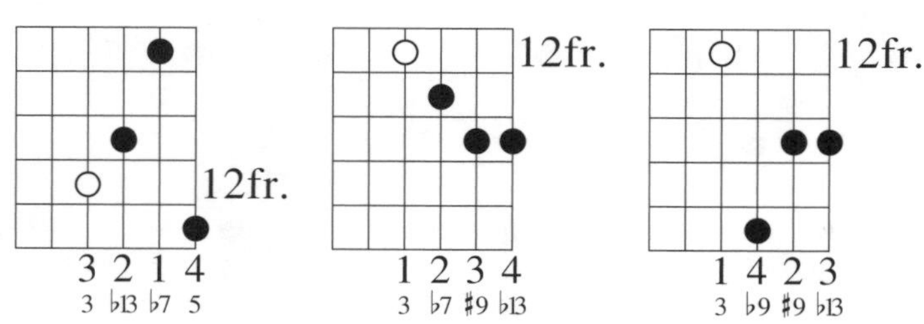

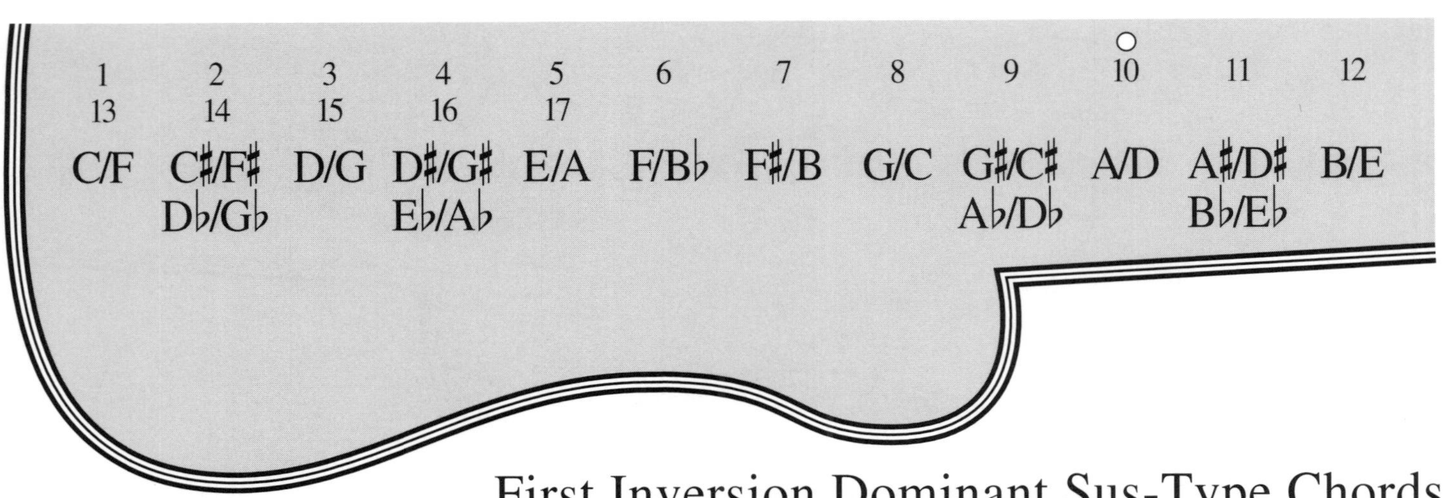

First Inversion Dominant Sus-Type Chords

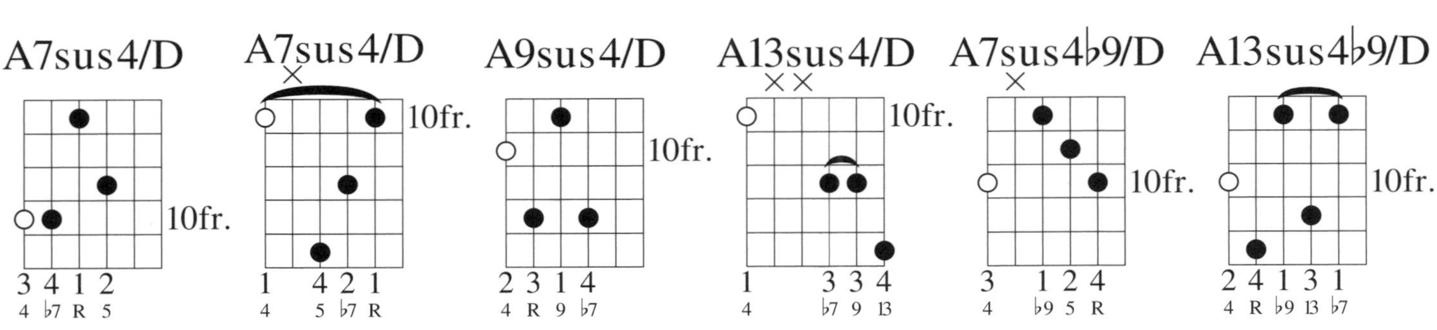

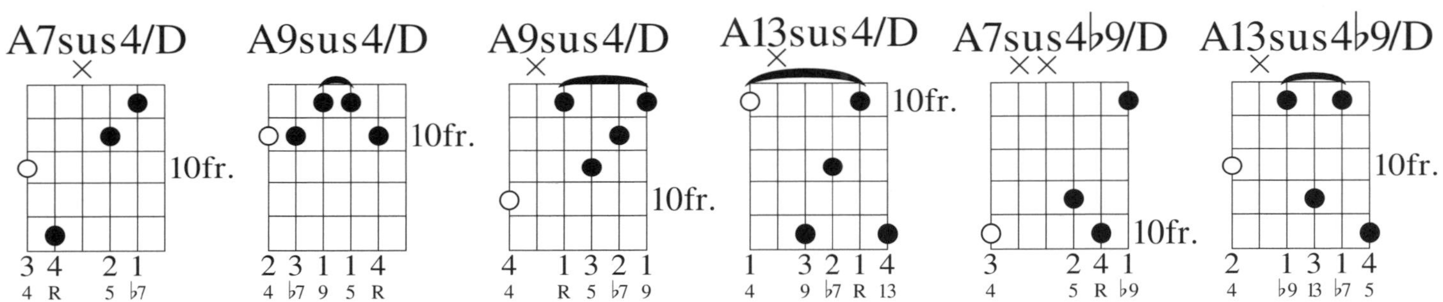

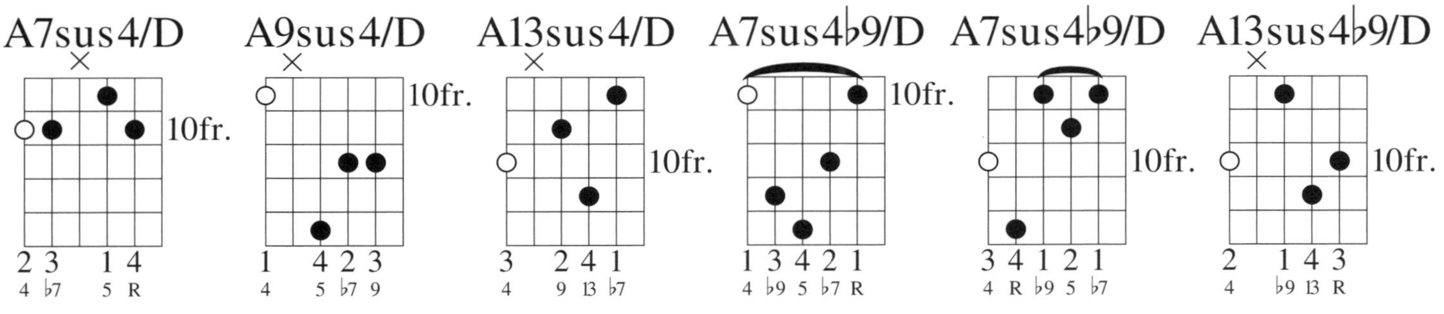

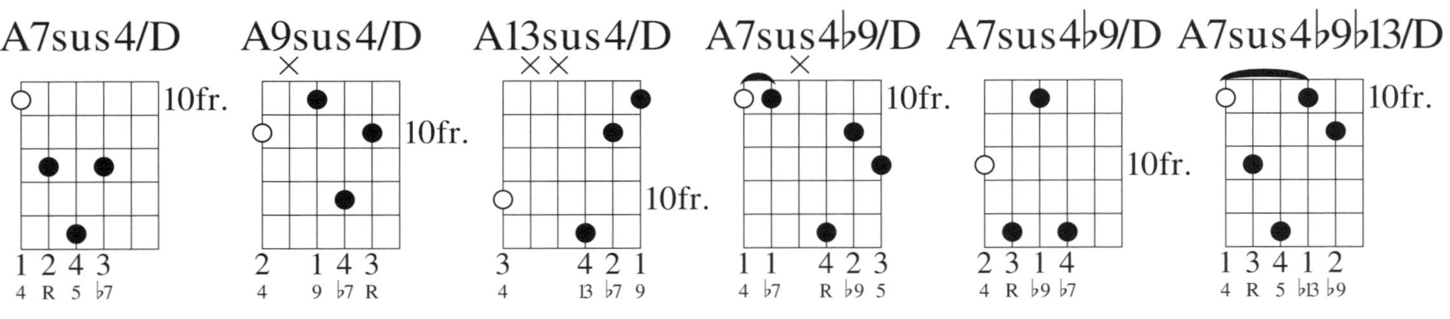

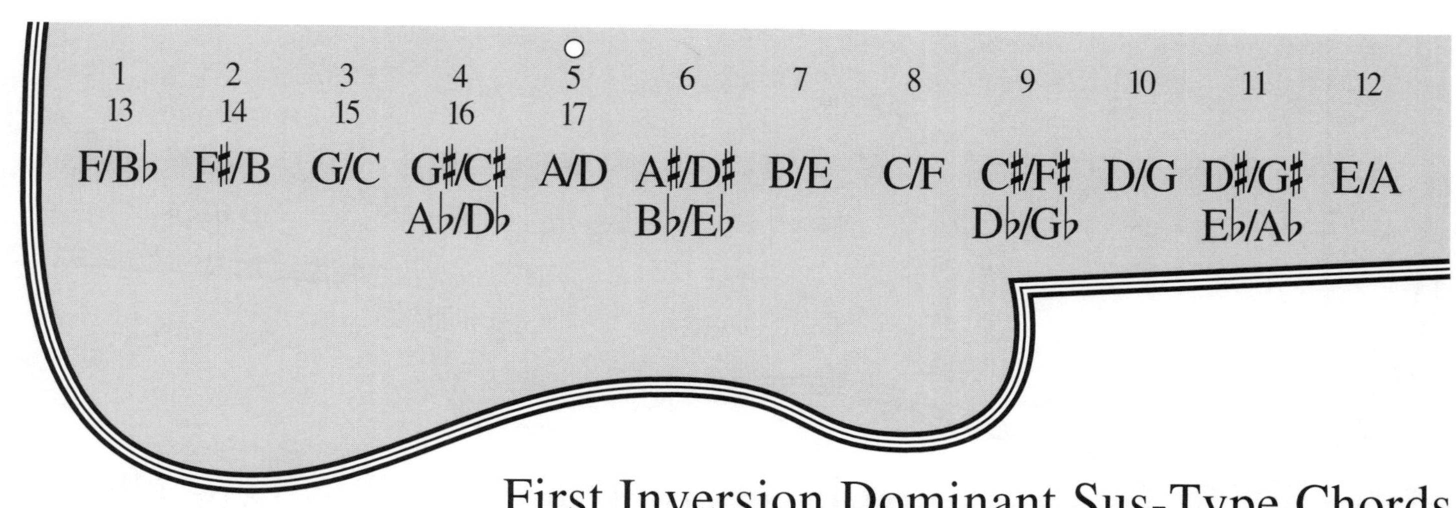

First Inversion Dominant Sus-Type Chords

A7sus4/D

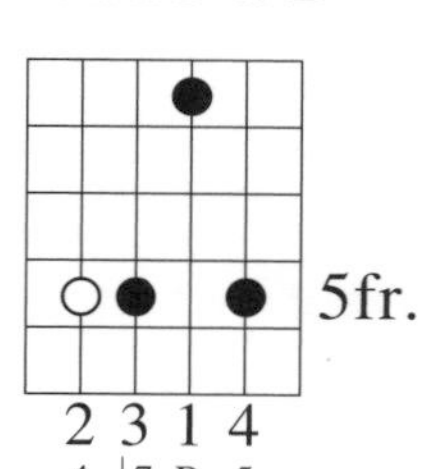

2 3 1 4
4 ♭7 R 5

A7sus4/D

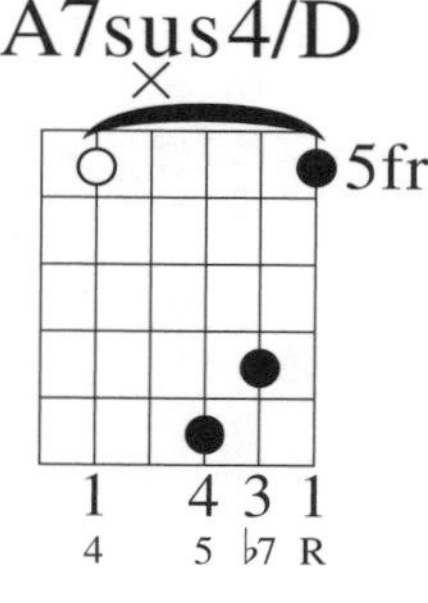

1 4 3 1
4 5 ♭7 R

A9sus4/D

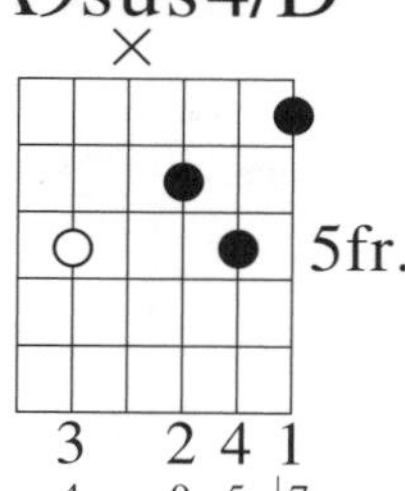

3 2 4 1
4 9 5 ♭7

A13sus4/D

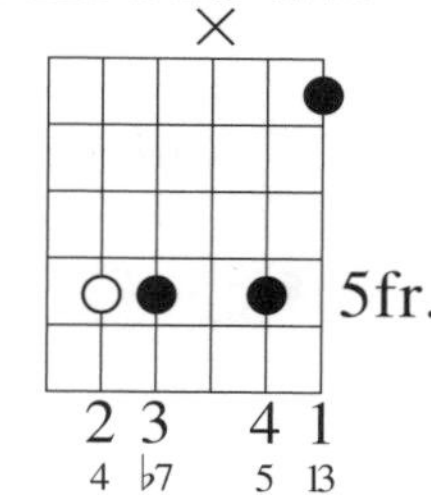

2 3 4 1
4 ♭7 5 13

A7sus4♭9/D

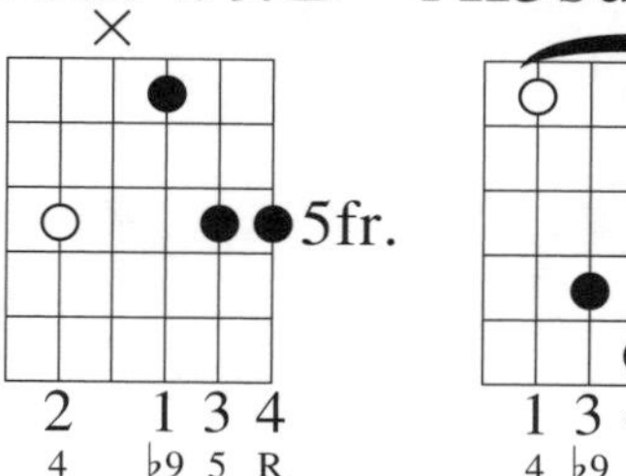

2 1 3 4
4 ♭9 5 R

A13sus4♭9/D

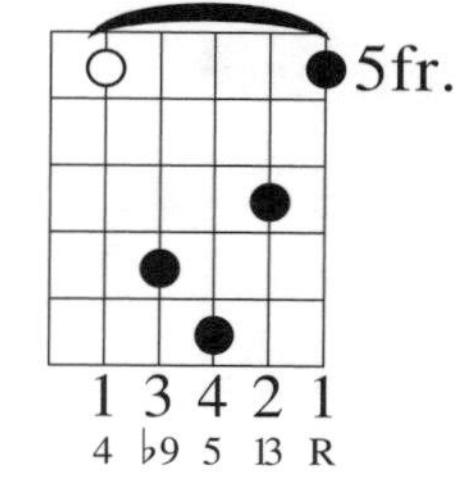

1 3 4 2 1
4 ♭9 5 13 R

A7sus4/D

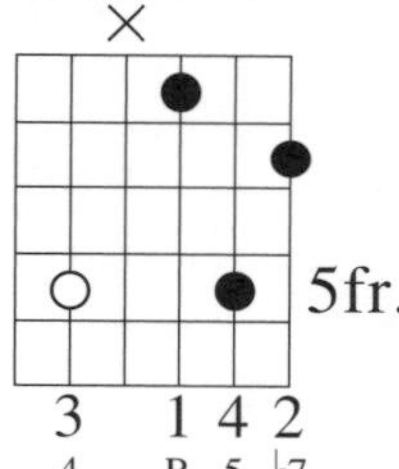

3 1 4 2
4 R 5 ♭7

A9sus4/D

5fr.

2 3 1 4 4
4 ♭7 9 5 R

A13sus4/D

5fr.

2 3 1 4
4 ♭7 9 13

A7sus4♭9/D

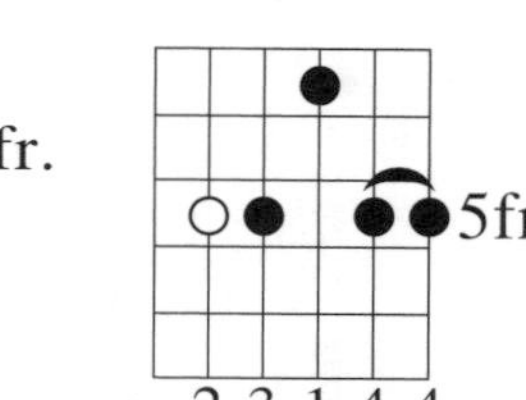

2 3 1 4 4
4 ♭7 ♭9 5 R

A7sus4♭9/D

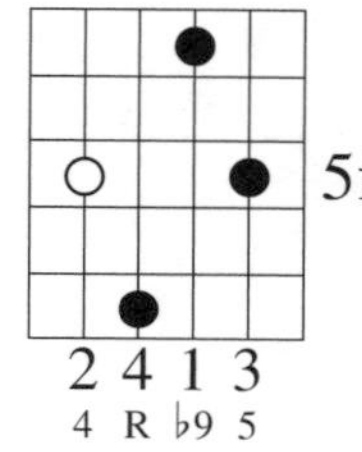

2 4 1 3
4 R ♭9 5

A13sus4♭9/D

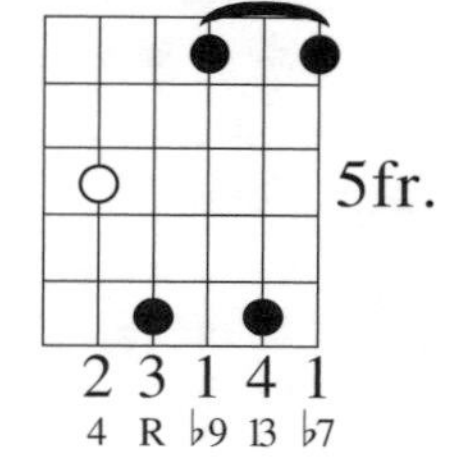

2 3 1 4 1
4 R ♭9 13 ♭7

A7sus4/D

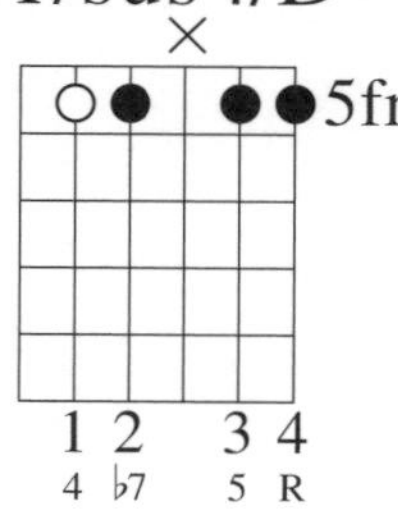

1 2 3 4
4 ♭7 5 R

A9sus4/D

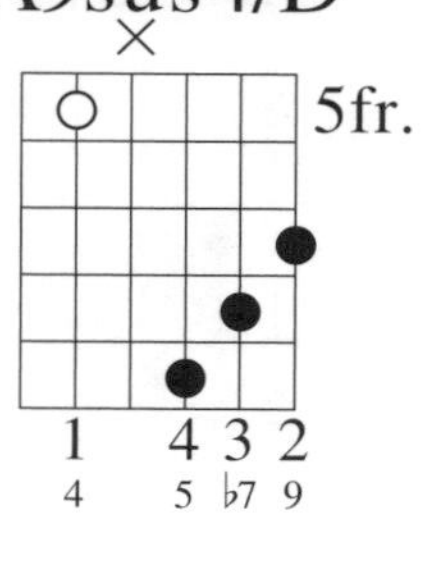

1 4 3 2
4 5 ♭7 9

A13sus4/D

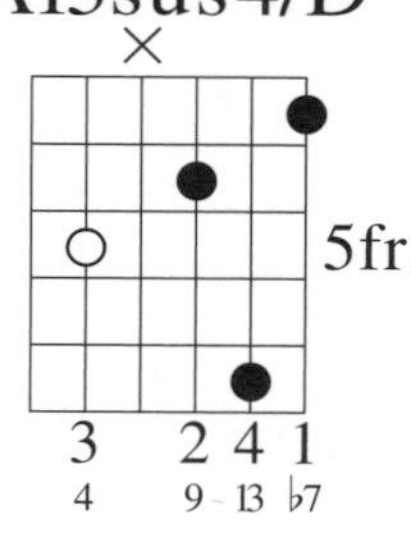

3 2 4 1
4 9 13 ♭7

A7sus4♭9/D

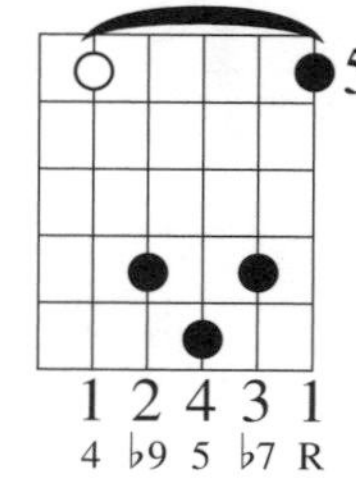

1 2 4 3 1
4 ♭9 5 ♭7 R

A13sus4♭9/D

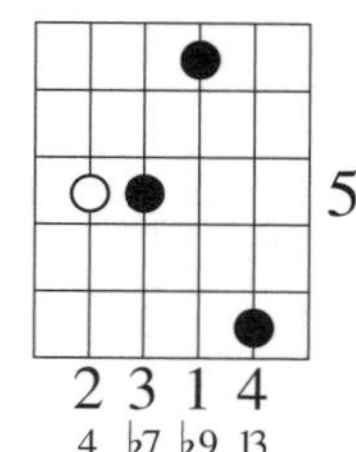

2 3 1 4
4 ♭7 ♭9 13

A13sus4♭9/D

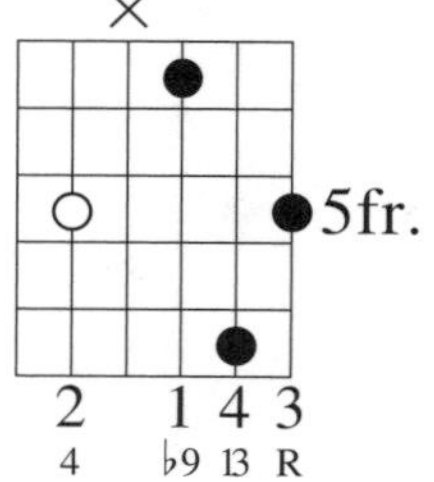

2 1 4 3
4 ♭9 13 R

A7sus4/D

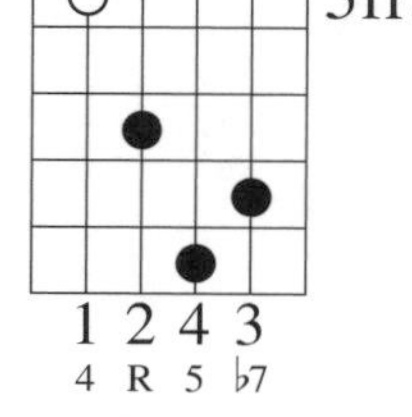

1 2 4 3
4 R 5 ♭7

A9sus4/D

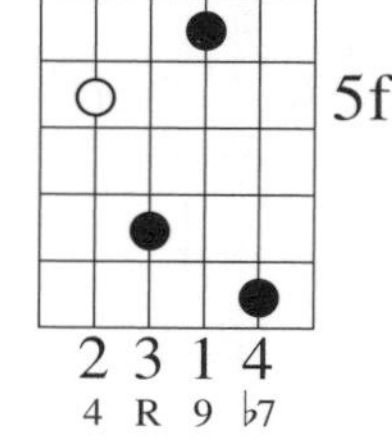

2 3 1 4
4 R 9 ♭7

A13sus4/D

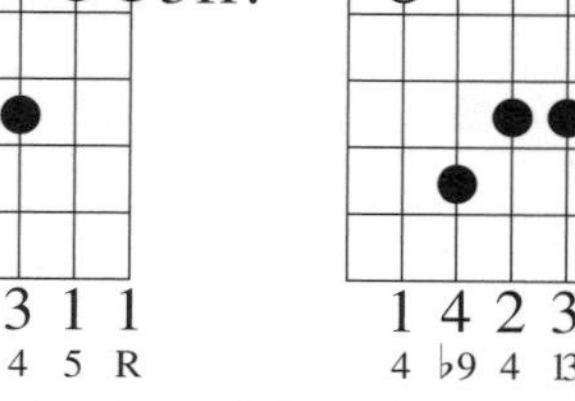

1 1 4 2 1
4 ♭7 5 13 R

A7sus4♭9/D

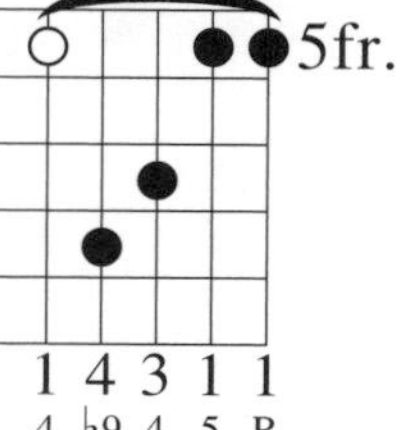

1 4 3 1 1
4 ♭9 4 5 R

A13sus4♭9/D

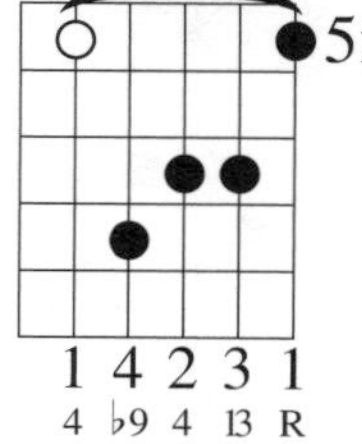

1 4 2 3 1
4 ♭9 4 13 R

A7sus4♭9♭13/D

5fr.

1 3 4 2 1
4 ♭9 5 ♭13 R

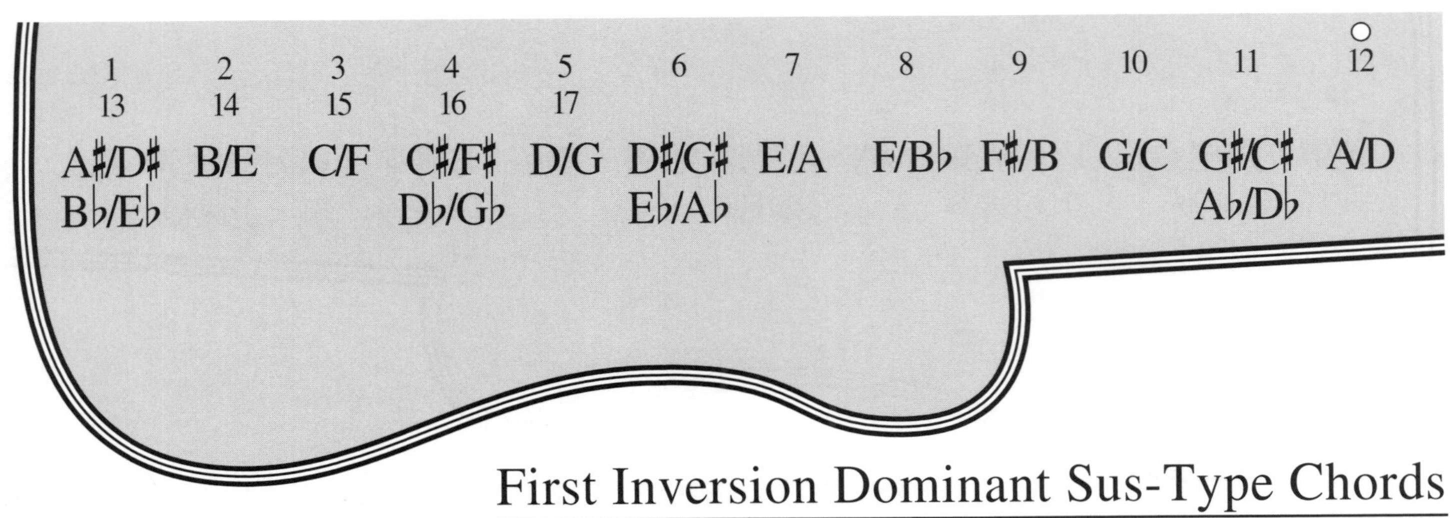

First Inversion Dominant Sus-Type Chords

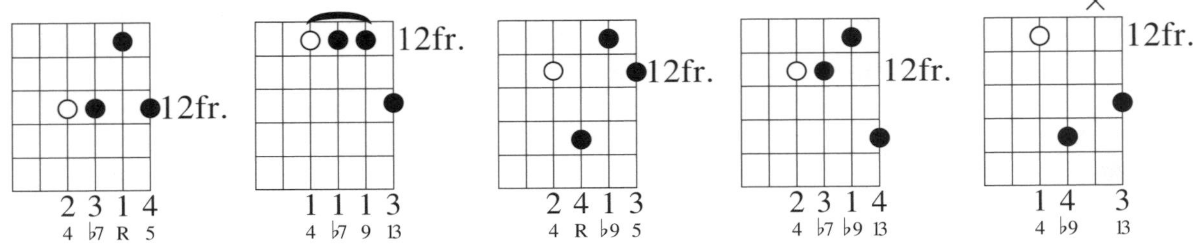

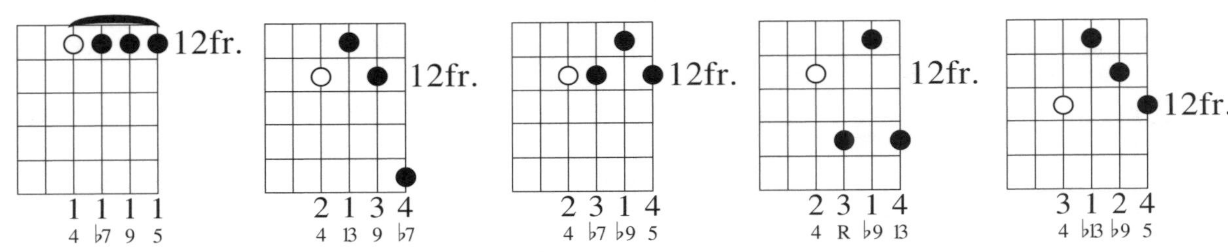

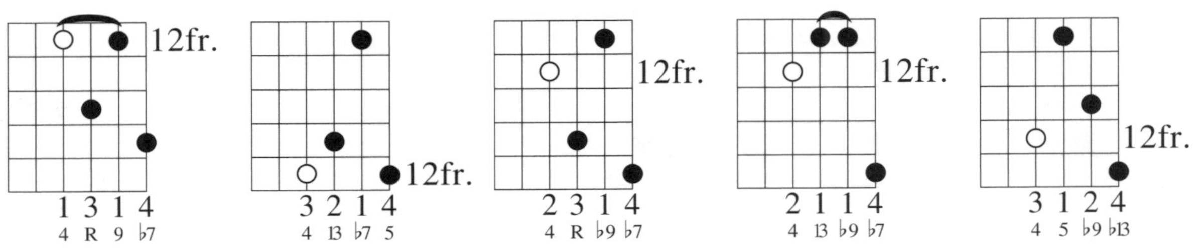

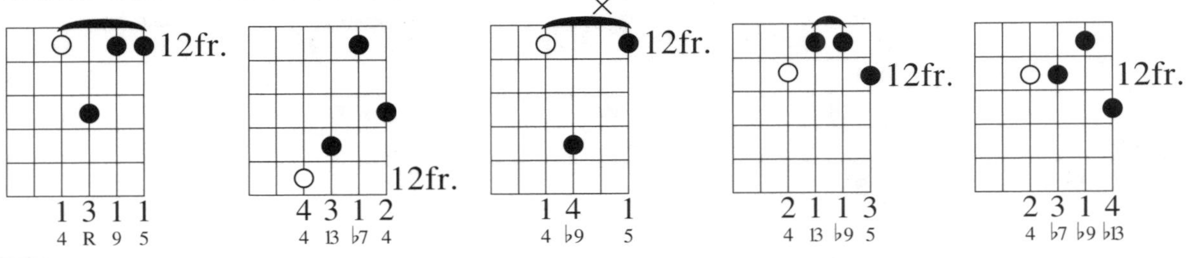

1 13 B♭/F A♯/E♯
2 14 B/F♯ C♭/G♭
3 15 C/G
4 16 C♯/G♯ D♭/A♭
5 17 D/A
6 D♯/A♯ E♭/B♭
7 E/B
8 F/C
9 F♯/C♯ G♭/D♭
10 G/D
11 G♯/D♯ A♭/E♭
12 A/E

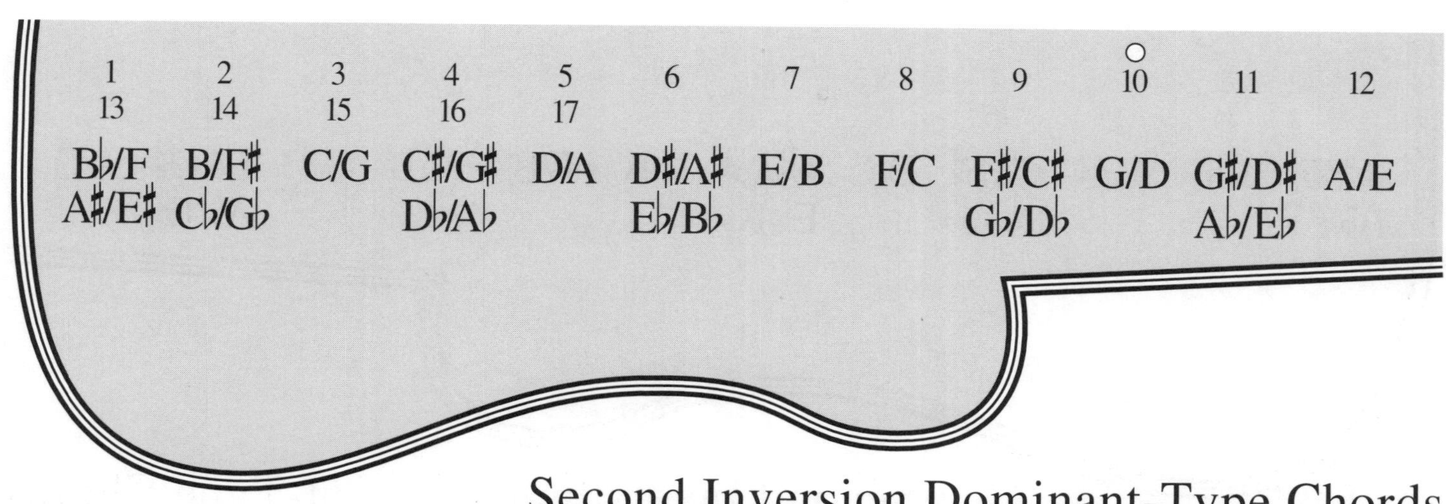

Second Inversion Dominant-Type Chords

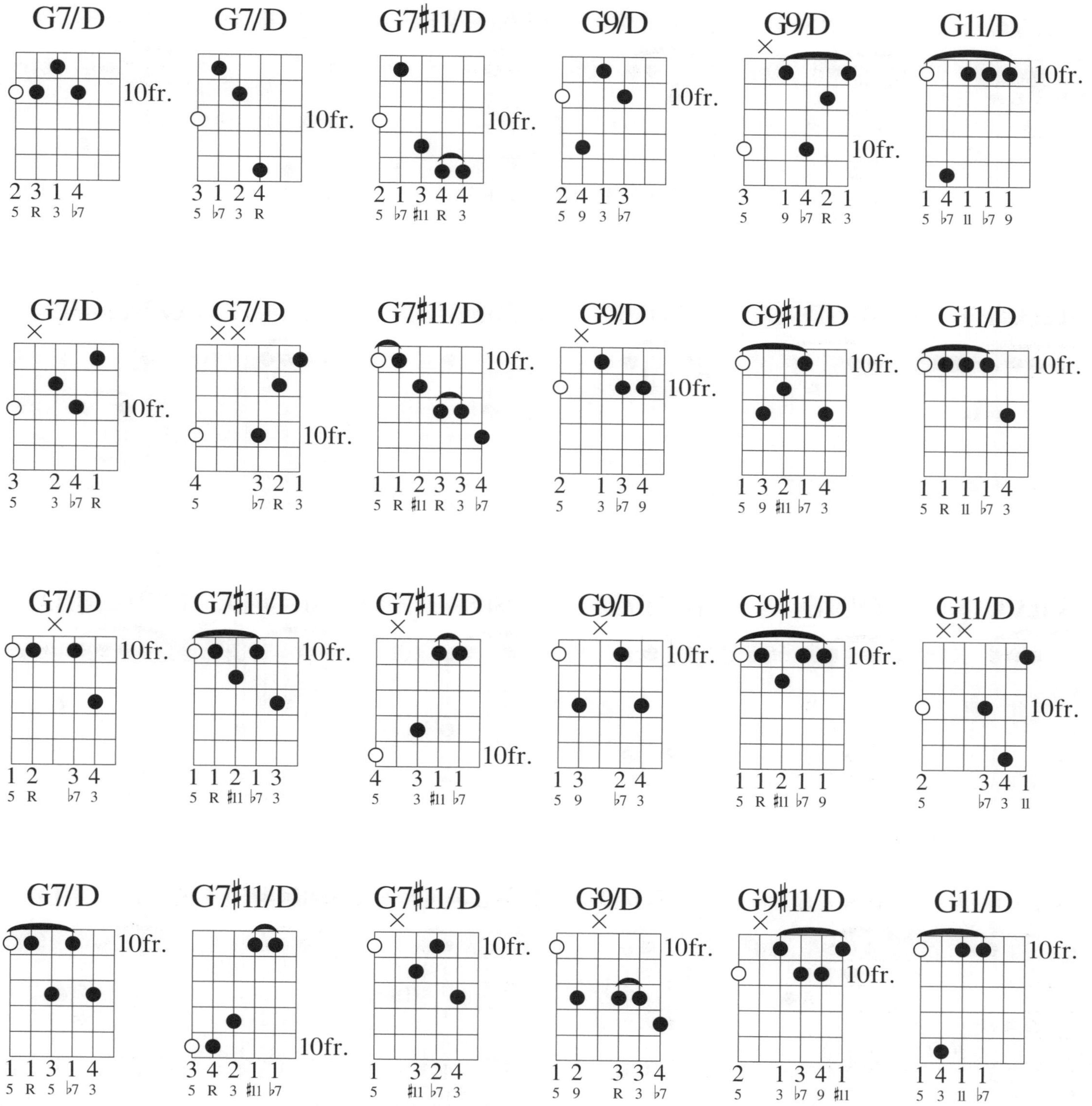

G7/D 10fr. 2 3 1 4 5 R 3 ♭7
G7/D 10fr. 3 1 2 4 5 ♭7 3 R
G7♯11/D 10fr. 2 1 3 4 4 5 ♭7 ♯11 R 3
G9/D 10fr. 2 4 1 3 5 9 3 ♭7
G9/D 10fr. 3 1 4 2 1 5 9 ♭7 R 3
G11/D 10fr. 1 4 1 1 1 5 ♭7 11 ♭7 9
G7/D 10fr. 3 2 4 1 5 3 ♭7 R
G7/D 10fr. 4 3 2 1 5 ♭7 R 3
G7♯11/D 10fr. 1 1 2 3 3 4 5 R ♯11 R 3 ♭7
G9/D 10fr. 2 1 3 4 5 3 ♭7 9
G9♯11/D 10fr. 1 3 2 1 4 5 9 ♯11 ♭7 3
G11/D 10fr. 1 1 1 1 4 5 R 11 ♭7 3
G7/D 10fr. 1 2 3 4 5 R ♭7 3
G7♯11/D 10fr. 1 1 2 1 3 5 R ♯11 ♭7 3
G7♯11/D 10fr. 4 3 1 1 5 3 ♯11 ♭7
G9/D 10fr. 1 3 2 4 5 9 ♭7 3
G9♯11/D 10fr. 1 1 2 1 1 5 R ♯11 ♭7 9
G11/D 10fr. 2 3 4 1 5 ♭7 3 11
G7/D 10fr. 1 1 3 1 4 5 R 5 ♭7 3
G7♯11/D 10fr. 3 4 2 1 1 5 R 3 ♯11 ♭7
G7♯11/D 10fr. 1 3 2 4 5 ♯11 ♭7 3
G9/D 10fr. 1 2 3 3 4 5 9 R 3 ♭7
G9♯11/D 10fr. 2 1 3 4 1 5 3 ♭7 9 ♯11
G11/D 10fr. 1 4 1 1 5 3 11 ♭7

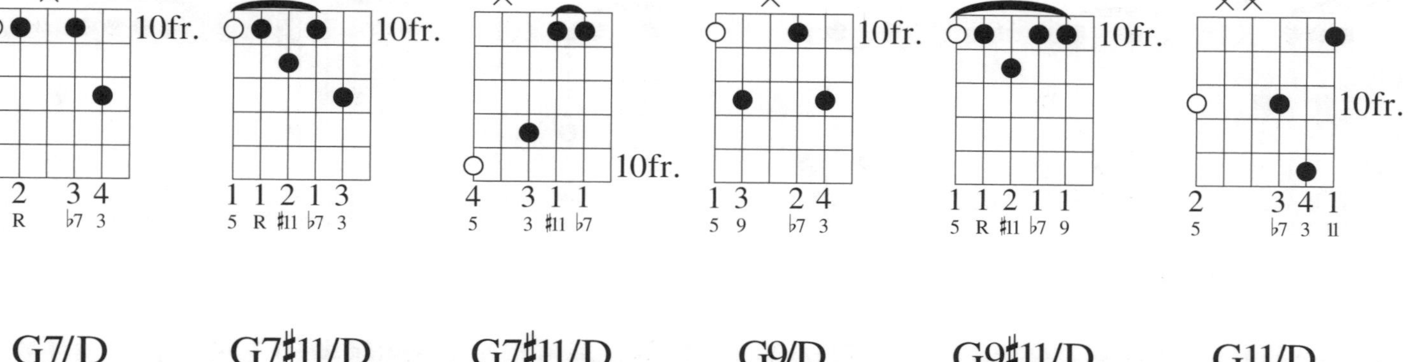

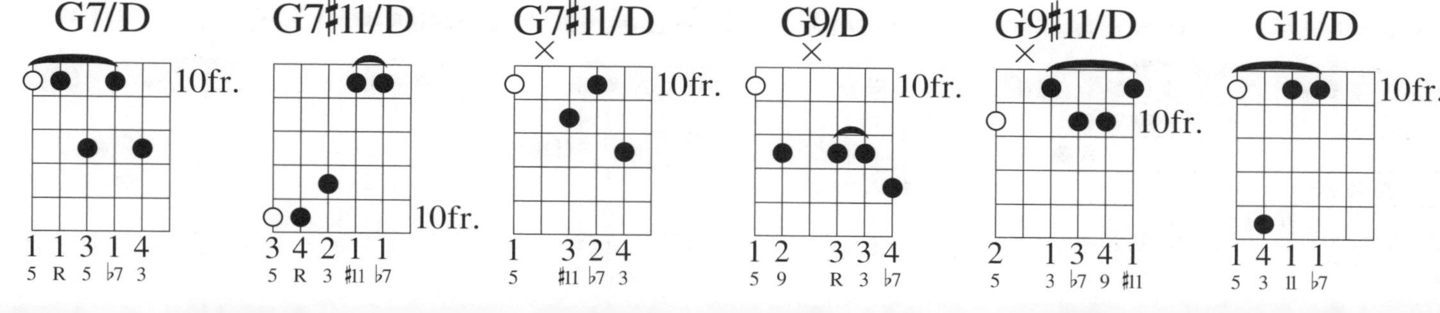

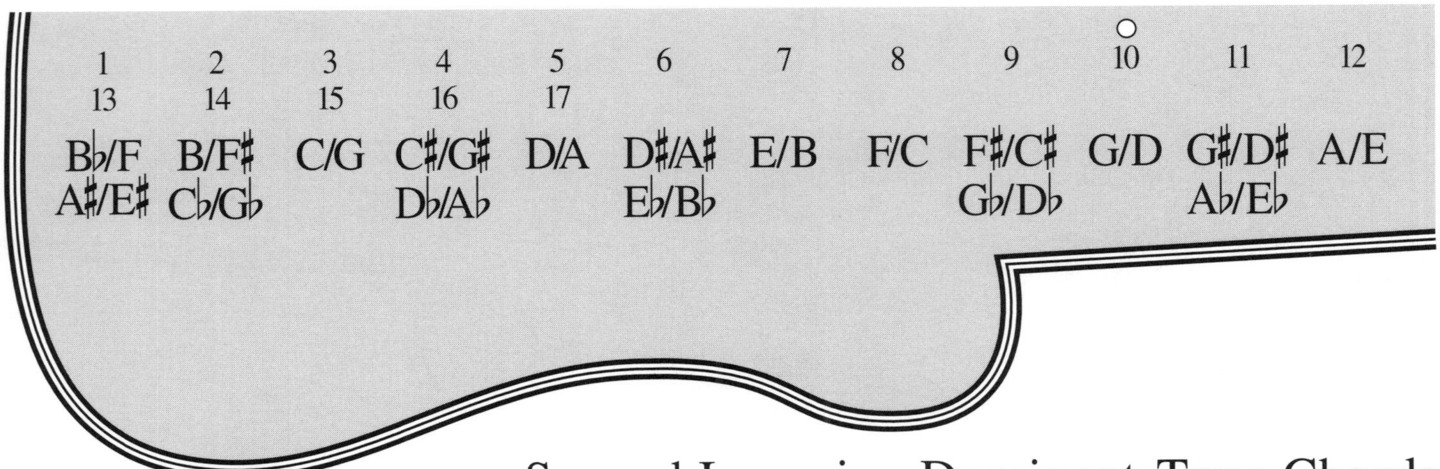

1 2 3 4 5 6 7 8 9 10 11 12
13 14 15 16 17
B♭/F B/F♯ C/G C♯/G♯ D/A D♯/A♯ E/B F/C F♯/C♯ G/D G♯/D♯ A/E
A♯/E♯ C♭/G♭ D♭/A♭ E♭/B♭ G♭/D♭ A♭/E♭

Second Inversion Dominant-Type Chords

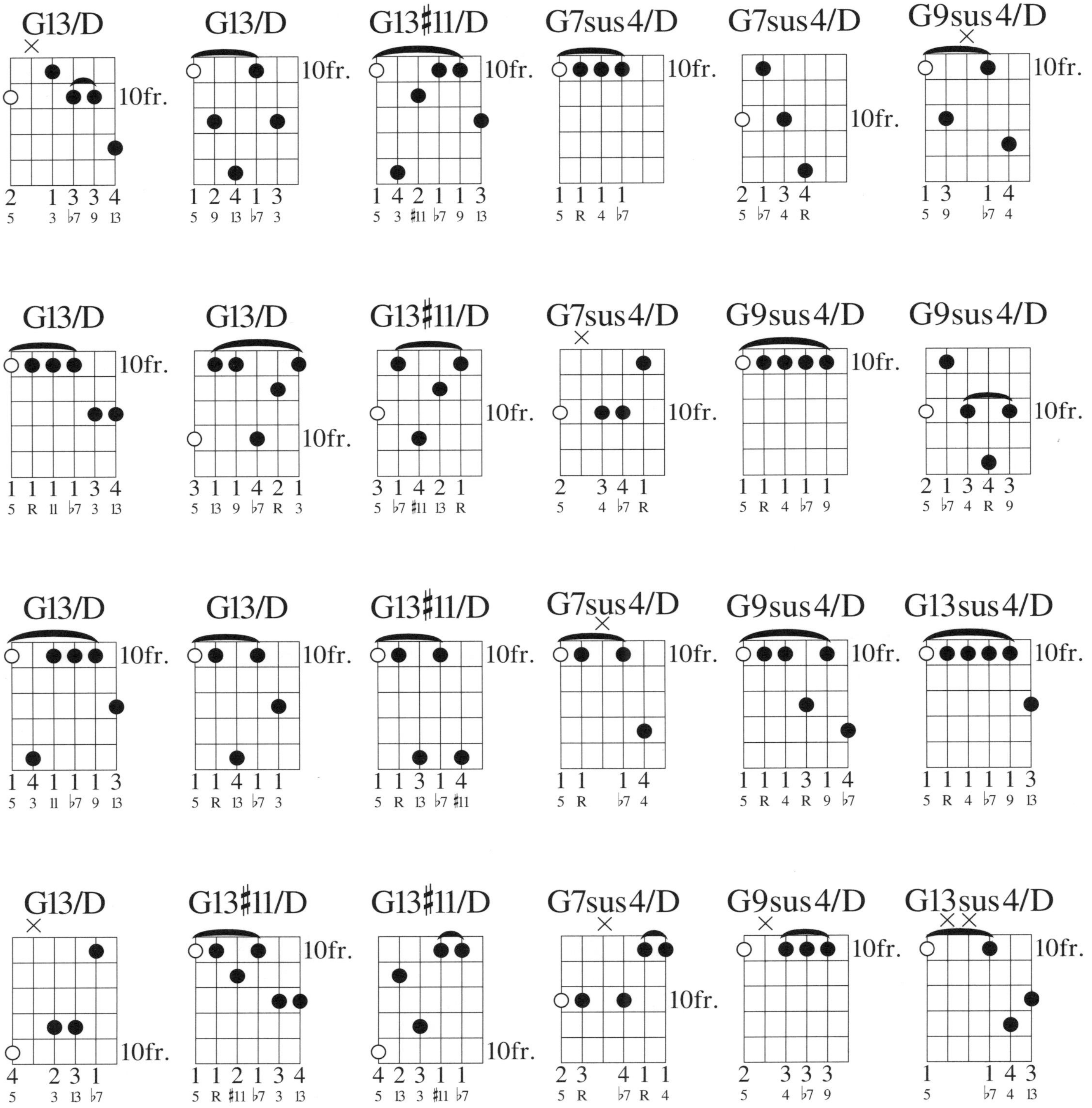

G13/D
10fr.
2 1 3 3 4
5 3 ♭7 9 13
G13/D
10fr.
1 2 4 1 3
5 9 13 ♭7 3
G13♯11/D
10fr.
1 4 2 1 1 3
5 3 ♯11 ♭7 9 13
G7sus4/D
10fr.
1 1 1 1
5 R 4 ♭7
G7sus4/D
10fr.
2 1 3 4
5 ♭7 4 R
G9sus4/D
10fr.
1 3 1 4
5 9 ♭7 4
G13/D
10fr.
1 1 1 1 3 4
5 R 11 ♭7 3 13
G13/D
10fr.
3 1 1 4 2 1
5 13 9 ♭7 R 3
G13♯11/D
10fr.
3 1 4 2 1
5 ♭7 ♯11 13 R
G7sus4/D
10fr.
2 3 4 1
5 4 ♭7 R
G9sus4/D
10fr.
1 1 1 1 1
5 R 4 ♭7 9
G9sus4/D
10fr.
2 1 3 4 3
5 ♭7 4 R 9
G13/D
10fr.
1 4 1 1 1 3
5 3 11 ♭7 9 13
G13/D
10fr.
1 1 4 1 1
5 R 13 ♭7 3
G13♯11/D
10fr.
1 1 3 1 4
5 R 13 ♭7 ♯11
G7sus4/D
10fr.
1 1 1 4
5 R ♭7 4
G9sus4/D
10fr.
1 1 1 3 1 4
5 R 4 R 9 ♭7
G13sus4/D
10fr.
1 1 1 1 1 3
5 R 4 ♭7 9 13
G13/D
10fr.
4 2 3 1
5 3 13 ♭7
G13♯11/D
10fr.
1 1 2 1 3 4
5 R ♯11 ♭7 3 13
G13♯11/D
10fr.
4 2 3 1 1
5 13 3 ♯11 ♭7
G7sus4/D
10fr.
2 3 4 1 1
5 R ♭7 R 4
G9sus4/D
10fr.
2 3 3 3
5 4 ♭7 9
G13sus4/D
10fr.
1 1 4 3
5 ♭7 4 13

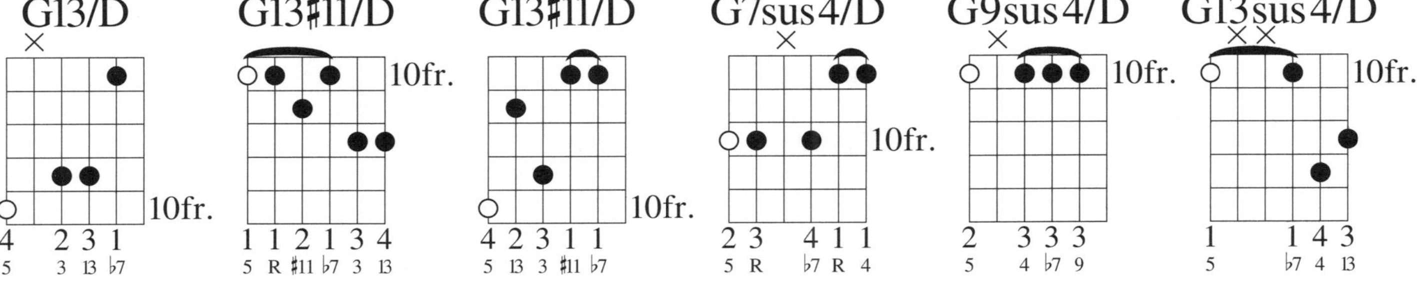

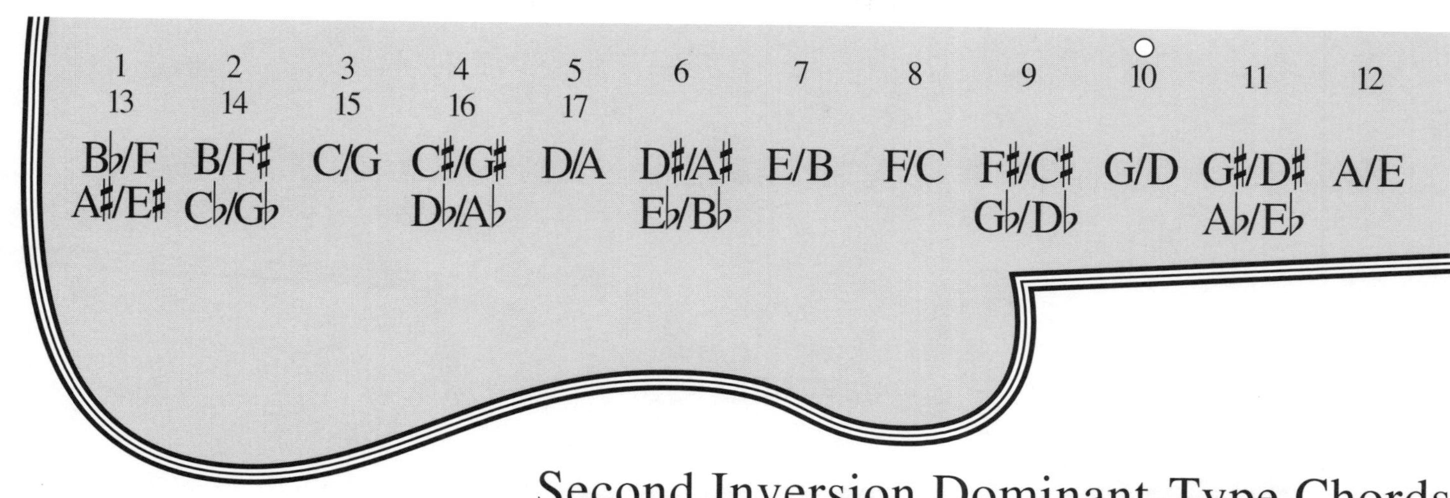

Second Inversion Dominant-Type Chords

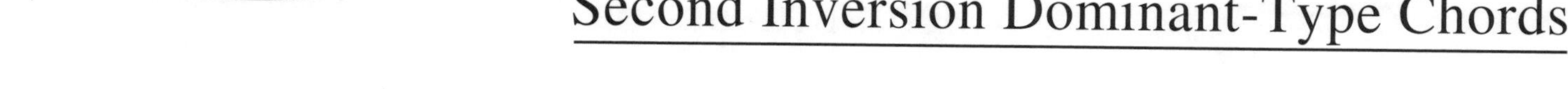

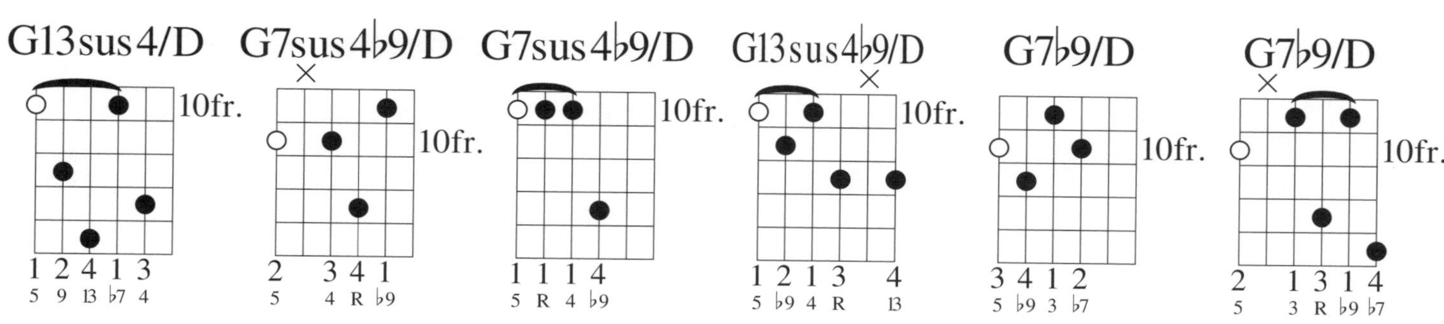

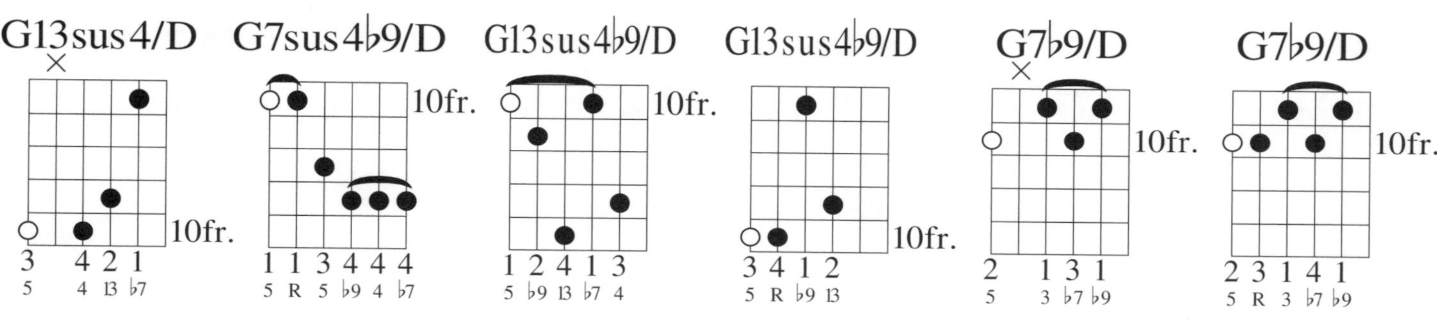

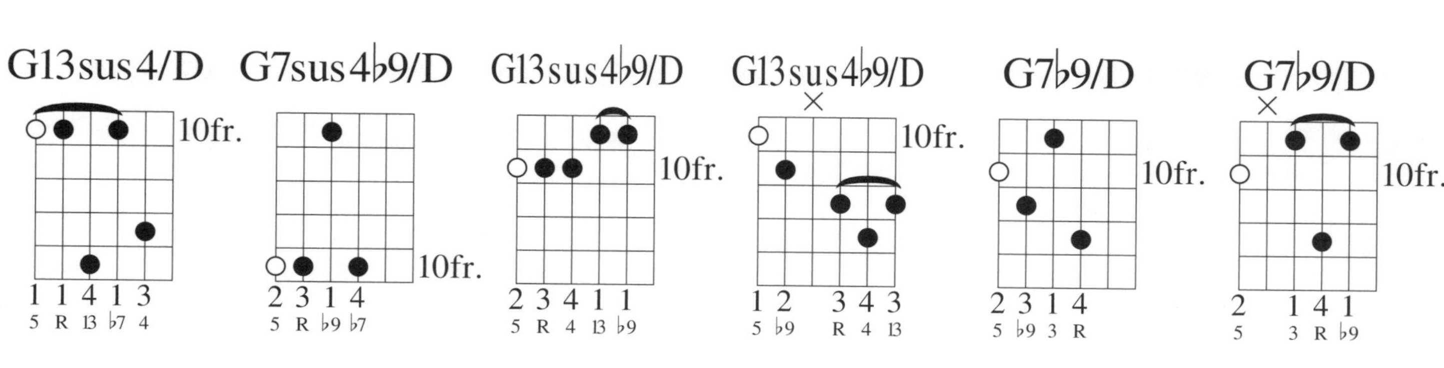

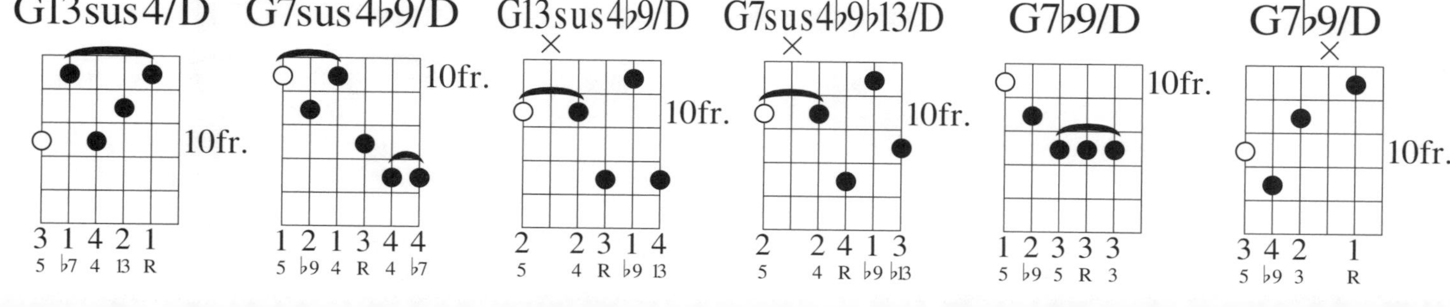

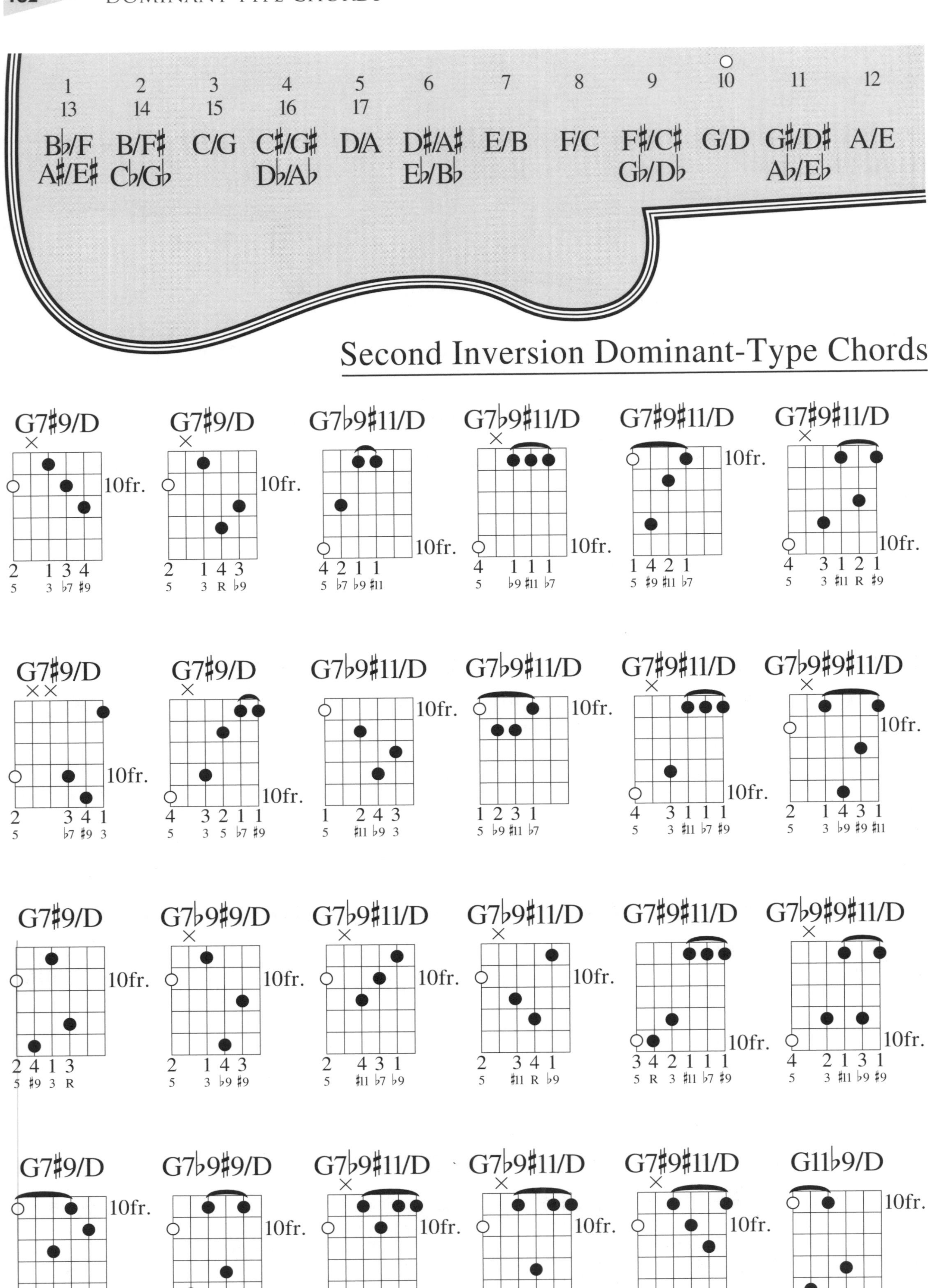
1 13 Bb/F A#/E#
2 14 B/F# Cb/Gb
3 15 C/G
4 16 C#/G# Db/Ab
5 17 D/A
6 D#/A# Eb/Bb
7 E/B
8 F/C
9 F#/C# Gb/Db
10 G/D
11 G#/D# Ab/Eb
12 A/E
Second Inversion Dominant-Type Chords
G7#9/D
G7#9/D
G7b9#11/D
G7b9#11/D
G7#9#11/D
G7#9#11/D
G7#9/D
G7#9/D
G7b9#11/D
G7b9#11/D
G7#9#11/D
G7b9#9#11/D
G7#9/D
G7b9#9/D
G7b9#11/D
G7b9#11/D
G7#9#11/D
G7b9#9#11/D
G7#9/D
G7b9#9/D
G7b9#11/D
G7b9#11/D
G7#9#11/D
G11b9/D
10fr.

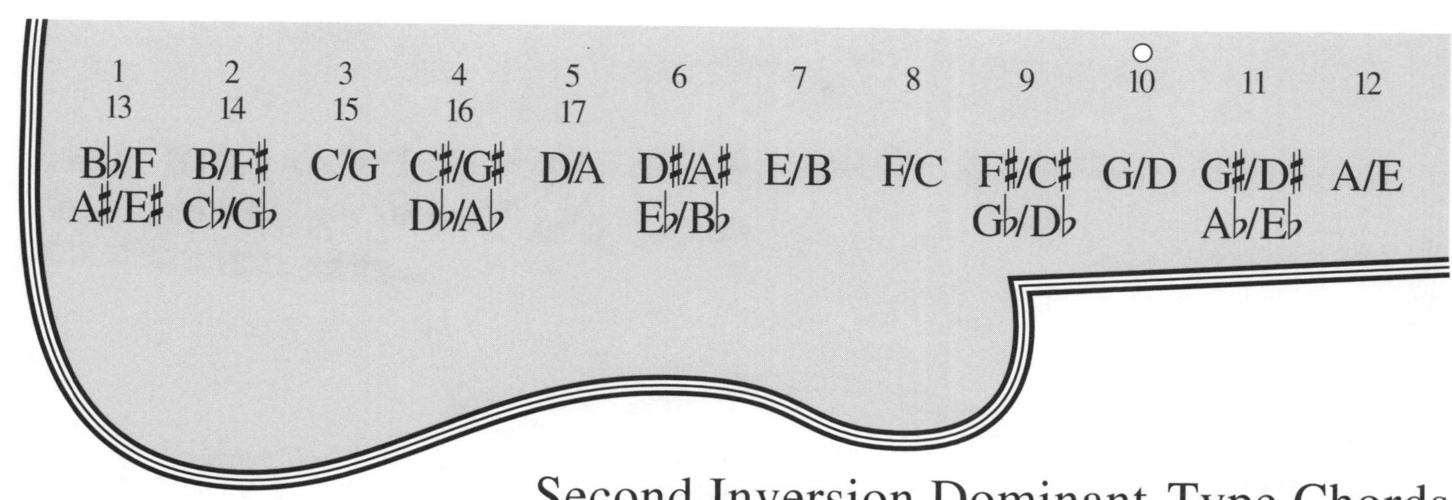

Second Inversion Dominant-Type Chords

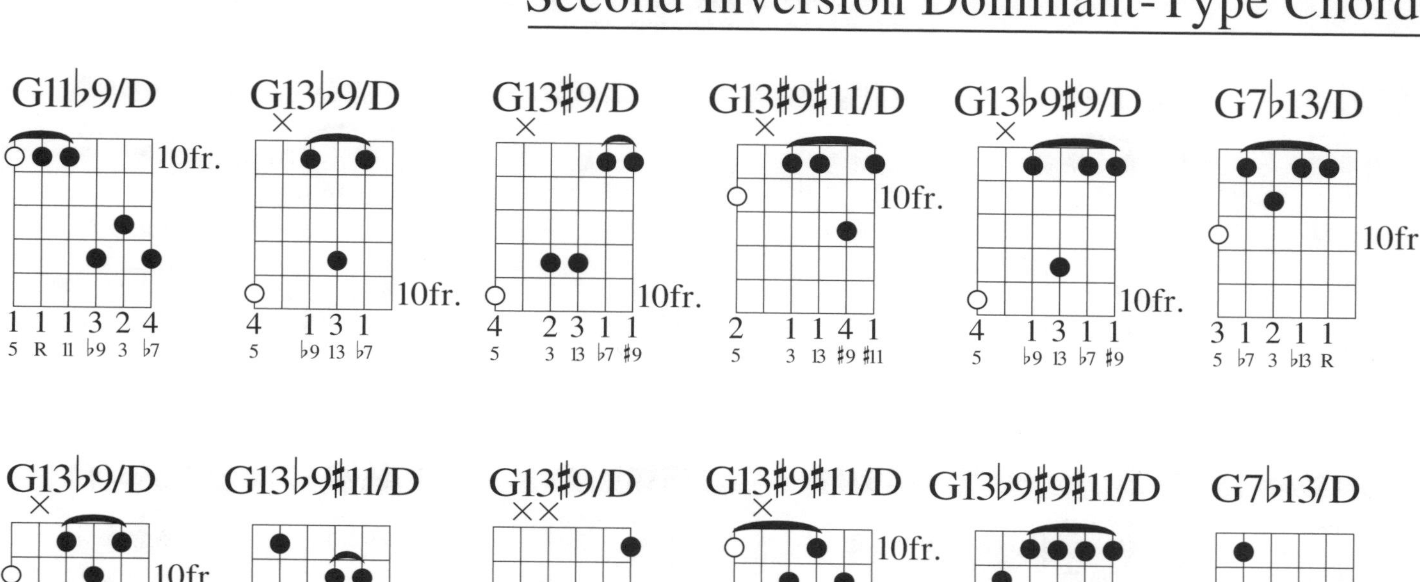

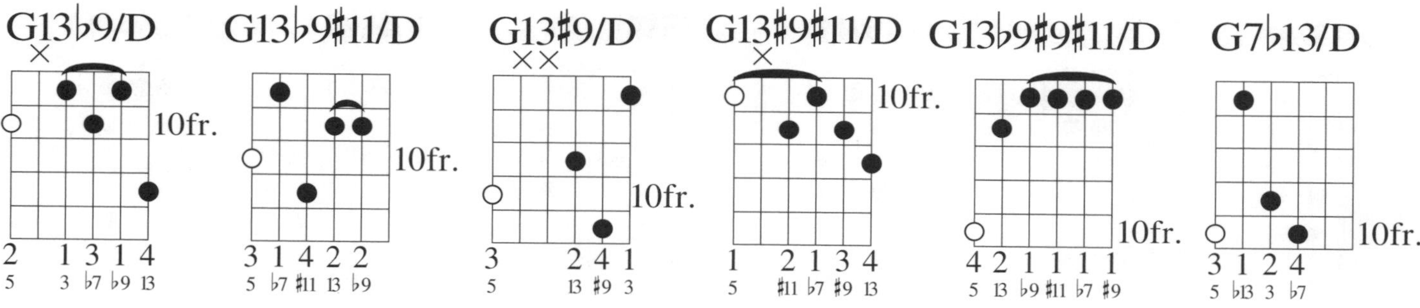

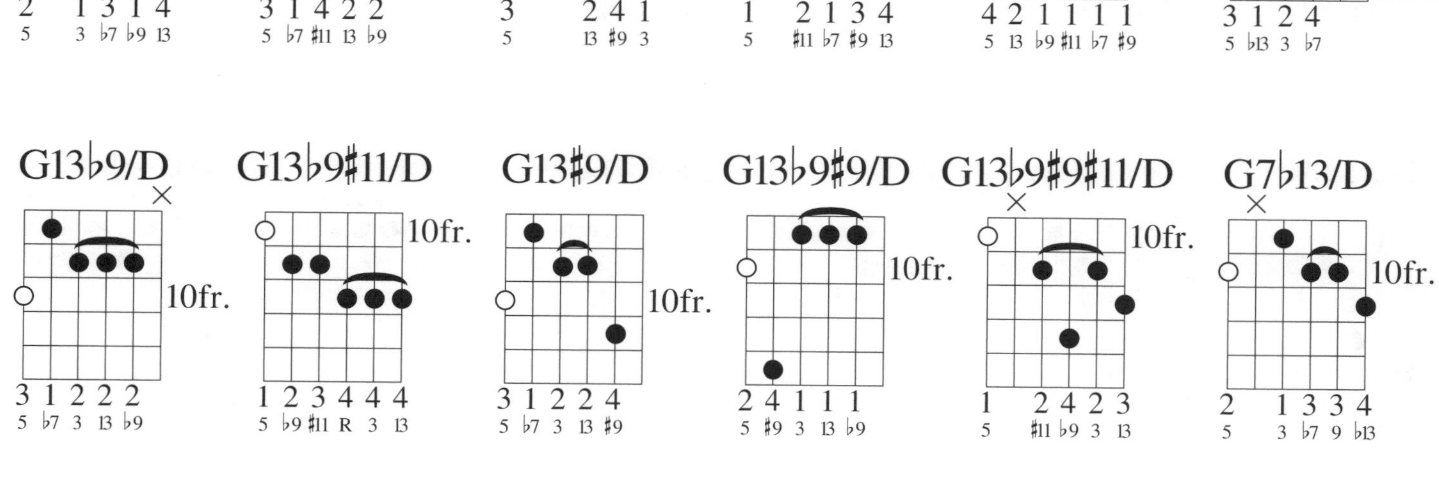

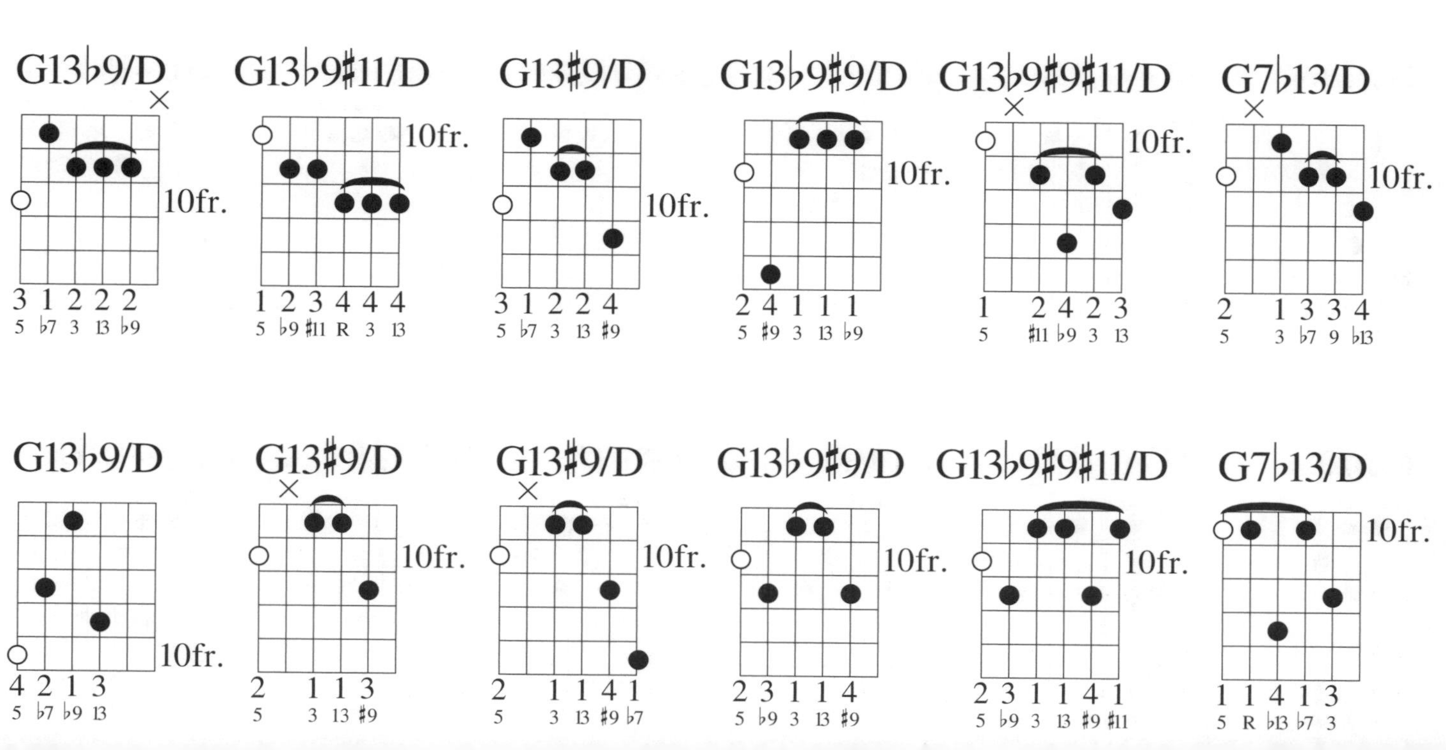

Second Inversion Dominant-Type Chords

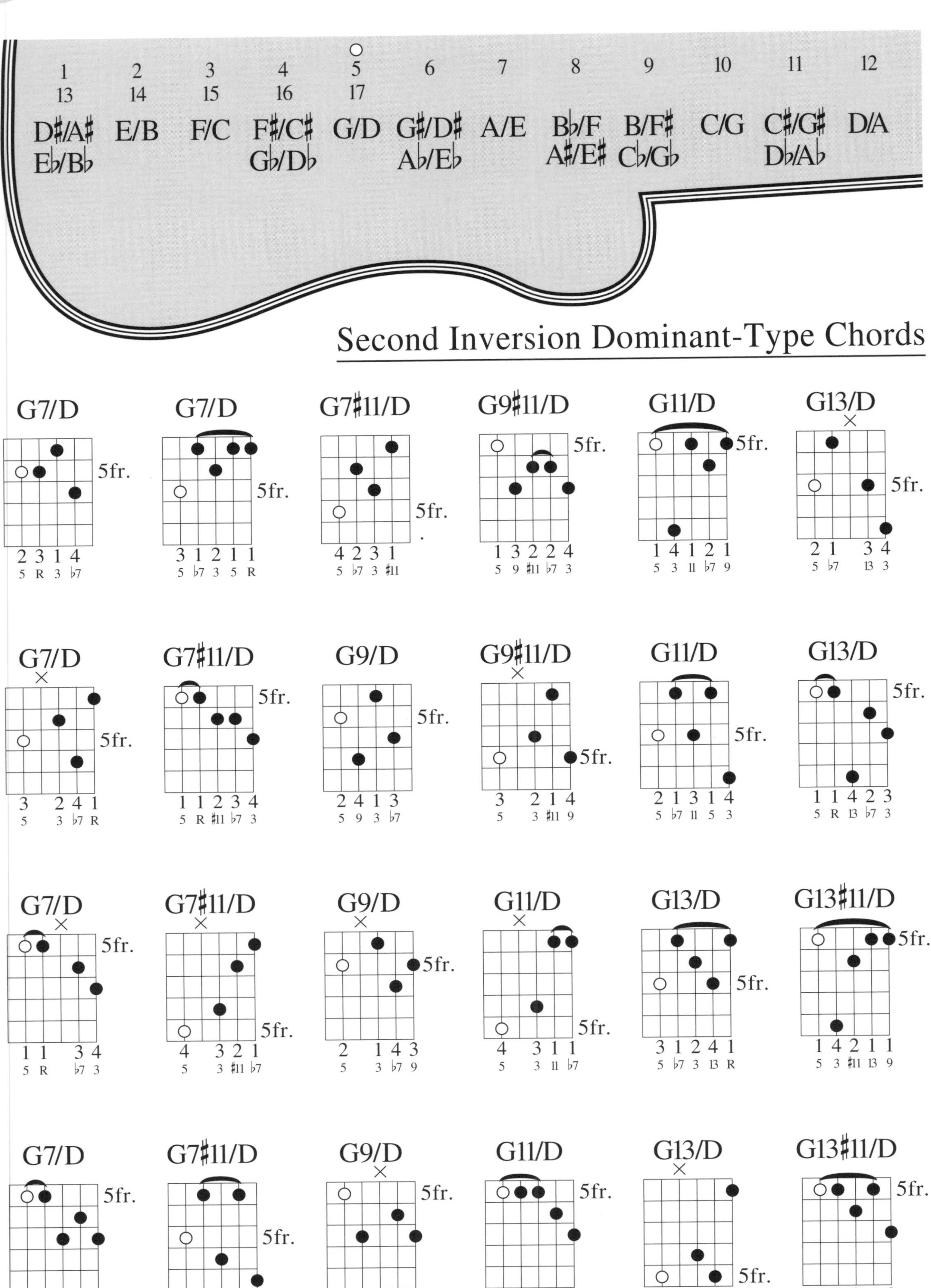

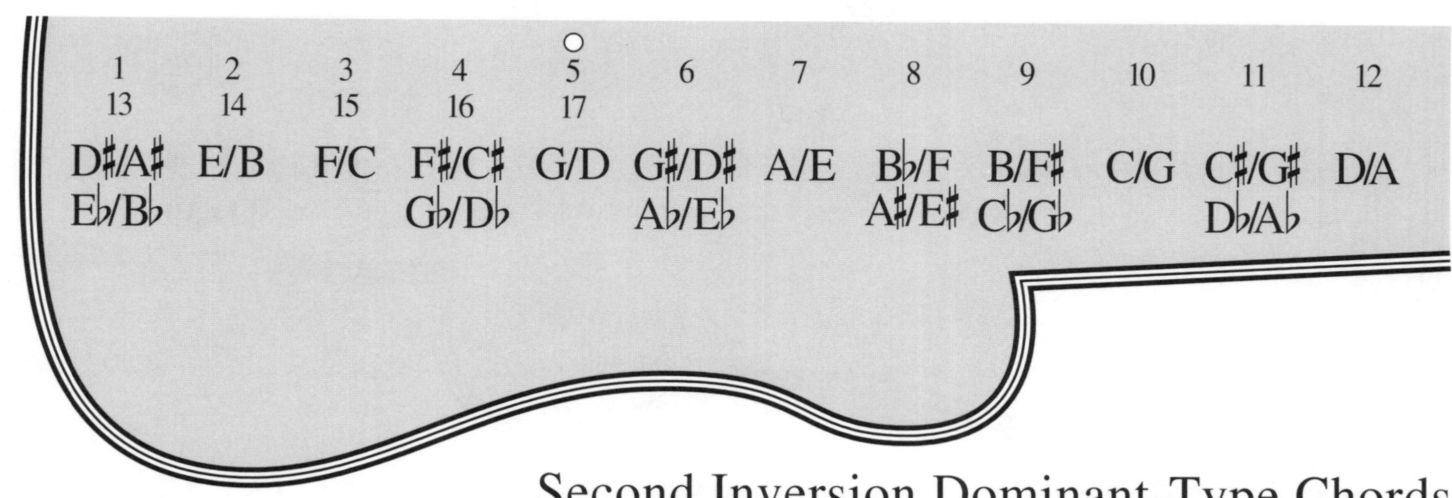

Second Inversion Dominant-Type Chords

G7sus4/D (5fr.)
1 1 1 2
5 R 4 ♭7

G7sus4/D (5fr.)
1 1 1 2 4
5 R 4 ♭7 4

G9sus4/D (5fr.)
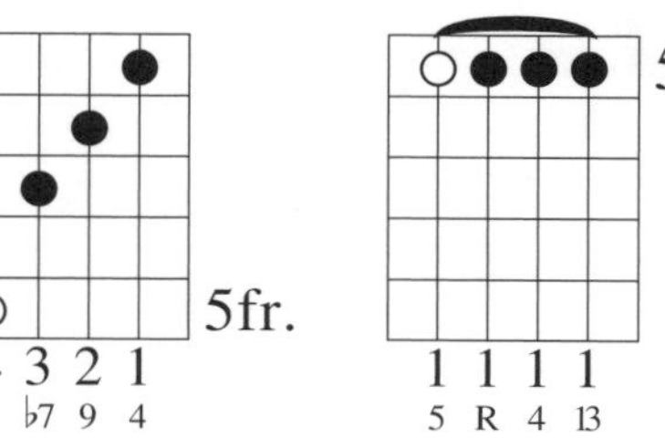
4 3 2 1
5 ♭7 9 4

G13sus4/D (5fr.)
1 1 1 1
5 R 4 13

G7sus4♭9/D (5fr.)
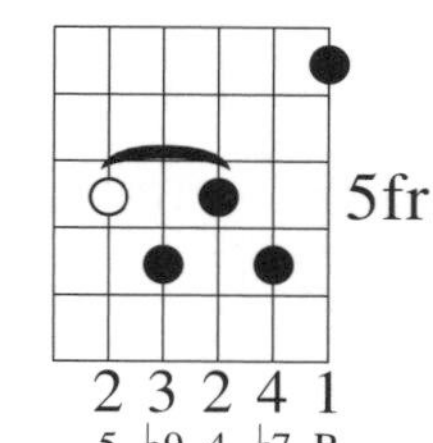
2 3 2 4 1
5 ♭9 4 ♭7 R

G13sus4♭9/D (5fr.)
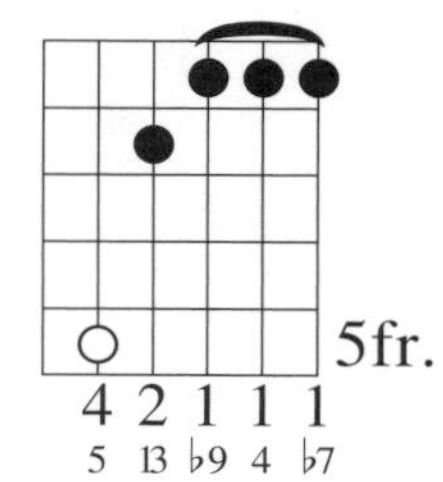
4 2 1 1 1
5 13 ♭9 4 ♭7

G7sus4/D (5fr.)
2 3 4 1
5 4 ♭7 R

G9sus4/D (5fr.)
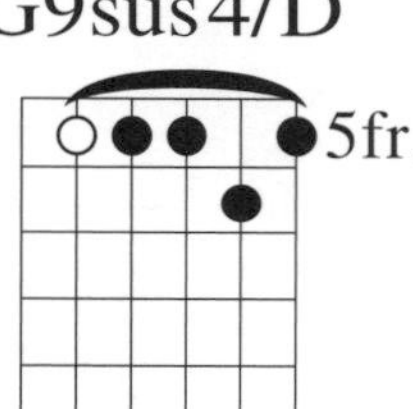
1 1 1 2 1
5 R 4 ♭7 9

G9sus4/D (5fr.)
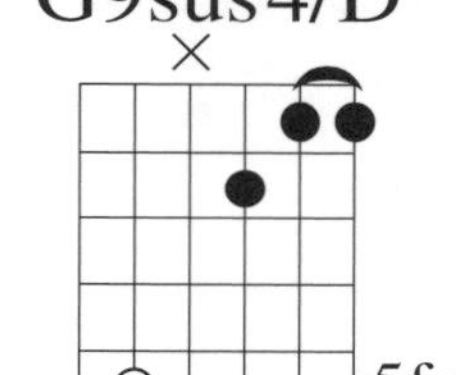
4 2 1 1
5 9 4 ♭7

G7sus4♭9/D (5fr.)
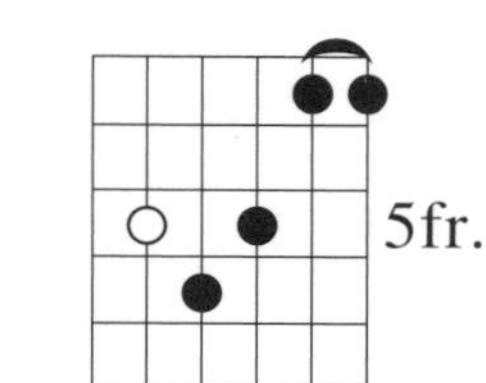
2 4 3 1 1
5 ♭9 4 5 R

G7sus4♭9/D (5fr.)
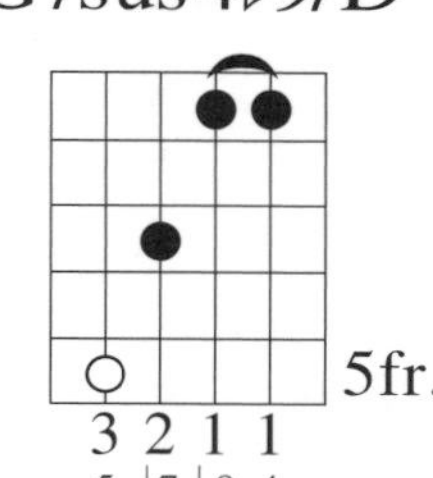
3 2 1 1
5 ♭7 ♭9 4

G13sus4♭9/D (5fr.)
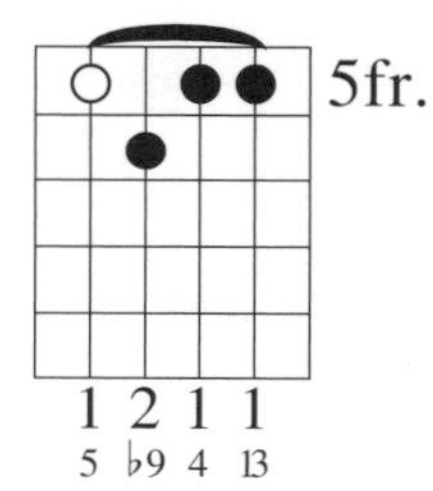
1 2 1 1
5 ♭9 4 13

G7sus4/D (5fr.)
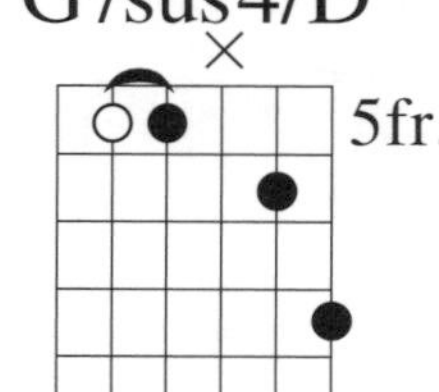
1 1 2 4
5 R ♭7 4

G9sus4/D (5fr.)
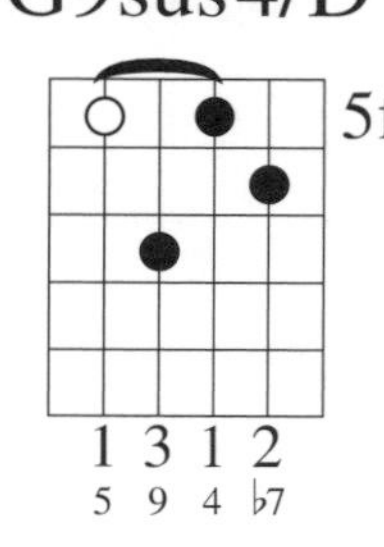
1 3 1 2
5 9 4 ♭7

G13sus4/D (5fr.)
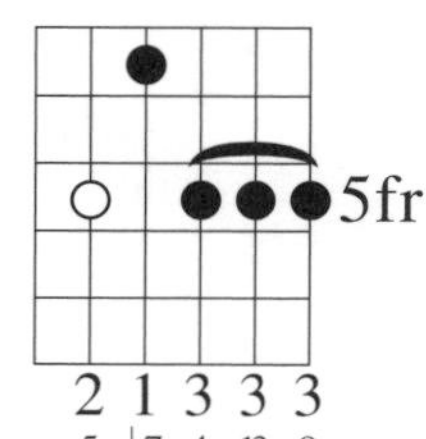
2 1 3 3 3
5 ♭7 4 13 9

G7sus4♭9/D (5fr.)
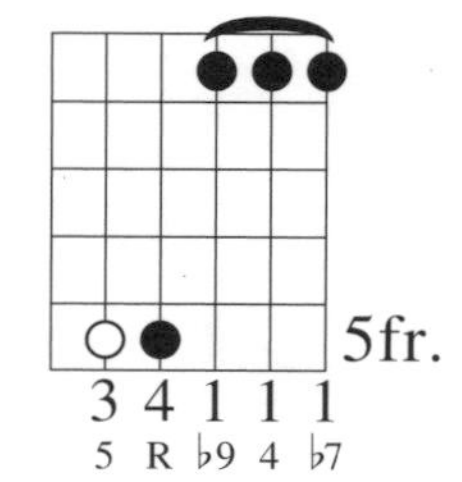
3 4 1 1 1
5 R ♭9 4 ♭7

G7sus4♭9/D (5fr.)
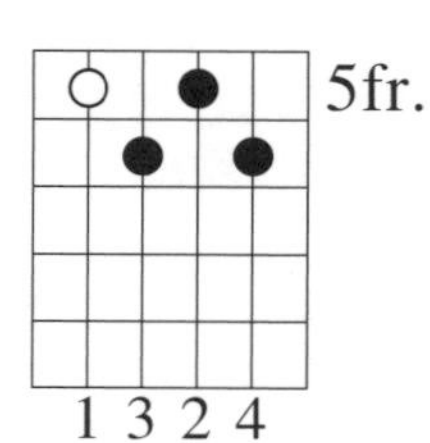
1 3 2 4
5 ♭9 4 ♭7

G13sus4♭9/D (5fr.)
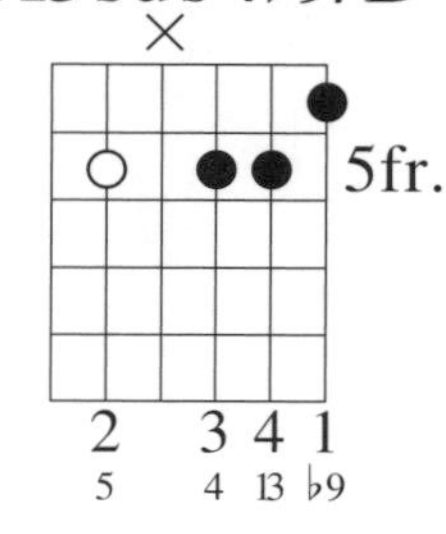
2 3 4 1
5 4 13 ♭9

G7sus4/D (5fr.)
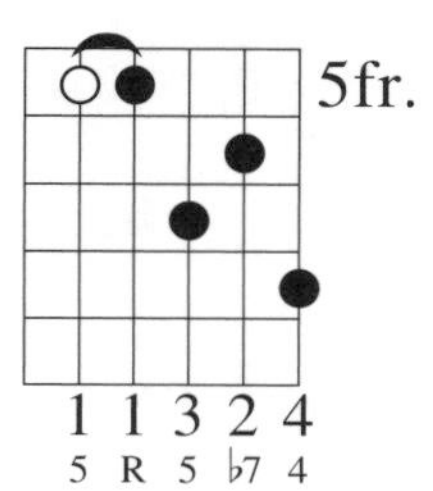
1 1 3 2 4
5 R 5 ♭7 4

G9sus4/D (5fr.)
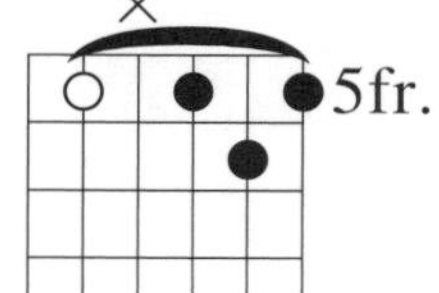
1 1 2 1
5 4 ♭7 9

G13sus4/D (5fr.)
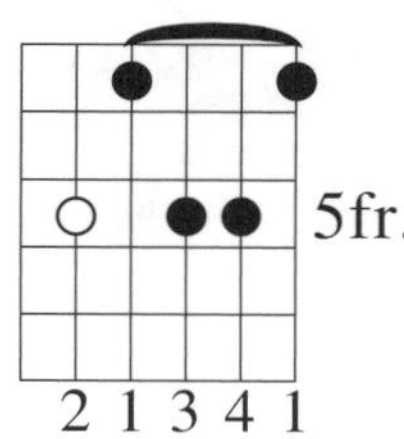
2 1 3 4 1
5 ♭7 4 13 R

G7sus4♭9/D (5fr.)
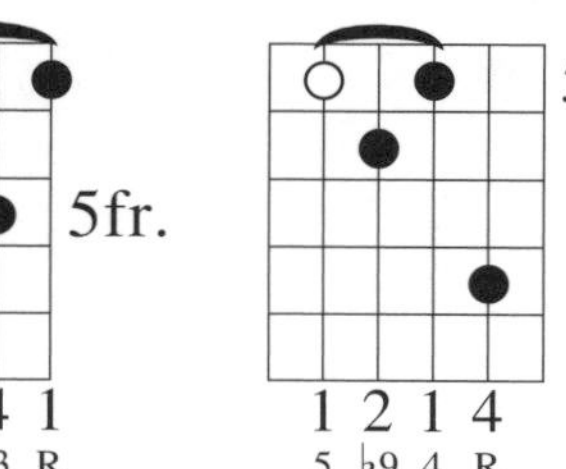
1 2 1 4
5 ♭9 4 R

G7sus4♭9/D (5fr.)
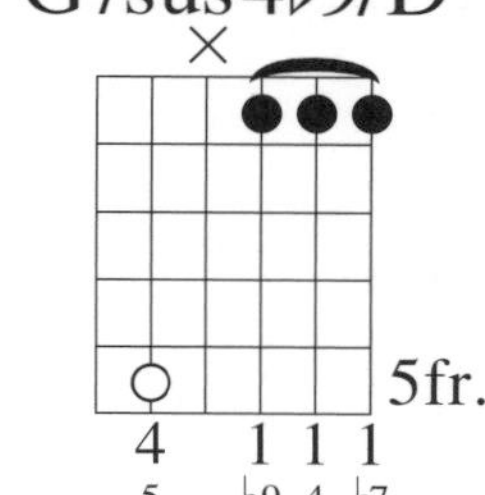
4 1 1 1
5 ♭9 4 ♭7

G7sus4♭9♭13/D (5fr.)
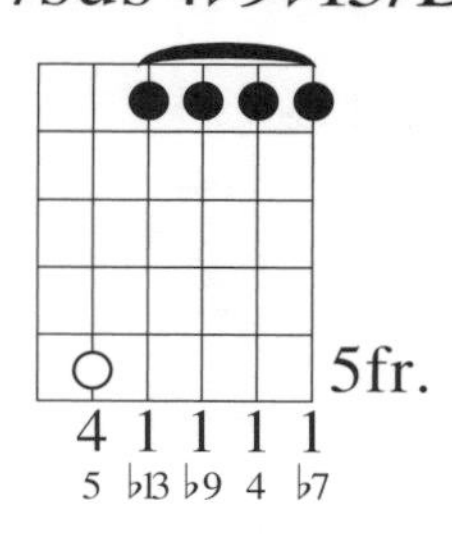
4 1 1 1 1
5 ♭13 ♭9 4 ♭7

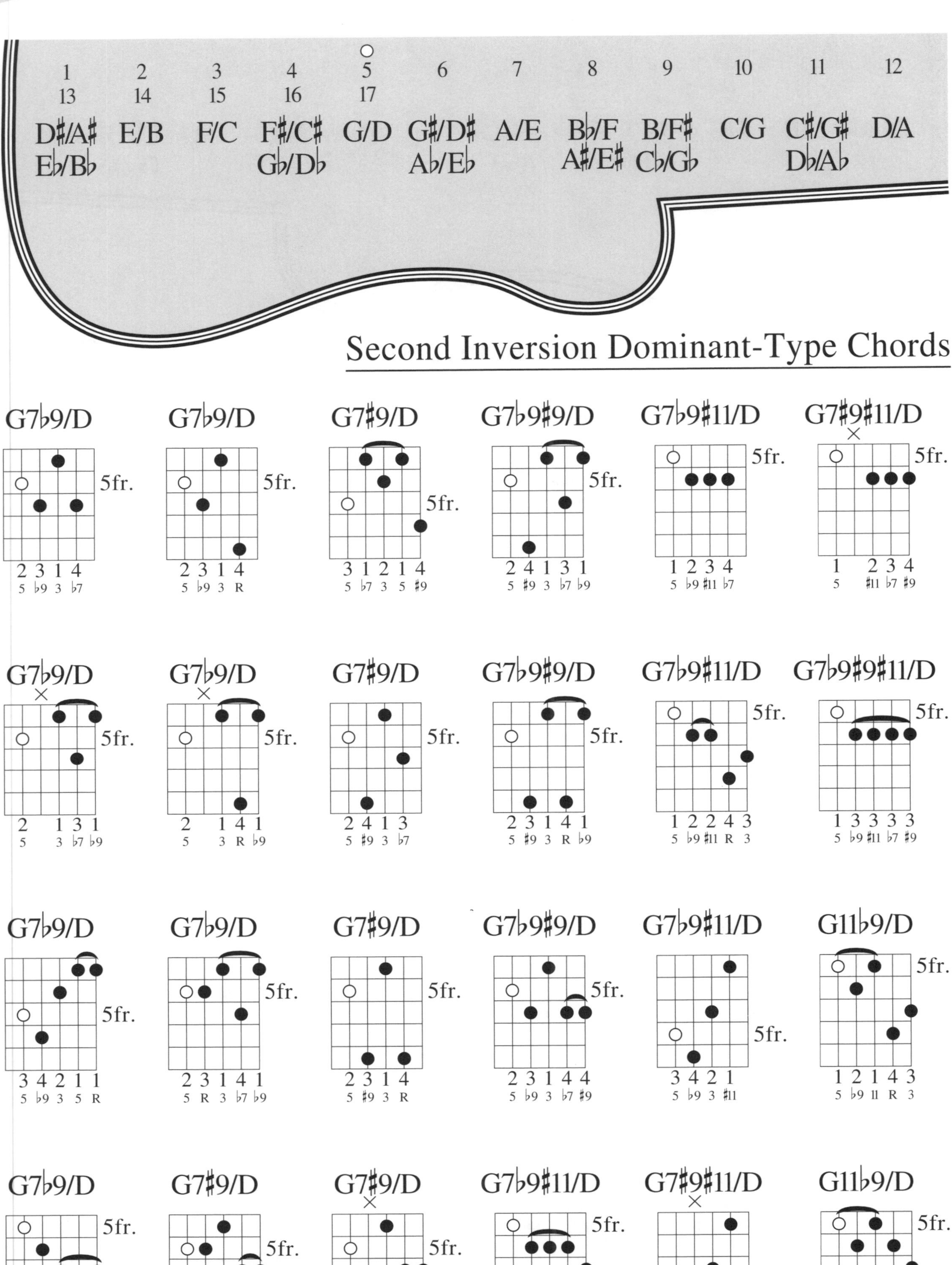
1 13 D♯/A♯ E♭/B♭
2 14 E/B
3 15 F/C
4 16 F♯/C♯ G♭/D♭
5 17 G/D
6 G♯/D♯ A♭/E♭
7 A/E
8 B♭/F A♯/E♯
9 B/F♯ C♭/G♭
10 C/G
11 C♯/G♯ D♭/A♭
12 D/A
Second Inversion Dominant-Type Chords
G7♭9/D 5fr. 2 3 1 4 5 ♭9 3 ♭7
G7♭9/D 5fr. 2 3 1 4 5 ♭9 3 R
G7♯9/D 5fr. 3 1 2 1 4 5 ♭7 3 5 ♯9
G7♭9♯9/D 5fr. 2 4 1 3 1 5 ♯9 3 ♭7 ♭9
G7♭9♯11/D 5fr. 1 2 3 4 5 ♭9 ♯11 ♭7
G7♯9♯11/D 5fr. 1 2 3 4 5 ♯11 ♭7 ♯9
G7♭9/D 5fr. 2 1 3 1 5 3 ♭7 ♭9
G7♭9/D 5fr. 2 1 4 1 5 3 R ♭9
G7♯9/D 5fr. 2 4 1 3 5 ♯9 3 ♭7
G7♭9♯9/D 5fr. 2 3 1 4 1 5 ♯9 3 R ♭9
G7♭9♯11/D 5fr. 1 2 2 4 3 5 ♭9 ♯11 R 3
G7♭9♯9♯11/D 5fr. 1 3 3 3 3 5 ♭9 ♯11 ♭7 ♯9
G7♭9/D 5fr. 3 4 2 1 1 5 ♭9 3 5 R
G7♭9/D 5fr. 2 3 1 4 1 5 R 3 ♭7 ♭9
G7♯9/D 5fr. 2 3 1 4 5 ♯9 3 R
G7♭9♯9/D 5fr. 2 3 1 4 4 5 ♭9 3 ♭7 ♯9
G7♭9♯11/D 5fr. 3 4 2 1 5 ♭9 3 ♯11
G11♭9/D 5fr. 1 2 1 4 3 5 ♭9 11 R 3
G7♭9/D 5fr. 1 2 3 4 3 5 ♭9 5 R 3
G7♯9/D 5fr. 2 3 1 4 4 5 R 3 ♭7 ♯9
G7♯9/D 5fr. 2 1 3 4 5 3 ♭7 ♯9
G7♭9♯11/D 5fr. 1 2 2 2 4 5 ♭9 ♯11 ♭7 3
G7♯9♯11/D 5fr. 3 2 1 4 5 3 ♯11 ♯9
G11♭9/D 5fr. 1 2 1 3 4 5 ♭9 4 ♭7 3

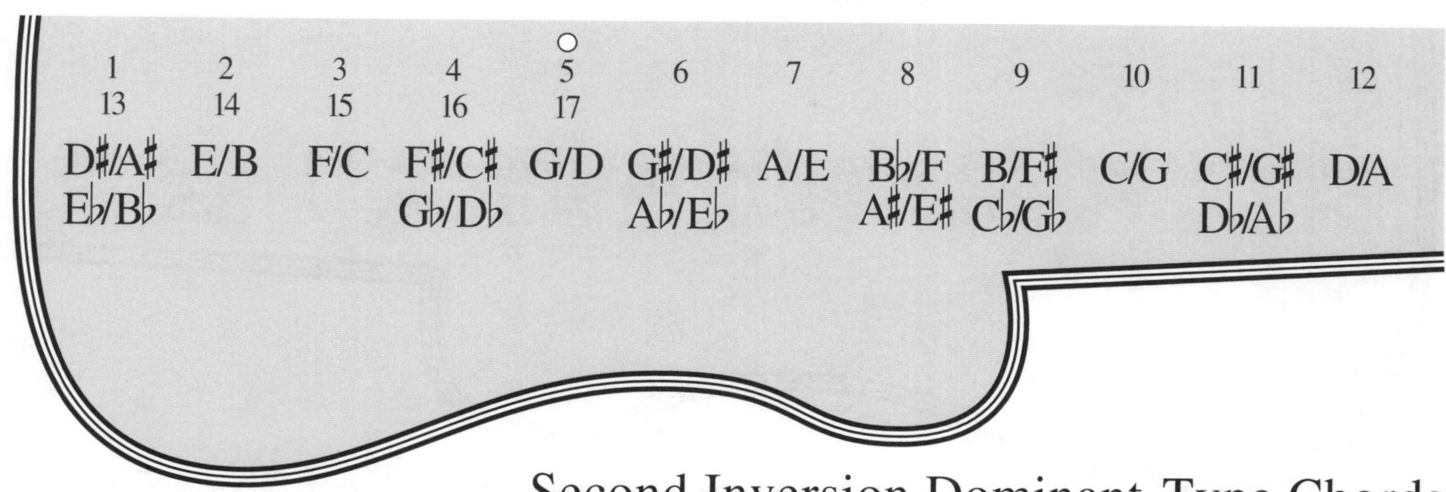

Second Inversion Dominant-Type Chords

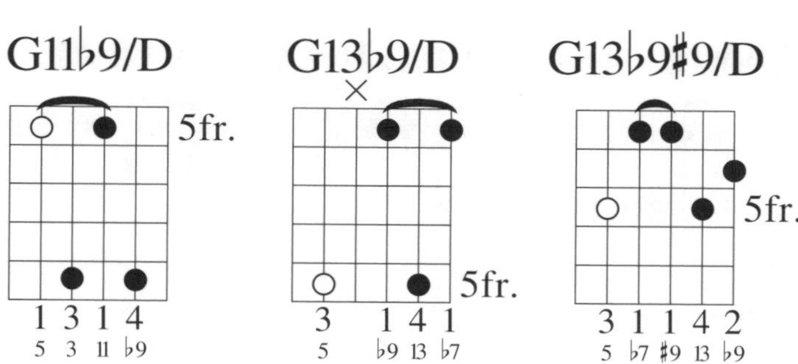

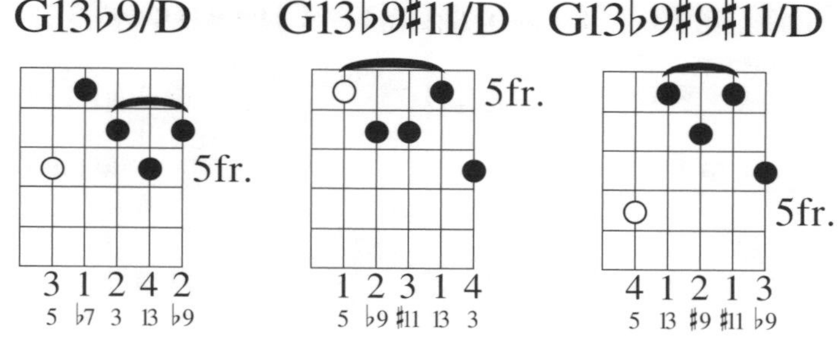

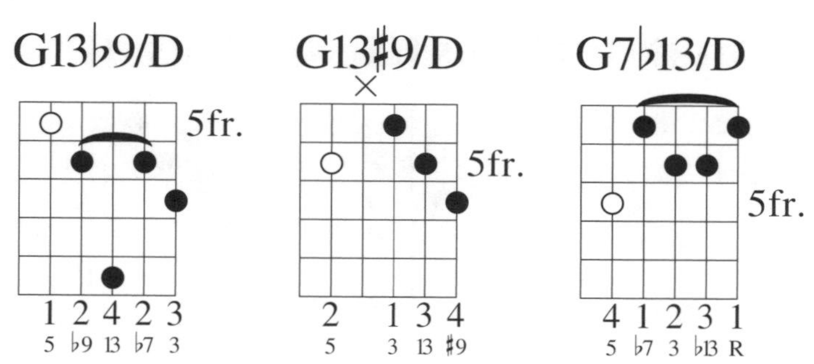

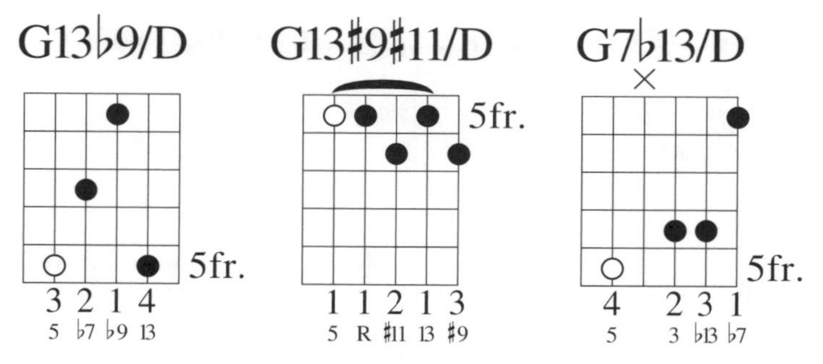

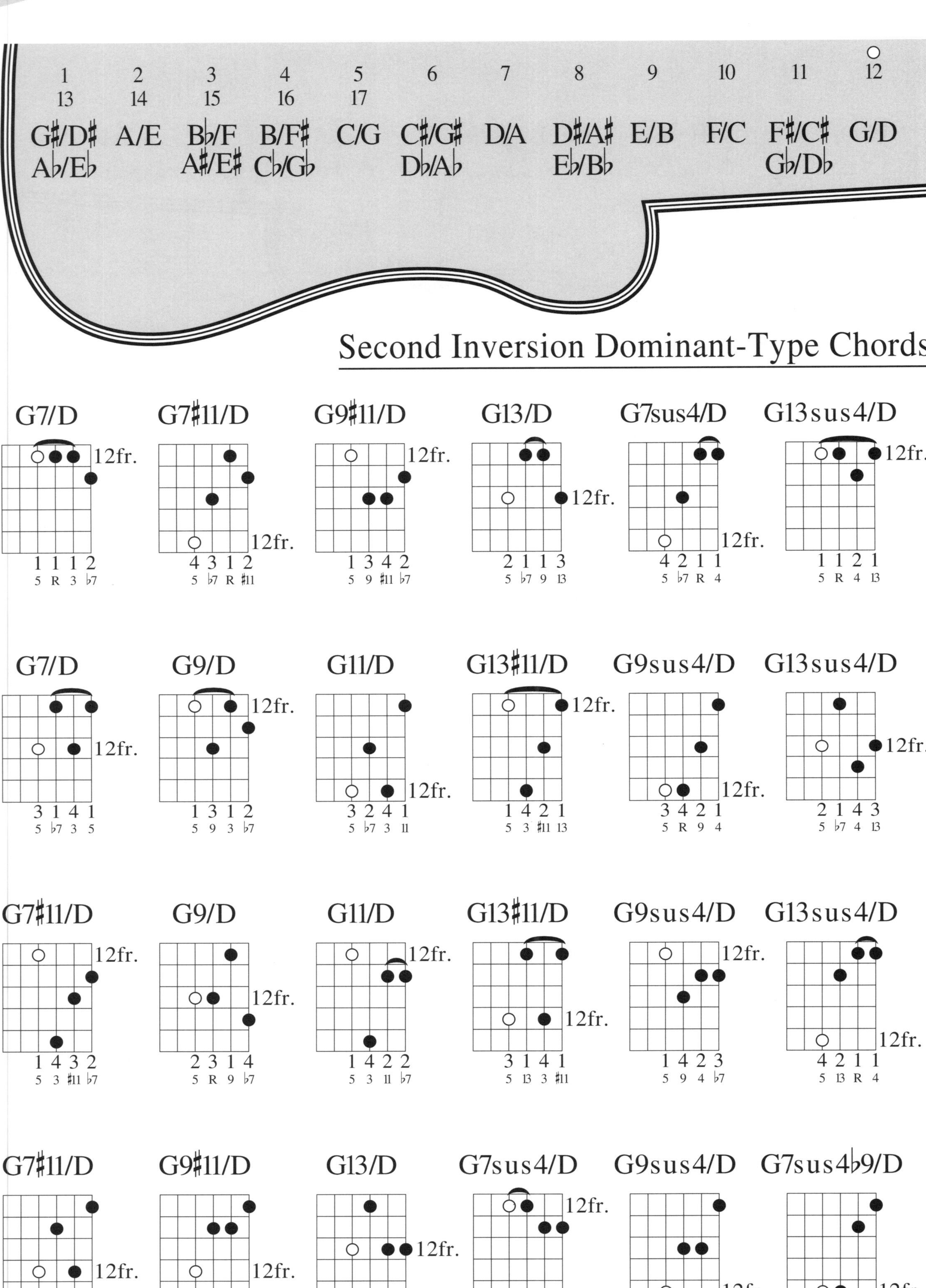
1 2 3 4 5 6 7 8 9 10 11 12
13 14 15 16 17
G♯/D♯ A/E B♭/F B/F♯ C/G C♯/G♯ D/A D♯/A♯ E/B F/C F♯/C♯ G/D
A♭/E♭ A♯/E♯ C♭/G♭ D♭/A♭ E♭/B♭ G♭/D♭
Second Inversion Dominant-Type Chords
G7/D 12fr. 1 1 1 2 5 R 3 ♭7
G7♯11/D 12fr. 4 3 1 2 5 ♭7 R ♯11
G9♯11/D 12fr. 1 3 4 2 5 9 ♯11 ♭7
G13/D 12fr. 2 1 1 3 5 ♭7 9 13
G7sus4/D 12fr. 4 2 1 1 5 ♭7 R 4
G13sus4/D 12fr. 1 1 2 1 5 R 4 13
G7/D 12fr. 3 1 4 1 5 ♭7 3 5
G9/D 12fr. 1 3 1 2 5 9 3 ♭7
G11/D 12fr. 3 2 4 1 5 ♭7 3 11
G13♯11/D 12fr. 1 4 2 1 5 3 ♯11 13
G9sus4/D 12fr. 3 4 2 1 5 R 9 4
G13sus4/D 12fr. 2 1 4 3 5 ♭7 4 13
G7♯11/D 12fr. 1 4 3 2 5 3 ♯11 ♭7
G9/D 12fr. 2 3 1 4 5 R 9 ♭7
G11/D 12fr. 1 4 2 2 5 3 11 ♭7
G13♯11/D 12fr. 3 1 4 1 5 13 3 ♯11
G9sus4/D 12fr. 1 4 2 3 5 9 4 ♭7
G13sus4/D 12fr. 4 2 1 1 5 13 R 4
G7♯11/D 12fr. 3 2 4 1 5 ♭7 3 ♯11
G9♯11/D 12fr. 4 2 3 1 5 ♭7 9 ♯11
G13/D 12fr. 2 1 3 4 5 ♭7 3 13
G7sus4/D 12fr. 1 1 2 3 5 R 4 ♭7
G9sus4/D 12fr. 4 2 3 1 5 ♭7 9 4
G7sus4♭9/D 12fr. 3 4 2 1 5 R ♭9 4

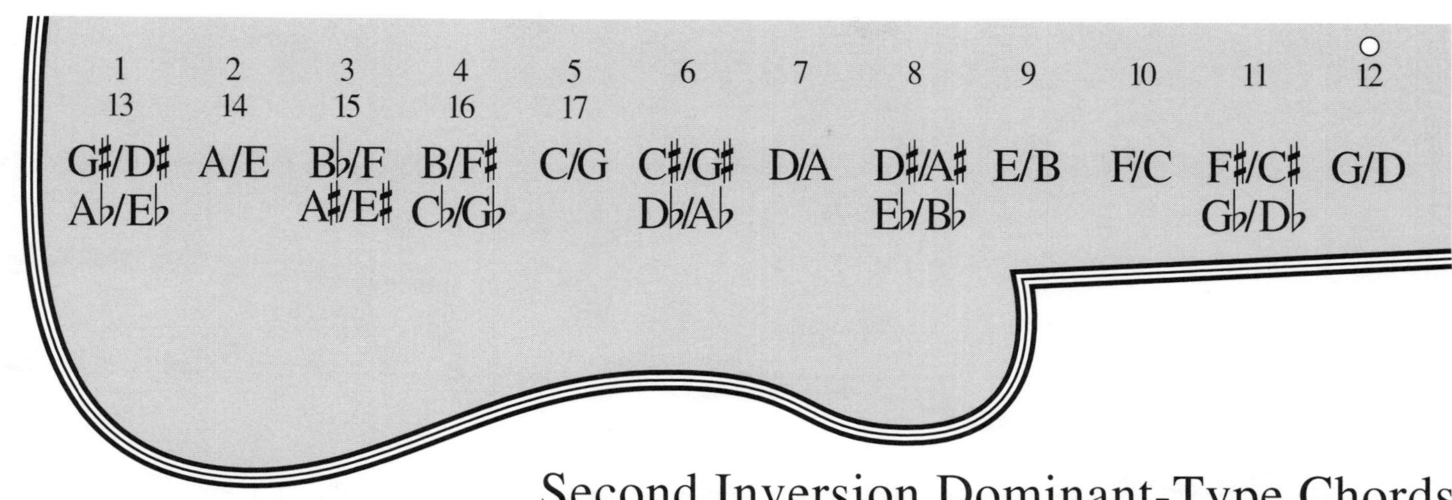

Second Inversion Dominant-Type Chords

G7sus4♭9/D
12fr.
1 2 2 4
5 ♭9 4 R

G7sus4♭9♭13/D
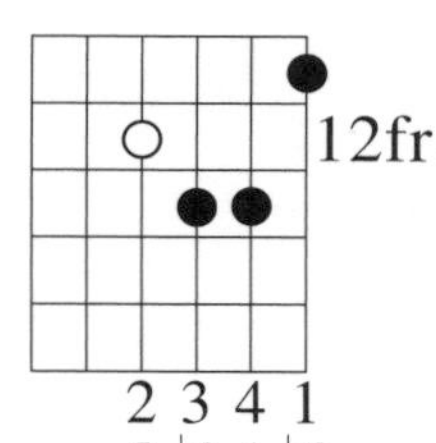
12fr.
2 3 4 1
5 ♭9 4 ♭13

G7♭9/D
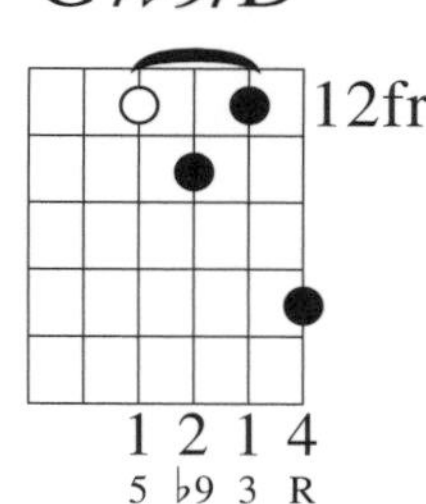
12fr.
1 2 1 4
5 ♭9 3 R

G7♭9♯11/D
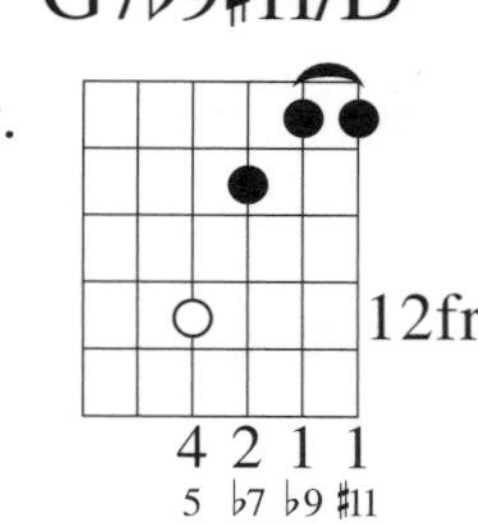
12fr.
4 2 1 1
5 ♭7 ♭9 ♯11

G7♭9♯9♯11/D
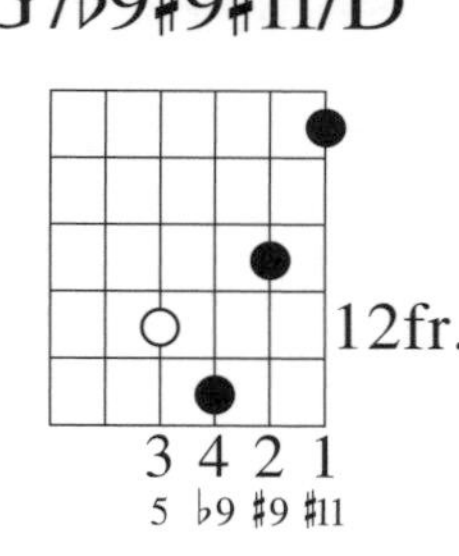
12fr.
3 4 2 1
5 ♭9 ♯9 ♯11

G13♭9♯11/D
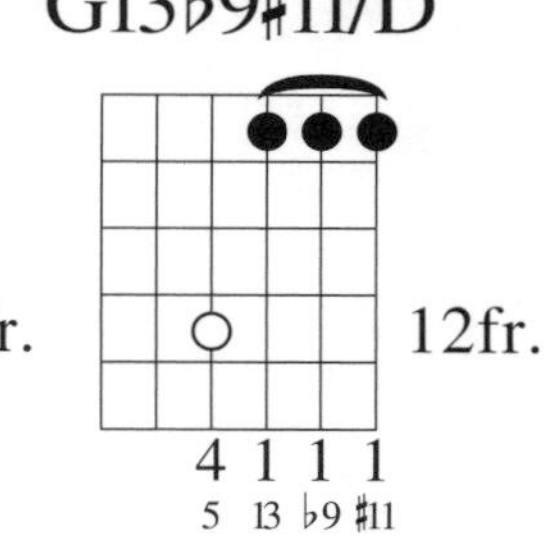
12fr.
4 1 1 1
5 13 ♭9 ♯11

G7sus4♭9/D
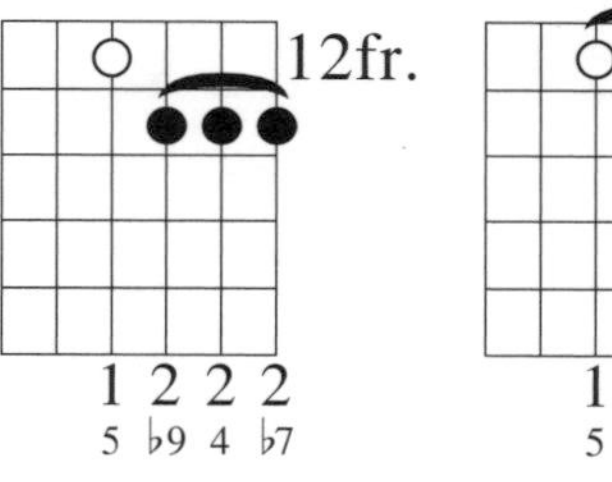
12fr.
1 2 2 2
5 ♭9 4 ♭7

G7♭9/D
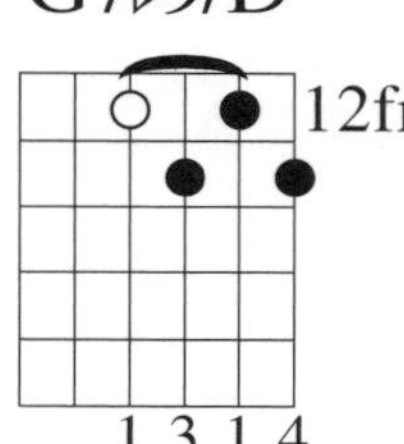
12fr.
1 3 1 4
5 ♭9 3 ♭7

G7♯9/D
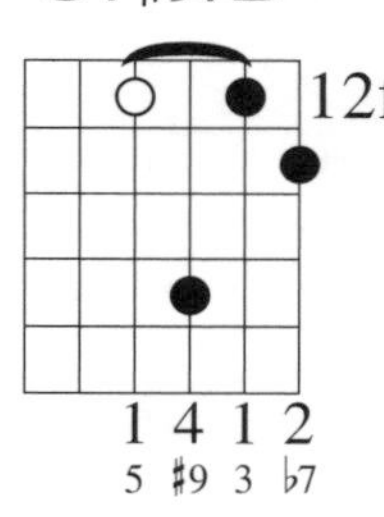
12fr.
1 4 1 2
5 ♯9 3 ♭7

G7♭9♯11/D
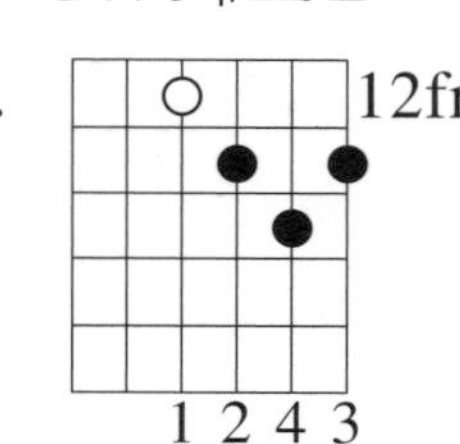
12fr.
1 2 4 3
5 ♭9 ♯11 ♭7

G11♭9/D
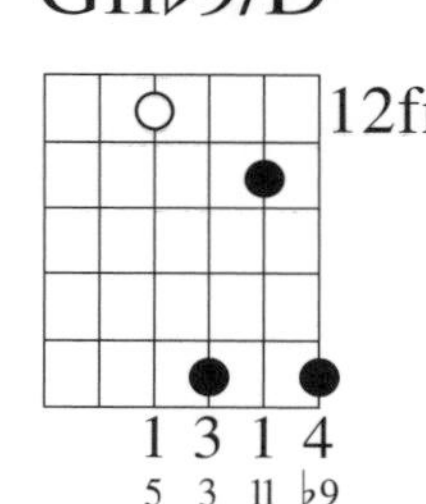
12fr.
1 3 1 4
5 3 11 ♭9

G13♯9/D
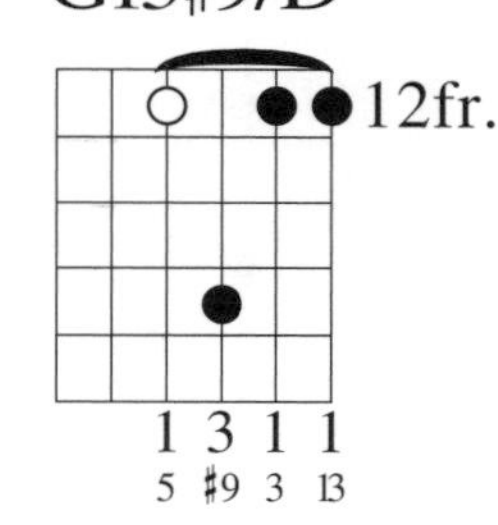
12fr.
1 3 1 1
5 ♯9 3 13

G13sus4♭9/D
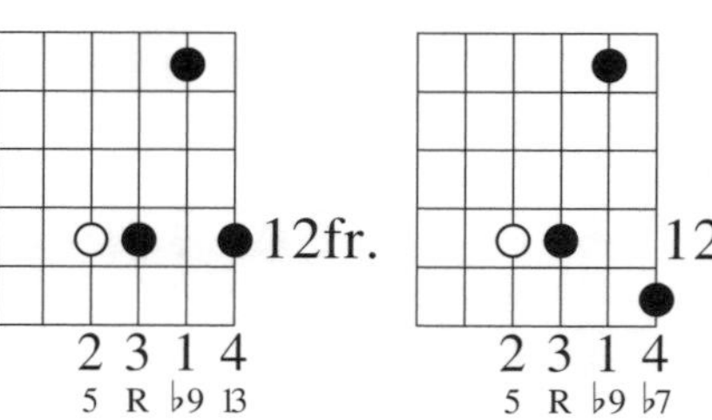
12fr.
2 3 1 4
5 R ♭9 13

G7♭9/D
12fr.
2 3 1 4
5 R ♭9 ♭7

G7♯9/D

12fr.
1 3 1 4
5 ♯9 3 R

G7♯9♯11/D
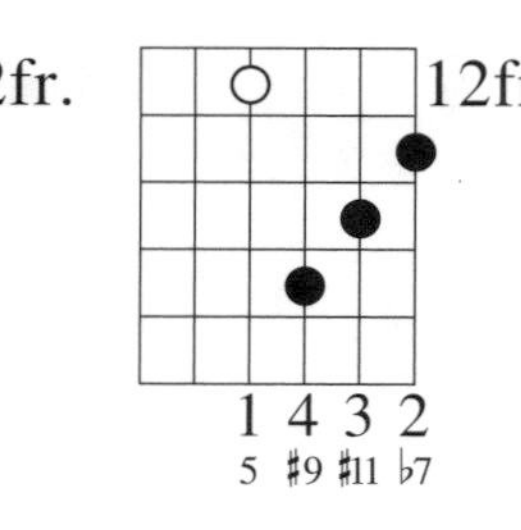
12fr.
1 4 3 2
5 ♯9 ♯11 ♭7

G13♭9/D
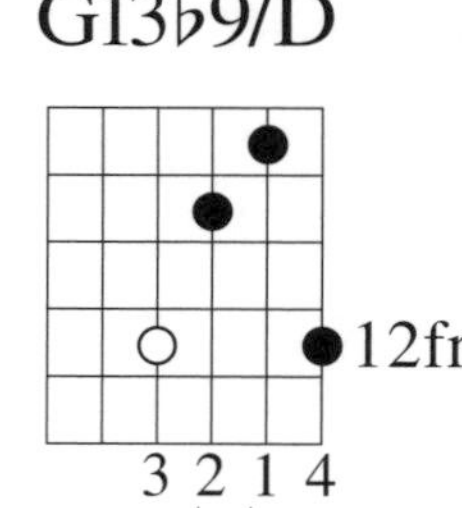
12fr.
3 2 1 4
5 ♭7 ♭9 13

G13♯9♯11/D
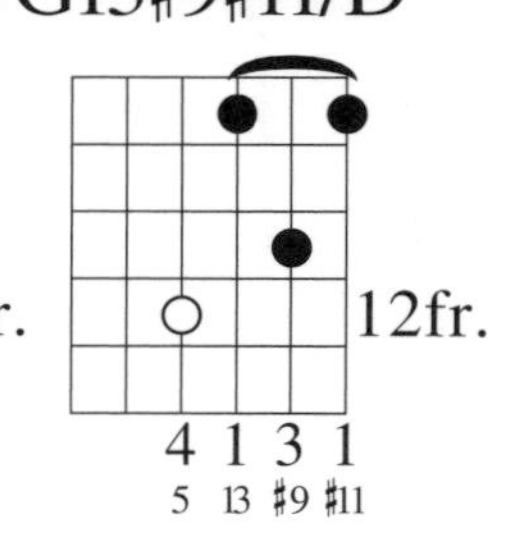
12fr.
4 1 3 1
5 13 ♯9 ♯11

G7sus4♭9♭13/D
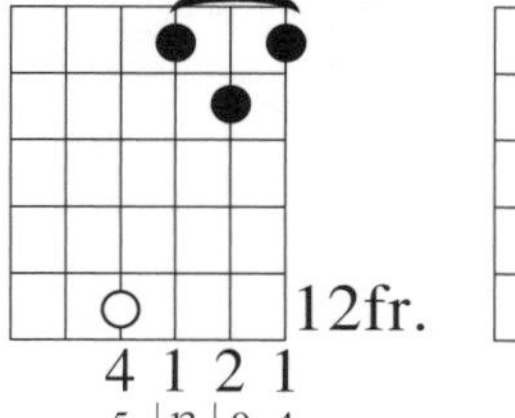
12fr.
4 1 2 1
5 ♭13 ♭9 4

G7♭9/D
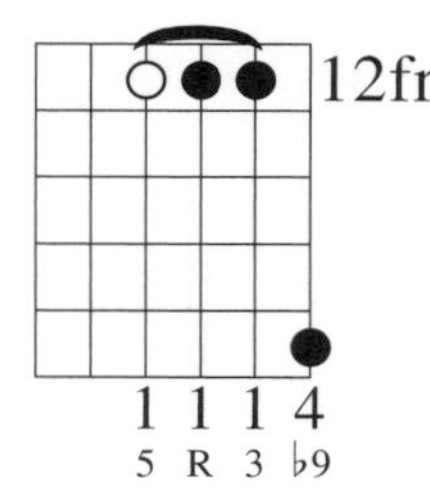
12fr.
1 1 1 4
5 R 3 ♭9

G7♭9♯9/D
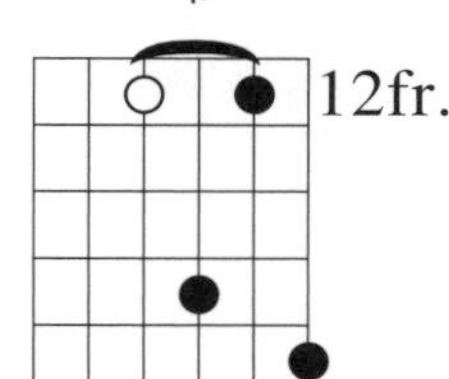
12fr.
1 3 1 4
5 ♯9 R ♭9

G7♯9♯11/D
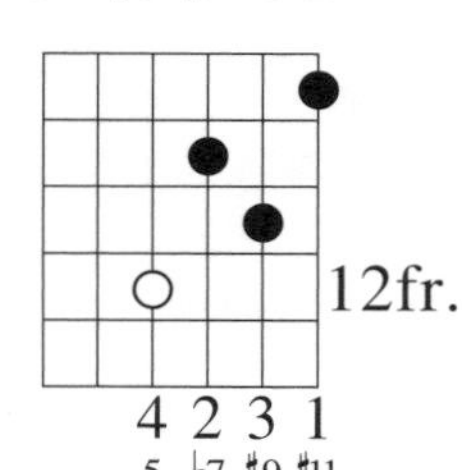
12fr.
4 2 3 1
5 ♭7 ♯9 ♯11

G13♭9♯11/D
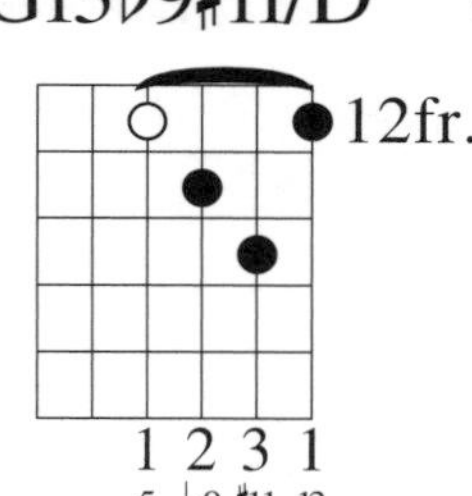
12fr.
1 2 3 1
5 ♭9 ♯11 13

G13♭9♯9/D
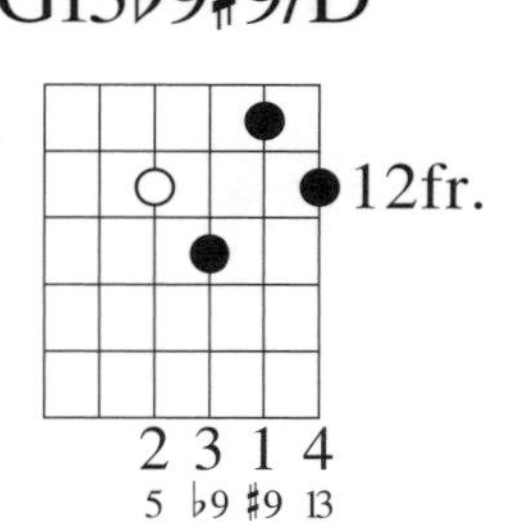
12fr.
2 3 1 4
5 ♭9 ♯9 13

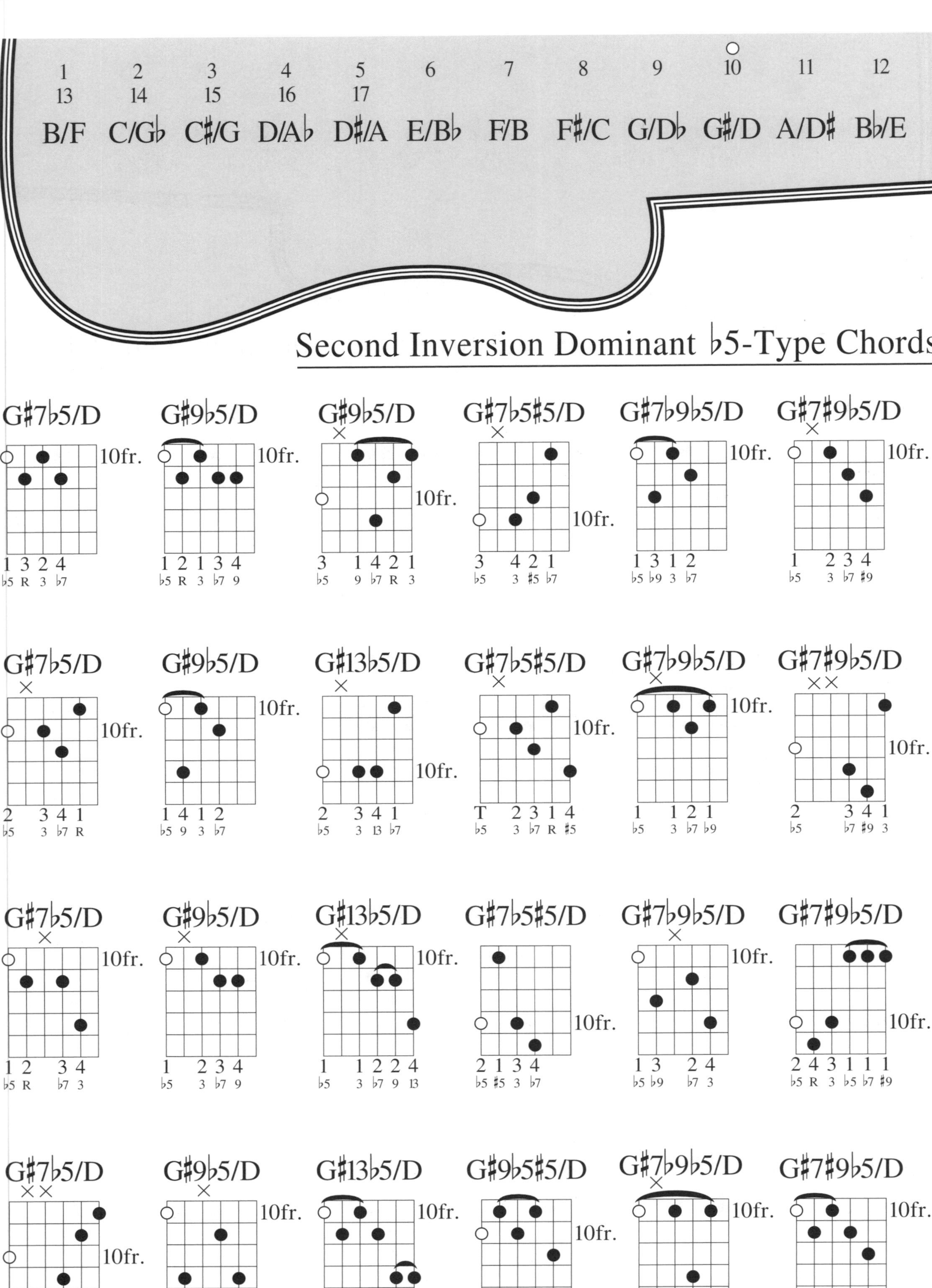
1 2 3 4 5 6 7 8 9 10 11 12
13 14 15 16 17
B/F C/G♭ C♯/G D/A♭ D♯/A E/B♭ F/B F♯/C G/D♭ G♯/D A/D♯ B♭/E
Second Inversion Dominant ♭5-Type Chords
G♯7♭5/D
G♯9♭5/D
G♯9♭5/D
G♯7♭5♯5/D
G♯7♭9♭5/D
G♯7♯9♭5/D
G♯7♭5/D
G♯9♭5/D
G♯13♭5/D
G♯7♭5♯5/D
G♯7♭9♭5/D
G♯7♯9♭5/D
G♯7♭5/D
G♯9♭5/D
G♯13♭5/D
G♯7♭5♯5/D
G♯7♭9♭5/D
G♯7♯9♭5/D
G♯7♭5/D
G♯9♭5/D
G♯13♭5/D
G♯9♭5♯5/D
G♯7♭9♭5/D
G♯7♯9♭5/D

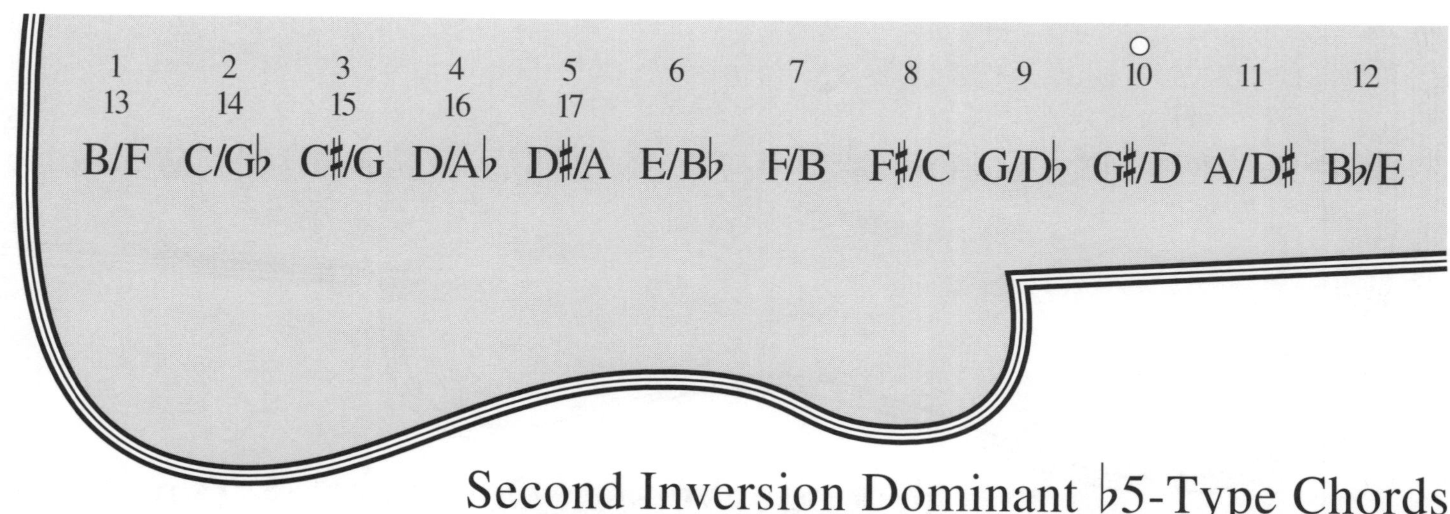

Second Inversion Dominant ♭5-Type Chords

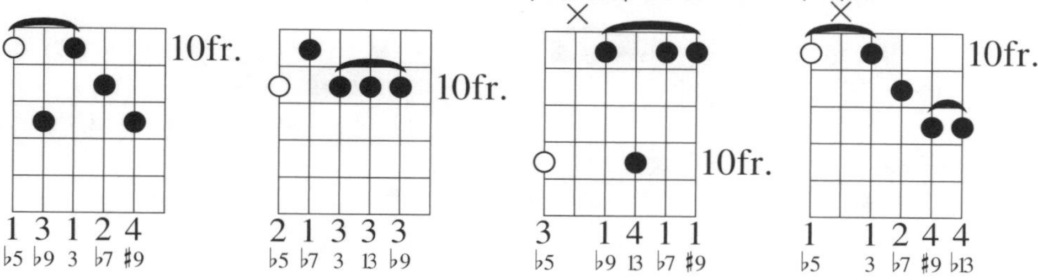

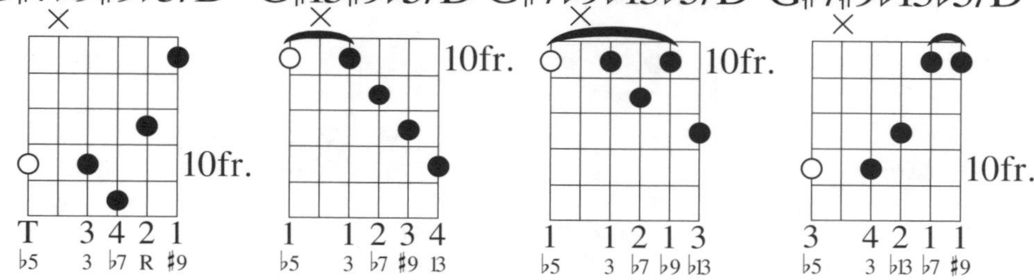

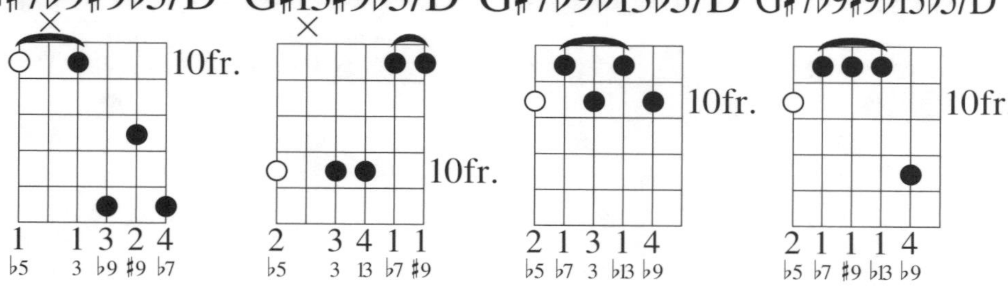

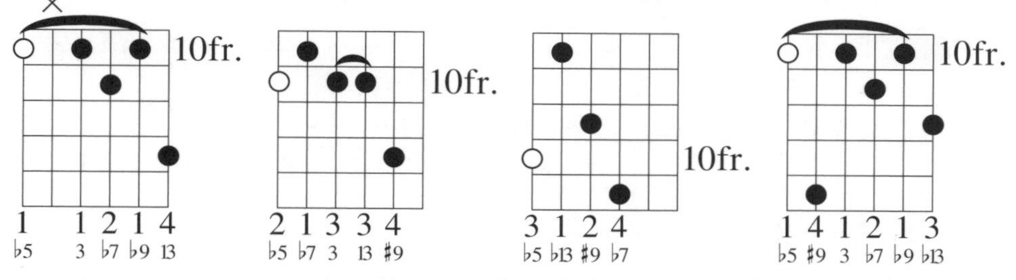

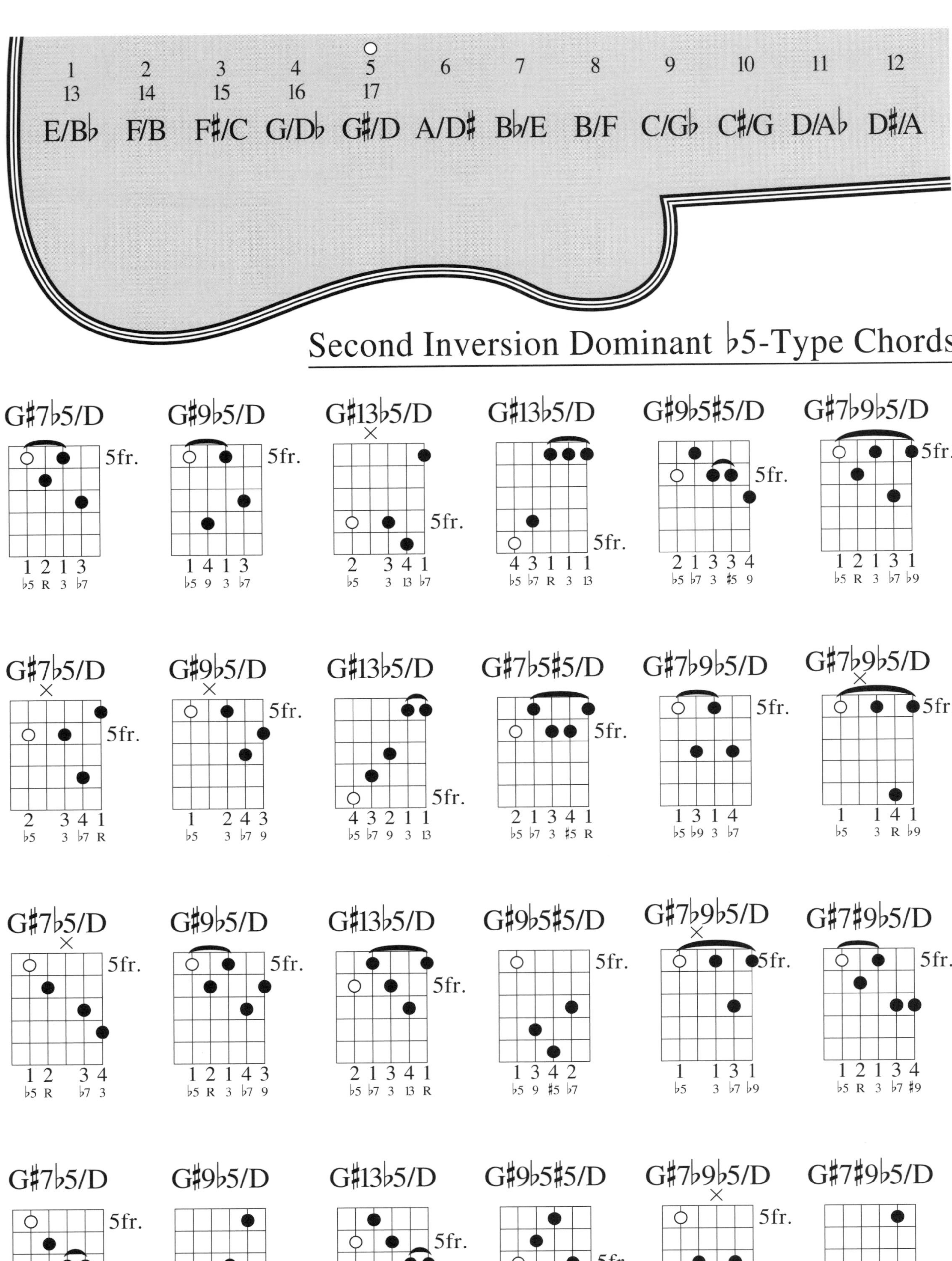

1 2 3 4 5 6 7 8 9 10 11 12
13 14 15 16 17
E/B♭ F/B F♯/C G/D♭ G♯/D A/D♯ B♭/E B/F C/G♭ C♯/G D/A♭ D♯/A
Second Inversion Dominant ♭5-Type Chords
G♯7♭5/D
G♯9♭5/D
G♯13♭5/D
G♯13♭5/D
G♯9♭5♯5/D
G♯7♭9♭5/D
G♯7♭5/D
G♯9♭5/D
G♯13♭5/D
G♯7♭5♯5/D
G♯7♭9♭5/D
G♯7♭9♭5/D
G♯7♭5/D
G♯9♭5/D
G♯13♭5/D
G♯9♭5♯5/D
G♯7♭9♭5/D
G♯7♯9♭5/D
G♯7♭5/D
G♯9♭5/D
G♯13♭5/D
G♯9♭5♯5/D
G♯7♭9♭5/D
G♯7♯9♭5/D
5fr.

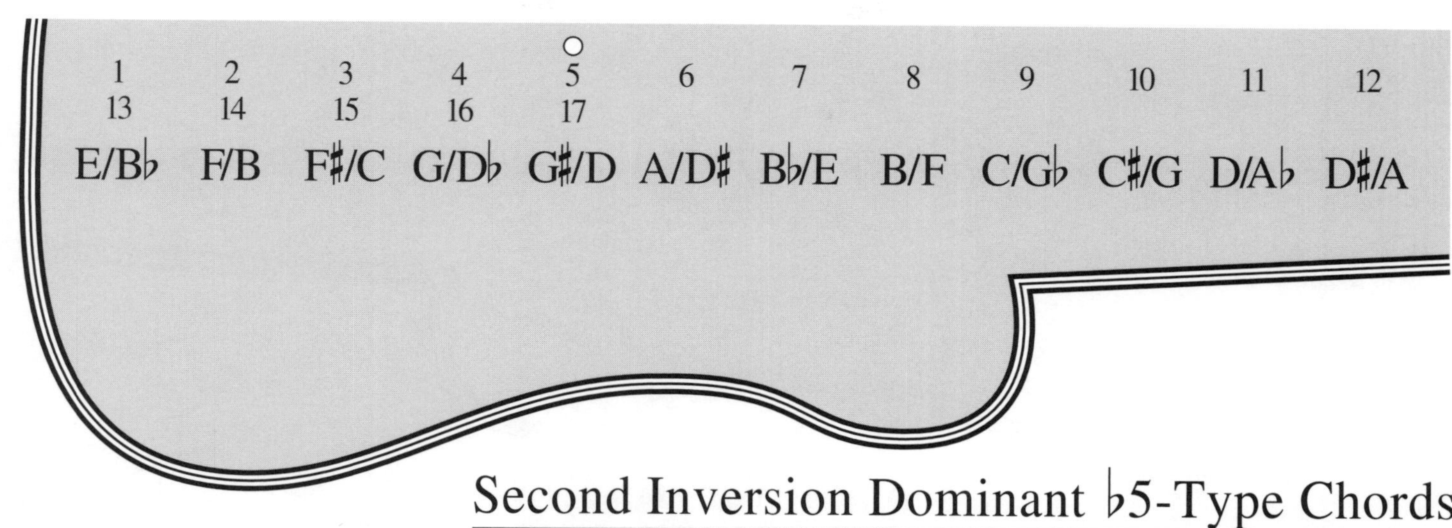

Second Inversion Dominant ♭5-Type Chords

G♯7♯9♭5/D G♯13♯9♭5/D G♯7♭9♭13♭5/D

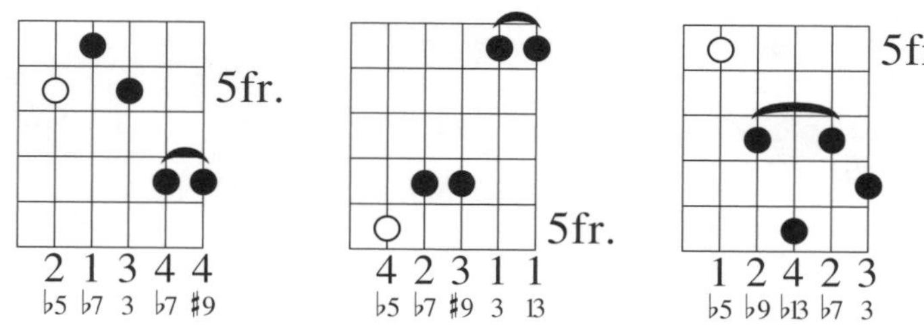

G♯7♭9♯9♭5/D G♯13♯9♭5/D G♯7♯9♭13♭5/D

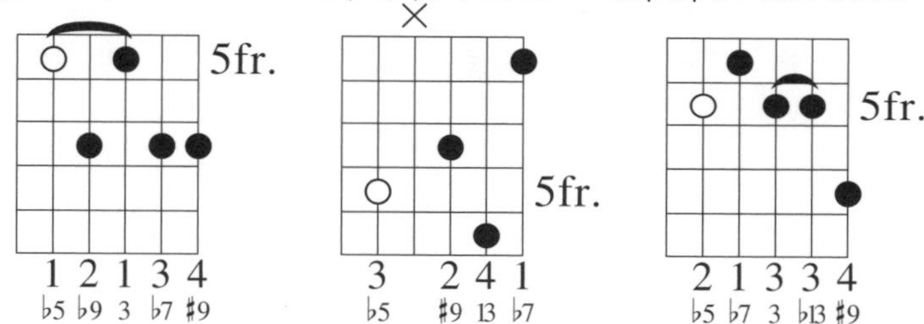

G♯7♭9♯9♭5/D G♯13♭9♯9♭5/D G♯7♯9♭13♭5/D

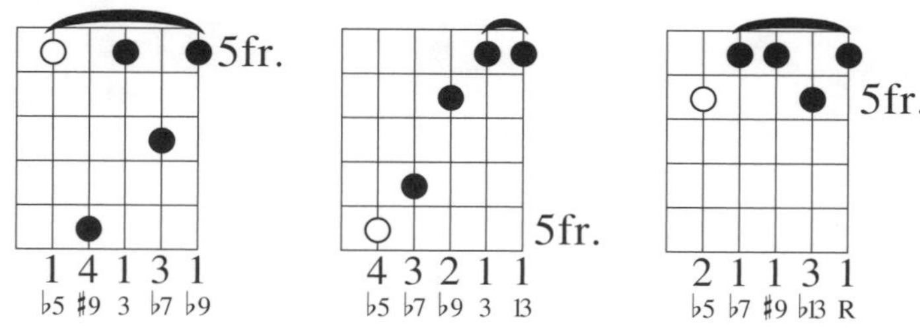

G♯13♭9♭5/D G♯13♭9♯9♭5/D G♯7♭9♯9♭13♭5/D

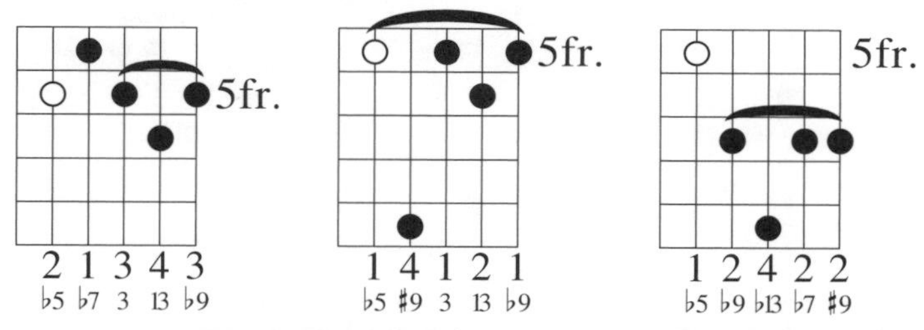

1 13	2 14	3 15	4 16	5 17	6	7	8	9	10	11	12
A/D♯	B♭/E	B/F	C/G♭	C♯/G	D/A♭	D♯/A	E/B♭	F/B	F♯/C	G/D♭	G♯/D

Second Inversion Dominant ♭5-Type Chords

G♯7♭5/D — 12fr. — 1 2 2 3 — ♭5 R 3 ♭7

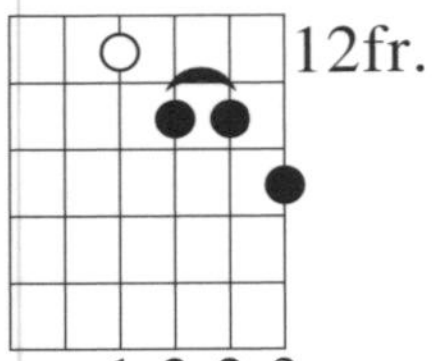

G♯13♭5/D — 12fr. — 2 1 3 4 — ♭5 ♭7 3 13

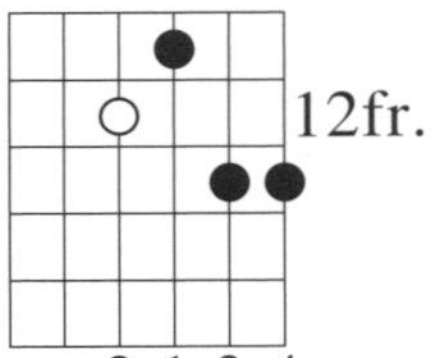

G♯7♭5♯5/D — 12fr. — 1 2 3 1 — ♭5 R 3 ♯5

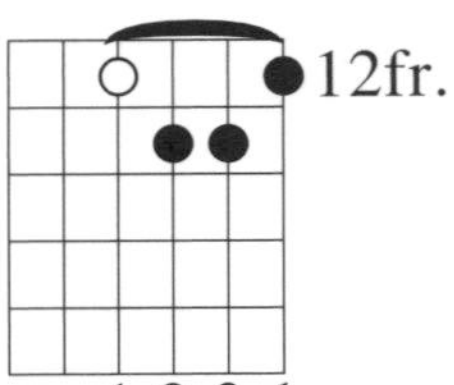

G♯7♭9♭5/D — 12fr. — 4 3 2 1 — ♭5 ♭7 ♭9 3

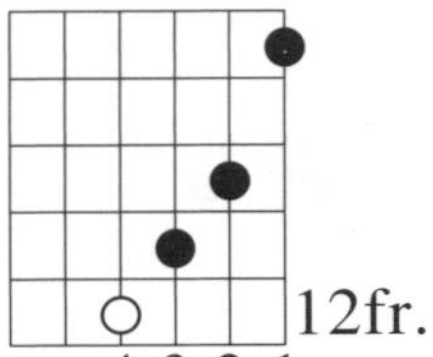

G♯7♭9♯9♭5/D — 12fr. — 1 3 1 4 — ♭5 ♭9 ♯9 ♭7

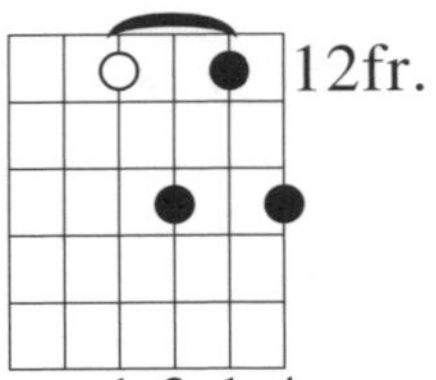

G♯7♭9♭13♭5/D — 12fr. — 3 2 1 4 — ♭5 ♭7 ♭9 ♭13

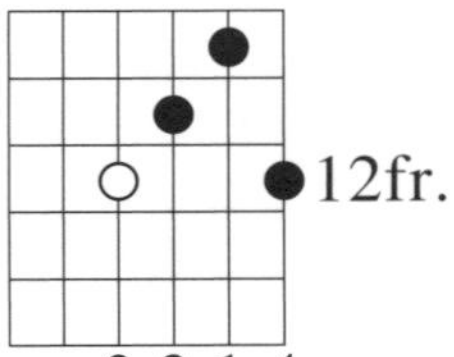

G♯7♭5/D — 12fr. — 4 3 2 1 — ♭5 ♭7 R 3

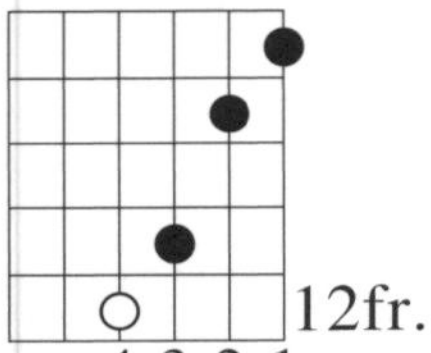

G♯13♭5/D — 12fr. — 3 2 1 4 — ♭5 ♭7 R 13

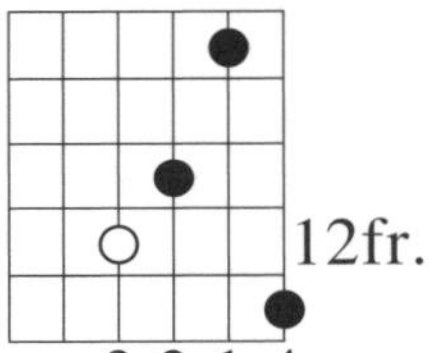

G♯9♭5♯5/D — 12fr. — 1 4 2 1 — ♭5 9 3 ♯5

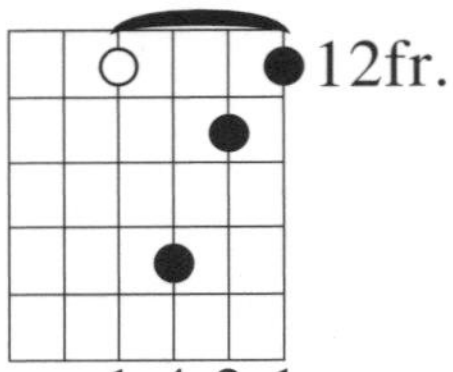

G♯7♭9♭5/D — 12fr. — 2 3 1 4 — ♭5 R ♭9 ♭7

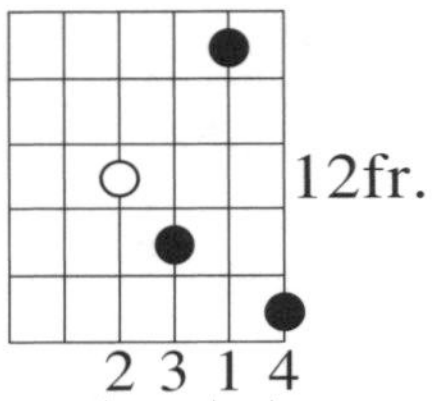

G♯13♭9♭5/D — 12fr. — 3 2 1 4 — ♭5 ♭7 ♭9 13

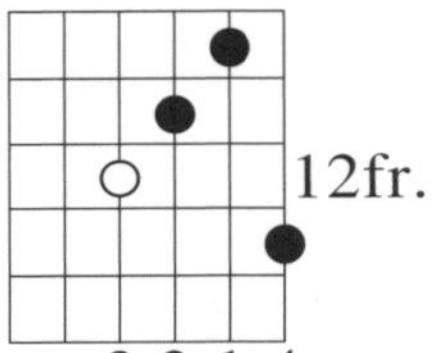

G♯7♯9♭13♭5/D — 12fr. — 3 2 4 1 — ♭5 ♭13 ♯9 3

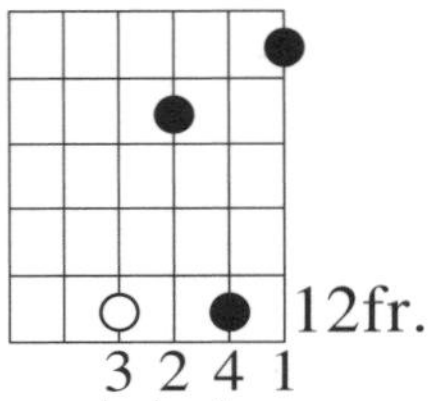

G♯9♭5/D — 12fr. — 1 4 2 3 — ♭5 9 3 ♭7

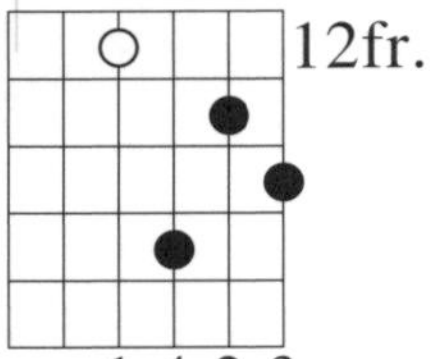

G♯13♭5/D — 12fr. — 2 1 1 3 — ♭5 ♭7 9 13

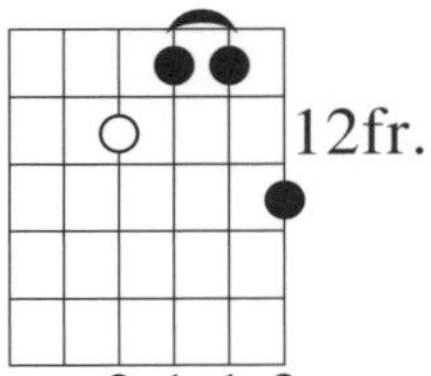

G♯9♭5♯5/D — 12fr. — 2 1 1 3 — ♭5 ♭7 9 ♯5

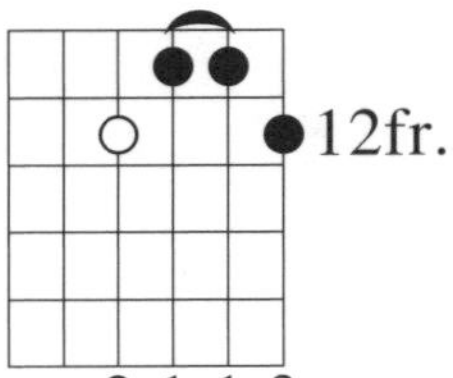

G♯7♯9♭5/D — 12fr. — 3 2 4 1 — ♭5 ♭7 ♯9 3

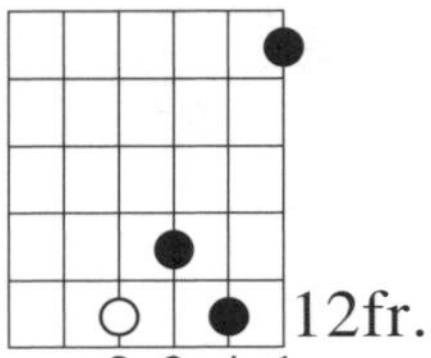

G♯13♯9♭5/D — 12fr. — 3 2 4 1 — ♭5 13 ♯9 3

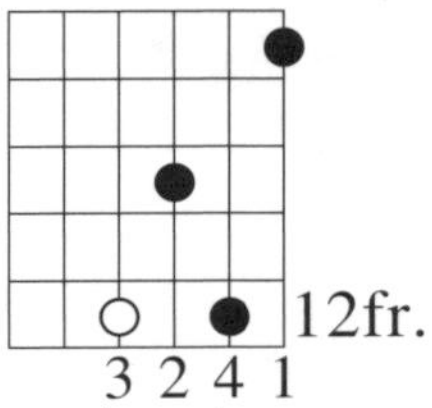

G♯7♯9♭13♭5/D — 12fr. — 2 1 3 4 — ♭5 ♭7 ♯9 ♭13

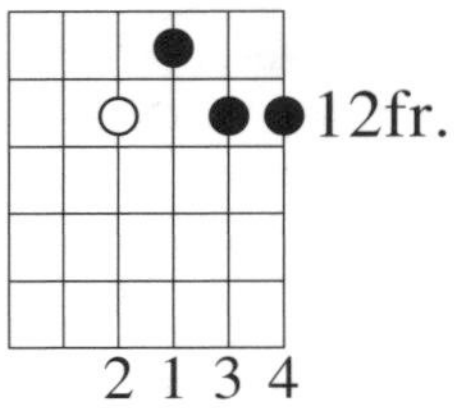

G♯9♭5/D **G♯7♭5♯5/D** **G♯7♭9♭5/D** **G♯7♯9♭5/D** **G♯13♭9♯9♭5/D** **G♯7♭9♯9♭13♭5/D**

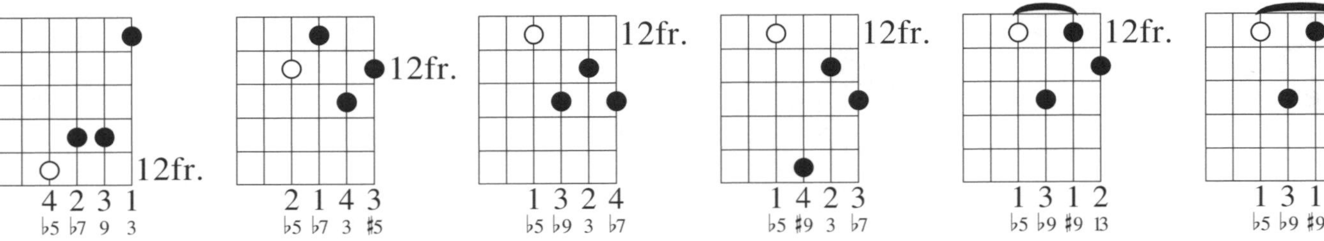

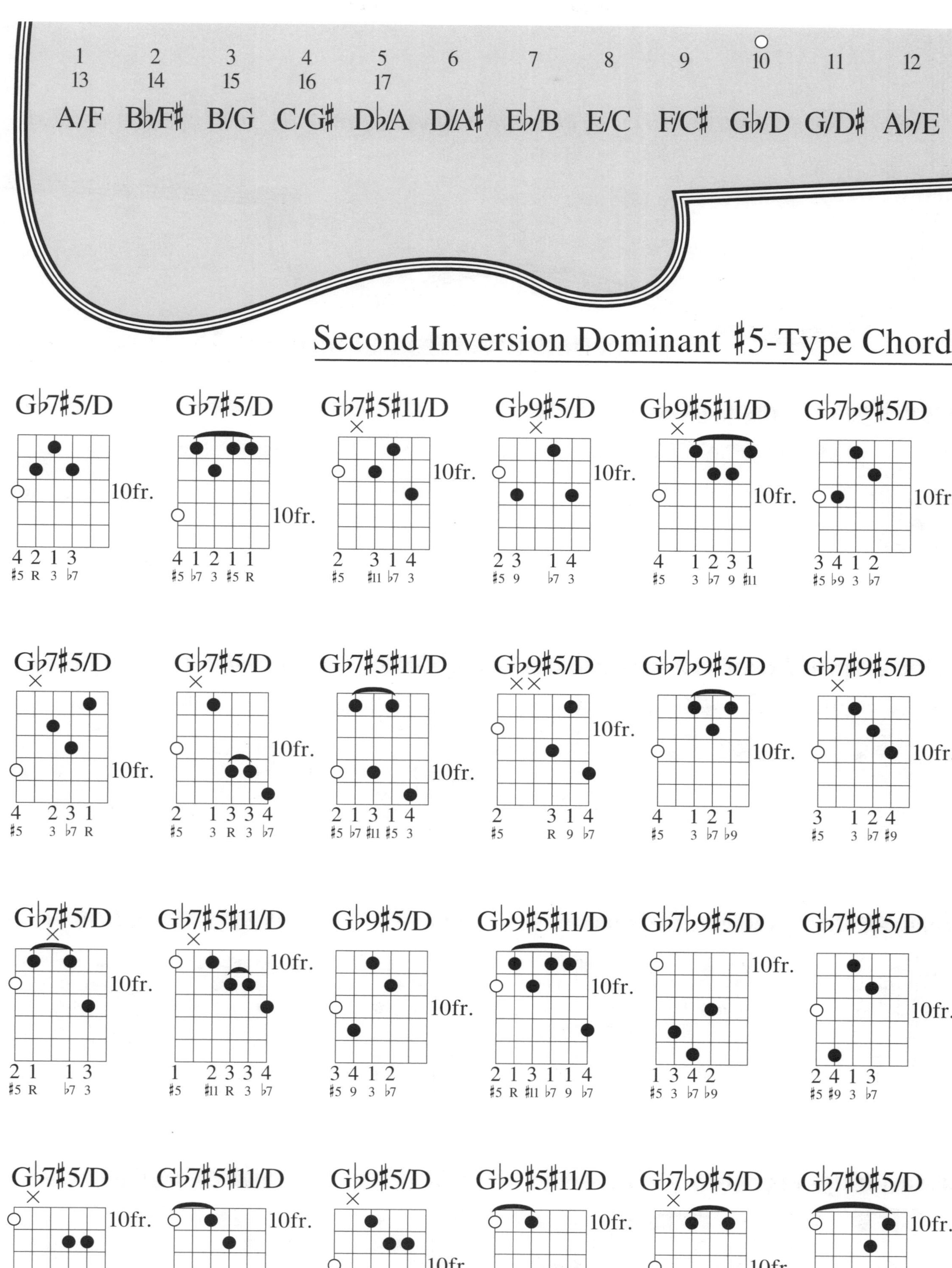
1 13 A/F
2 14 B♭/F♯
3 15 B/G
4 16 C/G♯
5 17 D♭/A
6 D/A♯
7 E♭/B
8 E/C
9 F/C♯
10 G♭/D
11 G/D♯
12 A♭/E
Second Inversion Dominant ♯5-Type Chords
G♭7♯5/D
G♭7♯5/D
G♭7♯5♯11/D
G♭9♯5/D
G♭9♯5♯11/D
G♭7♭9♯5/D
G♭7♯5/D
G♭7♯5/D
G♭7♯5♯11/D
G♭9♯5/D
G♭7♭9♯5/D
G♭7♯9♯5/D
G♭7♯5/D
G♭7♯5♯11/D
G♭9♯5/D
G♭9♯5♯11/D
G♭7♭9♯5/D
G♭7♯9♯5/D
G♭7♯5/D
G♭7♯5♯11/D
G♭9♯5/D
G♭9♯5♯11/D
G♭7♭9♯5/D
G♭7♯9♯5/D
10fr.

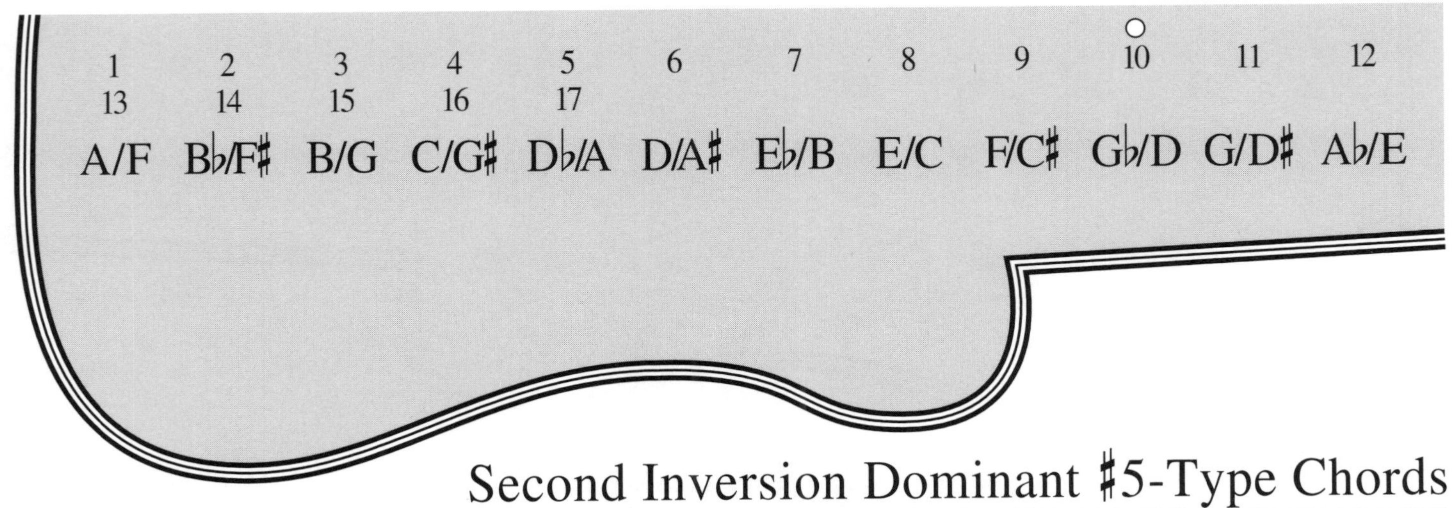

Second Inversion Dominant ♯5-Type Chords

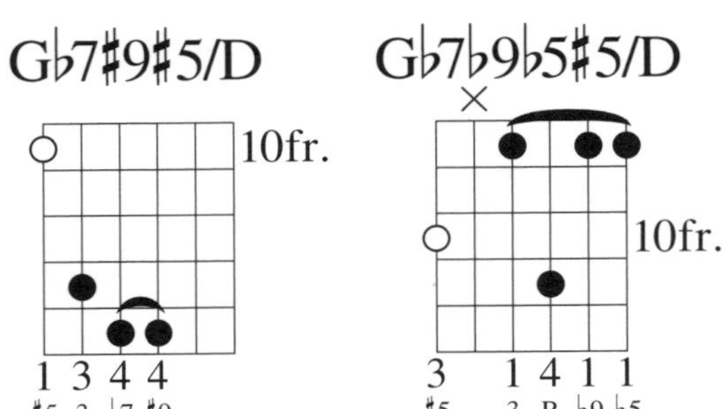

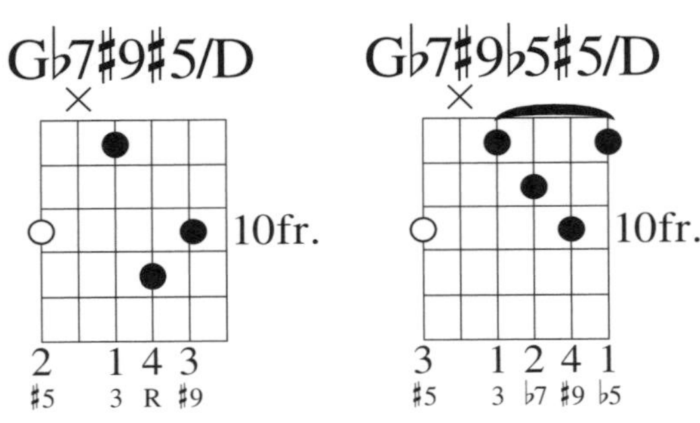

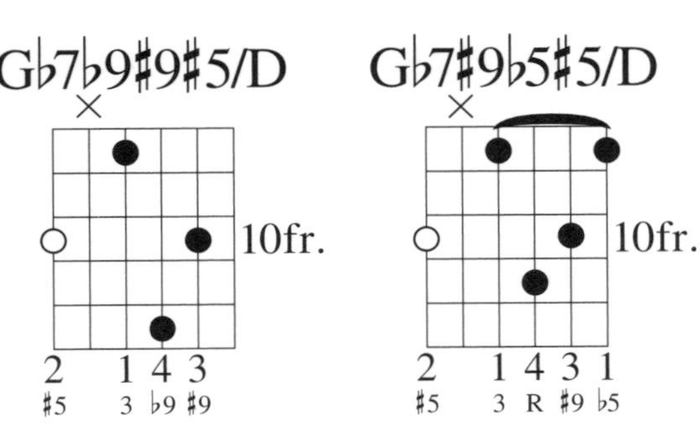

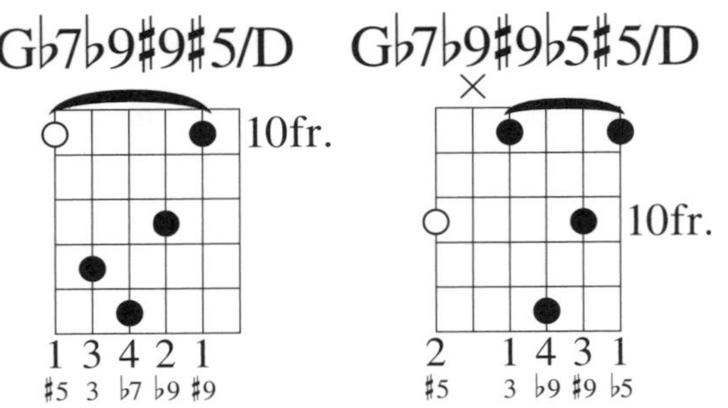

1 13	2 14	3 15	4 16	○ 5 17	6	7	8	9	10	11	12
D/A♯	E♭/B	E/C	F/C♯	G♭/D	G/D♯	A♭/E	A/F	B♭/F♯	B/G	C/G♯	D♭/A

Second Inversion Dominant ♯5-Type Chords

G♭7♯5/D

3 2 1 4
♯5 R 3 ♭7

G♭7♯5♯11/D

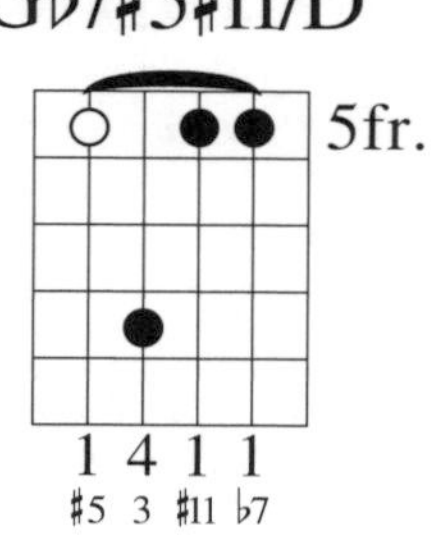

1 4 1 1
♯5 3 ♯11 ♭7

G♭9♯5/D

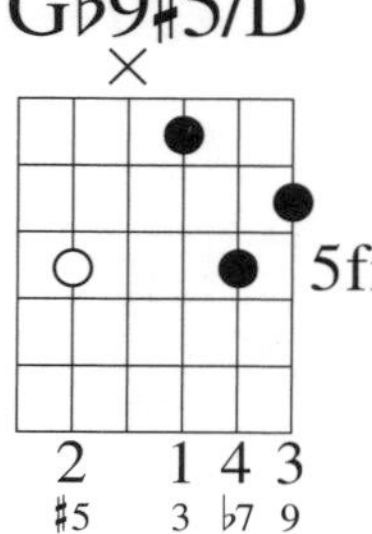

2 1 4 3
♯5 3 ♭7 9

G♭9♯5♯11/D

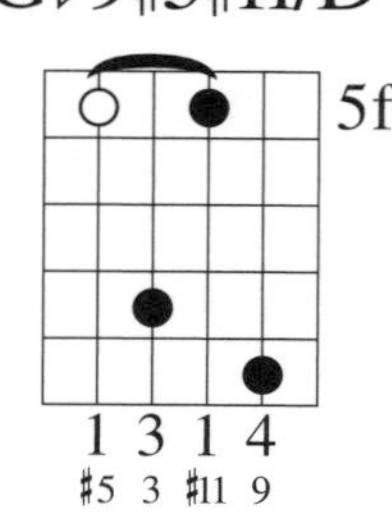

1 3 1 4
♯5 3 ♯11 9

G♭7♭9♯5/D

2 3 1 4
♯5 ♭9 3 ♭7

G♭7♭9♯9♯5/D

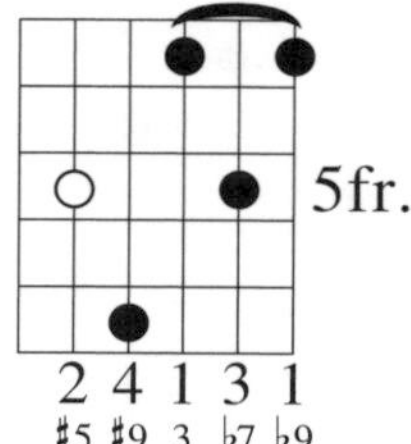

2 4 1 3 1
♯5 ♯9 3 ♭7 ♭9

G♭7♯5/D

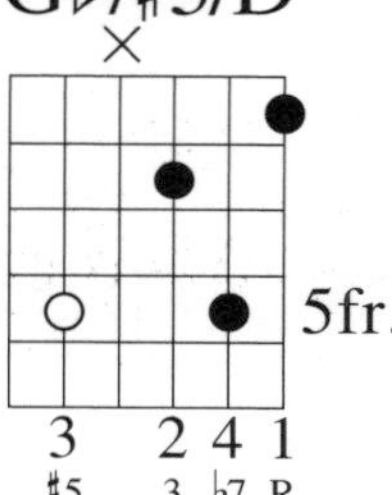

3 2 4 1
♯5 3 ♭7 R

G♭7♯5♯11/D

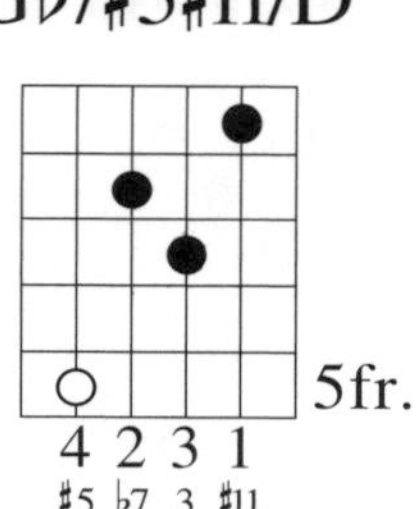

4 2 3 1
♯5 ♭7 3 ♯11

G♭9♯5/D

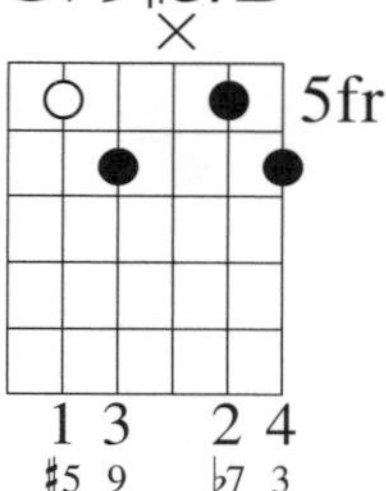

1 3 2 4
♯5 9 ♭7 3

G♭7♭9♯5/D

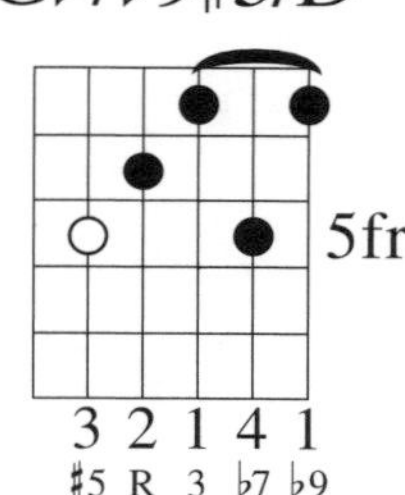

3 2 1 4 1
♯5 R 3 ♭7 ♭9

G♭7♯9♯5/D

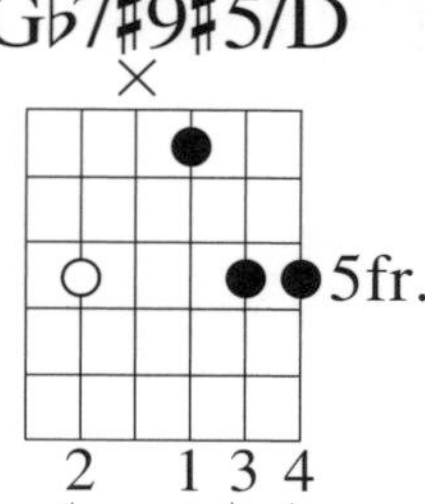

2 1 3 4
♯5 3 ♭7 ♯9

G♭7♭9♯9♯5/D

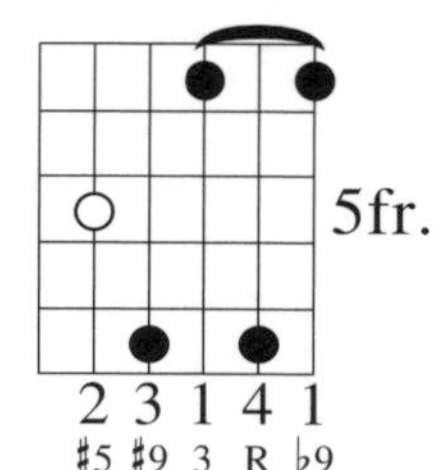

2 3 1 4 1
♯5 ♯9 3 R ♭9

G♭7♯5/D

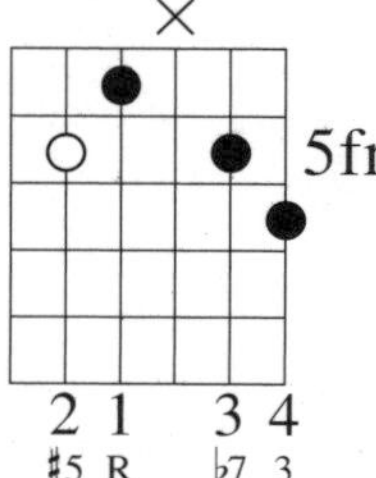

2 1 3 4
♯5 R ♭7 3

G♭7♯5♯11/D

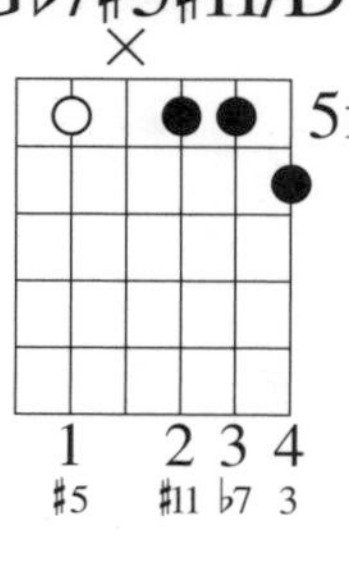

1 2 3 4
♯5 ♯11 ♭7 3

G♭9♯5/D

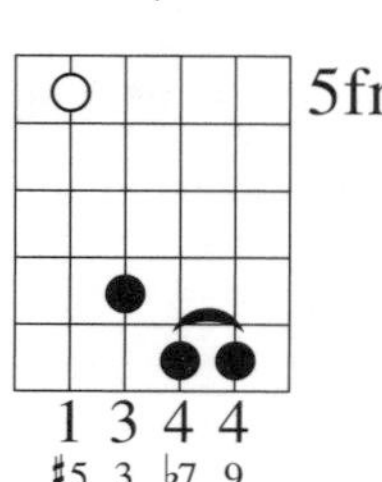

1 3 4 4
♯5 3 ♭7 9

G♭7♭9♯5/D

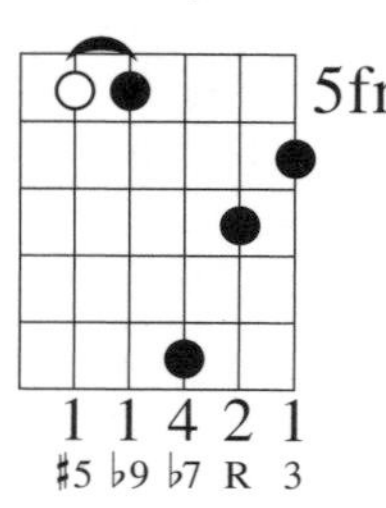

1 1 4 2 1
♯5 ♭9 ♭7 R 3

G♭7♯9♯5/D

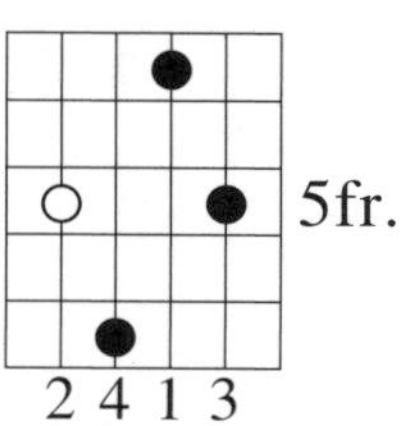

2 4 1 3
♯5 ♯9 3 ♭7

G♭7♯9♭5♯5/D

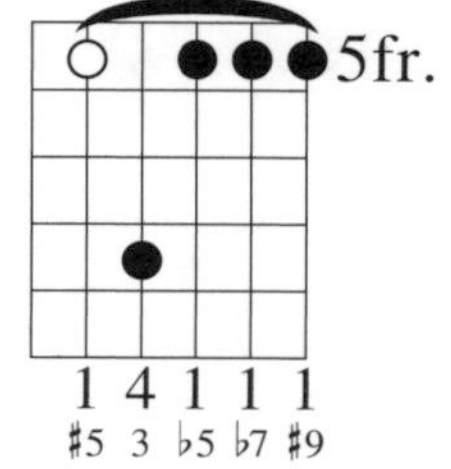

1 4 1 1 1
♯5 3 ♭5 ♭7 ♯9

G♭7♯5/D

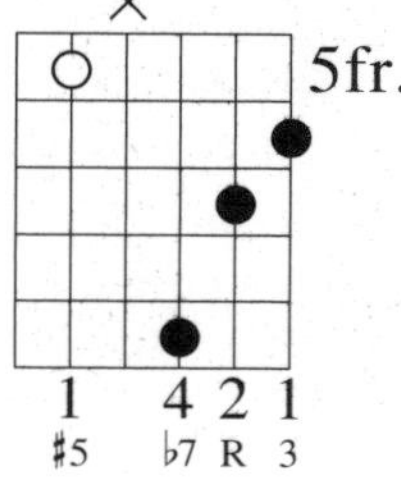

1 4 2 1
♯5 ♭7 R 3

G♭9♯5/D

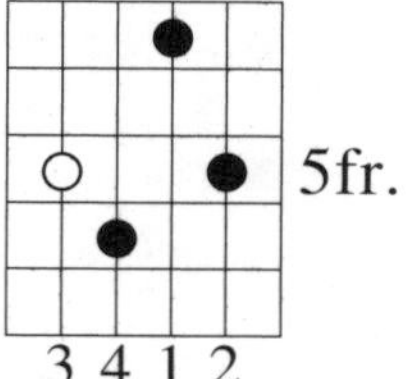

3 4 1 2
♯5 9 3 ♭7

G♭9♯5♯11/D

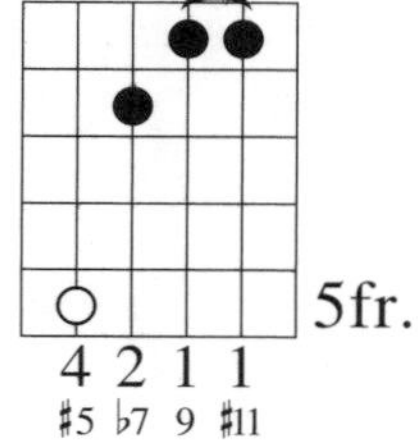

4 2 1 1
♯5 ♭7 9 ♯11

G♭7♭9♯5/D

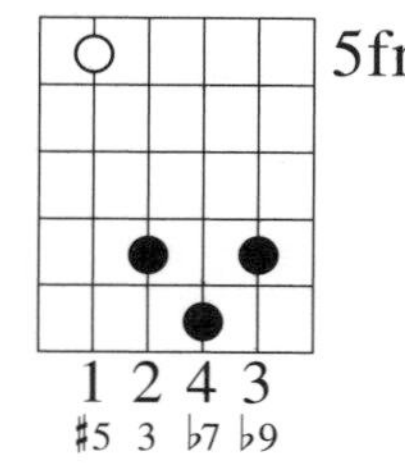

1 2 4 3
♯5 3 ♭7 ♭9

G♭7♯9♯5/D

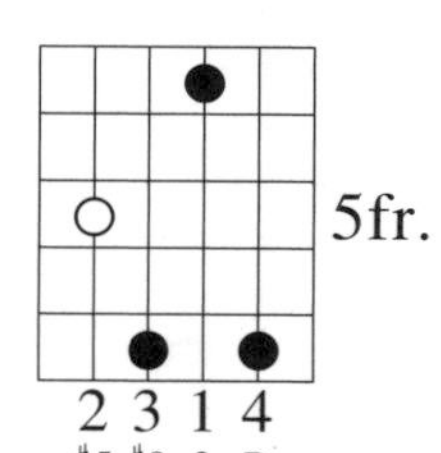

2 3 1 4
♯5 ♯9 3 R

G♭7♭9♯9♭5♯5/D

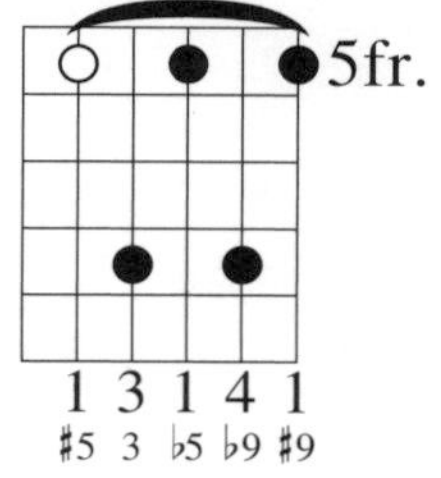

1 3 1 4 1
♯5 3 ♭5 ♭9 ♯9

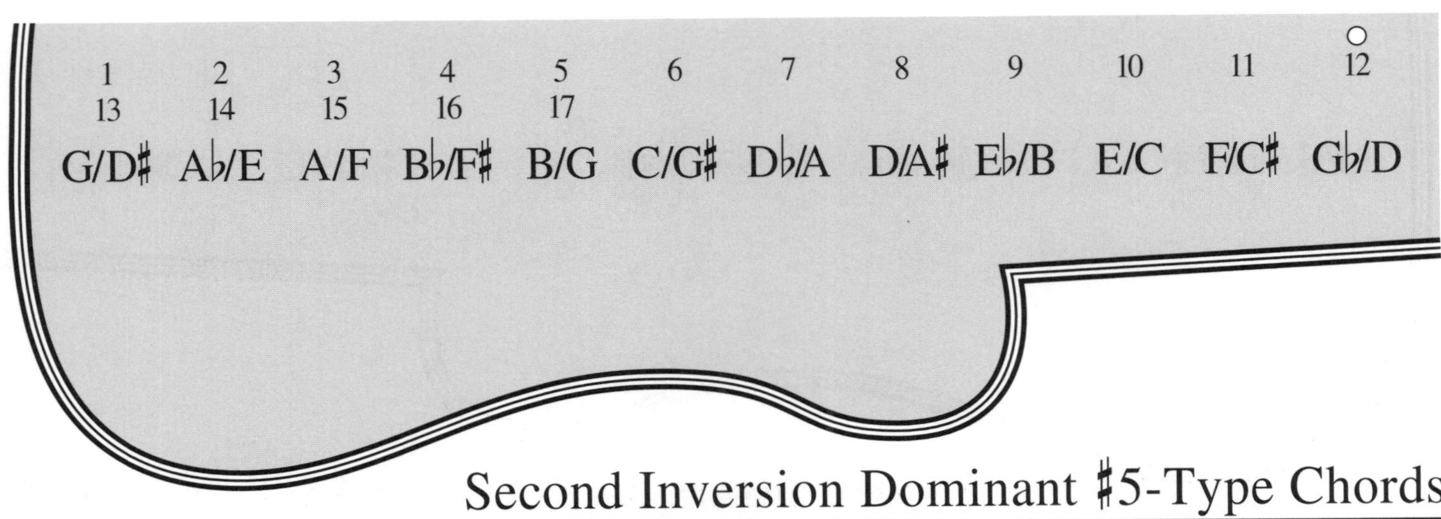

Second Inversion Dominant ♯5-Type Chords

G♭7♯5/D G♭9♯5/D G♭7♭9♯5/D G♭7♭9♯9♯5/D G♭7♭9♭5♯5/D

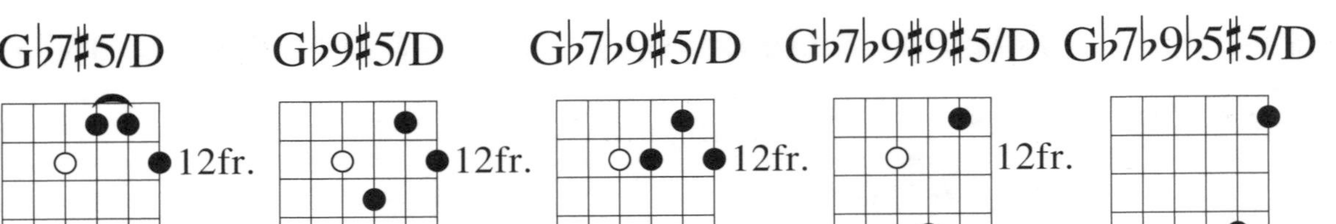

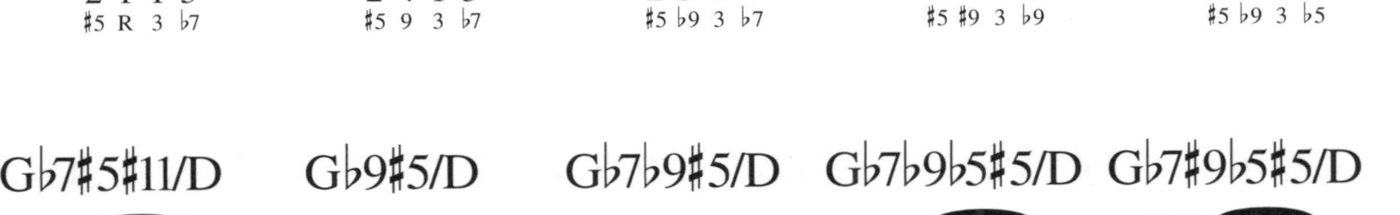

G♭7♯5♯11/D G♭9♯5/D G♭7♭9♯5/D G♭7♭9♭5♯5/D G♭7♯9♭5♯5/D

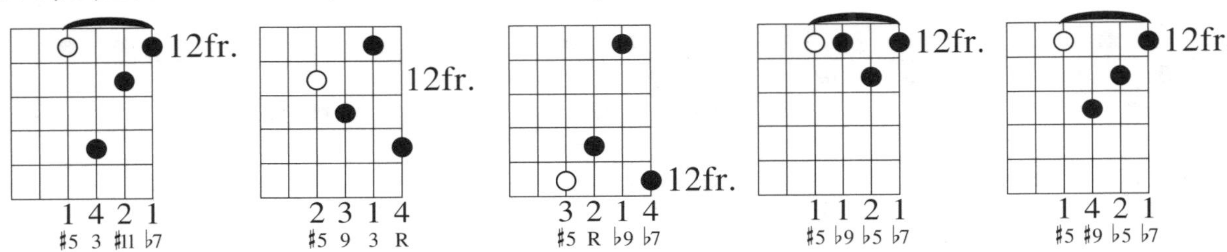

G♭7♯5♯11/D G♭9♯5♯11/D G♭7♯9♯5/D G♭7♭9♭5♯5/D G♭7♭9♯9♭5♯5/D

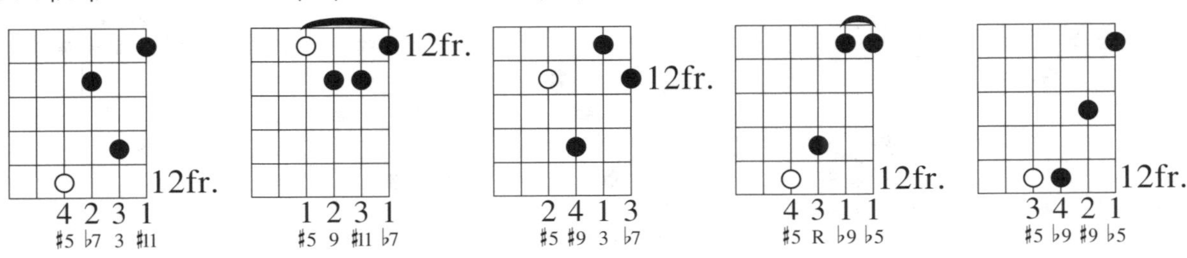

G♭7♯5♯11/D G♭9♯5♯11/D G♭7♯9♯5/D G♭7♭9♭5♯5/D G♭7♭9♯9♭5♯5/D

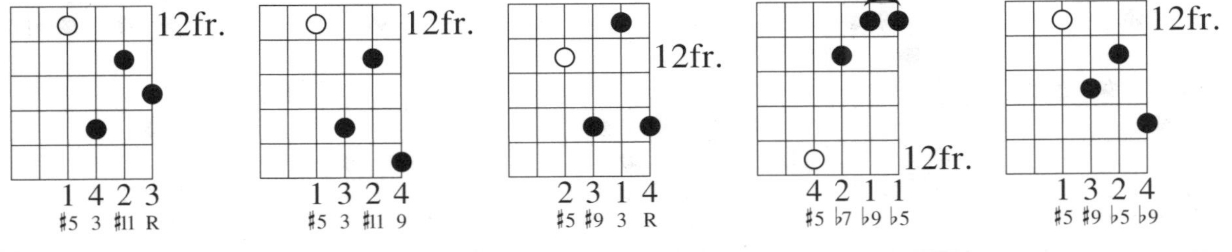

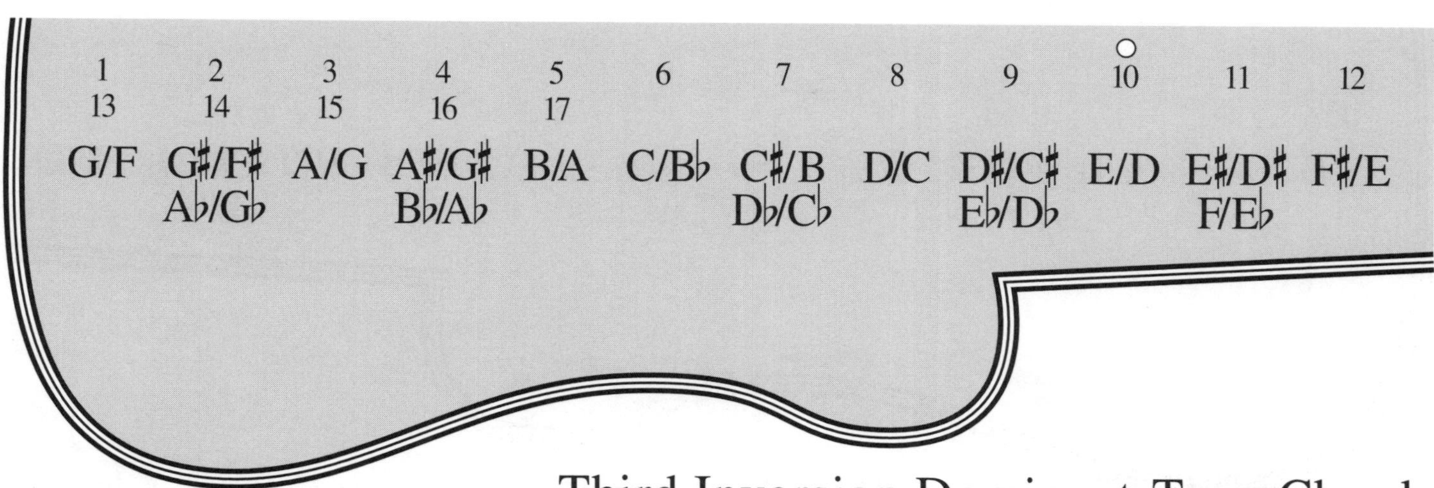

Third Inversion Dominant-Type Chords

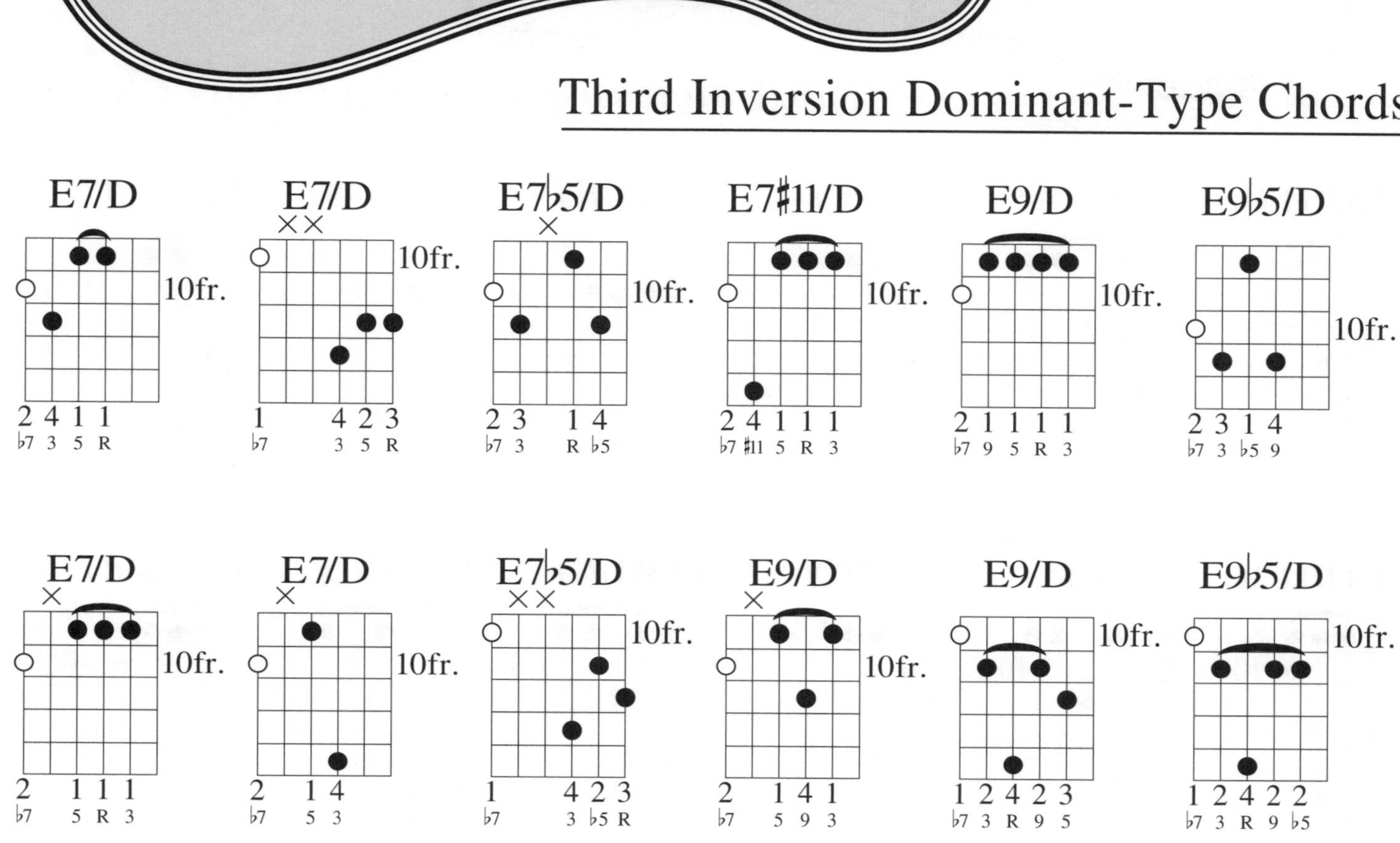

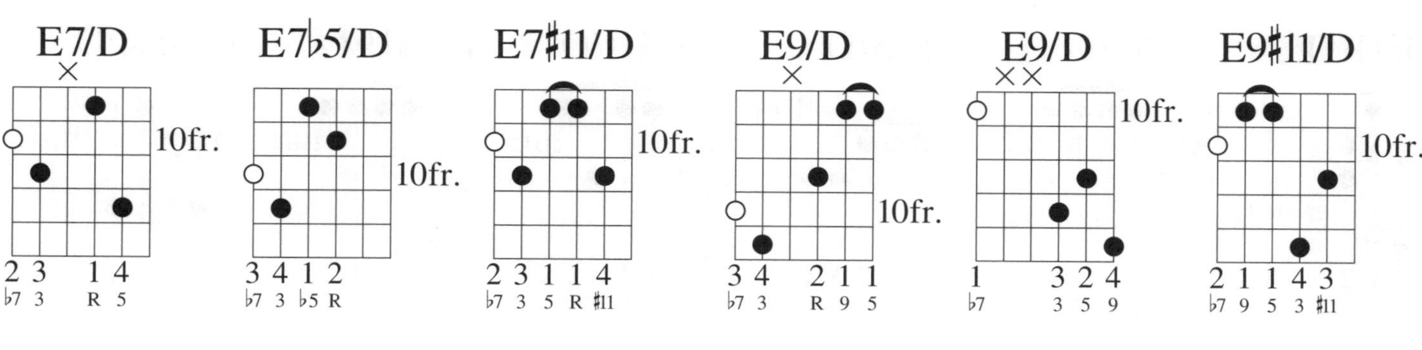

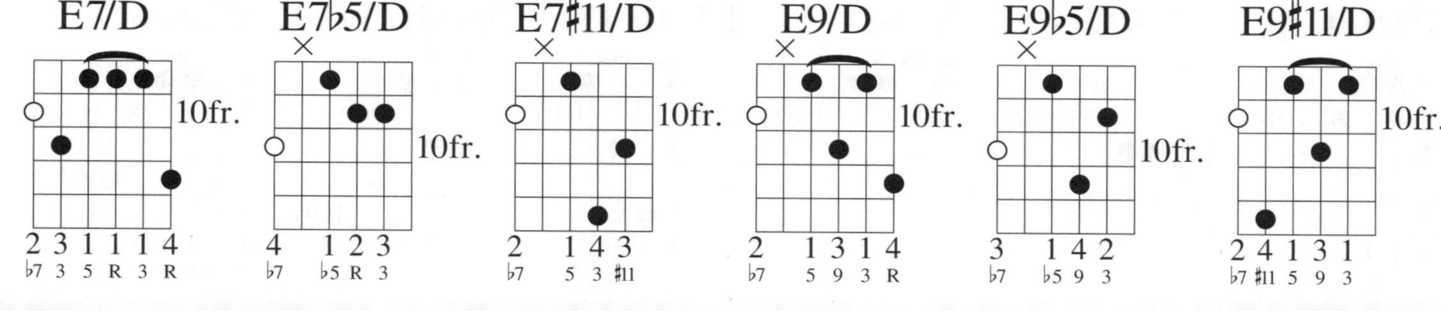

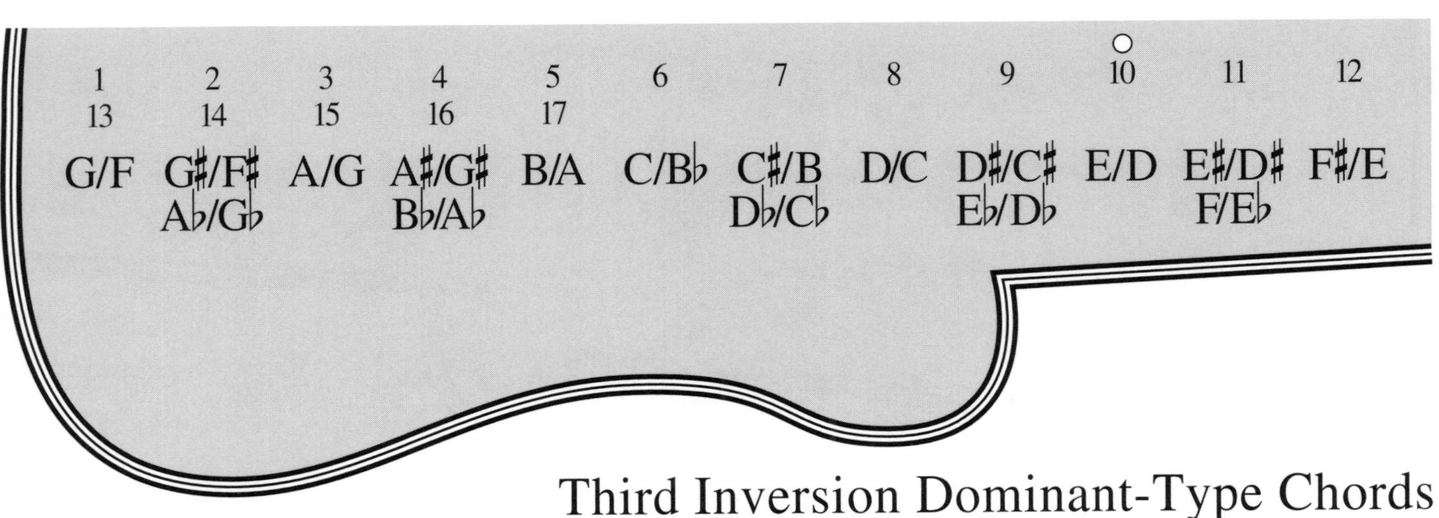

Third Inversion Dominant-Type Chords

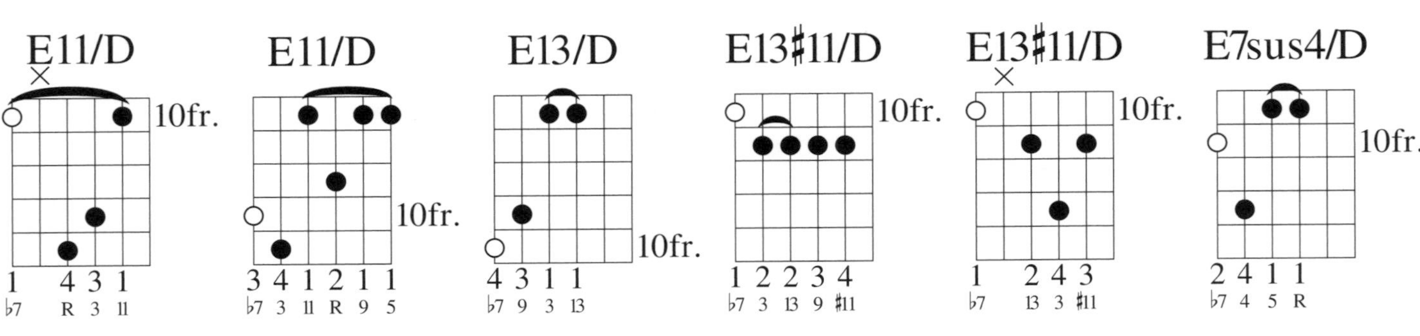

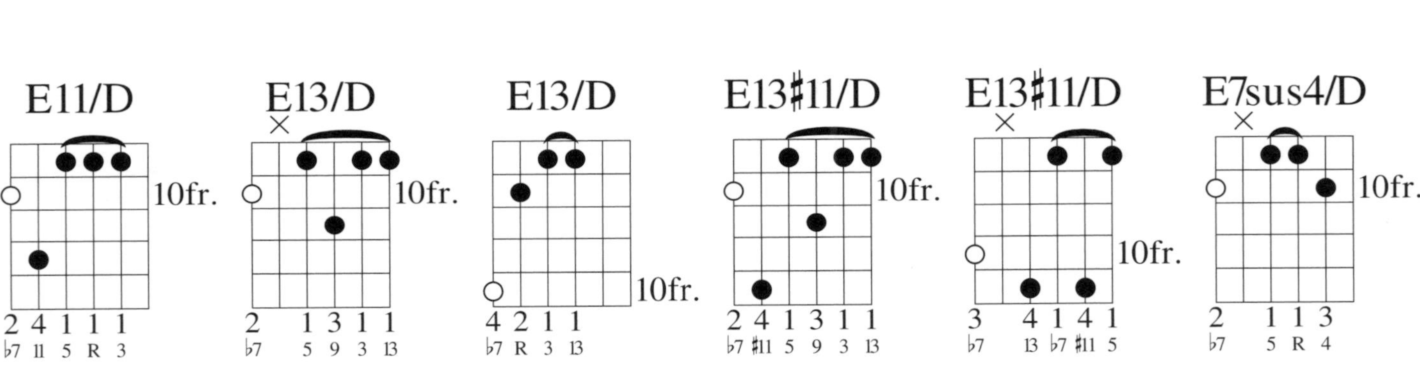

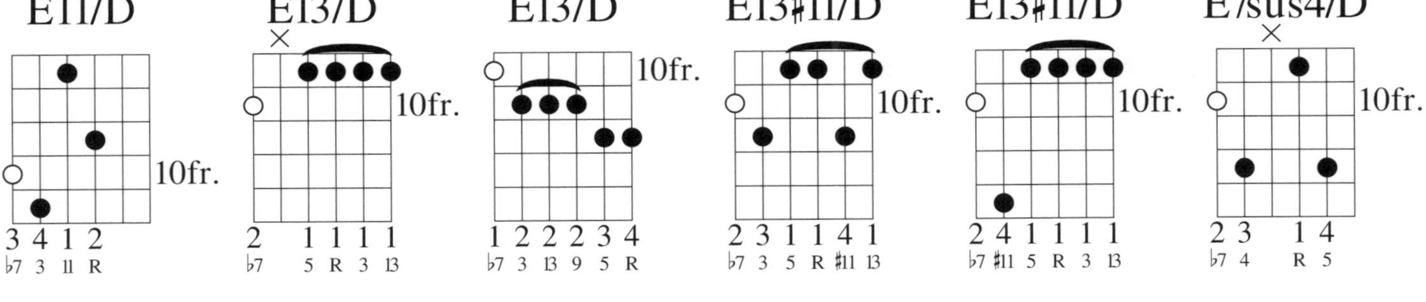

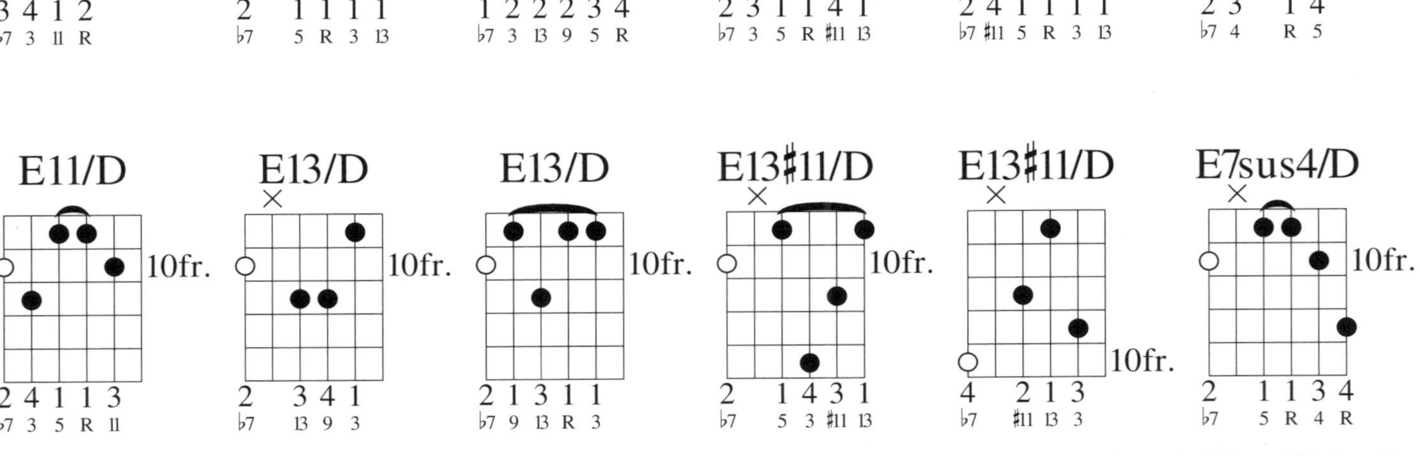

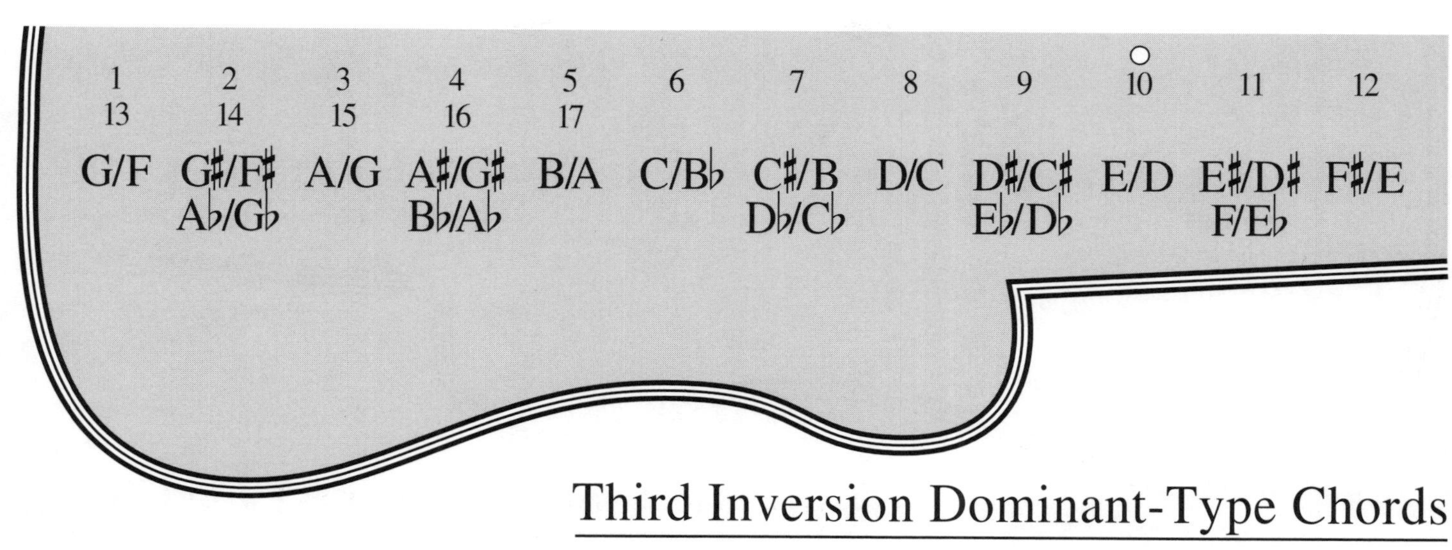

Third Inversion Dominant-Type Chords

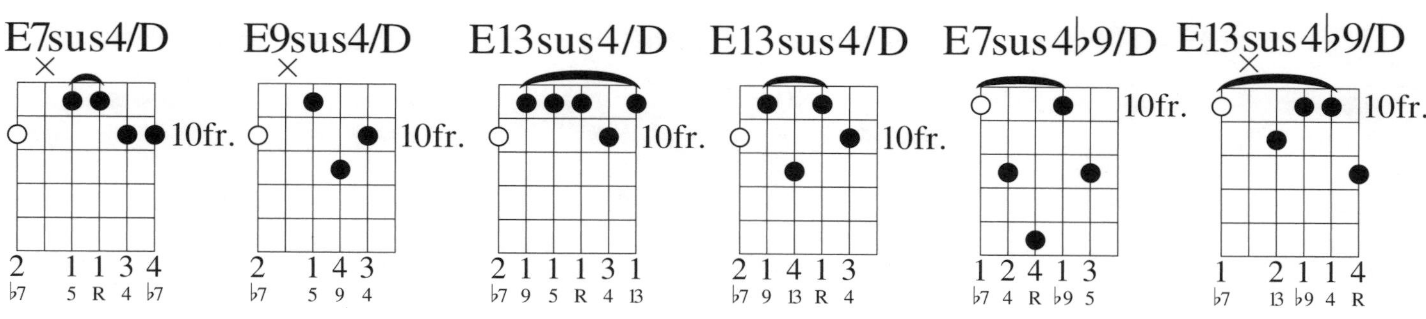

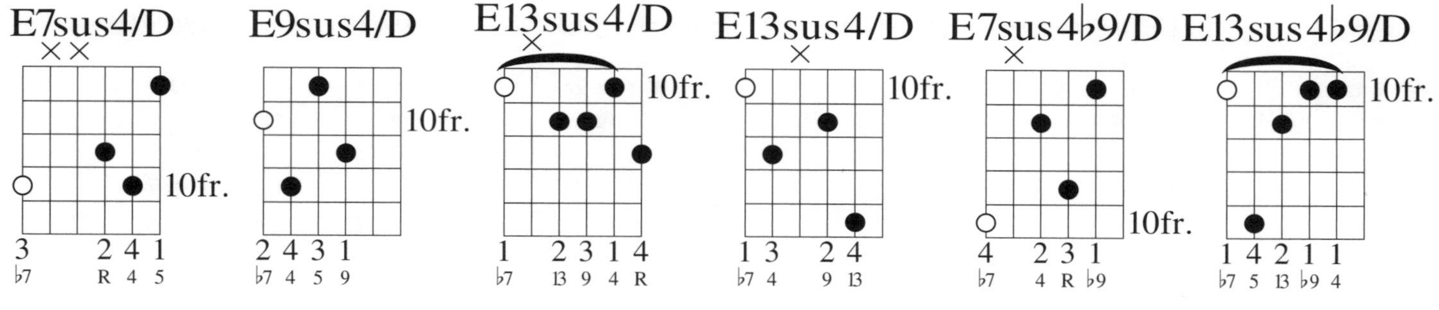

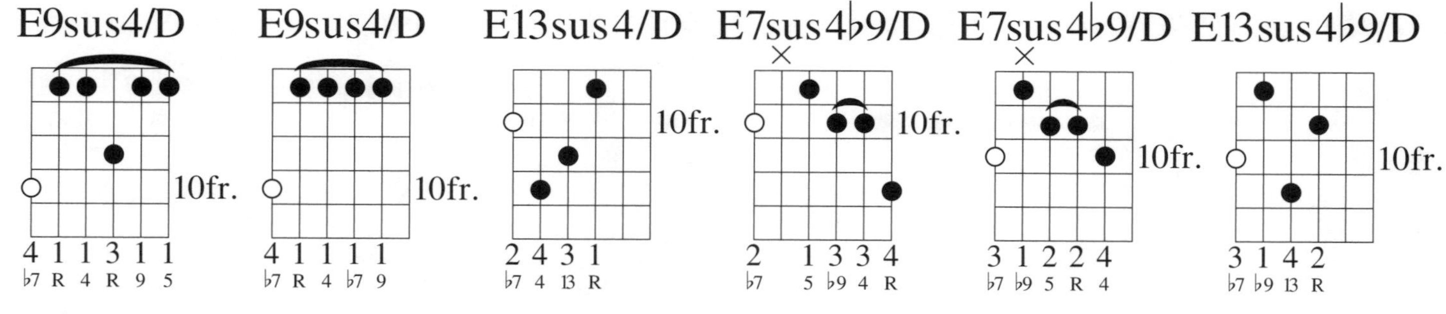

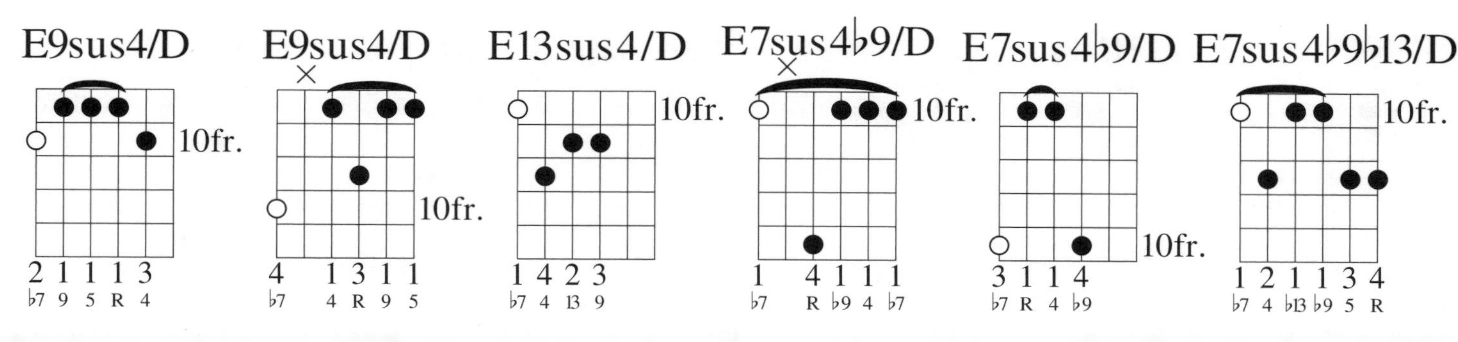

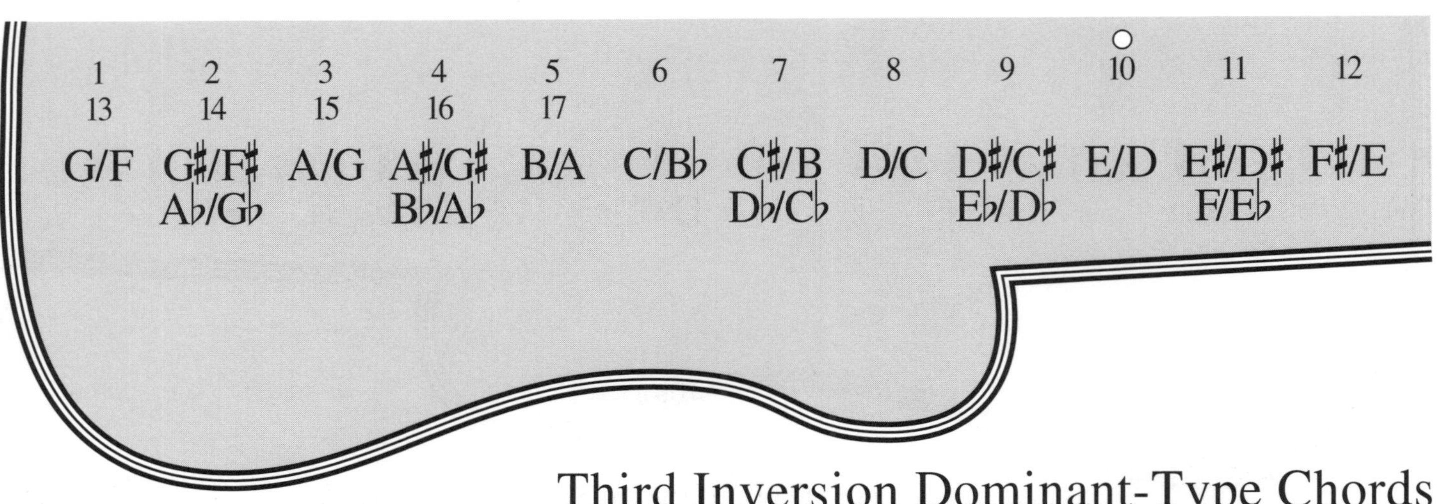

Third Inversion Dominant-Type Chords

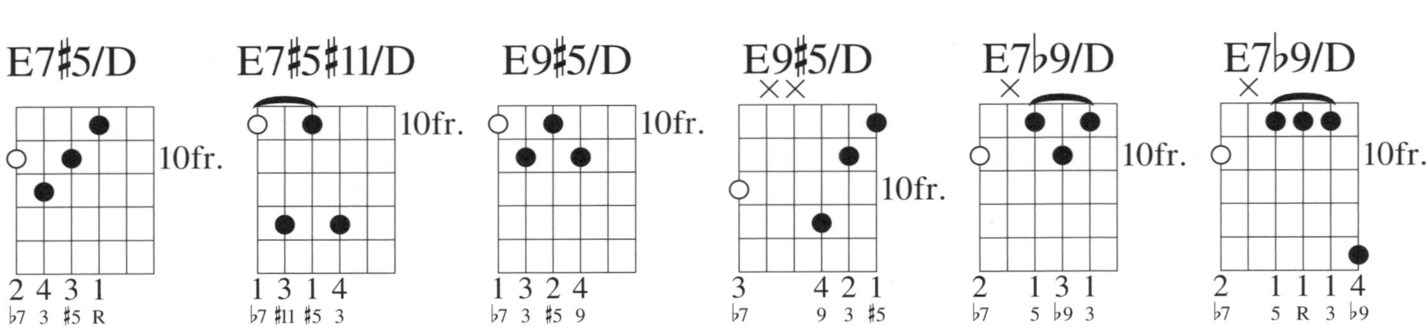

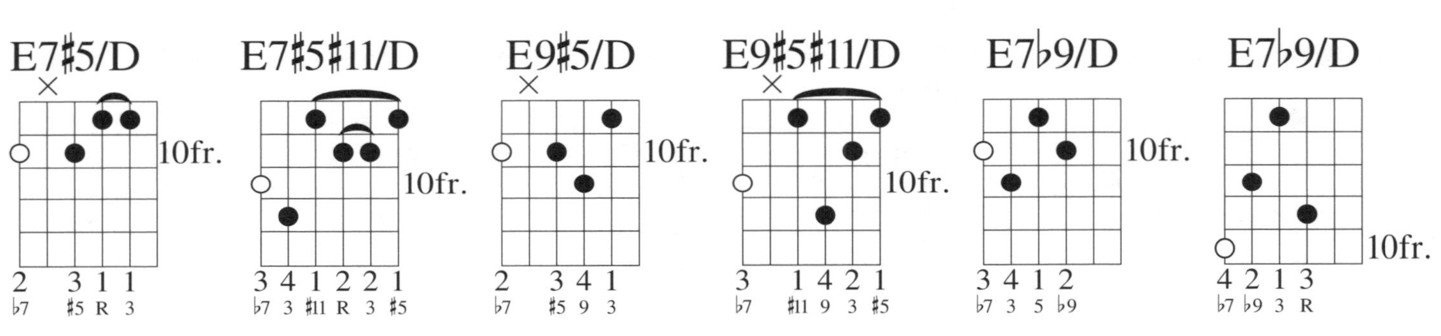

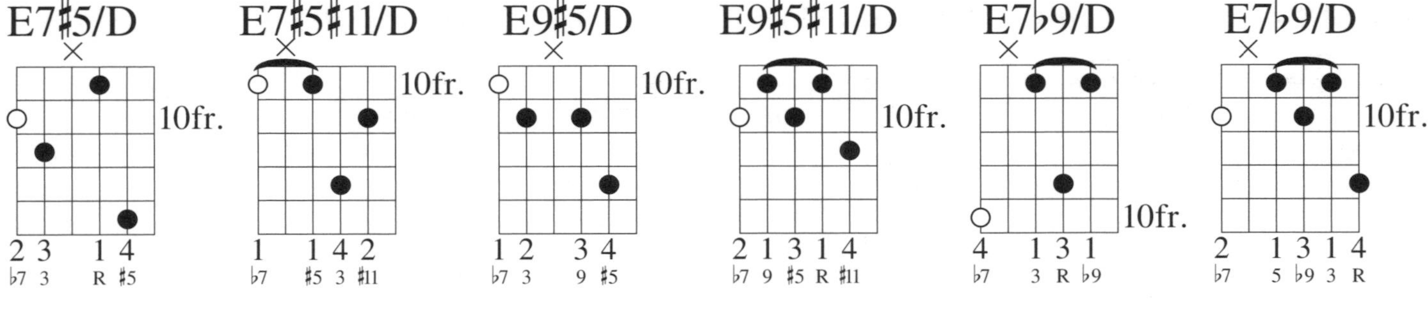

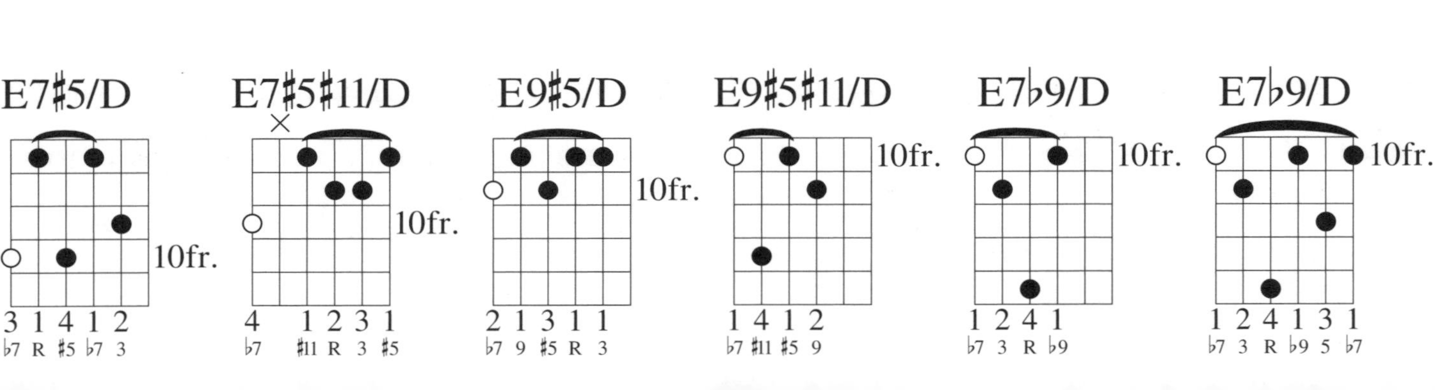

Third Inversion Dominant-Type Chords

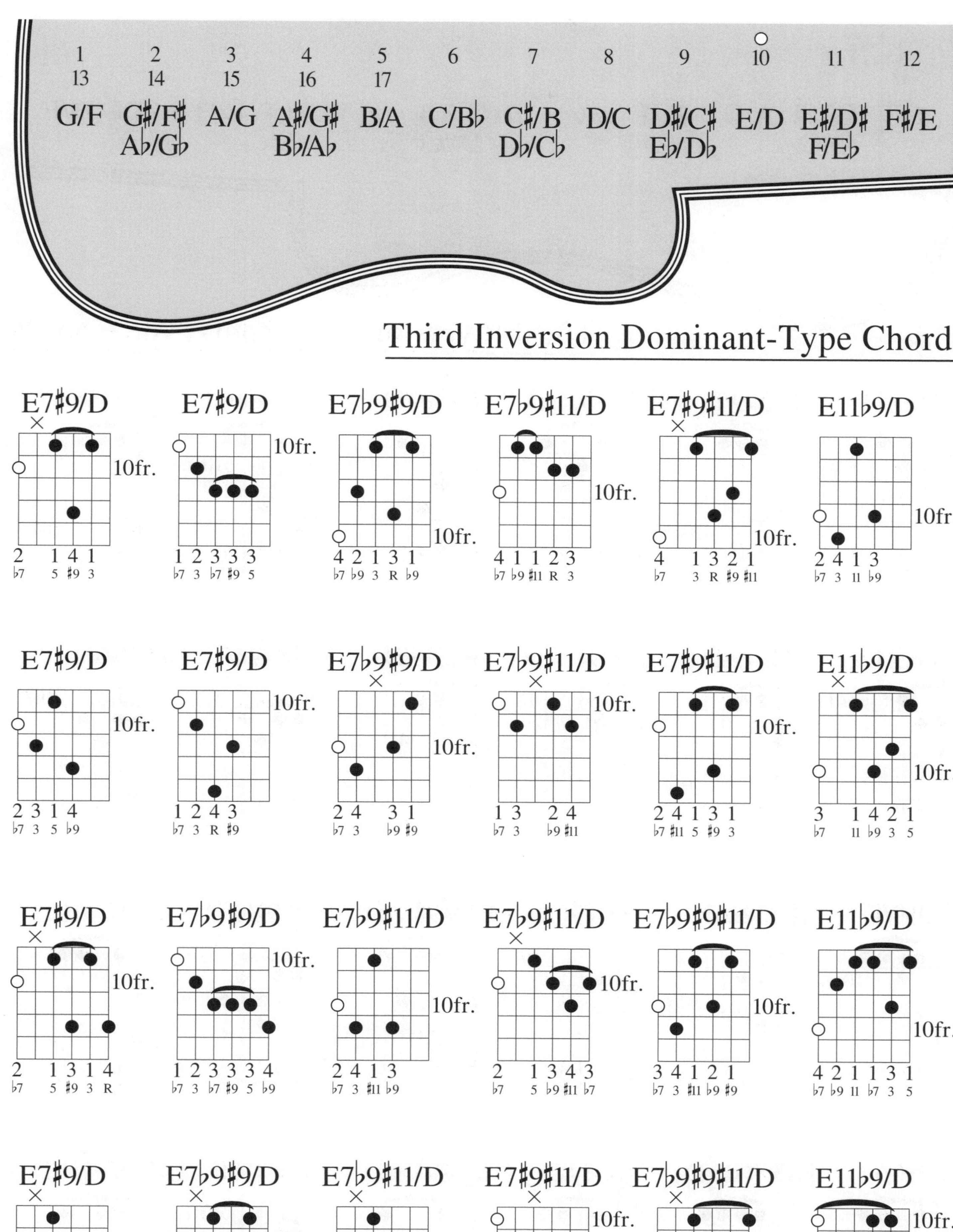

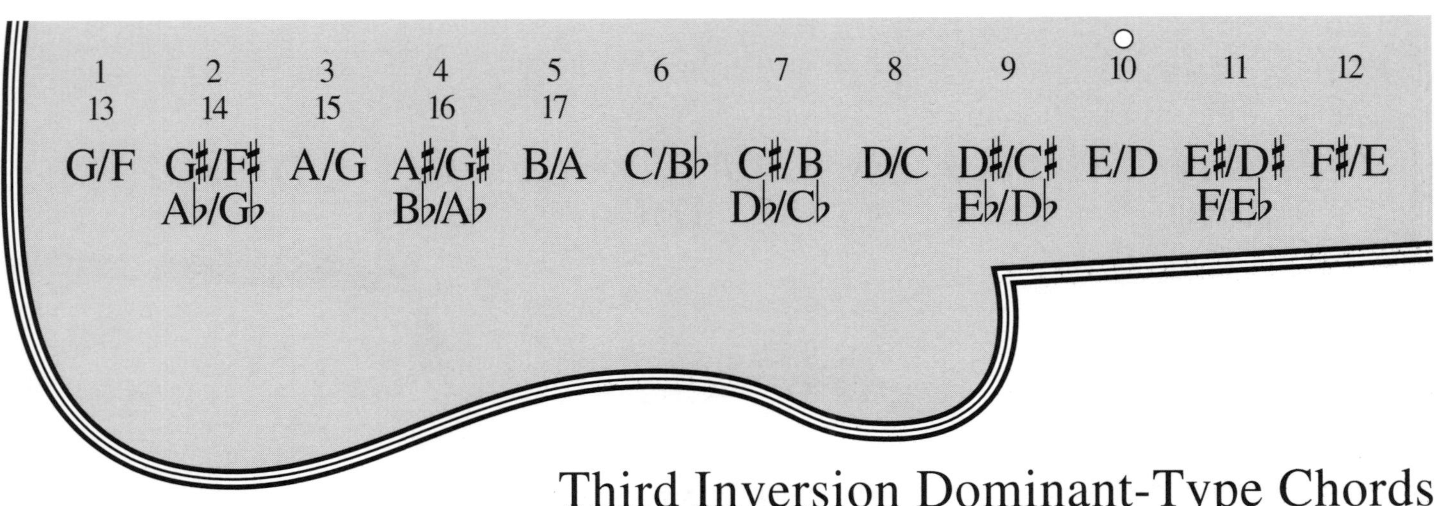

Third Inversion Dominant-Type Chords

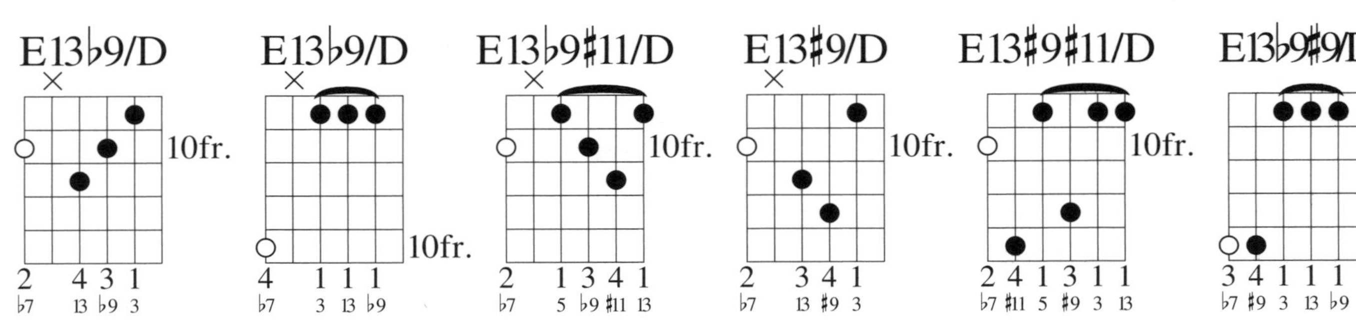
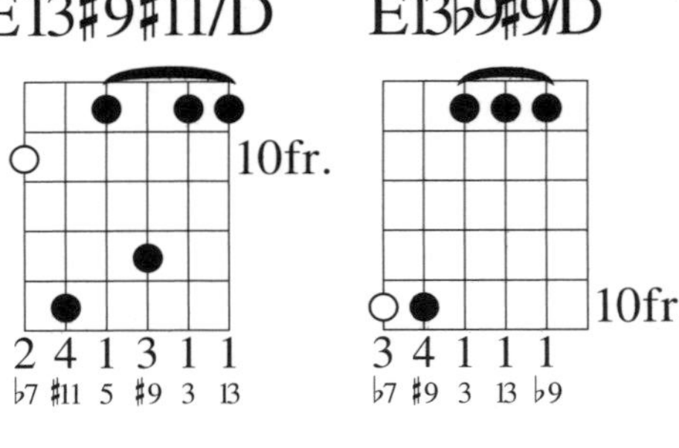

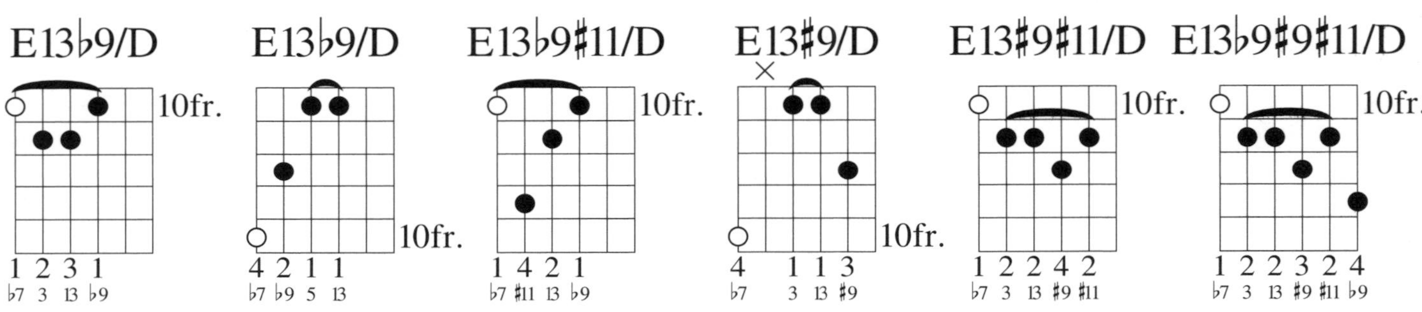

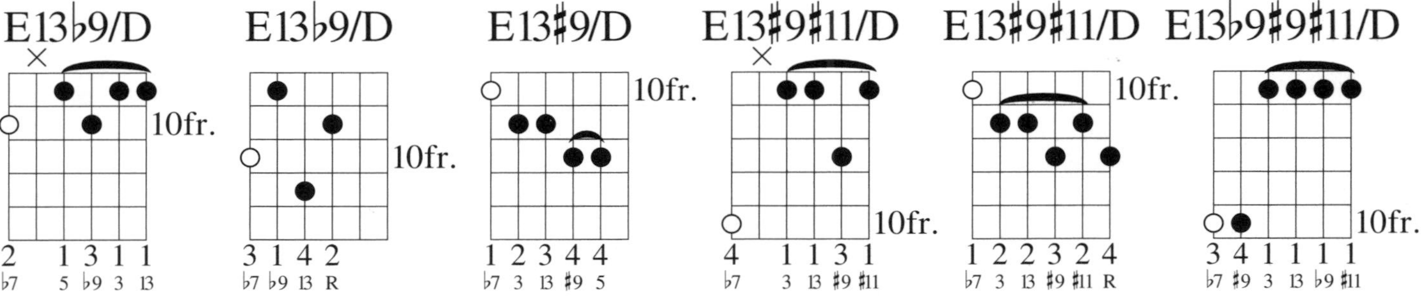

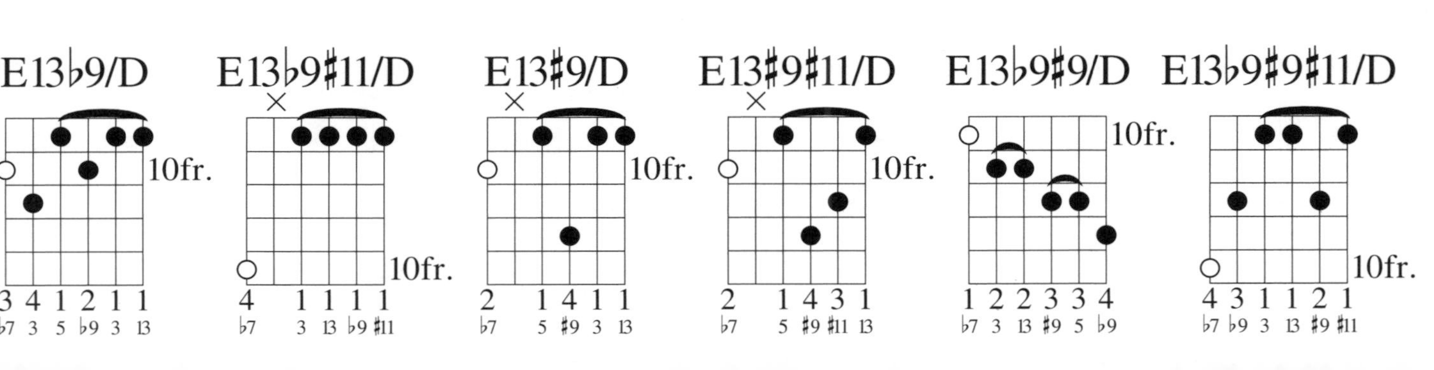

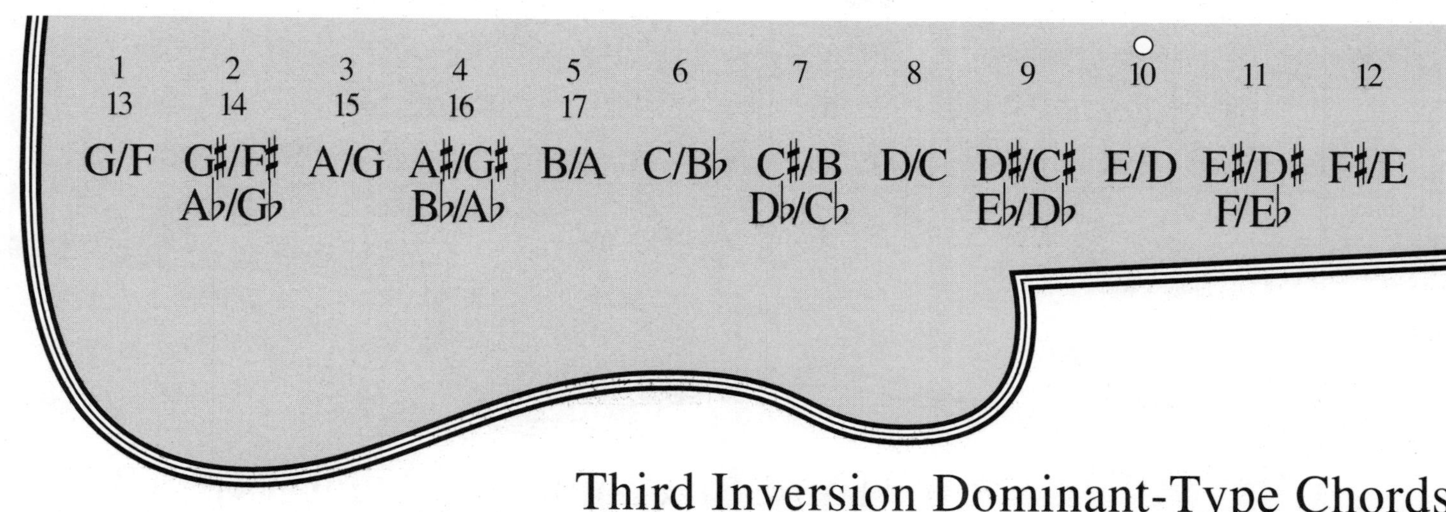

Third Inversion Dominant-Type Chords

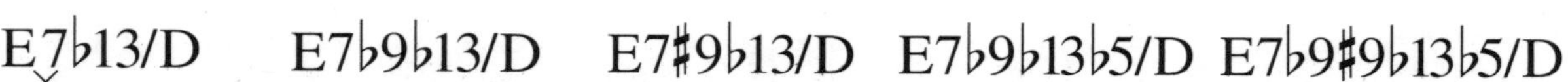

E7♭13/D

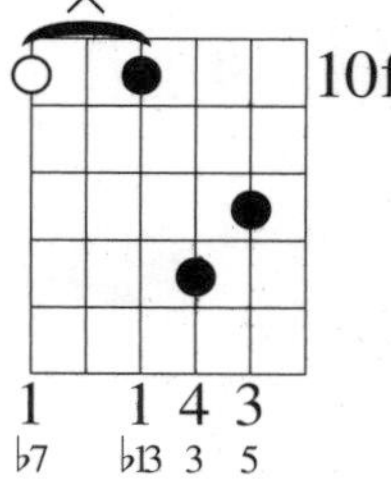

E7♭9♭13/D

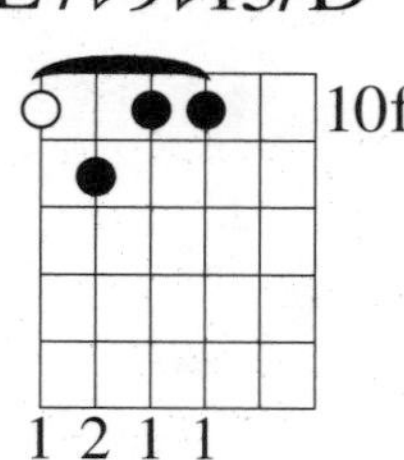

E7♯9♭13/D

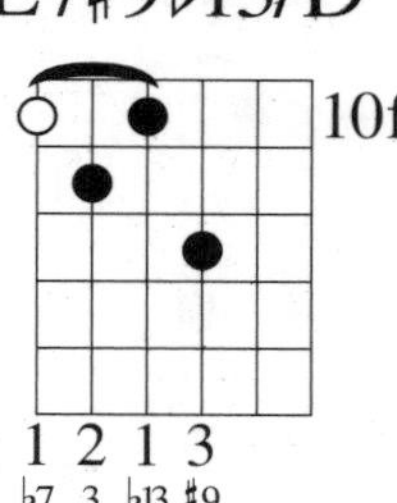

E7♭9♭13♭5/D

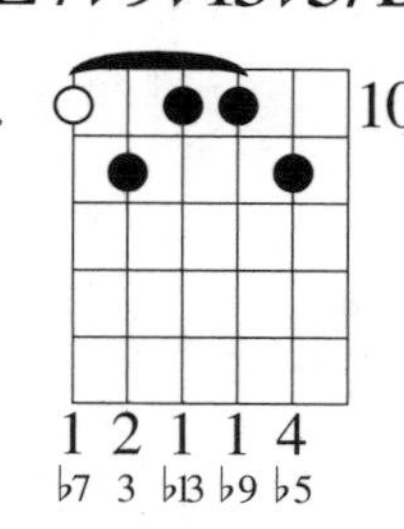

E7♭9♯9♭13♭5/D

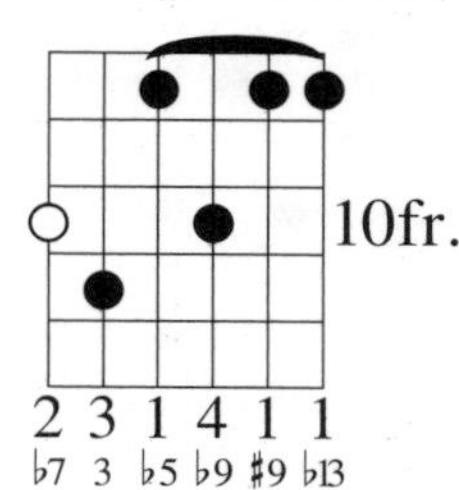

E7♭13/D

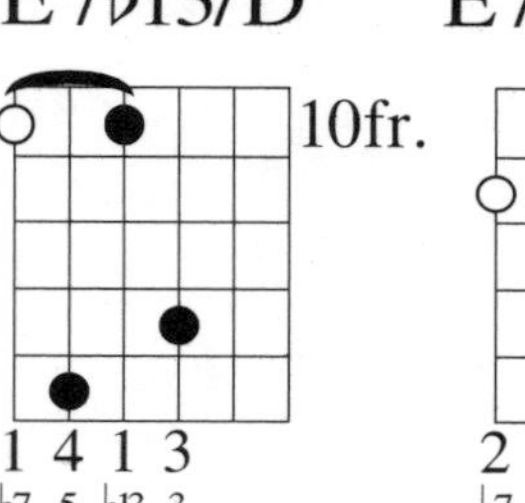

E7♭9♭13/D

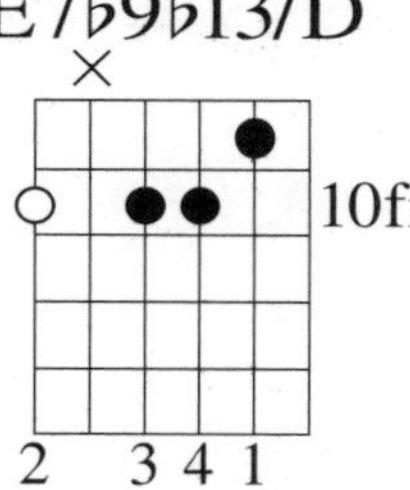

E7♯9♭13/D

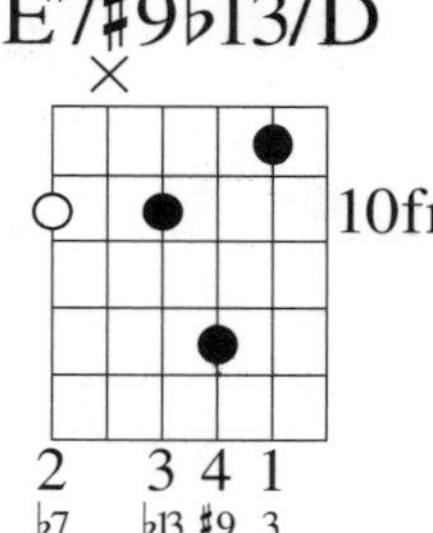

E7♭9♭13♭5/D

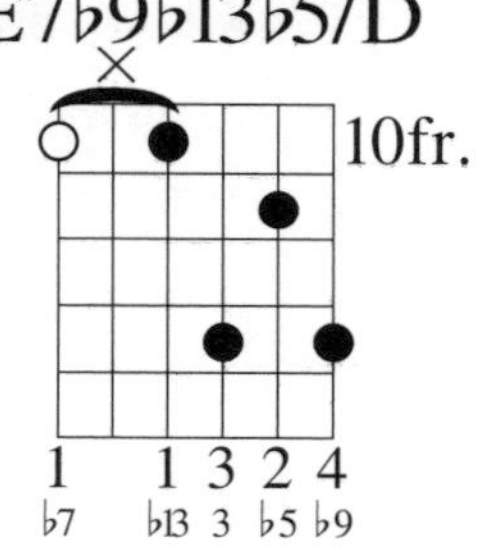

E7♭13/D E7♭9♭13/D

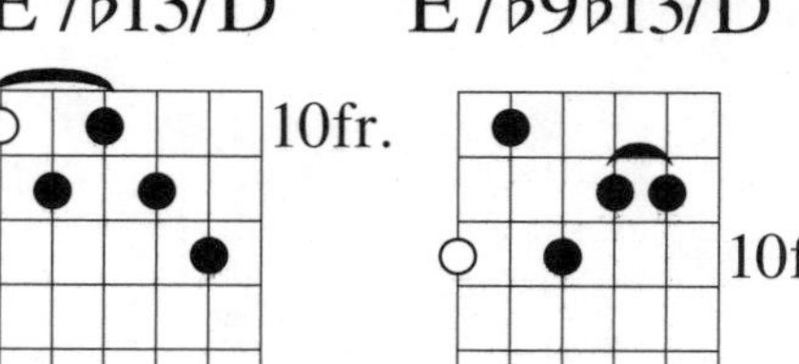

E7♯9♭13/D

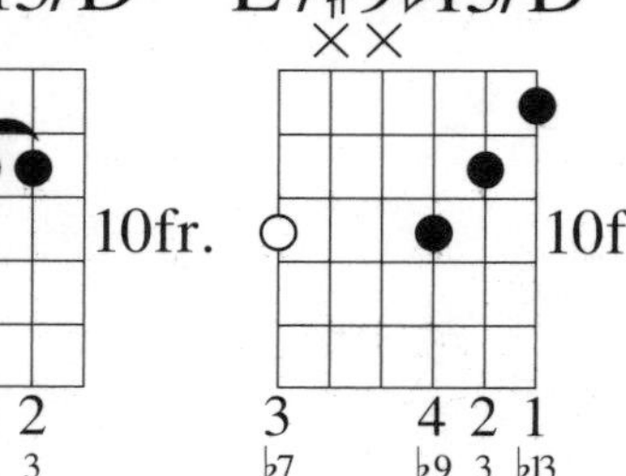

E7♯9♭13♭5/D

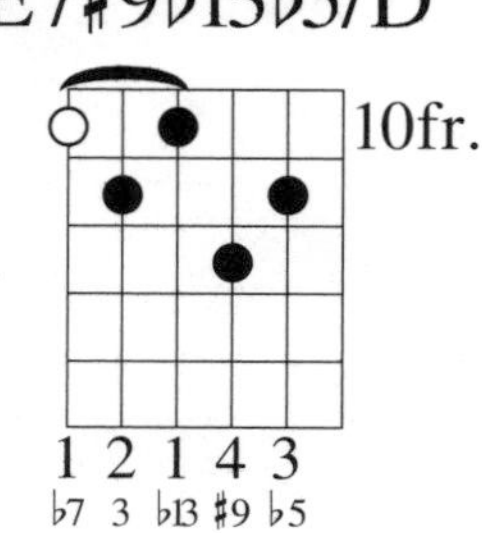

E7♭13/D

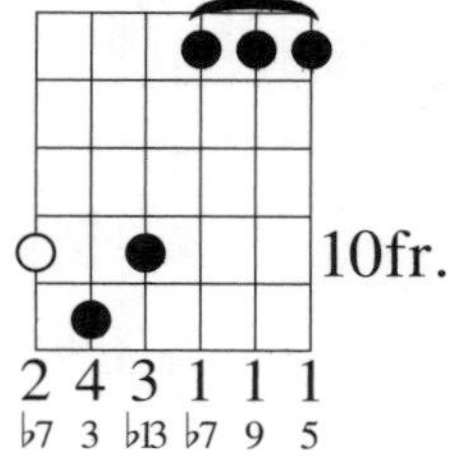

E7♭9♭13/D

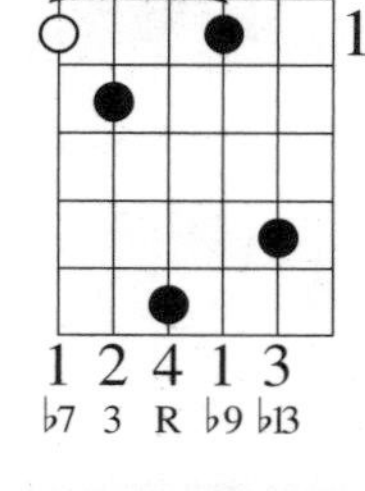

E7♭9♯9♭13/D

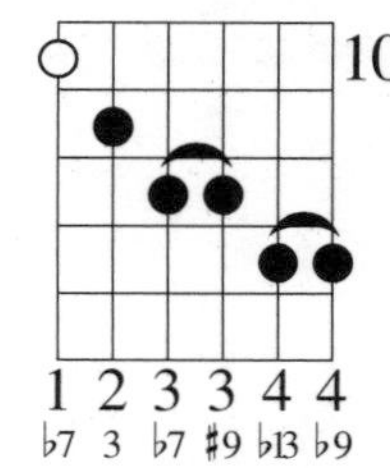

E7♯9♭13♭5/D

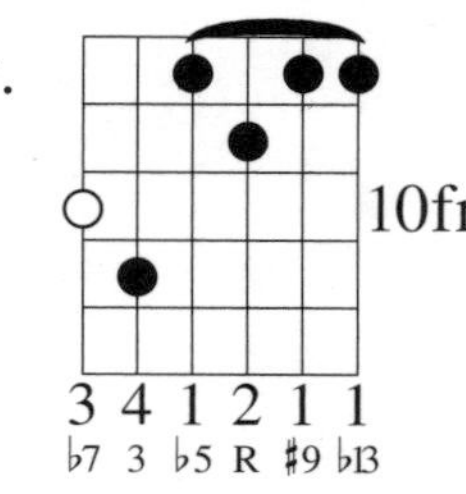

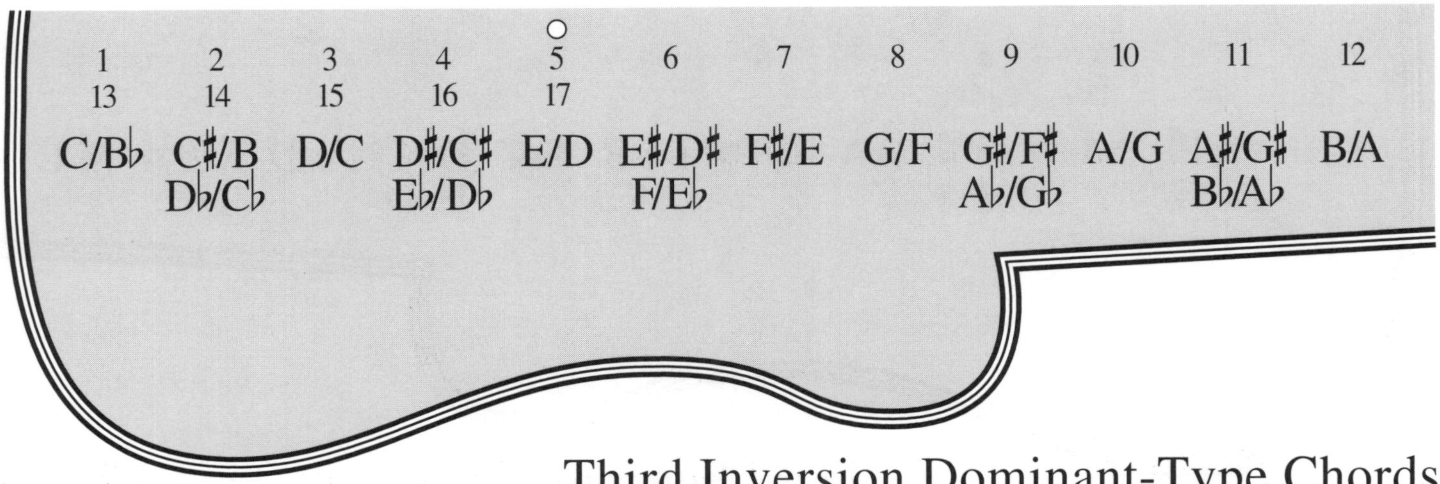

1 13	2 14	3 15	4 16	5 17	6	7	8	9	10	11	12
C/B♭	C♯/B D♭/C♭	D/C	D♯/C♯ E♭/D♭	E/D	E♯/D♯ F/E♭	F♯/E	G/F	G♯/F♯ A♭/G♭	A/G	A♯/G♯ B♭/A♭	B/A

Third Inversion Dominant-Type Chords

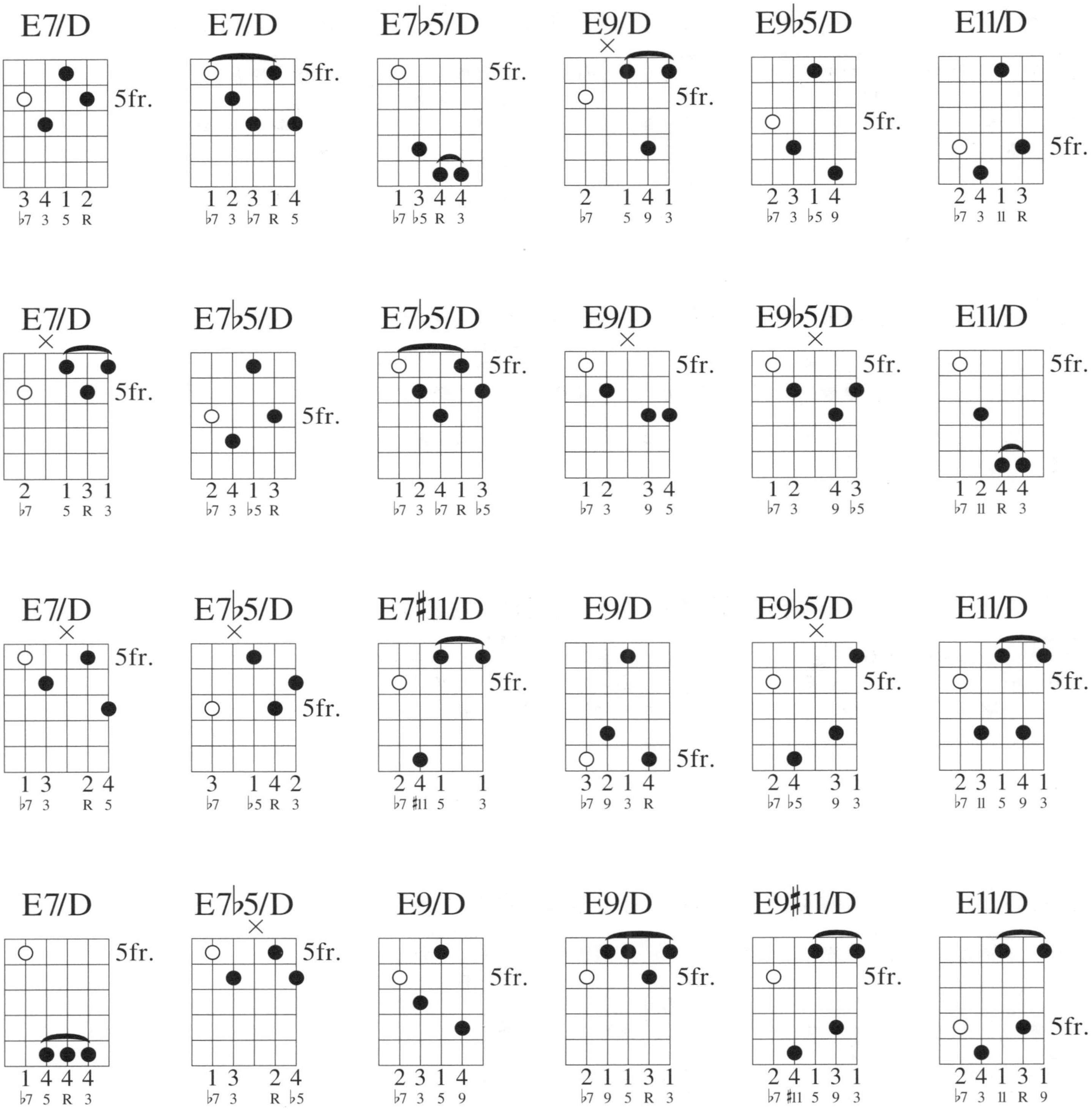

Chord	Fingering	Intervals
E7/D	3 4 1 2	♭7 3 5 R
E7/D	1 2 3 1 4	♭7 3 ♭7 R 5
E7♭5/D	1 3 4 4	♭7 ♭5 R 3
E9/D	2 1 4 1	♭7 5 9 3
E9♭5/D	2 3 1 4	♭7 3 ♭5 9
E11/D	2 4 1 3	♭7 3 11 R

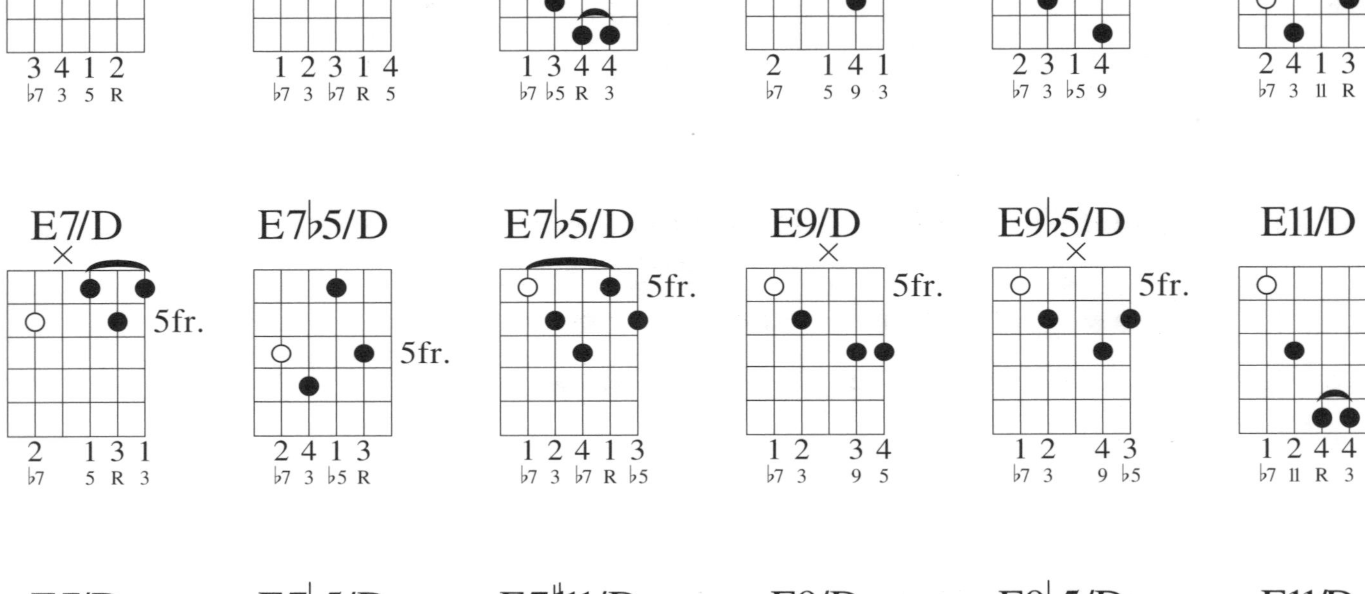

Chord	Fingering	Intervals
E7/D	2 1 3 1	♭7 5 R 3
E7♭5/D	2 4 1 3	♭7 3 ♭5 R
E7♭5/D	1 2 4 1 3	♭7 3 ♭7 R ♭5
E9/D	1 2 3 4	♭7 3 9 5
E9♭5/D	1 2 4 3	♭7 3 9 ♭5
E11/D	1 2 4 4	♭7 11 R 3

Chord	Fingering	Intervals
E7/D	1 3 2 4	♭7 3 R 5
E7♭5/D	3 1 4 2	♭7 ♭5 R 3
E7♯11/D	2 4 1 1	♭7 ♯11 5 3
E9/D	3 2 1 4	♭7 9 3 R
E9♭5/D	2 4 3 1	♭7 ♭5 9 3
E11/D	2 3 1 4 1	♭7 11 5 9 3

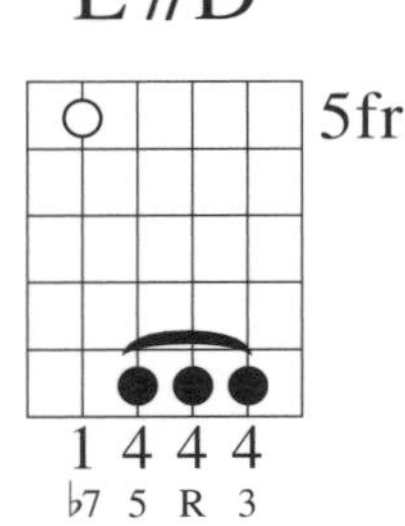

Chord	Fingering	Intervals
E7/D	1 4 4 4	♭7 5 R 3
E7♭5/D	1 3 2 4	♭7 3 R ♭5
E9/D	2 3 1 4	♭7 3 5 9
E9/D	2 1 1 3 1	♭7 9 5 R 3
E9♯11/D	2 4 1 3 1	♭7 ♯11 5 9 3
E11/D	2 4 1 3 1	♭7 3 11 R 9

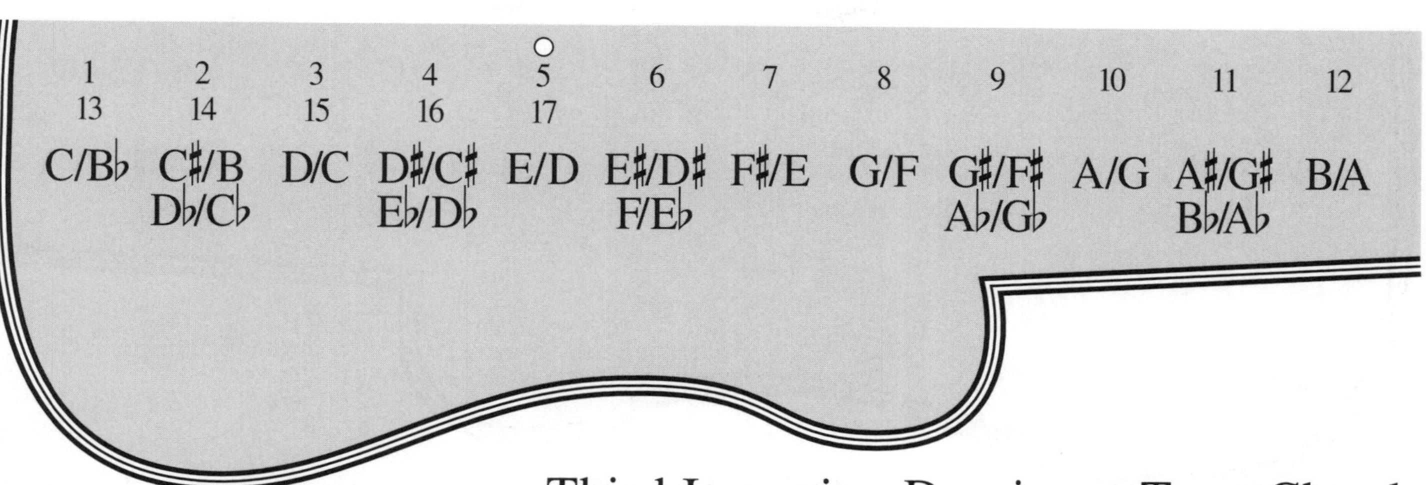

Third Inversion Dominant-Type Chords

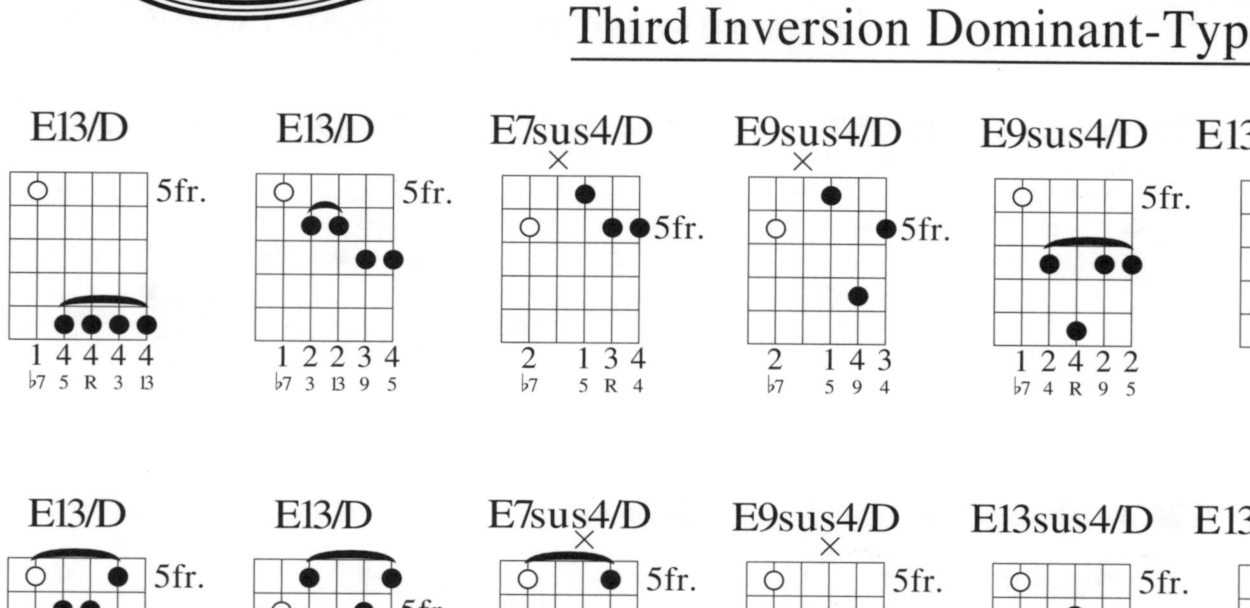

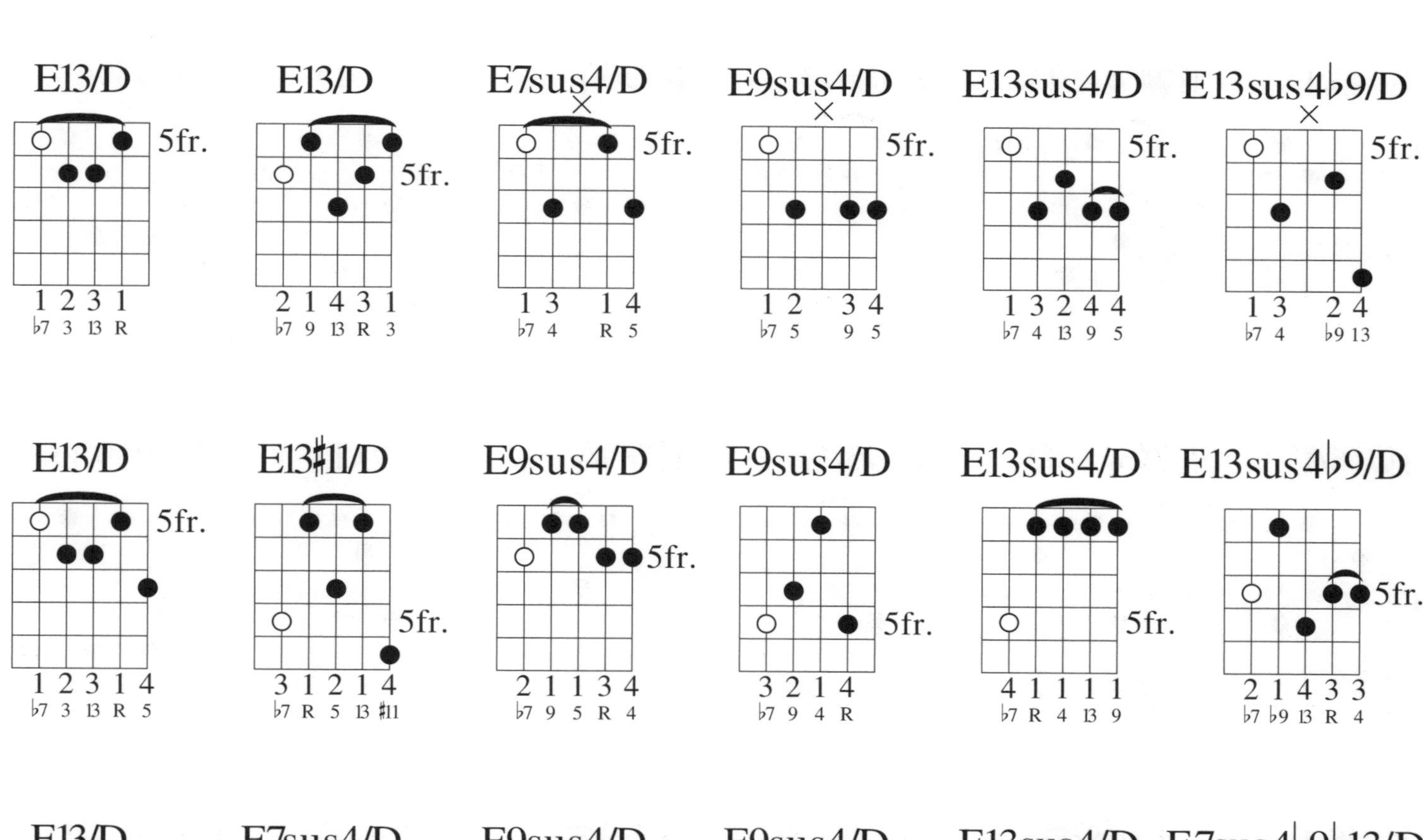

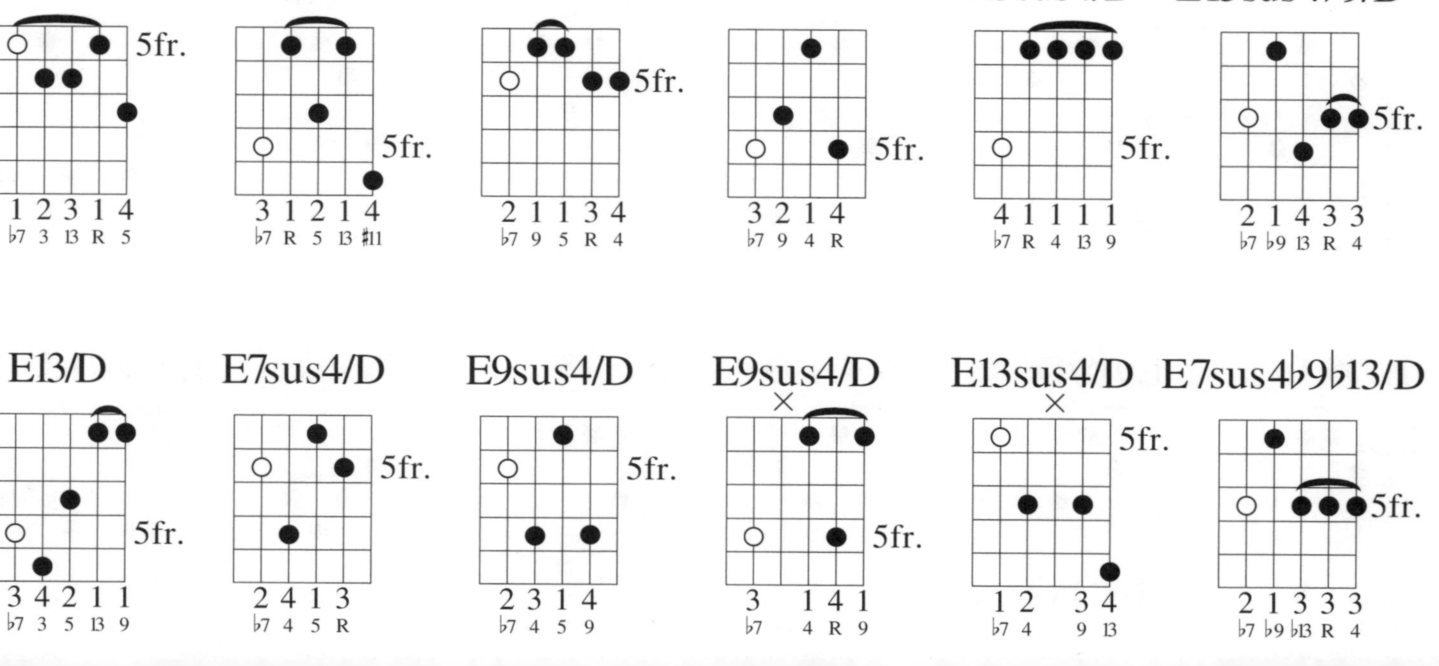

Third Inversion Dominant-Type Chords

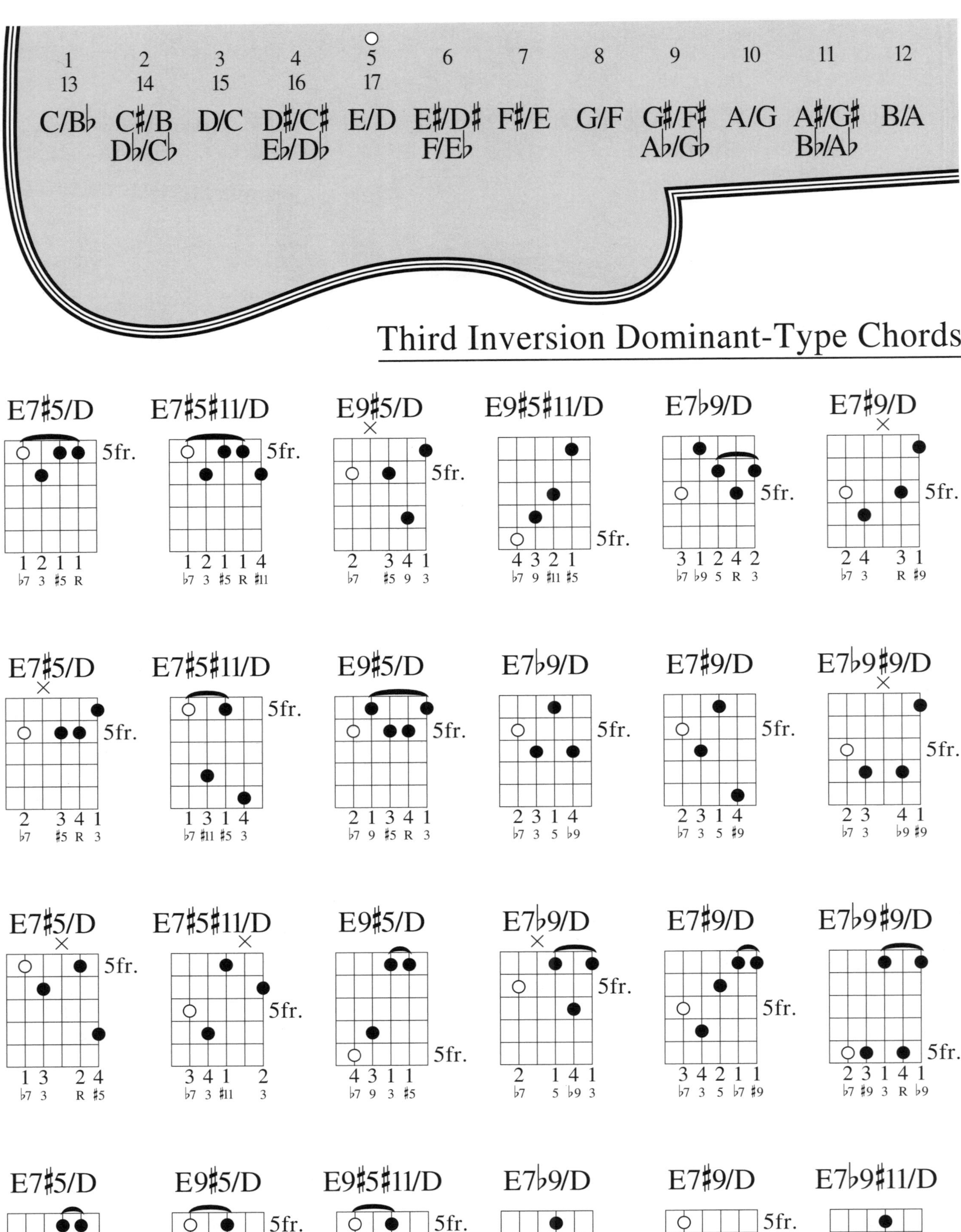

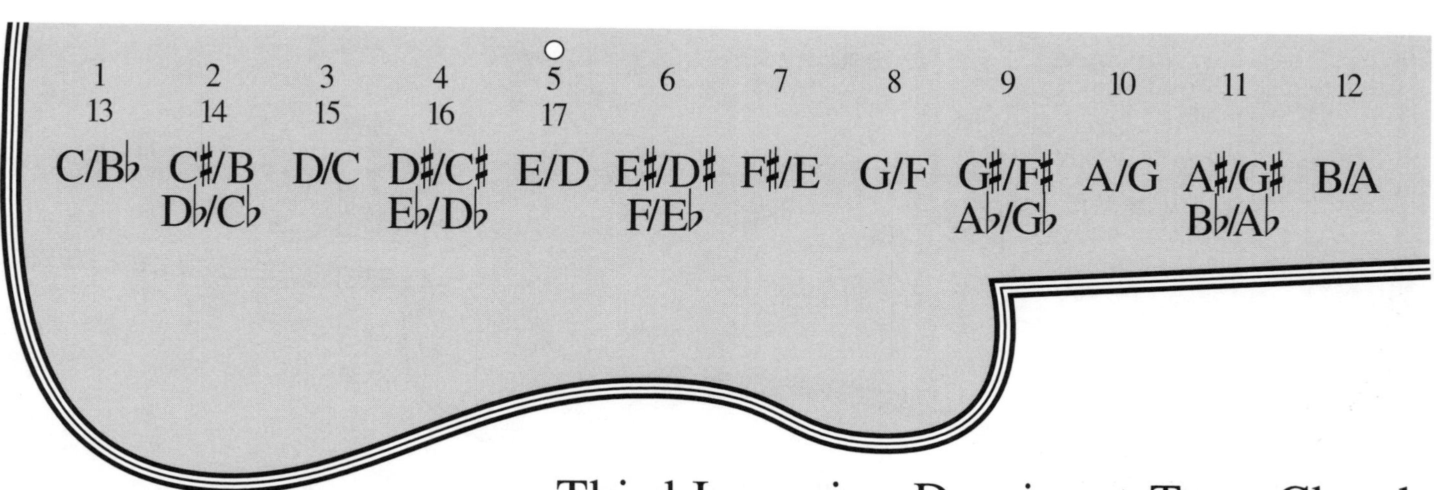

Third Inversion Dominant-Type Chords

E7♭9♯11/D

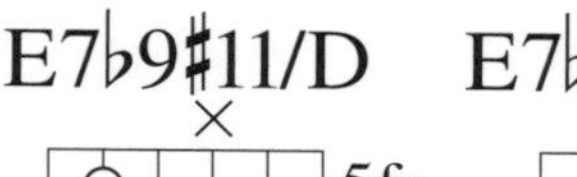

E7♭9♯9♯11/D

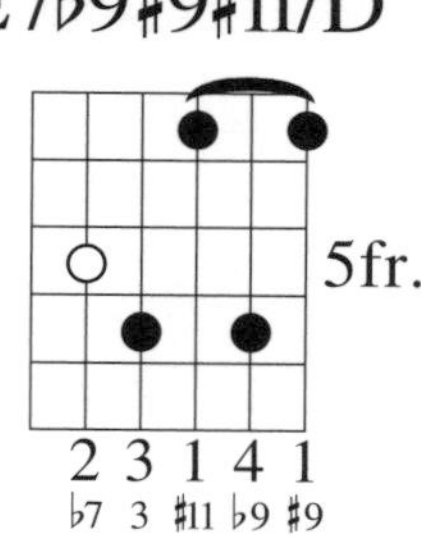

E13♭9/D

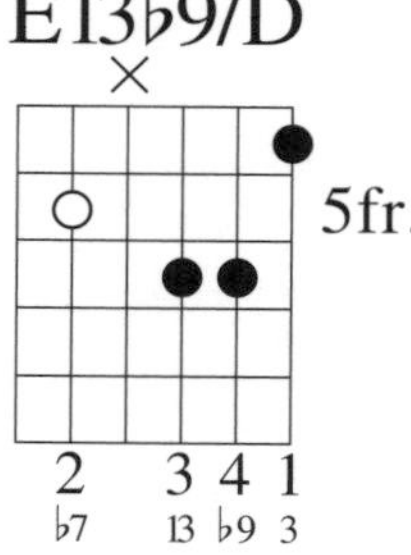

E13♯9/D

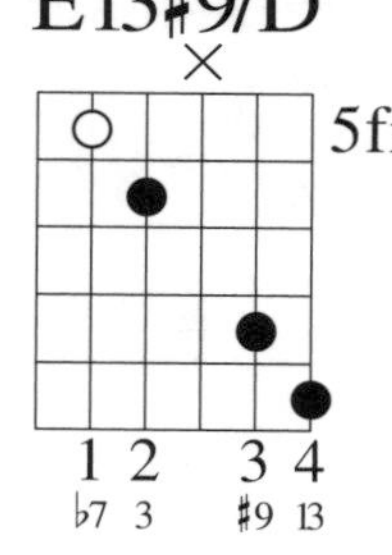

E7♭13/D

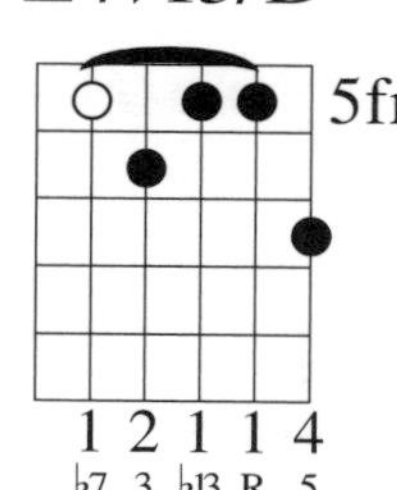

E7♭9♭13/D

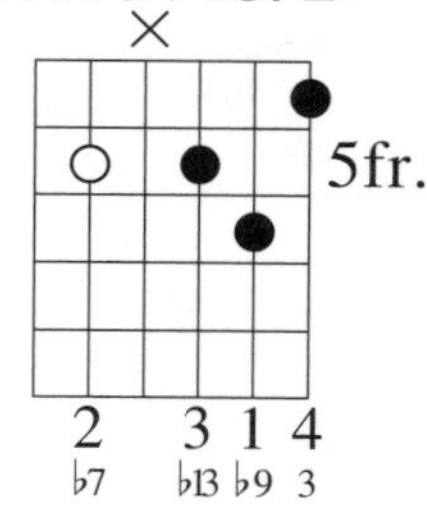

E7♭9♯11/D

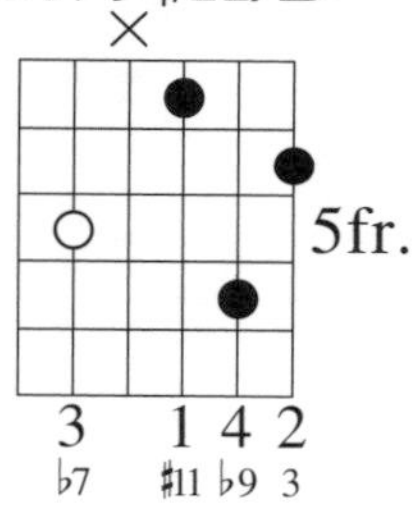

E11♭9/D

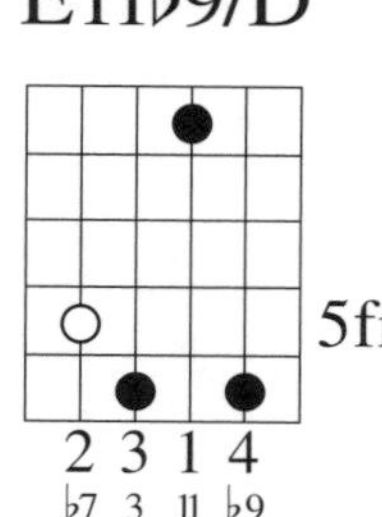

E13♭9/D

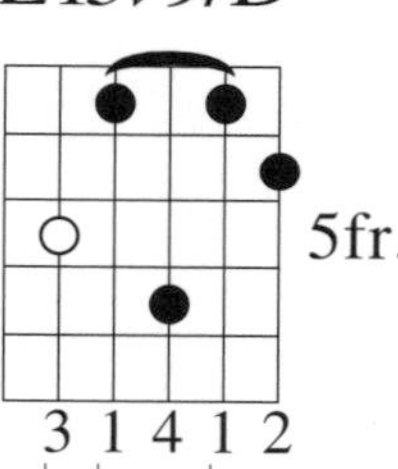

E13♯9/D

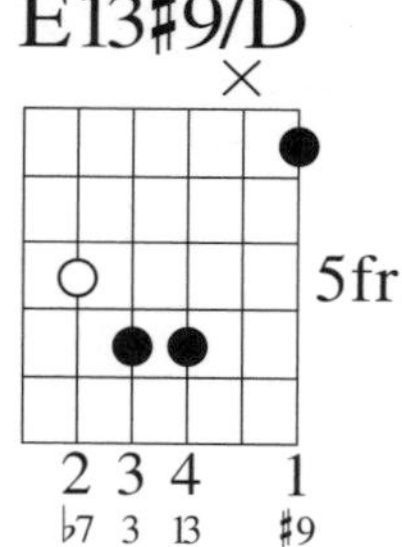

E7♭13/D

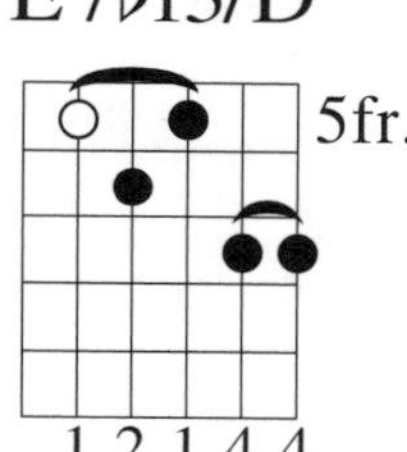

E7♭9♭13/D

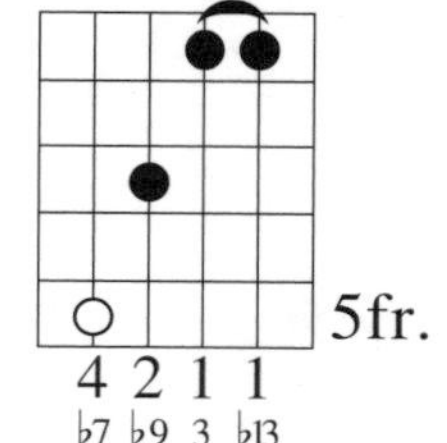

E7♯9♯11/D

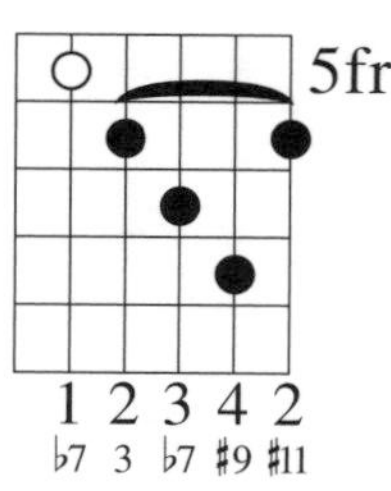

E11♭9/D

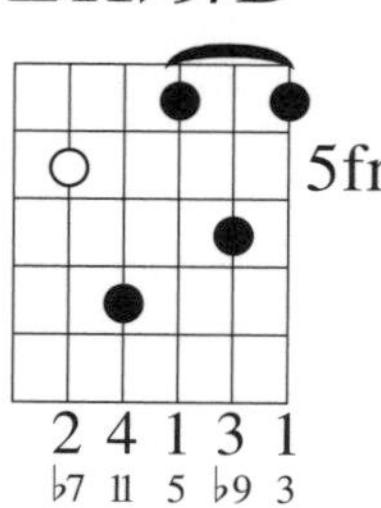

E13♭9♯11/D

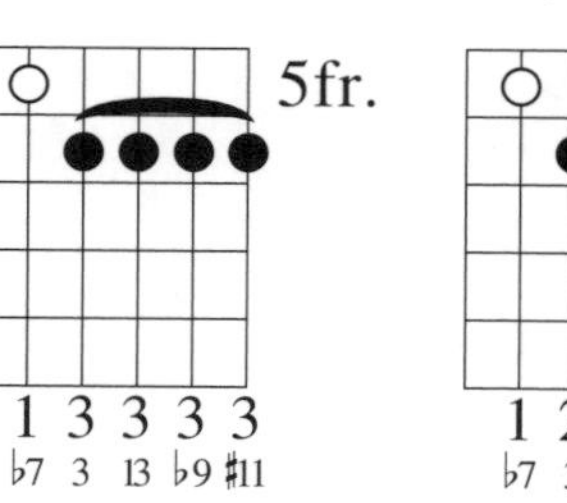

E13♯9♯11/D

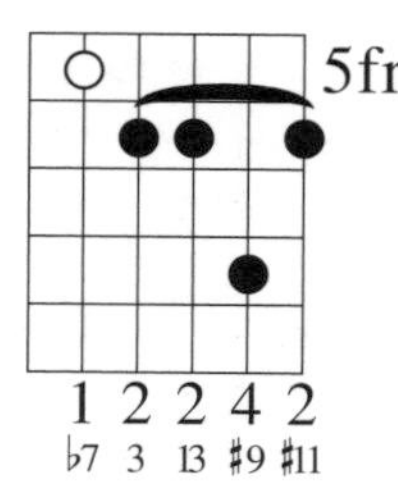

E7♭13/D

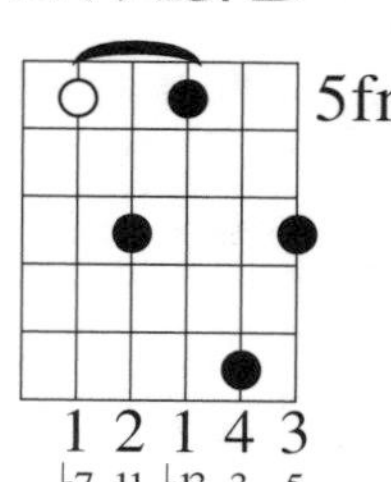

E7♭9♭13/D

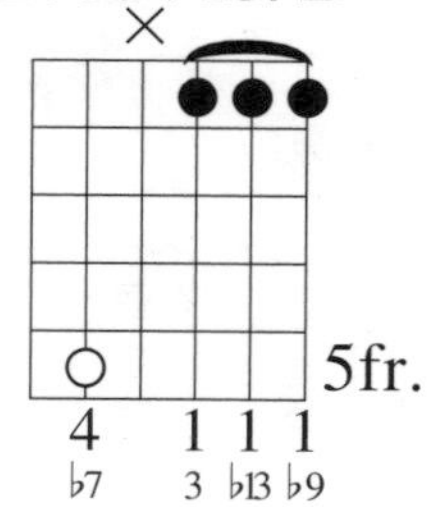

E7♯9♯11/D

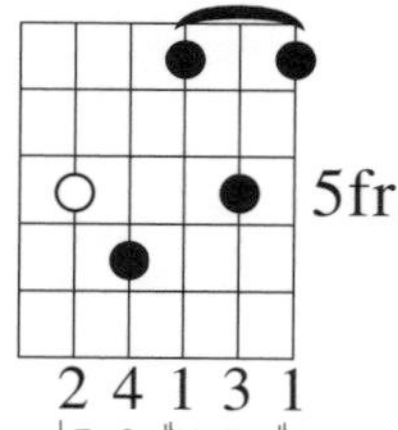

E13♭9/D

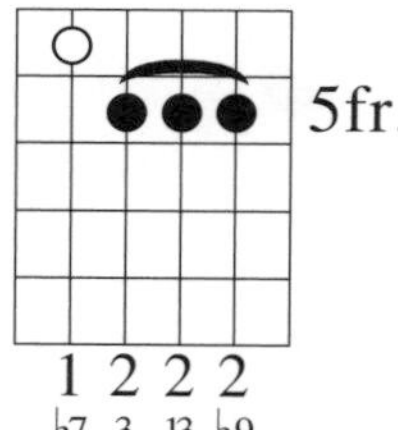

E13♯9/D

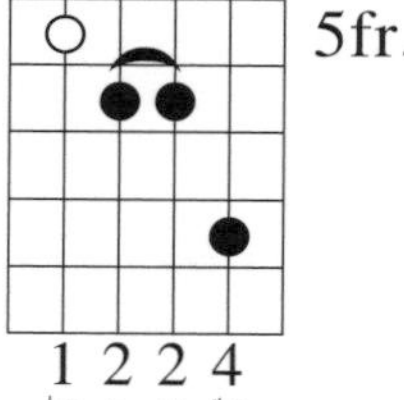

E13♭9♯9/D

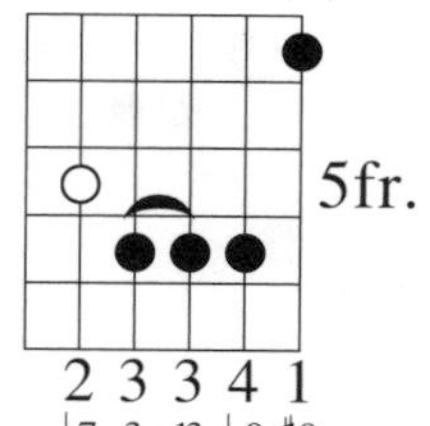

E7♭9♭13/D

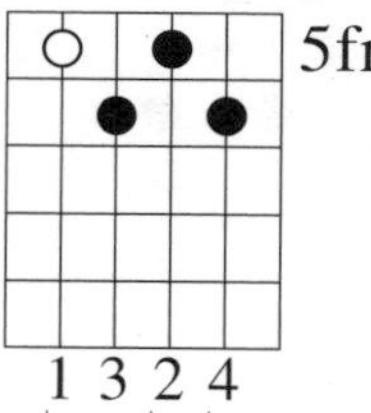

E7♭9♭13/D

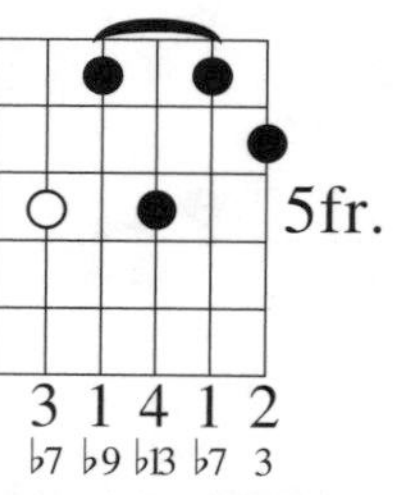

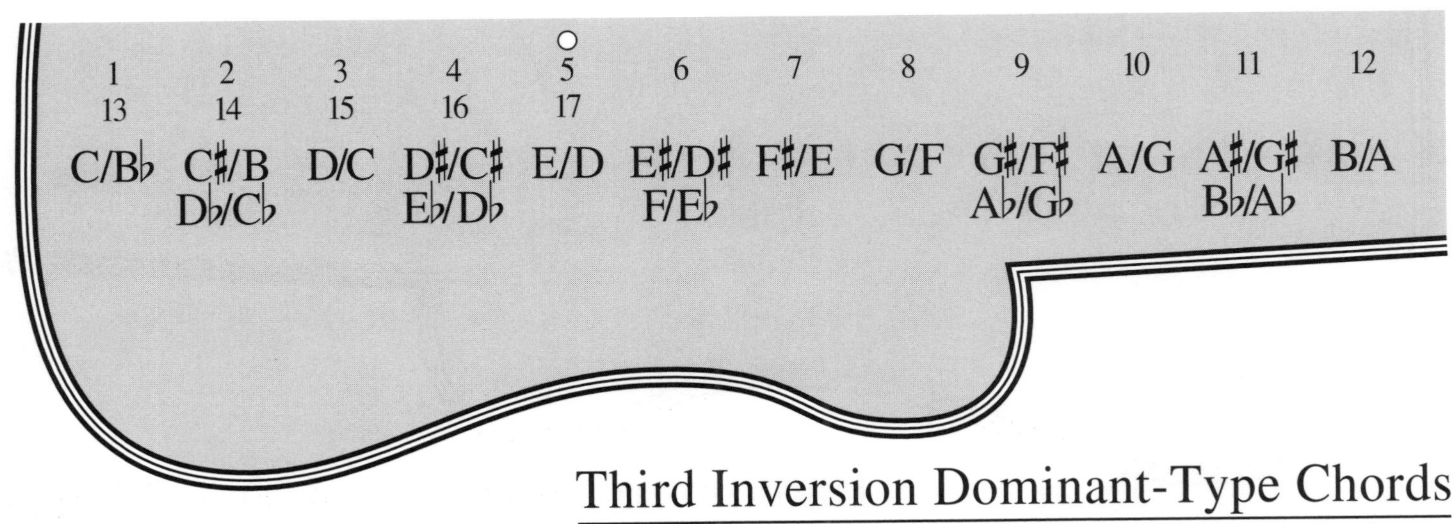

Third Inversion Dominant-Type Chords

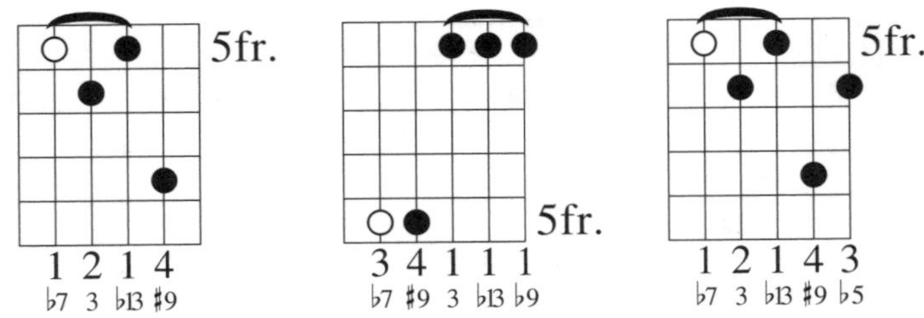

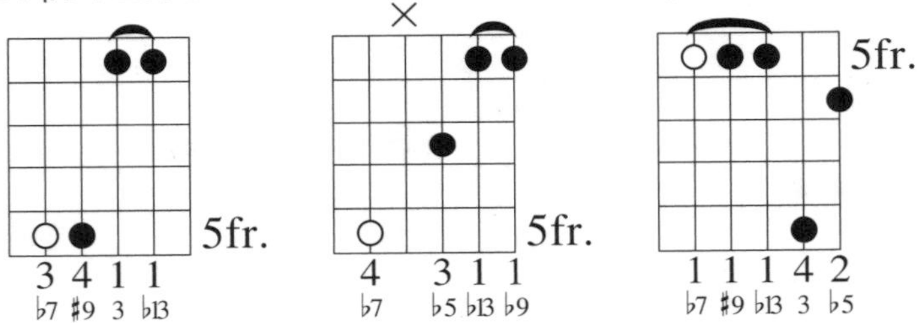

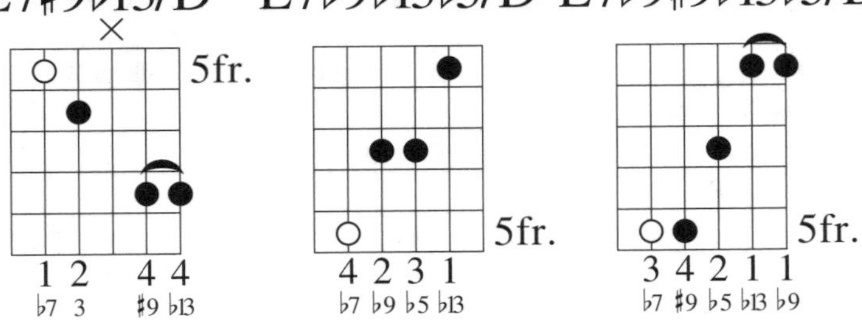

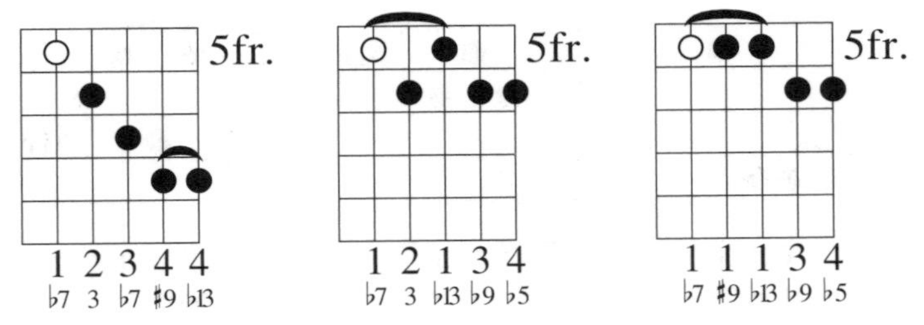

Third Inversion Dominant-Type Chords

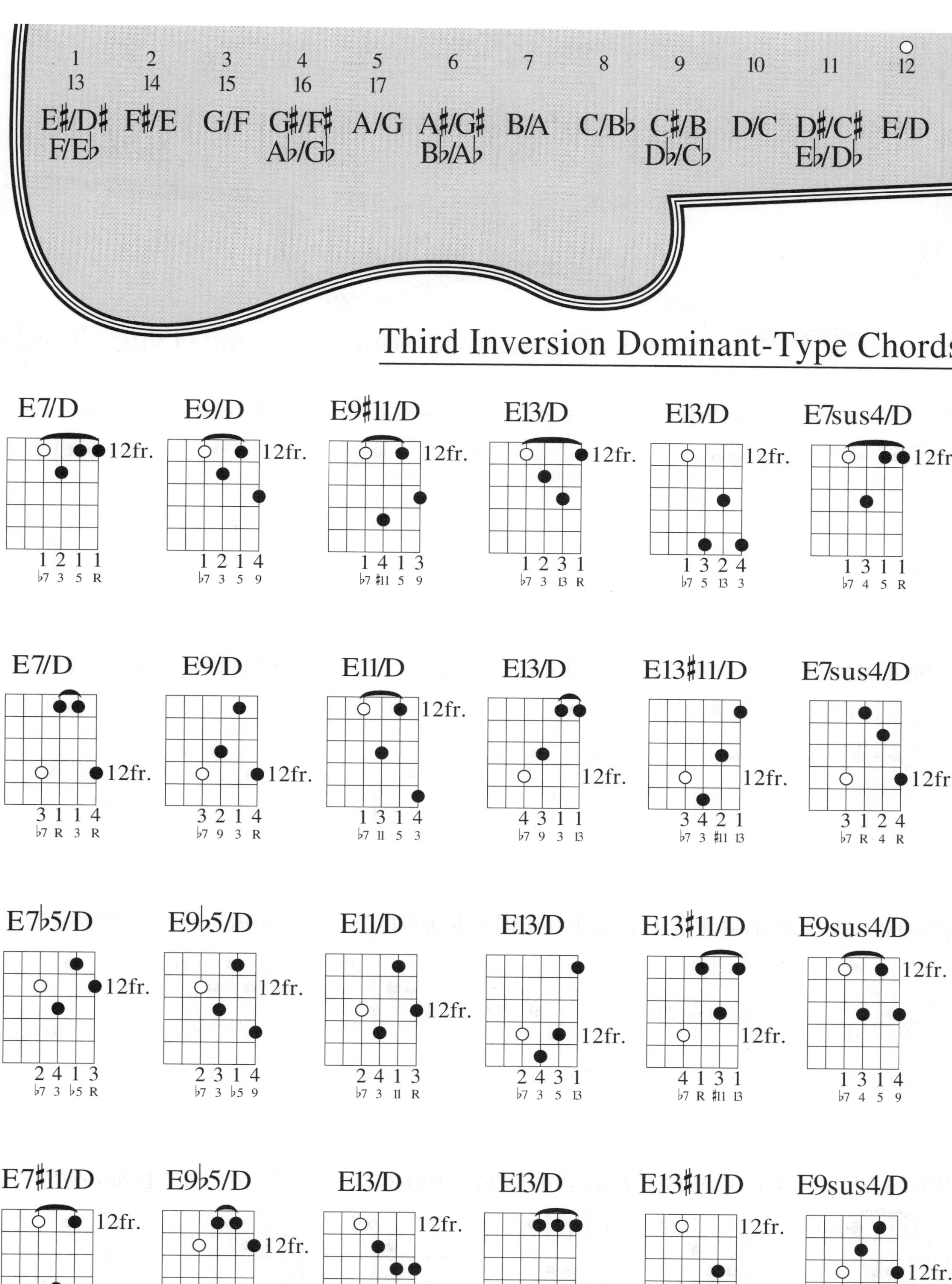

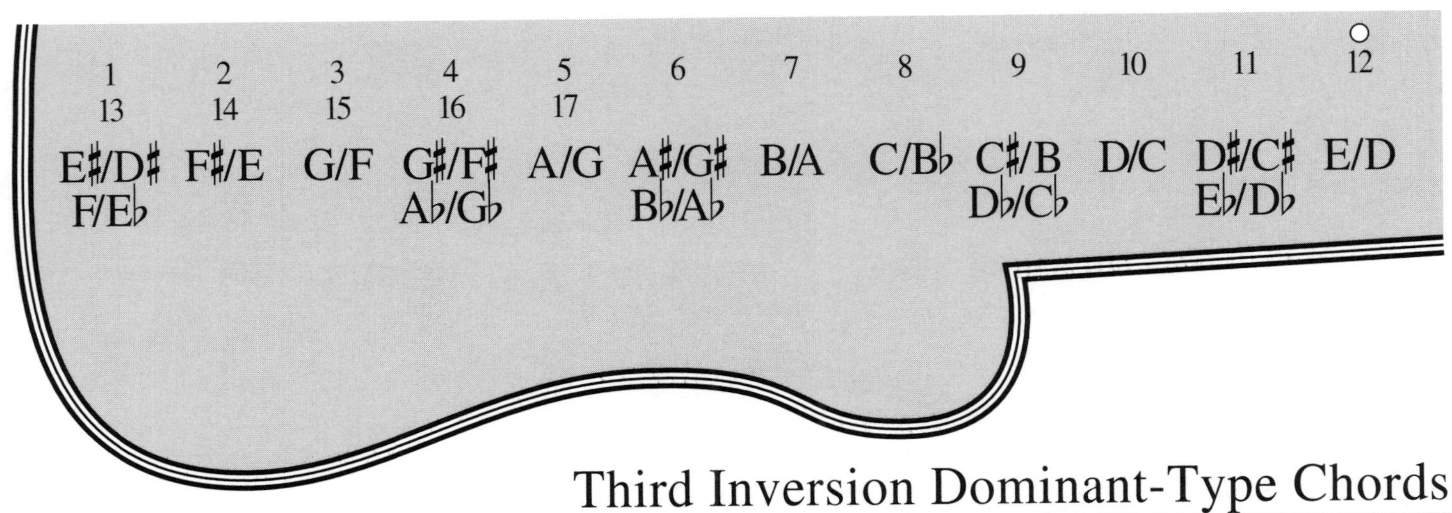

Third Inversion Dominant-Type Chords

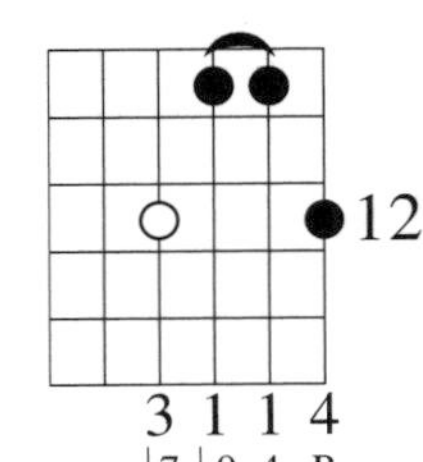
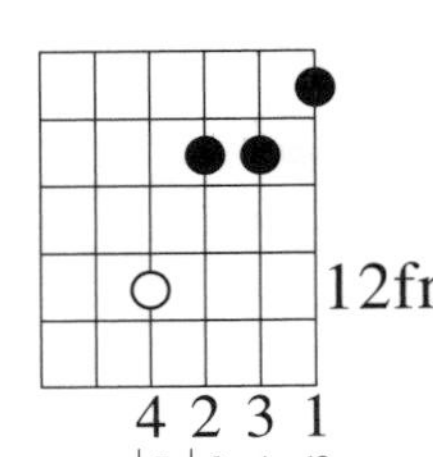
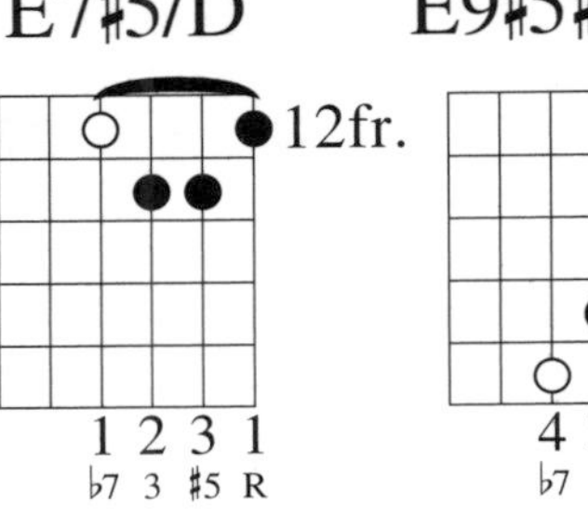
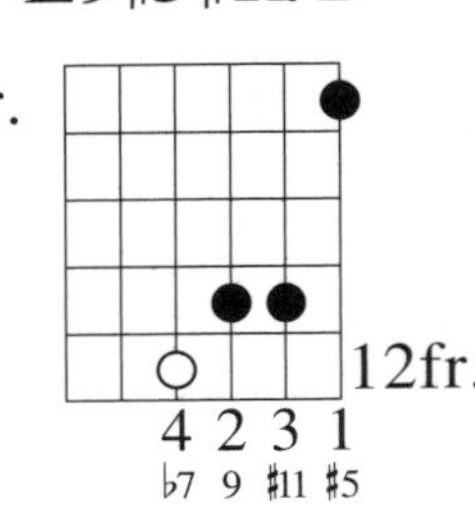
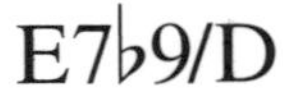
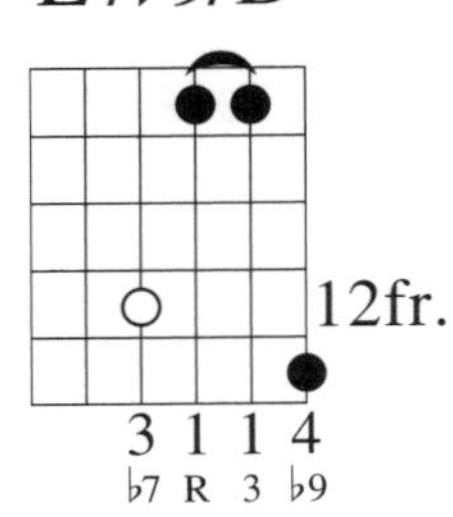

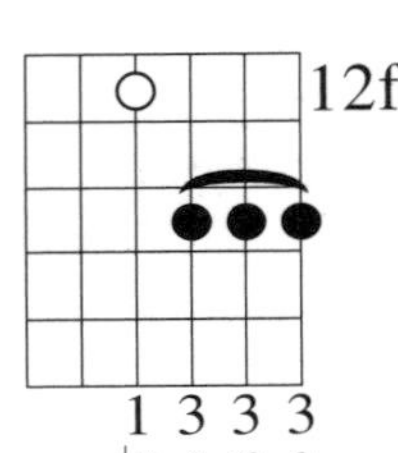
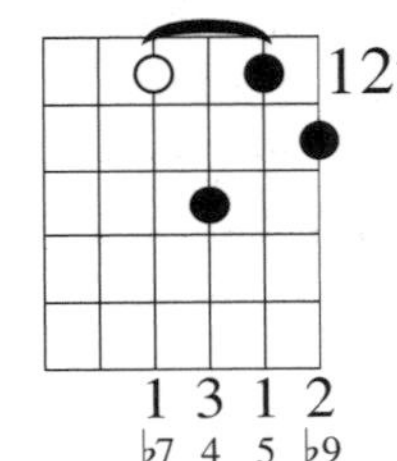
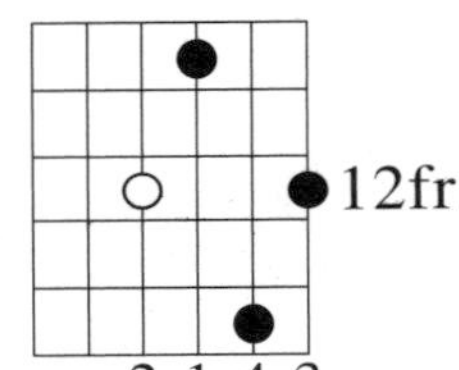
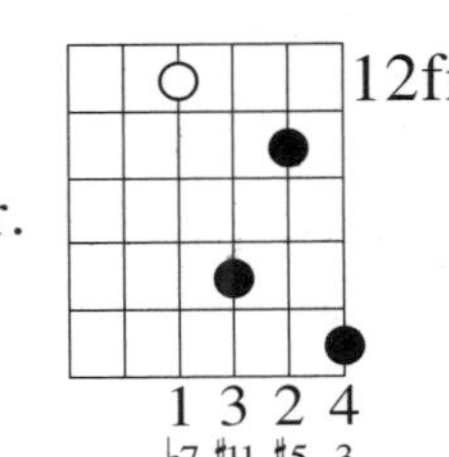

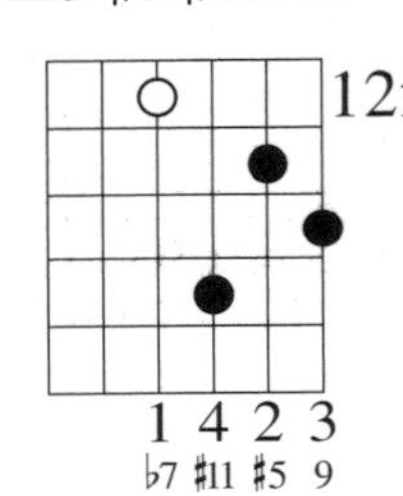

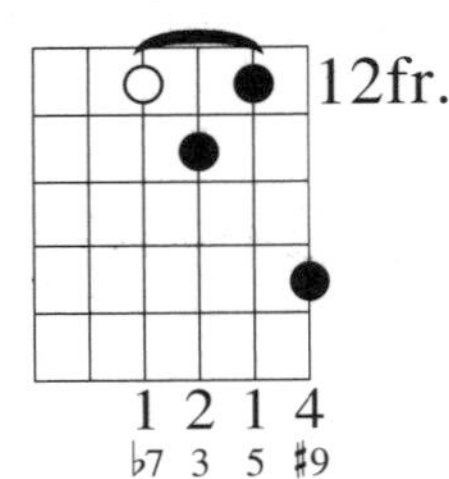

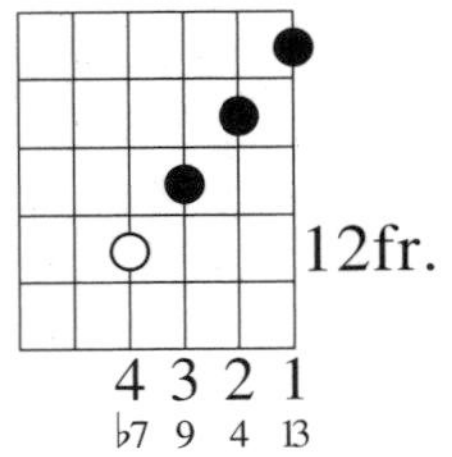
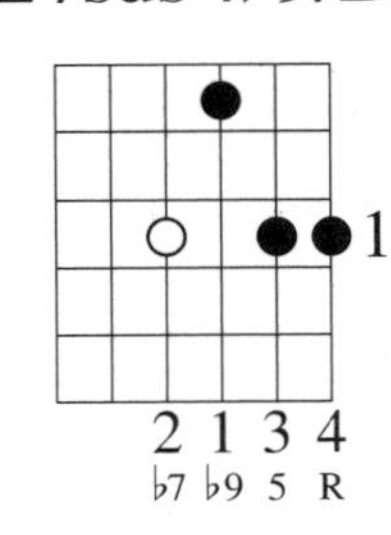
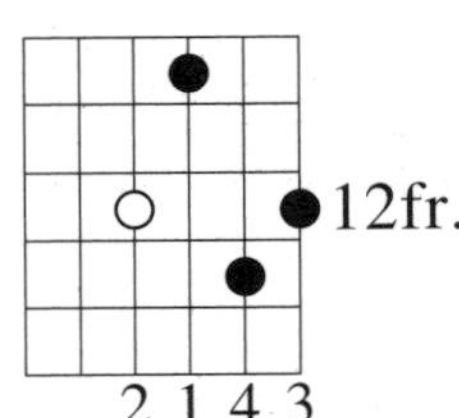
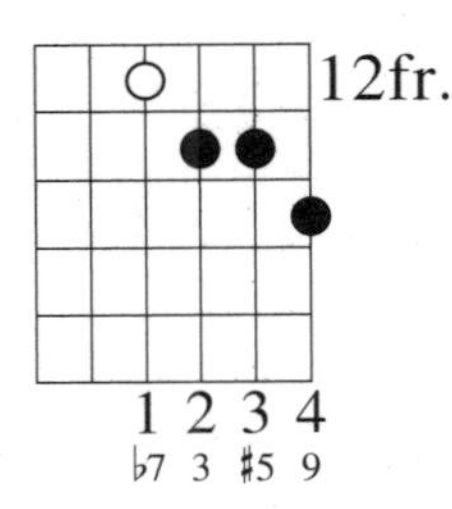
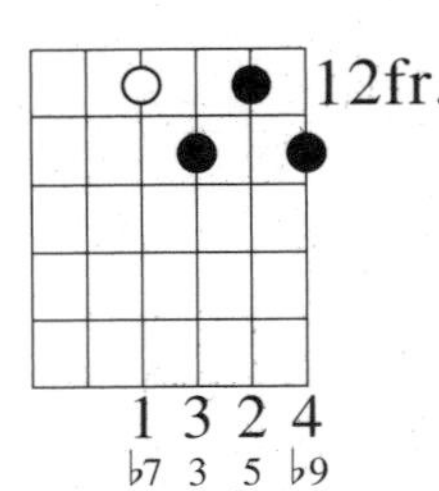
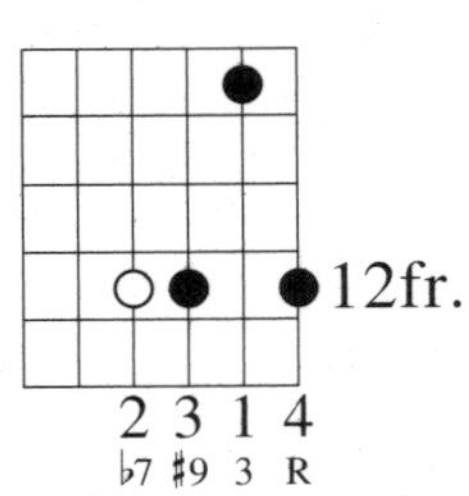

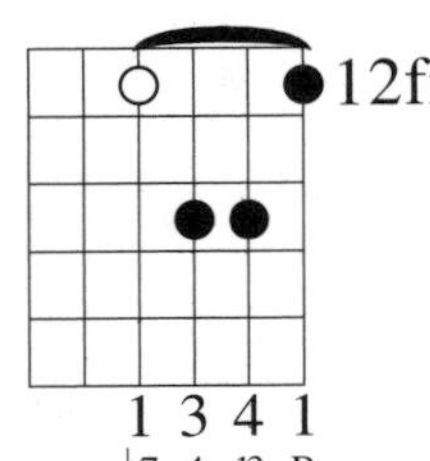
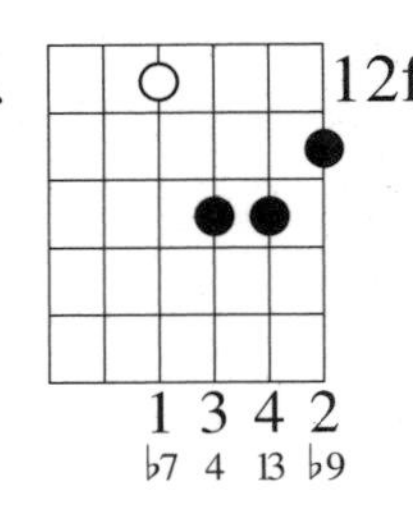
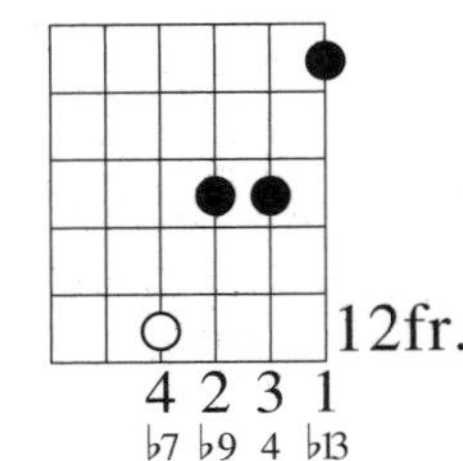
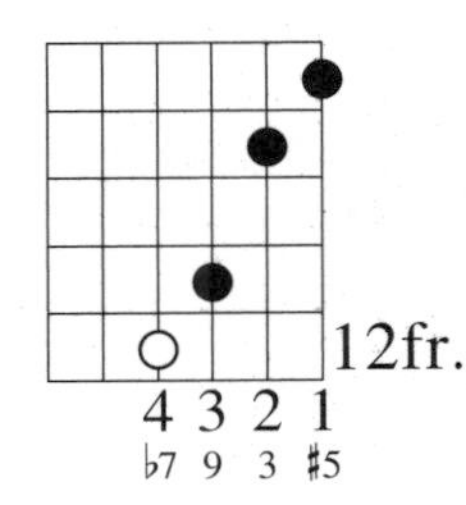
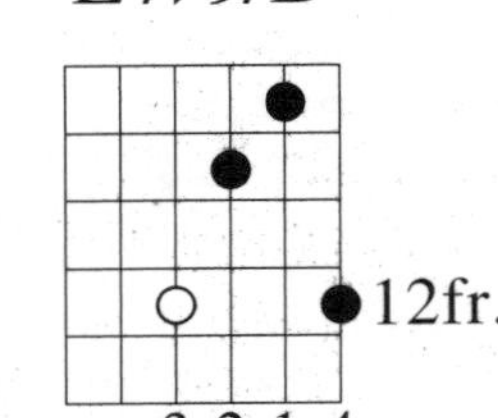
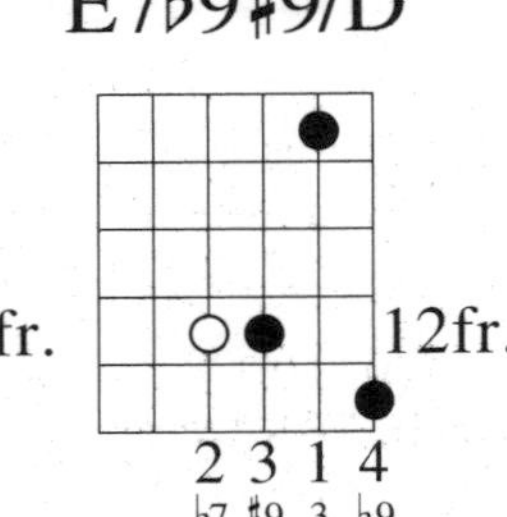

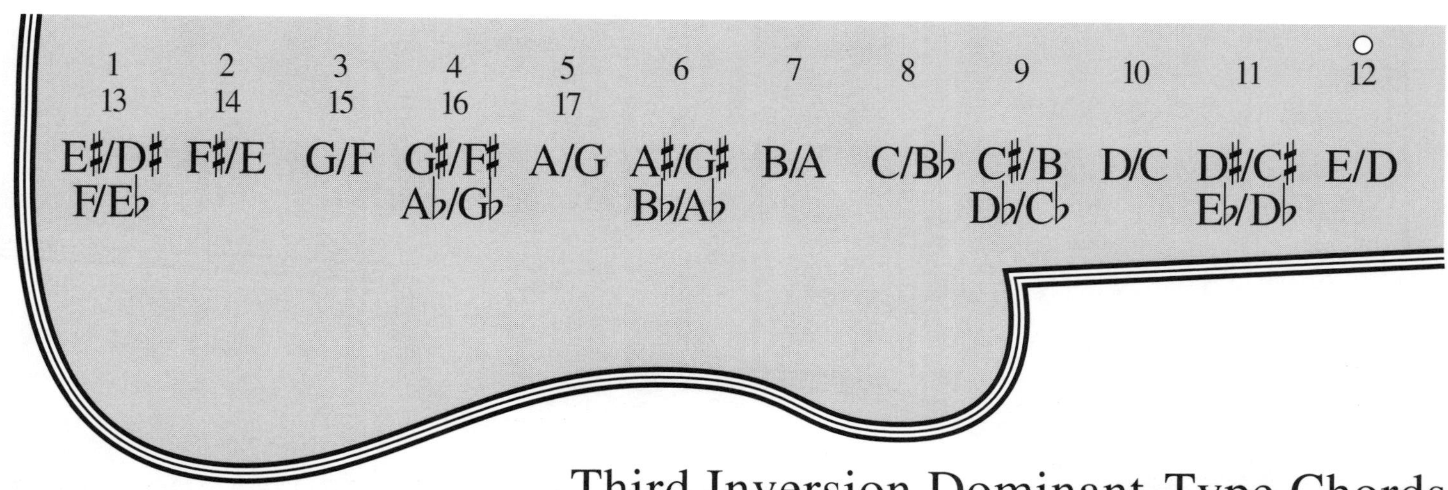

Third Inversion Dominant-Type Chords

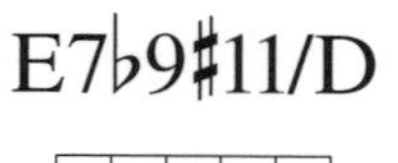

E7♭9♯11/D

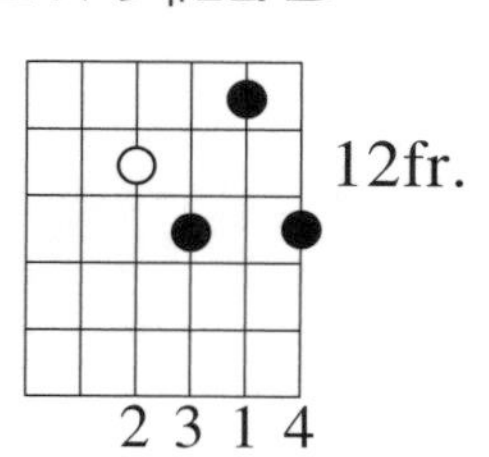

2 3 1 4
♭7 3 ♯11 ♭9

E11♭9/D — 12fr.
2 3 1 4
♭7 3 11 ♭9

E13♭9♯11/D — 12fr.
4 2 3 1
♭7 ♭9 ♯11 13

E13♯9♯11/D

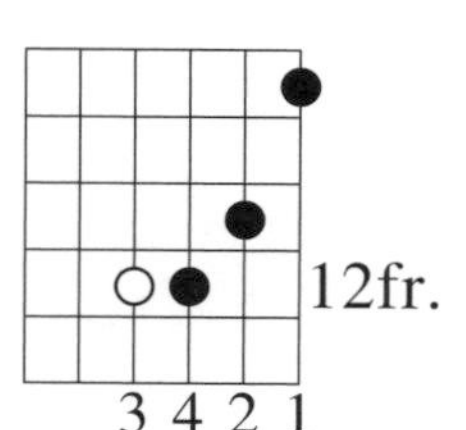

3 4 2 1
♭7 ♯9 ♯11 13

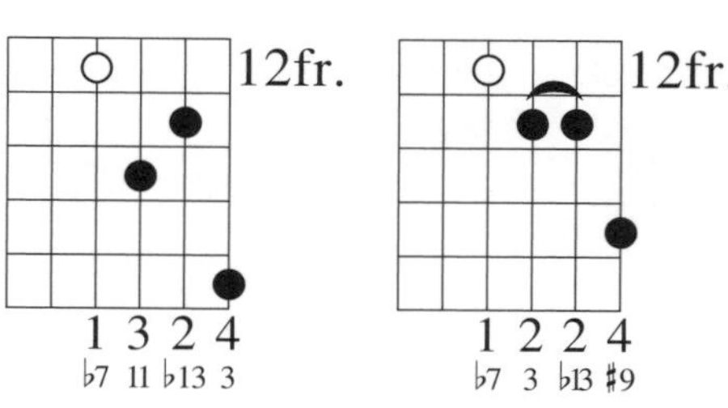

E7♭13/D — 12fr.
1 3 2 4
♭7 11 ♭13 3

E7♯9♭13/D — 12fr.
1 2 2 4
♭7 3 ♭13 ♯9

E7♭9♯11/D

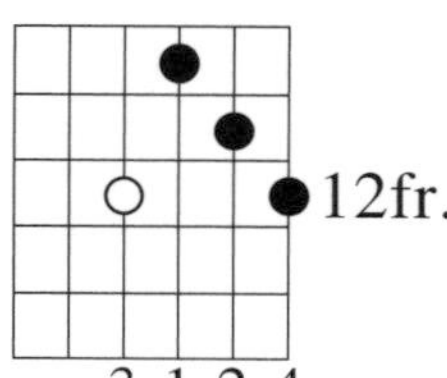

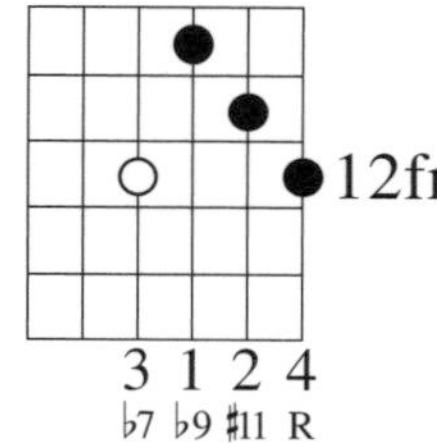

3 1 2 4
♭7 ♭9 ♯11 R

E13♭9/D

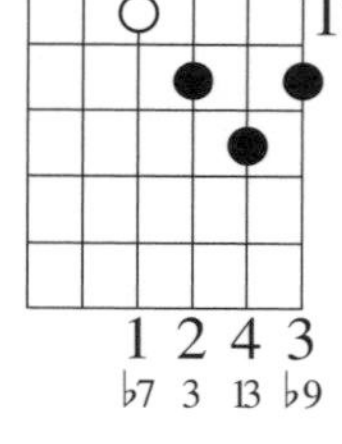

1 2 4 3
♭7 3 13 ♭9

E13♭9♯11/D

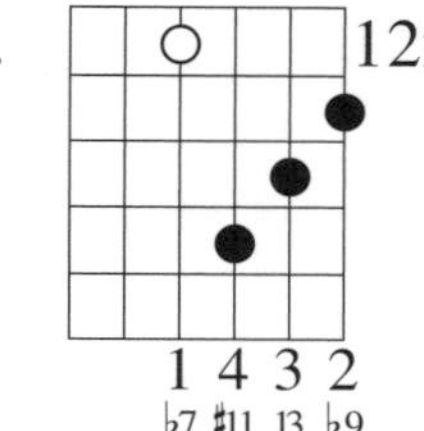

1 4 3 2
♭7 ♯11 13 ♭9

E13♯9♯11/D

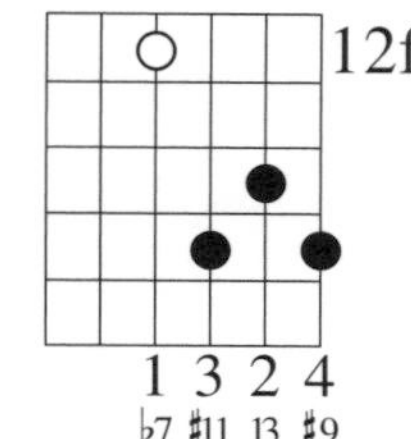

1 3 2 4
♭7 ♯11 13 ♯9

E7♭9♭13/D

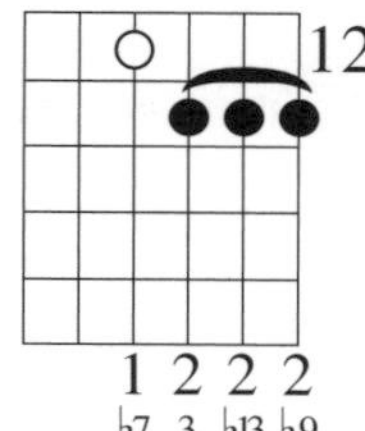

1 2 2 2
♭7 3 ♭13 ♭9

E7♯9♭13/D

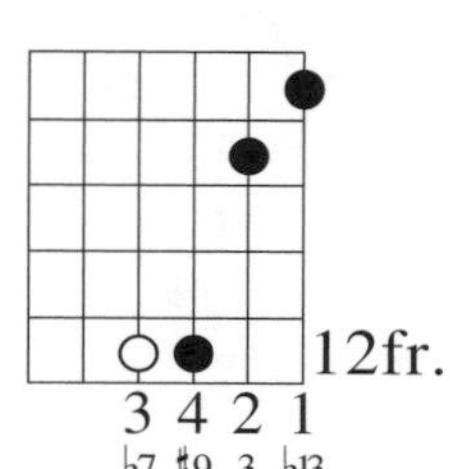

3 4 2 1
♭7 ♯9 3 ♭13

E7♯9♯11/D

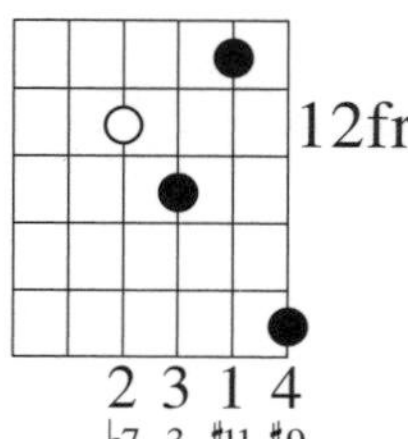

2 3 1 4
♭7 3 ♯11 ♯9

E13♭9/D

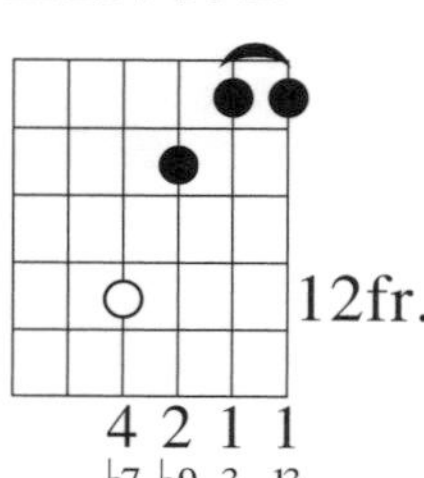

4 2 1 1
♭7 ♭9 3 13

E13♯9/D

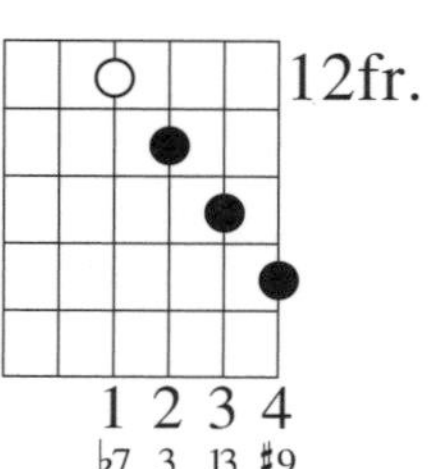

1 2 3 4
♭7 3 13 ♯9

E13♭9♯9/D

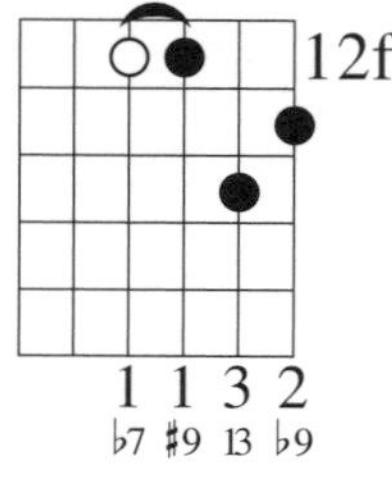

1 1 3 2
♭7 ♯9 13 ♭9

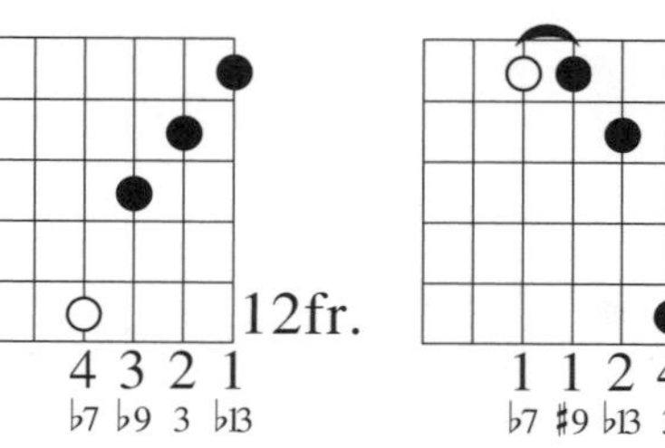

E7♭9♭13/D — 12fr.
4 3 2 1
♭7 ♭9 3 ♭13

E7♯9♭13/D — 12fr.
1 1 2 4
♭7 ♯9 ♭13 3

E7♭9♯9♯11/D

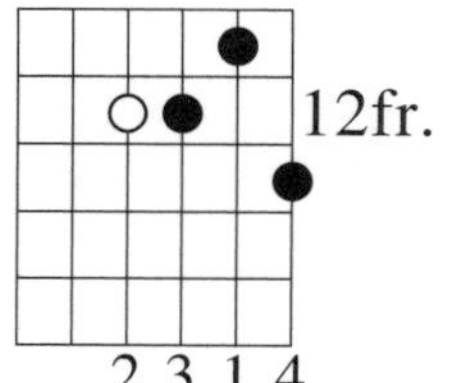

2 3 1 4
♭7 ♯9 ♯11 ♭9

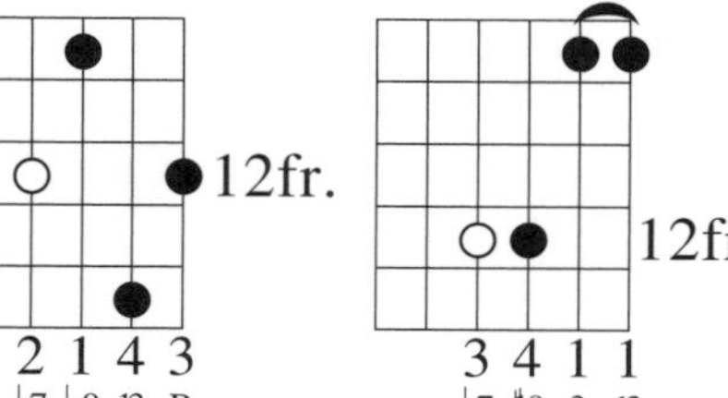

E13♭9/D — 12fr.
2 1 4 3
♭7 ♭9 13 R

E13♯9/D — 12fr.
3 4 1 1
♭7 ♯9 3 13

E13♭9♯9/D

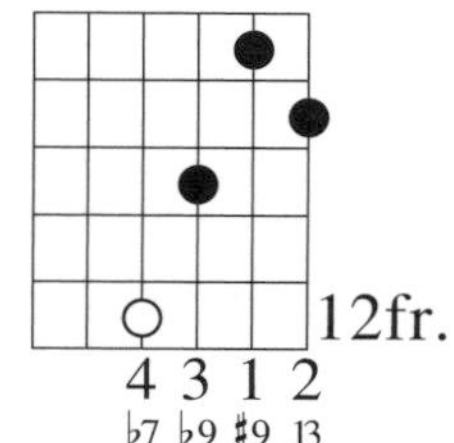

4 3 1 2
♭7 ♭9 ♯9 13

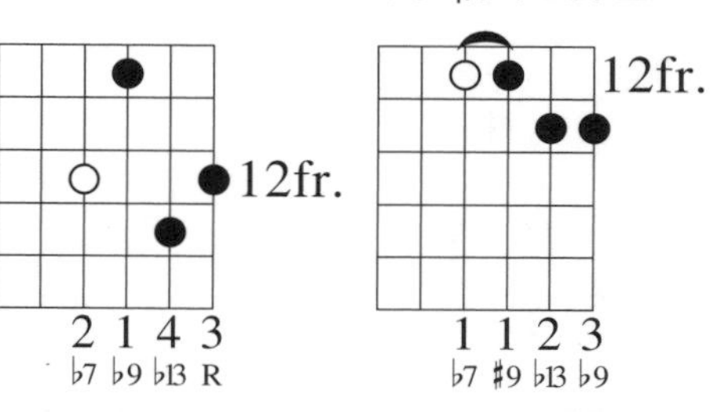

E7♭9♭13/D — 12fr.
2 1 4 3
♭7 ♭9 ♭13 R

E7♭9♯9♭13/D — 12fr.
1 1 2 3
♭7 ♯9 ♭13 ♭9

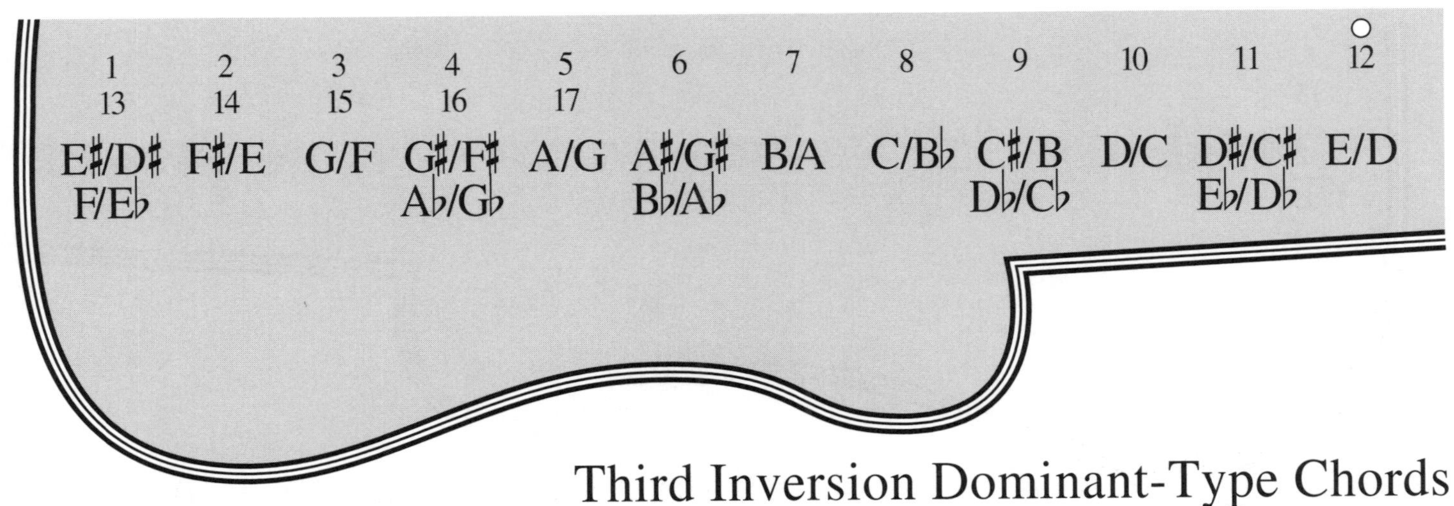

Third Inversion Dominant-Type Chords

E7♭9♭13♭5/D

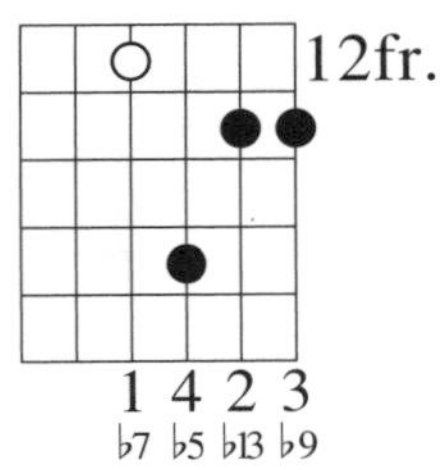

E7♭9♭13♭5/D

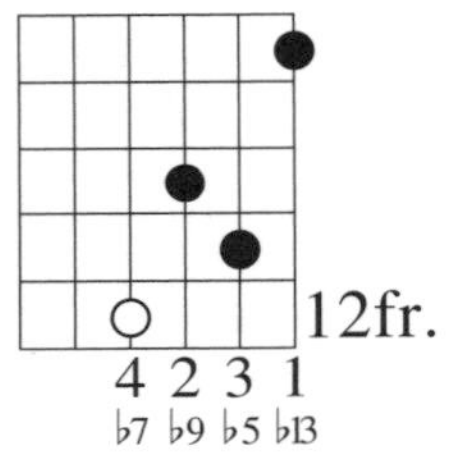

E7♭9♭13♭5/D

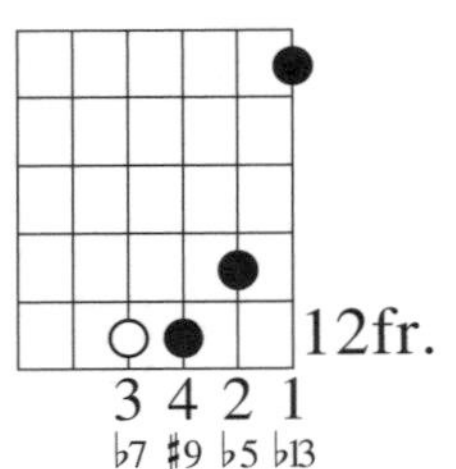

E7♯9♭13♭5/D

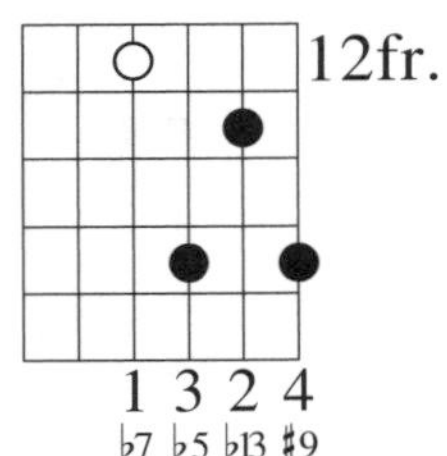

Non-Tertian Chords

D Major
(D E F♯ G A B C♯ D)
Four-Note Quartal

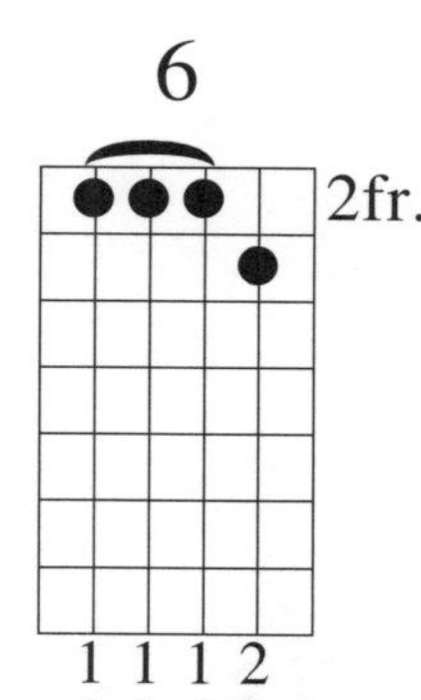

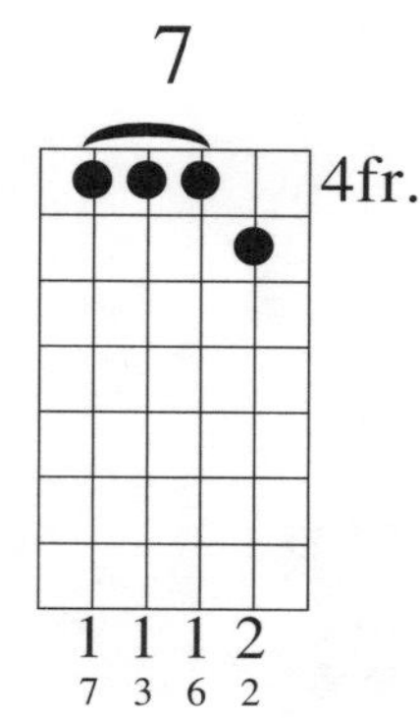

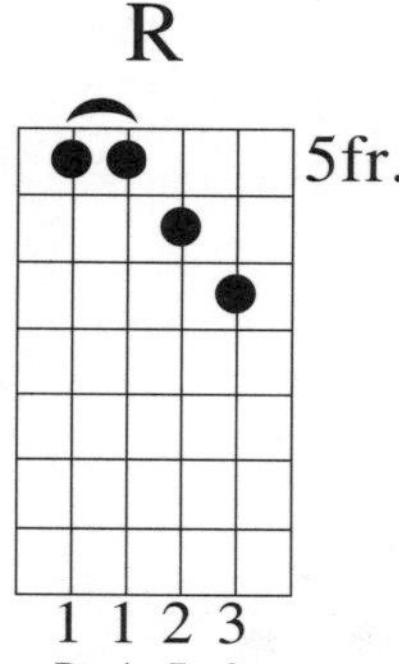

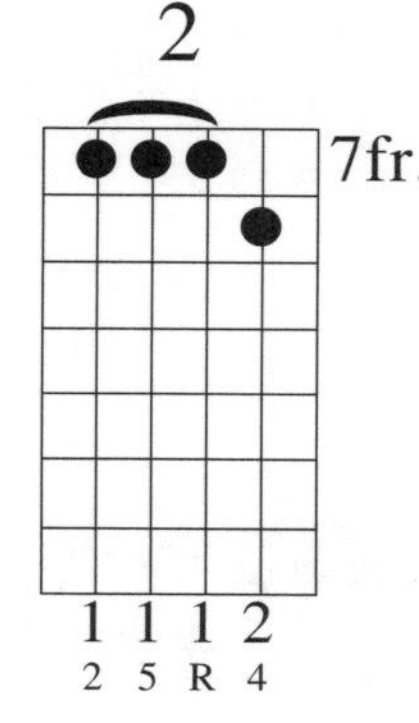

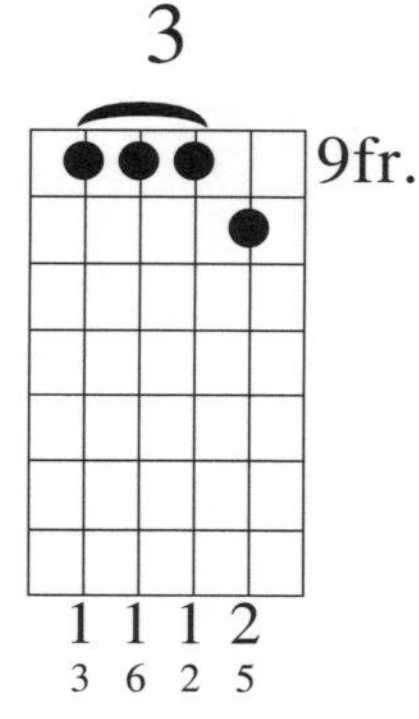

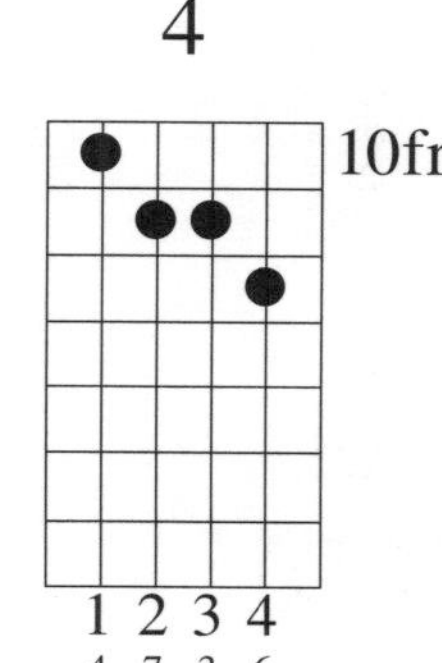

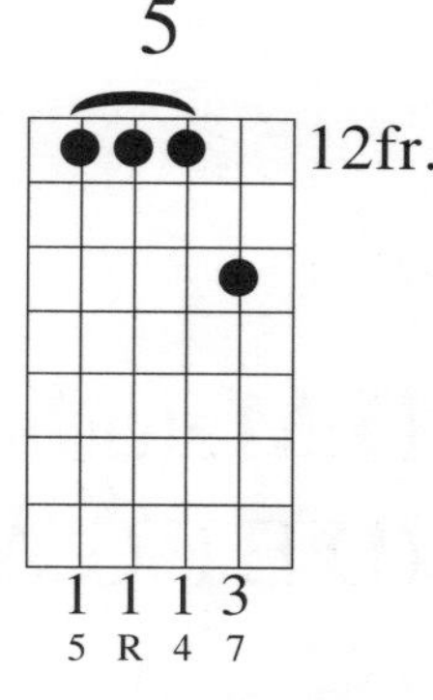

D Major
(D E F♯ G A B C♯ D)
Five-Note Quartal

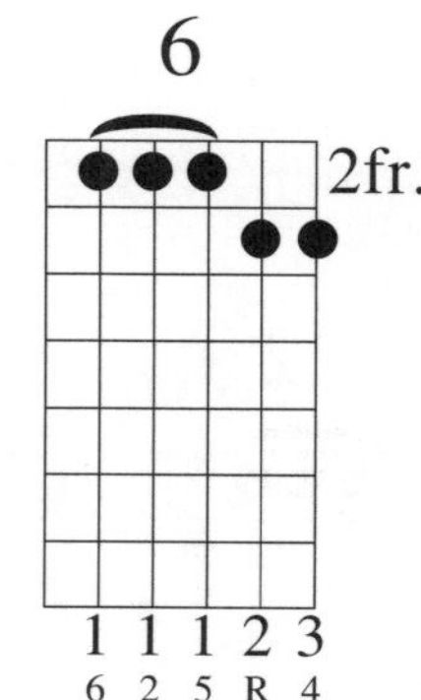

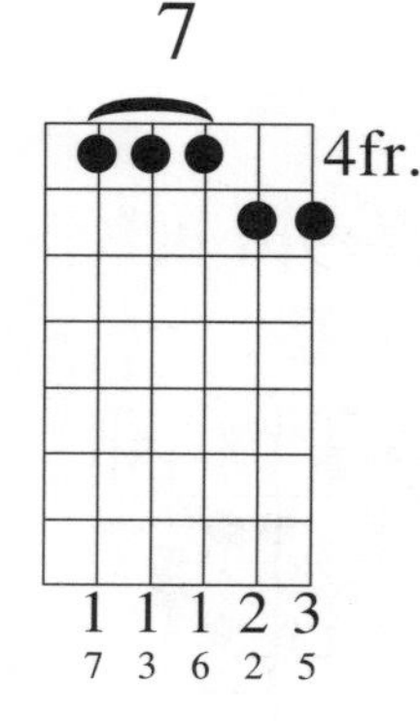

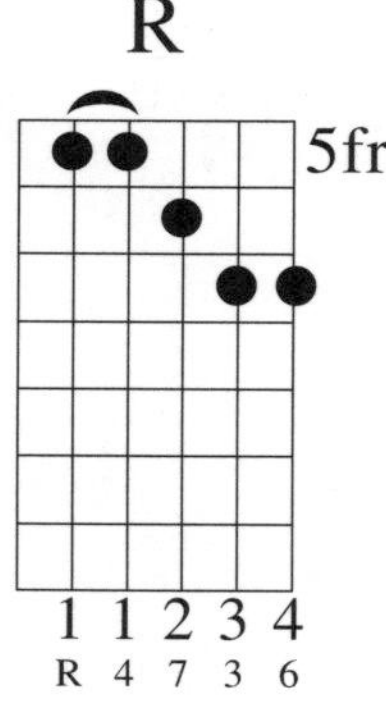

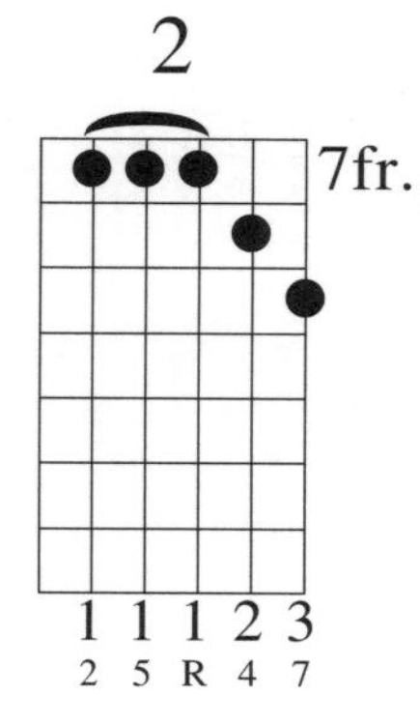

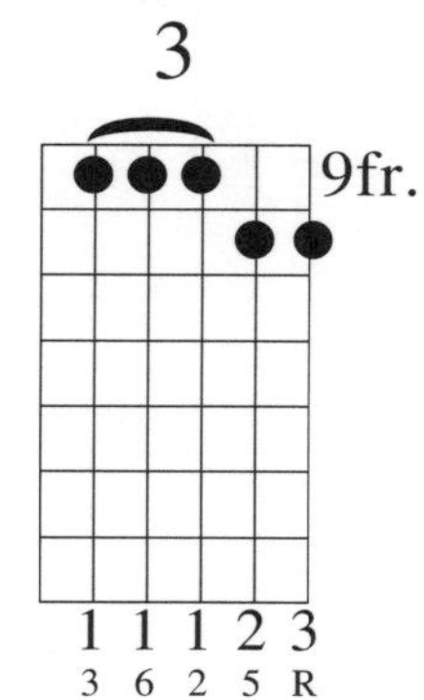

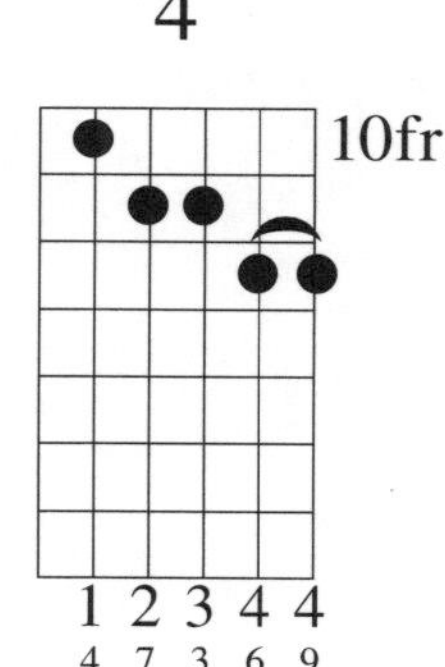

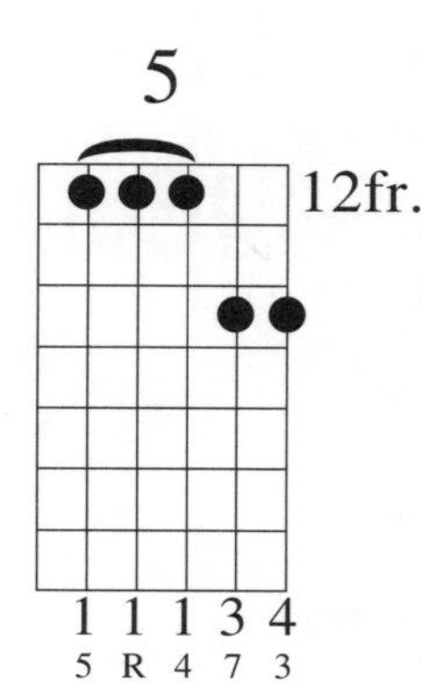

D Melodic Minor
(D E F G A B C♯ D)
Four-Note Quartal

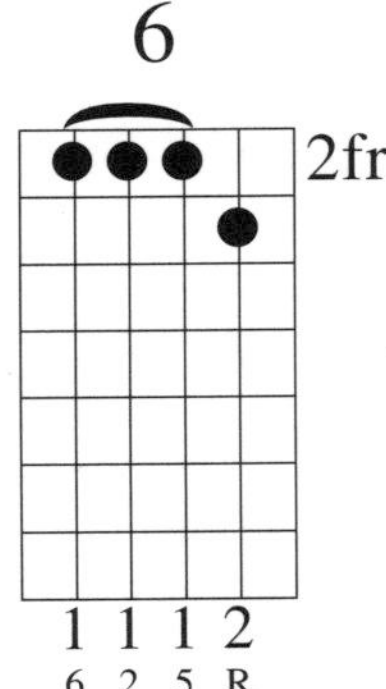

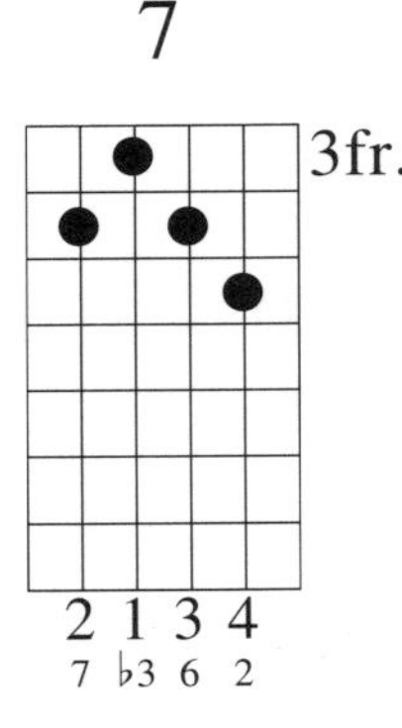

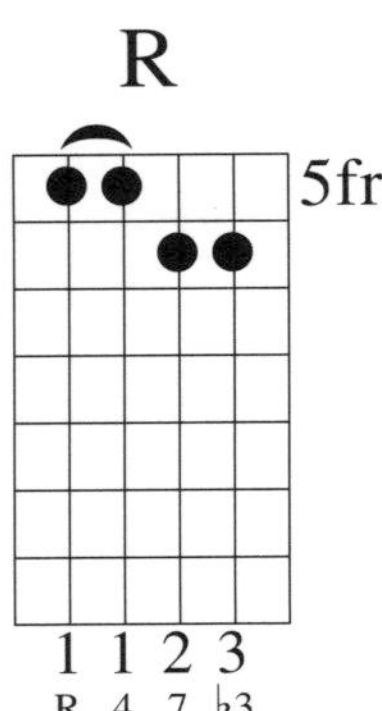

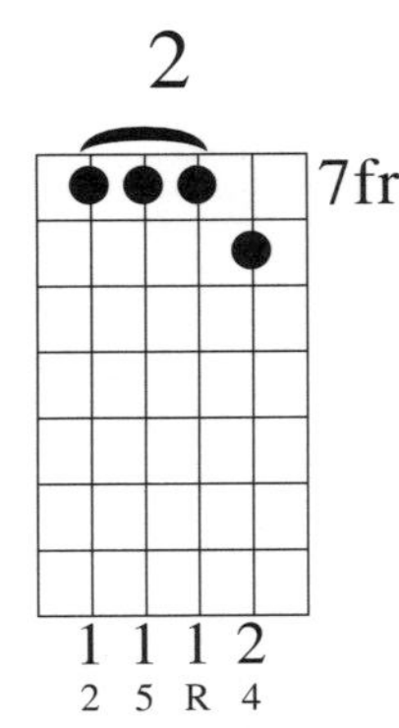

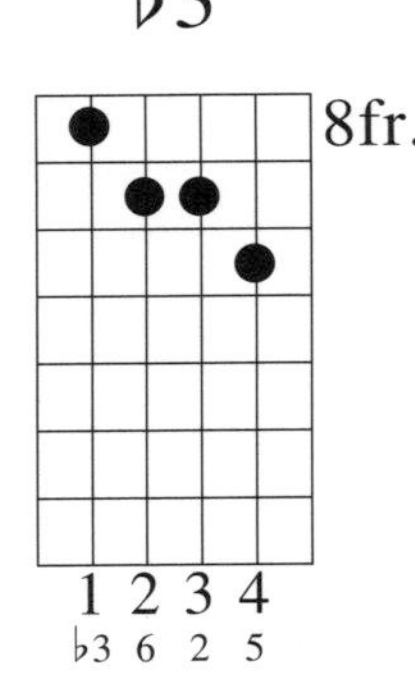

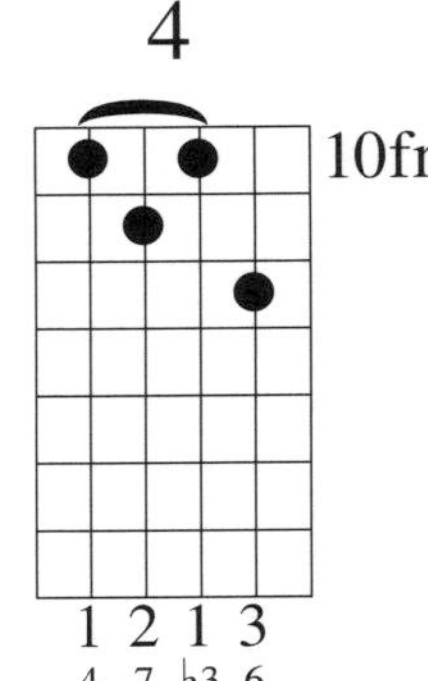

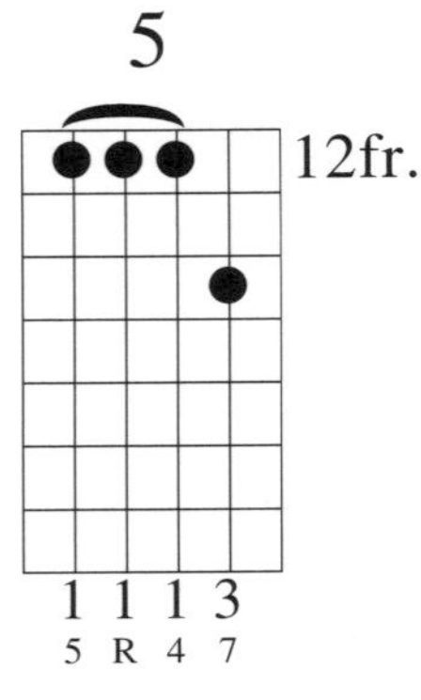

D Melodic Minor
(D E F G A B C♯ D)
Five-Note Quartal

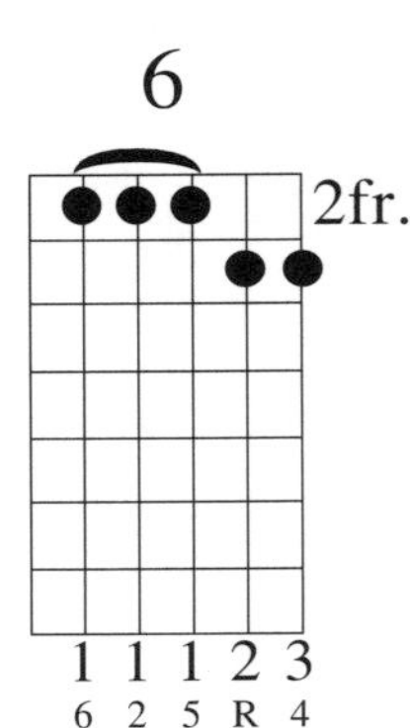

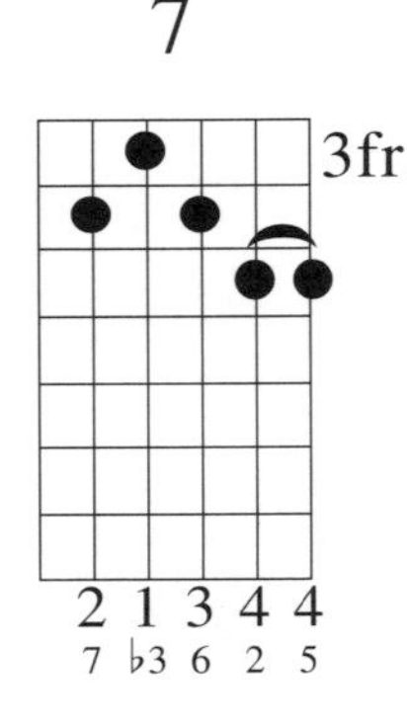

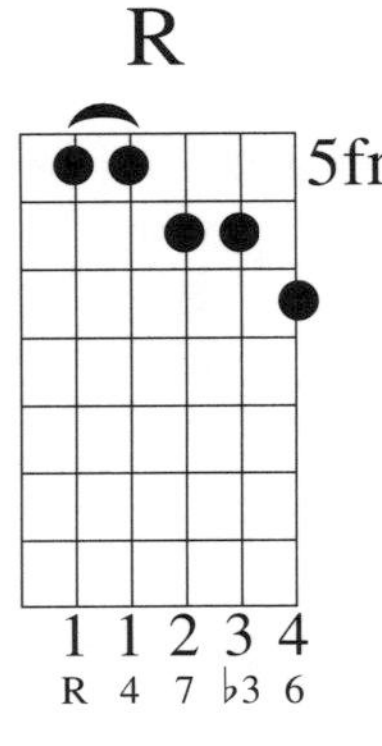

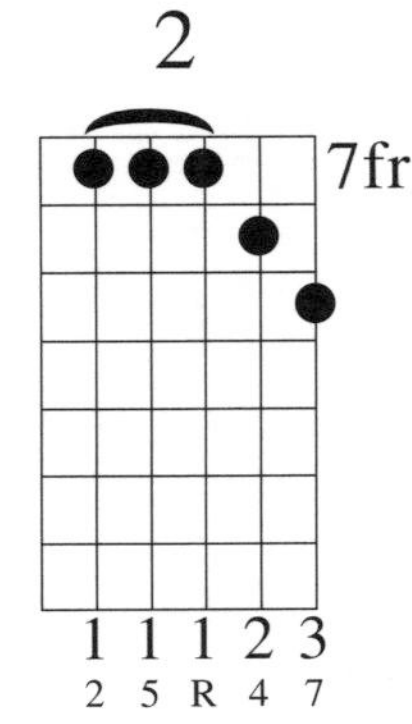

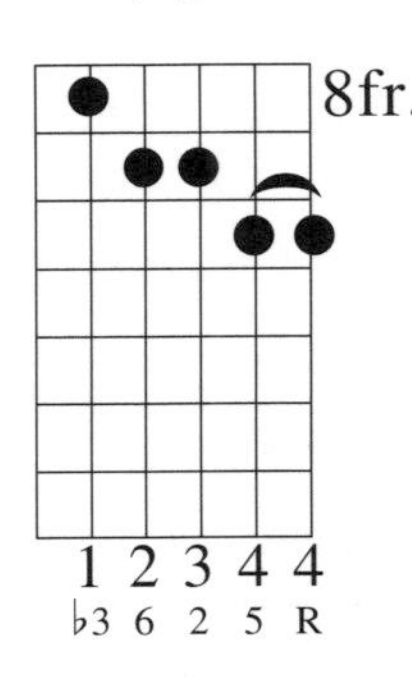

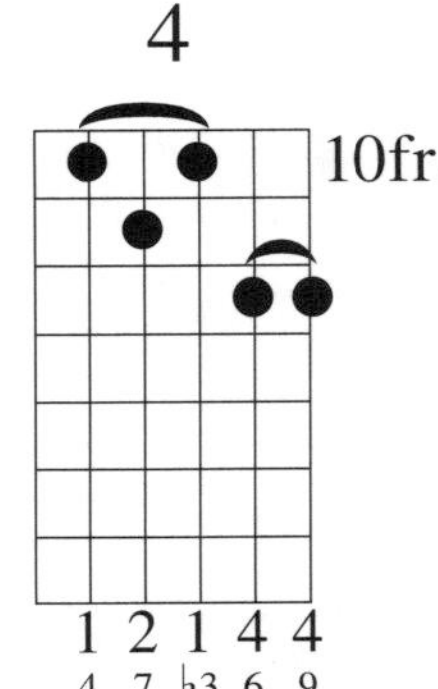

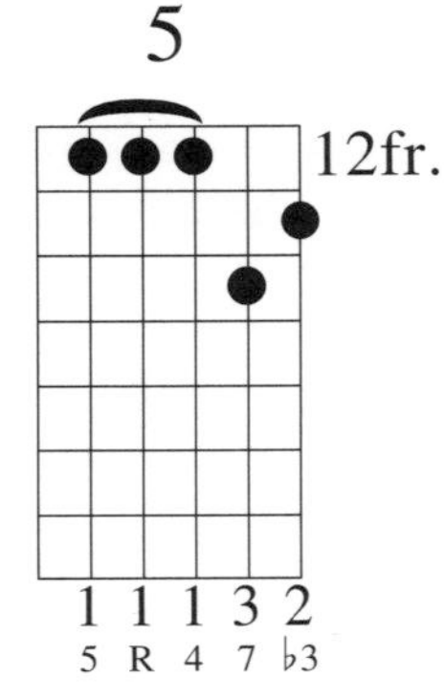

D Harmonic Minor
(D E F G A B♭ C♯ D)
Four-Note Quartal

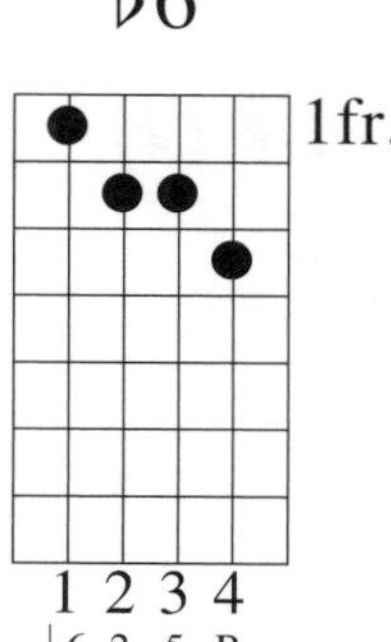

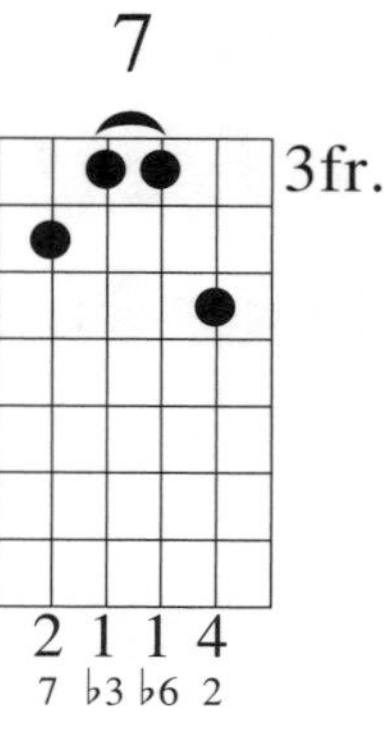

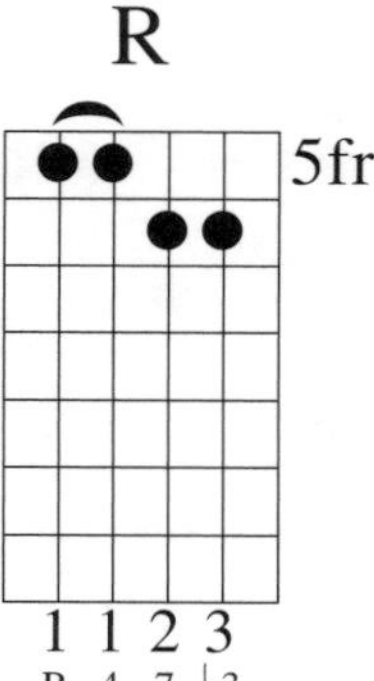

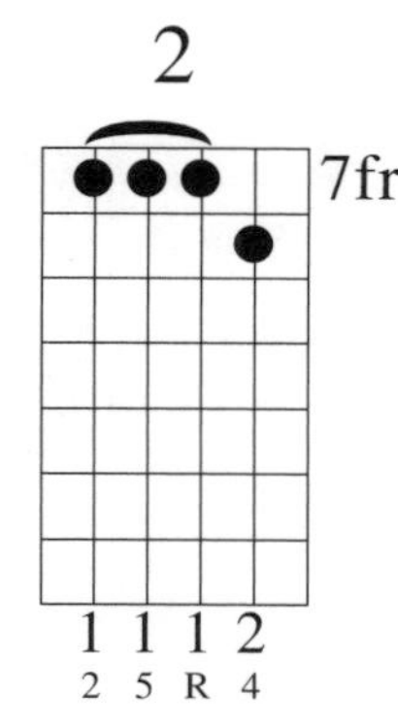

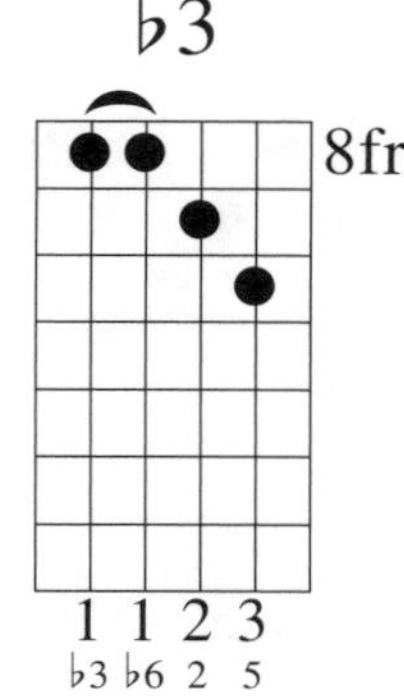

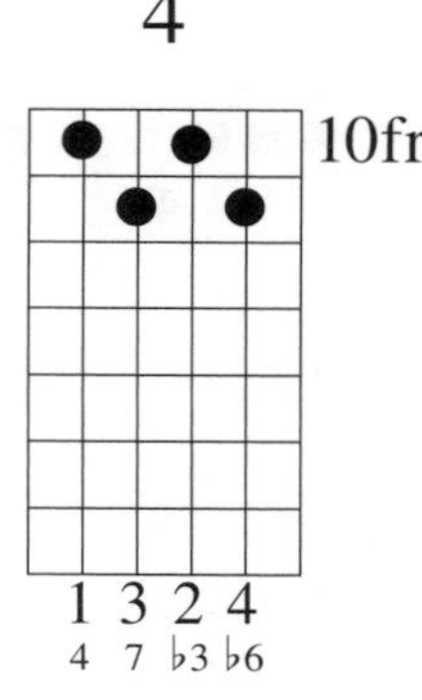

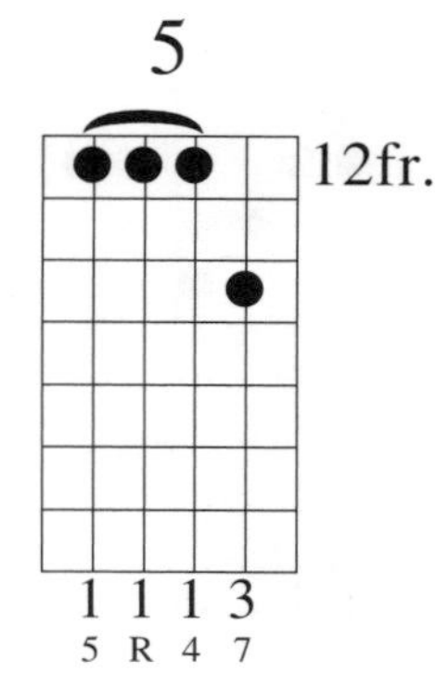

D Harmonic Minor
(D E F G A B♭ C♯ D)
Five-Note Quartal

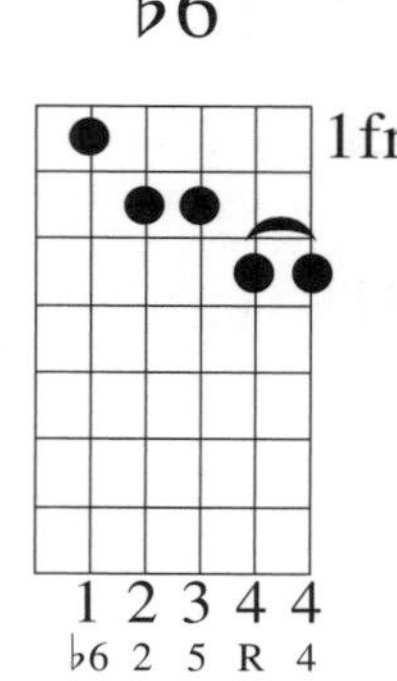

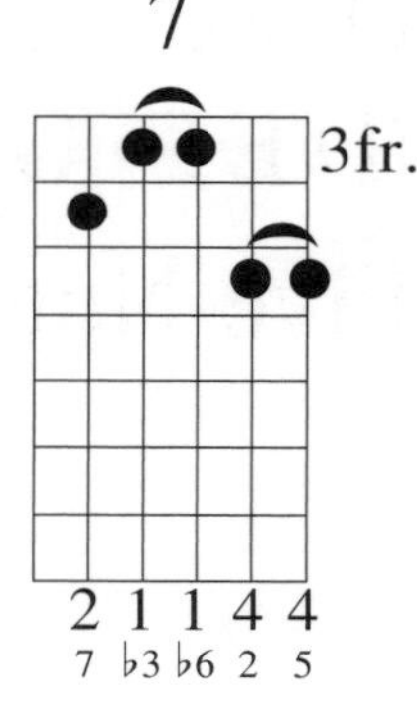

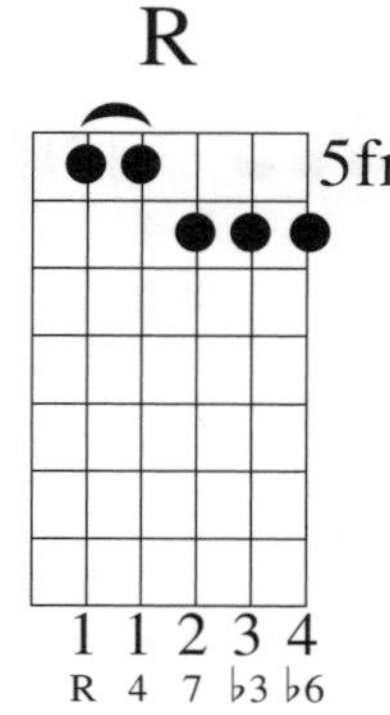

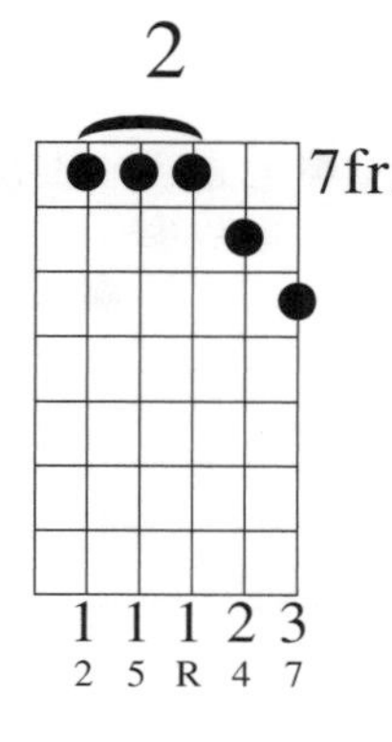

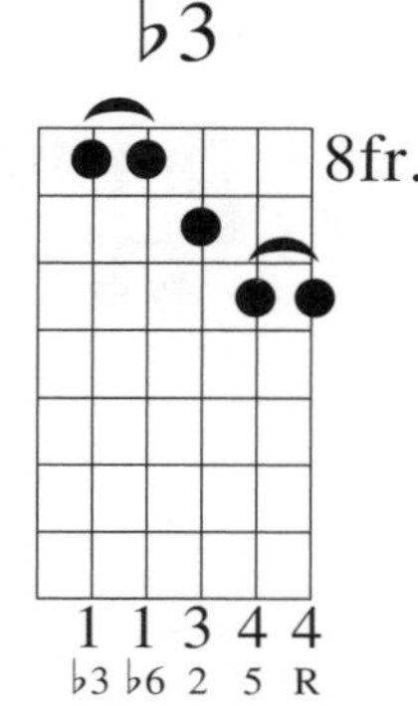

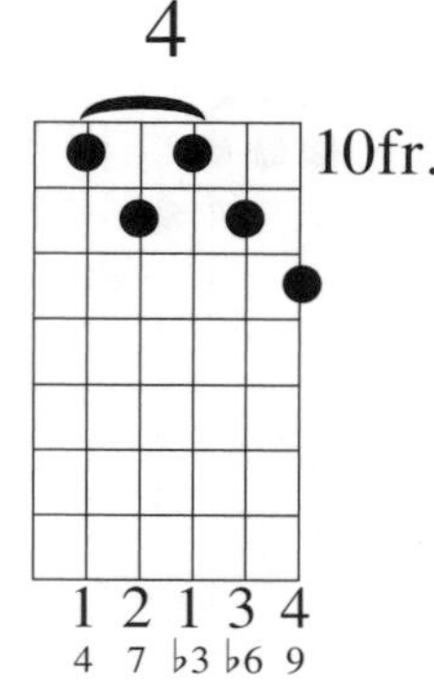

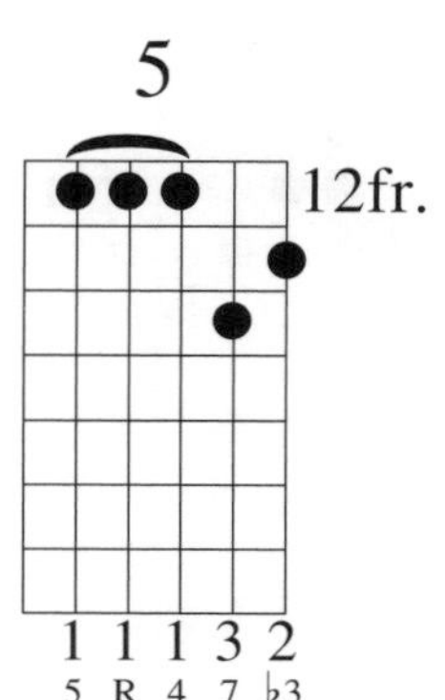

D Harmonic Major
(D E F♯ G A B♭ C♯ D)
Four-Note Quartal

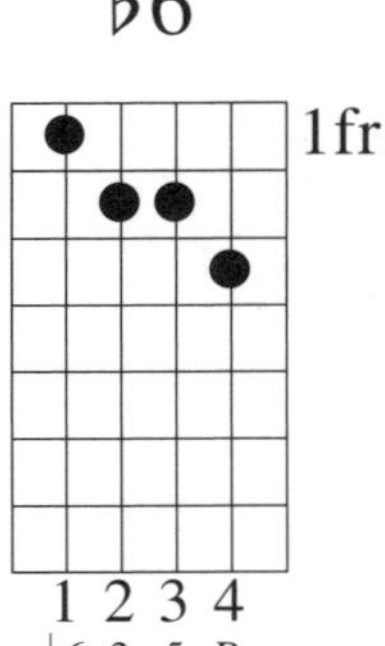

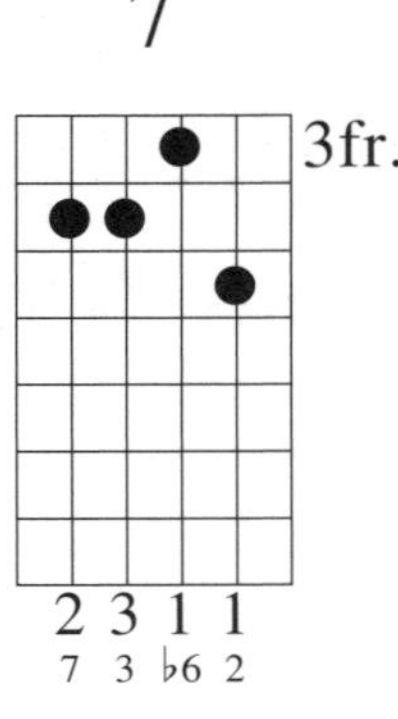

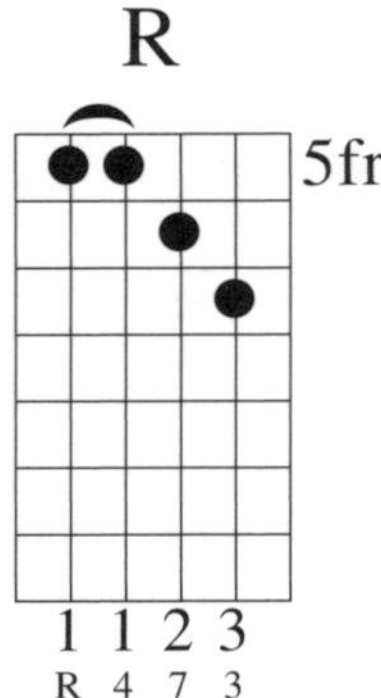

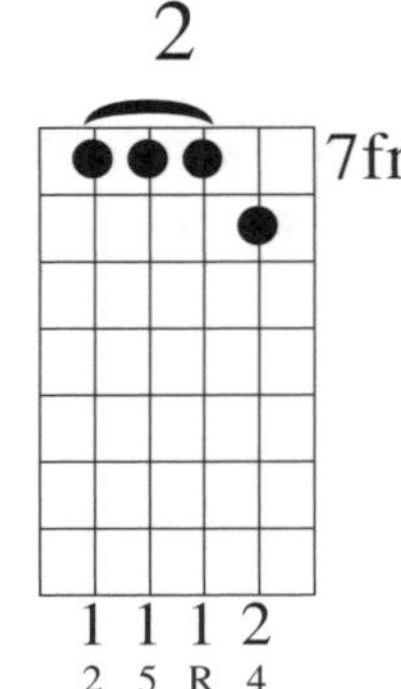

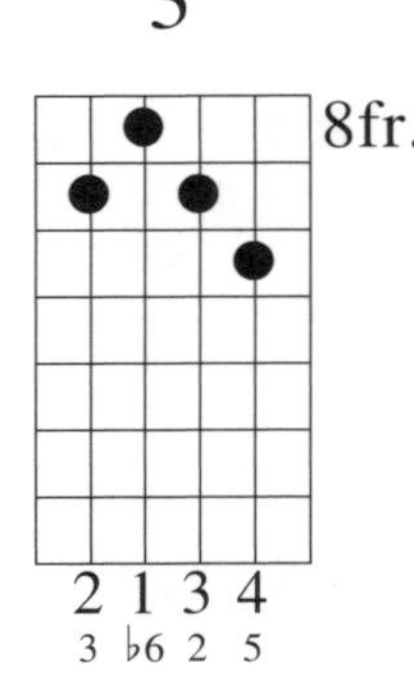

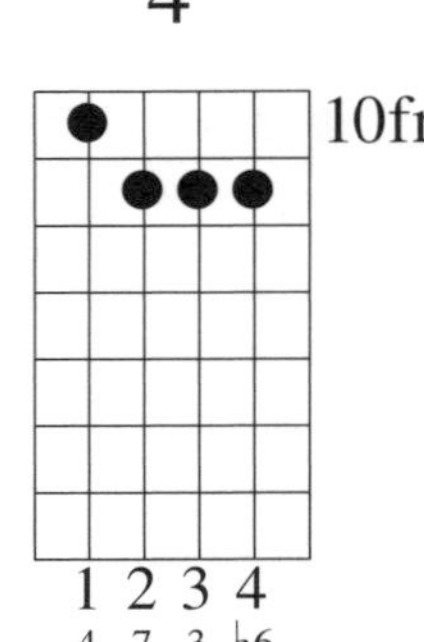

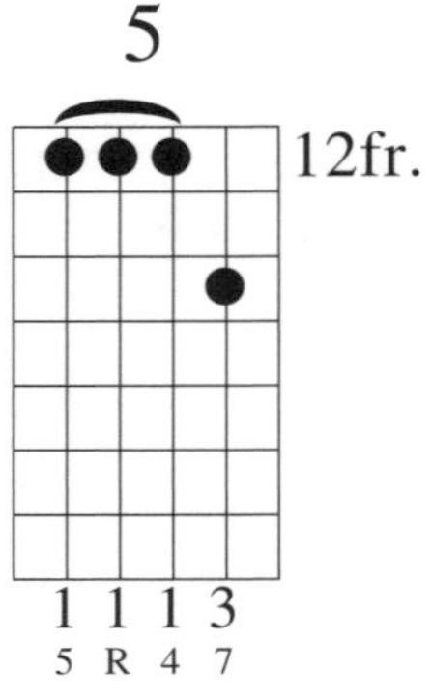

D Harmonic Major
(D E F♯ G A B♭ C♯ D)
Five-Note Quartal

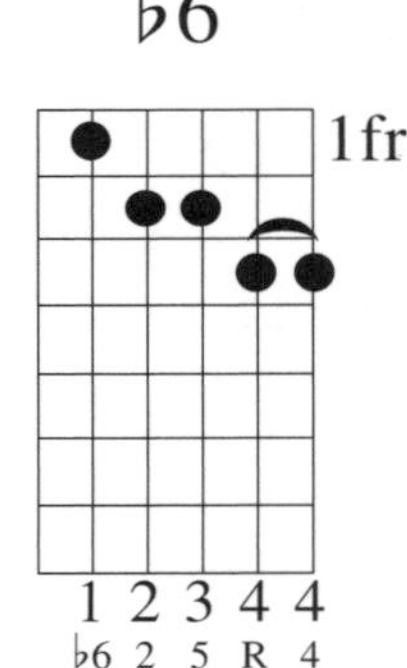

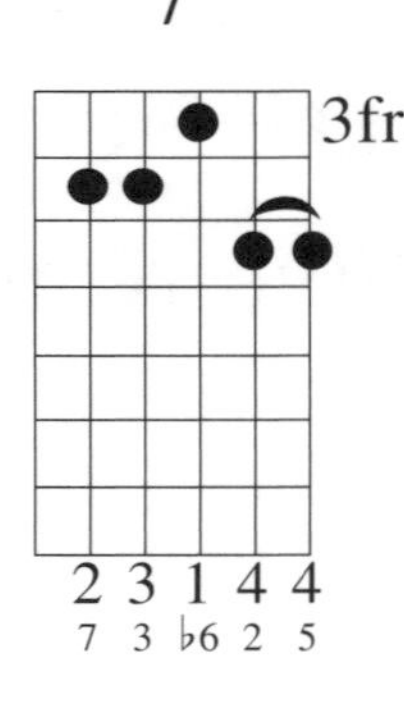

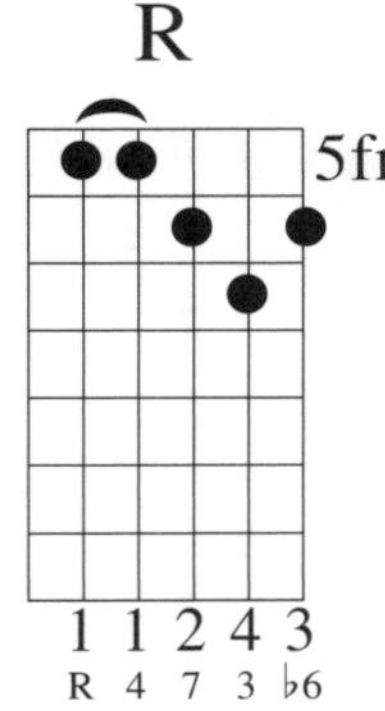

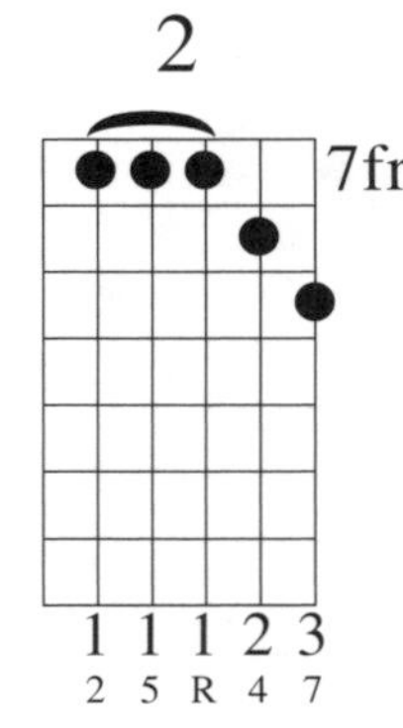

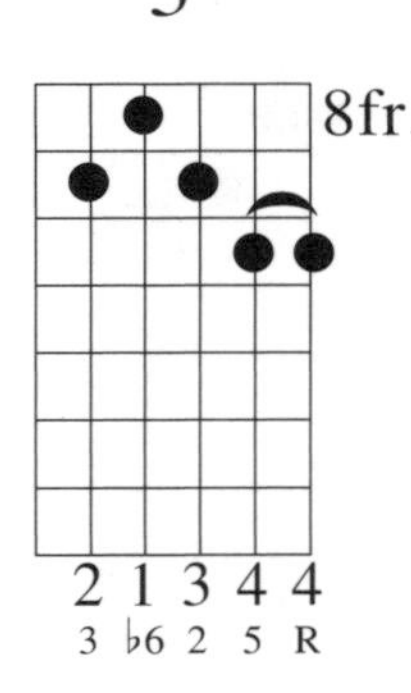

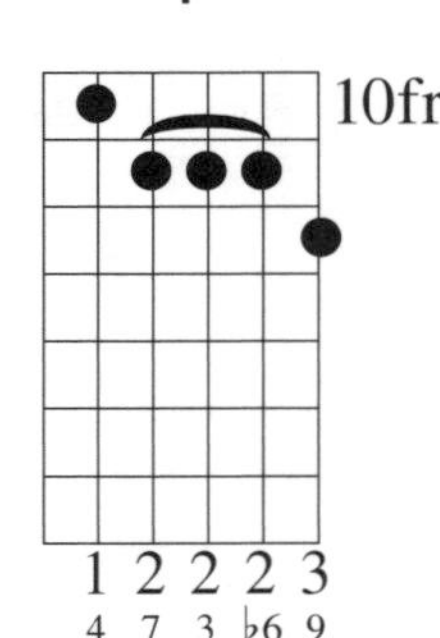

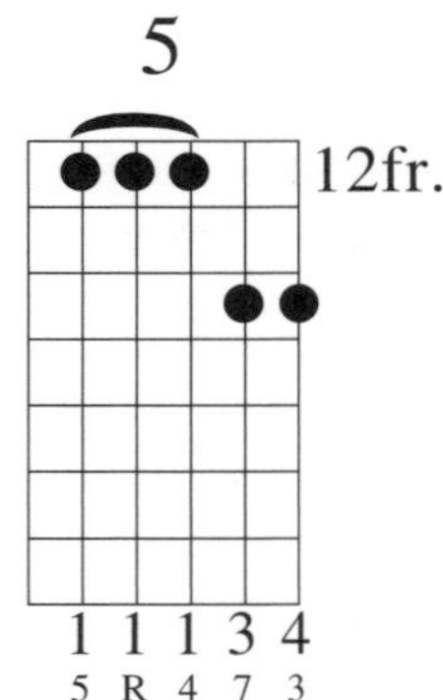

D Major
(D E F♯ G A B C♯ D)
Three-Note Quintal

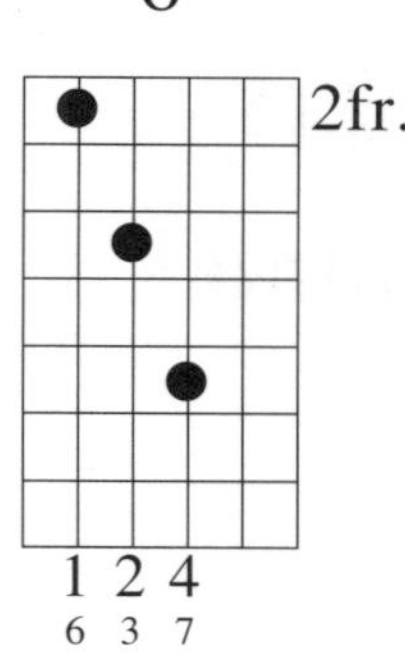

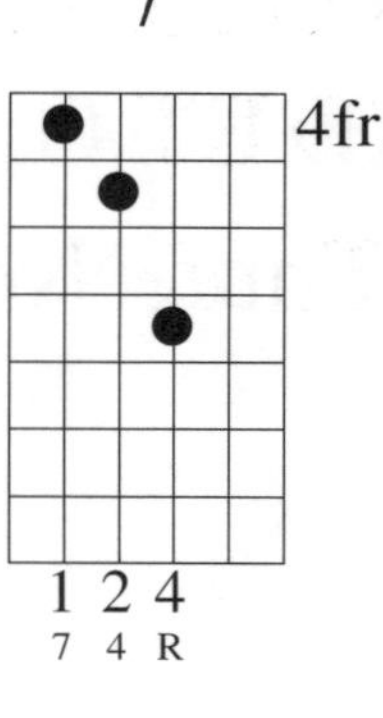

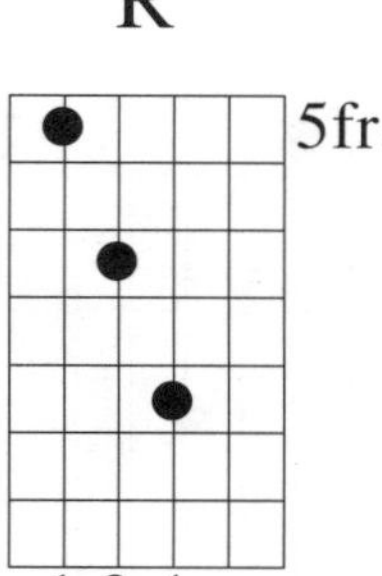

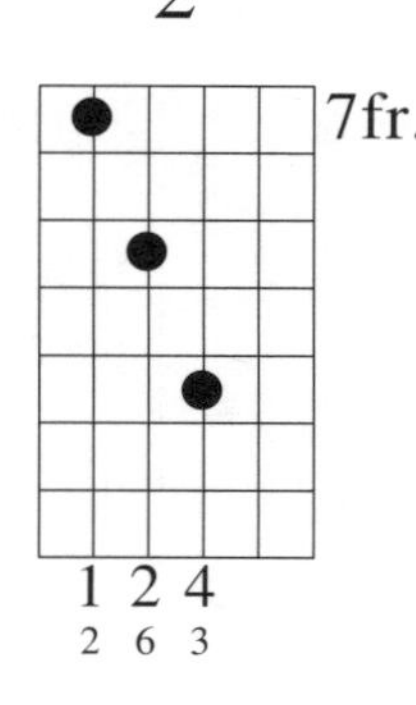

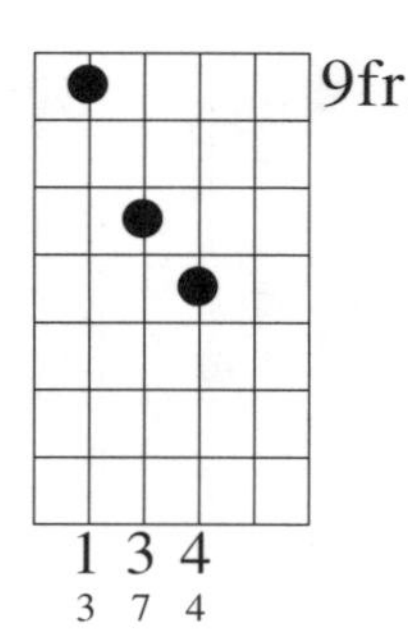

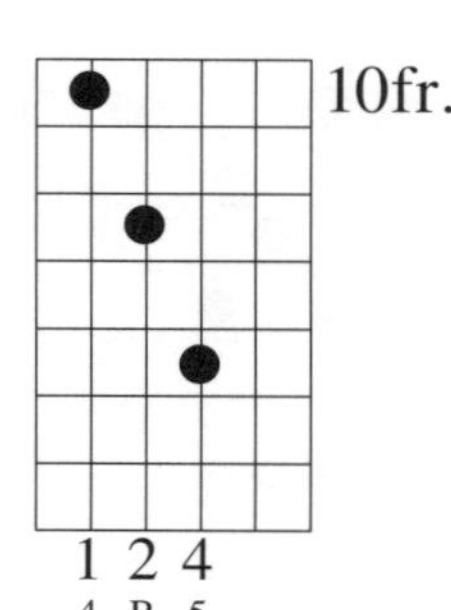

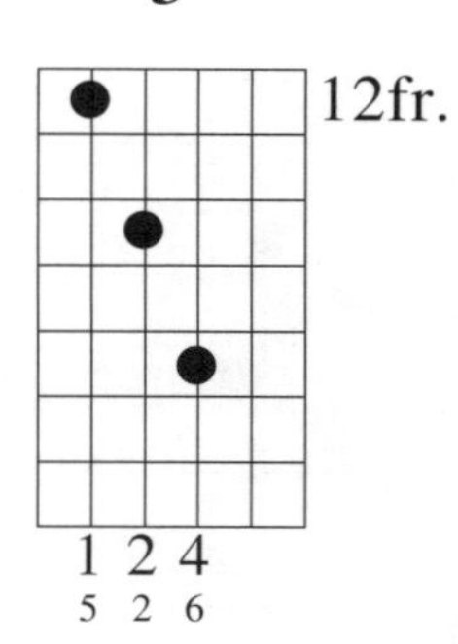

D Major
(D E F♯ G A B C♯ D)
Four-Note Quintal

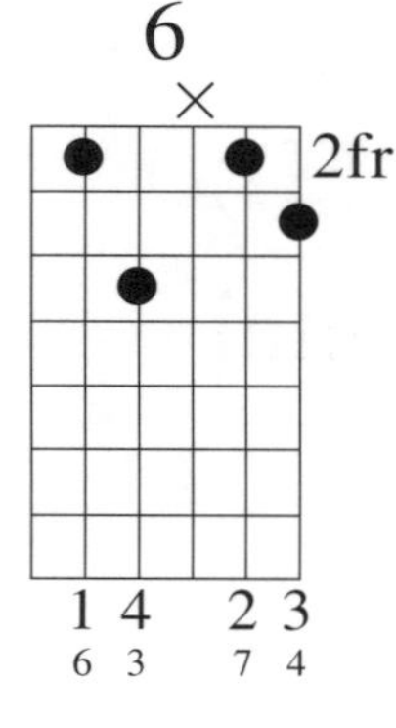

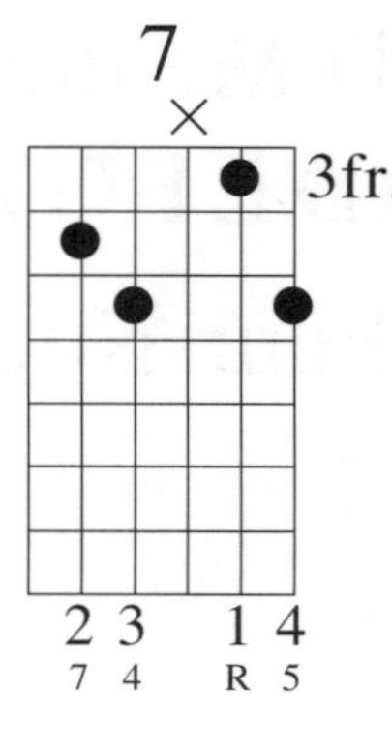

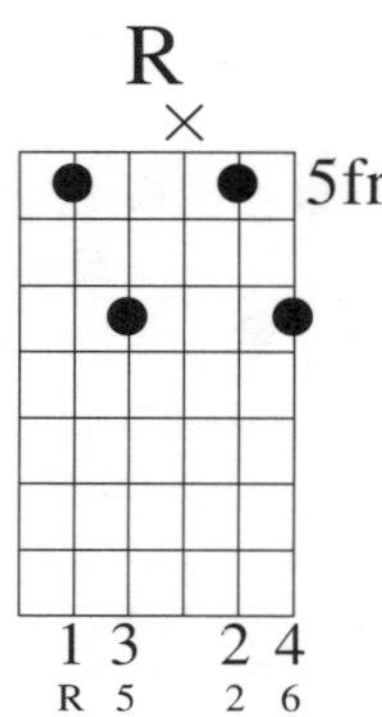

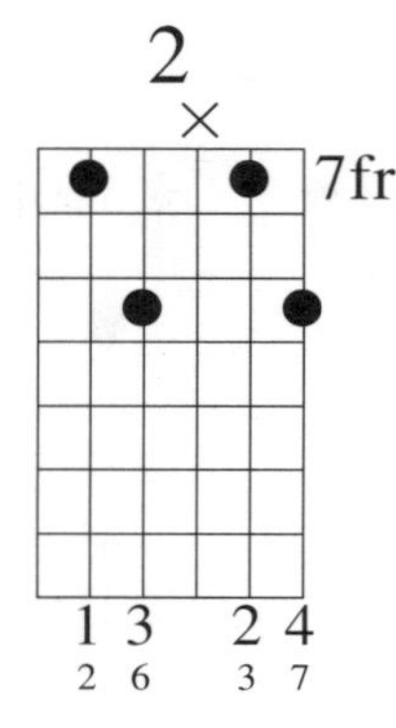

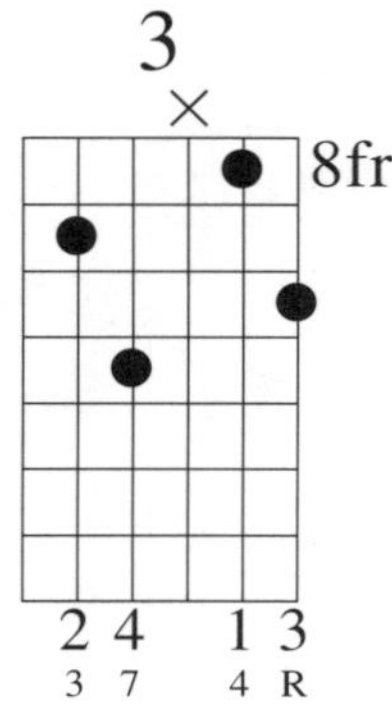

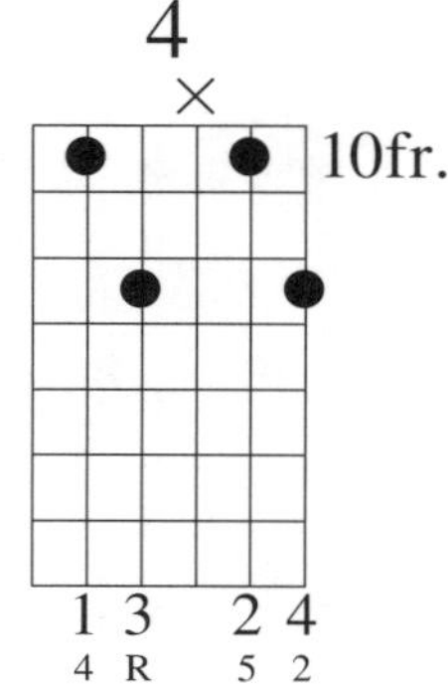

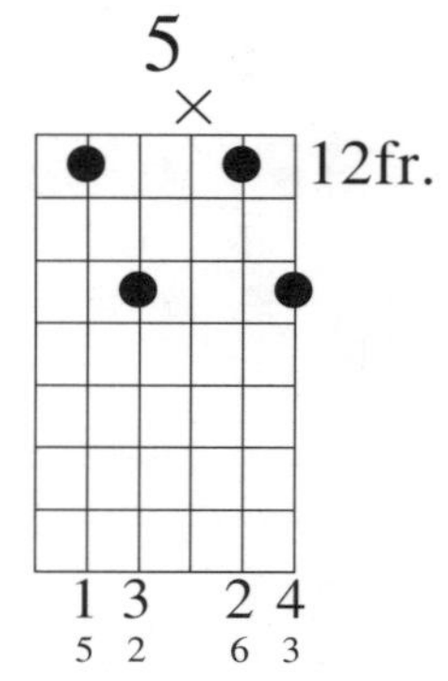

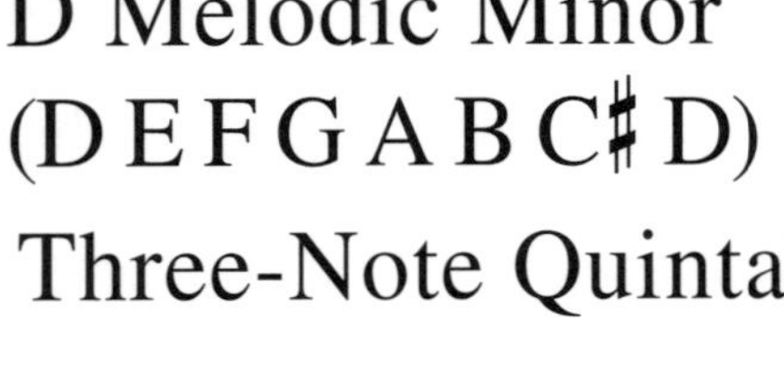

D Melodic Minor (D E F G A B C♯ D) Three-Note Quintal

6

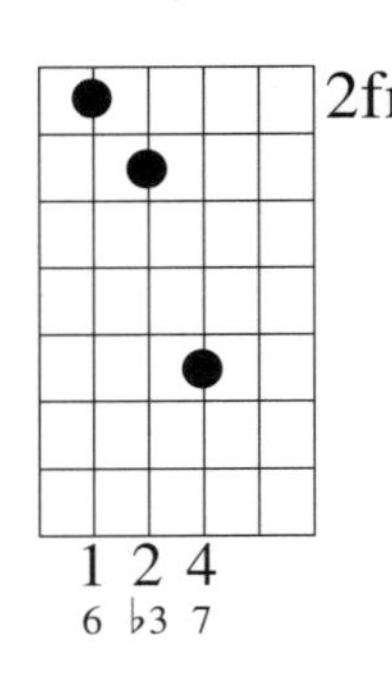

7

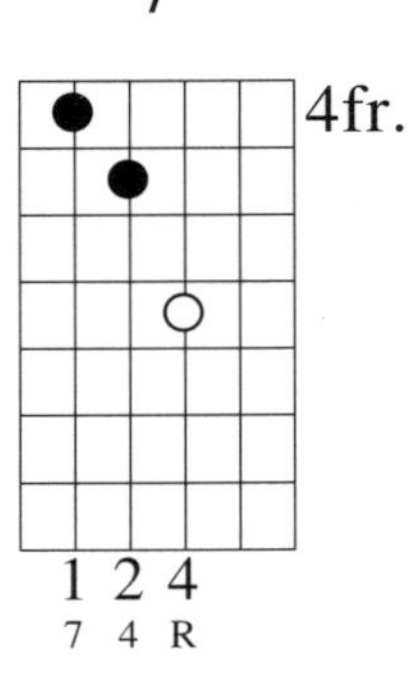

R

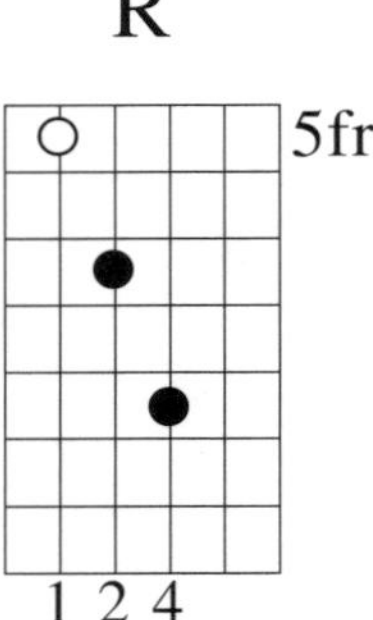

2

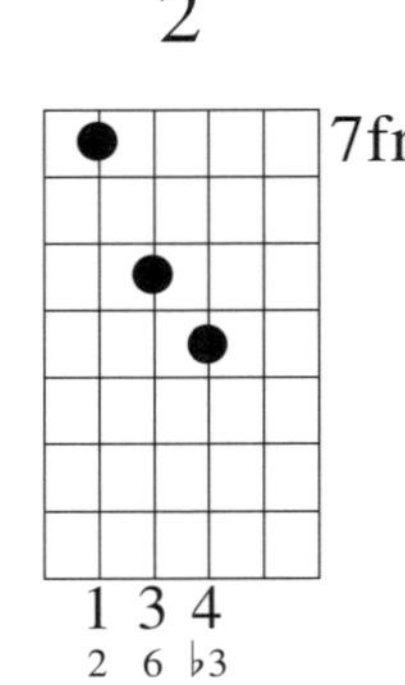

♭3

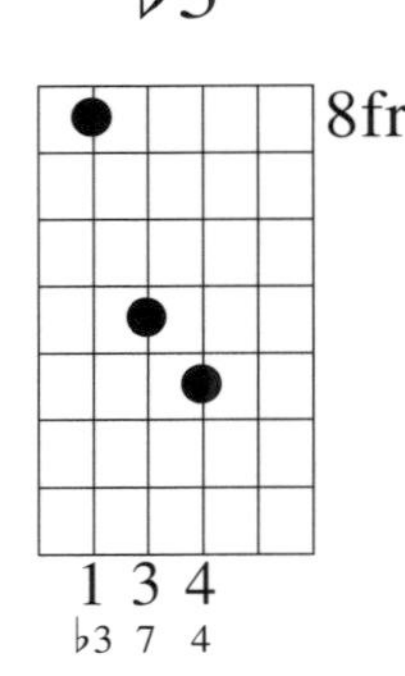

4

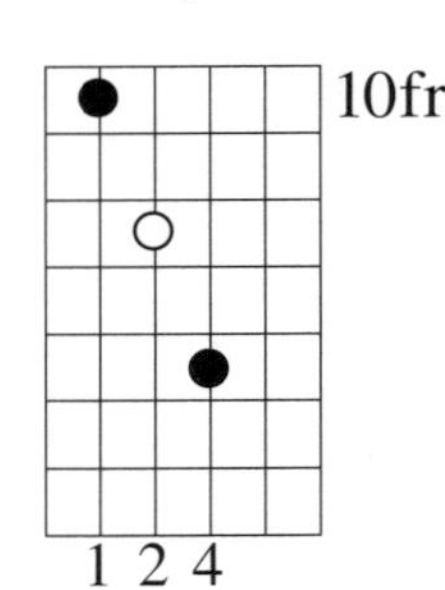

5

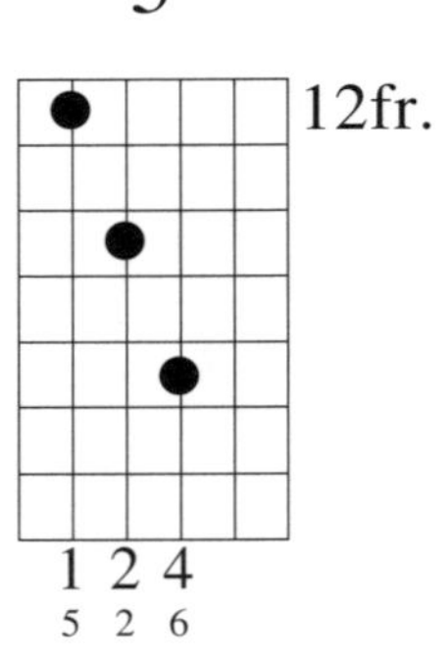

D Melodic Minor (D E F G A B C♯ D) Four-Note Quintal

6

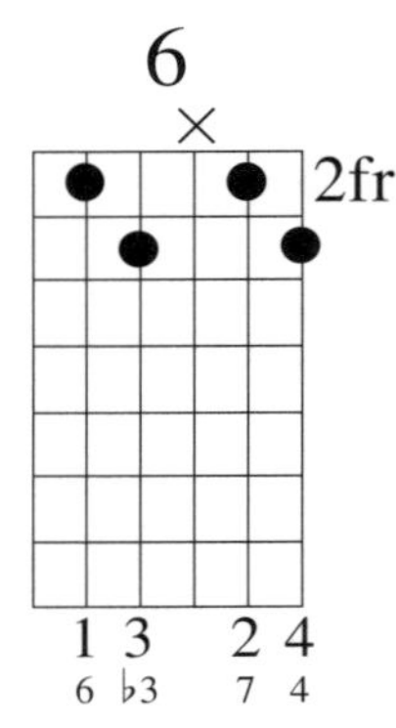

7

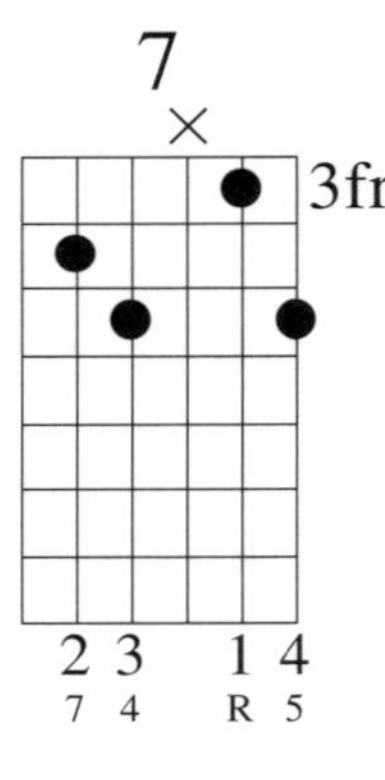

R

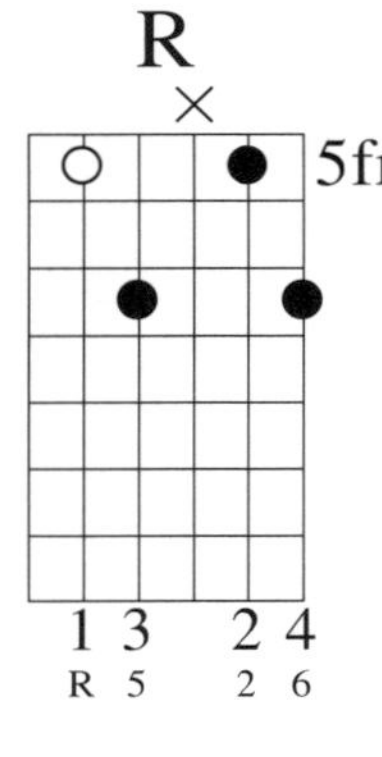

2

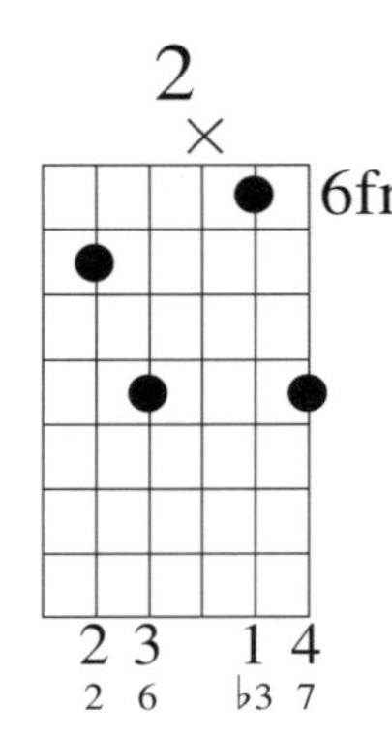

♭3

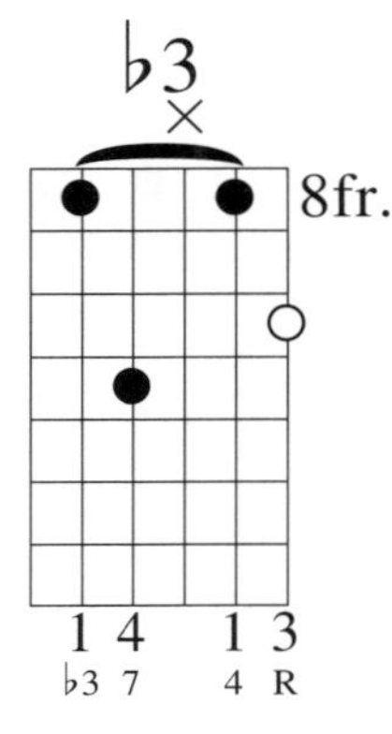

4

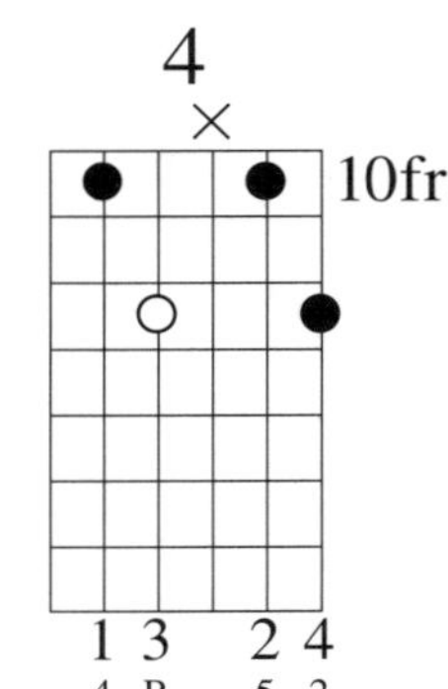

5

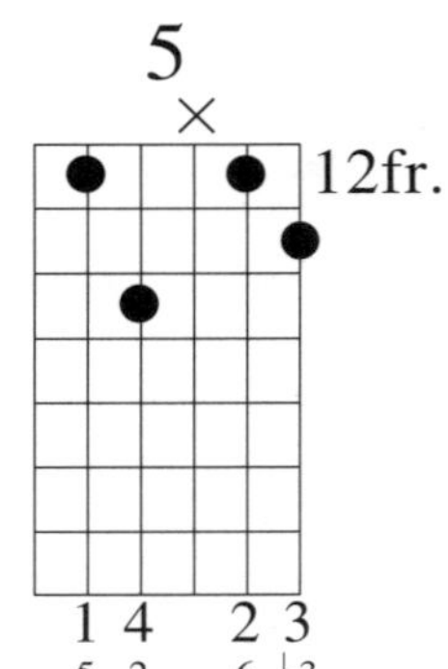

D Harmonic Minor (D E F G A B♭ C♯ D) Three-Note Quintal

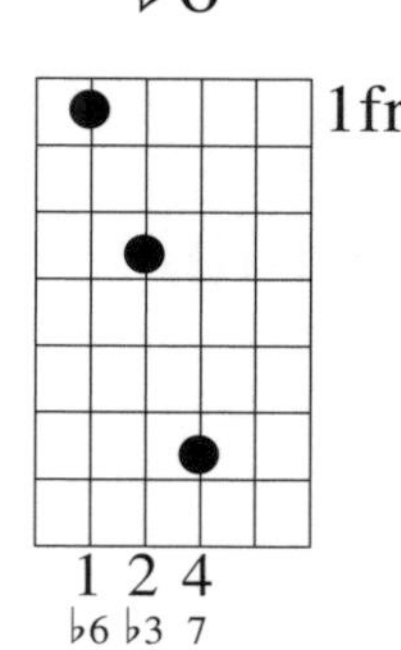

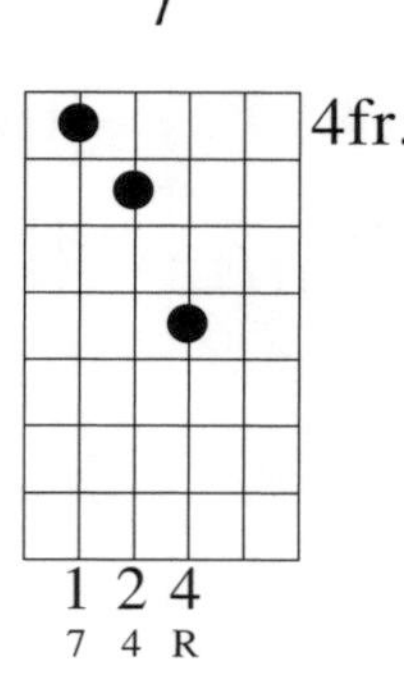

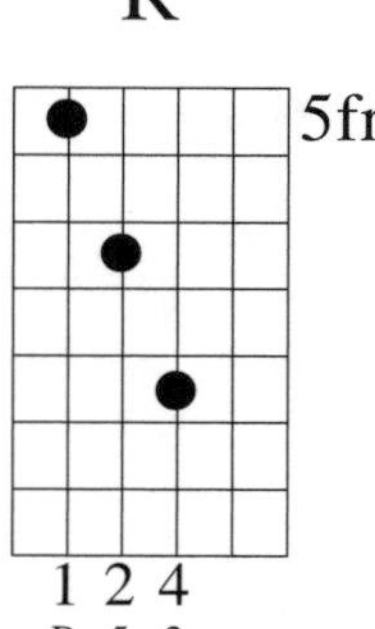

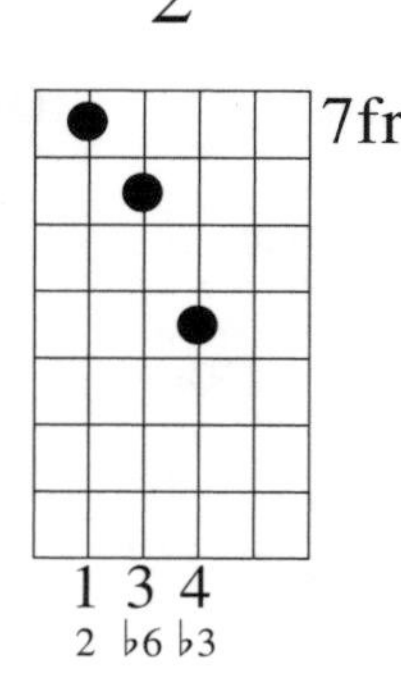

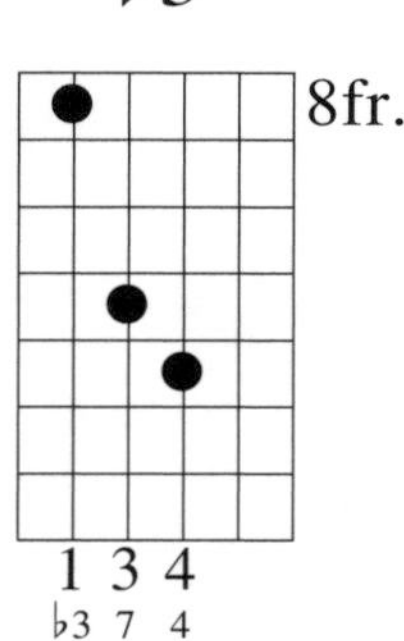

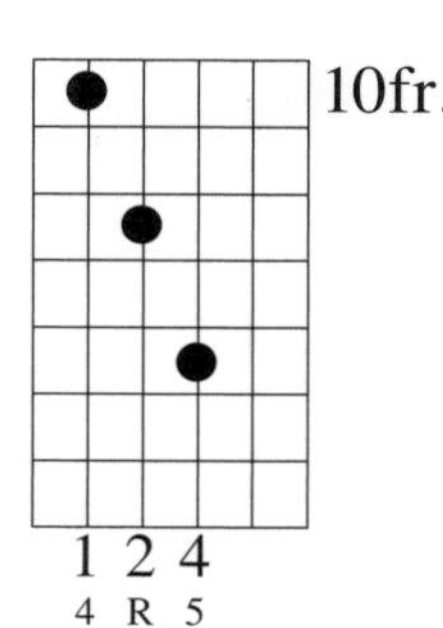

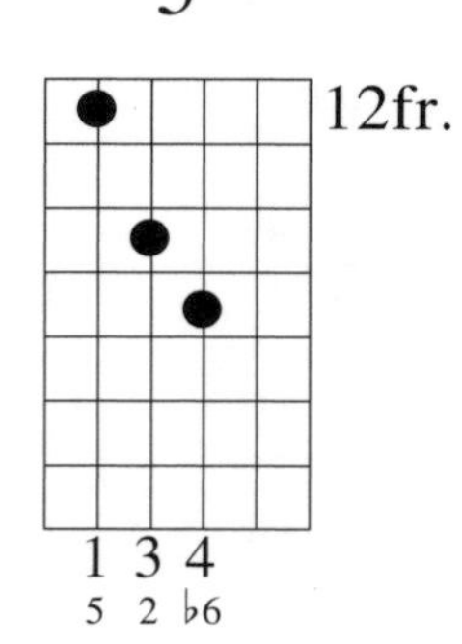

D Harmonic Minor (D E F G A B♭ C♯ D) Four-Note Quintal

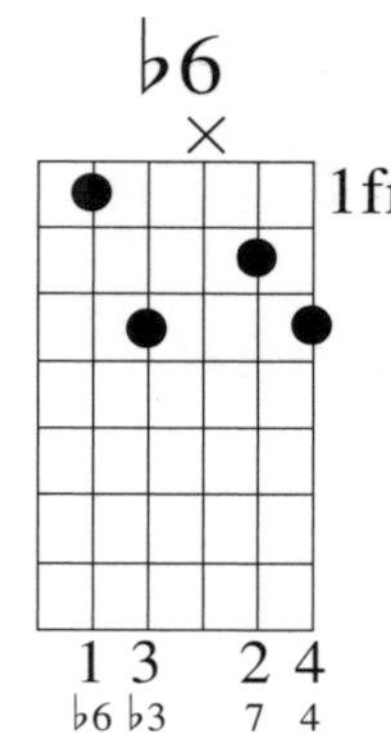

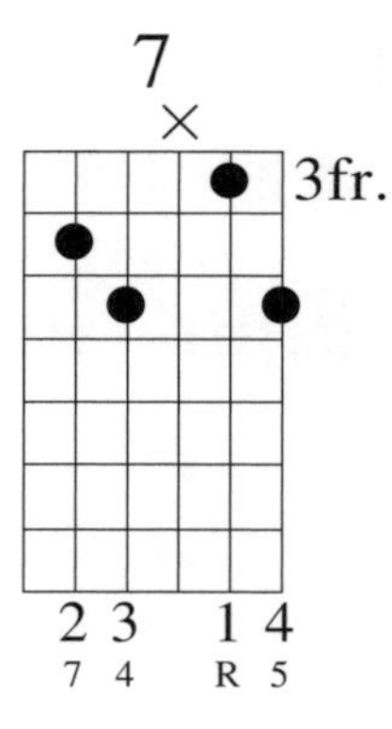

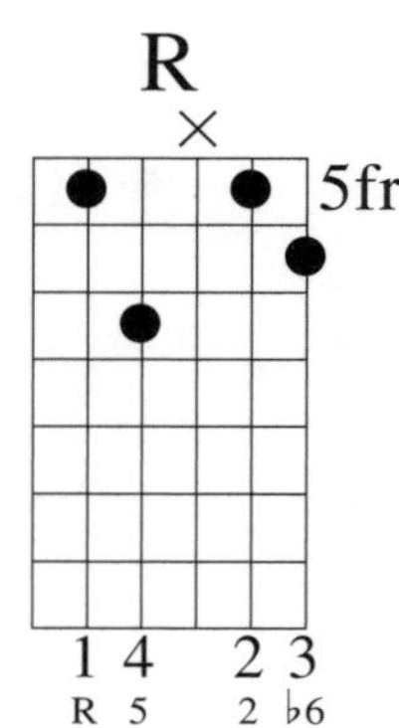

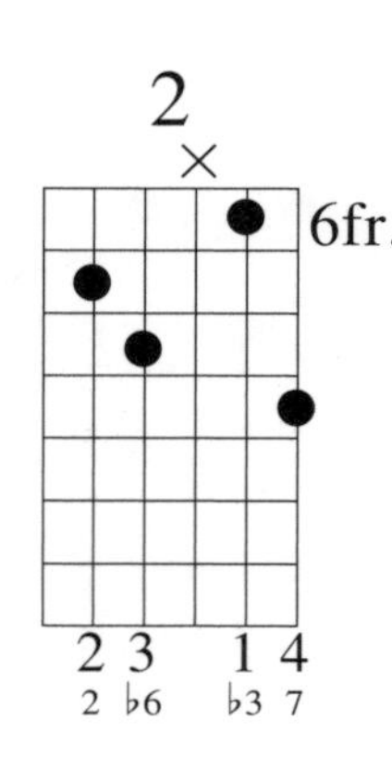

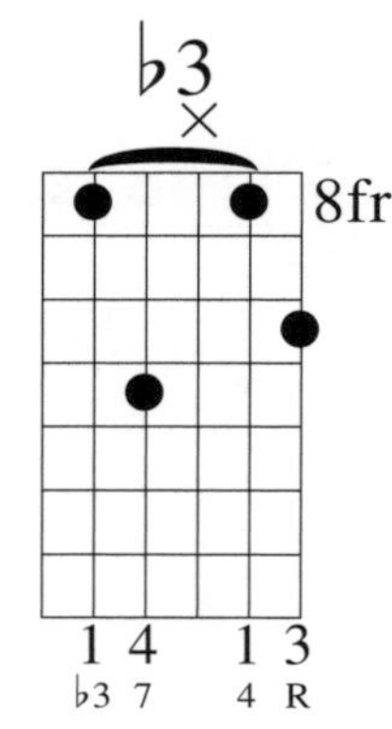

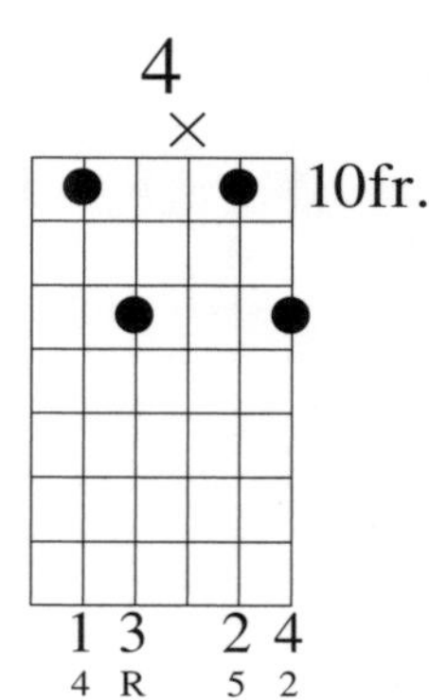

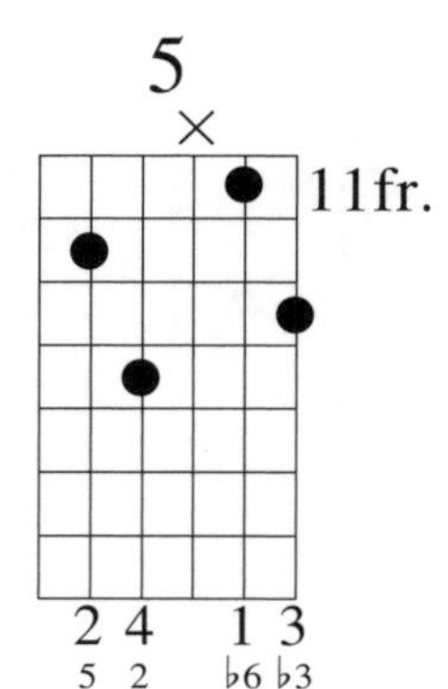

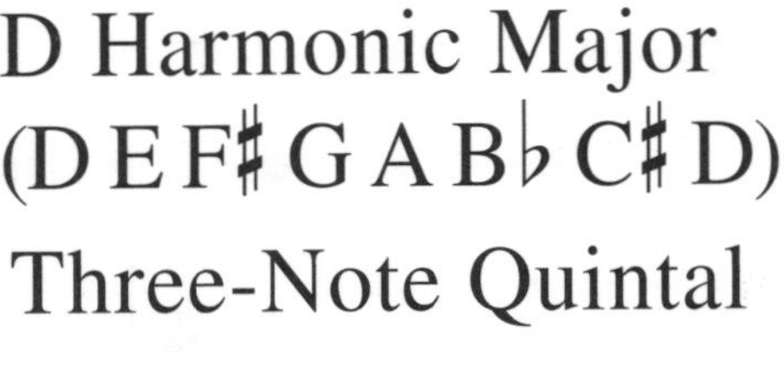

D Harmonic Major
(D E F♯ G A B♭ C♯ D)
Three-Note Quintal

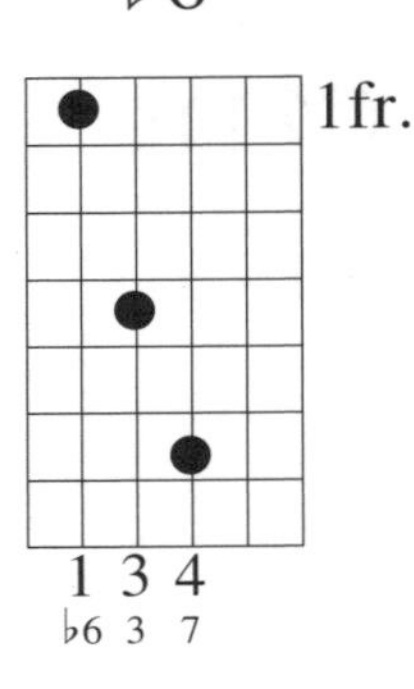

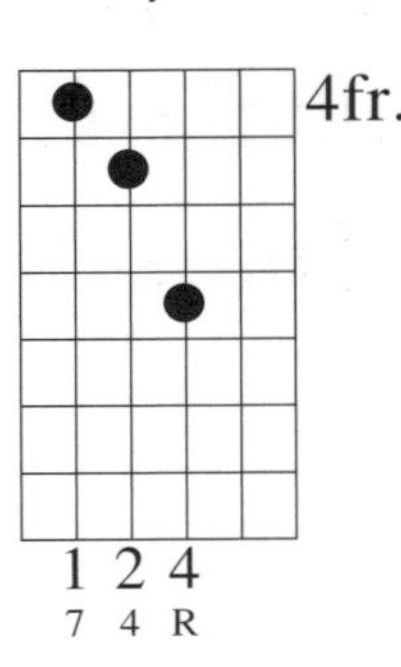

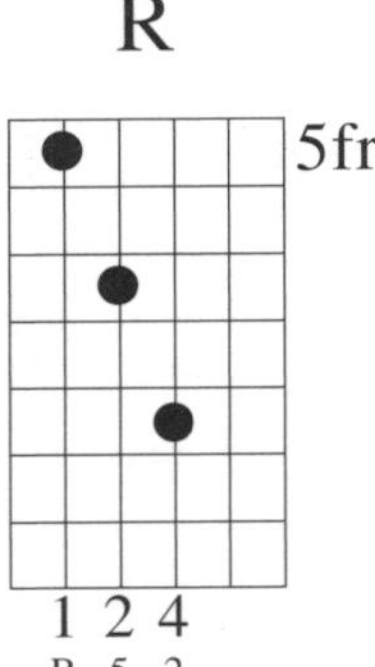

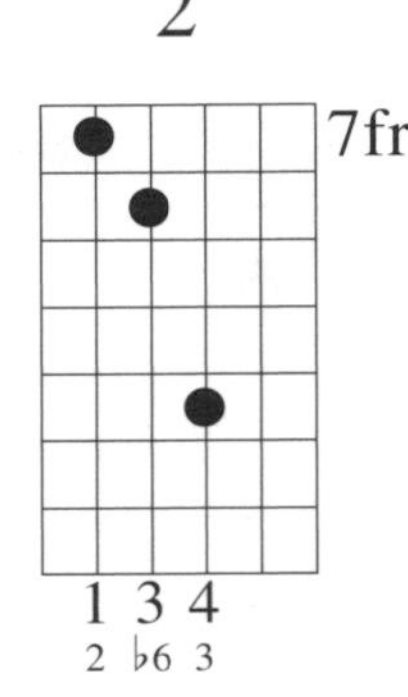

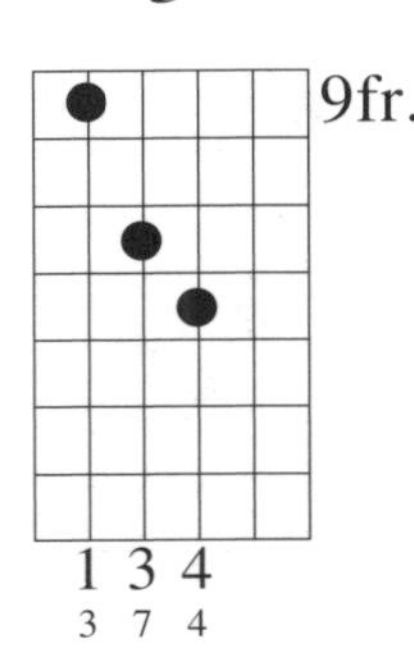

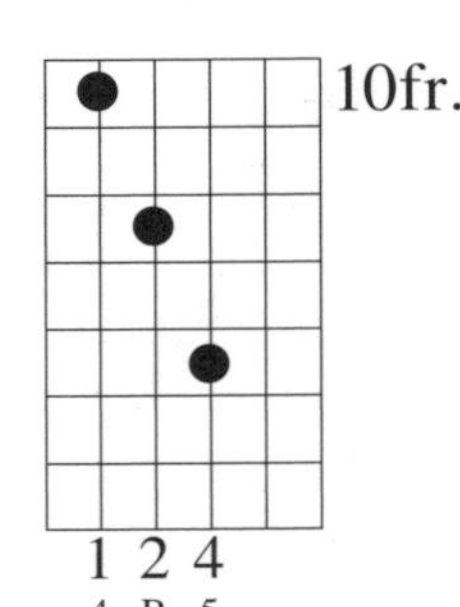

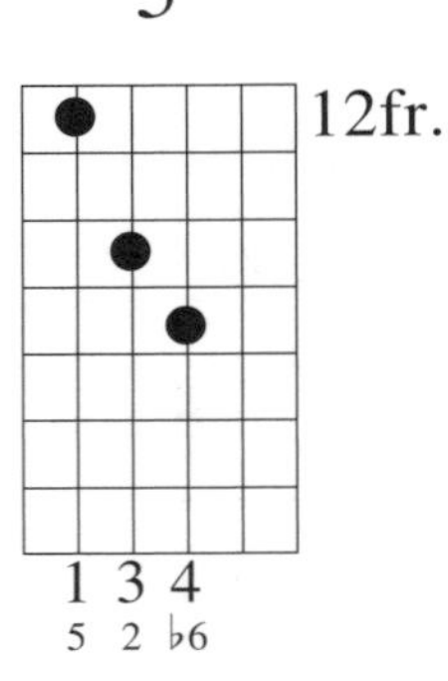

D Harmonic Major
(D E F♯ G A B♭ C♯ D)
Four-Note Quintal

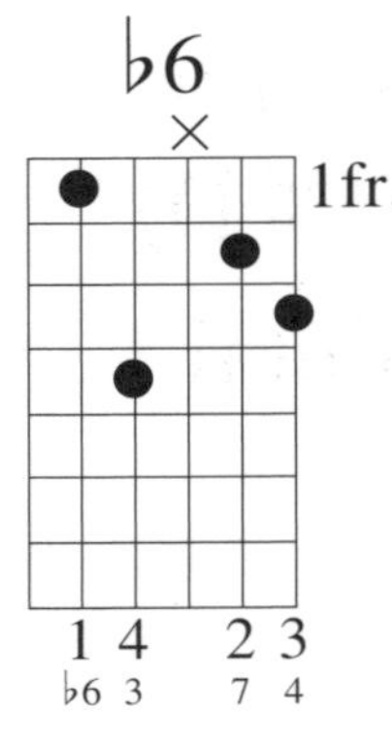

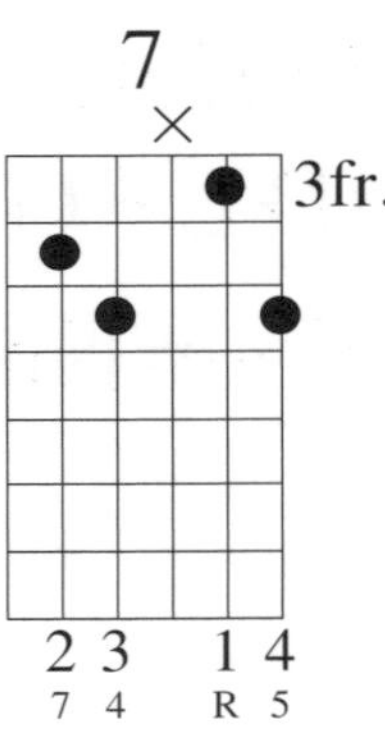

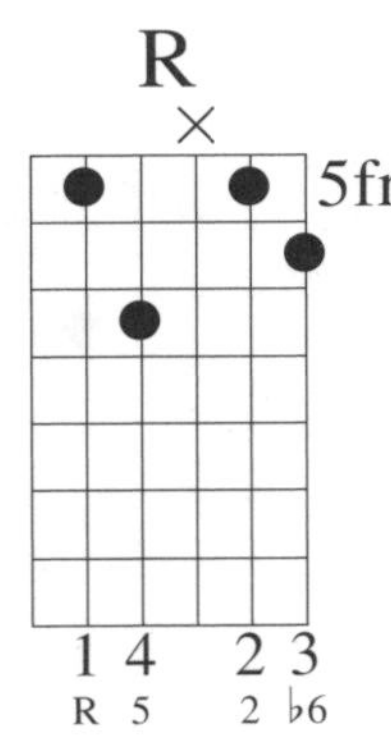

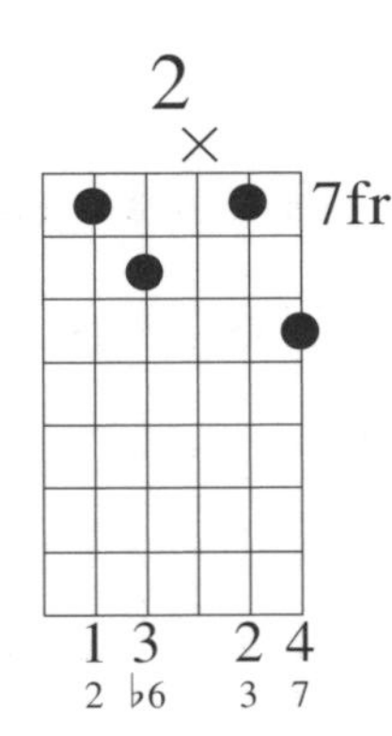

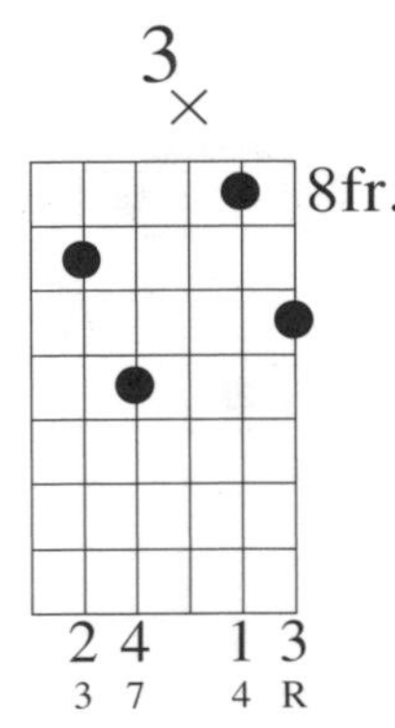

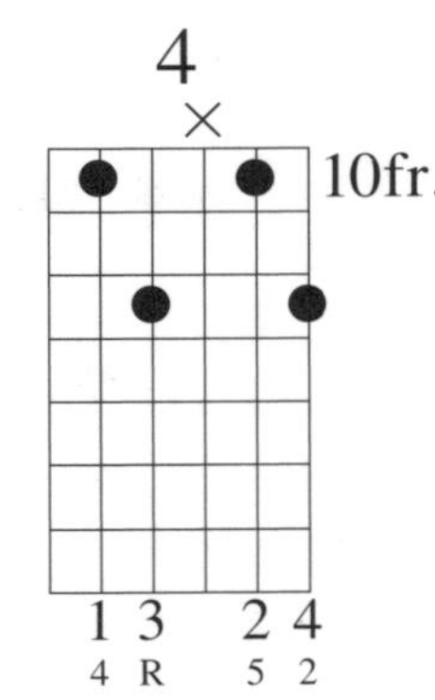

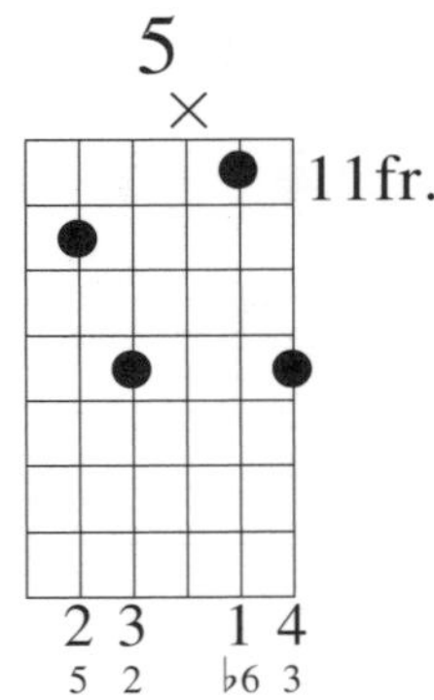

D Major
(D E F♯ G A B C♯ D)
Inverted Clusters

R

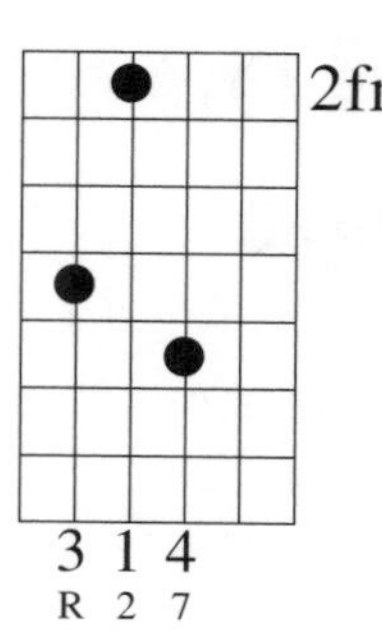

2

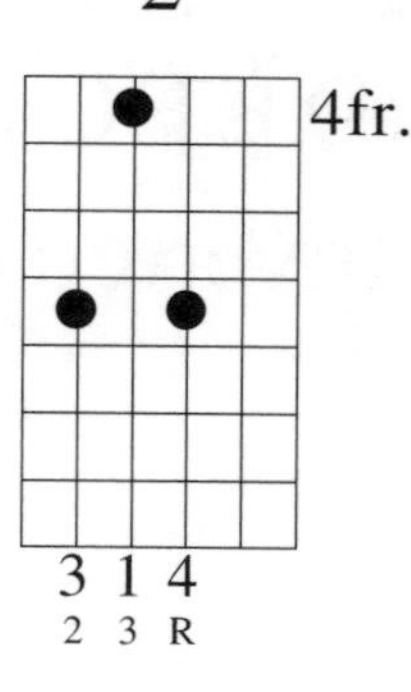

3

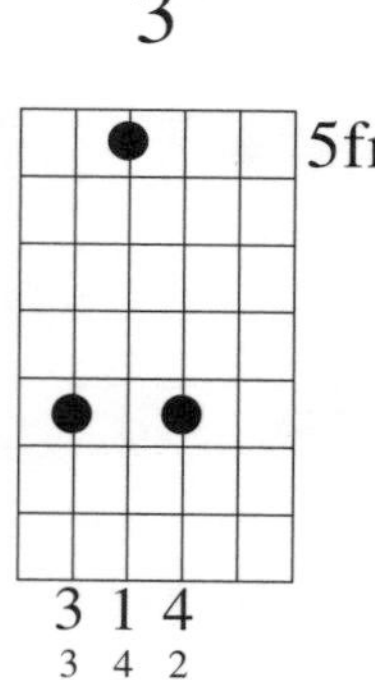

4

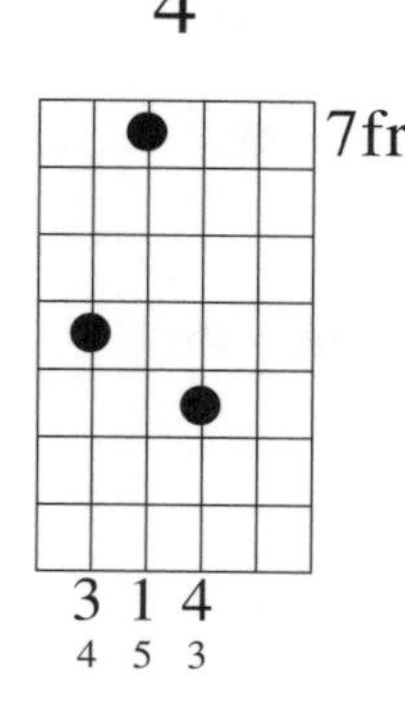

5

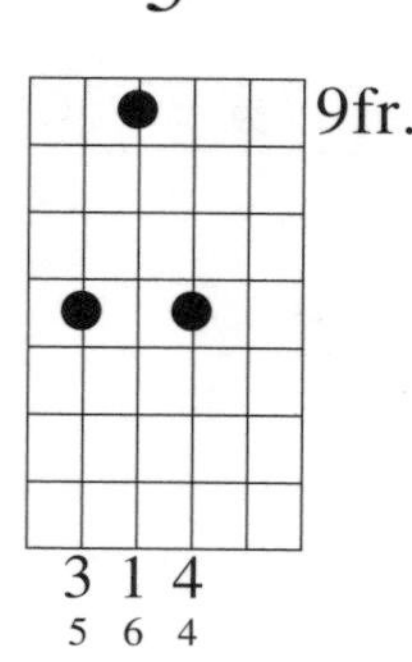

6

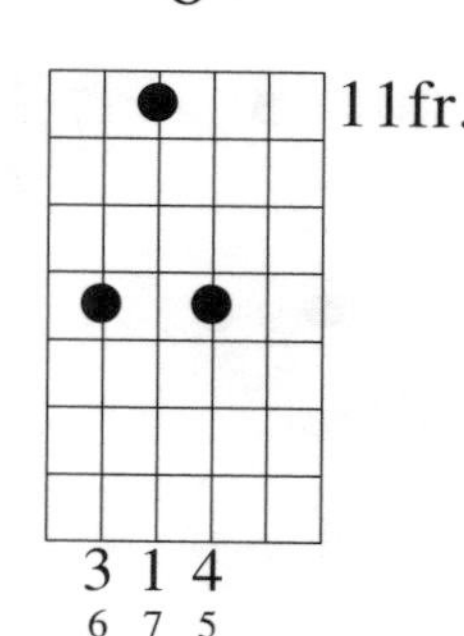

7

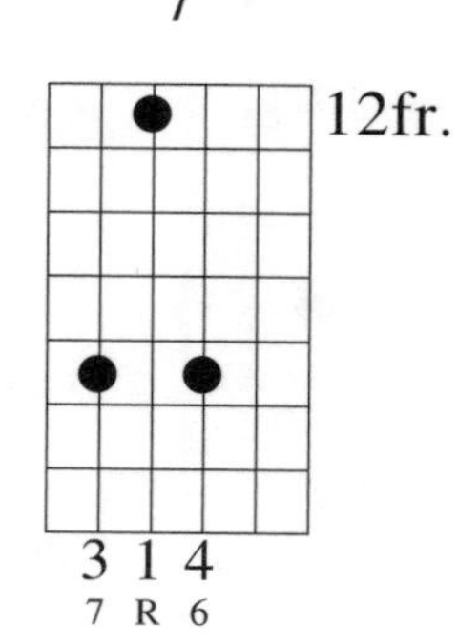

D Major
(D E F♯ G A B C♯ D)
Inverted Clusters

4

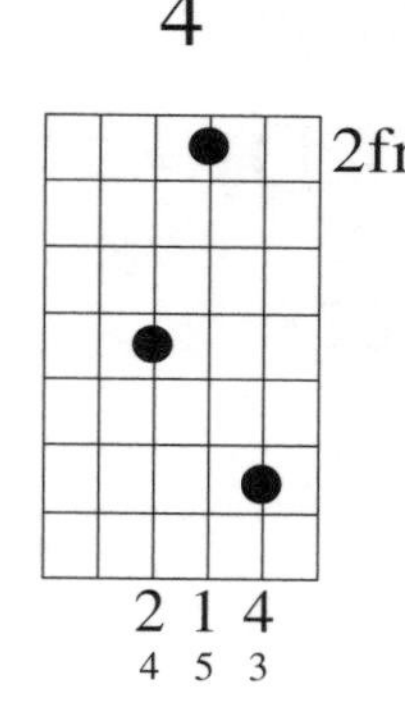

5

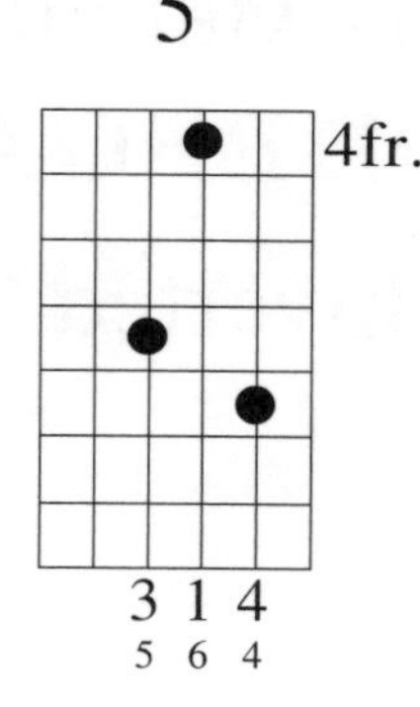

6

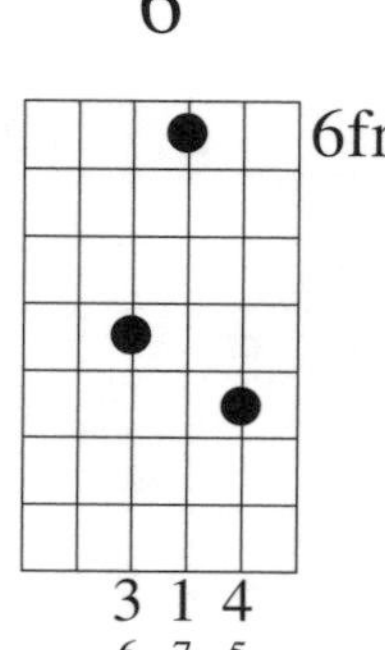

7

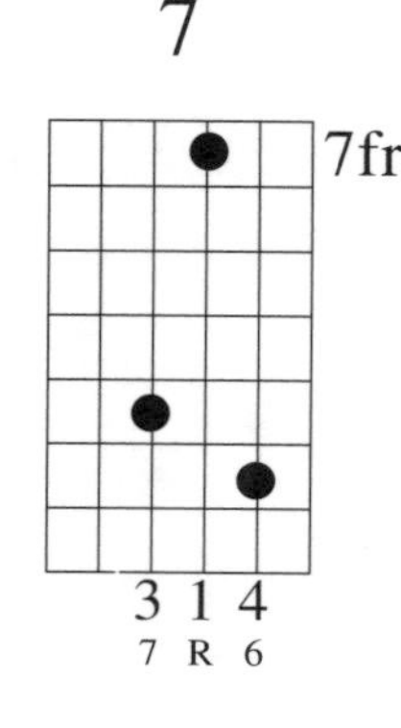

R

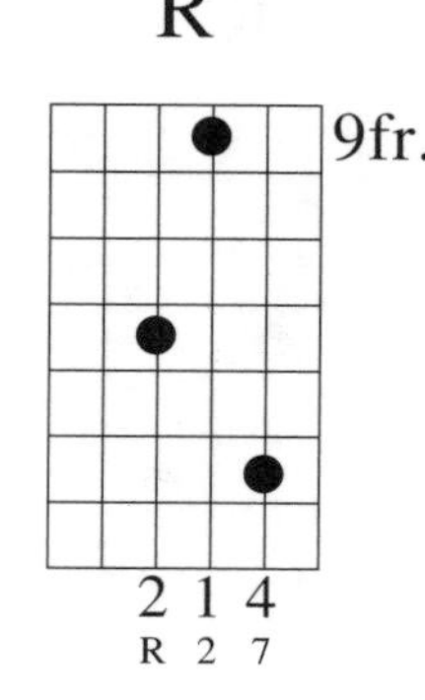

2

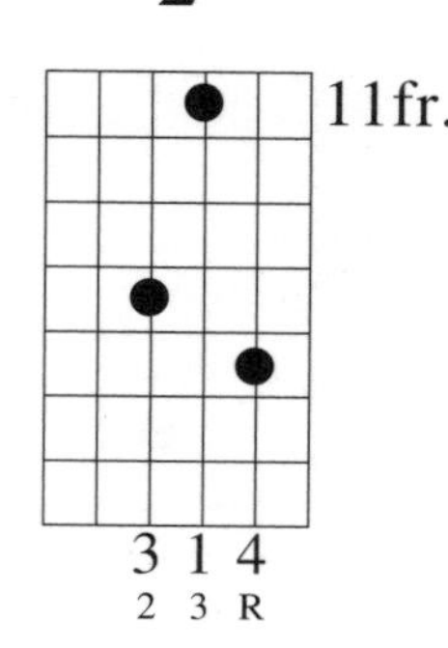

3

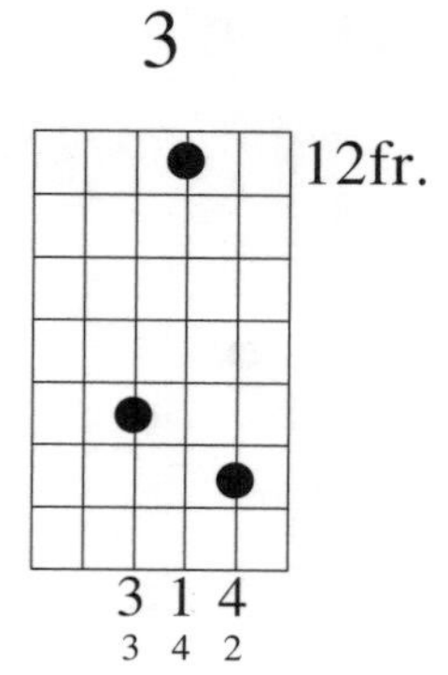

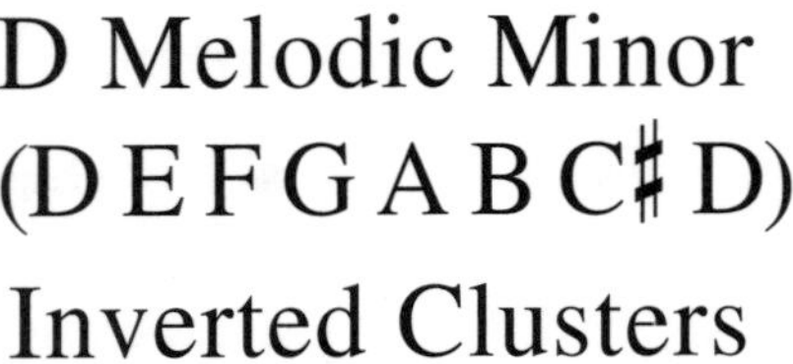

D Melodic Minor
(D E F G A B C♯ D)
Inverted Clusters

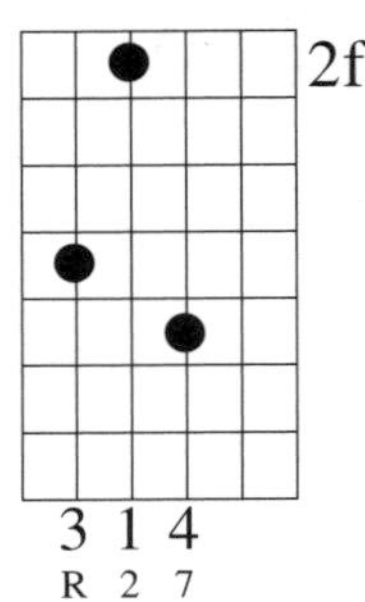

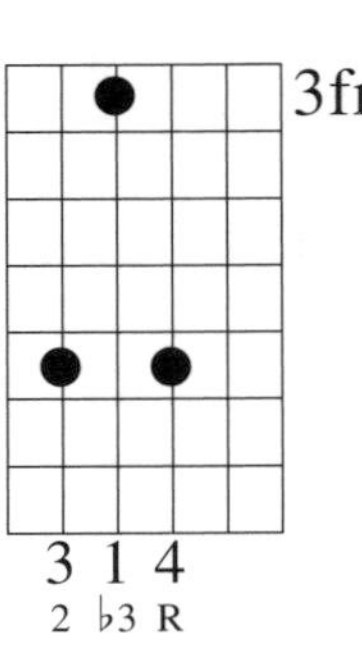

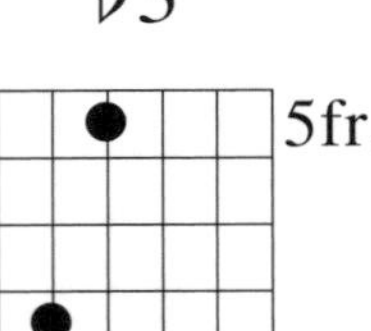

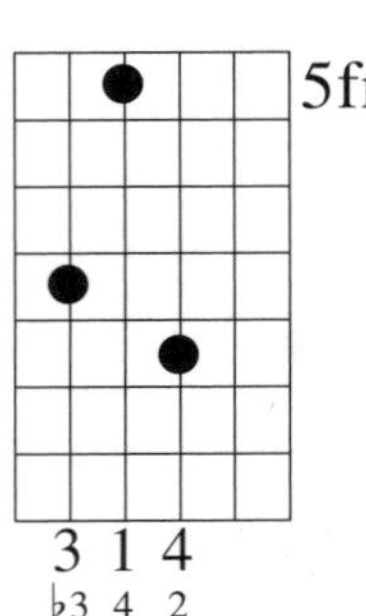

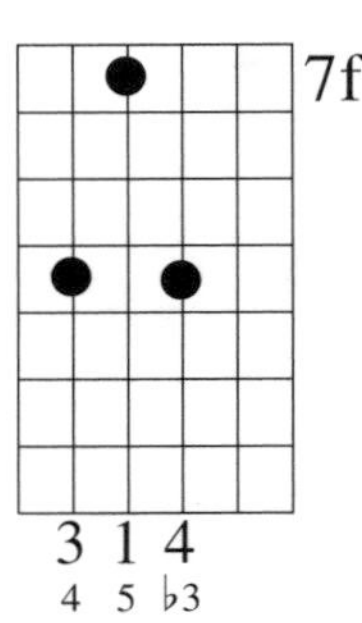

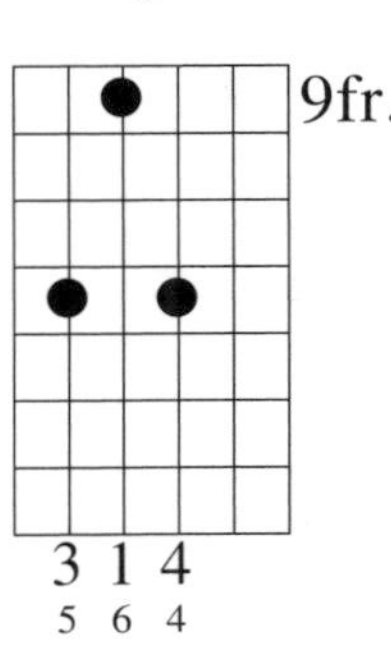

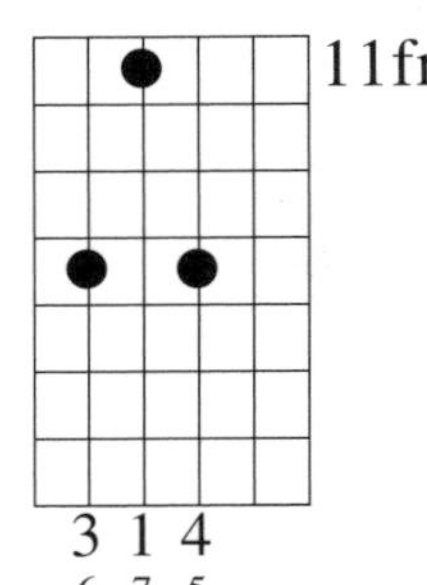

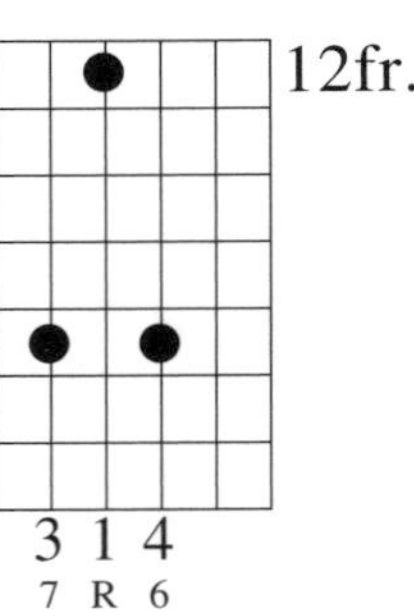

D Melodic Minor
(D E F G A B C♯ D)
Inverted Clusters

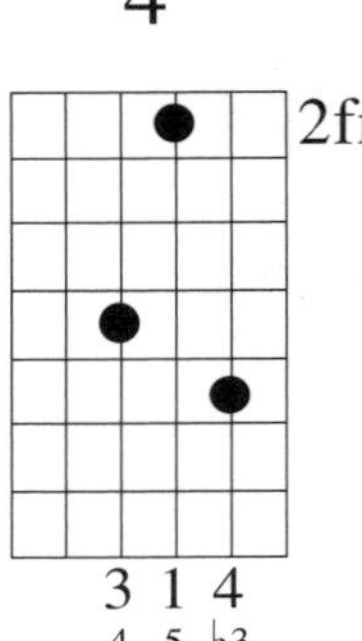

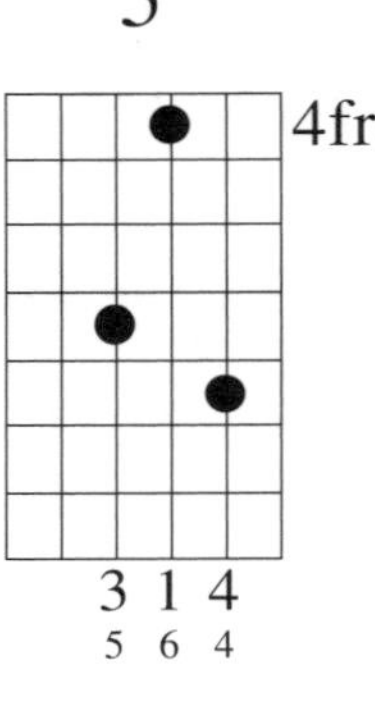

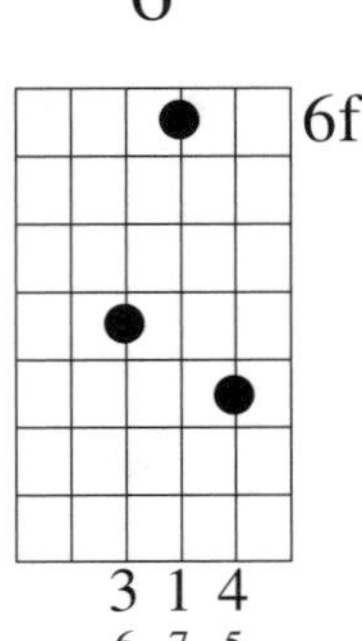

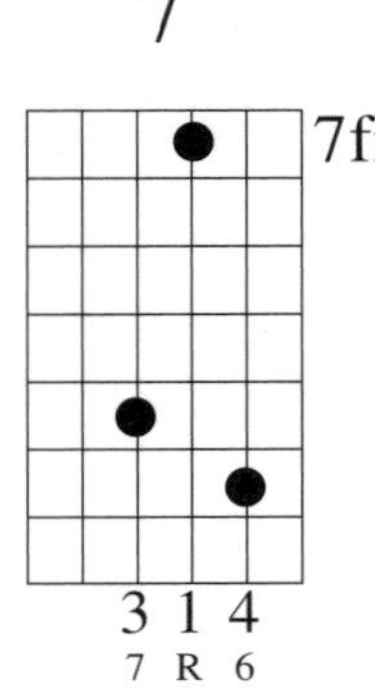

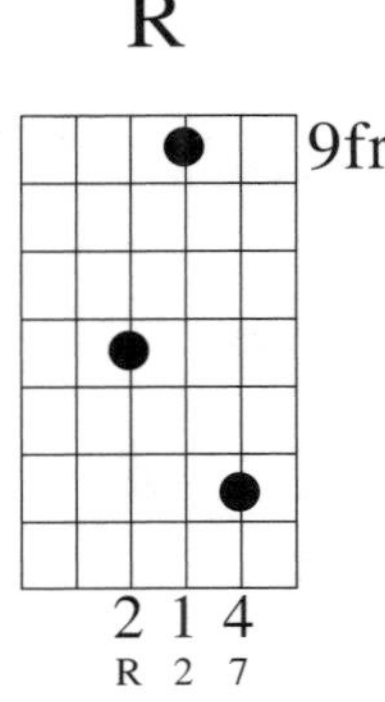

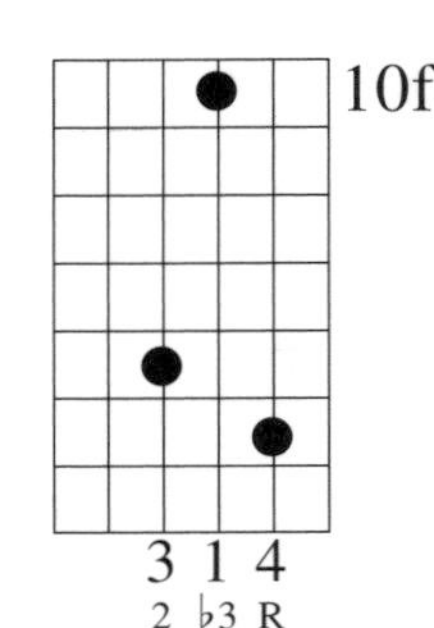

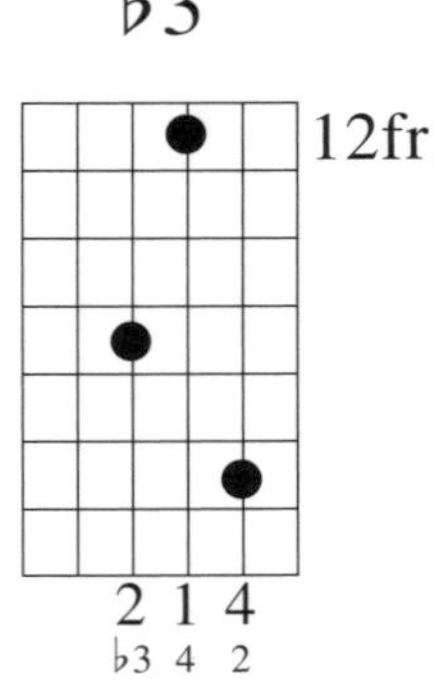

D Harmonic Minor
(D E F G A B♭ C♯ D)
Inverted Clusters

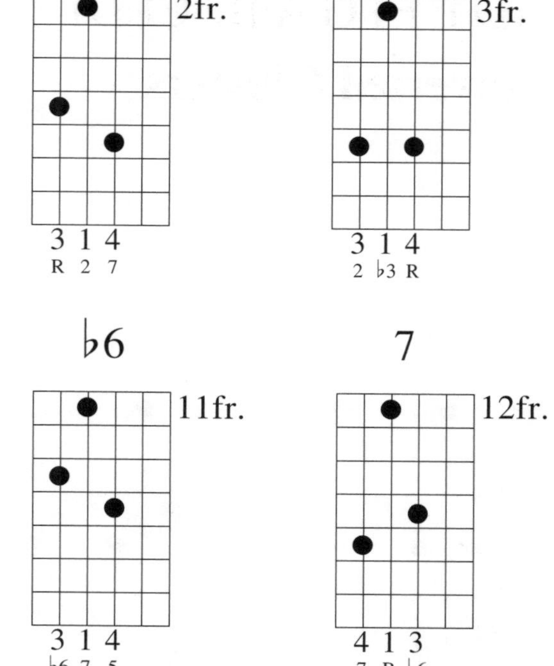

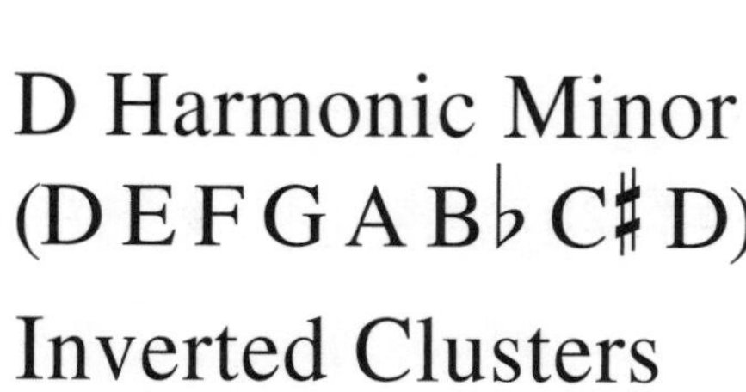

D Harmonic Minor
(D E F G A B♭ C♯ D)
Inverted Clusters

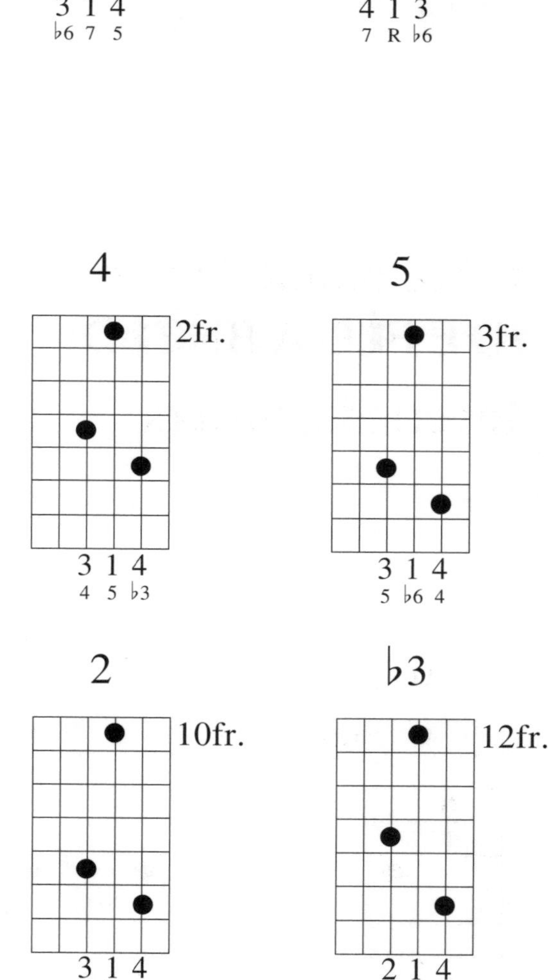

D Harmonic Major (D E F♯ G A B♭ C♯ D)

Inverted Clusters

R

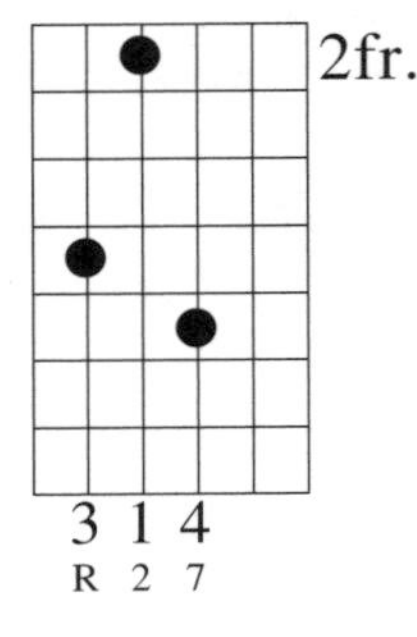

2

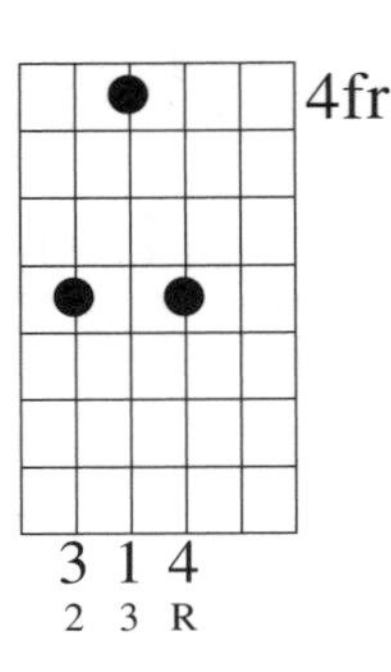

3

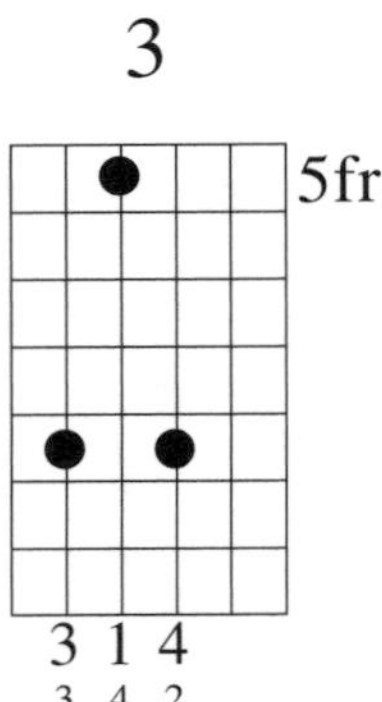

4

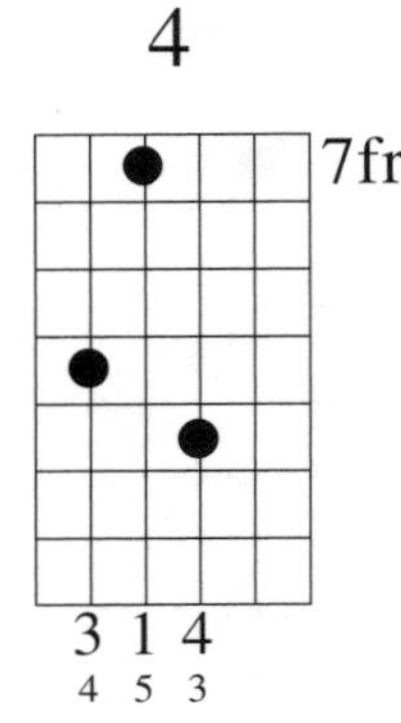

5

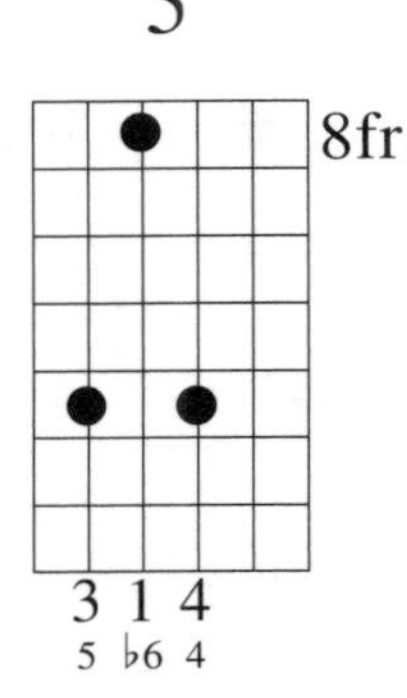

♭6

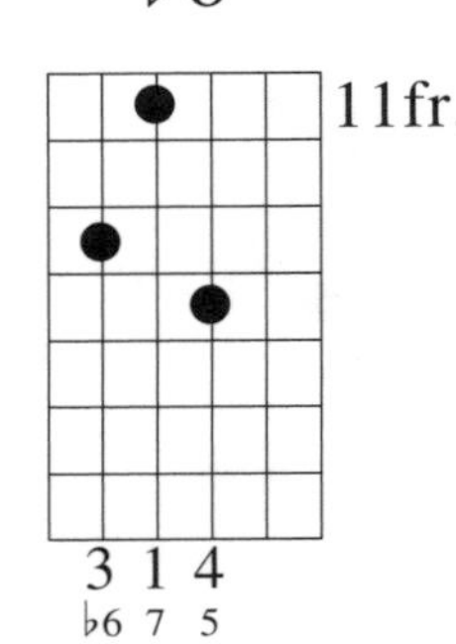

7

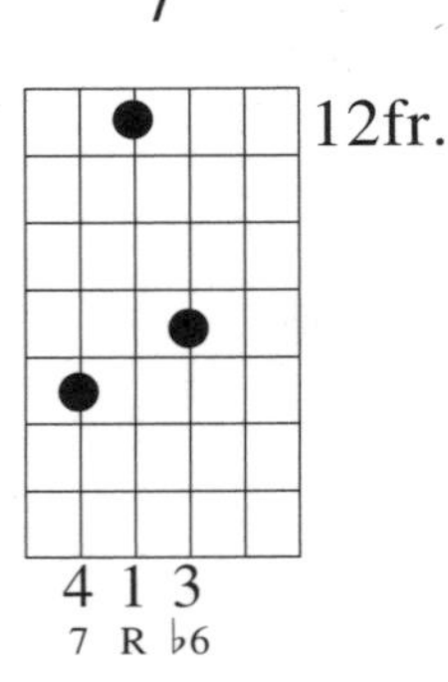

D Harmonic Major (D E F♯ G A B♭ C♯ D)

Inverted Clusters

4

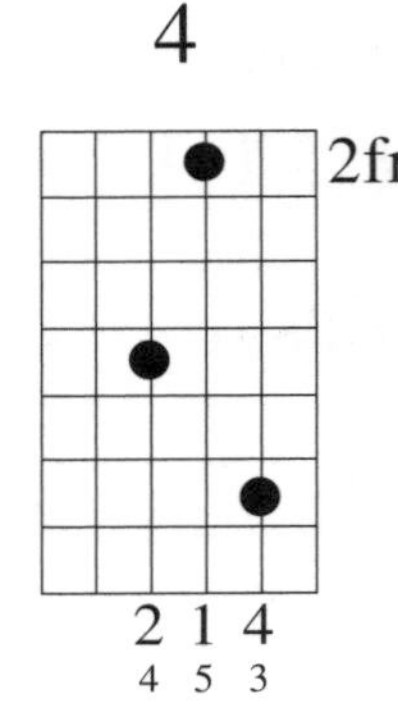

5

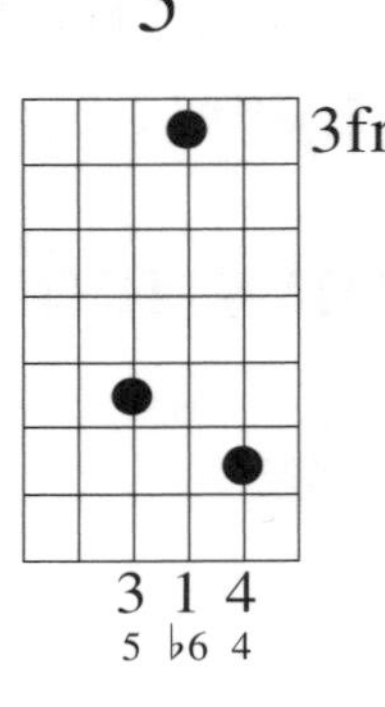

♭6

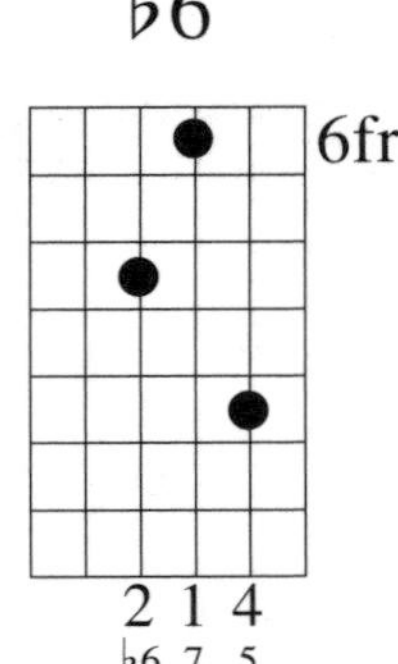

7

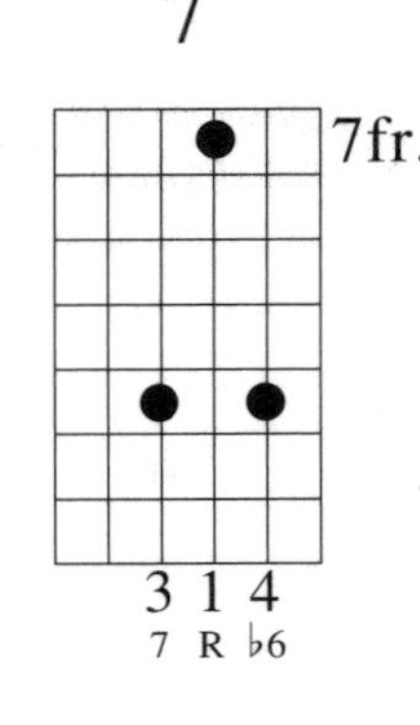

R

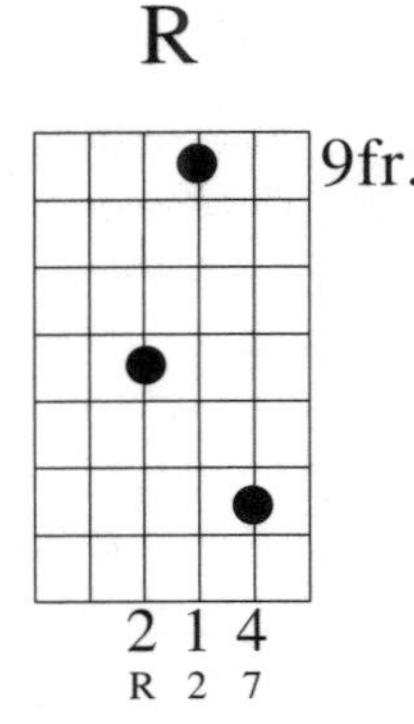

2

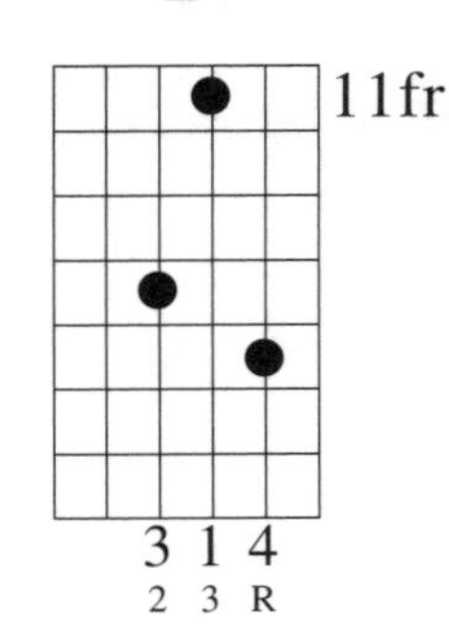

3

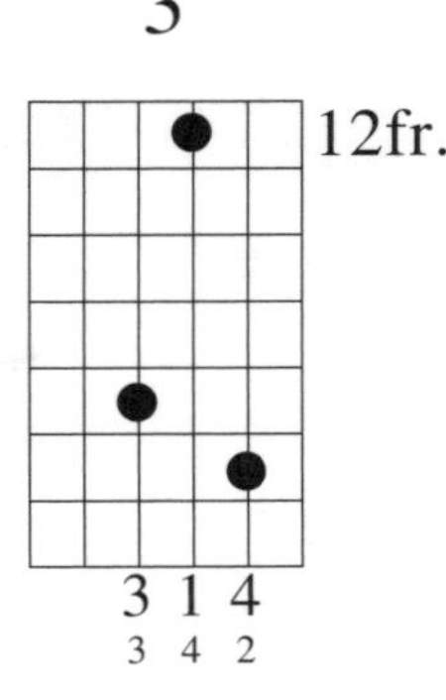